Emerging Research and Trends in Interactivity and the Human-Computer Interface

Katherine Blashki
Noroff University College, Norway

Pedro Isaias
Portuguese Open University, Portugal

A volume in the Advances in Human and Social Aspects of Technology Book Series (AHSAT) Book Series

Managing Director:	Lindsay Johnston
Editorial Director:	Myla Merkel
Production Manager:	Jennifer Yoder
Publishing Systems Analyst:	Adrienne Freeland
Development Editor:	Allyson Gard
Acquisitions Editor:	Kayla Wolfe
Typesetter:	Christina Barkanic
Cover Design:	Jason Mull

Published in the United States of America by
Information Science Reference (an imprint of IGI Global)
701 E. Chocolate Avenue
Hershey PA 17033
Tel: 717-533-8845
Fax: 717-533-8661
E-mail: cust@igi-global.com
Web site: http://www.igi-global.com

Library of Congress Cataloging-in-Publication Data

Emerging research and trends in interactivity and the human-computer interface /Katherine Blashki and Pedro Isaias, editors.
pages cm
Includes bibliographical references and index.
Summary: "This book addresses the main issues of interest within the culture and design of interaction between humans and computers,exploring the emerging aspects of design, development, and implementation of interfaces"-- Provided by publisher.
ISBN 978-1-4666-4623-0 (hardcover) -- ISBN 978-1-4666-4624-7 (ebook) -- ISBN 978-1-4666-4625-4 (print & perpetual access) 1. Human-computer interaction. 2. Human-computer interaction--Research. I. Blashki, Kathy, 1961- II. Isaias, Pedro.
QA76.9.H85E479 2014
004.01'9--dc23

2013025032

This book is published in the IGI Global book series Advances in Human and Social Aspects of Technology (AHSAT) (ISSN: 2328-1316; eISSN: 2328-1324)

British Cataloguing in Publication Data
A Cataloguing in Publication record for this book is available from the British Library.

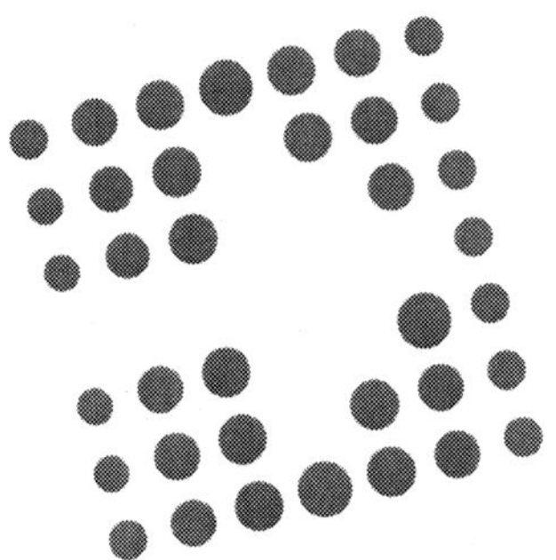

Advances in Human and Social Aspects of Technology (AHSAT) Book Series

Ashish Dwivedi
The University of Hull, UK

ISSN: 2328-1316
EISSN: 2328-1324

Mission

In recent years, the societal impact of technology has been noted as we become increasingly more connected and are presented with more digital tools and devices. With the popularity of digital devices such as cell phones and tablets, it is crucial to consider the implications of our digital dependence and the presence of technology in our everyday lives.

The **Advances in Human and Social Aspects of Technology (AHSAT) Book Series** seeks to explore the ways in which society and human beings have been affected by technology and how the technological revolution has changed the way we conduct our lives as well as our behavior. The AHSAT book series aims to publish the most cutting-edge research on human behavior and interaction with technology and the ways in which the digital age is changing society.

Coverage

- Activism & ICTs
- Computer-Mediated Communication
- Cultural Influence of ICTs
- Cyber Behavior
- End-User Computing
- Gender & Technology
- Human-Computer Interaction
- Information Ethics
- Public Access to ICTs
- Technoself

IGI Global is currently accepting manuscripts for publication within this series. To submit a proposal for a volume in this series, please contact our Acquisition Editors at Acquisitions@igi-global.com or visit: http://www.igi-global.com/publish/.

The Advances in Human and Social Aspects of Technology (AHSAT) Book Series (ISSN 2328-1316) is published by IGI Global, 701 E. Chocolate Avenue, Hershey, PA 17033-1240, USA, www.igi-global.com. This series is composed of titles available for purchase individually; each title is edited to be contextually exclusive from any other title within the series. For pricing and ordering information please visit http://www.igi-global.com/book-series/advances-human-social-aspects-technology/37145. Postmaster: Send all address changes to above address.

Titles in this Series

For a list of additional titles in this series, please visit: www.igi-global.com

Emerging Research and Trends in Interactivity and the Human-Computer Interface
Katherine Blashki (Noroff University, Norway) and Pedro Isaias (Portuguese Open University, Portugal)
Information Science Reference • copyright 2014 • 412pp • H/C (ISBN: 9781466646230) • US $175.00 (our price)

User Behavior in Ubiquitous Online Environments
Jean-Eric Pelet (KMCMS, IDRAC International School of Management, University of Nantes, France) and Panagiota Papadopoulou (University of Athens, Greece)
Information Science Reference • copyright 2014 • 325pp • H/C (ISBN: 9781466645660) • US $175.00 (our price)

Innovative Methods and Technologies for Electronic Discourse Analysis
Hwee Ling Lim (The Petroleum Institute-Abu Dhabi, UAE) and Fay Sudweeks (Murdoch University, Australia)
Information Science Reference • copyright 2014 • 546pp • H/C (ISBN: 9781466644267) • US $175.00 (our price)

Cases on Usability Engineering Design and Development of Digital Products
Miguel A. Garcia-Ruiz (Algoma University, Canada)
Information Science Reference • copyright 2013 • 470pp • H/C (ISBN: 9781466640467) • US $175.00 (our price)

Human Rights and Information Communication Technologies Trends and Consequences of Use
John Lannon (University of Limerick, Ireland) and Edward Halpin (Leeds Metropolitan University, UK)
Information Science Reference • copyright 2013 • 324pp • H/C (ISBN: 9781466619180) • US $175.00 (our price)

Collaboration and the Semantic Web Social Networks, Knowledge Networks, and Knowledge Resources
Stefan Brüggemann (Astrium Space Transportation, Germany) and Claudia d'Amato (University of Bari, Italy)
Information Science Reference • copyright 2012 • 387pp • H/C (ISBN: 9781466608948) • US $175.00 (our price)

Human Rights and Risks in the Digital Era Globalization and the Effects of Information Technologies
Christina M. Akrivopoulou (Democritus University of Thrace, Greece) and Nicolaos Garipidis (Aristotle University of Thessaloniki, Greece)
Information Science Reference • copyright 2012 • 363pp • H/C (ISBN: 9781466608917) • US $180.00 (our price)

Technology for Creativity and Innovation Tools, Techniques and Applications
Anabela Mesquita (ISCAP/IPP and Algoritmi Centre, University of Minho, Portugal)
Information Science Reference • copyright 2011 • 426pp • H/C (ISBN: 9781609605193) • US $180.00 (our price)

www.igi-global.com

701 E. Chocolate Ave., Hershey, PA 17033
Order online at www.igi-global.com or call 717-533-8845 x100
To place a standing order for titles released in this series, contact: cust@igi-global.com
Mon-Fri 8:00 am - 5:00 pm (est) or fax 24 hours a day 717-533-8661

Editorial Advisory Board

List of Reviewers

Ismael Ávila, *CPqD R&D Center in Telecommunications, Brazil*
Lulit Bezuayehu, *Oracle Inc., USA*
Julian Bowerman, *Loughborough University, UK*
Federico Cabitza, *Università degli Studi di Milano-Bicocca, Italy*
David Costa, *University of Lisbon, Portugal*
Randy Döring, *Technische Universität Dresden, Germany*
Carlos Duarte, *University of Lisbon, Portugal*
Lucia Vilela Leite Filgueiras, *Escola Politécnica da Universidade de São Paulo, Brazil*
Iade Gesso, *Università degli Studi di Milano-Bicocca, Italy*
Kim Nee Goh, *Universiti Teknologi Petronas, Malaysia*
Yinni Guo, *Purdue University, USA*
Rüdiger Heimgärtner, *Intercultural User Interface Consulting (IUIC), Germany*
Pirita Ihamäki, *University of Turku, Finland*
Tomayess Issa, *Curtin University, Australia*
Amalia Kallergi, *Leiden University, The Netherlands*
Ken Keane, *Madeira-Interactive Technology Institute (Madeira-ITI), Portugal*
Jari Laarni, *VTT Technical Research Centre of Finland, Finland*
Celina P. Leão, *University of Minho, Portugal*
Isabel F. Loureiro, *University of Minho, Portugal*
Mika Luimula, *University of Turku, Finland*
Cathie Marache-Francisco, *Université de Lorraine – Perseus, France*
Valentina Nisi, *Madeira-Interactive Technology Institute (Madeira-ITI), Portugal*
Johannes Pfeffer, *Technische Universität Dresden, Germany*
Soraia Silva Prietch, *Universidade Federal de Mato Grosso – Rondonópolis, Brazil*

Table of Contents

Section 4
Methodological Approaches

Section 5
Supporting Learning

Detailed Table of Contents

This chapter starts with an introduction illuminating the theoretical background necessary for taking culture into account in Human Computer Interaction (HCI) design. Definitions of concepts used are provided followed by a historical overview on taking culture into account in HCI design. Subsequently, a glimpse of the current state of research in culture-centered HCI design is derived from secondary literature providing the gist of the structures, processes, methods, models, and theoretic approaches concerning the relationship between culture and HCI design. Controversies and challenges are also mentioned. A short discussion of results from empirical studies and design recommendations for culture-centered HCI design lead to implications and trends in future intercultural user interface design research.

Developing icons has always been challenging, from the first appearance of icons on desktop computers to the current day mobile and tablet platforms. Many of the same challenges apply when designing icons for global enterprise software. Icons can easily be misinterpreted when the designer and user have differing cultural backgrounds. The purpose of this chapter is to demonstrate the various cultural implications of icon interpretations and misinterpretations by users in various regions around the world. The authors conducted several studies to understand the roles cultures play when icons are viewed and interpreted by users. By deploying global surveys and conducting focus groups with users from around the world, they collected data to help them understand some of the variations in understanding and interpretations of icons. The authors also looked into various cultures that might find certain icons culturally insensitive or even offensive. After extensive research, they found that some of their initial assumptions regarding taboos and cultural standards were skewed by antiquated research, and now, their more recent research data shows that there is a more accepting global view of iconic metaphors and graphical imagery.

In this chapter, the authors describe the design and implementation of an adaptive multimodal fission component integrated in the multimodal GUIDE framework. This component is able to adapt any HTML-based application's UI to a specific user's characteristics, making it possible for elderly and impaired users to interact by offering several output modalities that try to overcome possible interaction difficulties. They also present an evaluation of the proposed solution, conducted with more than 50 participants, that shows the efficiency of multimodal adaptation in increasing task perception and task execution.

An important issue in the capture of the real user experience while interacting with technology is the ability to assess emotional quality. There are several methods for emotional quality evaluation in the literature. However, when the target users are deaf participants, communication problems arise. A substantial part of the deaf community communicates in sign language. Because user experience researchers are seldom fluent in sign language, they require the assistance of an interpreter whenever users are deaf signers. Evaluation of emotional quality may lose accuracy because of the mediation of an interpreter; consequently, emotional quality evaluation requires a special instrument that can be used in an intuitive and independent way by researchers and their deaf subjects. The authors present the process of creation and improvement of Emotion-Libras, an instrument for assessing the emotional quality of people with hearing disabilities when interacting with technology.

Autism Spectrum Disorders (ASD) are a group of neuro-developmental disorders caused by brain abnormalities which result in impaired social story. Research on treatment in helping children with ASD to improve social story is growing as the cases of children diagnosed with ASD are on the rise. Social story is one of the proven methods of treatment in helping children with ASD to acquire social story through scenarios written in the form of stories. However, the current approaches to present the social story lack interactivity, consuming more intensive efforts to acquire the social story. Learning is most effectual when motivated; thus, the purpose of this study is to discover a learning tool that children with ASD will be motivated to learn independently, and it is achievable by combining elements that they are interested in. This research utilizes the interactivity of multimedia as a medium to present an interactive pedagogical tool for children with ASD to acquire social story. This combination is anticipated to be an effective tool in teaching social story to children with ASD, as they are naturally drawn to computers and visual cues, combined with the fact that Social Story™ has been effective in changing the social behavior of children with ASD. Thus, this study has contributed to the emergent research of treatment for children with ASD in social story acquisition. The result of this study is important as it presents a novel assistance that can be used effectively in assisting children with ASD to improve their main deficit, social story.

Geocaching is a multiplayer outdoor sports game. There is a lack of extensive research on this game, and there is a need for more academic research on this game and its application to other contexts worldwide. There are about 5 million people participating in the geocaching game in 220 different countries worldwide. The geocaching game is interesting because the players create it. The players' role in game design increases its value in human-centred design research. Digital games are a prevalent form of entertainment in which the purpose of the design is to engage the players. This case study was carried out with 52 Finnish geocachers as an Internet survey. The purpose of this conceptual analysis is to investigate how the geocaching sports game might inform game design by looking at player experiences, devices, and techniques that support problem solving within complex environments. Specifically, this analysis presents a brief overview of the geocaching sports game, its role in popular adventure game design, and an analysis of the underlying players' experiences and enjoyment as a structure to be used in game design.

Intuitive means of human-machine interaction are needed in order to facilitate seamless human-robot cooperation. Knowledge about human posture, whereabouts, and performed actions allows interpretation of the situation. Thus, expectations towards system behavior can be inferred. This work demonstrates a system in an industrial setting that combines all this information in order to achieve situation awareness. The continuous human action recognition is based on hierarchical Hidden Markov Models. For identifying and predicting human location, an approach based on potential functions is presented. The recognition results and spatial information are used in combination with a Description Logics-based reasoning system for modeling semantic interrelations, dependencies, and situations.

Current technological apparati have made it possible for natural input systems to reach our homes, businesses, and learning sites. However, and despite some of these systems being already commercialized, there is still a pressing need to better understand how people interact with these apparati, given the whole array of intervening contextual factors. This chapter presents two studies of how people interact with systems supporting gesture and speech on different interaction surfaces: one supporting touch, the other pointing. The naturally occurring commands for both modalities and both surfaces have been identified in these studies. Furthermore, the studies show how surfaces are used, and which modalities are employed based on factors such as the number of people collaborating in the tasks and the placement of appearing objects in the system, thus contributing to the future design of such systems.

Chapter 9
Reporting a User Study on a Visual Editor to Compose Rules in Active Documents........................ 182
Federico Cabitza, Università degli Studi di Milano-Bicocca, Italy
Iade Gesso, Università degli Studi di Milano-Bicocca, Italy

Researchers are exploring the feasibility of visual language editors in domain-specific domains where their alleged user-friendliness can be exploited to involve end-users in configuring their artifacts. In this chapter, the authors present an experimental user study conducted to validate the hypothesis that adopting a visual language could help prospective end-users of an electronic medical record define their own document-related local rules. This study allows them to claim that their visual rule editor based on the OpenBlocks framework can be used with no particular training as proficiently as with specific training, and it was found user-friendly by the user panel involved. Although the conclusions of this study cannot be broadly generalized, the findings are a preliminary contribution to show the importance of visual languages in domain-specific rule definition by end-users with no particular IT skills, like medical doctors are supposed to represent.

Section 2
Design Approaches

Chapter 10
The Gamification Experience: UXD with a Gamification Background 205
Cathie Marache-Francisco, Université de Lorraine, France
Eric Brangier, Université de Lorraine, France

Through this chapter, the authors aim at describing Gamification—the use of game elements in non-ludic environments—to identify its limits and lacks as well as its assets. Indeed, it has been developed to answer a need that arouses out of the Human Computer Interaction (HCI) field evolutions, and it could be valuable in that scope. The authors propose a definition of Gamification according to several different dimensions that are part of the HCI design field. They suggest it as a first step towards a guiding design framework aimed at designers. They mention future research directions that would help in going further and enriching the framework, leading to the creation of a design model for User Experience design through Gamification. The authors finally raise some ethical concerns about the meaning of Gamification itself.

Chapter 11
Experience Prototyping: Gathering Rich Understandings to Guide Design...................................... 224
Ken Keane, Madeira-Interactive Technology Institute (Madeira-ITI), Portugal
Valentina Nisi, Madeira-Interactive Technology Institute (Madeira-ITI), Portugal

In this chapter, the authors discuss Experience Prototyping as an appropriate research tool for capturing people's stories related to physical places. It is difficult to explore subjective experiences through strict conventional prototyping methods within a lab; therefore, the authors argue the need for innovative research techniques especially when designing interactive systems where mobility, context, and people play a fundamental role. They discuss the methodology of "Experience Prototyping," which is used to gather insight in a research project, and also what advantages such method brings to a user-centered process. The authors present some reflections and themes that emerged from using experience prototypes, and how they contribute to our understanding of the relationship between spatial narrative and place, and in particular how they may be used as an interaction resource towards discovery and sharing of "place." In doing so, they offer a basis for discussion on how to co-design technologically mediated experiences together with users of such spaces. Finally, the authors discuss how this method informed the design of "The Breadcrumbs" application.

of this decision tool includes several steps, such as conceptualization of the problem, definition of the three ETdA dimensions and observation tools, data collection, and weighting the results leading to ergonomic intervention proposal. The software, named ETdAnalyser, is proposed to provide the ergonomist or analyst a fast and simple way of collecting and analysing data. This system is considered to be a decision-making support tool for ergonomic intervention, representing a relevant contribution to the advance of the ergonomics field.

This chapter provides an introduction to a work that aims to apply the achievements of engineering psychology to the area of formal methods, focusing on the specification phase of a system development process. Formal methods often assume that only two factors should be satisfied: the method must be sound and give such a representation, which is concise and beautiful from the mathematical point of view, without taking into account any question of readability, usability, or tool support. This leads to the fact that formal methods are treated by most engineers as something that is theoretically important but practically too hard to understand and to use, where even some small changes of a formal method can make it more understandable and usable for an average engineer.

In the design of complex information systems and social practices for different domains a balance between theory-driven and practice-driven approaches is at best developed in a collaborative communication process between designers, researchers, and other actors. The authors have developed the Anticipation Design Dialogue method within the context of participatory design, which is based on dialogic communication between different stakeholders. A dialogic relationship between them takes place in future workshops in which experiences of different stakeholders are integrated in a way that makes it possible to illustrate the situation from different perspectives. The workshop participants develop in small groups a vision of the future state in which the situation is imagined from the future perspective by considering which kind of problems they have at the moment and by which way the problems could be managed in the future. Secondly, reflective thinking is promoted by letting each group at the time present their ideas while others are listening. The authors have found that the development of mutual understanding between different stakeholders in these kinds of workshops is a complex process that needs time, and therefore, an iterative series of workshops is recommended.

Interacting with mobile devices can be challenging in adverse working environments. Using hand gestures for interaction can overcome severe usability issues that users face when working with mobile devices in industrial settings. This chapter is dedicated to the design, implementation, and evaluation

This chapter introduces a new usability evaluation method, the axiomatic evaluation method, which is developed based on the axiomatic design theory – a formalized design methodology that can be used to solve a variety of design problems. This new evaluation method examines three domains of a product: customer domain, functional domain, and control domain. This method investigates not only usability problems reported by the users, but also usability problems related to customer requirements and usability problems related to control through checking the mapping matrix between the three domains. To determine how well this new usability evaluation method works, a between-subject experiment was conducted to compare the axiomatic evaluation method with the think aloud method. Sixty participants were randomly assigned to use either method to evaluate three popular consumer electronic devices (music player, digital camera, mobile phone) that represented different levels of complexity. Number of usability problems discovered, completion time, and overall user satisfaction were collected. Results show that the axiomatic evaluation method performed better in finding usability problems for the mobile phone. The axiomatic evaluation method was also better at finding usability problems about user expectation and control than the think aloud method. Benefits and drawbacks of using the axiomatic evaluation method are discussed.

Section 5
Supporting Learning

Chapter 19
Promoting Human-Computer Interaction and Usability Guidelines and Principles Through Reflective Journal Assessment 375
Tomayess Issa, Curtin University, Australia
Pedro Isaias, Portuguese Open University, Portugal

This chapter aims to examine the challenges to, and opportunities for, promoting Human Computer Interaction (HCI) and usability guidelines and principles through reflective journal assessment by information systems students from the Australian and Portuguese higher education sectors. In order to raise students' awareness of HCI and aspects of usability, especially in the Web development process, a new unit was developed by the first researcher called Information Systems 650 (IS650) in Australia. From this unit was derived the Web Site Planning and Development (WSPD) course introduced in Portugal. The reflective journal assessment approach was employed to enhance students' learning and knowledge of HCI and its usability aspects. This study provides empirical evidence from 64 students from Australia and Portugal, based on quantitative and qualitative data derived from three sources: students' formal and informal feedback and an online survey. Students confirmed that the use of reflective journal assessment consolidated their understanding of HCI and usability guidelines and principles and improved their reading, searching, researching, and writing skills, and their proficiency with the endnote software.

Chapter 20
The Impact of Visual Complexity on Children's Learning Websites in Relation to Aesthetic Preference and Learning Motivation 395
Hsiu-Feng Wang, National Chiayi University, Taiwan
Julian Bowerman, Loughborough University, UK

Websites in addition to being usable must also be pleasurable to look at. However, although much research has been conducted into usability, subjective issues have been far less explored. The purpose of this research is to look at the relationship between visual complexity, aesthetics, and learning motivation in children's learning websites. An experiment was set up that involved 132 11-12 year-old children using homepages taken from Websites designed for children as test materials. In the experiment, the children were randomly assigned into 3 groups and given a different visual complexity Website according to their group. The Websites given were: homepage with a low degree of visual complexity; homepage with a moderate degree of visual complexity; and homepage with a high degree of visual complexity. This study is guided by Berlyne's experimental theory, which suggests that there is an inverted-U shaped relationship between preference for a stimulus and its complexity. The study applies his theory and aims to understand the relationship between visual complexity, aesthetic preference, and learning motivation. The findings show that children prefer aesthetics of a medium level of perceived complexity, supporting Berlyne's theory. It also shows that children's aesthetic preferences and learning motivation are correlated. The findings have implications for Web designers working on children's Websites as they suggest that by manipulating visual complexity viewing pleasure can be enhanced or depreciated.

Chapter 21
Adapting Chatterbots' Interaction for Use in Children's Education 413
Antonio F. L. Jacob Junior, Federal University of Pará, Brazil
Eulália C. da Mata, Federal University of Pará, Brazil
Ádamo L. Santana, Federal University of Pará, Brazil
Carlos R. L. Francês, Federal University of Pará, Brazil
João C. W. A. Costa, Federal University of Pará, Brazil
Flávia de A. Barros, Federal University of Pernambuco, Brazil

The Web is providing greater freedom for users to create and obtain information in a more dynamic and appropriate way. One means of obtaining information on this platform, which complements or replaces other forms, is the use of conversation robots or Chatterbots. Several factors must be taken into account for the effective use of this technology; the first of which is the need to employ a team of professionals from various fields to build the knowledge base of the system and be provided with a wide range of responses, i.e. interactions. It is a multidisciplinary task to ensure that the use of this system can be targeted to children. In this context, this chapter carries out a study of the technology of Chatterbots and shows some of the changes that have been implemented for the effective use of this technology for children. It also highlights the need for a shift away from traditional methods of interaction so that an affective computing model can be implemented.

Chapter 22
A Framework for Designing Interactive Digital Learning Environments for Young People 429
Virgínia Tiradentes Souto, University of Brasilia, Brazil

In this chapter a descriptive framework for designing interactive digital learning environments for young people is proposed. The proposed framework aims to analyse and compare interactive digital learning environments. This framework may be useful to guide the design of digital learning environments for young people and also to provide a structure for understanding the interface characteristics of such environments and how users interact with them. Young people's characteristics are briefly discussed in relation to the learning process. The approach to creating the framework is presented with the related literature. The framework is described and consists of three main components: learning, user interaction, and visual. Finally, conclusions on the design of interactive digital learning environments are drawn.

Section 6
Reflection

Chapter 23
The Conceptual Pond: A Persuasive Tool for Quantifiable Qualitative Assessment 449
Christian Grund Sørensen, Aalborg University, Denmark
Mathias Grund Sørensen, Aalborg University, Denmark

"The Conceptual Pond" is a persuasive application designed to gather qualitative input through a multi-platform assessment interface. The process of using the application serves as a conceptual aid for personal reflection as well as providing a compilation and evaluation system with the ability to transform this input into quantitative data. In this chapter, a pilot study of this application is presented and discussed.

The aim of this chapter is the discussion of central issues in the system, the use of semantic fields, user freedom vs. default options, graphical interface, persuasive technology design, and the epistemological potential of the application. In this discourse, contextualized rhetorical and persuasive technology theories are implemented. Functionality and epistemological impact is exemplified through several use cases, one of these linked to the EUROPlot project. In a more comprehensive scope, this chapter adds to the discussion of the role of IT systems in experiencing the world and reflecting on it, thus breaking new ground for designing persuasive applications supporting human recognition.

Section 7
The Future

Chapter 24
Playful Interfaces for Scientific Image Data: A Case for Storytelling 471
Amalia Kallergi, Leiden University, The Netherlands
Fons J. Verbeek, Leiden University, The Netherlands

Recent developments in the field of HCI draw our attention to the potential of playful interfaces, play, and games. This chapter identifies a new but relevant application domain for playful interfaces (i.e. scientific practice involving image data). Given the thesis that play and playfulness are relevant for a researcher's interaction with scientific images, the question remains: How do we design playful interfaces that support meaningful ways to playfully engage with scientific images? This chapter introduces, investigates, and implements storytelling with scientific images as a worthwhile instance of playful interaction with scientific images. To better understand and further exemplify the potential of storytelling with scientific images, the chapter contributes both a review of utilitarian usages of storytelling with images and findings from a case study storytelling game.

Compilation of References..490

About the Contributors..539

Index..551

Preface

Human-Computer Interaction now occurs in every discipline, making it uniquely multi-disciplinary. Whilst we embrace this ubiquity, this pervasiveness of our discipline has led to its neglect. Despite the longevity of interest and the plethora of research activity in the field of Human-Computer Interaction, any cursory glance at the available applications suggests that the field has not progressed since Doug Engelbart was a graduate student.

That which constitutes the space we have routinely assigned as "the interface" has undergone a revolutionary change not seen since Gutenberg's press in the 1440s. Humans now interact with computers in ways never before imagined. It is this "imagined" space that we aim to explore. This book will range across a variety of emergent and innovative approaches, yet always with the active participation of the human element as the still point of the relationship between the human user and the digital realms with which they interact.

This book aims to address the main issues of interest within the culture and design of interaction between humans and computers at the interface. In particular, this book will emphasize emergent and innovative aspects of design, development, and implementation of interfaces for interactivity between humans and the technologies they routinely use.

In addition, this book aims to explore and discuss innovative studies of technology and its application in the implementation of interactivity in interface design and development and welcomes significant research in Interactivity and the Human Computer Interface (IHCI). This book aims to address a range of approaches including, but not limited to, the conceptual, technological, and design issues related to these developments.

This book is mainly intended to support an academic audience (academics, university teachers, researchers, and post-graduate students – both Master and Doctorate levels). In addition, this book will be of benefit to public and private institutions, HCI developers and researchers, HCI enterprise managers, professionals related to Information Systems and ICT sectors, and those who seek to reach an audience/user via media or technology.

The chapters were divided into seven sections for the purpose of structure and organization: "Users' Needs and Expectations," "Design Approaches," "Technological Approaches," "Methodological Approaches," "Supporting Learning," "Reflection," and "The Future."

The initial section, concerning users' needs and expectations is composed of nine chapters and explores a broad range of issues, such as global access, users with disabilities, and user experience.

Chapter 1, which introduces this section, "Intercultural User Interface Design," by Heimgärtner, explores the importance of culture in Human-Computer Interaction (HCI) design. It begins by providing a historical depiction of the role of culture in HCI design and then proceeds to analyse the current research being conducted in this area and the panoply of issues that it raises and unveils. The chapter concludes its argument by combining the outcomes of empirical studies with culture-centred design recommendations to forecast the consequences and trends of intercultural user design research.

"Icon Metaphors for Global Cultures," Chapter 2, authored by Bezuayehu, Stilan, and Peesapati, aims to scrutinise the multiple cultural consequences of interpretation and misinterpretation of icons by users around the world. It highlights the challenges of icon design, particularly in icons that are to be used globally and in situations where designers and users have different cultural contexts. The surveys and focus groups conducted by the authors concluded that, contrary to initial beliefs, there seems to be a more tolerant global scrutiny of iconic and graphical imagery

"Improving Interaction with TV-Based Applications through Adaptive Multimodal Fission," Chapter 3, authored by Costa and Duarte, depicts the design and application of an adaptive multimodal fission component integrated in the multimodal GUIDE framework, which has the ability to adapt any HTML-based application's UI to the needs of individual users. The empirical research of this proposition involved over 50 participants and intends to be an important element to surmount interaction difficulties by the elderly and the impaired.

"Developing Emotion-Libras 2.0: An Instrument to Measure the Emotional Quality of Deaf Persons while using Technology," Chapter 4, by Prietch and Filgueiras, addresses the challenge of the assessment of emotional quality of deaf users when they interact with technology. In this chapter, the authors present the procedure for the creation and perfection of Emotion-Libras, a tool for assessment of the emotional quality of people with hearing impairments when interacting with technology.

"Enhancing the Acquisition of Social Story through the Interactivity of Multimedia," Chapter 5, by Mandasari and Bee Theng, aims to develop a learning instrument for use by children with Autism Spectrum Disorders (ASD) that can assist in motivating them to learn in more independent ways by combining learning with the interests of the children. The authors use the interactivity of multimedia as a means to present an interactive pedagogical resource for the acquisition of social story by children with ASD.

"Players' Experience in a Sport Geocaching Game," Chapter 6, authored by Ihamäki and Luimula, analyses the multiplayer outdoor sports game, Geocaching. Specifically, this analysis presents a brief overview of the geocaching sports game, its role in popular adventure game design, and an analysis of the underlying players' experiences and enjoyment as a structure to be used in game design. The authors carried out a case study involving 52 Finnish geocachers who participated in an Internet survey.

"Seamless Interfacing: Situation Awareness through Action Recognition and Spatio-Temporal Reasoning," Chapter 7, by Puls and Wörn, attends to the need for intuitive human-machine interaction for the purpose of assisting seamless human-robot cooperation. The authors present a system in an industrial environment that combines information about human posture, location, and executed actions to capture situation awareness. In order to identify and envisage the human location, this chapter presents an approach based on potential functions.

"Studying Natural Interaction in Multimodal, Multi-Surface, Multiuser Scenarios," Chapter 8, by Duarte, Ribeiro, and Nunes, introduces two studies on how people interact with systems that support gesture and speech in different interaction surfaces. One of the studies concerns the support of touching and the other study relates to the support of pointing. The authors identify, in this chapter, the naturally occurring commands for these modalities and surfaces and demonstrate how surfaces were used and the modalities that were applied.

The chapter that concludes the first section, Chapter 9, is titled "Reporting a User Study on a Visual Editor to Compose Rules in Active Documents" and is authored by Cabitza and Gesso. It addresses the importance of visual languages in domain-specific rule definition by users with no IT proficiency. The authors describe an experimental user study conducted to assess the possibility of the positive impact of the adoption of visual language in potential users of an electronic medical record and delineate their own document-related local rules.

This next section, Section 2, concerns different design approaches.

"The Gamification Experience: UXD with a Gamification Background," Chapter 10, by Marache-Francisco and Brangier, presents a depiction of Gamification, the employment of game features in non-recreational settings. The authors propose a definition of the concept of Gamification that accounts for multiple and varied elements of the Human-Computer Interaction design area. They further analyse the notion of Gamification from the point of view of future research and ethical understandings.

"Experience Prototyping: Gathering Rich Understandings to Guide Design," Chapter 11, by Keane and Nisi, explores Experience Prototyping as a valuable research instrument for capturing people's stories related to physical places. The authors present the Experience Prototyping methodology employed to collect data in the research project conducted. Furthermore, they discuss the benefits that this method conveys to a user-centred process and how it facilitates an understanding of the rapport between spatial narrative and place.

Section 3 presents technological approaches.

"Strategy to Support the Memorization of Iconic Passwords," Chapter 12, by Ávila, Menezes, and Melo Braga, explores the employment of iconic passwords in authentication solutions for the use of smartphones as payment appliances. The authors intend to reach a compromise between security and usability by using memorization methods that are based on human memory abilities. Their proposition was assessed with users and compared with previous research.

"Location-Based Data Visualization Tool for Tuberculosis and Dengue: A Case Study in Malaysia," Chapter 13, by Goh, Chen, and Chow, intends to develop the prototype for an instrument of disease data visualisation on Google maps to assist Malaysian physicians and health centres to have a more clear and timely notion of where cases of diseases are located. The authors argue that this tool can be an asset in terms of following disease spreading patterns, helping with the isolation of diseases, and mobilising resources to the affected areas.

The chapters concerning methodological approaches were joined together in Section 4.

"ETdAnalyser: A Model-Based Architecture for Ergonomic Decision Intervention," Chapter 14, authored by Loureiro, Leão, Costa, Teixeira, and Arezes, discusses the Ergonomic Tridimensional Analysis (ETdA). ETdA is an innovative ergonomic method that enables the identification and description of numerous ergonomic settings characterized by common areas where consumers are subject to similar tasks as those normally carried out by professionals. The authors propose a software program, named ETdAnalyser, in order to provide ergonomists and analysts with a swift and straightforward technique for the collection and analysis of data.

"Design of Formal Languages and Interfaces: 'Formal' Does Not Mean 'unreadable'," Chapter 15, by Spichkova, offers a preliminary discussion to work that is aimed at applying the achievements of engineering psychology to the field of formal methods, with a particular emphasis on the specification stage of a system´s development process. The author intends to demonstrate that formal languages and interfaces can benefit from some improvement in terms of their usability and comprehension.

"Anticipation Dialogue Method in Participatory Design," Chapter 16, by Laarni and Aaltonen, develops a method within participatory design settings that is based on dialogic communication between distinct stakeholders. This method, the Anticipation Design Dialogue, was developed to facilitate the process of information systems' design in terms of its need to incorporate both theory- and practice-driven approaches. The authors employ this method, arguing that the design process can highly benefit from an efficient communication between the different actors in play, such as designers and researchers.

"Hand Gesture Recognition as Means for Mobile Human Computer Interaction in Adverse Working Environments," Chapter 17, by Ziegler, Döring, Pfeffer, and Urbas, focuses on the design, application, and assessment of mobile information systems with hand gesture recognition as tools for human computer interaction. The authors present and test with a case study a framework for the design of proficient and trustworthy user interfaces based on hand gestures.

"The Axiomatic Usability Evaluation Method," Chapter 18, authored by Guo, proposes an innovative usability evaluation method. The axiomatic evaluation method described by the author is based on the axiomatic design theory, and it contemplates three elements of a product: customers, functionality, and control. The empirical study the author conducted with 60 participants uncovered several advantages and disadvantages of this method.

This following section, Section 5, is dedicated to supporting learning.

"Promoting Human-Computer Interaction and Usability Guidelines and Principles through Reflective Journal Assessment," Chapter 19, authored by Issa and Isaias, intends to explore the challenges and opportunities of the promotion of Human-Computer Interaction (HCI) and usability guidelines and precepts via reflective journal assessment. To achieve this goal, the authors collected data from formal and informal feedback of 64 Information Systems students enrolled in Australian and Portuguese higher education and an online survey.

"The Impact of Visual Complexity on Children´s Learning Websites in Relation to Aesthetic Preference and Learning Motivation," Chapter 20, authored by Wang and Bowerman, examines the relationship between complexity, aesthetics, and learning motivation in Websites dedicated to children's learning. The authors conducted a study with 132 children aged 11 to 12 years old, where they were randomly divided in three groups and asked to use homepages with different levels of visual complexity: low, moderate, and high. The findings revealed a correlation between the children's aesthetics preferences and their learning motivation.

"Adapting Chatterbot Interaction for Use in Children's Education," Chapter 21, by Jacob Junior, da Mata, Santana, Francês, Costa, and Barros, is dedicated to the use of Chatterbots in children's learning. The authors conducted a study on the technology of Chatterbots and identify some of the modifications that have been employed for the proficient use of this technology for children. They underline the importance of moving away from conventional methods of interaction and investing in the implementation of affective computing models.

"A Framework for Designing Interactive Digital Learning Environments for Young People," Chapter 22, by Tiradentes Souto, proposes a descriptive framework for the design of interactive digital learning settings for young people. This framework intends to explore and compare different digital learning environments and is based on three core elements: learning, user interaction, and visual. The authors argue that the proposed framework has potential value in terms of guiding design and assisting the understanding of interfaces' features and the type of interaction users have with them.

The penultimate section of this publication, Section 6, is titled "Reflection."

"The Conceptual Pond: A Persuasive Tool for Quantifiable Qualitative Assessment," Chapter 23, by Sørensen and Sørensen, presents and discusses a pilot study of "The Conceptual Pond" persuasive application. The authors debate the core issues of this system, the employment of semantic fields, user's autonomy vs. default features, graphical interfaces, the design of persuasive technology, and the prospective epistemological value of "The Conceptual Pond."

This last section, Section 7, is about the future and looking forward in Human-Computer Interaction research.

"Playful Interfaces for Scientific Image Data: A Case for Storytelling," Chapter 24, by Kallergi and Verbeek, concludes this book. This chapter presents, explores, and applies storytelling with scientific images as a valuable illustration of playful interaction with scientific images. The authors substantiate their argument with a review of utilitarian utilization of storytelling with images and the data collected from a case study they conducted on a storytelling game.

Katherine Blashki
Noroff University College, Norway

Pedro Isaias
Portuguese Open University, Portugal

Section 1
Users' Needs and Expectations

Chapter 1
Intercultural User Interface Design

Rüdiger Heimgärtner
Intercultural User Interface Consulting (IUIC), Germany

ABSTRACT

This chapter starts with an introduction illuminating the theoretical background necessary for taking culture into account in Human Computer Interaction (HCI) design. Definitions of concepts used are provided followed by a historical overview on taking culture into account in HCI design. Subsequently, a glimpse of the current state of research in culture-centered HCI design is derived from secondary literature providing the gist of the structures, processes, methods, models, and theoretic approaches concerning the relationship between culture and HCI design. Controversies and challenges are also mentioned. A short discussion of results from empirical studies and design recommendations for culture-centered HCI design lead to implications and trends in future intercultural user interface design research.

BACKGROUND

Terminology

There are several concepts of "culture". For instance, the organizational anthropologist Geert Hofstede defines culture as collective programming of the mind (cf. G. H. Hofstede, Hofstede, & Minkov, 2010). According to the cultural anthropologist Edward T. Hall, culture co-occurs with communication. Culture is a "silent language" or "hidden dimension" which steers people unconsciously (cf. E. T. Hall, 1959). Difficulties in communication with members of other cultures arise from that. If one is not conscious of one's own motives, which are culturally influenced, one cannot understand the motives and actions of others (cf. Thomas, 1996). The position that is taken in this paper is that culture is a set of facts, rules, values and norms (structural conditions) representing an orientation system (cf. Thomas, 1996) established by collective programming of the mind (cf. G. H. Hofstede et al., 2010) within a group of individuals. This position is alternative to the one by which culture is rather seen as a "collection of practices" or in terms of "membership in a discourse community" (cf. Kramsch, 1998).

Cultural models describe the cultural distance, i.e. the differences between cultures and allow the comparison of them with each other (cf. Geert Hofstede, 1984). One of the best-known cultural models is the iceberg model of culture (cf. Hoft, 1996). Only some of the attributes of a culture

DOI: 10.4018/978-1-4666-4623-0.ch001

such as language and behavior are visible and conscious. Most of them such as beliefs and values are invisible and unconscious and hence, difficult to investigate. Cultural models help to overcome this methodological gap using cultural standards and dimensions to look beneath the water surface, i.e. to probe the unconscious areas of culture.

The organizational psychologist Alexander Thomas established the concept of "cultural standards", which expresses the normal, typical and valid attributes for the majority of the members of a certain culture regarding the respective kinds of perception, thought, judgment and action (cf. Thomas, 1996: 112). Cultural standards serve as an orientation system for the members of a group and regulate action. The individual grows into its culture by assuming and internalizing these cultural standards. This process encompasses learning basic human abilities in the social arena, control of one's own behavior and emotions, the satisfaction of basic needs, worldview, verbal and nonverbal communication and expectations of others as well as the understanding of one's role and scales for judgment.

Another key concept for describing a cultural system is that of "cultural dimension", which can serve as a basis for the identification of cultural standards (cf. Hodicová, 2007: 38). According to Hofstede, cultural dimensions are quantitative models to describe the behavior of the members of different cultures allowing the analysis and comparison of the characteristics of different groups quantitatively (cf. G. H. Hofstede et al., 2010) because the cultural imprint of cultural groups can be measured using quantitative questionnaires (cf. G. Hofstede, 1994). In my view, this can and should also be done for all other cultural dimensions in the future. They represent an aspect of a culture, which is measurable in relation to other cultures. Hence, cultural dimensions can be used to classify kinds of behavior between cultures. Cultural dimensions are indicators showing tendencies in the interaction and communication behavior of members of cultures.

There are similar concepts taking cultural aspects in HCI design into account. At least the following concepts exist:

- Intercultural HCI Design (P. Honold, 2000, K. Röse, Liu, & Zühlke, 2001, Rüdiger Heimgärtner, 2012.)
- Cross-Cultural HCI Design (A. Marcus, 2001, Rau, Plocher, & al., 2012.)
- Culture-Oriented HCI Design (K. Röse & Zühlke, 2001.)
- Culture-Centered HCI Design (Shen, Woolley, & Prior, 2006.)

Their connotations are different, which predisposes the concepts to be applied differently in diverse contexts. Intercultural HCI design means the process of HCI design in the cultural context (cf. Pia Honold, 2000b: 42-43). According to K. Röse & Zühlke, 2001, intercultural HCI design describes the user and culture oriented design of interactive systems and products taking the cultural context of the user into account with respect to the respective tasks and product usage (Kerstin Röse, 2002: 87). This approach has grown in academic literature from 1990 to 2000 and emerged from the processes of globalization, internationalization and localization of products. Localization (L10N) means the adaptation of the system to certain cultural circumstances for a certain local market, for example the adaptation of the look and feel of the user interface or the systems data structures to the culture dependent desires of the user (cf. VDMA, 2009) such as colors, layout, interaction frequency, date and currency format. Internationalization (I18N) of a product means that the product will be prepared for its usage in the desired (in the best case for all) countries (cf. International, 2003). The internationalization of a software product delivers a basic structure on which a later cultural customization (localization) can be carried out. Globalization (G11N) encompasses all activities with regard to the marketing of a (software) product outside a national market (including I18N and L10N of software). The objective is to run successful marketing in one or several regional markets by taking into account the technical, economic and legal conditions there (cf. Schmitz & Wahle, 2000). Marcus requested additionally that cross-cultural HCI design should account for dimensions of cultures relating them to user interface characteristics (cf. A. Marcus, 2001). Shen et al., 2006 introduced the culture-centered HCI design process based on research on cross-cultural interface design (Aaron Marcus, 2006, K. Röse & Zühlke, 2001 and others) and thereby applying iterative analysis to take the target users and their cultural needs into account. Therefore, the topic of intercultural HCI analysis is particularly interesting from the information sciences point of view since this can yield new knowledge, new requirements and goals for the design of information processing systems involving software engineering, software ergonomics / human factors and usability engineering.

Historical Overview

"Intercultural research in Information Systems is a relatively new research area that has gained increasing importance over the last few years [..]" (Kralisch, 2006: 17). Using the key words "cross-cultural HCI" when searching the ACM digital library reveals an exponential rise of publications in this area since 2000 (cf. Figure 1).

There are several "milestone" papers in the literature review concerning the usage of information systems in their cultural context. Two of the first important books regarding internationalization of HCI are *Designing User Interfaces for International Use* from Nielsen, 1990 and *International User Interfaces* from Del Galdo & Nielsen, 1996. Day, 1991 provided an introduction to the study of cross-cultural of HCI by a review of the research methodology, the technology transfer and the diffusion of innovation to shed light on the cross-cultural study of human-computer interaction. Another overview of culture and its effects on HCI is given by Cagiltay, 1999. There is also activity investigating the trends in intercultural HCI (cf. Jetter, 2004). Leidner & Kayworth, 2006 did a review of culture in information systems research to postulate a shift to a theory of information technology culture conflict. Vatrapu & Suthers, 2007 illuminated the relationship between culture and computers by a review of the concept of culture and implications for intercultural collaborative online learning. Clemmensen & Roese, 2010 provided an overview of a decade of journal publications about culture and HCI.

From this, several "waves" can be identified in this area. The first one happened in the early 1990ies. The next one was around 2000 and since about 2010 research in intercultural HCI design has steadily increased. In these "hypes", the number of publications is high indicating high research interest and effort:[1]

- **Before 1990:** Almost no publications available that would relate the concepts "culture" and "HCI."
- **1990-1999 (Pioneers):** Del Galdo & Nielsen, 1996, Aykin, 2004, Hoft, 1996, A. Badre & Barber, 1998.
- **2000-2004 (Basic Systematic Work):** P. Honold, 2000, K. Röse & Zühlke, 2001, Hermeking, 2001, Rößger & Hofmeister, 2003, A. Marcus, 2001, H. Sun, 2001, Vöhringer-Kuhnt, 2002.
- **2005-2010 (Evaluating the New Field and the Systematic Work):** Clemmensen & Goyal, 2004, Reinecke, Reif, & Bernstein, 2007, Rüdiger Heimgärtner, 2007, Shen et al., 2006, Clemmensen & Goyal, 2004; Thissen, 2008, Irani & th Annual Chi Conference on Human Factors in Computing Systems, 2010, I. Lee et al., 2008.
- **Since 2010 (Strongly Driving Research in this Field):** Abdelnour-Nocera et al., 2011, Dourish P., 2011, Rau et al., 2012, Rüdiger Heimgärtner, 2012, H. Sun, 2012.

Figure 1. Approximating exponential rise of publications regarding cross-cultural HCI design in the digital library of ACM

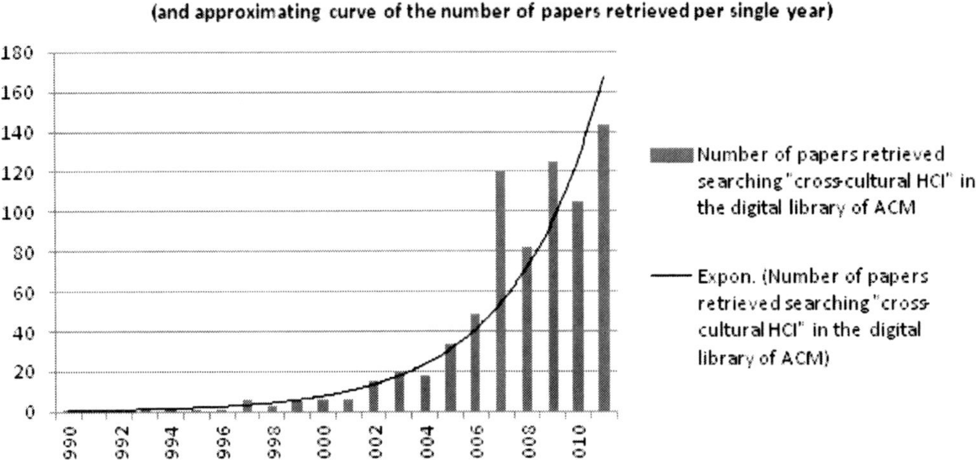

Sturm, 2002 suggested another kind of categorization of the field. The TLCC model was derived from the analysis of the history of examinining the cultural aspects in HCI design and contains four levels of depth and thereby takes cultural aspects in HCI design into account. This model shows the historical growth of internationalization and localization steps in HCI design represented by its four levels: technical affairs (T), language (L), culture (C and cognition (C). At the lowest level, certainly adequate programming languages, representation forms and character sets (Unicode), etc. must be used (as stated in the checklist by Esselink, 1998). Technical aspects have to be adapted so that the products can be used in every culture at least at national level (for example, power supply). Adapting software to Unicode is an example of a precondition to process Asian languages at the language level. Adaptation at cultural level concerns culture-specific aspects including format, currency, colors, modality, menu structure, content of the menu, help, number of messages, length of texts, number of hints, degree of entertainment or ratio of information to entertainment. At the highest level, cognitive styles that describe types of human thinking such as problem solving or making conclusions can be taken into account (cf. Nardi, 1996, Norman, 1986, Choong & Salvendy, 1998). These processes strongly affect not only the functionality and the user interface of the product (i.e., monitor, keyboard, soft and hard keys, control buttons, speech dialogs, within a graphical (GUI) or speech (SUI) user interface, etc.) but also interactive behavior. In cross-cultural HCI design cultural and cognitive aspects must be taken into account in addition to technical and linguistic aspects of localization, in any case. However, in industry, the usage of internationalization concepts beyond the technological and language level has only recently been initiated (cf. e.g., Kersten, Kersten, & Rakowski, 2002, Aykin, 2005, or for instance, Law & Perez, 2005 suggesting how to cross-culturally implement information systems). Hence, today, in industry at least technical and linguistic aspects are taken into account in designing products for other cultures. In contrast, academic reserach is also strongly concerned with cultural and cognitive aspects.

A GLIMPSE AT THE STATE OF THE RESEARCH

To capture the paradigms and newest aspects regarding methodology, technology transfer and the diffusion of innovation, one has to browse through the literature up to now to get an impression about what the most important tasks in intercultural HCI research can, should or must be in the future. The publications compiled by the author within this field of research connecting culture and HCI serve to determine the current state of research in this area and to categorize the main research topics in culture-centered HCI design. The most prominent results of this collection process by the author are presented in the following.

Methods and Approaches

Bourges-Waldegg & Scrivener, 1998 "developed an HCI cross-cultural design approach [called Meaning in Mediated Action (MMA)] which focuses specifically on how representations and meaning mediate action" (Bourges-Waldegg & Scrivener, 1998, p. 307) dealing with cultural diversity and differentiating between systems targeted for particular cultures and systems intended to be shared by culturally diverse users, because "existing approaches are inadequate for dealing with this issue." (Bourges-Waldegg & Scrivener, 1998, p. 287). This approach was referenced by several of the approaches that followed in the area of "HCI and culture". Yeo, 2001 found out that the global software development life cycle works efficiently for multicultural societies such as Malaysia in contrast to the Western driven usability assessment techniques.

"Cross-Cultural Design" as used by Plocher, Patrick Rau, & Choong, 2012 is rather a "headline" than an approach: the activities and methods used in this area were summarized and labeled by "cross-cultural design". Plocher et al., 2012 identified the following authors providing first milestones in cross-cultural HCI design: Fernandes, 1995 and Prabhu & Harel, 1999. A. Marcus, 2001, Aaron Marcus, 2001 extrapolated user interface design guidelines from the classic works of Hofstede (cf. G. H. Hofstede, 1991) and Hall (cf. E. T. Hall, 1959, E. T. Hall, 1976, Edward Twitchell Hall & Hall, 1990). "A less explored direction of cross-cultural design research has focused on cultural differences in cognition." (Plocher et al., 2012, p. 183). Choong & Salvendy, 1998 and Nisbett, 2003 worked on cultural differences in user interface information structures and in cognitive styles respectively.

Additional approaches are described in the recent work by Jensen & Bjørn, 2012 for intercultural software engineering. Finally, there is the trend to work on methods to take cross-cultural differences into account in design in general (cf. Dinet, Vivian, & Brangier, 2011). This trend is confirmed by augmenting general and systematic HCI design approaches such as design for use (cf. L. L. Constantine & Lockwood, 1999) to intercultural design for use, i.e. extending usage centered design by cultural aspects through integrating cultural models (cf. Windl & Heimgärtner, 2013).

Intercultural Variables and Method of Culture-Oriented Design

According to Kerstin Röse, 2002: 93-96, intercultural variables describe the differences in HCI design regarding the preferences of the users of different cultures. "Intercultural" variables represent knowledge that can be obtained only by observing at least two cultures and their differences, i.e. doing intercultural research (cf. Honold, 1999) to obtain relevant knowledge for internationalization of software and system platforms (Table 1).

Hence, "intercultural variables" are referred to in cases where the intercultural research character for obtaining the values of the variables is meant and "cultural variables" are denoted, when mainly the usage of the values of the variables themselves (concerning a specific culture) is important (cf. also P. Honold, 2000). However,

Table 1. Intercultural variables according to Röse 2002: 97 et. seqq. (estimated values regarding the difficulty to recognize the variables are added by the author)

Intercultural Variable	Level of Localization	Relation to HCI Design	Perceivability of the Variables	Estimated Difficulty to Recognize [0 (Easy) – 10 (Difficult)]
Dialog design	Interaction	Direct	Hidden/Over long time and deep analysis	10
Interaction design	Interaction	Direct	Hidden/Over long time and deep analysis	9
System functionality	Function	Indirect	Visible/Immediately	8
Service (Maintenance)	Function	Indirect	Visible/Immediately	7
Technical documentation	Function	Indirect	Visible/Immediately	6
Information presentation	Surface	Direct	Visible/Immediately	4
Language	Surface	Direct	Visible/Immediately	2
General system design	Surface	Indirect	Visible/Immediately	0

they can also be called simply "cultural" variables, because the values of those variables represent knowledge for a specific culture (relevant for system and software localization, cf. Windl & Heimgärtner, 2013). There are "direct" and "indirect" cultural variables affecting HCI parameters either directly (e.g., interaction, information presentation or language) or indirectly (e.g., via maintenance, documentation or technical surroundings). Direct cultural variables are the most important, because they have direct and essential influence on the design of HCI. According to Kerstin Röse, 2002, direct variables can be divided into "visible" variables concerning surface levels and "hidden" variables affecting interaction levels, together mirroring the concept of the iceberg metaphor. Both kinds of variables have strong influences on the design and determination of the usability and acceptance of the system. Visible intercultural variables concern presentation (colors, time and date format, icons, font size, window size, form, layout, widget position like the position of navigation bar) and language (font, direction of writing, naming) level of a product (appearing above "water surface" in the iceberg metaphor). They can be recognized very easily because they are directly accessible and less determined by cultural context. Non-visible or "hidden" intercultural variables (below the "water surface") affect dialog design (menu structure and complexity, changing of dialog form, layout, widget positions, information presentation speed, frequency of changing dialogs, screen transitions) and interaction design (navigation concept, system structure, interaction path, interaction speed, usage of navigation bar, etc.) which have strong correlations to the cultural context. These variables concern the interaction and dialog level of a product and need high research priority. Kerstin Röse, 2002: 108 used these cultural variables to develop an approach for the design of intercultural human-machine systems using the "method of culture-oriented design" (MCD) (Figure 2).

The MCD integrates factors from established concepts of culture-oriented design into existing concepts of HCI design. Thereby, knowledge about cultural differences is integrated into existing methods.

User Interface Characteristics

To make cultural dimensions available for user interface design, A. Marcus, 2001 developed characteristic factors for user interfaces and gives

Figure 2. Simplified version of the Method of Culture-oriented Design (MCD) (Source: Rüdiger Heimgärtner, 2012: 66)

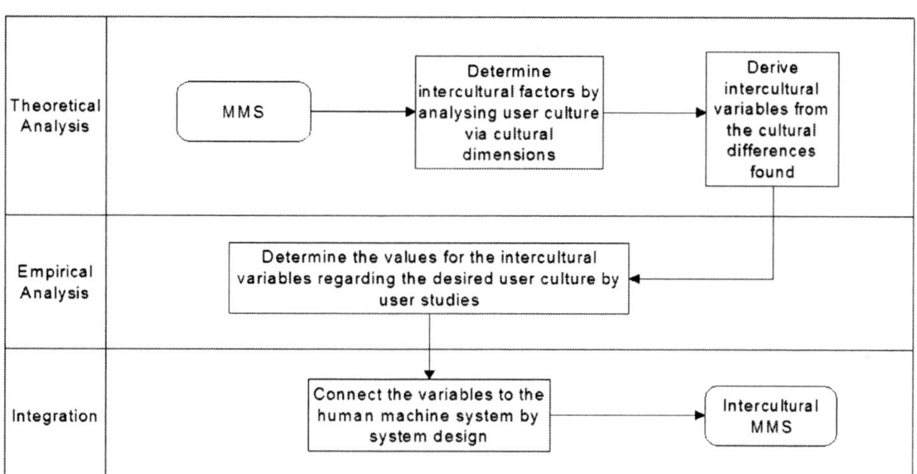

examples that can have an effect on user interface design. The user interface characteristics 'metaphor', 'mental model', 'navigation', 'interaction' and 'presentation' are connected to the cultural dimensions of Hofstede.[2] Marcus used a deductive approach to obtain these connections: many possible recommendations for web design have been derived by A. Marcus & Gould, 2000 mainly from Hofstede's knowledge without empirical foundation of all the connections. Therefore, this formulated model still needs empirical validation (even if, meanwhile, there is some empirical work from Marcus himself, cf. Aaron Marcus, 2006). According to A. Marcus, 2001 and K. Röse, Zühlke, & Liu, 2001, Chinese people (and hence users) are rather relationship and family oriented based on traditional powerful social hierarchical structures. In contrast, German users are described as event oriented regarding acts, tools, work, jobs and competition. Some tendencies regarding cultural differences can be used for the intercultural user interface design and further reflections and research. Table 2 shows a summary of general recommendations for intercultural user interface design based on K. Röse, 2002.

HCI Dimensions

Based on the work of Schlögl, 2005, G. H. Hofstede et al., 2010, Edward T Hall & Hall, 2004 and own studies, the author introduced the concept of HCI dimensions (following the concept of cultural dimensions) in order to support the determination of the relationship between culture and HCI (cf. Rüdiger Heimgärtner, 2007 and Heimgärtner, 2012). HCI dimensions (HCIDs) describe the "style of information processing" and the "interactional characteristics" of the user with the system. HCIDs are derived from the basic physical dimensions of space and time as well as from their sub-dimensions frequency, speed, duration; density and order (Table 3). HCIDs represent the characteristics of HCI by describing the HCI style of the user, i.e. the path of information processing and the interaction style exhibited by the user based on the concepts of "information" and "interaction" according to HCI dialogs that are characterized by transmitting pieces of information during user system interaction (cf. Bernsen, Dybkjær, & Dybkjær, 1998 and Jacko, 2007).

Table 2. Summary of recommendations for intercultural HCI design according to the user interface characteristics regarding China and Germany (summarized by the author in accordance to table 6-3 in Kerstin Röse, 2002: 138 as well as to Kerstin Röse, 2002: 305-317)

User Interface Characteristics	China	Germany
Metaphor	Use clear hierarchy and representation instead of abstraction	Use representation instead of abstraction
Mental model	Use many references without sequence of relevance, simple mental models, clear articulation, limited choice and binary logic	Use few references with sequence of relevance and fuzzy logic
Navigation	Use limited and predefined choice and navigation	Use open access and arbitrary choice and unique navigation
Interaction	Use personalized but team-oriented systems giving direct error messages, guided help and providing face-to-face interaction	Use distant but supportive (error) messages providing open and flexible interaction with the system (e.g., full text search)
Presentation	Use formal speech providing high contextual relationship-oriented information as well as feminine colors	Use informal speech providing low contextual task-oriented information as well as masculine colors

Table 3. HCI dimensions

Derived Physical Sub-dimensions [Basic Physical Dimension]	Information Related HCI Dimension	Interaction Related HCI Dimension
Frequency [Time]	Information frequency	Interaction frequency
Speed [Time]	Information speed	Interaction speed
Sequentiality / Priority / Order [Time and Space]	Information order / Information parallelism	Interaction order / Interaction parallelism
Density / Quantity [Time and Space] / Context [Time and Space]	Information density	

Frequency, density, order and structure are concerned particularly during information processing; frequency and speed are concerned during interaction behavior. HCI dimensions can be regarded as the main factors relevant for HCI design, because they denote the basic classes for variables useful in HCI design. The view of space, time and mental aspects is strongly culture dependent (cf. E. T. Hall, 1959). HCI is, therefore, also culture dependent, because HCI dialogs, interaction and information presentation and are strongly linked with time (interaction, communication) and space (layout, structure) as well as with mental aspects (relations, thoughts) (cf. Preim & Dachselt, 2010, Pia Honold, 2000b, Kerstin Röse, 2002). At least one potential indicator as a measurement variable is necessary to constitute the specifics of an HCI dimension. Table 4 shows examples of indicators for some HCI dimensions.

For example, the indicator "number of information units per space unit" belongs to the HCI dimension "information density" and can be expressed by the number of words displayed on the screen. The HCI dimension "interaction frequency" contains the variable "number of interactions per time unit" represented by the number of mouse clicks per second.

Table 4. HCI dimensions represented by specifics and indicators

HCI Dimension	Specifics	Indicator(s)
Interaction frequency	Number of interactions per time unit	Mouse clicks and mouse moves per second or per session
Information density	Number of information units per space unit	Number of words per message or on the display
Information / Interaction parallelism / order	Sequence of appearance of information units	Number and sequence of dialog steps (e.g. number of message boxes used to indicate one system error)

Semiotic Engineering

Semotic engineering of user interface languages was suggested by De Souza, 1993 as well as approach to HCI by De Souza, Barbosa, & Prates, 2001. Since then, the group of De Souza worked on this approach to make it useful for HCI design and suggested 2012 metaphors for guiding the design of cross-cultural interactive systems. Salgado, Leito, & Souza, 2012 considering semiotic engineering as relevant and promising framework in the intercultural field (cf. Salgado et al., 2012) as well as valuable approach to intercultural HCI (interface) design, because it can be combined with culture and HCI to take into account cultural aspects in HCI design (cf. Castro Salgado, Leitão, & Souza, 2013). In semiotic engineering, HCI is seen "as a two-tiered communicative process: one is the designer-to-user communication and the other is the user-system interaction. [..] HCI can only be achieved if both levels of communication are successfully achieved." (De Souza et al., 2001: 55). Prates, Souza, & Barbosa, 2000 developed the communicability evaluation method taking into account "that interactive systems are metacommunication artifacts, by telling designers, in a number of ways, how well their message is getting across." (De Souza et al., 2001: 56). The semiotic engineering approach complements cognitive and social theories useful for HCI design by providing new perceptions on the process and product of HCI design.

Usability Engineering

The usability of a system strongly depends on how the user can use the system. This knowledge can be obtained "simply" by observing and asking the user during his interactions with the system using methods such as "think aloud protocol" (cf. Clayton Lewis) and "protocol analysis" (cf. Ericsson & Simon). In this case the user articulates his desires and hence his needs regarding the usability of the system. This is trivial and easy, but unfortunately, this method is applied far too little in industrial HCI design even today. This is critical because, if that knowledge is missing in the final product, it is not wanted: the end-user cannot use it because important features are missing or it takes too long to do a certain task using this system because of wrong design. Probably, this is also, because these trivial and easy methods are criticized as too trivial (cf. Goguen & Linde, 1993), which led to develop more elaborated and adapted methods usable for the cultural context.

"Intercultural" usability engineering is a method for designing products of good usability for users from different cultures (Pia Honold, 2000b). The term "intercultural usability engineering" is commonly used by German usability engineers (cf. Detlef Zühlke, 2004). "Intercultural" in this context refers to the special methods that are necessary to do usability engineering for different cultures (cf. Honold, 1999). Bad or lacking intercultural usability engineering within the development process of the product increases the development and maintenance costs through requests for change. Detailed analysis of product requirements can save up to 80% of maintenance and implementation costs of such requests for change (cf. Mutschler & Reichert, 2004). Therefore, intercultural HCI design must already begin with the analysis of requirements before starting the design. The work of Pia Honold, 2000b deals with the question of whether there is a reduction of the fit between user and product if products of one culture are used in another. At the collection of culture specific user requirements and culture specific assessment of the concepts used, it must be determined how far approved methods of usability engineering are suitable. The existing cultural models should be taken into account in the process of product design in the context of intercultural usability engineering. First, the product developers must be sensitized to the difficulties of cultural influences on product development and product use. Then cultural factors influencing HCI must be provided to the developers and integrated into the product. Finally, the procedures, which serve to capture the knowledge acquired in concrete product design, must be institutionalized.

The preconditions for *intercultural* usability engineering are knowledge about the cultural differences in HCI and its considerations in product design and product realization (Pia Honold, 2000b; Kerstin Röse, 2002; Rüdiger Heimgärtner, 2005b). In addition to the common misunderstandings between developers and users, which lead to different product design, there are also misunderstandings because of cultural conditions. There is not only a different comprehension of the requirements of the product but also culturally dependent perspectives and views of them (cf. Jensen & Bjørn, 2012). Hence, the developer needs much intercultural knowledge to understand a user from another culture. Furthermore, he needs competency regarding intercultural communication to enable the exchange of information with the user and to know exactly which product the user is likely to have (cf. Honold, 1999). With this in mind Pia Honold, 2000a presented an empirical study for the development of a framework for the elicitation of cultural influence in product usage to take into account culture and context in HCI design.

After the pioneer research of Pia Honold, 2000b, several researchers have invested a great deal of effort to determine the best methods and settings to test the usability and user experience in cultural contexts. For instance, Clemmensen & Goyal, 2004 studied cross cultural think-aloud usability testing to make some suggestions for an experimental paradigm. Clemmensen et al., 2007 investigated usability constructs by doing a cross-cultural study of how users and developers experience their use of the information system. Clemmensen, 2010 discovered what is part of usability testing in three countries. Moreover, Clemmensen conferred with Apala Chavan, Anirudha Joshi, Dinesh Katre, Devashish Pandya, Sammeer Chabukswar and Pradeep Yammiyavar to describe interaction design and usability from an Indian perspective (cf. Clemmensen, 2008). Yammiyavar, 2008 investigated the influence of cultural background on non-verbal communication in a usability testing situation. Simon, 2000 investigated the impact of culture and gender on web sites. Shah, Nersessian, Harrold, & Newstetter, 2012 studied the influence of culture in global software engineering by thinking in terms of cultural models. Dasgupta & Gupta, 2010 did an empirical study concerning the organizational, cultural and technological use in a developing country. Paterson, Winschiers-Theophilus, Dunne, Schinzel, & Underhill, 2011 interpreted cross-cultural usability evaluation based on a case study of a hypermedia system for rare species management in Namibia. Bidwell, 2011b investigated situating media in the transfer of rural knowledge in Africa to enfranchise indigenous rural peoples. Röbig, Didier, & Bruder, 2010 published the results of the workshop on the international comprehension of usability the application of usability methods.

Research Directions, Related Work and Empirical Studies

The number of studies supporting the importance of taking cultural aspects into account in user interface design has been growing steadily since about 2000 (e.g., V. Evers, 2003; Smith & Chang, 2003).[3] Most studies concern the presentation of information on web pages (e.g., Hodemacher, Jarman, & Mandl, 2005, Aaron Marcus, 2003, Dormann & Chisalita, 2002, Baumgartner, 2003, A. Marcus & Gould, 2000, Stengers, Troyer, Baetens, Boers, & Mushtaha, 2004, H. Sun, 2001 and Callahan, 2005). There are already the first pragmatic guidelines for intercultural web design (cf. A. Marcus & Gould, 2000) or intercultural HCI design (cf. Kerstin Röse, 2001).[4] This is also supported by the overview of Sturm & Mueller, 2003 as well as Fitzgerald, 2004 presenting many activities and models for intercultural website design. As stated in the overview of Thissen regarding intercultural information design (cf. Thissen, 2008), it seems there are just few insights regarding intercultural interactive design beyond those presented in this work (cf. section "models and theories") – even if, for a short time, there have also been studies examining stand-alone systems and applications other than web applications (Kralisch, 2006, Kamentz, 2006, Lewandowitz, Rößger, & Vöhringer-Kuhnt, 2006, Braun, Röse, & Rößger, 2007). In addition, Kerstin Röse, 2002 and D. Zühlke & Röse, 2000 also explicitly mention intercultural HCI design as well as the design of global products for the Chinese market.

The cultural influences on the values of visible cultural variables of HCI is proven empirically in the literature on internationalization and partly implemented in products (cf. Nielsen, 1990, Vanessa Evers & Day, 1997) regarding surface level (presentation of information, speech and general design of machine) and functional level (machine functions, service and technical documentation) of localization. Most of these studies concentrate on "visible" cultural variables such as colors (NASA standard for colors (Currie & Peacock, 2002 or Ou, Luo, Woodcock, & Wright, 2004)), icons (use of pictorial or abstract icons (Kerstin Röse, 2002: 135)), date and time, phone numbers and address formats, spelling, typography, reading and writing directions, sorting methods (Shneiderman, Plaisant, Cohen, & Jacobs, 2009: 23-24), extension of texts, text processing, number of characters (Rätzmann, 2004: 77) and multimedia (cf. Krömker, 2000). Isa, Noor, & Mehad, 2009 contrasted cultural prescription and user perception of information architecture for a culture centered website by doing a case study on Muslim online users. Tateishi & Toma, 2010 asked why social media can cross seas but not nationalisms while doing a cross-cultural comparative study of user interface in social media. Endrass, Rehm, André, & Nakano, 2008 confirmed the proverb "talk is silver, silence is golden" in some cultural context by doing a cross cultural study on the usage of pauses in speech. Koda, Rehm, & Andre, 2008 did a cross-cultural evaluation of the facial expressions of avatars designed by Western designers. K.-P. Lee, 2007 investigated culture and its effects on human interaction design with emphasis on cross-cultural perspectives between Korea and Japan. Kankanhalli, Tan, Wei, & Holmes, 2004 concentrated on cross-cultural differences and information systems developer values.

In sum, in the area of intercultural HCI design there is much research regarding the design of cross-cultural web pages and research of international product design (cf. international workshops of internationalization of products and systems (IWIPS)) as well as many guidelines regarding the visible areas of graphic user interfaces for the internationalization and localization of software.

In contrast, some cultural variables have not been thoroughly investigated so far. Study of the literature does not reveal much about research on hidden intercultural variables at the interactional level. Cultural influence on HCI at the interactional level, for example with respect to navigation, system structure and mental models or varying functionality has not yet been investigated in detail to develop optimal products for the specific culture. In addition, there is still little literature about the connection between visible cultural aspects and hidden intercultural variables for HCI design.

Komlodi, 2005 investigated the cultural differences in the information seeking process. Guidelines are available on building IT architecture (cf. Koning, Dormann, & van Vliet, 2002). Nisbett, 2003 proposed that the thought patterns of East Asians and Westerners differ greatly (holistic vs. analytic). Holistically minded people have a tendency to perceive a scene globally considering the context; they are more field-dependent. Analytically minded people are more field-independent because they have a tendency to perceive an object separately from the scene and tend to assign objects to categories due to their narrow focus and ability to screen (cf. Witkin, Moore, Goodenough, & Cox, 1977). Y. Dong, & Lee, K., 2008 studied the relationship between cognitive styles and webpage perception and presented the culturally different behavior of eye movement. The different viewing patterns of Chinese, Korean and American people suggest that webpage designers should be aware of the cognitive differences existing among holistically minded people and analytically minded people, and that web pages should be designed to match the users' cognitive styles in order to enhance usability. Holistically minded people (e.g., Chinese people) scan the entire page non-linearly. Hence, the design of content should show the whole context of the website and the harmony between the foreground and background as well as the relationship among all the content areas. In contrast, the webpage design should be as clear and simple as possible for analytically minded people (e.g, German people). They tend to employ a sequential reading pattern among areas and to read from the center to the periphery of the page. Hence, the arrangement of all content areas must be considered carefully. Category titles and navigation items should be named as clearly as possible since analytically minded people tend to pay more attention to these items and gain an overall picture of the website from them. Y. Dong, & Lee, K., 2008 also intended to define the relationship between cognitive styles and webpage layout design. This indicates once more that most intercultural studies concentrate on examining web pages. I. Lee et al., 2008 investigated cultural dimensions for user experience doing a cross-country and cross-product analysis of users' cultural characteristics. Y. Lee, 2002 did a cross-cultural study on how users and developers experience their use of information systems and found differences in mobile Internet usage between users from Japan (e.g., high email traffic) and Korea (e.g., many downloads) depending on different value structures in Japan and Korea imprinted by culture. V. Evers, Kukulska-Hulme, & Jones, 1999 examined cultural differences in the understanding of metaphors applied in user interfaces. Since the real world changes from culture to culture, the metaphors referring to the real world that are used in HCI must also be considered for the localization of user interfaces. Examination has shown that test subjects from different cultures understand metaphors differently and their expectations, which they combine with the metaphors, are also different (cf. V. Evers et al., 1999). Moreover, an explorative study with French and Turkish users on an e-learning site by Rızvanoğlu & Öztürk, 2009 improved the cross-cultural understanding of the dual structure of metaphorical icons. Rüdiger Heimgärtner, 2012 investigated hidden cultural variables in HCI design such as information speed, information frequency, and interaction speed and interaction frequency.

However, all these issues can still be regarded as an open field for research in intercultural HCI design because there is still little empirical evidence for the results in this area. Hence, much effort must still be invested to investigate and consider hidden cultural variables in intercultural HCI design. Rüdiger Heimgärtner, 2007 showed that there are cultural differences in HCI concerning information presentation and interaction style. Detailed analysis of HCI dimensions in the cultural context has been done by Rüdiger Heimgärtner, 2012. However, interesting questions are not or only partly answered until now. How do different cultures interfere and affect the navigation within applications? Are there significant improvements when comparing an application without taking into account intercultural differences with the adapted version of the application? Can users from different cultures/regions have different experiences when interacting with applications from different cultures? Such questions must be answered by research to get useful hints for designers and developers of user interfaces in the cultural context. Some of the questions are already answered (cf. e.g. Rößger, 2003, Vöhringer-Kuhnt, 2002, Olaverri-Monreal, Draxler, & Bengler, 2011), but most of them are still open.

Models and Theories

Hoft, 1996 developed a cultural model (iceberg metaphor) relevant for international user interface design. A. G. Marcus, E. W., 2000 related user interface characteristics to Hofstede's cultural dimensions (as indicated above). Shi & Clemmensen, 2007 generated a relationship model in cultural usability testing. Kappos & Rivard, 2008 postulated a three-perspective model of culture, information systems and their development and use. Other authors based their approach on cultural models to study the relationship between culture and HCI. Shah et al., 2012 studied the influences of culture in global software engineering by thinking in terms of cultural models.

For instance, based on the results of Rüdiger Heimgärtner, 2012, the author formulated reflections on a preliminary model of culturally influenced human-computer interaction (HCI) to cover cultural contexts in HCI design which encompass the relationships between cultural and HCI dimensions. According to the results of an empirical study done by the author (cf. Rüdiger Heimgärtner, 2007), some of the correlations between the cultural dimensions and the HCI dimensions as well as their values were determined (cf. R. Heimgärtner, 2010) leading to the concept of HCI style scores, which can be computed for the designated cultural group from the Hofstede's indices. The HCI style score expresses the average degree of information density and frequency as well as interaction frequency and speed the members in the designated cultural group expect according to the model developed by the author (cf. Rüdiger Heimgärtner, 2013). For instance, the lower the normalized HCI style score (ranging from 0 to 100) the lower the expected amount of information and the lower the interaction frequency. The resulting HCI style scores permit the establishment of clusters of countries that have similar HCI scores. According to these cultural clusters identified in the HCI style score continuum it can be expected that the country clusters exhibit a similar HCI style because of their similar cultural characterization defined by power distance index (PDI), individualism index (IDV), masculinity (MAS), uncertainty avoidance index (UAI) and long term orientation (LTO) (Table 5).[5]

These taxonomic results partially resembles the findings of Galtung, 1981 on "Saxonic","Teutonic", "Gallic" and "Nipponic" styles. However, to generalize the postulated correlations many more studies with other cultural groups are required. To achieve this both the values of the cultural dimensions using Hofstedes value survey module (VSM) and the values of the HCI dimensions (such as pieces of presented information per minute, cf. Rüdiger Heimgärtner, 2012) must be determined for every desired culture / region. This can be done for indigenous groups as well by exploiting the same use cases and test settings in the arbitrary cultural groups of interest. A test tool developed by the author can be used to support this (cf. Rüdiger Heimgärtner, 2008). However, until there are no other values for the cultural dimensions than Hofstede's at the national level, those must be used to test

Table 5. HCI styles around the world

HCI Style	Cultural Characterization	Normalized HCI Style Score (Group Averaged)
Asian	PDI high, IDV low, MAS middle, UAI low, LTO high	90
Indian	PDI high, IDV middle, MAS middle, UAI middle, LTO middle	70
African	PDI high, IDV low, MAS middle, UAI middle, LTO low	60
Scandinavian	PDI low, IDV high, MAS low, UAI middle, LTO low	40
Slavic	PDI high, IDV middle, MAS middle, UAI high, LTO low	30
Angle-Saxon	PDI low, IDV high, MAS middle, UAI low, LTO low	20
German	PDI low, IDV middle, MAS high, UAI middle, LTO low	10

the model. In addition, to further confirm findings, factor analysis can be applied to statistically calculate the corresponding loadings to the HCI style by clustering Hofstede's indices according to their HCI style score. The findings should refine the currently assumed rules that describe the relationship between cultural imprint and HCI style of a group (with at least 20 members). The explanatory value of this descriptive model still must be worked out.

In addition to this model, there are several other approaches towards a theory of culturally influenced human computer interaction. Martinsons & Westwood, 1997 developed an explanatory theory for using management information systems in the Chinese business culture. Vatrapu outlined a theory of socio-technical interactions to explain culture. Wyer, Chiu, & Hong, 2009 integrated theory, research and application to understand culture. Faiola, 2006 worked towards a HCI theory of cultural cognition. Clemmensen, 2009 compared Cultural Models of Use (CM-U) theory with Artifact Development Analysis (ADA) theory to derive a theory for cultural usability. Using activity theory to tackle cultural contexts is very prominent (cf. Nardi, 1996, Kaptelinin, 2006, L. Constantine, 2009). E. Maier, 2005 applied activity theory as a framework for accommodating cultural factors in HCI studies. L. Constantine, 2009 integrated activity theory into a usage-centered design approach to cover environmental contexts. Windl & Heimgärtner, 2013 are working to extend this systematic usage-centered design approach to also cover cultural contexts by subjoining cultural models as new components. However, until now, there is no final theory that would explain all relevant factors necessary to derive design recommendations for culture-centered HCI design. This still remains a task for the future.

Processes, Standards and Tools

Bevan, 2001 described international standards for HCI and usability. The standard ISO 9241-171 can be used to integrate cultural aspects in intercultural HCI design processes. Rüdiger Heimgärtner, 2008 developed the intercultural interaction analysis tool (IIA tool) to determine the cultural differences in HCI at interaction level. Gould & Marcus, 2011 suggested a company culture audit to improve development team's collaboration, communication and cooperation. The working team "quality standards" of the German UPA (usability professionals association) carved out a usability engineering process that can be taken as a basis to be extended by the necessary roles, tasks, methods, documents and work products, which are necessary to take cultural aspects into account and to fit them into any cultural contexts.

Jagne & Smith-Atakan, 2006 developed a cross-cultural interface design strategy with four phases:

- **Investigation:** Determination of user behavior, identification of social and cultural factors and assessment of different indigenous user attitudes.
- **Translation:** Generation of a consistent cultural model based on the output of the investigation phase to identify and illuminate similarities and differences of the user groups.
- **Implementation:** Utilization of the cultural model to create internationalized/localized prototypes to perform usability tests with indigenous user groups.
- **Evaluation:** Analyzing results, optimizing the prototype using iterative loops in order to reach the final product.

Jagne & Smith-Atakan, 2006 emphasized the insights from V. Evers et al., 1999, Fernandes, 1995 and P. Honold, 2000 as vital and based their work on them along others such as Del Galdo & Nielsen, 1996, G. H. Hofstede et al., 2010, A. G. Marcus, E. W., 2000, Nielsen, 2006a, H. Sun, 2001, Trompenaars & Hampden-Turner, 2012, Yeo, 2001 and Zahedi & Bansal, 2011 and, in fact, their approach resembles the MCD-approach of Kerstin Röse, 2002. The simplified version of the culture-centered HCI design process developed by Shen et al., 2006 is partly similar to the standard user-centered HCI design process defined in ISO 9241-210 (cf. DIN, 2010) as well as in the emerging standard ISO 9241-220. However, the process by Shen et al., 2006 is focusing on social and cultural aspects. Within this process, Shen et al., 2006 focuses on culture-centered interface metaphors (e.g., V. Evers, 1998) as well as on iterative analysis taking into account Nielsen's usability engineering lifecycle model, Apple computer HCI guidelines as well as guidelines from ISO and W3C in order to cover the value of the user's cultural context.

PROBLEMS AND CONTROVERSIES

Methodological Challenges

According to E. T. Hall, 1976, the methodological problem in studying culture is that the transmission of simple systems is easier than the integration of complex systems, which can only be achieved by human creativity. This applies primarily to cultural questions, which encompass and integrate the complete context of a member of a culture. This problem also confronts intercultural user interface design, which makes it compellingly necessary to deal with the combination or linkage of culture with HCI design. Therefore, along with the common issues and challenges in HCI and in HCI design (cf. Chen, 2001, Reiterer, 2008) and in the usability engineering process (cf. Andreas Holzinger, 2005), problems also arise because they all must function in a cultural context (cf. P. Honold, 2000, Rüdiger Heimgärtner, Tiede, & Windl, 2011, Clemmensen, 2012 or Hertzum & Clemmensen, 2012). Rehm, Bee, Endrass, Wissner, & André, 2007 investigated the problems in adapting HCI to the cultural background of the user. Many aspects have to be taken into account simultaneously to obtain possible cultural explanations for their effect on HCI. Alternatively, the effects of culture on HCI cannot be explained by only one single aspect but by many different influences due to the complexity of culture. Another problem in cultural research is that one cannot predict how the single parts of the cultural puzzle will fit together (cf. E. T. Hall, 1976: 130). This has implications for the use of the appropriate methods in intercultural HCI design and intercultural usability engineering (cf. Janni Nielsen).

Different Approaches

Different approaches exist for determining intercultural variables and their values. For instance, cultural dimensions arise from cultural studies that can yield insight into the diversity of cultures. From cultural dimensions, intercultural factors for HCI design can be derived. The results thus acquired are supported argumentatively and deductively (cf. A. Marcus & Gould, 2000: 5 et seq.). Cyr & Trevor-Smith, 2004 state that the connection between cultural dimensions and HCI design has not yet been studied in depth. Either detailed empirical studies must follow or the results can only serve as exemplifications, but not as a scientific foundation for further research.

The complement to this deductive approach is the inductive approach: Cultural markers have been determined by empirical studies (e.g., A. Badre & Barber, 1998, Dormann, 2006, H. Sun, 2001), which are specific for a certain culture and which are preferably used within this certain culture. A. Badre & Barber, 1998 showed the direct influence of cultural markers on the performance of users interacting with the system and hence the connection between culture and usability (e.g., confirmed by the studies of H. Sun, 2001 or Vöhringer-Kuhnt, 2002). However, the results from these empirical studies often cannot be generalized because the sample sizes are too small and/or the limited representativeness of the test persons precludes statistical results of high quality.

This is one reason why there are just a few evident qualitative empirical studies and even fewer purely quantitative studies (cf. Smith, Dunckley, French, Minocha, & Chang, 2004 as well as Edith Maier, Mandl, Röse, Womser-Hacker, & Yetim, 2005, Rüdiger Heimgärtner, 2012) which treat the interaction of culturally different imprinted users with the system.

Missing Empirical Confirmation

Not all recommendations have yet been proved empirically according to the five postulated areas of user interface characteristics, even if there is some research in this area. Röse validated some of the aspects pointed out by Marcus by doing qualitative studies in China regarding different layouts for Chinese and German users (cf. K. Röse et al., 2001). Moreover, regarding metaphors, hierarchical taxonomies and classifying instruments are applied rather more in China than is the case in Germany because of the high power distance index in China compared to Germany (cf. G. H. Hofstede et al., 2010). Hence, most of the recommendations presented must be tested and confirmed empirically in detail by additional studies before being suggested as best practices or even useful guidelines, if not already done so. Furthermore, parallel to the research literature, empirical investigations regarding intercultural user interface characteristics are necessary, more specifically by comparing several systems of different cultures (benchmark tests) as well as usability evaluations (usability testing) to determine the usability of different systems.

High Research Effort

Hidden variables are difficult to identify because they are only recognizable over time. Therefore, the reason for the lack of results regarding direct hidden intercultural variables at the interaction level is also grounded in the difficulty of accessing and measuring them. To work against these methodological difficulties in studying hidden variables, it is reasonable, to a certain degree, to regard interaction and dialog design separately. First, the cultural differences in the interaction between a user and a system must be investigated, and then, how the interaction affects information flow between the user and the system must be considered. Finally, how dialog windows should be designed for culturally different users also needs investigation, which, in the end, should lead to preliminary design recommendations.

Usage of Cultural Dimensions

On the one hand, critics of Hofstede claim that the samples drawn from IBM's worldwide employee interview in their original study of 1967-72 are not representative. They do not provide data for actually measuring national culture differences between the countries but rather the differences within the corporate culture of IBM. Furthermore, Hofstede's approach ignores differences within a nation. The model treats a nation like a homogeneous collection of individuals who share the same structure of values. According to House & Aditya, 1997 and House, 2004, this is not correct in most cases. Moreover, some studies show inconsistencies in the values of Hofstede as presented by Komischke, McGee, Wang, & Wissmann, 2003: Power distance index (PDI) values for Japan, China and USA differ from those found by Hofstede. Furthermore, Komischke et al., 2003 pointed out that although much is said about what should be taken into account culturally, little empirical research is available on this topic. In addition, different behavior does not necessarily mean a different cultural (propositional) attitude, i.e. a different cognitive state in the web of belief. According to Rathje, 2003, restricted appreciation and mediation of cultural dimensions and models can lead to ineffective or even restricting action strategies. In this case, a little cultural understanding proves to be just as bad as, or even worse, than no cultural understanding at all. Therefore, Rathje, 2003 pleads for dimension independent cultural models because they make the derivation of concrete behavior patterns possible whose explanations are founded on concrete manifestations of the culture described in contrast to models that use cultural dimensions (cf. also Irani & th Annual Chi Conference on Human Factors in Computing Systems, 2010).[6]

On the other hand, supporters of Hofstede's theory reject these moves away from Hofstede because numerous independent repetition studies in subsequent years confirmed Hofstede's results. Moreover, Hofstede's results referred to different subgroups of the respective populations and nevertheless showed similar national differences, which agreed with Hofstede's dimension values. Furthermore, Hofstede points particularly to the different levels of culture whilst distancing himself from the list of questions (VSM) which was included with his explanations and designed for further use by the readers. According to G. Hofstede, 2006 this is also because one of the consequences of his research and its results (and a starting point for criticism) is the "not reflected" appropriation and assignment of his cultural model which is seen as a useful tool for research (cf. Bryan, McLean, Smits, & Burn, 1994) and a useful starting point to study user interfaces in the cultural context (especially if a well founded theory is the designated goal of the research). In my view, the benefit of Hofstedes approach is that it provides a quantitative characterization of cultural groups with more than 20 members (if the questions of the value survey module of Hofstede can be answered reasonably, cf. G. Hofstede, 1994 and G. Hofstede, Hofstede, Minkov, & Vinken, 2008). Thus, many culturally different end-user groups can be reached.

FUTURE RESEARCH DIRECTIONS

Research in intercultural HCI design is young and therefore there are just a few reliable recommendations or guidelines for intercultural user interface design that can be taken into account. Much research remains to reach a breakthrough. It is important to foster research in this area. Nevertheless, good solutions seem to be waiting in the wings and epoch making solutions can be expected. One expected solution is to develop a tool capable of automatically accessing applications concerning cultural guidelines. A first step in this direction has been done with the development of the intercultural interaction analysis (IIA) tool (cf. Rüdiger Heimgärtner, 2008) to determine cultural differences in the HCI on the dialog, information and interaction level. Combined with the tool "Reviser" for automatic determination of the usability of an application (cf. Hamacher, 2006), the IIA tool could be an approach to automatically derive recommendations for intercultural user interface design that can be used by the developers to create intercultural user interfaces.

The trend in research on culture and HCI is to verify preliminary models and theories by doing extensive empirical studies in various cultural contexts. Furthermore, the relationship between culture and HCI design must subsequently be elaborated upon in detail (cf. Rüdiger Heimgärtner, 2012). The focus of investigating cultural differences will shift from the national level to a regional level and even to any other situation to cover all cultural contexts. Thereby, methods, models and theories will be adapted and improved upon in the near future by taking the results from many empirical studies into account to derive and optimize processes for intercultural HCI design and intercultural usability engineering and thereby to establish international norms and to develop tools that finally augment the international standards of research covering user interface design in arbitrary (cultural) contexts.

At the moment, the relative differences in the expectations of UI designer and UI users reflecting their different cultural needs can be computed using cultural HCI scores (cf. Rüdiger Heimgärtner, 2013) to derive cultural design rules concerning colors, layout, and information presentation as well as interaction stlye. This could be very useful if implemented in mobile devices for daily usage by HCI designers, developers and managers. In addition, personalization and adaptation to the different user needs is necessary: "[..] Internet strategies should be localized or adjusted to unique cultures, since people want different values even from the same services across different cultures. [..] Mobile Internet services need to be personalized to individual users because value structures and usage patterns are influenced by various factors across countries. To develop personalized services, mobile Internet service providers need to segment user groups by cultural, demographical, or socio-economic factors and monitor them, which may enable them to chase users' fast changing needs or values efficiently." (Y. Lee, 2002: 237). User experience must also be taken into account (cf. Clemmensen & Clemmensen, 2012), which extends the research area to the experiences of the user during the whole product life cycle (including, e.g., also hedonic quality, cf. Hassenzahl & Tractinsky, 2006).

For successful (intercultural) user interface design and (intercultural) usability engineering it is necessary that the developer understands the user (cf. Nielsen, 2006b), because they have different points of view (cf. Eigenbrode et al., 2007). Only by taking the perspective of a user by the HCI designer into account in order to grasp their needs depending on their world view, general knowledge, context and purpose of usage can good user interfaces demonstrating high usability be achieved (cf. Paterson et al., 2011, Clemmensen, 2012). Excellent user experience design should be the ultimate goal (cf. Rüdiger Heimgärtner et al., 2011, Maguire, 2011, Biesterfeldt & Capra, 2011, Gould & Marcus, 2011). However, problems in intercultural communication ensuring empathic access to the user requirements inhibit good usability for system design and the related user experience (cf. E. T. Hall, 1959, Rüdiger Heimgärtner et al., 2011, LIU, WANG, YU, & WANG, 2009). This is because people and groups are shaped by many cultural systems, including religion, language and training as well as gender and life experience (cf. A. Marcus, 2001, Clemmensen & Clemmensen, 2010) representing a certain "culture", i.e. being a member of a group representing the same cultural characteristics.

"Reframing" HCI means to take cultural aspects into account in HCI design at the local level (cultural context/ indigeniously) in addition to the national level. For the last years the research and literature accounting for cultural contexts in Human Computer Interaction (HCI) design have grown quickly (Shen et al., 2006, Plocher et al., 2012). In addition, until recently, culture in HCI was considered a matter of internationalization or localization (cf. Clemmensen, 2009). As stated in Clemmensen, 2009, as computer use spreads around the world, these traditional approaches to culture and HCI have proven to be seriously insufficient approaches (cf. Bidwell, 2011b, Irani & th Annual Chi Conference on Human Factors in Computing Systems, 2010, Dourish & Mainwaring, 2012). According to Pia Honold, 2000b and Kerstin Röse, 2002, successful intercultural HCI design goes far beyond a regular design process by taking into account different mentalities, thought patterns and problem solving strategies that are anchored in culture. Usage patterns differ from culture to culture according to different power structures (cf. G. H. Hofstede et al., 2010), for example flat vs. hierarchical ones or problem solving strategies being linear vs. non-linear (cf. K. Röse et al., 2001, Pia Honold, 2000b). Hence, the designer must know exactly what the user needs or wants (e.g. why and in which context, cf. A. Holzinger, 2005). In addition, local designers must adapt general HCI methods to their needs (cf. Clemmensen, Hertzum, Hornbæk, Shi, & Yammiyavar, 2009, Röbig et al., 2010, Bidwell, 2011b).

RECOMMENDATIONS AND SOLUTIONS

Several researchers working in this area of taking cultural contexts into account in HCI design have already profited from the results of empirical studies to build well elaborated and comprehensible work products that end in complex but valuable models, theories and tools for further and broader fruitful future research. For instance, J. Dong & Salvendy, 1999 established the horizontal orientation of menus in layouts for the Chinese population. Y. Dong, & Lee, K., 2008 also conducted a cross-cultural comparative study of users' perceptions of a webpage with the focus on the cognitive styles of Chinese, Koreans and Americans. W. Dong & Fu, 2010 developed a culture-sensitive image tagging interface. Another example is H. Sun, 2001 who conducted an exploratory study of cultural markers based on A. Badre, 2000 to build a culturally competent corporate multilingual web site. X. Sun & Shi, 2007 performed a pilot study in china to clarify language issues in cross cultural usability testing. H. Sun, 2012 augmented the path to cross-cultural technology design by creating culture-sensitive technology for local users.

Feasible recommendations and guidelines for the conception, design and evaluation of issues when implementing standard HCI perspectives in local contexts, as exemplified by German developers generating products for Chinese people, can be found, for example, in R. Heimgärtner & Tiede, 2008. Related work on culture and HCI has been compiled along with Clemmensen & Roese, 2010, Aaron Marcus & Baumgartner, 2004, Röbig et al., 2010 and by the author (Rüdiger Heimgärtner, 2012). Within culturally different groups one must also consider dependence on context, situation and experience (cf. Bidwell, 2011b). This knowledge can be determined most precisely by using inquiry approaches or methods based on communication like interviews, focus groups or questionnaires (cf. Hampe-Neteler, 1994, Clemmensen & Clemmensen, 2009a, Clemmensen & Clemmensen, 2011).

Nevertheless, it is still important to take cultural context into account in designing HCI. For instance, Zhang, Chintakovid, Sun, Ge, & Zhang, 2006 found out by a cross-cultural study on knowledge sharing that saving face and sharing personal information is appropriate depending on the situation. A total of 197 Chinese undergraduate students and 111 American undergraduate students participated in the study. The first finding was that both Chinese and American students were more willing to share personal knowledge with in-group members than with member outside their group. Furthermore, the results showed that common work experience between group members was more important than common national cultural background in determining a people's attitude towards knowledge sharing. Another interesting finding was that Chinese participants were more willing to share personal information with an American stranger (out-group) than a Chinese stranger (in-group), while American participants showed no such difference. In summary, these findings indicate that a global organization should take both national culture and in-group/out-group factors into consideration to facilitate knowledge sharing.

In addition, as shown above, there is no systematic holistic approach integrating the benefits of all approaches to yield synergy effects being the basic universal approach that could be used by all researchers for intercultural user interface design. Therefore, the author suggests bundling efforts of the research community to establish a general framework and approach to profit from it in (applied) research as well as in industrial design in the future.

Furthermore, one of the most important objectives in intercultural user interface design is still to show developers of international products a way to develop their products such that they can be offered successfully in the global market. One of the most important tasks thereby is to explore the intercultural differences (e.g., different color meanings or cognitive styles) and then to consider the implications of the identified differences in designing intercultural user interfaces (e.g., different operation state colors, browsing style). Relevant cultural variables for intercultural user interface design have to be determined and specified by literature review and requirements analysis. The values of cultural variables show culture-dependent variations that can be exploited for intercultural user interface design. They can be found on all levels of user interface localization (surface, functionality, interaction) (cf. Kerstin Röse, 2002). Here, also cultural universals Schwartz, 2004 and universal design Stephanidis, 2009 should be taken into account in order to yield aspects for universal design and to reduce overall research efforts: the more universal aspects independent of culture can be applied the less cultural differences must be determined empirically. Finally, the empirical qualitative and quantitative analyses of the values of the cultural variables need to integrate the results into cross-cultural user interfaces.

Finally, the author recommends that "intercultural variables" are preferred in cases where the intercultural research character for obtaining the values of the variables is meant and "cultural variables", when mainly the usage of the values of the variables themselves (concerning a specific culture) is important. For instance, "Intercultural" usability engineering is a method for designing products of good usability for users from different cultures (Pia Honold, 2000b). "Intercultural" in this context refers to the special methods that are necessary to do usability engineering for different cultures (cf. Honold, 1999). However, the term "intercultural usability engineering" is commonly used by German usability engineers (cf. Detlef Zühlke, 2004) whereas outside Germany researches often use the concept of "cross-cultural usability testing" (cf. Clemmensen, Goyal, Clemmensen, & Goyal, 2005) that must be conducted in order to yield good "cultural usability" (cf. Clemmensen & Clemmensen, 2009b).

CONCLUSION

In the area of intercultural user interface design, the difficult investigation of methodological intercultural factors still stands at the beginning where it is acquiring results for phenomena like different habits of interacting with the system, different expectations regarding navigation within hyperspace or different mental models. It is still decisive in the area of intercultural user interface design to bridge the gap between general cultural aspects and those specific to user interface design. This is especially the case with respect to the current lack of research regarding culturally influenced interaction and dialog design based on empirical studies regarding hidden cultural variables. Even if the research concerning culture-centered HCI design is growing enormously, it is most important to integrate the results from empirical studies considering cultural contexts in user interface design and thereby provide both the basis of the data to feed models and construct theories and the basis of the graduated touchstone for their verification.

REFERENCES

Abdelnour-Nocera, J., Kurosu, M., Clemmensen, T., Bidwell, N., Vatrapu, R., Winschiers-Theophilus, H., & Yeo, A. (2011). *Re-framing HCI through local and indigenous perspectives.* Paper presented at the Lecture Notes in Computer Science. Berlin, Germany.

N. Aykin (Ed.). (2004). *Usability and internationalization of information technology*. Mahwah, NJ: Lawrence Erlbaum Associates Inc..

Aykin, N. (2005). *Usability and internationalization of information technology*. Mahwah, NJ: Erlbaum.

Badre, A. (2000). The effects of cross cultural interface design orientation on world wide web user performance. *GVU Technical Report,* 1-30.

Badre, A., & Barber, W. (1998). Culturabilty: The merging of culture and usabilty. In *Proceedings of the 4th Conference on Human Factors and the Web*. Basking Ridge.

Baumgartner, V.-J. (2003). *A practical set of cultural dimensions for global user-interface analysis and design.* Retrieved from http://www.mavas.at/val/education05_thesis00.asp

Bernsen, N. O., Dybkjær, H., & Dybkjær, L. (1998). *Designing interactive speech systems* (2nd ed.). London: Springer. doi:10.1007/978-1-4471-0897-9.

Bevan, N. (2001). International standards for HCI and usability. *International Journal of Human-Computer Studies International Journal of Human-Computer Studies, 55*(4), 533–552. doi:10.1006/ijhc.2001.0483.

Bidwell, N. J., Winschiers-Theophilus, H., Koch Kapuire, G., & Rehm, M. (2011b). Pushing personhood into place: Situating media in the transfer of rural knowledge in Africa. *International Journal of Human-Computer Studies, 69*(10), 618–631. doi:10.1016/j.ijhcs.2011.02.002.

Biesterfeldt, J., & Capra, M. (2011). Leading international UX research projects design, user experience, and usability. In A. Marcus (Ed.), *Theory, Methods, Tools and Practice* (Vol. 6769, pp. 368–377). Springer.

Bourges-Waldegg, P., & Scrivener, S. A. R. (1998). Meaning, the central issue in cross-cultural HCI design. *Interacting with Computers: The Interdisciplinary Journal of Human-Computer Interaction, 9*(3), 287–309. doi:10.1016/S0953-5438(97)00032-5.

Braun, B.-M., Röse, K., & Rößger, P. (2007). Localizing for the Korean market: Actually being there with a multi-method approach. In V. Evers, C. Sturm, M. Alberto, M. Rocha, E. Cambranes Martinez & T. Mandl (Eds.), *Proceedings of the Eighth International Workshop on Internationalisation of Products and Systems* (pp. 55-62). Product & Systems Internationalisation, Inc.

Bryan, N. B., McLean, E. R., Smits, S. J., & Burn, J. (1994). The structure of work perceptions among Hong Kong and United States IS professionals: A multidimensional scaling test of the Hofstede cultural paradigm. In *Proceedings of the 1994 Computer Personnel Research Conference on Reinventing IS: Managing Information Technology in Changing Organizations* (pp. 219-230). Alexandria, VA: ACM.

Cagiltay, K. (1999). Culture and its effects on human-computer-interaction. In B. Collis & R. Oliver (Eds.), *Proceedings of World Conference on Educational Multimedia, Hypermedia and Telecommunications 1999* (pp. 1626-1626). Chesapeake, VA: AACE.

Callahan, E. (2005). Cultural similarities and differences in the design of university web sites. *Journal of Computer-Mediated Communication, 11*(1), 239–273. doi:10.1111/j.1083-6101.2006.tb00312.x.

Castro Salgado, L. C., Leitão, C. F., & Souza, C. S. (2013). Semiotic engineering and culture. In *A Journey Through Cultures* (pp. 19–42). Springer. doi:10.1007/978-1-4471-4114-3_2.

Chen, Q. (2001). *Human computer interaction issues and challenges*. Retrieved from http://search.ebscohost.com/login.aspx?direct=true&scope=site&db=nlebk&db=nlabk&AN=60706

Choong, Y.-Y., & Salvendy, G. (1998). Design of icons for use by Chinese in mainland China. *Interacting with Computers, 9*(4), 417–430. doi:10.1016/S0953-5438(97)00026-X.

Clemmensen, T. (2008). *Interaction design & usability from an Indian perspective - Talks with: Apala Chavan, Anirudha Joshi, Dinesh Katre, Devashish Pandya, Sammeer Chabukswar, Pradeep Yammiyavar*. Retrieved from /z-wcorg/database

Clemmensen, T. (2009). Towards a theory of cultural usability: A comparison of ADA and CMU theory. *IFIP Advances in Information and Communication Technology, 316*, 98–112. doi:10.1007/978-3-642-11762-6_9.

Clemmensen, T. (2010). A comparison of what is part of usability testing in three countries. *International Federation for Information Processing,* (316), 31-45.

Clemmensen, T. (2012). Usability problem identification in culturally diverse settings. *Information Systems Journal, 22*(2), 151–175. doi:10.1111/j.1365-2575.2011.00381.x.

Clemmensen, T., & Clemmensen, T. (2009a). *A framework for thinking about the maturity of cultural usability*. Retrieved from http://openarchive.cbs.dk/cbsweb/handle/10398/7949

Clemmensen, T., & Clemmensen, T. (2009b). Towards a theory of cultural usability. *A Comparison of ADA and CM-U Theory,*(5619), 416-425.

Clemmensen, T., & Clemmensen, T. (2010). Regional styles of human-computer interaction. In *Proccedings of the 3rd ACM International Conference on Intercultural Collaboration (ICIS),* (pp. 219-222). Association for Computing Machinery.

Clemmensen, T., & Clemmensen, T. (2011). Templates for cross-cultural and culturally specific usability testing. *Results from Field Studies and Ethnographic Interviewing in Three Countries, 27*(7), 634–669. doi: doi:10.1080/10447318.2011.555303.

Clemmensen, T., & Clemmensen, T. (2012). *The human-computer domain relation in UX models*. Academic Press.

Clemmensen, T., & Goyal, S. (2004). *Studying cross cultural think-aloud usability testing: Some suggestions for an experimental paradigm*. Academic Press.

Clemmensen, T., & Goyal, S. (2005). *Cross cultural usability testing: The relationship between evaluator and test user*. Retrieved from http://openarchive.cbs.dk/cbsweb/handle/10398/6474

Clemmensen, T., Hertzum, M., Hornbæk, K., Kumar, J., Shi, Q., & Yammiyavar, P. (2007). *Usability constructs: A cross-cultural study of how users and developers experience their use of information systems*. Academic Press.

Clemmensen, T., Hertzum, M., Hornbæk, K., Shi, Q., & Yammiyavar, P. (2009). Cultural cognition in usability evaluation. *Interacting with Computers*, *21*(3), 212–220. doi:10.1016/j.intcom.2009.05.003.

Clemmensen, T., & Roese, K. (2010). An overview of a decade of journal publications about culture and human-computer interaction (HCI). *IFIP Advances in Information and Communication Technology*, *316*, 98–112. doi:10.1007/978-3-642-11762-6_9.

Constantine, L. (2009). *Human activity modeling: Toward a pragmatic integration of activity theory and usage-centered design human-centered software engineering*. Springer.

Constantine, L., & Lockwood, L. A. D. (1999). *Software for use: A practical guide to the models and methods of usage-centered design*. Reading, MA: Addison Wesley.

Currie, N. J., & Peacock, B. (2002). *International space station robotic systems operations: A human factors perspective*. Academic Press. doi:10.1177/154193120204600106.

Cyr, D., & Trevor-Smith, H. (2004). Localization of web design: An empirical comparison of German, Japanese, and United States web site characteristics. *Journal of the American Society for Information Science and Technology*, *55*(13), 1199–1208. doi:10.1002/asi.20075.

Dasgupta, S., & Gupta, B. (2010). *Organizational culture and technology use in a developing country: An empirical study*. Paper presented at the SIG GlobDev Third Annual Workshop. Saint Louis, MO.

Day, D. L. (1991). *The cross-cultural study of human-computer interaction: A review of research methodology, technology transfer, and the diffusion of innovation*. Academic Press.

De Souza, C. S. (1993). The semiotic engineering of user interface languages. *International Journal of Man-Machine Studies*, *39*, 753–773. doi:10.1006/imms.1993.1082.

De Souza, C. S., Barbosa, S. D. J., & Prates, R. O. (2001). *A semiotic engineering approach to HCI*. Paper presented at the CHI 2001. New York, NY.

Del Galdo, E. M., & Nielsen, J. (1996). *International user interfaces*. New York: Wiley.

DIN. (2010). *DIN EN ISO 9241-210 ergonomische anforderungen der mensch-system-interaktion teil 210: Prozess zur gestaltung gebrauchstauglicher systeme*. Berlin: BeuthVerlag.

Dinet, J., Vivian, R., & Brangier, E. (2011). Towards future methods to take into account cross-cultural differences in design: An example with the expert community staff (ECS). In *Proceedings of the 1st International Conference on Design, User Experience and Usability: Theory, Methods, Tools and Practice* (LNCS), (vol. 6769 LNCS, pp. 53-61). Berlin: Springer.

Dong, J., & Salvendy, G. (1999). Designing menus for the Chinese population: Horizontal or vertical? *Behaviour & Information Technology*, *18*(6), 467–471. doi:10.1080/014492999118887.

Dong, W., & Fu, W.-T. (2010). *Toward a cultural-sensitive image tagging interface*. Paper presented at the 15th International Conference on Intelligent User Interfaces. Hong Kong, China.

Dong, Y., & Lee, K. (2008). A cross-cultural comparative study of users' perceptions of a webpage: With a focus on the cognitive styles of Chinese, Koreans and Americans. *International Journal of Design*. Retrieved from http://www.ijdesign.org/ojs/index.php/IJDesign/article/view/267/163

Dormann, C. (2006). Cultural representations in web design: Differences in emotions and values. In T. McEwan, D. Benyon, & J. Gulliksen (Eds.), *People and computers XIX - The bigger picture* (pp. 285–299). London: Academic Press. doi:10.1007/1-84628-249-7_18.

Dormann, C., & Chisalita, C. (2002). *Cultural values in web site design*. Academic Press.

Dourish, P., & Bell, G. (2011). *Divining a digital future: Mess and mythology in ubiquitous computing*. Cambridge, MA: MIT Press.

Dourish, P., & Mainwaring, S. D. (2012). *Ubicomp's colonial impulse*. Paper presented at the 2012 ACM Conference on Ubiquitous Computing. Pittsburgh, PA.

Eigenbrode, S. D., O'Rourke, M., Wulfhorst, J. D., Althoff, D. M., Goldberg, C. S., Merrill, K., & Bosque-Pérez, N. A. (2007). Employing philosophical dialogue in collaborative science. *Bioscience*, *57*(1), 55–64. doi:10.1641/B570109.

Endrass, B., Rehm, M., André, E., & Nakano, Y. (2008). *Talk is silver, silence is golden: A cross cultural study on the usage of pauses in speech*. Academic Press.

Esselink, B. (1998). *A practical guide to software localization: For translators, engineers and project managers* (Vol. 3). Amsterdam: Benjamins.

Evers, V. (1998). Cross-cultural understanding of metaphors in interface design. In *Proceedings of Attitudes toward Technology and Communication*. CATAC.

Evers, V. (2003). Cross-cultural aspects of user understanding and behaviour: Evaluation of a virtual campus website by user from North America, England, The Netherlands and Japan. In V. Evers, K. Röse, P. Honold, J. Coronado & D. Day (Eds.), *Proceedings of the Fifth International Workshop on Internationalisation of Products and Systems* (pp. 189-210). Kaiserslautern, Germany: University of Kaiserslautern.

Evers, V., & Day, D. (1997). The role of culture in interface acceptance. In *Proceedings of the IFIP TC13 Interantional Conference on Human-Computer Interaction* (pp. 260-267). London: Chapman & Hall, Ltd.

Evers, V., Kukulska-Hulme, A., & Jones, A. (1999). *Cross-cultural understanding of interface design: A cross-cultural analysis of icon recognition*. Academic Press.

Faiola, A. (2006). *Toward an HCI theory of cultural cognition*. Academic Press.

Fernandes, T. (1995). *Global interface design*. Boston: AP Professional.

Fitzgerald, W. (2004). *Models for cross-cultural communications for cross-cultural website design*. Ottawa, Canada: National Research Council Canada.

Galtung, J. (1981). Structure, culture, and intellectual style: An essay comparing saxonic, teutonic, gallic and nipponic approaches. *Social Sciences Information. Information Sur les Sciences Sociales*, *20*(6), 817. doi:10.1177/053901848102000601.

Goguen, J. A., & Linde, C. (1993). *Techniques for requirements elicitation.* Paper presented at the Requirements Engineering, 1993. New York, NY.

Gould, E., & Marcus, A. (2011). Company culture audit to improve development team's collaboration, communication, and cooperation design, user experience, and usability. In *Proceedings of Theory, Methods, Tools and Practice (LNCS)* (Vol. 6769, pp. 415–424). Berlin: Springer.

Hall, E. T. (1959). *The silent language*. New York: Doubleday.

Hall, E. T. (1976). *Beyond culture*. New York: Anchor Books.

Hall, E. T., & Hall, M. R. (1990). *Understanding cultural differences*. Yarmouth, ME: Intercultural Press.

Hall, E. T., & Hall, M. R. (2004). *Understanding cultural differences*. Yarmouth, ME: Intercultural Press.

Hamacher, N. A. (2006). *Automatische kriterienorientierte bewertung der gebrauchstauglichkeit interaktiver systeme*. München, Germany: Dr. Hut.

Hampe-Neteler, W. (1994). *Software-ergonomische bewertung zwischen arbeitsgestaltung und softwareentwicklung* (Vol. 2). Frankfurt am Main, Germany: Lang.

Hassenzahl, M., & Tractinsky, N. (2006). User experience–A research agenda. *Behaviour & Information Technology*, *25*(2), 91–97. doi:10.1080/01449290500330331.

Heimgärtner, R. (2005b). Research in progress: Towards cross-cultural adaptive human-machine-interaction in automotive navigation systems. In D. Day & E. M. del Galdo (Eds.), *Proceedings of the Seventh International Workshop on Internationalisation of Products and Systems (IWIPS 2005)* (pp. 97-111). Amsterdam: Grafisch Centrum Amsterdam.

Heimgärtner, R. (2007). *Cultural differences in human computer interaction: Results from two online surveys*. Paper presented at the Open innovation. Konstanz, Germany.

Heimgärtner, R. (2008). A tool for getting cultural differences in HCI. In K. Asai (Ed.), *Human Computer Interaction: New Developments* (pp. 343–368). Rijeka, Germany: InTech. doi:10.5772/5870.

Heimgärtner, R. (2010). *Cultural differences in human-computer interaction - Towards culturally adaptive human-machine interaction.* (PhD Dissertation). Universitätsbibliothek der Universität Regensburg, Regensburg, Germany.

Heimgärtner, R. (2012). *Cultural differences in human-computer interaction. Oldenbourg*. Germany: Verlag.

Heimgärtner, R. (2013). Reflections on a model of culturally influenced human computer interaction to cover cultural contexts in HCI design. *International Journal of Human-Computer Interaction*. doi:10.1080/10447318.2013.765761.

Heimgärtner, R., & Tiede, L. W. (2008). Technik und kultur: Interkulturelle erfahrungen bei der produktentwicklung für China. In O. Rösch (Ed.), *Interkulturelle Kommunikation* (Vol. 6, pp. 149–162). Berlin: Verlag News & Media.

Heimgärtner, R., Tiede, L.-W., & Windl, H. (2011). *Empathy as key factor for successful intercultural HCI design*. Paper presented at the 14th International Conference on Human-Computer Interaction. Orlando, FL.

Hermeking, M. (2001). *Kulturen und technik*. München, Germany: Waxmann.

Hertzum, M., & Clemmensen, T. (2012). How do usability professionals construe usability? *International Journal of Human-Computer Studies*, *70*(1), 26–42. doi:10.1016/j.ijhcs.2011.08.001.

Hodemacher, D., Jarman, F., & Mandl, T. (2005). *Kultur und web-design: Ein empirischer vergleich zwischen grossbritannien und deutschland.* Paper presented at the Mensch & Computer 2005: Kunst und Wissenschaft – Grenzüberschreitungen der interaktiven ART., Wien, Austria.

Hodicová, R. (2007). *Psychische distanz und internationalisierung von KMU: Empirische untersuchung am beispiel des sächsisch-tschechischen grenzraumes*. Duv.

Hofstede, G. (1984). *Culture's consequences: International differences in work-related values*. Beverly Hills, CA: Sage.

Hofstede, G. (1994). *VSM94: Values survey module 1994 manual*. Tilberg, Netherlands: IRIC.

Hofstede, G. (2006). What did GLOBE really measure? Researchers' minds versus respondents' minds. *Journal of International Business Studies*, *37*(6), 882. doi:10.1057/palgrave.jibs.8400233.

Hofstede, G., Hofstede, G. J., Minkov, M., & Vinken, H. (2008). *Announcing a new version of the values survey module: The VSM 08*. Retrieved September 12, 2009, from http://stuwww.uvt.nl/~csmeets/VSM08.html

Hofstede, G. H. (1991). *Cultures and organizations: Software of the mind*. London: McGraw-Hill.

Hofstede, G. H., Hofstede, G. J., & Minkov, M. (2010). *Cultures and organizations: Software of the mind* (3rd ed.). Maidenhead, UK: McGraw-Hill.

Hoft, N. L. (1996). Developing a cultural model. In E. M. Del Galdo, & J. Nielsen (Eds.), *International users interface* (pp. 41–73). Hoboken, NJ: John Wiley & Sons, Inc..

Holzinger, A. (2005). Usability engineering for software developers. *Communications of the ACM*, *48*(1), 71–74. doi:10.1145/1039539.1039541.

Holzinger, A. (2005). Usability engineering methods for software developers. *Communications of the ACM*, *48*(1), 71–74. doi:10.1145/1039539.1039541.

Honold, P. (1999). Cross-cultural or intercultural - Some findings on international usability testing. In G. V. Prabhu & E. M. Del Galdo (Eds.), *Designing for Global Markets 1, First International Workshop on Internationalisation of Products and Systems* (pp. 107-122). Rochester, NY: Backhouse Press.

Honold, P. (2000a). Intercultural usability engineering: Barriers and challenges from a German point of view. In D. Day, E. D. Galdo, & G. V. Prabhu (Eds.), *Designing for Global Markets 2* (pp. 137–147). Academic Press.

Honold, P. (2000b). Culture and context: An empirical study for the development of a framework for the elicitation of cultural influence in product usage. *International Journal of Human-Computer Interaction*, *12*(3-4), 327–345. doi:10.1080/10447318.2000.9669062.

Honold, P. (2000c). *Interkulturelles usability engineering: Eine untersuchung zu kulturellen einflüssen auf die gestaltung und nutzung technischer produkte*. Düsseldorf, Germany: VDI Verl.

House, R. J. (2004). *Culture, leadership, and organizations: The globe study of 62 societies*. Thousand Oaks, CA: Sage.

House, R. J., & Aditya, R. N. (1997). The social scientific study of leadership: quo vadis? *Journal of Management*, *23*(3), 409. doi:10.1177/014920639702300306.

International, D. (2003). Developing international software (2. ed. ed.). Redmond, WA: Microsoft Press.

Irani, L. (2010). HCI on the move: Methods, culture, values. In *Proceedings of the Conference on Human Factors in Computing Systems*, (pp. 2939-2942). IEEE.

Isa, W. A. W. M., Noor, N. L. M., & Mehad, S. (2009). *Cultural prescription vs. user perception of information architecture for culture centred website: A case study on Muslim online user*. Paper presented at the 3rd International Conference on Online Communities and Social Computing: Held as Part of HCI International 2009. San Diego, CA.

Jacko, J. A. (Ed.). (2007). Human-Computer interaction: Interaction design and usability. In *Proceedings of the 12th International Conference, HCI International 2007*, (Vol. 4550). Berlin: Springer.

Jagne, J., & Smith-Atakan, A. (2006). Cross-cultural interface design strategy. *Universal Access in the Information Society*, *5*(3), 299–305. doi:10.1007/s10209-006-0048-6.

Jensen, R. E., & Bjørn, P. (2012). Divergence and convergence in global software development: Cultural complexities as social worlds. In J. Dugdale, C. Masclet, M. A. Grasso, J.-F. Boujut, & P. Hassanaly (Eds.), *From Research to Practice in the Design of Cooperative Systems: Results and Open Challenges* (pp. 123–136). London: Springer. doi:10.1007/978-1-4471-4093-1_9.

Jetter, H.-C. (2004). *Interkulturelles UI design und UI evaluation*. Universität Konstanz.

Kamentz, E. (2006). *Adaptivität von hypermedialen Lernsystemen: Ein Vorgehensmodell für die Konzeption einer Benutzermodellierungskomponente unter Berücksichtigung kulturbedingter Benutzereigenschaften*. Retrieved from http://d-nb.info/986457256/34

Kankanhalli, A., Tan, B. C. Y., Wei, K.-K., & Holmes, M. C. (2004). Cross-cultural differences and information systems developer values. *Decision Support Systems*, *38*(2), 183–195. doi:10.1016/S0167-9236(03)00101-5.

Kappos, A., & Rivard, S. (2008). A three-perspective model of culture, information systems, and their development and use. *Management Information Systems Quarterly*, *32*(3), 601–634.

Kaptelinin, V., & Nardi, B. (2006). *Acting with technologie: Activity theory and interaction design*. Cambridge, MA: MIT Press.

Kersten, G. E., Kersten, M. A., & Rakowski, W. M. (2002). Software and culture: Beyond the internationalization of the interface. *Journal of Global Information Management*, *10*(4), 86–101. doi:10.4018/jgim.2002100105.

Koda, T., Rehm, M., & Andre, E. (2008). Cross-cultural evaluations of avatar facial expressions designed by western designers. *Lecture Notes in Computer Science*, *5208*, 245–252. doi:10.1007/978-3-540-85483-8_25.

Komischke, T., McGee, A., Wang, N., & Wissmann, K. (2003). Mobile phone usability and cultural dimensions: China, Germany & USA. In L. Mühlbach (Ed.), *Human Factors in Telecommunication: Proceedings of the 19th International Symposium on Human Factors in Telecommunication (HFT 03)*. Berlin, Germany: Springer.

Komlodi, A. (2005). *Cross-cultural study of information seeking*. Paper presented at the International Conference on Human-Computer Interaction (HCII 2005). Las Vegas, NV.

Koning, H., Dormann, C., & van Vliet, H. (2002). *Practical guidelines for the readability of IT-architecture diagrams*. Academic Press. doi:10.1145/584955.584969.

Kralisch, A. (2006). *The impact of culture and language on the use of the internet empirical analyses of behaviour and attitudes*. (Dissertation). Berlin.

Kramsch, C. J. (1998). *Language and culture*. Oxford, UK: Oxford University Press.

Krömker, H. (2000). Introduction. *International Journal of Human-Computer Interaction*, *12*(3&4), 281–284.

Law, W. K., & Perez, K. (2005). Cross-cultural implementation of information system. *Journal of Cases on Information Technology*, *7*(2), 121–130. doi:10.4018/jcit.2005040108.

Lee, I., Choi, G. W., Kim, J., Kim, S., Lee, K., Kim, D.,... An, Y. (2008). Cultural dimensions for user experience: Cross-country and cross-product analysis of users' cultural characteristics. *People and Computers*, *1*(Edit 22), 3-12.

Lee, K.-P. (2007). *Culture and its effects on human interaction with design: With the emphasis on cross-cultural perspectives between Korea and Japan*. Retrieved from http://hdl.handle.net/2241/5979

Lee, Y. (2002). *Introduction*. Retrieved from http://www.csulb.edu/web/journals/jecr/issues/20024/paper3.pdf

Leidner, D. E., & Kayworth, T. (2006). Review: A review of culture in information systems research: toward a theory of information technology culture conflict. *Management Information Systems Quarterly*, *30*(2), 357–399.

Lewandowitz, L., Rößger, P., & Vöhringer-Kuhnt, T. (2006). Asiatische vs. europäische HMI Lösungen von Fahrerinformationssystemen. In *Proceedings of Useware 2006* (Vol. 1946, pp. 279–287). Düsseldorf, Germany: VDI.

Liu, C.-H., Wang, Y.-M., Yu, G.-L., & Wang, Y.-J. (2009). Related theories and exploration on dynamic model of empathy. *Advances in Psychological Science*, *5*, 14.

Maguire, M. (2011). Guidelines on website design and colour selection for international acceptance design, user experience, and usability. In *Theory, Methods, Tools and Practice* (Vol. 6769, pp. 162–171). Berlin: Springer.

Maier, E. (2005). Activity theory as a framework foraccommodating cultural factors in HCI studies. In A. Auinger (Ed.), *Workshops-Proceedings der 5: Fachübergreifenden Konferenz Mensch und Computer 2005: Internationalisierung von Informationssystemen: Kulturelle Aspekte der Mensch-Maschine-Interaktion* (pp. 69–79). Wien, Austria: Springer.

Maier, E., Mandl, T., Röse, K., Womser-Hacker, C., & Yetim, F. (2005). Internationalisierung von informationssystemen: Kulturelle aspekte der mensch-maschine-interaktion. In A. Auinger (Ed.), *Workshops-Proceedings der 5. fachübergreifenden Konferenz Mensch und Computer 2005* (pp. 57–58). Wien, Austria: Springer.

Marcus, A. (2001). Cross-cultural user-interface design. In M. J. S. G. Smith (Ed.), *Proceedings Human-Computer Interface Internat. (HCII)* (Vol. 2, pp. 502–505). New Orleans, LA: Lawrence Erlbaum Associates.

Marcus, A. (2001). International and intercultural user interfaces. In C. Stephanidis (Ed.), *User Interfaces for All: Concepts, Methods, and Tools* (pp. 47–63). Mahwah, NJ: Lawrence Erlbaum.

Marcus, A. (2003). User-interface design and China: A great leap forward. *Interaction*, *10*(1), 21–25. doi:10.1145/604575.604588.

Marcus, A. (2006). Cross-cultural user-experience design. In *Diagrammatic Representation and Inference* (pp. 16–24). Academic Press. doi:10.1007/11783183_4.

Marcus, A., & Baumgartner, V.-J. (2004). A practical set of culture dimensions for global user-interface development. In *Proceedings of Computer Human Interaction, 6th Asia Pacific Conference, APCHI 2004*, (pp. 252-261). APCHI.

Marcus, A., & Gould, E. W. (2000). *Cultural dimensions and global web user-interface design: What? So what? Now what?* Retrieved from http://www.amanda.com

Marcus, A., & Gould, E. W. (2000). Crosscurrents: Cultural dimensions and global web user-interface design. *Interaction*, *7*(4), 32–46. doi:10.1145/345190.345238.

Martinsons, M. G., & Westwood, R. I. (1997). Management information systems in the Chinese business culture: An explanatory theory. *Information & Management, 32*(5), 215–228. doi:10.1016/S0378-7206(96)00009-2.

Mutschler, B., & Reichert, M. (2004). *Usability-metriken als nachweis der wirtschaftlichkeit von verbesserungen der mensch-maschine-schnittstelle*. Academic Press.

Nardi, B. A. (1996). *Context and consciousness: Activity theory and human-computer interaction*. Cambridge, MA: MIT Press.

Nielsen, J. (1990). *Designing user interfaces for international use* (Vol. 13). Amsterdam: Elsevier.

Nielsen, J. (2006a). *Designing web usability*. Berkeley, CA: New Riders.

Nielsen, J. (2006b). *Usability engineering*. Amsterdam: Kaufmann.

Nisbett, R. E. (2003). *The geography of thought: How Asians and Westerners think differently..., & why*. New York: Free Press.

D. A. Norman, & S. Draper (Eds.). (1986). *User centered system design: New perspectives on human-computer interaction*. Hoboken, NJ: Lawrence Erlbaum Associates.

Olaverri-Monreal, C., Draxler, C., & Bengler, K. J. (2011). *Variable menus for the local adaptation of graphical user interfaces*. Paper presented at the Information Systems and Technologies (CISTI). New York, NY.

Ou, L. C., Luo, M. R., Woodcock, A., & Wright, A. (2004). A study of colour emotion and colour preference: Part I: Colour emotions for single colours. *Color Research and Application, 29*(3). doi:10.1002/col.20010.

Paterson, B., Winschiers-Theophilus, H., Dunne, T. T., Schinzel, B., & Underhill, L. G. (2011). Interpretation of a cross-cultural usability evaluation: A case study based on a hypermedia system for rare species management in Namibia. *Interacting with Computers, 23*(3), 239–246. doi:10.1016/j.intcom.2011.03.002.

Plocher, T., Patrick Rau, P.-L., & Choong, Y.-Y. (2012). Cross-cultural design. In *Handbook of Human Factors and Ergonomics* (pp. 162–191). Hoboken, NJ: John Wiley & Sons, Inc. doi:10.1002/9781118131350.ch6.

Prabhu, G., & Harel, D. (1999). *GUI design preference validation for Japan and China - A case for KANSEI engineering?* Paper presented at the HCI International (the 8th International Conference on Human-Computer Interaction) on Human-Computer Interaction: Ergonomics and User Interfaces. New York, NY.

Prates, R. O., de Souza, C. S., & Barbosa, S. D. J. (2000). Methods and tools: A method for evaluating the communicability of user interfaces. *Interaction, 7*(1), 31–38. doi:10.1145/328595.328608.

Preim, B., & Dachselt, R. (2010). Interaktive systeme: Vol. I. *Grundlagen, graphical user interfaces, informationsvisualisierung*. Berlin, Germany: Springer Verlag.

Rathje, S. (2003). Ist wenig kulturelles Verständnis besser als gar keins? Problematik der verwendung von dimensionsmodellen zur kulturbeschreibung. *Interculture-Online*. Retrieved from www.interculture-online.info

Rätzmann, M. (2004). *Software-testing & internationalisierung* (2nd ed.). Bonn, Germany: Galileo Press.

Rau, P.-L. P., & Plocher, T. A. et al. (2012). *Cross-cultural design for IT products and services*. Boca Raton, FL: Taylor & Francis. doi:10.1201/b12679.

Rehm, M., Bee, N., Endrass, B., Wissner, M., & André, E. (2007). *Too close for comfort? Adapting to the user's cultural background*. Academic Press. doi:10.1145/1290128.1290142.

Reinecke, K., Reif, G., & Bernstein, A. (2007). Cultural user modeling with CUMO: An approach to overcome the personalization bootstrapping problem. In *Proceedings of the First International Workshop on Cultural Heritage on the Semantic Web at the 6th International Semantic Web Conference (ISWC 2007)*. Busan, South Korea: ISWC.

Reiterer, H. (2008). *Seminar reader: Future challenges and trends in HCI*. University of Konstanz.

Rızvanoğlu, K., & Öztürk, Ö. (2009). *Cross-cultural understanding of the dual structure of metaphorical icons: An explorative study with French and Turkish users on an e-learning site*. Paper presented at the 3rd International Conference on Internationalization, Design and Global Development: Held as Part of HCI International 2009, San Diego, CA.

Röbig, S., Didier, M., & Bruder, R. (2010). *Internationales verständnis von usability sowie methodenanwendung im bereich der usability*. Paper presented at the Grundlagen - Methoden - Technologien, 5. VDI Fachtagung USEWARE 2010, Baden-Baden. Retrieved from http://tubiblio.ulb.tu-darmstadt.de/46312/

Röse, K. (2001). *Kultur als variable des UI design*. Paper presented at the Mensch & Computer 2001. Stuttgart, Germany.

Röse, K. (2002). Kulturmodelle und ihre anwendbarkeit beim user interface design. *Bedienen und Verstehen*, *4*, 305–317.

Röse, K. (2002). *Methodik zur gestaltung interkultureller mensch-maschine-systeme in der produktionstechnik* (Vol. 5). Kaiserslautern: Univ.

Röse, K., Liu, L., & Zühlke, D. (2001). Design issues in mainland china: demands for a localized human-machine-interaction design. In G. Johannsen (Ed.), *8th IFAC/IFIPS/IFORS/IEA Symposium on Analysis, Design, and Evaluation of Human-Machine Systems* (pp. 17-22). Kassel: Preprints.

Röse, K., & Zühlke, D. (2001). *Culture-oriented design: Developers' knowledge gaps in this area*. Paper Presented at the 8th IFAC/IFIPS/IFORS/IEA Symposium on Analysis, Design, and Evaluation of Human-Machine Systems. Kassel, Germany.

Röse, K., Zühlke, D., & Liu, L. (2001). Similarities and dissimilarities of German and Chinese users. In G. Johannsen (Ed.), *Preprints of 8th IFAC/IFIP/IFORS/IEA Symposium on Analysis, Design, and Evaluation of Human-Machine Systems* (pp. 24-29). Germany, Kassel: IFIP.

Rößger, P. (2003). An international comparison of the usability of driver-information-systems. In *Proceedings of the Fifth International Workshop on Internationalisation of Products and Systems* (pp. 129-134). University of Kaiserslautern.

Rößger, P., & Hofmeister, J. (2003). Cross cultural usability: An international study on driver information systems. *Human-Computer Interaction*.

Salgado, L. C. de C., Leito, C. F., & de Souza, C. S. (2012). *A journey through cultures: Metaphors for guiding the design of cross-cultural interactive systems*. Berlin: Springer Publishing Company, Incorporated.

Schlögl, C. (2005). Information and knowledge management: dimensions and approaches. *Information Research*, *10*(4), 10–14.

Schmitz, K.-D., & Wahle, K. (2000). *Softwarelokalisierung*. Tübingen: Stauffenburg-Verl.

Schwartz, S. H. (2004). Mapping and interpreting cultural differences around the world. In H. Vinken, J. Soeters, & P. Ester (Eds.), *Comparing cultures, Dimensions of culture in a comparative perspective* (pp. 43–73). Leiden, The Netherlands: Brill.

Shah, H., Nersessian, N. J., Harrold, M. J., & Newstetter, W. (2012). *Studying the influence of culture in global software engineering: thinking in terms of cultural models*. Paper presented at the 4th international conference on Intercultural Collaboration. Bengaluru, India.

Shen, S.-T., Woolley, M., & Prior, S. (2006). Towards culture-centred design. *Interacting with Computers*, *18*(4), 820–852. doi:10.1016/j.intcom.2005.11.014.

Shi, Q., & Clemmensen, T. (2007). Relationship model in cultural usability testing usability and internationalization. In *Proceedings of HCI and Culture*, (Vol. 4559, pp. 422-431). Berlin: Springer.

Shneiderman, B., Plaisant, C., Cohen, M., & Jacobs, S. (2009). *Designing the user interface: Strategies for effective human-computer interaction*. Reading, MA: Addison-Wesley Publishing Company.

Simon, S. J. (2000). The impact of culture and gender on web sites: An empirical study. *SIGMIS Database*, *32*(1), 18–37. doi:10.1145/506740.506744.

Smith, A., & Chang, Y. (2003). Quantifying hofstede and developing cultural fingerprints for website acceptability. In *Proceedings of the Fifth International Workshop on Internationalisation of Products and Systems* (pp. 89-102). University of Kaiserslautern.

Smith, A., Dunckley, L., French, T., Minocha, S., & Chang, Y. (2004). A process model for developing usable crosscultural websites. *Interacting with Computers*, *16*(1), 63–91. doi:10.1016/j.intcom.2003.11.005.

Stengers, H., Troyer, O., Baetens, M., Boers, F., & Mushtaha, A. (2004). *Localization of web sites: Is there still a need for it?* Paper presented at the International Workshop on Web Engineering. Santa Cruz, CA.

Stephanidis, C. (2009). Universal access in the information society. Universal Access in the Information Society, 8(2).

Sturm, C. (2002). *TLCC-towards a framework for systematic and successful product internationalization*. Paper presented at the International Workshop on Internationalisation of Products and Systems. Austin, TX.

Sturm, C., & Mueller, C. H. (2003). Putting theory into practice: How to apply cross-cultural differences to user interface design? In M. Rauterberg, M. Menozzi, & J. Wesson (Eds.), *Human-computer interaction: INTERACT '03, IFIP TC13 International Conference on Human-Computer Interaction, 1st-5th September 2003* (pp. 1051-1052), International Federation for Information Processing.

Sun, H. (2001). Building a culturally-competent corporate web site: An exploratory study of cultural markers in multilingual web design In *Proceedings of the 19th Annual International Conference on Computer Documentation* (pp. 95-102). Sante Fe, NM: ACM.

Sun, H. (2012). *Cross-cultural technology design: Creating culture-sensitive technology for local users*. Oxford, UK: Oxford University Press. doi:10.1093/acprof:oso/9780199744763.001.0001.

Sun, X., & Shi, Q. (2007). *Language issues in cross cultural usability testing: A pilot study in china*. Paper presented at the 2nd International Conference on Usability and Internationalization. Beijing, China.

Tateishi, M., & Toma, T. (2010). *A cross-cultural comparative study of user interface in social media: Why social media can cross seas but not nationalisms*. Retrieved from http://koara.lib.keio.ac.jp/xoonips/modules/xoonips/detail.php?koara_id=KO40002001-00002010-0037

Thissen, F. (2008). Interkulturelles informationsdesign. In W. Weber (Ed.), *Kompendium Informationsdesign* (pp. 387–424). Berlin, Germany: Springer. doi:10.1007/978-3-540-69818-0_15.

Thomas, A. (1996). *Psychologie interkulturellen Handelns*. Göttingen, Germany: Hogrefe.

Trompenaars, F., & Hampden-Turner, C. (2012). *Riding the waves of culture: Understanding diversity in business* (3rd ed.). London: Nicholas Brealey Publ..

Vatrapu, R., & Suthers, D. (2007). Culture and computers: A review of the concept of culture and implications for intercultural collaborative online learning. *Lecture Notes in Computer Science*, *4568*, 260. doi:10.1007/978-3-540-74000-1_20.

VDMA. (2009). *Software-Internationalisierung Leitfaden*. VDMA Fachverband Software.

Vöhringer-Kuhnt, T. (2002). *The Influence Of Culture On Usability.* (M.A. master Thesis). Freie Universität, Berlin, Germany.

Windl, H., & Heimgärtner, R. (2013). *Intercultural design for use - Extending usage-centered design by cultural aspects.* Paper presented at the HCII 2013. Las Vegas, NV.

Witkin, H. A., Moore, C. A., Goodenough, D. R., & Cox, P. W. (1977). Field-dependent and field-independent cognitive styles and their educational implications. *Review of Educational Research*, *47*(1), 1. doi:10.3102/00346543047001001.

Wyer, R. S., Chiu, C.-Y., & Hong, Y.-Y. (2009). *Understanding culture: Theory, research, and application*. New York: Psychology Press.

Yammiyavar, P., Clemmensen, T., & Kumar, J. (2008). Influence of cultural background on non-verbal communication in a usability testing situation. *International Journal of Design*. Retrieved from http://www.ijdesign.org/ojs/index.php/IJDesign/article/view/313

Yeo, A. W. (2001). *Global-software development lifecycle: An exploratory study*. Paper presented at the SIGCHI Conference on Human Factors in Computing Systems. Seattle, WA.

Zahedi, F., & Bansal, G. (2011). Cultural signifiers of web site images. *Journal of Management Information Systems*, *28*(1), 147–200. doi:10.2753/MIS0742-1222280106.

Zhang, Q., Chintakovid, T., Sun, X., Ge, Y., & Zhang, K. (2006). Saving face or sharing personal information? A cross-cultural study on knowledge sharing. *Journal of Information and Knowledge Management*, *5*(1), 73–80. doi:10.1142/S0219649206001335.

Zühlke, D. (2004). Useware-systeme für internationale märkte. In *Useware-Engineering für Technische Systeme* (pp. 142–164). Berlin, Germany: Springer.

Zühlke, D., & Röse, K. (2000). Design of global user-interfaces: Living with the challenge. In *Proceedings of the IEA 2000/ HFES 2000 Congress,* (Vol. 6, pp. 154-157). San Diego, CA: IEA.

KEY TERMS AND DEFINITIONS

Culture: A set of facts, rules, values and norms (structural conditions) representing an orientation system established by the collective programming of the mind within a group of individuals.

Cultural Dimension: Cultural model to describe/explain the behavior of the members of cultures allowing the analysis and comparison of the characteristics and relationships of different cultural groups.

Cultural HCI Style Score: The average degree of information density and frequency as well as interaction frequency and speed the members in a designated cultural group expect computed from the Hofstede's indices.

Cultural Model: Framework/mental tool to describe/explain a culture.

HCI Dimensions (HCID): Variables that describe the HCI Style of the user based on the concepts of "information" and "interaction" such as information presentation frequency, information density, information order, information presentation duration, interaction frequency, interaction speed and interaction style.

HCI Style: Path of information processing and the interaction style exhibited by the user based on the concepts of "information" and "interaction" according to HCI dialogs that are characterized by transmitting pieces of information during user system interaction.

Intercultural Model: Framework/mental tool to describe/explain the relationships between cultures, e.g. the commonalities or differences between cultures, comparison of cultures with each other as well as determining their cultural distance.

Intercultural Usability Engineering (IUE): Method mix/process for designing products of good usability for users from different cultures.

Intercultural User Interface Design (IUID): Method mix/process for designing user interfaces for users from different cultures.

User Interface Characteristics: Characteristic factors 'metaphor', 'mental model', 'navigation', 'interaction' and 'presentation' of user interfaces having an effect on user interface design.

ENDNOTES

1 I do not claim to provide a complete list.

2 Cf. section „Models and Theories" as well as Figure 5.

3 This is also the case for driver navigation systems (Rößger, 2003). However, there is relatively little literature and there are few guidelines for intercultural dialog and design for interaction (Kamentz, 2006, Kralisch, 2006) and very few especially for driver navigation systems (e.g., Rößger, 2003).

4 However, there are none for intercultural user interface design in driver navigation systems which could be used easily and effectively by HCI designers in this area even if some recommendations for designing driver navigation systems in the cultural context exist (cf. Heimgärtner 2012).

5 According to Hofstede, these indices can be computed for groups with more than 20 members being of the same culture.

6 For instance, marrying cultural interaction indicators (CIIs) with principles of neuro linguistic programming (NLP) means a "cultural" adaptation at the individual level as suggested by Rüdiger Heimgärtner, 2012. Furthermore, the criticism concerning the correctness of Hofstede's cultural dimensions and their indices reduces confidence in them, which then implies that it is probably better or at least advisable not to build an adaptive system based on these but on parameters that represent the immediate behavior of the user with the system. However, this approach by the author still needs to be further elaborated to be explained in detail and for its practical use (cf. Rüdiger Heimgärtner, 2012).

Chapter 2
Icon Metaphors for Global Cultures

Lulit Bezuayehu
Oracle Inc., USA

Eric Stilan
Oracle Inc., USA

S. Tejaswi Peesapati
Oracle Inc., USA

ABSTRACT

Developing icons has always been challenging, from the first appearance of icons on desktop computers to the current day mobile and tablet platforms. Many of the same challenges apply when designing icons for global enterprise software. Icons can easily be misinterpreted when the designer and user have differing cultural backgrounds. The purpose of this chapter is to demonstrate the various cultural implications of icon interpretations and misinterpretations by users in various regions around the world. The authors conducted several studies to understand the roles cultures play when icons are viewed and interpreted by users. By deploying global surveys and conducting focus groups with users from around the world, they collected data to help them understand some of the variations in understanding and interpretations of icons. The authors also looked into various cultures that might find certain icons culturally insensitive or even offensive. After extensive research, they found that some of their initial assumptions regarding taboos and cultural standards were skewed by antiquated research, and now, their more recent research data shows that there is a more accepting global view of iconic metaphors and graphical imagery.

INTRODUCTION

How do people from different cultures interpret icons used in software applications? How do the culturally significant ideas and imagery influence emotion and ability to associate these icons with real world principles? These important questions need answering as software applications transcend national boundaries. Intercultural icon-user encounters are becoming more and more common as the spread of technology reaches around the world.

First of all, what is an icon? An icon is a graphical representation of an object or idea. Icons have found their way into every aspect of modern life. We see icons on signs, consumer goods and products, and a wide variety of user interfaces.

DOI: 10.4018/978-1-4666-4623-0.ch002

The amount of electronic devices we use every day is growing and each device comes with its own custom-designed display. From television remote controls, car dashboard gauges, automated teller machines, in-store ordering kiosks, interactive alarm clocks, smart phones, tablets and e-readers, we see dozens of icons every day.

The spread of technology around the globe means that each of these devices needs to be quickly understood by many different and varied cultures and the icons must be easily recognizable in each of these locations. It is far more cost effective for a company to develop one central icon for each of its devices or application's functions rather than creating multiple versions of each icon that can be swapped out as a localization effort for different regions. How we find the perfect graphical metaphor or a symbolic representation of something that allows us to connect to all the users on a global scale is the challenge that every visual designer faces. The challenge has always been related to the information that is available to the designer.

In the era before the Internet, there was limited access to easy or affordable cultural information from various places around the world. The early information that supported decisions on what to include as metaphors for icon designs that different cultures understood or found acceptable was limited to a few books. These books were generally written by social anthropologists and from a business perspective. They recommended how one should conduct himself when they travel to other countries and interact with natives of that culture, without causing international incidents. For example, there is a story about how a president of the United States traveled to Australia and in an attempt to give a sign of peace to a crowd as he passed by; he had inadvertently used an offensive gesture. It is told that, when he gave the two finger "V" sign that is commonly used to represent "peace", he had the back of his hand facing the crowd, instead of having the palm of his hand facing out. The next day, he made headlines all across Australia, as the gesture he used is understood locally as "up yours, mate!" [1]

It is generally understood that certain graphical elements (like pictograms) often contain cultural elements in the form of people, places and things [2], but there are many questions on how people perceive these graphical elements [3] – especially from the perspective of culture. The mental model of an individual depends on the prior knowledge and experiences [5, 6]. Nisbett et. al studied the influence of culture on how people perceive photographs, and they found that there is a significant difference in the way Americans and Japanese perceive photographs [7]. A study by Peesapati et.al [8] studied the influence of culture on how Indians, Americans and Chinese perceive certain culturally relevant photographs and their study revealed that culture has a role in emotional and cognitive processes around picture perception. "There is no denying that culture influences human-product interaction" [10]. As icons provide a majority of interaction points on a user interface, cultural effectiveness of icons is an important aspect to consider when designing user interfaces for a multicultural user base.

While working on one of our ongoing research projects that deal with incorporating accessibility of icons [4], we found significant differences in the perceptions of certain icons used in our software applications. These differences, which we think are worth studying, led us to investigate the cross-cultural interactions on the icons, identifying the extent to which these interactions are influenced by the cultural background of the user. The following sections contain our research questions, a detailed description of the participants, the reasoning supporting our procedure and the measures used in our data analysis. Finally we will discuss our preliminary findings and possible directions for future work.

BACKGROUND

Icons are an essential part of today's graphical user interfaces. They are common on desktop machines, laptops, mobile and tablet devices as well as hundreds of consumer electronic devices. They allow users to understand and interact with complicated interfaces with ease and confidence. The success of these icons relies heavily on the metaphors used to communicate functions, objects and status. Icons and metaphors have developed as many different practices and cultures merged bringing both improvements and challenges as they extended the functions and interactions that users have with their devices.

There are many works in the literature focusing on the importance of designing for the specific needs of a particular culture [15,16, 17]. Culture centered design, as discussed by van der Veer [17], is a highly important parameter to be considered when designing for a global audience. Siu-Tsen Shen [18] conducted an online survey to understand the web browser icon preferences of Chinese users and their study results clearly state the importance of culture centered design. Icons play a vital role in the usage of an application they are used in. In instances where these icons fail to convey the message, it results in failure of the application as a whole. Metaphors are often culture sensitive [19] and when these metaphors, in the form of icons, are used to represent an action, culture plays a vital role in how these metaphors or icons are perceived. A study by Vanessa Evers et. al [20] investigated the role culture plays in how a website of a virtual university campus is perceived. Their results unearth the differences in how some metaphors are perceived and also suggest that these differences are potentially due to the various cultural background and societal experiences of the users.

In our research work, we looked at the history of various "cultures", such as Business Culture, Computer Culture, Global Culture, Internet Culture and Social Media Culture and how, as computers and icon metaphors evolved, they were both influenced by these new cultures. At each stage of development, and as new facets were added to these cultures, this appears to have expanded the design considerations of the current day systems as well as future development efforts. As cultures came together, there is a push for great advancements in application features, productivity and communication. However, there were also challenges in merging these cultures and ensuring these new resulting concepts could be successfully integrated into the existing taxonomy of icon metaphors and were still understood by a global culture. See Figure 1 for illustration of these "cultures" and how they evolved.

THE BUSINESS CULTURE

We define business culture as the model or style of business operations within a company that determines how different levels of staff communicate

Figure 1. Influence of new cultures on icon metaphors

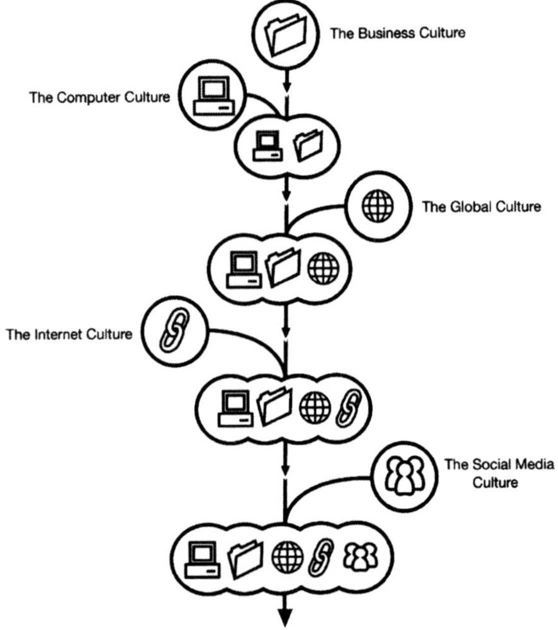

with one another as well as how employees deal with each other and their clients, customers, and day to day business. Many of the icons we see used in computer applications today have their roots in the pre-computer business culture. As much as current users identify the metaphors as from an old way of doing things, they are universally recognizable and still are useful today. For example, a file folder is used for filing information or paperwork in a business. And in the US, the "Rolodex" was commonly used for organizing and storing business cards. The Rolodex is a system of cards notched on the bottom to fit into a set of rails that hold the cards and allows them to be easily flipped through and contained while quickly removable and reorganized. Many of these early metaphors still play key roles on today's systems and, even if not currently used, they have themselves become iconic in their own right.

When the first computer interfaces adopted the desktop metaphor, they selected objects that matched functions to allow users to easily learn the underlying computer system. As more and more graphical interfaces developed, the desktop metaphor grew and included more objects and functions. Another example is the trashcan as a metaphor. Trashcan icons are common used for discarding files similar to how we would use them in an office to discard items. And as the business world began to expand with the use of computers, every maker of software around the world had to consider the use of icons and metaphors to ensure they could be understood by many users from different backgrounds.

THE COMPUTER CULTURE

The objects and tools used for generations in everyday offices became the base for metaphors of icons that were first used in the Xerox Star system and other first generation computers. Their evolution from the world of business to the computer screen happened in part due to the development of computer systems moving from terminal, character-based displays to bit-mapped displays. Terminal displays were favored due to limited and expensive memory at the time. As developers realized the future would bring less expensive memory, they saw bit-mapped displays and graphical interfaces as a more robust way to connect with users on a largely visual level. Taking advantage of bit-mapped displays, the concept of the "desktop metaphor" emerged using familiar office objects such as file folders, trashcans, pencils and paper documents to map to the same functions and uses on the computer. Computer systems even generated their own set of metaphors after they became a standard tool used in business. The 3.5 diskette became an icon to represent the "Save" function due to computer users relying on these diskettes to hold all of their data. As time has passed we are still using this same icon, even though the real world object has long since disappeared. This icon has become its own metaphor and although many have tried and discussed replacing it at great length, there still has been no better substitute for this iconic image.

THE GLOBAL CULTURE

"Global culture" is a term that is used to describe the habits and heritages of different societies around the world. As business became more global it was more apparent that the understanding of other cultures has to be taken into account. Graphic designers have always been aware of how metaphors and attributes can influence and convey messages to viewers without the use of words. This powerful and sometimes subtle form of communication can also easily bring with it unwanted meaning, if the designer is unaware of the background and context that its viewers comes from. Designers who developed software for foreign markets and web pages that could be viewed by a global audience looked for ways to understand these issues and turned to anthropologist and authors of books [12, 13, 14] for insight into these new and different cultures. There were issues of using many metaphors and objects of animals, faces, hand gestures and colors that designers took into account and avoided so as not to confuse or offend their potential customers.

Most designers were not able to experience a variety of cultures first hand and these meanings supplied through books and lectures became common knowledge when designing for global audiences. Without the means to test these taboo metaphors they became part of the designer's toolkit and influenced many generations of designers.

Today, many of these taboos are less severe and this has been witnessed by collecting user data through surveys and focus groups. Connecting with many different cultures and getting their understanding of modern metaphors and interpretations, we have been able to adopt many past taboo concepts, such as the "thumbs-up" gesture. Some design choices have also been rethought upon discovering through research that global audiences are unfamiliar with these object and metaphors. For example, a common metaphor to represent "user information" has been the Rolodex card. This staple of American business that has been used for decades in the past was unfamiliar to current computer users in focus groups we held in our offices in Hyderabad, India, as well as focus groups held in California with participants of many different cultural backgrounds and ages. This icon of a Rolodex card was seen as a folder or business card with some odd notches. Knowing that this metaphor is not connecting with users, we can now redesign these icons, removing the notches and using a more familiar and direct metaphor such as a business card. Armed with actual user data, design of icons becomes more informed and is closer to the goal of being globally accepted and understood.

THE INTERNET CULTURE

The Internet came into existence in the 1960s and ever since it has become more accessible to the public in the 1970s and since then, it has completely changed the way people communicate with each other. The public initially had access to the Internet via dial-up connections to Internet Service Providers (ISP). Companies like CompuServe and AOL advanced this technological movement by expanding the reach of the Internet inside the US including the most remote parts of the country. These companies dominated the Internet space in the 1980s and mid 1990s and with their wide spread usage, people had access to a powerful communication medium. Numerous websites came into existence all over the world from different cultures and on every imaginable topic. This allowed users to access infinite amounts of information, along with an opportunity to connect with people and companies across the globe.

This global infrastructure allowed ordinary folks to connect and interact with strangers through message boards and online chat rooms. The chat room phenomenon paved the way for a new communication language that favored abbreviated words such as BRB (Be Right Back), LOL (Laugh Out Loud), BTW (By The Way), and also introduced the use of text-based "Emoticons". People used emoticons to add feeling or emphasis to phrases and sentences. For example, "I am doing great:-)" has a different emotional value than "I am doing great". The first statement includes an "emoticon" (representing a smiley face), which conveys the mood of the sender. (An emoticon is a sequence of printable characters such as:) or ^_^, that is intended to represent a human facial expression and convey an emotion.)

In this new era of worldwide connectivity, there emerged many problems pertaining to the global views of icons and other graphical elements displayed on websites. As the Internet started spreading to remote corners of the world, information became more accessible by people from different cultures. Some of the graphical content used in the design of websites either had no understandable meaning in some cultures or was sometimes considered rude and or offensive.

The Internet also opened the door for traditional brick and mortar businesses to find and connect with new global customers via electronic commerce. With electronic commerce, the Internet also had its impact on the way business was being conducted. The concept of virtual markets, in which a person can buy goods from global sources and vendors, with just few clicks of a mouse, became common place. Although Internet commerce became popular, this is not to say it was always easy or well understood by the majority of novice users. These factors of usability were just the tip of the iceberg and did not even take into account the lack of cultural awareness in the design of websites and various graphical elements.

THE SOCIAL MEDIA CULTURE

The next major culture that influenced technology is Social Media. Social Media is the propagation and sharing of information through social networking sites such as Twitter and Facebook. It is a participatory media that allows for direct contact between participants. Social Media includes websites and applications that are accessed through computers, mobile devices, tablets and other such electronic gadgets. These applications enable users to connect more closely and on a personal level by allowing them to create, share and discuss information through words and pictures. This has exposed users around the world to a deluge of information about each others' lives, careers, interests, opinions and anything and everything that they wish to broadcast.

Traces of social media can be found as early as 1994 when Geocities offered a service that enabled users to build websites to share information about themselves in the form of text and photographs. Websites like MySpace and Friendster soon followed and dominated the social networking world until 2004. The social media game changed considerably when Facebook launched in 2004 and completely revolutionized the way people connected with each other offering a more streamlined experience with users posting status updates and photos more frequently. As of October 2012, Facebook has connected over a billion users across the world.

Other social media offerings added social flavor to most commonly used Internet services such as Pandora and Spotify for music and YouTube for video content sharing. All these applications primarily focus on enriching the user experience by adding social elements to their core services. For example, a person can like or dislike a video by clicking on thumbs-up or thumbs-down icons. A cumulative number of likes and dislikes are displayed on the video page which is used by other users to estimate the social rating and or popularity of that particular video content. Users can also engage in related discussions using the comments feature. (See Figure 2)

Adding to the unending list of social media applications, electronic commerce websites such as Amazon have also jumped on the bandwagon by adding social rating systems, where people can review and rate various products sold on their website. Users can take advantage of these social ratings for a product as a measure of quality and reliability in making purchasing decisions.

Figure 2. Example of an icon used for "Like"

This social media revolution completely changed the way people use the Internet. This also led to many cultural challenges. There are many underlying assumptions in the history of social media. As most of these applications/services were originated in the United States, designers and developers did not take into consideration potential users and consumers outside the United States. For example, usage of the gestural icon of thumbs-up and thumbs-down that are used to express like and dislike, were assumed to be acceptable worldwide. However, as in the case of social media culture discussed above, the thumbs-up icon that is used to represent 'like' is considered to be offensive in many Middle Eastern countries. The potential of offending or shunning a large portion of the world may have an undesirable consequence of loss of business and revenue.

Table 1 shows some of the common metaphors and global images and their potential meanings to people of various cultures around the world.

RESEARCH

We conducted several research studies in the course of one year that included three surveys and two focus groups. We designed each study with very specific research questions in mind. How do users from different cultures understand and interpret what they see in a user interface? Is their interpretation influenced and or biased by

Table 1. Images and Global Meanings

Metaphor/ Graphical Image	Potential Western Meaning	Global Issue	Country/Culture/Religion
Pointing finger	Direction	Rude gesture	Japan, Middle East Countries, Portugal, Singapore, Taiwan
Thumbs-up	Good, Okay, Yes	Rude gesture, offensive, "stick it"	Middle East Countries
Closed fist	Powerful, good	Obscene, black power	Pakistan, South Africa
Index and pinky extended	Hang Loose	Obscene gesture	Italy
Thumb and index circle	Okay, Good	Obscene, vulgar, zero, worth-less, money	Guatemala, Belarus, Paraguay, Russia, Spain,
Crossed index and middle finger	Good luck	Offensive gesture	Paraguay
Left hand	Lefty, weaker than right hand	Dirty, unclean hand used for personal hygiene	Middle East Countries, South Africa, Vietnam
Hand palm out	Stop, No	Rude gesture, "moutza" [11]	Greece
Fingers in "V" formation with palm facing inward	Victory, Peace	Rude gesture	Australia
Dog	Fetch	Unhygienic, dirty, dangerous	Islamic countries
Piggy bank	Savings	Greed, gluttony, and unclean/ swine	Judaism and Islam
Bomb	Remove, Delete	Danger, war	Areas of affect by war may be sensitive to such images
Flesh	Skin color	Person, but with limited cul-tural awareness (in general just "Caucasians" are represented)	Excludes other skin colors
Male figure	Person	Dismissing females / male-dominated	Excludes the opposite sex

their culture? Are people from different cultures able to connect to objects and metaphors used in our icons? We wanted to gather data that would help us understand some of the implications of a person's culture in the way he/she interprets and understands icons. Each of the three surveys that we administered included specific types of graphical images and was given to participants in various geographic locations around the world. Most of our participants were able to complete the surveys remotely via the Internet. However, some of the participants of our surveys were attendees to user group conferences where we also attended. This allowed us to reach participants as far away as Australia, China, Japan, India, Mexico, Brazil, and several countries in Europe, including the United Kingdom.

SURVEY DESIGN

In the first survey, a sample set of icons from a human resources application suite were selected due to their prevalence in the employee self-service portion of the enterprise software that we studied. The icons presented were meant to be understood by any non-domain expert users with minimal human resource knowledge. These icons are considered "compound icons" as they consist of multiple objects (Figure 3). In our study, we included a total of 6 compound icons and 15 individual icon objects that made up these 6 compound icons.

The primary goal of our first survey was to obtain the interpretations and first impressions of the compound icons. This information will help us determine their effectiveness. The second goal of the survey was to quantify the interpretation of the individual icon objects that compose a compound icon. Participants identified the individual objects (Figure 4) of each icon separately. This allowed us to identify the most important objects in a compound icon. It also allowed us to identify any icon objects not globally understood or unnecessary. Finally, we wanted to understand if any of our compound icons may be culturally offensive or insensitive to users from varying cultures.

In the second survey, we wanted to study the understandability of certain metaphors or graphical representations of objects in various regions around the world. Similar to the first survey, the metaphors included in this second survey were those that would be used in a Human resources application. We wanted to understand which of these metaphors would be best when designing the application for a global audience of users. Similar to our first survey, the images presented in the second survey were also meant to be understood by any non-domain expert users with minimal human resource knowledge.

In our study, we included a total of 12 icon metaphors. All of the images presented were photographs so as to eliminate any biases in the graphical design style that is used in an icon presented to participants. We wanted to make sure that that we did not introduce any other factors in

Figure 3. Compound icon sample

Figure 4. Three individual icon objects used in making a compound icon in Figure 3

how users were interpreting or understanding the images. For example, we asked users to identify which of the four presented images would best represent "Benefits" for an employee accessing a human resources application. Our goal here is to find out what would be a universally understood graphical representation of what would be considered as an employee benefit. From our experiences with global customers, we knew that "benefit" could mean very different things for people in Europe as it does to people in the US. In the US, the caduceus shown in Figure 5 is most commonly recognized to represent a medical symbol. Therefore, we used an image of a caduceus as one of the choices given under "Benefit".

For the third survey, we wanted to focus specifically on icons commonly used in social media interfaces. Specifically, we wanted to study the usage and acceptability of thumbs-up and thumbs-down and smiley face icons. From our literature reviews, we had several references regarding the usage of gestures and how they may be offensive to certain cultures. However, these icons (especially the "thumbs-up" icon) were used extensively in social media and even online shopping applications. We also wanted to gauge if any of these icons used casually in social media, would work in an enterprise application setting or if any of them would be considered offensive to certain cultures. We wanted to gather conclusive data on when and where these images were acceptable for usage. (See Figure 6 & 7 for the four icons tested)

Figure 5. Sample Photo of a "Caduceus" to represent Benefits

Figure 6. Icon Set 1 –thumbs-up/down

Figure 7. Icon Set 2 – Smiley Face

FOCUS GROUP DESIGN

Our final research activity was conducting focus groups with participants from various national origins. Participants were asked to come to one of the two of our usability lab locations in the Bay Area of California. The primary goal of the focus groups was to have a discussion on various icons with very specific research questions in mind. Namely:

1. Are people from different cultures able to connect to objects and metaphors used in our icons?
2. What kind of icons do they prefer to see in business applications? Why?
3. Do they think color will change their opinion?
4. Are there any common views across different cultures?
5. What influences do social media have on these views/perceptions?

PARTICIPANTS

For all of our various research activities, we recruited participants from different parts of the world and with various cultural backgrounds. Over the course of eighteen months, we conducted three online surveys and two focus groups to understand how people from around the world perceive icons. We had a total of 425 participants: 52 for Survey 1, 238 for Survey 2, 122 for Survey 3 and 13 for Focus Groups and participants came from countries such as US, UK, India, China, Ethiopia, Germany, Australia and Mexico. (For more detailed information on our participants, please refer to Table 2).

Participants for the Survey 1 were attendees of a global enterprise software user group conference. This conference was held in the UK and a total of 21 users from the following nationalities volunteered to participate in the study: Italian, American, Indian, British/Asian, Irish/American, and Estonian. We also administered the survey remotely with participants in India, Japan, France, Spain, Germany, Russia, South Korea, Sweden, Brazil, Argentina and Mexico. This diversified our participant sample and helped us get different cultural perspectives from Europe, Asia and Latin America. In addition, we had a total of 31 respondents who completed our icon survey remotely, which makes of total number or respondents 52. All participants were familiar with at least one of our enterprise software offerings, but had not seen any of the icons that we had designed for our enterprise applications prior to the study.

For the Survey 2, we wanted to reach an even wider range of participants and made efforts to distribute our survey to various regions in the world. We also traveled to global enterprise software user group conferences in the US, India and Australia and administered the survey to the conference attendees. With the second survey, we were able to get responses from a total of 238 participants in a period of 5 months (June to October of 2012).

The final survey, Survey 3, was very specific to icons used in social media applications and we distributed our survey to as many diverse cultures as possible. We specifically reached out to participants in North America, Europe, Australia, Africa, Latin America, Middle East and Asia. For this final survey, we had a total of 122 participants.

Our focus groups were conducted in our usability labs in northern California. Therefore, we recruited participants who live in or around the area and are from various global cultures. Our requirements for qualifications to participant in our research were:

Table 2. Research Activity Summary

Activity	Research Question	Participants	Research Timeframe
Survey 1	Study of compound and simple icons – how well are icon parts understood by users	UK and US participants Total = 52	Dec 2011 to March 2012
Survey 2	Identify metaphors that work globally	Global participants: US, India, and Australia Total = 238	June 2012 to Oct 2012
Survey 3	Social Media icons: Thumbs-up and Thumbs-down, smiley faces	Global participants: Oracle Open World Attendees, Oracle Usability Advisory Board (OUAB) Members, Global Oracle Employees Total Participants = 122	September 2012 to October 2012
Focus Groups	Icon design discussion	Global participants living in the US: Attendees from America, India, Ethiopia, Mexico, and Germany Total = 13	Run October 16th & 18th, 2012

1. Someone with non-American family origin.
2. Must have lived in the US no longer than 8 years.
3. Uses some sort of an enterprise or business application.
4. Uses or is familiar with social media applications such as Facebook.

PROCEDURES

Survey 1: There were two parts to Survey 1. Participants were asked to provide responses to a compound icon and to each of its icon objects. (See Figure 3 and Figure 4 for an example of a compound and the objects that make up the icon). In other words, participants were first shown a compound icon and instructed to advance to the next step asked to provide up to five ideas or concepts they perceived from the compound icon. Once complete, they advanced to the second part of the survey question where they were shown the individual icon objects that made up the compound icon. For each icon object, they had to first examine the icon object and were asked to provide up to five ideas or concepts that icon object portrayed to them. For example, if the compound icon consisted of three icon objects, they would have to provide up to five ideas or concepts for each of the three icon objects. (see Figure 8 for a sample page from Survey 1)

For the next step, participants were shown six compound icons and the icon objects that make up those compound icons. For each of these compound icons, they were given a brief description of the compound icon and where in the application it would be used. Participants then rated the ef-

Figure 8. Sample question page from Survey 1

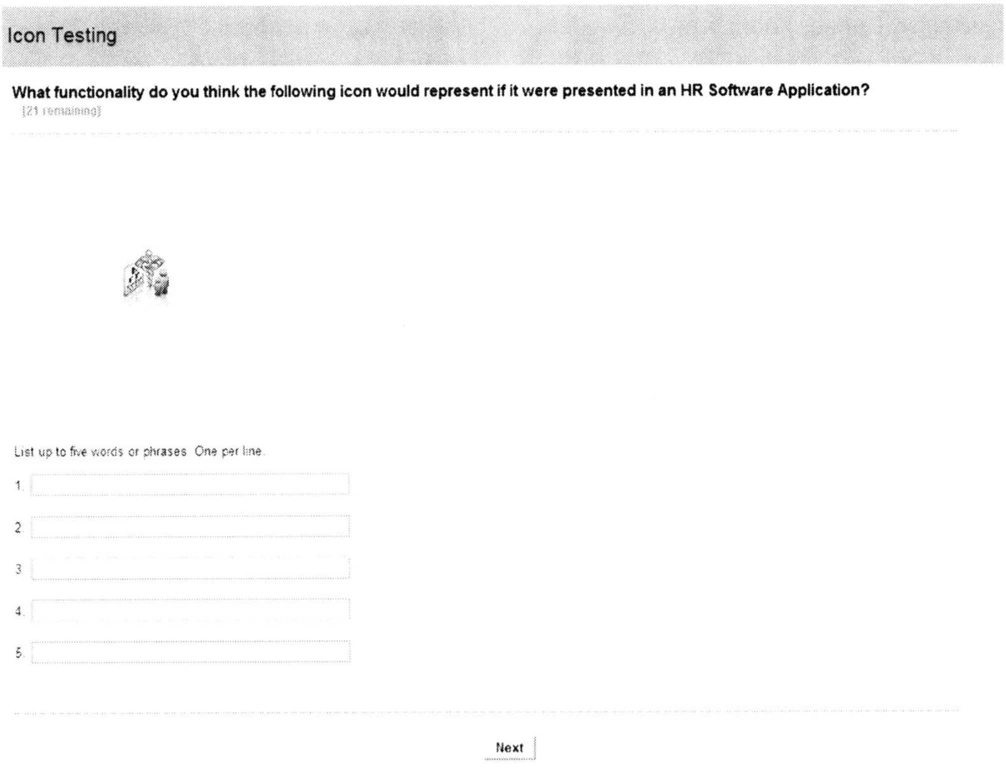

Icon Testing

What functionality do you think the following icon would represent if it were presented in an HR Software Application?

[21 remaining]

List up to five words or phrases. One per line.

1.

2.

3.

4.

5.

Next

fectiveness of each icon object in conveying the intended meaning of the compound icon. To capture the effectiveness, a 7 point Likert scale was used, with 1 being the least effective and 7 the most effective.

In the final portion of the study, participants were shown all compound icons included in the research. They then indicated their impressions of the compound icons and if they found any of them to be culturally offensive or insensitive. This question was intentionally asked at the end of the survey as we did not want to bias their first impressions of the icons and also clue them in to any sort of cultural sensitivity. If there were any emotions, positive or negative due to their cultural background, we wanted that to be expressed naturally without being made aware of it. In addition, we wanted to collect this data in order to understand if any of our icons were in any way offensive the various cultures where are products may be sold and used. Last, but not least, a demographic section was included to capture information regarding the cultural diversity of the participants.

Survey 2: In the second survey, participants were first asked to identify which region of the world they were originally from. Their choices were: Africa, Asia, Australia, Europe, Latin America, and Middle East. On the second page, participants were asked to select one image from a choice of four images (shown as photos) that best represented the concept that we wanted to test. We specifically chose to show photos instead of illustrations or icons to avoid influencing participants' choices based on reaction to design, style and other variables that may have been introduced by the graphic designer's interpretation of the concept. We also were very selective in the objects that we chose for the concepts tested in our survey. For example, for the "Benefits" concept, participants were shown the following photos: an umbrella, a caduceus, people, and a suitcase. We chose these images based on our domain knowledge of Human resources applications and the types of employee benefits that are offered. We selected images may represent a beach vacation (beach umbrella), medical symbol (caduceus), family benefits (people), and vacation travel (suitcase). In addition, if participant felt that none of the images fit the category or concept, then they had the choice to select "Other" and fill in a description of what other image would best represent the concept for them. We had a total of five concepts in Survey 2. Namely: "Benefits", "Medical Benefits", "Compensation" and "Experience & Qualifications".

Survey 3: As described above, the third survey was very specific to icons used in social media applications and included two sets of two icons. The first set of icons included a "thumbs-up" and a "thumbs-down" icon. And the second set included two face icons–happy and sad. When participants started the survey, they were asked to answer three demographic questions. Namely, what region of the world do you currently reside in, what is your region of origin, and what is your gender? Their choices of regions of origin were: Africa, Asia, Australia and New Zealand, Europe, Latin America, Middle East, and North America.

Once they advance to the second page, they were presented with the first icon ("thumbs-up"), and asked "What are the first words or ideas that come to mind when you see the following icon?", list up to five words or phrases. When they feel that they are done with this icon, they can advance to the next icon ("thumbs-down"), and are asked the same question and provided space to list up to five words or phrases. They can then continue to do the same for the other two face icons – happy and sad. Next, participants are presented with all four icons, and asked what they feel the icons would mean in the context of an enterprise application and if any of the icons have a negative or offensive connotation in their culture? If so, they were asked to provide a brief explanation.

On the next page, participants were shown an example screen from an enterprise application where a user is asked to "vote" and asked if they think these two pairs of icons ("thumbs-up" and "thumbs-down", and the face icon pair) are appropriate for use in an enterprise context similar to the one presented. They were provided a space so that they can explain their response. (See Figure 9)

After being given a chance to provide any additional comments about the survey or any of the materials within it, participants then completed the final step of the survey. On this final page, participants had the option to provide their name and email, should they wish to participate in future research activities.

Focus Groups: When participants arrived for our focus groups they were asked to fill out an icon survey. The survey was a hard copy and included icons from two different human resources applications. They were asked to work independently in completing the surveys. Once everyone was done, we presented and discussed some global icon design considerations, including icons for phones, microphones, banks, money, and post office. In this initial discussion, we wanted to understand how well users were able to connect to objects from different cultures.

The second part of our discussion was around icons commonly used in social media applications. Namely, thumbs-up/thumbs-down and smiley face/frowny face icons. We first asked if any of our participants found any of these icons offensive or culturally insensitive. In showing participants the thumbs-up/thumbs-down and smiley face/frowny face icons that are prevalent in social media, we wanted to understand if these icons would now be acceptable to be used in business applications. In our discussions, we also wanted to understand what kinds of icons users would prefer to see in business applications. We observed to see if there were any common views across the different cultures and also introduced the topic of color to see if our participants felt that the color of icons would change their opinions about these icons. We wrapped up our focus group by having a group discussion of the icons included in the paper survey that each of them completed individually at the beginning of the hour, and we revealed our answers to the participants to gather their feedback on the understandability and effectiveness of our icons.

MEASURES

Recall: Compound icons in Survey 1 were randomly presented without context. Participants were instructed to advance the survey when they felt ready to answer questions about the icon. Participants then recalled and listed as many concepts and ideas they could about the icon. This portion of the evaluation provided rich feedback and was

Figure 9. Sample survey question of icons in context of an application

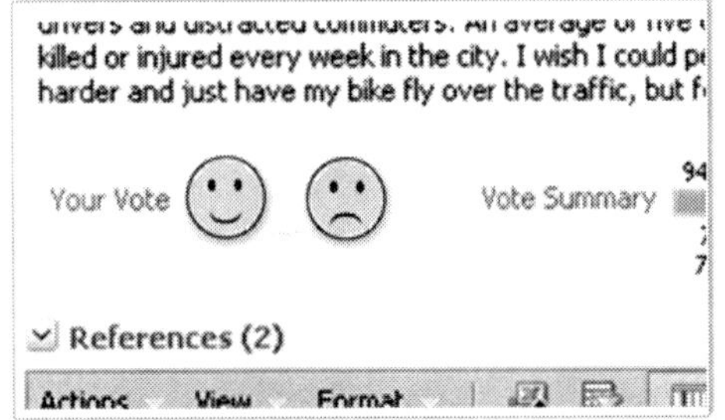

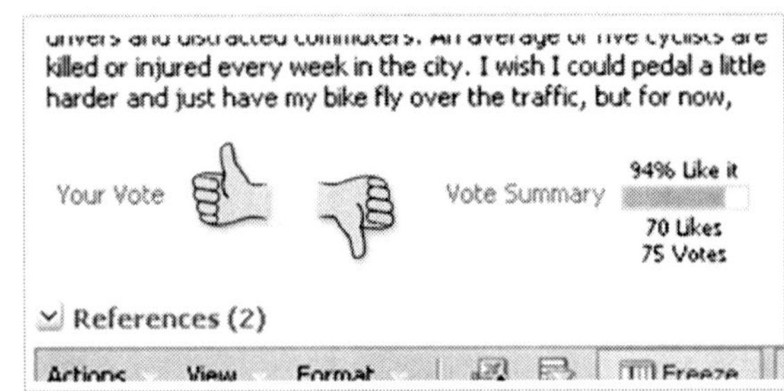

used to generate a word cloud highlighting the most commonly mentioned keywords.

Rating: For each compound icon presented in Survey 1, participants were given a brief description of the icon and where in the application it would be used. For example, one of the icons was designed to represent employee benefits, including health care. The brief description included with the icons was "employee benefits including health care." Based on this description participants were asked to rate each object on a scale of 1 to 7 on how effective it was in conveying the meaning of the compound icon, with 1 being the least effective and 7 the most effective.

Icon Metaphors: When presenting icons or images to participants, particularly in the second survey, participants selected or described the best metaphors for the given concept or idea. We captured the understandability and the appropriateness of each metaphor or graphical representation of the concept, taking into account the various cultural backgrounds of the participants.

Cultural Feedback: In all of the research activities, including the surveys and focus groups, participants were asked to provide feedback on the icons based on their impressions of the icons and if they found any of them to be culturally offensive or culturally insensitive.

Social Media Influence: How are social media applications influencing the acceptance of certain images or gestures? In our focus groups, we discussed if and when certain icons commonly used in social media may be used in enterprise applications. From our discussions with participants from various cultures, we were able to infer what influences social media have on the views and perceptions of certain, previously considered "taboo" imagery.

Table 2 shows the summary of the various research activities that we conducted.

RESULTS

The data we collected from Survey 1 indicates that our current compound icons are generally well understood by various cultures. However, there are some metaphors or object representations that are not globally known. For example, the Rolodex icon object was not understood and mistaken for a folder or ID card. (See Table 3). We also generated "word clouds" of the responses we received for the icons to understand the similarity and frequency of phrases mentioned by survey participants from various cultures. Figure 10 shows a word cloud that was generated for the "contact information" icon that was presented in the first survey.

Our data from Survey 1 showed that there were some icon objects and metaphors that were not well-understood by some of our participants. For example, the caduceus image that we used to represent a medical benefit was not understood by participants outside the United States. We also determined that we needed to use better objects or metaphors for some of our compound icons. For example, in the case of contact information, we can use an icon of an ID card rather than a Rolodex card as the Rolodex was only known to

Table 3. Icon sets with Popular Tags from Survey 1

Compound Icon with Popular Tags	Icon Object with Popular Tags
Business Card, Contact Information, Person Details	Business Card, Person Details
	Employee, Manager, Person

Figure 10. A word cloud of popular tags for "Contact Information" in the Survey 1

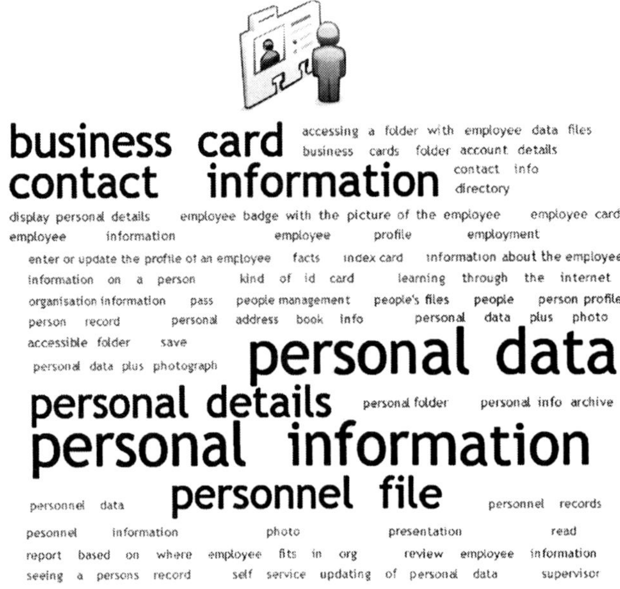

mostly US participants. Our results show that more data must be collected in order to obtain conclusive evidence as to how cultures vary in the way they perceive and understand a large collection of icons that will be used in enterprise software applications.

In the second survey, we wanted to see if there are any universally understood metaphors or graphical representations of objects that we could use for our Human Resource applications that are used by people in various regions around the world. Our second survey data indicated that it is indeed very challenging to find metaphors that can be used by all regions. For example, when we tried to find out what icon or metaphor would best represent the global concept for employee benefits, our participants could not come up with one conclusive item. When given four choices (as photos), participants' responses were not very conclusive and were split across all images. The caduceus and childcare images received a little over 30% of the votes, while the suitcase and umbrella images received 13% and 17% respective. (See Figure 11-Figure 14)

Figure 11. Data from Survey 2 – "Benefits"

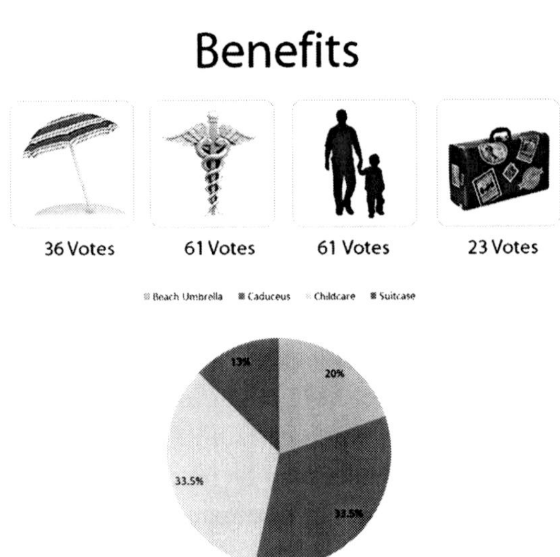

Overall, our data from the second survey helped us to conclude that designing universal icons for a global audience may not always be possible and needs more thorough research. In some cases, localization of these images and metaphors may be necessary to make them appropriate for a global culture. Another option may be to con-

Figure 12. Results from Survey 2 – "Medical Benefits"

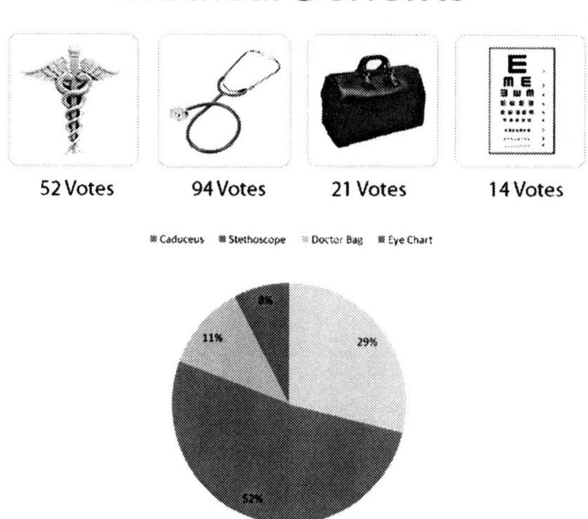

Figure 13. Results from Survey 2 – "Compensation"

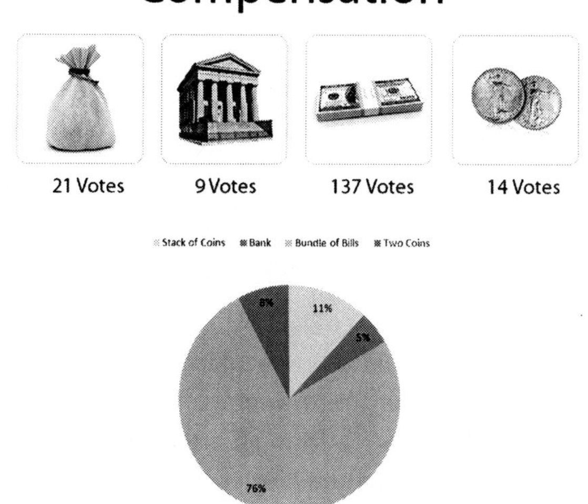

Figure 14. Results from Survey 2 – "Experience & Qualifications"

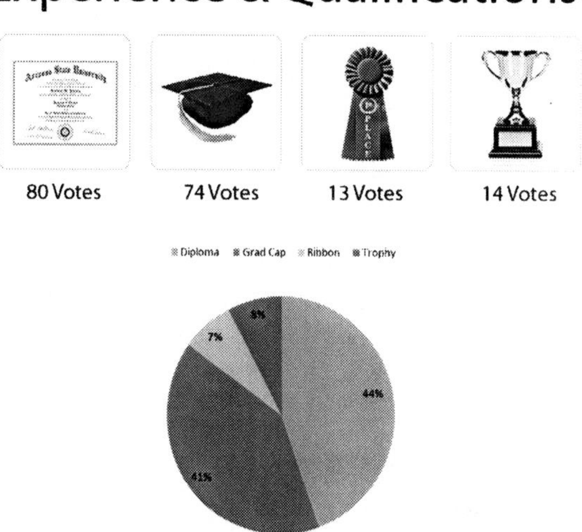

sider compound icons so multiple metaphors may be included in a single icon, which is one of our approaches in designing our icons, as explored in our initial survey.

Survey 3 was specifically designed to measure the acceptability of commonly used social media icons. We included two pairs of icons: thumbs-up and thumbs-down, and smiley face and frowny face. When we generated word clouds for each of these four icons, we found that the majority of our participants used very positive words and tags when asked to give three to five words that came to their minds when they saw the thumbs-up icon (See Figure 15). And when presented the thumbs-down icon, the word cloud we generated showed that they would use this icon to represent something that was bad, something that is wrong, or something they did not like (See Figure 16).

However, when asked about the potential cultural offensiveness of these icons, most indicated that they thought it was OK to use these icons in an application user interface. We also were able to find out that all our participants felt that the smiley and frowny face icons carry emotional value where as the thumbs-up and thumbs-down icons are more formal in nature.

After conducting our two focus groups, we were able to collect some preliminary data on the most common interpretations of our icons and we were also able to conclude that participants from various parts of the world may not find certain

Figure 15. Word Cloud for "thumbs-up" icon in Survey 3

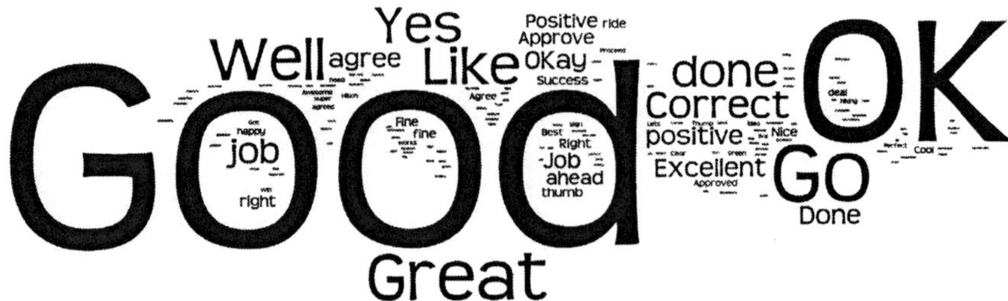

Figure 16. Word Cloud for "thumbs-down" icon in Survey 3

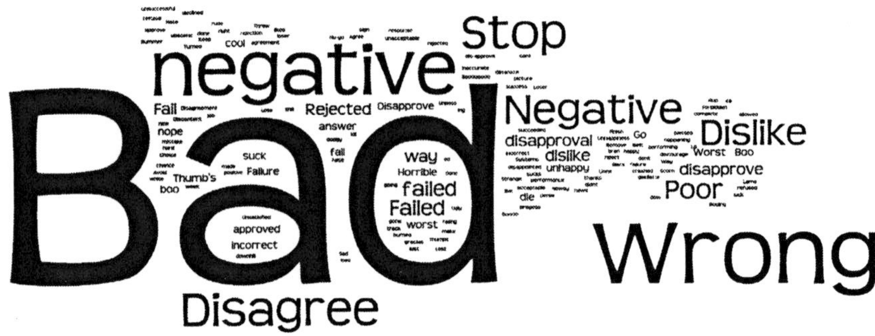

social networking icons as culturally offensive as we had initially assumed. However, more research is needed with participants living in various regions of the world, as our data was solely based on participants currently living in the US.

FUTURE RESEARCH DIRECTIONS

For future research on cross-cultural icon-user interactions, we plan to conduct research that includes the usage interpretation of emoticons. We also plan to conduct additional in-person and in-context research in various global regions. These studies will be similar to the focus groups that we conducted in the US and India. This additional research will help us make conclusions about usage of certain gestural icons and their potential offensiveness. Future research will also investigate the role of colors and shapes (such as lines, circles etc) in conveying the meaning of an icon to individuals from various cultural backgrounds.

CONCLUSION

The advancements in the current day technology make it common for an average user to be exposed to information from all around the world. We believe that culture has an important role in the way icons and other graphical elements are perceived. As one of the initial steps towards understanding the implications of culture in the way icons are perceived globally, we conducted extensive research in the form of global surveys and focus groups.

From our focus groups and global surveys, we learned that the compound icons we used in our surveys were well understood by various cultures. One of the interesting findings from our research is that some of the icons we use in our current enterprise applications, like the Rolodex for personal information, are just considered as an abstract representation rather than a metaphor for an actual concept. Our study participants indicated no familiarity with the Rolodex, but identified the "yellow folder" icon to be an abstract representation of an identity card or personal information.

We also learned that some of our initial assumptions about certain icons to be culturally offensive to some parts of the world were invalid as they were based on antiquated reference materials that had not been recently investigated. Our survey and focus groups informed us that due to the increased social media awareness among various cultures, some of the gestures and icons that were once considered offensive may now be acceptable. For example, the thumbs-up icon used in various social media websites was once considered offensive in some of the Middle Eastern countries, but in our focus groups and surveys, our study participants expressed a more accepting global view of iconic metaphors and graphical images. This also paves the way for an interesting research question to study the role of social media in decreasing the cultural gaps between various cultures of the world.

We hope that our work helps icon and graphic designers in making better design decisions when creating graphical elements for a global audience.

REFERENCES

Axtell, R. E. (1998). *Gestures: The DO's and TABOOs of body language around the world*. New York, NY: John Wiley & Sons, Inc..

Bourges-Waldegg, P., & Scrivener, S. (1998). Meaning, the central issue in cross-cultural HCI design. *Interacting with Computers*, *9*(3), 287–309. doi:10.1016/S0953-5438(97)00032-5.

Cho, H., Ishida, T., Yamashita, N., Inaba, R., Mori, Y., & Koda, T. (2007). Culturally-situated pictogram retrieval. In *Proceedings of the 1st International Conference on Intercultural Collaboration* (IWIC'07). Berlin: Springer-Verlag.

Evers, V., Kukulska-Hulme, A., & Jones, A. (1999). *Cross-cultural understanding of interface design: A cross-cultural analysis of icon recognition*. Paper presented at the International Workshop on Internationalization of Products and Systems. Rochester, NY.

Hoft, N. H. (1996). Developing a cultural model. In E. M. D. Galdo, & J. Neilson (Eds.), *International User Interfaces* (pp. 41–73). Hoboken, NJ: John Wiley & Sons, Inc..

Jones, N. A., Ross, H., Lynam, T., Perez, P., & Leitch, A. (2011). Mental models: An interdisciplinary synthesis of theory and methods. *Ecology and Society*, *16*(1), 46.

Kluwe, R. H., & Haider, H. (1990). Models of internal representations of complex systems. *Sprache & Kognition*, *4*, 173–190.

Lakoff, G., & Johnson, M. (1980). *Metaphors we live by*. Chicago: University of Chicago Press.

Lefevre, R. (2011). *Rude hand gestures of the world*. San Francisco, CA: Chronicle Books.

Morrison, T. (2006). *Kiss, bow, or shake hands*. Avon, MA: Adams Media. Barber, W., & Badre, A. (1998). Culturability: The merging of culture and usability. In *Proceedings of the 4th Human Factors and the Web Conference*. IEEE.

Nisbett, R. E., Peng, K., Choi, I., & Norenzayan, A. (2001). Culture and systems of thought: Holistic versus analytic cognition. *Psychological Review*, *108*, 291–310. doi:10.1037/0033-295X.108.2.291 PMID:11381831.

Peesapati, S. T., Wang, H.-C., & Cosley, D. (2010). Intercultural human-photo encounters: How cultural similarity affects perceiving and tagging photographs. In *Proceedings of ACM International Conference on Intercultural Collaboration* (ICIC 2010). ACM.

Schro¨ der. S., & Ziefle, M. (2006). Evaluating the usability of cellular phones' menu structure in a cross-cultural society. In E.A. Konigsveld (Ed.), *Proceedings IEA 2006: Meeting Diversity in Ergonomics*. Elsevier.

Shen, S.-T., Prior, S. D., Chen, K., & Fang, T. (2009). Chinese users' preference for web browser icons. *Design Principles and Practices, 3*(1), 115–128.

Stilan, E., Chen, A., & Bezuayehu, L. (2011). Accessible icon design in enterprise applications. In *Proceedings of the International Cross-Disciplinary Conference on Web Accessibility* (W4A '11). New York: ACM.

van der Veer, G. (2011). Culture centered design. In Proceedings of the 9th ACM SIGCHI Italian Chapter International Conference on Computer-Human Interaction: Facing Complexity (CHItaly). ACM.

Van House. N., Davis, M., Ames, M., Finn, M., & Viswanathan, V. (2005). The uses of personal networked digital imaging: an empirical study of cameraphone photos and sharing. In *Proceedings of CHI '05 Extended Abstracts on Human Factors in Computing Systems* (CHI EA '05). ACM.

ADDITIONAL READING

Ayouby, R., Croteau, A.-M., & Raymond, L. (2013). Impact of cultural influences on internet adoption. In *Proceedings of the 2013 46th Hawaii International Conference on System Sciences*, (pp. 2842-2851). IEEE.

Cho, H., Ishida, T., Yamashita, N., Koda, T., & Takasaki, T. (2009). Human detection of cultural differences in pictogram interpretations. In *Proceedings of the 2009 International Workshop on Intercultural Collaboration* (IWIC '09). ACM.

Creating a New Language for Nutrition: McDonald's Universal Icons for 109 Countries. (n.d.). Retrieved from http://www.translationdirectory.com/articles/article1387.php

Dreyfuss, H. (1984). *Symbol sourcebook: An authoritative guide to international graphic symbols.* New York, NY: McGraw-Hill.

Hall, E. (1976). *Beyond culture.* New York: Doubleday & Company.

Hicks, J. (2011). *The icon handbook.* Penarth, UK: Five Simple Steps.

History of Windows Icons. (n.d.). Retrieved from http://www.windows-icons.com/history.htm

Hofstede, G., & Hofstede, G. J. (2005). *Cultures and organizations: Software of the mind.* New York: McGraw Hill.

Horton, W. (1994). *The icon book.* New York, NY: John Wiley & Sons Inc..

International Business: International Symbol, Icon Blunders Can be Avoided. (n.d.). Retrieved from http://www.deseretnews.com/article/705370663/International-symbol-icon-blunders-can-be-avoided.html

Interview with Susan Kare. (n.d.). Retrieved from http://www-sul.stanford.edu/mac/primary/interviews/kare/trans.html

Johnson, J. (1989). *The xerox star: A retrospective.* Palo Alto, CA: IEEE Computer.

Kroeber, L., & Kluckhohn, C. (1952). Culture: A critical review of concepts and definitions. *Harvard University Peabody Museum of American Archaeology and Ethnology Papers, 47*, 181.

Laukkanen, T., & Cruz, P. (2012). Cultural, individual and device-specific antecedents on mobile banking adoption: A cross-national study. In *Proceedings of System Science (HICSS), 2012 45th Hawaii International Conference on System Sciences*, (pp. 3170-3179). IEEE.

Li, H., Sun, X., & Zhang, K. (2007). Culture-centered design: Cultural factors in interface usability and usability tests. In Proceedings of Software Engineering, Artificial Intelligence, Networking, and Parallel/Distributed Computing SNPD 2007 (Vol. 3, pp. 1084-1088). IEEE.

Marcus, A. (2003). Icons, symbols, and signs: Visible languages to facilitate communication. *Interaction*, *10*(3), 37–43. doi:10.1145/769759.769774.

McInnes, K. (2011). *Rockstar icon designer*. Melbourne, Australia: Rockable Press.

Perceptions of Animals Across Cultures: Man's Best Friend or Dirty Beast? (n.d.). Retrieved form http://blog.communicaid.com/cross-cultural-training/perceptions-of-animals-across-cultures-man's-best-friend-or-dirty-beast/

Pigs in Popular Culture. (n.d.). Retrieved from http://en.wikipedia.org/wiki/Pigs_in_popular_culture

Ping, T. P., Sharbini, H., Chan, C. P., & Julaihi, A. A. (2011). *Integration of cultural dimensions into software localisation testing of assistive technology for deaf children.* Paper presented at the Software Engineering (MySEC). New York, NY.

Rikakis, T., Kelliher, A., & Lehrer, N. (2013). Experiential media and digital culture. *Computer*, *46*(1), 46–54. doi:10.1109/MC.2012.391.

SanNicolas-Rocca, T., & Parrish, J. (2013). Using social media to capture and convey cultural knowledge: A case of chamorro people. In *Proceedings of System Sciences (HICSS), 2013 46th Hawaii International Conference on System Sciences*, (pp. 3386-3395). IEEE.

The Desktop Environment. (n.d.). Retrieved from http://www.guidebookgallery.org/articles/thedesktopenvironment

Tidwell, J. (2011). *Designing interfaces*. Sebastopol, CA: O'Reilly Media, Inc..

Usability in Icons. (n.d.). Retrieved from http://stiern.com/articles/usability/usability-in-icons/

KEY TERMS AND DEFINITIONS

Culture: The behaviors and beliefs characteristic of a particular group, based on social, ethnic or age group.

Emoticon: A sequence of printable characters such as:-) or ^_^, that is intended to represent a human facial expression and convey an emotion. An emoticon is also sometimes called a smiley.

Enterprise Software: Any software designed for and used by an enterprise (e.g. large businesses, government, or school).

Global: Worldwide.

Global Culture: A term used to describe the habits and heritages of different societies around the world.

Icon: Graphical representation of an object or idea.

Metaphor: Something that is regarded as a representative or symbol of something else.

Perception: An immediate or intuitive recognition.

Taxonomy: An ordered systematic grouping of items based on matching similar qualities or attributes.

Chapter 3
Improving Interaction with TV-Based Applications through Adaptive Multimodal Fission

David Costa
University of Lisbon, Portugal

Carlos Duarte
University of Lisbon, Portugal

ABSTRACT

In this chapter, the authors describe the design and implementation of an adaptive multimodal fission component integrated in the multimodal GUIDE framework. This component is able to adapt any HTML-based application's UI to a specific user's characteristics, making it possible for elderly and impaired users to interact by offering several output modalities that try to overcome possible interaction difficulties. They also present an evaluation of the proposed solution, conducted with more than 50 participants, that shows the efficiency of multimodal adaptation in increasing task perception and task execution.

INTRODUCTION

Nowadays, interaction with TV is no longer a passive viewing experience, where all the viewer does is choose what channel to watch or change volume settings. Today, with services like Google TV, Samsung smart TV or even Apple TV, viewers have active roles consuming and producing contents like browsing the web, uploading media such as images or videos, using different TV applications available or simply recording TV programs.

Since everyone can and should be able to access these new technologies regardless of their age, knowledge and physical, sensorial or cognitive abilities it makes sense to employ adaptation techniques and offer a wide range of possible interaction devices for both input and output feedback.

Given that it cannot be expected that software developers quickly become experts in designing and developing multimodal adaptive systems, the way to bring the benefits of adaptation and multimodality to end-users is to provide an easy way for application developers to include multimodal adaptation in their applications, or to integrate them into an existing adaptive multimodal framework.

Keeping in mind the e-inclusivity of all possible users of smart TVs and the feasibility for developers to apply those features, a framework was

DOI: 10.4018/978-1-4666-4623-0.ch003

envisioned with particular focus on elderly people and their specific impairments and preferences.

This chapter focuses on our approach to handle output adaptations based on users' abilities and characteristics. To do so, we demonstrate our implementation of a fission engine and its applicability on a specific project, a multimodal adaptive framework named GUIDE. This framework is a layer between the end-user and the application execution platform, which is capable of endowing applications with multimodal and adaptive features. The fission component uses an abstract description of the user interface (UI) to perceive what elements are displayed in the screen and adapts the UI to best suit the user and interaction context.

Although the approach designed can be applied to different execution environments, the GUIDE project focuses on TV as a channel to increase accessibility to Web application for older adults. As such, in this chapter, we will focus on the current implementation, that targets Web applications running on TVs. Consequently, the examples provided in the chapter will reflect this context.

In the following sections we describe what adaptive multimodal systems are and present earlier research work and projects on this subject. Next, we describe our results from earlier user studies to design and implement this user centered framework. In the main section we do an in depth description of the adaptive multimodal fission engine, by explaining the engine's process flow, the approaches and techniques used and its main sub-components. Later on, we present the conclusions of study made to evaluate the usability and adaptive capacities of the framework with more than 50 users from 3 different countries.

ADAPTIVE MULTIMODAL SYSTEMS

Dumas, Lalanne, and Oviatt (2009) define multimodal systems as "computer systems endowed with multimodal capabilities for human-computer interaction and able to interpret information from various sensory and communication channels". These systems offer users a set modalities to allow them to interact with machines and "are expected to be easier to learn and use, and are preferred by users for many applications" (Oviatt, 2003).

Adaptive multimodal systems enable a more effective interaction by adapting to different situations and different users according to their skills, physical or cognitive abilities.

The flexibility of these systems allows them to adapt not only to users but also to the environment (context awareness). For example, the system can use speech to warn or present information in an eyes-busy situation. Combining adaptation capabilities with multimodal interaction can result in an interface even more flexible and natural to the user. In the past, several works have tried to explore this combination as a way to improve interaction. Most of these have targeted adaptation within specific modalities, instead of adaptation across modalities (Duarte & Carriço, 2006).

Past attempts at designing adaptive systems have shown their potential and usefulness though they fail or are hard to be translatable to different types of applications or application execution environments. Examples of earlier projects include ELM-ART II (Weber & Specht, 1997) and I-Mailer (Kabassi & Virvou, 2003).

Other authors tried to address this issue and developed frameworks that are indeed able to perform adaptations, independently of the application. Examples of these systems are SmartKom (Reithinger et al., 2003) and SUPPLE (Gajos, Weld, & Wobbrock, 2008). The SUPPLE project considers the generation of personalized user interfaces as an optimization issue. It automatically generates a personalized user interface based on four types of input information: 1) Functional specification of the interface; 2) Device-specific constrains; 3) Usage trace and 4) Cost function. SUPPLE then generates the user interface that is the most efficient while satisfying all the constraints.

However, all of these mentioned frameworks require from application developers knowledge about the specificities of multimodality and adaptation. The framework presented in this chapter aims to achieve that goal, supporting interface adaptation, not only within but also across modalities, besides imparting applications with multimodal input capabilities.

GUIDE's architecture follows the "integration committee" approach introduced by Dumas et al. (2009) which is composed by: 1) A fusion engine (Feiteira & Duarte, 2011). Fusion engines are key components in multimodal systems, responsible for combining information from different sources and extract a semantic meaning from them; 2) A dialogue manager (DM) (Costa & Duarte, 2011a). The DM is responsible for coordinating the dialogue between human and machine; 3) A fission engine (Costa & Duarte, 2011b). This component is responsible for generating and adapting the UI of the application; and 4) A user model (Biswas et al., 2011) and a context model (UM and CM). These models manage user profile-data and environmental context respectively.

Figure 1 shows an overview of the framework and its communication system. Components 1), 2) and 3) described above are the main components that constitute the adaptive multimodal interaction layer in the framework. Components in 4) are the ones that gather information related to user and context interactions. These components altogether form the GUIDE core.

Applications are executed in environments (e.g. Web Applications in browsers, Java applications in java runtime environments, etc.). The framework abstracts this into the concept of Application Execution Environment (AEE). For each AEE, an Application Environment Interface (AEI) needs to be provided. The AEI is responsible for managing the communication between applications and framework. The main function of this interface is to translate the application's UI into a representation that is understood by the framework (UIML – User Interface Modeling Language). The AEI also exchanges events between the application and the framework.

Figure 1. Architectural overview of the framework

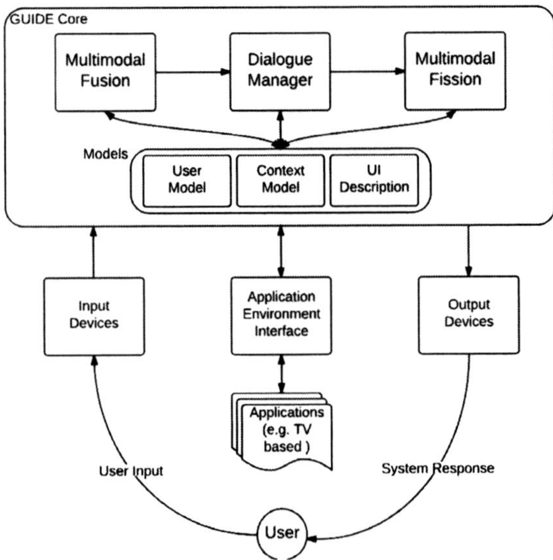

Based on the UIML, fission performs the UI adaptations in runtime. Some of these adaptations are adjusting text-size, colour schemes and adding other output modalities for interaction with the user. In the present, GUIDE offers support for applications based in HTML, Javascript and CSS, offering an implementation of the AEI for this application execution environment. This implementation is called the Web Browser Interface (WBI).

Multimodal Fission

This component is responsible for choosing the output to be presented to the user and how that output is channeled and coordinated throughout the different available output channels (based on the user's perceptual abilities and preferences). Dumas et al. (2009) states that a multimodal fission engine should follow three main tasks: message construction, modality selection and output coordination.

- **Message Construction:** The presentation content to be included must be selected and structured, i.e., it is necessary to decompose the semantic information issued from the dialogue manager into elementary data to be presented to the user. There are two main approaches for content selection and structuring that can be employed – schema-based (Fasciano & Lapalme, 2000) or plan-based (Duarte, 2008).

However, in GUIDE, this task begins before the Fission component process begins (it occurs in the Application Environment Interface). Schema-based systems like PostGraphe (Fasciano & Lapalme, 2000) determine from a set of existing schemas the best schema suitable for the user's intentions assigning a weight for each intention using heuristics. WIP (Wahlster, André, Finkler, Profitlich, & Rist, 1993) is a presentation generation system that follows this approach receiving as input a presentation goal and then tries to find a presentation strategy which matches the given goal.

- **Modality Selection:** After the message construction, the presentation must be allocated, i.e., each elementary data is allocated to a multimodal presentation adapted to the interaction context. This selection process follows a behavioural model that specifies the components (modes, modalities and medium) to be used. The available modalities should be structured according to the type of information they can handle or the perceptual task they permit, the characteristics of the information to present, the user's profile (abilities, skills, impairments and so on) and the resource limitations. Taking this into consideration is necessary for optimal modality selection. For the compliance of this goal there are three approaches: rule based (Bateman, Kleinz, Kamps, & Reichenberger, 2001), composite based (Fasciano & Lapalme, 2000) and agent based (Han & Zukerman, 1997).
- **Output Coordination:** Once the presentation is allocated, it needs to be instantiated, which consists in getting the lexical syntactic content and the attributes of the modalities. First, the concrete content of the presentation is chosen and then attributes such as modality attributes, spatial and temporal parameters, etc., are fixed. For a coherent and synchronized result of the presentation, all used output channels should be coordinated with each other.

Systems that combine outputs evolved since the early nineties where text and graphics were combined (e.g. COMET (Feiner & McKeown, 1993)). More recent systems combine speech, haptic, graphics, text, 2D/3D animations or avatars (e.g. SmartKon (Reithinger et al., 2003); MIAMM (Reithinger et al., 2005)). Although most applications use few output modalities and consequently straightforward fission techniques, dealing with the above-mentioned combination of outputs can make the presentations more complex and difficult to coordinate and be coherent.

Learning with Users

To be able to correctly exploit the possibilities of adaptive multimodal interaction, we need to learn about and characterize our users. We followed a user centered methodology to offer the best adaptive experience for the end users – focusing, in our case, in older adults, with the mild to moderate impairments that are typical of that age. To this end we conducted user trials to meet the users' requirements, behaviors and specificities, studying and analyzing their interaction with a multimodal application (Coelho, Duarte, Feiteira, Costa, & Costa, 2012).

These studies' conclusions had clear implications in the development of such an adaptive system as is GUIDE (Duarte, Coelho, Feiteira, Costa, &

Costa, 2011; Coelho, Duarte, Langdon and Biswas, 2011). In what concerns fission adaptation we learned that, no matter their characteristics, users prefer applications where there are short number of interactive elements for each screen, focusing on big buttons. If developers make complex UIs, GUIDE has to be capable of dividing one screen in multiple screens or present options to the user in alternative modalities.

Applications should make sure both text size and audio volume are configurable by the user at the beginning as well as in the middle of an interaction. If the application by itself doesn't offer this option, GUIDE UI adaptation should offer this possibility.

The existence of a strong relation between arm and item locations on the screen (e.g. users tended to use the left arm for pointing to menus located in the left side of the screen and right arm for the right side), will influence the way developers design the layout of their applications, as it also affects the configuration and parameterization of GUIDE presentation manager (fission module), as both have to contemplate the existence of this user-UI relation. For example, a user with impairments in the left arm should have interactive elements in the right side of the screen if he wishes to interact with hands in free air.

Users also prefer visual and audio channels to give redundant information on feedback interactions but it may differ in different applications and contexts.

Later on in this chapter we will describe an evaluation on the framework effectiveness with users from three different European countries.

MULTIMODAL ADAPTIVE FISSION

A multimodal adaptive system should be able to flexibly generate various presentations for the same information content in order to meet the individual user's requirements, environmental context, type of tasks and hardware limitations. Adapting the system to combine all this time changing elements is a delicate task.

The fission module is crucial to make that possible as it takes advantage of multimodalities to overcome sensory impairments that users may have.

Our implementation of the fission engine, although based on the aforementioned approaches, follows the What-Which-How-Then (WWHT) approach, a conceptual model of Rousseau, Bellik, and Vernier (2005). This component must know what information to present, which modalities to choose to present that information, how to present it using those modalities and coordinate the flow of the presentation.

Architecture

Figure 2 shows the architecture of the fission component, its subcomponents, the other framework components which it communicates with and output devices.

UIML, DM, UM and CM parsers are the classes responsible for parsing the information received from the corresponding components. The UIML parser gets the UI representation, i.e., all the visual elements (e.g. buttons, images, text, videos, etc.) and their properties (e.g. text size, color, width, height, location, volume, etc.) of the current application screen. The DM parser receives data whenever there are issues with users input recognition. For example, when the fusion component cannot understand a user's speech command (low confidence level on the words spoken), the fission component is responsible to render a message for the user to ask him to repeat the command. These messages are defined as User Framework Dialogues (UFDs), which are independent of the application running and will be described further. The UM parser gets the data from the user model such as the user's level of impairment on each modality and the range of recommended values for visual and audio attributes. The CM

Figure 2. Multimodal adaptive fission architecture

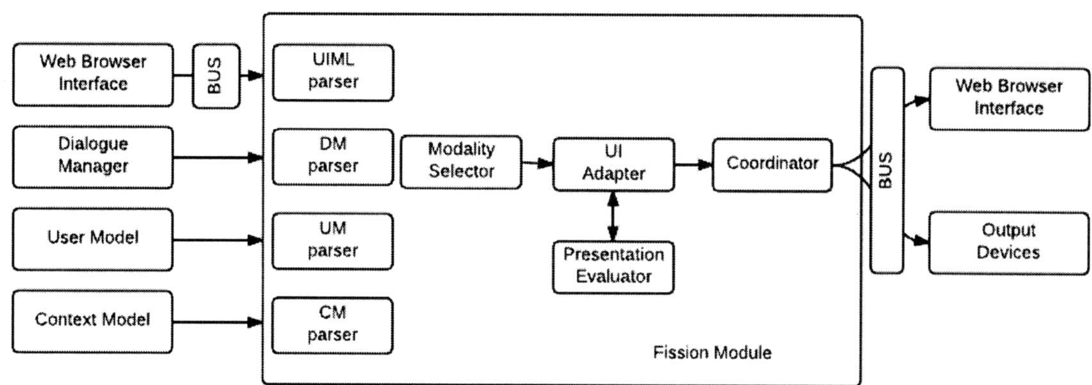

parser parses the information about the devices available and their configurations.

The Modality Selector (MS) class is responsible for selecting the modalities to use for a specific user. First the level of adaptation is chosen, inferred from the compatibility between the current user interface and the user's characteristics. Then, obtaining the impairment levels, this component decides which modalities to use.

The UI Adapter (UIA) adapts the presentation based on the user and context model values, while the Presentation Evaluator assesses the validity of the presentation.

The Coordinator component is responsible for laying out the output events in the right order and sending them to the respective output devices.

Output Features

In order to fulfill the objective of universal design, the fission module has at its disposal different types of equipment to perform the rendering of the presentation, thus allowing it to render content to a wide range of users.

The main medium used for visual rendering is the TV where the channels, the GUIDE interface and TV based applications such as Tele-learning, video conferencing or home automation are rendered. A tablet may also be used to clone or complement information displayed on the TV screen (e.g. context menus). Tablets are powerful tools for user adaptation purposes, although they essentially are used as secondary displays.

For these devices a virtual character will be also available (Ribeiro, Silva, José, & Iurgel, 2010) with the goal to illustrate, answer, advise and support the user. This virtual character plays a major role for elderly acceptance and adoption of the GUIDE system.

Audio feedback is available from the TV, tablet or remote control through audio speakers. Audio output can be from non-speech sounds such as rhythmic sequences that are combined with different tone, intensity, pitch and rhythm parameters to speech synthesizers that produce artificial human speech.

Haptic feedback is performed by vibration features from the remote control or tablet and is mainly used to complement other modalities (e.g. an alert message appears on the screen and the remote control vibrates to warn the user).

These are the devices available for the fission module to perform adaptation actions to TV applications based on the user characteristics. Visual modality can be complemented by auditory modality and/or haptic feedback. All elements of the presentation (e.g. text, images, buttons, videos, avatar, sounds, etc.) should be highly configurable and scalable, i.e., attributes such as size, font, location, color, volume and intensity should be able to be set by the fission module. Depending on the user, the depth of the adaption will change.

Adaptation Levels

In the past we decided to divide the different levels of adaptation into three categories of the interaction and presentation interface, which can be characterized as augmentation, adjustment and replacement.

Currently these adaptation levels are no longer explicitly selected or defined by the developer of the application or by the UM based on the user characteristics. Instead, the depth in the adaption is a consequence of a rule-based system located in the fission component that is inferred from UM and CM data.

Nevertheless these three levels represent the result from the MS decision making and are an increasing change to the visual presentation defined by the application, from no change to the visual rendering to a, possibly, complete overhaul. Given that the framework aims to support legacy applications, we must consider that these applications have been developed without accessibility concerns towards impaired users.

Augmentation is the first and lightest form of adapting the interface implemented by developers. In this case, visual elements are not subject of adaptation. Instead, what the fission module does is to complement the user interface with other modalities. The UI (its HTML/JavaScript-based embodiment, in the case of web applications) should be enriched with UI mark-up (e.g. WAI-ARIA), so that the framework can extract semantic information of UI elements and render a user-specific multimodal UI augmentation of it (fission would be able to perceive which elements are part of a menu, information text, etc. and then build an intelligent discourse for the virtual character).

Adjustment is the level of adaptation where the interface rendering is adjusted to the abilities of the user and can also be combined with augmentation. Considering applications are primarily developed using visual presentation mechanisms, this corresponds to be able to automatically adjust several parameters such as font size (e.g. myopia), color, contrast (e.g. for different type color blind diseases), etc. If other modalities are employed, their parameters can be also adapted (e.g. adjust audio volume of the speakers, vibration intensity of remote control, etc.). Other impairments such as physical ones (e.g. Parkinson's disease) can influence also the display of interactive elements on the screen. Fission considers this and applies wider spacing between buttons in order to ease the selection while using pointing input devices for example. Fission obtains all the recommended properties for a specific user from the different elements and compares with the application's settings, and then it sets the right values for those elements with possibly some small adjustments for presentation arrangement purposes.

Replacement level is the most complex adaptation scheme as it means a full control over the interface developed by the developer. Besides augmentation and adjustment it can also replace interactive elements by others (e.g. menus replaced by buttons) or distribute the screen content over different modalities and/or more screens. Users with cognitive impairments could experience a better navigation through the application by getting a simpler screen and not feel lost due to the tangle of menus and buttons displayed.

Replacement level has been left out of developments in the project so far, given the reluctance shown by application developers in having a foreign framework taking over the rendering of their applications. However, it is envisioned that new algorithms will have to be devised to that end, since the variables at play are substantially different than the ones for the first two adaptation levels.

Modality Selection and Evaluation

In this phase we need to know the user's characteristics and decide what modalities to use. Impairment levels are accessed and modalities are chosen to complement and/or be adapted. Figure 3 shows where Fission gets the information needed for modality selection.

Figure 3. Information for modality selection during multimodal fission process

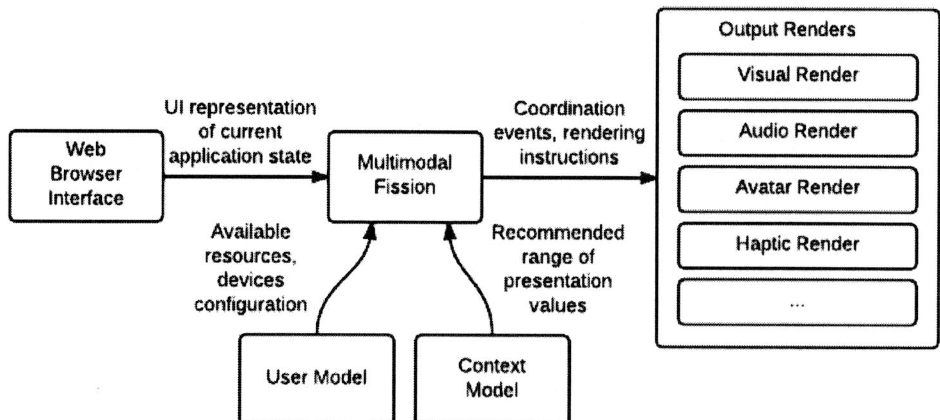

When the framework detects a user, the knowledge stored in the UM about the user is sent to fission. This information is split into two sets of data. The first one is the predicted preferred modalities. The second set, are more specific interface values (e.g. minimum font-size, color scheme, volume settings, etc.). Based on this data and the context environment (e.g. level of environmental noise, devices on and offline, distance of the user to the screen, etc.), fission will perform the first step of adaptation.

The MS follows a rule based system, which results from the analysis of the user studies (Coelho et al., 2011), to define which adaptations will be applied to the application's UI and which modalities will be added to complement the already existing ones. We decided to follow this approach due to hardware restrictions on performance derived from the need to execute the framework on a set-top-box. This modality decision approach is simple and takes less processing.

Table 1 presents the rules MS follows to select the output modalities from the received UM information. For example, for a user with both Visual and Auditive suggested modalities, the UI will be adapted and a Virtual Character (VC) will be rendered giving a description of the application's UI. For a user with only auditive modality suggested,

Table 1. Fission rules for selecting the modalities to render the output

	Active output features		
Predicted modality	Screen	Virtual character	Text-to-speech
Visual	Select		
Auditive			Select
Motor (Pointing & Gesture)	Select		
Visual & Auditive	Select	Select	
Visual & Motor	Select		
Auditive & Motor	Select	Select	
Auditive & Visual & Motor	Select	Select	

a text-to-speech solution will be used instead of the VC and no visual adaptions will occur.

The next step in fission is adapting the UI based on the modalities activated. In this process the specific data for each activated modality are taken into account and queried from the UM. Also the UI representation of the application is accessed, which contains detailed information on the visual elements of the current application's screen, i.e., for each element on the screen, fission knows its properties (e.g. position, width, height, font-size, color, etc.). Therefore, fission does not apply the UM recommended adaptations blindly, but optimizes the process. Regarding visual adaptations, for instance, the application element's properties can be compared with the ones recommended by the UM. Only elements that don't meet the requirements will be adapted and this adaptations will be still be validated by changes made to the UI. This prevents elements from overlapping each other, or to be placed outside of the device's screen resolution boundaries.

Coordination

To synchronize the presentation flow, coordination events will be sent to the bus in order to start or stop rendering, or to be notified when the rendering is completed. Figure 4 shows a simple example of render synchronization where the audio synthesis will only start after the visual rendering is completed.

These rendering instructions are handled by a buffer in the fission module, which sends one instruction for each device at a time. The device will then respond with a notification of completion or failure. By controlling the flow of events sent and notifications received, instructions that do not get a chance to be rendered because a new state needs to be loaded due to user intervention are not even sent to the rendering devices, saving bandwidth.

Coordination can be guaranteed by the fission component based on notifications of completion and failure. If all instructions were sent to render at once, coordination would be much more complex because output devices cannot be expected to be aware of the state of other devices.

Communication Events

The framework uses a publisher/subscriber communication system in which events from components outside the core flow through different buses. However, communication between components of the core is done through direct function calls and dealt by the DM. For example, the WBI sends to the framework new application states to be rendered (using the GUIDE Bus) and fission, which subscribes that type of events, will then request information from the user and context models by querying data of those components (direct function calls mediated by the DM). After the correct adaptation performed by the fission component, it publishes output events to the corresponding devices. A summary of the events produced and received is presented on Table 2.

User Interface Description Language

For the framework to understand applications' UI, we studied several abstract and concrete user interface mark-up languages that were taken into account to be used as the UI standard for GUIDE. We conducted a study on several languages and UIML was the best suited for our purposes (Costa, 2011, pp. 59-61).

The UIML specification does not define property names. This is a powerful concept, because it allows it to be extensible, as we can define any property appropriate for a particular element of the

Figure 4. Example of rendering synchronization

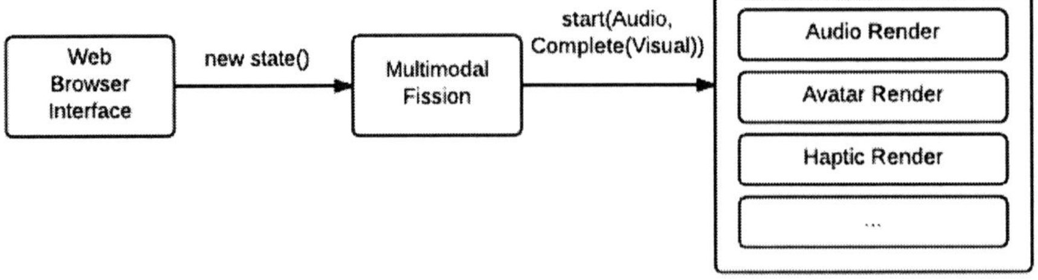

Web Browser Interface
new state()
Multimodal Fission
start(Audio, Complete(Visual))
Output Renders
Visual Render
Audio Render
Avatar Render
Haptic Render
...

Table 2. Communication events for multimodal fission

Name	In/Out	Description
UI Representation	IN	Published by WBI, Subscribed by all core components.
GUI Adaptations Required	OUT	Published by Fission, subscribed by visual renders (e.g. TV, Tablet, etc.).
VC Behavior	OUT	Published by Fission, Subscribed by VC. Contains scripted text and VC emotion/ intention.
VC Window	OUT	Published by Fission, Subscribed by VC. Contains VC window location and sizes.
VC Profile	OUT	Published by Fission, Subscribed by VC. Contains VC gender, appearance settings and camera shot.
Status	IN	Published by Output devices, Subscribed by Fission. Delivers the status of the rendering (Fail, Success).

UI. Additionally, they might be used to represent the information developers might provide using WAI-ARIA markup tags.

User Framework Dialogues

User Framework dialogues, or UFDs, are dialogues generated to solve a specific interaction issue related with the user. These dialogues are not generated in the application logic but in framework dialogue management and they are intended to unlock blocks in the interaction flow of the user. UFDs can be triggered by the user itself or by the framework. For instance we can have the case where the user asks for the list of possible voice commands and that list is then generated comprising the framework and current application state commands. On the other hand, the framework can detect if a user is lost in the interaction and promptly asks him if he wants to see an interaction tutorial video to instruct him on how to use the system capabilities.

To properly detect and solve these issues, the framework needs to make decisions in different scopes in the core components, i.e., each component has its own semantic knowledge and must share it with others components.

Therefore we followed an approach where we defined a chain of data objects carrying different levels of semantics in terms of derived knowledge and these objects are then handled by the corresponding core components.

For example, a user utters a speech command (e.g. "GUIDE HOME") and the fusion component does not recognize the input, due to low confidence level of the recognized command. This component will now proceed to generate an UFD requirement to the DM with the knowledge it has (e.g. recognized input "GUIDE HOME", confidence level low). The DM, based on the information received, will generate a "Confirm low input confidence" UFD and sends it to the Fission component (in Table 3 are listed all the defined UFDs). These dialogues are created using the same representation used for applications (UIML).

The fission component now knows the origin and type of UFD it is handling so, besides the normal adaptations based on the user characteristics, it will add more specific semantic information to the UFD.

Fission will make use of this information to personalize with great detail the VC component, i.e., the scripted text will be in a more natural language for the user (it is really different than just describing the content of an application), the emotions of the VC will be changed in order to accurately show the intention of the presented dialogue (e.g. VC will show concern and speak with a question tone).

Being generated in the framework, the WBI does not have yet access to the UIML, so the DM

Table 3. List of user framework dialogues

User Framework Dialogue	Description
Explain UI	User requests information about a UI element
Confirm Profile Update	System proposes a change on user profile
Confirm low confidence input	If an input has low confidence, the system seeks user confirmation
Wrong input	If a user does an unexpected input
Offer help	System recognizes a user is stuck during interaction
Tutorial	System detects problems using a certain modality
Speech Commands	User requests list of all available speech commands
Location	User requests a breadcrumb overview of the current location
Gestures	User requests list of gestures available
Go to home	User requests to go to the main screen of the application
Settings	User requests changes in user profile
Resolution of conflicting input	System detects conflict by user commands (e.g. clicking on one element but using a different speech command)

has to send the UIML to WBI in order to render the respective dialogue in the browser. Simultaneously fission sends the UI adaptations required and the VC specifications.

USER EVALUATION

As long foreseen, adapting the user interface and contents to the abilities and characteristics of the user is beneficial to the usability of applications. However, adaptive features are still lacking and falling short in adoption by application developers due to their inherent complexity.

Above, we have presented a framework (with particular focus on the multimodal adaptive fission component) able to sit between the system and the user and deploy the desired adaptability with minor effort required from the application developer.

To be able to evaluate the benefits of such approach and the underlying concepts, we have engaged on a user evaluation in the context of TV based applications

The main goal of this study was to validate our framework, in particular to what multimodal fission adaptation is concerned. We do so by assessing the benefits of multimodal adaptation in the interaction of older users with a user interface they are used to, a TV-based Electronic Program Guide (EPG) application.

Participants

We recruited 52 people (33 female and 19 male) with different disabilities, most of them age-related. Users were recruited in three countries, with 21 participants (17 male and 4 male) being recruited in Spain, 19 participants were from the UK (10 female and 9 male) and 12 Germans (6 female and 6 male).

The average age was 74.2 years old (SD=13.9). The large dispersion is justified by the inclusion of three young participants (25, 26 and 29 years old) with several physical and sensorial disabilities, which were included for us to assess if younger users with disabilities could also benefit from the proposed framework. The remaining participants had ages comprehended between 52 and 89 years old. All users had previous experience with EPG applications.

Procedure

An EPG application was implemented for the experiment, to simulate a realistic TV interaction setting (older users are, in general, familiarized with this type of applications). To achieve such a realistic scenario, the development started with mockup designs, which were then reviewed and implemented by experts in the development of TV and STB applications. Later, all elements were implemented using HTML, JQuery, CSS and JS languages. The EPG was fed with real information pertaining channels, shows and respective schedules.

The evaluation session, for each user, comprised:

- Running the User Initialization Application (UIA), an application developed with the main purpose of introducing the system to new users and trough a set of steps create his profile with his characteristics and preferences. Based on this information the user model will predict the adaptions needed for this particular user.
- Performing tasks with the adapted EPG version. Each user had its own version adapted by the framework based on the results collected in UIA.
- Performing tasks with the Non-adapted EPG version.

The order in which users performed both versions of the EPG was randomized to counteract learning effects. All users participated voluntarily and all activities in this study were logged and recorded on camera – both the TV screen and the user – for later analysis. All information was anonymized and privacy was taken in consideration.

Apparatus

The study was conducted in three locations, Spain, Germany and UK. Efforts were directed to create similar environment and technical conditions in all labs. Users were briefed about the framework, its goals and the tasks in hand. Given the specific character of the participants (mainly older adults), traditional usability unaided tasks were sometimes unfeasible. Although intervention was reduced to a minimum, to reduce anxiety, users were told they could ask for help if they felt lost. All help requests and interventions were logged and taken in consideration in the analysis. Concerning setup and specification, different modalities of interaction were configured: pointing resorted to the use of Microsoft Kinect; for speech recognition we used the Loquendo Speech engine; a simplified remote control, with less buttons than traditional ones and capable of controlling pointer coordinates using gyroscopic sensor was made available; an iPad was used for tablet interaction; and a full 1080p HDMI TV with integrated speakers and a 32'' screen was used for visual and audio output. User interactions and answers were video recorded.

Design and Analysis

We used a within-subjects design where all fifty-two (52) users ran the UIA and performed tasks in both adapted and non-adapted settings. Quantitative data was retrieved from the UIA (user profile and interface preferences). A satisfaction questionnaire composed of sentences to be rated according to a 5-point Likert scale was performed to assess the participants' understanding and acceptance of the UIA. Further, similar subjective procedures were deployed to assess the perceived benefits of adaptation and overall acceptance of the framework. Given the specificity of the population and the semi-supervised methodology (participants were motivated to perform the tasks on their own, but they were free to ask questions when they felt lost), as it is usual in the first contact of older users with novel technologies, objective comparisons were not performed (e.g. task times).

However, to enable a more concrete and objective analysis of user performance with and without adaptations, we performed a detailed video analysis to 15 randomly selected users (6 from Spain, 6 from the UK and 3 from Germany). These videos were coded according to pre-defined variables and categories within. Examples of such variables, for each task, were: task understanding, task completion, number of help requests, and number of errors.

Wilcoxon Signed rank tests were used in comparisons to subjective measures between both versions of the EPG. Differences in objective measures were evaluated with ANOVA procedures whereas normal distributions were found, while Wilcoxon Signed rank tests were used in the presence of non-normal data. We present statistical significant results at the $p<.05$ level. However, trends (or marginal effects) are also presented ($p<.1$) given the size of the sample and the exploratory scope of this research.

Evaluation and Results

GUIDE's framework aims to improve the usability of interactive systems by adapting the interaction between user and system. To enable this, besides the presented framework components, the user has to run a one-time calibration application (the UIA) which by turn feeds the user model component.

The results are presented firstly based on the measures collected from all 52 participants. This part comprises an analysis to the subjective measures pertaining perceived adaptation and its benefits, along with a qualitative assessment of the framework. Secondly we encompass a more detailed analysis based on the test footages of 15 participants. The latter is mainly focused on the benefits of adaptation and provides objective differences between the two versions of the EPG.

As mentioned before, an EPG approved by TV-based application developers was reproduced taking overall accessibility already in consideration. Moreover after running the UIA each user had an adapted version of the original EPG by GUIDE's framework.

Subjective acceptance to EPG adapted and non-adapted versions was evaluated through a statement to classify using a five-point Likert scale (1-the system has not supported me at all; 2-the system has supported me only in some parts of the task; 3-undecided; 4- the system has supported me in almost all the tasks; 5-the system has supported me at every moment). A Wilcoxon Signed Rank Test revealed a marginal significant difference between the EPG adapted (Mode=4, IQR=1.5) and non-adapted versions (Mode=3, IQR=2), $z=-1.665$, $p<.1$, with a medium effect size ($r=0.37$). This trend suggests that adaptations improve the relation between the participants and the interface. Once again, as the baseline EPG was already designed as an accessible version, this may be the reason for the participants to rate the non-adapted EPG as quite adapted to their needs as well. Also, since the goal of adaptation is to make the system perform in a subjective expected way, it is possible that participants did not even become aware of adaptation effects (Weibelzahl & Weber, 2002).

This experiment seeks to assess how people (in this case older and severe disabled people were considered) would react to the adaptable and flexible mechanisms present in our framework. While the aforementioned behaviors suggested that adaptation was positively seen and felt by the participants, we questioned them directly about their opinions on the presented system. We performed a self-rating post-questionnaire to assess their overall opinion and acceptance of the system (5-point Likert scale).

Overall, all items were positively rated by most users (Table 4). Regarding the opinion about the system, the overall satisfaction with it, the comfort and pleasure it guarantees were consistently highly rated as shown by the central tendency and low dispersion. The ratings with slightly larger dispersions were about the easiness, efficiency and recovering of errors of the system, although still on the positive end of the rating scale (Median 5, IQR = 2). This can be explained both by technical errors (e.g. speech recognition errors and tablet connection problems)

Table 4. Subjective ratings to the system. Median [IQR]

Overall Opinion about the System	Rating [1-5]
Overall, I am satisfied with how easy it is to use	4 [2]
I am able to efficiently complete the tasks using the system	4 [2]
I feel comfortable using the system	5 [1]
It was easy to learn to use it	4 [1]
Whenever I make a mistake, I recover easily and quickly	4 [2]
it is easy to find the information I needed	4 [1]
The interface of the system is pleasant	5 [1]
Overall, I am satisfied with the system	5 [1]

and by the difficulty when executing "select and confirm" tasks, which lead to errors and blocking situations. These users were unable to complete the tasks as they desired which translated in the mentioned lower ratings. Although these can be explained by technical and design glitches, they are still a relevant lesson learned as an unexpected, even localized, flaw, particularly in an adoption phase, is prone to damage the user's relationship with the system as a whole.

Detailed Evaluation

To be able to draw more conclusions from this experiment we delved further in the results and particularly, performed a detailed analysis of 15 randomly selected participants. Upon deciding a coding scheme, the videos were dissected to assess the behaviors of the participants in both versions of the EPG.

From the use of the EPG, a total of 160 tasks were analyzed in the adapted version, and 90 in the non-adapted one. We now describe results from the video analysis concerning the way users perceive (Figure 5) and execute (Figure 6) tasks on both versions.

In the adapted version, users managed to perceive the necessary interface elements before proceeding to the execution of the task in 94% of the tasks, while only 77% of the tasks were perceived without help in the non-adapted EPG. A Wilcoxon signed rank test showed this difference to be significant with a large effect size, $Z=-2.703$, $p<.01$, $r=0.5$. This can be justified first with the inclusion of the Virtual Character component in the explanation of every menu of the adapted EPG, and second, with the adaptations made to the GUI by the multimodal fission component.

In what relates to execution, 59% of the tasks were completed without any help on the adapted EPG, while in the non-adapted EPG the percentage

Figure 5. User perceive analysis

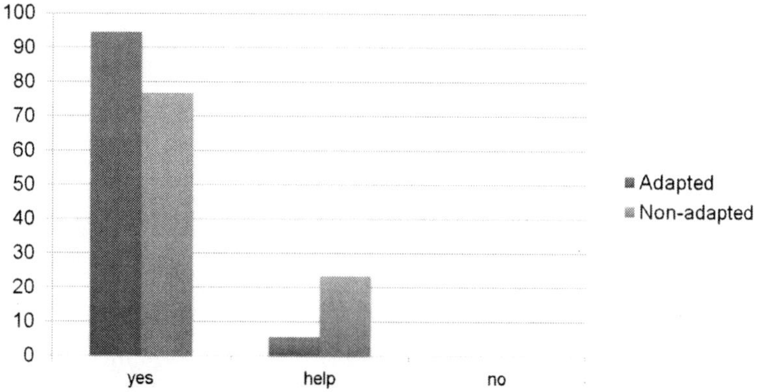

Figure 6. User execution analysis

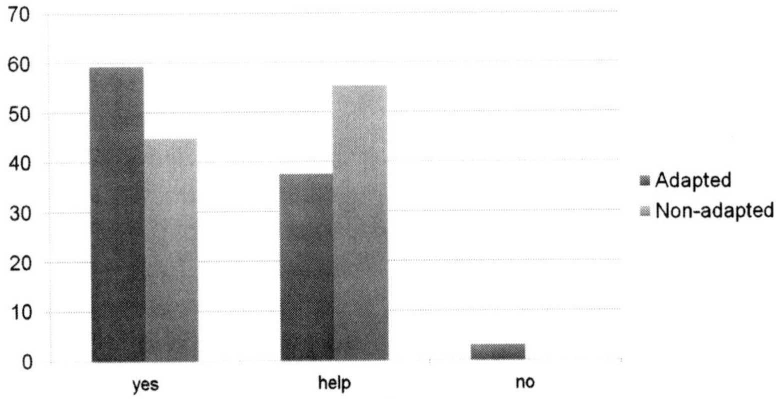

of unaided completed tasks was reduced to 45%, which was revealed as a significant difference (Wilcoxon signed rank test, Z=-1.978, p<.05, r=0.37, medium effect). Still, these percentages are lower than expected and largely different from the results pertaining perception of the task in hand. This is mostly related with the innovative aspects included in the system. For several times in the adapted version (47%), it was suggested to the users in the experiment process, the use of a certain modality (e.g. they never used a gyroscopic remote control before). Also, in both versions, users were asked to perform tasks they were not familiar with, like changing channels by navigating menus instead of pressing/selecting numbers, or tasks like "activating subtitles". Additionally, they were also frequently asked to change between modalities before proceeding to the next task. All these factors could lead to blocking and error situations, which in turn lead to explicit requests for help, or moderator interventions, as some devices and tasks did not act accordingly to the participants' mental model. This, together with some technological problems (e.g. pointing mechanism not sharp enough, or tablet disconnected from network) when using miss-configured modalities (like speech and tablet), contributed to the low completion rate.

Other variables (Figure 7) like the amount of user requests for help, the number of times users got stuck or the amount of user errors per task are worth exploring towards an understanding of the benefits of the adaptive framework.

Concerning the amount of times users got stuck in the middle of a task, results suggest that the adapted version (11%) helped the users when compared to the non-adapted version (16%).

Figure 7. User interaction issues

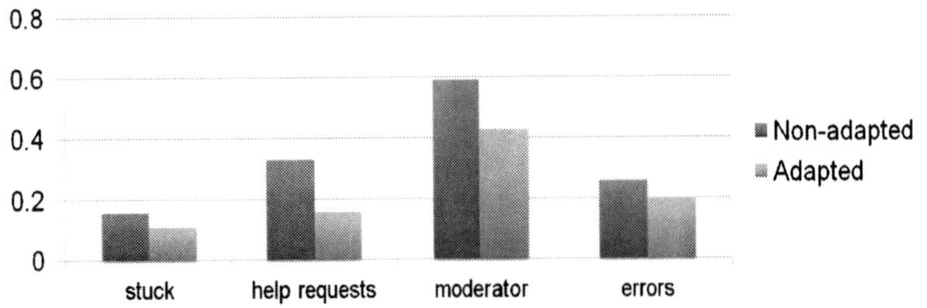

Looking at the number of users who accomplished the tasks without any help, in the non-adapted version, users accomplished an average of 49% of the tasks on their own while in the adapted version 61% of the tasks were accomplished without help. As this data showed a normal distribution (Shapiro-Wilk, $p>.05$), a parametric test (One-Way Within-Subjects ANOVA) was employed and revealed significant differences ($F(1,13)=4.66$, $p=.05$, $r^2=0.35$, large effect).

In what relates to the amount of times users asked for help, we can also verify that, without adaptation, users made an average of 0.33 requests per task while with adaptation they reduced drastically to 0.16 requests per task. This metric also showed a normal distribution (Shapiro-Wilk, $p > .05$), and differences were once again revealed as significant ($F(1,13)=7.164$, $p<.05$, $r^2=0.35$, large effect).

This is even more relevant if taking into consideration that more help was given by trial moderators in the non-adapted EPG tasks (about 0.59 times per task) than in the adapted EPG tasks (about 0.43 times per task).

However, and contrary to the tendency of the previous findings, no significant differences were found in terms of the number of errors (non-normal distribution, Shapiro-Wilk, $p<.05$) per task between the adapted and non-adapted versions (Wilcoxon Signed Rank Test, $Z=-.667$, $p=.505$). Nevertheless, there is still a tendency for performing more errors in the non-adapted version than in the adapted one, especially if we again take into consideration that some errors in the latter version were caused by malfunctions in modality recognition.

Therefore, the results obtained denoting less errors, less requests for help, less blocking situations, and higher rates in the perception and execution of tasks without help in the adapted version of the EPG, show that adaptations performed by the framework (and more specifically the Fission component) helped in the interaction between users with age-related (or other severe) impairments and the tested platform (TV).

Finally, 47% of the users agreed with the adaptation provided by the EPG. Only 13% disagreed, and 40% stated they would like even more adaptation. As examples of additional adaptation, users stated they would prefer if UI elements were bigger (buttons and text font), and also wished for different colours on the interface.

CONCLUSION

GUIDE tries to deliver accessibility features to TV based applications without requiring much effort from developers as the multimodality features and adaptations are transparent to them. Taking advantage of a set of multimodal devices provided by the system, the framework allows users with some kind of functional limitation or impairment to continue enjoying interaction with TV based applications.

Thanks to the knowledge gained in user studies conducted with end-users in the early phases of GUIDE implementation, the Fission component is capable to choose the best modalities to perform adaptation based on the user model using a simple binary rule method. It evaluates the content in order to change the visual properties with compatible values. It also coordinates the presentation flow, ordering which and when devices should start rendering.

An evaluation was performed with 52 participants with a variety of age related impairments which compared two versions of a TV-based application (EPG). Results showed that they perceived adaptations and are positive about them. An in-depth analysis with a reduced set (15) of participants showed that in an adapted version the users are more effective both in understanding and completing the tasks, perform fewer errors, and require less help. Still, to fully assess the impact of adaptation, a longitudinal evaluation is required as the real value of adaptation is proven over time.

In the overall, even such a challenging audience as are older people (due to their individual differences and reluctance in adopting novel technologies) showed to be positive about the adaptations provided by the framework and eager to experiment its full potential on the long run. Future work includes refining multimodal fission algorithms based on the user trials findings and a longitudinal deployment of the adaptive framework in older people's homes to fully assess the potentialities of our approach.

REFERENCES

Bateman, J., Kleinz, J., Kamps, T., & Reichenberger, K. (2001). Towards constructive text, diagram, and layout generation for information presentation. *Computational Linguistics, 27*, 409–449. doi:10.1162/089120101317066131.

Biswas, P., Robinson, P., & Langdon, P. (2012). Designing inclusive interfaces through user modeling and simulation. *International Journal of Human-Computer Interaction, 28*(1), 1–33. doi:10.1080/10447318.2011.565718.

Coelho, J., Duarte, C., Feiteira, P., Costa, D., & Costa, D. (2012). Building bridges between elderly and TV application developers. In *Proceedings of the International Conference on Advances in Computer-Human Interactions*, (pp. 53-59). IEEE.

Coelho, J., Duarte, C., Langdon, P., & Biswas, P. (2011). Developing accessible TV applications. In *Proceedings of the International ACM SIGACCESS Conference on Computers and Accessibility,* (pp. 131– 138). ACM. doi:10.1145/2049536.2049561

Costa, D. (2011). *Self-adaptation of multimodal systems*. (Master Thesis). University of Lisbon, Lisbon, Portugal.

Costa, D., & Duarte, C. (2011a). Self-adapting TV based applications. In C. Stephanidis (Ed.), *Universal Access in Human-Computer Interaction: Design for All and eInclusion* (pp. 357–364). Springer. doi:10.1007/978-3-642-21672-5_39.

Costa, D., & Duarte, C. (2011b). Adapting multimodal fission to user's abilities. In C. Stephanidis (Ed.), *Universal Access in Human-Computer Interaction: Design for All and eInclusion* (pp. 347–354). Springer. doi:10.1007/978-3-642-21672-5_38.

Duarte, C. (2008). *Design and evaluation of adaptive multimodal systems*. (Doctoral Dissertation). University of Lisbon, Lisbon, Portugal.

Duarte, C., & Carriço, L. (2006). A conceptual framework for developing adaptive multimodal applications. In *Proceedings of the International Conference on Intelligent User Interfaces*, (pp. 132–139). IEEE. doi: 10.1145/1111449.1111481

Duarte, C., Coelho, J., Feiteira, P., Costa, D., & Costa, D. (2011). Eliciting interaction requirements for adaptive multimodal TV based applications. In C. Stephanidis (Ed.), *Universal Access in Human-Computer Interaction: Design for All and eInclusion* (pp. 42–50). Springer. doi:10.1007/978-3-642-21672-5_6.

Dumas, B., Lalanne, D., & Oviatt, S. (2009). Multimodal interfaces: A survey of principles, models and frameworks. In D. Lalanne, & J. Kohlas (Eds.), *Human Machine Interaction* (pp. 3–26). Springer. doi:10.1007/978-3-642-00437-7_1.

Fasciano, M., & Lapalme, G. (2000). Intentions in the coordinated generation of graphics and text from tabular data. *Knowledge and Information Systems, 2*, 310–339. doi:10.1007/PL00011645.

Feiner, S., & McKeown, K. (1993). Automating the generation of coordinated multimedia explanations. In M. T. Maybury (Ed.), *Intelligent multimedia interfaces* (pp. 117–138). American Association for Artificial Intelligence.

Feiteira, P., & Duarte, C. (2011). Adaptive multimodal fusion. In C. Stephanidis (Ed.), *Universal Access in Human-Computer Interaction: Design for All and eInclusion* (pp. 373–380). Springer. doi:10.1007/978-3-642-21672-5_41.

Gajos, K. Z., Weld, D. S., & Wobbrock, J. O. (2008). Decision-theoretic user interface generation. In *Proceedings of the National Conference on Artificial Intelligence* (vol. 3, pp. 1532–1536). IEEE.

Han, Y., & Zukerman, I. (1997). A mechanism for multimodal presentation planning based on agent cooperation and negotiation. *Human-Computer Interaction*, *12*, 187–226. doi:10.1207/s15327051hci1201&2_6.

Kabassi, K., & Virvou, M. (2003). Adaptive help for e-mail users. In J. Jacko, & C. Stephanidis (Eds.), *Human-Computer Interaction: Theory and Practice* (pp. 405–409). CRC Press.

Oviatt, S. (2003). Multimodal interfaces. In J. Jacko, & A. Sears (Eds.), *The Human-Computer Interaction Handbook: Fundamentals, Evolving Technologies and Emerging Applications* (pp. 286–304). Lawrence Erlbaum Associates Inc..

Reithinger, N., Alexandersson, J., Becker, T., Blocher, A., Engel, R., & Lockelt, M. … Tschernomas, V. (2003). Smartkom: Adaptive and flexible multimodal access to multiple applications. In *Proceedings of the International Conference on Multimodal Interfaces*, (pp. 101–108). IEEE. doi:10.1145/958432.958454

Reithinger, N., Fedeler, D., Kumar, A., Lauer, C., Pecourt, E., & Romary, L. (2005). Miamm – A multimodal dialogue system using haptics. In J. Kuppevelt, L. Dybkjaer, N. Bernsen, & N. Ide (Eds.), *Advances in Natural Multimodal Dialogue Systems* (Vol. 30, pp. 307–332). Springer. doi:10.1007/1-4020-3933-6_14.

Ribeiro, P., Silva, T., José, R., & Iurgel, I. (2010). Combining explicit and implicit interaction modes with virtual characters in public spaces. In *Proceedings of the Joint Conference on Interactive Digital Storytelling*, (pp. 244-247). IEEE.

Rousseau, C., Bellik, Y., & Vernier, F. (2005). WWHT: Un modéle conceptuel pour la présentation multimodale d'information. In *Proceedings of the 17th International Conference on Francophone sur l'Interaction Homme-Machine*, (pp. 59–66). IEEE. doi:10.1145/1148550.1148558

Wahlster, W., André, E., Finkler, W., Profitlich, H.-J., & Rist, T. (1993). Plan-based integration of natural language and graphics generation. *Artificial Intelligence*, *63*, 387–427. doi:10.1016/0004-3702(93)90022-4.

Weber, G., & Specht, M. (1997). User modeling and adaptive navigation support in www-based tutoring systems. In *Proceedings of the International Conference on User Modeling*, (pp. 289-300). IEEE.

Weibelzahl, S., & Weber, G. (2002). Advantages, opportunities, and limits of empirical evaluations: Evaluating adaptive systems. *Künstliche Intelligenz, 3*, 17–20.

ADDITIONAL READING

Biswas, P., & Langdon, P. (2011).Towards an inclusive world – A simulation tool to design interactive electronic systems for elderly and disabled users. In *Proceedings of the Annual Global Conference of Service Research and Innovation Institute (SRII)* (pp.73-82). SRII. doi: 10.1109/SRII.2011.18

Biswas, P., & Langdon, P. (2011). Investigating the accessibility of program selection menus of a digital TV interface. In *Proceedings of the 14th International Conference on Human-Computer Interaction: Users and Applications.* Berlin: Springer. doi: 0.1007/978-3-642-21619-0_52

Coelho, J., Biswas, P., Duarte, C., Guerreiro, T., Langdon, P., & Feiteira, P. et al. (2012). Involving all stakeholders in the development of TV applications for elderly. *International Journal on Advances in Intelligent Systems*, *5*(3-4), 427–440.

Coelho, J., Costa, D., Duarte, C., Feiteira, P., & Costa, D. (2012). From low to high fidelity prototypes: Challenges when developing for elderly. In *Proceedings on Developing Intelligent User Interfaces for e-Accessibility and e-Inclusion Workshop at Intelligent User Interfaces*. Lisbon, PortugalL IEEE.

Coelho, J., & Duarte, C. (2011). Building supportive multimodal user interfaces. In *Proceedings of the 1st International Workshop on Supportive User Interfaces (SUI 2011) at the 3rd ACM SIGCHI Symposium on Engineering Interactive Computing Systems*. Pisa, Italy: ACM.

Costa, D., & Duarte, C. (2011). Adapting multimodal fission to user's abilities. In *Proceedings of the 6th International Conference on Universal Access in Human-Computer Interaction: Design for All and eInclusion*. Springer. Doi: 10.1007/978-3-642-21672-5_38

Costa, D., Fernandes, N., Duarte, C., & Carriço, C. (2012). Accessibility of dynamic adaptive web TV applications. In *Proceedings of the 13th International Conference on Computers Helping People with Special Needs*. DOI=10.1007/978-3-642-31522-0_52

Emery, V., Edwards, P., Jacko, J., Moloney, K., Barnard, L., & Kongnakorn, T. et al. (2003). Toward achieving universal usability for older adults through multimodal feedback. *ACM SIGCAPH Computers and the Physically Handicapped*, *73-74*, 46–53. doi: doi:10.1145/957205.957214.

Feiteira, P., & Duarte, C. (2011). Adaptive multimodal fusion. In Proceedings of the 6th International Conference on Universal Access in Human-Computer Interaction: Design for All and eInclusion - Volume Part I. Springer. Doi: 10.1007/978-3-642-21672-5_41

Feiteira, P., & Duarte, C. (2012). Evaluating fusion engines through simulation of interaction scenarios. In *Proceedings of the Developing Intelligent User Interfaces for e-Accessibility and e-Inclusion Workshop*. Lisbon, Portugal: IEEE.

Foster, M. (2005). Interleaved preparation and output in the COMIC fission module. In *Proceedings of the Workshop on Software*. Stroudsburg, PA: ACL.

Hamisu, P., Heinrich, G., Jung, C., Hahn, V., Duarte, C., Langdon, P., & Biswas, P. (2011). Accessible UI design and multimodal interaction through hybrid TV platforms: Towards a virtual-user centered design framework. In *Proceedings of the 6th International Conference on Universal Access in Human-Computer Interaction: Users Diversity*. Springer.

Hamisu, P., Jung, C., Duarte, C., Biswas, P., & Langdon, P. (2012). An open-source software framework for adaptive multi-modal user interfaces in web TV applications. In *Proceedings of the Developing Intelligent User Interfaces for e-Accessibility and e-Inclusion Workshop*. Lisbon, Portugal: IEEE.

Han, Y., & Zukerman, I. (1997). A mechanism for multimodal presentation planningbased on agent cooperation and negotiation. *Human-Computer Interaction*, *12*, 187–226. doi:10.1207/s15327051hci1201&2_6.

Jung, C., Hamisu, P., Duarte, C., Biswas, P., & Almeida, L. (2012). GUIDE: Personalisable multi-modal user interfaces for web applications on TV. In *Proceedings of the NEM Summit*. NEM.

Jung, C., Hamisu, P., Duarte, C., Frid, L., Almeida, L., & Biswas, P. (2012). Personalised interactive TV: An open-source software framework for adaptive multi-modal user interfaces. In *Proceedings of IBC (International Broadcasting Convention)*. IBC.

Lee, J., & Spence, C. (2009). Feeling what you hear: Task-irrelevant soundsmodulate tactile perception delivered via a touch screen. *Journal on Multimodal User Interfaces*, *2*(3-4), 145–156. doi:10.1007/s12193-009-0014-8.

McTear, M. (2002). Spoken dialogue technology: Enabling the conversational user interface. *ACM Computing Surveys*, *34*(1), 90–169. doi:10.1145/505282.505285.

Noy, D., Ribeiro, P., & Iurgel, I. A. (2012). *Virtual emotions for the elderly population: Emotional expressions guidelines for virtual characters*. Paper presented at the 17th International Conference of Intelligent User Interfaces. Lisbon, Portugal.

Oviatt, S. (1999). *Mutual disambiguation of recognition errors in a multimodel architecture*. ACM Press. doi:10.1145/302979.303163.

Oviatt, S. (2003). The human-computer interaction handbook: Fundamentals, evolving technologies and emerging application. In *Multimodal Interfaces* (pp. 286–304). Hillsdale, NJ: L. Erlbaum Associates Inc..

Oviatt, S., & Cohen, P. (2000). Multimodal interfaces that process what comes naturally. *Information Systems Journal*, *43*(3), 1–23. doi: doi:10.1145/330534.330538.

Oviatt, S., Coulston, R., Tomko, S., Xiao, B., Lunsford, R., Wesson, M., & Carmichael, L. (2003). Toward a theory of organized multimodal integration patterns during human-computer interaction. In *Proceedings of the 5th International Conference on Multimodal Interfaces*, (pp. 44–51). New York, NY: ACM. Doi: 10.1145/958432.958443

Reithinger, N., Fedeler, D., Kumar, A., Lauer, C., Pecourt, E., & Romary, L. (2005). Miamm - A multimodal dialogue system using haptics. In J. Kuppevelt, L. Dybkjaer, & N. O. Bernsen (Eds.), *Advances in Natural Multimodal Dialogue Systems*. Springer. doi:10.1007/1-4020-3933-6_14.

KEY TERMS AND DEFINITIONS

Active Inputs: Inputs are issued deliberately by the user, e.g., speech, text.

Medium: A channel or the mean used to express the modality, i.e., the peripheral devices such as monitor or TV screen, sound columns and so on. All these three components are dependent of each other's.

Modality: Defined by the structure of the information that is perceived by the user (text, sound, vibration, etc.)

Modes: The sensorial system of a human with which he perceives the world.

Multimodal Fission: Divides or selects the output channels to distribute that information throughout the available outputs and usually according to the user profile and context.

Multimodal Interfaces: Process more than one combined input mode such as speech, manual gestures and head and body movements in a coordinated manner with multimedia output" which can be adaptive, enabling a more natural and effective interaction whichever mode or combination of modes are best suitable to a given situation, context and according to user's preferences and abilities (user profile).

Multimodal System: Means to provide input using one or multiple modalities such as speech, key pressing with keyboard or mouse, gestures, etc. and receiving information and feedback from the system by a modality or combination of modalities such as visual, audio or other output modality.

Parallel or Sequential Input Modalities: These systems can combine various modalities in the recognition process, this is called multimodal fusion. These combinations can be made at several different levels in the recognition process.

Passive Inputs: Inputs that are monitored by the system without requiring explicit command from the user, e.g., facial expression or manual gesturing.

Chapter 4
Developing Emotion-Libras 2.0:
An Instrument to Measure the Emotional Quality of Deaf Persons while Using Technology

Soraia Silva Prietch
Universidade Federal de Mato Grosso – Rondonópolis, Brazil

Lucia Vilela Leite Filgueiras
Escola Politécnica da Universidade de São Paulo, Brazil

ABSTRACT

An important issue in the capture of the real user experience while interacting with technology is the ability to assess emotional quality. There are several methods for emotional quality evaluation in the literature. However, when the target users are deaf participants, communication problems arise. A substantial part of the deaf community communicates in sign language. Because user experience researchers are seldom fluent in sign language, they require the assistance of an interpreter whenever users are deaf signers. Evaluation of emotional quality may lose accuracy because of the mediation of an interpreter; consequently, emotional quality evaluation requires a special instrument that can be used in an intuitive and independent way by researchers and their deaf subjects. The authors present the process of creation and improvement of Emotion-Libras, an instrument for assessing the emotional quality of people with hearing disabilities when interacting with technology.

INTRODUCTION

Designers depend on knowledge about users' emotions when interacting with technological products (e.g., mobile applications, virtual learning environments) to enhance acceptance and to design more intense experiences.

Our literature research so far has shown that there are many studies about Emotional Design and User eXperience (UX), and several emotional measurement methods have been proposed (e.g., Russell (1980); Bradley & Lang (1994); Ekman (2003); Desmet (2003); Scherer (2005); Isbister *et al* (2007); Agarwal & Meyer (2009); Broekens, Pronker & Neuteboom (2010); Elokla, Hirai & Morita (2010)). These methods have been applied in a variety of contexts, with different user profiles; nevertheless, none of these literature findings has shown researches concerned with verifying

DOI: 10.4018/978-1-4666-4623-0.ch004

the emotional user experience of people with hearing disabilities interacting with technology (e.g., computational systems or software, mobile applications).

We here present the process of creation and improvement of an instrument called Emotion-Libras. Emotion-LIBRAS was conceived from the need of an evaluation instrument with a natural communication interface to be used by - and with - people with hearing disabilities, so that they would be able to easily understand the instrument and to know how to manipulate it. LIBRAS is the Brazilian sign language, because the instrument was developed to be used with Brazilian signers. Despite that, we believe that localization can allow the application of Emotion-LIBRAS in other sign languages.

Developing Emotion-Libras required a five-phase research methodology: literature review, ethnographic study, design of the first version of Emotion-Libras, test with users and improvement, resulting in Emotion-Libras 2.0.

This paper is organized as follows: first, we present the theoretical background to emotional quality evaluation methods; next, we report the steps towards the first proposal of Emotion-Libras; after this, the improvement of Emotion-Libras is shown.

EMOTIONAL QUALITY EVALUATION METHODS: BACKGROUND

In this section, we depart from the definition of the word "emotion" and the expression "emotion quality" adopted in this paper. As stated by Scherer (2005, p. 696), "The number of scientific definitions [for the word emotion] proposed has grown to the point where counting seems quite hopeless (Kleinginna & Kleinginna already reviewed more than one hundred in 1981)". Ekman (2003, p. 13), for example, states that "emotion is a process, a particular kind of automatic appraisal influenced by our evolutionary and personal past, in which we sense that something important to our welfare is occurring, and a set of physiological changes and emotional behaviors begins to deal with the situation".

In this sense, adapting from Scherer's definition (2005), we assume that emotion is the situation in which a person is affected by one or more feelings, either positive and/or negative, driven by a set of factors that influence actions and reactions, for example, past experiences, personal tastes, external factors, desires, and needs. Thus, considering this definition, emotional quality was defined as a value generated from the qualitative measure of a person's emotions.

Emotional quality evaluation methods intend to find out what the target user feels while he/she interacts with products, such as computational systems. Evaluation of emotional quality is important in product design and is often a part of User Experience (UX) analysis. While emotions can be positive or negative, solutions are often expected by their designers to provide a positive experience to the user. Negative emotions are deleterious to UX and must be avoided carefully in product design. As Van Gorp & Adams (2012, p. 11) found, "in software, unpleasant error messages can cause people to remember and focus on negative experiences over positive ones, potentially distorting how they think and feel about the application". UX evaluation, according to Bargas-Avila & Hornbæk (2011), must assess dimensions of "emotions and affect", "enjoyment and fun", and "aesthetics and appeal" besides other traditional usability attributes. However, Bargas-Avila & Hornbæk mentioned that despite many researches involving the use of emotional measurements to assess UX, they mostly found the use of simplistic instruments.

Van Gorp & Adams (2012) were concerned about the issues related to design for emotion; in this sense, the authors explored why, when, where, and how to do it. Several researchers of this area were studied by Van Gorp & Adams, such as: Russell (1980), Csikszentmihalyi (1990),

McLean (1990), Desmet (2002), Norman (2004); their conclusions indicate that these early methods are still important to current studies linked to the design of products and systems, and user experiences' evaluations.

Our literature review indicated several works on emotional evaluation, many of which were developed and applied to the experience with technology:

- Lera & Garreta-Domingo (2007) proposed a method which included a guideline with ten emotion-heuristics to help researchers through the process of interface evaluation, based on facial or bodily movements, such as frowning; brow raising; gazing away; smiling; compressing the lip; moving the mouth; expressing vocally; hand touching the face; drawing back on the chair; and leaning the trunk forward.
    - The Computer Emotion Scale was a method proposed by Kay & Loverock (2008), which uses four emotions as parameters of evaluation: anger, anxiety, happiness, and sadness. The goal of this work was to evaluate what people feel when they are learning how to use new software. Besides emotions, data were also collected on computer knowledge, attitude, university use, and field use about the participants; the emotions were thus co-related to these other data. The authors found out that the scale has moderate reliability and good validity.
- Burmester *et al* (2010, p. 1) proposed a valence evaluation method of the user experience, which was created to identify positive and negative emotions during the use of an interactive product. The method provided two phases: one for a 236-valence marker to capture quantitative data; and, another for a retrospective interview to capture qualitative data. The authors considered that the qualitative data enabled "a better understanding of the design and can serve as the starting point for design improvements". (p. 3).
- Shahriar (2011) analysed two emotional user evaluation methods: the GAQ (Geneva Appraisal Questionnaire), by Scherer (2002) and 3E (Expressing Experiences and Emotion), by Tähti & Niemelä (2005). For comparison purposes, the author chose Facebook as an application. The first method follows a quantitative approach and the second a qualitative approach of data gathering.

The methods referred above were tested with people without disabilities. There are, however, other studies that focused on the emotional evaluation with people with hearing disabilities, but in the psychology field. None of them addressed interaction with technology as the source of emotion.

- Wallbott & Seithe (1993) presented the results of experiments regarding the perception of hearing impaired persons in recognizing visual emotional expression. Within this investigation, the authors mentioned that "[...] persons with high impairment have to compensate in order to manage interaction and communication by paying closer attention to visual emotion information" (Wallbott & Seithe, 1993, p. 7), but this perception is not so different from the perception of hearing persons. Moderately impaired persons demonstrated "less focus of attention to visual stimuli".
- Goldstein, Sexton & Feldman (2000) compared the facial expression of hearing persons who were fluent signers in ASL (American Sign Language) with hearing non-signer persons while they were given a task to communicate a list of words with emotional meaning. As a conclusion, the authors mentioned that "as predicted, signers were more successful than were non signers at encoding facial expressions of

emotion", and complemented reporting that "because facial expression is the primary mode of transmitting grammatical and affective information in ASL, signers should be particularly adapted to using the face to transmit information" (p. 73).

- Cambra (2005) investigated the feelings and emotions of deaf adolescents in Spain, comparing the results expressed by the deaf and hearing participants of the same sex and age, and also comparing answers within the group of deaf participants. The author reported that the results "indicate that social and educational activities for the deaf should not only aim at encouraging interaction with hearing and deaf peers [which make them happy] so as to improve self-perception and identity but also for enabling them to learn about their wider milieu and developing critical judgment and feelings of solidarity [instead of worrying mostly about themselves]".
- Dyck (2011) reported the development and validation of the Emotional Recognition Scales (ERS), which was tested with participants of several populations of impaired persons, including people with hearing disabilities. According to Dyck (2011, p. 1), the ERS allows one "to recognise facial and vocal expressions of common emotions, to understand the meaning of emotion terms, to understand relationships between emotions and the experiences that elicit them, and to use reasoning skills and knowledge of emotion–event relationships to resolve apparently incongruous emotional outcomes". As a result of the tests with people with hearing disabilities, an increase in ability was noticed at the "emotion understanding tests, but not the emotion recognition ones". (p. 7).

The following studies address the emotional quality evaluation in the use of technology by people with hearing disabilities.

- Hiraga & Kato (2009, p. 39) "conducted a series of experiments on recognizing emotions conveyed on the hearing of musical performances as a means of building a musical performance assistance system with which deaf and hard of hearing people could communicate through musical performance". Since the authors "believed that visual information can assist in listening to music", they "used several types of stimuli to understand recognition of emotions that music can elicit". Following these premises, the authors compared the emotions recognized by deaf and hearing students, using as stimuli: (i) music only; (ii) music with drawings; (iii) music with performing scenes; (iv) music with video sequences intended to convey no emotion; and, (v) music with video sequences intended to convey the same emotion as a musical performance. However, the results could not strongly confirm their hypothesis.
    - Within their research about meta-communication in inclusive scenarios, Hayashi & Baranauskas (2010) analyzed Norman's three levels of emotion considering the observation of participant responses, the users' interaction with the mechanism, and reflective responses on colored papers. As a result, the authors mentioned that this kind of evaluation is effective in assessing "other factors that influence people's choice" of a product. It is relevant to say that the authors adopted usual data collection and usability concepts to apply the principles of Norman's theory, making it simple for the deaf participants to understand, and efficient for the researchers to obtain important information.

FIRST VERSION OF EMOTION-LIBRAS

In this section, we describe the steps towards the first proposal of the instrument: selecting emotions, interview with potential users, and instrument design.

Before proposing a new instrument, we asked ourselves if existing methods and instruments could be used in this research to identify deaf people's emotions instead of creating a new instrument. To answer this question, a field study with deaf participants was accomplished by Alves & Prietch (2012), in which the following instruments were tested: SAM by Bradley & Lang (1994); GEW by Scherer (2005); and Kansei Sheet-1 by Elokla, Hirai & Morita (2010). GEW and Kansei Sheet-1 were freely translated from English to Brazilian-Portuguese. Because of the known difficulty of deaf people with written words, the results indicated that (1) SAM was the easiest instrument for them to understand, due to its graphic presentation; (2) GEW had to be explained by a Libras interpreter frequently, due to its verbosity; and, (3) the circular shape and information organization of the Kansei Sheet-1 made it confusing for the participants to mark their options.

Selecting Emotions

In order to understand how Deaf subjects express their emotions, we proposed an experiment in which Deaf subjects would relate an emotion to an experience of using technology. We planned to present a set of images with Libras signs representing emotions to the Deaf subjects and ask them to recall a situation of technology usage in which they felt as represented in each image.

In order to develop this set of images, we first had to select which emotions were significant to evaluate a technology experience; and for the selection of emotions (words), we departed from the 36 affect categories of Scherer (2005)'s work and the three bipolar dimension (PAD), from Bradley & Lang (1994). A list of words expressing emotions was produced and translated from English to Brazilian Portuguese by an English teacher for Brazilian students. It is worth mentioning that the translation of words expressing emotion, from one language to another, is not a trivial task. Desmet (2003) had already noticed that verbal instruments are difficult to apply between cultures. In emotion research, translating emotion words is known to be difficult because often a one-to-one, straight translation is not available. In this case, some arrangements had to be made in order to find a word that expressed the sense of another, for example, the English word "Amusement" was translated into Portuguese as "Fun/Funny" (considered as a pertinent word or word stem in Scherer's work (2005)).

We had the help of one Libras teacher and interpreter, and six Libras advanced students to produce the equivalent set of emotions expressions in Libras, which resulted in videos of the corresponding expressions. Due to its large acceptance within the Brazilian Deaf community, we used Capovilla, Raphael & Mauricio's (2010) trilingual dictionary to check the signs/words in the recorded videos at the Libras course. It is worth noticing that as the signs/words were searched in the dictionary, (i) more than one of the written Brazilian Portuguese emotion words were represented by the same Libras sign. The difference between them is expressed as intensity (e.g. "Sadness" ("Sad" sign) and "Disappointment" (the same sign of "Sad", but intensified), by communicating the sign/emotion using facial and corporal expression; (ii) some of the written Brazilian Portuguese words had too similar meanings, even though the written words were translated differently in Libras, "Happiness" and "Contentment" and "Joy", or "Joy" and "Pleasure/Enjoyment", or "Anxiety" and "Tension/Stress", or "Anger" and "Hatred", or "Being touched" and "Feeling". In these cases, only one word of each was chosen to represent the types of emotion so as to reduce ambiguity. At that moment, we were not interested yet in identifying the range between opposite emotions (e.g., Happy/Sad) to specify its intensity, or in developing Desmet's (2003) mixed emotions. Additionally, two words were excluded because they would not be representative for this investigation, specifically, "Lust" and "Jealousy".

Thus, from the initial 36-word list, eight words were removed by similarity criteria, and three new words were included (from SAM instrument (Self Assessment Manikin - Bradley & Lang, 1994)), resulting in a list of words composed of 31 emotions, denoting 16 positive and 15 negative emotions: Admiration; Alert/Awake; Amusement; Anxiety; Boredom; Compassion; Contempt; Desperation; Disappointment/Sadness; Disgust; Dissatisfaction; Dominance; Envy; Fear; Feeling; Gratitude; Guilt; Happiness/Happy; Hatred; Hope; Humility; Interest/Enthusiasm; Irritation; Longing; Pleasure/Enjoyment; Pride; Relaxation/Serenity; Relief; Shame; Submission; and, Surprise. The transition from the 36-word list to the 31-word list is illustrated in Figure 1.

Elaborating the Interview Script

The proposed instrument is meant to receive non-verbal responses through sign language, but the words in Portuguese were kept for two reasons. First, because Libras has its regionalisms, for example, the word "Fun" in one region of the country can be represented by one sign, and in another region the same word can be communicated by another sign, so the written word could help the individual to read what was unknown as a sign; and, second, to help the researchers and the interpreter to understand what the sign meaning is. If the researchers want to observe the participant during the process, he/she can keep up by reading the words, and the interpreter can explain the sign to the Deaf subject if he/she does not understand it.

For this purpose, a script with images was elaborated, so that the Deaf subjects could identify the words (emotions) in Libras and in written Brazilian Portuguese, by making the relation between the words/signs and their remembrances of the technology use (situation, object, place or people).

The decision of using images of a static avatar signing in Libras to identify words (emotions) was taken, instead of only written words in Brazilian Portuguese, because the number of Deaf Brazilians who can read written Brazilian Portuguese is small (Hayashi & Baranauskas, 2010). Also, it was decided not to use, at that moment, written words in Brazilian Portuguese with pictures of someone's facial expressions, because of the dif-

Figure 1. Filter of words

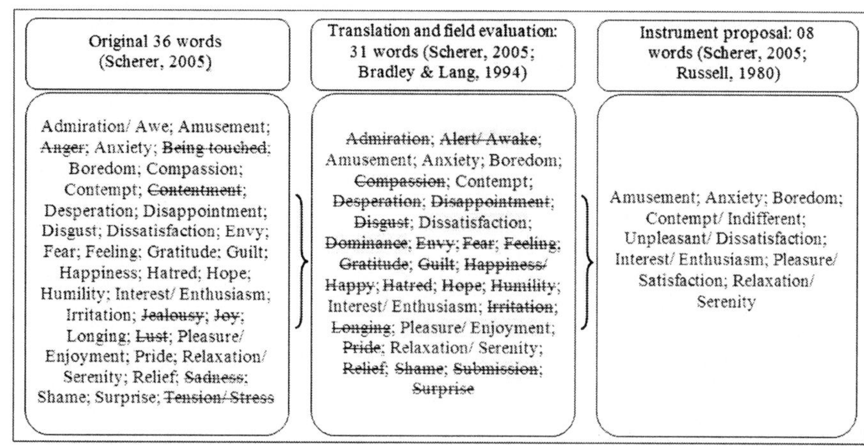

ficulty in finding pictures or in creating images that would express and differentiate between similar emotions, for example, "Fun" and "Happy".

The interview instrument was composed of four parts: (i) explanation of the research objectives; (ii) ten direct questions (yes/no) about the use of technology; (iii) one table with two columns corresponding to the list of words in Libras and in Brazilian Portuguese, in column 1, and a blank space for the Deaf participant to write (or "dictate" in Libras for the interpreter to write) his/her answer about a/an situation, object, place or person that reminded him/her of the use of technology, in column 2; and, (iv) one open question asking if the participant wanted to include one or more words (emotions) that were not mentioned in the table.

Reporting the Interview

The interview intended to motivate Deaf subjects to reflect on their previous experience with the use of technology and to refer to emotions associated with this usage.

The participants were two students, over 18 years-old. A Libras interpreter mediated the explanation, and the questioning between the researcher and the participants, if any questions arose. Although they consented to participate, they did not consent to be filmed during the meeting.

It was clear that the participant recall of technology use was very different, as was their manner of speaking about it. While one reports about family, work, religion, and friendship, the other is restricted to the subject matter and to the perception he had about himself. Nevertheless, the language issue was brought up by both participants, stressing the need to focus on solutions that enhance the use of sign language, and texts that are provided in simple written language. They related this issue to the following emotions: "Being touched" and "Feeling" when a movie or drama is available in Libras; "Grateful" when somebody helps them; "Hope" to access more materials in Libras available on the Internet; "Submission" when a text message is not understandable; and "Surprise" when a text message is understandable. In general, it was possible to observe that the their experiences of using technology were positive for both, highlighting that one answered "does not apply" to the word "Hatred", and the other participant informed the same answer to the word "Desperation". Another point to note is the fact that both demonstrated a desire for communicating with others via MSN, and social networks on the Internet, and text messages on the cell phone, as well as watching videos and playing on the Internet, associating this activity with the emotions: "Being touched", "Feeling", "Happiness/Happy", and "Pleasure/Enjoyment".

With respect to the words representing emotions on the table of the interview, it was found that: (i) the answers for "Being touched", "Feeling", and "Happiness/Happy" are very similar feelings, they could be used as synonymous of "Pleasant/Satisfaction/Enjoyment"; (ii) the words "Disappointment/Sadness" could be easily replaced by "Dissatisfaction/Unpleasant"; (iii) "Irritation" and "Anxiety" could be represented by only one word in a new instrument; (iv) the words "Disgust", "Humility", "Hatred", "Hope", "Desperation", and "Relief" could be suppressed from the table, because they were not representative for this research; (v) the word "Surprise" can represent both positive or negative emotions, and to avoid ambiguity this word was suppressed; (vi) the words "Pride", "Shame", "Gratitude", "Dominance", "Submission", "Compassion", "Admiration", "Longing", and "Envy" only make sense if there are two or more participants involved during the interview, in other words, interpersonal emotions, felt from interacting with others; and, (vii) the words "Fear" and "Alert" should be excluded from the list, since, accordingly to Pôrto (2006, p. 93, our translation) "the methodologies currently employed to evoke states of alertness and fear in humans are limited by ethical issues when compared with animal studies".

The remaining word selection from Scherer's list was confronted with the eight words of Russell's Circumplex Model of Affect to reduce the number of words for the instrument proposal, specially because the more the instrument has visual information, the worse for the Deaf participant to focus and to choose between the displayed words, his/her emotions. After all the filtering made in the list of original words, Figure 1 presents the final 08-word list.

In order to explain some details of Figure 1, it is necessary to point out that the strikethrough words, in the first and second columns, mean that they were removed from the list; in the second column, some words were marked with gray background to highlight the words taken from Bradley & Lang (1994)'s instrument.

Proposing the Emotion-Libras 1.0

We have considered the following set of requirements for an emotional quality evaluation instrument, proposed to collect the user's emotion at the visceral level:

- The technology solution and the evaluation instrument would be installed in two different computers; the Deaf participant is instructed to use the technology and to express his/her emotion through one-word in sign language, and facial and corporal expression; and the interpreter is instructed to use the evaluation instrument to mark the option expressed by the Deaf participant;
- The evaluation instrument should:
    - Follow the idea of Russell's Circumplex Model of Affect, in which emotions are organized by quadrants, and level of affinity.
    - Use the visual model by Elokla, Hirai & Morita (2010)'s Kansei Sheet, but instead of static images to reference the emotions, including an animated avatar, following Desmet (2003)'s proposal, communicating the emotions words in sign language.
    - Be an explicit[1] kind of emotional quality evaluation instrument, the non-verbal aspect prevailing to facilitate understanding by the participant, and to reduce interference from others in responses.
    - Keep few words to facilitate the choice of options made by the Deaf Students at the moment of using the instrument.

Thus, the words kept to propose the Emotional Quality Evaluation Instrument for Interviewing People with hearing disabilities, named Emotion-Libras, make a total of eight, four being positive emotions (Interest/Enthusiasm - to learn, to know -; Amusement; Pleasure/Satisfaction/Enjoyment; Relaxation/Serenity), and four negative emotions (Contempt/Indifferent, Boredom; Dissatisfaction/Unpleasant; Anxiety). The choice of words considered the field study made with the words extracted from Scherer's paper, and the Circumplex Model of Affect by Russell (1980), combining one another. Hence, placing the words on a Kansei Sheet-like layout, the first version of the instrument was produced, which can be seen in Figure 2.

The images in Figure 2 were scanned from Capovilla, Raphael & Mauricio (2010)[2], noting that, on the paper form instrument, each drawing represent a static sequence of images, but the intention was to produce an animated avatar to perform the words in Libras. Also, it is worth noting that: (i) the idea of the Circumplex Model of Affect was kept, placing the antagonistic words (positive = blue (right side), and negative = red (left side)) on each side of the circle; and, (ii) the placement of the three grey circles in the center were not random, because the intention was to create the illusion of intensity, as exposed in the Elokla, Hirai & Morita (2010)'s Kansei Sheet.

The words representing emotions, in Figure 2, were not translated into English, because the

Figure 2. Emotion-Libras

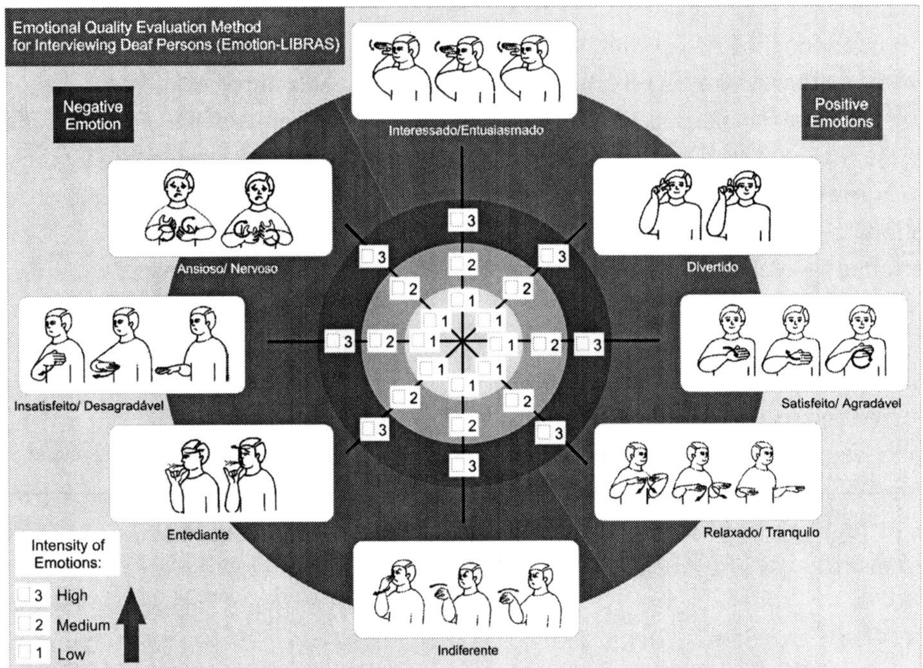

Brazilian Sign Language images mean only the Brazilian-Portuguese written word. Each country has its own Sign Language for the Deaf community, for example: the Deaf community of the United States of America communicates using the American Sign Language; in France, their Deaf community uses French Sing Language, and so on.

FIELD STUDY WITH EMOTION-LIBRAS 1.0

This section refers to the usage of emotion Libras 1.0 regarding the evolution of our instrument.

Questions Raised

Because none of the works mentioned in the literature review was originally created to evaluate the emotional quality for people with hearing disabilities, we performed a field study aimed to answer to six research questions.

Question 1: What is more emotionally expressive in an instrument to assess the emotional quality: photographs of someone's facial expressions, or drawings of an avatar signing in Libras?

An example of the first option mentioned was reported by Elokla, Hirai & Morita (2010), who presented two "Kansei Sheets" ([a] how do you feel?; [b] what do you complain about?) to assess the emotional quality of the research participants. The Kansei Sheets grouped, respectively, eight and nine photographs of an actress representing emotion by making different facial expressions. Also, the written words were disposed in the instrument. The facial expressions were very representative and allowed easy identification of emotions. Studies about facial expression have been the interest of many researchers, such as: Wallbott & Seithe (1993); Goldstein, Sexton & Feldman (2000); and, Ekman (2003).

An example of the second option was presented earlier in this paper in Figure 2, using 08 static images copied from Capovilla, Raphael & Mauricio (2010) Libras dictionary. Even though the images were static, they represented a set of sequential images to form each sign. Each sign represents a word (emotion). The image from the dictionary is a drawing. A drawing can hardly represent the exact facial expression of a person.

Thus, looking at these two possibilities, a deadlock was found: which one would People with hearing disabilities find easier to understand? For a good observer, the first option makes it easy to read the facial expression, if you either are a Deaf or a hearing person. In the second option, the drawings present the signs in Libras, which, for a person who knows the language, is straightforward to understand.

Question 2: What would be better understood by the Deaf user: the image followed by a written word (in Brazilian Portuguese), or only the image, without any text)?

Bradley & Lang (1994) did not use texts to identify the images in the SAM instrument. The idea was a visual semantic differential scale, in which the participant should, for example, look at the presented IAPS (Lang, Bradley & Cuthbert, 1999) images and mark one choice for each one of the three bipolar options: pleasure, arousal and dominance. This difference between the SAM and the other instruments (e.g. Kansei Sheets by Elokla, Hirai & Morita (2010), and PrEmo by Desmet (2003)) raised the doubt about the need of a text with the image or not.

As for the SAM instrument, also the instruments presented by Russell (1980), and Scherer (2005) do not link the words with images. The latter has a circular shape, composing the words around in a bipolar order (positive and negative words on opposite sides of the circle), but neither present images associated to the words.

On the one hand, we can think that to include a lot of displayed information (text, and images) would facilitate the assimilation; on the other hand, too much displayed information could be confusing.

Question 3: What is the most appropriate instrument shape for the Deaf user to handle: a circular shape, or a rectangular shape?

Russell (1980); Scherer (2005); and, Elokla, Hirai & Morita (2010) proposed their instrument in a circular shape; on the other hand, Bradley & Lang (1994); and Desmet (2003) proposed their instrument in a rectangular shape. At first, one can imagine that the instrument shape would not matter; however, it is interesting to know what the user target prefers.

Question 4: Additional information, besides the image, should be given in SignWriting, in manual Alphabet, or in written Brazilian-Portuguese?

In case the participant preferred the image accompanied by extra information, if the Deaf person had difficulties with written language, then one option could be the use of SignWriting, which is asserted by some authors (e.g., Sutton (2004); Ahmed & Seong (2006); Bianchini *et al* (2012)) to be the written version of the sign languages (each country has its own SignWriting). It is worth informing that, in the schools of Rondonopolis, Mato Grosso/Brazil (city where these researches took place), they do not teach SignWriting to Deaf students. In Martins & Filgueiras (2010) paper, the result of 14 interface evaluations was shown, by People with hearing disabilities, one of them being a SignWriting tool. The authors reported that one Deaf participant informed to know SignWriting, but his/her answers told otherwise, resulting in only one right answer out of four.

Another option would be the use of manual Alphabet (dactylology) instead of written language (Portuguese or SignWriting). However, the use of manual Alphabet is specific to communicate a proper name (e.g. firm name, brand name, people's name). The written Brazilian-Portuguese would be straightforward; nevertheless, even though Libras is the official language of People with hearing disabilities in Brazil, there are still many Deaf or hard of hearing persons who do not know how to communicate in this language, especially those who did not learn sign language in their early age and/or have hearing parents, or who experienced late auditory deprivation (Dye, Hauser & Bavelier (2009)).

Question 5: Would he/she prefer several or few options for choosing emotional words/signs disposed on an evaluation instrument?

The human being can feel several kinds of emotions, at different moments of his/her life, negative or positive or mixed ones. If an emotional quality evaluation instrument is composed of several words/signs, the participant can get confused when he/she has to select his/her emotions. Ekman (2003, p. 7) carried out several researches in New Guinea, with participants who spoke Fore language. The author reported that "they had no written language, so I couldn't ask them to pick a word from a list that fit the emotion shown. If I were to read them a list of emotion words, I would have to worry about whether they remembered the list, and whether the order in which the words were read influenced their choice". If the participant has a long list to choose from, could he/she forget what about the emotion felt by him/her, or even forget about what he/she was doing before starting to read?

On the other hand, if an instrument contains few options of emotional words/signs choice, how can someone, for example, summarize several types of emotions in one? One example of this situation is described by Pôrto (2006, p. 93): "In IAPS, a large number of basic emotions such as anger, envy, fear, sadness, joy, [...] among others, were reduced to general situations of pleasure and displeasure, situations of alert and relaxation, and finally dominance situation. In short, to access emotions, it can vary in three major dimensions: affective valence, arousal and dominance level [using SAM]". In this sense, would there be a correct number of words/signs to represent the human being emotion during a product evaluation?

Question 6: Would he/she prefer the communication of Libras using a video, or a digital animated avatar?

Considering that an emotional quality assessment instrument was developed in a digital format, would a Deaf person prefer the sign language to be expressed by a video of a filmed person, or a digital animated avatar?

Both are images are in movement and include someone communicating the emotional words in Libras. The video shows the image of the person who is signing. This is not a problem if the person agrees to sign a consent document to disclose his/her image.

The animated avatar brings the concern about the facial expression, as mentioned in Question 1. The facial expression is one of the parameters of sign languages structure (McCullough & Emmorey (1997); Stokoe Jr. (2005); Easterbrooks & Huston (2007)), if this aspect is missing, then communication may be hampered.

Field Study Plan

To answer the research questions raised, a field study was planned and executed. The planning stage was composed of the following six steps:

Step 1: Photographs of Facial Expressions of an Amateur Actress

To answer Question 1, a two-hour section of photos to take pictures of the actress representing the emotional words by making facial expression occurred. A range between three and five photos was taken for each emotional word, so the most representative photo could be chosen later. Three examples of facial expression photos of the actress can be seen in Figure 3.

We expanded the list of emotion words and defined three sets of emotional types (described at Step 4 in this subsection). In Figure 3, one example of each set is presented. A consent term was signed by the actress in order to provide the use of her image in scientific papers.

During the section, it was noticed that the words "Relaxation/Calm" and "Relief" from Part I, and the words "Dominance" and "Pride" from Part II converged to a similar facial expression. We thus removed "Relief" and "Pride", and kept "Relaxation" and "Dominance".

Step 2: Creating another Shape for the Emotion-Libras

Preparing to respond Question 2, two details of the Emotion-Libras 1.0 (Figure 2) were changed. One of the changes is at the center of the image, in which the radio button format was prioritized rather than the checkbox format,which may help the interviewee to remember that only one option can be marked. The second change was accomplished in the font size of the written words under each image; they were amplified to facilitate the reading. Figure 4 presents the altered Emotion-Libras.

Informally showing the circular shaped Emotion-Libras to three Brazilian-Portuguese/Libras interpreters, they informed that it was hard to understand the bipolarity of the images disposed on each side of the circle. From that information, the doubt about the shape of the instrument was raised, and a rectangular shaped version was created. The rectangular shaped version of the Emotion-Libras can be viewed in Figure 5.

The drawing images, in Figure 4 and Figure 5, were copied from Capovilla, Raphael & Mauricio (2010) Libras dictionary. The words underneath each image are in written Brazilian-Portuguese, since they represent the Libras signs, from the same country.

Also, in both Figures, 4 and 5, the set of words formed four subsets of bipolar dimensions. For each positive emotion, there is a negative emotion; they are displayed on opposite sides and three different levels of intensity (low/mid/high) can be exclusively marked.

Step 3: Separating Samples of SignWriting and Manual Alphabet Words

In order to answer Question 4, we needed to search for illustrations in SignWriting and in Libras Alphabet. The first one, we found in Capovilla, Raphael & Mauricio (2010), whose trilingual dictionary, besides the signs in Libras and the Brazilian-Portuguese written words, there is the illustration of the SignWriting of each word. Figure 6 presents two examples of words in Brazilian SignWriting.

The word "Interessado" (means Interested, in English) is illustrated in manual Alphabet in Figure 7. When a hearing person is not a Libras signer and is trying to communicate with a Deaf

Figure 3. Three examples of facial expression of the actress from Sets: I, II and III

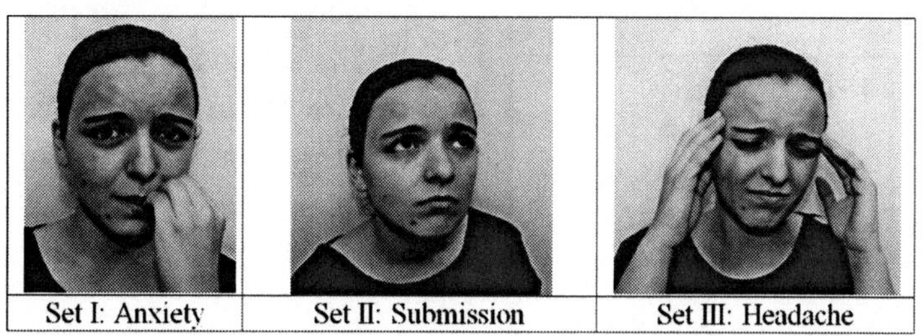

Figure 4. Emotion-Libras: Circular shape version

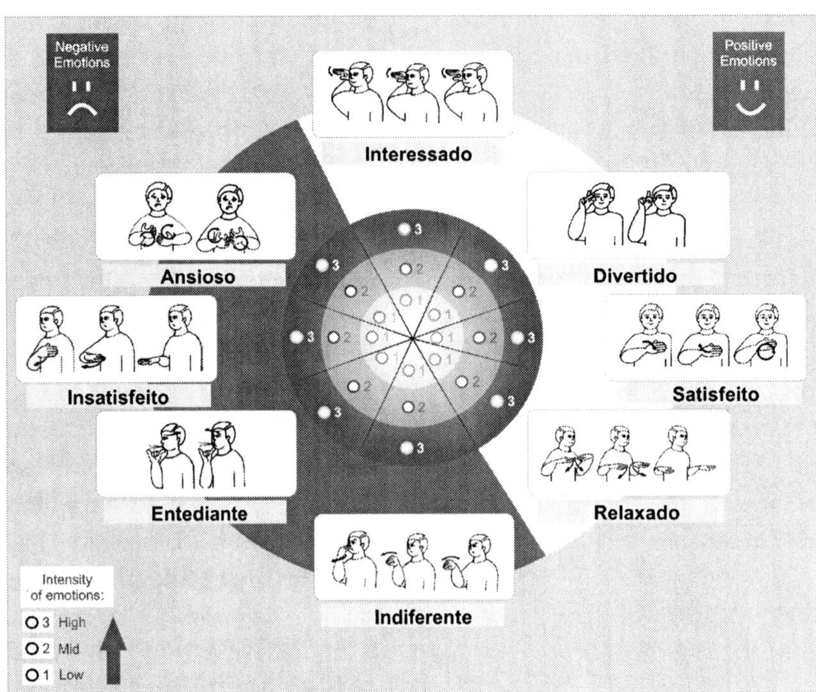

Figure 5. Emotion-Libras: Rectangular shape version

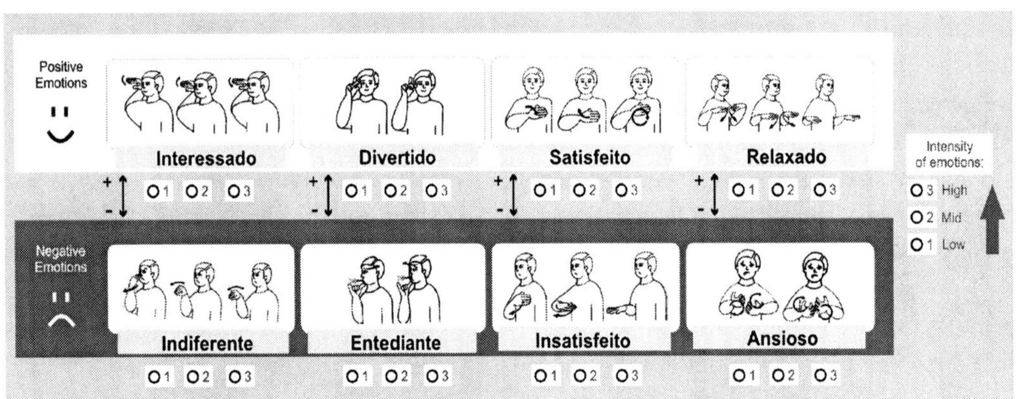

Figure 6. Two examples of words in Brazilian SignWriting

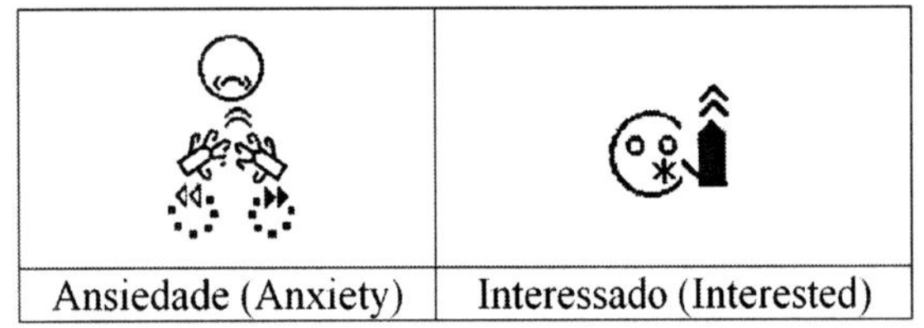

Ansiedade (Anxiety)	Interessado (Interested)

person, this resource is commonly used. However, as it was prior mentioned, this kind of communication is used for proper names.

The images in Figure 7 were copied from the website Smartkids[3], which offers online educational games for kids (login not needed). The words in manual Alphabet were built by editing a manual Alphabet sheet found in this website.

Figure 7. The word "Interessado" (Interested) in manual alphabet of Libras

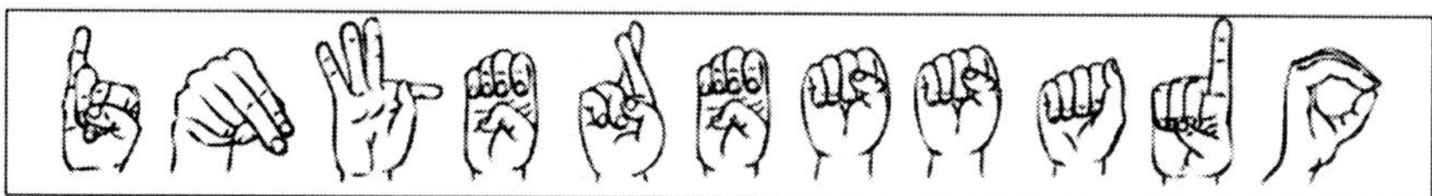

Step 4: Emotional Words Selection

When Question 5 arose, another round of selection was made. Thus, from Russell (1980); Bradley & Lang (1994); Desmet (2003); Scherer (2005); and, Elokla, Hirai & Morita (2010) papers, one set of 34 emotional words was selected (contemplating the previously selected eight words), which was grouped into three categories:

- **Set I:** Personal emotions felt without the need of interaction with others (14 words): Interest/Enthusiasm (to learn, to know); Satisfaction/Pleasure; Contempt; Dissatisfaction/Unpleasant; Irritation; Surprise (positive); Guilt; Amusement; Relaxation/Calm; Boredom; Anxiety; Confusion; Fear; Relief.
- **Set II:** Interpersonal emotions felt from the interaction with others (10 words): Admiration (positive, by someone's action); Dominance (feeling superior to someone); Envy (of someone); Pride ("I do not need help!"); Distrust (of someone); Compassion (will to help someone); Submission (feeling inferior to someone); Gratitude (thanking someone); Shame ("someone saw that I do not know how to do something that I think I should"); Will to Share (something with someone).
- **Set III:** Personal emotions felt physically (10 words), feeling: Cold body; Dizziness; Rapid heartbeat; Body pain; Sleepy; Hot body; Difficulty in breathing; Headache; Hungry; Thirsty.

Step 5. Drawing and Editing the Digital Animated Avatar

To prepare the material to answer Question 6, first, several possibilities of humanoid appearance were drawn on paper. At this stage, cultural and racial differences were not taken into account to design the animated avatar, because it was created for test purposes; if research findings point to an avatar preference, this issue will be addressed in a further investigation. One of them was chosen, and edited using CorelDraw. To do the sample animation, the iSpring tool was used (a free PowerPoint to Flash Converter). Figure 8 shows the sequence of images that form the animation of the sign "Interessado" (Interested, in English) in Libras.

To help with the animation development process, a video of a Libras interpreter signing the word "Interessado" was used. For the preparation of the opinion research questionnaire, a print-screen of the video was taken, and then this image was edited by placing a blue stripe over the interpreter's face to prevent the participants from identifying him/her.

Step 6: Preparation of the Opinion Research Questionnaire and Consent Document

The date and time of the opinion research was previously scheduled with the Director of a state school of Rondonopolis, and the teacher/interpreter responsible for the resource room was committed to inviting Deaf students who would like to contribute to the research.

Figure 8. Sequence of images representing the sign for "Interessado" in Libras

The opinion research questionnaire, with a brief script, was composed of eight questions with images. The questions were the same presented at the beginning of Section 4, only with the difference that Question 4 was subdivided into three: "Do you prefer the use of SignWriting or written Portuguese?"; "Do you prefer the use of SignWriting or manual Alphabet?"; "Do you prefer the use of manual Alphabet or written Portuguese?". An example of the questions included in the opinion research questionnaire can be seen in Figure 9.

Also, the consent document was elaborated, explaining the research goal, the participant contributions, and the ethical aspects.

Execution of the Field Study

The field study took place at a resource room of a state school, in which three Deaf students answered the opinion research questionnaire. The intention here was not focused on a quantitative approach; on the contrary, the assumptions made before were verified during observations of a small group of deaf persons, which led to the questions to confirm their preferences.

The participants' ages were, respectively, 18, 19 and 24 (named here as Student1, Student2, and Student3, respectively), and they were interviewed with the help of three different interpreters individually. All the interviewed Deaf students are male, the youngest is taking the 3rd grade of high school, and the others the 2nd grade of high school. Student3 can hear 30% with one ear and uses oralism; Student1 and Student2 are profoundly deaf, and do not use oralism. They study at the same school, but they are not close friends.

In Table 1, the answers of the three participants for the eight questions are displayed.

In Question 1, two out of the three participants answered they preferred the photographs of some-

Figure 9. Question 5 of the opinion research questionnaire

Table 1. Answers to the opinion research questionnaire

Questions	Question1		Question2		Question3		Question4		Question5		Question6		Question7		Question8	
Options	(a)	(b)	(a)	(b)	(a)	(b)	(a)	(b)	(a)	(b)	(a)	(b)	(a)	(b)	(a)	(b)
Answers	2	1	3	0	0	3	0	3	2	1	1	2	3	0	3	0

one's facial expressions instead of the drawings of an avatar signing in Libras. Contrary to what one might think, their official language was placed as a second option. This can highlight the relevance of the facial expression as a sign language parameter. Also, the static sequence of drawings which should represent a dynamic sign (incorporating movement) showed not to be well understood by People with hearing disabilities.

The answer was unanimous for Question 2, in which the participants informed that it would be better understood if there was the presence of written language (Brazilian-Portuguese) accompanied by an image. Therefore, if he could not understand one type of information, he could use the other one available. This can suggest that the more diversified the types of information can be displayed the better for the respondent; it can be thought of as a simple form of multimodality presented in one single media (paper or screen).

For Question 3, three votes were obtained for a rectangular shape of an instrument model. The participants found it easier to understand what they were supposed to mark.

As an answer to Question 4, the three participants expressed their opinion concerning the preference of Libras manual Alphabet instead of SignWriting. For Question 5, two of them preferred Brazilian SignWriting over written Brazilian-Portuguese; and, in Question 6, two preferred written Brazilian-Portuguese rather than Libras manual Alphabet. Observing the answers of these three questions, certain confusion can be perceived. Perhaps it would be more interesting to have kept the three options information in a single question. For this matter, we analyzed the answers of each one of the participants separately (Table 2).

Looking at Table 2, one can see that the Student1 kept a coherent line of thought to inform his answer, being evident that his preference among all the three options is the Libras manual Alphabet. However, despite the confusing preference between written Brazilian-Portuguese and Brazilian-SignWriting, the two other students also showed their preference towards the Libras manual Alphabet.

Considering Question 7, the three participants voted for the fewer options for choice of emotional words/signs presented in an evaluation instrument. In this question, it was specifically asked if they preferred an 08-word or a 32-word instrument. They mentioned that, with too many options, they would get tired of answering; they preferred something that would quickly be done.

To conclude, Question 8 also obtained three answers to the same option, the one with the communication of the Libras using a video. This answer is consistent with the responses of Question 1, in which both include facial expressions, and in

Table 2. Specific answers to the Questions 4, 5 and 6

Participants	Question4	Question5	Question6
Student1	Libras manual Alphabet	Written Brazilian-Portuguese	Libras manual Alphabet
Student2	Libras manual Alphabet	Brazilian SignWriting	Written Brazilian-Portuguese
Student3	Libras manual Alphabet	Brazilian SignWriting	Libras manual Alphabet

this case the Libras signs and facial expression are grouped together, facilitating the understanding of the emotion words.

FILMING THE VIDEOS WITH A DEAF NATIVE LIBRAS SIGNER

From the results of the last field study, the modifications were carried out. Thus, the Emotion-Libras 2.0 was elaborated, which is exposed in Figure 10.

The eight pictures of the person in Figure 10 were captured by the one frame of each video filmed with his consent document signed for the use of his image. The man in the video is a Deaf native Libras signer, who performed the eight emotion words/signs to compose this new instrument version. At the day, time and location of the filming, two Libras interpreters were present, and they voluntarily helped to instruct how he should position himself in front of the camera, or how facial expressions could be more exaggerated to better convey the idea of emotion.

In Figure 10, all the top rated answers from the questionnaire were verified to be taken into account, and they could thus be represented in the new version of the Emotion-Libras. For the purposes of this paper, this new version is a static one, but the real instrument is supposed to be digital in order to show the videos with signs in Libras.

FUTURE RESEARCH DIRECTIONS

As future research directions, many segments can be continued, such as: (a) test other emotional evaluation methods (e.g., 3E, Emotion Cards, GAQ, FACS) with People with hearing disabilities during their interactions with technology solutions ([i] this can be performed in different environments such as educational settings or work places; or [ii] could focus on different age ranges and compare the results; or [iii] different types of technology devices or software); and, (b) test the Emotion-Libras 1.0 and 2.0 in different regions of Brazil to verify: [i] their ability to identify people with hearing disabilities' emotions in the context of technology use; [ii] if the regionalism of the language can influence the final results.

Also, it is important to mention that no works were found, for example, in the Web of Science base search using these keyword topics: "quality in use" AND "user experience" AND emotion; or even: "quality in use" AND "emotional user experience" AND "people with hearing disabilities". Hence, this can be an evidence of lack of works in the area.

Figure 10. New version of the Emotion-Libras

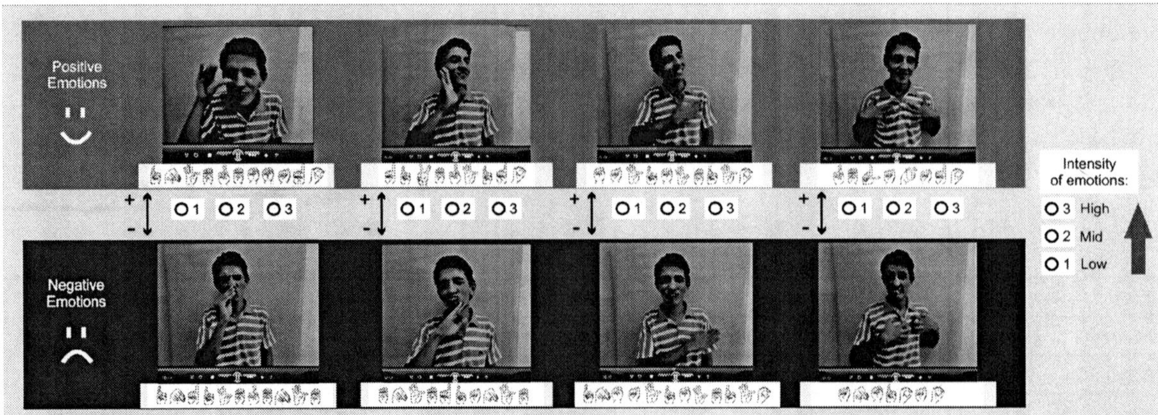

CONCLUSION

This paper presented the planning and the results of an interview with deaf participants aiming to find out about their remembrance of emotions concerning technology use, and also to discuss features of an emotional quality evaluation method for interviewing people with hearing disabilities at the moment they are using some technological solution.

It is relevant to know about the emotional experience of the people with hearing disabilities in relation to technology use, because the researchers that propose improvement and new technologies for this specific target user can include qualities in their design that enhance user experience. Knowing the positive and negative emotions during an evaluation process, one can gather all the positive aspects, and avoid the negative aspects when producing a technology really desired by that Community.

Notice that we carried out the field studies with high school deaf students. That was not random. The reason for inviting this specific public to participle, in the research was that we can already make contact with the subjects of future researches. The Emotion-Libras conception was conceived inside the TApES project (Prietch & Filgueiras, 2012a), which it is concerned about the process of designing through evaluation of an assistive technology prototype to support Deaf students in classroom settings.

ACKNOWLEDGMENT

The authors thank FAPEMAT and CAPES for their financial support, the deaf students interviewed, the interpreters: Samadar Polinati Lopes, Thais Polinati Lopes, Shirley Lopes Maidana de Oliveira, and Hélder Henrique Silva Siqueira; and the actress Josilaine Melo.

REFERENCES

Ahmed, A. S., & Seong, D. S. K. (2006). *SignWriting on mobile phones for the deaf.* Paper presented at Mobility 06. Bangkok, Thailand.

Alves, N. S., & Prietch, S. S. (2012). *Analysis and discussion of methods for assessment of emotional experience with deaf people: A practical approach (Tech. Rep.).* Rondonópolis, Brazil: Universidade Federal de Mato Grosso.

Bargas-Avila, J., & Hornbæk, K. (2011). Old wine in new bottles or novel challenges? A critical analysis of empirical studies of user experience. In *Proceedings of CHI 2011, User Experience.* ACM.

Bevan, N. (2009). Extending quality in use to provide a framework for usability measurement. In *Proceedings of HCI International 2009.* San Diego, CA: ACM.

Bianchini, C. S., Borgia, F., Bottoni, P., & de Marsico, M. (2012). *Swift – A signwriting improved fast transcriber.* Paper presented at AVI '12. Capri Island, Italy.

Bradley, M. M., & Lang, P. J. (1994). Measuring emotion: The self-assessment manikin and the semantic differential. *Journal of Behavior Therapy and Experimental Psychiatry, 25*(1). doi:10.1016/0005-7916(94)90063-9 PMID:7962581.

Broekens, J., Pronker, A., & Neuteboom, M. (2010). Real time labeling of affect in music using the affectbutton. In *Proceedings of AFFINE'10.* AFFINE.

Burmester, M., Mast, M., Jäger, K., & Homans, H. (2010). *Valence method for formative evaluation of user experience.* Paper presented at DIS 2010. Aarhus, Denmark.

Cambra, C. (2005). Feelings and emotions in deaf adolescents. *Deafness & Education International, 7*(4), 195–205.

Capovilla, F., Raphael, W., & Mauricio, A. (2010). *Dicionário enciclopédico ilustrado trilíngue*. São Paulo, Brazil: EdUSP.

Desmet, P. M. A. (2003). *Measuring emotions: Development and application of an instrument to measure emotional responses to products*. Boston: Kluwer Academic Pub..

Dyck, M. J. (2011). The ability to understand the experience of other people: Development and validation of the emotion recognition scales. *Australian Psychologist*.

Dye, M. W. G., Hauser, P. C., & Bavelier, D. (2009, May). Is visual selective attention in deaf individuals enhanced or deficient? The case of the useful field of view. *PLoS ONE. Visual Attention and Deafness*, *4*(5), e5640. PMID:19462009.

Easterbrooks, S. R., & Huston, S. G. (2008). The signed reading fluency of students who are deaf/hard of hearing. *Journal of Deaf Studies and Deaf Education*, *13*(1). PMID:17607020.

Ekman, P. (2003). *Emotions revealed: Recognizing faces and feelings to improve communication and emotional life* (2nd ed.). New York, NY: St. Martin's Press.

Elokla, N., Hirai, Y., & Morita, Y. (2010). A proposal for measuring user's kansei. In *Proceedings of the International Conference on Kansei Engineering and Emotion Research (KEER2010)*. KEER.

Goldstein, N. E., Sexton, J., & Feldman, R. S. (2000). Encoding of facial expressions of emotion and knowledge of american sign language. *Journal of Applied Social Psychology*, *30*(1). doi:10.1111/j.1559-1816.2000.tb02305.x.

Hayashi, E. C. S., & Baranauskas, M. C. C. (2010). Meta-communication in inclusive scenarios: Issues and alternatives. In *Proceedings of the IX Simpósio de Fatores Humanos em Sistemas Computacionais*. Academic Press.

Hiraga, R., & Kato, N. (2009). Is visual information useful for music communication? In *Proceedings of MSIADU'09*. Beijing, China: MSIADU.

Kay, R. H., & Loverock, S. (2008). Assessing emotions related to learning new software: The computer emotion scale. *Computers in Human Behavior*, 24.

Lang, P. J., Bradley, M. M., & Cuthbert, B. N. (1999). *International affective picture system (IAPS), instruction manual and affective ratings* (Tech. Rep. A-4). Gaithersburg, FL: The Center for Research in Psychophysiology, University of Florida.

Lera, E., & Garreta-Domingo, M. (2007). Ten emotion heuristics: Guidelines for assessing the user's affective dimension easily and cost-effectivelly. In *Proceedings of the 21st BCS HCI Group Conference*. BCI. Freitas-Magalhães, A. (2011). *A psicologia das emoções: O fascínio do rosto humano*. Porto, Portugal: Universidade Fernando Pessoa.

Mandryk, R. L., Atkins, M. S., & Inkpen, K. M. (2006). A continuous and objective evaluation of emotional experience with interactive play environments. In *Proceedings of CHI 2006*. ACM.

Marschark, M. (2007). *Raising and educating a deaf child: A comprehensive guide to the choices, controversies, and decisions faced by parents and educators* (2nd ed.). Oxford, UK: Oxford University Press.

Martins, S., & Filgueiras, L. V. L. (2010). Avaliando modelos de interação para comunicação de deficientes auditivos. In *Proceedings of IHC 2010 – IX Simpósio de Fatores Humanos em Sistemas Computacionais*. Belo Horizonte, Brazil: IHC.

Masip, L., Oliva, M., & Granolles, T. (2011). User experience specification through quality attributes. In P. Campos et al. (Eds.), *INTERACT 2011, (LNCS)* (Vol. 6949). Berlin: Springer. doi:10.1007/978-3-642-23768-3_106.

McCullough, S., & Emmorey, K. (1997). *Face processing by deaf ASL signers: Evidence for expertise in distinguishing local features*. Oxford, UK: Oxford University Press. doi:10.1093/oxfordjournals.deafed.a014327.

Norman, D. A. (2004). *Emotional design: Why we love (or hate) everyday things*. New York, NY: Perseus Books Group.

Pôrto, W. G. (2066). *Emoção e memória*. São Paulo, Brazil: Artes Médicas.

Prietch, S. S., & Filgueiras, L. V. L. (2012a). Assistive technology in the classroom taking into account the deaf student-centered design: the TApES project. In *Proceedings of Educational Interfaces, Software, and Technology (EIST)/ ACM SIGCHI Conference on Human Factors in Computing Systems (CHI)*. Austin, TX: ACM.

Prietch, S. S., & Filgueiras, L. V. L. (2012b). Emotional quality evaluation method for interviewing people with hearing disabilities (emotion-libras). In *Proceedings of IADIS International Conference Interfaces and Human Computer Interaction (ICHI)*. Lisbon, Portugal: IADIS.

Russell, J. A. (1980). A circumplex model of affect. *Journal of Personality and Social Psychology*, *39*(6), 1161–1178. doi:10.1037/h0077714.

Scherer, K. R. (2005). *What are emotions? And how can they be measured?* Thousand Oaks, CA: SAGE Publications. doi:10.1177/0539018405058216.

Shahriar, S. D. (2011). *A comparative study on evaluation of methods in capturing emotion*. (Master Degree Thesis). UMEA Universitet, Umea, Sweden.

SmartKids. (2012). *Passatempo: Alfabeto em libras*. Retrieved June, 18, 2012, from http://www.smartkids.com.br/

Stokoe, W. C. Jr. (2005). Sign language structure: An outline of the visual communication systems of the American deaf. *Journal of Deaf Studies and Deaf Education*, *10*(1). doi:10.1093/deafed/eni001 PMID:15585746.

Sutton, V. (2004). *The signwriting site*. Retrieved June, 18, 2012, from www.signwriting.org

Van Gorp, T., & Adams, E. (2012). *Design for emotion*. Waltham, MA: Morgan Kaufmann.

Wallbott, H. G., & Seithe, W. (1993). Sensitivity of persons with hearing impairment to visual emotional expression: Compensation or deficit? *European Journal of Social Psychology*, 23.

KEY TERMS AND DEFINITIONS

Deaf Persons: Persons that do not hear, and can communicate through written text, sign language, or lip-reading and speaking.

Emotional Design: This technique considers the user's emotions the main point of a project, or an advertising, or an evaluation of products/systems.

Emotional Quality Evaluation: Through the use of specific instruments of data collection, be able to identify what kinds and level of intensity of emotions the research subjects are feeling during the moment of a product/system use.

Evaluation Instrument: A paper or digital tool for data collection, which can be, for example, a questionnaire (with Likert Scale, or Semantic Differential Scale, or open questions, or images, or videos, among others), or a device that measures someone's heartbeat, or a system that automatically identifies someone's facial expression.

Sign Languages: They are visual-spatial languages used by Deaf persons all around the world. However, each country has its own sign language, in Brazil, it is called LIBRAS (Brazilian Sign Language).

User eXperience: UX takes into account the user felt experience, which (i) during the design stage, can be predicted to cause a desired response, or (ii) during the evaluation stage, can be identified. Experiences can be good or bad; but the good ones are memorable and can influence user's behavior during decision making.

ENDNOTES

1 Definitions about explicit and implicit methods are described by Broekens, Pronker & Neuteboom (2010).

2 The images from Capovilla, Raphael & Mauricio's (2010) trilingual dictionary, used in Figures 2, 4, 5, 6 and 9 in this Chapter, are the following: (1) Volume 1: (a) "Angustiar (2)", p. 244; (b) "Curioso(a)", p. 725; (c) "Divertido(a) (2)", p. 848; and, (d) "Não gostar (desgostar)", p. 1568; (2) Volume 2: (a) "Indiferente (2)", p. 1267; (b) "Satisfeito(a) (2)", p. 1993; (c) "Tédio (1)", p. 2090 (Volume 2); and, (d) "Tranquilo(a)", p. 2142.

3 Available in: http://www.smartkids.com.br/desenhos-para-colorir/alfabeto-libras.html.

Chapter 5
Enhancing the Acquisition of Social Skills through the Interactivity of Multimedia

Vivi Mandasari
Swinburne University of Technology, Malaysia

Lau Bee Theng
Swinburne University of Technology, Malaysia

ABSTRACT

Autism Spectrum Disorders (ASD) are a group of neuro-developmental disorders caused by brain abnormalities which result in impaired social story. Research on treatment in helping children with ASD to improve social story is growing as the cases of children diagnosed with ASD are on the rise. Social story is one of the proven methods of treatment in helping children with ASD to acquire social story through scenarios written in the form of stories. However, the current approaches to present the social story lack interactivity, consuming more intensive efforts to acquire the social story. Learning is most effectual when motivated; thus, the purpose of this study is to discover a learning tool that children with ASD will be motivated to learn independently, and it is achievable by combining elements that they are interested in. This research utilizes the interactivity of multimedia as a medium to present an interactive pedagogical tool for children with ASD to acquire social story. This combination is anticipated to be an effective tool in teaching social story to children with ASD, as they are naturally drawn to computers and visual cues, combined with the fact that Social Story™ has been effective in changing the social behavior of children with ASD. Thus, this study has contributed to the emergent research of treatment for children with ASD in social story acquisition. The result of this study is important as it presents a novel assistance that can be used effectively in assisting children with ASD to improve their main deficit, social story.

INTRODUCTION

Today, ASD is a neurodevelopmental disorder with high prevalence rates of 90 to 110 per 10000 children (Matson & Kozlowski, 2011). There has been evidence of growing rates in cases of ASD in the past decade (Fambonne, 2003; Bogdashina, 2006; Shattuck, 2007; Stillman, 2009; Kaufmann & Silverman, 2010; Lewandowski, 2010; Williams & Williams, 2011). There have been many controversies in identifying the causes of the brain abnormalities in children with ASD, among which

DOI: 10.4018/978-1-4666-4623-0.ch005

are environmental contributions, genetics, drug therapy/vaccine, onset in infancy, onset in prenatal period or complications in pregnancy (Kaufmann & Silverman, 2010; Lewandowski, 2010; Roullet & Crawley, 2011; Burstyn et al., 2011). Autism Spectrum Disorders (ASD) include Asperger's Syndrome, Pervasive Developmental Disorder-Not Otherwise Specified, Autistic Disorder, Rett Syndrome and Childhood Disintegrative Disorder. The broad spectrum makes a wide variation of symptoms among the children with ASD, each with his own individual pattern of autism.

There are many treatments claimed to be effective for children with ASD, but each child has his/her own unique profile. Therefore, a treatment that is suitable for one child might not be suitable for another child (Ball, 2008). As the case with the cause, there have been controversies in the search for an effective treatment for children with ASD, which has branched into a wide variety of treatment approaches (Williams & Williams, 2011). Lack of knowledge in the specific causative factors of ASD is the reason behind the controversies that surround the treatment for children with ASD (Williams & Williams, 2011).

SOCIAL SKILL DEFICIT

Social skill deficits in children with ASD lay the concepts of *Theory of Mind* and *Triad of Impairment*, which both entered the literature around the same time (Doherty, 2009). This elicited Baron-Cohen et al. (2009) to hypothesize that the two concepts might be related.

Deficits in Theory of Mind

Theory of Mind (ToM) could be referred to as empathy in general. However, this term has been popularly used to define the concept that is lacking in children with ASD and it explains the social challenges they are having (Bogdashina, 2006; Doherty, 2009; Baron-Cohen et al. 2009). ToM, or empathy, is crucial for social awareness in a complex social environment.

ToM is defined as the ability to take and surmise perspectives such as belief, desire, emotion, perception and intention of self and others to interpret behavior. This ability involves making a distinction between the real world and the mental representation of the world. ToM can be explained as the ability to understand other people as mindful beings who have their own mental states that are different from self (Lantz, 2002; Elzouki et al., 2007).

Normal children are said to have ToM because of their ability to explain and predict others' behavior by attributing them to independent mental states (Gallagher & Frith, 2003). In contrast, children with ASD often rely on a backup system like intellectual reasoning and experiences for their daily decision making and social interaction, which could lead a simple social interaction into a complex social calculation for them (Hickson & Khemka, 1999).

The development of ToM begins within the first year of life, such as by gaze following, joint attention, drawing attention of others with pointing, ability to understand if an object is animate or inanimate, and an awareness of others as intentional agents (Weiss et al., 2009).

The inability to impute mental states of self and others that underpins the essential human ability to communicate and interact in a meaningful way (Parsons & Mitchell, 2002) has caused children with ASD to have a difficult time in understanding and interacting with other people. They find it difficult to understand that other people have their own point of view of things that is different from their own point of view. They also cannot understand that a comment could embarrass or offend other people and that an apology would help to make a person feel better (Sicile-Kira & Grandin, 2006).

These inabilities cause children with ASD to have problems in communication and social relation as they may not be able to anticipate what other people will say or do in various situations (Chen, 2008). In addition, based on his personal experience as an individual with ASD, Chen (2008) also states that people with ASD have no instinct to share their world and are unconscious of the world around them.

From a study of a first birthday party at home, children with ASD paid less attention to other people, and to the faces of others, failed to respond when their names were called and did not see the gaze of others to guide their actions (Osterling & Dawson, 1994; Dawson et al., 2010). This is an evidence that children with ASD often fail to develop the essential prerequisite of ToM.

Triad of Impairment

The original concept of *Triad of Impairment* as defined by Wing & Gould (1979) is impairment in the areas of (1) social interaction (impaired relationship); (2) social communication/language (verbal and non-verbal); and (3) imagination/rigidity of thought (Wing, 1988; Wing, 2006; Wing, 1998; Wing & Wing, 1976; Bowen & Plimley, 2008; Macintyre, 2009). However, imagination is now replaced in the triad by behavior inflexibility that is characterized by restricted, repetitive, stereotyped and narrow range of interests/behaviors and activities/actions (rigidity of thought/lack of imagination) (Doherty, 2009; Boucher, 2009; Eyal, 2010).

Triad of impairment translates the difficulty that children with ASD have in understanding/ conveying meaning, expressing/reading emotion, using non-verbal behavior and participating in interpersonal imaginative play (Tartaro & Casell, 2008; Tartaro, 2007). Social interaction and communication are the critical features in children with ASD, as stated by many authors (Howlin, 2003; Schreibman, 2005; Schreibman, 2008). Language and communication pattern in children with ASD reflect their failure to understand the nature of another person. Another deficit includes restricted interest as identified by Howlin (2003) and Schreibman (2005).

The symptoms included in the *Triad of Impairment* differ among children with ASD; some children with ASD would have a mild combination of symptoms while symptoms in other children with ASD are more obvious (Sicile-Kira, 2004). Schreibman (2005) states that there are heterogeneous nature and complexity in ASD; therefore, it is frustrating to identify the core and primary deficit in ASD, as it is unlikely that a single core deficit would explain all features of ASD. However, he identifies that the behavior problems featured in children with ASD are in the areas related to social story, communication and restrictive, repetitive and stereotype behavior and interests.

Social Interaction Impairment

The inability to form a normal social relationship is the exceptional characteristic of children with ASD. Their inability to interact normally with other individuals includes: no desire to make friends, lack of eye contact, showing the trait of gullibility (LeBlanc & Volker, 2007), less likely to develop peer relationships or personal friendships, and lack of the urge to share interests or achievements. Added to that, they hardly point out objects of interest, are lacking in cooperative play, they spend an unusual amount of time unoccupied or in ritualistic activities, have lack of empathy, and lack of coordination of social behavior to signify social intention (Schopler & Mesibov, 1986).

They also possess abnormality in voice and speech intonation, impairment in non-verbal behavior such as eye gaze, facial expressions and gestures (Weiss et al., 2009). The lack in social/ emotional reciprocity (such as discrimination between parents and other adults or repeating behavior that are laughed at) and their difficulty in initiating, maintaining and terminating social interactions in an appropriate manner or failure to respond properly in social situations are among the symptoms as well (Brassard & Boehm, 2007).

Children with ASD are insensitive in responding to social stimuli such as name calling or play group participation. They have circumscribed and obsessive interests in the physical aspect of the social situation rather than in being engaged in the social experiences. For instance, in a setting where two or more children are playing with toys, children with ASD will not be drawn to join but will rather have a fixation on other physical elements such as on the toy itself.

Howlin (2003) refers to people with ASD as having social dyslexia, as they show direct avoidance of social situations and do not actively seek out social interaction, often failing in perceiving and appreciating others' thoughts and feelings, failing in perceiving the impact of someone's behavior on others, and having difficulty in reading facial and body expressions of other people.

Regardless of their inability to form normal social relationships, Bogdashina (2006) argues that many children with ASD have a strong desire to be with others. They interact and form relationships with others, but of a different nature. Thus, isolation from social situations will increase their feelings of loneliness and of being different (Joan & Rich, 1999).

Social Communication Impairment

Social situations can be very confusing for children with ASD as they tend to pre dominantly interpret language literally without interpreting the accompanied body language (Myles et al., 2004). This makes them very vulnerable and dysfunctional in certain situations (Bogdashina, 2006).

Symptoms of social communication inability in children with ASD are: inability to sense people who are not sincere, or when someone is lying (Bogdashina, 2006), inability to grasp different idiosyncrasies of language/signs, monotonous speech in intonation and volume, overly formal speeches, taking phrases literally, and delayed responses to questions (LeBlanc & Volker, 2007). They face difficulties in understanding and using forms of communication (such as speech, sign language, body language, tone of voice and vocalization), and difficulties with the form/content/use of verbal language (Dodd, 2005).

Some children with ASD, especially those with AS, may be extremely verbal with vast vocabularies, however, their usage of words is not appropriate for social communication. They speak in monotonous or pedantic style, lacking in melody and intonation. Other children with ASD who are verbally delayed may have some typical language problems which are consistent with a language disorder (Howlin, 2003), such as delayed or lack of functional language, impairment in initiating or sustaining conversations, repetitive use of language, lack of varied and spontaneous make-believe play, using idiosyncratic language, and a tendency to echo the last few words heard (Brassard & Boehm, 2007). Children at the lower functioning level may throw tantrums, make noises or physical activities as the way infants do when they feel discomfort, have a fixation on an object, or as an initiation of interaction (Schopler & Mesibov, 1985), may listen selectively to familiar words, and may point and use gestures to get something that they want (Brassard & Boehm, 2007).

Social communication difficulties can trigger challenging behavior in children with ASD, such as self-injury, aggression and tantrums. There is evidence shown that when children with ASD are taught functional communication skills, there is a reduction in these challenging behaviors (Schreibman, 2005).

Deficit in social communication results in a difficulty to learn through peer social interaction, which normally provides many benefits of learning. They will not only miss the valuable learning opportunities, but these deficits will affect their future especially in personal relationships, education and employment opportunities (Tartaro & Cassell, 2008).

Behavioral Inflexibility

Rigidity of thought and an impoverished imagination causes children with ASD to have narrow and repetitive patterns of activities/behavior (Macintyre, 2009; Feinstein, 2010). This results from a lack of social imagination and creativity or a lack of novel, imaginative behavior (Boucher, 2009).

Behavioral inflexibility in children with ASD is also indicated by their inability to pretend and hence they have a hard time trying to play games with peers, they have difficulties in relating with others and in forming friendships. They find it hard to transfer/generalize skills learnt from one situation to another similar situation (Bowen & Plimley, 2008).

Other typical behaviors of children with ASD include stereotype (known as self-stimulatory behavior, referring to repetitive movement of body or object); hypersensitivity to environment; tunnel vision, which is strictly following rules and routines in highly specific orders everyday as repetitive behavior; and finding it difficult to cope with a sudden change in daily routine (Bowen & Plimley, 2008). They seldom play spontaneously, instead, they simply manipulate toys and do not engage with them in any meaningful way (Slater & Bremmer, 2003).

They are also preoccupied with a restricted pattern of interest, adhere to non-functional routines, engage in repetitive gestures and have a persistent preoccupation with parts of objects. They also show stereotyped behavior such as body rocking, hand flapping, finger flicking and object spinning and twirling with a lack of obvious purpose (Slater & Bremmer, 2003). According to Schreibman (2005), this occurs up to 100% in children and adults with ASD.

Children with ASD are often fascinated with regular patterns of objects and may collect and arrange objects they find in a systematic and repetitive way for no apparent reason and they may be distressed when these arrangements are disturbed (Slater & Bremmer, 2003). Their interest is restricted and narrow, and most of them show affinity to one special interest that can be all-absorbing and dominating. This causes problems in social interaction especially when they are with people who do not share the same interest (Howlin, 2003; Bowen & Plimley, 2008).

SOCIAL STORY

Social story is one of the effective methods in learning social story (Gray & Garand, 1993; Rogers & Myles, 2001; Brownell, 2002; Agosta et al., 2004; Schneider & Goldstein, 2009). Social story is a short story containing description of the social situation, including introduction of the event, possible reaction of others and the expected behavior from the child. Social story aims to help children with ASD to understand the social situation which they do not learn naturally. *Social story*™ (SS) was first developed by Carol Gray (Gray & Garand, 1993) as an intervention strategy that taught social story to children with ASD. SS is a promising approach and the effectiveness has been proven by numerous studies that have reported improvement in children's behavior after a systematic exposure to SS (Hagiwara & Myles, 1999; Scurlock, 2008; Bledsoe et al., 2003; Rogers & Myles, 2001). Social story has been used independently or in combination with other methods of intervention. For instance, Schneider and Goldstein (2009) combined social story with visual cues, Agosta et al. (2004) used social story in partnership with classroom teacher, Rogers & Myles (2001) used social story as comic strip conversation and Brownell (2002) integrated social story with music.

SS is a brief, written story that explains a social situation that is causing difficulty in a person's life due to the lack of information or cognitive confusion (Scurlock, 2008), and it is used to provide concrete information to help improve social story and appropriate behavior. Therefore, the objective of SS is to describe rather than to direct, and it provides a child with information through text and visual images. In each story it provides concise and accurate information about what is happening in a specific social situation, what people do, why they do it, and what the common responses (expected behavior) are to help children with ASD to feel more relaxed and comfortable in social situations. The child's improved understanding of events and expectations from the story could lead to a more effective response (The Gray Center, 2010).

SS is a great tool for teaching skills through direct instructions, giving a better understanding of other people's thoughts, feelings and views, the areas where children with ASD are unable to pick up naturally. Therefore, providing SS to children with ASD before an event could help them predict actions, behavior and assumptions of others (Gabbert, 2010). This could lead to a decrease in a child's anxiety, improve his/her behavior and help him/her understand an event from the perspective of others (Heward, 2006).

SS attempts to address the *Theory of Mind* impairment by helping children with ASD to be able guess beliefs, thoughts, feelings, emotions and behaviors of others (Wallin, 2009). This will help strengthen their intuitive skill and instill in them a sense of ethics (Gabbert, 2010). Therefore, SS should inculcate concrete and clear information on the social situation, expected behavior from characters involved, in order to improve their reactions and responses in the situation. It should also explain simple steps for achieving certain goals or outcomes.

The main goal of SS is not to change behavior, rather to increase the understanding of social situations and expectations in these situations, by describing the social situation in detail and translating the goal of the social event into understandable steps including appropriate responses. This would help the child to be more comfortable in the situation and could facilitate the opportunity to learn more effective responses to the social situation (Ball, 2008; Wallin, 2009).

The traditional method of teaching children with ASD is often monotonous, laborious and not effective (Sharmin et al., 2011). Therefore, for this reason and concerning the natural interest in computer of children with ASD, many developers have been led to produce interactive software to assist their play and learning activities. The interactive computer software is also effective in increasing intelligibility in children with ASD (Sharmin et al., 2011). An improved way of developing social story for the children with ASD should be investigated to enhance the efficiency of social story intervention for social skill deficit.

WAYS TO IMPROVE SOCIAL STORY INTERVENTION

As mentioned, social story deficit is one of the core deficits where every child with ASD shares. This includes the impairment in the area of social interaction, verbal and non-verbal communication and repetitive behavior and interest. There has been much research conducted on helping children with ASD to improve their social story.

Studies found that children with ASD are visual learners (Odom & Watts, 1991; Grandin, 1992; Gray, 1994; Quill, 1995; Quill, 1997; Twachtman-Reilly et al, 2008) and naturally attracted to computer (Strickland, 1997; Elzouki et al, 2007; Tartaro and Cassell, 2008; Eliasz, 2009), as a result. Hagiwara and Myles (1999) were the first to implement social story in the computerized format. Following them, there were few more computerized social stories being researched by Sansosti and Powell-Smith (2008). The studies showed that the combination of social story and the visual image on computer-based format is effective in helping children with ASD to acquire social story.

Interactive multimedia provides the visual cues that attract children with ASD (Howlin, Baron-Cohen & Hadwin, 1999; Myles et al, 2004; Wells, 1998; Bernard-Opitz et al, 2001; Howlin et al,

1999; Herskowitz, 2009). Using computerized animation, children with ASD are able to learn problem solving techniques (Herskowitz, 2009). It has also been proven in helping children with ASD to recognize human emotions (Golan et al, 2009; Baron-Cohen et al, 2009; Baron-Cohen et al, 2007). Bosselar & Massaro (2003) showed that children with ASD are capable in learning vocabulary with the help of computer-animated agent. Positive results on using it to teach children with ASD was proven by Baron-Cohen et al (2009), their research showed that an animated movie improve understanding and emotion recognition in children with ASD.

ANIMATION AS A SOLUTION

Computer presented animation is a type of visual support that children with ASD are attracted to, and this technique has already been implemented for many years in helping children with ASD to enhance their understanding of language (Myles et al. 2004). Animation figures can play an integral role in a number of intervention techniques, such as pragmatism (Arwood & Brown 1999), mind reading (Howlin et al. 1999), and comic strip conversation (Gray 1995). Each of these techniques promotes social understanding by using simple figures and other symbols. Visual cues enhance the ability of children with ASD to understand their environment (Gray 1995; Rogers & Myles 2001; Myles et al. 2004). Visual symbols found in animation/cartoon often enhance the social understanding of children with ASD by turning an abstract and elusive event into something tangible and static that a person can reflect upon (Dunn et al. 2002; Hagiwara & Myles 1999; Myles et al. 2004).

The use of computer presented animation as a treatment approach for children with ASD has been widely supported by various authors, such as Wells (1998), Bernard-Opitz et al. (2001), Howlin et al. (1999), Herskowitz (2009) and Baron-Cohen et al. (2009). Children with ASD are capable of learning a new language within a program that is centered on a computer-animated agent, multimedia, to encourage active participation. Compared to video modeling, the use of this method shows that there is a transfer and use of language learned in a natural and untrained environment, as suggested by Bosselar & Massaro (2003).

A research by Bosselar & Massaro (2003) showed that children with ASD are capable of learning vocabulary with the help of a computer-animated agent. Positive results using animation to teach children with ASD have also been shown by Baron-Cohen et al. (2009), whose research shows that an animated movie has improved the understanding and emotion recognition in children with ASD. Using computerized animation, children with ASD are able to learn problem solving techniques (Herskowitz 2009); animation has also been proven effective in helping children with ASD to recognize human emotions (Golan et al. 2009; Baron-Cohen et al. 2009; Baron-Cohen et al. 2007). As noted by Herskowitz (2009), animation can be used for several purposes: Firstly, animation can be used as a reinforcer, for example when a child performs a task correctly in the computer program, an animated character will display and congratulate the child for the job well done. The second function of the character animation is that it can be used as a prompt device. And thirdly, the use of animation as the actual characters in the program can increase the child's attention and focus on the task.

Despite the fact that 2D animation has been widely used in many areas, there has not been much scientific research conducted on the effects of 2D animation, particularly on children with ASD, except for a few like Boraston et al. (2007) who studied the effect of 2D abstract animation on children with ASD, in identifying simple emotions. However, there has been much feedback from real-life experiences from the families of children with ASD who claimed that 2D animation was enjoyed by most of the children with ASD. Therefore, we aim to explore on how children with ASD could acquire social story by combining 2D animation with a social story.

RESEARCH PROBLEM

Social skill deficit is one of the core deficits of the children diagnosed with ASD. There have been many ways to acquire social story. Social story, computer and visual cues through interactive multimedia, play an important role as treatment tool for children with ASD in social story learning. Each of these subjects has been used positively whether individually or in combination with others. It also evidences that social story is more effective when used in combination with visual schedules.

The use of visual schedules, such as picture has been found useful in structuring the learning of children with ASD, as well as improving their understanding and comprehension of conversation. Social story in combination with visual schedules has also been presented using PowerPoint software where it produced higher positive results when compared to normal paper-based social story.

However, the static visual schedule failed to portray the non-literal components in communication, such as body language, facial expression and gestures. Another problem with the current social story methods is intensive teacher assistance or supervision for them to be effective. In fact, children should acquire social story more independently to cope with their daily routines.

Studies described in the background has illustrates social story, computer and animation could greatly engage children with ASD. However, there is no related research on the combination of social story and animation to improve the social story acquisition of children with ASD as to date. Therefore, this paper presents the improved social story intervention through the interactivity of multimedia to enhance the social story acquisition of children with ASD.

METHODOLOGY

This study employed quantitative research design that is ABA Reversal design from single subject design. Single subject design is a rigorous scientific methodology used to define behavior and it offers features that are useful for use in the field of special education research (Hopkins, 2000; Homer et al, 2005). Based on findings listed in Appendix 2, reversal design is the most powerful of single subject design which shows a strong reversal from baseline (A) to intervention (B) and back again to baseline (A).

To ensure the validity of the experimental study, there are a few criteria in participant selection:

1. He/she has a diagnosis of Autism Spectrum Disorders, identified by a psychological assessment or psychiatric diagnosis, as reviewed from the medical record documented in the school database.
2. His/her age is between 4 to 17 years of age and currently a student in the school.
3. He/she demonstrates behavioral problem and/or has impaired verbal/social communication (currently or in the past) for the targeted behavioral problems.
4. He/she is able to look at a computer screen, without necessary to be able to operate the computer.
5. He/she is willing to participate in the study with parents' consent.

Parents of the students who met the inclusion criteria were invited through the school management. The parents who were interested to allow their children participating in this research would sign for the consent forms circulated. The management of the school compiled the list of students for the researcher. The classroom teachers were also informed regarding the study and asked for help and cooperation in assisting researcher with the selected participants.

Participant Selection

There were thirty participants selected to participate in the study. Appendix 1 shows the summary of the participants' profile, including their gender, age, diagnosis, basic communication skills, cognitive functioning, home-class, mother tongue and special notes if any. It had been anticipated that the number of male participants would be significantly more than the female participants, as statistic has shown that the diagnosis of ASD is more prominent in males (Fambonne 2003). In this study, there were 4 female participants and 26 male participants. The average age of the participants was 9.8 years old. There was only one participant with a diagnosis of *Rett's Syndrome*, three participants with *Asperger Syndrome*, eleven participants with *Pervasive Developmental Disorders – Not Otherwise Specified*, fifteen participants with *Autistic Disorders* and none with *Childhood Disintegrative Disorders*. Basic communication skill was defined from the ability of the students to communicate in an appropriate way using verbal or non-verbal languages (such as gestures). Students without basic communication skills were the ones who often did not respond to others verbally or gesturally in an appropriate way. Cognitive functioning was defined from the students' competency to understand the materials taught by the teacher and be able to join in the teaching activities. Students afflicted with this problem would not also participate in the teaching activities, and were thus often excluded from the teaching sessions.

Data Measures and Collection

For data collection and analysis, each social behavior was categorized as appropriate, inappropriate and no interaction, as suggested in Thiemann and Goldstein (2001). There were three phases in the data collection: Baseline (A), Intervention (B) and Reversal Baseline (A). To conceal the children's privacy, data collection was not recorded with any video camera. Instead, data collection sheet was prepared specifically for the data collection suggested in Norris and Datillo (1999) with the response column of appropriate, inappropriate and no interaction. Data was collected when it occurred during the observation sessions; the data was marked with a "1" in the appropriate column of the data collection sheet. The duration of each session of data collection was set to 10 minutes. In a regular one day class, there will be 2 to 8 sessions of data collection.

Data Processing and Analysis

Data was collected in handwritten form. Thus, for the processing and analysis purpose, it was compiled and computed using Microsoft Excel. In Microsoft Excel, data collected during all phases was combined and tabulated to generate the mean and standard deviation of behavioral changes of 'appropriate', 'inappropriate' and 'no interaction' for each participant. This generated the number of interaction in average per session (10-minutes). The overall data of behavioral changes was also tabulated by combining all the data generated from all of the participants. Data was analyzed anonymously without using the name of participant, instead, a number ID were given, and their collected data were analyzed using this ID. This was to prevent conscious or unconscious prejudiced interpretation (Hopkins, 2000).

Ethical Consideration

As this study required human participation that is children with ASD, some ethical issues were addressed to ensure privacy and safety of the participants. Among the significant ethical issues that were considered in the study includes the consent from parents, as well as the confidentiality of the participation. To secure the consent of the participants, all important details of the study, including its aim and purpose was explained to the parents and children. The participants were also advised that they could withdraw from the study if they wish to, at any point of the study process without any obligation. The confidentiality of the participants was ensured by not disclosing their names or any personal information in any presentation or publications. They were not photographed or video recorded throughout the study.

DESIGN

From the observation performed at the special school and also discussions made with the teachers at school, the identification of target behaviors for the thirty participants was confirmed. Five social stories were developed for them based on Gray's guidelines. The developed social stories were constructed into 2D animation with narration and music using Adobe Flash CS3 and ActionScript 3.0. 2D animation was chosen over 3D animation or real-human video as studies suggested that children with ASD have greater interest in the 2D cartoon compared to 3D animation or real-human video as suggested in Rosset et al (2008), van der Geest et al (2002) and Grelotti et al (2005).

The prototype, namely *iLearn Social story* was designed to engage children with ASD in their acquisition of social story with 2D animations, narrations and music throughout the learning. Figure 1 illustrates the introduction scene of the interactive multimedia based social story; it is a simple animation for 8 seconds before the program displays the list of the Social Stories to choose from, with English and Bahasa Malaysia options. Figure 1 also shows that when a social story is selected to be played, the respective target behavior will be displayed for 10-20 seconds; there is also a "Skip", where user can press to skip the scene. Finally, after the target behavior scene, the animation for the respective story chosen will be displayed. Figure 2 illustrates four screenshots of the different social stories content. At the end of each story, there is "Another Story" which will bring the user back to the Story List scene as in Figure 1.

How to Greet Someone at School

'How to greet someone at school' story teaches student in initiating or responding to greetings verbally or non-verbally. This story was adapted from ASD Concepts LLC (2009), as it is appropriate for the use in the school's context, thus it was not modified. The appropriate behaviors include (1) student could initiate and/or respond to greetings verbally, physically or through gesture. Inappropriate behaviors includes student initiate greetings in inappropriate way such as pushing or yelling, (2) student responds to greetings in an inappropriate way such as pushing or yelling. No interaction behavior includes (1) student has no any response to the social greetings.

Figure 1. Sample screenshots for Introduction (left), social story list in English and Malay languages (center) and target behavior (right) with 2D animations, narrations and music

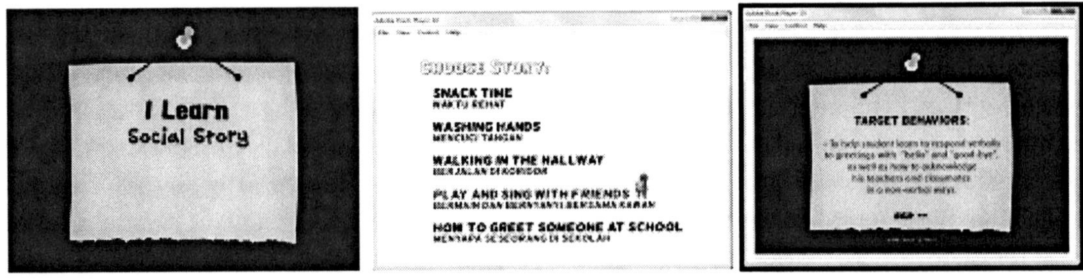

Figure 2. Sample of multimedia based learning materials with 2D animations, narrations and music

Play and Sing with Friends

The targeted behavior in this story is to engage the student in an activity with other students. Therefore, the appropriate behavior included (1) student could play, sing or have any other social interaction with their friends, such as share stationery and ask/respond to help in an appropriate way. Inappropriate behaviors include (1) student refuses to play or share his/her toys/stationery with the friends, (2) student refuses to sing together with the friends, (3) student refuses to borrow or help the friends in an inappropriate way. No interaction behavior includes student has no response to the social invitation by their friends.

Snack Time

'Snack time' story targeted on encouraging students to interact with their friends, teacher or class helpers during snack time. Appropriate behaviors include (1) students could initiate or responding to others verbally, physically or though some body gesture during snack time, (2) students could share their snack with others, (3) students could ask for snacks from their friends or teacher/class helper, or (4) students refuse to share their snack in an appropriate way. Inappropriate behaviors include: (1) student takes other's snack without permission, (2) students refuse to share their snack in an improper way such as pushing him/her. No interaction behavior includes (1) student has no response when being offered snack (2) student has no response when he/she is being invited for social interaction during snack time.

Walking in the Hallway

'Walking in the Hallway' story's target behavior is to teach students to socialize with their friends while walking in the hallway as well as to encourage students to walk appropriately in the school hallway. Appropriate behaviors include (1) students could initiate or respond to social interaction while walking in the hallway, such as holding hands or talking softly, (2) students could walk slowly and do not put up noises while walking in the hallway. Inappropriate behaviors include: (1) student initiates or responds to social interaction in an inappropriate manner, (2) student runs or makes noises while walking in the hallway. No interaction behavior include student does not have any responses when he/she is being invited into social interaction during walking in the hallway.

Washing Hands

The targeted behavior in 'Washing Hands' story is to encourage the students to ask their friends to wash hands, brush teeth or go to washroom together. This story also promotes healthy living lifestyle to the student by teaching them to wash hands before meals. The appropriate behavior for this story includes (1) students are able to ask their friend(s) to wash hands, brush teeth or go to washroom together, (2) student is able to accept or reject in appropriate way of the friend's request to wash hands, brush teeth or go to washroom together and (3) without prompt, student is able to wash hands before the meals or after activity that would make the hands dirty. The inappropriate behaviors included (1) students reject their friend's request of washing hands, brushing teeth or going to washroom together in an inappropriate way, such as pushing or shouting, (2) wash hands only after a few prompts from teacher or the class helper. No interaction means the student's has no responses to teacher, class helper or friend's request to wash hands, brush teeth or go to washroom together.

EVALUATION

The setting of the intervention was in the school, included the participants' respective classrooms which contains a maximum of 30 students of mixed disabilities, the hall, the kitchen, the book room and the open area where they do their daily school activities. Each class is managed by classroom teacher with one to two assistants. The prototype of interactive multimedia based social story was created for the intervention purpose, and a laptop computer was used to present the interactive multimedia based social stories to the participants; data collection sheet (Appendix 3) was also created to mark each social interaction as it occurred.

In the baseline (A), the initial condition of the participants were observed from a close distant while they engage in their daily school activities. There was no intervention, inappropriate behavior was not corrected and correct behavior was not cued in this phase. Each participant engaged in 10-minutes social activity in each session. In the baseline, each participant was observed for 12 to 20 sessions in total, depending on their attendance and the stability of the baseline data. Social activities were conducted based on the current classroom curricular topic, familiar routines and the children's preferences whenever possible.

In the intervention (B), interactive multimedia based social story was shown to the participant prior to the activity of interest. In this phase, participant and researcher sat (side by side) on chairs with a table where the researcher assisted him/her in using the prototype for 10-20 minutes. Immediately after the learning, the participant was allowed to get back to his/her regular school activities. The observation for data collection for the intervention phase began after that. There were 10 to 16 sessions of data collection in the intervention phase, depending on the participant's attendance. Sometimes, to ensure the social story was understood by the participant, the researcher asked comprehension questions to confirm that participant understand the social story and behavior recommended. Then the social story was being repeated to him. Once the data was stable or sixteen sessions had been completed, the reversal baseline phase began.

In the reversal baseline (A), interactive multimedia based social story intervention was completely withdrawn from the participant, and reversal baseline phase began for 16 to 32 sessions (depending on the participant's attendance and the stability of the data) after the intervention phase ended. The procedure used in the reversal baseline was the same procedure used in the baseline sessions. The purpose of the reversal baseline phase was to access the short-term skills maintenance of the participant after they learn the social story.

RESULTS AND DISCUSSIONS

The effectiveness of the interactive multimedia based social story was identified by comparing the average of occurrences for the 'appropriate', 'inappropriate' and 'no interaction' behaviors on each of the phases (pre-intervention, intervention and post-intervention) for each participant per social story. The average was obtained by the number of occurrence divided by the number of sessions as each participant had different number of sessions. The result of each participant was compiled and tabulated to generate the average of 'appropriate', 'inappropriate' and 'no interaction' in each phase, which is summarized in Table 1 to Table 5. The behavioral change is measured by the number of occurrences in each 10-minute session.

These overall behavioral changes from baseline to reversal baseline were the increment in appropriate behavior by 0.88 occurrences per 10 minutes session, decrement in inappropriate behavior by 0.89 occurrences in 10 minutes session, and increment in social interaction by 0.89 numbers of occurrences per 10 minutes session.

These overall behavioral changes were increment in appropriate behavior by 1.16 per 10 minutes session, decrement in inappropriate behavior by 0.95 in 10 minutes session, and increment in social interaction by 0.90 per 10 minutes session of social interaction.

These overall behavioral changes were increment in appropriate behavior by 0.96 occurrences per 10 minutes session, decrement in inappropriate behavior by 0.75 occurrences in 10 minutes session, and increment in social interaction by 0.86 numbers of occurrences per 10 minutes session.

These overall behavioral changes were increment in appropriate behavior by 0.85 occurrences per 10 minutes session, decrement in inappropriate behavior by 0.58 occurrences per 10 minutes session, and increment in social interaction by 0.82 numbers of occurrences per 10 minutes session.

Table 1. How to greet someone at school

	Baseline	**Intervention**	**Reversal Baseline**
Average of appropriate	0.78	1.74	1.59
Average of inappropriate	1.96	1.09	1.07
Average of No Interaction	2.35	1.43	1.49

Table 2. Play and sing with friends

	Baseline	**Intervention**	**Reversal Baseline**
Average of appropriate	0.75	2.01	1.81
Average of inappropriate	2.32	1.38	1.35
Average of No Interaction	2.38	1.49	1.48

Table 3. Snack time

	Baseline	**Intervention**	**Reversal Baseline**
Average of appropriate	0.90	1.92	1.79
Average of inappropriate	1.96	1.20	1.23
Average of No Interaction	2.24	1.35	1.40

Table 4. Walking in the hallway

	Baseline	**Intervention**	**Reversal Baseline**
Average of appropriate	0.73	1.65	1.53
Average of inappropriate	2.12	1.50	1.58
Average of No Interaction	2.40	1.56	1.60

Table 5. Washing hands

	Baseline	**Intervention**	**Reversal Baseline**
Average of appropriate	0.64	1.49	1.41
Average of inappropriate	2.01	1.28	1.26
Average of No Interaction	2.34	1.54	1.72

The overall behavioral changes were the increment in appropriate behavior by 0.81 occurrences per 10 minutes session, decrement in inappropriate behavior by 0.75 occurrences per 10 minutes session, and increment in social interaction by 0.71 numbers of occurrences per 10 minutes.

Overall Behavioral Changes

Table 6 presents the summary of intervention results with average and standard deviation (SD). For *How to greet someone at school*, there was an overall increment of 0.88 occurrence for appropriate behaviors (SD 0.62), inappropriate behavior was reduced to 0.89 (SD 0.64), and the number of social interaction was increased by 0.89 (SD 0.70). For *Play and sing with friends*, averagely there was an increment of 1.16 occurrences of appropriate behaviors (SD 0.76), decrement of 0.95 occurrences of inappropriate behaviors (SD 0.74), and increment of 0.90 occurrences of social interaction made (SD 0.77). In *Snack time*, overall there was an increment in appropriate behavior by 0.96 occurrences (SD 0.64), decrement in inappropriate behavior by 0.75 occurrences (SD 0.56), and increment in the number of social interaction by 0.86 occurrences (SD 0.70). *Walking in the hallway* had an increment of 0.85 occurrences for appropriate behavior (SD 0.74), decrement of 0.58 occurrences in inappropriate behavior (SD

Table 6. Overall results obtained from multiple intervention sessions

Participant	Social Story															Overall Behavioral Changes		
	How to greet someone at school			Play and sing with friends			Snack time			Walking in the hallway			Washing hands					
	Appropriate	Inappropriate	No Interaction	Appropriate	Inappropriate	No Interaction	Appropriate	Inappropriate	No Interaction	Appropriate	Inappropriate	No Interaction	Appropriate	Inappropriate	No Interaction	Appropriate	Inappropriate	No Interaction
1 (4 yrs)	0.45	-1.05	-1.60	1.90	-0.85	-2.75	1.15	-1.80	-1.90	na	na	na	1.45	-1.05	-2.70	1.24	-1.19	-2.24
2 (5 yrs)	1.10	-1.50	-1.95	1.70	-1.75	-1.30	1.35	-1.05	-1.40	na	na	na	1.10	-1.55	-1.65	1.31	-1.46	-1.58
3 (5 yrs)	1.15	-0.10	-1.60	1.50	-0.75	-2.00	1.60	-0.25	-1.90	na	na	na	0.60	-1.25	-1.40	1.21	-0.59	-1.73
4 (6 yrs)	1.85	-1.90	-1.10	2.00	-1.60	-1.15	1.85	-0.95	-2.25	na	na	na	1.65	-1.60	-1.45	1.84	-1.51	-1.49
5 (6 yrs)	1.75	-1.35	-2.10	1.85	-1.45	-2.15	1.55	-0.80	-1.35	1.15	-1.35	-1.05	1.15	-0.80	-1.50	1.49	-1.15	-1.63
6 (6 yrs)	1.35	-1.40	-0.70	1.10	-1.45	-1.20	0.75	-1.00	-1.25	na	na	na	1.00	-0.40	-1.30	1.05	-1.06	-1.11
7 (7 yrs)	0.95	-0.25	-2.05	1.90	-0.95	-0.90	1.60	-1.25	-1.10	na	na	na	0.90	-0.65	-0.80	1.34	-0.78	-1.21
8 (7 yrs)	1.30	-1.50	-1.05	2.35	-1.70	-0.75	1.15	-1.25	-0.65	1.30	-1.45	-0.75	1.15	-0.10	-0.45	1.45	-1.20	-0.73
9 (8 yrs)	0.45	-0.50	-0.10	2.25	-3.20	0.00	1.15	-0.65	-0.65	1.25	-0.90	0.05	1.25	-2.45	0.00	1.27	-1.54	-0.14
10 (8 yrs)	0.60	-1.80	-1.60	0.60	-0.55	-1.85	1.80	-0.30	-1.00	1.15	-0.15	-1.85	1.20	-1.00	-1.50	1.07	-0.76	-1.56
11 (9 yrs)	0.10	-0.95	0.20	0.55	-0.65	0.35	0.25	-1.40	0.65	0.05	-0.55	-0.20	0.20	-0.15	-0.05	0.23	-0.74	0.19
12 (9 yrs)	0.85	-0.40	-1.10	0.75	-0.25	-1.00	0.35	-0.75	-1.55	0.60	-0.65	-0.90	0.25	-0.30	-1.60	0.56	-0.47	-1.23
13 (9 yrs)	1.25	-0.40	-0.50	1.55	-0.55	-0.75	1.40	-0.45	-0.70	0.85	-0.75	-0.90	0.65	-0.55	-0.40	1.14	-0.54	-0.65
14 (9 yrs)	1.05	-0.65	-0.30	1.00	-1.30	-0.65	1.10	-0.85	-0.60	0.90	-0.60	-1.50	1.15	-0.85	-0.75	1.04	-0.85	-0.76
15 (10 yrs)	2.20	-0.90	-2.25	1.80	-0.85	-2.05	1.20	-0.40	-1.75	3.00	-0.75	-2.95	1.45	-0.25	-0.60	1.93	-0.63	-1.92
16 (10 yrs)	1.45	-1.35	-1.25	1.75	-1.65	-1.60	1.90	-2.50	-0.15	2.00	-2.00	-0.55	1.35	-1.55	-0.65	1.69	-1.81	-0.84
17 (10 yrs)	0.05	0.05	-0.05	-0.05	-0.15	0.15	0.10	0.10	-0.05	0.05	0.05	0.00	0.05	-0.15	-0.05	0.04	-0.02	0.00
18 (10 yrs)	1.30	-1.70	-1.00	1.80	-1.55	-1.50	1.10	-1.15	-1.30	1.25	-0.80	-1.95	1.40	-1.85	-0.75	1.37	-1.41	-1.30
19 (10 yrs)	0.25	-0.30	-1.30	0.15	-0.15	-0.45	0.15	-0.25	-0.35	0.30	-0.30	-0.25	0.30	-0.15	-0.35	0.23	-0.23	-0.54
20 (11 yrs)	0.00	-0.40	0.00	0.00	0.25	0.10	0.05	-0.20	0.05	-0.05	0.30	-0.15	0.00	0.00	0.05	0.00	-0.01	0.01
21 (11 yrs)	0.70	-0.75	-1.05	0.90	-0.25	-0.55	0.40	-0.85	-0.55	1.00	-0.30	-1.00	0.90	-1.35	2.00	0.78	-0.70	-0.23
22 (11 yrs)	1.10	-0.75	-0.75	1.30	-1.10	-1.00	0.65	-0.55	-1.90	1.45	-0.50	-1.55	1.10	-1.40	-0.70	1.12	-0.86	-1.18
23 (11 yrs)	0.40	-0.45	-0.70	0.55	-0.45	-0.60	0.45	-0.65	-0.40	0.50	-0.35	-0.65	0.20	-0.35	-0.35	0.42	-0.45	-0.54
24 (11 yrs)	0.00	0.10	-0.20	-0.10	-0.15	-0.35	0.05	-0.10	-0.30	-0.10	0.10	-0.05	-0.05	0.25	-0.15	-0.04	0.04	-0.21
25 (12 yrs)	1.30	-1.50	-0.65	1.00	-1.50	-0.70	1.05	-0.40	-1.20	0.60	-0.65	-0.45	0.95	-0.70	-1.05	0.98	-0.95	-0.81
26 (13 yrs)	-0.05	-0.15	-0.05	-0.05	-0.25	0.30	0.05	-0.10	0.00	0.05	-0.05	0.15	0.00	-0.10	0.05	0.00	-0.13	0.09
27 (15 yrs)	1.30	-1.95	-0.35	2.00	-1.25	-0.55	1.95	-0.90	-0.55	1.00	-0.75	-0.80	0.90	-0.50	-1.10	1.43	-1.07	-0.67
28 (16 yrs)	0.90	-1.30	-1.15	1.20	-1.55	-1.25	0.95	-1.15	-0.65	0.55	-0.95	-0.95	0.90	-1.05	-1.00	0.90	-1.20	-1.00
29 (17 yrs)	-0.05	0.00	0.10	0.10	0.15	-0.10	0.05	-0.05	-0.10	0.00	-0.15	-0.20	0.00	0.00	-0.05	0.02	-0.01	-0.07
30 (17 yrs)	1.40	-1.50	-0.50	1.45	-1.05	-0.65	1.55	-0.45	-1.05	1.60	-0.45	-1.25	1.20	-0.55	-1.05	1.44	-0.80	-0.90
Average	0.88	-0.89	-0.89	1.16	-0.95	-0.90	0.96	-0.75	-0.86	0.85	-0.58	-0.82	0.81	-0.75	-0.71	*0.95*	*-0.80*	*-0.87*
Std Deviation	0.62	0.64	0.70	0.76	0.74	0.77	0.64	0.56	0.70	0.74	0.52	0.75	0.52	0.65	0.83	*0.59*	*0.50*	*0.65*

0.52), and increment off 0.82 occurrences in social interaction made (SD 0.75). *Washing hands* had an increment of 0.81 occurrences in appropriate behavior (SD 0.52), decrement in inappropriate behavior by 0.75 occurrences (SD 0.65) and the number of social interaction was increased by 0.71 occurrences (SD 0.83).

Highest increment in appropriate behavior was obtained by P15 with increment of 1.93 appropriate behaviors per ten-minute session, lowest by P24 with slightly decrement in appropriate behavior by 0.04 per ten-minute session. Average of appropriate behavior changes made by all participants was an increment of 0.95 occurrences of appropriate behaviors per 10-minute session, with SD of 0.59 occurrences.

Highest decrement in inappropriate behavior was obtained by P16 with decrement of 1.81 occurrences of inappropriate behaviors per ten-minute session, lowest by P24 with slightly increment in inappropriate behavior by 0.04 occurrences per 10-minute session. Average of inappropriate behavior changes made by all participants was decrement of 0.80 occurrences of inappropriate behaviors per ten-minute session, with SD of 0.50 occurrences.

Highest increment in social interaction made was obtained by P1, with increment of social interaction by 2.24 occurrences of interaction per ten-minute, lowest by P11, whom number of social interaction made was reduced by 0.19 per 10 minutes session. The average change in social interaction was 0.87 increment in number of social interaction made per 10 minute session with SD of 0.65 occurrences.

These numbers, as illustrated in the bottom part of right side of Table 6, will make the summary of overall behavioral changes of 0.95 increment of appropriate behaviors, decrement of 0.80 occurrences of inappropriate behavior and increment of 0.87 occurrences in social interaction made. The standard deviation for appropriate behavior was 0.59 occurrences, inappropriate was 0.50 occurrences and no interaction was 0.65 occurrences across participants.

Statistical Significance

Only two previous studies on SS have had a sufficiently large cohort for a statistical analysis (Appendix 2). Pettigrew (1998) had the highest number of participants, she tested SS on 69 children with language impairment. She divided them into three groups: an experimental group of 31 who used SS with scaffolding activities; a control group of 24 who read library book with no social meaning; and a comparison group of 14 who read a library book and participated in scaffolding activities. In this study, teachers were asked to complete the pre- and post-test ratings of the students. Result showed that the experimental group had an increase in social competence. However, it is statistically confusing and inconsistent. There was disagreement between the data presented in the figures and the texts, as argued by Washburn (2006). The numbers used for Chi-square analysis were inconsistent with the number in the text. Another suspect source of inconsistency is due to the fact that the teachers, instead of the researcher, rated the behaviors. On the other hand, Feinberg (2001) tested SS to a control group of 14 normally developed children and experimental group of 34 children with ASD. SS was read to the experimental group while regular story was read to the control group. Result show there is a significant change for the experimental group only in certain behaviors ($p<0.005$).

The current study showed statistically significant improvements, especially in the high functioning group. The *t*-test results shown in Table 7, Table 8, Table 9, Table 10 and Table 11 show that the results observed in participants with high cognitive functioning group are significant with $p<0.01$. From these significance values, it is proven that the proposed intervention using the prototype is effective in assisting the participants with high cognitive functioning in improving

Table 7. Behavioral changes observed in high cognitive functioning group for 'How to greet someone at school'

Average of behavioural changes during baseline (A), Intervention (B) and Reversal Baseline (A)

Participant	Baseline (A)				Intervention (B)				Reversal Baseline (A)			
		Average of Appropriate	Average of Inappropriate	Average of No Interaction		Average of Appropriate	Average of Inappropriate	Average of No Interaction		Average of Appropriate	Average of Inappropriate	Average of No Interaction
1 (4 yrs)	16	0.10	1.60	2.40	16	0.60	0.60	0.80	32	0.50	0.50	0.80
2 (5 yrs)	16	0.80	2.30	2.60	16	2.20	0.80	0.60	32	1.60	0.80	0.70
3 (5 yrs)	12	0.70	1.30	2.90	14	2.10	1.20	1.10	22	1.60	1.20	1.50
4 (6 yrs)	16	0.60	2.40	1.40	16	2.60	0.60	0.30	32	2.30	0.40	0.30
5 (6 yrs)	16	0.40	2.40	2.90	16	2.20	1.10	0.80	32	2.10	1.00	0.80
6 (6 yrs)	16	1.30	2.50	1.20	16	2.80	1.00	0.40	32	2.50	1.20	0.60
7 (7 yrs)	16	1.50	1.10	2.90	16	2.50	0.90	0.80	32	2.40	0.80	0.90
8 (7 yrs)	16	0.30	2.80	2.00	16	1.60	1.40	0.90	32	1.60	1.20	1.00
9 (8 yrs)	16	2.70	0.80	0.30	16	3.40	0.30	0.10	32	2.90	0.30	0.30
10 (8 yrs)	16	2.50	2.50	2.00	16	3.10	0.80	0.50	32	3.10	0.60	0.30
12 (9 yrs)	16	0.20	1.80	4.00	16	1.30	1.60	2.90	32	0.80	1.20	2.90
13 (9 yrs)	16	0.90	0.90	1.20	16	2.10	0.40	0.60	32	2.20	0.60	0.80
14 (9 yrs)	16	1.70	1.00	0.50	16	2.70	0.30	0.20	44	2.80	0.40	0.20
15 (10 yrs)	20	0.60	1.20	2.40	16	2.90	0.30	0.10	44	2.70	0.30	0.20
16 (10 yrs)	20	0.70	2.70	1.60	16	2.30	1.40	0.30	40	2.00	1.30	0.40
18 (10 yrs)	16	0.60	2.80	1.80	16	1.90	1.00	0.80	32	1.90	1.20	0.80
19 (10 yrs)	16	0.10	1.70	5.50	16	0.40	1.40	4.10	36	0.30	1.40	4.30
21 (11 yrs)	16	0.30	2.40	1.60	16	1.10	1.50	0.50	32	0.90	1.80	0.60
22 (11 yrs)	16	1.80	1.00	0.90	16	3.10	0.20	0.20	32	2.70	0.30	0.10
23 (11 yrs)	16	0.90	1.20	1.40	16	1.40	0.80	0.70	36	1.20	0.70	0.70
27 (15 yrs)	14	0.60	2.80	1.10	14	2.10	0.90	0.90	28	1.70	0.80	0.60
28 (16 yrs)	16	0.50	2.60	1.90	16	1.30	1.40	0.80	32	1.50	1.20	0.70
30 (17 yrs)	16	1.20	2.10	0.80	16	2.80	0.40	0.30	40	2.40	0.80	0.30
Average		0.91	1.91	1.97		2.11	0.88	0.81		1.90	0.87	0.86
SD		0.71	0.71	1.17		0.81	0.44	0.91		0.78	0.41	0.94

Overall Bahavioral Changes

Participant	Appropriate			Inappropriate			No Interaction		
	a to b	a to a	Overall	a to b	a to a	Overall	a to b	a to a	Overall
1 (4 yrs)	0.50	0.40	**0.45**	-1.00	-1.10	**-1.05**	-1.60	-1.60	**-1.60**
2 (5 yrs)	1.40	0.80	**1.10**	-1.50	-1.50	**-1.50**	-2.00	-1.90	**-1.95**
3 (5 yrs)	1.40	0.90	**1.15**	-0.10	-0.10	**-0.10**	-1.80	-1.40	**-1.60**
4 (6 yrs)	2.00	1.70	**1.85**	-1.80	-2.00	**-1.90**	-1.10	-1.10	**-1.10**
5 (6 yrs)	1.80	1.70	**1.75**	-1.30	-1.40	**-1.35**	-2.10	-2.10	**-2.10**
6 (6 yrs)	1.50	1.20	**1.35**	-1.50	-1.30	**-1.40**	-0.80	-0.60	**-0.70**
7 (7 yrs)	1.00	0.90	**0.95**	-0.20	-0.30	**-0.25**	-2.10	-2.00	**-2.05**
8 (7 yrs)	1.30	1.30	**1.30**	-1.40	-1.60	**-1.50**	-1.10	-1.00	**-1.05**
9 (8 yrs)	0.70	0.20	**0.45**	-0.50	-0.50	**-0.50**	-0.20	0.00	**-0.10**
10 (8 yrs)	0.60	0.60	**0.60**	-1.70	-1.90	**-1.80**	-1.50	-1.70	**-1.60**
12 (9 yrs)	1.10	0.60	**0.85**	-0.20	-0.60	**-0.40**	-1.10	-1.10	**-1.10**
13 (9 yrs)	1.20	1.30	**1.25**	-0.50	-0.30	**-0.40**	-0.60	-0.40	**-0.50**
14 (9 yrs)	1.00	1.10	**1.05**	-0.70	-0.60	**-0.65**	-0.30	-0.30	**-0.30**
15 (10 yrs)	2.30	2.10	**2.20**	-0.90	-0.90	**-0.90**	-2.30	-2.20	**-2.25**
16 (10 yrs)	1.60	1.30	**1.45**	-1.30	-1.40	**-1.35**	-1.30	-1.20	**-1.25**
18 (10 yrs)	1.30	1.30	**1.30**	-1.80	-1.60	**-1.70**	-1.00	-1.00	**-1.00**
19 (10 yrs)	0.30	0.20	**0.25**	-0.30	-0.30	**-0.30**	-1.40	-1.20	**-1.30**
21 (11 yrs)	0.80	0.60	**0.70**	-0.90	-0.60	**-0.75**	-1.10	-1.00	**-1.05**
22 (11 yrs)	1.30	0.90	**1.10**	-0.80	-0.70	**-0.75**	-0.70	-0.80	**-0.75**
23 (11 yrs)	0.50	0.30	**0.40**	-0.40	-0.50	**-0.45**	-0.70	-0.70	**-0.70**
27 (15 yrs)	1.50	1.10	**1.30**	-1.90	-2.00	**-1.95**	-0.20	-0.50	**-0.35**
28 (16 yrs)	0.80	1.00	**0.90**	-1.20	-1.40	**-1.30**	-1.10	-1.20	**-1.15**
30 (17 yrs)	1.60	1.20	**1.40**	-1.70	-1.30	**-1.50**	-0.50	-0.50	**-0.50**
Average	1.20	0.99	1.09	-1.03	-1.04	-1.03	-1.16	-1.11	-1.13
SD	0.51	0.49	0.49	0.58	0.59	0.58	0.62	0.60	0.61
P	< 0.001	< 0.001	-	< 0.001	< 0.001	-	< 0.001	< 0.001	-

Table 8. Behavioral changes observed in high cognitive functioning group for 'Play and sing with friends'

Average of behavioural changes during baseline (A), Intervention (B) and Reversal Baseline (A)

Participant	Baseline (A)				Intervention (B)				Reversal Baseline (A)			
		Average of Appropriate	Average of Inappropriate	Average of No Interaction		Average of Appropriate	Average of Inappropriate	Average of No Interaction		Average of Appropriate	Average of Inappropriate	Average of No Interaction
1 (4 yrs)	16	0.30	1.30	3.80	16	2.30	0.40	1.20	32	2.10	0.50	0.90
2 (5 yrs)	16	0.80	2.50	2.10	16	2.70	0.70	0.70	32	2.30	0.80	0.90
3 (5 yrs)	12	0.50	1.60	3.40	14	2.00	0.90	1.50	22	2.00	0.80	1.30
4 (6 yrs)	16	0.40	2.50	1.60	16	2.60	0.80	0.40	32	2.20	1.00	0.50
5 (6 yrs)	16	0.80	2.10	3.40	16	2.90	0.70	1.20	32	2.40	0.60	1.30
6 (6 yrs)	16	2.30	2.30	1.90	16	3.60	0.80	0.50	32	3.20	0.90	0.90
7 (7 yrs)	16	1.20	2.00	2.00	16	3.30	1.10	1.00	32	2.90	1.00	1.20
8 (7 yrs)	16	0.60	3.10	1.10	16	3.00	1.60	0.30	32	2.90	1.20	0.40
9 (8 yrs)	16	0.60	5.20	0.60	16	3.10	2.10	0.70	32	2.60	1.90	0.50
10 (8 yrs)	16	2.70	0.90	2.80	16	3.40	0.40	0.90	32	3.20	0.30	1.00
12 (9 yrs)	16	0.30	1.20	3.80	16	1.10	0.80	2.90	32	1.00	1.10	2.70
13 (9 yrs)	16	0.90	1.10	1.40	16	2.60	0.60	0.60	32	2.30	0.50	0.70
14 (9 yrs)	16	1.10	1.80	0.90	16	2.20	0.60	0.20	44	2.00	0.40	0.30
15 (10 yrs)	20	1.00	1.10	2.40	16	2.90	0.10	0.30	44	2.70	0.40	0.40
16 (10 yrs)	20	0.30	2.80	2.80	16	2.10	1.20	1.20	40	2.00	1.10	1.20
18 (10 yrs)	16	0.40	2.30	3.00	16	2.10	0.70	1.60	32	2.30	0.80	1.40
19 (10 yrs)	16	0.10	2.90	3.40	16	0.30	2.70	2.90	36	0.20	2.80	3.00
21 (11 yrs)	16	0.30	1.30	1.90	16	1.20	1.10	1.40	32	1.20	1.00	1.30
22 (11 yrs)	16	1.70	1.80	1.50	16	3.30	0.60	0.60	32	2.70	0.80	0.40
23 (11 yrs)	16	1.10	1.10	1.30	16	1.70	0.60	0.80	36	1.60	0.70	0.60
27 (15 yrs)	14	0.70	1.90	0.90	14	2.90	0.60	0.40	28	2.50	0.70	0.30
28 (16 yrs)	16	0.60	2.60	2.20	16	1.90	1.10	1.00	32	1.70	1.00	0.90
30 (17 yrs)	16	1.20	1.70	1.30	16	2.80	0.80	0.60	40	2.50	0.50	0.70
Average		0.87	2.05	2.15		2.43	0.91	1.00		2.20	0.90	0.99
SD		0.64	0.94	0.98		0.82	0.57	0.72		0.71	0.54	0.69

Overall Bahavioral Changes

Participant	Appropriate			Inappropriate			No Interaction		
	a to b	a to a	Overall	a to b	a to a	Overall	a to b	a to a	Overall
1 (4 yrs)	2.00	1.80	**1.90**	-0.90	-0.80	**-0.85**	-2.60	-2.90	**-2.75**
2 (5 yrs)	1.90	1.50	**1.70**	-1.80	-1.70	**-1.75**	-1.40	-1.20	**-1.30**
3 (5 yrs)	1.50	1.50	**1.50**	-0.70	-0.80	**-0.75**	-1.90	-2.10	**-2.00**
4 (6 yrs)	2.20	1.80	**2.00**	-1.70	-1.50	**-1.60**	-1.20	-1.10	**-1.15**
5 (6 yrs)	2.10	1.60	**1.85**	-1.40	-1.50	**-1.45**	-2.20	-2.10	**-2.15**
6 (6 yrs)	1.30	0.90	**1.10**	-1.50	-1.40	**-1.45**	-1.40	-1.00	**-1.20**
7 (7 yrs)	2.10	1.70	**1.90**	-0.90	-1.00	**-0.95**	-1.00	-0.80	**-0.90**
8 (7 yrs)	2.40	2.30	**2.35**	-1.50	-1.90	**-1.70**	-0.80	-0.70	**-0.75**
9 (8 yrs)	2.50	2.00	**2.25**	-3.10	-3.30	**-3.20**	0.10	-0.10	**0.00**
10 (8 yrs)	0.70	0.50	**0.60**	-0.50	-0.60	**-0.55**	-1.90	-1.80	**-1.85**
12 (9 yrs)	0.80	0.70	**0.75**	-0.40	-0.10	**-0.25**	-0.90	-1.10	**-1.00**
13 (9 yrs)	1.70	1.40	**1.55**	-0.50	-0.60	**-0.55**	-0.80	-0.70	**-0.75**
14 (9 yrs)	1.10	0.90	**1.00**	-1.20	-1.40	**-1.30**	-0.70	-0.60	**-0.65**
15 (10 yrs)	1.90	1.70	**1.80**	-1.00	-0.70	**-0.85**	-2.10	-2.00	**-2.05**
16 (10 yrs)	1.80	1.70	**1.75**	-1.60	-1.70	**-1.65**	-1.60	-1.60	**-1.60**
18 (10 yrs)	1.70	1.90	**1.80**	-1.60	-1.50	**-1.55**	-1.40	-1.60	**-1.50**
19 (10 yrs)	0.20	0.10	**0.15**	-0.20	-0.10	**-0.15**	-0.50	-0.40	**-0.45**
21 (11 yrs)	0.90	0.90	**0.90**	-0.20	-0.30	**-0.25**	-0.50	-0.60	**-0.55**
22 (11 yrs)	1.60	1.00	**1.30**	-1.20	-1.00	**-1.10**	-0.90	-1.10	**-1.00**
23 (11 yrs)	0.60	0.50	**0.55**	-0.50	-0.40	**-0.45**	-0.50	-0.70	**-0.60**
27 (15 yrs)	2.20	1.80	**2.00**	-1.30	-1.20	**-1.25**	-0.50	-0.60	**-0.55**
28 (16 yrs)	1.30	1.10	**1.20**	-1.50	-1.60	**-1.55**	-1.20	-1.30	**-1.25**
30 (17 yrs)	1.60	1.30	**1.45**	-0.90	-1.20	**-1.05**	-0.70	-0.60	**-0.65**
Average	1.57	1.33	1.45	-1.13	-1.14	-1.14	-1.16	-1.16	-1.16
SD	0.62	0.56	0.58	0.65	0.71	0.68	0.66	0.68	0.66
P	< 0.001	< 0.001	-	< 0.001	< 0.001	-	< 0.001	< 0.001	-

Table 9. Behavioral changes observed in high cognitive functioning group for 'Snack time'

Average of behavioural changes during baseline (A), Intervention (B) and Reversal Baseline (A)

Participant	Baseline (A)				Intervention (B)				Reversal Baseline (A)			
		Average of Appropriate	Average of Inappropriate	Average of No Interaction		Average of Appropriate	Average of Inappropriate	Average of No Interaction		Average of Appropriate	Average of Inappropriate	Average of No Interaction
1 (4 yrs)	16	0.70	2.70	3.00	16	1.90	0.90	1.00	32	1.80	0.90	1.20
2 (5 yrs)	16	0.80	1.90	2.40	16	2.30	0.80	1.00	32	2.00	0.90	1.00
3 (5 yrs)	12	0.70	1.80	3.80	14	2.40	1.60	1.80	22	2.20	1.50	2.00
4 (6 yrs)	16	0.80	1.60	2.70	16	2.80	0.60	0.40	32	2.50	0.70	0.50
5 (6 yrs)	16	0.60	1.60	2.30	16	2.30	0.60	0.90	32	2.00	1.00	1.00
6 (6 yrs)	16	2.10	1.80	1.90	16	2.90	0.80	0.50	32	2.80	0.80	0.80
7 (7 yrs)	16	1.40	2.40	2.00	16	3.10	1.10	1.00	32	2.90	1.20	0.80
8 (7 yrs)	16	0.60	2.40	1.50	16	1.90	1.10	0.70	32	1.60	1.20	1.00
9 (8 yrs)	16	2.90	1.50	1.60	16	4.30	0.90	1.00	32	3.80	0.80	0.90
10 (8 yrs)	16	1.80	0.40	1.80	16	3.70	0.10	0.80	32	3.50	0.10	0.80
12 (9 yrs)	16	0.90	1.90	3.70	16	1.40	1.10	2.10	32	1.10	1.20	2.20
13 (9 yrs)	16	0.80	0.90	1.50	16	2.10	0.50	0.90	32	2.30	0.40	0.70
14 (9 yrs)	16	1.90	1.40	0.90	16	3.10	0.50	0.30	44	2.90	0.60	0.30
15 (10 yrs)	20	1.00	0.50	2.40	16	2.20	0.10	0.60	44	2.20	0.10	0.70
16 (10 yrs)	20	0.20	3.60	0.50	16	2.10	1.00	0.30	40	2.10	1.20	0.40
18 (10 yrs)	16	0.80	1.90	3.10	16	2.00	0.80	1.90	32	1.80	0.70	1.70
19 (10 yrs)	16	0.40	3.10	2.60	16	0.50	2.80	2.20	36	0.60	2.90	2.30
21 (11 yrs)	16	1.00	2.10	1.50	16	1.50	1.30	0.90	32	1.30	1.20	1.00
22 (11 yrs)	16	1.60	0.80	2.40	16	2.20	0.20	0.40	32	2.30	0.30	0.60
23 (11 yrs)	16	0.80	1.30	1.20	16	1.40	0.70	0.90	36	1.10	0.60	0.70
27 (15 yrs)	14	0.90	1.90	1.40	14	2.90	0.80	0.70	28	2.80	1.20	1.00
28 (16 yrs)	16	0.70	2.20	1.20	16	1.60	1.00	0.60	32	1.70	1.10	0.50
30 (17 yrs)	16	0.50	0.90	1.70	16	2.20	0.40	0.60	40	1.90	0.50	0.70
Average		1.04	1.77	2.05		2.30	0.86	0.93		2.14	0.92	0.99
SD		0.63	0.79	0.85		0.82	0.56	0.55		0.76	0.57	0.55

Overall Bahavioral Changes

Participant	Appropriate			Inappropriate			No Interaction		
	a to b	a to a	Overall	a to b	a to a	Overall	a to b	a to a	Overall
1 (4 yrs)	1.20	1.10	**1.15**	-1.80	-1.80	**-1.80**	-2.00	-1.80	**-1.90**
2 (5 yrs)	1.50	1.20	**1.35**	-1.10	-1.00	**-1.05**	-1.40	-1.40	**-1.40**
3 (5 yrs)	1.70	1.50	**1.60**	-0.20	-0.30	**-0.25**	-2.00	-1.80	**-1.90**
4 (6 yrs)	2.00	1.70	**1.85**	-1.00	-0.90	**-0.95**	-2.30	-2.20	**-2.25**
5 (6 yrs)	1.70	1.40	**1.55**	-1.00	-0.60	**-0.80**	-1.40	-1.30	**-1.35**
6 (6 yrs)	0.80	0.70	**0.75**	-1.00	-1.00	**-1.00**	-1.40	-1.10	**-1.25**
7 (7 yrs)	1.70	1.50	**1.60**	-1.30	-1.20	**-1.25**	-1.00	-1.20	**-1.10**
8 (7 yrs)	1.30	1.00	**1.15**	-1.30	-1.20	**-1.25**	-0.80	-0.50	**-0.65**
9 (8 yrs)	1.40	0.90	**1.15**	-0.60	-0.70	**-0.65**	-0.60	-0.70	**-0.65**
10 (8 yrs)	1.90	1.70	**1.80**	-0.30	-0.30	**-0.30**	-1.00	-1.00	**-1.00**
12 (9 yrs)	0.50	0.20	**0.35**	-0.80	-0.70	**-0.75**	-1.60	-1.50	**-1.55**
13 (9 yrs)	1.30	1.50	**1.40**	-0.40	-0.50	**-0.45**	-0.60	-0.80	**-0.70**
14 (9 yrs)	1.20	1.00	**1.10**	-0.90	-0.80	**-0.85**	-0.60	-0.60	**-0.60**
15 (10 yrs)	1.20	1.20	**1.20**	-0.40	-0.40	**-0.40**	-1.80	-1.70	**-1.75**
16 (10 yrs)	1.90	1.90	**1.90**	-2.60	-2.40	**-2.50**	-0.20	-0.10	**-0.15**
18 (10 yrs)	1.20	1.00	**1.10**	-1.10	-1.20	**-1.15**	-1.20	-1.40	**-1.30**
19 (10 yrs)	0.10	0.20	**0.15**	-0.30	-0.20	**-0.25**	-0.40	-0.30	**-0.35**
21 (11 yrs)	0.50	0.30	**0.40**	-0.80	-0.90	**-0.85**	-0.60	-0.50	**-0.55**
22 (11 yrs)	0.60	0.70	**0.65**	-0.60	-0.50	**-0.55**	-2.00	-1.80	**-1.90**
23 (11 yrs)	0.60	0.30	**0.45**	-0.60	-0.70	**-0.65**	-0.30	-0.50	**-0.40**
27 (15 yrs)	2.00	1.90	**1.95**	-1.10	-0.70	**-0.90**	-0.70	-0.40	**-0.55**
28 (16 yrs)	0.90	1.00	**0.95**	-1.20	-1.10	**-1.15**	-0.60	-0.70	**-0.65**
30 (17 yrs)	1.70	1.40	**1.55**	-0.50	-0.40	**-0.45**	-1.10	-1.00	**-1.05**
Average	1.26	1.10	1.18	-0.91	-0.85	-0.88	-1.11	-1.06	-1.08
SD	0.54	0.52	0.53	0.54	0.51	0.52	0.62	0.58	0.59
P	<0.001	<0.001	-	<0.001	<0.001	-	<0.001	<0.001	-

Table 10. Behavioral changes observed in high cognitive functioning group for 'Walking in the hallway'

Average of behavioural changes during baseline (A), Intervention (B) and Reversal Baseline (A)

Participant	Baseline (A)				Intervention (B)				Reversal Baseline (A)			
		Average of Appropriate	Average of Inappropriate	Average of No Interaction		Average of Appropriate	Average of Inappropriate	Average of No Interaction		Average of Appropriate	Average of Inappropriate	Average of No Interaction
1 (4 yrs)	0	na	na	na	0	na	na	na	0	na	na	na
2 (5 yrs)	0	na	na	na	0	na	na	na	0	na	na	na
3 (5 yrs)	0	na	na	na	0	na	na	na	0	na	na	na
4 (6 yrs)	0	na	na	na	0	na	na	na	0	na	na	na
5 (6 yrs)	16	0.60	2.60	2.00	16	1.80	1.10	0.80	32	1.70	1.40	1.10
6 (6 yrs)	0	na	na	na	0	na	na	na	0	na	na	na
7 (7 yrs)	0	na	na	na	0	na	na	na	0	na	na	na
8 (7 yrs)	16	0.70	3.50	1.80	16	2.10	2.00	0.90	32	1.90	2.10	1.20
9 (8 yrs)	16	0.80	1.90	0.60	16	2.10	1.10	0.70	32	2.00	0.90	0.60
10 (8 yrs)	16	1.80	0.20	2.80	16	2.80	0.00	1.10	32	3.10	0.10	0.80
12 (9 yrs)	16	0.30	2.00	4.90	16	0.90	1.40	3.80	32	0.90	1.30	4.20
13 (9 yrs)	16	1.00	2.10	2.30	16	1.90	1.20	1.30	32	1.80	1.50	1.50
14 (9 yrs)	16	1.30	1.10	1.80	16	2.30	0.50	0.40	44	2.10	0.50	0.20
15 (10 yrs)	20	0.60	0.90	3.20	16	3.80	0.10	0.30	44	3.40	0.20	0.20
16 (10 yrs)	20	0.30	2.90	0.90	16	2.40	0.80	0.30	40	2.20	1.00	0.40
18 (10 yrs)	16	0.80	1.60	3.10	16	2.30	0.60	1.10	32	1.80	1.00	1.20
19 (10 yrs)	16	0.40	4.60	3.20	16	0.80	4.30	2.80	36	0.60	4.30	3.10
21 (11 yrs)	16	0.50	1.60	2.00	16	1.60	1.30	1.10	32	1.40	1.30	0.90
22 (11 yrs)	16	1.70	0.90	2.40	16	3.30	0.30	1.00	32	3.00	0.50	0.70
23 (11 yrs)	16	0.90	1.10	1.70	16	1.60	0.80	1.00	36	1.20	0.70	1.10
27 (15 yrs)	14	0.60	2.10	1.40	14	1.60	1.30	0.50	28	1.60	1.40	0.70
28 (16 yrs)	16	1.10	2.00	1.80	16	1.60	1.00	0.80	32	1.70	1.10	0.90
30 (17 yrs)	16	0.90	1.10	1.80	16	2.60	0.60	0.40	40	2.40	0.70	0.70
Average		0.84	1.89	2.22		2.09	1.08	1.08		1.93	1.18	1.15
SD		0.44	1.07	1.01		0.77	0.97	0.91		0.75	0.95	1.02

Overall Bahavioral Changes

Participant	Appropriate			Inappropriate			No Interaction		
	a to b	a to a	Overall	a to b	a to a	Overall	a to b	a to a	Overall
1 (4 yrs)	na	na	**na**	na	na	**na**	na	na	**na**
2 (5 yrs)	na	na	**na**	na	na	**na**	na	na	**na**
3 (5 yrs)	na	na	**na**	na	na	**na**	na	na	**na**
4 (6 yrs)	na	na	**na**	na	na	**na**	na	na	**na**
5 (6 yrs)	1.20	1.10	**1.15**	-1.50	-1.20	**-1.35**	-1.20	-0.90	**-1.05**
6 (6 yrs)	na	na	**na**	na	na	**na**	na	na	**na**
7 (7 yrs)	na	na	**na**	na	na	**na**	na	na	**na**
8 (7 yrs)	1.40	1.20	**1.30**	-1.50	-1.40	**-1.45**	-0.90	-0.60	**-0.75**
9 (8 yrs)	1.30	1.20	**1.25**	-0.80	-1.00	**-0.90**	0.10	0.00	**0.05**
10 (8 yrs)	1.00	1.30	**1.15**	-0.20	-0.10	**-0.15**	-1.70	-2.00	**-1.85**
12 (9 yrs)	0.60	0.60	**0.60**	-0.60	-0.70	**-0.65**	-1.10	-0.70	**-0.90**
13 (9 yrs)	0.90	0.80	**0.85**	-0.90	-0.60	**-0.75**	-1.00	-0.80	**-0.90**
14 (9 yrs)	1.00	0.80	**0.90**	-0.60	-0.60	**-0.60**	-1.40	-1.60	**-1.50**
15 (10 yrs)	3.20	2.80	**3.00**	-0.80	-0.70	**-0.75**	-2.90	-3.00	**-2.95**
16 (10 yrs)	2.10	1.90	**2.00**	-2.10	-1.90	**-2.00**	-0.60	-0.50	**-0.55**
18 (10 yrs)	1.50	1.00	**1.25**	-1.00	-0.60	**-0.80**	-2.00	-1.90	**-1.95**
19 (10 yrs)	0.40	0.20	**0.30**	-0.30	-0.30	**-0.30**	-0.40	-0.10	**-0.25**
21 (11 yrs)	1.10	0.90	**1.00**	-0.30	-0.30	**-0.30**	-0.90	-1.10	**-1.00**
22 (11 yrs)	1.60	1.30	**1.45**	-0.60	-0.40	**-0.50**	-1.40	-1.70	**-1.55**
23 (11 yrs)	0.70	0.30	**0.50**	-0.30	-0.40	**-0.35**	-0.70	-0.60	**-0.65**
27 (15 yrs)	1.00	1.00	**1.00**	-0.80	-0.70	**-0.75**	-0.90	-0.70	**-0.80**
28 (16 yrs)	0.50	0.60	**0.55**	-1.00	-0.90	**-0.95**	-1.00	-0.90	**-0.95**
30 (17 yrs)	1.70	1.50	**1.60**	-0.50	-0.40	**-0.45**	-1.40	-1.10	**-1.25**
Average	1.25	1.09	1.17	-0.81	-0.72	-0.76	-1.14	-1.07	-1.11
SD	0.67	0.61	0.64	0.50	0.45	0.47	0.67	0.76	0.71
P	<0.001	<0.001	-	<0.001	<0.001	-	<0.001	<0.001	-

Table 11. Behavioral changes observed in high cognitive functioning group for 'Washing hands'

Average of behavioural changes during baseline (A), Intervention (B) and Reversal Baseline (A)

Participant	Baseline (A)				Intervention (B)				Reversal Baseline (A)			
	n	Average of Appropriate	Average of Inappropriate	Average of No Interaction	n	Average of Appropriate	Average of Inappropriate	Average of No Interaction	n	Average of Appropriate	Average of Inappropriate	Average of No Interaction
1 (4 yrs)	16	0.20	1.90	3.70	16	1.50	0.90	1.30	32	1.80	0.80	0.70
2 (5 yrs)	16	0.10	2.00	2.30	16	1.20	0.40	0.70	32	1.20	0.50	0.60
3 (5 yrs)	12	0.40	2.20	2.30	14	1.20	0.90	0.90	22	0.80	1.00	0.90
4 (6 yrs)	16	0.90	2.40	1.80	16	2.80	0.90	0.30	32	2.30	0.70	0.40
5 (6 yrs)	16	0.30	2.10	3.80	16	1.40	1.40	2.30	32	1.50	1.20	2.30
6 (6 yrs)	16	0.50	0.80	2.00	16	1.50	0.40	0.60	32	1.50	0.40	0.80
7 (7 yrs)	16	0.80	1.80	1.80	16	1.80	1.20	0.90	32	1.60	1.10	1.10
8 (7 yrs)	16	1.00	1.80	1.30	16	2.10	1.80	0.90	32	2.20	1.60	0.80
9 (8 yrs)	16	1.10	5.10	0.30	16	2.70	2.50	0.30	32	2.00	2.80	0.30
10 (8 yrs)	16	1.90	1.50	1.90	16	2.90	0.60	0.50	32	3.30	0.40	0.30
12 (9 yrs)	16	0.80	1.80	3.90	16	1.00	1.50	2.30	32	1.10	1.50	2.30
13 (9 yrs)	16	1.50	1.30	1.30	16	2.20	0.90	0.80	32	2.10	0.60	1.00
14 (9 yrs)	16	0.60	1.30	1.10	16	1.70	0.50	0.40	44	1.80	0.40	0.30
15 (10 yrs)	20	0.90	0.40	0.80	16	2.40	0.10	0.10	44	2.30	0.20	0.30
16 (10 yrs)	20	0.70	2.20	0.80	16	2.30	0.60	0.10	40	1.80	0.70	0.20
18 (10 yrs)	16	0.50	3.00	2.30	16	1.90	1.10	1.90	32	1.90	1.20	1.20
19 (10 yrs)	16	0.20	3.00	4.60	16	0.60	2.80	4.20	36	0.40	2.90	4.30
21 (11 yrs)	16	0.20	2.20	1.30	16	1.00	0.90	0.60	32	1.20	0.80	6.00
22 (11 yrs)	16	1.60	1.90	2.10	16	2.90	0.60	1.20	32	2.50	0.40	1.60
23 (11 yrs)	16	1.10	0.80	1.20	16	1.30	0.40	0.90	36	1.30	0.50	0.80
27 (15 yrs)	14	0.70	1.20	2.00	14	1.60	0.60	1.00	28	1.60	0.80	0.80
28 (16 yrs)	16	0.70	2.00	2.00	16	1.70	0.90	1.00	32	1.50	1.00	1.00
30 (17 yrs)	16	0.90	0.90	1.60	16	2.30	0.30	0.60	40	1.90	0.40	0.50
Average		0.77	1.90	2.01		1.83	0.97	1.03		1.72	0.95	1.24
SD		0.47	0.96	1.08		0.65	0.67	0.91		0.61	0.70	1.38

Overall Bahavioral Changes

Participant	Appropriate			Inappropriate			No Interaction		
	a to b	a to a	Overall	a to b	a to a	Overall	a to b	a to a	Overall
1 (4 yrs)	1.30	1.60	**1.45**	-1.00	-1.10	**-1.05**	-2.40	-3.00	**-2.70**
2 (5 yrs)	1.10	1.10	**1.10**	-1.60	-1.50	**-1.55**	-1.60	-1.70	**-1.65**
3 (5 yrs)	0.80	0.40	**0.60**	-1.30	-1.20	**-1.25**	-1.40	-1.40	**-1.40**
4 (6 yrs)	1.90	1.40	**1.65**	-1.50	-1.70	**-1.60**	-1.50	-1.40	**-1.45**
5 (6 yrs)	1.10	1.20	**1.15**	-0.70	-0.90	**-0.80**	-1.50	-1.50	**-1.50**
6 (6 yrs)	1.00	1.00	**1.00**	-0.40	-0.40	**-0.40**	-1.40	-1.20	**-1.30**
7 (7 yrs)	1.00	0.80	**0.90**	-0.60	-0.70	**-0.65**	-0.90	-0.70	**-0.80**
8 (7 yrs)	1.10	1.20	**1.15**	0.00	-0.20	**-0.10**	-0.40	-0.50	**-0.45**
9 (8 yrs)	1.60	0.90	**1.25**	-2.60	-2.30	**-2.45**	0.00	0.00	**0.00**
10 (8 yrs)	1.00	1.40	**1.20**	-0.90	-1.10	**-1.00**	-1.40	-1.60	**-1.50**
12 (9 yrs)	0.20	0.30	**0.25**	-0.30	-0.30	**-0.30**	-1.60	-1.60	**-1.60**
13 (9 yrs)	0.70	0.60	**0.65**	-0.40	-0.70	**-0.55**	-0.50	-0.30	**-0.40**
14 (9 yrs)	1.10	1.20	**1.15**	-0.80	-0.90	**-0.85**	-0.70	-0.80	**-0.75**
15 (10 yrs)	1.50	1.40	**1.45**	-0.30	-0.20	**-0.25**	-0.70	-0.50	**-0.60**
16 (10 yrs)	1.60	1.10	**1.35**	-1.60	-1.50	**-1.55**	-0.70	-0.60	**-0.65**
18 (10 yrs)	1.40	1.40	**1.40**	-1.90	-1.80	**-1.85**	-0.40	-1.10	**-0.75**
19 (10 yrs)	0.40	0.20	**0.30**	-0.20	-0.10	**-0.15**	-0.40	-0.30	**-0.35**
21 (11 yrs)	0.80	1.00	**0.90**	-1.30	-1.40	**-1.35**	-0.70	4.70	**2.00**
22 (11 yrs)	1.30	0.90	**1.10**	-1.30	-1.50	**-1.40**	-0.90	-0.50	**-0.70**
23 (11 yrs)	0.20	0.20	**0.20**	-0.40	-0.30	**-0.35**	-0.30	-0.40	**-0.35**
27 (15 yrs)	0.90	0.90	**0.90**	-0.60	-0.40	**-0.50**	-1.00	-1.20	**-1.10**
28 (16 yrs)	1.00	0.80	**0.90**	-1.10	-1.00	**-1.05**	-1.00	-1.00	**-1.00**
30 (17 yrs)	1.40	1.00	**1.20**	-0.60	-0.50	**-0.55**	-1.00	-1.10	**-1.05**
Average	1.06	0.96	1.01	-0.93	-0.94	-0.94	-0.97	-0.77	-0.87
SD	0.43	0.40	0.39	0.63	0.60	0.61	0.56	1.36	0.86
P	<0.001	<0.001	-	<0.001	<0.001	-	<0.001	0.006	-

their social story. For the low functioning group, the result of the *t*-test were not significant that is $p>0.05$. Thus, the effectiveness of SS for this group is not proven. The lack of statistical significance may be due, at least in part, to the small number of participants (i.e. seven participants) in this group. These results were consistent with majority of the previous studies (presented in Appendix 2) which resulted with positive change in social behaviors after the SS intervention.

Treatment Integrity

Data for the treatment integrity for each participant was collected everyday by the researcher, and the classroom teacher/class helper using the checklist that detailed the steps of the experimental study. The number of steps completed correctly was divided by the total number of steps, and then multiplied by 100. A score of 100% meant that the treatment integrity had been achieved. If the score was less than 100%, the researcher thus corrected any deficiencies before the following session. In average, the treatment integrity achieved 100% on the 3rd day of intervention for all of the participants.

Social Validity and Acceptability

Variables such as teacher's time and motivation hold an important role on the success or failure of intervention for working in the school setting (Sansosti and Powell-Smith, 2008), thus teacher satisfaction is one way to investigate the social validity of an intervention program.

At the end of the study, classroom teachers and assistant teachers were interviewed on their comments and perception on the intervention. Generally, they were happy and satisfied with the intervention. Furthermore, they commented that there were noticeable behavioral changes of the students after intervention, which provided further evidence of the social validity of the intervention.

When researcher first introduced the method of social story to teachers, most of the teachers were aware of the effectiveness of this intervention. However, it has not been used at the school due to the difficulties of the traditional method to deliver social story, which is time consuming to be implemented in a large classroom setting. However, interactive multimedia based social story presented in computer is highly accepted by the teachers as they can easily play it in the classroom with the computer.

Inter-Observational Agreement

For inter observational agreement purpose, either classroom teacher or the classroom helper was asked by the researcher to be the second observer to validate the target behaviors performed by the participants. Prior to the data collection, the target behavior of each story were explained to them.

The researcher as the first observer was responsible for the main data collection, using traditional tally method count, by marking with an "I" on the appropriate column in the Data Collection Sheet for each of target behavior performed by the participant. Once data collections is completed for one session, the first observer then ask the second observer if they agree to the data collected by the first observer.

The score for the inter-observational agreement was calculated on a session-by-session basis on the target behaviors occurrence on each session, by first and second observer agreeing on the target behaviors occurred. The calculation is done by summing the number of agreement divided by the numbers of agreement and the number of disagreements, and multiplying it by 100, as suggested by Kazdin (1982).

A minimum percentage of 80% is needed to support the inter-observational agreement. If the inter agreement had ever been less than 80%, which is not in this study, the definition of the appropriate, inappropriate and no interaction target behaviors would have been reviewed by the first observer with the second observer, and the inter-observer calibration procedure would have continued until the inter-observational agreement was at least 80%.

The results generated from the study indicated that acquisition of social story through social story presented in interactive multimedia form increased the appropriate behavior, decreased the inappropriate behavior and increased the social interaction made by children with ASD. The evaluation was not conducted in the experimental laboratory as the participants preferred to be in their usual learning environment. Hence, they often got distracted during the intervention session.

Discussions

In view of the rising cases of ASD, remedial aid has to be developed to provide adequate support for children diagnosed with ASD to learn social story in order to provide them with the opportunity to lead a normal social life within an inclusive environmental setting.

SS is an old, yet effective intervention in teaching social story to children with ASD by describing specific social situations in words in order to help them resolve related cognitive confusion. To increase the effectiveness of SS, this study introduced computer-presented SS in the form of 2D animation; social stories enacted in computerized 2D animation are more appealing and engaging especially for children as they are visual learners and this could in turn accelerate their learning process and stimulate their curiosity in exploring exciting ideas.

In the study, this novel approach of intervention was developed and tested on the targeted users. As expected, the results of the intervention produced positive outcomes, and teachers were ready to accept interactive 2D animated social story as part of their teaching materials, especially when dealing with students with ASD. However, there are still some problems for the prototype to be acquainted in the classroom, such as the issues with implementation.

The results of the study suggest that the intervention developed through interactive 2D animated social story offer a positive and relatively unobtrusive type of intervention for children with

ASD. Certainly, it offers several advantages over the traditional method used for children with ASD in social skill learning. Interactive 2D animated social story is technologically friendly and has the benefit of producing results relatively quickly; the results are seemingly effective and generalizable across settings. The social skill literacy level increases naturally when the participants successfully apply the skills they have learnt into their daily activities. This positive generalization and quick acquisition of social story may be due to the result of stimulus control of animation and the use of the computer, and as said earlier that learning is best when motivated. If they are motivated to learn, they would pay attention and acquire the knowledge presented in the content, thus, they would be able to present the skills learned in a real life situation when the behavior or skill is called for.

In short, this study has contributed to the emerging research on SS by supporting the clinical recommendations of using SS in combination with other methods, in teaching social story to children with ASD (Attwood 2000; Rogers 2000; Gray 1998). This study has also made a contribution to literature by the establishment of a novel intervention which combines SS with 2D animation and the computer to help children with ASD learn social story.

CONCLUSION AND FUTURE WORKS

This study has contributed to the emergent research utilizing the interactivity of multimedia to assist children with ASD to acquire social story and supporting the clinical recommendations by Attwood (2000), Rogers (2000) and Gray (1998). This study developed an intervention which combines social story and interactive multimedia for acquisition of social story. The study followed Rust and Smith's (2006) guidelines to conduct the large population experimental design of social story intervention. The results presented in the study suggest that the interactive multimedia based social story offer a positive and relatively unobtrusive type of intervention for children with ASD. It offers several advantages over the traditional method used for children with ASD in social skill acquisition. These findings are in accord with previous research demonstrating positive effect of using social story in teaching social story (Adams et al, 2004; Bledsoe et al, 2003; Crozier & Tincani, 2005, Crozier & Tincani, 2007, Delano & Snell, 2006; Demiri, 2004, Kuoch & Mirenda, 2003; Ozdemir, 2008; Sansosti & Powell-Smith, 2006, Sansosti & Powell-Smith, 2008; Scattone et al, 2002, Scattone et al, 2006, Schneider & Goldstein, 2009) and interactive multimedia in teaching and learning for children (Bosselar & Massaro, 2003; Baron-Cohen et al, 2009; Rosset et al, 2008; van der Geest et al, 2002; Grelotti et al, 2005; Mayer & Moreno, 2002; Mayer, 2003).

In future, researcher would work on interactive multimedia in the form of 3D animations and linear photorealism walkthrough combined with narrations and music to promote the eagerness to acquire social story. Most of the children with ASD are said to be able to focus better on interactive graphics rather that texts during learning. We would also evaluate the impacts of future design on different cohorts representing various spectrums of the autism.

ACKNOWLEDGMENT

We would like to thank Assoc. Professor Dr Lee Seldon and Dr Margaret Seldon for their valuable advice and support. We would also like to express our gratitude to the principal, teachers and participants from PERKATA for their kind assistance and participation.

REFERENCES

Adams, L., Gouvousis, A., vanLue, M., & Waldron, C. (2004). Social story intervention: Improving communication skills in a child with an autism spectrum disorder. *Focus on Autism and Other Developmental Disabilities*, *19*, 87–94. doi:10.1177/10883576040190020301.

Agosta, E., Graetz, J. E., Mastropieri, M. A., & Scruggs, T. E. (2004). Teacher-researcher partnership to improve social behavior through social stories. *Intervention in School and Clinic*, *39*(5), 276–287. doi:10.1177/10534512040390050401.

Arwood, E. L., & Brown, M. M. (1999). *A guide to cartooning and flowcharting*. Portland, OR: Apricot Inc..

ASD Concepts LLC. (2009). *Social story: How to greet someone at school*. Available at http://www.child-autism-parent-cafe.com/How-To-Greet-Someone-At-School.html

Attwood, T. (2000). Strategies for improving the social integration of children with Asperger syndrome. *Autism*, *4*(1), 85–100. doi:10.1177/1362361300004001006.

Ball, J. (2008). *Early intervention and autism: real-life questions, real-life answers*. Arlington, TX: Future Horizons.

Baron-Cohen, S., Golan, O., & Ashwin, E. (2009). Can emotion recognition be taught to children with autism spectrum conditions? *Philosophical Transactions of the Royal Society of Biological Sciences*, *364*, 3567–3574. doi:10.1098/rstb.2009.0191 PMID:19884151.

Baron-Cohen, S., Golan, O., Chapman, E., & Granader, Y. (2007). Trasported to a world of emotion. *The Psychologist UK*. Available at http://www.thepsychologist.org.uk/archive/archive_home.cfm/volumeID_20-Ed.ID_144-ArticleID_1140-getfile_getPDF/thepsychologist%5C0207baro.pdf

Bernard-Opitz, V., Sriram, N., & Nakhoda-Sapuan, S. (2001). Enhancing social problem solving in children with autism and normal children through computer-assisted instruction. *Journal of Autism and Developmental Disorders*, *31*(4), 377–384. doi:10.1023/A:1010660502130 PMID:11569584.

Bledsoe, R., Myles, B. S., & Simpson, R. L. (2003). Use of a social story intervention to improve mealtime skills of an adolescent with Asperger Syndrome. *Autism*, *7*, 289–295. doi:10.1177/13623613030073005 PMID:14516061.

Bogdashina, O. (2006). *Theory of mind and the triad of perspective on autism and Asperger Syndrome: A view from the bridge*. London: Jessica Kingsley Publishers.

Boraston, Z., Blakemore, S., Chilvers, R., & Skuse, D. (2007). Impaired sadness recognition is linked to social interaction deficit in autism. *Neuropsychologia*, *45*(7), 1501–1510. doi:10.1016/j.neuropsychologia.2006.11.010 PMID:17196998.

Bosselar, A., & Massaro, D. W. (2003). Development and evaluation of a computer-animated tutor for vocabulary and language learning in children with autism. *Journal of Autism and Developmental Disorders*, *33*(6). PMID:14714934.

Boucher, J. (2009). *The autistic spectrum: Characteristics, causes, and practical issues*. London: SAGE Publications Limited.

Bowen, M., & Plimley, L. (2008). *The autism inclusion toolkit: Training materials and facilitator notes*. London: SAGE Publications Limited.

Brassard, M. R., & Boehm, A. E. (2007). *Preschool assessment: Principal and practices*. New York: The Guilford Press.

Brownell, M. D. (2002). Musically adapted social stories to modify behaviours in students with autism: four case studies'. *Journal of Music Therapy*, *39*(2), 117–144. PMID:12213082.

Chen, E. (2008). *Autism aspergers myths – The theory of mind.* Retrieved from http://iautistic.com/autism-myths-theory-of-mind.php

Crozier, S., & Tincani, M. J. (2005). Using a modified social story to decrease disruptive behavior of a child with autism. *Focus on Autism and Other Developmental Disabilities, 20*, 150–157. doi:10.1177/10883576050200030301.

Crozier, S., & Tincani, M. J. (2007). Effects of social stories on prosocial behaviors of preschool children with autism spectrum disorders. *Journal of Autism and Developmental Disorders, 37*, 1803–1814. doi:10.1007/s10803-006-0315-7 PMID:17165149.

Dawson, G., Rogers, S., Munson, J., Smith, M., Winter, J., & Greenson, J. et al. (2006). The effects of social stories on the social engagement of children with autism. *Journal of Positive Behavior Interventions, 8*, 29–42. doi:10.1177/10983007060080010501.

Demiri, V. (2004). *Teaching social story to children with autism using social stories: An empirical study.* (PhD Thesis). Hofstra University, Hempstead, NY.

Dodd, S. (2005). *Understanding autism.* London: Elsevier.

Doherty, M. J. (2009). *Theory of mind: How children understand others' thoughts and feelings.* New York: Taylor & Francis.

Donaldson, A., & Varley, J. (2010). Randomized, controlled trial of an intervention for toddlers with autism: The early start Denver model. *Pediatrics, 125*, e17–e23. doi:10.1542/peds.2009-0958 PMID:19948568.

Eliasz, A. W. (2009). Not just teaching robotics but teaching through robotics. In J. H. Kim, S. S. Ge, P. Vadakkepat, N. Jesse, & A. Al Manum (Eds.), *Proceedings of communication in computer and information sciences series.* Springer. doi:10.1007/978-3-642-03986-7_25.

Elzouki, S., Fabri, M., & Moore, D. (2007). Teaching severely autistic children to recognise emotions: Finding a methodology. In *Proceedings of the twenty-first British Computer Society on Human Computer Interaction Group Conference,* (vol. 2, pp. 137-140). IEEE.

Eyal, G. (2010). *The autism matrix.* Cambridge, MA: Polity Press.

Fambonne, E. (2003). The prevalence of autism. *Journal of the American Medical Association, 289*(1), 87–89. doi:10.1001/jama.289.1.87 PMID:12503982.

Feinstein, A. (2010). *A history of autism: Conversations with the pioneers.* Hoboken, NJ: John Wiley and Sons. doi:10.1002/9781444325461.

Gabbert, C. (2010). *Using social stories to teach kids with Asperger's disorder: The hub for bright minds.* Retrieved from http://www.brighthub.com/education/special/articles/29487.aspx

Gallagher, H. L., & Frith, C. D. (2003). Functional imaging of theory of mind. *Trends in Cognitive Sciences, 7*, 77–83. doi:10.1016/S1364-6613(02)00025-6 PMID:12584026.

Golan, O., Ashwin, E., Granader, Y., McClintock, S., Day, K., Leggett, V., & Baron-Cohen, S. (2009). Enhancing emotion recognition in children with autism spectrum conditions: an intervention using animated vehicles with real emotional faces. *Journal of Autism and Developmental Disorders, 40*(3), 269–279. doi:10.1007/s10803-009-0862-9 PMID:19763807.

Grandin, T. (1992). An inside view of autism. In E. Schopler, & G. B. Mesibov (Eds.), *High-functioning individuals with autism.* New York: Plenum Press. doi:10.1007/978-1-4899-2456-8_6.

Gray, C. A. (1994). *Comic strip conversations.* Future Horizons.

Gray, C. A. (1998). Social stories and comic strip conversation with students with Asperger syndrome and high functioning autism. In *Asperger Syndrome or High-Functioning Autism?* New York: Plenum. doi:10.1007/978-1-4615-5369-4_9.

Gray, C. A., & Garand, J. D. (1993). Social stories: Improving responses of students with autism with accurate social information. *Focus on Autistic Behavior*, *8*(1), 1–10.

Gray Center. (2010). *The gray center*. Retrieved from http://www.thegraycenter.org/

Grelotti, D. J., Klin, A. J., Gauthier, I., Skudlarski, P., Cohen, D. J., & Gore, J. C. et al. (2005). fMRI activation of the fusiform gyrus and amygdala to cartoon characters but not to faces in a boy with autism. *Neuropsychologia*, *43*(3), 373–385. doi:10.1016/j.neuropsychologia.2004.06.015 PMID:15707614.

Hagiwara, T., & Myles, B. S. (1999). A multimedia social story intervention: Teaching skills to children with autism. *Focus on Autism and Other Developmental Disabilities*, *14*, 82–95. doi:10.1177/108835769901400203.

Hanley-Hochdorfer, K., Bray, M. A., Kehle, T. J., & Elinoff, M. J. (2010). Social stories to increase verbal initiation in children with autism and Asperger's disorder. *School Psychology Review*, *39*(3), 484–492.

Herskowitz, V. (2009). *Autism and computers: Maximizing independence through technology*. Researcher House.

Hickson, L., & Khemka, I. (1999). Decision making and mental retardation. In L. M. Glidden (Ed.), *International Review of Research in Mental Retardation*. Academic Press.

Hopkins, W. G. (2000). Quantitative research design. *Sportscience*, *4*(1). Retrieved from http://sportsci.org/jour/001/wghdesign.html

Horner, R. H., Carr, E. G., Halle, J., McGee, F., Odom, S., & Wolery, M. (2005). The use of single-subject research to identify evidence-based practice in special education. *Exceptional Children*, *71*(2), 165–179.

Howlin, P. (2003). Outcome in high-functioning adults with autism with and without early language delays: Implications for the differentiation between autism and Asperger syndrome. *Journal of Autism and Developmental Disorders*, *33*(1), 3–13. doi:10.1023/A:1022270118899 PMID:12708575.

Howlin, P., Baron-Cohen, S., & Hadwin, J. (1999). *Teaching children with autism to mind-read: A practical guide for teachers and parents*. Hoboken, NJ: John Wiley and Sons.

Joan, S., & Rich, R. (1999). *Facing learning disabilities in the adult years: Understanding dyslexia, ADHD, assessment, intervention, and research*. Oxford, UK: Oxford University Press.

Kaufmann, W. E., & Silverman, W. (2010). Searching for the causes of autism. *Exceptional Parent*, *40*(2), 32–33.

Kazdin, A. (1982). *Single-case research designs: Methods for clinical and applied settings*. New York: Oxford University Press.

Kuoch, H., & Mirenda, P. (2003). Social story interventions for young children with autism spectrum disorder. *Focus on Autism and Other Developmental Disabilities*, *18*, 219–227. doi:10.1177/10883576030180040301.

Lantz, J. (2002). Theory of mind in autism: development, implications, and interventions. *The Reporter*, *7*(3), 18–25.

LeBlanc, R., & Volkers, H. (2007). *What you should know about Autism spectrum disorders: Signs, symptoms, diagnosis, treatment and effects on life*. Cranendonck Coaching.

Lewandowski, T. A. (2010). Evolving understanding of the relationship between mercury exposure and autism. In L. I. Simeonov, M. V. Kochubovski, & B. G. Simeonova (Eds.), *Environmental heavy metal pollution and effects on child mental development: Risk assessment and prevention strategies*. Springer. doi:10.1007/978-94-007-0253-0_4.

Lorimer, P. A., Simpson, R. L., Myles, B. S., & Ganz, J. B. (2002). The use of social stories as a preventative behavioral intervention in a home setting with a child with autism. *Journal of Positive Behavior Interventions*, *4*(1), 53–60. doi:10.1177/109830070200400109.

Macintyre, M. S. (2009). *Play for children with special needs: Supporting children with learning differences*. New York: Taylor & Francis.

Mandasari, V. (2012). *Learning social story with 2D animated social stories for children with autism spectrum disorders.* (Dissertation for Masters of Science by Research). Swinburne University of Technology.

Mayer, R. E. (2003). The promise of multimedia learning: Using the same instructional design methods across different media. *Learning and Instruction*, *13*(2), 125–139. doi:10.1016/S0959-4752(02)00016-6.

Mayer, R. E., & Moreno, R. (2002). Animation as an aid to multimedia learning. *Educational Psychology Review*, *14*(1), 87–99. doi:10.1023/A:1013184611077.

Myles, B. S., Trautman, M. L., & Schelvan, R. L. (2004). *The hidden curriculum: Practical solutions for understanding unstated rules in social situations*. Autism Asperger Publishing Company.

Norris, C., & Datillo, J. (1999). Evaluating effects of a social story intervention on a young girl with autism. *Focus on Autism and Other Developmental Disabilities*, *14*(3), 180–186. doi:10.1177/108835769901400307.

Odom, S. L., & Watts, P. S. (1991). Reducing teacher prompts in peer-initiation interventions through visual feedback and corresponding training. *The Journal of Special Education*, *25*, 26–43. doi:10.1177/002246699102500103.

Osterling, J., & Dawson, G. (1994). Early recognition of children with autism: A study of first birthday home videotapes. *Journal of Autism and Developmental Disorders*, *24*(3), 247–257. doi:10.1007/BF02172225 PMID:8050980.

Ozdemir, S. (2008). The effectiveness of social stories on decreasing disruptive behaviors of children with autism: Three case studies. *Journal of Autism and Developmental Disorders*, *38*, 1689–1696. doi:10.1007/s10803-008-0551-0 PMID:18373187.

Parsons, S., & Mitchell, P. (2002). The potential of virtual reality in social story training for people with autistic spectrum disorders. *Journal of Intellectual Disability Research*, *46*(5), 430–443. doi:10.1046/j.1365-2788.2002.00425.x PMID:12031025.

Quill, K. A. (1995). Visually cued instruction for children with autism and pervasive developmental disorders. *Focus on Autism and Other Developmental Disabilities*, *10*(3), 10–20. doi:10.1177/108835769501000302.

Quill, K. A. (1997). Instructional consideration for young children with autism: The rationale for visually cued instruction. *Journal of Autism and Developmental Disorders*, *27*(6), 697–714. doi:10.1023/A:1025806900162 PMID:9455729.

Rogers, M. F., & Myles, M. F. (2001). Using social stories and comic strip conversations to interprest social situations for an adolescent with Asperger syndrome. *Intervention in School and Clinic*, *36*(5), 310–313. doi:10.1177/105345120103600510.

Rogers, S. J. (2000). Interventions that facilitate socialization in chldren with autism. *Journal of Autism and Developmental Disorders*, *30*(5), 399–409. doi:10.1023/A:1005543321840 PMID:11098875.

Rosset, D. B., Rondan, C., Da Fonseca, D., Santos, A., Assouline, B., & Deruelle, C. (2008). Typical emotion processing for cartoon but not for real faces in children with autistic spectrum disorders. *Journal of Autism and Developmental Disorders*, *38*, 919–925. doi:10.1007/s10803-007-0465-2 PMID:17952583.

Roullet, F. I., & Crawley, J. N. (2011). Mouse models of autism: Testing hypothesis about molecular mechanisms. *Current Topics in Behavioral Neurosciences*, *7*, 187–212. doi:10.1007/7854_2010_113 PMID:21225409.

Rowe, C. (1999). Do social stories benefit children with autism in mainstream primary schools? *British Journal of Special Education*, *26*(1), 12–14. doi:10.1111/1467-8527.t01-1-00094.

Rust, J., & Smith, A. (2006). How should the effectiveness of social stories to modify the behaviour of children on the autistic spectrum be tested? Lessons from the literature. *Autism*, *10*(2), 125–138. doi:10.1177/1362361306062019 PMID:16613863.

Sansosti, F. J., & Powel-Smith, K. A. (2008). Using computer-presented social stories and video models to increase the social communication skills of children with high-functioning autism spectrum disorders. *Journal of Positive Behavior Interventions*, *10*(3), 162–178. doi:10.1177/1098300708316259.

Sansosti, F. J., & Powell-Smith, K. A. (2006). Using social stories to improve the social behavior of children with Asperger syndrome. *Journal of Positive Behavior Interventions*, *8*, 43–57. doi:10.1177/10983007060080010601.

Scattone, D., Tingstrom, D. H., & Wilczynski, S. M. (2006). Increasing appropriate social interaction of children with autism spectrum disorders using social stories. *Focus on Autism and Other Developmental Disabilities*, *21*(4), 211–222. doi:10.1177/10883576060210040201.

Scattone, D., Wilczynski, S. M., Edwards, R. P., & Rabian, B. (2002). Decreasing disruptive behaviors of children with autism using social stories. *Journal of Autism and Developmental Disorders*, *32*(6), 535–543. doi:10.1023/A:1021250813367 PMID:12553590.

Schneider, N., & Goldstein, H. (2009). Using social stories and visual schedules to improve socially appropriate behaviors in children with autism. *Journal of Positive Behavior Interventions*, *11*, 1–12.

E. Schopler, & G. B. Mesibov (Eds.). (1986). *Social behavior in autism*. New York: Plenum Press. doi:10.1007/978-1-4899-2242-7.

Schreibman, L. E. (2005). *The science and fiction of autism*. Boston: Harvard University Press.

Schreibman, L. E. (2008). Treatment controversies in autism. *Zero to Three*, *28*(4), 38–45.

Scurlock, M. (2008). *Using social stories with children with Asperger syndrome*. (MSc thesis). Ohio University, Athens, OH.

Sharmin, M. A., Rahman, M. M., Ahmed, S. I., Rahman, M. M., & Ferdous, S. M. (2011). Teaching intelligible speech to the autistic children by interactive computer games. In *Proceedings of the Twenty-Sixth ACM Symposium on Applied Computing*. Tai Chung, Taiwan: ACM.

Sicile-Kira, C. (2004). *Autism spectrum disorders: The complete guide to understanding autism, Asperger's syndrome, pervasive developmental disorder, and other ASDs*. New York: Penguin.

Sicile-Kira, C., & Grandin, T. (2006). *Adolescents on the autism spectrum: A parent's guide to the cognitive, social, physical and transition needs of teenagers with Autism Spectrum Disorders*. New York: Penguin.

Single-Subject Research. (2011). Retrieved form http://en.wikipedia.org/wiki/Single-subject_research

Slater, A., & Bremner, J. G. (2003). *An introduction to developmental psychology*. London: Wiley-Blackwell Publishing.

Stillman, W. (2009). *Empowered autism parenting: Celebrating (and defending) your child's place in the world.* San Francisco, CA: Jossey-Bass.

Strickland, D. (1997). Virtual reality for the treatment of autism. In G. Riva (Ed.), *Virtual reality in neuro-psycho-physiology: Cognitive, clinical, and methodological issues in assessment and rehabilitation*. Amsterdam: IOS Press.

Tartaro, A. (2007). Authorable virtual peers for children with autism. In *Proceedings of the Conference on Human Factors in Computing Systems*. ACM.

Tartaro, A., & Cassell, J. (2008). Playing with virtual peers: Bootstrapping contingent discourse in children with autism. In *Proceedings of the Eighth International Conference for Learning Sciences*, (vol. 2, pp. 382-389). IEEE.

Thiemann, K. S., & Goldstein, H. (2001). Social stories, written text cues, and video feedback: Effects on social communication of children with autism. *Journal of Applied Science*, *34*(4), 425–446. PMID:11800183.

Twachtman-Reilly, J., Amaral, S. C., & Zebrowski, P. P. (2008). Addressing feeding disorders in children on the autism spectrum in school-based setting: Physiological and behavioral issues. *Language, Speech, and Hearing Services in Schools*, *39*, 261–272. doi:10.1044/0161-1461(2008/025) PMID:18420528.

Van der Geest, J. N., Kemner, C., Camfferman, G., Verbaten, M. N., & van Engeland, H. (2002). Looking at images with human figures: Comparison between autistic and normal children. *Journal of Autism and Developmental Disorders*, *32*(2). doi:10.1023/A:1014832420206 PMID:12058845.

Wallin, J. M. (n.d.). *Social stories: An introduction to social stories*. Retrieved from http://www.polyxo.com/socialstories/introduction.html

Weiss, M. J., LaRue, R. H., & Newcomer, A. (2009). Social story and autism: Understanding and addressing the deficits. In J. L. Matson (Ed.), *Applied Behavior Analysis for Children with Autism Spectrum Disorders*. Springer. doi:10.1007/978-1-4419-0088-3_7.

Wells, P. (n.d.). *Undestanding animation.* London: Routledge.

Williams, B. F., & Williams, R. L. (2011). *Effective programs for treating autism spectrum disorder: Applied behavior analysis models*. New York: Taylor & Francis.

Wing, L. (1981). Asperger's syndrome: A clinical account. *Psychological Medicine*, *11*(1), 115–129. doi:10.1017/S0033291700053332 PMID:7208735.

Wing, L. (1988). The continuum of autistic characteristics. In E. Schopler, & G. B. Mesibov (Eds.), *Diagnosis and assessment in autism*. New York: Plenum Press. doi:10.1007/978-1-4899-0792-9_7.

Wing, L. (1998). The history of Asperger syndrome. In E. Schopler, G. B. Mesibov, & L. J. Kunce (Eds.), *Asperger syndrome or high-functioning autism?* New York: Springer. doi:10.1007/978-1-4615-5369-4_2.

Wing, L. (2006). *What's so special about autism?* National Autistic Society.

Wing, L., & Gould, J. (1979). Severe impairments of social interaction and associated abnormalities in children: Epidemiology and classification. *Journal of Autism and Developmental Disorders*, *9*(1), 11–29. doi:10.1007/BF01531288 PMID:155684.

Wing, L., & Wing, J. K. (1976). *Early childhood autism: Clinical, educational, and social aspects*. Pergamon Press.

ADDITIONAL READING

Alvin, J. (1978). *Music therapy for the autistic child*. Oxford, UK: Oxford University Press.

American Psychiatric Association. (2000). *Diagnostic and statistical manual for mental disorders* (4th ed.). Washington, DC: American Psychiatric Association.

Audet, L. R. (2007). Augmentative and alternative communication. In (Eds.), Autism Spectrum Disorders: A Handbook for Parents and Professionals. Greenwood Publishing Group.

Autism Society. (2008). *What causes autism.* Retrieved from http://www.autism-society.org/site/PageServer?pagename=about_whatcauses

Autism Society Canada. (2005). *What are autism spectrum disorders?* Retrieved from http://www.autismsocietycanada.ca

Bernard-Opitz, V., & Hauber, A. (2011). *Visual support for children with autism spectrum disorders*. AAPC Publishing.

Burstyn, I., Wang, X., Yasui, Y., Sithole, F., & Zwaigenbaum, L. (2011). Autism spectrum disorders and fetal hypoxia in a population-based cohort: Accounting for missing exposures via estimation-maximization algorithm. *BMC Medical Research Methodology*, *11*(2), 1–9. PMID:21208442.

Matson, J. L., & Kozlowski, A. M. (2011). The increasing prevalence of autism spectrum disorders. *Research in Autism Spectrum Disorders*, *5*(1), 418–425. doi:10.1016/j.rasd.2010.06.004.

Murphy, E. (2011). *Welcoming linguistic diversity in early childhood classroom: Learning from international school*. Multilingual Matters.

Shattuck, P. T., & Grosse, S. D. (2007). Issues related to the diagnosis and treatment of autism spectrum disorders. *Mental Retardation and Developmental Disabilities Research Reviews*, *13*(2), 129–135. doi:10.1002/mrdd.20143 PMID:17563895.

Stahmer, A. C., Suhrheinrich, J., Reed, S., Schreibman, L., & Bolduc, C. (2011). *Classroom pivotal response teaching for children with autism*. New York: Guilford Press.

Test, D. W., Richter, S., Knight, V., & Spooner, F. (2011). A comprehensive review and meta-analysis of the social stories literature. *Focus on Autism and Other Developmental Disabilities*, *26*(1), 49–62. doi:10.1177/1088357609351573.

Wadley, G., & Ducheneaut, N. (2009). The out-of-avatar experience: Object-focused collaboration in second life. In *Proceedings of the Eleventh European Conference on Computer Supported Cooperative Work*. IEEE.

Waltz, M. (2003). *Pervasive developmental disorders: Diagnosis, options, and answers*. Arlington, TX: Future Horizons.

Washburn, K. P. (2006). *The effects of a social story intervention on social story acquisition in adolescents with Asperger's syndrome*. (PhD Thesis). University of Florida, Gaithersburg, FL.

Wasson, J. B. (2005). *Single subject design.* Retrieved from http://www.practicalpress.net/updatenov05/SingleSubject.html

Weathington, B. L., Cunningham, C. J. L., & Pittenger, D. J. (2010). *Research methods for the behavioral and social sciences*. Hoboken, NJ: John Wiley and Sons.

Weiss, P. L. T., & Klinger, E. (2009). Moving beyond single user, local virtual environments for rehabilitation. In A. Gaggioli, E. A. Keshner, P. L. Weiss, & G. Riva (Eds.), *Advanced technologies in rehabilitation: Empowering cognitive, physical, social and communicative skills through virtual reality, robots, wearable systems and brain-computer interfaces*. Amsterdam: IOS Press.

Wempen, F. (2004). *Microsoft Windows XP: Simply visual*. Alameda, CA: SIMPEX.

Werry, I., Dautenhahn, K., & Harwin, W. (2001a). Investing a robot as a therapy partner for children with autism. In C. Marincek (Ed.), *Assistive technology: Added value to the quality of life*. Amsterdam: IOS Press.

Werry, I., Dautenhahn, K., Ogden, B., & Harwin, W. (2001b). In M. Beynon, C. L. Nehaniv, & K. Dautenhahn (Eds.). Lecture Notes in Computer Science: Vol. 2117. *Can social interaction skills be taught by a social agent? The role of a robotic mediator in autism therapy*. Berlin: Springer. doi:10.1007/3-540-44617-6_6.

Westwood, P. S. (2007). *Commonsense methods for children with special educational needs* (5th ed.). New York: Taylor & Francis.

White, H. (2002). Combining quantitative and qualitative approaches in poverty analysis. *World Development*, *30*(3), 511–522. doi:10.1016/S0305-750X(01)00114-0.

Yale School of Medicine. (2008). Retrieved from http://www.med.yale.edu/chldstdy/autism/pdd-nos.html

Yildirim, Z., Ozden, M. Y., & Aksu, M. (2001). Comparison of hypermedia learning and traditional instruction on knowledge acquisition and retention. *The Journal of Educational Research*, *94*(4), 207–214. doi:10.1080/00220670109598754.

Zhao, Y., & Wang, W. (2008). Attribution of human-avatar relationship closeness in a virtual community. In M.D. Lytras et al. (Eds.), *Proceedings of the first World Summit on the Knowledge Society*. Springer-Verlag.

KEY TERMS AND DEFINITIONS

2D Animation: One type of visual cue, it is a rapid display of a sequence of images in order to create an illusion of movement.

Autism Spectrum Disorders: A range of developmental disorders that are characterized by problems in areas of social development, communication and stereotypic behaviors.

Baseline Phase: A phase of collecting information of a subject's behavior before the treatment/intervention.

Experimental Design: Research design to investigate cause-and-effect relationships between interventions and outcomes.

Intervention Phase: A phase where the subject is exposed to treatment/intervention.

Intervention: The act of intervening, treatment.

Reversal Baseline Phase: A phase of collecting information on a subject's behavior after the treatment/intervention.

Single-Subject Design: A research design where the subject serves as his/her own control, rather than using that of another individual/group.

Social Behavior: Behavior directed towards society.

Social Story: Set of skills that is used to facilitate interaction and communication with one another.

Social Story™: Short stories written for children with ASD with the purpose of helping them to understand social situations and to behave appropriately in such situations.

Visual Cues: Illustrations using visual objects such as images, graphics, or colors.

APPENDIX 1

Table 12.

ID	Gender	Age	Diagnosis	Basic Communication Skill	Cognitive Functioning	Class	Mother Tongue	Notes
1	F	4	Rett's Syndrome	-	√	1	English	
2	F	5	Asperger Syndrome	-	√	1	Mandarin	
3	M	5	PDD/NOS	-	√	2	Mandarin/ English	
4	M	6	Asperger Syndrome	-	√	1	English	Interest in drawing and computer
5	M	6	PDD/NOS	√	√	2	English	
6	M	6	PDD/NOS	√	√	1	BM	
7	M	7	Autistic Disorder	√	√	1	English	
8	M	7	Autistic Disorder	-	√	2	BM	Severe type
9	M	8	PDD/NOS	√	√	2	Mandarin/English	Hyperactive
10	M	8	PDD/NOS	√	√	3	Mandarin	
11	M	9	Autistic Disorder	-	-	2	BM	
12	M	9	Autistic Disorder	-	√	3	Mandarin	
13	F	9	Autistic Disorder	√	√	3	English	
14	M	9	PDD/NOS	√	√	3	English	
15	M	10	Asperger Syndrome	√	√	4	BM/English	Interest in computer and math
16	M	10	PDD/NOS	√	√	4	Mandarin	Special interest in computer
17	M	10	Autistic Disorder	-	-	2	BM	Severe type
18	M	10	PDD/NOS	-	√	3	Mandarin/ BM	
19	M	10	Autistic Disorder	-	√	3	BM	Hyperactive
20	M	11	Autistic Disorder	-	-	4	English	Severe type
21	M	11	PDD/NOS	-	√	4	English	
22	M	11	PDD/NOS	√	√	4	BM	Interest in phones and computer
23	M	11	Autistic Disorder	-	√	4	BM/English	

continued on following page

Table 12. Continued

ID	Gender	Age	Diagnosis	Basic Communication Skill	Cognitive Functioning	Class	Mother Tongue	Notes
24	M	11	Autistic Disorder	-	-	4	Mandarin	
25	M	12	Autistic Disorder	-	-	5	BM	
26	M	13	Autistic Disorder	-	-	5	BM	Severe type
27	F	15	PDD/NOS	√	√	5	Mandarin	
28	M	16	Autistic Disorder	√	√	5	BM	
29	M	17	Autistic Disorder	-	-	5	English	Severe type
30	M	17	Autistic Disorder	√	√	6	Mandarin/BM	

APPENDIX 2

Table 13.

Study	Number of participant	Variation of SS	Design	Duration	Result/Effectiveness	Statistical Significance
Agosta et al (2004)	1	Teacher as active researcher	ABCA	>22 days	Positive behavioral changes, counted in occurrences per session.	Not tested
Brownell (2002)	4	Musical social story	ABAC	>8 days each	Reading (B) and singing (C) phase were significantly more effective than control phase (A)	*t*-test $p<.05$
Crozier & Tincani (2005)	1	Drawing illustration	ABAC	Unknown	Reduction in disruptive behavior, counted in occurrences per observation session.	Not tested
Crozier & Tincani (2007)	3	Color icon illustration	ABAB ABACBC	Unknown	Overall, there was a reduction in inappropriate behavior and increase in appropriate behavior, counted per session. However, SS alone insufficient for one participant.	Not tested
Delano & Snell (2006)	3	Picture symbols	Multiple baseline	Unknown	Increase in the duration of social engagement, counted duration (seconds) and frequency of social engagement	Not tested
Haggerty et al (2005)	1	Drawing illustration	AB	4 weeks	Maladaptive behaviors decreased in frequency, duration and intensity	Not tested
Hagiwara & Myles (1999)	3	Visual symbol on computer (multimedia)	Multiple baseline	15-24 days	Increased the skills level of some participants in certain settings, counted by percentage of completion day-by-day	Not tested
Ivey & Alberto (2004)	3	Digital photographs	ABAB	11 weeks	Increase in participation during novel event, counted in number of targeted skills occurrences.	Not tested

continued on following page

Table 13. Continued

Study	Number of participant	Variation of SS	Design	Duration	Result/Effectiveness	Statistical Significance
Kuttler et al (1998)	1	Prize reinforcer	ABAB	19 days	Behavior improve further after the second intervention phase	Not tested
Kuoch & Mirenda (2003)	3	Cartoon pictures, Verbal reminder	ABA(2) ACA-BA(1)	Unknown	Reduction in rate of problem behaviors, counted in number of behavior per minute	Not tested
Litras et al (2010)	1	Video self-modeling	Multiple baseline	Unknown	Effective in improving target behaviors, counted in frequency in percentage per session	Not tested
Lorimer et al (2002)	1	Picture illustration	ABAB	24 days	Behavior returned to baseline when intervention withdrawn	Not tested
Norris & Dattilo (1999)	1	Picture symbols	AB	18 days	Reduction in inappropriate behavior, however no effect in increasing appropriate behavior	Not tested
Rowe (1999)	1	Support assistant	Case Study	12 weeks	Immediate response, however it is anecdotal, as it is an extremely informal and brief case study	Not tested
Roger & Myles (2001)	1	Comic Strip Conversation	Case study/AB	5 days	CSC show greater effects than SS alone	Not tested
Swaggert et al (1995)	3	Verbal prompting	AB	27-28 days	Increase in appropriate behaviors	Not tested
Sansosti & Powell-Smith (2008)	3	Computer and video modeling	Multiple baseline	Unknown	Effective in improving the rates of social communication, counted by percentage of intervals of social communication.	Not tested
Scattone et al (2006)	3	None	Multiple baseline	11 weeks	SS alone may be effective for some children with ASD, counted in percentage of intervals during 10-min session.	Not tested
Scattone (2008)	1	Video modeling	Multiple baseline	15 weeks	Increase in 2 out of 3 targeted skills, counted in percentage of intervals per 5-min session	Not tested
Schneider & Goldstein (2009)	3	Pictures illustration	Multiple baseline	Unknown	Modest improvement in classroom on-task behaviors, counted in percentage of intervals of behaviors	Not tested
Thiemann & Goldstein (2001)	5	Card cues, video feedback and verbal prompting	Multiple baseline	15-19 weeks	Increases in target social communication skills, counted in number of behaviors per 10-min session	Not tested
Pettigrew (1998)	69	Scaffolding activities	Experiment design	Unknown	Increase in social competence	Chi-square test
Feinberg (2001)	34	Verbal prompting	Pre- post-test	Unknown	Significant change in certain behaviors	*t*-test

Source: Mandasari, 2012

APPENDIX 3

Figure 3.

***I Learn Social Story* Data collection sheet**

Phase: (Baseline/Intervention/Reversal)

Participant ID :__________________

Date :__________________

SWIN BUR NE

Session	How to greet someone at school			Play and sing with friends			Snack time			Walking in the hallway			Washing hands			Note/Comment
	A	I	NI	A	I	NI	A	I	NI	A	I	NI	A	I	NI	
1																
2																
3																
4																
5																
6																
7																
8																
9																
10																
11																
12																
13																
14																
15																
16																
17																
18																
19																
20																

<u>Legend</u>

A = Appropriate

I = Inappropriate

NI = No Interaction

<u>How to use this data collection sheet:</u>

For every behaviour occurred for appropriate (A), inappropriate (I) or no interaction (NI), Mark with | in the appropriate column.

Chapter 6
Players' Experience in a Sport Geocaching Game

Pirita Ihamäki
University of Turku, Finland

Mika Luimula
University of Turku, Finland

ABSTRACT

Geocaching is a multiplayer outdoor sports game. There is a lack of extensive research on this game, and there is a need for more academic research on this game and its application to other contexts worldwide. There are about 5 million people participating in the geocaching game in 220 different countries worldwide. The geocaching game is interesting because the players create it. The players' role in game design increases its value in human-centred design research. Digital games are a prevalent form of entertainment in which the purpose of the design is to engage the players. This case study was carried out with 52 Finnish geocachers as an Internet survey. The purpose of this conceptual analysis is to investigate how the geocaching sports game might inform game design by looking at player experiences, devices, and techniques that support problem solving within complex environments. Specifically, this analysis presents a brief overview of the geocaching sports game, its role in popular adventure game design, and an analysis of the underlying players' experiences and enjoyment as a structure to be used in game design.

INTRODUCTION

This chapter introduce geocaching sport game and how to use player experiences to game design process to development pervasive games. Geocaching is sports game: partly a treasure hunt, and partly an outdoor exploration based on principles of orientation. It was created around 2000 and owes its birth to human ingenuity, the Internet and Global Position System (GPS) technology. (Flintman, 2007) The growing practice of geocaching is as a hide-and-seek game, except the seeking is done using hand-held GPS devices, and the hiding is done by geocachers who have their favourite places around the world. The global game is a growing trend with families of all ages. Adventurous geocachers, armed with GPS devices and co-ordinates found on the geocaching website, search for a box, take a trinket and replace it, or record their visit while enjoying someone's special

DOI: 10.4018/978-1-4666-4623-0.ch006

spot. Treasure hunts are games where players try to find certain objects in an unlimited game space. Treasure hunts are the oldest genre of pervasive games and the one with the most well established format. (Sherman, 2004) Geocaching is a pervasive multiplayer game that is currently played in 220 different countries. Massive multiplayer online games (MMOGs) are lauded as the newest and fastest-growing genre of digital games (The Editors and Staff of Geocaching.com, Peter, 2004, 7).

This chapter we will describe and evaluate the player experiences that we gathered in our geocaching survey. The main research questions in this study are: *what are these players' most memorable and positive geocaching experiences? How can players' experiences in the geocaching game be used to develop adventure games?* First, we will briefly explain the research related to the geocaching game. Then, we will describe the theoretical background of player experiences. We will describe our method Internet survey in this case study. Then, we will introduce our results, which are based on the features of pervasive games and empirical findings. Our focus in this research is emphasising player experiences for designers and researchers when designing new adventure games. It is important to evaluate players' experiences in popular games like geocaching, as designers and researchers can draw upon them when designing new games. Taking the paradigm of user-centred design as a starting point means that the potential software players or future game users are considered a major source of information throughout the design process.

RELATED RESEARCH

This section describes some of the earlier work that has been done on the geocaching sports game. The related literature presented in this chapter contains the studies where geocaching is the main focus of the research. The study of geocaching has only recently begun, and the game has extended to many social media forms and contexts, adding to the meaningfulness of this geocaching study. Our study presents of brief overview of the geocaching sport game, its role in popular adventure game design and an analysis of the underlying players' experiences and enjoyment as a structure to be used in pervasive game design.

In their study, Reimann and Paelke (2005) describe how mobile gaming has begun expanding into the domain of physical movement where players take gaming into the real world. They presented the prototype of a mobile mixed-reality game that adapts the game presentation and content to the user's context. (Weiser, 1999) Muessing and Price (2007) present EarthCaching, which is a form of geocaching. They describe EarthCaching as a geological twist; the player finds a site of geological interest. (Muessig et al. 2007) Ihamäki (2007) describes what geocaching is and presents an analysis of a case study on how geocaching can be used as a rewarding approach in teaching GPS technology in education. (Ihamäki, 2007) In her study, O'Hara (2008) presents geocaching game practices and motivations that can be built up around a location-based activity field. (O'Hara, 2008) Neufeld et al. (2008) describe an autonomous robot system designed to solve the challenging task of geocaching. Robot geocaching requires addressing three key issues: map building, navigation and local search. (Neufeld et al. 2008) Ihamäki (2008) presents an analysis of a case study discussing how and where to use geocaching as experience tourism products. This study deals with a case study, "Geocaching – A New Experience for Sport Tourism in Pori", which was a service for tourists using geocaching in experience production. (Ihamäki, 2008) Furthermore, Gram-Hansen (2009) argues that the computing technologies involved in the activity, such as websites, desktop applications, GPS units and mobile software, together constitute a persuasive environment along with the physical artefacts that are central to the activity of geocaching. (Gram-Hansen, 2009) Ihamäki and Tuomi (2009) presented a qualitative study of the 21st century's mobile device-based forms of game culture and described different aspects around marginal games. They argue that geocaching can be seen as an updated, technology-enhanced version of the treasure hunt games, and at the same time, a physical variant of popular digital adventure games. (Ihamäki & Tuomi, 2009) Ihamäki (2012a) describe interactive communication channel, which has extend of the multi-player geocaching game. Ihamäki (2012b) study extend the approach of studying geocaching player experiences and creative tourism experience content with research focusing on geocachers creativity in tourism context.

Studies of geocaching game are incoherent and phenomenon of studies depends of authors background. However all studies try to understand geocaching game nature. Our study passed on design perspective and expanding opinion mobile gaming as Reimann and Paelke do they study. O'Hara presented geocaching game in motivation perspective which is near for our prove enjoyment in geocaching game. Our studies expand adventure game design by looking at player's experiences, devices and techniques to support problem solving within complex environments.

PLAYER EXPERIENCE

This section will summarize recent HCI studies in player experience point of view. Significant work in the HCI community has focused on designing games that support human values. The main purpose of a player experience study is to understand what aspects constitute the enjoyment of playing the game, what kinds of experiences the game can elicit and how to design something that elicits a certain type of experience. (Korhonen et al. 2009) Enjoyment is arguably the single most important motivation for people to play digital games. Game developers would like to understand it more fully in order to optimize game design. Here, enjoyment is considered the core experience of entertainment (Vordere, Klimmt & Rittefeld, 2004), defining the sum of positive reactions toward geocaching experiences as being both as cognitive and affective. This view is consistent with empirical evidence in psychology indicating that the motivational basis of human activity. (Elliot & Thrash, 2002) Pioneering work by Csikszentmihalay (1975, 1990) found that many elements of enjoyment are universal. Forlizzi and Ford's (2000) present theory of experience in three phenomenons. Three ways of viewing experience are: experience, an experience and experience as a story. The purest form of reference is experience, the constant stream that happens during moments of consciousness. An experience is more than experience and enjoyment emphasize when players get an experience. Another way to discuss having a specific experience, as philosopher John Dewey (1980) referred to in his book Art as Experience. The third way deals with experience as a story, an idea that has been discussed at length by Roger Schank and AI Researcher 1990. Current research has been performed on user-centred design for productivity software within the general computing domain, e.g. office applications, but ideas and theories that specifically address user-centred game design are only beginning to be constructed. Pagulayan et al. (2004) highlight some of the crucial aspects of effective user-centred game design. The process is the ISO 13407 (1999) standard for human-centred design which is divided into four stages: 1) understanding and defining the context of use, 2) making up a definition of the user, 3) producing the design solutions, and 4) evaluating the solutions. The process treats the understanding and definition of the context and creates a definition of the user as detached from design. Human factors specialists as a rule define the context of use; the designers handle the ideation; and the relevant experts do the evaluation, such as usability testing. (Mattelmäki, 2006, pp. 62.) As designers trying to craft an experience, we can only design situations, or levers that people can interact with, rather than nearly predicted outcomes. A product offers a story of use that invites engagement. If the product happens to be encountered in an unfamiliar context for a user, the product may be experienced in ways other than the designer intended. (Forlizzi & Ford 2000.) Ermi & Mäyrä (2005) divided experience into four dimensions: entertainment (absorption and passive participation), educational (absorption and passive participation), aesthetic (immersion and passive participation) and escapist (immersion and active participation). In terms of this categorisation, gameplay experiences can be classified as escapist experiences, where in addition to active participation, also immersion plays a central role.

The experience gained from geocaching surveys is that an improved understanding of the player's context can, and should, take place in a parallel dialogue. In this study, we try to link design thinking and the understanding of the players' experience. Attributes such as fun and pleasure are abstractly defined and there are uncertainties as to how the different possibilities for supporting player experiences can be addressed in design. (Korhonen et al. 2009) However, there are significant variations between players in what they find pleasurable or fun. Games need to find a balance to be enjoyable on main segment of player and game design need to understand that player enjoyment is the most important goal for digital games. The research was used to develop a concrete understanding of what constitutes good design and player enjoyment in strategy games. Digital games are a prevalent form of entertainment in which the purpose of the design is to engage players. Game designers incorporate a number of strategies and tactics for engaging players in 'gameplay'. Game design is at the forefront of cultivating innovative techniques for interactive design. (Dickey, 2005) A treasure hunt game is a good opportunity for game designers to explore how to design something that focuses on player experience aspects, already during the design phase. Competition in the game industry is hard and the gaming experience becomes a crucial factor in differentiating similar kinds of games and game titles. (Korhonen et al. 2009)

Based on our extensive review of current literature, we find that the nature game playing is an entertainment experience. This is a perplexing situation, because the understanding of its intrinsic nature can significantly enhance studies on the consequences of concept. The intrinsic motivation to play a game results from promoting enjoyable experiences (approach state) and from preventing boredom or failure (avoidance state). Lee, Sheldon and Turban (2003) demonstrate how enjoyment and performance in achievement settings depend on the individual's capability to focus mentally on the task given. We believe that if we want to have a fuller understanding of this new form of media entertainment, we have to understanding of what players actually experience while they are playing games.

Research by Koivisto and Wenninger (2005) had explored how current massively multi-player online games can use mobile features for enhancing players' experiences and increasing the pervasiveness of these games. Pervasive games have a tendency to play wildly with different contexts and mindsets, leading to various different activities. They identify six different categories for how this can be done and review their findings with multi-player online game players and developers. Research categorization is based on how the players can interact with or influence the virtual game world and other players by using their mobile phones. The categories that they identified are: *communications access*, *event notifications*, *asynchronous gameplay*, *synchronous player-to-player interaction*, *passive participation* and *parallel reality*. (Koivisto et al. 2005) Sweetser and Wyeth's (2005) GameFlow model consists of eight elements, which are: *concentration, challenge, skills, control, clear goals, feedback, immersion and social interaction*. Each element includes a set of criteria for achieving enjoyment in games. (Sweetser et al., 2005) Korhonen, Montola and Arrasvuori (2009) discuss playful experience in

18 to 19 categories, with which they extended the GameFlow model and give a wide perspective for playful experiences. (Korhonen et al. 2009) This case study used features that emerged in this data and have meaning for the results of geocaching games. We started this qualitative study with an initial set of categories for pervasive multi-player online game features and extend enjoyment of game design framework.

METHOD

Participants Background Information

This section describe method has used to collect the player experience on geocaching game. The methodology proposed was for a descriptive empirical case study carried out by an Internet survey, in which 52 Finnish geocaching players participated. These consisted of 36 male players and 16 female players. The participants completed a structured enquiry over the Internet. The average age of the geocachers who participated was 37. The participators in this case study were between 14 and 63 years old. Player activity is indicated by how many caches they have found.

Geocaching players' activity can be seen in Table 1 which describes the number of places where participants have visited to log or to find caches and they get one point per cache. There were 5 participants out of 52 who have found more than 1000 caches. Table 2 below, in turn, shows participants' activity. That is to say, the number of caches they have hidden.

From the number of caches hidden, we can see the participants' activity for the geocaching game. Geocachers have founded of caches less than finding caches in environment. One reason could be that always every cache has one owner and that owner has to take care of their own cacheplace and the containers, logbook and pencil in the container. There were 3 participants out of 52 who have hidden more than 30 caches. The following data describes how many times geocaching players have had visits in geocaching events (Table 3.).

Table 1. Cache places found by participants

100	101-200	201-400	401-600	600-800	801-1000	1090	1450	1474	2450	3000
88	88	111	99	55	66	11	11	11	11	11

Table 2. Geocaching players: number of caches hidden

0-10	11-20	21-30	37	45	48
30	13	6	1	1	1

Table 3. Geocaching players visits during geocaching events

No	Once or twice	3-5 times	6 time or more
24	16	8	4

Half of the participants have not had visits during geocaching events. Half of participants in this study describe that geocaching events appear the same around the world.

Survey

For this study, we used a semi-structural geocaching online survey – the Implications of Geocaching to Social Interaction and Tourism - administered over the Internet during October and November 2009. The Tampere University of Technology, Unit of Human-Centred Technology, approved the study. Geocaching players were told that their responses would be kept confidential. This qualitative study was carried out as an Internet survey for geocachers during October and November 2009, and is based on an Internet survey of 52 responses.

The survey consisted of (1) background information, (2) the implication of geocaching and (3) the social elements in geocaching. The questions in the survey consisted of both quantitative and qualitative items. Background information consisted of the geocachers nickname (not necessary), age, gender, nationality, country and education. Background information consisted of nine claims of how player use technology in daily life. Background information also consisted of quantitative data, for example how many geocaches players had found and hidden. Examples of open questions were: in what kind of situations and contexts do you do geocaching? What kind of technology and devices are involved in players' geocaching trips? The implication of geocaching consisted of open questions, asking players to describe their most memorable and positive geocaching experiences and what impact geocaching has had on the players and their everyday lives. Questionnaires had a quantitative component, which ask how many caches players have found, how many caches they have hidden and how often geocachers play geocaching game in season time. The questionnaire consisted of 22 open questions for geocaching game itself, the technology of the game, tourism and the future of geocaching games.

Internet survey was sent to the Groundspeak Forum with a request for geocachers to participate in this case study. In addition, the survey was sent via email to a randomly selected set of players. With this survey we aim to understand what implications geocaching has as a hobby, for example, for the social interactions of people, for travelling, lifestyle and behaviour in general. This case study analyses a part of 6 pages of survey material.

Procedure

This article analysed the data using a research technique called qualitative content analysis. Qualitative content analysis is "a research technique for the objective, systematic, qualitative description of the manifest content of communication". (Berelson, 1952 p. 519) The main idea of the procedure of analysis is, thereby, to preserve the advantages of quantitative content analysis as developed within communication science and to transfer and further develop them to qualitative interpretative step of analysis.

Specifically, this analysis presents a brief overview of the geocaching sports game and its role in popular adventure game design. It also involves an analysis of the underlying players' experience and enjoyment as a structure to be used in game design. Secondary material is based on geocaching stories in magazines around the world that are all linked to the geocaching.com website. These stories are used in this study to expand the description of players' experiences in the geocaching sport game and can be used to develop adventure games. Accordingly, in this study, the description of geocacher experiences is highlighted as stories created by different geocachers. The purpose of this case study is to find out about players' experiences and positive geocaching experiences to provide potential users of the design process with information that can inform and inspire game design.

RESULT

Social Interaction and Communication Access

This subsection provides an overview of geocacher's player enjoyable experiences and enjoyment as a structure to be used in game design in pervasive games. Social interaction in Geocaching game has important role in gameplay. For instance, geocaching players can access an in-game chat when they are not logged into the game with the PC game client. Geocachers describe how they enjoy meeting players for face-to-face and using cross-media access: *"I met many new people in person and electronically, from around the world. Have become exposed to new ways of life.* (Geocaching player, Blue Man) Geocachers' equipment describes the interaction of the user between devices and other players, which is why it is regarded as important in this study. The geocaching hobby has motivated participants to use technology in geocaching; some players have even created services for the game. This could be compared to a product designer choosing and combining specific product features, i.e, content, presentational style, functionality, interactional style. However, the character is subjective and only intended by the designer. There is no guarantee that players will actually perceive and appreciate the product the way designers wanted it to be and 'clear' will not necessarily be perceived as 'clear'. (Hassenzahl 2003, 33.) Geocaching is a game that is created by players and new services develop around the game, which are created by players and companies like Nokia and Apple. Geocaching players have created websites and map services for geocaching. Participants' equipment in the geocaching game usually consists of a GPS, mobile phone, mini-PC, map, digital camera and flashlight. Some players also used, for example, the Geocaching Live program, the GSAK- program and other geocaching programs on their mobile phones and PCs. For example, the dajaq geocaching player describes his equipment's in geocaching trips: *"Garmin GPSMap 60cx which has maps. Sometimes also Ausu EEE mini PC is with me, which has the GSAK-program"*. (Geocaching player dajaq, 2009.) Access to communication can allow one to search for elements of enjoyment like Sweetser and Wyeth's (2005) summaries that the games must maintain the player's concentration through a high workload; however, the tasks must be sufficiently challenging to be enjoyable. (Sweetser et al., 2005) To be enjoyable, a game has to require concentration, and the player must be able to concentrate on the game. In terms of concentration, player quasz has a memorable experience *"One cache place I had already seeking one place for 45 minute and I almost give up. I got frustrated and kicked a mound of dirt on the ground and I noticed that under the mound have trapdoor and under the earth have cache what I was hunting for long time."* The player should not be burdened with tasks that feel unimportant (Dickey, 2005). It will be interesting to see to what extent geocaching and treasure hunt games create new applications, depending upon the relationship, especially those in which virtual content is attached to existing physical landmarks rather than being overlaid on an empty space or moving through the game environment. Design level includes designing the spaces and places for interaction, environmental cues and affordances for actions. This phase provides a more concrete illustration and plan of the mixed reality environment that forms the scene for action. The level design overlaps with the interaction design, the environment affords certain interactions and some interactions require specific features from the environment.

Event Notifications as Clear Goal

This subsection presented on result event notification as clear goal in Geocaching events. Event notifications allow the players to contact each other face-to-face at the same place. Like communication access with other players, event notifications do not necessarily require many changes in the game design. However, the feature needs to be well integrated in the game, the idea of the game being part of one's everyday life can be quite new to many people. (Sweetser et al., 2005) An event cache is set up much like a regular cache, except participants follow coordinates to the party. An event cache chooses a date and time and then saves the coordinates of the location. One first logs on to the geocaching.com to post the cache, selecting the Event Cache option. The future date places the cache at the top of the cache search and places it on the geocaching.com Event Cache calendar. (The Editors and Staff of Geocaching.com, Peter, 2004, pp. 223.) Geocachers say their motivation consists of a desire for adventure, outdoor activity and finding new places. On the other hand, geocachers also like to meet similar minded players and spend time together, for example at geocaching events. "It was nice to see that there were many different kinds of geocaching players. Before I participated in the first event, I was afraid that the other participants would all be 25 year old male nerds. Thanks I look for last year pictures for events and see that I was totally wrong. Both of events which I has participate has been fun and geocacher been relaxed people." (Geocache player Minneli, 2009.) One of the top reasons why people play is to participate in a social activity they can enjoy with their friends.

Geocaching events are usually organised by players, not professionals. Geocaching events are always special events because they are situated in different places (even different countries); every time is new for those who organise the events. It is possible for players to know others well within Internet forums, but to never meet face-to-face. That is why geocaching events provide the possibility of meeting other players together. Sweetser and Wyeth's (2005) GameFlow element of Clear Goals should provide players at appropriate times on games. (Sweetser et al., 2005) "At the neighbourhood FTF (First to Find) hunting are very spontaneous. If caches are more far away and I need to travel for hunting caches, I will look what kind of caches have in long with my trip and sometimes solving for puzzles before the cache place." Each level should also have multiple goals and games often describe a mission that outlines the immediate goals of the current part of the game and suggest some of the obstacles that the players might face. (Fullerton, Swain & Hoffman, 2004)

To look at design perspective an event cache defines the physical environment and the playing field within which a game is played at a certain time. It is affected by a variety of other factors, such as when and how people want to join the game, the level of publicity and user control over the application as well as the number of players attending the game. Communication is affected by the smoothness of human-human and human-machine communication during the game, and the level of real world activity. Both of these drivers can be related to any form of application of social activity, and have special features in mobile gaming. Convivial systems encourage players to be actively engaged in generating creative extensions to the artefacts given to them, and have the potential to break down the strict counterproductive barriers between players and designers (Fischer, 1998). As a result of the social interaction of geocaching, participants have made numerous friends and enjoyed attending caching events: "I have made many new friends/acquaintances and enjoyed a few events with local and not-so-local cachers. Caching in Mexico was fun and we met lots of nice people" (Cowboneneck, 2009). When geocachers meet at events, interaction between players happens face-to-face. We have discussed the technical background of social and physical interactive paradigms and provided examples where users interacted both socially and physically in a physical or virtual environment; nonetheless, thousands and thousands of people continue to geocache each day. In at least this portion of their lives, players are rejecting the discourse of fear and mistrust of others, instead developing new ways to promote trust and extend community. The geocaching version of trust is facilitated by some of the specific regulating mechanisms built into the game. Geocachers are adding to the store of social capital by behaving in ways that increase social cohesiveness, interpersonal trust and community.

Asynchronous Gameplay as Challenges on the Game

This subsection describe for result of asynchronous gameplay as challenges on the geocaching game. Implementing the same kind of gameplay for mobile phones as that used by PCs or consoles does not often make sense for a typical multi-player online game. However, many of the activities in these games do not really require rapid interaction. (Koivisto et al., 2005) Players of event caches while online are quite interested in mobile skill development access. Geocachers enjoy the create something new in geocaching game. Kuukkelit (2007) suggests that geocaching events "could have action on radio amateur perspective and other player could get ideas from that and understand for radio amateur action in geocaching game. Also we suggest that someone's could present different GPS devices and mobile applications, what has existence in the moment". (Geocacher Kuukkelit, 2007.) Participants always play geocaching games when they have leisure time, holidays or even during work and just need to be in the town Centrum having time. "I play geocaching mostly in my home town while bicycling, sometimes with my friend in the car while visiting other environments. In other countries, I like walking and finding caches in the evening more than going out to bars." (Geocachers Itiq, 2009.) This is one reason why mobile phones with GPS have become more important for playing different pervasive games like geocaching. Sweetser and Wyeth (2005) have noted that the GameFlow element of challenge is consistently identified as the most important aspect of good game design. (Sweetser et al. 2005) "The best cache places are the most difficult in terms of accessibility. For example, Store Blåmann cache, which many geocacher can't find." (Geocacher Itiq 2009.) A game should be sufficiently challenging, match the player's skill level, vary the level of difficulty and keep an appropriate pace. In Sweetser and Wyeth's (2005) GameFlow element of player skills means that for the game to be enjoyable, it must support player skill development and mastery. In order for a player to experience flow, their perceived skills must match the challenge provided by the game, and both challenge and skills must exceed a certain threshold. (Sweetser et al., 2005) "15 km wayfaring in the middle of nowhere and back, only because we could visit on certain waypoints to take a GPS coordinates picture. That was a beautiful walking trip in nature. Also, in Greece we visit up to 2 km high mountains to seeking for cacheplace, where we will never visit otherwise. It was beautiful place". (Geocacher dajag 2009.) Therefore, it is necessary that players develop their skills at playing the game to truly enjoy the game. Sweetser and Wyeth's (2005) GameFlow element of immersion means that a player should experience deep but effortless involvement in the game. The element of flow that describes immersion is important in game design and research. (Sweetser et al., 2005) "I remember one time we went with my friend to one cache place, where we had to walk along the inside of tube for long way. You couldn't request the time of walking there or even how long you walked there. I guess it was an even one half kilometre. The cache place was a nice and exciting place". (Geocacher Henrik, 2009.) Games should entice the player to linger and become immersed in the experience.

Designers should include features that the players appreciated such as context awareness in terms of an intelligent location. Natural contexts for a mobile multiplayer game with a public display were seen for the ones where people have spare time to do things that they enjoy, or the ones where they are forced to wait for a specific event or a service. The extensions created in the context of specific design projects should be incorporated in future versions of the generic design environment. As such, the geocaching game offers the possibility to create local communities that players can contribute to. The trigger can be earlier experiences of games (fun and joy), a hint or invitation from a friend, or the person can join the game just out of plain curiosity towards a specific game. This study analysis addresses the "what" of player behaviour, and the data prove why is important to understand player experiences, and what values users appreciate in the geocaching game and future adventure games.

Synchronous Player-to-Player Interaction as Concentration Certain Gameplay

This subsection describe the problem with synchronous player-to-player interaction in the multi-player online game world is that players who use different platforms for playing the same game need to be equal. Mixing players using different platforms becomes feasible in multi-player online games where a critical part of the gameplay is tick or turn-based. (Koivisto et al. 2005) The geocaching game introduces possibilities for making experimental technical applications for the game. For example Trimble (Nasdaq: TRMB) announced the availability of a free, ad-supported version of its Geocache Navigator (TM) application for selected Nokia devices with integrated Global Positioning System (GPS) capabilities. Geocache Navigator application brings geocaching capabilities to the mobile phone and provides real-time access to Groundspeak's geocaching.com, the largest geocaching database in the world. (Erns, 2008) Players can also use Apple's iPhone for geocaching and access the Groundspeak forum with a geocaching iPhone application. Groundspeak's iPhone application then queries the geocaching.com database in real-time and provides a list of geocaches near you. (Geocaching.com) Users also share their own software at the Groundspeak forum. Geocaching.com has provided an online platform for players where they can share their own software with other players, but also the largest device companies like Nokia, Apple and Garmin share their own applications with players.

Because geocaching gives possibilities to use different platforms to play the game, players have easily to use familiar platforms for them. Player's want's to share geocaching community for them own software's. Open software are included well in geocaching community, example Open Cache Manager (OCM) is open source geocache manager for Linux operating system. This software allows users to important geocache listings from GPS or Loc file formats, add notes and waypoints to cache listings. OCM works with Geocaching.com, Terracaching.com, Navicaching.com and Open Caching site. (Geocaching software 2011) Sweetser and Wyeth's (2005) GameFlow element of concentration should support and create opportunities in the game. (Sweetser et al. 2005) "Always hunting for geocaching is fun, but it is also nice to follow on the internet how Travel Bugs move from some cache places to others and follow all kinds of geocaching happenings on the internet and interact there..." (Geocacher Salemmi 2009.) To support concentration certain gameplay element, games should create opportunities for player competition, cooperation and connection (Pagulayan, 2008). Sweetser and Wyeth's (2005) GameFlow element of feedback means that players must receive appropriate feedback at appropriate times. "It was nice to meet those players that I had a conversation with in the IRC-network". (Geocacher player, Hukka1974.)

Games design should provide immediate feedback for player actions and games should reward players with feedback on their progress and success. Joining the group or the community (even ad-hoc) should be easy and effortless. Designers should consider how players with different needs or problems could benefit from the community effects of a mobile multi-user application and use the public display e.g. for boosting their confidence, either personally or anonymously on the public display. The public display itself can have different functions, containing e.g. information of the service, advertisements, sponsor ads, and chat possibilities. Data prove that enjoyment is arguably the single most important motivation for geocachers to play the game and engagement the geocaching game comes from player's creativity to novel solutions. This indicates that game developers should understand the player's experience more fully, as well as player's co-designers role, what enjoyment means to players and how to create an enjoyable experience for players. For example players engagement on Geocaching game, 'In the Netherlands, the first people I met were geocachers, and we went geocaching as a group on several occasions. Outside of geocaching we haven't had a lot of contact, barring over Christmas and New Year's. In South Africa, I'm still too new on the scene to have made any social contact of note. I have, however, had semi-regular email contact with some of the local cachers (besem, 2009).

Passive Participation as Control of Gameplay

This subsection describes passive participation as control of gameplay meaning on game design. Passive participation means that the player does not need to actively play the game, but can instead observe the game world or influence the game by voting or rating with his mobile device. (Koivisto et al., 2005) Certainly, the geocaching game presents episodes requiring intense interactive engagement (this is what we most commonly think of as the game). Importantly, however, these sections are punctuated and usually framed by periods of far more limited interaction, and quite often, no interaction. Interaction here can be seen as a simple, mechanical measure of inputting controls or commands in order to influence on-screen action as opposed to players finding caches by GPS alone. (Newman, 2002)

The constitution of the on-line/off-line model of engagement as an interactive continuum allows for accommodation of transitional states of interaction, and states of interested but non-interactive engagement. For example, despite their frequent designation as solitary experiences, even the ostensibly single-player geocaching game is often played by more than one individual. A common arrangement is a primary player (interactively controlling and engaged on-line) assisted and supported by one or more co-pilots. These support players perform important tasks such as map-reading, puzzle solving and provide additional sets of vigilant senses primed to spot danger. While these players cannot be seen as having any interactive control because they possess no direct link to the interface of the game and can neither perform nor execute commands, they nonetheless demonstrate a level of interest and experimental engagement with the game that, while mediated through the primary player, exceeds that of the bystander or observer. (Newman 2002)

Geocachers have different roles in the geocaching community. Some people like to hunt for caches themselves but avoid participating in any geocaching forums, chat conversations or event caches. Still other players might be members of a geocaching community. "I am a lonely geocacher; I don't know any other players and nobody knows me". (Geocacher qasz, 2009.) "I am a fresh geocacher and I am not yet participating in Internet conversations and have not been so much invisible. I indeed like hunt for difficult places' caches and some could be recognising me for that." (Geocacher Tapelo, 2009) Sweetser and Wyeth's (2005) GameFlow element of control in order to experience flow means that a player must be allowed to exercise a sense of control over their actions. (Sweetser et al. 2005) "Geocaching become a very important part of my life. First geocaching was only a hobby and now I make software for the geocaching game on both PCs and GPS-devices." (Geocacher, Man60.) Players should feel a sense of control over the game interface and game controls, with mastery of the control system being an important part of most games (Johnson and Wiles, 2003). Players can choose to be passive player without the chance gameplay itself. Other words player's can also be very social and take part of different platforms to play and connect other players without to chance gameplay itself. Designer's needs to give different player's passive participate or social participate possibilities without chance the basic gameplay.

Design need to consider passive participation in game design, which involves having engagement, competing experiences and rich media content. Game design determines what win or loss criteria the game might include, how users will be able to control the game, and what information the game will communicate to them, and it establishes how hard the game will be.

Parallel Reality as Immersion on Game

This subsection presented parallel reality, as immersion on game should take on account game design process. In a parallel reality, the game takes place in two different worlds: the real world and the virtual world. A good example of this involves location-based games and mixed-reality games. In parallel reality games, the players should be motivated to take action in real life but not feel forced to do so. (Koivisto et al., 2005) The geocaching game has an amplified reality content within virtual cache places in the real world. Geocaching.com shares virtual cache locations on web pages, which means that each cache place is in a place in the real world but there is no plastic box hidden, as usually is the case at cache locations. Players have made virtual cache places where you cannot hide boxes at the location. The particular focus in this study is definite on a mobile mixed reality game, geocaching, which is a boundary game among mixed reality games because the playing field exists both in the real and in the Internet environment, and they serve different game functions. Geocaching has multi-player online game elements, such as players' global competition for points, and a determination of how many caches they have found in order to get an FTF-award (in other words, to be the first one to find a cache and get a special merit). FTF (First To Find) is more than a merit. Usually in capital cities, it is truly a race to get an FTF prize. (Horsman, 2005) The geocaching game has spread to many areas in the mixed reality games field and player interaction levels depend on the players' needs. The Geocachers gets immersion experiences during the game for example "One time I surrounding on geocache place for least 45 minute and I almost give up. I was frustrated and same time I kick on the dust in the land and I notice, that anthill have a hatch and under the earth have a cache what I was looking for long". (Geocacher qasz). Geocachers forget time, when they are looking for geocaches in real world and sometimes not have a clue how long they where even looking for the cache.

Game design in co-located game settings, opportunities for communication and immediacy behaviours are structured by the game interface, and characteristics of the players' physical environment. Game characteristics such as the vs. real-time competition formats, (like geocaching FTF competition), determine whether players have the opportunity to interact at all during a game. The case of co-located play vs. mediated play can also be extended to play against virtual others, simulated social actors rather than avatars. (De Kork, Ijsselsteijn 2008.)

CONCLUSION

This section make conclusion for player experience of geocaching game and emergence the result in game design. Technology is influencing all aspects of our lives. Like Geocaching game has engagement players the game giving players enjoyment experiences, which they create themselves and have active participation on gameplay. Players' most positive geocaching experiences are usually in memorable places (beautiful landscapes, nature and extreme cache places). The game takes geocachers to unexpected places. In geocaching players share their own experiences and creativity that show that the player is not a viewer but an agent of action, a creator of their own world. It should be noted that computer mediated communication in the geocaching game being in tool for around the game and same time expression tool for technological orientated people. The geocaching game's media are also identity devices that affect the player's worldview and the subjectivity of an individual. The geocaching sports game was once derided as orienteering for nerds but has become mainstream, attracting thousands of enthusiasts and presenting marketing opportunities for outdoor providers.

A move into player-centred game design is an important step in the development of more systematic and evaluated game design processes. The paradigm of player-centred design as a starting point is that the potential players of the game are considered a major source of information throughout the design process. To summarize, player-centred game design is not only for players' ideas for fun games, but potential user experiences and game ideas providing the design process with references to inform and inspire the design to develop new adventure games. This study's findings prove that computational media have the unique potential to let players be designers or co-designers in game design projects. Learning to create game experiences for players is one of the goals of successful game design, perhaps the most important one. As a result, the more experienced geocaching game players know from experience that they have really enjoyed the game. It makes sense that more experienced players should find freedom of expression more enjoyable, as their experience means that they are more likely to want to experiment, try different strategies and try to play the geocaching game in their own way. Design is the process by which a designer creates a context to be encountered by a participant, from which meaning emerges. This study also identified a number of interesting points that are worthy of further exploration in future player-centred studies.

FUTURE RESEARCH

The literature review has shown that players are interested in testing new technologies in geocaching. In fact, new technologies such as RFID and wireless sensor network technologies could provide innovative approaches to geocaching.

First of all, these technologies could be applied to virtual caches. In the case of unique objects, such as monuments, they could be attached with RFID tags. The use of mobile devices with RFID can provide better end-user experiences (Luimula et al. 2007) In addition, RFID tags assigned to physical objects and locations can be seen as a realisation of a ubiquitous computing society (T-Engine Forum, 2007). That is to say, RFID can be seen as one of the technology enablers of smart objects and an Internet of things.

Secondly, RFID and wireless sensor network technologies could offer new possibilities for implementing mystery geocaches. According to Hawking et al. (2005), there is an evident need for services in tourism, which are pervasive or ubiquitous. (Hawking, 2005) These services should enrich experiences while simultaneously remaining invisible. For example, the use of pressure or motion detecting sensors as a part of the infrastructure of a mystery geocache location would provide information about the user's behaviour in an invisible manner, and thus enrich geocaching experiences, for example in sport geocaching. (Luimula et al., 2009)

Thirdly, wireless sensor networks could be used for creating alarm systems in the case of caches located in challenging or even dangerous areas such as mountains or water areas. Sensors could, in this case, provide information about alarms related to weather conditions, for example. NASA has created many successful earth monitoring and alarm systems, such as in the National Snow and Ice Data Center, and in Cascade Volcano Observatory (Chien et al. 2007).

Fourthly, the use of RFID or wireless sensor networks could enlarge the use of geocaching from outdoors to indoor conditions as well. On the other hand, in indoor conditions, the challenges are more complicated and different kinds of wireless technologies have to be tested and combined to achieve a convenient solution. If the environment contains wireless technologies such as WLAN, a suitable indoor positioning technology can be WLAN positioning (Ekahau, 2008).

The previously described technologies can be used, for example, in geocaching sports games. In sport exercises could be monitored when visiting caches. It could thus be possible to monitor how fast geocachers are able to visit caches, or how geocachers are able to execute the sports-related tasks in the current cache. The use of wireless sensor networks, in turn, would give geocaching sports game developers opportunities to not only identify, but also sense players' activities. For example, sensors as a part of geocachers' accessories would provide wellness and stress information such as heart rate, ECG, and acceleration. In the case of sensors that are situated in the geocaching location, the system could in turn analyse conditions and rate geocachers' activities based on current information. This information could, for example, be used for calculating times. The system could now take this information into account when comparing results for other players who have visited a cache at a different time in better conditions.

Thus, to summarize, new technologies already offer developers significant opportunities to create innovative geocaching services, which could provide better end-user experiences. Geocaching as a business area is still quite young and often quite unknown when compared to other service areas with millions of users. Innovations can be provided with the technologies that are currently on the market. Therefore, we suggest that the geocaching game will chance the more ubiquitous game side. The geocaching game to find treasure hints could utilise a mobile phone screen as a mixed reality mode. At a game location, the player could interact with the real environment more intensively than merely navigating and looking for only hints to find caches.

ACKNOWLEDGMENT

We thank all participants of the study. We thank Timo Partala in Tampere University of Technology, who provided helpful comments on previous versions of this document.

REFERENCES

Battarbee, K. (2003). Co-experience: The social user experience. In *Proceedings of CHI 2003*. ACM.

Berelson, B. (1952). *Content analysis in communication research*. Free Press.

Buchenau, M., & Fulton Suri, J. (2000). Experience prototyping. In *Proceedings of the Conference on Designing Interactive Systems: Processes, Practices, Methods, and Techniques*. ACM Press.

Chien, S., Tran, D., Davies, A., Johnston, M., Doubleday, J., Castano, R., et al. (2007). Lights out autonomous operation of an earth observing sensorweb. In *Proceedings of the 7th International Symposium on Reducing the Cost of Spacecraft Ground Systems and Operations*. Moscow, Russia: AIAA.

Cziksentimihalyi, M., & Rochberg-Halton, E. (1981). *The meaning of things*. Cambridge, UK: Cambridge University.

Desmet, P. M. A. (2002). *Designing emotions*. (Doctoral Thesis). Technical University of Delft, Delft, The Netherlands.

Dewey, J. (1980). *Experience and education*. New York: Perigee.

Dickey, M. D. (2005). Engaging By design: How engagement strategies in population computer and video games can inform instructional design. *Education Teach Research Dev.*, *53*(2), 67–83. doi:10.1007/BF02504866.

Dyer, M. (2004). *The essential guide to geocaching, tracking treasure with your GPS*. Golden, CO: Fulcrum Publishing.

Ekahau. (2008). *Positioning engine 4.2 datasheet*. Retrieved from http://www.ekahau.com/file.php?id=99419

Ermi, L., & Mäyrä, F. (2005). Fundamental components of the gameplay experience: analysing immersion. In *Proceedings of DIGRA 2005 Conference: Changing Views – World in Play*. DIGRA.

Fisher, G. (1998). Beyond couch potatoes: From consumers to designers. In *Proceeding of the Third Asian Pacific Computer and Human Interaction*. AMC.

Flintman, M. (2007). *Supporting mobile mixed-reality experiences*. (Doctoral dissertation). The University of Nottingham, Nottingham, UK.

Forlizzi, J., & Shannon, F. (2000). The building blocks of experience: An early framework for interaction designers. In *Proceedings of DIS'00*. Brooklyn, NY: DIS.

Gram-Hansen, L. B. (2009). Geocaching in a persuasive perspective. In *Proceedings of Persuasive '09*. Persuasive. doi:10.1145/1541948.1541993.

Hassenzahl, M. (2003). The thing and I: Understanding the relationship between user and product. In *Funology: From Usability to Enjoyment*. Dordrecht, The Netherlands: Kluwer Academic Publishers.

Hawking, P., Stein, A., Zeleznikow, J., Pramod, S., Devon, N., Dawson, L., & Foster, S. (2005). Emerging issues in location based tourism systems. In *Proceedings of the International Conference on Mobile Business*, (pp. 75-81). IEEE.

Ihamäki, P. (2007). Geocaching at the institute of paasikivi – New ways of teaching GPS Technology & basics of orientation in local geography. In *New Trends in Information and Communication Technology & Accessibility*. Academic Press.

Ihamäki, P. (2008). Geocaching – A new experience for sport tourism. In *Selling or Telling? Paradoxes in tourism, culture and heritage*. Atlas Reflections.

Ihamäki, P. (2012a). Geocaching: Interactive communication instruments around the game. *Eludamos Journal for Computer Game Culture, 5*(2).

Ihamäki, P. (2012b). Geocachers the creative tourism experience. *Journal of Hospitality and Tourism Technology, 3*(3). doi:10.1108/17579881211264468.

Ihamäki, P., & Tuomi, P. (2009). Understanding 21st century's mobile games within boundaries. In *Breaking New Ground: Innovation in Games, Play, Practice and Theory*. Brunel University.

ISO. (1999). *Human-centred design processes for interactive systems*. Geneva: international Standards Organisation.

Jääskeläinen, K. (2001). *Strategic questions in the development of interactive television programs*. (Doctoral Dissertation). University of Art and Design Helsinki, Helsinki, Finland.

Johnson, D., & Wiles, J. (2003). Effective affective user interface design in games. *Ergonomics, 46*, 1332–1345. doi:10.1080/00140130310001610865 PMID:14612323.

Koivisto, E. M. I., & Wenninger, C. V. (2005). Enhancing player experience in MMORPGs with mobile features. In *Proceedings of DIGRA 2005 Conference: Changing Views – Worlds in Play*. DIGRA.

Korhonen, H., Montola, M., & Arrasvuori, J. (2009). Understanding playful user experience through digital games. In *Proceedings of the International Conference on Designing Pleasurable Products and Interfaces*. DPPI.

Luimula, M., Pieskä, S., Pitkäaho, T., & Tervonen, J. (2009). Ambient intelligence in mobile field work. In *Proceedings of the 8th International Conference and Workshop on Ambient Intelligence and Embedded Systems*. IEEE.

Luimula, M., Sääskilahti, K., Partala, T., & Saukko, O. (2007). A field comparison of techniques for location selection on a mobile device. In *Proceedings of the Wireless Applications and Computing, International IADIS Conference*. Lisbon, Portugal: IADIS.

Mattelmäki, T. (2006). *Design probes*. (Doctoral Dissertation). University of Art and Design Helsinki, Helsinki, Finland.

Montola, M., Stenros, J., & Waern, A. (2009). *Pervasive games, theory and design*. San Francisco, CA: Morgan Kaufmann Publishers.

Muessig, K., & Price, J. G. (2007). *International viewpoint and news*. Berlin: Springer-Verlag.

Newman, J. (2001). *Reconfiguring the videogame player*. Paper presented at GameCulture International Computer and Videogame Conference. Bristol, UK.

Newman, J. (2002). In search of the videogame player: The lives of Mario. *New Media & Society*, *4*, 405.

O'Hara, K. (2008). Understanding geocaching practices and motivations. In *Proceedings of CHI 2008*. ACM.

Pagulayan, R., Keeker, K., Wixon, D., Romero, R., & Fuller, T. (2003). User-centered design in games. In J. A. Jacko, & A. Sears (Eds.), *The Human-Computer Interaction Handbook: Fundamentals, Evolving Techniques and Emerging Applications*. Mahwah, NJ: Lawrence Eribaum Associates.

Pagulayan, R. J., & Steury, K. R. Fulton, B., & Romero, R.L. (2004). Designing for fun: User-testing case studies. In M. Blythe, K. Overbeeke, A. Monk, & P. Wright (Eds.), Funology: Form Usability to Enjoyment. Boston: Kluwer Academic Publishers.

Peter, J. W. (2004). The complete idiot's guide to geocaching. New York: Peguin Group (USA), Inc.

Schank, R. (1998, July-August). Narrative and intelligence economy. *Harvard Business Review*, 97.

Sherman, E. (2004). *Geocaching hike and seek with your GPS*. New York: Springer.

Sweetser, P., & Wyeth, P. (2005). GameFlow: A model for evaluating player enjoyment in games. *ACM Computers in Entertainment, 3*(3).

T-Engine Forum. (2007). *Ucode tag lineup significantly expanded*. Ubiquitous ID Center.

Weiser, M. (1999). The computer for the 21st century. *Mobile Computing and Communications Review*, *3*(3), 3–11. doi:10.1145/329124.329126.

KEY TERMS AND DEFINITIONS

Adventure Game: Have game genre, which has mainly puzzle solving, exploring and memorization activities.

Geocaching: Technology-supported treasure hunt activity that uses a Global Positioning System (GPS) receiver or a smartphone with a Geocaching application to find something hidden by other players (Geocaching.com).

Pervasive Game: A game that has one or more salient features that expand the contractual magic circle of play spatially, temporally or socially. (Montola et al. 2009, 12)

Player Experience: A balance to be enjoyable on main segment of player and game design need to understand that player enjoyment is the most important goal for digital game design. Digital games are a prevalent form of entertainment in which the purpose of the design is to engage players. Game designers and researchers incorporate a number of strategies and tactics for engaging players in 'gameplay'. Game design is at the forefront of cultivating innovative techniques for interactive design. (Dickey, 2005)

Social Interaction: The possibility of co-experiencing and co-creation the game through. Social interaction offers players an element that supports the occurrence of meaningful experiences (Battarbee, 2003)

Synchronous Player-to-Player Interaction: The multi-player online game world is that players who use different platforms for playing the same game need to be equal. Mixing players using different platforms becomes feasible in multi-player online games where a critical part of the gameplay is tick or turn-based. (Koivisto et al. 2005)

User-Centred Design: Concerned with incorporating the user's perspective into the software development process in order to achieve a usable system. According to the ISO 13407 standard on user-centred design (ISO, 1999) there are five essential processes, which should be undertaken in order to incorporate usability requirements into the software development process. There are as follows: 1) Plan the user-centred design process, 2) Understand and specify the context of use, 3) Specify the user and organizational requirements, 4) Produce design and prototypes, 5) Carry out user-based assessment.

Chapter 7
Seamless Interfacing:
Situation Awareness through Action Recognition and Spatio-Temporal Reasoning

Stephan Puls
Karlsruhe Institute of Technology (KIT), Germany

Heinz Wörn
Karlsruhe Institute of Technology (KIT), Germany

ABSTRACT

Intuitive means of human-machine interaction are needed in order to facilitate seamless human-robot cooperation. Knowledge about human posture, whereabouts, and performed actions allows interpretation of the situation. Thus, expectations towards system behavior can be inferred. This work demonstrates a system in an industrial setting that combines all this information in order to achieve situation awareness. The continuous human action recognition is based on hierarchical Hidden Markov Models. For identifying and predicting human location, an approach based on potential functions is presented. The recognition results and spatial information are used in combination with a Description Logics-based reasoning system for modeling semantic interrelations, dependencies, and situations.

INTRODUCTION

Bringing together human intelligence and industrial robotics in effective productive systems is a challenging task. Due to safety concerns, fences are installed to separate human workers and robots. Consequently no time and space sharing cooperation is feasible and interaction is restricted to the usage of specialized, complex input devices.

In some cases, modern working cells replace safety fences by laser scanners performing foreground detection in order to slow down robot motion if foreground movement is detected. This approach does not allow for meaningful analysis of the scene and appropriate reasoning about human actions. Thus, the contribution towards challenging tasks like safe human-robot cooperation is limited. We are conducting research in the realm of human centered production environment in order to enable interactive and cooperative scenarios. In previous work, a framework for human-robot-cooperation (MAROCO) was introduced (Puls et al., 2012a). This work expands the framework and

DOI: 10.4018/978-1-4666-4623-0.ch007

previous work (Puls & Wörn, 2012) by merging three components: (1) continuous human action recognition, (2) human location identification and prediction, and (3) spatio-temporal reasoning about situations.

In interaction, knowledge about performed actions of one agent is necessary when the other agent has to decide on a corresponding action. In case of bringing humans and technical systems together, recognizing human actions is compulsory in order to identify possible intentions and reason about expectations towards system behavior. Moreover, actions can be considered in context of the location of its performance. Thus, different reactions by the system are possible, either due to spatial constrains or due to differing interpretations of the action in context. In order to achieve situation awareness, general knowledge about actions, locations, their semantic interrelations and temporal dependencies needs to be modeled. Using this knowledge and the recognition results it is possible to reason about situations and, thus, expectations towards system behavior can be assumed. Consequently, explicit and tedious interaction procedures can be avoided.

The continuous human action recognition is based on hierarchical Hidden Markov Models. For identifying and predicting the human location an approach based on potential fields is presented. A Description Logic (DL) based reasoning system is used to model the general knowledge and infer information about situations and expectations. The remainder of this chapter is organized as follows. In the next section, selected research work on action recognition, location awareness and reasoning about situations is presented. Also, a short overview of the underlying MAROCO framework is given to clarify the foundations of this work. Thereafter, HMMs, potential functions and DLs are briefly introduced. Also, the recognition module and its impact on the DL module are presented in detail. In the end, experimental evaluation is explained, results are discussed and, finally, a summary is given and some hints for future work are mentioned.

BACKGROUND

The idea of achieving seamless interaction between human and machine has motivated research for a long time. Many research groups have dedicated their work to this idea and many research subfields have developed. In the following, some of these related works are presented.

Human Action Recognition

Human action recognition is a very active research area. The diversity in action classification methods is ordered in the survey by Poppe (2010) into three categories: (1) classification without an explicit model of variations in time, (2) temporal state-space approaches and (3) action detection without modeling the action. The latter category, according to Poppe (2010), tries to correlate observations to labeled video sequences and, thus, uses similar techniques as approaches in the other categories. Due to the assumption that in industrial settings practicable actions and processes are known the remainder of this section concentrates on related works in the realm of category (1) and (2). Also, in case of process variations including new and unknown actions means of concrete modeling of these actions is assumed to be more feasible than comprehensive sensor data annotation which would be required by category (3).

Fitting the first category, Sun and Wang (2010) use the k-nearest neighbor algorithm to classify binary images according to pixel projection and mass center movement features. Classification without movement features is reported to be poor for similar actions with differing speeds, e.g., running and walking (Sun and Wang, 2010). Thus the incorporation of temporal information is needed and achieved through the use of mass center movement features. This measure increases the classification rate greatly.

In order to capture directly the temporal nature of actions lots of research is based on Bayes Networks (Loccoz et al., 2003; Park & Aggarwal, 2004; e.g.) or HMMs. All these approaches fit into category (2) and try to correlate observations with probabilistic temporal action models. Especially HMMs are a popular means for the recognition task (Krüger et al., 2007) as their theoretic foundations are well understood and applications in speech recognition and other domains have shown their capabilities.

In the work of Elmezain et al. (2008) a hand gesture recognition system is presented. They argue that the orientation is the best feature compared to location and velocity in order to describe hand gestures. Thus, their system relies solely on orientation features of the tracked hand. Discretizations of observed orientations are used as input for a HMM recognition module. For achieving recognition of continuous gestures a zero-codeword detection with static velocity motion is introduced. Through the integration of 3D information about hand location and movement the recognition results are improved in (Elmezain et al., 2009).

For the recognition of actions of the upper body Wu et al. (2008) utilize layered HMMs. Local and global features, regarding the human body and the image scene respectively, are separately used in different HMMs. These HMMs compose the lower layer and are responsible for the recognition of individual arm actions. The outcomes of the lower layer are combined into a new feature vector and used as input for the upper layer which models the interrelationship of two arms. Thus, this approach can also be regarded as hierarchical modeling of the resulting action as sub-actions performed by each arm.

In the work of Junxia et al. (2008) the goal is to recognize human actions based on full body tracking. Similar to Wu et al. (2008) local and global features are used to represent the state of the human body. Through a model based representation of the human agent global movement information and local configuration features can be obtained. For classification different HMMs are used in parallel but not in a hierarchical manner. The classification result is a combined maximum of the HMMs results.

Location Awareness

A human's position is especially interesting when location based services target possible consumers. In the work of Marmasse & Schmandt, (2002), GPS coordinates are used to track a person and to learn so called virtual places which resembles semantic mapping. Based on these places information, like reminders, emails or web content can be passed to the user. Different approaches are evaluated to learn about place-correlations and to predict future movement of the user, namely Bayes classifier, histogram models and Hidden Markov Models. In their findings, histogram models were best suited to abstract the data and allow prediction.

A similar approach is used by Ashbrook & Starner (2002), where wearable computers are argued to assist users using context to determine on how to act. A user's tasks are related to the location and through prediction of a user's movement tasks can be scheduled or influenced beforehand. The number of places is determined by clustering the GPS data based on the duration the user stayed at each place. The correlations between places are modeled using Hidden Markov Models which are also used for prediction.

In (Eagle et al., 2009), cellular tower data is analyzed to gather position information on cellphone users. The data is used with unsupervised clustering by means of graph segmentation for identifying salient locations in the network of cellular towers. The inferred locations are used as states in multiple dynamic Bayesian networks (DBN) to predict a user's movement. Also, abnormal human behavior can be determined through adaption of the DBNs.

Using semantics of the human's current location for recognizing human activities is proposed by Yamada et al. (2007). It is argued, that on the one side locations can invoke different activities, but on the other side, these activities are closely related to utilized objects. Thus, locations are defined as activity spaces and can be modeled indirectly through usage of objects. Based on these activity spaces different services can be proactively offered to the user, thus, avoiding explicit service request procedures.

Using prediction of human position for adapting a robot's trajectory is accomplished by Tadokoro et al. (1993). The human motion is modeled as a Markov process and the prediction is used to compute an estimation of danger. Accordingly, the velocity of the robot's path traversal is proactively adapted. In the work of Puls et al. (2012b), situational risk estimation is used to adapt the path of an industrial robot. Besides head orientation and direction of movement, the relative position of the human co-worker towards the robot is used for risk evaluation.

Situation Awareness

Shi et al. (2004) argue that HMMs are not suitable for recognition of parallel activities. Thus, they introduced propagation networks. In such networks an action primitive, which incorporates a probabilistic duration model, is associated to each node. For enforcing temporal and logical constraints conditional joint probabilities are used. In analogy to HMMs, many propagation networks are evaluated in order to approximate the observation probability.

In contrast, Minnen et al. (2003) argue that purely probabilistic methods are not adequate enough for recognition of prolonged activities. Consequently, an approach is devised using parameterized stochastic grammars.

The application of knowledge based methods for action recognition tasks is scarce, but work on scene interpretation using DLs has been conducted. DLs are used by Hummel et al. (2007) for reasoning about traffic situations and understanding of intersections. For reduction of the intersection hypotheses space deductive inference services are used. These services are also utilized to retrieve useful information for the driver.

The application of knowledge processing in the context of robotic control is presented in Tenorth & Beetz (2009). The system is especially designed for use with personal robots. Prolog is used for the underlying system to process knowledge. The knowledge representation itself is based on DLs and processed via a Web Ontology Language (OWL) Prolog plug-in. The approach is used to query on its environmental model. Due to the fact that actions and events are observed by the processing framework and used as knowledge facts, the system is not applicable for recognition of activities or for reasoning about situations. The knowledge base can be extended by using embedded classifiers in order to search for groups of instances that have common properties.

DLs are also used by Neumann & Möller (2008) for establishing scene interpretation. Spatial and temporal relations of visually aggregated concepts are the foundation of the analysis and interpretation of table cover scenes. The proposed interpretation approach resembles a stepwise process which uses visual evidence and contextual information for guidance. Moreover, probabilistic information is integrated within the knowledge based framework in order to generate preferred interpretations. This approach yielded in a general interpretation framework based in DLs which can cope with general multimedia data (Möller & Neumann, 2008).

A comprehensive approach for situation-awareness is introduced in (Springer et al., 2010). The system incorporates context capturing, context abstraction and decision making into a generic framework. Different sensing devices and reasoning components are managed by the framework. Thus, different reasoning facilities and as such DLs can be used for high level decision making.

These last examples and our previous work show that the usage of DLs bears great potential. Hence its adoption for the situation awareness incorporated into the MAROCO framework.

The MAROCO Framework

In our previous research a framework for human-robot-cooperation was developed. The goal is to realize a comprehensive cognitive cycle which consists of (1) sensing, (2) cognition, and (3) acting. The sensing is done by a photon mixer device (PMD) camera which captures directly a 3D point cloud of the scene. Through 3D image sequence analysis the work space of an industrial robot is observed and the kinematics of a human worker is reconstructed (see Figure 1).

The reconstruction of the human kinematics is based purely on depth image analysis and does not require marker attached to the human agent (Graf & Wörn, 2009). During the process of reconstruction many parameters of the human kinematics are estimated, e.g., head orientation, upper body orientation, arm configurations, etc. Due to the position of the camera above the work cell some parameters, like leg configurations, cannot be identified.

The camera fixation at the ceiling is mandatory in respect to safety concerns. For one thing, dirt which is inevitable in a production environment is less prone to stick to the lens system of the camera. Furthermore, manipulation of the camera position is difficult to achieve. Thus, its calibration in the environment is constant. Last but not least, occlusions through the movement of the robots and production materials are avoided.

In order to achieve seamless interaction and an intuitive human-machine interface an activity recognition and situation awareness system based on Description Logics was implemented (Graf et al. 2010, Puls et al. 2011). Extracted features of the human kinematics are directly mapped onto semantic relations of DL concepts. Moreover, context information about the environment, e.g. robot state, is represented as DL concepts and their relations. Through reasoning over these related concepts inferences about occurring activities and situations are made. Also, expectations towards robotic behavior are inferred based on situation and context. Thus, these results can be used to guide a task planning module for completing the cognitive cycle.

Even though safety relevant systems, like kinematics reconstruction, risk estimation, and robot motion control, are processed with more than 15 frames per second, the DL based module has longer cycle times (Puls et al. 2011). It can be argued that higher cognitive functions like activity and situation recognition do not necessarily have to be processed in real time as their duration can be assumed to be longer than a few milliseconds. Nevertheless, accelerating the processing will enable better responsiveness and, thus, allow for better human-machine interaction.

In order to capture actions with short durations and their temporal relationships the MAROCO framework is extended. Accordingly, one goal of this work is to use HMM based computation for fast recognition of basic continuous human actions which can be interpreted in context by the situation awareness module. Another goal is

Figure 1. Reconstructed human model from depth images (left). Environmental scene model consisting of several kinematical chains (right).

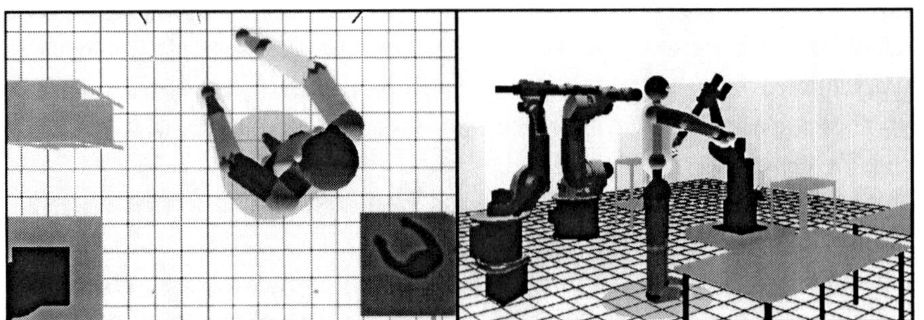

to enrich the available context information with location information. Thus, true spatio-temporal reasoning can be achieved.

Hidden Markov Models

In the following, HMMs will be briefly introduced. A thorough introduction to HMMs can be found in (Rabiner, 1989).

Hidden Markov Models describe two probabilistic processes. One process constitutes a so called Markov chain which consists of states and transition probabilities. It can be represented as a probabilistic state machine. These states are not observable, hence the attribution *hidden*. The second process generates observable symbols according to a state depending probability distribution. Thus, by observing symbols the current underlying state of the hidden model can be probabilistically inferred. This can be achieved by using the Viterbi algorithm.

If there are many different models and an observation sequence of symbols, one can determine the specific Markov model which fits the observation best. For evaluation of the probability $P(O|\lambda)$ of an observation sequence O and a given model λ the Forward algorithm is used. In order to learn the parameters of a HMM based on given observations the Baum-Welch algorithm can be applied.

For the purpose of action recognition the evaluation of different HMMs is done through the Forward algorithm. Each action is represented by its own Markov model and the specific action whose model has highest probability is considered to be recognized.

Potential Functions

Potential fields originate from describing gravity and magnetic fields. They were first used by Hwang & Ahuja (1992) for robot path finding by defining electric charges onto objects in the scene and the same charges onto the robot. The goal was defined as being the opposite charge, so that attractive forces were guiding the robot towards the goal. Repelling forces kept the robot at a safe distance to obstacles. Thus, potential functions create a landscape in which robots move from a *high-value* state to a *low-value* state. By following the negative gradient of the potential function the robot can reach its goal. The robot follows a path *downhill* which is called *gradient descent*. A detailed introduction to potential fields in the realm of robot motion can be found in (Choset et al., 2005).

Description Logics

In the MAROCO framework, DLs are used to formalize knowledge about situations, actions and expectations. Theoretic foundations of DLs and a comprehensive overview of their applications are given in (Baader et al., 2010). Due to the fact that DL is a 2-variable fragment of First Order Logic and that most DLs are decidable, sound, complete and terminating reasoning algorithms exist.

A DL knowledge base is composed of two parts: (1) general knowledge and (2) knowledge about individuals in a domain. Part (1) defines the terminology of the domain and its axioms are declared in the terminology box, hence TBox. Part (2) defines the assertion box or ABox which incorporates assertions about individuals. As argued by Hummel et al. (2007) this allows for modular and reusable knowledge bases and, thus, for more efficient coding of knowledge. DLs can deal naturally with incomplete information due to their open world assumption. This is essential in reasoning when taking sensor data into account.

ACHIEVING SITUATION AWARENESS

The overall system for action recognition and situation awareness involves different modules that need to exchange information with each other. An

Figure 2. System overview of the different components involved

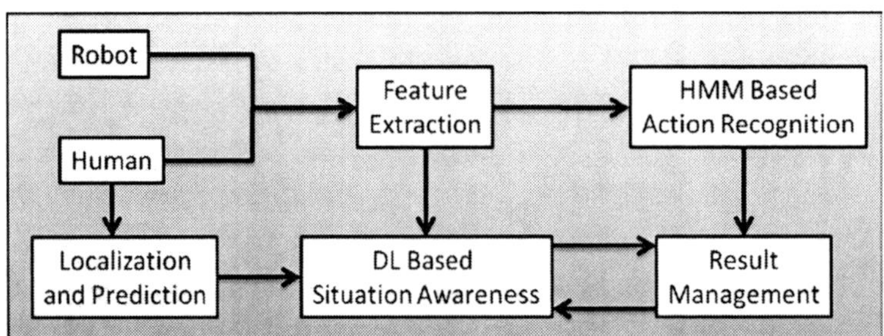

overview is given in Figure 2. In the following these modules and methods will be explained in detail.

Continuous Action Recognition

The purpose of the action recognition module is to identify basic human actions such as *walking forwards*, *backwards* and *sideways*, *left* and *right* respectively. Also, the actions *standing still*, *crouching down*, *sitting down* and *standing up* are recognized. Furthermore, some complex actions which are composed of consequent basic actions need to be identified, such as *lifting up* and *standing up after sitting*. The compound action *lifting up* consists of *crouching down* and *standing up*. Thus, the HMMs build up a two layer hierarchical network in which recognized actions in the first layer are used as observations for the second layer (see Figure 3). All recognized actions are fed into the result management module which stores all system wide recognition and reasoning results for retrieval.

The selection of appropriate features to use as observations is the foundation for successful action recognition. Based on the experience reported by Elmezain et al. (2008) orientations of movements are best suited for distinguishing actions. Accordingly, in our approach the three dimensional direction of movement of the upper body is mapped onto a set of discrete directions (see Fig. 3 right), thus, the observation is a function of the appropriate angles, $O = f(\alpha, \beta)$.

In order to account for body movement and global orientation changes the direction of movement needs to be computed in respect of the local frame of reference. Consequently, a movement to the left side needs to generate the same observation regardless of the global facing direction of the human agent. Due to the kinematics reconstruction the global orientation of the upper body is known and can directly be used for compensation.

Figure 3. Processing of the two layered HMM architecture (left), Orientation mapping of a 3D direction (right)

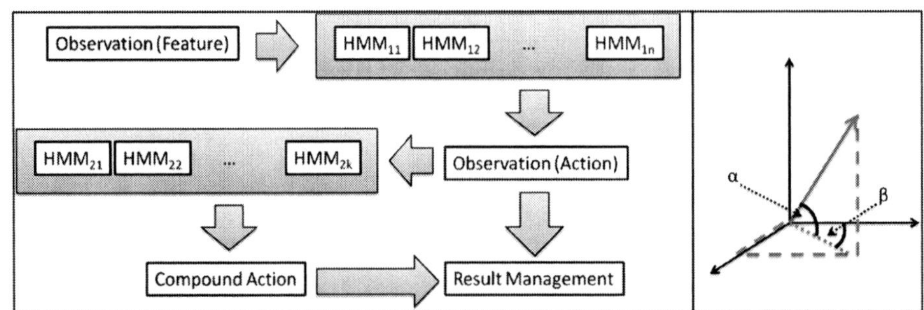

Continuity of the action recognition is achieved by evaluating all models each time step. In case unknown actions are performed this way of evaluation still comes up with a model which has highest probability of all models. In order to deal with such occurrences, the resulting maximal probability needs to be above a certain threshold or else it will be included in the result management as *unknown action.*

Location Identification, Localization and Prediction

In this work, Gaussian functions are used to define potentials in the work space in order to identify and predict the human co-worker's location. The main advantage of Gaussian functions is the ability to represent locations as position distributions in contrast to singular points in space. Figure 4 shows an example tracking result of a human co-worker (left, scaled to the interval [-1, 1]) in the work space of the robot (right). In this case, the work space includes three different locations, of which two are cooperation areas where human and robot might work jointly.

Knowledge about the location of the human is based on a semantic mapping of the tracking coordinates onto the concepts of locations. This mapping is the foundation for further interpretations and reasoning about situations. The mapping process differs according to its task: localization or prediction.

As can be seen in Figure 4, the tracking coordinates form different clusters that correspond to different locations. Thus, the idea is to identify locations based on unsupervised clustering techniques and use the extracted clusters to build attracting potential functions. These functions are then used for mapping purposes in localization and prediction.

The algorithm DBSCAN allows clustering of data points without prior knowledge about the expected number of clusters (Ester et al., 1996). Thus, the location identification is independent on the use-case, resulting in an overall general approach. The result of the clustering is a mapping for each data point to its cluster. Also, points that do not belong to a group are considered to be noise and discarded. Such points might be tracking positions between locations when the human co-worker walks through the work space. In order to compute Gaussian functions, all data points of each cluster are examined: the mean and covariance are computed. Afterwards, these functions are normalized (see Figure 5).

Figure 4. Tracking result of a human co-worker (left) in the work space of the robot (right)

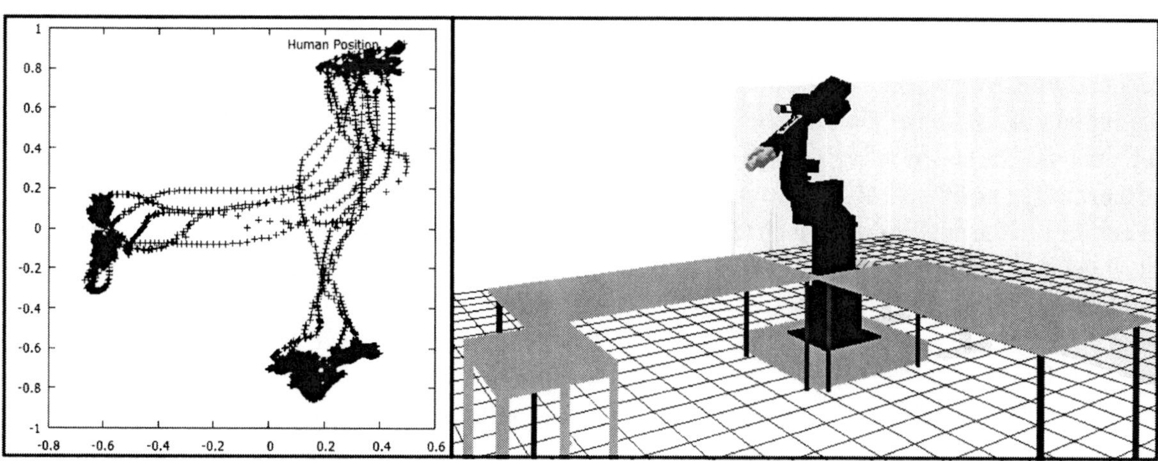

Figure 5. Gaussian functions representing each cluster

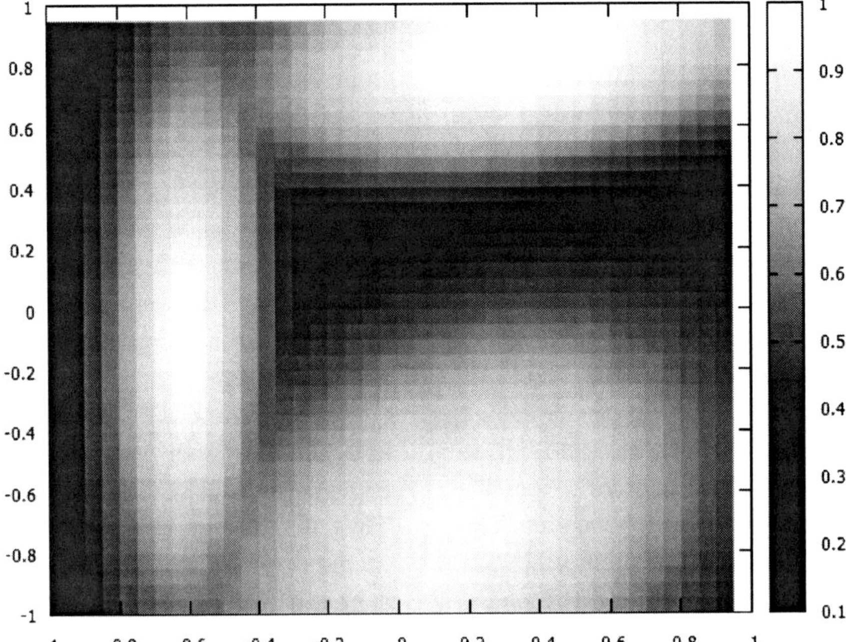

For localization purposes, the Gaussian functions represent position distributions and define the certainty of a tracking position belonging to a location. Thus, the localization of the human co-worker is achieved by thresholding the value of each Gaussian function. If a value is above the threshold, the person is assumed to reside at the corresponding location.

The prediction is based on two factors: movement direction and attractive force of the potential functions. The attraction of a potential function is defined by its gradient given the movement. Consequently, the next location can be predicted with the initial observation of motion. The movement direction is obtained by using Kalman prediction of the tracking position (Bar-Shalom et al., 2001). In contrast to the application of path finding, the maximal gradient in movement direction is used for determining the future location.

The Reasoning System

As stated above, in previous research a knowledge base was engineered which models concepts of situations, activities and expectations. In order to incorporate the results of the HMM action recognition and location awareness into this knowledge base new concepts were defined and others were refined (see Table 1).

The concepts about situations, activities, actions and expectations were augmented with newly added sub-concepts. Furthermore, concepts related to places and predictions are introduced. Recognized actions and results of the location awareness are incorporated as individual instantiations of the corresponding sub-concepts. All other concepts are inferred by the reasoning system and are therefore indirectly linked with observed action individuals. These are also correlated with other actions and reasoning results through roles which capture temporal relationships of actions.

Table 1. A listing of newly added and refined concepts

Concepts	Added sub-concepts	Refined concepts
Action	Sit Down Crouch Down Stand Up Walk	
Activity	Sitting Crouching	Standing Walking
Situation	Having A Break	Walking By Distraction Monitoring
Expectation	Get Beverage Change Workplace	
Place	Cooperative Place Manual Workplace In Between	
Predicted Place	Stay Enter Coop. Space Leave Coop. Space	

One major requirement for effective reasoning in a DL system is the consistency of the knowledge base. If contradicting observations are instantiated during run time the DL system is not capable to cope and reports the inconsistency without further reasoning. Consequently, some concept definitions needed refinement, e.g., the activity walking needs to consider if the person sat down sometime before. Using a bureau chair with wheels, a person can move horizontally without being upright. This should not be regarded as walking.

In order to demonstrate the interleaving of combined action recognition and spatio-temporal reasoning the situation *having a break* and the expectations *get beverage* are introduced. This situation is implied by the fact that the person is sitting down due to the simplifying assumption that in productive environments working agents are standing upright. The expectation that the robot should get a beverage for the worker can only be fulfilled if the person is located in the reach of the robot. Otherwise, the robot is expected to continue its work and follow a defined path of motion. Additionally, for demonstration purposes the expectation *change workspace* is incorporated which is triggered by prediction results and is based on an assumption about the production process. Thus, the idea is, that robot and human co-worker share the same workspace but not at the same time. When the human co-worker intends to enter a cooperative workspace the robot is expected to leave that particular space and continue with other tasks.

Experimental Evaluation

For the experimental analysis of the HMM based continuous action recognition different courses of action were executed by three different persons experienced with and novices to the system. The recognition results were recorded (see Table 2). The total of all executed actions has a length of 20 minutes at a frame rate of 15 fps. Actions were performed in no particular order and arbitrarily by the human agent. For evaluation reasons, the sensor data was also recorded and manually annotated. During comparison of recorded results and annotated data correctly detected, not detected and falsely detected actions were noted.

Overall 121 actions were performed of which 101 were correctly detected, 14 were not detected and 6 were falsely detected. Consequently a precision of 83.47% was achieved.

In order to evaluate the localization and prediction, a production process was imitated in which the human co-worker needed to handle objects at

Table 2. Example of the generated output of the multi-layered HMM action recognition

1	16-3-3-0	Observation sequence
2	Standing Up	Detected action
3	0.1225	Probability action
4	1	Generated symbol
5	Sitting >> Standing	Detected compound action
6	0.9704	Probability compound action

different work places. These places correspond to the setting as shown in Figure 4. Due to the modeling of locations as Gaussian distributions based on actual data the localization achieves a high rate of 100% accuracy. This is also due to the clear distinction between locations which allows for accurate clustering results of the DBSCAN algorithm. In productive environments this distinction is highly likely due to organizational structure of processes and equipment. In some respect this is also true for domestic environments, e.g. kitchens, where utensils and furniture define a structure in the environment and impose constraints on locations (Tenorth & Beetz, 2009).

Regarding the evaluation of the location prediction the predicted value was compared with the corresponding actual occurrence. During the process imitation the predictions and localization results were recorded for comparison. Thus, a prediction accuracy of 90.9% was achieved. Especially challenging are diagonal movements. As can be seen in Figure 4, the actual trajectory resembles more of a corner than a direct approach. This can lead to false intermediate predictions. Also of interest is the earliest possible time of prediction. On average, 29.63 processing cycles before reaching a new location a prediction was established. This relates to about 1.98 seconds with a frame rate of 15fps.

In Figure 6, different examples are presented which demonstrate the capability of the overall system. Icons symbolize the recognized actions, localization and prediction results, inferred situations and expectations.

The upper two images of Figure 6 show the influence of the location of the person. If the person is close to a table that the robot can reach the expectation *get beverage* is generated after the action *sit down* is recognized. The middle two images of Figure 6 depict the change of situations after the action *stand up* is identified. The situation *having a break* switches to the situation *distraction*. The generated expectations alternate accordingly from *get beverage* to *follow predefined path*. The bottom two images of Figure 6 demonstrate the expectation generation according to prediction results. As the human co-worker walks towards the workspace in which the robot is situated the corresponding expectation *change workspace* is emitted. If the human is walking towards the manual workspace this expectation cannot be concluded.

It is noteworthy that the system is so far not capable of object recognition. Thus, all reasoning about situations and expectations are purely based on recognized actions and spatial awareness. This renders the system prone to possible false reasoning based on misclassifications of actions. Consequently, the achieved precision of about 83% needs to be increased. Also, premature predictions might cause conclusions about expectations which might not be congruent with the actual situation. Thus, means of verification are needed to ensure error tolerance of the system. Nevertheless, the effectiveness of the integration of action recognition and spatio-temporal reasoning is demonstrated.

Figure 6. Different examples of recognized actions, locations, situation, and expectations

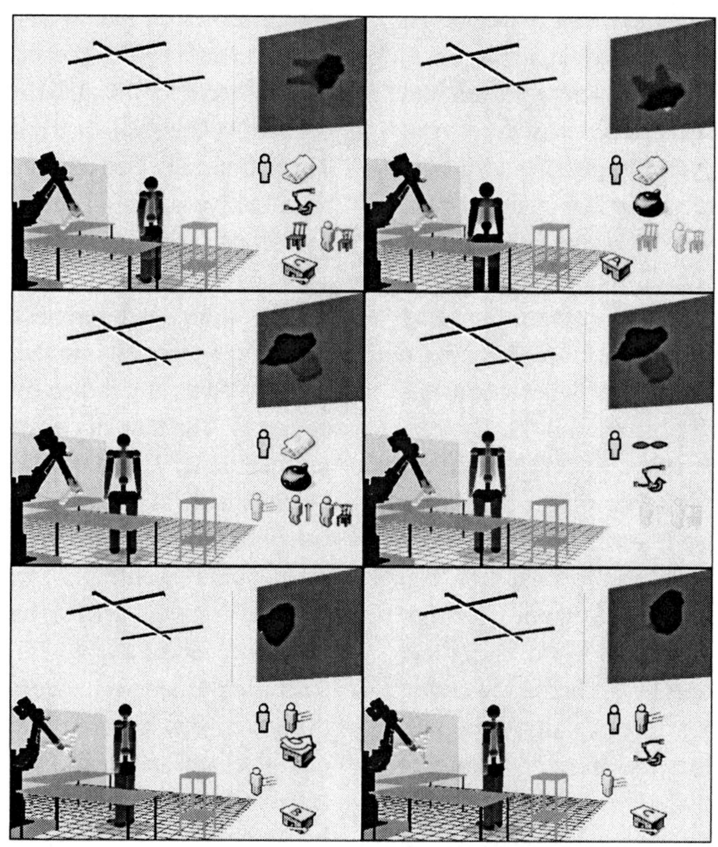

FUTURE RESEARCH DIRECTIONS

As demonstrated with the presented work and related research, using comprehensive approaches to situation awareness is the key for easier and seamless human-machine interfacing. Regardless of the scenario, e.g. industrial appliances or domestic services, it is necessary to take overall context information into account when interpreting human intentions and actions.

Considering specifically the presented work, there are a few main direction future researches will take. Incorporating more context information is also the basic principle. In order to cope with action recognition errors means need to be devised to validate the results. One such mean can be the incorporation of object recognition into the environment model and DL knowledge base. Recognition of *sitting down* might be inappropriate when no chair was recognized beforehand. Also more accurate spatial relations need to be modeled. Walking forwards is not feasible if a table is in front of the human – in contrast to table positions beside or behind the human. Moreover, objects and constraints on their usage can be incorporated into the knowledge base, e.g., a chair is not usable for sitting if the backrest is between human and seating area.

For encountering premature conclusions about expectations due to prediction inaccuracy context information about the production process can be used. Gaussian functions are well suited for incorporating additional knowledge. Through adjustment of co-variances and weighting of the overall function according to a process plan further knowledge can be exploited for a more robust prediction. By examining the localization results such a process plan could be extracted and enriched with knowledge about actions and situations. Thus, process identification and plan recognition can also enhance the user experience with the overall system. For example, during training of a new worker the steps could be checked against a plan and abnormalities could be registered and used as feedback for the trainee.

In the realm of production systems the trend towards robots being side by side with humans is emerging. On the one side, robots become available that are small, flexible and inherently safe, e.g. KUKA lightweight robot, ABB Frida robot or Rethink Robotics Baxter robot. On the other side, the interaction process is made safer and more intuitive for process engineers and workers, e.g. through companies like MRK-Systeme GmbH or research such as the presented work. Still, there are many open challenges before human and robot cooperation becomes a fact of daily work life. The here presented work has uncovered some of these challenges but there are numerous others, e.g. in the fields of data acquisition, data mining, machine learning and human cognitive processes to name a few.

CONCLUSION

Merging human intelligence and robotic capabilities in a productive system is a challenging task. The here presented work demonstrates a comprehensive approach to situation awareness in order to enable seamless interfacing between human and machine. As a part, a module for continuous action recognition was presented. It is based on the evaluation of multi-layered hierarchical Hidden Markov Models which model different actions through observation of motion direction.

Localizing the human co-worker in the workspace is important for defining the context in which actions take place. An approach is presented which allows for identifying dominant locations based on unsupervised clustering. This information is used for localization by modeling and evaluating Gaussian distributions of each cluster. These Gaussian distributions are also interpreted as attractive potential functions which serve for prediction through gradient ascending.

The results of both modules are used as input for the situation awareness module. Identified actions are inserted into the DL knowledge base as individuals and linked by relations with other concepts. The human co-worker is set in context of locations. Thus, the system for inferences about situations and expectation towards robotic behavior is augmented and allows for extended substantial reasoning.

The achieved HMM based action recognition precision of about 83% allows for confident reasoning. Due to reliance on recognition results the system can be prone to false reasoning based on misclassifications. The location prediction achieves over 90% accuracy in a production setup but is prone to erratic movement of the human co-worker. Still, the achievements allow already sophisticated interpretations of context and state of the scene.

The combination of each presented subsystem lays the foundation for seamless interfacing between human co-workers and robots. Achieving understanding for human behavior and situations enables intuitive human-robot interaction and cooperation. Thus, the achieved results are promising and encourage further research.

ACKNOWLEDGMENT

This work was supported in part by Baden-Württemberg Stiftung through the research project SILIA.

REFERENCES

Ashbrook, D., & Starner, T. (2002). Learning significant locations and predicting user movement with GPS. In *Proceedings of the Sixth International Symposium on Wearable Computers*, (pp. 101-108). IEEE.

Baader, F., Calvanese, D., McGuinness, D. L., Nardi, D., & Patel-Schneider, P. F. (2010). *The description logic handbook* (2nd ed.). Cambridge, UK: Cambridge University Press.

Bar-Shalom, Y., Li, X. R., & Kirubarajan, T. (2001). *Estimation with applications to tracking and navigation: Theory, algorithms, and software*. New York: Wiley. doi:10.1002/0471221279.

Choset, H., Lynch, K. M., Hutchinson, S., Kantor, G., Burgard, W., Kavraki, L. E., & Thrun, S. (2005). *Principles of robot motion*. London: MIT Press.

Delius, D. M., Plagemann, C., & Burgard, W. (2009). Probabilistic situation recognition for vehicular traffic scenarios. In *Proceedings of the IEEE International Conference on Robotics and Automation*. IEEE.

Elmezain, M., Al-Hamadi, A., Appenrodt, J., & Michaelis, B. (2008). A hidden Markov model-based continuous gesture recognition system for hand motion trajectory. In *Proceedings of the 19th International Conference on Pattern Recognition*. IEEE.

Elmezain, M., Al-Hamadi, A., & Michaelis, B. (2009). Improving hand gesture recognition using 3D combined features. In *Proceedings of 2nd International Conference on Machine Vision*. IEEE.

Ester, M., Kriegel, H. P., Sander, J., & Xu, X. (1996). A density-based algorithm for discovering clusters in large spatial databases with noise. In *Proceedings of the 2nd Int. Conf. on Knowledge Discovery and Data Mining (KDD-96)*. AAAI Press.

Graf, J., Puls, S., & Wörn, H. (2010). Recognition and understanding situations and activities with description logics for safe human-robot cooperation. In *Proceedings of Cognitive* (pp. 90–96). Cognitive.

Graf, J., & Wörn, H. (2009). Safe human-robot interaction using 3D sensor. In *Proceedings of VDI Automation*, (pp. 445-456). VDI.

Hummel, B., Thiemann, W., & Lulcheva, I. (2007). Description logics for vision-based intersection understanding. In Proceedings of Cognitive Systems with Interactive Sensors. Stanford.

Hwang, Y. K., & Ahuja, N. (1992). A potential field approach to path planning. *IEEE Transactions on Robotics and Automation*, *8*(1). doi:10.1109/70.127236.

Junxia, G., Xiaoqing, D., Shengjin, W., & Wu Youshou, W. (2008). Full body tracking-based human action recognition. In *Proceedings of the 19th International Conference on Pattern Recognition*. Tampa, Finland: IEEE.

Krüger, V., Kragic, D., Ude, A., & Geib, C. (2007). The meaning of action: A review on action recognition and mapping. *Proceedings of Advanced Robotics*, *21*, 1473–1501.

Lavee, G., Rivlin, E., & Rudzsky, M. (2009). Understanding video events: A survey of methods for automatic interpretation of semantic occurrences in video. *IEEE Transactions on Systems, Man and Cybernetics. Part C, Applications and Reviews*, *39*(5), 489–504. doi:10.1109/TSMCC.2009.2023380.

Loccoz, N. M., Brémond, F., & Thonnat, M. (2003). Recurrent Bayesian network for the recognition of human behaviours from video. In *Proceedings of the 3rd International Conference on Computer Vision Systems (ICVS'03)*. Graz, Austria: ICVS.

Mahajan, D., Kwatra, N., Jain, S., Kalra, P., & Banerjee, S. (2004). A framework for activity recognition and detection of unusual activities. In *Proceedings of ICVGIP*. Kolkata, India: ICVGIP.

Marmasse, N., & Schmandt, C. (2002). A user-centered location model. *Personal and Ubiquitous Computing*, *6*, 318–321. doi:10.1007/s007790200035.

Minnen, D., Essa, I., & Starner, T. (2003). Expectation grammars: Leveraging high-level expectations for activity recognition. [CVPR]. *Proceedings of Computer Vision and Pattern Recognition*, *2*, 626–632.

Möller, R., & Neumann, B. (2008). Ontology-based reasoning techniques for multimedia interpretation and retrieval. In *Semantic Multimedia and Ontologies* (pp. 55–98). London: Springer. doi:10.1007/978-1-84800-076-6_3.

Neumann, B., & Möller, R. (2008). On scene interpretation with description logics. *Image and Vision Computing*, *26*, 81–101. doi:10.1016/j.imavis.2007.08.013.

Park, S., & Aggarwal, J. K. (2004). A hierarchical Bayesian network for event recognition of human actions and interactions. *Multimedia Systems*, *10*(2), 164–179. doi:10.1007/s00530-004-0148-1.

Poppe, R. (2010). A survey on vision-based human action recognition. *Image and Vision Computing*, *28*, 976–990. doi:10.1016/j.imavis.2009.11.014.

Puls, S., Betz, P., Wyden, M., & Wörn, H. (2012b). Path planning for industrial robots in human-robot interaction. *IEEE/RSJ IROS Workshop on Robot Motion Planning: Online, Reactive, and in Real-Time*.

Puls, S., Graf, J., & Wörn, H. (2011). Design and evaluation of description logics based recognition and understanding of situations and activities for safe human-robot cooperation. *International Journal on Advances in Intelligent Systems*, *4*, 218–227.

Puls, S., Graf, J., & Wörn, H. (2012a). Cognitive robotics in industrial environments. In *Human Machine Interaction – Getting Closer*. Rijeka, Croatia: Academic Press. doi:10.5772/28130.

Puls, S., & Wörn, H. (2012). Combining HMM-based continuous human action recognition and spatio-temporal reasoning for augmented situation awareness. In *Proceedings of the IADIS International Conference on Interfaces and Human Computer Interaction* (pp. 133-140). IADIS.

Rabiner, L. R. (1989). A tutorial on hidden Markov models and selected applications in speech recognition. *Proceedings of the IEEE*, *77*(2), 257–286. doi:10.1109/5.18626.

Shi, Y., Huang, Y., Minnen, D., Bobick, A., & Essa, I. (2004). Propagation networks for recognition of partially ordered sequential action. [CVPR]. *Proceedings of Computer Vision and Pattern Recognition*, *2*, 862–869.

Springer, T., Wustmann, P., Braun, I., Dargie, W., & Berger, M. (2010). A comprehensive approach for situation-awareness based on sensing and reasoning about context. *Lecture Notes in Computer Science*, *5061*, 143–157. doi:10.1007/978-3-540-69293-5_13.

Sun, X., & Wang, J. (2010). Human action recognition based on projection and mass center movement features. In *Proceedings of the 8th World Congress on Intelligent Control and Automation*. Jinan, China: IEEE.

Tadokoro, S., Takebe, T., Ishikawa, Y., & Takamori, T. (1993). Control of human cooperative robots based on stochastic prediction of human motion. In *Proceedings of the 2nd IEEE International Workshop on Robot and Human Communication* (pp. 387-392). IEEE.

Tenorth, M., & Beetz, M. (2009). KNOWROB – Knowledge processing for autonomous personal robots. *IEEE International Conf. on Intelligent Robots and Systems (IROS)*. IEEE.

Wu, Y. C., Chen, H. S., Tsai, W. J., Lee, S. Y., & Yu, J. Y. (2008). Human action recognition based on layered-HMM. In *Proceedings of the IEEE International Conference on Multimedia and Expo*. Hannover, Germany: IEEE.

Yamada, N., Sakamoto, K., Kunito, G., Isoda, Y., Yamazaki, K., & Tanaka, S. (2007). Applying ontology and probabilistic model to human activity recognition from surrounding things. *IPSJ Digital Courier, 3*.

Zaidenberg, S., Brdiczka, O., Reignier, P., & Crowley, J. (2006). Learning context models for the recognition of scenarios. In *Artificial Intelligence Applications and Innovations*. Boston: Springer. doi:10.1007/0-387-34224-9_11.

ADDITIONAL READING

Baader, F., Calvanese, D., McGuinness, D. L., Nardi, D., & Patel-Schneider, P. F. (2010). *The description logic handbook*. Cambridge University Press.

Choset, H., Lynch, K. M., Hutchinson, S., Kantor, G., Burgard, W., Kavraki, L. E., & Thrun, S. (2005). *Principles of Robot Motion*. MIT Press.

Poppe, R. (2010). A survey on vision-based human action recognition. *Image and Vision Computing, 28*, 976–990. doi:10.1016/j.imavis.2009.11.014.

Rabiner, L. R. (1989). A tutorial on hidden markov models and selected applications in speech recognition. *Proceedings of the IEEE, 77*(2), 257–286. doi:10.1109/5.18626.

Russell, S., & Norvig, P. (2010). *Artificial intelligence: A modern approach*. New York: Prentice Hall.

KEY TERMS AND DEFINITIONS

Action Recognition: Recognizing human actions is a vivid research topic. Especially in the realm of human-computer interaction knowledge about performed actions can ease the interaction mechanisms.

Description Logics: DLs represent a logical formalism based on a fragment of first order logic. Due to the existence of sound, complete and terminating reasoning algorithms and underlying open world assumption DLs are have high potential in robotics applications.

Hidden Markov Models: Hidden Markov Models describe probabilistic processes and can be used to model human actions. They are well known based on the successful application in speech recognition.

Location Awareness: Locations are often linked to tasks or actions. Being aware of a user's location can imply spatial constraints or provide context and guide lines when identifying human actions.

Potential Field: Potential fields originate from describing gravity and magnetic fields. They can also be used for robot navigation and path planning.

Situation Awareness: Taking all information about actions, their temporal relationships, and spatial information for extracting knowledge about activities and the overall situation.

Spatio-Temporal Reasoning: Drawing conclusions and reasoning about spatial and temporal information, usually regarding human actions.

Chapter 8
Studying Natural Interaction in Multimodal, Multi-Surface, Multiuser Scenarios

Carlos Duarte
University of Lisbon, Portugal

Andreia Ribeiro
University of Lisbon, Portugal

Rafael Nunes
University of Lisbon, Portugal

ABSTRACT

Current technological apparati have made it possible for natural input systems to reach our homes, businesses, and learning sites. However, and despite some of these systems being already commercialized, there is still a pressing need to better understand how people interact with these apparati, given the whole array of intervening contextual factors. This chapter presents two studies of how people interact with systems supporting gesture and speech on different interaction surfaces: one supporting touch, the other pointing. The naturally occurring commands for both modalities and both surfaces have been identified in these studies. Furthermore, the studies show how surfaces are used, and which modalities are employed based on factors such as the number of people collaborating in the tasks and the placement of appearing objects in the system, thus contributing to the future design of such systems.

INTRODUCTION

Natural interaction technologies are becoming widely available nowadays. Gesture recognition is available in tablets and smartphones, but also in entertainment systems like Microsoft's Kinect. Speech recognition, available in some desktop operating systems for some time now, is also becoming mainstream in more recent smartphones. Traditionally, the major driving force for the development work in these systems has been the field of entertainment (Silva & Bowman, 2009). However, these technologies are reaching a maturing point that makes them available and desirable for other fields (Hinrichs & Carpendale, 2011; Morris, Wobbrock, & Wilson, 2010; Voida, Tobiasz, Stromer, Isenberg, & Carpendale, 2009).

To further strengthen this adoption process, a continuous process of understanding user interac-

DOI: 10.4018/978-1-4666-4623-0.ch008

tion in these scenarios is required. This chapter addresses this need by adopting the following complementary approaches. First, by exposing users to an interactive prototype, without imposed command languages or other technical restrictions, it is possible to elicit the language users naturally employ in different modalities when interacting with the system. Second, by deploying a prototype based on the elicited commands, it is possible to study natural interaction in scenarios characterized by diverse surfaces and number of users.

In this chapter, we present two studies aiming to increase the knowledge regarding gestural and speech interaction in scenarios with interactive surfaces. In the first study, a single surface out of the participants' reach is used. In the second study, we added an interactive touch surface to the initial set-up.

These studies focused initially on understanding how the characteristics of the performed action influenced the way modalities were used. This was followed by analyzing what is the impact on the usage of different surfaces and different modalities of the number of people interacting with the system, and of the application behavior when it comes to rendering new objects.

This chapter is organized in the following way. It starts by reviewing relevant work related to gesture and speech interaction, and to previous efforts on finding how users interact with this technology. It then briefly motivates to the use of the aforementioned two stages approach. The following section presents the first study, conducted with only a single surface. The ensuing section describes the second study, with two surfaces with different characteristics. In each of these sections, the findings and results from the two stages are presented and discussed. The last two sections consider future directions for this technology, and conclude the chapter proposing some design recommendations on the use of multiple modalities and multiple surfaces.

BACKGROUND

Gestural interaction is becoming pervasive. It can be found in tablets and smartphones, who offer their users touch based interfaces, supporting direct manipulation and semaphoric gestures (Quek et al., 2002). Microsoft Kinect and other entertainment systems support deictic and semaphoric gestures also. While people interact naturally with each other through gestures, gesture dictionaries are still required for HCI. This has been acknowledged in several works that tried to understand how people interact with computers through gestures (Kurdyukova, Redlin, & André, 2012; Miki, Miyajima, Nishino, Kitaoka, & Takeda, 2008; Wobbrock, Morris, & Wilson, 2009; Yin & Davis, 2010).

While some gestures have become standard for performing actions (e.g. pinch for zooming), there is still a need to characterize the way people perform general actions in a computing environment (Dang, Straub, & André, 2009; Epps, Lichman, & Wu, 2006; Neca & Duarte, 2011). These studies show that people not only present variability in the gestures they make for each command, but also in how they make it (e.g. by using different hand posture). This impacts the interaction design of applications that want to make use of gestures, but also the way gesture recognizers need to perform. Two of the major problems identified are: (1) people perform the same gesture for different actions; and (2) people find it very difficult to come up with gestures for actions that can not be addressed through direct manipulation (e.g. deleting an object in an interactive space without a recycle bin to drop the object into).

One way to address these problems is to combine gestural with speech interaction (Bourguet & Ando, 1998; Neca & Duarte, 2011; Tse, Greenberg, & Shen, 2006). When speech is available as an input modality, the way gestures are used changes, assuming more of a supporting role, providing arguments for the action specified in the speech command (e.g. pointing at an object while speaking the command "delete"). While the variability in the use of gestures is diminished with the introduction of spoken commands, the variability in speech commands needs now to be addressed also.

A further problem that needs to be attended to when supporting speech interaction, in scenarios with more than one interactive surface, is how to disambiguate between possible target surfaces for each command. A common strategy is to name each surface and precede the command with the surface's name, a strategy already used naturally by people (Sung, Grinter, & Christensen, 2009). Without such a solution, this problem would even be more serious in collaborative scenarios, which can be expected to happen when multiple surfaces are available. While it is hard to predict how groups coordinate their actions when supported by an interactive table (Tang, Tory, Po, Neumann, & Carpendale, 2006), it has been shown that integrating gestures, speech and interactive surfaces can improve the efficiency in collaborative scenarios (Cunningham, Close, Thomas, & Hutterer, 2010; Müller-Tomfelde, Cheng, & Li, 2011; Shaer et al., 2011; Voida et al., 2009).

The studies presented in this chapter expand on this body of knowledge, by exploring natural interaction languages, initially without imposing command dictionaries to the study participants, and then by deploying fully interactive prototypes, where the recognizers have been trained to understand the natural commands elicited before. We conducted studies focused on understanding the problems raised above, with a special emphasis on interactive surfaces, with or without touch support, and considering the impact of actions available, number of surfaces, number of users, and some specific application behaviors related to surface usage, on the way that people use the available modalities and surfaces.

DEALING WITH CONSTRAINTS WHEN STUDYING NATURAL MODALITIES

In order to better understand how people interact using gestural and speech modalities, we decided to first observe how people interact without technology imposed constraints, in such scenarios. By technology imposed constraints we refer to the need of current gesture and speech recognizers to resort to a command dictionary. Consequently, each of our studies consisted of two experiments. The first experiment relied on a Wizard of Oz approach, where the role of the recognizers was played by a researcher that interpreted the trial participant's commands, and initiated the corresponding action in the interface. This was applied to both gesture and speech commands. All other support was provided by the prototype (e.g. cursor tracking was supported by a Kinect). In the second experiment, all interaction was fully supported by the prototype. Command dictionaries for the recognizers were built based on the results from the previous experiment. No participant took part in both experiments of the same study. This allowed us to verify if the natural interaction language that was elicited in the initial study holds up in a fully working prototype, with different users, and, consequently, if we can have any guarantee that those commands are general enough, for applications with the same characteristics.

Furthermore, we wanted to understand how other constraints like the number of surfaces available, or the number of people interacting, impact the way modalities are used. To this end we envisaged two studies: an initial study to better understand how people interact through gestures and speech with a single interactive surface out of their physical reach; and a second study, expanding on the knowledge gained in the first study, by including a second, touchable, surface that communicates with the first surface. In the following sections we describe both studies and the lessons learned.

THE SINGLE SURFACE STUDY – UNDERSTANDING THE USE OF SPEECH AND GESTURES

The first study aims at understanding how tasks with different characteristics influence the way people interact with gestures as a single modality, or with gestures and speech combined. Actions were characterized by requiring, or not, manipulation of interface objects. This study focused on perceiving what tasks are more easily done with a single modality or with a combination of modalities, and the way modalities are used changes. For this purpose, we considered a projected surface, with which the users were allowed to interact with through gestures and speech.

First Experiment

Initially we designed an experiment where participants were asked to perform tasks in two photo browsing and manipulation applications. The experiment was setup as a Wizard of Oz experiment, where the participant and the Wizard controlled applications jointly. The participant was in control of a cursor through pointing recognition. Cursor control was implemented resorting to a Microsoft Kinect. Commands issued by the participant were interpreted by the Wizard, who was responsible for inputting them using keyboard shortcuts. We opted to use two applications instead of one to understand the possible impact of a 3D space in the tasks performed. One application was purely 2D, with non-overlapping photos that could be browsed and zoomed in and out. The other application worked in a 3D space, where photos could overlap and be freely moved in the 3 dimensions (e.g. zooming in meant bringing the photo closer to you).

Experimental Set-Up

The experiments were conducted in a spacious and evenly lit room. The participants stood about 2 meters (7 feet) from the wall where the applications were being projected. The Wizard stood behind and to the side of the participant, with a clear view to both participant and projection. Ten participants, with an average age of 22 years, took part in this experiment. We tried to sample a population that was representative of future users of these interactive systems. Eight out of the ten had more than 10 years' experience using computers. All knew at least one device capable of gestural interaction and two were regular users of such devices. Eight out of the ten knew at least one device with voice input capabilities, and one used it regularly.

In order to keep from influencing the gesture and speech commands used, we asked participants to perform general (e.g. find the white daisy and count its petals) instead of specific tasks (e.g. browse 3 times to the left and zoom in on the white daisy picture). This allowed us to learn what gestures are made and what speech commands are uttered without leading the participants in any direction.

Sessions were videotaped and later analyzed to identify the different gestures and speech commands issued by participants.

Discussion

In this analysis we are not going to focus on which gestures were performed and what speech commands were issued for each action that had to be performed (see (Neca & Duarte, 2011) for that kind of analysis). Instead, here we aim to abstract those behaviors, and try to find the task characteristics that make people use one modality or the other, or use them in a combined fashion. In the following paragraphs a discussion on three dimensions of this analysis is presented: how the nature of the task impacts modality combination; how modality usage influences the content transmitted in each modality; how the spatial nature of the task impacts the gestures performed.

The first finding is that actions which do not imply object manipulation (e.g. delete, undo or redo) require the use of voice commands in combination with pointing. Otherwise, our observations showed that participants face great difficulty in completing the action, and the gestures made were too diverse to be manageable by a recognition based system. When using speech (combined with pointing when deleting) no difficulties were felt and the response was homogeneous. Actions that manipulated objects (e.g. move, rotate) were primarily performed through gestures, with speech, when used, conveying redundant information. It was also observed that people perform the same gesture with different meanings. When this happened, speech used redundantly proved valuable in disambiguating the intended meaning.

The information transmitted in one modality changes based on whether it is used alone or combined with other. When solely using gestures, these convey the action made and the target of the action. When speech is combined with gestures, speech is used almost exclusively to convey the action, while the gesture conveys the target of the action (e.g. by pointing) or an argument of the action (e.g. the amount which an object should be rotated). Almost no use of speech alone was observed, which can be explained by the graphical nature of the applications. This information was used to good advantage in the optimization of the different recognizers and the configuration of the multimodal fusion engine employed in the system.

Depth was only relevant in interpreting the gesture made when the action manipulated the depth of the object. This showed that a direct mapping between gesture and action extends to the 3D space. But it also showed that depth was not used to convey other types of information. For instance, there are approaches (Liu & Fujimura, 2004) where depth information is used for selection (e.g. point to an object and then stretch or retract the arm to select it). In our unconstrained environment, participants did not feel the need to resort to depth information unless they were manipulating the depth of the object in the 3D space.

Second Experiment

After the first experiment, a second experiment, with full technological support was conducted. Speech and gesture recognizers, trained with the commands learned in the first experiment were deployed. In order to assess if these commands are scalable to other domains, we added another scenario to the experiment. The new scenario consisted in browsing the Google Earth application with gesture and speech commands.

For the second experiment a total of 15 people participated, with an average age of 24 years. No participant took part in both experiments. Technical details and set-up were similar to the first experiment. The major difference was that a Wizard was not required anymore. Similarly to the first experiment, sessions were also videotaped for later analysis.

Discussion

The most important conclusion from this experiment was that the findings from the unconstrained environment translated without a problem to a technically constrained environment. Different participants were able to interact and perform the requested tasks without difficulties. Gesture and speech recognizers performed as requested with the given vocabularies and the fusion engine was capable of correctly interpreting the user commands. A couple of interesting observations are discussed in the following paragraphs.

Approximately half of the test participants (6 out of 15) switched pointing hands during the trials depending on the placement of the target. If a picture was on the left side of the projection surface they used their left hand. If it was on the right side, they used their right hand. The remainder participants used always their dominant hand, independently of the target placement. This kind of knowledge can be useful for an adaptive system. It can be exploited in two manners: to optimize the operation of the gesture recognizer; and to optimize item placement by favoring placement of selectable objects on the side of the user's dominant hand.

Another trend that was observed in this experiment was how the number of targets of the action seemed to influence the use of modalities. Whenever the action encompassed several images (e.g. moving a group of images from one side of the projection surface to the other) participants employed both modalities redundantly. If the target of the action was a single image it was more likely that only a gesture was performed without any spoken command.

THE MULTIPLE SURFACE STUDY – STUDYING THE IMPACT OF MULTIPLE USERS AND MULTIPLE SURFACES ON MODALITY USE

In order to continue studying the usage of speech and gestures in interactive scenarios we introduced an extra surface, touchable, in addition to the existing one. Similarly to what was done in the previous study, two experiments were conducted. In the initial experiment, the goal was to identify what commands, in each modality and in each surface, people naturally use. In the second experiment, the goal was to study the impact of certain factors on the usage of multi-surface, multiuser, multimodal applications. Both experiments resorted to a prototype of a collaborative vacation planning application.

First Experiment

In the first experiment, the prototype was deployed on two surfaces: (1) a multitouch table; and (2) a projected surface with a Kinect for gesture recognition. Objects could be exchanged between surfaces. It was possible to create copies of objects that could then be synchronized, so that operations performed in one copy were replicated in the other.

Given the aim of the first experiment, no gesture recognition nor speech recognition was performed, and a Wizard of Oz technique was employed. The table was capable of processing touch selections, and the Kinect was able to track pointing in the projected surface. Both gesture and speech recognition were performed by the Wizard. In this experiment it was possible to: identify and compare the gestures made in each of the surfaces; identify and compare the speech commands used in combination with gestures; improve the graphical icons used to describe the actions that can be performed on each object.

As aforementioned, the application used in these experiments was a vacation planning application. It was supported by the architecture presented in Figure 1. Touch based interaction is directly processed in the application controlling the interactive table. Gesture and speech commands are recognized by a Kinect, and then processed in a multimodal fusion component. The recognized commands are then dispatched to the table application, where they can be fused with touch

Figure 1. Architecture of the multi-surface prototype

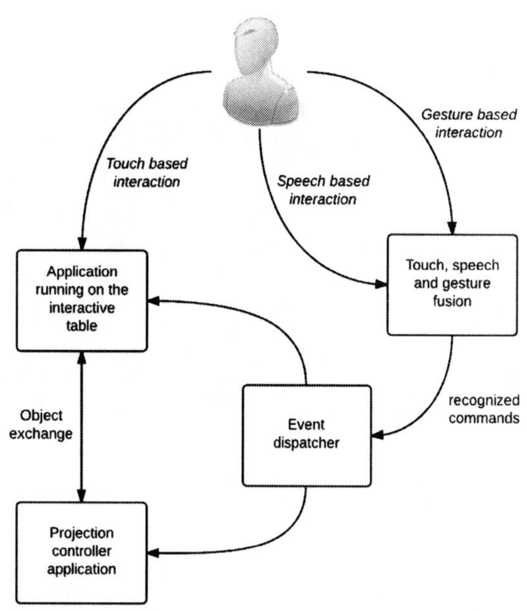

events, or to the projection application, depending on their target. Both the table and the projection applications are capable of exchanging objects between themselves.

The application supports browsing of hotels, restaurants, photos and information about specific sites of a city. This information is organized hierarchically and can be browsed in independent objects or displayed spatially in a map. Figure 2 presents a view of the interactive table's interface. It shows a map with interesting spots highlighted, one of them presented in the object to the right of the map. The projected surface is rendered in the same fashion. Objects can be created by interacting with existing objects (e.g. selecting one of the items highlighted in the map creates an object with the description of the item). Copies of objects can be created from the objects themselves and then synchronized if the user wishes. Objects can also be moved (including to the other surface), minimized (and restored) and destroyed. All the options can be achieved through any of the available modalities or combinations of modalities.

In order to understand what gestures and speech commands people make when interacting without command dictionary restrictions, an experiment with this prototype was conducted using the aforementioned Wizard of Oz technique. Technically, the prototype followed the architecture presented in Figure 1, without the recognition components, which were replaced by a human operator. Kinect was still used to track pointing.

Procedure

The trial begun with an explanation of the application and its purpose. The participant's profile was then collected. Participants were then asked to perform three groups of tasks. In group A, participants were asked to identify the meaning of each graphical control displayed in the interface. In group B, participants were asked to perform a series of tasks in both surfaces using only gestures. In group C, participants were asked to perform the same tasks in both surfaces, but they were now allowed to use speech commands if they wished. All participants began by performing group A

Figure 2. Example view of the interactive table surface

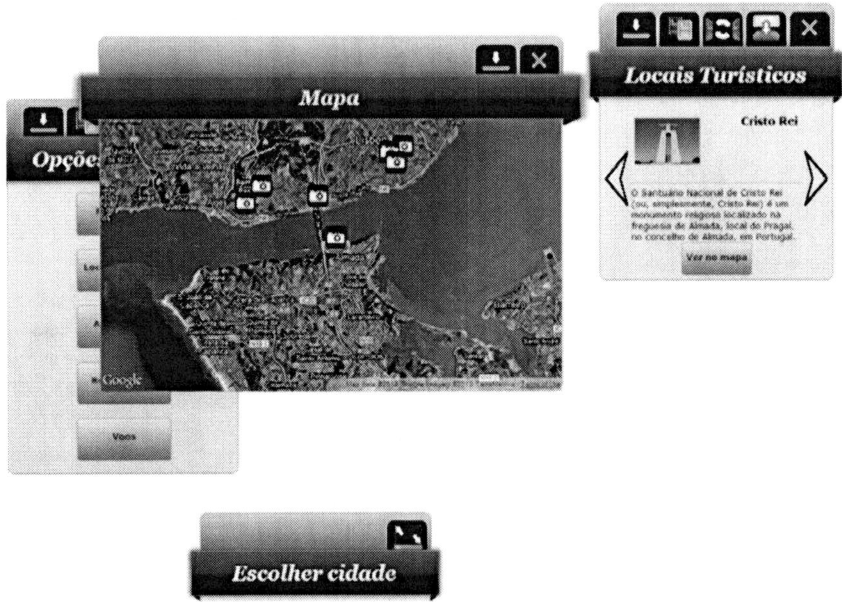

tasks. Half of the participants then performed group B tasks before performing group C tasks, while the other half did these tasks in reverse order. The tasks participants were requested to perform included: (1) move an object from one surface to the other; (2) synchronize two objects; (3) minimize an object; (4) copy an object; and (5) move an object inside the same surface.

Participants

A total of 19 people participated in this experiment. Their average age was 25 years, and four of them were female. Eighteen reported to have prior experience with some kind of touch based interaction device (smartphones and tablets). Only one reported to have experience with an interactive table. Fourteen reported to have experience with gesture based devices like Nintendo's Wii, Sony's PS3 Move and Microsoft's Kinect. Twelve of the participants reported having prior experience with voice based interfaces in smartphone applications.

Results and Discussion

Group A tasks supported the improvement of the graphical icons used, since it was found that the meaning of the icon used for synchronization was not understandable for the trial participants.

Gestures Only

Table 1 presents the most common gesture performed for each of the tasks in the interactive table and the projection surface, together with the percentage of users that performed it and the number of alternatives proposed by the users that performed other gestures. As can be easily perceived from the table, there is no doubt about how to minimize, maximize or send objects to other surfaces. However, performing copy and synchronization actions is not clear, in particular in the projection surface. Additionally, minimize and maximize gestures are difficult to distinguish from the send to other surface gestures.

Gestures and Speech

Table 2 presents the most common gesture and speech commands performed for each of the tasks in the interactive table and projection surface, together with the percentage of users that performed it and the number of alternatives proposed by the participants that performed other gestures. Comparing with the gestures only results, it can be seen that there are no longer any actions with low agreement rates, and the previously most troublesome action (synchronize) is now the only one with full agreement between all participants. However, the number of actions that have more alternatives has grown due, mainly, to variability in the speech commands used, not in the gestures

Table 1. Gestures performed on the interactive surface without speech

	Interactive Surface			Projection Surface		
Action	**Gesture**	**Agreed**	**Alternatives**	**Gesture**	**Agreed**	**Alternatives**
Minimize	Swipe down	100%	0	Swipe down	100%	0
Maximize	Drag up	100%	0	Drag up	100%	0
Copy	Double tap	78.9%	3	Grab with one hand and pull with the other	47.4%	3
Synchronize	Overlap objects	68.4%	2	Overlap objects	42.1%	2
Send to surface	Swipe up	100%	0	Swipe down	100%	0

Table 2. Gestures performed on the interactive surface with speech

	Interactive Surface			Projection Surface		
Action	Command	Agreed	Alternatives	Command	Agreed	Alternatives
Minimize	Touch object and speak "hide"	84.2%	2	Grab object and speak "hide"	84.2%	2
Maximize	Touch object and speak "show"	73.7%	3	Grab object and speak "show"	73.7%	3
Copy	Touch object and speak "copy"	73.7%	1	Grab object and speak "copy"	73.7%	1
Synchronize	Touch both objects and speak "sync"	100%	0	Grab both objects and speak "sync"	100%	0
Send to surface	Touch object and speak "send"	84.2%	1	Grab object and speak "send"	84.2%	1

(e.g. for the maximize action most participants used "show", but "reveal" and "restore" were also used).

Another important aspect that was observed was the shorter time required by participants to complete the command when they could complement gestures with speech commands. This was due to the difficulty to come up with a gesture for the "copy" and, especially, the "synchronize" actions. This difficulty was no longer felt when speech was a possibility.

Besides contributing to the identification of gestural and speech commands, this first experiment contributed to strengthen the decision to support multimodal interaction, since it became clear that having multiple modalities to complete available actions helps users by giving them options that best fit their mental models for each action.

Second Experiment

In the second experiment, the same setup was used, but the prototype was endowed with gesture and speech recognition (also performed by the Kinect) capabilities. The gesture and speech command dictionaries were built based on the results of the previous experiment. With this fully interactive system we investigated how factors related to the use and the design of a multimodal, multi-surface, multiuser application can impact the usage of modalities and surfaces by their users.

Three independent variables were controlled in this study:

- **Number of Users:** Groups of 1, 2 or 3 users participated in the trial.
- **Surface for Copied Objects:** In one condition copies of objects appeared in the same surface as the object being copied, while in the other condition they appeared in the other surface.
- **Surface for New Objects:** In the first condition new objects always appeared in the interactive table, in the second condition they always appeared in the projection surface, and in the third condition they appeared in the same surface of the object that created the new object (in this condition, the first object appeared in the interactive table).

The prototype logged and measured: 1) to what surface was a command issued to; and 2) in what modality was a command issued. Every command could be issued in the modality, or combination of modalities, participants wished to. For the remainder of this section, the modalities will be referred to as pointing (for pointing at targets or selecting targets by touch), gestures (for performing gestures in either of the surfaces) and speech (for every command including speech).

The study was designed as a between subjects experiment. This resulted in a total of 18 runs (3 conditions for the number of users, times two conditions for the surface of copies, times 3 conditions for the surface of new objects).

Procedure

Each trial begun with an explanation of the application's goal (plan a vacation) and of the interactive system. The available gesture and speech commands were not presented to the participants. The participants' profiles were collected after this introduction. Then, the group was asked to perform several tasks: (1) pick a city as the travel destination; (2) browse the city's photographs and pick the two most interesting ones; (3) browse the city's tourist attractions and pick three as a travel priority; (4) find a 3 star hotel in a given district; (5) find the cheapest hotel in three adjoining districts; (6) look for restaurants near that hotel; (7) select the restaurants to visit together with your travel partners that are sitting at the back of the room (role played by members of the research team); and (8) book a flight to that destination. After the tasks were completed, each participant of the group was asked to fill a questionnaire with questions regarding their experience with the application.

Participants

A total of 36 participants took part in the experiment. Their age ranged from 18 to 30 years old, and eleven of them were female. Thirty-four participants reported having experience with touch devices, and ten with gestural interaction. Eight reported experience with speech interaction. Neither of the participants that took place in the first experiment participated in the second experiment.

Results

In the following paragraphs we present the statistical analysis of the collected results. Distributions of commands per surface and per modality, according to the different independent variables, were analyzed with MANOVA tests. Prior to MANOVA testing, univariate normality was assessed with Kolmogorov-Smirnov tests, and multivariate normality tested with Mahalanobis distance at an alpha level of *0.001*. The analysis of participant's answers to the questionnaire was conducted with non-parametric tests, namely χ^2 and Kruskal-Wallis tests.

Figure 3 shows the distribution of commands issued in each of the surfaces, according to the number of people in the group. To assess this effect a MANOVA analysis was conducted and found the number of people in the group had a significant effect on the number of commands issued in each surface ($F(5,28)=22.495$, $P<0.0005$, Wilk's $\lambda=0.03$, partial $\eta^2=0.828$).

Testing between subjects effects showed that this effect was significant both in the interactive table ($F(3,15)=150.74$, $P<0.0005$) and the projection surface ($F(3,15)=16.84$, $P<0.0005$). Tukey's HSD tests with Bonferroni adjustments did not find significant differences in the interactive table between groups of one and two people ($P=0.359$), one and three people ($P=0.05$) and two and three people ($P=0.48$). For the projected surface no significant effects were felt between groups of one and two people ($P=0.588$), one and three people ($P=0.176$) and two and three people ($P=0.655$).

Figure 4 shows the effect of the number of people in the group on the number of commands issued in each modality. Once again a MANOVA analysis was conducted and found the number of people in the group had a significant effect on the number of commands issued in each modality ($F(8,45)=15.123$, $P<0.0005$, Wilk's $\lambda=0.017$, partial $\eta^2=0.741$).

Figure 3. Effect of the number of people in a group on the number of commands issued in each surface

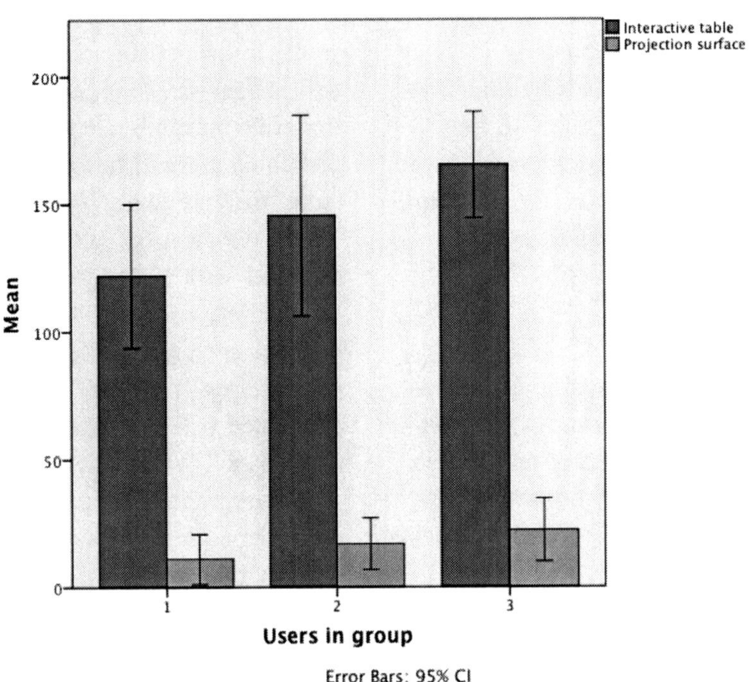

Figure 4. Effect of the number of people in a group on the number of commands issued in each modality

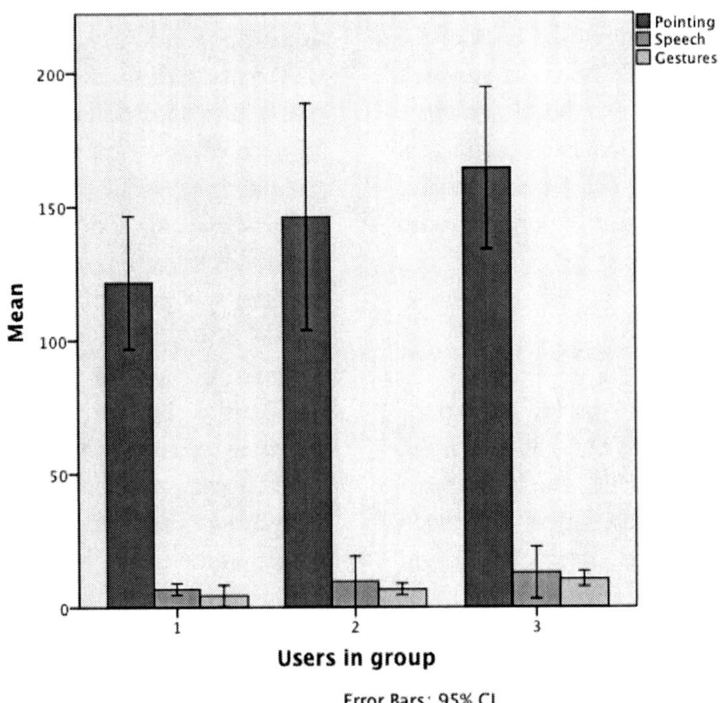

Similar to the previous analysis, tests of between subjects effects found statistical significance on the effect of the number of people in the group in the commands issued through pointing ($F(3,15)=125.563$, $P<0.0005$), through speech ($F(3,15)=10.822$, $P<0.0005$) and through gestures ($F(3,15)=40.605$, $P<0.0005$). Tukey's HSD with Bonferroni adjustments tests were used to search for significant effects in each of the modalities. No significant effects were found for pointing between groups of one and two persons ($P=0.397$), one and three ($P=0.082$) and two and three ($P=0.593$). For speech commands no significant effects were found between groups of one and two persons ($P=0.793$), one and three ($P=0.373$) and two and three ($P=0.749$). For gestural commands a statistically significant difference was found between groups of one and three participants ($P=0.006$), but not between groups of one and two ($P=0.374$) and two and three ($P=0.091$).

Afterwards we assessed the impact of the surface where copies appeared. Figure 5 shows whether participants agreed with the behavior or not, as collected in the questionnaire. All the participants for whom the copies appeared in the same surface of the object being copied agreed with the behavior. On the other hand, only one third of the participants who experienced the contrary behavior agreed with it. A χ^2 test found a significant effect of the surface where a copy appears on the participants' satisfaction with the behavior ($\chi^2(1,36)=18$, $P<0.0005$).

Figure 6 shows how the surface where new objects appear impacts the surface usage. A MANOVA analysis failed to find any statistical significance ($F(5,28)=1.344$, $P=0.278$, Wilk's $\lambda=0.704$, partial $\eta^2=0.161$).

Figure 7 shows the effect of the same variable on modality usage. A MANOVA analysis failed once again to find any statistical significance

Figure 5. Participants opinion regarding copies behavior

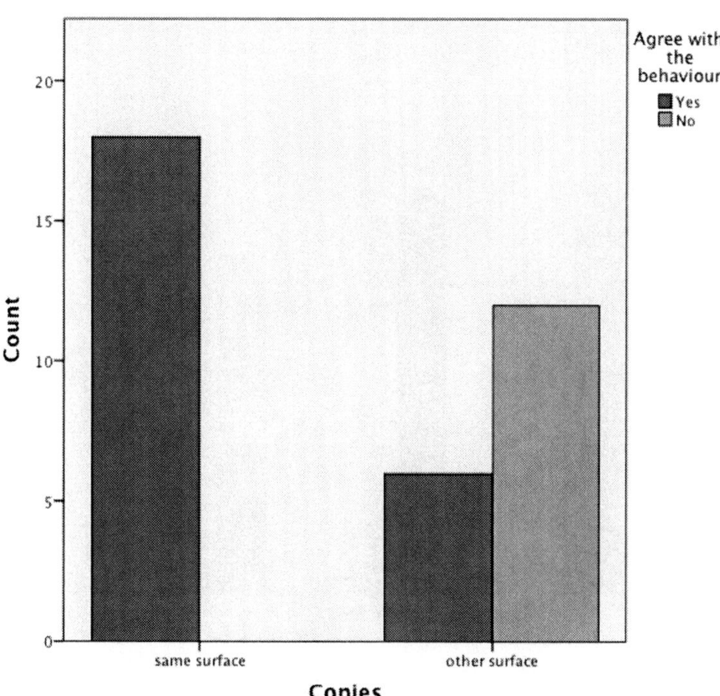

Figure 6. Effect of the surface where new objects appear on the number of commands issued in each surface

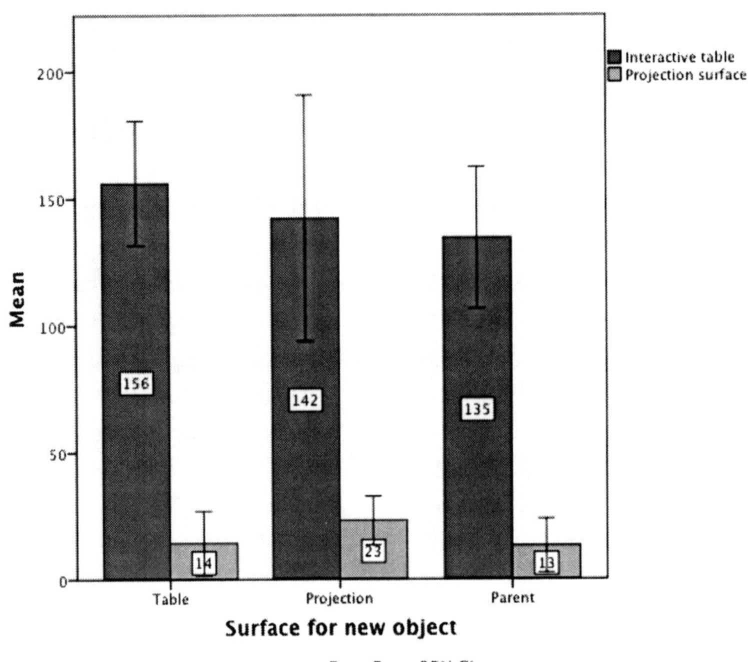

Figure 7. Effect of the surface where new objects appear on the number of commands issued in each modality

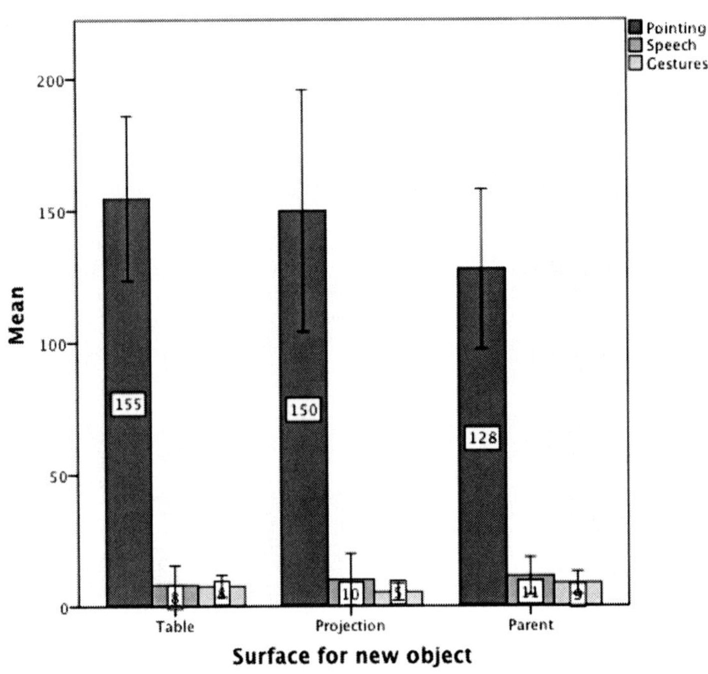

($F(5,26)=1.073, P=0.404$, Wilk's $\lambda=0.643$, partial $\eta^2=0.198$).

Figure 8 shows the participants opinion about the behavior for presenting new objects. The tendency is for the majority of the participants to agree with the behavior they experienced. A χ^2 test failed to find any effect of the surface where new objects appear on the participants agreement with the behavior ($\chi^2(2,36)=3.938$, $P=0.14$).

Figure 9 shows general satisfaction metrics. As can be seen both speech and gesture commands were evaluated positively by the study participants. Speech commands were more satisfactory, nevertheless. Still, such a positive evaluation validates the results of the first experiment, meaning the dictionaries built from those results proved adequate for use by different people. Additionally, it can be seen that both values for general satisfaction with the application, and the desire to use a system like this again in the future were also evaluated positively.

A Kruskal-Wallis test was applied to try to find any effect of the number of people in the group in any of the satisfaction variables. No significant effect was found.

Discussion

Based on the results found in this experiment, it is possible to gain extra knowledge that might prove useful when designing multi-surface, multiuser applications.

The first set of results concerns the number of people interacting with an application. Even though the tasks performed were exactly the same for all groups, it was possible to observe that the number of commands issued for the same group of tasks increases with the number of elements in the group performing the tasks. Moreover, it was possible to conclude that this effect is significant both when considering the surfaces used and the modalities used. This result is of importance to

Figure 8. Participants opinion regarding new objects behavior

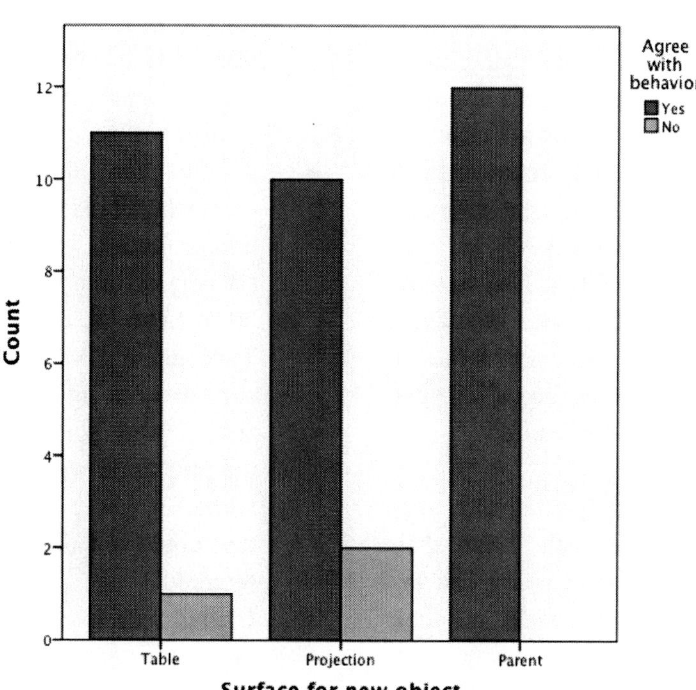

Figure 9. General satisfaction metrics

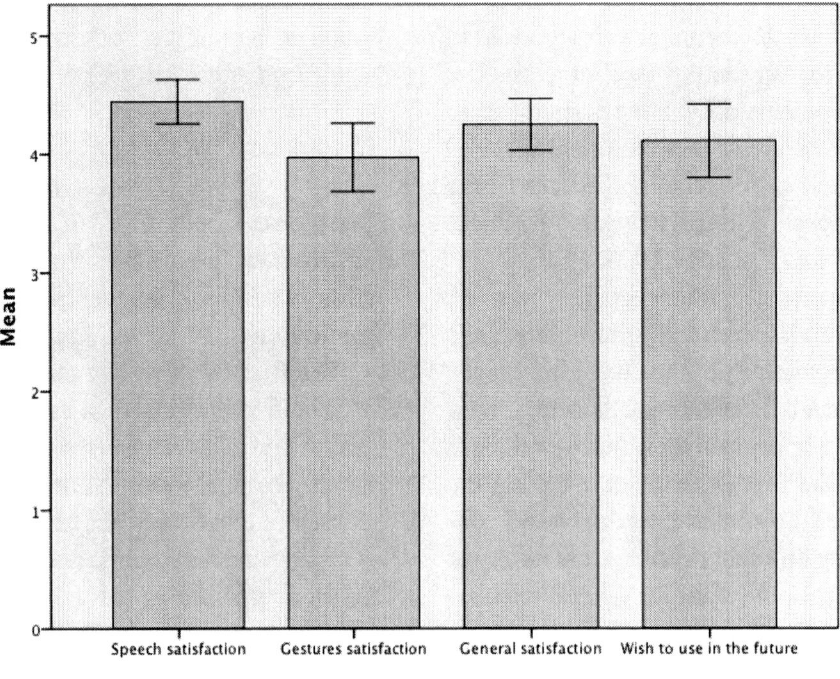

interactive system designers. If the system is to be used collaboratively, it should be prepared for an increasing load when the number of users increases. Users will tend to distribute responsibilities between themselves, but not in a clear and exclusive manner. This means that some users will repeat what others are already doing, resulting in an increased number of commands.

From the first set of results it also became obvious that, given the surfaces and modalities available, all participants largely opted for touch interaction in the interactive surface. There can be various explanations for this result:

- This was the modality participants were already more familiar with. From their reports, a large majority already had experience with touch interfaces on their smartphones or tablets. They easily translated this experience to the touch surface available, thus justifying the preference for the interactive table over the projection surface, and for direct manipulation through touch, over speech commands or semaphoric gestures.
- Touching an interactive surface is more comfortable than pointing at an interactive projection, especially for long periods (Banerjee, Burstyn, Girouard, & Vertegaal, 2012; Schmidt, Block, & Gellersen, 2009; Tuddenham, Kirk, & Izadi, 2010). This can contribute to understand why most interactions were performed on the table, and the projection was mostly reserved for the scenarios where a discussion with people that could not directly see the table was required.
- Using speech commands in multiuser interactive scenarios where you expect verbal communication to occur between

group members can be confusing (Tse, Greenberg, Shen, Forlines, & Kodama, 2008). This, together with not wanting to interrupt ongoing conversations, contributes to a lower usage of speech commands. Still, even in the single participant condition, speech was used as frequently as in the multi participant conditions. This is an indication that the speed of interaction that direct manipulation through touch allows, combined with the lower cognitive demand of direct touch when compared to discourse preparation, makes speech a less desired modality for tasks similar to the ones that were performed in this experiment.

The second and third group of results are more relevant to application designers, since they directly relate to the behavior of application elements, in particular where application elements should appear. Although no impact on the surface and modalities usage was found, it is important to stress out that the participants' reaction to the elements behavior was different depending on whether new elements or copied elements were considered.

When considering copies, it was clear that participants felt that copies should appear in the same surface of the object being copied. However, when considering new objects, there was not a clear indication as to what should be the default behavior. Participants positively assessed the three conditions in the experiment. A small tendency could be perceived in the fact that the only condition that had no negative feedback was the one where the behavior was similar to the discussed above for copies. The participants' behavior observed in the trials is consistent with the analysis of their answers to the questionnaire. It was observed that copies were frequently moved to the same surface of the original element when appearing in the other surface. It was also observed that new objects were often moved to the surface that was being used when not appearing there. Still, reactions about the place of appearance of new objects in different surfaces did not evoke the same feelings of frustration that appearance of copies in different surfaces did.

One of the application's features that was deemed relevant by participants, and which probably is the least common of all features, is the capability to synchronize objects. It was possible to recognize, from the comments made, but also from direct observation, how synchronization was important, particularly in multiple user scenarios. When something needed to be discussed inside the group, or between the group and the audience, the most common observed behavior consisted in creating a copy of the object, synchronizing it with the original, sending the copy to the projection surface, and then manipulate the original in the table, with the results of the manipulation being available to the audience or the rest of the group's elements through the projection. This was obviously useful for sharing information with the audience that had no access to the interactive table. More surprising was that it was also used to present information to group elements that were standing across the table, and that, in the table, would see the manipulated object upside down. If the object was projected in the projection surface that problem was solved.

The fact that participants preferred to copy and synchronize an object, instead of manipulating it directly on the projection surface, is also a clear indication of the preference for using the interactive table. Even though they could perform the same actions in both surfaces, the efficiency of direct manipulation through touch on the table, made participants adopt this behavior.

Other contributions for application development are, on the one hand, the gesture and speech commands dictionaries that have been elicited in the first experiment (which were used without any complaints by a different population in the second experiment – without informing that population of what commands were available), and, on the other hand, the command elicitation process.

For applications with similar characteristics to the one used in this experiment, the command dictionaries here described can be adopted. But, more importantly, the command elicitation process presented in this chapter can be applied to discover what are the most appropriate commands in other domain areas, or in settings with different interaction possibilities.

Finally, it is worth noticing, not only the positive indicators of satisfaction, but, more importantly, the response regarding the perceived usefulness of the collaborative multi-surface setup. Almost all participants found it useful, and several suggested possible real world scenarios where they envisioned this technology being applied, including business meetings, training actions and medical appointments among others.

FUTURE RESEARCH DIRECTIONS

Multimodal interaction is coming out of the labs and entering our homes, with entertainment systems (e.g. gaming consoles, and more recently, TV systems) being the main culprit. As such, it is of paramount importance that the way people interact with such systems is studied in order to improve their adoption. Current technical advances make it easier to deploy multiple interaction modalities. These have the advantage of being more natural to use than the traditional keyboard and mouse, so, it can be expected that for non-office tasks, they will be quickly adopted.

One particular way that multimodal interaction can be explored is adaptation to users and context of use, in order to increase both the user experience, and the accessibility to services and information. Research on multimodal interaction needs to address the selection of the most appropriate modality (or combination of modalities) considering both user characteristics and context of interaction. Past research has focused on answering each of these questions in an independent manner. Future research needs to consider the impact each dimension has on the overall usability of the services.

Furthermore, multimodal interaction is starting to incorporate into its processing, information that cannot be directly associated to the human senses. At the signal interpretation level, current state-of-the-art research is including emotional, affective and psychological cues. Extending the research to behavioral cues has the potential to further the context comprehension required to improve multimodal interaction. By relying on implicit and explicit cues for interpretation, we can aim to improve current activity and behavior detection mechanisms. These will then be explored, in the context of multimodal interaction, to increase intent recognition and recognizers performance by endowing them with enriched context information. Additionally, these interpretation mechanisms can be explored in the context of multimodal fission, to improve on current multimodal output generation mechanisms. By reasoning on emotional, affective, social and behavioral states, multimodal fission engines can be endowed with mechanisms to present the desired output in a more natural and convincing manner.

CONCLUSION

This chapter presented two studies of multimodal interaction, focusing on speech and pointing, with one of the studies considering multiuser, multi-surface scenarios. Both studies contribute to further the understanding of how people interact with speech and pointing systems, with or without the support of touch based surfaces, focusing on an array of different factors.

The first study considered speech and pointing interaction with a projection surface and analyzed how modalities are combined based on task characteristics, what information is conveyed in each modality, and how presentation aspects can impact user's input.

The second study combined an extra touch aware surface. In this iteration the study confirmed that the number of people interacting collaboratively with support from the system impacts the number of commands issued, independent of the tasks they are asked to perform. Such impact is felt in all available surfaces, and in all available input modalities. This results from users failing to clearly distribute tasks among themselves, ending with replicated tasks.

Furthermore, it was possible to identify direct manipulation of objects in the interactive table as the preferred and most used interaction method. Several factors can contribute to justify this finding: users are becoming more familiar with touch based devices and touch interaction is more comfortable than pointing and more expedite than speech.

The behavior of an application when rendering created objects over multiple surfaces was also studied. Two ways to create an object were considered: copy of an existing object and creating a novel object. It was possible to detect a tendency that users prefer created objects to appear in the surface they are already working in. While this was not clear for novel objects, it was very clear for copied objects.

The possibility to synchronize copies of the objects was also found to be relevant, particularly for multiuser scenarios. It was also important to understand that participants clearly preferred to create and synchronize a copy to display in the projected surface, while manipulating the original in the interactive table, than manipulating the original directly in the projected surface.

All the presented findings contribute to improve the current knowledge about the design of multimodal, multiuser and multi-surface systems and applications, hopefully fostering their continued adoption in real life deployments.

ACKNOWLEDGMENT

This work has been financed by National Funds through FCT – Fundação para a Ciência e a Tecnologia in the scope of project PTDC/EIA-EIA/105061/2008.

REFERENCES

Banerjee, A., Burstyn, J., Girouard, A., & Vertegaal, R. (2012). Multipoint: Comparing laser and manual pointing as remote input in large display interactions. *International Journal of Human-Computer Studies*, *70*(10), 690–702. doi:10.1016/j.ijhcs.2012.05.009.

Bourguet, M.-L., & Ando, A. (1998). Synchronization of speech and hand gestures during multimodal human-computer interaction. In *Proceedings of the Conference Summary on Human Factors in Computing Systems,* (pp. 241 – 242). doi: 10.1145/286498.286726

Cunningham, A., Close, B., Thomas, B., & Hutterer, P. (2010). Design and impressions of a multi-user tabletop interaction device. In *Proceedings of the Eleventh Australasian Conference on User Interface* (pp. 71 – 79). IEEE.

Dang, C. T., Straub, M., & André, E. (2009). Hand distinction for multi-touch tabletop interaction. In *Proceedings of the ACM International Conference on Interactive Tabletops and Surfaces,* (pp. 101 – 108). ACM. doi: 10.1145/1731903.1731925

Epps, J., Lichman, S., & Wu, M. (2006). A study of hand shape use in tabletop gesture interaction. In Proceedings of Extended Abstracts on Human Factors in Computing Systems, (pp. 748 – 753). doi: doi:10.1145/1125451.1125601.

Hinrichs, U., & Carpendale, S. (2011). Gestures in the wild: studying multi-touch gesture sequences on interactive tabletop exhibits. In *Proceedings of the SIGCHI Conference on Human Factors in Computing Systems,* (pp. 3023 – 3032). ACM. doi: 10.1145/1978942.1979391

Kurdyukova, E., Redlin, M., & André, E. (2012). Studying user-defined ipad gestures for interaction in multi-display environment. In *Proceedings of the ACM International Conference on Intelligent User Interfaces,* (pp. 93 – 96). ACM. doi: 10.1145/2166966.2166984

Liu, X., & Fujimura, K. (2004). Hand gesture recognition using depth data. In *Proceedings of the IEEE International Conference on Automatic Face and Gesture Recognition,* (pp. 529 – 534). IEEE.

Miki, M., Miyajima, C., Nishino, T., Kitaoka, N., & Takeda, K. (2008). An integrative recognition method for speech and gestures. In *Proceedings of the International Conference on Multimodal Interfaces,* (pp. 93 – 96). IEEE. doi: 10.1145/1452392.1452411

Morris, M. R., Wobbrock, J. O., & Wilson, A. D. (2010). Understanding users' preferences for surface gestures. In *Proceedings of Graphics Interface* (pp. 261–268). IEEE.

Müller-Tomfelde, C., Cheng, K., & Li, J. (2011). Pseudo-direct touch: interaction for collaboration in large and high-resolution displays environments. In *Proceedings of the Australian Computer-Human Interaction Conference,* (pp. 225 – 228). IEEE. doi: 10.1145/2071536.2071572

Neca, J., & Duarte, C. (2011). Evaluation of gestural interaction with and without voice commands. In *Proceedings of IADIS International Conference Interfaces and Human Computer Interaction,* (pp. 69 – 76). IADIS.

Olivier, P., Xu, G., Monk, A., & Hoey, J. (2009). Ambient kitchen: Designing situated services using a high fidelity prototyping environment. In *Proceedings of the International Conference on Pervasive Technologies Related to Assistive Environments,* (pp. 47:1 – 47:7). doi: 10.1145/1579114.1579161

Quek, F., McNeill, D., Bryll, R., Duncan, S., Ma, X.-F., & Kirbas, C. et al. (2002). Multimodal human discourse: gesture and speech. *ACM Transactions on Computer-Human Interaction, 9*(3), 171–193. doi:10.1145/568513.568514.

Schmidt, D., Block, F., & Gellersen, H. (2009). A comparison of direct and indirect multi-touch input for large surfaces. In *Proceedings of the IFIP TC 13 International Conference on Human-Computer Interaction: Part I,* (pp. 582 – 594). IFIP. doi: 10.1007/978-3-642-03655-2_65

Shaer, O., Strait, M., Valdes, C., Feng, T., Lintz, M., & Wang, H. (2011). Enhancing genomic learning through tabletop interaction. In *Proceedings of the SIGCHI Conference on Human Factors in Computing Systems,* (pp. 2817 – 2826). ACM. doi: 10.1145/1978942.1979361

Silva, M. G., & Bowman, D. A. (2009). *Body-based interaction for desktop games* (pp. 4249–4254). Extended Abstracts on Human Factors in Computing Systems.

Sung, J., Grinter, R. E., & Christensen, H. I. (2009). Pimp my roomba: Designing for personalization. In *Proceedings of the SIGCHI Conference on Human Factors in Computing Systems,* (pp. 193 – 196). ACM. doi: 10.1145/1518701.1518732

Tang, A., Tory, M., Po, B., Neumann, P., & Carpendale, S. (2006). Collaborative coupling over tabletop displays. In *Proceedings of the SIGCHI Conference on Human Factors in Computing Systems,* (pp. 1181 – 1190). ACM. doi: 10.1145/1124772.1124950

Tse, E., Greenberg, S., & Shen, C. (2006). GSI demo: Multiuser gesture/speech interaction over digital tables by wrapping single user applications. In *Proceedings of the International Conference on Multimodal Interfaces*, (pp. 76 – 83). doi: 10.1145/1180995.1181012

Tse, E., Greenberg, S., Shen, C., Forlines, C., & Kodama, R. (2008). Exploring true multi-user multimodal interaction over a digital table. In *Proceedings of the ACM Conference on Designing Interactive Systems,* (pp. 109 – 118). ACM. doi: 10.1145/1394445.1394457

Tuddenham, P., Kirk, D., & Izadi, S. (2010). Graspables revisited: Multi-touch vs. tangible input for tabletop displays in acquisition and manipulation tasks. In *Proceedings of the SIGCHI Conference on Human Factors in Computing Systems,* (pp. 2223 – 2232). ACM. doi: 10.1145/1753326.1753662

Voida, S., Tobiasz, M., Stromer, J., Isenberg, P., & Carpendale, S. (2009). Getting practical with interactive tabletop displays: Designing for dense data, fat fingers, diverse interactions, and face-to-face collaboration. In *Proceedings of the ACM International Conference on Interactive Tabletops and Surfaces,* (pp. 109 – 116). ACM. doi: 10.1145/1731903.1731926

Wobbrock, J. O., Morris, M. R., & Wilson, A. D. (2009). User-defined gestures for surface computing. In *Proceedings of the SIGCHI Conference on Human Factors in Computing Systems,* (pp. 1083 – 1092). ACM. doi: 10.1145/1518701.1518866

Yin, Y., & Davis, R. (2010). Toward natural interaction in the real world: Real-time gesture recognition. In *Proceedings of the International Conference on Multimodal Interfaces and the Workshop on Machine Learning for Multimodal Interaction,* (pp. 15:1 – 15:8). doi: 10.1145/1891903.1891924

ADDITIONAL READING

Bolt, R. (1980). Put-that-there: Voice and gesture at the graphics interface. In *Proceedings of the 7th Annual Conference on Computer Graphics and Interactive Techniques,* (pp. 262–270). ACM. doi: 10.1145/800250.807503

Buxton, B. (2008). Surface and tangible computing, and the small matter of people and design. *IEEE International Solid-State Circuits Conference Digest of Technical Papers, 51*, 24-29. doi: 10.1109/ISSCC.2008.4523043

Cochet, H., & Vauclair, J. (2010). Pointing gesture in young children: Hand preference and language development. *Gesture, 10*(2), 129–149. doi:10.1075/gest.10.2-3.02coc.

Dohse, K. C., Dohse, T., Still, J. D., & Parkhurst, D. J. (2008). Enhancing multi-user interaction with multi-touch tabletop displays using hand tracking. In Proceedings of Advances in Computer-Human Interaction, (pp. 297-302). doi: doi:10.1109/ACHI.2008.11.

Duarte, C., Carriço, L., & Guimarães, N. (2007). Evaluating usability improvements by combining visual and audio modalities in the interface. In *Proceedings of Human-Computer Interaction. Interaction Design and Usability 12th International Conference,* (pp. 428-437). doi: 10.1007/978-3-540-73105-4_47

Duarte, C., & Neto, A. (2009). Gesture interaction in cooperation scenarios. In *Proceedings of the 15th International Conference on Groupware: Design, Implementation, and Use, CRIWG'09,* (pp. 190–205). CRIWG. doi: 10.1007/978-3-642-04216-4_16

Eisenstein, J., & Davis, R. (2004). Visual and linguistic information in gesture classification. In *Proceedings of the 6th International Conference on Multimodal Interfaces*, (pp. 113-120). doi: 10.1145/1027933.1027954

Fikkert, W., Hakvoort, M., Vet, P., & Nijholt, A. (2009). Experiences with interactive multi-touch tables. In Intelligent Technologies for Interactive Entertainment, (pp. 193-200). doi: doi:10.1007/978-3-642-02315-6_19.

Grifoni, P. (2009). *Multimodal human computer interaction and pervasive services*. Hershey, PA: IGI Global. doi:10.4018/978-1-60566-386-9.

Gutwin, C., & Greenberg, S. (1998). Design for individuals, design for groups: Tradeoffs between power and workspace awareness. In *Proceedings of the 1998 ACM Conference on Computer Supported Cooperative Work, CSCW '98*, (pp. 207–216). ACM. doi: 10.1145/289444.289495

Han, J. Y. (2006). Multi-touch interaction wall. In *Proceedings of ACM SIGGRAPH 2006 Emerging Technologies*. doi: 10.1145/1179133.1179159

König, W., Rädle, R., & Reiterer, H. (2010). Interactive design of multimodal user interfaces: Reducing technical and visual complexity. *Journal on Multimodal User Interfaces*, *3*(3), 197–213. doi:10.1007/s12193-010-0044-2.

Mähr, W., Carlsson, R., Fredriksson, J., Maul, O., & Fjeld, M. (2006). Tabletop interaction: research alert. In *Proceedings of the 4th Nordic Conference on Human-Computer Interaction: Changing Roles, NordiCHI '06*, (pp. 499–500). doi: 10.1145/1182475.1182551

Malik, S., Ranjan, A., & Balakrishnan, R. (2005). Interacting with large displays from a distance with vision-tracked multi-finger gestural input. In *Proceedings of the 18th Annual ACM Symposium on User Interface Software and Technology, UIST '05*, (pp. 43–52). doi: 10.1145/1095034.1095042

Nehaniv, C. (2005). Classifying types of gesture and inferring intent. In *Proceedings of the AISB 05 Symposium on Robot Companions: Hard Problems and Open Challenges in Robot-Human Interaction*, (pp. 74–81). AISB.

Peltonen, P., Kurvinen, E., Salovaara, A., Jacucci, G., Ilmonen, T., Evans, J., & Saarikko, P. (2008). It's mine, don't touch! Interactions at a large multi-touch display in a city centre. In *Proceedings of the Twenty-Sixth Annual SIGCHI Conference on Human Factors in Computing Systems*, (pp. 1285-1294). ACM. doi: 10.1145/1357054.1357255

Ringel, M., Ryall, K., Shen, C., Forlines, C., & Vernier, F. (2004). Release, relocate, reorient, resize: Fluid techniques for document sharing on multi-user interactive tables. In *Proceedings of CHI'04 Extended Abstracts on Human Factors in Computing Systems*, (pp. 1441-1444). ACM. doi: 10.1145/985921.986085

Ryall, K., Morris, M. R., Everitt, K., Forlines, C., & Shen, C. (2006). Experiences with and observations of direct-touch tabletops. In *Proceedings of Horizontal Interactive Human-Computer Systems*. IEEE. doi:10.1109/TABLETOP.2006.12.

Schüssel, F., Honold, F., & Weber, M. (2012). Influencing factors on multimodal interaction during selection tasks. *Journal on Multimodal User Interfaces*, *6*(3-4). doi: doi:10.1007/s12193-012-0117-5.

Thiran, J.-P., Marqués, F., & Bourlard, H. (2010). *Multimodal signal processing: Theory and applications for human-computer interaction*. Elsevier.

Tzovaras, D. (2008). *Multimodal user interfaces: From signals to interaction*. Berlin: Springer. doi:10.1007/978-3-540-78345-9.

Wigdor, D., Jiang, H., Forlines, C., Borkin, M., & Shen, C. (2009). WeSpace: The design development and deployment of a walk-up and share multi-surface visual collaboration system. In *Proceedings of the 27th International Conference on Human Factors in Computing Systems*, (pp. 1237-1246). doi: 10.1145/1518701.1518886

Wilson, A., & Bobick, A. (1999). Real-time online adaptive gesture recognition. In *Proceedings of the International Workshop on Recognition, Analysis, and Tracking of Faces and Gestures in Real-Time Systems, RATFG-RTS '99*, (p. 111). RATFG-RTS. ISBN:0-7695-0378-0

Wobbrock, J., Wilson, A., & Li, Y. (2007). Gestures without libraries, toolkits or training: a $1 recognizer for user interface prototypes. In *Proceedings of the 20th Annual ACM Symposium on User Interface Software and Technology*, (pp. 159–168). ACM. doi: 10.1145/1294211.1294238

Wu, M., & Balakrishnan, R. (2003). Multi-finger and whole hand gestural interaction techniques for multi-user tabletop displays. In *Proceedings of the 16th Annual ACM Symposium on User Interface Software and Technology, UIST '03*, (pp. 193–202). ACM. doi: 10.1145/964696.964718

KEY TERMS AND DEFINITIONS

Multimodality: Multimodality is the ability to interact using multiple modalities (channels to exchange information between the user and the system) in a coordinated or independent fashion. While it can be applied to both input and output, in this chapter we are chiefly concerned with multimodal input. Specifically, this chapter deals with the usage of speech and gestures in an interactive environment.

Multi-Surface: Interactive application with the capability to distribute its interface over several surfaces. In the context of this chapter, a prototype is presented that is able to exchange objects between the projection surface and the touchable surface.

Natural Interaction Modalities: Interaction modalities that are naturally used by humans in human to human interaction. In this chapter, this refers to speech and gestural interaction.

Pointing: In this chapter pointing is used to mean selection of an interaction object by pointing at it (in the projection surface) or by touching it (in the touchable surface).

Projection Surface: Surface where interactive elements are projected. In the experiments reported in this chapter we projected onto a wall surface. Participants could interact with the projected elements using both speech and gestures.

Semaphoric Gestures: Gestures drawn from a dictionary of hand or arm gestures, with a predefined meaning.

Touchable Surface: Interactive surface capable to interpret touch events. In our prototype, the table could interpret touch events for selection purposes, but also as gestural commands (e.g. swipe). Additionally, speech could also be used to interact with the table.

Chapter 9
Reporting a User Study on a Visual Editor to Compose Rules in Active Documents

Federico Cabitza
Università degli Studi di Milano-Bicocca, Italy

Iade Gesso
Università degli Studi di Milano-Bicocca, Italy

ABSTRACT

In the last years, researchers are exploring the feasibility of visual language editors in domain-specific domains where their alleged user-friendliness can be exploited to involve end-users in configuring their artifacts. In this chapter, the authors present an experimental user study conducted to validate the hypothesis that adopting a visual language could help prospective end-users of an electronic medical record define their own document-related local rules. This study allows them to claim that their visual rule editor based on the OpenBlocks framework can be used with no particular training as proficiently as with specific training, and it was found user-friendly by the user panel involved. Although the conclusions of this study cannot be broadly generalized, the findings are a preliminary contribution to show the importance of visual languages in domain-specific rule definition by end-users with no particular IT skills, like medical doctors are supposed to represent.

INTRODUCTION

During the past years we conducted a number of observational studies in the healthcare domain (Cabitza & Simone, 2012; Cabitza, Simone, & Sarini, 2009) to elicit requirements for the successful introduction of electronic document-based information systems in organizational settings that presented features of criticality and complexity that are typical of hospital settings, especially the feature of heavily relying on paper-based documents and hence typically exhibiting a strong resistance to change. In such settings, documents (i.e., forms, charts, reports, spreadsheets) provide end-users with the natural interface by which to interact with the underlying information system.

The main finding of these studies is that traditional electronic document management systems are often too rigid with respect to the local needs of end-users and to how the corresponding requirements can change over time. For this reason, unlike

DOI: 10.4018/978-1-4666-4623-0.ch009

what happens in traditional software engineering approaches toward software adaptivity (e.g., see (Weyns, Malek, & Andersson, 2010) and (de Lemos et al., 2012) for an overview), which are aimed at providing software engineers with a set of tools that allow them to design and configure self-adaptive systems, we believe that end-users should be left being autonomous in making their document-based information systems "on their own" (Cabitza, Gesso, & Corna, 2011); this means that users should become as much as possible independent of IT providers (e.g., software specialists and application vendors) in tweaking and adapting their systems to their ever changing functional needs.

In this light, we conceived the WOAD framework (Cabitza & Gesso, 2011; Cabitza & Simone, 2010), which encompasses an End-User Development (Lieberman, Paternò, & Wulf, 2006) environment. In particular, WOAD is aimed at making end-users autonomous in their customization efforts in regard to two distinct aspects by means of two specific visual editors: the *Template Editor* (Cabitza et al., 2011) to build and maintain templates of digital documents; and the *Mechanism Editor*, to augment those documents with simple rules (i.e., mechanisms in WOAD) and make it active. In particular, mechanisms make documents able to react to the users' interaction and to changes in the execution context in an asynchronous and proactive manner, and to modulate how the document content should "look like" (i.e., its layout affordances), in order to promote the end-users' *collaboration awareness* (Gutwin & Greenberg, 1997) of what is going on and help them cope with the current situation. Mechanisms are simple *if-then* constructs that couple a set of document-related conditions with a set of actions that act on the documents' structure and content. Despite their simplicity, defining rules can result to be a hard task for end-users: indeed, these latter ones are usually experts of their work domain and setting, but can have relatively low confidence with formalized languages and, in general, with programming concepts and the related constraints. In this light, our point is that visual languages are useful to fill in this gap and make end-users able to "program" the active behavior of their electronic artifacts in order to fulfill the requirement of autonomy we mentioned above.

In what follows, after a short survey of the main visual languages we considered to express rule-based mechanisms, we present the main aspects of our rule visual editor, and we describe an experimental user study that we conducted to evaluate the usability of the editor and, hence informally, the feasibility of the whole EUD-oriented approach. The research question that motivated this user study is whether a visual language can make "programming" an interface as easy as a child's play, i.e., akin to using simple building blocks in order to accomplish simple tasks that do not require a specific training or a long acquired competence in programming.

BACKGROUND

Within the healthcare domain, i.e., the reference domain of our research activities, the need to make the definition of the user interfaces of an *Electronic Patient Records* (*EPR*) more flexible, typically more or less structured forms, so that these can be adjusted to better meet the local needs of each single group of practitioners has been recognized long ago and confirmed in a number of recent field studies (e.g., (Bringay, Barry, & Charlet, 2006; W. Chen & Akay, 2011; Mamlin et al., 2006; Morrison & Blackwell, 2009)). Nevertheless, despite this recognition, the necessary tailoring activities to this aim still require that IT professionals work together with the end-users of such systems, i.e., the clinicians, in order to be able to perform the due customizations in a timely and aptly manner. In other words, clinicians can not autonomously tailor their EPRs. Mamlin et al. (2006), for instance, proposed *OpenMRS*, an open-source, modular solution to allow the implementation of EPRs that are flexible with respect to the fact that they can be tailored to meet the specific needs of different healthcare institutions. OpenMRS relies on a fixed patient-centric data model that is compliant with the *Health Level 7* (*HL7*) standard (Dolin et al., 2006, p. 7). In OpenMRS, clinical records can be defined using the template engine of the Velocity project[1]. Moreover, OpenMRS encompasses both a decision support module employing the Arden syntax[2] and a compliant rule builder module. On the other hand, OpenMRS adopts a data-driven approach in order to perform data entry operations: forms are collections of data pointers; this allows for the creation of flexible data entry forms, without requiring any programming activity to be created. In (Morrison & Blackwell, 2009) two commercially available EPRs are described that provide clinicians with advanced customization features: i.e., *Centricity Electronic Medical Record*[3] and *MetaVision*[4]. The customizability of Centricity concerns the possibility of clinicians to generate their unstructured textual reports by selecting the contents that they need through menus and checkboxes. Moreover, Centricity allows clinicians to customize both terminology and boilerplate sections of their reports through a "medical specification language"; yet this approach requires them to learn general purpose programming skills. MetaVision allows for the definition of customized forms and operations, by means of an ad-hoc scripting language. In this light, performing MetaVision customizations requires that clinicians work in collaboration with IT professionals. A more lightweight approach to EPRs customizability is proposed in (W. Chen & Akay, 2011). The proposed approach is to adopt FileMaker[5] to develop flexible EPRs for small- and medium-size clinical settings. Such an approach leverages the FileMaker's capability of generating databases on the basis of the composition of intuitive form-like GUIs through simple drag'n'drop interactions. In this project, EPRs can be dynamically updated to meet the constantly evolving needs of clinicians with little effort as modifications performed at interface level are seamlessly reflected in the underlying data structures. Moreover, the authors corroborate their idea by arguing that FileMaker has already been extensively adopted in a number of Japanese hospitals to develop flexible frontends for their institutional EPRs. Nevertheless, even if FileMaker provides its users with a user-friendly graphical interface, deep customizations, like those related to active behaviors to attach to the defined interfaces, still require the involvement of IT professionals to be accomplished and deployed safely.

On the other hand, the concept of *rule* is quite common within the healthcare domain, since many rule-based expert systems and decision support systems have been developed in the last thirty years with the explicit aim to support clinicians in their decision making and care activities, e.g., see (Seto et al., 2012; Wong, Moore, Cooper, & Wagner, 2002). In these systems, adding new rules is not a task that usually clinicians can autonomously perform; rather, these operations require to be performed by knowledge engineers that elicit the behaviors related to these rules by involving key representative of the clinicians, the so called domain experts and then passing these specifications to professional programmers to develop corresponding computational structures that could be interpreted by an inference engine. Nevertheless, at least in the healthcare domain, some attempts to empower clinicians in defining and maintaining their rules autonomously have been done, although with different purposes other than the WOAD mechanisms. H.-T. Chen, Ma, and Liou (2002), for instance, proposed a visual editor to create rules for a real-time alerting system, which has been tailored to be used within an Intensive Care Unit (ICU). The editor helps clinicians in defining the textual representation of rule conditions, which allow to monitor some physiological parameters of the inpatients. Nevertheless, this editor is not actually a visual editing solution, rather it is a wizard-like textual editor. On the other hand, *MARBLS* (Krebs, Conrad, &

Wang, 2012), i.e., *Medical Alert Rule BuiLding System*, is an end-user programming environment that allow to design and test clinical alert rules in a visual manner. MARBLS user interface encompasses two relevant components, i.e., the rule workspace and the query explorer. MARBLS allows end-users to define rules in two ways: by (i) composing visual blocks in the rule workspace; and by (ii) acting directly on the charts in the query explorer (to update rules in the rule workspace). The MARBLS visual language relies on the MIT OpenBlocks library (Roque, 2007) that will be better described in the next section as this is what we also used for our visual rule editor.

PRESENTING THE WOAD EDITOR AND THE EVALUATION USER STUDY

In this section we will delve into the main focus of the chapter, that is the presentation of our rule editor and of the user study in which we evaluated its usability and the user-friendliness of the visual notation proposed to a sample panel of users to express simple rule-based tasks in computational terms. Before dealing with the user study, we will outline the main characteristics of the reference architecture of the WOAD framework, the visual language we adopted and the related visual editor that we tested in the user study. Subsequently, we will describe the user study and discuss its results.

A Concise Review of the State of the Art in Visual Language Systems

Since the 1990s, visual languages met an ever increasing interest in both the research community and the sector of commercial software. This interest has led some researchers to investigate whether visual languages are any better than traditional text-based programming approaches (e.g., see (Navarro-Prieto & Cañas, 2001; Whitley & Blackwell, 2001)). In particular, Navarro-Prieto and Cañas (2001) present an experiment that shows how a visual approach can result to be more intuitive and easy to understand than a purely textual approach to programming, as it allows users to focus also on the flow of data rather than only on the control flow that their code must follow. On the other hand, the results of this study showed that, despite their intuitiveness, visual languages can not completely replace textual programming languages for the sake of expressive power.

Nevertheless, visual languages have continued to gain popularity in virtue of their immediate appeal for non-professional users, so that at present they have been adopted within a heterogeneous set of application domains, ranging from software development to multimedia compositions (e.g. the cases of *Buzz Manchines* and *vvvv*[6] as well as *Pure Data* (Puckette, 1996)), up to the educational field (e.g., see (Maloney, Resnick, Rusk, Silverman, & Eastmond, 2010; Repenning et al., 2011; Stolee & Fristoe, 2011)). In this section, we will present a concise but to our aims comprehensive survey of the most notable visual languages.

The education domain has adopted the visual approach to support users, and in particular kids, in learning computer programming concepts and techniques. *AgentSheets* (Repenning et al., 2011), for instance, is aimed at teaching students programming skills through the creation of web-based games. AgentSheets provides a drag'n'drop programming interface that allows end-users to create computational grids, like spreadsheets, in which they can put numbers and strings, but also agents. Those agents are represented through pictures, and can be animated, produce sounds, react to mouse and keyboard interactions, and so forth. *Microsoft Kodu* (Stolee & Fristoe, 2011) is another educational visual programming language, endowed with a developing environment: end-users learn programming concepts by creating their own Xbox video games, defining both world (i.e., environments) and characters. Kodu is an interpreted, rule-based language: rules are simple *when-do* clauses that are grouped, and evaluated, by pages. Pages are the "place" where users define the behaviors of their video game characters. Also *Scratch* (Maloney et al., 2010) is a visual tool that allows kids to learn computer programming through the creation of interactive animated stories or simple games. Scratch associates programming formal constructs (e.g., *if-then* or loop constructs) with corresponding graphic building blocks, which can be arbitrarily composed to define the intended behaviors.

Besides the educational domain, visual approaches have been undertaken also in other ambits. In some cases, visual languages have been adopted to create industrial and embedded software (see, for instance, *LabVIEW*[7] and *Minibloq*[8]). In recent years, the diffusion of smartphones and smart mobile devices allowed for the adoption of visual programming languages also on this kind of devices. Puzzle (Danado & Paternò, 2012), for instance, is a visual language that is based on the jigsaw puzzle metaphor, i.e., a metaphor by which, similarly to the "building block" metaphor, language constructs are represented through composable jigsaw pieces; users can create applications directly on their mobile devices through composing pieces together in any size, and hence complexity, puzzles according to composition constraints that are rendered in terms of physical slot shapes.

SourceBinder (Conradi, Serényi, Kranz, & Hussmann, 2010) is a general purpose visual tool that empowers end-users to develop their own applications. It is based on web standard technologies and it is aimed at creating dynamic *Adobe Flash* applications. SourceBinder creates a mapping between most of the standard *ActionScript* classes and the concept of a corresponding node; in so doing writing a program in this language means to literally "wired" up nodes together so as to define the control "flow" in a visual manner. Moreover, in order to support different levels of complexity, each node can be managed accordingly as a distinct entity: from the simple capability of being composed with certain nodes and not to others, up to the possibility of being fully customized by editing the source code of the node.

With the advent and diffusion of Web 2.0 platforms, as in the case of traditional applications also visual languages have moved from the traditional desktop environment to Web-based ones. *Lively Fabrik* (Lincke, Krahn, Ingalls, & Hirschfeld, 2009) is a web-based environment that integrates Fabrik (Ingalls, Wallace, Chow, Ludolph, & Doyle, 1988) with the Lively Kernel[9] with the aim to allow end-users to create their own web applications and mashups within their web browser. Users can define the application logic by visually wiring up the scriptable blocks of the language, similarly to the more widely known *Yahoo Pipes*[10].

Besides the standalone visual applications and environments, also a set of visual libraries and frameworks has been developed and refined over time. These solutions are conceived to make the task of endowing software systems with new visual languages easier and faster. For instance, the MIT OpenBlocks (Roque, 2007) is a Java library aimed at creating visual languages that are based on the "building block" metaphor (further details about OpenBlocks will be provided in the next section). Nevertheless, the ever increasing trend toward the Web-based tools has led the MIT researchers to drop the development of OpenBlocks and to reuse the acquired expertise to start the creation of ScriptBlocks[11], the web-based evolutions of OpenBlocks. Similarly, Google Inc. started the development of Blockly[12], which apparently seems to be based on OpenBlocks, at least from the merely visual point of view.

This cursory and necessarily partial survey shows that visual languages usually rely on a finite set of recurrent metaphors and concepts: most of these are traceable back to the "building block" metaphor, while others allow the definition of the application logic through connectors, like pipes, and some others combine these two approaches in some way. In any case, visual languages that rely exclusively on the concept of rule are relatively few (e.g., Microsoft Kodu).

The WOAD Framework Architecture

The WOAD framework encompasses a reference architecture, which is depicted in Figure 1. For the sake of brevity we will focus only on those components of the architecture that are responsible for the definition and the execution of the WOAD mechanisms as well as those components with which they need to interact (a complete description of the architecture is reported in (Cabitza & Gesso, 2011)).

As mentioned, when end-users need to create a new WOAD mechanism in order to add some active behaviors to their existing documents, they accomplish this task through the Mechanism Editor (see below for an extensive description of this component). The Mechanism Editor queries both the *Template Manager* and the *Didget Manager* in order to obtain the list of the existing document templates and the related sets of didgets making them available to create a new WOAD mechanism or to modify an existing one. When end-users wants to make their WOAD mechanisms executable, they need to make them available to the component devoted to this task, i.e., the *Mechanism Interpreter*. This latter component interacts with both the Didget Manager and the *Document Builder* in order to obtain all the needed data to trigger the WOAD mechanisms. When a WOAD mechanism is triggered, the Mechanisms Interpreter interacts with the *Markup Tagger*, which is the component responsible for changing the affordances of the documents that are displayed to the users through the *Layout Engine*, in order to convey additional awareness information.

The WOAD Visual Language

Also the WOAD Visual Language adopts the "building block" metaphor; accordingly, language constructs are rendered in terms of a set of composable visual blocks. The language constructs have been defined according to the findings of the field studies that we conducted in the healthcare domain. Despite the simplicity of this small set of constructs, users can define mechanisms that can reach an arbitrary level of complexity through it.

The meaning of the mechanism construct is quite obvious: it provides users with the visual representation of an *if-then* mechanism, allowing users to connect other blocks to define both the *when-* and the *then-part* of the rule. Since to define mechanisms users have to make an explicit

Figure 1. The UML Composite Structure diagram of the WOAD reference architecture (source (Cabitza & Gesso, 2011))

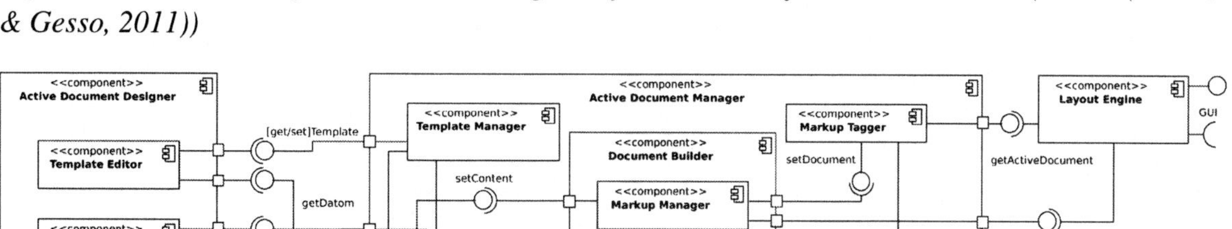

reference to the data fields of their document templates, both within *when-* and *then-part* of the mechanism, the set of language constructs is augmented with a dynamically populated set of all the available data fields previously defined in the document templates using the Template Editor. Each of these constructs is labeled according to a positional notation (more specifically, in terms of `template_id.didget_id.field_id` where didgets represent reusable groups of fields). Moreover, users may need to specify some constant value (like, e.g., a number, a string of characters or a Boolean value); to this aim, the visual language encompasses four specific constructs: two of them represent the true and false Boolean values respectively, while the other two constructs provide users with the possibility to customize textual or numeric variables and constants. To define the conditions within the *when-part* of their mechanisms, users can select the language constructs from a predefined list of available items, which includes comparators, arithmetical operators and aggregators. The first two are intuitive constructs and therefore we will not linger on describing them; moreover, arithmetical operators can be recursively combined to reach the necessary level of complexity. On the other hand, aggregators require a more detailed description. Users may need to define conditions on sets of values. For instance, clinicians may need to check if an allergy is in the list of the allergies suffered by a patient or to check if a patient suffers more than one allergy. Aggregators allow users to define these complex conditions. More in details, aggregators allow users to define conditions over sets of fields, which are referenced through the template_id.didget_id.* notation, and encompass both a two spreadsheet-like constructs (i.e., count and avg) and the 'in' operator. In the WOAD Visual Language conditions are evaluated as in strictly logical conjunction (i.e., in AND) and hence all of them must be satisfied for the mechanism to be executed and the actions defined in the *then-part* applied to their operands. If users need to define a disjunctive set of conditions (i.e., using the OR logic operator), they have simply to compose a set of distinct mechanisms. At the current time, the *then-part* allows only to compose together a set of constructs that modify the content appearance and layout affordances as we purposely did not want users define mechanisms by which the content itself of the document could be automatically corrected/imputed or modified (obviously, implementing these constructs is just a matter of connecting a visual block to a certain application behavior). For instance, when a clinician needs to proactively convey an awareness-related information to make her colleagues aware of a critical situation, she just needs to pick the set of constructs denoted with the label "criticality" and to connect it with both the mechanism construct and the construct that refers to the data field to which she wants to apply that kind of information (what we defined *Criticality Awareness Promoting Information* in (Cabitza et al., 2009)). In some cases, the aspect of each kind of awareness-related information can be modulated by a specific style sheet, in order to give more specificity to the message conveyed: to reach this goal, users need just to specify the value of some optional parameter of the corresponding construct, and set a specific constant value (e.g., the safety set can get a parameter in input, called "risk level" that allows users to modulate the related affordances, e.g., by having the system display different icons associated to different levels of risk).

The WOAD Mechanism Editor

Our visual rule editor has been developed on the basis of the MIT OpenBlocks demonstration project[13]. We chose OpenBlocks mainly because it was conceived as a simplified environment to teach children the basics of computer programming and, for its intended simplicity, it is also used by Google as a part of *App Inventor for Android* (now *App Inventor Edu* at the *MIT Media Lab*)[14], which is a web environment that helps non-programmer end-users in developing their own Android applications.

In order to use OpenBlocks as a visual language, we customized the OpenBlocks demo project in two distinct, but strictly intertwined ways. The former way consisted in finding a way to associate both the WOAD document components (which are automatically connected with the resulting output of our visual document template editor) and the related rule language constructs (which are statically defined within the rule editor) and the OpenBlocks language original primitives. Then we customized the user interface of the OpenBlocks demonstration project (see Figure 2) by adding a set of features aimed at improving its intuitiveness and convenience: e.g., we added the preview of existing document templates and the ability to clone groups of blocks that have been previously defined).

We also defined an intermediate, XML-based rule language. This language is used to translate the OpenBlocks XML-based output format, which contains blocks core features, connections and topological arrangement, into a simplified format that stores only the core features of the rules (i.e., conditions and actions). The intermediate language can be translated into the different rule languages that are provided by the rule engines which one wants to employ (e.g., the DRL language provided by *JBoss Drools*[16]); this contributes in making our visual editor independent of the underlying system implementation.

The Mechanism Editor is a standalone, window-based application, which is implemented using Java 7.0, and the Swing library and Java graphic primitives. The Mechanism Editor's main components are located in the main window, and they are the *block palette*, which takes up the left side of the window, and the editing area, which fills the central part of the window.

Figure 2. The Mechanism Editor user interface[15]

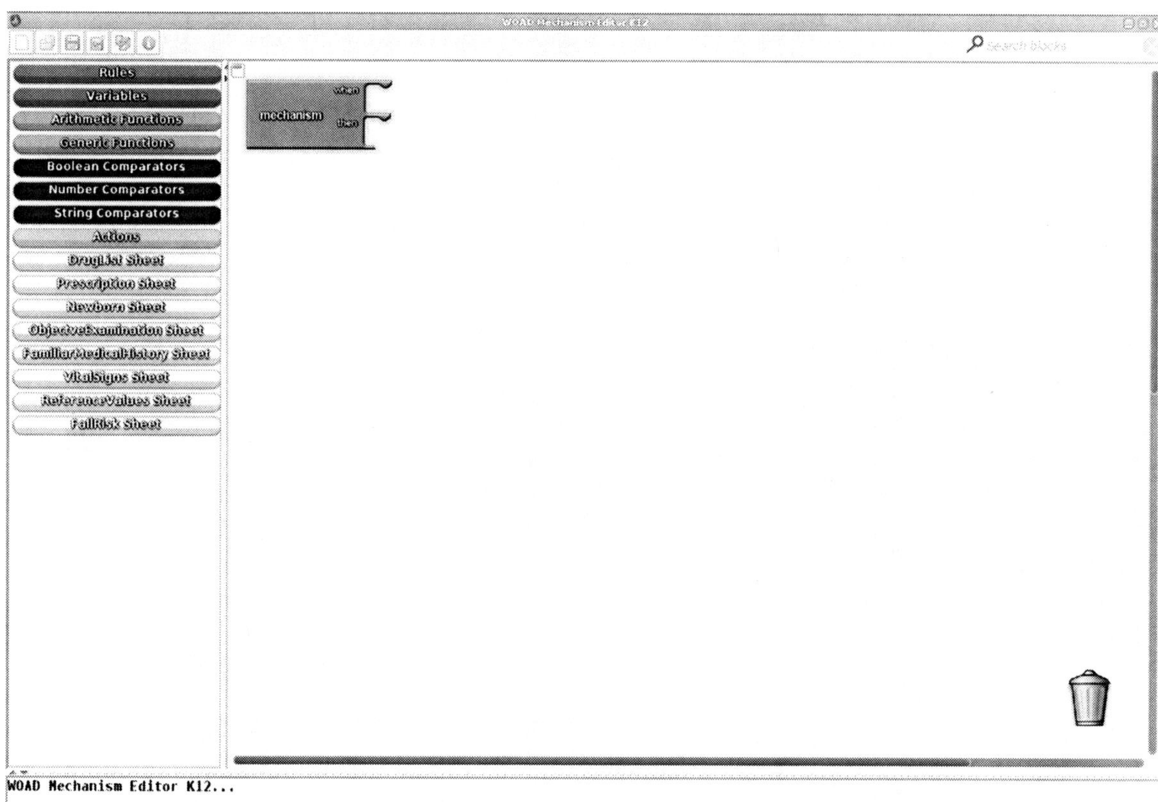

The blocks palette is composed by a set of buttons, which represent homogeneous group of blocks (see Figure 3). The first ten buttons regard the WOAD rule language blocks according to their semantic (i.e., comparison operators for numeric values, actions and constant values). Moreover, buttons in the palette, and the related language blocks, are colored so that the user can quickly distinguish those that have a similar semantic (e.g., all the comparison operators and the related palette buttons are colored in blue). The set of language-related buttons is followed by an arbitrary set of white colored buttons (the last two in Figure 3) that groups together document data fields according to the document template that contains them.

Each palette button gives access to its set of language blocks by showing a scrollable panel. Inside these panels, language blocks are presented to the user directly in their graphical layout. In a set of preliminary tests this proved to make easier to recognize whether a block could be attached to another block that has been already inserted in the mechanism logic, or not. This has been possible since the OpenBlocks language primitives allow to define if and how a block can be connected with other blocks, and also what is the data type of each connector (e.g., to manage strings, numbers or boolean values).

In the case of those palette buttons that group together blocks that are related to the data fields of a specific document template, the panel icon is a small thumbnail representing the document template, and allows users to open a preview window (see Figure 4).

The main use of the editing area is trivial: it manages all the drag'n'drop operations that users perform on the language blocks with the aim to compose or modify the mechanisms. Nevertheless, the editing area is also responsible of managing delete actions, which can be visually enacted through the widely diffused metaphor of the trash icon, which takes place at the lower right corner of the editing area (see Figure 2 and Figure 3, bottom side).

Figure 3. The WOAD rule language operators and data fields mapped with OpenBlocks visual constructs

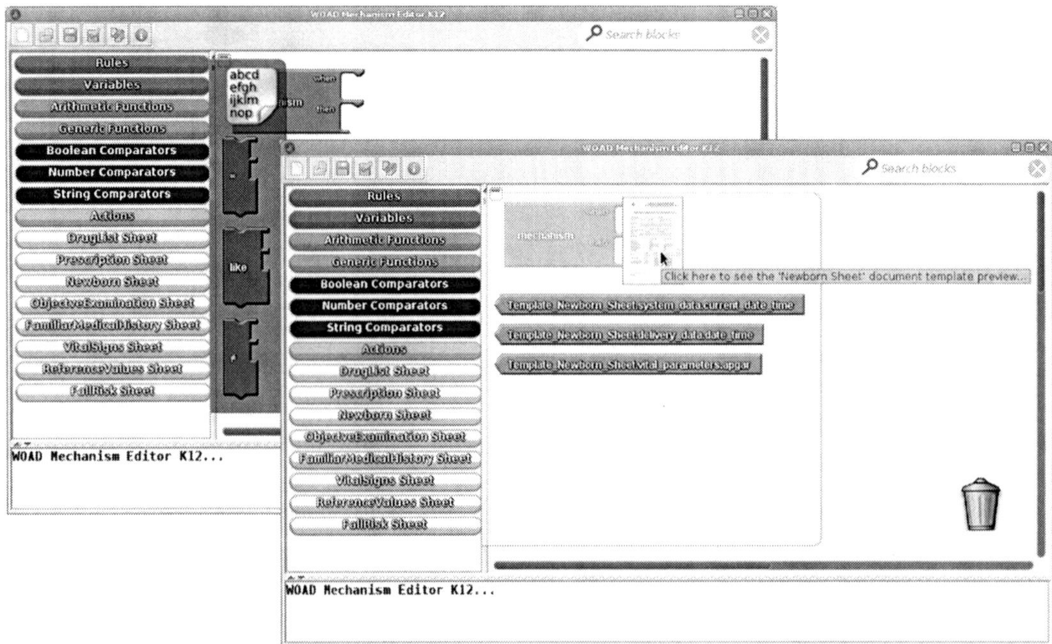

Figure 4. The document template preview window

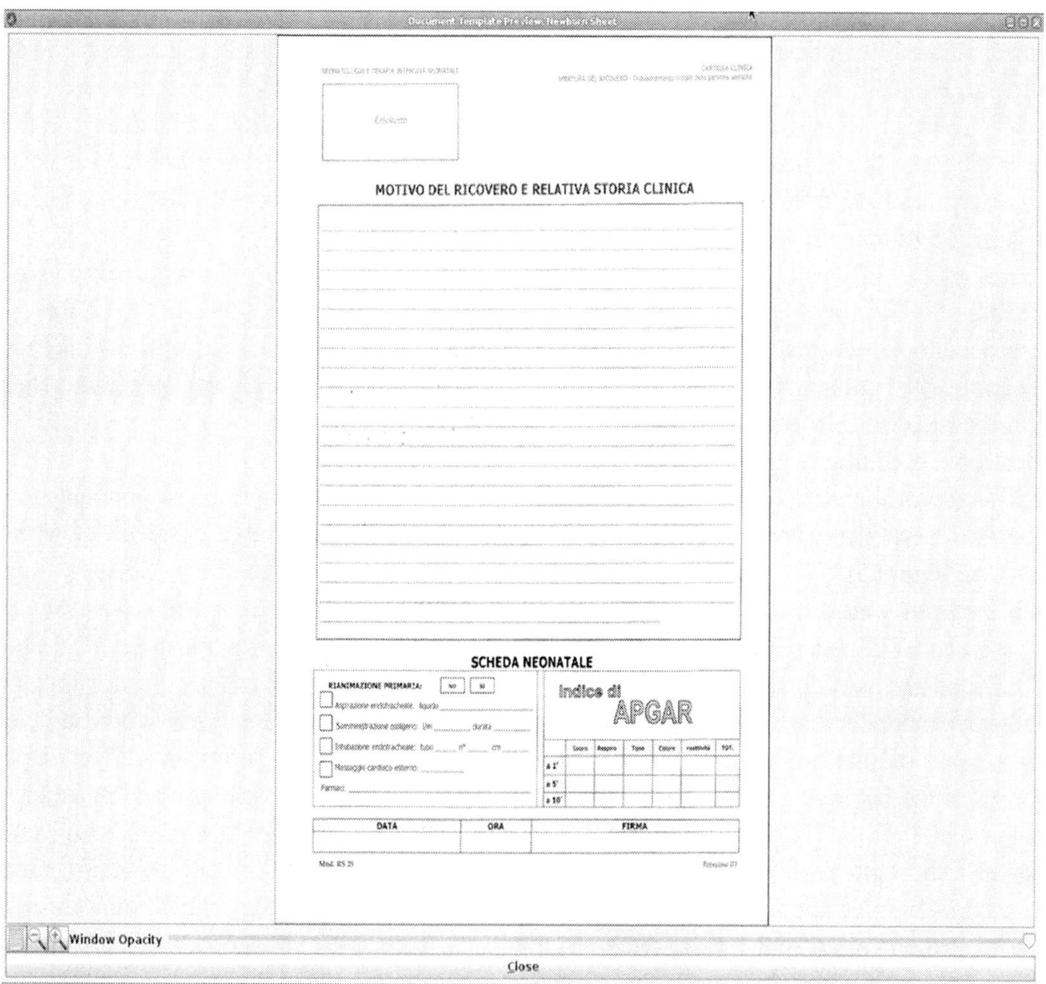

User Study

The goal of our study was to test the *perceived usability*, or user-friendliness, of our visual rule editor, with a particular focus on the extent end-users perceived its use intuitive. In what follows, we will briefly describe the main aspects of the method that we adopted to perform our study.

First of all, on the basis of the general structure of empirical studies that has been suggested in (Perry, Porter, & Votta, 2000), the first activity we undertook has been the design of the user study. This resulted in five step study: (i) we spent some time in formulating and refining the hypothesis to test with the collaboration of two senior doctors; (ii) we gathered the clinicians who claimed to be interested in participating in the study, divided this panel in two even groups; (iii) we conducted the test sessions; (iv) we performed a statistical analysis of the data we had collected and measured during the test sessions; and, finally, (v) starting from the above mentioned analysis, we drew some remarks about the possibility to reject or not our initial hypothesis.

The hypothesis under test can be expressed as follows: "the participants that received the training session (i.e., in what follows denoted as U1 group) and those who did not receive such a training (i.e., the U2 group) will take an equal time, on average, to perform each of the three tasks we ask them to perform through the same video clip" (more formally put, H_0: $\mu Ti_{U1} = \mu Ti_{U2}$ for each task T1, T2 and T3). The study was then aimed at collecting sufficient evidence that H_0 can be either rejected or, conversely, confirmed. In this latter case, we would claim that untrained users can use the editor as much as proficiently as users that received a specific and effective training.

The procedure we adopted to perform the third step (see above) of the study was articulated in four shorter activities. In the first activity, we administered a preliminary questionnaire to get information about the participants, their education level, their work experience and their self-assessed IT skills (see Figure 5).

Then, we briefly outlined the scope and aims of the research to all the participants. We randomly divided the participants in two evenly-matched groups and administered a comprehensive training session only to one group (namely, the U1 group), as the latter was supposed to be the "control group" (i.e., the U2 group). In this training session, a short movie showed how to use the editor and how to solve simple tasks by creating a couple of pertinent rules. At the end of the training session, we administered a questionnaire to assess the perceived satisfaction with the training received in terms of efficacy. The third activity encompassed the test session, where participants were required to perform three different tasks (in what follows, T1, T2 and T3) of increasing complexity. In the fourth and last activity, we administered a short post-test questionnaire with the aim to collect a qualitative feedback on the user experience, both in terms of ordinal scale assessments and in terms of free-text comments and suggestions.

The three tasks were structured to involve no more than two documents, not to be too complicated but, at the same time, reproducing a realistic situation. In what follows, we outline each task briefly.

T1: This task required the respondents to check if the weight of a newborn is within the reference range (i.e., 2500g $\leq$ Newborn Weight $\leq$ 4500g), and otherwise to convey an awareness information of a critical situation. The task involved only one document that is called 'Objective Examination' and contains the 'newborn_summary' didget). Since the condition can be expressed as a disjunctive boolean expression, i.e., newborn_summary.weight < 2500g OR newborn_summary.weight > 4500g, clinicians were asked to compose two distinct mechanisms: the former to check if newborn_summary.weight was lower than 2500g and the latter to check if newborn_summary.weight was higher than 4500g; both mechanisms, if activated, would

Figure 5. The charts of user sample characteristics

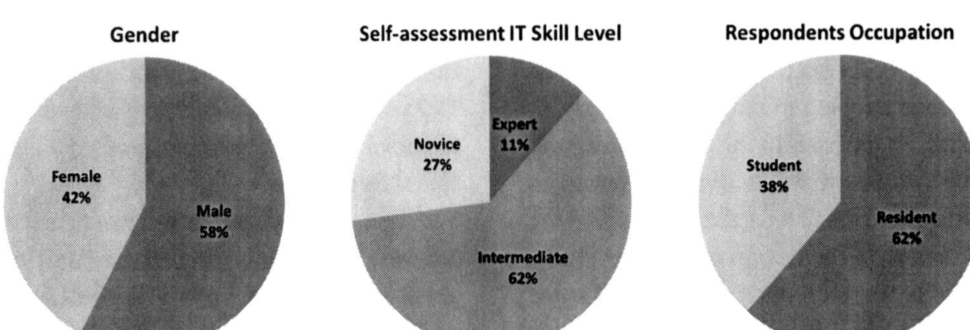

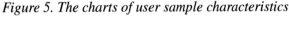

have to convey a *Criticality information*, which has been previously defined to show a red border around the weight data field in the newborn_summary section.

T2: This second task required the respondents to check if a newborn has at least a malformation, and in this case to convey awareness information to make evident that there is some risk for the safety of the newborn. Even in this case, clinicians were asked to compose a mechanism that involved a single document: the 'FAMILIAR MEDICAL HISTORY'. The related document template contains a group of fields that pertains to 'malformations'; this is a check list reporting the most common congenital malformations. Notably, this task required to use the 'count' aggregator. The test participants were asked to compose a mechanism that counts the number of checked malformations in the malformation didget and, if the resulting value is greater than zero (i.e., count(malformations.*) > 0), to convey a *Safety information* near to the first data field of this didget. In order to convey the *Safety information* for a medium risk, clinicians were also asked to specify the `medium' value for the `risk level' parameter of the corresponding *Safety* construct. The resulting mechanism can be seen in Figure 6.

T3: The third and last task required clinicians to check if a drug that they prescribed to an inpatient is in the official list of drugs of the hospital pharmacy, and otherwise to convey an indication to make their colleagues aware of the need of reviewing the name of the prescribed drug. This task involved two distinct documents: the 'PRESCRIPTION SHEET', which contains the drugs that doctors have prescribed to an inpatient; and the 'DRUG LIST', which contains the list of drugs of the hospital pharmacy. For the sake of simplicity, the 'PRESCRIPTION SHEET' has been defined so as to contain four distinct 'drug' didgets, while the `PRESCRIPTION SHEET' is composed of a single didget pertaining to the 'drug_list'. The task required clinicians to compose a mechanism that uses the 'in' aggregator to check that the name of the first drug is *not* in the list of drugs, and accordingly to convey a *Revision information* close to the drug name to revise (and correct) in the `PRESCRIPTION SHEET'.

A total of 34 participants were enrolled in this study. These were considered as "proxy users" (Friedman & Wyatt, 2006) of our visual rule editor. Proxy users are users that sufficiently represent the typical users of the system being tested. Enrolling proxy users is useful in those situations in which it is difficult to involve the actual users directly, in this case doctors and nurses actually working in a hospital setting full time. To this aim, the enrolled participants were students of both medicine and nursing as well as post-graduate residents. According to the proxy user framework, we could consider medicine

Figure 6. A block rule taken from Task 2

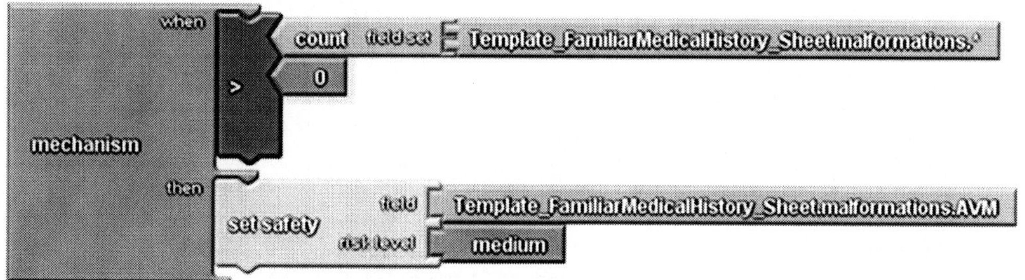

practitioners to be representative of a type of user not professionally focused on programming language, and rule definition. Indeed, the enrollment criteria that we defined required participants to have some experience with computers, but no particular skill in either programming or visual programming editors. For this reason, we discarded 4 potential subjects from the initial sample of 38 who declared to have good programming skills. Participants were between 25 and 32 year old; 19 of them (56%) were already graduated. Most of the participants defined themselves as intermediate computer users, while 9 of the other defined themselves as beginners (27%) and only 4 as experts (11%); moreover, 8 of them (24%) declared to have some basic experiences in computer programming, but only 2 (6%) declared to have had previous experiences with *visual* editing environments. The average job experience was 2.5 years.

As said before, this sample of potential respondents was splitted into two groups: who received a 5 minute long individual training session by means of a video clip (i.e., trained) and who did not (not trained); the training session was conveyed through a video clip to be sure that the training was exactly the same for each single respondent. A Chi-squared test on the proportions of the two groups allowed to state that the two groups were equal with respect to Gender, IT skills and Occupation. Of the 34 participants that were asked to perform the three tasks mentioned above, 3 of them dropped out before completion. This results in a final sample of 31 participants. At the subsequent questionnaire to assess the quality of the training session, 12 out of 17 participants found the training session at least effective ("effective" or "very effective"): notably, only these 12 participants were considered for the actual execution of the tasks so as to consider only those that thought to have been benefitted from receiving the training and therefore maximize the potential differences between the trained vs. no-trained groups. Our aim here was to discard who could perform as if they did not receive the training just because they could not exploit the training as an advantage for their performance. We also considered only those respondents that could accomplish the tasks correctly or, at least, with minor mistakes. In doing so, we purposely did not consider those respondents that, irrespective of the training received, did a bad performance of the tasks. In Table 1 we report the results of the test that are represented also in Figure 7.

We preliminarily set the significance level of the test at the conventional threshold of the probability to discard the initial hypothesis (H_0) if this is actually true (i.e., alpha = 0.05). The usual

Table 1. Statistical comparisons between the two subgroups (Student's T-test for independent samples for equality of means)

	Groups	N	Mean (seconds)	Standard Deviation	Mean Std. Error	p-Value
Task 1	Trained – T_{U_1}	12	391.00	173.41	48.10	0.077
	Not trained – T_{U_2}	14	510.92	157.28	43.62	
Task 2	Trained – T_{U_1}	12	280.31	128.62	35.67	0.658
	Not trained – T_{U_2}	14	260.15	99.03	27.47	
Task 3	Trained – T_{U_1}	12	295.08	87.66	24.31	0.380
	Not trained – T_{U_2}	14	257.69	122.75	35.05	

Figure 7. The chart of the mean times of performance of the two groups of users, for each task

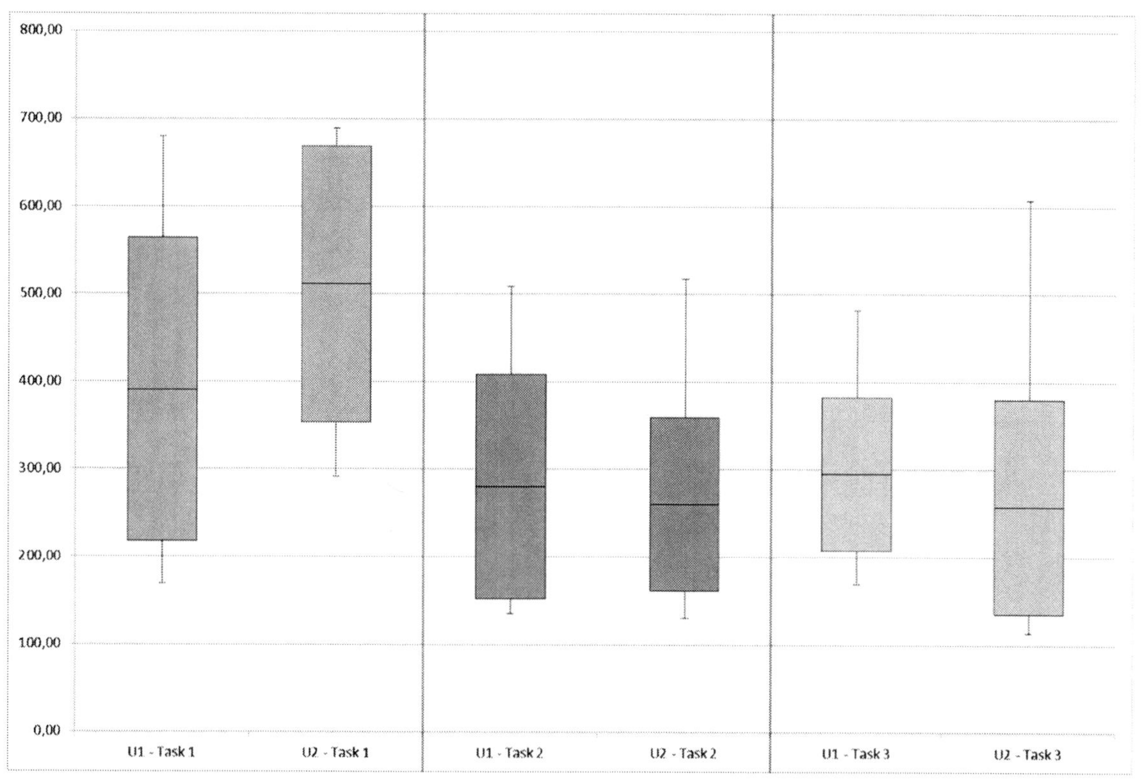

approach undertaken here is then to confirm the initial hypothesis to be true (as initially assumed) if and only if the probability of observing data at least as extreme as that observed is greater than 5%. According to the time measures that we collected during the execution of the test, and hence to the so called "mean time to performance" (in seconds) for each task, we cannot reject either H_{0T1}, H_{0T2} or H_{0T3} (see p-Value > 0.05 for all three tasks in Table 1). Therefore, H_0 can be considered true for all three tasks; this makes us confident that our visual rule editor can be profitably used also without a specific (and effective) training session. In other words, the visual rule editor under test does not require specific skills to support realistic tasks of computational augmentation of regular clinical documents.

In regard to the post-test evaluation, we show the results regarding the subjective assessment of the overall value of the user experience, of the user-friendliness of the graphical user interface, and on the extent the visual language was found intuitive, i.e., easy to comprehend and apply to the requested cognitive tasks. These assessments were solicited asking the participants to choose one possible value in an ordinal scale from 1 to 4, with explicit anchors being "very low", and "very high". As we purposely avoided the middle option to limit central tendency bias, we provided the opportunity to select a "don't know option". In Figure 8, the corresponding results are shown. Calculated means, which we report for descriptive (i.e., not inference) purposes only, are respectively: Overall value: 2.78 (Standard Error of the Mean or SEM: .13); GUI user-friendliness: 2.57 (.14); language intuitiveness: 2.63 (.17). This can be taken as an informal indication that respondents found the editor usable and the visual language intuitive enough for their purposes (since the mean was always greater than 2.5). A two sample

Figure 8. The charts of the evaluations of the two groups of participants

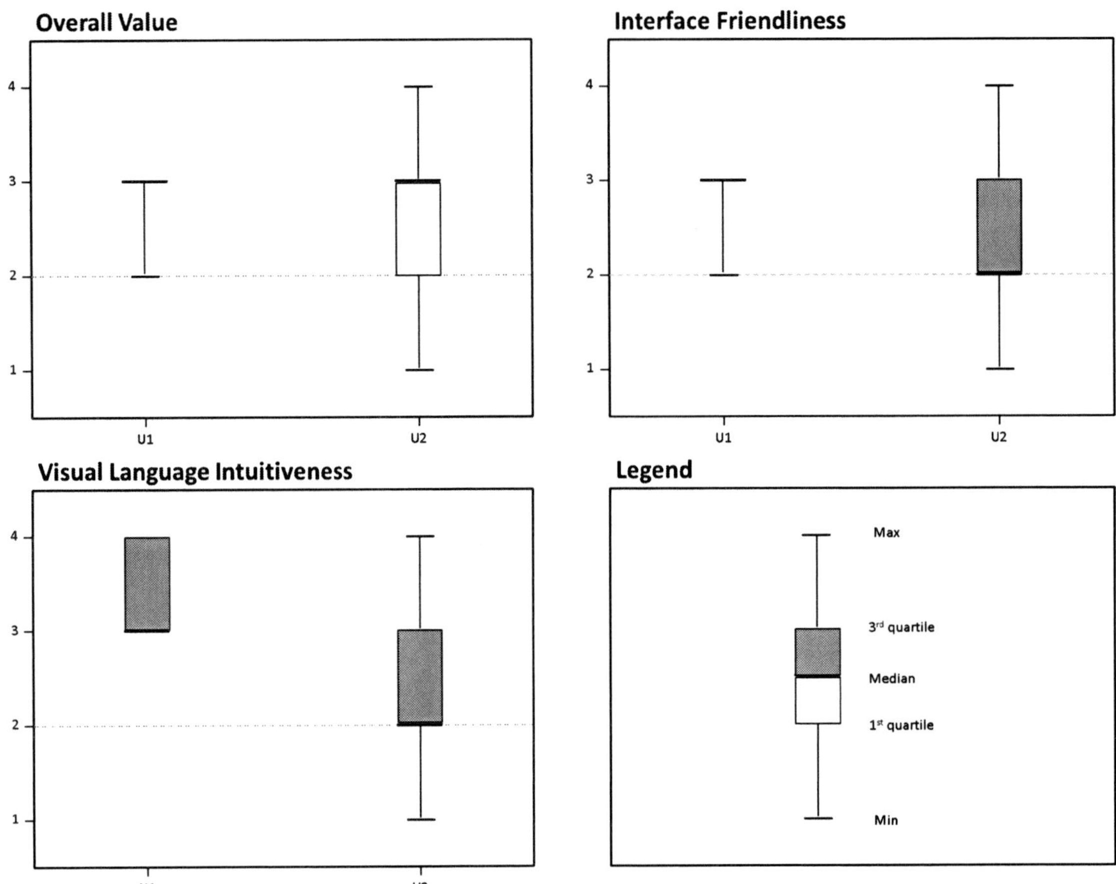

Kolmogorov-Smirnov Test (performed with SPSS v. 17.0) provided insufficient evidence to reject the assumption that the median assessments from the two distinct groups were not uniform (overall value: Z=.53, p-value=.94; GUI user-friendliness: Z=1.1, p=.18; language intuitiveness: Z=1.24, p=.09), that is we can claim that user satisfaction did not depend on having received the training or not (which, we recall it, was nevertheless considered effective by whom received it).

FUTURE RESEARCH DIRECTIONS

The promising results coming from the validation user study reported in this chapter encourages us in getting further confirmation that visual languages and related editor can be used in order to empower end-users and make them autonomous in the customization of a document-based information system, like WOAD is. To this aim, we are planning to perform other validation sessions within the healthcare domain, which for many reasons is our reference domain, but we are also considering other collaborative domains like the archaelogical one, that already provided us with a similarly promising feedback from the end-users involved (Locatelli, Ardesia, & Cabitza, 2010). Anyway, although the document-related rules employed in this user study had to be familiar to the users involved, and hence are certainly domain specific, the editor features and the language expressiveness that is here under investigation are general enough to submit that a similar tool could result to be user-friendly also in other application domains. Further similar user studies have to be performed to confirm this claim.

In regard to our future works, we will follow two different, but complementary directions that will improve the WOAD framework: (i) supporting users in collaboratively annotating their documents; and (ii) improving the support for tasks of collaborative tailoring of their WOAD-compliant application.

Annotations play a key role in supporting cooperation among the cooperating members of a group of practitioners (Cadiz, Gupta, & Grudin, 2000; Luff, Heath, & Greatbatch, 1992; Nobarany, 2012). In particular, as also shown in the user studies reported in (Bringay et al., 2006; Cabitza, Colombo, & Simone, 2013), annotations are a fundamental feature in enabling and promoting collaboration among the users of document-based EPRs and clinicians exhibit the requirement of being able to annotate their electronic documents like they could do with their paper-based ones. At present, the WOAD framework does not support document annotations, although we have already developed an editor that allows to attach annotations to both text and images in Web content management systems (currently Drupal). We have then applied these prototypes in the field studies reported in (Cabitza, Simone, & Locatelli, 2012), and got a first positive feedback on the need to integrate such capability in terms of a Recursive Annotation Tool (i.e., RAT) that will make end-users able to annotate any part of a document (e.g., texts, data fields and images) in their electronic documents. Annotations could be of two types: (i) a free text object, i.e., what is usually denoted as "comment"; and (ii) a label, i.e., what it is commonly denoted with the term 'tag'. To be more precise, tags could be either system-defined or user-defined keywords as well as dates (in a standard format), URLs and any string that the system can interpret and associate with specific behaviors. The recursiveness of annotations emerged as a precise requirement from our interaction with the end-users involved in the field studies mentioned above, as they appreciated the possibility to annotate existing annotations and create sort of thread-like discussions, in a sort of forum thread where the first target represents the "topic" to discuss. In this way, annotations allow for a distributed and asynchronous communication process among users, as well as the further improvement of their collaborative practices and promotion of knowledge creation and sharing. Doctors and nurses, for instance, used to discuss the trajectory of an inpatient's illness or the response of the inpatient to a particular drug through the recursive annotation of some documents, and told us that this contributed in the continuous improvement of their common understanding of the inpatient's health problems. Other field studies we conducted in the healthcare domain (e.g., Cabitza et al., 2013) also showed that clinicians often use annotations to define some relationships among documents, contributing in building a web of documental artifacts in a bottom up and emerging (that is not expected or plannable) manner. To this aim, users of the WOAD framework will be enabled to share annotations among different documents, in order to support them in defining relationships involving multiple documents.

Moreover, we observed some collaborative conventions that involved how practitioners used to annotate their documents (Cabitza et al., 2009) or the conventional meaning associated to specific annotations (Cabitza et al., 2013); this urges us to integrate annotations both in the definition and in the application of the WOAD mechanisms, that is to allow users to both use annotations to collaboratively edit their mechanisms, as well as to allow them to define mechanisms that refer to annotations' content either in their *if-part* or in their *then-parts*. Including annotations in the *when-part* will allow users to define WOAD mechanisms to convey a specific affordance or awareness-related information whenever one or more conditions involving either the content or the existence of annotations are verified. On the other hand, including annotations in the *then-part* would allow WOAD mechanisms to be able to change the affordances of the involved annotations in a similar way as to how we described above in relation to regular content.

The development and refinement of conventions is a continuous and collaborative process in which each member of the group in which it takes place give her contribution. The need of considering the collaborative dimension of the end-users' tailoring activities has been widely recognized long ago (see (Nardi, 1993)). Since end-users perform their tailoring activities in order to adapt the system to meet the needs related to their local conventions, the WOAD framework should be improved in order to support end-users in performing tailoring activities in a collaborative manner. With respect to the document templates, the WOAD framework partially addresses this requirement through the adoption of the Repository application that is a part of the Oryx Editor. The adoption of the Repository helped us in providing end-users with a shared space within which they can store their own document templates, and allowed us to endow the WOAD framework with a set of basic collaborative features, e.g., comments and ratings as well as a real-time lock strategy to avoid concurrent changes on the same document template. On the other hand, the WOAD framework still does not support cooperation in the definition of the WOAD mechanisms. In this light, the WOAD framework should be improved in two ways. On the one hand, the Mechanism Editor should be integrated with the Repository applications in order to provide end-users with a unique storage space in which they could be able to store both document templates and the related WOAD mechanisms. On the other hand, the Mechanism Editor should be further improved making end-users able to collaboratively annotate the WOAD mechanisms with the aim of promoting a process of communication among end-users who progressively modify WOAD mechanisms.

CONCLUSION

The paper illustrated two core functionalities of the applications we developed under the tenets of the WOAD framework: these regard enabling end-users to both define simple rules, and associate those rules to electronic documents so that their content can be visually and textually enriched (e.g., in terms of different affordances) according to the context and at various levels of scope.

This feature can be also seen as a demonstrator of a wider class of applications designed to support collaborative work, whereas documents can be used to mediate collaboration and articulate cooperative tasks. In WOAD compliant applications, coordination is achieved mainly through electronic documents (e.g., forms, charts, shared documents) with respect to both their visible structure and to that particular kind of additional information that can be conveyed through the user interface to promote "collaboration awareness" (Cabitza et al., 2009). In particular, this information is conveyed according to simple rules that end-users can create, tune and progressively refine in a visual manner, even if they have no specific computer skill, let alone programming skills. This is the most challenging part of our research program, which places it within the scope of both the End-User Development (EUD) and Interaction Design fields.

On the basis of the experimental results that we presented and discussed in this chapter, we have also outlined our future works on how to further improve the usability of the visual rule editor due to the importance of this latter aspect in the EUD perspective. Usability is a different dimension with respect to either "easiness to learn" or "easiness to use" and these latter ones regard both performance only, not satisfaction in its broadest sense. The next improvement steps will take into account the users' suggestions collected by means of the feedback questionnaire and the users' behaviors that we observed during the execution of the test sessions. In this line, we will try to improve the visual editor usability and intuitiveness in two ways: on one hand, we will improve the GUI, e.g., by making a more clear separation between the visual language blocks and the blocks that represent the document fields; on the other hand, we will try to extend and improve the original OpenBlocks visual language in order to make it even more intuitive (e.g., by making the different data types available, and corresponding "blocks", more evident).

REFERENCES

Bringay, S., Barry, C., & Charlet, J. (2006). Annotations: A functionality to support cooperation, coordination and awareness in the electronic medical record. In *Proceedings of the 7th International Conference on the Design of Cooperative Systems*. COOP.

Cabitza, F., Colombo, G., & Simone, C. (2013). Leveraging underspecification in knowledge artifacts to foster collaborative activities in professional communities. *International Journal of Human-Computer Studies*, *71*(1), 24–45. doi:10.1016/j.ijhcs.2012.02.005.

Cabitza, F., & Gesso, I. (2011). Web of active documents: An architecture for flexible electronic patient records. In A. Fred, J. Filipe, & H. Gamboa (Eds.), *Biomedical Engineering Systems and Technologies: Third International Joint Conference, BIOSTEC 2010,* (Vol. 127, pp. 44–56). Springer.

Cabitza, F., Gesso, I., & Corna, S. (2011). Tailorable flexibility: Making end-users autonomous in the design of active interfaces. In K. Blashki (Ed.), *MCCSIS 2011: IADIS Multi Conference on Computer Science and Information Systems*. IADIS.

Cabitza, F., & Simone, C. (2010). WOAD: A framework to enable the end-user development of coordination oriented functionalities. *Journal of Organizational and End User Computing*, *22*(2), 1–20. doi:10.4018/joeuc.2010101905.

Cabitza, F., & Simone, C. (2012). Affording mechanisms: An integrated view of coordination and knowledge management. *Computer Supported Cooperative Work*, *21*(2), 227–260. doi:10.1007/s10606-011-9153-z.

Cabitza, F., Simone, C., & Locatelli, M. P. (2012). Supporting artifact-mediated discourses through a recursive annotation tool. In *Proceedings of the 17th ACM International Conference on Supporting Group Work* (pp. 253–262). New York, NY: ACM.

Cabitza, F., Simone, C., & Sarini, M. (2009). Leveraging coordinative conventions to promote collaboration awareness. *Computer Supported Cooperative Work*, *18*(4), 301–330. doi:10.1007/s10606-009-9093-z.

Chen, H.-T., Ma, W.-C., & Liou, D.-M. (2002). Design and implementation of a real-time clinical alerting system for intensive care unit. In *Proceedings of the AMIA Symposium* (p. 131). AMIA.

Chen, W., & Akay, M. (2011). Developing EMRs in developing countries. *IEEE Transactions on Information Technology in Biomedicine*, *15*(1), 62–65. doi:10.1109/TITB.2010.2091509 PMID:21075735.

Conradi, B., Serényi, B., Kranz, M., & Hussmann, H. (2010). SourceBinder: Community-based visual and physical prototyping. In V. Pipek, M. Rohde, S. Budweg, S. Draxler, S. Lohmann, A. Rashid, & G. Stevens (Eds.), *ODS 2010: Proceedings of the 2nd International Workshop on Open Design Spaces*, (Vol. 7, pp. 23–35). International Institute for Socio-Informatics.

Danado, J., & Paternò, F. (2012). Puzzle: A visual-based environment for end user development in touch-based mobile phones. In M. Winckler, P. Forbrig, & R. Bernhaupt (Eds.), *Human-Centered Software Engineering, (LNCS)* (Vol. 7623, pp. 199–216). Berlin: Springer. doi:10.1007/978-3-642-34347-6_12.

de Lemos, R., Giese, H., Müller, H. A., Shaw, M., Andersson, J., & Baresi, L. et al. (2012). *Software engineering for self-adaptive systems: A second research roadmap. Software Engineering for Self-Adaptive Systems II*. Dagstuhl, Germany: Schloss Dagstuhl - Leibniz-Zentrum fuer Informatik, Germany.

Friedman, C. P., & Wyatt, J. (2006). Evaluation methods in biomedical informatics. In K. J. Hannah, & M. J. Ball (Eds.), *Health Informatics* (2nd ed.). Berlin: Springer.

Gutwin, C., & Greenberg, S. (1997). Workspace awareness, position paper. In S. E. McDaniel & T. Brinck (Eds.), *Proceedings of the ACM CHI'97 Workshop on Awareness in Collaborative Systems*. Atlanta, GA: ACM.

Ingalls, D., Wallace, S., Chow, Y.-Y., Ludolph, F., & Doyle, K. (1988). Fabrik: A visual programming environment. In *Proceedings on Object-Oriented Programming Systems, Languages and Applications* (pp. 176–190). New York, NY: ACM.

Krebs, D., Conrad, A., & Wang, J. (2012). Combining visual block programming and graph manipulation for clinical alert rule building. In *Proceedings of the 2012 ACM Annual Conference Extended Abstracts on Human Factors in Computing Systems Extended Abstracts*, (pp. 2453–2458). New York, NY: ACM.

H. Lieberman, F. Paternò, & V. Wulf (Eds.). (2006). *End user development*. Springer Netherlands. doi:10.1007/1-4020-5386-X.

Lincke, J., Krahn, R., Ingalls, D., & Hirschfeld, R. (2009). Lively fabrik - A web-based end-user programming environment. In *Proceedings of the 2009 Seventh International Conference on Creating, Connecting and Collaborating through Computing*, (pp. 11–19). IEEE.

Locatelli, M. P., Ardesia, V., & Cabitza, F. (2010). Supporting learning by doing in archaeology with active process maps. In *Proceedings of the IADIS International Conference on e-Learning*, (Vol. 1, pp. 218–225). IADIS.

Maloney, J., Resnick, M., Rusk, N., Silverman, B., & Eastmond, E. (2010). The scratch programming language and environment. *Transactions on Computing Education, 10*(4), 16:1–16:15.

Mamlin, B. W., Biondich, P. G., Wolfe, B. A., Fraser, H., Jazayeri, D., Allen, C., et al. (2006). Cooking up an open source EMR for developing countries: OpenMRS - A recipe for successful collaboration. In *Proceedings of AMIA Annual Symposium* (p. 529). AMIA.

Morrison, C., & Blackwell, A. (2009). Observing end-user customisation of electronic patient records. In V. Pipek, M. Rosson, B. de Ruyter, & V. Wulf (Eds.), In *Proceedings of the 2nd International Symposium on End-User Development*, (LNCS), (Vol. 5435, pp. 275–284). Springer.

Nardi, B. A. (1993). *A small matter of programming: perspectives on end user computing*. Cambridge, MA: MIT Press.

Navarro-Prieto, R., & Cañas, J. J. (2001). Are visual programming languages better? The role of imagery in program comprehension. *International Journal of Human-Computer Studies, 54*(6), 799–829. doi:10.1006/ijhc.2000.0465.

Perry, D. E., Porter, A. A., & Votta, L. G. (2000). Empirical studies of software engineering: A roadmap. In *Proceedings of the Conference on The Future of Software Engineering*, (pp. 345–355). New York, NY: ACM.

Puckette, M. (1996). Pure data: Another integrated computer music environment. In *Proceedings of the Second Intercollege Computer Music Concerts*, (pp. 37–41). IEEE.

Repenning, A., Ahmadi, N., Repenning, N., Ioannidou, A., Webb, D., & Marshall, K. (2011). Collective programming: Making end-user programming (more) social. In M. Costabile, Y. Dittrich, G. Fischer, & A. Piccinno (Eds.), *End-User Development, (LNCS)* (Vol. 6654, pp. 325–330). Springer. doi:10.1007/978-3-642-21530-8_34.

Roque, R. V. (2007). *OpenBlocks: An extendable framework for graphical block programming systems.* (Master Thesis). Massachusetts Institute of Technology, Cambridge, MA.

Seto, E., Leonard, K. J., Cafazzo, J. A., Barnsley, J., Masino, C., & Ross, H. J. (2012). Developing healthcare rule-based expert systems: Case study of a heart failure telemonitoring system. *International Journal of Medical Informatics, 81*(8), 556–565. doi:10.1016/j.ijmedinf.2012.03.001 PMID:22465288.

Stolee, K. T., & Fristoe, T. (2011). Expressing computer science concepts through Kodu game lab. In *Proceedings of the 42nd ACM Technical Symposium on Computer Science Education*, (pp. 99–104). New York, NY: ACM.

Weyns, D., Malek, S., & Andersson, J. (2010). FORMS: A formal reference model for self-adaptation. In *Proceedings of the 7th International Conference on Autonomic Computing*, (pp. 205–214). New York, NY: ACM.

Whitley, K. N., & Blackwell, A. F. (2001). Visual programming in the wild: A survey of LabVIEW programmers. *Journal of Visual Languages and Computing, 12*(4), 435–472. doi:10.1006/jvlc.2000.0198.

Wong, W.-K., Moore, A., Cooper, G., & Wagner, M. (2002). Rule-based anomaly pattern detection for detecting disease outbreaks. In *Proceedings of the Eighteenth National Conference on Artificial Intelligence* (pp. 217–223). Menlo Park, CA: American Association for Artificial Intelligence.

ADDITIONAL READING

Atkinson, P. A. (1995). *Medical talk and medical work.* Thousand Oaks, CA: Sage Publications Ltd..

Banâtre, J.-P., Fradet, P., & Le Métayer, D. (2001). Gamma and the chemical reaction model: Fifteen years after. In C. Calude, G. Paun, G. Rozenberg, & A. Salomaa (Eds.), *Multiset Processing, (LNCS)* (Vol. 2235, pp. 17–44). Springer. doi:10.1007/3-540-45523-X_2.

Bardram, J., & Hansen, T. (2010). Context-based workplace awareness. *Computer Supported Cooperative Work, 19*(2), 105–138. doi:10.1007/s10606-010-9110-2.

Blackwell, A. F. (2006). Ten years of cognitive dimensions in visual languages and computing: Guest editor's introduction to special issue. *Journal of Visual Languages and Computing, 17*(4), 285–287. doi:10.1016/j.jvlc.2006.04.001.

Bringay, S., Barry, C., & Charlet, J. (2005). Annotations for managing knowledge in the electronic health record. In *Proceeding Workshop Knowledge Management and Organizational Memories IJCAI-2005*. IJCAI.

Buneman, P., & Steedman, M. (2002). Annotation – The new medium of communication. In *Proceedings of the UKCRC Grand Challenge Workshop*. Edinburgh, UK: UKCRC.

Carroll, J. M., Kellogg, W. A., & Rosson, M. B. (1991). The task-artifact cycle. In J. M. Carroll (Ed.), *Designing interaction: Psychology at the human-computer interface* (pp. 74–102). New York, NY: Cambridge University Press.

Dourish, P., & Bellotti, V. (1992). Awareness and coordination in shared workspaces. In *Proceedings of the 1992 ACM Conference on Computer-Supported Cooperative Work* (pp. 107–114). New York, NY: ACM Press.

Fischer, G. (2003). Meta-design: Beyond user-centered and participatory design. *Human-Computer Interaction: Theory and Practice, 1*, 88.

Fischer, G., & Giaccardi, E. (2006). Meta-design: A framework for the future of end-user development. In H. Lieberman (Ed.), *End User Development -- Empowering people to flexibly employ advanced information and communication technology* (pp. 427–457). Dordrecht, The Netherlands: Kluwer Academic Publishers. doi:10.1007/1-4020-5386-X_19.

Fischer, G., Giaccardi, E., Ye, Y., Sutcliffe, A. G., & Mehandjiev, N. (2004). Meta-design: A manifesto for end-user development. *Communications of the ACM, 47*(9), 33–37. doi:10.1145/1015864.1015884.

Hague, R., & Robinson, P. (2006). End-user programming of reconfigurable systems. *Software, Practice & Experience, 36*(11-12), 1285–1306. doi:10.1002/spe.758.

Hovorka, D. S., & Germonprez, M. (2009). Tinkering, tailoring, and bricolage: Implications for theories of design. In *Proceedings of the 15th Americas Conference on Information Systems*. AMCIS.

Lewis, D. K. (1969). *Convention: A philosophical study*. Boston: Harvard University Press.

Mørch, A. I., & Mehandjiev, N. D. (2000). Tailoring as collaboration: The mediating role of multiple representations and application units. *Computer Supported Cooperative Work, 9*(1), 75–100. doi:10.1023/A:1008713826637.

Sellen, A. J., & Harper, R. H. R. (2003). *The myth of the paperless office*. Cambridge, MA: MIT Press.

Strauss, A., Fagerhaugh, S., Suczek, B., & Wiener, C. (1985). *The social organization of medical work*. New York, NY: University of Chicago Press.

Wachter, R. M. (2010). Patient safety at ten: Unmistakable progress, troubling gaps. *Health Affairs, 29*(1), 165–173. doi:10.1377/hlthaff.2009.0785 PMID:19952010.

Whitley, K. N. (1997). Visual programming languages and the empirical evidence for and against. *Journal of Visual Languages and Computing, 8*(1), 109–142. doi:10.1006/jvlc.1996.0030.

KEY TERMS AND DEFINITIONS

Awareness (Promoting) Information: A graphic cue that is proactively conveyed on top of documents with the aim of supporting and improving convention-based work practices.

Datom: A reusable set of data fields, which defines the visual arrangement and the underlying data model of a relevant piece of information that can be used to create document templates.

Didget: A reusable instance of a datom; didgets are created when users drop a datom within a document template and can be reused within different document templates.

Document Template: A spatial arrangement of didgets.

Electronic Patient Record (EPR): Also known as Electronic Medical Record, a set of electronic records, charts and documents that are used in a healthcare setting to collect and organize health-related information of single inpatients.

Mechanism: A document-related proactive rule aimed at conveying suitable Awareness Information (see above) to users.

Proxy User: A user that can be considered sufficiently representative of the actual intended users of a system that is undergoing validation.

ENDNOTES

1. http://velocity.apache.org/
2. http://www.hl7.org/special/Committees/arden/index.cfm
3. http://www3.gehealthcare.com/
4. http://www.imd-soft.com/
5. http://www.filemaker.com/
6. See http://www.buzzmachines.com/ and http://vvvv.org/, respectively.
7. http://www.ni.com/labview/
8. http://blog.minibloq.org/
9. http://www.lively-kernel.org/
10. http://pipes.yahoo.com/pipes/
11. http://code.google.com/p/scriptblocks/
12. http://code.google.com/p/blockly/
13. http://education.mit.edu/openblocks
14. http://appinventoredu.mit.edu/.
15. The whole set of screenshots can be found at http://tinyurl.com/medit-ihci-2012
16. http://www.jboss.org/drools

Section 2
Design Approaches

Chapter 10
The Gamification Experience:
UXD with a Gamification Background

Cathie Marache-Francisco
Université de Lorraine, France

Eric Brangier
Université de Lorraine, France

ABSTRACT

Through this chapter, the authors aim at describing Gamification—the use of game elements in non-ludic environments—to identify its limits and lacks as well as its assets. Indeed, it has been developed to answer a need that arouses out of the Human Computer Interaction (HCI) field evolutions, and it could be valuable in that scope. The authors propose a definition of Gamification according to several different dimensions that are part of the HCI design field. They suggest it as a first step towards a guiding design framework aimed at designers. They mention future research directions that would help in going further and enriching the framework, leading to the creation of a design model for user experience design through Gamification. The authors finally raise some ethical concerns about the meaning of Gamification itself.

INTRODUCTION

The Human Computer Interaction (HCI) design field has tremendously evolved from accessibility to emotional design and persuasive technology (Brangier & Bastien, 2010). This has lead designers to create more and more intuitive and hedonic interactions (Figure 1). That trend is not meant to come to an end as technologies and users are constantly evolving. In that scope, Gamification appeared as a new way to design for successful leisure and work systems.

It can be defined as "an informal umbrella term for the use of video game elements in non-gaming systems to improve user experience (UX) and user engagement" (Deterding, Sicart, Nacke, O'Hara & Dixon, 2011b, p.2). The goal is to modify regular human-machine interactions and turn it into more engaging and motivating ones through the use of game elements in non-game contexts.

Albeit seductive, this idea is very controversial nowadays as it mixes user experience and game design, as well as activity tracking. Its attraction power might come from the game industry success. Indeed, many talks – whether marketing or scientific-oriented – do introduce that topic by mentioning stunning numbers. For instance, Mc-

DOI: 10.4018/978-1-4666-4623-0.ch010

Figure 1. Technological change and evolution of software ergonomics (adapted from Brangier & Bastien, 2010)

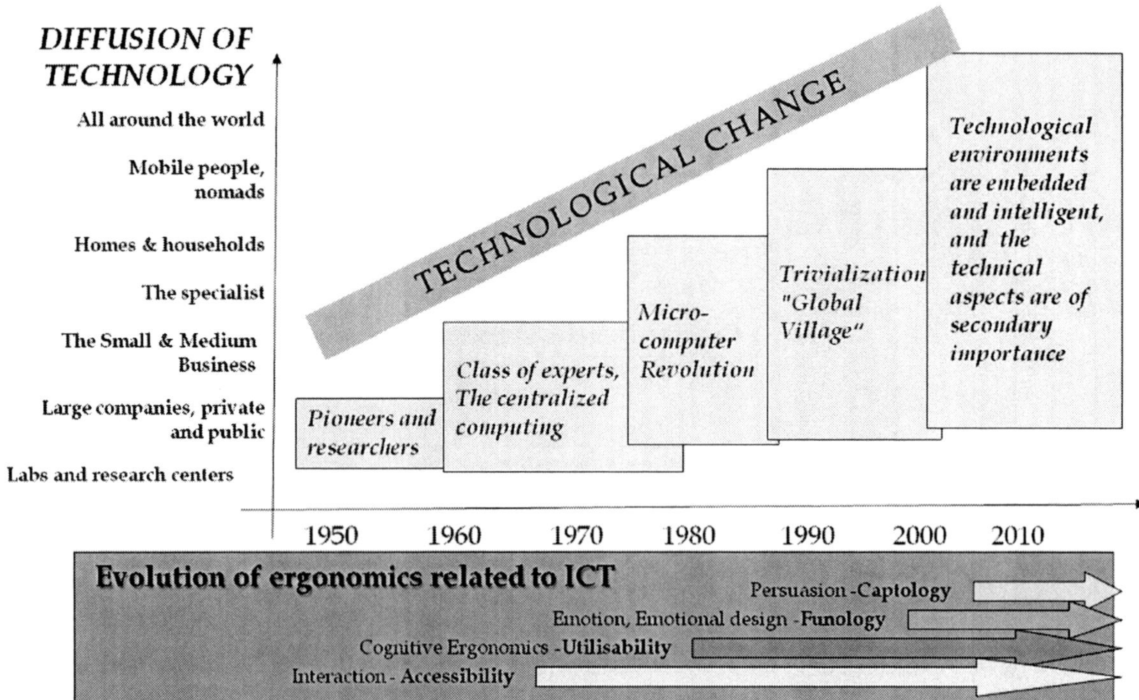

Gonigal's book (2011, p. 3-4) starts with: "Globally, the online gamer community — including console, PC, and mobile phone gaming — counts more than 4 million gamers in the Middle East, 10 million in Russia, 105 million in India, 10 million in Vietnam, 10 million in Mexico, 13 million in Central and South America, 15 million in Australia, 17 million in South Korea, 100 million in Europe, and 200 million in China". Besides, beyond those impressive figures, the immersive game experience is seductive. Being able to decipher and transfer Flow (Csikszentmihalyi, 1990) to non-ludic systems could be a tremendous asset for companies, whether by helping them sell more or by having more productive employees. A Gartner's study (technology research and consulting) reflects that keen interest. Indeed, according to it (Gartner, 2011), more than 50% of innovative companies will take Gamification into account by 2015.

This chapter aims at describing Gamification through its definition, goal, underlying concepts and design methods. We first introduce it the way it is described in the literature to then highlight its limits and put it into its context of emergence. Indeed, Gamification is here to answer a need that arouses out of the HCI field evolutions and it can be valuable if well done. As a step further, we stand back in order to assess Gamification. This leads us to point out several lacks in its concept and design guidance. We finally define it according to several different dimensions as an answer to those lacks. We then mention potential research directions and open the debate of the underlying meaning of Gamification.

BACKGROUND

Gamification Design

There currently exist several different definitions of the concept of Gamification in the literature (Table 1). The common idea is the fact that game elements are introduced in non-ludic systems with the main goal to increase user engagement and motivation.

In order to illustrate what is sought-after, we can quote Liu, Alexandrova and Nakajima (2011) who define a "so-called game-like behavior: focus on the task at hand, multitasking under pressure, work overtime without discontented attitude, always keep retrying when fails, etc.". However, as reflected on the above-mentioned definitions, some authors focus on reaching a better user experience – even fun and devouring – while others concentrate on issue-resolution.

Table 1. Gamification definitions

Authors	Definition
Deterding & al (2011b)	An informal umbrella term for the use of video game elements in nongaming systems to improve user experience (UX) and user engagement.
Thom, Millen & DiMicco (n.d.)	The use of game mechanics in non-gaming applications (…) aims to create a sense of playfulness in non-game environments so that participation becomes enjoyable and desirable.
Zichermann & Cunningham (2011)	The process of game-thinking and game mechanics to engage users and solve problems.
Witt, Scheiner & Robra-Bissantz (2011)	Implementing principles and mechanics of games (like points, leaderboards or levels) in a serious context is called "Gamification" and illustrates one possibility to increase the level of enjoyment and flow and hence, to address these challenges [encourage customers to submit ideas].
IActionable (2012) (gamification platform)	Gamification increases engagement by leveraging feedback mechanisms traditionally found in games.

Deterding, Khaled, Nacke & Dixon (2011a) positioned Gamification amongst the past tentative to use game as an inspiration for HCI design (e.g., Malone, 1984; funology; playfulness; serious games). Four components characterize gamification according to the authors:

- **Game:** The focus is on game and not play, as differentiated by Caillois (1967) through the two poles Ludus (rules and goals) and Païda ("tumultuous".)
- **Elements:** Gamification does not aim at creating a full game as in serious games but at reusing elements of it. This raises the issue of the frontier between games and game elements and it also questions the possibility to define what a game element is. The authors suggest as a first step to talk about "elements that are characteristic to games."
- **Design:** Gamification implies the use of five levels of game design (game interface design patterns ; game design patterns and mechanics ; design principles, heuristics or 'lenses' ; conceptual models of game design units ; game design methods and design processes.)
- Non game context.

There is currently no consensus concerning Gamification theoretical background as several authors mention several different theories. It may be explained by the fact that Gamification is a very trendy concept nowadays and that a lot of people share their insight on it, coming from interactive marketing, user experience or game design fields. Robert (2011) even talked about Gamification *slideshareatture* as this kind of communication mostly consist of live presentation or downloadable slides. Very often, the authors mention a gathering of motivational psychology theories and game design theories, leading to the conclusion that game elements must fit the user's profiles (social style, motivators, skills), and that the emphasis must be on status, progression elements, rewards, social connection and challenges.

As an example, Zichermann and Cunningham (2011) list several different theories: Flow (Csikszentmihalyi, 1990), conditioning, neuropsychology (reinforcement through dopamine), Bartle's players types (Killers, Achievers, Socializers, Explorers, 2005), intrinsic/extrinsic motivation (the authors state that both are valuable), Dreyfus' steps to mastery, MDA by Hunicke & al., 2004, the social engagement loop. They also introduce their own theories: SAPS rewarding system (Status, Access, Power and Stuff) and a classification of the reasons why people play: mastery, relaxation, fun, socialization. Finally, they describe the Gamification process as a reward system adapted to the users, based on their SAPS theory. Status is obtained through badges, levels (and progression elements) and leaderboards. The authors also mention the use of points and virtual economy, the need for a social system and customization.

Another Gamification contributor, Kim (Casual Games Association, 2011), is a social game designer. In order to create a "multi-player" Gamification experience, she has advised to take into account the social style of the users (based on Bartle's players types, 2005) and his/her level of expertise (Newbie, Regular or Enthusiast). She mentioned the motivational model PERMA (Positive emotions, Engagement and flow, Relationships, Meaning and purpose, Accomplishments by Seligman, 2011) as well as Maslow's work (1970). She defines a Gamification design loop based on the workflow: "Action - Visible Progress - Positive Emotions - Call to Action - Action...". As her talk focuses on social systems, she gives design tips based on the users' social styles: Competition (e.g., points, badges and leaderboard), Expression (e.g., choose, customize, layout, design), Exploration (e.g., view, read, search, collect, complete) and Cooperation (e.g., join, share, exchange, gifting). She also insists on the need for an interaction that evolves through time and that would induce intrinsic motivation through autonomy, mastery and purpose.

Academic researchers are also working on that topic, creating Gamification systems and analyzing its effects on the users' activity. Based on a literature review, Flatla (& al., 2011) have identified four main elements to add to their calibration system in order to gamify it: challenging goals, rewards and behavior reinforcement (through animations and sounds), progress units (e.g., levels) and markers (e.g., badges, score, time pressure) and finally a theme. Gnauk (& al., 2012) states that hedonic aspects of games consist of points, levels and badges as well as social comparison/ challenges that trigger motivation. They also mention more generic concepts: usability, stimulating visuals and input techniques. Law, Kasirun and Gan (2011) use roles missions and Epic Meaning as well as rewards (point, badges and status), leaderboards and statistics on the users' performance. Knautz (& al., 2012) has created an avatar that would grow from egg to pet through the winning of levels and experience points. He also mentions achievements, leaderboards and social comments. As a last example, Singer and Schneider (2012) have designed a motivational system for team work based on news feeds, comments, avatar, leaderboards, and congratulation.

In order to specify further what Gamification design consists of, Liu, Alexandrova and Nakajima (2011) define what they call the "Gamification Loop". This consists of a cycle that is initiated by a challenge defined by specific winning conditions. Every time a sub goal is achieved, a reward system is triggered, underlined by a point system. A leaderboard is then filled with that new entry and badges are offered to the user. As a consequence, the user's social and network status are modified. On top of that point-system-centered Gamification loop, the authors mention the importance of what they call a "game-like surface". However, they don't provide any further design specification on that matter.

Several real Gamification examples can be found on the Internet. They are aimed at several different topics such as the promotion of a healthy lifestyle or sustainable environment practices, social relationships and knowledge sharing, marketing, education or productivity. They all share a common set of Gamification design techniques that we will introduce briefly, knowing that this is a non-exhaustive list of the Gamification components that are part of those systems.

We can mention the cases of the non-productive systems such as HealthMonth, a website that allows setting and monitoring health goals through time. It consists of game vocabulary, point systems, iconography, gifts, statistics, progression bar and goals. Foursquare, a mobile application to share one's knowledge of places in a city (like restaurants, hanging out places) uses avatars, points, goals, progression bar, leaderboard, social network, statistics, badges and rewards. Finally, MindBloom, a website that allows to set and monitor healthy goals, whether physical, psychological or financial efforts, uses thematic, game-like surface, goals, metaphor, social network, levels and points.

About productivity, a lot of attempts have been released such as DevHub, a Website that allows creating and managing websites and blogs aimed at professionals and casual people. We can identify a Game-like surface, avatar, points systems, virtual monetary system, trophies, progression image, game vocabulary and the use of metaphor. We can also mention Ribbon Hero 2, a plugin that is aimed at the Microsoft office suite. It integrates learning modules inside of each tool in order to teach it to the users which use a Game-like surface, virtual playmate avatar, story, game vocabulary, goals and sub goals, points, hints, extra-content. Finally, Nitro, a website for selling team where its members can log on that website and manage their efforts uses points, levels, progression bars, challenges, iconology, game vocabulary, leaderboards, teams, customizable pictures.

What is Behind the Concept?

Gamification designed at its apex could lead to a real feeling of gaming while using a non-ludic system. This raises several concerns.

First, researchers don't perceive games as a collection of game elements. Contrarily to Gamification, it is not only about adding points and leaderboards: it generates an experience (Schell, 2008). Scholars (Caillois, 1967; Winnicott, 1971; Triclot, 2011; Juul, 2005) thus define games as leading to an absorbing experience detached from reality and production matters, set in a space aside. As an example, Juul (2005) mentions the fact that "the consequences of the activity are negotiable", while Salen and Zimmerman (2004) state that "players engage in an artificial conflict". By designing for pleasurable interactions and a globalized interactive hedonism which provide a game-like atmosphere, professional users could thus be diverted from productivity matters and grow away from work.

A second concern is about Efficiency. Indeed, the notion of efficiency at work differs utterly from games characteristics. Work requires minimum effort for maximum productivity while games, as described by Suits (1990), limit the player's efficiency: "To play a game is to engage in activity directed towards bringing about a specific state of affairs, using only means permitted by rules, where the rules prohibit more efficient in favour of less efficient means, and where such rules are accepted just because they make possible such activity" (p.34). This definition emphasizes the fact that games limit the player's behavior. Nevertheless, players accept those limiting rules, those "unnecessary obstacles", as it is what makes it meaningful.

Following a review of game definition led by Salen and Zimmerman (2004, 80): "A game is a system in which players engage in an artificial conflict, defined by rules, that results in a quantifiable outcome". Indeed, according to the authors, "All games embody a contest of powers" (whether using cooperation or competition). Games are thus mostly about challenging the player. This could raise a concern when applied to work as according to Apter (1991), arousal could be pleasant when it is related to an activity without external goal, but stressful when its goal is work-related.

Most elements used on Gamification rely on competition and rewards. The underlying idea is that people are competitive and seek payment, which does not reflect the current population. Indeed, about competition games, Adams (2010) reminds us that there are several different kinds of players, not all being motivated by competition. This questions the efficacy of such a method. About the role of rewards, a meta-analysis conducted by Deci, Koestner and Ryan (2001) revealed the fact that "tangible rewards do significantly and substantially undermine intrinsic motivation" (p.2). The Cognitive Evaluation Theory explains that phenomena: elements decreasing perceived self-determination by offering external reasons for actions will consequently have a negative effect on intrinsic motivation. Nicholson (2012) relates that study to current gamification practices and call for a meaningful gamification that would be a user-centered and relevant use of game design elements that would not rely on external rewards. This concept is fundamental; especially at work where having employees motivation not directed towards "doing the job right" could potentially harm the organization.

Gamification is not neutral. This concept conveys a certain meaning as Caillois (1967) says that "[Games] illustrate (…) a moral and intellectual value of a culture" (p.76). Current characteristics of Gamification question the underlying value of it: it is used by managers to track the user activity, work and leisure are being monetized, workplaces are turned into competition areas and the main goal is to change people's behavior. We seem to be far from what he calls "a universe that is kept aside, closed, protected: a pure area" (p.38). Triclot (2011) also mentions that ambiguous aspect of Gamification. According to him, it is a transcription of anything into indicators that are to be optimized. It sets an ideal of perfect equality with public indicators and the end of cheating.

Thus, by trying to unite productivity and pleasure within a same system, Gamification can be thought as an ideology rather than a technique. It would thus rely on three main points:

1. **A Pivot Concept for Technology Acceptance:** A gap can be witnessed between the success of games and mobile devices and the painful interactions employees experience everyday with professional software. Gamification does not consider work as associated with constraints but through ludic interactions, going beyond usefulness and usability.
2. **Promoting a Successful Professional Model of Interaction:** Gamification is about implementing aesthetic elements, ludic and appealing interactions still successfully filling a function in a professional context. It would thus be a requisite to professional technologies use.
3. **An Ambiguous Method:** Gamification, as a set of HCI methods, compounds practices that are both helpful and harmful for the final users. Indeed, by trying to create simplified and more appealing systems for novice users and the GenYers, it can complicate what was straightforward and efficient to experts.

Despite all those potential issues that can be raised on Gamification, we cannot deny the fact that it appears at the edge of the HCI evolution. It is an answer to the need for more hedonic and motivational interactions and could be valuable in that scope.

Why does Gamification Matter?

According to Brangier and Bastien (2010) the HCI Design field is no longer the one it used to be. It has evolved tremendously through those last years as designers are creating systems that are more and more engaging. Indeed, by taking into account the final user and his relationship with the system, we have shifted from accessibility to persuasive technology.

First, accessibility helps the designers getting focused on a primary concern: guaranteeing the access of the users to the system. Despite the fact that it is very often about designing for users with disabilities, accessibility is also aimed at casual users.

Beyond accessibility, the notion of usability arose to emphasis the need for simple interactions. This ergonomics concept arose out of HCI studies that took place during the 70's. Those were focused on operators reasoning modes, workload and constraints with the final goal to guarantee that systems fitted their cognitive and motor characteristics. It is defined by the ISO norm 9241-11 (1998) as "the effectiveness, efficiency and satisfaction with which specified users can achieve specified goals in particular environments":

- **Effectiveness:** Accuracy and completeness with which users achieve specified goals.
- **Efficiency:** Resources expended in relation to the accuracy and completeness with which users achieve goals.
- **Satisfaction:** Freedom from discomfort, and positive attitudes towards the use of the product.

The concept of usability has been fundamental for decades. Indeed, classic theories of technology adoption and use state that usability coupled with usefulness are requisite for a successful Human-machine interaction. In fact, according to Brangier, Hammes-Adelé and Bastien (2010), the first HCI design approaches were focused on the operatory acceptance of systems, which can be guaranteed through compatibility between the triad "user, task and software". Subsequently, social acceptance theories such as the TAM (Technology Acceptance Model by Davis, 1989) state that the perceived use and ease of use are primary factors on users' acceptance of a NICT (New Information and Communications Technology).

Afterwards, the field of emotional design has added a new layer to those two key concepts: it implies thinking about the non-instrumental qualities of a system. The goal is to fulfill a user's need beyond mere usability, such as the wish for social bounds or for a hedonic experience, leading to positive experiences. Indeed, user centered design fields of practice seek for compatibility between the users' characteristics and the systems they interact with. This can be studied from several different angles: technical, social integration or appropriation. All those aspects are not covered by usability and usefulness, hence the need for a new concept. Several authors have worked on that topic such as Foxall and Goldsmith (1994), Jordan (1999), Norman (2004), Hassenzahl (2004) or Desmet, Hekkert and Hillen (2004). Several different categorizations of users' needs exist nowadays, yet having common concepts. First, usefulness and usability are root needs. When fulfilled, non-functional needs can be looked for: aesthetic (through all senses), value and prestige, social needs, accomplishment, learning, expression and then evocation.

In the end, Persuasive technology is at the apex of this HCI evolution. The goal of this set of techniques is to take advantage of the characteristics of new technologies in order to modify the users' attitudes and/or behavior. Indeed, as NICT are ubiquitous and interactive, it is easy to create an adaptive and continuous persuasive dialogue. Several authors have suggested design guidelines for persuasive technology such as Fogg (2003), Oinas-Kukkonen and Harjumaa (2009) and Nemery, Brangier and Kopp (2010). We can also mention Lockton, Harrison and Stanton (2010) who have created a Design with Intent toolkit that comprises persuasive technology techniques.

Finally, a broader concept can be mentioned: we all design for a user experience. This field of practice aims at gathering instrumental and non-instrumental aspects of a system under the same model, as well as the emotions felt by the users during the interaction. This "Umbrella Topic" (Instone, 2005) is still not consensual amongst researchers, as there is a variety of disciplinary, methodological and conceptual points of view on that topic. However, it is valuable as it links several disciplines' contributions. Every definition of user experience emphasizes the idea that it results from the interaction of several factors. Hassenzahl and Tractinsky's definition (2006, p. 95) illustrates this concept well: it is "a consequence of a user's internal state (e.g., predispositions, expectations, needs, motivation, mood), the characteristics of the designed system (e.g. complexity, purpose, usability, functionality) and the context (or the environment) within which the interaction occurs (e.g. organizational/social setting, meaningfulness of the activity, voluntariness of use)". That trend is not meant to come to an end as NICT are constantly evolving towards interfaces that are always simpler and more engaging. The world of Web 2.0 is thus offering user experiences of an increasing quality, especially since mobile devices development. Indeed, it implies numerous constraints that are directly bound to its characteristics. The device itself, through its size or the interaction model and the context of use (mobility) imply necessarily different needs and design answers. Finally, the interfaces are more and more streamlined, user-friendly, attractive and immersive. Besides, it leads to more ubiquitous user experiences since those devices (computers, tablets and smartphones) are linked and share information. Through that continuous channel and transversal experience, the host device is becoming secondary (Saha & Mukherjee, 2003).

Finally, the users are not the same as before. New generations are born with the internet, Gameboys and PlayStations. They are familiar with these devices and their interaction modes, which leads them to expect always more from a user experience point of view. Besides, they were born while deep human-machine interaction modifications were happening and intend to testimony even more innovation.

Furthermore, workplaces are currently facing a staff reconfiguration. Through lifespan expansion, numerous generations work together (veterans, baby-boomers, X generation and Y generation), each and every one of them carrying their own attitudes and expectations towards companies (Dejoux & Wechtler, 2011). The Y generation is the focus of many concerns as numerous myths are attached to it: lack of loyalty and efficiency, search for quick rise in the hierarchy scheme in parallel of a wish to live fully one's personal life. It implies rethinking current management techniques as well as non-user-friendly numeric working tools.

Finally, Gamification is said to be able to answer those concerns by transferring the habits the new generations have about gaming to non-ludic systems. Indeed, Gamification aims at triggering the users' needs for accomplishment and social bounds as well as for hedonic interactions. By doing this, it could help going even further than current practices and it would become a requisite for a successful human-technology interaction.

USER EXPERIENCE DESIGN AND GAMIFICATION DESIGN

A Need for Clear Concepts and Design Specifications

Through that Gamification literature review, we can note that despite the fact that a lot has been said and written about Gamification, this field of practice is still not mature enough to constitute a concrete and clearly defined user experience design method. Concerning its definition in itself, Gamification seems to differ from one author to another. Indeed, even if the core principle is similar – using game elements and game thinking into non-ludic systems – its goal is not clearly set. Gamification is said to be used to improve user experience, user engagement, motivation, but also to generate fun, flow and enjoyment while using regular systems. However, this idea of fun is not shared amongst every authors and Gamification upholders. For instance, IActionable (2012), which is a Gamification platform, claims that Gamification is a way to provide game-inspired feedbacks and rewards in order to engage people. According to them, fun is nothing more than a side-effect to those who are sensitive to the chosen game elements:

We know you may want to take a common task and make it "fun" – but that's not what we do – not directly. What we do is help users see how well they are performing or contributing, how they compare to other people, and provide goals for them to work towards. Now, some people may find that fun (...) [it] is a nice side effect, but incidental. It is not the primary goal. (...) It's all wrapped up in a game-like interface, but no one is going to think they are playing Space Invaders.

Those two different and complementary goals imply different ways of thinking and designing for Gamification. Indeed, game feedback elements are only rewards attached to pre-defined goals, which does not reflect the core game experience but a mere feedback system. On the contrary, trying to create fun out of a system implies a more high-level design time – what some authors call: "game-thinking". But game-thinking does not necessarily mean fun. It is about designing for an experience that drives the user through a journey. Indeed, the social game designer Kim (Casual Game Association, 2011) insists on the need for a meaningful Gamification that would fit the user's profile and create a catchy and increasing challenging system based on what makes sense for him. When looking at how Gamification is currently being applied, those ideas are mostly operationalized through point-based systems attached to goals and the use of social dynamics – mostly competition ones through the use of leaderboards. The Gamification loop is a good example of the way games are reduced to in the Gamification scope.

Several issues arise from that point. To begin with, Gamification thought as a "game-like experience" does not seem that easy to design for. Indeed, according to Kim (Casual Game Association, 2011), adding points, badges and leaderboards is not what makes the core of game design – and thus a good Gamification design. The author claims for the use of Gamification as a way to create positive emotions through Autonomy, Mastery and Purpose. Those concepts are appealing and imply the "high-level design time" we have already mentioned before. The author mentions a few tips to take that into account but no clear design framework has been suggested: it implies to think like a game designer which requires a full game design process (and thus a very specific expertise). This could be thought as contradictory to Gamification itself as the goal is not to create a game but to extract simple game elements that will then be dusted over a non-ludic system. Indeed, Gamification, as Bogost (2011) says, suggests through the "-ification" part of it a simple, repeatable and efficient process. Therefore, there seems to be an ambiguity as it is both said that game elements must be carefully chosen and organized through game thinking, but also that the Gamification process can be easy to reproduce.

The fact that the game journey is not present on Gamification – thus questioning the efficacy of the game elements that are being reused – is a first level of concern. But when examining current Gamification design a second level of concern arises. Indeed, beyond that "to be or not to be" consideration, the current (and simplified) way to design for Gamification is not clear as well. For instance, the Gamification loop that comprises a lot of common Gamification practices does not clearly define the several different elements that it consists of, especially concerning the visual design part. Furthermore, several articles mention the need for a nice experience, such as Gnauk (& al., 2012) who calls for "stimulating visuals and input techniques" – which is hard to define.

Beyond that nice-visual-elements hazy concept, the listing of other game elements that can be reused is not clearly set. Authors mostly mention goal-based rewards and reinforcement systems as well as progression and social elements. One issue is that there is currently no exhaustive method of Gamification design and designers must apply those broad concepts to their own project or transpose existing Gamification systems to their own. They have to choose which element to use and how (e.g., sub goals granularity and badges). There is thus a need for more systematic framework. Besides, this could also lead to confusion. Indeed, elements that are part of casual non-ludic systems and that have been more recently added to games are mentioned and used, such as newsfeeds, social sharing and comments (Facebook assets). We can wonder whether those elements are game elements or not, thus questioning the boundaries of Gamification as such: can any element used in games be labeled as Gamification?

Finally, a theoretical plethora is characteristic of that concept: Gamification authors make reference to recent (and outdated) motivational and game theories. It reveals the fact that Gamification is a broad concept that everyone wants to seize, coming from several different fields of practices (marketing, user experience, design, game design, etc.) and bringing their own insight and sources. It is also characteristic of the fact that Gamification is not yet mature as a concept.

The Dimensions of Gamification

This analysis of Gamification lacks brought us to an exercise of categorization. Indeed, we can identify several different dimensions out of Gamification existing definitions and practices as presented in Figure 2. We believe that pointing those out can help establishing a clear framework for Gamification definition and design.

We claim that three main aspects underlie Gamification design. First, the most prominent element of Gamification is related to its sensory-motor dimension. Indeed, the output modes are specific to this kind of systems. Second, the motivational part of it – through emotional engagement –is central as it is one of the most consensual goals of it. Thirdly, we call attention to the cognitive dimension of Gamification. Indeed, some authors aim at using Gamification as a goal-resolution method, and some elements are directly related to the task, helping the users resolve it in an efficient manner. We will see through that discussion that the Gamification elements overlap those categories as they all carry several different meaning and functions.

Figure 2. The three dimensions of gamification design

Gamification through Sensory-Motor Modalities

The sensory-motor dimension is related to the input and output modes of the interaction. Indeed, Gamification always implies having a Game-like surface (Liu & al, 2011) which is applied either to the whole user interface (e.g., Mindbloom and its immersive country environment where the user progress is symbolized through a growing tree) or to single elements that are part of a professional-looking user interface (e.g., eccentric challenge icons on the SalesForce Nitro portal).

Games offer a very wide range of output methods by stimulating visually, through the audition and the touch. It helps communicating an atmosphere, a theme or needed information.

The most obvious sensory part of a game is its visual elements (Fox, 2005): its logo, color palette, pictures and symbols, the dimension used (2D or 3D) or typography. Concerning the color palette, classical design principles are to be applied (e.g., harmonious color choice through the color wheel). The visual elements must be consistent through the whole game and, most importantly, fit the public and kind of game. For example, we can find similar visual characteristics across the video games Silent Hill and Resident Evil: dark unsaturated colors including the complimentary red and green.

Audio is used a lot as well to provide feedback and help creating an atmosphere. It can take shape of sound effects, music or verbal discourse.

Haptic feedback is provided through joysticks or mobile devices. Albeit not often used on gamified systems, vibrations could help providing an immersive environment just like the audio.

Perceptive coding is not only a matter of static elements: animations are intrinsically part of games. It can either be about visual coding animations (e.g., flash, twinkling, highlight, transparency) or the movement of game elements. Fox (2005) mentions several different animations that are inspired from real behavior: Squash and stretch (imitating the movement of a gum ball bouncing on the floor), Anticipation (adding a slight movement in the opposed direction of the movement before its start), Ease in and ease out (progressively starting and ending animation movements), Follow-through (animating an object a little bit after its end point then bringing it back to it), Arcs (imitating natural nonlinear movements), Exaggeration, Translation, Rotation and Scale Variation.

Concerning perceptive organization, Fox (2005) insists on the need to follow – again – fundamental and elementary design principles. He provides us with some examples: the elements must be aligned and uniformly spaced; there must be a good balance between variations and unity elements; the user's eye must be guided by the composition through lines, forms, colors and shapes; the whole must be balanced (whether through symmetry or asymmetry); a short list must be composed of an odd number of elements. Finally, Fox (2005) states that usability matters such as legibility and grouping/distinction between items (Bastien & Scapin, 1993).

Game-to-player communication must be straightforward with non-intrusive but constantly available indicators (Desurvire & Wiberg, 2008). Game designer have thus adopted specific perceptive organization principles. HUDs (Heads Up Display) are a good example of it: those are every piece of information displayed to support the player task. A sub layer that is located above the current gaming area contains radars, health metrics or scores that are constantly available, generally on the border of the screen. It is characterized by its small size, its potential transparency and its very visual and simplified representation (e.g., Zelda the Ocarina of Time always displays the available inventory elements and health information through images).

Besides, Dyck (& al., 2003) mentioned what they call fluid system-human interaction. It means that games deliver information to the player without interrupting his task and immersion, in a way that implies less attention and effort. The authors mention three types of communication strategies: calm messaging, attention-aware interface elements and finally context-aware view behaviors:

- **Calm Messaging:** The information is delivered on a non-intrusive way. No action is needed from the user part, whether to reject it, explicitly acknowledge it or process it. Games communicate through sounds, ephemeral exits or animations.
- **Attention-Aware Interface Elements:** The elements on an interface are displayed differently according to the importance granted by the user. This frees space for relevant items. For examples, elements can be set half-transparent when not focused on.
- **Context-Aware View Behaviors:** The workspace is dynamically self-adapted through zoom, panoramic view and rotation. The goal is to automatically focus on relevant information to the user for a given task sequence.

Furthermore, games can give the user the possibility to modify themselves the organization of their interface so that it could be adapted to their current task (Dyck & al., 2003).

Gamification to Drive Motivation

As Gamification's first mission is to engage the users and to motivate them working on the gamified tool, two main dimensions are gathered under that will: playing on the users' Emotions and triggering Persuasion.

HCI evolutions leading to emotional design and the consideration of the users' non-functional needs that go beyond usability can be directly related to Gamification. Indeed, as already mentioned, its upholders claim being inspired by players' profiles and needs (e.g., Bartle's players types, 2005; PERMA by Seligman, 2011; Maslow's work, 1970). It thus orients the kind of game elements that are going to be reused in a Gamification scope.

Primarily, the need for hedonism through senses stimulation can be directly related to the Sensory-motor dimension of Gamification. Indeed, games communicate through visual, audio and haptic elements.

Concerning value and prestige, several different elements answer these concerns: mission accomplishment, badges and privileges or leaderboards all reflect certain skills and status. The game thematic and the concept of Epic Meaning (having a goal that goes beyond oneself and serve a greater purpose) can also add certain values to a system. For example, the players' points reaching a given level can lead to a charity donation, thus adding value to the system and the users' actions.

The need for accomplishment is filled through task completion, sub-goals and challenge resolutions as well as through associated rewards (e.g., point systems, virtual money, and gifts) and new levels reached. Indeed, it leads to a gratifying increasing use and learning curve.

Lastly, social needs are central on Gamification design. Kim (Casual Game Association, 2011) illustrates that through corresponding game elements: competition (e.g., leaderboards), cooperation (e.g., sharing, gifting, helping), exploration (e.g., collecting, voting) or expression (e.g., personalizing, creating, decorating).

Persuasive technology inspires a lot of techniques that are perceived as belonging to the Gamification field of study. On this point, Nemery, Brangier and Kopp (2010) introduce a set of ergonomics criteria for persuasive technology that consists of 4 static criteria and 4 dynamic ones.

Two static criteria are relevant concerning Gamification: Personalization and Attractiveness. Personalization is two-sided: it first concerns the possibility for the user to personalize his content, which can be found on Gamification systems through goal personalization, voting or user interface personalization. Second, it deals with tailored content which can be attained through the use of difficulty-increasing goals that help novice users through easy first steps and the suggestion of tailored steps. Attractiveness deals with visually appealing elements that have a guiding and call-to-action function as well as a hedonic function (e.g., look and feel, attractive talking avatar).

The dynamic criteria stage an evolutionary interaction: 1) Priming: initiating the interaction; 2) Commitment: easy, not demanding and thus engaging baby-step actions and encouragement and 3) Freely accepted compliance: increasing and more demanding actions to engage the user more deeply. First, games gratification rhetoric (Järvinen, 2008) helps Priming the interaction. Second, every light first action to take and game-like motivational message lead to Commitment (e.g., avatar configuration, goal setting and congratulation). Finally, more demanding goals and tasks help engaging the user deeper in the interaction leading to Freely accepted compliance. The feeling of freedom of choice must underlie all those steps in order to guarantee persuasion.

Oinas-Kukkonen and Harjumaa (2009) have suggested four sets of persuasive techniques, of which three are relevant on a Gamification scope: Primary Task Support, Dialogue Support and Social Support. Concerning Primary task support techniques, several of them are reused on Gamification: Tunneling is operated by making explicit guiding goals and sub goals; Self-monitoring through any progression element (e.g., level or progress bar) and statistics and Reduction through the splitting of complex tasks into more simple ones. Tailoring and Personalization are linked to Nemery, Brangier and Kopp (2010)'s Personalization criteria while Rehearsal is used when the user have the possibility to "replay" a task to improve it. Seven Dialogue support techniques are close to current Gamification techniques: Praise through excessively positive textual, visual and sound-based feedback; Rewards through any points, badges, trophies or gift system; Social role through the use of a main theme and an interactive avatar; Similarity through its vocabulary and Reminders and Suggestion through games goal and mean rhetoric (Järvinen, 2008). Finally, Liking corresponds to Nemery, Brangier and Kopp (2010, 2011)'s Attractiveness criteria. Social support is a core element for Gamification upholders. Competition and Cooperation are extensively used through teams, team goals and leaderboards. Social comparison and facilitation, Recognition and Normative influence are triggered through the use of public indicators and social game mechanics such as the use of sharing and comments within a social network. The dimensions of persuasive technology that are not considered in the scope of Gamification are about credibility and privacy (Oinas-Kukkonen & Harjumaa, 2009; Nemery, Brangier & Kopp, 2010, 2011).

Gamification to Support Cognitive Process

Gamification, beyond its visual aspect and motivational techniques, is meant to drive the users' behavior towards task completion. To do so, it uses elements from games that aim at going along with the user and guiding his progression through the system.

First, as Desurvire and Wiberg (2009) said, games are characterized by their adaptability to the user. It is possible through the increasing levels system and expertise modes that provide interactions and tasks that fit the users' skills and needs at a given time. Concerning expertise modes, it both has implication on the tasks and the functionalities provided. Furthermore, the first minutes of a game are always extremely simple so that anyone can learn the basics in a positive manner (tutorials are other examples of this approach).

Second, the gaming systems massively communicate with the players through what Järvinen (2008) calls "game rhetoric". It describes the way the system communicates information to the player about the game and its rules system, using in particular its thematic. We will briefly describe what these three game components are about and then describe the several different rhetoric types:

- **Information:** About the events (outcomes), the agents (roles and attributes), the objects (attributes) and finally the system (procedures and game state). Providing those information enhances the knowledge and understanding of the user concerning the whole system and its evolutions through the interaction.
- **Rules:** About the goals, sub goals and tasks of the players as well as the conditions (options and constraints) that drive the game. It helps guiding the user through a chosen path, still letting him choices, given that he learns the rules when experiencing the system.
- **Thematic:** Help contextualizing and giving meaning to the rules, information and game elements by liking it under the theme. It is especially done through the use of metaphors.

Game rhetoric describes the way the system links up those three game components. There exist 6 game rhetoric types, 4 directly dealing with guiding and enhancing the understanding the user has of the system.

The Goal rhetoric is about communicating the several different goals and tasks of the user. It comprises both the global target and the sub tasks that guide the user through the global target resolution. This helps both explaining what is to be done and what the system has been created for and also to decrease the complexity of the global target resolution by splitting it into several different sub targets and thus providing a gratifying journey through the use of the system.

The Mean rhetoric communicates about the procedures of the game. It implies explaining what kind of actions is available in order to complete a given task. This helps increasing the user's understanding of the system and the interaction that takes place within it. It is akin to help systems when the messages are explicit, but it can also be conveyed through the design of an element (e.g., GuitarHero: the shape of the joystick matches the user interface that matches the thematic of the game, all that explicitly stating that the buttons must be pressed as if it were real guitar strings). It is important to note that the communication of the means of a game are generally contextual and delivered whenever it is needed.

The Feedback rhetoric provides feedback about the actions of the players on the system. It keeps him aware of his progress and helps him monitoring his evolution towards the final goal of the game. Two kind of feedback are provided: Valence feedback (to praise or condemn a player on his performance) and Goal Resolution feedback (to explicit the player status regarding the final goal.

Finally, the Outcome rhetoric communicates both about the End of the game (whether when getting close to it or when reaching it) and the Victory conditions (gathering information about the outcome of the several different participants of the game). It helps the user understanding the way his actions have impacted the system

We can thus note that through game rhetoric and the selection of relevant information to provide regarding the task of the user, Gamification is a biased way to guide the user through his interaction with the system. Indeed, it provides an oriented set of elements and metrics that is aimed at increasing the task resolution capacities and performance of the user.

CONCLUSION

General Synthesis

Through the categorization that arose out of the HCI concepts (from usability to persuasive technology), we have been able to point out the several different dimensions of Gamification:

1. **Sensory-Motor Modalities:** Gamification is using extensively games multimodal coding (visual, audio and haptic) for aesthetic

purpose as well as to communicate an atmosphere, a theme or needed information.

2. **Motivation Elements:** Gamification first drives motivation through the triggering of emotions. It implies using game elements that answer users' needs beyond usability (e.g., value, accomplishment, social). Second, it exploits game elements that are part of the persuasive technology set of tools in order to create engagement.
3. **Cognitive Process Support Elements:** Finally, Gamification uses game elements that are guiding for the player in order to support task resolution. It both implies adapting the interaction to the user profile and communicating relevant and useful information (goal, mean, feedback and outcome).

At last, we can state that Gamification implies a bias as all those dimensions imply a selection of elements and processes that will enhance certain aspects of a task and/or add other dimensions to it (e.g., competition).

Through this chapter, we have taken stock of Gamification. By analyzing its definitions, claimed goals, underlying concepts and design elements, we have come to the conclusion that it was lacking clear concepts and guidance. We have also pointed out its limits, still explaining through the HCI evolutions why it could become an essential concept for successful HCI design.

We have tried to contribute to the Gamification field of practice by providing a categorization of Gamification elements through HCI design concepts. Those three dimensions – *Sensory-Motor modalities, Motivation elements* and *Cognitive process support element* – are a first attempt to provide a clear and guiding framework for Gamification design which needs to be evaluated. We plan to enrich it through a confrontation of Gamification platforms to designers and final users in order to create a Gamification toolkit alike Lockton's research (2010).

This will to provide a contribution to Gamification upholders should not make us forget that this concept is questionable from an ethical point of view. Indeed, it is biased through the selection of game elements to inject into non-gaming systems and it thus conveys a certain intention.

FUTURE RESEARCH DIRECTIONS

This chapter has led us to envision future research directions on Gamification. Our next step is to conduct a study with designers in order to refine our classification. They will be asked to identify and then classify the ludic elements of existing gamified systems. This would help us providing a Gamification guide that would fit the designers' mental models. It could also be interesting to compare the designers and final users' perception of Gamification design in order to obtain a conception versus use logic confrontation.

Finally, the outcome of those researches will lead to the creation of a design method for user experience design through Gamification. We will use the Design with Intent concept developed by Lockton (2010) as inspiration source. Indeed, he has created a toolkit that gathers elements from several different fields of study united under one goal: shaping people's behavior when using a product. Design patterns have thus been identified and categorized through "Lenses", leading to an easy to understand and to reuse method. Both our concept of Gamification dimensions and the interviewees' answers will be used in order to generate such a tool.

REFERENCES

Adams, E. (2010). *Fundamentals of game design* (2nd ed.). Berkeley, CA: New Riders.

Apter, M. J. (1991). A structural-phenomenology of play. In *Adult Play: A Reversal Theory Approach* (pp. 13–22). Amsterdam: Swets & Zeitlinger.

Avedon, E., & Sutton-Smith, B. (1971). *The study of games*. New York: John Wiley & Sons.

Bartle, R. (2005). Hearts, clubs, diamonds, spades: Players who suit MUDs (1996). In K. Salen, & E. Zimmerman (Eds.), *The Game Design Reader: A Rules of Play Anthology*. Cambridge, MA: The MIT Press.

Bastien, J. M. C., & Scapin, D. L. (1993). Ergonomic criteria for the evaluation of human-computer interfaces. *International Journal of Human-Computer Interaction*, *4*(156), 183–196.

Bogost, I. (2011). *Gamification is bullshit*. Retrieved April 2, 2012 from http://www.bogost.com/blog/Gamification_is_ bullshit.shtml

Brangier, E., & Bastien, J. M. C. (2010). L'évolution de l'ergonomie des produits informatiques: Accessibilité, utilisabilité, émotionnalité et persuasivité. In G. Vallléry, M. C. Le Port, & M. Zouinar (Eds.), *Ergonomie des produits et des services médiatisés: Nouveaux territoires, nouveaux enjeux* (pp. 307–328). Paris: Presses Universitaires de France.

Brangier, E., Hammes-Adelé, S., & Bastien, J.-M. C. (2010). Analyse critique des approches de l'acceptation des technologies: De l'utilisabilité à la symbiose humain-technologie-organisation. *Revue Européenne de Psychologie Appliquée*, *60*(2), 129–146. doi:10.1016/j.erap.2009.11.002.

Caillois, R. (1967). *Les jeux et les hommes*. Paris: Gallimard.

Casual Games Association. (2011). *Smart gamification: Seven core concepts for creating compelling experiences*. Retrieved February 2, 2012 from http://casualconnect.org/lectures/business/smart-Gamification-seven-core-concepts-for-creating-compelling-experiences-amy-jo-kim

Csikszentmihalyi, M. (1990). *Flow: The psychology of optimal experience*. New York: Harper and Row.

Davis, F. D. (1989). Perceived usefulness, perceived ease of use, and user acceptance of information technology. *Management Information Systems Quarterly*, *13*, 319–340. doi:10.2307/249008.

Deci, E., Koestner, R., & Ryan, R. (2001). Extrinsic rewards and intrinsic motivations in education: Reconsidered once again. *Review of Educational Research*, *71*(1), 1–27. doi:10.3102/00346543071001001.

Dejoux, C., & Wechtler, H. (2011). Diversité générationnelle: Implications, principes et outils de management. *Management et Avenir*, *43*, 227–238. doi:10.3917/mav.043.0227.

Desmet, P. M. A., Hekkert, P., & Hillen, M. G. (2004). *Values and emotions, an empirical investigation in the relationship between emotional responses to products and human values*. Paper presented at Techné: Design Wisdom 5th European Academy of Design conference. Barcelona, Spain.

Desurvire, H., & Wiberg, C. (2008). Master of the game: Assessing approachability in future game design. In *Proceedings of CHI '08 Extended Abstracts on Human Factors in Computing Systems (CHI EA '08)*. ACM.

Deterding, S., Khaled, R., Nacke, L., & Dixon, D. (2011a). Gamification: Toward a definition. In *Proceedings of CHI 2011 Workshop Gamification: Using Game Design Elements in Non-Game Contexts* (pp. 6-9). Vancouver, Canada: ACM.

Deterding, S., Sicart, M., Nacke, L., O'Hara, K., & Dixon, D. (2011b). Gamification: Using game design elements in non-gaming contexts. In *Proceedings of CHI 2011 Workshop Gamification: Using Game Design Elements in Non-Game Contexts* (pp. 2-5). Vancouver, Canada: ACM.

Dyck, J., Pinelle, D., Brown, B., & Gutwin, C. (2003). Learning from games: HCI design innovations in entertainment software. In *Proceedings of Graphics Interface*. IEEE.

Flatla, D., Gutwin, C., Nacke, L. E., Bateman, S., & Mandryk, R. L. (2011). Calibration games: Making calibration tasks enjoyable by adding motivating game elements. In *Proceedings of the 24th Annual ACM Symposium on User Interface Software and Technology 2011*. Santa Barbara, CA: ACM.

Fogg, B. J. (2003). *Persuasive technology: Using computers to change what we think and do*. San Francisco, CA: Morgan Kaufmann.

Fox, B. (2005). *Game interface design*. Boston: Thomson Course Technology PTR.

Foxall, G. R., & Goldsmith, R. E. (1994). *Consumer psychology for marketing*. New York, NY: Routledge Chapman & Hall Inc..

Gartner. (2011). *Gartner says by 2015, more than 50 percent of organizations that manage innovation processes will gamify those processes*. Retrieved February 2, 2012 from http://www.gartner.com/it/page.jsp?id=1629214

Gnauk, B., Dannecker, L., & Hahmann, M. (2012). Leveraging gamification in demand dispatch systems. In *Proceedings of the 1st Workshop on Energy Data Management, 15th International Conference on Extending Database Technology*. Berlin, Germany: IEEE.

Hassenzahl, M. (2004). Emotions can be quite ephemeral: We cannot design them. *Interaction, 11*(5), 46–48. doi:10.1145/1015530.1015551.

Hassenzahl, M., & Tractinsky, N. (2006). User experience – A research agenda. *Behaviour & Information Technology, 25*(2), 91–97. doi:10.1080/01449290500330331.

Hunicke, R., Leblanc, M., & Zubek, R. (2004). MDA: A formal approach to game design and game research. In *Proceedings of the Challenges in Games AI Workshop, Nineteenth National Conference of Artificial Intelligence* (pp. 1-5). San Jose, CA: IEEE.

IActionable. (2012). *What is gamification?* Retrieved January 16, 2013 from http://iactionable.com/gamification/what-is-gamification/

Instone, K. (2005). User experience: An umbrella topic. In *Proceedings of CHI '05 Extended Abstracts on Human Factors in Computing Systems* (pp. 1087-1088). New York, NY: ACM.

Järvinen, A. (2008). *Games without frontiers: Theories ans methods for game studies and design*. (Doctoral Dissertation). University of Tampere, Tampere, Finland. Retrieved April 2, 2012 from http://ocw.metu.edu.tr/pluginfile.php/4468/mod_resource/content/0/ceit706/week3_new/AkiJarvinen_Dissertation.pdf

Jordan, P. W. (1999). Pleasure with products: Human factors for body, mind and soul. In W. S. Green, & P. W. Jordan (Eds.), *Humans factors in Product Design: Current practice and future trends* (pp. 206–217). London: Taylor & Francis.

Juul, J. (2005). *Half-real: Video games between real rules and fictional worlds*. Cambridge, MA: The MIT Press.

Knautz, K., Guschauski, D., Miskovic, D., Siebenlist, T., Terliesner, J., & Stock, W. (2012). Incentives for emotional multimedia tagging. In *Proceedings of the ACM 2012 Conference on Computer Supported Cooperative Work Companion*. New York, NY: ACM.

Law, Kasirun, & Gan. (2011). Gamification towards sustainable mobile application. In *Proceedings of the 5th Malaysian Conference in Software Engineering* (pp. 349-353). IEEE.

Liu, Y., Alexandrova, T., & Nakajima, T. (2011). Gamifying intelligent environments. In *Proceedings of the 2011 International ACM Workshop on Ubiquitous Meta User Interfaces, Ubi-MUI '11* (pp. 7-12). ACM.

Lockton, D., Harrison, D., & Stanton, N. (2010). The design with intent method: A design tool for influencing user behaviour. *Applied Ergonomics*, *41*(3), 382–392. doi:10.1016/j.apergo.2009.09.001 PMID:19822311.

Malone, T. W. (1984). Heuristics for designing enjoyable user interfaces: Lessons from computer games. In J. C. Thomas, & M. L. Schneider (Eds.), *Human Factors in Computer Systems*. Norwood, NJ: Ablex.

Maslow, A. H. (1970). *Motivation and personality* (3rd ed.). New York, NY: Harper & Row.

McGonigal, J. (2011). *Reality is broken*. New York: The Penguin Press.

Nemery, A., Brangier, E., & Kopp, S. (2010). Proposition d'une grille de critères d'analyses ergonomiques des formes de persuasion interactive In B. David, M. Noirhomme, & A. Tricot (Eds.), *Proceedings of IHM 2010*. New York: ACM.

Nemery, A., Brangier, E., & Kopp, S. (2011). First validation of persuasive criteria for designing and evaluating the social influence of user interfaces: justification of a guideline. In A. Marcus (Ed.), *Design, User Experience, and Usability, (LNCS)* (Vol. 6770, pp. 616–624). Berlin: Springer. doi:10.1007/978-3-642-21708-1_69.

Nicholson, S. (2012). A user-centered theoretical framework for meaningful gamification. Paper Presented at Games+Learning+Society 8.0. Madison, WI.

Norman, D. A. (2004). *Emotional design*. New York, NY: Basic Books.

Oinas-Kukkonen, H., & Harjumaa, M. (2009). Persuasive systems design: Key issues, process model, and system features. *Communications of the Association for Information Systems*, *24*(1), 485–500.

Robert, T. (2011). *Gamification: La slideshare-atture*. Retrieved February 2, 2012 from http://www.ludicite.ca/2011/10/ Gamification-la-slideshareatture

Saha, D., & Mukherjee, A. (2003). Pervasive computing: A paradigm for the 21st century. *Computer*, *36*(3), 25–31. doi:10.1109/MC.2003.1185214.

Schell, J. (2008). *The art of game design: A book of lenses*. Burlington, MA: Morgan Kaufmann.

Seligman, M. E. P. (2011). *Flourish: A new understanding of happiness and well-being - And how to achieve them*. New York, NY: Free Press.

Singer, L., & Schneider, K. (2012). It was a bit of a race: Gamification of version control. In *Proceedings of the 2nd International Workshop on Games and Software Engineering (GAS)*. Zürich, Switzerland: GAS.

Suits, B. (1990). *Grasshopper: Games, life, and utopia*. Boston: David R. Godine.

Thom, J., Millen, D. R., & DiMicco, J. (n.d.). Removing gamification from an enterprise SNS. In *Proceedings of the Fifteenth Conference on Computer Supported Cooperative Work 2012*. Seattle, WA: IEEE.

Triclot, M. (2011). *Philosophie des jeux vidéo*. Paris: La Découverte.

Winnicott, D. W. (1971). *Playing and reality*. New York: Basic Books.

Witt, M., Scheiner, C., & Robra-Bissantz, S. (2011). Gamification of online idea competitions: Insights from an explorative case. In H.-U. Heiß, P. Pepper, B.-H. Schlingloff, & J. Schneider (Eds.), *Informatik schafft Communities, (LNIS)* (p. 192). Berlin: Springer.

Zichermann, G., & Cunningham, C. (2011). *Gamification by design: Implementing game mechanics in web and mobile apps*. Sebastopol, CA: O'Reilly Media, Inc..

ADDITIONAL READING

Alvarez, J., & Michaud, L. (2008). *Serious games : Advergaming, edugaming, training and more*. Retrieved November 17, 2011 from http://www.ludoscience.com/ EN/diffusion/285-Serious-Games.html

Arhippainen, L., & Tähti, M. (2003). Empirical evaluation of user experience in two adaptative mobile application prototypes. In *Proceedings of the 2nd International Conference on Mobile and Ubiquitous Multimedia (MUM)* (pp. 27-34). Norrköping, Sweden: MUM.

Barcenilla, J., & Bastien, J. M. C. (2009). L'acceptabilité des nouvelles technologies: Quelles relations avec l'ergonomie, l'utilisabilité et l'expérience utilisateur? *Le Travail Humain*, *72*(4), 311–331. doi:10.3917/th.724.0311.

Blythe, M., Overbecke, C., Monk, A. F., & Wright, P. C. (2003). *Funology: From usability to enjoyment*. Dordrecht, The Netherlands: Kluwer.

Brandtzæg, P. B., Følstad, A., & Heim, J. (2003). Enjoyment: Lessons from karasek. In M. Blythe, C. Overbeeke, A. F. Monk, & P. C. Wright (Eds.), *Funology: From Usability to Enjoyment* (pp. 55–65). Dordrecht, The Netherlands: Kluwer.

Costello, B., & Edmonds, E. (2007). A study in play, pleasure and interaction design. In *Proceedings of Designing Pleasurable Products and Interfaces* (pp. 76–91). Helsinki, Finland: IEEE. doi:10.1145/1314161.1314168.

Mahlke, S. (2008). Visual aesthetics and the user experience. In M. Hassenzahl, G. Lindgaard, A. Platz, & N Tractinsky (Eds.), *Dagstuhl Seminar Proceedings : The Study of Visual Aesthetics in Human-Computer Interaction*. Dagstuhl, Germany: Schloss Dagstuhl - Leibniz-Zentrum fuer Informatik.

Reeves, B., & Read, J. L. (2009). *Total engagement*. Boston: Harvard Business Press.

Tractinsky, N. (1997). Aesthetics and apparent usability: Empirically assessing cultural and methodological issues. In *Proceedings of the SIGCHI Conference on Human Factors in Computing Systems* (pp. 115-122). New York, NY: ACM.

KEY TERMS AND DEFINITIONS

Cognitive Process Support Gamification Elements: Game elements that are guiding for the player in order to support task resolution (i.e., adapting the interaction to the user profile and communicating relevant and useful information).

Emotional Design: Designing a product so that it answers the users' needs beyond usefulness and usability.

Gamification: Using Sensory-Motor, Motivation and Cognitive Process Support elements from games in non-ludic environments.

Game-Like Experience: Using game design spirit and elements in non-ludic environments in order to create an experience of Flow and thus triggering emotions and motivation.

Motivation Gamification Elements: Game elements that answer users' needs beyond usability and thus create positive emotions and game elements that are part of the persuasive technology set of tools.

Persuasive Technology: Designing a product to induce behaviors and or attitudes.

Sensory-Motor Gamification Elements: Games multimodal coding (visual, audio and haptic) for aesthetic purpose as well as to communicate an atmosphere, a theme or needed information.

User Experience Design: Designing a product by taking into account the users, the system and the context, both through its functional and non-functional characteristics.

Chapter 11
Experience Prototyping: Gathering Rich Understandings to Guide Design

Ken Keane
Madeira-Interactive Technology Institute (Madeira-ITI), Portugal

Valentina Nisi
Madeira-Interactive Technology Institute (Madeira-ITI), Portugal

ABSTRACT

In this chapter, the authors discuss Experience Prototyping as an appropriate research tool for capturing people's stories related to physical places. It is difficult to explore subjective experiences through strict conventional prototyping methods within a lab; therefore, the authors argue the need for innovative research techniques especially when designing interactive systems where mobility, context, and people play a fundamental role. They discuss the methodology of "Experience Prototyping," which is used to gather insight in a research project, and also what advantages such method brings to a user-centered process. The authors present some reflections and themes that emerged from using experience prototypes, and how they contribute to our understanding of the relationship between spatial narrative and place, and in particular how they may be used as an interaction resource towards discovery and sharing of "place." In doing so, they offer a basis for discussion on how to co-design technologically mediated experiences together with users of such spaces. Finally, the authors discuss how this method informed the design of "The Breadcrumbs" application.

INTRODUCTION

In this paper, we discuss the methodology of Experience Prototyping (EP) and how it helped us gather meaningful insights on people's experiences of places to inform design interventions. We refer to work we have conducted on the island of Madeira, that seeks to motivate and facilitate social activities in both local communities and visitors to the region. An initial phase of the investigation was dedicated to user research to increase our understanding of the local communities through the employment of design based research methods such as cultural probes (McCarthy, J, P Wright, 2004). Insights gathered, such as the importance of preserving the past and fostering authentic

DOI: 10.4018/978-1-4666-4623-0.ch011

experiences while roaming the city and the difficulties and importance of encountering local culture and community for tourists for tourists, inspired us to design the "Breadcrumbs" (BC) application and adopt Experience Prototypes (EP) to explore and how to capture people engagement in rich activities such as serendipitous discovery of new places. Serendipity is a very desirable quality, bringing surprise, a sense of discovery and adventure. We wanted to capture some aspects of this phenomenon and facilitate it during the use of the BC experience. Thus we began to question how people like to discover, explore, and interpret places. The EP's helped us to understand how participants use the physical environment as a source of information and how it shapes their experiences of place through the hearing of stories. Results have informed the design choices for the Breadcrumbs application as well as novel user Interface (UI) design.

In this paper we present our methodology and show how it has helped our project progress. Inspiration is taken from Gaver (Gaver et al. 2001), who discusses the difficulty of applying scientific design theories to the experience design where problems and solutions are unclear, stating that designing for user experience is not about problem solving but about creating opportunities for users. We are also motivated by Hassenzahl (Hassenzahl, M. 2005), who states that experience design is an opportunity for designers to provide platforms that encourage users' personal growth and self-expression. We argue that our use of EP as a research method can provide deep insights into user behavior outside of a lab setting, as well as opportunities for creativity. In doing so it can contribute to real knowledge (the ethnographic studies produced by anthropologists and design researchers), according to Zimmerman's 'research-through-design' model (Zimmerman et al. 2007). As a tool EP differs from Ethnography, which focuses on uncovering design requirements through observations and direct engagement in situ. EP investigations are not just to interested in facts from settings but also scopes for insights, identifying specific areas to focus on terms of user experience. Being more open-ended their flexibility encourages creativity to emerge, resulting in insights rather then user requirements.

The Breadcrumbs Experience

The "Breadcrumbs" mobile application focuses on motivating and facilitating social interaction between local communities and visitors to the region. The application allows users to leave trails of mediated information (photographs, text and sound) in the form of short media segments (virtual breadcrumbs) while exploring spaces. These segments can be discovered by other users than the creators of such media themselves, by enabling all the Breadcrumbs users to navigate the spatially distributed content left by others. The breadcrumbs experience focuses on such things as spatial orientation, experiences, memories, conversations, and stories that people attach to places. It supports people's exploration of space, and casts its users in two interlinked roles: explorers and storytellers, and asks how it may be used towards serendipitous discovery and sharing of "places". A series of EP's enabled us to iteratively refine our concepts with participants in different settings. We adopted an investigation method that takes into account the dynamic relationship between physical space and the lived world in order to observe user behavior in context.

Experiencing Space and Place

An understanding of how people experience the world and relate to concepts, such as space/place is an increasingly important consideration in the design of technologies. Jacucci et al. (Iacucci, G. & Kuutti, K., 2002) suggests that the vision of Ubiquitous Computing from Weiser (Weiser M. 1991) and Abowd and Mynatt (Abowd, GD and Myatt, 2000) have not materialized as expected. They argue that social implication has driven technological innovation rather then making social use the target of design.

New forms of locative media, such as Foursquare, Instagram, Path to name a few are bringing digitally mediated experiences directly into physical spaces. However, digitally mediated or not, our interaction with space is highly subjective. Erickson (Erickson, T., 1993) notes how people read meaning into space and used the term "place" to describe spaces where people develop understandings, meanings, and memories. He proposes that space is a trigger for social and individual human interaction. Harrison and Dourish (Harrison, S. and Dourish, P., 1996) state that place is: " a space which is invested with understandings of behavioral appropriateness, cultural expectations, and so forth. We are located in space, but we act in place". Ciolfi and Bannon (Ciolfi, L. and Bannon, L., 2005) suggest that "place describes spaces invested with understandings, meanings, and memories [...] that place and human action are inextricable linked so when actions take place, the particular places in which they occur make a difference". McCullough (McCullough M, 2005) states that "Place begins with embodiment. Body is place, and it shapes your perceptions".

As living actors in the world, narrative enables us make sense of our place through our interactions and our position within. Work that looks at narrative and place are seen with Miskelly (Miskelly, C. Cater, K, 2005) who focuses on stories to relate to communities' sense of place. He states that community stories cannot be interpreted as a single narrative thread with a definable end but is an ongoing process of telling from which different parts can be drawn out and told at different times for different purposes. Linde's (Linde, C. 1993) discussion on individual life stories often discontinuous, informal and fragmented suggests that we use coherence principles to understand them against what we believe to be a coherent life. Lippard (Lippard, L. 1997) proposes that rather than having a single sense of place we experience "serial senses of place", that both producing and experiencing story fragments can be seen as a process of creating story of place somewhere between the making, locating or listening to the recording and being in that place.

Understanding Experiences

Understanding the role of user experience, in terms of understanding our selves, our culture, and our lives is becoming a crucial for the purpose of design (Leong et al. 2010). Understanding how to design technologically mediated experiences, requires informative research in settings where the experience occurs. We already see how ethnography helps to understand user requirements by observing in situ. However, recently more innovative methodologies have emerged that not only document people's practices and activities but also inspire and motivate design activities. Gaver's et al.'s (1999, 2001, 2003, 2004) demonstrates such methods through their work with Cultural Probes (CP). They originally deployed CP as an alternative method to gain a rich understanding of people 's everyday lives and environments and opportunities for design through engaging users in discussions toward "unexpected ideas."

Macaulay, Iacucci, O'Neill, Kankainen and Simpson (2006) propose that role-playing methods in design process are motivated by three different research fields: user experience, participatory design and embodied interaction. User experience looks for methods that support designing for user experience and considers pleasure, enjoyment, emotional and cultural aspects; participatory design aims to facilitate participation from users in the design process through lived experience. While Embodied interaction research focuses on the physical environment, and "the role of body, beyond ergonomics, for its' increased relevance as a presentational, representational, and experimental medium" (ibid. p.946).

According to Boess, Saakes and Hummel (2007), role-playing has been used in design to communicate complexity of the experience and empathy of designers, the tangibility of interaction, and attentiveness to social change". Seland (2006) argues that role-playing is needed to "explore and understand users, context, and to test and communicate ideas, by involving users in the design process. Role-playing methods help to explore of contexts where the physical and mobile aspects play a role in use of technology (Iacucci & Kuutti, 2002; Strömberg, Pirttilä, & Ikonen, 2004).

Bedwell et al. (Bedwell et al. 2009) use role playing to research elements of experience through performance and play with 'Anywhere', an application where participants are guided over the phone by unseen on-the-street performers to explore a city's history through hidden places and seldom told stories embedded into physical places. They analyze the engaging and unique personalized paths through content by a performer participant pair in the city as they accessed location based activities and staged performances in multiple locations.

Aiello et al. (Aiello, G. and Gendelman, I., 2008) offer a critical analysis of narrative construction of Seattle's Pike Place Market through institutional and amateur sources, including travel guides and tourists photographs revealing certain dimensions of place. They argue that public space is not merely geographical but a narrative construction helped/enhanced by technology. They examine the dynamic relationship between institutional and amateur texts about popular public spaces, and the narratives that help reproduce a celebrated place. They articulate the appeal of the market and how tourists internalize institutional narratives, and reproduce in their own narratives, what they add, ignore and how they transgress.

Leong et al. (Leong et al. 2010) discuss their adoption of McCarthy and Wright's "Technology as Experience" framework to research the richness of serendipity. They used three themes: life as lived and felt, the whole person, and dialogical sense making to understand strategies, tools and techniques required in the design of an empirical study of the experience of serendipity. They describe how they interpreted McCarthy and Wright's three themes to shape the strategy, the specific methods, tools/techniques used to gather the experiential data, and how they approached the analysis and interpretation of this data.

This section has shown the relevance of a deep understanding of experiences when designing interactive systems and some innovative approaches used to gather insights on people's experiences in richer and more inspirational ways. Informed by the work reviewed here, and to realize our design concept, time invested towards understanding the dimensions of space/place and its relationship with narrative requires a methodological tool that accurately fits with our research goals. Thus applying EP's aimed to help our understanding of the social, spatial, cultural, and personal dimensions that contribute to people's experiences in space, informing the refinements of the BC application.

Experience Prototyping

Experience prototyping is a method that takes your research outside the lab to give you an understanding of how your users will actually interact with your designs, by considering mobility, context, people and culture. It differs slightly to paper prototyping, which aims to simulate and test the concepts with users using lo fidelity materials and observe their behavior with the proposed system before starting its construction. Experience Prototyping has a very exploratory function if used early in the design process even when just at the concept stage. It's strength lies in being able to investigate the important touch points within the experience as it unfolds and helps the observer and designer understand how to design for it.

Similar in nature, Ethnography as a tool also allows researchers to uncover design requirements for existing or proposed systems through details observations and direct engagement in situ. These investigations are organized not just to extract facts from settings but to stage encounters between cultures that they may then be supporting of appropriate interpretive analysis [4]. However the main distinction between the two is that Experience prototyping is much more open-ended approach. For our research we were not just looking for design requirements but scoping for insights in the experience itself, that would lead to ideation and clarification of our already existing core concept. This is an important distinction that supports our decision to deploy such a method. EP allowed us to observe the dynamic relationship between narrative, the physical space and the lived world while helping us to identify specific areas to focus on terms of user experience. We began to understand the design space through a more open exploration in situ through role-playing and mock ups while allowing flexibility for creativity to emerge, resulting in insights rather then user requirements. Hence we decided to adopt a tailored made series of Experience Prototypes, where users were engaged in multiples roles and fitted with a wide range of low fi to high fi prototyping tools in order to carry out the experience we were co designing with them.

To frame the presentation of EP, the following sections will discuss relevant related work referring to key issues for our research. Firstly it is important to clarify aspects of the experience of space and place in order to convey the motivations behind our EP's.

Buchenau et al. (Buchenau, M. and Suri, J F., 2000) remind us that "The experience of even simple artifacts does not exist in a vacuum but, rather, in dynamic relationship with other people, places and objects. They state the best way to understand the experiential qualities of an interaction is toexperience it subjectively, fostering empathy with users. They describe EP as, "emphasizing the experimental aspect of whatever representations are needed to successfully (re) live or convey an experience with a product, space or system" (Buchenau, M. and Suri, J F., 2000). EP can be used in three critical design activities: understanding existing experiences, exploring ideas, and communicating design concepts. We built on this definition and use EP's to advance the design and understanding of our existing concept by encouraging participants to externalize their sense of place and uncover stories important to their relationship with the island, neighborhoods and communities. The EP's helped us to understand the basic needs and flow of events for storyteller and explorer roles in the BC experience and helped gather seed content for the application such as stories from local inhabitants, common/uncommon routes, places, and hidden physical locations.

Deploying Experience Prototypes

We deployed five EP's, each refined and re-arranged based on lessons learned from the previous one. These ranged from low fidelity prototyping: role-playing and paper based tools, to a high fidelity prototype. All EP's were documented using shadowing, note taking and pictures. For each, participants were asked to take the role, either as "storyteller" or "explorer". The goal was to get the storyteller to describe and share their experience of the island and relationships with certain places, while allowing the explorer to discover these. We wanted to see how people explore, attach, and interpret stories, memories of places. The following section describes the EP's, and presents main findings and insights that emerged. We specifically looked to gather three main categories of insights: those related to the design of the experience, interaction design issues leading to possible design specs, and insights helping us to design the evaluation of the application.

EP 1: One Local Storyteller/ One Foreign Explorer

The first EP focused on a scenario of a local (storyteller) preparing a trail and taking a foreigner (explorer) around the city (see Figure 1). Through stories and facts related to places the local was asked to share "his city". The foreigner was requested to search out anything of interest as

Figure 1. First EP in the main city of Funchal. The two recruited users take on the two different roles identified for the experiment: one plays the role of the explorer and one plays the role of the storyteller.

they roamed around, and to deviate from the trail whenever they wished. The goal was to observe how people go about discovering places and the role that stories play in the process, whether as a point of interest or a springboard for decision-making.

Findings

The storyteller felt pressure in delivering information that was accurate and felt a responsibility to provide an informative experience rather than following serendipitous variations of the tour proposed at multiple stages by the foreigner. Asking to prepare a trail in advance resulted in the local participant adopting a role of a "tour guide" and a strictly historical approach and lacked personal content, resulting in a predominately one-way conversation. Sometimes the explorer preferred factual information to stories and memories, when she didn't know the place at all for example, while other times they preferred more informal and personal accounts to connect to a place, when some monuments or historical building were insight for example. This identifies a typology of users and a level at which they might wish to engage in the experience. Moments of spontaneous engagement with places from the explorer and the storyteller happened only when there was no knowledge of the place from both sides, so they openly explored it further. Throughout, the way information was experienced had a nonlinear quality: questions raised during a certain conversation were often answered later in the tour in a different, but related context.

EP 2: One Local Storyteller/ Two Foreign Explorers

This time a location where the storyteller grew up and had more affinity to was chosen (see Figure 2). The storyteller was given no tools and asked not to prepare anything beforehand, so to encourage a more impromptu storytelling experience. Two explorers accompanied him, questioning as they roamed and relived each story. Again the explorers were asked to divert anytime they wished and the storyteller would accommodate.

Findings

This time, with the second EP, a much warmer, less rigid tour was enacted. The shared experience co created between the explorer and the storyteller included personal anecdotes mixed with local history, folk stories and characters from the past. The

Figure 2. The second EP. The experiment takes place in the local storyteller's hometown of Canico.

explorer was particularly interested in the personal accounts of place as well as the folkloristic aspects and anecdotes of some locations rather than the 'historical' facts, raising questions about when and how to deliver both aspects of a place, the historical and the personal. The importance of physical artifacts in revealing as well as triggering curiosity about a place was identified through the questions the explorer raised, regarding ruins, cobblestones, and abandoned buildings and roads. Even though the area had changed dramatically some artifacts were still standing and raising curiosity. This revealed the role artifacts play in helping people explore, interpret and [re] live places. For example, an old stone road we were walking on sparked a conversation about its age, materials and building techniques in the past. Furthermore, the local found that being somewhere personal enticed more personal recollections, while the explorer wanted to be able to complement stories with official information of the area.

EP 3: One Local Storyteller/ One Local Explorer/Two Foreign Explorers

The third EP involved four people, a storyteller, one local and two explorers. Initially we focused on the local storyteller, we observed how, where and what kind of stories they leave in places and the spaces /objects they chose to use in their activity. We explicitly decided to continue to avoid technology at this stage and rather mimic the activity or writing and leaving digital content through physical tangible artifact, such a index cards and orange helium inflated balloons. The storyteller wrote stories and comments on index cards and left them around the place tied with a string to a bright orange balloon, filled with helium. The balloon was then tied to the location where the proposed digital breadcrumb and content would be left and geo stamped by the GPS coordinates. (See Figure 3). In our opinion, using balloons, paper notes and writing/drawing tools would be the best way to capture the experience and intentions of the storyteller that is in the task of producing and disseminating content, without presenting already the constrain of a technological interface to the task. Subsequently, explorers could discover these traces (the cards containing content, signaled by the bright orange balloons), read its content and add more comments on the cards if they wished to do so. We observed in this way, how different explorers looked and interacted with the content left by the storyteller. Furthermore we observed what, where, and how explorers interpreted the cards, if and when they found them.

Figure 3. Third EP. Using physical props to support the prototyping: orange balloons and index cards as the means to leave and find content in the exact location.

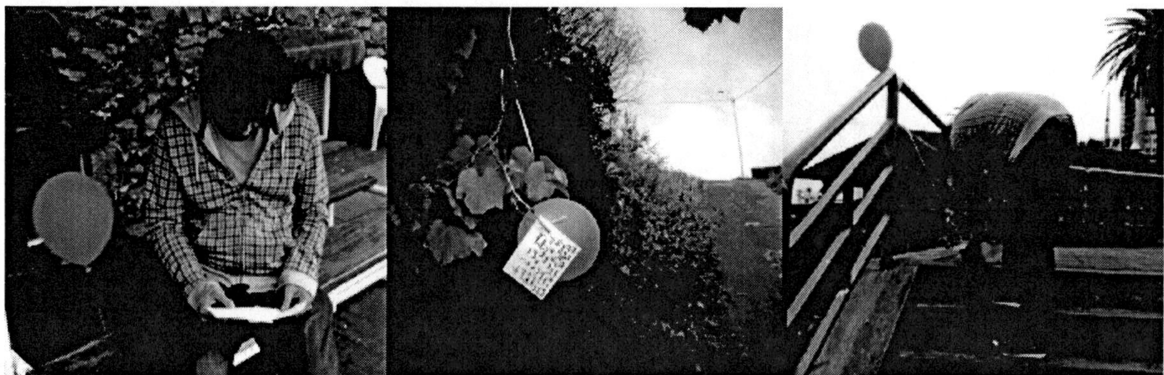

Findings

With this third EP we observed that not all explorers wanted historical information about places and were equally interested in everyday stories and thoughts left around by the local storyteller. Some explorers enjoyed reflecting and wondering while exploring, as they left long comments on the initial notes left by the storyteller. The local explorer, on the other hand, had no desire to reply to any of the stories as he felt that the conversations were private and personal. Though he mentioned that he would like to be able to bookmark locations so he could re-visit certain places later.

One of the foreign explorers stated that often the stories were more intriguing not knowing whom they were from and what they were entirely about, who the other characters were and what their lives like were like. Regarding the local storyteller, this time he felt more comfortable recollecting stories around his local environment, without the pressure of the explorer next to him. The storyteller enjoyed the time spent on location, reflecting and writing up his comments and memories on the cards, without having to think of how the explorer felt next to him, listening to his stories live. The choice of using props to leave and retrieve content proved to be a step closer to what the storyteller's and explorers would enjoy doing. Comparing to the first EP where the storyteller reminded the explorer: "This it is not my world" (referring to the city of Funchal) this time he said, "Here there is always something to say." He explained further: "to entice more personal stories it is better to be alone, to reflect without pressure.

EP 4: One Foreign Explorer/ One Local Participant Mirroring the System

This Fourth EP was designed mainly to explore how the system could support the explorer in its activities. A local participant was asked to imitate the application and its content already filled up by the local (storyteller), while a foreigner (explorer) roamed around. A series of BC trail had previously been distributed around a location using orange balloons tagged with cardboard notes displaying text and images (see Figure 4). For this activity the two participants were recorded using notes and photographs.

One location presented a BC in the form of an audio clip that the person acting like the BC system would play back for the explorer when found. The explorer was asked to roam the area, look for BC and experience the encountered content. The local acting as the BC system was asked to follow the explorer but only interact when the explorer asked him.

Figure 4. Forth EP. The storyteller performs like the application, only upon the explorer probing for information.

Findings

The physical attributes of places offered the explorer cues for enquiry and conversation with the system, such as evocative street names and ruins of buildings. The sound recording at one location proved to be very evocative for the explorer. The sound of fishermen, in from of the rocky beach helped the explorer to effectively engage with the story as it reminded him of home and various memories attached to it: "This reminds me of Scotland. I recognize this sort of community". The explorer wanted to be able to calculate his options in advance using the stories and physical attributes of places to see if the content was relevant for him to follow. He expressed interest for a sneak preview of what would lay ahead of him. However the act of following pre prepared trails quickly took over and didn't entice the explorer to physically explore the spaces for themselves but only experience them through the existing predefined route.

EP 5: One Foreign Explorer Testing a Working Prototype of the Breadcrumbs Application

Finally the BC working prototype was introduced into the fifth and final EP. Using some of the insights and inspirations derived from the previous prototyping exercises we designed this one to test mainly how the technological artifact and the map based interface would influence the users experience (see Figure 5 and Figure 6).

In this EP the participant (Undistinguished as storyteller or explorer) was encouraged to explore a pre prepared trail of BC using the working prototype. He could also add his own content to the trail if he felt so inclined. We purposely stirred from any detailed explanation of the technology in order to identify any major usability issue. We wanted to check how well the UI complemented and suited the experience we wanted our users to have, which was one of pleasurable exploration and engagement with a new location.

Findings

With this EP we noticed that the user had problems engaging with certain stories due to time related factors: some stories were positioned were ultimately the places had changed very much, or people would not be around anymore. Contrary to the expectation that this kind of miss match of timing would re-live the old times or generate curiosity, the user felt frustrated. An example is when the explorer was disappointed when she encountered a BC describing local fishermen's activities around the peer, but could not see them anymore. The user found it disappointing not to be able to see this when she encountered the story

Figure 5. Interface of the first iteration of the breadcrumbs prototype

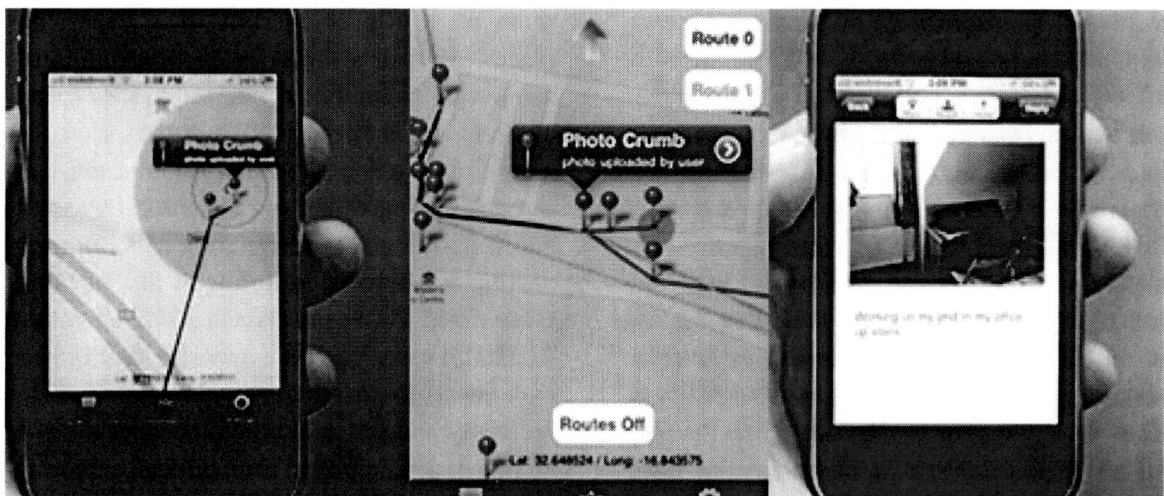

Figure 6. The redesign of the breadcrumb interface

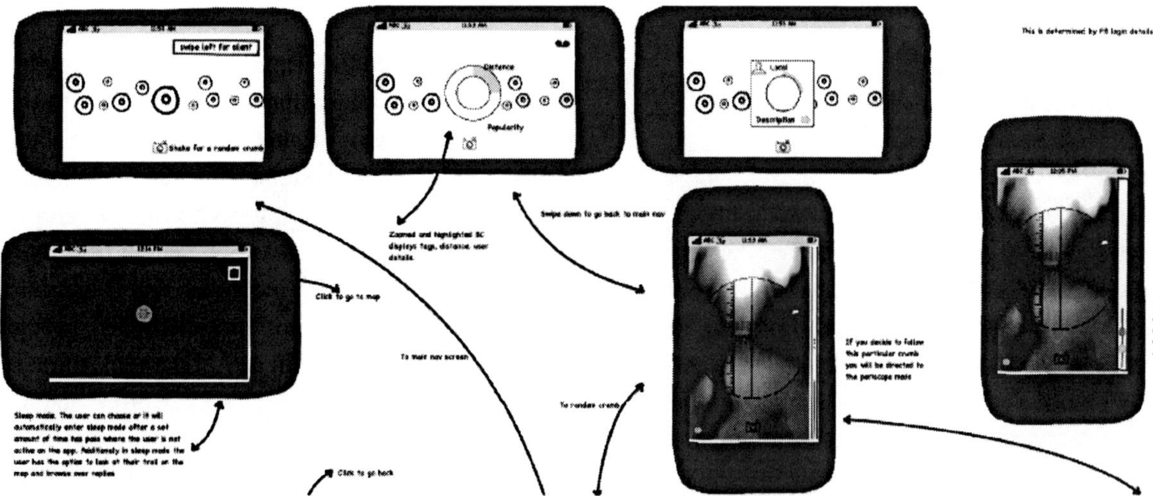

and wanted to know at what times of the day these fishermen would normally be around.

An important observation made was that the user quickly became preoccupied with certain elements of the application, such as using the map to orient, and locating existing trails and rather then physically and naturally exploring the surroundings. This ultimately affected each story that was uncovered due to the user continuously checking with the technology before the physical place and locating the story content in the real environment. In fact, while navigating the map, the explorer felt anxious following a trail as she felt she was not driving the experience, "I feel like I am hunting". After turning the trail off, she felt more comfortable and began to enjoy, stating, "This feels like I am fishing". We also observed during this EP that using a map based UI had a significant impact on how users interacted with and experienced the BC. This was also an observation made during the fourth EP, when the explorer user began to prefer to follow trails, neglecting to explore or contribute with its own content to the BC's. This ultimately affected how users observed the physical environment and experience places. If the map based interface pushes users only to follow someone's trail rather then using the BC to interpret and [re] live places, then we are co creating a different experience from the one we intended to. These last observations leads us to think that the use of trails is questionable as people's exploration and interpretation of places is not always linear. Thus there is a need to step away from the map UI and explore alternative metaphors that more accurately match our research questions: how to support serendipitous discovery of places, based on story based user generated content.

DISCUSSION AND REFINEMENTS AND FUTURE RESEARCH DIRECTIONS

The EP'S helped us to acquire real knowledge in terms of how participants observe the physical environment and use it to shape their experience of places through stories. Identifying the importance of non-linearity with discovery reveals an interesting design space with opportunities for synchronous and asynchronous exchange of stories. We became aware of the unique opportunity offered by mobile technologies in combining exploration of new and [re] living of old places through storytelling by local and foreign visitors, who are present or have since left the island. By offering an online extension of the BC experience, users who have left the island are provided with the possibility to re-visit their personal trails and BC, reflect and re-connect with previously formed communities and form new ones. This offers a space that enables them to observe the relationship between the media they have left and subsequent encounters by other in those locations. It allows them to observe, reflect and respond, in real-time to encounters people have with their BC enabling them to influence others as they experience places. We believe this is a step forward towards supporting serendipitous interaction with spaces and people. The EP enabled us to understand that serendipity is a very subjective phenomenon, born through the individual and their worldly experiences, desires and to design for it will ultimately destroy it. However in line with that of Gaver (Gaver et al. 2001) and Hassenzahl (Hassenzahl, M., 2005) we can provide opportunities for such experiences to emerge by providing a platform for creativity and self expression, opening the possibility of serendipity to form through exploring, discovery and sharing of places.

Refining our Concept: Moving Away from the Map Interface

Time was spent re-defining the design metaphor from that of a linear map-based interface to one that matches with the insights mentioned above was needed. The metaphor of searching through a periscope, and encountering content through the phone interface led to the design of a more engaging and intuitive metaphor that fitted more accurately with the experience identified through our research so far. Figure 7 illustrates some of the wireframes that bring the Periscope metaphor to life.

Currently, to inform this re-design, we are asking participants to take part in a participatory design process that seek to iteratively clarify which aspects of the newly proposed design metaphor do and do not work. Two pilot sessions have been conducted to identify design issues and also help refine the concept validation study itself, which would be delivered to eight other participants: three local and five foreign participants in the main user study. The refined study consisted of a further eight participants and used hi-fi wireframes to deliver the refined design metaphor. Both sets of wireframes consisted of paper mockups where the participant was given specific tasks and asked

Figure 7. Screenshots from the final interface of breadcrumbs after the feedback of the pilot sessions

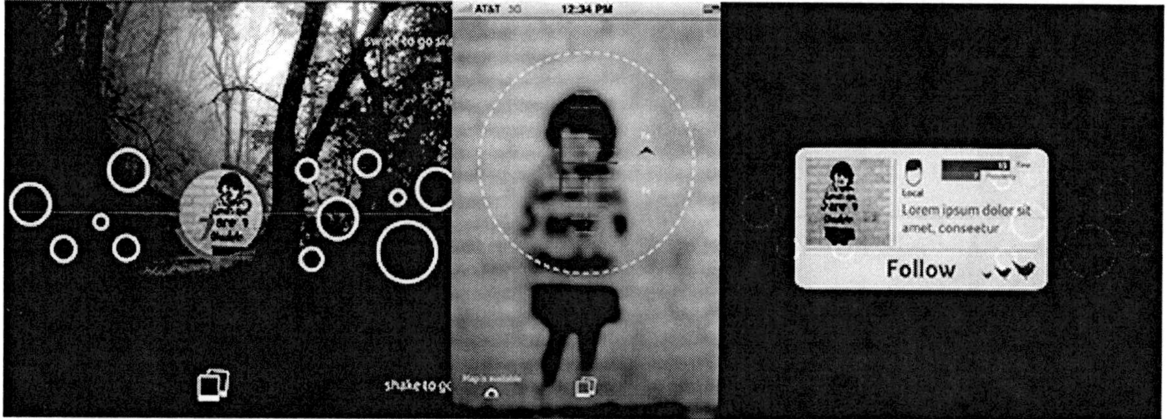

to act out each stage of the user experience. These were conducted around the University campus. This participatory design method involved a combination of role playing, body storming and paper prototyping to aid a design process through users perception and acceptance of a proposed design. Results are under analysis, and qualitative results will drive the finalization of the new interface design.

CONCLUSION

New forms of locative media are bringing experiences into physical spaces. EP have helped us understand the multi dimensions of how people tell stories in space and insights gathered have informed the design of 'Breadcrumbs' application. In this paper, we provided a frame to our process in terms of place experience, personal narratives and the connection between them. Subsequently, we presented the methodology of EP. We focused on narrative as a resource to reveal the relationship between people, community, and physical locations that they inhabit. The five EPs showed the importance of spatial orientation, the personal histories that people bring with them as they locate and orient themselves in space, and the role of the physical environment in both constructing narrative in space but also reliving past places shared by others. Finally we looked at how people might use the spatially distributed narrative fragments to build three-dimensional spaces that supports their interpretation and perspective of places encountered. The paper aims to make a contribution to the current stream of research on design for experience, by showing how EP can be used to gather rich accounts of human activities and inspire design decisions.

ACKNOWLEDGMENT

The authors are very grateful to the volunteers participating in the Experience Prototypes: Lucio Quintal, Nuno Santos and Raffaella Nisi. The authors would like to thank the other project team members: Mayur Karnik, Roberto Sousa, and Ian Oakley. The project received support from the Madeira Interactive Technologies Institute and the CCM research centre of the University of Madeira.

REFERENCES

Abowd, G.D., & Myatt. (2000). Charting past, present and future research in ubiquitous computing. *ACM Transactions*.

Aiello, G., & Gendelman, I. (2008). Seattle's pike place market (de) constructed: An analysis of tourist narratives about a public space. *Journal of Tourism and Cultural Change*, *5*(3), 158–185. doi:10.2167/jtcc093.0.

Bedwell., et al. (2009). In support of city exploration. In *Proceedings of the 27th International Conference on Human Factors in Computing Systems*. ACM.

Boess, S., Saakes, D. P., & Hummels, C. (2007). When is role-playing really experiential? Case studies. In *Proceedings of Tangible and Embedded Interaction* (pp. 279–282). IEEE. doi:10.1145/1226969.1227025.

Buchenau, M., & Suri, J. F. (2000). Experience prototyping. In *Proceedings of the Conference on Designing Interactive Systems Processes, Practices, Methods, and Techniques*. DIS.

Ciolfi, L., & Bannon, L. (2005). *Space, place and the design of technologically enhanced physical environments: Spaces spatiality and technology*. Boston: Kluwer.

Erickson, T. (1993). From interface to interplace: The spatial environment as medium for interaction. In *Proceedings of Conference on Spatial Information Theory*. Cupertino, CA: Kluwer.

Gaver, et al. (1999). Cultural probes. *Interaction*, *6*(1), 21–29. doi:10.1145/291224.291235.

Gaver, et al. (2001). *The presence project*. London: Royal College of Art.

Gaver., et al. (2003). Ambiguity as a resource for design. In *Proceedings of the Conference on Human Factors in Computing Systems*. ACM.

Gaver, et al. (2004). Cultural probes and the value of uncertainty. *Interaction*, *9*(5), 53–56. doi:10.1145/1015530.1015555.

Harrison, S., & Dourish, P. (1996). Re-place-ing space: The roles of place and space in collaborative systems. In *Proceedings of the ACM Conference on Computer Supported Cooperative Work*. ACM.

Hassenzahl, M. (2005). The quality of interactive products: Hedonic needs, emotions and experience. In *Encyclopaedia of Human Computer Interaction*. Hershey, PA: Idea Group Inc. doi:10.4018/978-1-59140-562-7.ch042.

Iacucci, G., & Kuutti, K. (2002). Everyday life as a stage in creating and performing scenarios for wireless devices. *Personal and Ubiquitous Computing Journal*, *6*, 299–306. doi:10.1007/s007790200031.

Leong., et al. (2010). Understanding experience using dialogical methods: The case of serendipity. In *Proceedings of OZCHI*. Brisbane, Australia: OZCHI.

Linde, C. (1993). *Life stories, the creation of coherence*. Oxford, UK: Oxford University Press.

Lippard, L. (1997). *The lure of the local: Senses of place in a multicentered society*. New York: New Press.

Macaulay, C., & Jacucci, G., ONeill, S., Kankainen, T., & Simpson, M. (2006). The emerging roles of performance within HCI and interaction design. *Interacting with Computers*, *18*(5), 942–955. doi:10.1016/j.intcom.2006.07.001.

McCullough, M. (2005). *Digital ground, architecture, pervasive computing, and environmental knowing*. Cambridge, MA: MIT Press.

Miskelly, C., & Cater, K. (2005). *Locating story: Collaborative community-based located media production*. Cambridge, MA: MIT.

Paay, J. (2005). Where we met last time. In *Proceedings of OZCHI*. Canberra, Australia: OZCHI.

Seland, G. (2006). System designer assessments of role play as a design method: A qualitative study. In *Proceedings of the 4th Nordic Conference on Human-Computer Interaction: Changing Roles* (NordiCHI '06) (pp. 222-231). ACM.

Strömberg, H., Pirttilä, V., & Ikonen, V. (2004). Interactive scenarios—Building ubiquitous computing concepts in the spirit of participatory design. *Personal and Ubiquitous Computing*, *8*(3), 200–207.

Weiser, M. (1991). The computer for the 21st century. *Scientific American*, *265*(3), 94–104. doi:10.1038/scientificamerican0991-94 PMID:1675486.

Zimmerman., et al. (2007). Research through design as a method for interaction design research in HCI. In *Proceedings of SIGCHI Conference on Human Factors in Computing Systems.* ACM.

ADDITIONAL READING

Boehner, K., Vertesi, J., Sengers, P., & Dourish, P. (2007). How HCI interprets the probes. In *Proceedings of the SIGCHI Conference, CHI 2007*, (pp. 1077-1086). ACM.

Dourish, P. (2006). Implications for design. In *Proceedings of the SIGCHI Conference – CHI 2006*, (pp. 541-550). ACM.

Gaye, L., & Holmquist, L. E. (2004). In duet with everyday urban settings: A user study of sonic city. In *Proceedings of NIME '04.* NIME.

Goffman, E. (1963). *Behavior in public places, notes on the social occasion of gatherings.* New York: The Free Press.

Reid, J., Hull, R., Cater, K., & Fleuriot, C. (2005). Magic moments in situated mediascapes. In *Proceedings of the 2005 ACM SIGCHI International Conference on Advances in Computer Entertainment Technology - ACE '05*, (pp. 290–293). ACM.

Tuan, Y.-F. (1977). *Space and place: The perspective of experience.* Minneapolis, MN: University of Minnesota Press.

KEY TERMS AND DEFINITIONS

Experience Design: Uses techniques that allow designers to both discover and explore design spaces with the aim of understanding how to encourage users' personal growth and self-expression.

Experience Prototypes: Enable designers to develop greater empathy with user by offering a tool that help explore and understand the subjective experience of user's in a given context.

Narrative: Helps people to understand the world around them as it presents itself through a series of physical events.

Participatory Design: Puts the participant at the center of the design process by actively involving them through various design-oriented workshops.

Place: Is embedded into physical Space and represents it's meaning through events, conversations, memories that have occurred within.

Role Playing: Is used as a method to immerse ones self in the context of a given situation or problem and helps to better understand the problem space.

Space: Helps us enact the stories that get presented to us and to helps us to eventually create personal accounts of spaces.

Section 3
Technological Approaches

Chapter 12
Strategy to Support the Memorization of Iconic Passwords

Ismael Ávila
CPqD R&D Center in Telecommunications, Brazil

Ewerton Menezes
CPqD R&D Center in Telecommunications, Brazil

Alexandre Melo Braga
CPqD R&D Center in Telecommunications, Brazil

ABSTRACT

In this chapter, the authors discuss the application of iconic passwords in authentication solutions aimed at the use of smartphones as payment devices. They seek a trade-off between security and usability by means of memorization strategies based on human memory skills. The authors present a first approach to the authentication solution, which was tested with users and compared with a previous scheme that lacked the strategies. The advantages and limitations of the proposed solution, along with future research directions, are then discussed.

INTRODUCTION

According to many technological trend forecasts, in a near future, smartphones will be widely used for payments, replacing many of the current uses of cash or credit cards. This scenario highlights the need to equip smartphones with authentication solutions that are both reliable and usable.

In this context, as commented by Biddle et al. (2011), the use of passwords (PWs) for user authentication has several advantages, including the elimination of the privacy issues normally associated with biometric authentication, and also avoiding the need to carry a token, such as a chip card.

However, while alphanumeric passwords are supposed to provide a high theoretical security level, they tend to be predictable whenever they are chosen by users and, conversely, they tend to be difficult to memorize if they are generated by the system (Morris and Thompson, 1979; Klein, 1990; Mallows and Bentley, 2005; Sasse et al.,

DOI: 10.4018/978-1-4666-4623-0.ch012

2001, Yan et al. 2004). Besides, the input modalities available in virtual keyboards of mobile devices hinder typing long alphanumeric PWs.

System-defined alphanumeric PWs are hard to memorize mainly when the resulting strings have no semantic or phonetic values, as those in conformance with the best security practices. This occurs because, in order to expand the theoretical space, the PWs are required to explore the entire keyboard, to be formed by a sequence of random characters (uppercase and lowercase letters, digits and special characters). This produces strings such as *XP5sW8mN%&#* or *9(yUt5$#c*m*, which represent a challenge for the human memory, then forcing many users to resort to workarounds that can compromise the security of the application, such as writing down the password in a way that it makes it usable, but also vulnerable to capture.

On the other hand, if users are allowed to choose the PW, they will often adopt unsafe coping strategies, such as the use of real words or significant dates (vulnerable to dictionary and pattern-based attacks) or even the reuse of PWs across accounts to help with memorability, in which case "the decrease in security cannot be addressed by simply strengthening, in isolation, the underlying technical security of a system" (Biddle et al., 2011).

Finally, even when the user is asked to create an alphanumeric PW, while respecting the above-mentioned best practices, he or she still can circumvent these guidelines, for instance by creating a PW with no semantic value, but composed with adjacent keyboard keys, in order to memorize the movements for typing the string, instead of having to memorize the PW itself. By doing so, the user unconsciously creates a PW that is more vulnerable to shoulder-surfing attacks (as well as totally dependent on that particular keyboard standard).

Nevertheless, the main reason for those bad practices in the creation and handling of PWs is the legitimate attempt to overcome memorization difficulties, something totally justifiable from the usability perspective. But since authentication solution creators have no control over such workarounds, these can actually be considered unsafe behaviors that compromise the overall system security, making it susceptible to attacks.

The core of the problem lies then in the usability/security trade-off. While this trade-off needs to be carefully addressed and balanced, what occurs quite often is that, from a naïve security standpoint, most of the usability requirements are only regarded as likely to cause security breaches or to create loopholes for attacks, whereas from a non-informed usability perspective, the more usable a solution is, the better, regardless of the security implications of the evaluated alternatives. So, when it comes to proposing and developing an authentication mechanism for such a critical application as the use of smartphones as "digital money", security and usability need to be considered on equal footing, otherwise they could undermine one another.

Hence, the use of graphic and iconic PWs in user authentication mechanisms draws more attention due to its potential benefits in terms of usability and security, and it is mainly motivated by the fact that the human memory is more effective in storing pictures than alphanumeric strings, as seen, for example, in Paivio et al. (1968).

However, the alternative represented by iconic PWs does not necessarily solve all the questions. In a comprehensive review of the first twelve years of authentication mechanisms based on graphic PWs, since 1999, Biddle et al. (2011) concluded that the graphic nature of such schemes does not avoid, *per se*, the problems found in alphanumeric PWs. In other words, even a graphical or iconic PW authentication mechanism could encourage memorization practices and improvisations that result in low-quality PWs. Examples of that occur when users reduce the universe of possible PWs from the repertoire by detecting and selecting some explicit variables, such as choosing icons from a single category (e.g. only icons of animals), or picking icons that share a common characteristic, such as color, or icons that are located in the same row or column in the grid of icons. All the potential weaknesses originating from such easily guessed (degenerated) PWs need to be addressed by the proposed solution, so that the authentication mechanism can reduce the risk of successful attacks.

Hence, the hypothesis investigated in this study is that the adoption of rules and guidelines for the creation of iconic PWs, combined with an organization of the icon repertoire based on cognitive criteria, can underpin the use of memorization strategies. Such strategies, as a consequence, could enable the users to choose better PWs than those they would have chosen without the support of these strategies. It is assumed, therefore, that this means better usability, and that this feature, rather than worsening the authentication security, would improve it by eliminating degenerated PWs or other bad practices.

In this chapter we review the rationale for using iconic PWs, as well as the main security issues that need to be considered when it comes to conceiving an authentication solution for smartphones. We also summarize some basic aspects of the human memory and point out the cognitive and practical reasons that support our proposal of memorization strategies for iconic PWs in smartphones. To illustrate the potential of the solution, we advance some initial results from user tests in which such strategies are compared with a previous authentication mechanism in which the strategies were not employed.

A RATIONALE FOR GRAPHIC AND ICONIC PASSWORDS

Textual or alphanumeric PWs, as well as the iconic ones, are mechanisms for knowledge-based authentication, where users enter a secret (which they share with the authentication system) as proof of their identity. However, textual PWs have either security or usability disadvantages, in the first case because they become predictable whenever the user is allowed to choose them, and in the second case because they tend to be difficult to memorize if they are generated by the system, as discussed in (Bentley and Mallows, 2005; Klein, 1990; Morris and Thompson, 1979; Sasse et al 2001, Yan et al, 2004). These disadvantages are indeed closely related, since the bad practices in choosing PWs are, to a large extent, due to the users' attempt to ease the memorization of alphanumeric PWs by providing them with some semantic value. Hence, the attempt to enhance usability by permitting the creation of PWs with semantic value (words, dates or sentences) besides limiting the maximum character repertoire also opens loopholes for pattern-based attacks.

One way to add semantic value to PWs is using icons instead of alphanumeric symbols. In addition to the reduction of security risks, it is also beneficial from a usability point of view, as suggested by decades of studies (Kirkpatrick, 1894; Madigan, 1983; Paivio et al, 1968; Shepard, 1967) showing that our brain is more adapted to recognize and recall visual than textual information.

The use of icon-based PWs can increase the security of the solution, including through the expansion of the theoretical space of PWs, which is, in principle, unlimited, but fixed for alphanumeric characters. What limits the repertoire of icons is indeed the usability, since a too extensive icon repertoire would make it more time-consuming for the users to locate in the grid the right icons of the PW. Moreover, the available space on the smartphone screen largely determines the maximum number of icons that can be simultaneously displayed, since small icons are less intelligible and harder to distinguish and to point with the finger. And although it is possible to split the repertoire of icons in more than one grid, this implies adding a mechanism for flipping between screens and the additional number of interaction steps, incurring some usability cost. But before describing the authentication scheme, it is worth discussing the security threats that the scheme is supposed to reduce. The following section covers this aspect.

SECURITY ASPECTS OF KNOWLEDGE-BASED AUTHENTICATIONS

Attacks on knowledge-based authentications can be classified into two general categories: guessing and capture attacks. According to Biddle et al. (2011), in the former, attacks are successful (in obtaining an acceptable success rate within a manageable number of guesses) when it is possible to either exhaustively search through the entire theoretical PW space, or predict higher probability PWs. Guessing attacks may be conducted online or offline (if some verifiable text can be used to assess the guesses). Authentication systems with identifiable patterns in PW choices or small theoretical PW spaces are especially vulnerable to such attacks.

Still according to Biddle et al. (2011), PW capture attacks involve "directly obtaining the PW, or part thereof, by capturing login credentials when entered by the user, or by tricking the user into divulging their password". Among the most common forms of capture attack, those based on shoulder-surfing, phishing or malware are worth mentioning. Table 1 summarizes the main types of attack and assigns them into either category.

Table 2 correlates possible solutions for the weaknesses listed in Table 1. Existing systems often tend to focus on one particular aspect, for example, shoulder-surfing (C1), but usually prove to be vulnerable to other types of attack. Table 2 also correlates the types of attack with their implications on the overall usability of the authentication process. Our purpose here is then to discuss how a solution can cope with all (or most of) these security issues without neglecting the usability aspects of the interaction. In other words, we aim to achieve an optimal trade-off between security and usability.

Table 1. Main types of attack and the explored weaknesses

Category	Type of Attack	Explored Weaknesses
Guessing	G1) Brute-force (online / offline)	PW with small theoretical space
	G2) Dictionary (online / offline)	PW with identifiable patterns
	G3) Social engineering	PW elements can be verbalized by users
	G4) Smudge (phone's surface)	Grid-based system with fixed positions
Capture	C1) Shoulder surfing (direct / camera)	PW input vulnerable to observation
	C2) Direct access to the PW file	PW processing vulnerable to violation
	C3) Phishing (fraudulent login site)	Non-secure website authentication
	C4) Malware (screen scrapers / mouse loggers)	Breaches in the underlying input system
	C5)Theft of the written PW	Improvising on a hard-to-memorize PW

As discussed previously, in practice the alphanumeric schemes allowing user choice are susceptible to dictionary attacks that exploit "skewed password distributions" where "certain subsets of PWs are more attractive to non-negligible sets of users" (Biddle et al., 2011). Hence, the so-called weak PW subspaces occur when users select PWs from predictable, relatively small subsets of the theoretical PW. This reduces the effective theoretical spaces of alphanumeric PWs unless they are chosen by the system or are forced to comply with strict guidelines, which make them unusable.

Being an alternative to alphanumeric PWs, iconic PWs aim at opening a larger theoretical space for the PW (SG1) and at reducing the risk of too explicit patterns (SG2), as the dictionaries of images or icons are not very common, although

Table 2. Solutions for the weaknesses and usability implications

Attack	Possible Solution for the Weaknesses	Usability Implications
G1	SG1) Larger theoretical space	Longer interaction to find the PW elements
G2	SG2) Avoid patterns through strict PW rules	Lack of semantic clues (in alphanumeric PWs)
G3	SG3) Non-verbalizable elements	Lack of semantic clues (in any PWs)
G4	SG4) Permutation (shuffling) of PW elements	A little more time-consuming PW typing
C1	SC1) PW elements hidden among decoys	Longer interaction to complete de PW
C2	SC2) One-way cryptographic hash	None
C3	SC3) No authentication from non-secure sites	None: the smartphone is the only entry
C4	SC4) Avoid alphanumeric PWs	None, if the alternate PW solution is usable
C5	SC5) Avoid hard-to-learn/easy-to-annotate PWs	None, if the alternate PW solution is usable

it remains to be investigated if there may be identifiable patterns based on conditional probability in the choice of icons. Additionally, the icon grid also allows a straightforward permutation of elements, what eliminates the risk of smudge attacks (SG4) and also enables hiding the PW elements among decoys, reducing the shoulder surfing threat (SG5). Considering the solution against verbalization of the PW (SG3), an iconic PW does not eliminate the risk completely, as it is the case with graphical solutions based on abstract images (e.g. fractals), but, to some extent, it does seem a little cumbersome to verbalize an entire 8-icon PW, in comparison with an alphanumeric PW such as "abracadabra". Finally, the option to use non-verbalizable images instead of icons would in fact produce harder-to-memorize PWs, something reproachable from a usability perspective.

In what refers to the theoretical space for the PW, that is, the number of all possible PWs, our baseline here is that of alphanumeric PWs, to which the proposed scheme intends to be a viable alternative. Table 3 shows a comparison between iconic and alphanumeric PWs in terms of mathematical security (disregarding here the effective space due to predictable alphanumeric strings). In this table we take into account the size of the repertoire of icons, the length of the iconic PW and whether PW icons are sorted or not. The security level is mathematically estimated from the bit length of PWs by means of the formula $\log_2$ (length). The parameter k represents the length of the iconic PW, whereas N represents the grid or the extension of the repertoire. The alphanumeric PWs are represented in the contexts of some known PW policies. The column "# bit" stands for the entropy of PWs and the minimum number of bits according to a given PW policy. For instance, in the case of a 4-element PW (where elements can be digits from 0 to 9), the entropy is $\log_2(9999) = 13.3$ bits. The iconic PWs for an equivalent security level should be: 3 icon-long non-ordered with a 41-icon repertoire or 4-icon long non-ordered with a 24-icon repertoire or 3-icon long ordered with a 23-icon repertoire, and so forth, as shown in Table 3.

The scheme discussed here was meant to support the use of an 8-icon PW because in a previous iconic scheme Tambascia et al. (2011), that wasn't designed to assist memorization strategies, it was observed that iconic PW with similar length led to more cases of low-quality combinations. Thus, according to Table 3, to achieve entropy of about 35 bits, the scheme had to work with a repertoire of nearly 80 icons, if they are entered in an unordered way. In fact, as discussed below, due to usability requirements, the repertoire had to be divided into four distinct and non-inter-

Table 3. Comparison of theoretical spaces of alphanumeric and iconic PWs

	Password Policies		Unsorted Icons							Sorted Icons						
#	**k = Iconic Password Length**	**#bits**	**U3**	**U4**	**U5**	**U6**	**U7**	**U8**	**U9**	**S3**	**S4**	**S5**	**S6**	**S7**	**S8**	**S9**
1	4 digits "9999" (0-9)	13.3	41	24	19	17	16	16	17	23	12	9	8	8	8	9
2	Date (DDMMYY) 365D x 100Y	15.2	62	32	24	20	19	18	18	35	16	11	9	8	8	9
3	4 letters "AAAA" (A-Z)	18.8		60	38	29	25	23	22		28	16	12	10	10	10
4	6 digits "999999" (0-9)	19.9		72	44	33	28	25	24		34	18	13	11	10	10
5	4 alphanumeric (A-Z I 0-9)	20.7		82	44	36	30	27	25		39	20	14	12	10	10
6	8 digits "99999999" (0-9)	26.6				68	51	42	37			42	25	18	14	13
7	6 letters "AAAAAA" (A-Z)	28.2				81	59	48	41			52	29	20	16	14
8	6 alphanumeric (A-Z I 0-9)	31.0					78	60	50				40	26	19	16
9	6 letters with M != m	34.2						77	62				55	33	23	19
10	6 alphanumeric with M != m	35.7						87	70					38	26	20
11	8 letters (A-Z)	37.6							80					45	30	23
12	8 alphanumeric (A-Z I 0-9)	41.4													40	29
13	PCI: 7 alphanumeric (26+10+26)	41.7													41	30
14	8 letters with M != m	45.6													56	38
15	8 alphanumeric with M != m	47.6														44
16	Corporate PW (8): 52+10+24	51.4														57
			N = grid size													

changeable grids. In addition, as the user was free to select the icons in any order in a given grid, provided that respecting the order of the grids, this put the proposed scheme somewhere in between the unordered and the ordered extremes, therefore altering the above-mentioned entropy calculation a little bit.

Additional information on protection aspects of iconic PWs can be found in Braga et al. (2012). In the following sections we summarize aspects of the human memory that could shed light on our quest for an authentication solution that combines usability and security.

ASPECTS OF HUMAN MEMORY

As the memory is needed in the real world, the ability to remember is just as important as the ability to learn. When we find something that reminds us of a past experience, the memory connections related to that event "light up" the corresponding areas in the cortex.

Within our scope of interest, the ability to memorize a PW, whether alphanumeric or iconic, depends upon neural mechanisms of our memory. According to Baars & Gage (2010), such mechanisms are not fully known yet. Several cellular and molecular processes have been proposed to explain the biological bases of memory, including mechanisms of synaptic plasticity and other phenomena of dynamic modification of shape and function of the nervous system, in response to environmental changes.

Still according to Baars & Gage (2010), transitory and lasting information is stored in different cortical areas, according to their function: motor memories in motor cortex, visual memories in visual cortex and so on. From these regions they can be mobilized as working memory by the prefrontal areas, in connection with areas of parietal cortex and occitotemporal. In addition, the explicit (declarative or conscious) memory may be consolidated in a process that can be strongly influenced by systems modulators, particularly those involved with the emotional processing.

The human memory can be functionally divided into two parts: the working memory (WM) and long-term memory (LTM). Figure 1 shows how the sensory data is first kept in the working memory and later transferred into the long-term memory, from where it can be retrieved when required.

The WM can handle explicit memories, like words, numbers, facts and semantic autobiographical episodes. However, it turns out that the WM has a very limited storage capacity: in the renowned study from the fifties, George Miller concluded that only seven (plus or minus two) items can be kept in the immediate memory at any given time. A more recent work suggests that the effective capacity of the WM can be even smaller, being around four items when no training is possible (Cowan, 2001). In addition, according to Baars & Gage (2010), the duration of time in which an item is available in WM is of the order of a few seconds. Because of that, if that informa-

Figure 1. Functional division of WM and LTM (adapted from Baars and Gage, 2010)

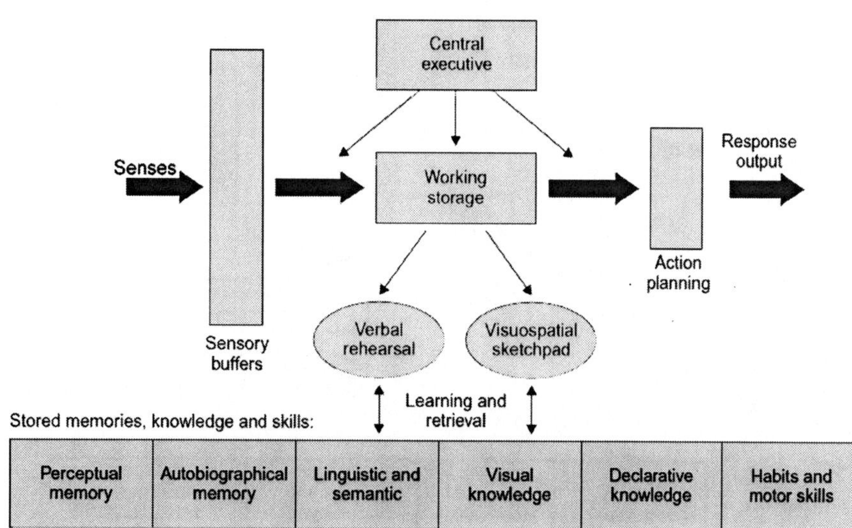

tion is not transferred into the LTM, it is soon replaced by newer information and consequently lost.

Every learning process, including of PWs, starts by entering data into the WM and then encoding them into the LTM, whether through an explicit (conscious) process, or through an implicit (largely unconscious) one as shown in Figure 2. In the former, the learning process leads to the formation of declarative semantic memories (for facts) and episodic memories (for episodes and events of life). In the latter, the process creates non-declarative memories: motor skills or habits.

In our scope, the creation and memorization of an iconic PW can rely on the conscious memory, not only on its semantic part, but also on its episodic counterpart. The semantic memory is mandatory because, as the users are expected to choose the icons of their PWs, that choice will be largely based on the meaning that the users assign to each icon. What matters here is that the users can attach a (stable) meaning to every icon, so that this (semantic) information is used to create their PWs, and later recall these very meanings.

Then again, the use of the episodic memory is optional, but it may come in handy whenever the users attempt to support their own memories by imagining events or situations that bind the chosen icons together, in a sort of "short story" or "narrative" involving the PW icons. This natural tendency originates in our cognitive apparatus, as discussed in the following subsection, which can then provide a safe path to balance usability and security.

Memorization of Social Episodes

Our cognitive apparatus has an innate ability to quickly retain letter/phoneme strings with semantic meaning, i.e., linguistic signs, if transmitted through social interaction. Unfortunately, this ability does not extend to the memorization of strings without semantic value (as those recommended by the best practices of creation of alphanumeric PWs).

Additionally, Bloom (2000) reports empirical results that proved the existence, both in children and in adults, of an innate fast mapping mechanism through which we are able to memorize arbitrary facts that have been presented to us in an incidental context. This ability can be credited to the human capacity to quickly retain information interpreted by social cognition. But it seems that it only applies to historical and social facts, which are accessible through attention to what occurs or is said around us and, if forgotten, could never be accessible again. In contrast, any information perceived as being "stored in the world" tends not to be quickly memorized, because that information supposedly will be available in a more persistent way in the environment.

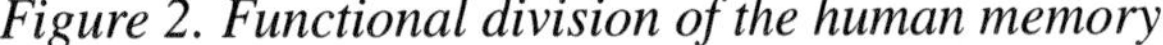

Figure 2. Functional division of the human memory

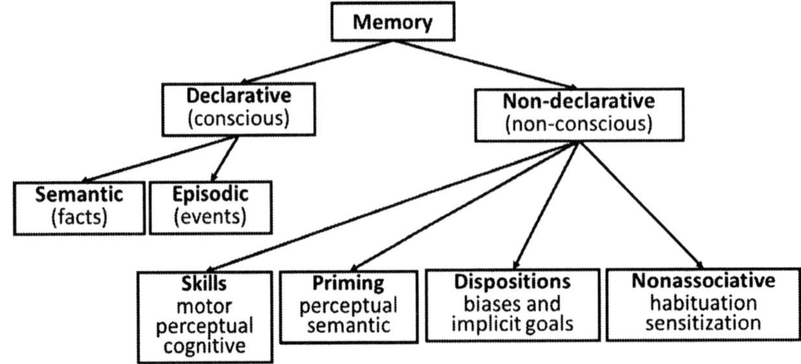

Hence, the modality of episodic memory can be present in the memorization of PWs if the users, when choosing the PW, are able to encode some elements that picture an episode of their own lives or are able to *imagine an episode* applicable to the available icons. As explained later in this article, the resource to the episodic memory is helpful because of our innate ability to memorize "social facts" (Bloom, 2000). The challenge for designers of authentication solutions is to find out how to offer a repertoire of icons that not only does it allow but also encourages such strategies. In addition, it is important to find a repertoire that does not favor PWs that could be inferred based on easily obtained information, such as user preferences (colors, food, places and so on).

In the alternative scenario in which the system chooses the user's iconic PW, the semantic memory may still be necessary as the users have to interpret the meaning of the icons assigned to them. Still, also the episodic memory can play a role in the PW memorization as long as the icon sequence provided by the system suggests events with subject, action and context, i.e., the generated PW encompasses a plausible "social episode".

Motor Memory

Finally, regarding non-declarative (unconscious) memory, it is unlikely to be considered as a memorization strategy for the PW. Specifically for the case of the motor memory, this can be used when PWs are formed by a group of keys on a keypad with fixed key positions or when the users draw their PW on a fixed grid, such as in the Android device screen-unlock. In such cases, the users memorize a sequence of keystrokes or movements rather than the PW itself.

In the context of an iconic PW on a smartphone, however, this is not useful because the icons need to be shuffled (permuted) between successive authentications, mainly to minimize the risk of shoulder surfing attacks. Since it is not possible to repeat the same movements every time one types the PW, the motor memory cannot be of any use.

Memorization of Images

Another remarkable ability of human beings is the recognition of previously seen images, including those seen very quickly (Baars and Gage, 2010, p. 180). Moreover, this ability seems to be particularly higher for some image types, such as faces and places. Some brain areas, specialized in those recognitions, have already been identified, in contrast with the inexistence of such specialization for other types of objects. And just like with the language, this may also be credited to the key role of social recognition of faces of known people, as well as the perception of affective states from subtle changes in facial expressions. Analogously, the social importance of the recognition of familiar places is also clear. This suggests that an authentication mechanism that employs images of faces and places could somewhat facilitate the users' memorization task.

It seems then valid to take advantage of these specificities of the human memory in memorization strategies to facilitate the retention of the iconic PWs by the users, both during creation as well as in the use, in order to avoid or reduce security breaches resulting from degenerate PWs, such as those observed in a previous study, when no strategies were suggested to the users.

The above-mentioned memory skills suggest that an authentication system based on images could be more usable if the image repertoire included faces and places to create social facts and that these specificities of the human memory could be used to support memorization strategies to facilitate both creation and retention of the iconic PWs. The following section presents a memorization strategy based on episodic and semantic memories and on the human ability to quickly retain "social facts or episodes".

AN EXAMPLE OF SOLUTION

In view of the human capacity in recognizing and memorizing faces and in making fast mappings of socially transmitted (factual and episodic) information, and taking into account the benefits of allowing users to resort to their episodic memory when creating their PWs, in a more consistent way, an example of strategy for selection and distribution of the icons in the grid is described here. It consists, as shown in Figure 3, in arranging spatially the repertoire of icons in such a way that the users can easily identify some characters, some actions and some contexts. These three icon categories allow the users to imagine a social fact involving some characters, in which some actions occur in some context, according to what the users consider more relevant or appealing. The first category has 20 faces of men and women. This gives the users many possible characters for the imagined episodes. The two following grids have 40 icons of objects whose relation to an action is expected to be intuitive. This allows users to associate actions to the chosen characters: for instance, "Irene rides her bike and carries a bag" or "Gloria plays tennis with Carmita". Finally, the third category has 20 icons of spatial, temporal or meteorological contexts, with themes such as "time" (date, hour, etc.), "place" (Rio, Rome, etc.) and "weather" (rainy and cloudy).

However, nothing prevents users from interpreting the icons in their own way and thereby creating episodes based on this interpretation. In the example seen above, based on the same set of icons another user could image the episode where "Irene buys a bike with the money she had in the bag". The main point here is that, whatever the iconic interpretation and the episode it induces, this will serve as a memorization aid for the users to retain more easily their PWs.

The character faces were produced through a composite drawing application, with the selection and adjustment of some basic elements such as eyes, nose, mouth, hair, etc. Twenty faces were created, ten female and ten male, as illustrated in Figure 3(a). We attempted to create the faces as different from one another as possible, in order to minimize the risk that users could be confused by too similar faces when trying to recognize the characters that participate in their PWs. We also avoided producing too much aesthetic discrepancy among the faces, in order to reduce any tendency

Figure 3. The three icon categories divided into four grids

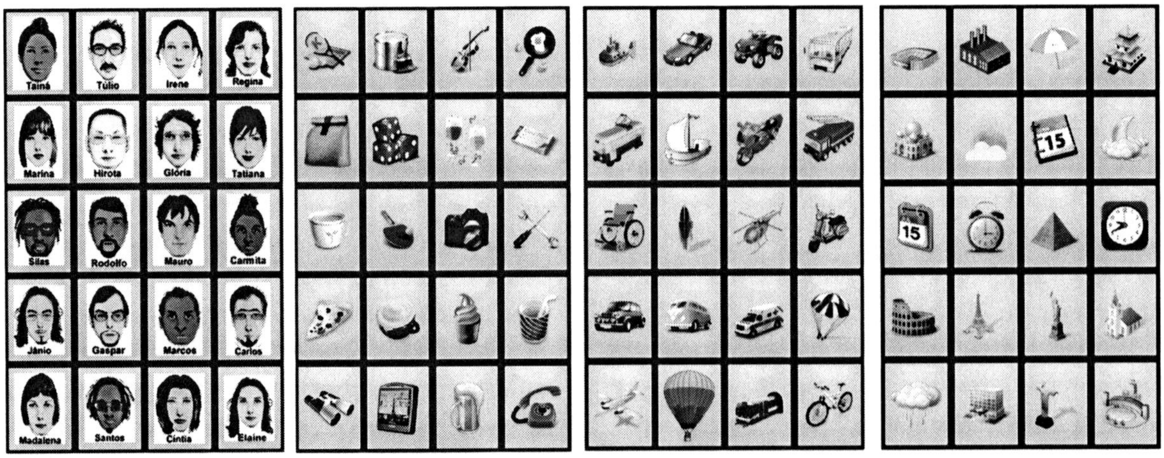

(a) (b) (c) (d)

of users choosing more often faces they considered prettier. Both these issues, i.e., ease distinction and aesthetic balance, were investigated in the user tests.

The option of using drawings instead of photos of faces was due to some practical considerations. First of all, based on cognition data, in order to enhance memorization easiness it seems sufficient for the images to look like real people, i.e., to be anthropomorphic. Thus it doesn't seem necessary to use photos of real people. Furthermore, this facilitates the development of the solution since it does not require the production of real photos of such a varied group of people. Although the composite drawings were originally generated in black and white, they were later colorized to look more natural and consistent with the other icons.

The second consideration was that an alternative strategy, such as the creation of the face grid taking advantage of the pictures from personal phone contacts on the smartphones, would have a clear drawback because the use of photos of the users' acquaintances could lead to PWs much more susceptible to guessing attacks, since the attacker could guess, with relative ease and based on information obtained from social networks, what would be the more likely stories with those people. Yet, the use of photos of the users' acquaintances could still bring some advantage for memorization, even though this does not necessarily outweigh the mentioned weakness.

Also, in order to reproduce as close as possible the users' daily experience, the characters were given names. The reason for that decision is simply because in episodes of social interaction we usually know the names of people around us. In addition, the association between name and face can help the memory, given the human ability to retain names in contexts of social cognition. Moreover, as discussed in Ávila & Gudwin (2009), the combination of icon and text can have a reinforcing effect that helps recognition and memorization.

The presence of characters on the first screen is aimed at allowing the users to create PWs based on imagined episodes for one or some of those characters. Most importantly, when reviewing the face(s) at subsequent authentications, the users should be able to remember the episode (action and context) imagined for a/some given character(s). But in the process of creating his/her PW the user must be presented with all the action and context icons before opting for one or a few characters from the first screen, otherwise he/she would tend to imagine an episode that is not supported by the icons in the following screens.

Additionally, as mentioned previously, the solution offered the functionality of suggesting a theme to help the users attach meaningful stories to their PWs. Even if the users were not obliged to accept the suggestions, this strategy added more randomness in the choice of PW themes, thus reducing its susceptibility to guessing attacks. This technique, as proposed here, is the middle ground between the system creating the PWs for the users and the users creating their own PWs. The themes were randomly chosen from a list including: "adventure", "work", "romance", "party", "unforeseen events", "travel", "good luck" and "bad luck". We investigated if this mechanism would stimulate some variability in the universe of PWs.

In the tests where the users chose their own PW, they were not prevented from selecting a PW without one or some icons from the categories. However, they were not allowed to pick all the icons from a single category (character, action or context). As a means to avoid low-quality PWs, the system imposed some rules to the users, such as accepting a maximum of three icons from each grid.

In order to produce a more homogeneous repertoire where each icon has equal chance of being chosen, we avoided low contrast and grey-shaded icons, because a previous study had shown they were less popular. We also avoided icons with very strong cultural appeal in the Brazilian context, such as the national flag or football icons.

The discoverability and navigation in the repertoire of icons proved to be a very important feature in previous tests and played an important role in the users memorization strategies. With that in mind, we eliminated all the unnecessary elements of the screen, such as toolbars and buttons, leaving more space for the icons. Smartphone users are already familiar with touch screen gestures, such as swipe, so we applied an interaction similar to the application grid presented in most of touchscreen smartphones.

In short, users were presented with a total of 80 icons, divided into four grids. The icons were permuted between two subsequent authentications. As the PW length was established to include eight icons, a typical PW would involve two icons from each grid. Finally, the order of the selected icons inside a given grid is free, but the order of the grids must be obeyed: "icons of faces" + "action icons" + "icons of context".

DESIGN OF THE TEST

The described solution was tested with 30 volunteers, all of which are employees at our Research Center, but none directly connected with the study. Eleven of the 30 participants had no prior experience with smartphones and 12 of those who had experience were considered advanced users. In terms of genre, 57% of them were female and 43% male; 36% were less than 30 years old, 47% were between 30 and 45, and 17% were over 45. The participants also had different cultural backgrounds, coming from several different hometowns.

The participation was voluntary and the test did not represent any risks to the participants. An initial interview was performed in order to characterize the participants, including in terms of their previous experiences with the use of smartphones. The first steps were taken in a usability lab, but as the test involved the use of smartphones (Figure 4a), the following steps could be made in the usual workplaces of the participants.

To test the initial hypotheses a prototype of the solution was developed in a smartphone, as well as in a desktop emulator (Figure 4b), in order to test the authentication memorization strategies both in real use conditions as in a more controlled environment, with all the necessary recording and analysis tools, including a Tobii T60 eye tracker device.

The test began with the exploration phase, where the repertoire of icons was presented to users on an Android emulator displayed on a 17-inch monitor, in order to allow us to record the eye movements through the eye tracker. With this eye- tracking data we were able to determine the more fixated icons during the exploration process and then trace a "heat map" of every icon, in every

Figure 4. (a) The authentication screen on a smartphone and (b) the desktop emulation

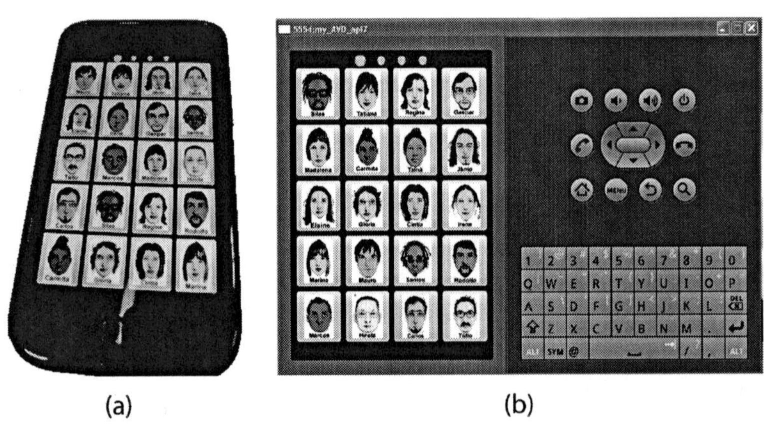

screen. The eye tracker also allowed us to trace patterns of visual exploration of each screen as users interacted with the emulated device.

After that, the participants were divided into 6 groups, as shown in Figure 5a. Three of the six groups had a training period during which they were asked to enter the PW three times, regardless of entering it correctly or not. The other three groups did not undergo that training step. Each of the three groups (both from the trained as from the untrained half) underwent a different process for creating the iconic PW: the first was asked to create a PW with a free theme, the second was asked to create a PW from a suggested theme, and the third received a system generated PW. For the four groups that were asked to create their own PWs, the time needed to accomplish this task was registered.

Once PWs were created or received (and in some cases also trained), users were prompted to authenticate with a smartphone four times within a period of thirteen days, with an increasing interval between authentications, as shown in Figure 5b. The time required to accomplish these tasks, the mistakes that were made, the number of attempts to enter the correct PW and other user experience metrics were registered. Finally, the study was completed with an in-depth interview to gather every user's impressions on the authentication solution and other pertinent information.

The obtained results were compared to those from a previous 8-icon PW solution tested by our team some months earlier, as reported in (Tambascia et al, 2011), which neither stimulated the use of memorization strategies nor imposed any restriction in the PW creation, and therefore produced many low-quality PWs.

TEST RESULTS

As shown in Table 4, the scheme described here had success rates slightly better than those produced by the previous solution. An as shown in Figures 6 and 7, the time needed for the users to create their PWs and to authenticate into the application were very similar. On the other hand, no low-quality PWs were produced in the new scheme.

As shown in Figure 8, users acquainted with the use of smartphones, to whom the proposed solution is primarily aimed, performed noticeably better than novice users in all the test phases.

As for the comparison between the groups, the best performances were found in the group with PW chosen by the user and initial training (UCWT) and in the group with system-generated PW and initial training (SGWT), as illustrated in Figure 9.

The eye tracker showed that, as illustrated in Figure 10, Figure 11, Figure 12, and Figure 13,

Figure 5. (a) Division of the users into six groups and (b) distribution of the test rounds

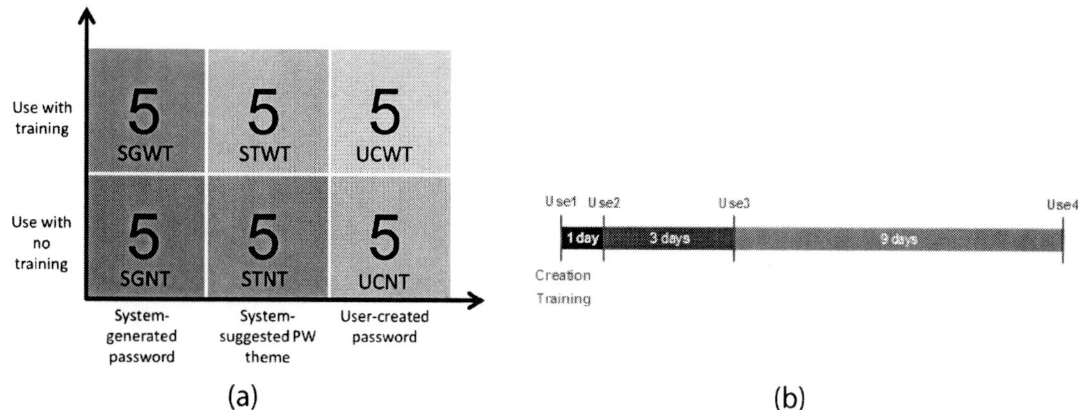

Table 4. Success rates for iconic PWs with and without memorization aids

	Without Memorization Aids			With Memorization Aids		
	1st Attempt	2nd Attempt	3rd Attempt	1st Attempt	2nd Attempt	3rd Attempt
1 day	80%	90%	90%	67%	77%	90%
5 days	70%	80%	90%	80%	93%	97%
9 days	80%	90%	90%	73%	90%	100%

Figure 6. Time without memorization support

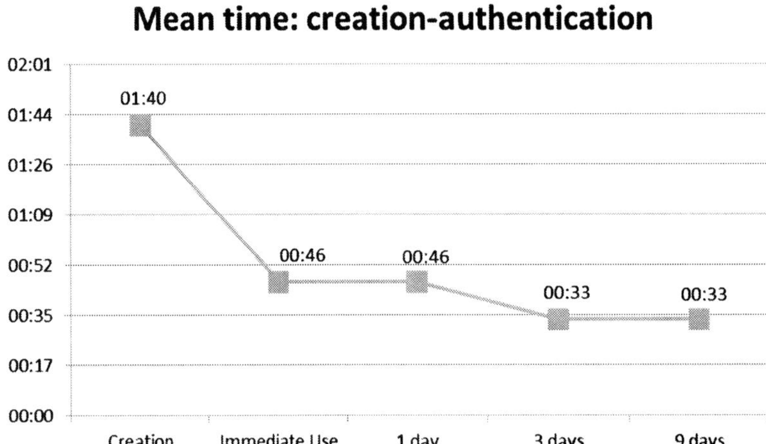

Figure 7. Time with memorization support

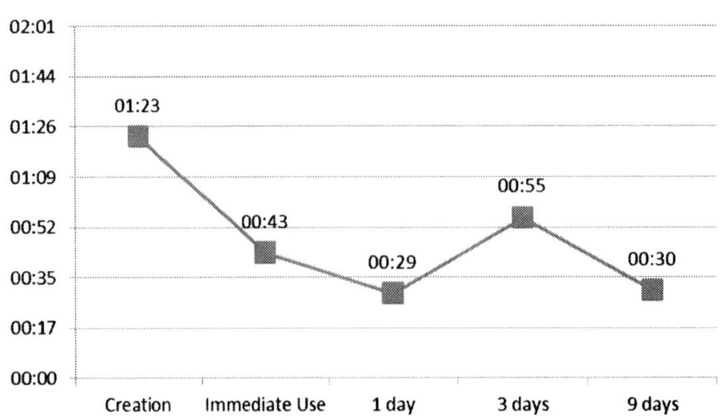

Figure 8. Expert versus novice users

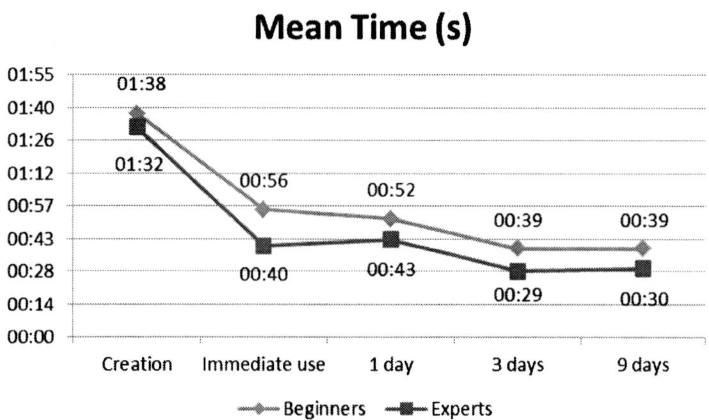

Figure 9. Authentication times per group

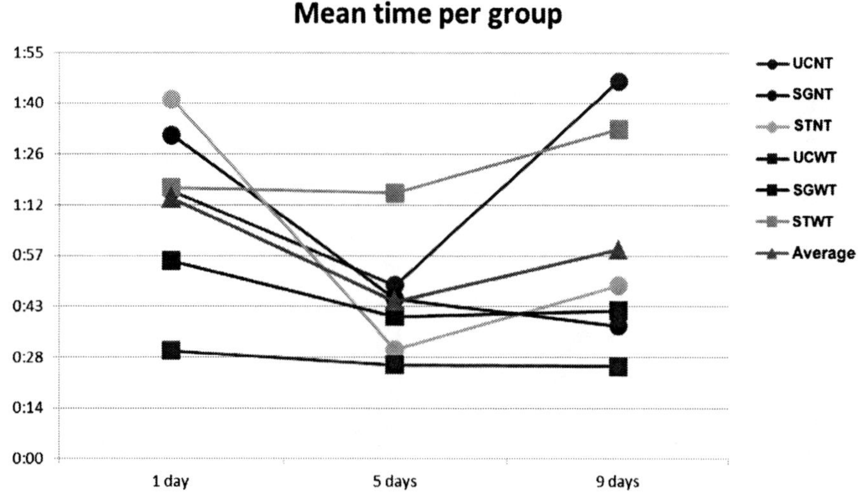

some icons tended to draw the attention of most users, but this also depended on the position of those icons on the grid, with the hotspots consistently located more often in the upper left part of the grid. This probably reflects the reading direction to which the participants are accustomed. On the other hand, no clear correlation was found between the more fixated icons and the more frequently chosen ones (the X's indicate the faces or icons that were not chosen). This suggests that a longer fixation on a given icon can be caused by the reading habits or by a greater difficulty in identifying that icon, and not necessarily by the user's attempt to create a story with that icon.

FUTURE RESEARCH DIRECTIONS

It is important to emphasize that the solution described in this chapter was proposed during the development of a prototype for secure authentication in smartphones, in which iconic PWs are

Figure 10. Eye tracker heat map for the first grid versus the icons not chosen

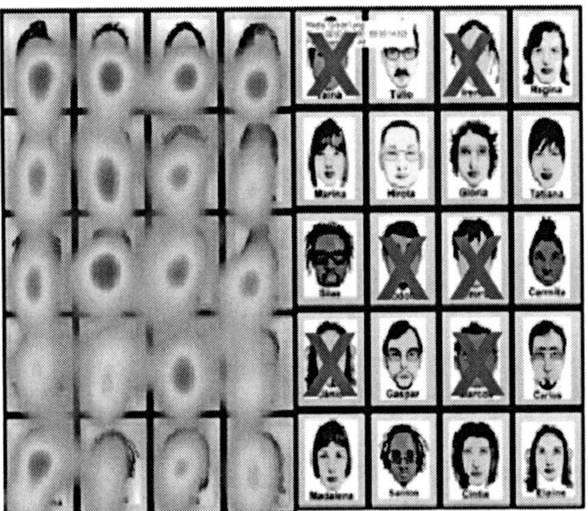

Figure 11. Eye tracker heat map for the second grid versus the icons not chosen

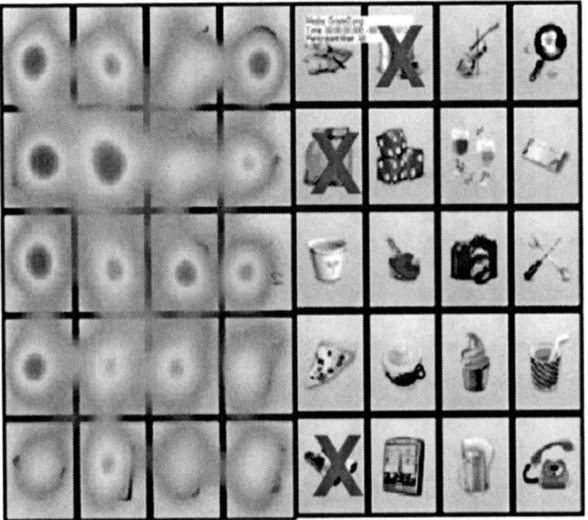

used together with two biometric (face and voice) authentication solutions. This particular development context and the strict timeframe asked for systemic test scenarios, instead of more detailed evaluations of isolated features of the proposed solution. As stated, the first phase of our study was aimed at testing a broad range of aspects related to the basic idea of an iconic PW authentication scheme with support of a memorization strategy.

Figure 12. Eye tracker heat map for the third grid versus the icons not chosen

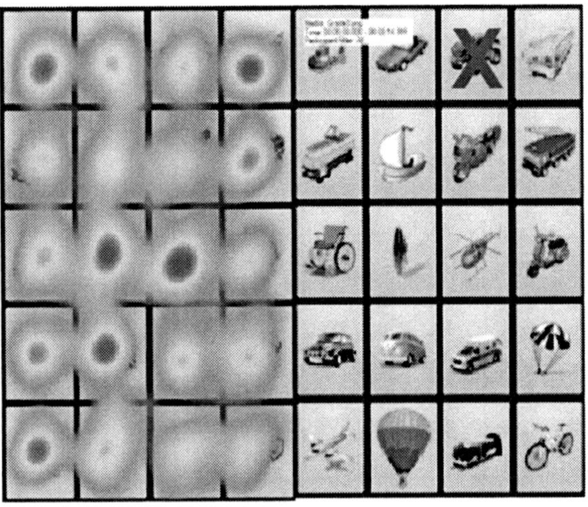

Figure 13. Eye tracker heat map for the fourth grid versus the icons not chosen

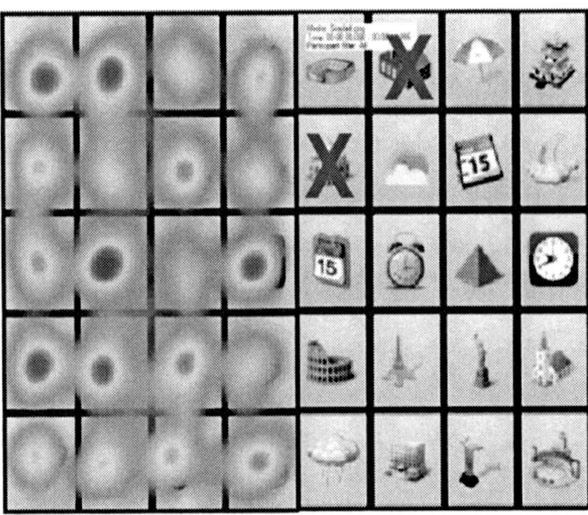

We evaluated a first instance of such scheme, along with some pertinent variables, such as the PW creation policy (if user defined or system generated), or the effect of an initial training session on the users' performances. The main goal was to evaluate the overall feasibility of the scheme and, additionally, gather some initial evidence on what should be the direction of its future evolution.

That means that more in-depth investigations of the tested hypothesis would be necessary, but they were not in the initial scope of our systemic research. Therefore, the next step of the study will be to apply the results of the first phase in order to improve the repertoire and then repeat the test with other users. In order to produce more conclusive results, this second phase will focus on fewer security and usability aspects, concentrating on the best performing scenarios found in the first phase (PW chosen by the user + initial training or system generated + initial training) and testing these scenarios with a larger number of users, instead of testing many different variables with smaller groups of users.

Another necessary development refers to the evaluation of conditional probabilities in the choice of icons, because, if such probabilities do occur, this means they tend to create patterns that could be explored in attacks. Ideally, the study should find a suitable iconic repertoire in which every combination is equally probable and with no detectable pattern in the choice of icons.

Finally, the following steps of this research should evaluate the use of the proposed solution for shorter PWs, with 4 or 6 icons, in order to check if it is still possible to retain a plausible social episode with less elements, and how this reflects in the time necessary for authenticating, since for many situations a faster mechanism would be desirable, provided that the required security level is not as critical as in the "digital money" scenario.

CONCLUSION

We presented here a memorization strategy aimed at facilitating the creation and the memorization of iconic PWs. The employed strategies are based on known skills and abilities of the human brain to recognize and retain faces and places, and make a fast mapping of information obtained through social cognition. This information includes facts and episodes that our cognitive system perceives as not "stored" in the environment. Accordingly, as the authentication solution favors the creation of episodes involving characters (faces), actions and contexts, this was expected to stimulate the users to create good PWs (or to memorize high-quality system-generated PWs), differently from what was found in the previous usability tests with a repertoire that lacked aids to ease memorization and with characteristics that favored low-quality PWs based on explicit variables such as colors or grid positions.

From a usability perspective, an iconic PW solution, based on the choice of icons from a pre-established universe, has some advantage over alphanumeric PWs. For instance, the number of screens and of elements on every screen can be chosen, allowing the creation of various scenarios with the desired security and usability levels for the application.

The proposed strategy takes advantage of the easiness that the socially meaningful icon repertoire brings to the creation and memorization of the PW. Furthermore, the organization of these categories in the form of a sequence "subject + action + context", combined with some restrictions on the number of icons chosen by category, avoids the creation of low-quality PWs, such as those observed in previous tests.

When comparing the six user groups that undertook the test, it was remarkable to see that the best performing group was the one whose members created their own PWs and then underwent a training phase. This suggests that these users chose meaningful PWs and also had the opportunity to retain them during the training. The second best performing groups were those whose members received their PWs from the system and had time to train the use of that PW; However the group with no training performed noticeably worse on the first day, then, on the 5th day they matched the members of the group that had training and later even slightly outperformed them on the 9th day.

Surprisingly enough, the group that received suggested themes and had time to train the PWs had a poor performance in all the three days of test, whereas the group that received suggested themes but had no training showed the poorest performance on the 1st day, but remarkably improved it on the 5th and 9th days. The worst performance on the 9th day was shown by the group that created the PWs but had no time to train. These results suggest that the best overall option is letting the users create their own PWs and undergo a training phase prior to starting using them in a real application, provided that the memorization solution imposes some rules in the creation process to avoid low-quality PWs.

With respect to the PW creation, the study sought to test what the best strategy would be, whether the automatic generation of a PW by the system, or the creation of PW by the user. The disadvantage of a PW entirely created by the user is the risk that he/she will choose a low-quality combination. On the other hand, the generation of PWs with no involvement of the users could reduce the memorability of the generated PW.

Thus, an intermediate approach was proposed and tested here: some users chose their PWs after receiving a random theme suggested by the system from a set of themes compatible with the icons available in the repertoire. So, the test evaluated three scenarios: users freely creating their own PWs, users receiving a preset PW from the system, and users receiving a suggested theme from the system but being free to take it into consideration or not. Some users acknowledged having followed the theme suggestion, and other simply ignored it, but PWs created by users based on a suggested theme seemed more balanced among the categories.

The interviews with the participants revealed that the 7% who experienced difficulty with the solution belonged to the group of non-users of smartphones. This was expected because both the PW creation and the authentication process required a good understanding of browsing on touchscreen smartphones. Users without this previous knowledge needed a much longer time to accomplish the tasks. As the proposed solution is aimed at smartphone users, it is likely that these target users will not face that kind of difficulty.

Finally, 87% of the tested participants reported that the experience with the iconic PW was satisfactory, mostly for smartphone users, and 60% of the participants said they would accept changing an alphanumeric PW mechanism for an iconic one. The visibility of faces and their respective names was considered satisfactory in the used smartphone, the Samsung Galaxy model.

In what refers to the main research question of the study, the results showed that the memorization solutions were effective in eliminating the low-quality PWs, and that this occurred without any degradation of the mean times necessary to create the PWs and to use them during the authentication processes.

Even though 33 seconds to authenticate in a smartphone could seem much slower than authenticating by means of a few alphanumeric symbols, it is important to notice that the necessary number of alphanumeric items to produce the same level of mathematical security as produced by 8 icons from an 80-element repertoire is rather large, and entering an equivalent textual PW, according to the mentioned best practices, should be much slower than typing four numbers in a single grid. In other words, if one is using the smartphone to replace the wallet or the credit card, it is advisable to assure a minimal security level, while keeping the whole process as usable as possible. That was precisely our initial goal.

In short, the memorization strategy for iconic PWs produced the result for which it was designed, namely, the elimination of low-quality PWs, and yet lead to slightly better success rates in the use of the created PWs. The solution proved to be effective in offering wider possibilities for the creation of stories, in eliminating the low-quality PWs and in producing less observable errors. Some additional conclusions are that the training phase did not significantly influence performances for system-created PWs, but seemed to be effective with PWs created by the users.

The most popular icons (e.g. pizza and beer) had a strong cultural appeal as well as a colorful design. The least popular icons usually had shades of grey and low contrast and therefore were harder to identify. Finally, some faces proved to be harder to distinguish by some users, and some others proved to be very popular. As a result, improvements in the icon repertoire have already been devised to improve it in the near future by avoiding or reducing these unbalances among icons. These improvements may encompass the inclusion of faces of children or elderly characters, in order to expand the universe of possible stories.

In short, the use of memorization aids and the application of stricter rules for the PW creation in the described authentication scheme stimulated the creation of best PWs, without worsening the users' performances when compared to the previous test.

REFERENCES

Abdullah, R., & Hübner, R. (2006). *Pictograms, icons, and signs*. London, UK: Thames & Hudson.

ADDITIONAL READING

Anderson, R. J. (2008). Usability and psychology. In *Security Engineering: A Guide to Building Dependable Distributed Systems* (pp. 17–62). Indianapolis, IN: Wiley Publishing Inc..

Ávila, I., & Gudwin, R. (2009). Icons as helpers in the interaction of illiterate users with computers. In *Proceedings of the Interfaces and Human Computer Interaction 2009*. IHCI.

Baars, B. J., & Gage, N. M. (2010). *Cognition, brain and consciousness – Introduction to congnitive neuroscience*. Elsevier.

Bentley, J., & Mallows, C. (2005). How much assurance does a PIN provide? In Baird & Lopresti, (Ed.), Human Interactive Proofs (HIP), (LNCS) (vol. 3517, pp. 111-126). Berlin: Springer-Verlag.

Biddle, R., Chiasson, S., & Van Oorschot, P. C. (2012). Graphical passwords: Learning from the first twelve years. *ACM Computing Surveys*, *44*(4), 1–41. doi:10.1145/2333112.2333114.

Bloom, P. (2000). *How children learn the meanings of words*. Cambridge, MA: The MIT Press.

Bowman, M. et al. (1993). Reasoning about naming systems. *ACM Trans. Program. Lang. Syst.*, *15*(5), 795–825. doi:10.1145/161468.161471.

Braga, A., Cividanes, R., Ávila, I., & Tambascia, C. (2012). Protection aspects of iconic passwords on mobile devices. In Y. Xiang et al. (Eds.), *CSS 2012, (LNCS)* (Vol. 7672, pp. 21–32). Berlin: Springer-Verlag. doi:10.1007/978-3-642-35362-8_3.

Chiasson, S., Biddle, R., & Oorschot, P. C. (2007). A second look at the usability of click-based graphical passwords. In *Proceedings of the 3rd Symposium on Usable Privacy and Security* (SOUPS '07). ACM.

Chin, E., Felt, A. P., Sekar, V., & Wagner, D. (2012). Measuring user confidence in smartphone security and privacy. In *Proceedings of the Eighth Symposium on Usable Privacy and Security* (SOUPS '12). ACM.

Cowan, N. (2001). The magical number 4 in short-term memory: A reconsideration of mental storage capacity. *The Behavioral and Brain Sciences*, *24*, 87–114. doi:10.1017/S0140525X01003922 PMID:11515286.

Cranor, L. F., & Garfinkel, S. (2005). *Security and usability: Designing secure systems that people can use*. Sebastopol, CA: O'Reilly Media.

De Angeli, A., Coventry, L., Johnson, G., & Renaud, K. (2005). Is a picture really worth a thousand words? Exploring the feasibility of graphical authentication systems. *International Journal of Human-Computer Studies*, *63*(1–2), 128–152. doi:10.1016/j.ijhcs.2005.04.020.

De Luca, A., Denzel, M., & Hussmann, H. (2009). Look into my eyes! Can you guess my password? In *Proceedings of the 5th Symposium on Usable Privacy and Security* (SOUPS '09). ACM.

Dunphy, P., Heiner, A. P., & Asokan, N. (2010). A closer look at recognition-based graphical passwords on mobile devices. In *Proceedings of the Sixth Symposium on Usable Privacy and Security* (SOUPS '10). ACM.

Everitt, K. M., Bragin, T., Fogarty, J., & Kohno, T. (2009). A comprehensive study of frequency, interference, and training of multiple graphical passwords. In *Proceedings of the SIGCHI Conference on Human Factors in Computing Systems* (CHI '09). ACM.

Hayashi, E., Hong, J., & Christin, N. (2011). Security through a different kind of obscurity: Evaluating distortion in graphical authentication schemes. In *Proceedings of the SIGCHI Conference on Human Factors in Computing Systems* (CHI '11). ACM.

Horton, W. K. (1994). *The ICON book: Visual symbols for computer systems and documentation*. New York: John Wiley & Sons, Inc..

Hosie, J. A., & Milne, A. B. (1995). Distinctiveness and memory for unfamiliar faces. In T. Valentine (Ed.), *Cognitive and Computational Aspects of Face Recognition: Explorations in face space*. New York, NY: Routledge.

Johnston, J., Eloff, J. H. P., & Labuschagne, L. (2003). Security and human computer interfaces. *Computers & Security*, *22*(8), 675–684. doi:10.1016/S0167-4048(03)00006-3.

Johnston, R. A., & Ellis, H. D. (1995). The development of face recognition. In T. Valentine (Ed.), *Cognitive and Computational Aspects of Face Recognition: Explorations in face space*. New York, NY: Routledge.

Kirkpatrick, B. (1894). An experimental study of memory. *Psychological Review*, *1*, 602–609. doi:10.1037/h0068244.

Klein, D. (1990). Foiling the cracker: A survey of, and improvements to, password security. In *Proceedings of the 2nd USENIX Security Workshop*. USENIX.

Lampson, B. (2009). Privacy and security: Usable security: how to get it. *Communications of the ACM*, *52*(11), 25–27. doi:10.1145/1592761.1592773.

Liu, K. (2009). *Semiotics in information systems engineering*. New York, NY: Cambridge University Press.

Madigan, S. (1983). Picture memory. In J. Yuille (Ed.), *Imagery, Memory, and Cognition: Essays in Honor of Allan Paivio* (pp. 65–89). Hoboken, NJ: Lawrence Erlbaum Associates.

Mathiasen, N. R., & Bødker, S. (2011). Experiencing security in interaction design. In *Proceedings of the SIGCHI Conference on Human Factors in Computing Systems (CHI '11)*. ACM.

Menezes, A. J., Oorschot, P. C., & Vanstone, S. (1996). Overview of cryptography. In K. H. Rosen (Ed.), *Handbook of Applied Cryptography* (pp. 1–45). Boca Raton, FL: CRC Press. doi:10.1201/9781439821916.ch1.

Moncur, W., & Leplâtre, G. (2007). Pictures at the ATM: exploring the usability of multiple graphical passwords. In *Proceedings of the SIGCHI Conference on Human Factors in Computing Systems* (CHI '07). ACM.

Morris, R., & Thompson, K. (1979). Password security: A case history. *Communications of the ACM*, *22*(11), 594–597. doi:10.1145/359168.359172.

Mullet, K., & Sano, D. (1994). *Designing visual interfaces: Communication oriented techniques*. Englewood Cliffs, NJ: SunSoft Press.

Paivio, A. etal. (1968). Why are pictures easier to recall than words? *Psychonomic Science*, *11*(4), 137–138.

Payne, B. D., & Edwards, W. K. (2008). A brief introduction to usable security. *IEEE Internet Computing*, *12*(3), 13–21. doi:10.1109/MIC.2008.50.

Sasse, M. A. etal. (2001). Transforming the 'weakest link' - A human/computer interaction approach to usable and effective security. *BT Technology Journal*, *19*(3), 122–131. doi:10.1023/A:1011902718709.

Schneier, B. (2008). Psychology of security. In *Schneier on Security* (pp. 169–188). Indianapolis, IN: Wiley Publishing Inc..

Shepard, R. (1967). Recognition memory for words, sentences, and pictures. *Journal of Verbal Learning and Verbal Behavior*, *6*, 156–163. doi:10.1016/S0022-5371(67)80067-7.

Tambascia, C., et al. (2011). *Usability evaluation using eye tracking for iconographic authentication on mobile devices*. Paper presented at the Mobility 2011. Barcelona, Spain.

Tari, F., Ozok, A. A., & Holden, S. H. (2006). A comparison of perceived and real shoulder-surfing risks between alphanumeric and graphical passwords. In *Proceedings of the Second Symposium on Usable Privacy and Security* (SOUPS '06). ACM.

Vokey, J. R., & Read, J. D. (1995). Memorability, familiarity and categorical structure in the recognition of faces. In T. Valentine (Ed.), *Cognitive and Computational Aspects of Face Recognition: Explorations in face space*. New York, NY: Routledge.

Yan, J. etal. (2004). Password memorability and security: Empirical results. *IEEE Security & Privacy Magazine*, *2*(5), 25–31. doi:10.1109/MSP.2004.81.

Zakaria, N. H., Griffiths, D., Brostoff, S., & Yan, J. (2011). Shoulder surfing defense for recall-based graphical passwords. In *Proceedings of the Seventh Symposium on Usable Privacy and Security* (SOUPS '11). ACM.

KEY TERMS AND DEFINITIONS

Alphanumeric Password: A password formed by a sequence of characters, such as uppercase and lowercase letters, digits and special characters.

Degenerated Password: The same as low-quality password, i.e., a password that can be guessed or predicted based on typical patterns or on easily acquired information.

Episodic Memory: One of the two modalities of the declarative (conscious) memory; the episodic memory is responsible for registering autobiographical events (times, places, associated emotions, and other contextual knowledge).

Iconic Password: A password formed by a sequence of icons or pictograms, also referred to as graphic password; but in the definition adopted here this does not include sequences of meaningless images, such as fractals or any abstract images.

Memorization: In the scope of this research memorization refers to the mental process of deliberately storing in the memory a password for a given computational system so as to later be able to recall it during an authentication to enter that system.

Theoretical Security (a.k.a. Mathematical Security): Is here understood as the security derived from mathematical assumptions about the space of valid passwords, without considering the feasibility of brute-force attacks. In a broad sense, is a somewhat loose definition that does not comprehend the formal notion of Information-theoretic security.

Usability: In the context of this research it refers to the learnability and ease of use of a software application designed to authenticate a user in a smartphone.

User Authentication: Process through which a user proves his/her identity by entering a pattern or secret that he/she shares with the system.

Chapter 13
Location-Based Data Visualisation Tool for Tuberculosis and Dengue: A Case Study in Malaysia

Kim Nee Goh
Universiti Teknologi PETRONAS, Malaysia

Yoke Yie Chen
Universiti Teknologi PETRONAS, Malaysia

Cheah Hui Chow
Universiti Teknologi PETRONAS, Malaysia

ABSTRACT

Malaysians suffer from both communicable and non-communicable diseases. Tuberculosis (communicable disease) is common in rural places and dengue (non-communicable disease) is a popular vector-borne disease in Malaysia. Health centres record information of the victims, but merely recording the address in a Microsoft Excel file does not provide much insight to viewers. Currently, an easy to use tool is not available for doctors, officers from the Ministry of Health, and also the public to analyse and visualise the data. It is difficult and time consuming to analyse and interpret raw data tabulated through Microsoft Excel. This research aims to develop a prototype tool that visualises disease data on a Google map. An interpretation is then generated along with the visualisation to give an impartial description about the data. This prototype obtained favourable feedback from a health officer as it can help them in analysing data and assist in the decision making process. The benefit of such application is helpful in tracking diseases' spreading patterns, how to isolate diseases, as well as mobilising personnel and equipment to the affected areas.

DOI: 10.4018/978-1-4666-4623-0.ch013

INTRODUCTION

With the immense power of computing these days, data can now be given 'treatment' in order to transform it into usable information. Health centres have a lot of data that are not fully utilized. In our research work, we developed a prototype system to visualise data, as it is easier to interpret an image rather than text (Jin & Liu, 2009). Visualization reduces the extra cognitive effort needed to understand raw data and data mining results besides allowing comparisons and testing to be done on the results. It will also make data mining algorithms more understandable to users and thus enable them to be involved in their decision analysis (Kantardzic, 2002). Our location of study is situated in Kinta District, within the Perak state of Malaysia. Two diseases were chosen: 1. tuberculosis, as it is contagious and common in rural parts of Kinta District and 2. dengue, as it is a very common vector borne disease in Malaysia. From interviews conducted with the health officer of Kinta District, data were obtained, requirements were gathered and a prototype was developed. It is envisaged that this prototype will assist health officers in managing new disease cases, monitoring the spread of diseases and to make more informed decisions in terms of mobilizing resources such as health personnels and equipment that may be needed in a particular area. In the long run, it is hoped that it will be able to assist health centres in discovering spreading patterns, isolating diseases and mobilizing personnel and equipment to such areas.

BACKGROUND

As people become more mobile with travelling due to various accessible transportation modes and affordability, the risk of influenza or other communicable diseases increases (Merler et. al., 2006). In Malaysia, both inbound and outbound tourism has been rapidly increasing as the global economy in Asia strengthens. In 2007, the top five diseases in Malaysia were dengue fever, tuberculosis, food poisoning, hand food and mouth disease (HFMD) and HIV/AIDS. As stated by the World Health Organisation (WHO) (2010), the incidence rates for Malaysia were 80.6 per 100,000 population for dengue fever, 61.9 per 100,000 for tuberculosis, 52.6 per 100,000 for food poisoning, 46.1 per 100,000 for HFMD, and 16.0 per 100,000 for HIV/AIDS. Dengue fever, which is a vector borne disease, topped the rank. All of the top five diseases are communicable diseases which indicate that transmission could happen between humans through direct or indirect contact (Hawker et. al., 2000). One of the strategies that will guide the health sector development is by enhancing research and development to support evidence-based decision-making and strengthening health information and management systems (Ali, 2010).

Communicable diseases are diseases that can be passed from one person to the other. If we are able to inform and educate the public to help contain and prevent the spread of communicable diseases by taking some precautionary steps, the number of death and also the money spent on curing such diseases can be reduced tremendously. Pandemic influenza is also threatening the health of not only Malaysians but also many people around the world. Pandemic influenza arrives with little warning and can cause huge damage in a short period of time. The risk of influenza had also increased as the mobility of the population becomes greater. The outbreak of a new disease is reminded by the Spanish flu pandemic, which happened between 1918 and 1919 and was estimated to have killed 40 million people worldwide. This perception had caused panic and weakened the world economy. The areas that were adversely affected by this situation were air travel, tourism and meat imports and exports, although WHO relaxed the travel restrictions that were recommended earlier and meat was proven not as a medium where the virus could spread. The circumstance above showed that the panic caused by the virus seemed to be more destructive than the virus itself. In order to overcome this problem, it is crucial for us to analyse the spread of a virus so that action proper to the risk level of the virus can be taken (Richards, 2004). Because of the West Nile Virus reported in 1999 at New York State, it required rapid mobilization and coordination of hundreds of public health workers, equipment, medicine and others and this has cost millions of dollars on an emergency basis as immediate surveillance is necessary to control this outbreak (Zeng et. al., 2004).

Early prevention of these diseases will save the money spent on combating them later. According to Richards (2004), mathematical models can predict the way communicable diseases will spread and possibly prevent them from spreading. Google Flu Trend is a project by Google that is able to estimate flu activity in particular vicinity. It is said that the number of people query for flu related topics using Google search and the number of people experiencing flu symptoms are closely related. When compared, the popularity of flu related queries with the official data that were released two weeks later than the queries statistic, the numbers actually matched although there are some small variations (Google Flu Trends, n.d.).

However, in order to analyse the spread of diseases, sufficient amount of data and information is necessary. WHO publishes information in regards to communicable diseases but this is only done on an annual basis. A hospital within a particular locality would have more up to date information but the information is not publicly available. Public release of such information is very rare. Thus, it is near impossible for the public to be informed of the spread of diseases within the particular vicinity that they are located. Even though data is available, proper presentation of such data is necessary. Reporting statistics alone does not help in knowing whether the area you are located at is of risk. It just gives you an averaged overall picture of an area. Large amount of data becomes useless when no visual treatment is given when there are a lot sitting around (Yau, 2011). Shneiderman (1996) mentioned that exploring information collection becomes increasingly difficult as volume grows. A page of information is easy to explore, but when the information becomes the size of a book, or library, or even larger, it may be difficult to locate known items or to browse to gain an overview. With the current disease data available in Malaysia, it is difficult and time consuming to analyse as data exist in raw form and no visual representation is available to see its density and geographical location of a particular disease. There is no simple automatic map plotting system which can plot addresses to enable visualization of data. As quoted from Shneiderman (2008), "The purpose of visualization is insight, not pictures." Tools that support a process of information-seeking will help lead users to important insights and it becomes valuable if it contributes to solving significant problems. It is very useful to visualise health data as such application will be helpful in tracking infectious diseases' spreading tendency, in building up isolation for the infectious disease and also in establishing the best transportation line for the personnel and the equipment supply in the infectious region (Lu, 2009). As mentioned by Lu (2009), web GIS based visualization information can be used for warning, monitoring, processing and controlling an emergent event with its visible spatial information.

By introducing a system which can visualise the data obtained from hospitals and generate an interpretation, it will certainly make it easier to know and learn about the locality of the disease, prompting quicker investigation and thus lowering the possibilities of communicable disease spread. According to Palaniappan and Awang (2008), useful information can be retrieved if the data contained in the health care industry can be processed and analysed. The objective of this research is to develop a prototype system that could ease the analysis of disease data by visualising them on a map and to generate an interpretation of the data based on the visualised map. This system is meant for doctors, officers from the Ministry of Health Malaysia and also the public to better understand disease spread and patterns.

PREVIOUS WORKS

Impact of Environmental Factors on Vector Borne Diseases

Malaysia records high number of dengue fever and malaria cases as they are both vector borne diseases. Zeng et. al. (2006) assessed the impact that environmental factors have on vector borne diseases and conclude that the relationship is valid. However, it was mentioned that remote sensing and GIS method used in identifying and monitoring environmental factors would not be a reliable epidemiological technique if the understanding of the relationship between the factors are not sound (Tsui et. al., 2010). Previous researches were done by Syahman (2006) and Omar (2007) to find out how GIS factors in Batu Gajah area, a town that is situated 30km off our study area affects the number of dengue cases in the year 2006 and 2007. MapInfo Map software was used to create and edit a map. MapInfo also allowed embedding maps in their word processor and edit it using MapInfo functions. The authors collected GIS information and placed it on their map. A comparison was done with the suspected dengue cases data that the authors obtained from Batu Gajah Hospital. Hypotheses were developed: mosquito bit the victim 1. when they were walking on the road, 2. when their house location is nearby a drain and 3. when there is a toilet bowl, as it is a mosquito breeding ground. These hypotheses were proven to be true since all the dengue cases that happened at least fulfilled one of the three assumptions. Studies also found that temperature will affect the population of mosquitoes, in effect the incidence rate of dengue and other vector borne diseases. The changes in climate due to global warming may increase the population of mosquitoes which results in more dengue cases. The area that used to be dengue safe might be affected by this factor. Identifying factors that effects the spread is important in containing and combating it.

Visualising Data

Amar and Stasko (2005) defined the word 'visualise' as the creation of static presentations built to convey a message around a particular selected subset of data. Two types of goals for visualization techniques are geometric and symbolic. When deciding the visualization technique, we also need to determine whether the stimulus will be 2D or 3D and also decide to have either dynamic or static stimulus. Examples of data representation using geometric techniques are scatter plot, lines, surfaces or volume and are usually used to display the relationship between some elements of the data. Symbolic representations use pixels, icons, array or graphs to display data. Both geometric and symbolic representation can be presented as 2D or 3D, hence it is more important to decide the goals of the representation first. Lastly, it is also equally important to decide whether the representation should be dynamic or static (Fayyad, Grinstein & Wierse, 2001). Dynamic representation will be more interactive and interesting but developing it could be more complex.

Work by Hansen et. al. (2010) developed a multi-touch display to visualise simulation of the spread of disease in a hospital. Much attention was given to this concern as there were more than 100,000 lives lost in a year in United States due to high rates of infection in hospitals. The visualization will allow users to see and manipulate the view of the hospital building and see how its workers move around within the building. Users can 'infect' health workers and see how the infection spreads throughout the hospital based on vaccination rates and chances of infection.

Research done by Lu (2009) visualises the number of disease cases in different states of China using colour. Figure 1 shows the different colours that represent different number of cases. Users can click on the map if they want to know more about the trend of the disease over time. The visualization of the trend of disease over a period of time is shown in Figure 2. When partial data of GIS and infectious disease information are combined, infectious disease distribution information can be communicated through maps. Information such as number of infected persons and the source of the virus can be presented visually to geographically show the affected areas at a certain time period.

As this research combines disease data, medical information and GIS data, it allows users to track the spreading tendency of infectious disease. It can also be used to find the best route for health personnel to use to travel into the affected area. However, this system was built based on Java GIS applet technology and web GIS. Other means should be researched to enable easily available technology to be used to produce similar results, as what we have done using Google API and Google Map. SmartGIS is another similar system done by Zeng et. al. (2006). This system integrates SVG, WebGIS and data visualisation techniques, which continuously visualises and monitor SARS outbreak status. Users can also view it on the web to better understand its movement so that potential life-lost could be reduced.

One of the more popular visualisation applications is Google Flu Trends by Google. This application trends flu activities in various parts of the world. A sample snapshot is shown in Figure 3.

Trending is mapped based on what users searched on Google's search engine. A close relationship was found between the number of people that searched for flu-related topics and the number of people who actually have flu symptoms. Although there are some very minor discrepancies between the actual data and the estimates, Google is quite accurately visualising the trends based on users' search. In our prototype, we will use markers to mark the exact point of location where a case has been reported based on the victim's given address where they are suspected to have caught the disease.

In Zhang et. al. (2012) work, he states that there are two kinds of visualisation: science and information visualisation. Science visualisation

Figure 1. Visualization of a disease developing tendency in a map

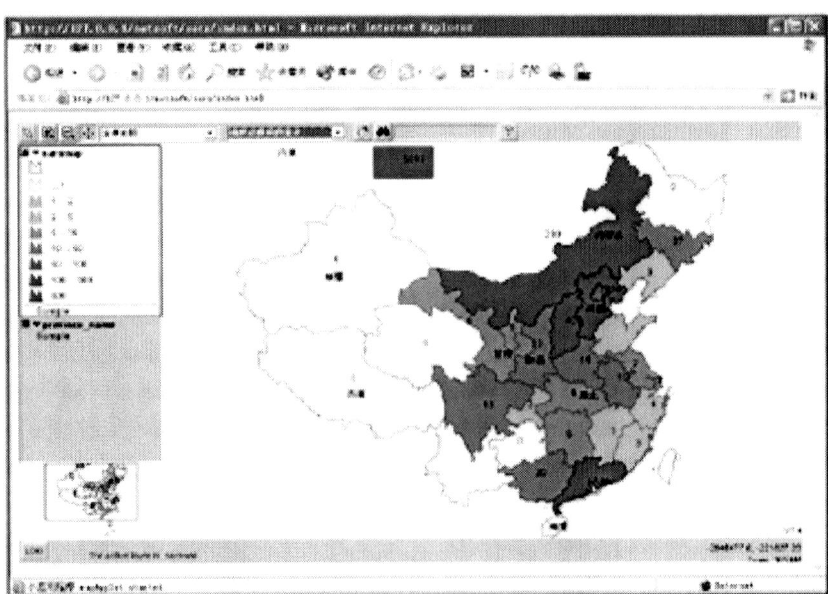

Figure 2. Visualisation of the number of persons infected with the disease, died from the disease as well as recovered from the disease over a period of time

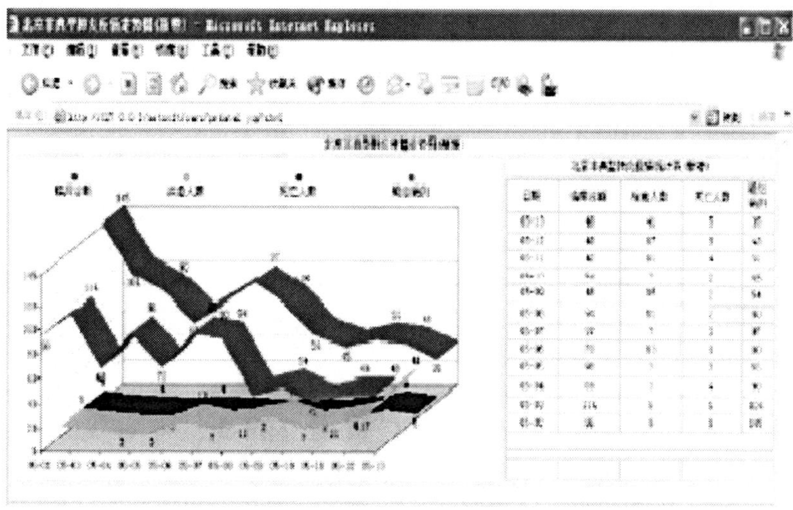

Figure 3. Google Flu Trends in various parts of the world

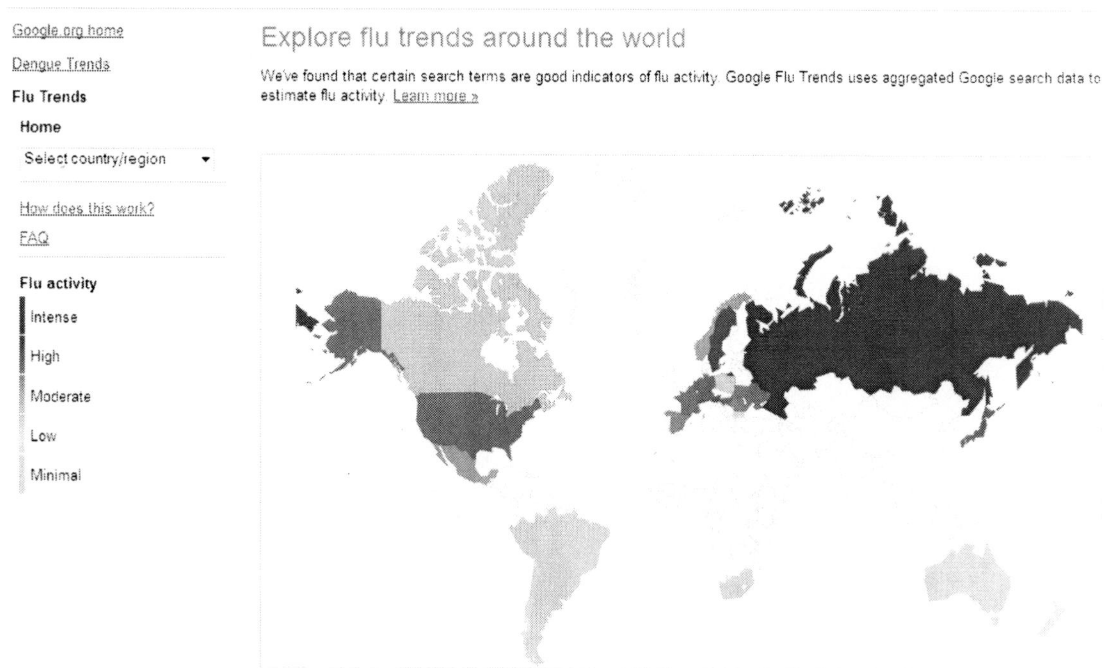

is merely simulating real world to explore more information, which we are not able to see on the surface. Information visualisation on the other hand is to visualise information sets of data in a more understandable graphic form using various tools. This research uses information obtained from the government to learn the region's macro-distribution of diseases. It is then used to be compared with a patient's condition, to show how influential the environment is to his or her condition. Figure 4 shows the region's macro-distribution of diseases, which is used to visualise pattern of diseases in a particular area.

Cesario et. al. (2012) discussed visualising communicable diseases in remote areas to assist epidemiologists and other health care professionals in mapping the spread. They introduced a time-based visualisation technique on geographical maps in which data of patients are collected via mobile devices. Because of the advancement of technology, mobile devices have enabled field workers to remotely collect data, provide up-to-date information and display spatial and time-based information. A good point made in Cesario et. al. was that most disease maps are based on patient's home address while ignoring the fact that people and animals move around which weakens location of diagnosis (Robertson et. al., 2010). Thus, Robertson et. al. (2010) mentioned that with the usage of GPS-enabled devices, personal location can be identified accurately, making surveillance on patients timelier. However, obtaining real-time data can be tedious if field workers are insufficient. In addition, hospitals record patients' home addresses, without taking into account mobility. Thus, there are no known sources to obtain credible information other than hospital records.

Zeng et. al. (2004) developed WNV/BOT, a collaborative infectious disease informatics which provides sharing, analysis and visualisation of infectious West Nile Virus and Botulism disease. It consisted of three components: 1. web portal, which has user interface in which visualisation will be displayed, 2. data store, which enables users from various organisations to share data and 3. communication backbone, which obtains data from different sources to enable visualisation of data. Zeng et. al. embedded Spatial Temporal Visualizer (STV), which helps users to explore data and summarize query results. STV has three different views namely, periodic, timeline and GIS. This is helpful for users to see what is relevant for them and from different perspectives.

Shenson and Joshi (2012) developed DiseaseTrends, a visualisation tool that explores eco-

Figure 4. A region's macro-distribution of diseases

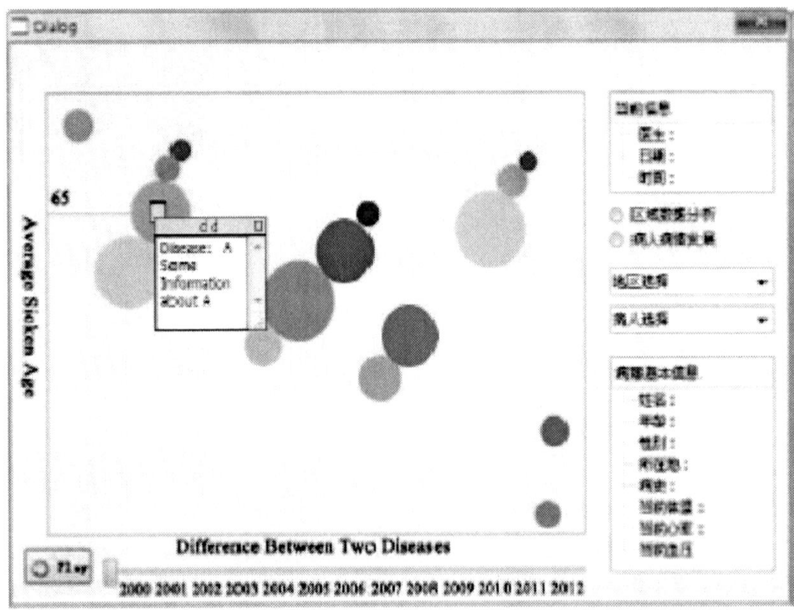

nomic, educational and environmental factors are associated with diabetes and cancer occurrence across United States. Geographic visualisation in cartographic form was used as it is proven to easily visualise geocoded data. Other approaches like choropleth maps were reportedly used by Symanzik et. al. (1997), Carr et al. (2001) and Chen et. al. (2008). Statistical approach was taken by Chen et. al. (2008), who used algorithms of large datasets to generate useful data to be visualising in on choropleth maps. Even Harle, Neill and Padman (2012) used statistical approach to visualise diseases information on many health relevant dimensions including risk classification across different risk factors.

The area of visualising large amounts of data has been rapidly growing in importance. Much research has been done in this area of utilising data to make useful representations for purposeful decision-making process. However, little works was done in the context of using data the from health sector in Malaysia to create visualisation that would assist personnel in making critical decisions. Users are familiar in using mapping tools like Google Maps. Thus, we are utilising this open source to identify reported cases to see if a pattern exist.

As mentioned by Andrienko et. al. (2011), one major challenge is to understand the visualisation presented and provide adequate support for different types of users. Thus, it is important to be able to interpret correctly visualisation shown in order for an analyst to have the same understanding and common grounds. In our prototype, we generate an interpretation based on the visualisation generated to assist in understanding the case shown.

Usage of Social Networks

Online Social Networks (OSNs) are synonymous with the daily lives of the current younger generation. Because it is easily accessible and allows sharing of information within group of friends, this medium has proven that individuals are willing to share a vast array of information with close or even distant connections (Dearman, Kellar & Truong, 2008). Some literature below shows the power of OSNs in changing health behaviours of individuals.

Chen et. al. (2010) aimed to achieve faster and near real time detection and prediction of influenza epidemic through OSNs data. Authorities would need the earliest possible warning method to ensure effective intervention by adopting a more efficient and timely method in estimating influenza incidences quickly. They designed and created a Social Network Enabled Flu Trends (SNEFT) in which it will collect and aggregate OSNs data, extract the required information and integrate it with their mathematical models. It was reported that also Centres for Disease Control and Prevention (CDC) reports Influenza-Like Illness (ILI) cases, the report is delayed for one or two weeks due to heavy manual process. Although individual results collected on OSN data is noisy, collectively however, it did reveal the necessary findings.

Kamal, Fels and Ho (2010) developed a preliminary prototype that uses survey of literature on the models for the use of OSN and health behaviour change. Since social network services are becoming a popular medium to obtain and share information, they leveraged this platform to promote personal health management. In their research, a Health Belief Model Dimension, adapted from Janz and Becker (1984), it tabled that stimulus, either internal (symptoms) or external (media, reminder postcards), could be used to promote health behaviour change. Thus, a good stimulus in our situation today would be social medias. Ma, Chen and Xiao (2010) studied how effective OSNs are in influencing weight-change health behaviours of people. In the five-month data collected from 107,000 users, it was reported that users' weight changes correlate positively with the number of their friends and their friends' weight-change performance. Users with similar weight who want to achieve similar weight-change goals are more likely to make positive progress.

This goes to show that there is a strong rippling effect in OSN, which is greater than real-world social network.

As people move towards communicating on OSNs, we must realise that they are collective voices of people rather than bodies of authority. It was raised by Bowler, He and Hong (2011) in a study conducted on 16 health blogs, to discover who are referring teens to reliable health information. It was found that there is a weak level of referrals from health-related groups as compared to schools and public libraries. Thus, teens may not be accessing accurate, reliable and necessary health information. Gavgani (2010) reported receiving reliable health information and information prescription is remarkably demanded by patients. Of the surveyed 139 patients, 40% to 50% of them would prefer information be viewed via the World Wide Web (WWW). Other methods were Short Messaging Service (75.4%) and phone calls (72%). To reach the masses, WWW would be the most convenient and cost effective method. However, there are drawbacks to technologies, for example, no access to Internet service at remote locations. Gavgani (2010) added that even with WWW, despite its potential in delivering and disseminating mass amount of information in various formats, it has not gained as much popularity as mobile phones. This reflects that people would like to receive information at their convenience as soon as they can get hold of it, rather than to search for information online.

Usage of Twitter during times of emergency has been unknowingly widely practiced in the recent years. A study by Scanfeld, Scanfeld and Larson (2010) looked at communication practices during the H1N1 outbreak. Broadcasting information through this method seems to work, provided information broadcasted comes from a reliable source. It was also found that Twitter was used to ask fitness-related questions and provide recommendations and resources (Kendall et. al., 2011). Patients use social software more often to obtain advice from similar patients, rather than for emotional support (Sarasohn-Kahn, 2008). It was also reported in this paper that 30% of tweets originated from mobile devices, or even higher as some 17% of the tweets were sent via applications that could operate on multiple platforms. This goes to show that mobility is the essence in obtaining real-time information, especially for people who are always on the move.

These examples prove that social networks are used by the public as one of the mediums to obtain information, advice and to seek comfort for various situations a person could be in. However, the reliability of such a source is questionable. Above all, information should come from reliable data source to ensure accuracy and reliable information is disseminated so as to not cause panic among people.

METHODS

We are focusing the mapping of diseases that happened at Kinta District. This district is located in the state of Perak Darul Ridzuan in Malaysia and it covers a few towns, namely, Tanjung Rambutan, Tronoh, Chemor, Gunung Rapat, Gopeng, Kampar, Malim Nawar, Menglembu, Pasir Pinji, Manjoi, Ulu Kinta and Ipoh. An interview was done with a health officer at the Health Centre of Kinta District on 21st March 2012. He is the domain expert and officer in charge of Kinta District area. The interview was meant to obtain information on which disease should be mapped, to get data and find out what the system should encompass. He also said it was hard to keep track of disease movement as there are no tools available for him to easily visualise the data he obtains.

Card et. al. (1999) described how visualisations are created. Firstly, raw data are processed and transformed into data tables, known as data transformation. The raw data obtained from the health officer needed to be processed as some addresses were incomplete, for example, no postcodes. Cleaning up was necessary so that geocoding could be done. Data tables were then transformed by filtering, adding calculations and merging. The resulting data tables are mapped to become visual structures (visual mappings) which are visual representations to be rendered and displayed to the user. Two tools that were vital in completing this research work was Google Maps API, database and PHP.

Geocoding is the process of converting geographic related data, such as street names and zip codes, into a set of latitude and longitude coordinates so that it can be plotted on a map. Google Maps API Geocoder is a free geocoding service provided by Google. After geocoding, we used scripts to specify the icon size and shapes and other details and use Google Maps API to display the map. A database is needed to store and appropriately manipulate the data before it is visualised. phpMyAdmin was used as the database tool. PHP is used to interact with Google Geocoder, generate XML, access the database, analyse the results and generate interpretation.

RESULTS

Google Correlate is a web application developed by Google that allows the public to retrieve the frequency of search keywords when the public uses the Google search engine to look for something. The duration of the data can be as early as 2003 until recent. The graph shown by Google Correlate are normalized search activity, which means normalized amount = amount of people query the keywords/amount of people using Google search over time. Figure 5 shows an example of using Google Correlate to find the frequency of the keyword 'dengue' in Malaysia for the year of 2009 and 2010. The graph also shows similar search with the keyword 'dengue fever'.

The real statistic of cases of dengue in Malaysia during 2009 – 2010 is shown in Figure 6, obtained from the Ministry of Health, Malaysia (Pejabat Kesihatan Wilayah Persekutuan Putrajaya, n.d.).

Figure 5. Google Correlate

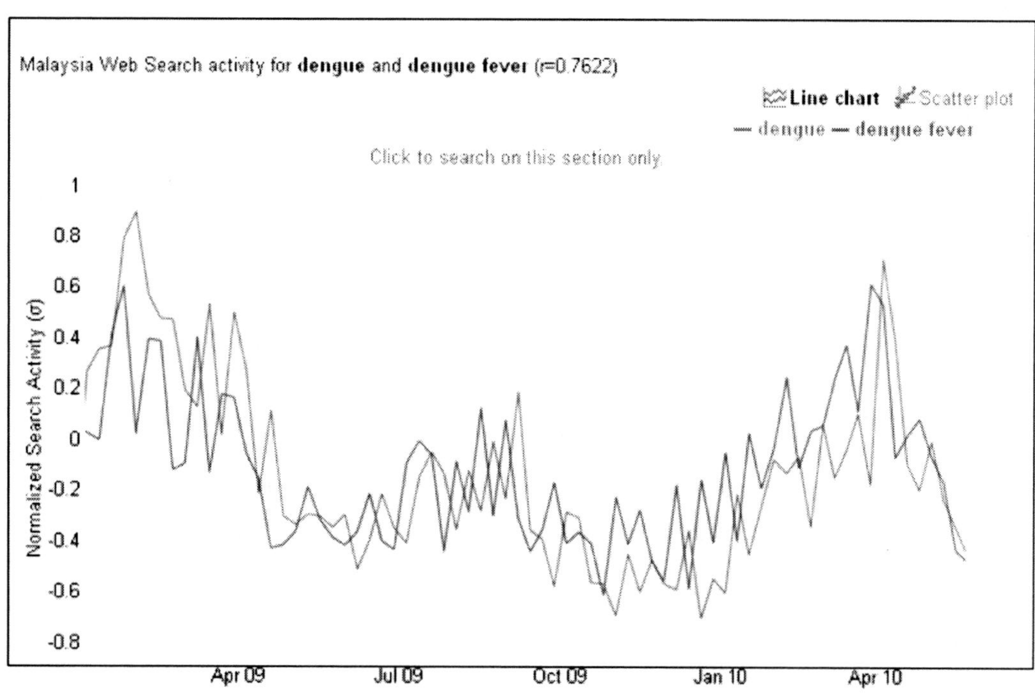

Figure 6. Number of registered cases according to Putrajaya Epidemiology Week in 2010 (until week 18) compared to 18 years median and year 2009. The x-axis is Epidemiology Week, y-axis is Number of Cases.

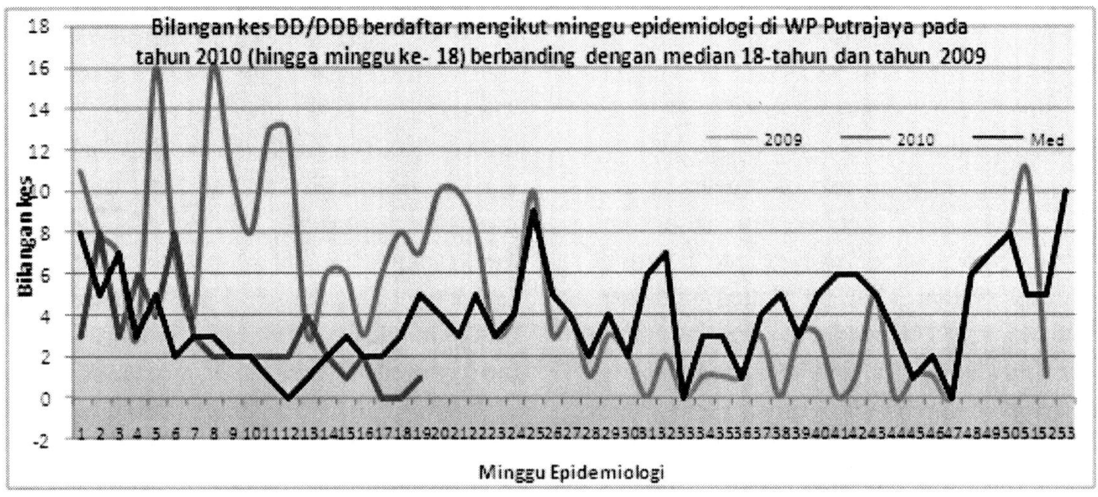

The amount of searches at the beginning of 2009 and 2010 for the Google Correlate and the real statistic has a similar pattern. The intention of showing this example is to show how health data can be made visual and tools like Google Correlate and Google Trends can be used as comparison methods. Since it is more tedious to make the comparison like this, we are motivated to develop a prototype system, which can combine all the data and visualise it in a more feasible and standard scale.

One disadvantage of Google Trends is that the graph cannot be generated when the Search volume is too little. Since the author planned to conduct this research in Kinta District, Perak, the author had tried to use Google Trends to search for some diseases in Perak state. The result is all of the keywords have too little search volume to show the graph. When the volume is too little, the Excel file downloaded will show zero hits. As a result, Google Trends can only be used as input when the amount of search volume is high enough.

Figure 7 is the use case diagram of the system. The users choose the duration of the data that they wish to view. They also need to choose the disease type that they wish to view. Then they will be able to view the map visualisation and also a paragraph of interpretation of the data.

Figure 8 depicts the raw data that was obtained from the health centre. Figure 9 shows the clean up that has been done to the raw data. The disease type, column F, is also added in order to align the table to have the same column with the table in the database. This will allow phpMyAdmin to import the data into the database. The author will put zeroes for the value of longitude and latitude in Excel file and put TB for the type if the disease is tuberculosis and dengue for the type if the disease is dengue. Moreover, since the date format in phpMyAdmin database is year-month-date, the author need to change the date format in Excel file to this format before importing. The author has to clean up the addresses from Figure 7 so that it can be marked on the map by geocoding process. After running the Geocoding script, it is found that not all addresses are successfully geo-coded. To successfully obtain all longitude and latitude of these addresses, the author needs to append the state, Perak, and country, Malaysia, behind the addresses to get a more accurate result.

Figure 7. Use case diagram

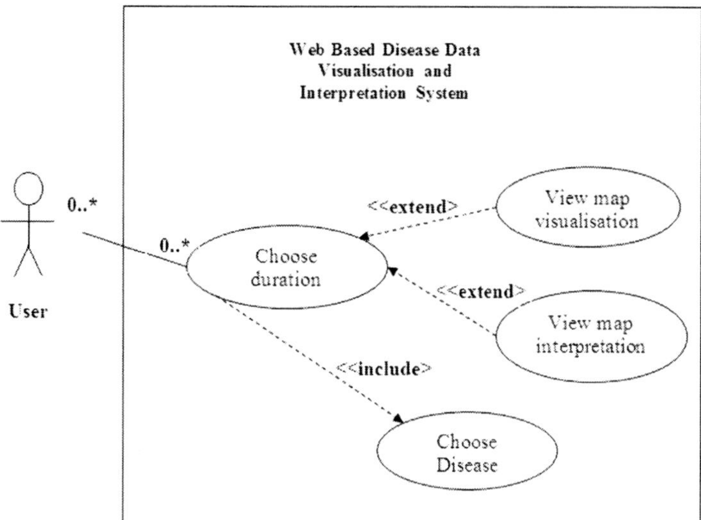

Figure 8. Raw tuberculosis disease data

A	B	C
Bil.	Kediaman Semasa (Seperti Dalam CDCIS)	Tarikh rawatan dimulakan
1	LOT 4228 KAMPUNG TERSUSUN KAMPUNG PULAI GOPENG	2009-10-29
2	NO. 39 PSRN. SARI 15 TAMAN CEMPAKA IPOH	2009-08-20
3	NO. 28 LALUAN HULU BERCHAM 4 BANDAR BARU PUTRA IPOH	2009-11-11
4	B-11 TKT. 11 PANGSAPURI SRI KEPAYANG, IPOH	2009-10-06
5	43, PERSIARAN RISHAH 7, KAWASAN PERINDUSTRIAN SILIBIN	2009-11-16
6	C25 JLN BENUS STARPARK IPOH PERAK	2009-11-16
7	357 A KAMPUNG BARU MAMBANG DIAWAN KAMPAR	2009-11-25
8	NO 460 JALAN BIDOR BUNTONG IPOH	2009-08-10
9	707, LALUAN SIMEE 1,KG SIMEE IPOH PERAK	2009-11-10
10	BLOK C-29, NO. D-16, LENGKOK BERCHAM TIMUR 4, TMN PAKATAN IP	2009-11-11
11	NO. H10, PERUMAHAN AWAM 2,LAWAN KUDA BARU	2009-12-24
12	NO. 4 PSRN WIRA JAYA BARAT 29 TAMAN DESA INDAH IPOH	2009-11-19
13	NO. 58 CEMPAKA SARI 20 TAMAN CEMPAKA IPOH	2009-12-15

This Excel file is saved in .csv extension. The author then truncates the table in the database and imports this .csv file. Figure 10 shows the screen shot of the table before the Geocoding script is done.

Figure 11 shows that the longitude and latitude has already been populated.

In order to display the visualisation of diseases on Google map, we need to create markers for each disease case by using Google Maps API. Clicking on the markers will give the user the full address of the disease case. Note that the markers in Figure 13 and Figure 14 are red and blue markers respectively, to show different time period that has been chosen. Thus, it is possible to show disease data from different years on the same map where the disease data from different years are represented by different colour markers. Figure 12 shows how to query the database by dates for visualising disease cases.

Figure 9. Appended data

A	B	C	D	E	F
1	NO. 74, JALAN TAWAS, BATU 19, TAMAN EHSAN, IPOH ,PERAK, MALAYSIA	10/2/2007	4.65184	101.0972	TB
2	36 LANDASAN TASEK TIMUR 7 TAMAN CAHAYA BERCHAM IPOH ,PERAK, MALAYSIA	12/19/2007	4.646719	101.1256	TB
3	71 BUKIT MERAH NEW VILLAGE, LAHAT ,PERAK, MALAYSIA	12/20/2007	4.543161	101.0407	TB
4	LOT 38007 JALAN BESAR SPG. PULAI KG. KEPAYANG IPOH ,PERAK, MALAYSIA	12/27/2007	0	0	TB
5	8G KAMPUNG JAMBU TANJUNG RAMBUTAN, IPOH ,PERAK, MALAYSIA	12/27/2007	0	0	TB
6	A7 JALAN LASAM GREENTOWN, IPOH ,PERAK, MALAYSIA	12/27/2007	4.597343	101.0942	TB
7	24 HALA PKLN TIMUR 22 TAMAN PASIR PUTEH SELATAN IPOH ,PERAK, MALAYSIA	12/27/2007	0	0	TB
8	23 JALAN TAWAS BARU 3 TAMAN TASEK DAMAI IPOH ,PERAK, MALAYSIA	12/27/2007	0	0	TB
9	244, TAMAN SENTOSA KAMPAR ,PERAK, MALAYSIA	7/4/2007	4.586623	101.0847	TB
10	53 PSRN. RAPAT BARU 20 TMN. LAPANGAN PERMAI, IPOH ,PERAK, MALAYSIA	12/8/2006	0	0	TB
11	5589 KG. AIR RAPAT TG. TUALANG ,PERAK, MALAYSIA	12/26/2006	0	0	TB
12	52 KG. BT. 9 TAMBAHAN JALAN JELAPANG ,PERAK, MALAYSIA	12/17/2006	0	0	TB
13	56 JALAN LEONG LOH BOH ,PERAK, MALAYSIA	1/4/2007	0	0	TB
14	56 JALAN LEONG LAH BOH ,PERAK, MALAYSIA	1/4/2007	0	0	TB
15	NO. 63 KG. SINDU, KG. KEPAYANG ,PERAK, MALAYSIA	1/5/2007	0	0	TB
16	NO.2 JALAN PEKELILING TASEK ,PERAK, MALAYSIA	1/3/2007	4.606427	101.117	TB
17	3 BULATAN CHERRY TAMAN CHERRY ,PERAK, MALAYSIA	1/7/2007	4.607386	101.0747	TB
18	NO. 37 HALA KLEDANG EMAS 6, TAMAN KLEDANG EMAS, IPOH ,PERAK, MALAYSIA	1/9/2007	4.546847	101.074	TB
19	BLOK B,30-4 KEM PGA ULU KINTA ,PERAK, MALAYSIA	1/9/2007	35.11926	-95.2377	TB
20	D/A PENJARA BATU GAJAH ,PERAK, MALAYSIA	1/9/2007	0	0	TB
21	40 PRSN ORKID 2, DESA CHANGKAT,BT GAJAH ,PERAK, MALAYSIA	1/16/2007	0	0	TB
22	KG CHANGKAT LEGONG GOPENG ,PERAK, MALAYSIA	1/16/2007	0	0	TB
23	57713 KG TASEK PERMAI,JLN GOPENG,BT GAJAH ,PERAK, MALAYSIA	1/13/2007	0	0	TB
24	NO. 35 3552 KG TERSUSUN TANAH HITAM CHEMOR ,PERAK, MALAYSIA	1/17/2007	0	0	TB
25	B-11 TKT. 11 PANGSAPURI SRI KEPAYANG, IPOH ,PERAK, MALAYSIA	1/18/2007	0	0	TB
26	NO. 16 ULU KAMPAR, GOPENG ,PERAK, MALAYSIA	1/11/2007	4.584835	101.1161	TB
27	NO. 16 ULU KAMPAR ,PERAK, MALAYSIA	1/16/2007	0	0	TB

Figure 10. Before Geocoding script

id	address	Date	lat	lng
1	NO. 74, JALAN TAWAS, BATU 19, TAMAN EHSAN, IPOH ,P...	2007-10-02	0.000000	0.000000
2	36 LANDASAN TASEK TIMUR 7 TAMAN CAHAYA BERCHAM IPO...	2007-12-19	0.000000	0.000000
3	71 BUKIT MERAH NEW VILLAGE, LAHAT ,PERAK, MALAYSIA	2007-12-20	0.000000	0.000000
4	LOT 38007 JALAN BESAR SPG. PULAI KG. KEPAYANG IPOH...	2007-12-27	0.000000	0.000000
5	8G KAMPUNG JAMBU TANJUNG RAMBUTAN, IPOH ,PERAK, MA...	2007-12-27	0.000000	0.000000
6	A7 JALAN LASAM GREENTOWN, IPOH ,PERAK, MALAYSIA	2007-12-27	0.000000	0.000000
7	24 HALA PKLN TIMUR 22 TAMAN PASIR PUTEH SELATAN IP...	2007-12-27	0.000000	0.000000
8	23 JALAN TAWAS BARU 3 TAMAN TASEK DAMAI IPOH ,PERA...	2007-12-27	0.000000	0.000000
9	244, TAMAN SENTOSA KAMPAR ,PERAK, MALAYSIA	2007-07-04	0.000000	0.000000
10	53 PSRN. RAPAT BARU 20 TMN. LAPANGAN PERMAI, IPOH ...	2006-12-08	0.000000	0.000000
11	5589 KG. AIR RAPAT TG. TUALANG ,PERAK, MALAYSIA	2006-12-26	0.000000	0.000000
12	52 KG. BT. 9 TAMBAHAN JALAN JELAPANG ,PERAK, MALAY...	2006-12-17	0.000000	0.000000
13	56 JALAN LEONG LOH BOH ,PERAK, MALAYSIA	2007-01-04	0.000000	0.000000
14	56 JALAN LEONG LAH BOH ,PERAK, MALAYSIA	2007-01-04	0.000000	0.000000

Based on Figure 12 query, Figure 13 shows the visualisation of disease cases, which happened within the period as entered by the user. Figure 14 shows tuberculosis cases in Kinta District for the year 2009.

After visualising the data, an interpretation based on the Ministry of Health Malaysia standard, is generated based on the mapping done. To generate the interpretation, we first calculate the number of diseases in a chosen period. Next,

Figure 11. After running geocoding

id	name	address	lat	lng	type	date
1	NO. 74, JALAN TAWAS, BATU 19, TAMAN EHSAN, IPOH, P...	NO. 74, JALAN TAWAS, BATU 19, TAMAN EHSAN, IPOH, P...	4.651840	101.097153	bar	2007-10-02
2	36 LANDASAN TASEK TIMUR 7 TAMAN CAHAYA BERCHAM IPO...	36 LANDASAN TASEK TIMUR 7 TAMAN CAHAYA BERCHAM IPO...	4.646719	101.125633	bar	2007-12-19
3	71 BUKIT MERAH NEW VILLAGE, LAHAT, Perak, Malaysia	71 BUKIT MERAH NEW VILLAGE, LAHAT, Perak, Malaysia	4.543161	101.040733	bar	2007-12-20
4	LOT 38007 JALAN BESAR SPG. PULAI KG. KEPAYANG IPOH...	LOT 38007 JALAN BESAR SPG. PULAI KG. KEPAYANG IPOH...	4.611750	101.113503	bar	2007-12-27
5	8G KAMPUNG JAMBU TANJUNG RAMBUTAN, IPOH, Perak, Ma...	8G KAMPUNG JAMBU TANJUNG RAMBUTAN, IPOH, Perak, Ma...	4.619038	101.118439	bar	2007-12-27
6	A7 JALAN LASAM GREENTOWN, IPOH, Perak, Malaysia	A7 JALAN LASAM GREENTOWN, IPOH, Perak, Malaysia	4.597343	101.094177	bar	2007-12-27
7	24 HALA PKLN TIMUR 22 TAMAN PASIR PUTEH SELATAN IP...	24 HALA PKLN TIMUR 22 TAMAN PASIR PUTEH SELATAN IP...	4.611750	101.113503	bar	2007-12-27
8	23 JALAN TAWAS BARU 3 TAMAN TASEK DAMAI IPOH, Pera...	23 JALAN TAWAS BARU 3 TAMAN TASEK DAMAI IPOH, Pera...	4.660385	101.111389	bar	2007-12-27
9	244, TAMAN SENTOSA KAMPAR, Perak, Malaysia	244, TAMAN SENTOSA KAMPAR, Perak, Malaysia	4.327390	101.139595	bar	2007-07-04
10	53 PSRN. RAPAT BARU 20 TMN. LAPANGAN PERMAI, IPOH,...	53 PSRN. RAPAT BARU 20 TMN. LAPANGAN PERMAI, IPOH,...	4.611750	101.113503	bar	2006-12-08
11	5589 KG. AIR RAPAT TG. TUALANG, Perak, Malaysia	5589 KG. AIR RAPAT TG. TUALANG, Perak, Malaysia	4.807294	100.800003	bar	2006-12-26

Figure 12. Choose start and end date

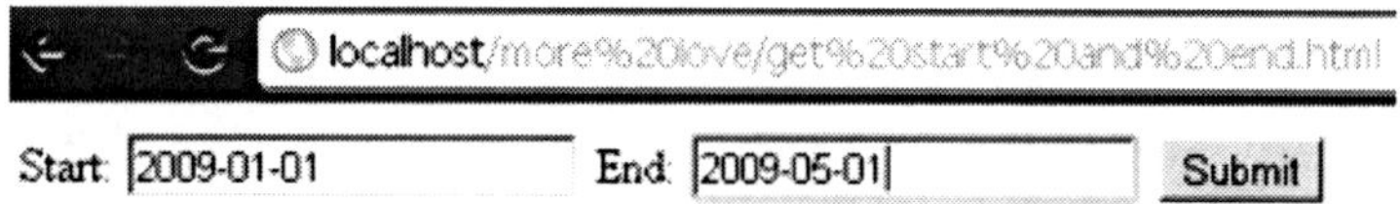

Figure 13. Visualisation of disease cases happened within the period the user entered

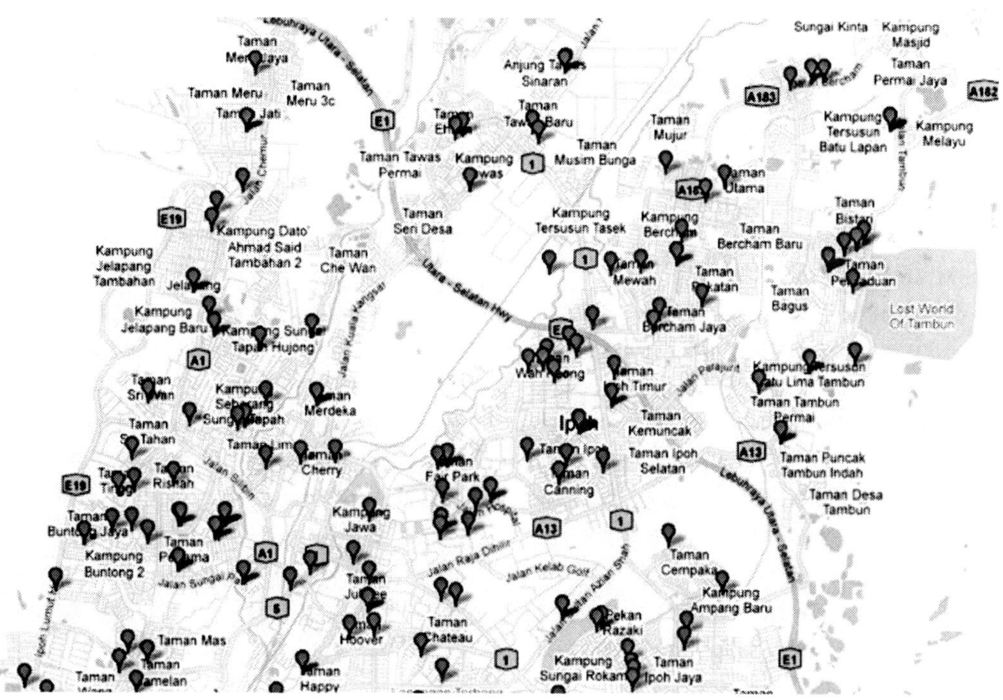

Figure 14. Tuberculosis cases in year 2009

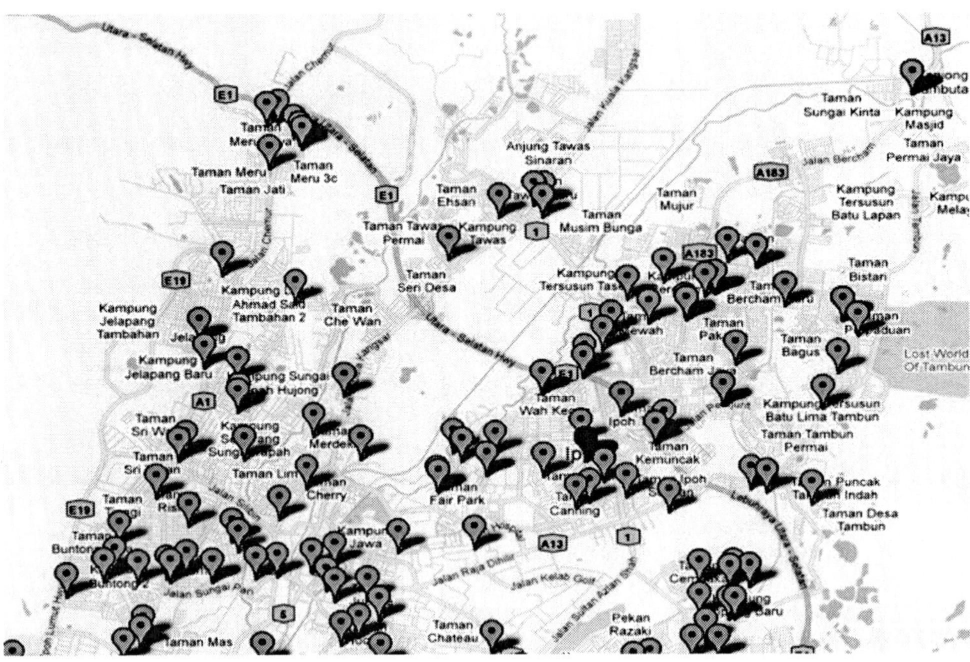

average of disease cases per week or days is calculated, depending on the standard given by the Health Centre of Kinta District for that particular disease. For tuberculosis, the standard is weekly. As a result, the number of days within the period chosen by the user is calculated. Then the number is divided by seven (7) to get the number of weeks during that period. The number of disease cases will be divided by the number of weeks to get the average number of disease cases per week. This average number will be compared with the numbers provided by the health centre to determine the risk level for the particular area.

Some development has been done to make the system prototype more usable and aesthetic. The prototype has evolved to be more robust. New interface have been designed to enhance the system's look. The new prototype allows users to add in a new case directly into the database, without needing to append or amend from the Excel file and import into phpMyAdmin.

Figure 15 and 16 show the new interface, which will allow users to view disease cases in Google Map. More diseases can also be added into the database as shown in Figure 20.

Figure 17 shows an example of tuberculosis that happened between the period of 1st January 2006 to 31st December 2010. Clicking on a marker will allow exact address information to be displayed, as shown in Figure 18.

As expected, the map will allow a more detailed view of a particular area, as in Figure 19. Users can zoom in and out to see at road level details. This will be useful in creating a new algorithm by calculating frequency of cases based on certain square meter of an area.

Figure 20 shows the interface of the system that allows users, for example health officers, to add in new disease cases easily. Once information is submitted, it will be inserted into the database, which allows the system to use that data to populate the disease on the map as soon as possible. This can eliminate the usage of Microsoft Excel, in which we eliminate the trouble of importing data from Excel to be extracted into a database. Real time data can also be accessed and viewed.

Figure 15. New interface to view mappings

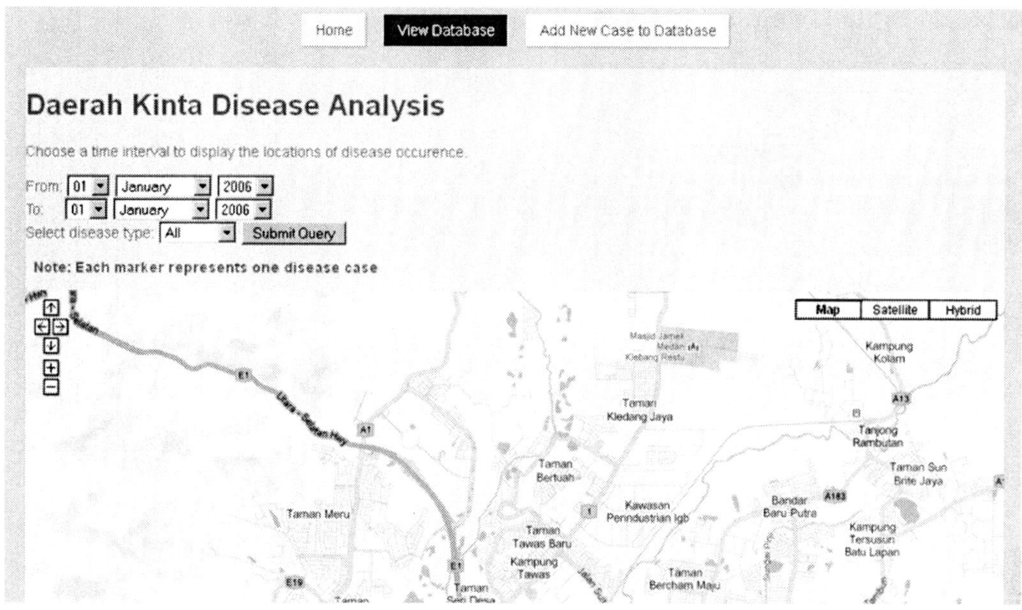

Figure 16. Drop down menu to select different diseases

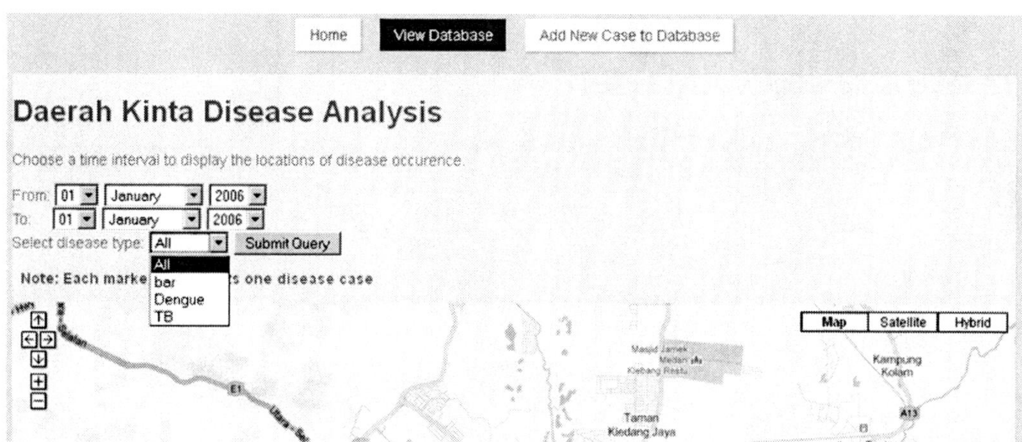

Once a case is added through this system, geocoding is automatically done so that it can be used for mapping a marker on the map instantly.

According to the health officer, this system is very useful for them to track the outbreak of communicable diseases on a timely basis. The health officer gave an example where there used to be high density of diarrhea and vomiting cases in an area, which was related to communicable disease a few years ago. The health centre investigated the matter and realised the existence of a broken underground water pipe, which allowed microorganisms to enter. Thus, if such an incident happens again, they would know where to spot the problem immediately by looking at the visualisation on the map. It would otherwise be very difficult for them to link past incidents to the current situation as it is difficult to visualise raw data (address) and

Figure 17. Tuberculosis cases from 1st January 2006 until 31st December 2010

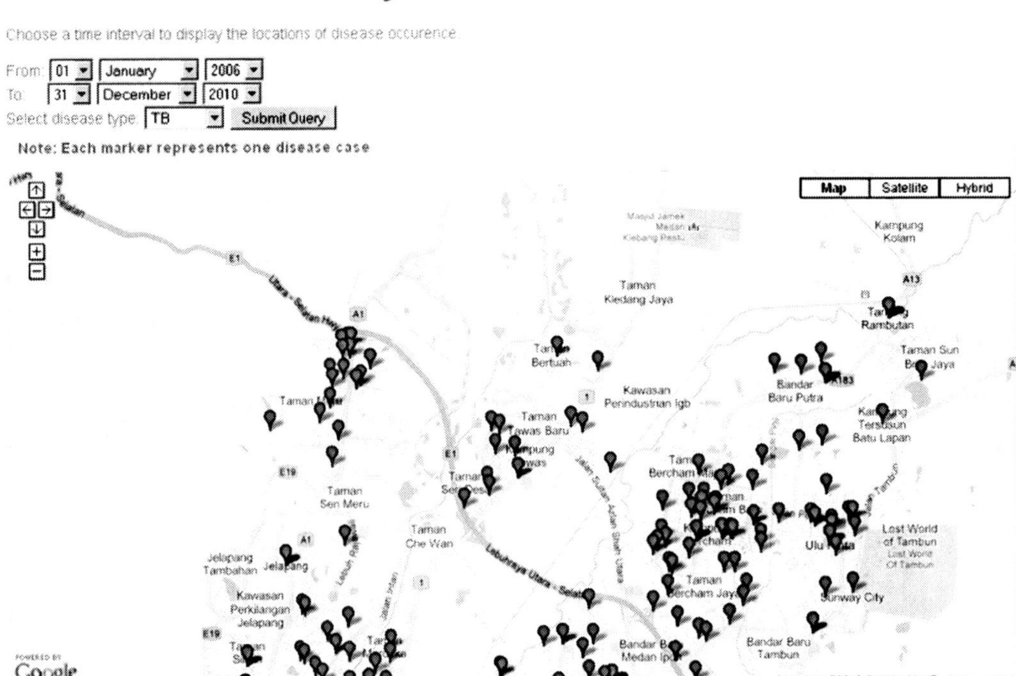

Figure 18. Exact location information is displayed

density of cases just by looking at the disease record containing only words. Past data can show trends, in which users can deduce and estimate when the problem might occur and why. In addition, new staff could also use this to learn trends and refer past historical incidences that could have happened within an area.

Figure 19. Detailed view of diseases at road level

Figure 20. Add new disease case

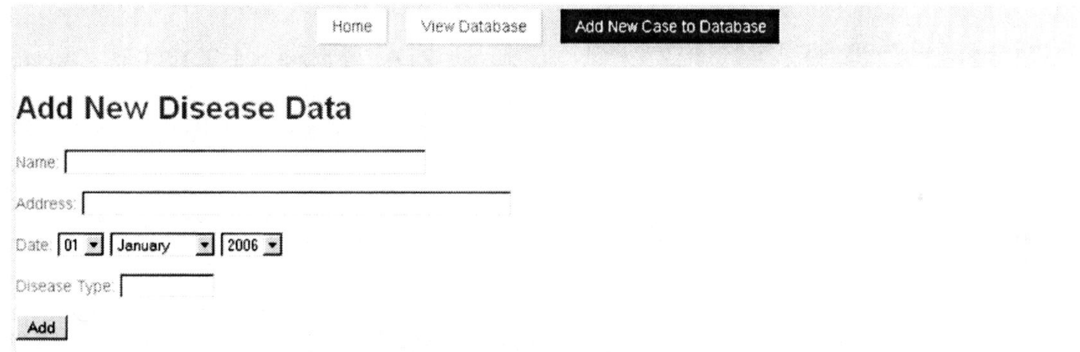

This research aims to provide a means for doctors, officers from the Ministry of Health Malaysia and also the public to understand and relate diseases data to assist them in the decision making process. Malaysia Health Profile, which is published by WHO, showed that 28% of Malaysians died due to communicable diseases during 2008 (World Health Organization, 2010). It will allow us to educate the public in preventing the spread of communicable diseases by taking some precautionary steps or avoid travelling to high-risk areas. Health officers can issue warnings to areas that are prone to catch the disease. The Ministry of Health could mobilise and allocate their resources to infected areas, depending on severity. Health centres can use this system to visualise past disease cases and compare with the current disease cases to find out the trend of disease density, thus allowing them to analyse the disease better.

FUTURE RESEARCH DIRECTION

There are various kinds of visualisation that can be used to represent data. Further research is necessary to study the effectiveness of different kinds of visualisation techniques that could be used to represent similar data. A more accurate algorithm could be developed to produce a more accurate interpretation. Currently, the formulae given by the health department allows basic calculation to know the average of cases per week in a particular area. Generating appropriate and accurate interpretation could help recommend the next best steps. Thus, a more accurate algorithm can be developed in addition to what was given would strengthen the interpretation to produce a more accurate suggestion. A more robust system could be developed to ensure the system serves it purpose. The data obtained from the health centre is limited to certain years. In addition, data are not updated as often. Thus, this system could help in entering new data into the database directly, with minimal manual labor. We would also like to expand the database to include different kinds of diseases. However, sufficient number of years of data is necessary to allow users to see trends and predict future outlook. In addition, we can obtain and consolidate data from various locations to be added into this system. We could also extend this system to include other diseases, communicable or non-communicable, and to include factors like weather.

CONCLUSION

This research developed a system that aims to ease the analysis of disease data by visualising them on a map. An interpretation is also generated to give an impartial explanation of the data being visualised and it will allow a standard understanding of what the data means as set by the Ministry of Health. This system will enable relevant authorities to make more informed decisions given a certain scenario. Although further testing is needed to strengthen the claims of the usefulness of such system, preliminary results tested with the health officer revealed satisfaction. Future works would include connecting the application to the local hospital database to obtain real time update of the disease data. This tool can assist the users by allowing them access to the most recent disease information and be able to avoid the high-risk areas. The system can also be enhanced to show the different types of diseases in one map by using different icons to represent different types of disease. With this, we can find the relationship between diseases, to find if there is any way that the occurrence of one disease will affect the occurrence of other diseases.

REFERENCES

Ali, S. N. S., Razali, A. M., Suradi, N. R., Abu Bakar, A., & Ramli, S. A. (2010). A framework for continuous outpatient health care delivery improvement through treatment plan support. In *Proceedings of the Regional Conference on Statistical Sciences*, (pp. 93-102). IEEE.

Amar, R. A., & Stasko, J. T. (2005). Knowledge precepts for design and evaluation of information visualizations. *IEEE Transactions on Visualization and Computer Graphics*, *11*(4), 432–442. doi:10.1109/TVCG.2005.63 PMID:16138553.

Andrienko, G., Andrienko, N., Keim, D., MacEachren, A. M., & Wrobel, S. (2011). Challenging problems of geospatial visual analytics. *Journal of Visual Languages and Computing*, *22*(4), 251–256. doi:10.1016/j.jvlc.2011.04.001.

Bowler, L., He, D., & Hong, W. Y. (2011). Who is referring teens to health information on the web? Hyperlinks between blogs and health web sites for teens. In *Proceedings of the 2011 iConference*, (pp. 238-243). iConference.

Card, S., Mackinlay, J., & Shneiderman, B. (1999). *Readings in information visualization: Using vision to think*. San Fransisco, CA: Morgan Kaufmann.

Carr, D. B. (2001). Designing linked micromap plots for states with many counties. *Statistics in Medicine*, *20*(9-10), 1331–1339. doi:10.1002/sim.670 PMID:11343354.

Cesario, M., Jervis, M., Luz, S., Masoodian, M., & Rogers, B. (2012). Time-based geographical mapping of communicable diseases. In *Proceedings of the 6th International Conference on Information Visualization*, (pp. 118-123). IEEE.

Chen, J., Roth, R. E., Naito, A. T., Lengerich, E. J., & MacEachren, A. M. (2008). Geovisual analytics to enhance spatial scan statistics interpretation: an analysis of U.S cervical cancer mortality. *International Journal of Health Geographics*, *7*(57).

Chen, L., Achrekar, H., Liu, B., & Lazarus, R. (2010). Vision: Towards real time epidemic vigilance through online social networks: introducing SNEFT - Social network enabled flu trends. In *Proceedings of the 1st ACM Workshop on Mobile Cloud Computing & Services: Social Networks and Beyond*. ACM.

Dearman, D., Kellar, M., & Truong, K. N. (2008). An examination of daily information needs and sharing opportunities. In *Proceedings of the 2008 ACM Conference on Computer Supported Cooperative Work*, (pp. 679-688). ACM.

Fayyad, U., Grinstein, G., & Wierse, A. (2001). *Information visualization in data mining and knowledge discovery*. San Francisco, CA: Morgan Kaufmann.

Gavgani, V. Z. (2010). Health information need and seeking behavior of patients in developing countries' context, an Iranian experience. In *Proceedings of the 1st ACM International Health Informatics Symposium*, (pp. 575-579). ACM.

Google Correlate. (n.d.). Retrieved November 5, 2012 from http://www.google.com/trends/correlate

Google Flu Trends. (n.d.). *How does this work?* Retrieved November 5, 2012 from http://www.google.org/flutrends/about/how.html

Hansen, T. E., Hourcade, J. P., Segre, A., Hlady, C., Polgreen, P., & Wyman, C. (2010). Interactive visualization of hospital contact network data on multi-touch displays. In *Proceedings of the 3rd Mexican Workshop on Human Computer Interaction*, (pp. 15-22). ACM.

Harle, C. A., Neill, D. B., & Padman, R. (2012). Information visualization for chronic disease risk assessment. *IEEE Intelligent Systems*, *27*(6), 81–85. doi:10.1109/MIS.2012.112.

Hawker, J., Begg, N., Blair, I., Reintjes, R., & Weinberg, J. (2000). *Communicable disease control handbook*. Boston: Wiley-Blackwell.

Janz, N. K., & Becker, M. H. (1984). The health belief model: A decade later. *Health Education & Behavior*, *11*(1), 1–47. doi:10.1177/109019818401100101 PMID:6392204.

Jin, H., & Liu, H. (2009). Research on visualization techniques in data mining. In *Proceedings of the International Conference on Computational Intelligence and Software Engineering*. IEEE.

Kamal, N., Fels, S., & Ho, K. (2010). Online social networks for personal informatics to promote positive health behavior. In *Proceedings of the 2nd ACM SIGMM Workshop on Social Media*, (pp. 47-52). ACM.

Kantardzic, M. (2002). *Data mining: Concepts, models, methods, and algorithms*. New York, NY: IEEE Press & John Wiley. doi:10.1109/9780470544341.

Kendall, L., Hartzler, A., Klasnja, P., & Pratt, W. (2011). Descriptive analysis of physical activity conversations on Twitter. In *Proceedings of CHI '11 Extended Abstracts on Human Factors in Computing Systems*, (pp. 1555-1560). ACM.

Lu, X. (2009). Web GIS based information visualization for infectious disease prevention. In *Proceedings of the Third International Symposium on Intelligent Information Technology Application*, (pp. 148-151). IEEE.

Ma, X., Chen, G., & Xiao, J. (2010). Analysis of an online health social network. In *Proceedings of the 1st ACM International Health Informatics Symposium* (IHI '10), (pp. 297-306). ACM.

Merler, S., Jurman, G., & Furlanello, C. (2006). Strategies for containing an influenza pandemic: The case of Italy. In *Proceedings of the 1st International Conference on Bio-Inspired Models of Network, Information and Computing Systems*, (pp. 1-7). IEEE.

Omar, S. (2007). *Geographical information system for dengue management system.* (Final Year Dissertation). Universiti Teknologi Petronas, Petronas, Malaysia.

Palaniappan, S., & Awang, R. (2008). Intelligent heart disease prediction system using data mining techniques. In *Proceedings of the International Conference on Computer Systems and Applications,* (pp. 108-115). IEEE.

PD-Downloads: Pejabat Kesihatan Wilayah Persekutuan Putrajaya. (n.d.). Retrieved November 5, 2012 from http://pkpj.moh.gov.my/modules/PDdownloads/viewcat.php?cid=2

Richards, G. (2004). Don't panic! [control medical]. *Engineering & Technology*, *4*(10), 45–47. doi:10.1049/et.2009.1007.

Robertson, C., Nelson, T. A., MacNab, Y. C., & Lawson, A. B. (2010). Review of methods for space-time disease surveillance. *Spatial and Spatio-temporal Epidemiology*, *1*(23), 105–116. doi:10.1016/j.sste.2009.12.001 PMID:22749467.

Sarasohn-Kahn, J. (2008). *The wisdom of patients: Health care meets online social media*. Retrieved November 5, 2012 from http://www.chcf.org/publications/2008/04/the-wisdom-of-patients-health-care-meets-online-social-media

Scanfeld, D., Scanfeld, V., & Larson, E. (2010). Dissemination of health information through social networks: Twitter and antibiotics. *American Journal of Infection Control*, *38*(3), 182–188. doi:10.1016/j.ajic.2009.11.004 PMID:20347636.

Shenson, J., & Joshi, A. (2012). Visualizing disease incidence in the context of socioeconomic factors. In *Proceedings of the 5th International Symposium on Visual Information Communication and Interaction*, (pp. 29-38). IEEE.

Shneiderman, B. (1996). The eyes have it: A task by data type taxonomy for information visualizations. In *Proceedings of the IEEE Symposium on Visual Languages*, (pp. 336-343). IEEE.

Shneiderman, B. (2008). Extreme visualization: Squeezing a billion records into a million pixels. In *Proceedings of the 2008 ACM SIGMOD International Conference on Management of Data*, (pp. 3-12). ACM.

Syahman, A. M. (2006). *GIS for dengue epidemic management for ipoh/ batu gajah.* (Final Year Dissertation). Universiti Teknologi Petronas, Petronas, Malaysia.

Symanzik, J., Klinke, G., Klinke, S., Schmelzer, S., Cook, D., & Lewin, N. (1997). The acrview/xgobi/xplore environment: Technical details and applications for spatial data analysis. In *Proceedings of the Section on Statistical Graphics American Statistical Association,* (pp. 73-78). ASA.

Tsui, K. L., Goldsman, D., Jiang, W., & Wong, S. Y. (2010). Recent research in public health surveillance and health management. In *Proceedings of the Prognostics and Health Management Conference*. IEEE.

World Health Organization. (2010). *Country cooperation strategy at a glance – Malaysia.* Retrieved 22nd March 2012 from http://www.who.int/countries/mys/en/

Yau, N. (2011). *Visualize this – The flowingdata guide to design, visualization and statistics*. Indianapolis, IN: Wiley.

Zeng, D., Chen, H., Tseng, C., Larson, C. A., Eidson, M., & Gotham, I. ... Ascher, M. (2004). Towards a national infectious disease information infrastructure: A case study in west nile virus and botulism. In *Proceedings of the 2004 Annual National Conference on Digital Government Research,* (pp. 1-10). IEEE.

Zeng, W., Cui, X., Liu, X., Cui, H., & Wang, P. (2006). Remote sensing and GIS for identifying and monitoring the environmental factors associated with vector-borne disease: An overview. In *Proceedings of the IEEE International Conference on Geoscience and Remote Sensing Symposium 2006,* (pp. 1443-1446). IEEE.

Zhang, N., Hong, W., Zheng, S., & Tao, L. (2012). A solution for an application of information visualization in telemedicine. In *Proceedings of the 7th International Conference on Computer Science & Education (ICCSE),* (pp. 407-411). ICCSE.

ADDITIONAL READING

Amar, R. A., & Stasko, J. T. (2005). Knowledge precepts for design and evaluation of information visualizations. *IEEE Transactions on Visualization and Computer Graphics, 11*(4), 432–442. doi:10.1109/TVCG.2005.63 PMID:16138553.

Andrienko, G., Andrienko, N., Keim, D., MacEachren, A. M., & Wrobel, S. (2011). Challenging problems of geospatial visual analytics. *Journal of Visual Languages and Computing*, 22(4), 251–256. doi:10.1016/j.jvlc.2011.04.001.

Bederson, B. B., & Shneiderman, B. (2003). *The craft of information visualization: readings and reflections (interactive technologies)*. San Francisco, CA: Morgan Kaufmann.

Card, S., Mackinlay, J., & Shneiderman, B. (1999). *Readings in information visualization: Using vision to think*. San Francisco, CA: Morgan Kaufmann.

Cesario, M., Jervis, M., Luz, S., Masoodian, M., & Rogers, B. (2012). Time-based geographical mapping of communicable diseases. In *Proceedings of the 6th International Conference on Information Visualization*, (pp. 118-123). IEEE.

Chen, L., Achrekar, H., Liu, B., & Lazarus, R. (2010). Vision: Towards real time epidemic vigilance through online social networks: Introducing SNEFT - Social network enabled flu trends. In *Proceedings of the 1st ACM Workshop on Mobile Cloud Computing & Services: Social Networks and Beyond*. ACM.

Chi, E. H. (2002). *A framework for visualizing information*. Secaucus, NJ: Springer-Verlag. doi:10.1007/978-94-017-0573-8.

Fayyad, U., Grinstein, G., & Wierse, A. (2001). *Information visualization in data mining and knowledge discovery*. San Francisco, CA: Morgan Kaufmann.

Gavgani, V. Z. (2010). Health information need and seeking behavior of patients in developing countries' context, an Iranian experience. In *Proceedings of the 1st ACM International Health Informatics Symposium*, (pp. 575-579). ACM.

Hansen, T. E., Hourcade, J. P., Segre, A., Hlady, C., Polgreen, P., & Wyman, C. (2010), Interactive visualization of hospital contact network data on multi-touch displays. In *Proceedings of the 3rd Mexican Workshop on Human Computer Interaction*, (pp. 15-22). IEEE.

Kamal, N., Fels, S., & Ho, K. (2010). Online social networks for personal informatics to promote positive health behavior. In *Proceedings of the ACM SIGMM Workshop on Social Media,* (pp. 47-52). ACM.

Lu, X. (2009). Web GIS based information visualization for infectious disease prevention. In *Proceedings of the Third International Symposium on Intelligent Information Technology Application*, (pp. 148-151). IEEE.

Ma, X., Chen, G., & Xiao, J. (2010). Analysis of an online health social network. In *Proceedings of the 1st ACM International Health Informatics Symposium* (IHI '10), (pp. 297-306). ACM.

Robertson, C., Nelson, T. A., MacNab, Y. C., & Lawson, A. B. (2010). Review of methods for space-time disease surveillance. *Spatial and Spatio-temporal Epidemiology*, *1*(23), 105–116. doi:10.1016/j.sste.2009.12.001 PMID:22749467.

Scanfeld, D., Scanfeld, V., & Larson, E. (2010). Dissemination of health information through social networks: Twitter and antibiotics. *American Journal of Infection Control*, *38*(3), 182–188. doi:10.1016/j.ajic.2009.11.004 PMID:20347636.

Shenson, J., & Joshi, A. (2012). Visualizing disease incidence in the context of socioeconomic factors. In *Proceedings of the 5th International Symposium on Visual Information Communication and Interaction*, (pp. 29-38). IEEE.

Shneiderman, B. (1996). The eyes have it: A task by data type taxonomy for information visualizations. In *Proceedings of the IEEE Symposium on Visual Languages*, (pp. 336-343). IEEE.

Shneiderman, B. (2008). Extreme visualization: Squeezing a billion records into a million pixels. In *Proceedings of the 2008 ACM SIGMOD International Conference on Management of Data*, (pp. 3-12). ACM.

Tufte, E. R. (1997). *Visual explanations*. Cheshire, CT: Graphic Press.

Tufte, E. R. (2001). *The visual display of quantitative information*. Cheshire, CT: Graphics Press.

Yau, N. (2011). *Visualize this – The flowingdata guide to design, visualization and statistics*. Indianapolis, IN: Wiley.

Zeng, D., Chen, H., Tseng, C., Larson, C. A., Eidson, M., & Gotham, I. … Ascher, M. (2004). Towards a national infectious disease information infrastructure: A case study in west nile virus and botulism. In *Proceedings of the 2004 Annual National Conference on Digital Government Research,* (pp. 1-10). IEEE.

Zeng, W., Cui, X., Liu, X., Cui, H., & Wang, P. (2006). Remote sensing and GIS for identifying and monitoring the environmental factors associated with vector-borne disease: An overview. In *Proceedings of the IEEE International Conference on Geoscience and Remote Sensing Symposium 2006,* (pp. 1443-1446). IEEE.

Zhang, N., Hong, W., Zheng, S., & Tao, L. (2012). A solution for an application of information visualization in telemedicine. In *Proceedings of the 7th International Conference on Computer Science & Education (ICCSE),* (pp. 407-411). ICCSE.

KEY TERMS AND DEFINITIONS

Communicable Disease: Also known as infectious or transmissible disease as it spreads from person to person.

Decision Making: The cognitive process of selecting a choice based on the options known and available.

Interpretation: To explain the meaning of certain things.

Non-Communicable Disease: Diseases which are not infectious and not transmissible among people.

Prototype: A preliminary working model of a system.

Spreading Pattern: Propagation over an area following a certain design.

Visualization: Visual representation of data into information made useful for human understanding.

Section 4
Methodological Approaches

Chapter 14
ETdAnalyser:
A Model-Based Architecture for Ergonomic Decision Intervention

Isabel F. Loureiro
University of Minho, Portugal

Fábio Costa
University of Minho, Portugal

Celina P. Leão
University of Minho, Portugal

José Teixeira
University of Minho, Portugal

Pedro M. Arezes
University of Minho, Portugal

ABSTRACT

Ergonomic Tridimensional Analysis (ETdA) is a new ergonomic approach that makes possible the identification and description of several ergonomic contexts defined by common areas where clients or consumers are subject to similar activities normally carried out by professionals. The development of this decision tool includes several steps, such as conceptualization of the problem, definition of the three ETdA dimensions and observation tools, data collection, and weighting the results leading to ergonomic intervention proposal. The software, named ETdAnalyser, is proposed to provide the ergonomist or analyst a fast and simple way of collecting and analysing data. This system is considered to be a decision-making support tool for ergonomic intervention, representing a relevant contribution to the advance of the ergonomics field.

INTRODUCTION

Commercial Areas with Free Circulation of People (CAFCP) are characterized by large open spaces where Professionals and Clients share the same space and have different interactions. In modern society, the differentiation of the ergonomic context is the result of a market customization, where Clients are becoming intrinsically linked to the organizations. Nowadays, most of the traditional commercial activities have been replaced by common areas where Clients' interactions are related not only to Professionals but also to other levels of the socio-technical system, such as the organization, manager, technological, and governmental levels. In a narrower sense, it is possible to say that an ergonomic approach aims to characterize the working areas, by identifying the risk factors.

DOI: 10.4018/978-1-4666-4623-0.ch014

This allows the definition of the priorities regarding the identified factors. This priority list gives the diagnosis of the studied conditions (Stanton, Hedge, Brookhuis, Salas & Hendrick, 2005). In order to provide an effective system approach in terms of ergonomic analysis, it is important to characterize the ergonomic context. This can be made by describing the workers' activities and the work organization, by identifying the system participants, and by defining the importance of the relations between the different levels of the system. Through the study and understanding of the real work activities, it is possible to observe Clients' influence on many aspects of the worker performance. Considering a system approach, Clients may interact directly with the personal subsystem and, through this, they may have influence on the environment subsystem and, in a certain way, they command the strategies of the organizational subsystem. The strategies defined by managers will certainly have influence on workers' activities. Clients, or in a broad sense consumers, patients, students, etc. must be integrated in a system approach not only from an organization management perspective but also as being a part of the system. Taking this into consideration, organizations must have both social and economical goals to achieve the optimization of the performance of the overall system. Therefore, it is important to study and characterize, not only the situation and working conditions related to these areas (occupational goal), but also from the Clients' comfort and wellbeing perspective, as well as Professionals and Clients attendance in the area (usability goal). In these situations, the ergonomic approach must also recognize that Clients are an active part of the ergonomic context. Based on Zink's (2000) research, it is possible to say that (1) most of the ergonomic approaches are focused on specific topics or ergonomic contexts, (2) usually ergonomics is developed under an outside-in approach, where problems are not properly analysed, and (3) a balance between research and real work context is not always achieved. According to this line of thinking, challenges can be transformed into opportunities.

Indeed, the existent strategies for ergonomics data collection have not evolved during the past decade. Traditional ergonomics data collection methods are usually based on systematic indirect observation, direct measurements and workers' perceptions and subjective judgments. This type of data collection is time-consuming and subjective (Van Der Beek, Mathiassen & Burdorf, 2013; Lee & Lee, 2012). Much has been done in terms of simulation and 3D modelling to aid the ergonomic analysis. Nevertheless, advances on technologies that provide a faster way of performing data collection and generation of reports including the decision-making process for the ergonomic interventions, are necessary.

Cacciabue (2008) identified three decisive aspects that can be defined as new challenges on the ergonomics domain: the constant and continuous advance in technology, the variety of application domains (ergonomic context), and the diversity of users. The advances in technology are related to several identified situations, for example, the development of sensors and instruments to be used in the nanotechnologies field. Simulators and virtual reality are used to test new technologies, training and testing human interactions with control systems and new design concepts and solutions (Cacciabue, 2008). The main advantage of the use of virtual reality is to develop interfaces that are as much "user friendly and realistic" as possible. In both situations, the use of ergonomics is very relevant. In a technological context, depending on the specificity and complexity of the interfaces and control systems developed, a variety of domains may be identified. The complexity of the systems may affect work organization, worker performance and worker interrelations with the environment. Another important issue to consider is related to the diversification of technology users. In fact, the general public is not trained to use the technology, interfaces are not standardized and the variety of users is enormous and should be considered. In both situations, the variety of domains of application and the variety of users, ergonomics has an important role to ensure the systems usability (Baillie, Benyon, Bodker, & Macaulay, 2003; Stanton & Young, 2003).

Ergonomic Tridimensional Analysis (ETdA) is a new approach developed specifically for ergonomic assessments and redesign of CAFCP (Loureiro, Leão, & Arezes, 2012). This model presents a realistic, in occupational and usability terms, overview of the CAFCP. This line of research is an evolution of the traditional ergonomic occupational analysis involving all the system participants through a system approach. In this approach workplaces are analysed as an integrated part of a complex and dynamic socio-technical system, where all the participants are identified, as well as the interrelations among them. The proposed analysis is multidimensional since it considers all the organizational participants, namely the Analyst, Clients, Professionals and in a broader sense, the Managers. The conceptualization of the ETdA methodology is in line with customer relationship management strategies that contribute to companies' success. According to Chalmeta (2006), a customer-focused strategy is leading to a strong demand by companies for methodologies and solutions capable of allowing them to consider customers' satisfaction as their ultimate aim. In this particular case, Clients' ergonomic evaluation can be used as an indicator of some situations that otherwise would not be a priority. It can be useful to improve the Analyst evaluation when there is agreement in the ratings (Analyst, Clients, Professionals), or to be used as an advice-guide if ratings are inconsistent. It is authors' believe that any of these situations will have greater impact on the manager decision for the ergonomic intervention (Loureiro, Leão, & Arezes, 2012). Indeed, this persistent concern about the wellbeing of the Clients will reproduce adjustments, which will also benefit the Professionals' ergonomic context, by facilitating the ergonomic intervention. ETdA model follows these emerging challenges by increasing the population awareness regarding ergonomics, allowing the participation of the entire organization in critical situations' identification and proposals of intervention (Caple, 2010; Dul & Newmann, 2009).

The establishment of a system called ETdAnalyser was developed to help the Analyst to implement this ergonomic model. This system should allow data collection and simplification of the massiveness of the studied variables (Kettenring, 2009). Folmer & Bosch (2004) mentioned that "Software is developed with a particular purpose, to provide specific functionality to allow a stakeholder to support a task in a specific context". Taking this into consideration, a model framework, ETdAnalyser, is proposed. This will result in an efficient interaction by providing the Analyst with a fast and simple way of collecting and analysing data. Ultimately, this system is considered to be a decision-making support tool to an ergonomic intervention, representing also a relevant contribution to the advance of the ergonomics field.

The research opportunity to develop a decision-making support computational tool for an ergonomic intervention is in line with the need and the opportunities of development in ergonomics domain. The next two sections introduce the new ergonomic system approach by identifying the general guidelines to reach the ergonomic decision intervention, and the identification of the system requirements for the ergonomic tool development. The subsequent three sections describe the development, implementation and verification of described tool by addressing the user requirements identified and considering the most recent developments on Interactivity and the Human-Computer Interface, and the final section provides final considerations and some future research directions.

ETDA: ERGONOMIC TRIDIMENSIONAL ANALYSIS

As above mentioned, ETdA development was based upon a system approach. In the following sections, the variables that are assessed by the ETdA methodology, as well as the observation tools used to collected data upon a tridimensional perspective, are identified. The ETdA implementation regarding the use of the software ETdAnalyser is also defined.

The Ergonomic Factors (EFs) that allow the ETdA operability are intrinsically (individual: postures, general physical activity, communication/inter-relation, attentiveness) or extrinsically linked to Professionals. In the latter case, they are divided in environmental or occupational EFs. If they are enclosed in the organizational schemes of the social-technical systems they will be occupational (Professional training quality, decision-making, restrictiveness, job content, work space or common area), otherwise, environmental, when related to the physical aspects of the work (noise, lighting, thermal environment, risk of accident). In the ETdA model, different observation tools are considered: a questionnaire, an evaluation form and a checklist for the Clients, Professionals and Analyst dimensions, respectively (Loureiro, Leão & Arezes, 2010a). Professionals and Analyst observation tools are presented in the Ergonomic Workplace Analysis, EWA (Ahoen, Launis, & Kuorinka, 1999), and were correctly adapted to be applied in ETdA model. This methodology allows a systematic and careful description of the task or workplace and has been planned to serve as a tool to provide the Analyst with a more sophisticated "picture" of the work situation. According to Hakkarainen, Ketola & Nevala (2010), the EWA is suitable for observing the ergonomics of sedentary, standing and physically active work. Due to its simplicity, it can help the Analyst in the EF assessments'. The Analyst defines the procedure for the analysis, according to the work organization and relevance of the EFs. Regarding the work organization, the analysis can be made using two different approaches: (1) restricted to a section where the Professionals activities are performed, or (2) consider the commercial area as a whole if the Professionals' activities are developed across the common area. The definition of the EFs set is flexible and can be chosen according to the area under analysis.

Through a general checklist with criteria for ergonomic evaluation and safety, the Analyst rates the EF using a three-category scale representing health risks (1 to 3). A rating of (1) indicates a negative evaluation representing a critical situation; (2) represents an acceptable situation but with suggestions to be implemented and (3) is related to a positive evaluation with no relevant identified risk. It is important to mention that not only the workplace is under analysis but also the Clients' attendance area. Professionals use evaluation forms to carry out the assessments of the commercial area, both by analysing a specific task or a particular sector. The evaluation form was based on the EWA checklist developed by the Finnish Institute of Occupational Health (reference for EWA). Thus, if necessary the Analyst can associate a critical identified situation to a specific area or Professional activity. The form is a simple sheet on which Professionals evaluate the EFs in a subjective scale, with the following options: "very poor (- -)", "poor (-)", "fair (+)", and "good (++)". According to the recommendations from Hakkarainen, Ketola & Nevala (2010), a new item was included allowing the Professional to summarize the work conditions and prioritize the identified needs for development and improvement.

To complete the tridimensional analysis, a questionnaire was developed for the Clients' dimension. The questionnaire was previously tested in order to be used in the survey (Khalid & Helande, 2004), and the results of the tests (sensibility, validity and reliability) contributed to its improvement (Hedlund, Åteg, Andersson, & Rosén, 2010; Loureiro, Leão & Arezes, 2012). In general terms, the ETdA questionnaire allows not only the evaluation of the ergonomic issues but also to collect information about factors not directly related to work but which might contribute to define the Clients dimension profile (Macdonald & Bendak, 2000). It is a direct administration tool, which presents as main advantage the possibility to quantify a variety of data and consequent establishment of multiple correlations. The ETdA questionnaire is divided in three major parts: (1) Clients' characterization, (2) Clients' ergonomic evaluation, and (3) open question. In the first part, two groups of questions can be identified: Questions Clients (Qc) and, Questions Clients/store relationships (Qcs) (Loureiro, Leão & Arezes, 2010b). The first one is related with Clients' socio-demographic characteristics like gender, age, academic qualifications and professional activity. To contextualize the Clients on the ergonomic analysis issue it is also asked about the Client's meaning about the ergonomic aims and the reasons for the preference for that specific establishment. These variables are considered supplementary as it does not have a main role in Clients' EFs assessment. The Qcs questions are related with service quality and the reasons why Clients choose that specific establishment for shopping. Service quality is accessed through a set of multiple questions related to Clients' wellbeing (Professionals' kindness, Cost/quality relation and Hospitality).

The second part consists on Client's perception and evaluation of EFs. This Clients' ergonomic evaluation is done through a set of Ergonomic questions (Qe - Clients' ergonomic questions) related with noise, lighting quality, thermal environmental and risk of accident assessments. Anthropometrics limitations related to the balconies and the height of the shelves help in the evaluation of the Clients' adopted postures and movements EF. The restrictiveness was also accessed through a question that evaluates the efficiency of the software used by the Professional when a Client/Professional interrelation is implicated. The existence of a question where Clients must evaluate the general appearance of the establishment intends to focus their attention in the commercial area itself. Clients are also asked to express their opinion about the quality of the Professional training and the physical effort of the Professional activity.

The EF evaluation is done using a three or five level scale (frequency, probability or opinion scales).

In the third part, it can be set an open-ended question where Clients may express their general opinion about the establishment. Respondents can state, in their own words, what could be improved in the service provided and in the establishment general appearance. This issue can have high importance for total quality management, as it will reveal if the establishment is, or not, in line with the Clients' expectations.

The final task of the ETdA methodology is the weighting table assembly to support the Analyst in the ergonomic intervention decision. The dimensions' results obtained through the proposed three level analyses are added and the obtained value is related to a colour within the weighting table supporting the Analyst in the ergonomic intervention decision-making. The weighting table assembly to support the Analyst in the ergonomic intervention decision will simplify and summarize the results of the dimensions, leading to the 3-dimension matrix assembling (Kettenring, 2009). A methodology of colours is used: red (R), representing a critical situation, yellow (Y), representing a medium-term intervention, and green (G), identifying a non-critical situation. The final results for each dimension are average values and each one is associated with a colour within the weighting table. This procedure will support the Analyst on the ergonomic intervention decision-making. Since the scores are integer numbers and the individual results are higher or equal to 1 and lower or equal to 3, a 3-point scale is proposed as follows: the values ranged [1, 1.5[are scored as 1; the values ranged [1.5, 2.5[are scored as 2, and values [2.5, 3] are scored as 3.

The general guidelines for ETdA use on common areas with free circulation of people are presented in Figure 1.

Figure 1. ETdA general guidelines

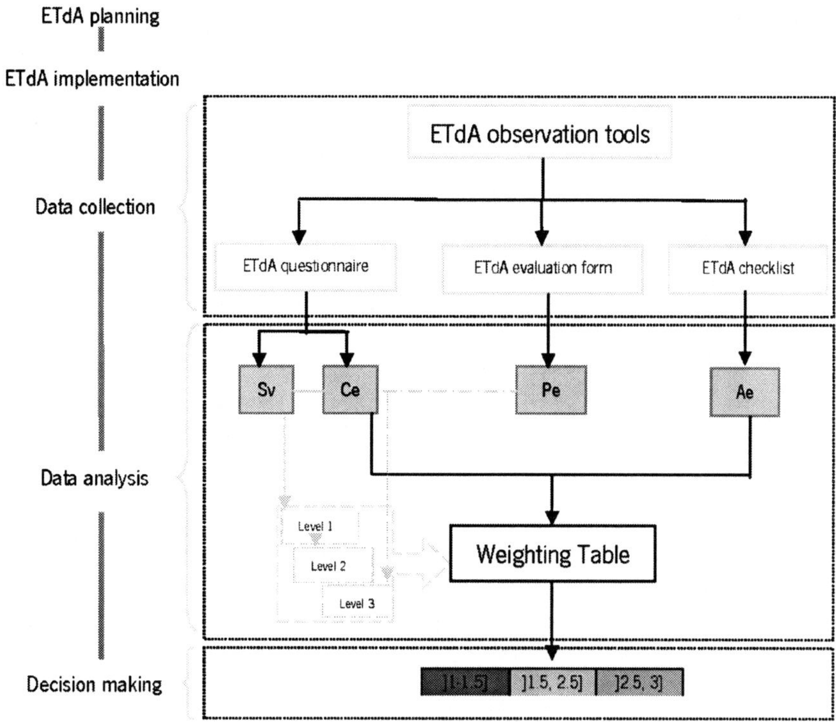

The ETdAnalyser software is used to support the Analyst on the implementation, analysis and decision-making steps.

ETDA: REQUIREMENTS ANALYSIS

ETdAnalyser is the software that was developed to be used by an Analyst, helping him/her on the implementation of the ETdA model. That is, the development of a decision-making support tool that helps the Analyst to characterize the actions needed towards each defined item. Thus, this software must assist the Analyst in all the steps of the model, providing an intuitive and efficient interface. This contributes to automatically collect and analyse data in an easier and faster way, minimizing also the probability of making errors.

Considering the ETdAnalyser development, the system requirements are related to the analysis of the main tasks that the Analyst performs and the time that each one takes. The main tasks related to this subject are identified in Figure 2.

The identified tasks that can be automatically executed contribute to saving time and improving efficiency.

The conception of the analysis, (a) in Figure 2, consists in creating a project for each of the analysed establishments. Inside those projects, several analyses can be defined. This fact is very useful as an ergonomic analysis is a continuous process meaning that during the time several analyses can be performed for each of the establishments under analysis. The main advantage of the multiple project analysis is that the Analyst can have a report of all the analysis made as well a comparison of the results. To create the project, the Analyst just needs to introduce the establishment name. The analysis and the type of analysis also should be named. By default, the analysis is

Figure 2. System requirements - ETdA main tasks

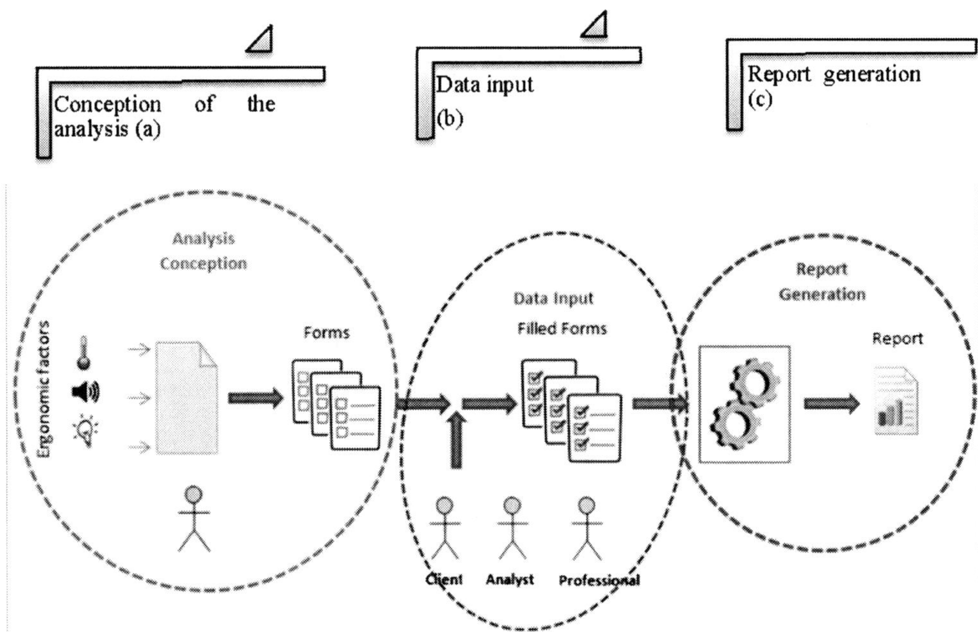

under the name of the date on which the report was set up. The setup and the information provided will be according the type of the analysis to be performed. The setup consists on the definition of EFs relevant to the analysis, the evaluation scale and the weighting assigned to each dimension. If the analysis is to be made by common are, no more information is required.

Completed the conception of the analysis, the forms must be created before any data importation. If the default forms are available this step can be more rapidly processed. As previously mentioned, three types of forms could be used according to the three ETdA observation tools. Regarding the ETdA questionnaire and the evaluation forms, the Analyst must adjust the type of questions and corresponding evaluation scale. The ergonomic checklist, as it is always the same, independently of the analysis, is automatically generated.

Data importation, (b) in Figure 2, can be done by three different ways: (1) file importation, (2) web forms and (3) direct submissions. The file importation option (1) is used when the Analyst has data in a digital format. In this case, it is necessary that the software imports it to the system. In this importation process, an error detection mechanism was developed. In this way, the Analyst scans the data values and when an error is found, it is automatically revised. This action can be made by three different options: stop the importation; ignore the form with the detected errors; or ignore the value that is incorrect. The web forms importation option (2) is accomplished through a web based platform. This platform allows the Clients and the Professionals to submit the forms (web forms) into the system. Thus, the Analyst does not need to manually insert them, which reduces the likelihood of error occurrences and is less time consuming. The last data importation option is the direct submission (3). In order to minimize the length related to the fulfilment of the forms process an intuitive graphical interface should be used.

The report generation, (c) in Figure 2, should be automatically generated by the ETdAnalyser. The report contents the (1) partial results of the analysis for each dimension, (2) the weighting and/or (3) the final result of each EFs. A section for allowing the Analyst to insert comments about the result generated was included.

One advantage of the ETdAnalyser it is its multi-user features that is, multiple Analysts can simultaneously use the application. The same should be applied to the others dimensions, Clients and Professionals. These last two use the application with a different objective that is; they only fulfil the forms created by the Analyst.

The web-based platform has to be simple, intuitive, and provide a quick operation. This is a very important issue since Professionals will fill the forms on labour time and Clients would not agree to participate on the ergonomic analysis if it takes much of their time. Considering that the main application of the ETdAnalyser is for the Analyst' use, a concise language with an accurate technical terminology must be applied, leaving no place for misunderstandings. ETdAnalyser is a good example of the importance of the engagement of all the end-users of the application due to its different characteristics strengthening the need of a balance in the relation design/optimization of the system (Young, Bisset, Grant, Williams, Sell, & Haslam, 2012).

ETDANALYSER DEVELOPMENT

System Architecture

In order to consider all the requirements previously specified, a high level of abstraction had to be taken into consideration for the development of all components of the system architecture. To create an automatic way of distribution and form collection and their corresponding data, a centralized database accessed by either a native application or a web-based application were developed. By choosing this type of architecture, all the information can be always updated, independently of the workstation in use, and can be accessed from all around the world as long as an internet connection is available. This also allows supporting multiple users whilst keeping their management sufficiently flexible and adaptable.

The native application is one of the most important components to the Analyst. The application allows the Analyst to access/modify all the information on the Database Engine regarding his/her account, as well as creating a new one. All the management of the projects and analysis are done from here, including managing the web-based application (its availability) and who as access to it. In one specific case the native application can access the web-based application, but just in order to allow the manual insertion of the paper-based forms.

Considering that the application is designed for the exclusive use of the Analyst, a unique/single environment where the Analyst was able to perform all the needed tasks was provided, reducing Analyst distraction through the application.

This component of the system architecture is responsible for the accesses of all the three dimensions, allowing the preparation and submission of the web forms. It communicates directly with the Database Engine to get the correspondent forms of each dimension and to check their permission to view and to submit. It is able to support every kind of form predicted in the ETdA model, thus being very flexible without losing its accuracy.

Special attention must be given to the development of this component interface in order to enable a quick operation. This is a very important issue since Professionals will fill the forms during their work time and Clients would not agree to participate if this is very time-consuming or if it is too complex. It is authors' believe that by providing a digital way of filling and submitting the forms assisted by an intuitive input device (for example, through a tablet or a mobile phone), users will be more willing to participate.

The Database Engine is the core of the system architecture, as it contains all the information required for either the native or the web-based application to operate. It also manages the users' access to the information, considering every user's privacy. All communication between both applications passes through the Database Engine, which stores the information so the other one can access it when needed.

All the information management in the Database Engine is automatically performed by both applications, although in case of an emergency, a manual intervention is allowed.

Supporting the Main Tasks

This section describes the mechanisms that were implemented to support the Analyst throughout his/her ergonomic assessment, namely: a) analysis conception, and b) data input.

The analysis conception (a) requires a great interaction with the Analyst. In order to help the Analyst planning, a "concept - project" was created, where a project correspond to a work/commercial space. In this way, a registered Analyst may have several defined projects, and several analyses for each of them.

To create the analysis (which belongs to a project), as defined by the ETdA Model, the Analyst must select the type of analysis (by section, activity or common area), as well as the EFs. By default 14 EFs where added and the weights of each dimension set to 0.333 (one of them to 0.334 – so the sum can be equals to 1), aiming to speed up the whole process. A simple mechanism of error prevention was added to the sum of the probabilities of each dimension, so it is always equals to 1. As the Analyst can also change the limits of each colour in the colour scale, an automatic mechanism to reject an overlapping of the range limits was also implemented.

To be able to proceed in the Ergonomic Assessment, the forms must be created. To support the Analyst in this task the checklist is automatically created, without any human intervention needed, as this only comprises the ergonomic values (previously specified) and a fixed scale.

As for the other ergonomic tools, in the questionnaire, default characterization questions are added, as well as the default questions regarding the ergonomic values. This last feature also applies to the evaluation form, but with specific questions to the Professionals. In both cases it is possible to change the current answer scale. By default 10 different types of answers were created some with different scales.

Besides all the default questions and types of answers, new scales of answers can easily be added.

Data input (b) was carefully designed and many possibilities were identified. The main aim of the Web Forms creation was to reduce the amount of work that is time-consuming regarding the Analyst tasks. The main advantage of using a web format is related to the fact of the Analyst can virtually provide a link to the manager of the commercial area the link, preventing unnecessary visits to the site. Since the forms are submitted directly, the answers automatically go to Database Engine (Figure 3). With the Web Forms the mandatory questions cannot be unanswered, thus providing at first site a better accuracy.

In case some data is already in a digital format, file Importation is another feature that allows the Analyst to save time. The format .csv (comma separated values) is supported by most programs dealing with large amounts of data; therefore, this format was selected to support this task. Besides allowing the direct insertion of data form files, it also does verifications and automatic corrections of the data values. In case of unexpected values, the Analyst can manually correct them or can define an action to be taken each time this error occurs (see section above entitled "system requirements").

As sometimes the Analyst may have paper-based forms, it was necessary to develop an intuitive way of making the submission. To accomplish this issue, the web-based application, previously

Figure 3. Data input - information flow

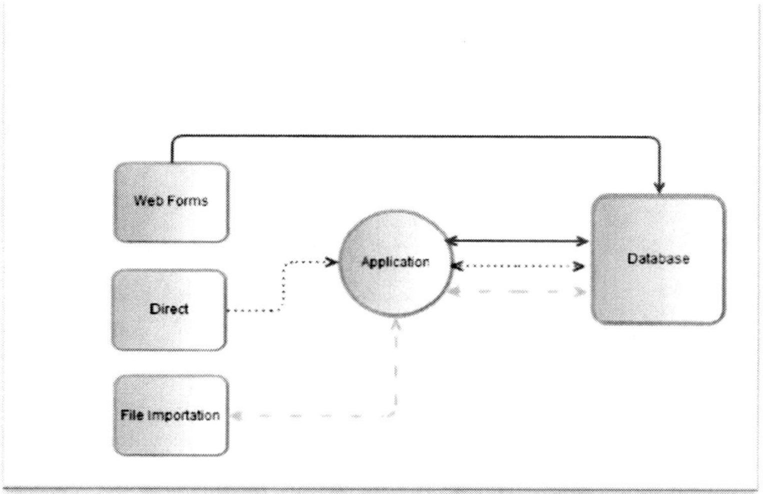

mentioned was used. A basic browser was included in the native application. The browser automatically accesses the Web Form correspondent to the dimension chosen by the Analyst, so they are then submitted through the web-based application.

The report generation assumes two phases: (1) since all the answers from all the forms are computed, a numeric result for each section and for each EF is generated; (2) after the computation of all the results, a new document containing all the results is created.

The graphical interface allows the Analyst to see, for each section and for each EFs, all the partial results (correspondent to each dimension), the weight attributed, the final result and a colour scale showing in which interval the final result is in. It is authors' believe that the graded colour scale is the most effective way to show the results (has also indicated by the ETdA model conceptualization), allowing an easy reading and identification of the dimension that contribute negatively or positively to the final ergonomic decision. In this interface it is also possible for the Analyst to insert comments regarding the EFs and the results obtained.

The native application allows the generation of a Microsoft Word document containing all the information presented in the previous phase. This means that the Analyst remarks are automatically included in the document.

It is also possible to include statistical data concerning the non-ergonomic factors (questions that allow the characterization of the Clients). Then, using the Microsoft Word program, different graphics can be used, which will help to better understand a particular situation. For example, the perception of the accident risk can be associated with Clients' gender. In order to make more focused decisions regarding safety measures it is important to study if these two variables are associated.

The Analyst can also choose to include, or not, the partial results regarding each dimension (if they are thought to be relevant to the ergonomic assessment).

System Overview

The system consists of a web-based application (available from the website) and the original application, both associated to the database that contains all the information (Figure 4) (Nunes & O'Neill, 2000; Sommerville, 2006). Through the website, the Professionals, Clients, and even

Figure 4. ETdAnalyser system overview

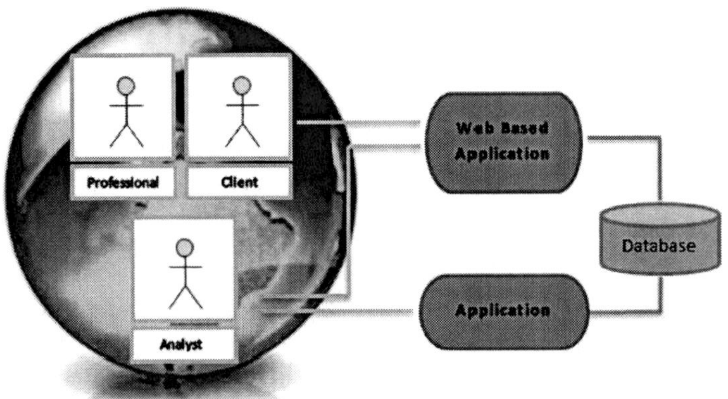

the Analyst can submit the corresponding forms. Presently, the application itself allows the Analyst to access all the data to generate the report, and to submit new forms consider three different types: file importation, web forms, and direct submission. In addition, it is possible to select the type of the analysis and the corresponding items to be considered.

System Functionalities

The system functionality is accomplished if software enables the user to perform specified goals in a specified context of use. The proper study of the ETdAnalyser application and website definition are made through a concept map. Briefly, the systems functionalities are described in the following paragraphs.

After the data input step, the Analyst selects the type of analysis to be performed: by activity, by zone, or by commonplace. The EF to be analysed is also selected so that the computed results values can be presented by EF. The results are displayed in text or/and in graphical way. A colour scale by item and by activity/zone/commonplace is presented.

For the website definition, three types of forms are defined (Professional, Client and Analyst), with the possibility of adjustments. This option is only available to the Analyst. Finally, the form is filling out and the corresponding data included in the database.

ETDANALYSER IMPLEMENTATION

In this phase of the project everything that was specified in the preceding steps must be fully implemented: a database to store all the information, a website to facilitate the insertion of the forms, and a project management application with result calculation

The use of the .NET Framework was the option since two different systems with access to centralized data would be developed. It provides similar interaction, even with different programming languages and paradigms. The text editor used was the Microsoft Office, being possible the integration with the .NET Framework and to generate the report directly from the application. The choice of the programming languages inside the .NET Framework was, somehow, evident. The use of an object oriented programming language was already defined by the modulation phase. Also the vast .NET Framework library was a feature taken into consideration. Thus, the choice for the application was C#. This language together with the Microsoft Visual Studio (MVS) formed a “great pair", i.e. the implementation of the application was simpler, mainly in the interface development (allowing a better and faster development). The MVS allows the creation of windows forms in a simple and intuitive way, reducing considerably the amount of time in its implementation. Finally, the MVS debugger was also of great help in testing the application behaviour.

For the website it was adopted ASP.NET, due to its simplicity. It allows reusing classes previously created, for the application to access the database, as it separates the presentation from the logic, facilitating the organization and eventual, make changes. Since .NET Framework was going to be used, opting for a database engine outside the Microsoft tools would not make sense. The choice was SQL Server, because once again, the support offered is good, and it made easier the integration with the two sub-systems.

To implement the application, the MVC (Model View Controller) development model was used as it allows the development and testing each part of the application independently. Furthermore, for a small change in a part, it will be unnecessary to modify the entire application.

The obtained results from the application are presented in a very intuitive and simple way. The final report contains all the features described previously. In order to illustrate this description several screenshots of the ETdAnalyser application are provided in Figure 5: a) Data Input, b) Analysis Management, c) a part of the report generation. As observed in Figure 5c), a colour scale is used with the corresponding numerical result. This allows a quick and easy way to identify the decision-making that will lead to the ergonomic intervention.

ETDANALYSER VERIFICATION

Software testing or verification can be stated as the process of validating and verifying that a software program/application/product (1) meets the requirements that guided its design and development; (2) works as expected; (3) can be implemented with the same characteristics and; (4) satisfies the needs of stakeholders. The ETdAnalyser verification and validation were carried out by the supervision of an expert advisor on Ergonomics and with knowledge of the ETdA methodology.

To verify that all the requirements where accomplished, each feature of the identified main tasks was tested through an experimental study. This study was conducted with data being manually collected from the ETdA model application in a commercial area. The first step of the ETdAnalyser verification was related to the analysis creation, i.e., the creation of a project with the corresponding analysis. This was accomplished, as previously defined (see section "analysis creation").

Although the data have been collected manually, a file was created and saved as (*.sav) file. Therefore the data input was done by file importation (see "system requirements" section).

The data used for this experimental study included 206 ETdA questionnaires and 107 evaluation forms. Only one ergonomic checklist was used, as this analysis was conducted by one Analyst.

It is important to refer that data used to perform this experimental study was previously analysed according to the ETdA guidelines. The analysis of the results obtained from the ETdA implementation on this commercial area involved exploratory data analysis, inference and decision-making. Firstly, it was calculated the average of each ETdA variable. Then, a weight was assigned to each dimension and finally, a weighted value was obtained. After weighting the ETdA variables, the obtained value was associated to a colour within the weighting table, representing a possible decision regarding an intervention.

The obtained results from the generated report were comparable with the report generated by the ETdAnalyser. It was verified that the results produced were accurate and that it helped to detect incorrect values that possibly may have been im-

Figure 5. ETdAnalyser application screenshots (in Portuguese): a) data input, b) analysis management, c) report generation

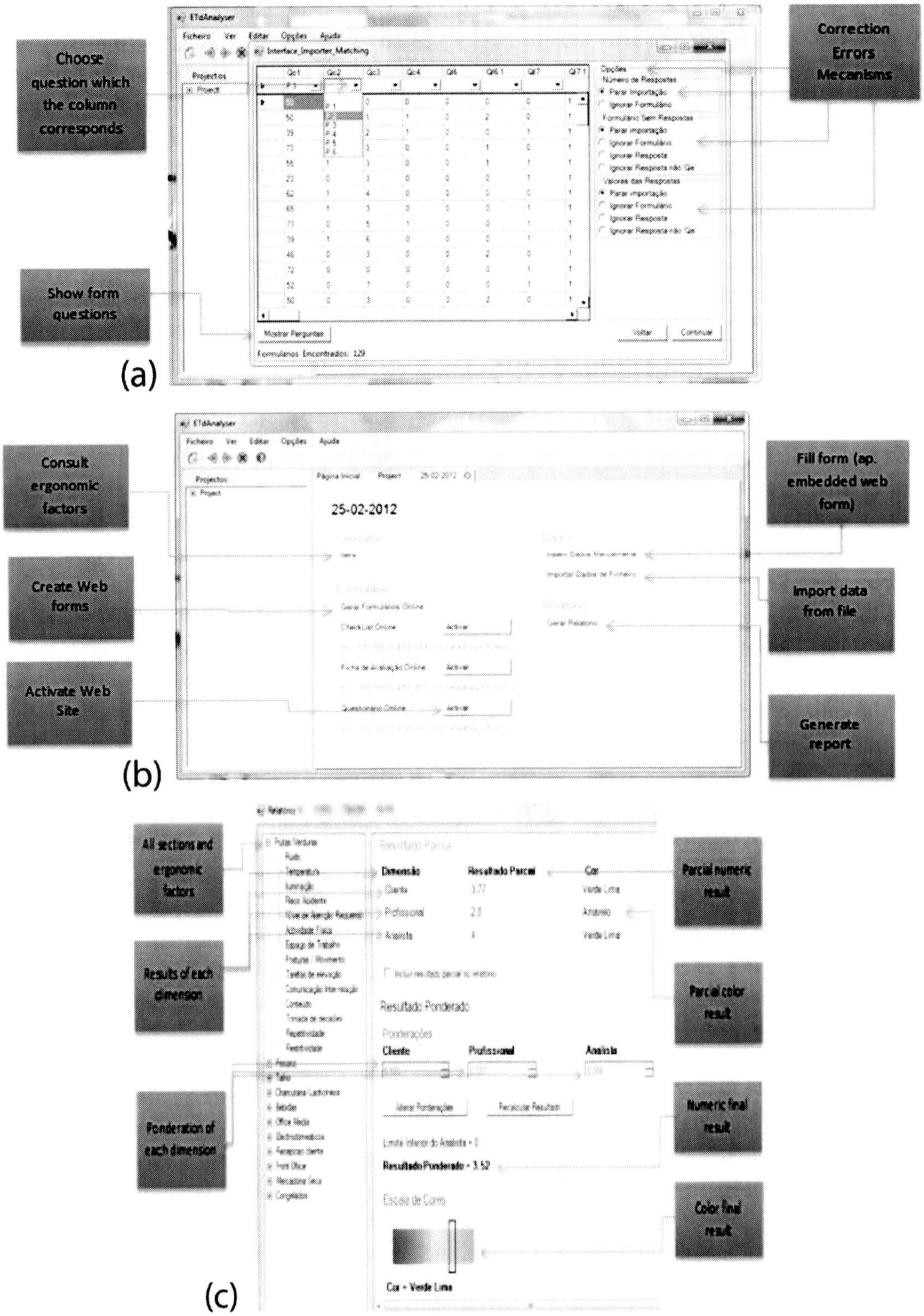

properly inserted on the (*.sav) file. This largely contributes to guarantee that no error occurred on the file import step, allowing the ETdAnalyser validation, as the obtained results were exactly the same. It was possible to conclude that in terms of decision-making results no differences were obtained from both reports. Concerning the user interaction and how it may affect the model, the web-based application effectively presented the forms in an intuitive way, which has motivated the participation. Similarly for the application, it was verified that the integration of all features into one working environment has allowed the user to focus on the ergonomic analysis. The use the Microsoft Word to generate the report was an advantage, as most of the people use it daily.

FINAL CONSIDERATIONS AND FUTURE WORK

The field of application of the ETdAnalyser is within the ergonomics workplace analysis providing a supporting tool for the decision to take any action or not. Considering the Ergonomic Tridimensional Analysis, ETdA, designed specifically for commercial areas with free circulation of people, it is considered that the users of the developed software are the Analyst, the Clients and the Professionals. The application helps the Analyst on the ergonomic analysis and in decision-making regarding any needed intervention. The Clients and Professionals have a more restrictive use, as they only fulfil the correspondent forms with their ergonomic evaluation. The ETdAnalyser development take into consideration that the final product must be easy to learn, simple, intuitive and that it carry out the proposed tasks in an efficient way. The architecture of the application was the major concern at this point of time. That is, it must present a level of functionality that allowed the Analyst to collect data and analyse the results of three dimensions together (Analyst, Professionals and Clients). The report generated by the ETdAnalyser is an important tool in the identification of critical situations that need any type of ergonomics intervention. Specific attributes of the application, such as performance and usability, are being currently analysed and will contribute to the quality of the ETdAnalyser. Future work will also be focused in the adaptation of the ETdA observations tools to more intuitive and easy-to-use digital platforms, such as tablets and mobile phones, which are expected to facilitate its use and, hopefully, increase users' willingness to participate.

REFERENCES

Ahonen, M., Launis, M., & Kuorinka, T. (1989). *Ergonomic workplace analysis*. Helsinki, Finland: Finnish Institute of Occupational Health.

Baillie, L., Benyon, D., Bodker, S., & Macaulay, C. (2003). Special Issue on Interacting with technology in household environments. *Cognition Technology and Work*, *5*(1), 2–3.

Cacciabue, P. C. (2008). Role and challenges of ergonomics in modern societal contexts. *Ergonomics*, *51*(1), 42–48. doi:10.1080/00140130701800878 PMID:18097829.

Caple, D. C. (2010). The IEA contribution to the transition of ergonomics from research to practice. *Applied Ergonomics*, *41*, 731–737. doi:10.1016/j.apergo.2010.03.002 PMID:20392433.

Chalmeta, R. (2006). Methodology for customer relationship management. *Journal of Systems and Software*, *79*, 1015–1024. doi:10.1016/j.jss.2005.10.018.

Dul, J., & Neumann, W. P. (2009). Ergonomics contributions to company strategies. *Applied Ergonomics*, *40*, 745–752. doi:10.1016/j.apergo.2008.07.001 PMID:18775532.

Folmer, E., & Bosch, J. (2004). Architecting for usability: A survey. *Journal of Systems and Software*, *70*, 61–78. doi:10.1016/S0164-1212(02)00159-0.

Hakkarainen, P., Ketola, R., & Nevala, N. (2011). Reliability and usability of the ergonomic workplace method for assessing working environments. *Theoretical Issues in Ergonomics Science*, *12*(4), 367–378. doi:10.1080/14639221003736339.

Hedlund, A., Åteg, M., Andersson, I. M., & Rosén, G. (2010). Assessing motivation for work environment improvements: Internal consistency, reliability and factorial structure. *Journal of Safety Research*, *41*, 145–151. doi:10.1016/j.jsr.2009.12.005 PMID:20497800.

Kettenring, J. R. (2009). Massive datasets. *Wiley Interdisciplinary Reviews: Computational Statistics*, *1*(1), 25–32. doi:10.1002/wics.15.

Khalid, H. M., & Helander, G. H. (2004). A framework for affective customer needs in product design. *Theoretical Issues in Ergonomics Science*, *5*(1), 27–42. doi:10.1080/1463922031000086744.

Lee, K. W., & Lee, Y. C. (2012). Design and validation of an improved graphical user interface with the 'Tool ball'. *Applied Ergonomics*, *43*(1), 57–68. doi:10.1016/j.apergo.2011.03.004 PMID:21555114.

Loureiro, I., Leão, C. P., & Arezes, P. (2012). Ergonomic tridimensional analysis: Critical ergonomic factors identification in a commercial environmental. *Work (Reading, Mass.)*, *41*(S1), 636–641. PMID:22316794.

Loureiro, I., Leão, C. P., & Arezes, P. M. (2010a). Management of the benefits on the client's involvement on ergonomic analysis. In T. de Magalhães et al. (Eds.), *Communications in Computer and Information Science* (pp. 1–8). Berlin, Germany: Springer. doi:10.1007/978-3-642-15717-2_1.

Loureiro, I., Leão, C. P., & Arezes, P. M. (2010b). Tabela de ponderação: Construção de uma metodologia para intervenção ergonómica. In P. Arezes et al. (Eds.), *SHO 2010: Occupational Safety and Hygiene* (pp. 299–303). Guimarães, Portugal: Academic Press.

Macdonald, W., & Bendak, S. (2000). Effects of workload level and 8- versus 12-h workday duration on test battery performance. *International Journal of Industrial Ergonomics*, *26*(3), 399–416. doi:10.1016/S0169-8141(00)00015-9.

Nunes, M., & O'Neill, H. (2000). *Fundamental de UML*. Lisbon, Portugal: FCA - Editora de Informática.

Sommerville, I. (2006). *Software engineering*. Harlow, UK: Pearson Education.

Stanton, N. A., Hedge, A., Brookhuis, K., Salas, E., & Hendrick, H. (2005). *Handbook of human factors and ergonomics methods*. Boca Raton, FL: CRC Press.

Stanton, N. A., & Young, M. S. (2003). Giving ergonomics away? The application of ergonomics methods by novices. *Applied Ergonomics*, *34*(5), 479–490. doi:10.1016/S0003-6870(03)00067-X PMID:12963333.

Van der Beek, A. J., Mathiassen, S. E., & Burdorf, A. (2013). Efficient assessment of exposure to manual lifting using company data. *Applied Ergonomics*, *44*(3), 360–365. doi:10.1016/j.apergo.2012.09.006 PMID:23069188.

Young, M. S., Bisset, F. J., Grant, L., Williams, B., Sell, R., & Haslam, R. (2012). An ergonomically designed ergonomics exhibition: Lessons from and for public engagement. *Theoretical Issues in Ergonomics Science*, *13*(1), 75–91. doi:10.1080/1463922X.2010.491875.

Zink, K. (2000). Ergonomics in the past and the future: From a German perspective to an international one. *Ergonomics*, *43*(7), 920–930. doi:10.1080/001401300409116 PMID:10929827.

ADDITIONAL READING

Baillie, L., Benyon, D., Bodker, S., & Macaulay, C. (2003). Special issue on interacting with technology in household environments. *Cognition Technology and Work*, *5*(1), 2–66. doi: doi:10.1007/s10111-002-0110-y.

Boivie, I., Åborg, C., Persson, J., & Löfberg, M. (2003). Why usability gets lost or usability in in-house software development. *Interacting with Computers*, *15*(4), 623–639. doi:10.1016/S0953-5438(03)00055-9.

Cacciabue, P. C. (2008). Role and challenges of ergonomics in modern societal contexts. *Ergonomics*, *51*(1), 42–48. doi:10.1080/00140130701800878 PMID:18097829.

Chalmeta, R. (2006). Methodology for customer relationship management. *Journal of Systems and Software*, *79*, 1015–1024. doi:10.1016/j.jss.2005.10.018.

Dockrell, S., O'Grady, E., Bennett, K., Mullarkey, C., Mc-Connell, R., & Ruddy, R. et al. (2012). An investigation of the reliability of rapid upper limb assessment (RULA) as a method of assessment of children's computing posture. *Applied Ergonomics*, *43*(3), 632–636. doi:10.1016/j.apergo.2011.09.009 PMID:22018838.

Dul, J., Bruder, R., Buckle, P., Carayon, P., Falzon, P., & Marras, W. et al. (2012). A strategy for human factors/ergonomics: Developing the discipline and profession. *Ergonomics*. doi:10.1080/00140139.2012.661087 PMID:22332611.

Folmer, E., & Bosch, J. (2004). Architecting for usability: A survey. *Journal of Systems and Software*, *70*, 61–78. doi:10.1016/S0164-1212(02)00159-0.

Hakkarainen, P., Ketola, R., & Nevala, N. (2011). Reliability and usability of the ergonomic workplace method for assessing working environments. *Theoretical Issues in Ergonomics Science*, *12*(4), 367–378. doi:10.1080/14639221003736339.

Han, S. H., Yun, M. H., Kim, K.-J., & Kwahk, J. (2000). Evaluation of product usability: Development and validation of usability dimensions and design elements based on empirical models. *International Journal of Industrial Ergonomics*, *26*(4), 477–488. doi:10.1016/S0169-8141(00)00019-6.

Hornbæk, K., & Stage, J. (2004). Improving the Interplay between usability evaluation and user interface design. In *Proceedings of the NordiCHI Workshop on Improving the Interplay Between Usability Evaluation and User Interface Design*. Aalborg University.

Jayarama, U., Jayarama, S., Shaikha, I., Kima, Y., & Palmer, C. (2006). Introducing quantitative analysis methods into virtual environments for real-time and continuous ergonomic evaluations. *Computers in Industry*, *57*(3), 283–296. doi:10.1016/j.compind.2005.12.005.

Karwowski, W. (2005). Ergonomics and human factors: The paradigms for science, engineering, design, technology and management of human-compatible systems. *Ergonomics*, *48*(5), 436–463. doi:10.1080/00140130400029167 PMID:16040519.

Kettenring, J. R. (2009). Massive datasets. *Wiley Interdisciplinary Reviews: Computational Statistics*, *1*(1), 25–32. doi:10.1002/wics.15.

Khalid, H., Hedge, A., & Ahram, T. Z. (2010). *Advances in ergonomics modeling and usability evaluation*. Boca Raton, FL: CRC Press.

Khalid, H. M., & Helander, G. H. (2004). A framework for affective customer needs in product design. *Theoretical Issues in Ergonomics Science*, *5*(1), 27–42. doi:10.1080/1463922031000086744.

Lee, K. W., & Lee, Y. C. (2012). Design and validation of an improved graphical user interface with the 'Tool ball'. *Applied Ergonomics*, *43*(1), 57–68. doi:10.1016/j.apergo.2011.03.004 PMID:21555114.

Molich, R., Ede, M. R., Kaasgaard, K., & Karyukin, B. (2004). Comparative usability evaluation. *Behaviour & Information Technology*, *23*(1), 65–74. doi:10.1080/0144929032000173951.

Norros, L. L., & Savioja, P. J. (2007). Towards a theory and method for usability evaluation of complex human-technology systems. *@ctivités*, *4*(2), 143-150.

Nunes, M., & O'Neill, H. (2000). *Fundamental de UML*. Lisbon, Portugal: FCA - Editora de Informática.

Sommerville, I. (2006). *Software engineering*. Harlow, UK: Pearson Education.

Sonderegger, A., & Sauer, J. (2010). The influence of design aesthetics in usability testing: Effects on user performance and perceived usability. *Applied Ergonomics*, *41*, 403–410. doi:10.1016/j.apergo.2009.09.002 PMID:19892317.

Stanton, N. A., Hedge, A., Brookhuis, K., Salas, E., & Hendrick, H. (2005). *Handbook of human factors and ergonomics methods*. Boca Raton, FL: CRC Press.

Wilpert, B. (2009). Impact of globalization on human work. *Safety Science*, *47*, 727–732. doi:10.1016/j.ssci.2008.01.014.

Womack, S. K., & Armstrong, T. J. (2005). Use of a computerized decision support system for primary and secondary prevention of work-related MSD disability. *Journal of Occupational Rehabilitation*, *15*(3), 313–328. doi:10.1007/s10926-005-5939-5 PMID:16119223.

Young, M. S., Bisset, F. J., Grant, L., Williams, B., Sell, R., & Haslam, R. (2012). An ergonomically designed ergonomics exhibition: Lessons from and for public engagement. *Theoretical Issues in Ergonomics Science*, *13*(1), 75–91. doi:10.1080/1463922X.2010.491875.

KEY TERMS AND DEFINITIONS

Ergonomic Factors (EFs): The factors that allow the ETdA operability. They can be individual (postures, general physical activity, communication/inter-relation, attentiveness) or extrinsically linked to Professionals (environmental or occupational). If they are enclosed in the organizational schemes of the social-technical systems they will be occupational (Professional training quality, decision-making, restrictiveness, job content, work space or common area), otherwise, environmental, when related to the physical aspects of the work (noise, lighting, thermal environment, risk of accident).

Ergonomic Tridimensional Analysis (ETdA): New ergonomic approach developed specifically for ergonomic assessments and redesign of Commercial Areas with Free Circulation of People (CAFCP) characterized by large open spaces where Professionals and Clients share the same space and have different interactions. It is a multidimensional analysis since it considers all the organizational participants: Analyst, Clients, Professionals and in a broader sense, the Managers.

ETdAnalyser: Software to be used by Analyst as a support tool in the implementation, analysis and ergonomic decision-making to an ergonomic intervention in the CAFCP, based on the ETdA model.

Software Verification: The process of evaluating work-products of a development phase to ensure that the product is being built according to the requirements and design specifications.

System Architecture: The conceptual model that defines the structure, behaviour, and more views of the system.

System Requirements: The necessary specifications that the software must have in order to run well and to meet all the Analyst's requirements.

Chapter 15
Design of Formal Languages and Interfaces:
"Formal" Does Not Mean "Unreadable"

Maria Spichkova
RMIT University, Australia

ABSTRACT

This chapter provides an introduction to a work that aims to apply the achievements of engineering psychology to the area of formal methods, focusing on the specification phase of a system development process. Formal methods often assume that only two factors should be satisfied: the method must be sound and give such a representation, which is concise and beautiful from the mathematical point of view, without taking into account any question of readability, usability, or tool support. This leads to the fact that formal methods are treated by most engineers as something that is theoretically important but practically too hard to understand and to use, where even some small changes of a formal method can make it more understandable and usable for an average engineer.

INTRODUCTION

There are many definitions of human factors, however most of them are solely oriented on human-machine operations in terms of system and program usability, i.e. on those parts that are seen by the (end-)user, but not by the requirements, specification and verification engineers. Nevertheless, many problems during the engineering phase are completely the same as by using the final version of a system just because of a simple fact that many people sometimes forget: engineers, even those who are working on verification or formal specification, are humans too and have the same human abilities and weaknesses as people working in any other areas, from arts to construction. Moreover, developing safety-critical systems using formal methods means much harder constraints and stress than using a completed version of software application (e.g., using an entertainment software, typing a personal e-mail using a smartphone, etc.) because of consequences of

DOI: 10.4018/978-1-4666-4623-0.ch015

any mistake: a typo in an e-mail can lead to misunderstanding which is easy to clear up, where a specification or verification error by developing of a safety-critical system, like a fly-by-wire system for airlines or pre-crash safety functionality for vehicles, can cost many human lives.

Nowadays, the research of human factors and of Human Computer Interface (HCI) mostly concentrates on the development of entertainment or every-day applications, but it was initiated and elaborated exactly because of mistakes in usage and development of safety-critical systems. For example, one of the widely cited HCI-related accidents in safety-critical systems are the accidents involved massive radiation overdoses by the Therac-25 (a radiation therapy machine used in curing cancer) that lead to deaths and serious injuries of patients which received thousand times the normal dose of radiation (Miller, 1987; Leveson & Turner, 1993). The causes of these accidents were software failures as well as problems with the system interface.

The Therac-25 was an extension of the two previous models, the Therac-6 and the Therac-20, but the upgrade was unsafe: the software was not correctly updated and adapted to the elaborated extensions in the system architecture. In this model, in comparison to the previous ones, the company tried to mix two system modes, a low-energy mode and a high-energy mode, together. In the high-energy mode the filter plate must be placed between the patients and the X-ray machine, so that a radiation beam is used in a correct way. Because of some software failures the high-energy mode was used in the Therac-25 without the filter plate. This kind of failures occurred also in the old models, but it did not lead to overdosed accidents due to hardware interlocks. In the Therac-25 the company replaced the hardware interlocks with software checks, this result in a deathly overdosed treatment.

The HCI-related problem with this machine was that the Therac-25 in some cases displayed system states incorrectly and showed just some error codes instead of full warning or error messages, and, moreover, these codes were not even well documented. As the result, the operator of the Therac-25 was not able to recognise a dangerous error situation and continued the treatment even after the machine showed warning messages, which did not look like a warning or a signal to stop the treatment. Together with very little training, this caused the operators not aware of the importance of keeping the safety guideline and as a result, they violated many of the safety guidelines. In some case, the operators conducted the treatment even when the video and audio monitoring, which were the only method to observe the patient in separated room, were not working. These accidents have shown that studying the human errors and their causation should be a significant part of software and system engineering at least in the case of safety-critical systems.

An appropriate system interface which allows a correct human computer interaction is just as important as correct, errorfree behaviour of the developed system: even if the system we develop behaves in an ideal correct way, this does not help much in the case the system interface is unclear to the user or is too complicated to be used in a proper way. According to statistics presented in (Dhillon, 2004), the human is responsible for 30% to 60% the total errors which directly or indirectly lead to the accidents, and in the case of aviation and traffic accidents, 80% to 90% of the errors were due to human. Thus, it is necessary to take human factors into account by developing safety-critical systems.

The fundamental goal of human factors engineering, as claimed in (Wickens, Hollands 2000), is to reduce errors, increase productivity and safety when the human interacts with a system. Engineering psychology applies psychological perspective to the problems of system design and focuses on the information-processing capacities of humans. The goals of formal methods are almost the same: to reduce errors, increase productivity and safety of the developed systems, however, the formal methods does not focus on the user of the system and the interface between the user and the system – they focus on the system itself, but only in very rare cases they take into account information-processing capacities of engineers.

In our approach *Human Factors of Formal Methods*, HF^2M, we focus on human factors in formal methods used within formal specification phase of a system development process (Feilkas et al., 2011; Feilkas et al., 2009): on (formal) requirements specification and on the developing of a system architecture that builds a bridge between requirements and the corresponding system.

The main ideas of the approach are language and framework independent, but for a better readability and for better understanding of these ideas we show them based on formal specification presented in the Focus (Broy & Stølen, 2001), a framework for formal specifications and development of interactive systems.[1] We can also see this methodology as an extension of the approach "Focus on Isabelle" (Spichkova, 2007) integrated into a seamless development process, which covers both specification and verification, starts from informal specification and finishes by the corresponding verified C code (Hölzl et al., 2010; Spichkova et al., 2012).

BACKGROUND

There are many applications of formal methods to analyse human computer interaction and to construct user interfaces, e.g., (Shackel & Richardson, 1991; Følstad et al., 2012), as well as a number of approaches on the integrating human interface engineering with software engineering, e.g., (Volpert, 1991; Heumann, 2002; Constantine, 2003), but the field of application of human factors to the analysis and to the optimization of *formal methods* area is still almost unexplored. To our best knowledge there are no other works on this field, the nearest area is only the application of human factors to the development of engineering tools, however, there are many achievements in the HCI research that could be applicable within the formal languages as well as verification and specification engineering tools, for example, the ideas of the usage-centered approach for presentation and interaction design of software and Web-based applications were introduced in (Constantine & Lockwood, 1999; Constantine & Lockwood, 2002).

Speaking of any kind of science and research, one can say that a lot of new ideas are just well forgotten old ones, and a lot of newly developed methodologies are, in fact, the reinvention of the wheel. Leaving the research results solely in the area they are introduced, or just forgetting them does not have any benefit, vice versa, application of old ideas on a new field brings them to a new level and gives them new power to improve safety or, even more general, living standards.

Unfortunately, we should acknowledge that dealing with formal methods often assumes that only two factors must be satisfied: the method must be sound and give such a representation, which is concise and beautiful just from the mathematical point of view, without taking into account any question of readability, usability, or tool support. This leads to the fact that formal methods are treated by most engineers as "something that is theoretically important but practically too hard to understand and to use", and, moreover, the term "formal" is for many people just some kind of synonym for "unreadable", however, even small syntactical changes of a formal method can make it more understandable and usable for an average engineer.

Looking on the matter from a different standpoint, we can see that most of programming languages have a formal background, even if this is not mentioned to programmers and engineers explicitly. For example, the Structured Query Language (SQL) is nowadays a standard for managing data in relational database management systems, however it is originally based upon relational algebra and relational calculus – this side of the programming language is generally unimportant to the SQL-programmers, being an important feature for the developers of the language itself.

Using natural languages, e.g., English, to specify a system we profit by their flexibility and power, we do not have any special learning efforts, because we can write the specification directly, without encoding. These advantages sounds very attractive, but considering a specification of a safety-critical system, their all are exceeded by the disadvantage that a natural language is ambiguous, vague, and imprecise. A formal language, even if it requires an initial learning effort and uses a notation unfamiliar to an average engineer, is unambiguous and precise, and, moreover, due a predefined syntax and semantics a formal language is machine processible, i.e. using such a specification we could do some development steps (semi-)automatically.

Because of this image of formal methods, some approaches try to cover the fact they have formal background and "simulate" the appearances of informal representation to look user-friendly. In some cases it implies that the approach becomes semiformal or introduces extra specification ambiguity. For example, controlled natural languages (CNL) try to avoid disadvantages of both natural and formal languages and being a subset of a natural language have a well-defined syntax and semantics (Macias & Pulman,1993; Fuchs & Schwitter,1995). Their syntax is unambiguous, but engineers can interpret the semantics of some sentences in wrong way just because the language looks like a natural one and this gives a feeling it can be also used according to all rules of the natural language, i.e. the restriction can be ignored through lack of attention which is "provoked" by the visual similarity to the natural language.

A famous example of the misinterpretation is the sentence "I see the girl with the telescope". In English, this sentence allows not only the interpretation "I see the girl via the telescope" but also the interpretation "I see the girl which has a telescope". Which one should be correct in the case of CNL? If we want to have an unambiguous syntax, we should take a choice. E.g., in Attempto Controlled English (Kuhn, 2010; Fuchs & Schwitter, 2007) only the first interpretation is allowed, but reading such a specification it is very easy to forget this rule. Moreover, looking at the specification in controlled language, an engineer can consider that he does not need to know *any* rules, because he *consider* he can understand the specification without spending time on any additional training, whereas he misunderstand it.

Specifying safety-critical systems, it is not enough to use controlled languages and semiformal languages – the precise formal specification is essential to ensure that the safety properties of the system really hold. Speaking about human factors according to the safety-critical systems we focus mostly on technical aspects; this idea, applied to the formal methods, is often called *Engineering Error Paradigm* (Redmill & Rajan, 1997). Human factors that are targeted by the Engineering Error Paradigm typically include the design of HCI as well as the corresponding automatization: by this paradigm humans are seen as they are almost equivalent to software and hardware components in the sense of operation with data and other components, but at the same time humans are seen as "the most unreliable component" of the total system. This implies also that designing humans out of the main system actions through automatization of some system design steps is considered as a proposal for reducing risk. In the case of design of safety-critical systems, this means automatic translation from one representation kind to another one, e.g., between two formal languages or between two internal representation within some tools.

Another important view of the Engineering Error Paradigm is that human errors often occur as a result of mismatch in HCI and overestimation of physical capabilities of a person. With other words, human performance and reliability need to be considered in the design process (Klare, 2000); in our case, we have to focus on clearness – up to obviousness – and readability of formal specifications. For these reasons we have to analyse the achievements of HCI approaches to apply their ideas on another kind of HCI – interface between (verification, software) engineer and the applied formal method or tool. *The Individual Error Paradigm* (Redmill & Rajan, 1997) focuses on understanding the reasons why people make mistakes or commit unsafe acts, and then tries to eliminate those reasons. The same idea should be applied to analyse the syntax of a formal method: Which kind of specification mistakes and misreading is prevailing? How can we prevent them? Can we do it automatically or, at least, semi-automatically?

HUMAN FACTORS + FORMAL METHODS = HF²M

One of the common mistakes by writing a system specification, particularly writing a requirement specification, is the omission of assumptions about the system's environment. The concentration on the question *"What we want our system can do?"* is very natural, but it leads to the point that the question *"Under which constraints the correct work of the system can be ensured?"* is ignored, however, the answer to this question gives us a crucial property of the system. To make this kind of mistake is even easier if we have additional efforts through concentration on a formal syntax, but it is also even more disappointing in this case, after devoting much effort in the precise and unambiguous specification. However, the solution to this problem can be really simple and uses the same principle as enriching an email client by an alert like "The attachment keyword is found. Do you want to add the attachment now or should we remind you later?"

Specifying a system formally we should have special alerts that remind us to cover this part of the system description. In the case of the Focus specification language this means to restrict all the specification styles (both textual and graphical) to the variants using the Assumption/Guarantee representation, where a component is specified in terms of an assumption and a guarantee: whenever input from the environment behaves in accordance with the assumption, the specified component is required to fulfil the guarantee. Thus, it will be impossible to overlook the question about the necessary properties of the environment, and if the system does not have any constraints under which it provides the correct functionality, the corresponding field of the specification should be filled out by the constraint "true" representing the property that the system should work correctly in any environment. The probability that an engineer signs this property without checking the corresponding system constraints is much smaller than in the case the engineer do not get any reminder to check these constraints.

As mentioned in our previous work (Spichkova, 2007), during requirements specification phase and the phase of a system architecture development we need to care about later phases (modelling, simulation, testing, formal verification, implementation) already doing the formal or, even, semiformal specification of a system – that is, choosing an appropriate abstraction and modelling technique. A crucial question is here how we can optimize the formal representation and formal methods with respect to human factors. In our approach we focus on the following aspects:

- Representation of the formal specification in more readable way, optimisation of the specification layout/formatting.
- Unification of the representation of different specification views and artefacts by using an integrated specification language.
- Automatization of several aspects of the specification and verification process.

Let discuss these issues in more detail.

Layout/Formatting of a Formal Specification

The main aspect of HF²M is the representation, i.e. layout/formatting and visualization including graphical representation, of formal specification.

The first results of visual optimization of specifications are presented in (Spichkova, 2011b). That work covers all specification styles of the Focus framework – from textual to graphical representation, also covering on the timing aspects of the specification. The notion of time takes central stage for many kinds of safety-critical systems, especially in the case of embedded real-time ones: abstracting from the timing aspects we may lose the core properties of a system we represent, e.g. the causality property. To help an engineer to concentrate on the timing properties of the system to be specified and verified, we introduced so-called timed state transition diagrams (TSTDs). Specifying system behaviour by TSTD we can use three specification styles: classical diagram (automaton), table and also textual style. Inter alia, we suggest to simplify the timed specification in the way to get shorter specifications that are more readable and clear: specifying a component we have often such a case where for some time intervals both conditions hold: local variables are still unchanged and there is no output. This can occur, e.g., if at this time interval the component gets no input or if some preconditions don't hold. In classical Focus, as well as in Isabelle/HOL, we need to specify such cases explicitly otherwise we get an underspecified component that has no information how to act in these cases.

In many cases even not very complicated optimization changes of a specification method can make it more understandable and usable. Moreover, taking into account the Individual Error Paradigm, we can extend specification templates in order to get not only more readable, but also more correct specification, e.g. by introducing an obligatory assumption-part of the specification.

The simplest optimization steps are often overlooked just because of their obviousness, and it would be wrong to ignore the possibility to optimize the language without much effort. For example, simply adding an enumeration to the formulas in a large formal specification as well as extending the specification template by general rules makes its validation on the level of specification and discussion with co-operating experts much easier.

Figure 1 presents an example of this kind of optimisation. The first (basic) specification layout leads to the situation where even a very short specification is hardly readable. In the example we have a specification which guarantee-part consists of just six properties, where even in middle-size case studies an average size of the guarantee-part is at least thirty properties; it is easy to imagine how unreadable could be a large formal specification written using this kind of layout. The second specification has only tiny modifications in formatting vs. the first one, but even adding empty lines between properties of different kind makes the guarantee-part of the specification more readable. In the third specification we number all properties in the guarantee-part with the aim not only to improve the readability but also to make the discussion of the specification more concrete and free of misunderstandings.

1. Basic specification layout.
2. Specification layout with tiny optimizations.
3. Optimized specification layout.

In the HF^{2}M approach, we see a formal specification as a ground to the discussion of the system properties, requirements, and structure, therefore the specification itself plays here a role of an interface between engineers of different disciplines (e.g., software and electrical engineers) and dealing with requirements, system, software, architecture, verification and many other aspects of the development. Thus, applying one of the basic design rules to a formal specification we get very similar results as in the case of development of webpages, interfaces, newspapers, etc. because of the nature of the problem that we are aiming to solve: problems in the information representation are very similar in any area, and the solutions from one area could be adopted to another one.

Figure 1. Comparing different specifications layouts

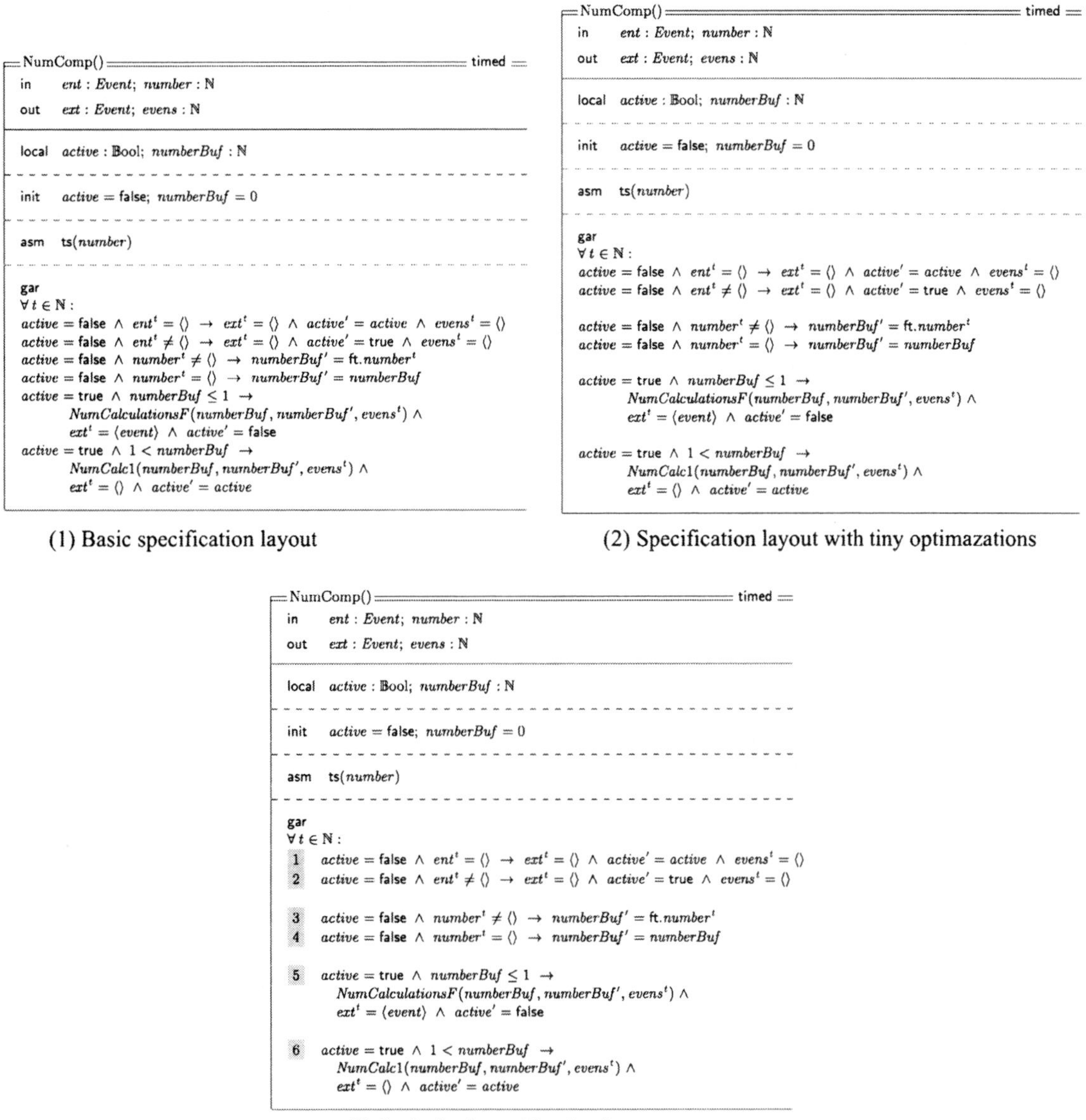

NumComp() timed

in $ent : Event;\ number : \mathbb{N}$

out $ext : Event;\ evens : \mathbb{N}$

local $active : \mathbb{B}ool;\ numberBuf : \mathbb{N}$

init $active = \mathsf{false};\ numberBuf = 0$

asm $\mathsf{ts}(number)$

gar

$\forall t \in \mathbb{N}:$

$active = \mathsf{false} \wedge ent^t = \langle\rangle \rightarrow ext^t = \langle\rangle \wedge active' = active \wedge evens^t = \langle\rangle$

$active = \mathsf{false} \wedge ent^t \neq \langle\rangle \rightarrow ext^t = \langle\rangle \wedge active' = \mathsf{true} \wedge evens^t = \langle\rangle$

$active = \mathsf{false} \wedge number^t \neq \langle\rangle \rightarrow numberBuf' = \mathsf{ft}.number^t$

$active = \mathsf{false} \wedge number^t = \langle\rangle \rightarrow numberBuf' = numberBuf$

$active = \mathsf{true} \wedge numberBuf \leq 1 \rightarrow$
$NumCalculationsF(numberBuf, numberBuf', evens^t) \wedge$
$ext^t = \langle event\rangle \wedge active' = \mathsf{false}$

$active = \mathsf{true} \wedge 1 < numberBuf \rightarrow$
$NumCalc1(numberBuf, numberBuf', evens^t) \wedge$
$ext^t = \langle\rangle \wedge active' = active$

(1) Basic specification layout

NumComp() timed

in $ent : Event;\ number : \mathbb{N}$

out $ext : Event;\ evens : \mathbb{N}$

local $active : \mathbb{B}ool;\ numberBuf : \mathbb{N}$

init $active = \mathsf{false};\ numberBuf = 0$

asm $\mathsf{ts}(number)$

gar

$\forall t \in \mathbb{N}:$

$active = \mathsf{false} \wedge ent^t = \langle\rangle \rightarrow ext^t = \langle\rangle \wedge active' = active \wedge evens^t = \langle\rangle$
$active = \mathsf{false} \wedge ent^t \neq \langle\rangle \rightarrow ext^t = \langle\rangle \wedge active' = \mathsf{true} \wedge evens^t = \langle\rangle$

$active = \mathsf{false} \wedge number^t \neq \langle\rangle \rightarrow numberBuf' = \mathsf{ft}.number^t$
$active = \mathsf{false} \wedge number^t = \langle\rangle \rightarrow numberBuf' = numberBuf$

$active = \mathsf{true} \wedge numberBuf \leq 1 \rightarrow$
$NumCalculationsF(numberBuf, numberBuf', evens^t) \wedge$
$ext^t = \langle event\rangle \wedge active' = \mathsf{false}$

$active = \mathsf{true} \wedge 1 < numberBuf \rightarrow$
$NumCalc1(numberBuf, numberBuf', evens^t) \wedge$
$ext^t = \langle\rangle \wedge active' = active$

(2) Specification layout with tiny optimazations

NumComp() timed

in $ent : Event;\ number : \mathbb{N}$

out $ext : Event;\ evens : \mathbb{N}$

local $active : \mathbb{B}ool;\ numberBuf : \mathbb{N}$

init $active = \mathsf{false};\ numberBuf = 0$

asm $\mathsf{ts}(number)$

gar

$\forall t \in \mathbb{N}:$

1 $active = \mathsf{false} \wedge ent^t = \langle\rangle \rightarrow ext^t = \langle\rangle \wedge active' = active \wedge evens^t = \langle\rangle$
2 $active = \mathsf{false} \wedge ent^t \neq \langle\rangle \rightarrow ext^t = \langle\rangle \wedge active' = \mathsf{true} \wedge evens^t = \langle\rangle$

3 $active = \mathsf{false} \wedge number^t \neq \langle\rangle \rightarrow numberBuf' = \mathsf{ft}.number^t$
4 $active = \mathsf{false} \wedge number^t = \langle\rangle \rightarrow numberBuf' = numberBuf$

5 $active = \mathsf{true} \wedge numberBuf \leq 1 \rightarrow$
$NumCalculationsF(numberBuf, numberBuf', evens^t) \wedge$
$ext^t = \langle event\rangle \wedge active' = \mathsf{false}$

6 $active = \mathsf{true} \wedge 1 < numberBuf \rightarrow$
$NumCalc1(numberBuf, numberBuf', evens^t) \wedge$
$ext^t = \langle\rangle \wedge active' = active$

(3) Optimized specification layout

Unification of the Representation

Another point, which is seen as obvious if we are speaking about interfaces and interaction, is the unification of the representation of any information we are dealing with (cf. also Figure 2). Specifying components and system in a formal language is helpful to have a possibility to change the view on the system or the kind of its description to cover several problem areas by a single specification language: this helps to simplify representation of different views on a system as well as to switch between them. However, it does not make any sense to extend the core of a (formal) language/ framework, because this can decrease readability of a specification – an overflow of additional information, which is not really needed to specify a concrete system on a concrete level, can distract from the important properties and aspects. Thus, we need another solution of this problem. Instead of the reinvention of existing approaches, it is more sufficient to reuse within the formal methods some successful ideas from other areas. Analysing the similar problems within general software engineering, we can see that one of the effective ways is an extension of the core framework by a number of several add-ons covering different application areas and different functionality. According to this idea, we made the following "add-ons like" extension of the Focus formal language:

- Specification of processes and matching to the representation of components.
- Specification of security-critical systems with respect to secrecy properties.

Specifying systems in a formal language, we often need to present not only components but also processes within the system. Even if the common practice to describe system parts is to use a component view, the representation of system processes becomes more and more important: nowadays the process view and the data flow representation are a typical part of the development of interactive or reactive systems. Specifying both components and processes within the same language, without changing the framework, we not only increase the readability of a system specification but also can easier ensure consistency among these different views on a system: this extension of the language functionality allows us to have more precise and at the same time more flexible representation of the system.

For these reasons we extend the formal language Focus by the theory of processes described in (Leuxner, 2010). A process is understood there as "an observable activity executed by one or several actors, which might be persons, components, technical systems, or combinations thereof". Each process has one *entry (activation, start) point* and one *exit (end) point*. An entry point is a special kind of input signal/channel that activates the process, while an exit point is a special kind of output signal/channel that is used to indicate that the process is finished. We treat a process as a special kind of a Focus component having additionally two channels (one input and one output channel) of a special kind. These channels represent the entry and exit points of the process.

Dealing with *security-critical systems* we have another question in the foreground: how we can combine system components that each enforce a particular security requirement in a way that allows us to predict which properties the combined system will have (Apostolopoulos et al., 1999). Formal verification of software systems and es-

Figure 2. Unification of the information representation on the level of languages

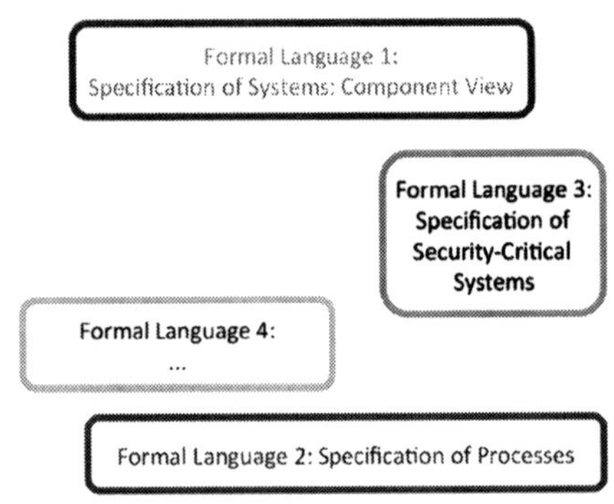

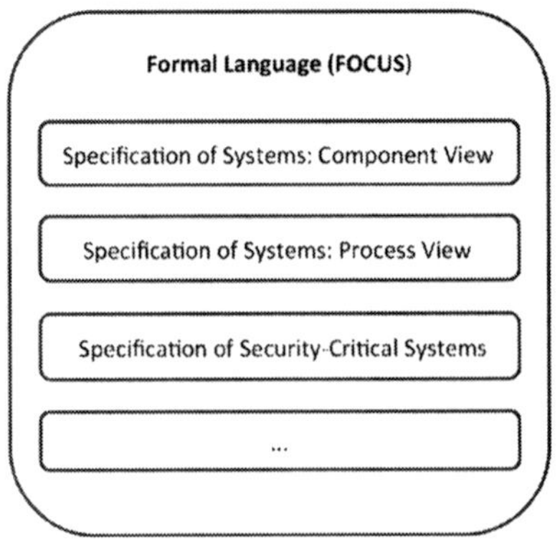

pecially reasoning about compositional properties is a challenge in particular important in the area of security-critical systems: combining system components which have a number of security/secrecy properties, the most important and the most difficult question is to predict which of these properties the composed system will have. For this purpose we introduced in (Spichkova, 2012) a representation methodology for crypto-based software, such as cryptographic protocols, and their composition properties. Having such a formal representation, one can argue about the protocol properties as well as the composition properties of different cryptographic protocols in a methodological way and make a formal proof of them using a theorem prover.

Using these extensions, on the one hand, we do not need to switch between languages, the representation is unified to make the communication between different development team easier and the accurate specifications of different system's parts more understandable, on the other hand, if, for example, the representation of cryptographic properties is irrelevant for the system we specify and verify, the engineer do not need to study the aspects of the formal language related to the security-critical systems. Extending the formal language in the add-ons manner we increase the specifications' readability without the rapid increase of learning effort required by the formal language.

Automatization

Last but not least point in of HF^{2}M is an appropriate automatization of a number of steps within the specification and verification process, because the automatization not only saves time but also excludes (at least partially) the human element as the most "unreliable" in failure, according to the *Engineering Error Paradigm* (Redmill & Rajan, 1997). As the next step of or research, we are currently proving all the theoretical ideas of HF^{2}M practically, using the AutoFocus CASE tool.

AutoFocus is a scientific prototype[2] implementing on top of the Eclipse platform[3] a modelling language based on a graphical notation. This prototype uses a restricted version of the formal semantics of the Focus specification and modelling language (Schätz, 2004; Schätz & Huber, 1999; Huber et al., 1996). Specifying a system in AutoFocus, we obtain an executable mode, which can be validated by means of the AutoFocus simulator to get a first impression of the system under development and possibly find implementation errors that we introduced during the transformation of the requirements into an AutoFocus model.

The following extensions of the AutoFocus CASE tool are in progress (Spichkova et al., 2013): the add-ons that allow

- To generate formal Focus specification from the CASE tool representation.
- To edit in the user-friendly[4] way a (generated) Focus specification represented in LaTeX.
- To write a specification using the predefined templates.

The Focus generator produces a specification of the model by representing the formal specification in LaTeX according to the predefined templates restricting all specification styles to the Assumption/Guarantee variant to exclude the loss of the constrains on the system's environment. Using this generator we can, on the one hand, get a readable formal specification developed according the suggested optimisations, on the other hand, apply the HCI development methods within the common application area, development of the tools, focusing this time on the formal methods are „hidden" by the modelling tool.

Even a readable formal specification is hard to keep up to date if the system model is frequently changing during the modelling phase of the development. This causes the situation where the system documentation is often outdate and does not describe the latest version of the system: system requirements documents and the general systems description are not updated according to the system's or model's modifications, sometimes because this update is overseen, sometimes on purpose, because of the timing or costs constraints on the project. This problem could be also be solved by using this add-on: we simply generate new (updated) formal specification from the model. The current version of the editor inherits the most of the functions an open source plugin TeXlipse[5] (e.g., the syntax check of the specification as well as syntax highlighting, code folding, etc.), and is extended by additional features such as

- Focus operators as well as the main Focus frames: component and function specification.
- Several specification tables.
- Predefined data types and streams.
- Tool box for the predefined Focus operators, which allows a quick access to the most important features of the formal language.

This add-on is oriented on the features of the Focus language, but it does not require any special sophisticated knowledge, and this point leads us to the next step of our research: how can we represent the element of formal language in such a way that the language learning effort is minimized.

FUTURE RESEARCH DIRECTIONS

As mentioned in the previous section, one of the future research directions is to investigate the possibilities of formal language optimization in order not only to increase the readability of the specification, but also to minimize the learning effort needed to be fluent using the formal language.

Another interesting direction is the tool-support of the methodology "Focus on Isabelle" (Spichkova, 2007). This methodology allows verifying properties of the system using the semi-automatical theorem prover Isabelle/HOL. Using "Focus on Isabelle" we can influence the complexity of proofs and their reusability already during the specification phase, because the specification and verification/validation methodologies are treated here as a single joint methodology with the main focus on the specification part. Moreover, using it we can perform automatic correctness proofs of syntactic interfaces for specified system components. Having an automatic translation of formal specifications from Focus to Isabelle/HOL we can apply the methodology not only in theory but also in practice.

CONCLUSION

In our work "Human Factors of Formal Methods" we aim to apply the engineering psychology achievements to the design of formal methods, focusing on the specification phase of a system development process. The main ideas discussed in this chapter are language independent, but for better readability and for better understanding of these ideas we show them on the base of formal specifications presented in the Focus specification framework.

According to the Engineering Error Paradigm we optimize representation of formal specification, which corresponds to the classical HCI design, as well as add a corresponding automatization of a number specification and verification steps of system design. This approach demonstrates that even small changes within a formal method can make it much more understandable, usable, and also safe. Moreover, in many cases it is sufficient to reuse within the formal methods some successful ideas from other areas where the similar representation or design problems were already solved.

REFERENCES

Apostolopoulos, G., Peris, V., & Saha, D. (1999). Transport layer security: How much does it really cost? In *Proceedings of the Conf. on Computer Communications (IEEE Infocom)*. IEEE Computer Society.

Broy, M., & Stølen, K. (2001). *Specification and development of interactive systems: Focus on streams, interfaces, and refinement*. Berlin: Springer. doi:10.1007/978-1-4613-0091-5.

Constantine, L. (2003). Canonical abstract prototypes for abstract visual and interaction design. In *Proceedings of Interactive Systems: Design, Specification, and Verification* (Vol. 2844). Berlin: Springer. doi:10.1007/978-3-540-39929-2_1.

Constantine, L. L., & Lockwood, L. A. D. (1999). *Software for use: A practical guide to the models and methods of usage-centered design*. Reading, MA: Addison-Wesley.

Constantine, L. L., & Lockwood, L. A. D. (2002). Usage-centered engineering for web applications. In *Proceedings of IEEE Software*. IEEE.

Dhillon, B. (2004). *Engineering usability: Fundamentals, applications, human factors, and human error*. American Scientific Publishers.

Feilkas, M., Hölzl, F., Pfaller, C., Rittmann, S., Schätz, B., Schwitzer, W., et al. (2011). *A refined top-down methodology for the development of automotive software systems – The keylessentry system case study* (Technical Report TUM-I1103). Munich, Germany: TU München.

Feilkas, M., Fleischmann, A., Hölzl, F., Pfaller, C., Scheidemann, K., Spichkova, M., & Trachtenherz, D. (2009). *A top-down methodology for the development of automotive software* (Technical Report TUM-I0902). Munich, Germany: TU München.

Følstad, A., Law, E., & Hornbæk, K. (2012). Analysis in practical usability evaluation: A survey study. In *Proceedings of the SIGCHI Conference on Human Factors in Computing Systems*. ACM.

Fuchs, E. N., & Schwitter, R. (1995). Specifying logic programs in controlled natural language. In *Proceedings CLNLP 95, ELSNET/COMPULOG-NET/EAGLES Workshop on Computational Logic for Natural Language Processing*. Edinburgh, UK: University of Edinburgh.

Fuchs, E. N., & Schwitter, R. (2007). Web-annotations for humans and machines. In *Proceedings of the 4th European Semantic Web Conference (ESWC 2007)*, (LNCS). Berlin: Springer.

Heumann, J. (2002). Use cases, usability requirements, and user interfaces. In *Proceedings of Object-Oriented Programming, Systems, Languages, and Applications (OOPSLA 2002)*. ACM.

Huber, F., Schätz, B., Schmidt, A., & Spies, K. (1996). AutoFocus - A tool for distributed systems specification. In *Proceedings of of FTRTFT'96, (LNCS)* (Vol. 1135). Berlin: Springer.

Hölzl, F., & Spichkova, M. & Trachtenherz. D. (2010). *Safety-critical system development methodology* (Technical Report TUM-I1020). Munich, Germany: TU München.

Klare, G. R. (2000). Readable computer documentation. *ACM Journal of Computer Documentation, 24*(3), 148–168. doi:10.1145/344599.344645.

Kuhn, T. (2010). *Controlled English for knowledge representation*. (PhD Thesis). University of Zurich, Zurich, Switzerland.

Leuxner, C., Sitou, W., & Spanfelner, B. (2010). A formal model for work flows. In *Proceedings of the 8th IEEE International Conference on Software Engineering and Formal Method* (pp. 135–144). IEEE.

Leveson, N. G., & Turner, C. S. (1993). An investigation of the therac-25 accidents. *IEEE Computer*, *26*(7), 18–41. doi:10.1109/MC.1993.274940.

Macias, B., & Pulman, S. (1993). Natural language processing for requirements specifications. In F. Redmill, & T. Anderson (Eds.), *Safety-Critical Systems, Current Issues, Techniques and Standards*. London: Chapman & Hall.

Miller, E. (1987). The therac-25 experience. In *Proceedings of the Conf. State Radiation Control Program Directors*. IEEE.

Redmill, F., & Rajan, J. (1997). *Human factors in safety-critical systems*. London: Butterworth-Heinemann.

Schätz, B. (2004). Mastering the complexity of reactive systems: The AUTOFOCUS approach. In *Formal Methods for Embedded Distributed Systems: How to Master the Complexity* (pp. 215–258). Boston: Kluwer Academic Publishers. doi:10.1007/1-4020-7997-4_7.

Shackel, B., & Richardson, S. J. (1991). *Human factors for informatics usability*. Cambridge, UK: Cambridge University Press.

Spichkova, M. (2007). *Specification and seamless verification of embedded real-time systems: Focus on isabelle*. (PhD Thesis). Munich, Germany: TU München.

Spichkova, M. (2011). Architecture: Requirements + decomposition + refinement. *Softwaretechnik-Trends, 32*(4).

Spichkova, M. (2011). *Focus on processes* (Technical Report TUM-I1115). Munich, Germany: TU München.

Spichkova, M. (2012). *Component composition: Formal specification and verification of cryptographic properties* (Technical Report TUM-I124). Munich, Germany: TU München.

Spichkova, M., Hölzl, F., & Trachtenherz, D. (2012). Verified system development with the autofocus tool chain. In *Proceedings of the 2nd Workshop on Formal Methods in the Development of Software (WS-FMDS)*. WS-FMDS.

Spichkova, M., Zhu, X., & Mou, D. (2013). Do we really need to write documentation for a system? CASE tool add-ons: Generator+editor for a precise documentation. In *Proceedings of the International Conference on Model-Driven Engineering and Software Development (MODELSWARD'13)*. MODELSWARD.

Volpert, W. (1991). Work design for human development. In C. Floyd et al. (Eds.), *Software Development and Reality Construction*. Berlin: Springer-Verlag.

Wickens, C. D., & Hollands, J. G. (2000). *Engineering psychology and human performance*. Englewood Cliffs, NJ: Prentice Hall.

ADDITIONAL READING

Abrial, J.-R. (1996). *The b-book: Assigning programs to meanings*. Cambridge, UK: Cambridge University Press. doi:10.1017/CBO9780511624162.

Broy, M. (1991). Towards a formal foundation of the specification and description language SDL. *Formal Aspects of Computing*, *3*(1), 21–57. doi:10.1007/BF01211434.

Broy, M., Fox, J., Hölzl, F., Koss, D., Kuhrmann, M., Meisinger, M., & Wild, D. (2007). Service-oriented modeling CoCoME with focus/autofocus. In *The Common Component Modeling Example: Comparing Software Component Models (LNCS)* (Vol. 5153, pp. 177–206). Berlin: Springer. doi:10.1007/978-3-540-85289-6_8.

Bauer, V., Broy, M., Irlbeck, M., Leuxner, C., Spichkova, M., Dahlweid, M., & Santen, T. (2013). *Survey of modeling and engineering aspects of self-adapting & self-optimizing systems* (Technical Report TUM-I130307). Munich, Germany: TU München.

Campetelli, A., Hölzl, F., & Neubeck, P. (2011). User-friendly model checking integration in model-based development. In *Proceedings of International Conference on Computer Applications in Industry and Engineering*. IEEE.

Dekker, S. (2006). *The field guide to understanding human error* (2nd ed.). Lund, Sweden: Lund University School of Aviation.

Dekker, S. (2011). *Drift into failure*. London: Ashgate.

DeMarco, T. (1979). *Structured analysis and system specification*. Englewood Cliffs, NJ: Prentice Hall.

Dhillon, B. S. (2009). *Human reliability, error, and human factors in engineering maintenance: with reference to aviation and power generation*. Boca Raton, FL: CRC Press. doi:10.1201/9781439803844.

Dhillon, B. S. (2012). *Safety and human error in engineering systems*. Boca Raton, FL: CRC Press. doi:10.1201/b12534.

Fuchs, N. E., & Schwertel, U. (2003). Reasoning in attempt to controlled English. In F. Bry, N. Henze, & J. Maluszynski (Eds.), *Principles and Practice of Semantic Web Reasoning, International Workshop PPSWR* (LNCS), (Vol. 2901). Berlin: Springer.

Kaljurand, K. (2009). Paraphrasing controlled english texts. In *Proceedings of the CEUR Workshop*. CEUR.

Klein, C., Prehofer, C., & Rumpe, B. (1997). Feature specification and refinement with state transition diagrams. In P. Dini (Ed.), *Fourth IEEE Workshop on Feature Interactions in Telecommunications Networks and Distributed Systems*. Boca Raton, FL: IOS-Press.

Kuhn, T. Royer, L., Fuchs, N. E., & Schroeder, M. (2006). Improving text mining with controlled natural language: A case study for protein interactions. In U. Leser, B. Eckman, & F. Naumann (Eds.), *Proceedings of the 3rd International Workshop on Data Integration in the Life Sciences 2006 (DILS'06)*, (LNBI). Berlin: Springer.

Kuhn, T. (2010). Codeco: A grammar notation for controlled natural language in predictive editors. In *Proceedings CEUR Workshop*. CEUR.

Kuhn, T. (2013). A principled approach to grammars for controlled natural languages and predictive editors. *Journal of Logic Language and Information*, *22*(1). doi:10.1007/s10849-012-9167-z.

Morgan, C. (1994). *Programming from specifications*. Englewood Cliffs, NJ: Prentice Hall.

Mosses, P. D. (1997). CoFI: The common framework initiative for algebraic specification and development. In M. Bidoit & M. Dauchet (Eds.), *Theory and Practice of Software Development (TAPSOFT '97), 7th International Jiont Conference CAAP/FASE* (LNCS), (Vol. 1214). Berlin: Springer.

Potter, B., Sinclair, J., & Till, D. (1996). *An introduction to formal specification and Z*. Englewood Cliffs, NJ: Prentice Hall.

Ratiu, D. (2009). *Intentional meaning of programs*. (PhD Thesis). Munich, Germany: TU München.

Schätz, B., & Giese, H. (2007). Models of reactive systems: communication, concurrency, and causality. In H. Giese, G. Karsai, E. Lee, B. Rumpe, & B. Schätz (Eds.), *Proceedings of the 2007 International Dagstuhl conference on Model-based engineering of embedded real-time systems (MBEERTS'07)*. Berlin: Springer.

Schätz, B. (2011). 10 years model-driven - What did we achieve? In *Proceedings of the 2011 Second Eastern European Regional Conference on the Engineering of Computer Based Systems* (ECBS-EERC '11). IEEE Computer Society.

Schwitter, R. (1998). *Kontrolliertes Englisch für anforderungsspezifikationen*. (PhD thesis). University of Zurich, Zurich, Switzerland.

Spichkova, M. (2012). Towards focus on time. In *Proceedings of the 12th International Workshop on Automated Verification of Critical Systems (AVoCS'12)*. AVoCS.

Spichkova, M. (Ed.). (2012). *Seminar: Human factors in software engineering* (Technical Report TUM-I1216). Munich, Germany: TU München.

Spivey, M. (1988). *Understanding Z: A specification language and its formal semantics*. Cambridge, UK: Cambridge University Press.

KEY TERMS AND DEFINITIONS

Controlled Natural Language (CNL): A subsets of a natural language, obtained by restricting its grammar and vocabulary in order to eliminate (or, at least, to reduce) ambiguity and complexity of the specification written in this language.

Engineering Error Paradigm: A particular kind of Human Error Paradigms, which focuses on the technical aspect of the system and interact between the human factor and the system. This paradigm sees the human factor as one part of the system.

Focus on Isabelle: A specification and verification framework, which is the result of the coupling of the formal specification framework Focus in the generic theorem prover Isabelle/HOL.

Formal Method: A particular kind of techniques (based on logic and mathematics) for the specification, development and verification of software and hardware systems.

Human Computer Interface (HCI): An interface between a user and a (software and/or hardware) system.

Readability: The ease in which text can be read and understood without ambiguity and misinterpretation.

Safety-Critical System: A system which failure could result in loss of human life or damage to the environment or valuable objects.

Specification: A system's description representing the set of requirements to be satisfied by the system.

ENDNOTES

1 See http://focus.in.tum.de.

2 http://af3.fortiss.org

3 http://www.eclipse.org

4 A "user" means here a "software engineer".

5 http://texlipse.sourceforge.net

Chapter 16
Anticipation Dialogue Method in Participatory Design

Jari Laarni
VTT Technical Research Centre of Finland, Finland

Iina Aaltonen
VTT Technical Research Centre of Finland, Finland

ABSTRACT

In the design of complex information systems and social practices for different domains a balance between theory-driven and practice-driven approaches is at best developed in a collaborative communication process between designers, researchers, and other actors. The authors have developed the Anticipation Design Dialogue method within the context of participatory design, which is based on dialogic communication between different stakeholders. A dialogic relationship between them takes place in future workshops in which experiences of different stakeholders are integrated in a way that makes it possible to illustrate the situation from different perspectives. The workshop participants develop in small groups a vision of the future state in which the situation is imagined from the future perspective by considering which kind of problems they have at the moment and by which way the problems could be managed in the future. Secondly, reflective thinking is promoted by letting each group at the time present their ideas while others are listening. The authors have found that the development of mutual understanding between different stakeholders in these kinds of workshops is a complex process that needs time, and therefore, an iterative series of workshops is recommended.

BACKGROUND

Two trends have been identified in design practice that challenge the role of technical products as the only target of design work. Firstly, it has been widely acknowledged that we should pay more attention to social aspects of technologies so that we not only passively adapt to technological systems but focus more on how human activities can be supported by them. The aim is that technologies should be integrated into human activities and habits, and they should help us to participate in activities that are socially rewarding (Nardi & O'Day, 1999). A critical question is how technologies should be designed so that they can support the activities for which they are intended to. A common

DOI: 10.4018/978-1-4666-4623-0.ch016

answer is that participatory design methods are needed to explore people's motivations, desires, objectives and values (Buur & Matthews, 2008; Bødker et al., 2004 Muller et al., 2003). According to the principles of participatory design, we have to start the design process in the practice field of the users in order to identify the goals of their activity and the physical environment, the objects and the tools used in this activity (Bødker et al., 2004; Muller et al., 2003). Secondly, it has been widely realized that new technologies and products are not necessarily at all the answer to the many of the present day problems (e.g., Buur & Larsen, 2011). For example, according to the service design framework, it is even more important to shape behaviour of different stakeholders than to develop new technologies.

In this novel situation, the more acute task is thus to define the problems carefully than to create the perfect solution to a particular design task. It also has to be accepted that people's environments are continuously changing, and the design work is never completed. Since there is not one perfect solution, diversity of design solutions is preferred. In addition, emphasis is placed in the future in the design work, not on the past, and the aim is to move beyond people's current problems. A special task is to envision future work situations to allow the users to experience how emerging designs may affect their activities and to define how to get from the current situation to the desired situation, and consider consequences, alternatives and possible obstacles in the chosen path.

The big question is how to support this kind of co-creation process that involves different stakeholders in a collaborative framework. A quite common view in participatory design is that new ideas can only be emerged in negotiations between people with different intentions, and design work must be based on dialogues in which different stakeholders collaborate in order to obtain new understandings concerning a particular topic. Dialogue is a special kind of conversation in which each participant is willing to listen to the contributions of others and respond reflectively to each others' statements. In a dialogue, the aim is to achieve new insights and a new kind of understanding of the topic at hand, and therefore listening is typically more important than speaking. The final aim is to help us to understand better how other people see the topic and why they see it in a particular way. Real dialogue in design work is thus based on a two-way communication, in which all people have the same status; ideas are investigated in a dialogue framework, and their acceptance or rejection is based on discussions. This kind of approach requires that people really listen to each other, recognize agreements and disagreements and elaborate their own point of view. This is only possible in a communicative and collaborative environment in which the facilitator's role is important.

It is also suggested that in design work we have to foster people to envision the future and develop scenarios of the future. Future anticipation is thought to be some kind of mental testing in which we consider what will happen in the future and what the consequences of current actions would be. We perform anticipation all the time in our lives, and we normally are not consciously aware of doing it. Often we become aware of our anticipations when they are incorrect, and we have to make corrections to our visions.

There are different methods and approaches to explore the future in strategic planning and in design work. Some of these methods are quantitative, some of them are qualitative; some methods and approaches are expert-based, some others are participatory. Typical methods that are used in future anticipation are, among others, Delphi survey and scenario planning. These methods, however, have their limitations in terms of applying them in design studies and in participatory design. For example, they are typically not dialogic in nature, and they thus cannot be of any help in fostering dialogue between different stakeholders.

We have developed a workshop method that provides the grounds for interaction and co-operation, support the interplay between participants and provide tools for contextual/ecological design of product and services. The ecological framework aims at, among other things, identifying the activity and goal of activity of the user, identifying the physical surroundings and objects as well as the tools used in different activities, and analysing the affordances provided by the surroundings, and the digital system elements for the activity (Laarni et al., 2008).

OTHER VISIONING APPROACHES

The aim of the paper is to present our approach within the context of participatory design which is based on anticipation dialogues between different participant groups. Our approach is based on useful features of similar other approaches some of which are briefly described in the following.

Future workshop is a method for helping people to participate in the decision making process in workplaces. Future workshops were introduced in the 1960's, but the special technique was developed by Jungk and Müllert (1987) in order to foster different citizen groups to participate in the decision making processes of public planning authorities. Kensing (1991) applied the technique in the envisioning of information and communication technology (ICT) tools for future work situations. The technique includes a description of a problematic social situation, development of visions about the future and discussions how the visions can be realized (e.g., Kensing & Madsen, 1991). The work is divided into four main phases: In preparation phase of the method, its rules and the scheduled course of the workshop is introduced; in the critique phase, critical and thorough investigation of the problem is carried out; in the fantasy phase future possibilities are envisioned, and in the implementation phase they are realized. Another version of future workshops, proposed by Inayatullah (2006), is based on action research/learning and future studies traditions. The main aim has been to develop a method for questioning the future with the aim to transform organizations and society in large (see also Stevenson, 2002; 2006). Future workshop is some kind of "model example" of the future anticipation methods, against which other methods can be compared.

Work or dialogue conference is a dialogically structured joint activity fostering the emergence of new relationships between participants (e.g., Shotter & Gustavsen, 1999), and it is based on a set of orientating statements providing guidance and advice. The discussions are democratic, which means that all participants are considered equal, and possible rejections of arguments have to be based on careful consideration. This kind of dialogue should also be able to integrate diverse views, and it should promote decisions that provide starting points for joint action. The aim of the work and dialogue conferences is to provide a forum for facilitating collaboration among members, e.g., the different members of the labour market parties. Work conference has been used in the development of work practices in different domains, and it is not a design method as such, but its applicability to that purpose is worth to consider. Different forms of work conferences have been developed (e.g., Tavistock/Leicester conference, Tavistock working conference, search conference, and dialogue conference).

Anticipation dialogue is a set of methods to approach today's problems by developing solutions of the future (e.g., Arnkil, 2004). Participants are urged to envision the future and make reflections about future challenges and opportunities. They are, for example, asked to anticipate how things are if it is moved forward in time and things have gone well with the challenging situation the participants are just discussing. The participants are also asked to make thoughtful reflections how they moved from the current situation to the desired future situation. Different participant groups are involved, and dialogue is typically facilitated by a group placed between these groups. Anticipation dialogue-method has been used in the development of social services and in psychosocial work in general, and it has been successfully applied in different settings of psychosocial work, e.g., in crisis service and in child care consultations (Eriksson & Arnkil, 2009).

In prompted reflections freehand drawings are used to elicit potentials for new technology (Kensing, 1998). It includes the preparation stage in which freehand drawings are generated, workshops in which the drawings are explained and reflected, the analysis stage in which the produced documents are analyzed, and finally the discussion stage in which the results are discussed (Kensing, 1998). Prompted reflections are considered as a part of the MUST method which is quite similar to future workshop. The method has shown to be useful in the analysis of complex work domains and in generations of visions and reflections of the desired future.

In future technology workshop people envision and design the interactions between current and future technology and interaction through a series of structured workshop sessions (Vavoula & Sharpes, 2007). Vavoula and Sharpes presented a series of seven sessions in which the participants approached the design task from different perspectives. In these sessions participants generated visions of future activities that were related to the topic of the design task; generated prototypes of future usage contexts; played scenarios of use for the above-mentioned scenarios; modified the scenarios so that they could be realized by using present-day technologies; identified problems and challenges with implementing the scenarios; analyzed the differences between current and future technology and activity; and defined requirements for future technology (Vavoula & Sharpes, 2007). Vavoula and Sharpes have successfully tested the technique in several projects by using both children and adult participants.

It is characteristic to all these methods that there is a dialogue between designers, multiple voices are heard and accepted, and commitment to decisions is supported (Pulkkis & Ala-Laurinaho, 2007). There is also room for reflection and inner dialogue, in which the facilitator plays an important role. All of them emphasize future anticipation and future consciousness in design, including holistic reasoning, critical and reflective thinking and open-mindedness. The first three methods are mainly applied in social work and in the development of workplace; the latter two are mainly used in product design. Therefore, it seems to be that the first three methods are not very well suited to product and service design, whereas the latter two are not well suited for the development of social innovations.

DESCRIPTION OF THE ANTICIPATION DESIGN DIALOGUE METHOD

Our starting point has been that new meanings and innovative ideas emerge in conversations between participants of different social worlds (cf. Buur & Larsen, 2011). Comparing to the above-mentioned approaches, our method has some similarities with the fantasy phase of the future workshop method where the participants envision a future free of the previously identified problems, and with the anticipation dialogue method where participants are urged to anticipate the future in dialogic settings. Backcasting and recollecting the future is also a key element of the futures workshop approach developed by Inayatullah (2006).

Our primary aim has been to combine the useful features of the above-mentioned future anticipation methods. The key features of our method are:

- Presentation of (new) technological and social opportunities to aid the participants to imagine what might be possible in the future.
- Discussions in small groups aiming at developing a plan in which the actual state is imagined from the future perspective by considering, what problems there are at the

moment, and by which way the problems could be managed within a longer term perspective. Sometimes also freehand drawings are used to promote the development of new technical solutions (see Figure 1).
- Generate visions of preferred futures that foster hope among participants.
- Description of a migration path and identification of possible challenges and obstacles. The aim is to ask questions such as, how to get from the current situation to the desired situation, what kind of challenges can be expected along the way, and what alternative migration paths are available.
- Each group is allowed, one at the time, to present their ideas and views while others are listening which should promote reflective thinking. Listening is considered to be a prerequisite for real understanding the meaning of people's anticipations.
- Other participants have an opportunity to comment on the presented ideas.
- Generated visions are elaborated into scenarios that are discussed, e.g., with the different stakeholders of the client organization.

The aim of the proposed Anticipation Design Dialogue workshop is to facilitate dialogues between different stakeholders and encourage each participant to elaborate his/her own point of view. Due to a diversity of opinions, high tolerance for uncertainty is required. Participants' work is future-oriented, and the past and present worries are not emphasized.

The technique focusses on the idea generation, and it is therefore best suited for the first steps of the design process. The aim is to identify and conceptualize potential new technologies and services, and develop concepts and models that provide a foundation for more detailed design work. The aim is that the workshop should provide new innovative ideas on a particular topic and help people to reassess the way a particular topic is seen. What is the best possible outcome depends on how the results are used; it also depends on whether there is a series of workshops in which the topics can be elaborated stepwise.

We have trained people in our organization to apply this technique in their daily work with clients. Their feedback has been useful in further development of the method. There have also been discussions to enrich the Anticipation Design Dialogue method with other techniques that have been used at VTT to promote the design of complex socio-technical systems.

APPLICATION EXAMPLES

The method has been tested in several workshop sessions in different application areas ranging

Figure 1. Examples of illustrations generated in the workshops

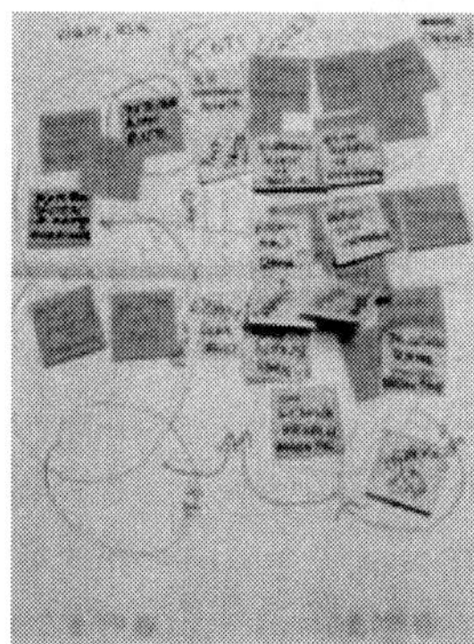

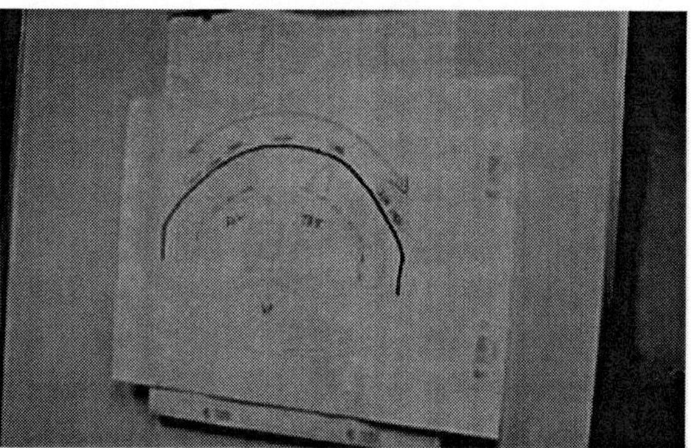

from ICT usage in judicial administration to the development of large-screen display design concept for nuclear power plant control rooms. In the following five examples of the application of the method are provided.

In the first three cases we have applied the technique for developing scenarios of the future; in the two more specific cases the aim has been to support the design of ICT tools for complex work systems. The results of the five applications of the technique are briefly evaluated according to originality, fluency and elaboration (see, e.g., van Vliet et al., 2012). Originality refers to the novelty, fluency to the number, and elaboration to the detailedness of the new ideas generated.

Enrichment of the Concept of Smart Environment

The first example describes a case where participants had to discuss what properties are important for a good smart environment. The workshop was conducted in a cross-disciplinary project, Ecological Design of Intelligent Environments (EASE), during 2005-2006 (Kaasinen & Norros, 2007). The purpose of the project was to investigate the design topics related to the smart environments and to provide some general guidelines for the design of smart environments in different application areas (Kaasinen & Norros, 2007). The aim was that the method could help the participants to enrich their conception of the basic term, and the dialogue was based on the hypotheses of the characteristics of smart environments that were developed by the research group (Pulkkis & Ala-Laurinaho, 2007). Five discussion groups were built, two consisted of representatives of the research group and three consisted of representatives of companies and other organizations. In order to support communication within a group and between groups, there were two pairs of groups, one member of each pair represented one kind of context and the other one another kind. Each of the two pair of groups discussed with each other while the other groups listened in turn, and the fifth group gathered material from discussions.

All the themes were presented to all participants, and they were presented in a question form. The schedule comprised the following questions: 1) what kind of activity is in question; 2) to whom the activity appears as smart; 3) what makes the environment smart; and 4) what kind of properties make the environment smart (Pulkkis & Ala-Laurinaho, 2007). The discussion proceeded as a dialogue between the two groups while the other groups concentrated on listening. The aim was that when a particular topic was expressed, the members of the other group could continue the discussion and express their own reflections on the topic. By this way each group's own ideas and experiences were prepared for discussion and reflection. (Pulkkis & Ala-Laurinaho, 2007).

The dialogue proceeded as planned, and a rich view of the common topic emerged that was based on people's reflections. Each partner examined and developed during the discussion their own view from the topic, and as a result the smart environment was defined both from technical and human point of view. Since the topic of the workshop was quite challenging, participants' elaborations were not very concrete, but some novel and original ideas were raised. As a result of the workshop the concept of smart environment was enriched, and its different aspects were identified and specified. The dialogue shows that the same target can be structured at the same time in different ways that do not rule out each other. (Pulkkis & Ala-Laurinaho, 2007). The results have been utilized in the refinement of our conceptual basis concerning the design of smart environments.

Future Perspectives in Indoor Space Usage

The goal of the iM-project is to develop visions of the indoor space usage in the future. As a result of the project, it will be possible to bring new insights and inspiration to indoor space design and use. Several workshops are conducted during 2012-2013, some of which have already been undertaken. In one of these workshops, experienced researchers and other professionals participated in the Anticipation Dialogue Workshop. The participants were divided into three groups presenting three different environments, Home (living environment), Service (service environment) and Work (work environment). They had to imagine that it is the year 2023, and all the main challenges concerning their environment have been resolved. Their task was to imagine what this desired future would look like, and they had to concentrate on ordinary everyday things and not describe technologies that would make this future possible. After that, they had to describe their future vision to other participants who were allowed to comment the presented visions. In the next phase of the workshop, the participants had to think about what has made this desirable future possible and what has happened in the last ten years in order for this desirable state to be achieved. Once again, they had to present their visions to other participants which had a possibility to present comments to the vision. At the third phase, the participants had to get familiar with trend slides presenting futures challenges and opportunities, and their task was to select those slides that are important in the accomplishment of their vision and sort them out according to their importance.

Lively discussions were held on the desirable futures, and that was the most promising contribution of the workshop to the project. It was found that there were large differences between groups in their ability to generate visions of the future. Some groups were able to generate a rich set of novel ideas; it was, however, difficult for some of the professionals to avoid thinking about technical solutions. The task seems to be easier if the participants are familiar with the environment they had to elaborate.

In the next phase of the project, similar workshops have been arranged with non-professionals (i.e., college students). The participants were divided into three groups representing the three environments, and again they had to imagine that it is the year 2023, and all the main challenges concerning their environment have been resolved. It was found that college students quite easily repeat what they have presumably heard in lessons at school. More detailed and innovative solutions were generated by the "home" and "school" groups. Some of the students were quite active to comment the anticipations and reflect them, but overall the discussions were not very extensive and there were no big discrepancies between the groups on any of the topics that were raised.

In all the workshops, the participants' visions were not very concrete and articulated, and their originality and fluency vary quite much depending on the issue in question. It seemed to be that people's anticipations mostly reflect what they have read on newspapers or heard from TV news. Some differences were found between the anticipations of the researcher and student groups: e.g., researchers tend to focus on how to improve their well-being at work; students, in turn, thought how schools would be improved to make them a better place to study. There were also some differences between students representing different colleges. For example, in one of the collages in which social sciences and economics are emphasized, the students generated somewhat more elaborated visions.

Challenges of New Lifestyle

There are several obstacles in our path to the welfare society 2.0 such as aging and decline of physical and psychic well-being. In one of our recent workshops, the starting point was a new book on future challenges by Finnish philosopher Pekka Himanen and coworkers in which they have analyzed global economic changes and solutions to sustainable development (Himanen, 2012). The aim of the workshop was to discuss how the obstacles can be solved and what role ICT plays in solving these problems. A group of researchers from our company participated in the workshop.

There were three participant groups that discussed these questions from different point of views: One group put them in the role of personnel of a kindergarten, a second group in the role of senior citizens, and the third group in the role of the researchers participating in the workshop. Firstly, they had to imagine that all the challenges of the new lifestyle have been resolved, and they had to describe what this desirable future would look like. Secondly, they had to think about what has made this desirable future possible, and finally they had to describe one concrete technical solution that would be helpful in the realization of the desirable future and which was not available in 2012. After each group discussion session the group had to present their visions to other groups that had a possibility to comment these visions.

The groups could quite easily get rid of old thoughts, and they mainly generated visions of social innovations. It was quite surprising that at the third phase, when they had to generate technical solutions, they had some problems to find suitable technologies that could support the accomplishment of the ideas they had earlier presented.

The results of the workshop have been summarized to obtain a general view of the main solutions to the above-mentioned obstacles. Some methodological issues were also addressed: For example, it was discussed with participants how strictly the procedures should be followed in the workshop. It was thought that common sense should be used in this issue, and the procedures of the workshop have to be tailored to the goals of the workshop.

ICT Usage in Judicial Administration

In the fourth example workshop it was envisioned how ICT can be utilized in the management of crime cases. As a general background of the project, since work life is changing in the public sector, all possible means to reduce costs have to be considered because of savings requirements. One possibility is to cut real estate costs by developing new workspace concepts based on flexible multifunctional spaces. At the same time new ways of working are emerging characterized by, e.g., knowledge work, teleworking, mobile working, and flexible working hours blurring the boundary between work and life.

The work was done in a project titled New Ways of Working (NewWoW), the aim of which is the creation of concepts, management models as well as methods and metrics for high-performance and sustainable new ways of working. Since knowledge work is increasingly carried out as an interaction work, there is a growing need to achieve a comprehensive understanding of the changing nature and requirements of knowledge and collaborative work, their productivity drivers, and their workplace management needs. In the NewWoW project the companies and public authorities use pilots to test new scenarios and concepts. The pilots compare and analyze different types of working practices and processes of knowledge work, different ways of organizing collaborative work and different workspace solutions.

The aim of the workshop was to study, how the management of a crime scene could proceed fluently in the future through the management chain from the police to the verdict or to the transfer to higher courts. The police and the preliminary investigation were considered to a degree their tasks were related to the prosecutor's work. The workshop focussed on work practices, work tools and arrangements of a court session and topics related to the session procedure. In the arrangement of the workshop it was utilized issues that were raised in the preliminary survey interviews, in the literature review and the interim report and in the results of benchmarking company visits. In addition, there has been a discussion of the role of the different stakeholders in the crime case's management chain.

It was decided to limit the turnout of the workshop so that all the participants would have a possibility to present their views. Members of the different phases of the management chain (i.e., magistrates, clerks of court, prosecutors, judges from the appellate court, presenters and secretaries) were participated. None of the participants had special experiences in the field of ICT, but half of them had participated in the document management project or were familiar with previous ICT development projects. All the participants used information technology and computer systems daily outside their work, and they were coming from different parts of Finland. The aim was to recruit people who use different types of work practices and whose travelling needs differ from each other.

The workshop was realized in two places online via videoconferencing. It was divided into three stages. In the first stage, the participants were urged to imagine that it is year 2015. This year was selected, since at that time the document management project will be finished and the electronic case management system will be available for all the stakeholders. They were asked to imagine that law and supply of computer equipment do not restrict their anticipations. They were presented a picture of the management process of a crime case, and they had to place themselves in a role of one of the stakeholders. In the second stage, the participants were told to remember "back" and consider how this desirable state was achieved. There were three questions presented to the participants: 1) What were the main challenges in 2011? 2) What has changed during the past four years? 3) What has enabled these changes? In the third stage, the participants were presented pictures and videos from different sources the aim of which was to promote their anticipations. One part was gathered from benchmarking visits including material of new ICT technologies and work practices, computer-supported decision making tools, electronic law literature, videoconferencing tools, possibilities in video hearing and electronic filing, subtitling and interpretation and new court room and user interface technologies. The participants were asked to think which of these technical solutions might be promising and useful in the future from the perspective of their work. It was also discussed the challenges and prerequisites how the ideal state can be achieved by using these technologies.

The workshop went on fluently, and the video connections between the two places worked smoothly. Video conferencing did not seem to affect the quality of conversations to a larger extent. A lot of information was collected providing useful knowledge for further activities. Key ICT needs could be successfully identified, at least in part, since many of the participants were already familiar with the technologies that were surveyed, and they had a quite realistic view of their strengths and weaknesses. One additional reason for the success was that the workshop was arranged at the end of the project, and therefore a lot of background work was already conducted. There were only few differences in the participants' opinions and attitudes, and they agreed on most of the issues. Perhaps because of this consensus, extensive and intensive dialogues did not emerge in the workshop.

Overall, the participants' visions were rich in detail and quite elaborated, and since the conversations were focussed on the present-day problems, they were quite practical and realistic. Even though there was a consensus at a general level, each stakeholder generated visions of the future that reflected the challenges they have in their work. Our task has been to synthetisize these fragmentary visions into a coherent view of the management of a crime case in the near future.

Based on the workshop, a vision of the fluent management of crime cases has been defined from the perspectives of the different stakeholders. A preliminary workplace concept and a concept for the usage of ICT tools in the judicial administration have been elaborated, and several challenges and obstacles have also been identified. According to the participants, the way of working may somewhat change, but the amount of work is not diminished. ICT may, however, create new secondary tasks. Workspaces, tools and systems should form an integrated whole, instead of a collection of separate systems. Systems in all organizations must be on the same level, or else information can be lost with the weakest link. Sufficiently long piloting is required to confirm that incomplete systems are not introduced. It is also required appropriate and timely training when new systems are put into use. Additionally, one of the key requirements is that the new systems are well functioning and user-friendly so that professionals can focus on their main task.

After these preliminary workshops had been arranged, a sequence of workshops have been conducted in which the aim has been to develop an overall corporate real estate management model for the judicial administration and to develop workplace concept and guidelines for 10.000 employees working for the judicial administration in Finland.

Development of a Large Screen Display Concept for Control Rooms

We have arranged large-screen display design workshops in two Finnish nuclear power plants (Laarni et al., 2008). Operators, trainers, and designers participated in these workshops. Participants have to generate a design solution for the use of large-screen displays in the main control room, for the information content of the large-screen displays and for the way of presentation of information on large-screen displays. The key discussion topics were: why large screen, what is presented on it, and how it is presented. The main result of the workshop sessions was a large-screen display concept for digital control rooms.

Firstly, participants had to think about the role of large-screen displays (why large screen) and generate a design solution for the use of large-screen displays in the control room (i.e., layout of the control room equipped with large screens, arrangement of workstations in the control room). Secondly, they had to think about the information content of large-screen displays in different plant states (what is presented) and properties of the user interface (how it is presented). Finally, they had to think about the usage practices of large-screen displays and generate a practical design solution for the use of large screens.

In general, the workshops were a success, and they produced a lot of material that is useful in the design of large-screen displays. It was found that profound expertise is required in the design work, and also researchers should be experts in the nuclear field. The development of mutual understanding was shown to be a slow process. Technologies have to be presented in a quite detailed fashion, since the users had often difficulties to get rid of old thoughts. It was shown to be difficult to generate ideas that are concrete enough and promote detailed design work. Operators had conflicting hopes of what should be done and what is important. There were also some doubts about their ability to have an effect on design. In addition, many of the participants had no clear visions of the endpoint.

The participants thought that one of the most important tasks is to develop a large-screen display concept for digitalized control rooms that should describe the usage practices of large-screen displays and provide suggestions of what information should be presented on these displays. A general framework for the large-screen display concept was elaborated based on the results of the workshops.

Based on the findings of these workshops, we suggest that an iterative series of workshops is needed (Laarni et al., 2008). In the first workshops, since present problems dominate participants' minds, the main task is to promote positive thinking and encourage the participants to anticipate the future positively. In later workshops, anticipations and suggestions for the future can be more critically evaluated and prioritized. It would also be useful to expand and enrich the current method by using other kind of artefacts such as photographs, animations and virtual reality or augmented reality simulations in generation of ideas (Laarni et al., 2008). In addition, it was found that it may constrain creativity and thinking, if possible future technologies are presented in the beginning stage of the workshop. It is better to let the participants explore first themselves how the control room would look like in the future before presenting the new technologies.

EVALUATION

All the workshops have been arranged within a period of seven years. The topics of the projects have been varied, and also the participant groups have been diverse. All of them have been successful in their own right, and in general they have been helpful in the fulfillment of the project goals. It has, however, shown to be difficult to analyze the outputs of the workshops according to their originality, fluency and elaboration. The findings suggest that there seems to be a trade-off between the different evaluation criteria: e.g., the more focused is the topic, the more elaborated, but not necessarily very innovative, views can be generated. Fluency and originality, in turn, seem to be highly correlated. These findings suggest that we have to develop more specialized and sophisticated tools for analyzing people's anticipations and future visions in order to better identify the strengths and weaknesses of the method.

We think that the Anticipation Design Dialogue -method provides possibilities to build up a common language between different stakeholders that facilitate the mutual understanding between them. The method could be seen as one element in a participatory and co-creative design process, and it is useful in the early stages of design and innovation activities both in product and service design projects and in developing social innovations.

The method is flexible and it is easily tailorable to different purposes. It is also quite cost-effective, since special participant training is not required, nor is it required special facilities for the workshops. In an iterative series of workshops different participant groups are typically used, but it is also possible to take advantage of participants from earlier iterations which can then reflect on their ideas that they had generated in previous workshops.

It has been found that envisioning of the future is not an easy task: it is difficult to forget the present worries and to evaluate the prospects and weaknesses of new technologies. We have also found that people have sometimes difficulties to articulate their visions, and sometimes they have problems to get rid of old thoughts. We think that resistances and fears must be confronted and treated. To the degree these fears are considered, alternatives can emerge which will reduce people's resistance.

What has also been found in some of the above-mentioned workshops is that participants that are experts in their field quite easily start to use technology jargon in their anticipations and consider only technology-based remedies to present-day problems. Therefore, it is important to ask them to focus in the beginning stage of the workshop on everyday activities and practical means to support these activities. In the later stages, more technical issues can be addressed.

Even though the anticipation of the future is emphasized at the cost of present problems, there is always an interaction between the present and the future in people's anticipations, since people simply cannot neglect and forget present problems and worries. However, in order to prevent them to dominate participants' thinking, one of the main ideas of the method is that the present problems are approached from the future's perspective.

We have emphasized the exchange and negotiation of views between different stakeholders, but since people are not typically familiar with dialogic methods and approaches, this aim is difficult to achieve. We have found that the development of mutual understanding between different stakeholders is a slow process. Since listening is often more difficult than speaking, strict procedures are needed in order to ensure that all the participant groups have an equal opportunity to present their views. People also have quite easily doubts about their ability to have an effect on design. Due to all these reasons, the facilitator's role is important. His/her main task is to help dialogues to emerge and facilitate the process of dialogue.

Typically, a diverse set of views emerge in people's anticipations that can be combined to each other in different ways. This is not necessarily a problem: It is more important to start to develop ideas and carry through a number of plans than to develop a unified vision of the future. We are convinced that diverse intentions can be fruitful and provide a starting point for the emergence of new solutions. The aim is not to urge the participants to look in the same way at something but to promote the elicitation of a number of visions. Sometimes conflicts and discrepancies can be key drivers for the emergence of novel ideas and innovation. Therefore, Anticipation Design Dialogues can be considered as a relationship-building event the task of which is to promote the highlighting of a multitude of opinions that can be linked to together in different ways (cf. Gustavsen, 2011). Even though discrepancies should not be avoided, and in some cases they can be even useful, in our example workshops no conflicts have been detected. This may reflect the fact that the issues have not been personally significant and involving for the participants.

We think that an iterative series of workshops is needed which form a cycle within cycles process and progressively generate design solutions and decisions that provide a starting point for joint action (List, 2006). The importance of iterations has been acknowledged by several action researchers. It is proposed that since the future is difficult to anticipate, the cyclical paradigm can be used to foster to develop multiple perspectives of the future.

The material gathered in these workshops provides us valuable insights into prospects and challenges that are faced in a particular work system or insights into the perspective and thoughts of a particular group of people. All the material is helpful in building scenarios that are useful in the design process. Visions that participants in these workshops generate can be considered as fragments of scenarios that can be linked together in different ways. How they are combined depends on the way they are applied in the design work. One of our next steps is to consider how we move from conversations and exchange of opinions to actual practice of creating and implementing change.

CONCLUSION

Five example cases of the application of the Anticipation Design Dialogue method were given. Envisioning of the future state is a key element in the development of new technologies and services, and in general the proposed method provides useful information for further discussions. But, as our examples have shown, it is very difficult to jump into the unknown future and try to define one's future work settings and situations. The method could be seen as one element in a participatory and co-creative design process and in our efforts to see technology development in a larger context, develop new ideas and integrate them into more holistic concepts. But it is only one element: before the discussions with different stakeholders, it is necessary to model the action environment; and after visioning, possible obstacles and solutions to the obstacles have to be discussed, and the whole development program has to be tested and evaluated.

ACKNOWLEDGMENT

We would like to thank Arja Ala-Laurinaho, Hanna Koskinen, Leena Norros, Esa Nykänen and Anneli Pulkkis for their participation in the development of the method, and two anonymous reviewers for their valuable comments.

REFERENCES

Arnkil, H. (2004). The Finnish workplace development programme — A small giant? *Concepts and Transformation*, *9*(3), 249–278. doi:10.1075/cat.9.3.03arn.

Bødker, K., Kensing, F., & Simonsen, J. (2004). *Participatory IT design: Designing for Business and Workplace Realities*. Cambridge, MA: MIT Press.

Buur, J., & Larsen, H. (2010). The quality of conversations in participatory innovation. *CoDesign: International Journal of CoCreation in Design and the Arts*, *6*(3), 121–138.

Buur, J., & Matthews, B. (2008). Participatory innovation. *International Journal of Innovation Management*, *12*, 255–273. doi:10.1142/S1363919608001996.

Eriksson, E., & Arnkil, T. A. (2009). *Taking up one's worries: A handbook on early dialogues*. Jyväskylä: Gummerus.

Gustavsen, B. (2011). Theory and practice: the mediating discourse. In P. Reason, & H. Bradbury (Eds.), *The Handbook of Action Research*. London: Sage.

Himanen, P. (2012). *Sininen kirja: Suomen kestävän kasvun malli: Luonnos kansalliseksi tulevaisuushankkeeksi*. Retrieved from http://valtioneuvosto.fi/tiedostot/julkinen/pdf/2012/sininen-kirja/fi.pdf.

Inayatullah, S. (2006). Anticipatory action learning: Theory and practices. *Futures*, *38*, 656–666. doi:10.1016/j.futures.2005.10.003.

Jungk, R., & Müllert, N. (1987). *Futures workshops: How to create desirable futures*. London: Institute for Social Inventions.

E. Kaasinen, & L. Norros (Eds.). (2007). *Älykkäiden ympäristöjen suunnittelu: Kohti ekologista systeemiajattelua*. Helsinki: Teknologiateollisuus.

Kensing, F. (1998, January-February). Prompted reflections: A technique for understanding complex work. *Interaction*. doi:10.1145/268986.268988.

Kensing, F., & Madsen, K. H. (1991). Generating visions: Future workshops and metaphorical design. In J. Greenbaum, & M. Kyng (Eds.), *Design at work: Cooperative design of computer systems*. Mahwah, NJ: Lawrence Erlbaum.

Laarni, J., Koskinen, H., & Norros, L. (2008). *Activity-driven design of collaborative tools for nuclear power plant control rooms*. Paper presented at International Ergonomic Association Symposium. Helsinki, Finland.

List, D. (2006). Action research cycles for multiple futures perspectives. *Futures*, *38*, 673–684. doi:10.1016/j.futures.2005.10.001.

Muller, M. J. (2003). Participatory design: The third space in HCI. In J. A. Jacko, & A. Sears (Eds.), *The Human-Computer Interaction Handbook: Fundamentals, Evolving Technologies and Emerging Applications*. Mahwah, NJ: Lawrence Erlbaum.

Nardi, B., & O'Day, V. L. (1999). *Information ecologies: Using technology with heart*. Cambridge, MA: MIT Press.

Pulkkis, A., & Ala-Laurinaho, A. (2007). Dialogiset menetelmät suunnittelussa. In E. Kaasinen, & L. Norros (Eds.), *Älykkäiden ympäristöjen suunnittelu: Kohti ekologista systeemiajattelua* (pp. 215–220). Helsinki: Teknologiateollisuus.

Ramos, J. (2002). Action research as foresight methodology. *Journal of Futures Studies*, *7*, 1–24.

Robinson, J. (1988). Unlearning and backcasting: Rethinking some of the questions we ask about the future. *Technological Forecasting and Social Change*, *33*, 325–338. doi:10.1016/0040-1625(88)90029-7.

Seikkula, J., Arnkil, T. E., & Eriksson, E. (2003). Postmodern society and social networks: Open and anticipation dialogues in network meetings. *Family Process*, *42*, 185–203. doi:10.1111/j.1545-5300.2003.42201.x PMID:12879593.

Shotter, J., & Gustavsen, B. (1999). *The role of dialogue conferences in the development of learning regions: Doing from within our lives together what we cannot do apart*. Stockholm: Centre for Advanced Studies in Leadership, Stockholm School of Economics.

Stevenson, T. (2002). Anticipatory action learning: conversations about the future. *Futures*, *34*, 417–425. doi:10.1016/S0016-3287(01)00068-4.

Stevenson, T. (2006). From vision into action. *Futures*, *38*, 667–672. doi:10.1016/j.futures.2005.10.009.

van Vliet, M., Kok, K., Veldkamp, A., & Sarkki, S. (2012). Structure in creativity: An exploration study to analyse the effects of structuring tools on scenario workshop results. *Futures*, *44*, 746–760. doi:10.1016/j.futures.2012.05.002.

Vavoula, G. N., & Sharples, M. (2007). Future technology workshop: A collaborative method for the design of new learning technologies and activities. *Computer-Supported Collaborative Learning*, *2*, 393–419. doi:10.1007/s11412-007-9026-0.

ADDITIONAL READING

Andersen, T. (1990). *The reflecting team: Dialogues and dialogues about dialogues*. New York: Norton.

Andersen, T. (1995). Reflecting processes: Acts of informing and forming. In S. Friedman (Ed.), *The Reflective Team in Action* (pp. 11–37). New York: Guilford Publication.

Arnkil, T. E., Eriksson, E., & Arnkil, R. (2000). *Anticipation dialogues: Vertical and horizontal dialogue methods for strategic management and smart networking*. Helsinki: Stakes Themes from Finland 3.

Bødker, K. (1991). *Through the interface: A human activity approach to user interface design*. Hillsdale, NJ: Lawrence Erlbaum.

Burns, C., Cottam, H., Vanstone, C., & Winhall, J. (2006). *Transformation design*. London: Design Council.

Ehn, P. (1989). *Work oriented design of computer artefacts*. Hillsdale, NJ: Lawrence Erlbaum.

Ehn, P. (1993). Scandinavian design: On participation and skill. In D. Schuler, & A. Namioka (Eds.), *Participatory design: Principles and practices* (pp. 41–78). New York: Lawrence Erlbaum.

Emery, M., & Purser, R. E. (1996). *The search conference: Theory and practice*. San Francisco: Jossey-Bass.

Gustavsen, B. (1992). *Dialogue and development*. Assen: van Gorcum.

Gustavsen, B. (2001). Theory and practice: The mediating discourse. In P. Reason, & H. Bradbury (Eds.), *Handbook of Action Research*. London: SAGE.

Inayatullah, S. (2005). *Questioning the future*. Tamsui: Tamkang University Press.

Kensing, F., & Blomberg, J. (1998). Participatory design: Issues and concerns. *Computer Supported Cooperative Work*, *7*, 167–185. doi:10.1023/A:1008689307411.

Kensing, F., Simonsen, J., & Bödker, K. (1998). MUST - A method for participatory design. *Human-Computer Interaction*, *13*, 167–198. doi:10.1207/s15327051hci1302_3.

Kujala, S. (2003). User involvement: A review of the benefits and challenges. *Behaviour & Information Technology*, *22*, 1–16. doi:10.1080/01449290301782.

Kyng, M. (1998). Users and computers: a contextual approach to design of computer artifacts. *Scandinavian Journal of Information Systems*, *10*, 7–44.

List, D. (2003). Three maps for navigating the ocean of alternatives. *Journal of Future Studies*, *8*, 55–64.

Luck, R. (2003). Dialogue in participatory design. *Design Studies*, *24*, 523–535. doi:10.1016/S0142-694X(03)00040-1.

B. A. Nardi (Ed.). (1996). *Context and consciousness: Activity theory and human-computer interaction*. Cambridge, MA: MIT Press.

Nardi, B. A., & Engeström, Y. (1999). A web on the wind: The structure of invisible work. *Computer Supported Cooperative Work*, *8*, 1–8. doi:10.1023/A:1008694621289.

Pasmore, W. (2001). Action research in the workplace: The socio-technical perspective. In P. Reason, & H. Bradbury (Eds.), *Handbook of Action Research* (pp. 38–47). London: SAGE.

Roser, T., & Samson, A. (2009). *Co-creation: New paths to value*. London: Promise/LSE Enterprise.

Sanders, E. B.-N. (2000). Generative tools for CoDesigning. *Proceedings of CoDesigning*, *2000*, 3–12.

Sanoff, H. (2008). Multiple ways of participatory design. *International Journal of Architectural Research*, *2*, 57–69.

Schuler, D., & Namioka, A. (1993). *Participatory design: Principles and practices*. Hillsdale, NJ: Lawrence Erlbaum.

Sharples, M., Jeffery, N., du Boulay, J. B., Teather, D., Teather, B., & du Boulay, G. H. (2002). Sociocognitive engineering: A methodology for the design of human-centred technology. *European Journal of Operational Research*, *136*, 310–323. doi:10.1016/S0377-2217(01)00118-7.

KEY TERMS AND DEFINITIONS

Action Research: Research aiming to solve social and economic problems by actively participating in those settings and activities where changes will be made.

Anticipation Dialogue: Approach supporting people to envision the future and make reflections about future challenges and opportunities.

Dialogue: Special kind of conversation in which each participant is urged to listen to the contributions of others and respond reflectively to each others' statements.

Future Anticipation: Some kind of mental testing in which we consider what will happen in the future and what the consequences of current actions would be.

Future Studies: Set of approaches and methodologies to study different possible futures and prospects and challenges related to them.

Future Technology Workshop: Technique in which people envision and design the interactions between current and future technology and interaction through a series of structured workshop sessions.

Future Workshop: Methodology for helping people to actively participate in the development of their work.

Participatory Design: Research methodology and approach to the design and evaluation of technical and organizational systems aiming to start the design process in the practice field of the users in order to identify the goals of their activity and the physical environment, the objects and the tools used in this activity.

Prompted Reflections: Technique in which freehand drawings are used to elicit potentials for new technology.

Work Conference: Dialogically structured joint activity fostering the emergence of new relationships between participants which is based on a set of orientating statements providing guidance and advice.

Chapter 17
Hand Gesture Recognition as Means for Mobile Human Computer Interaction in Adverse Working Environments

Jens Ziegler
Technische Universität Dresden, Germany

Randy Döring
Technische Universität Dresden, Germany

Johannes Pfeffer
Technische Universität Dresden, Germany

Leon Urbas
Technische Universität Dresden, Germany

ABSTRACT

Interacting with mobile devices can be challenging in adverse working environments. Using hand gestures for interaction can overcome severe usability issues that users face when working with mobile devices in industrial settings. This chapter is dedicated to the design, implementation, and evaluation of mobile information systems with hand gesture recognition as means for human computer interaction. The chapter provides a concise theoretical background on human gestural interaction and gesture recognition, guidelines for the design of gesture vocabularies, recommendations for proper implementation, and parameterization of robust and reliable recognition algorithms on energy-efficient 8-bit architectures. It additionally presents an elaborated process for participatory design and evaluation of gesture vocabularies to ensure high usability in the actual context of use. The chapter concludes with a case study that proves the suitability of the proposed framework for the design of efficient and reliable hand gesture-based user interfaces.

DOI: 10.4018/978-1-4666-4623-0.ch017

INTRODUCTION

Mobile IT-supported workis becoming a key competitive advantage in factories of the future. As nearly the entire enterprise data is available in digital form, business processes and workflows increasingly rely on information technology. This dependency is obvious in office work, but is also increasing for mobile work. Maintenance personnel, engineers, site managers, transporters or building inspectors – the entire mobile workforce of a company requires information to do their job. Mobile information systems provide data, workflow support, documentation and reporting services, access to plant equipment or the control system, and even augmented reality for specific purposes. Coming from the area of mobile consumer products, prominent pioneers of mobile interaction have helped to bring mobile devices of all sizes in all areas of daily life, and increasingly into office routine. Today, direct interaction styles such as touch-and-swipe interaction, speech recognition and tilt interfaces supplemented by haptic or acoustic feedback, and also combined as a multi-modal user interface, dominate interaction with mobile devices. The mentioned user interfaces enable users to choose the most appropriate interaction style for their specific context of use. Because of their widespread use, these concepts have usually been directly adopted for mobile information systems. However, this has quickly led to problems, as the demands on robustness and usability are significantly different from those for the consumer market. For example, adverse environmental conditions with challenging features such as changing light, high humidity, dirt, dust, grease and liquids require protective clothing including helmet and working gloves. Users have to use one or even both hands to accomplish various physical tasks at least temporarily. Long distances between different work locations lead to occasional and frequently interrupted usage of the system. Mobile information systems need to be operable under all these conditions. When conventional user interfaces fail, they must be substituted by alternatives that have been designed for the particular context of use. Alternative visual displays such as head-mounted displays have already been successfully tested and implemented (e.g. Witt, 2007). However, more interaction concepts for input devices need to be developed and evaluated in industrial environments. Without such input devices, reliable mobile IT-support under adverse environmental conditions will remain impossible.

This book chapter is devoted to *hand gesture recognition*using on-body sensors, a promising input style for working environments where the above-mentioned ways of interaction are impossible or improper, e.g. in cleanrooms in the semiconductor industry, process plants or factories in the manufacturing industry. Hand gesture recognition has the potential to meet the requirements of professional working environments. It allows one-handed work while operating the mobile device and two-handed work when not. Being wearable, self-contained, lightweight and robust, it forms a reliable, efficient and inexpensive intelligent user interface. Especially wearable systems with head mounted displays, pico projectors or wearable flexible display screens can benefit from hand gesture based interaction.

The remainder of this book chapter is structured as follows. In section *Hand Gesture Based Interaction with Mobile Devices*, a concise discussion of the theoretical foundations of human gestural interaction and gesture recognition highlights current challenges and gives valuable guidelines for the design of gesture recognition systems and gesture vocabularies. A literature review grounds the topic in the current state of research on hand gesture recognition using Hidden Markov Models (HMM). Section *Gesture Recognition using Hidden Markov Models* goes into the details of HMM based gesture recognition algorithms and gives recommendations for proper implementation and parameterization of robust and reliable recognition algorithms on energy-efficient 8-bit architectures. The following section *Case Study: A wearable dynamic hand gesture recognition system* presents a case study which was conducted as part of a development project to demonstrate the suitability of the proposed framework for the design of efficient and reliable hand gesture based user interfaces. The section provides a description of an actual implementation of a hand-gesture based user interface for a wearable system and a two-step participatory design process (Schuler & Namioka, 1993) for gesture vocabularies used in mobile support applications. The chapter concludes with an outlook on future research directions.

HAND GESTURE BASED INTERACTION WITH MOBILE DEVICES

Literature Review

The gesture sets investigated in existing research reach from simple directions (Kallio, Kela & Mäntyjärvi 2003) and geometrical forms like triangle, rectangle and circle (Kendon, 1996) to highly application specific gestures. Gestures are, for example, used to interact with a virtual environment or to control slideshow presentations. However, multimedia control is one of the most obvious and simplistic application domains for gestural interfaces. Studies on usable gesture sets for mobile information systems for IT-supported work are still rare.

A proper design of the gesture set is crucial for the success of any gestural user interface. Designing gesture sets for particular use cases requires a sophisticated user-centered design process that addresses both the technical limitations of the system and the expectations of its prospective users. Several procedures have been proposed in current literature (e.g. Henze et al., 2010; Ruiz, Lee & Lank, 2011). However, most procedures use existing and well-known use cases such as controlling a DVD player or navigating through a list of contacts. For a weakly specified design space, those procedures tend to fail quickly due to the vast number of possible design solutions. The development of an integrated methodology for participatory, task-oriented design of gesture vocabularies for mobile applications is still subject of ongoing research.

Theoretical Background

In technical terms a *gesture* is defined as "a motion of the body that contains information" (Kurtenbach & Hulteen, 1990). In general, gestures are performed to either convey meaningful information, or to interact with the environment. Mostly, gestures supplement other means of communication like oral speech and have a culture-specific and context-dependent meaning. According to Mitra & Acharia (2007), gestures can be classified as either static or dynamic. Static gestures are characterized by the configuration of the involved body parts (*posture*); dynamic gestures are defined by a specific motion sequence (*trajectory*). Complex gestures, may have both static and dynamic elements. Depending on the involved body parts, gestures can further be classified as *hand & arm gestures*, *head & face gestures* and *body gestures*.

Gesture recognition is the process in which the gestures performed by the sender are recognized by the receiver. While the sender is typically a human, the receiver can either also be a human or a technical system that is able to perceive, identify and interpret a set of gestures. In the simplest case, the receiver has to recognize the temporal and spatial change of the involved body parts in order to identify a gesture. However, gestures are usually ambiguous and incompletely specified because they depend on the current context of the communication, the emotional states of the sender and the receivers, and the relationship between them. Gesture recognition is usually also affected by subconscious communication. Depending on these factors, in different situations gestures may be mapped to different concepts. Further, the meaning of a gesture can be affected by the preceding or following gesture (Mitra & Acharya, 2007).

For the development of gesture recognition systems, it is therefore essential to properly define the socio-cultural and organizational working context of the sender and the interpersonal relations to the receiver to clearly delimit the set of relevant gestures and concepts, and to disambiguate the gesture-based interaction by creating a natural and convenient interaction design.

Design Considerations for Hand and Arm Gesture Vocabularies

Hand and arm gestures are often the most expressive and most frequently used class of gestures. Mitra & Acharia (2007) define five categories of gestures, which are shown in Figure 1. Almost no interpersonal communication occurs without some kind of gesticulation. In fact, 90% of human gestures are gesticulation. Sign languages and artificial gesture sets interfere with the continuous communication stream, which results in additional cognitive load for the user and high demands on the recognition system. The exact determination of the start and end point of a gesture pattern and the correct segmentation of the relevant gesture (gesture spotting) are technically demanding due to segmentation ambiguity and the spatio-temporal variability of the stream (Mitra & Acharya, 2007). Limiting the variety and ambiguity of the hand gesture set may significantly increase reliability and efficiency of a gesture recognition system. In the remainder of this section, a number of design guidelines for on-body gesture recognition systems are presented that help designing robust hand and arm gesture vocabularies. These guidelines should be seen as tradeoffs between expressiveness and power of the gesture set.

Design Guideline 1: Use Dynamic Gestures Only

The most basic restriction is to only use dynamic gestures. Static gestures are only observable by vision-based approaches or by indirect posture estimation from motion tracking using complex intrinsic sensor technology. Dynamic hand gestures, however, are comparatively easy to record using mobile or wearable sensor platforms, without the need for additional technical equipment.

Design Guideline 2: Avoid Using Finger Gestures

Hand gestures may include finger motion or posture as well. However, additional technical equipment like instrumented data gloves (CyberGloveSystems, 2012) or surface electromyography (SEMG) (Zhiyuan et al., 2011) is required to track finger gestures. Reducing the gesture set to whole-hand gestures may significantly reduce the necessary technical effort.

Figure 1. Classification of hand gestures (Adapted from (Mitra & Acharia, 2007)

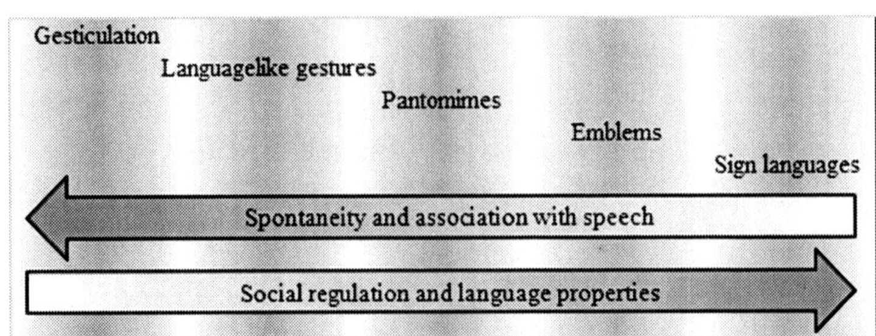

Design Guideline 3: Normalize Dynamic Gestures

Because of the before-mentioned continuous gestural or artisanal activity of human users, it is challenging to recognize a certain gesture from a gesture set. The effort for detection of too subtle or too complex gestures can quickly increase dramatically. It may also be risky to use very common everyday gestures. Although their recognition may be rather easy, it is difficult to discriminate whether the gesture was made to actually operate the device or rather unconsciously. As a consequence, Kendon (1996) has restricted dynamic gestures by defining four key characteristics:

1. Dynamic gestures always start from and return to a rest position (gestures are excursions).
2. Gestures have a peak structure, in which the part containing the information is located in the middle of the sequence.
3. Gesture phrases are organized symmetrically.
4. Gestures are well-bounded having clear onsets and offsets.
5. Gestures are disjunctive to other gestures (no gesture is contained within another gesture.)

Considering these characteristics can significantly improve the expressiveness of a gesture set and decrease the algorithmic effort for gesture recognition.

Design Guideline 4: Use Metaphoric Mappings Between Gestures and Concepts

Interaction with mobile devices requires mapping of artificial concepts (*enter* or l*eave a menu*, *confirm an input*, *shortcut to menu*) to a defined vocabulary of gestures. Hand gesture vocabularies should always be task-oriented, efficient, ergonomic, minimal and intelligible. Metaphoric mappings adapt shared experience such as basic physics, biomechanics, social conventions and already familiar interaction techniques to gain advantage from existing mental models, which is crucial for the *learnability* and *memorability* of an interaction technique (Hurtienne et al., 2010). For example, vertical and horizontal movement can be directly transferred from a hand gesture to a panning operation on a large picture. The movement of the hand when opening a book (turning the right hand from backside-up to backside-down while moving it sideways to the right) can be used for switching between overview and detail view in an application.

Design Guideline 5: Use Contrary Gestures Redundantly

In some cases, there is no meaningful metaphoric mapping of a concept to a gesture. In this case, users must extend their mental model with the new mapping. Considering the symmetric design of the gestures (*design guideline 3*), gestures usually have a semantically contrary counterpart (e.g. clockwise rotation around the x-axis vs. counterclockwise rotation; translation in the direction of the x-axis vs. against its direction). Studies have shown that such gesture pairs frequently cause confusion (Ziegler et al., 2012). Hence, if a concept is mapped to both opposite gestures, the number of erroneous inputs can be significantly reduced.

GESTURE RECOGNITION USING HIDDEN MARKOV MODELS

Literature Review

Basically, there are two basic approaches of gesture recognition: camera-based systems, which have no direct contact with the user, and body-mounted systems, where the sensors are fixed to the body of the user. Camera-based systems apply techniques of image processing, especially pattern recognition and motion tracking to detect movements of the user (Rigoll, Kosmala & Eickeler, 1998). Stationary cameras, however, are inadequate for most mobile use cases. On-body systems, in contrast, are portable without significant additional effort and do not need remote equipment. For body-mounted systems, the most common sensors are accelerometers (e.g. Kurtenbach & Hulteen, 1990; Hofmann, Heyer & Hommel, 1998, Geer, 2004; Pylvänäinen, 2005). Various algorithms for gesture classification can be found in the literature. Rubine (1991) gives a general classification of such algorithms. The most common types of algorithms for gesture recognition are *Dynamic Time Warping* (DTW) (Min et al. 2010), *Neural Networks* (NN) (Bailador et al. 2007), and *Hidden Markov Models* (HMM) (Schlömer et al. 2008). Liu et al. (2009) have shown that DTW is not suitable for user-independent recognition.

Numerous studies have investigated the utility of HMM for gesture classification, in particular for accelerometer-based input devices. The variety of input devices ranges from hand movement recognition (Rao et al., 2009) to systems that detect motions of single fingers (Zhang et al., 2009). Recent studies increasingly use off-the-shelf sensor platforms like the *Nintendo Wii* controller (e.g. Kratz & Rohs, 2010; Schlömer et al. 2008), the *Microsoft Kinect* (Zhou et al., 2011) or the *iPhone* (Klingmann, 2009). Several contributions have a focus on the need for robust and cost-effective recognition systems (e.g. Zappi et al., 2009; Kratz & Rohs, 2010). Usually, the HMM algorithm runs on the mobile device itself, or, if necessary, on a remote machine in order to provide sufficient computational performance and memory for the algorithm. This is because common implementations of the HMM-algorithm require floating-point arithmetic because of scaling and arithmetic underflow effects caused by repeated multiplications of probabilities in the so-called forward algorithm. Floating-point arithmetic on embedded architectures without a separate floating-point unit, however, is computationally expensive. For this reason, current embedded intelligent user interfaces rarely use HMM for real-time gesture classification.

Zappi et al. (2009) have presented an implementation of the forward algorithm that is optimized for fixed-point operation. An evaluation of a tangible user interface called SMCube has shown that the results of an algorithm that uses 16-bit fixed-point arithmetic are comparable to the results of one that uses common floating-point arithmetic. This algorithm has been extensively evaluated with the SMCube user interface by Milosevic, Farella & Benini (2010). However, the presented implementation left room for further improvements (Ziegler et al. 2012).

Theoretical Background

Hidden Markov Models (HMM) belong to the class of statistical classifiers (Rabiner, 1989). An HMM consists of hidden states that emit symbols. Transitions between the states are described by a matrix containing a discrete probability function for each state. The emitted symbols only depend on the current state and are described by a discrete probability function. An HMM is a *doubly embedded stochastic process* (Mitra & Acharia, 2007). Formally, an HMM can be described by a 5-tuple $» = (S, V, p, A, B)$ with

S: Set of *N* possible states
V: Set of *M* possible observation symbols
p: Initial distribution of states:

$$p_i = P(q_1 = s_i), \qquad À \in \mathbb{R}^{N\times 1}$$

A: Probability distribution of state transitions:

$$a_{ij} = P(q_{t+1} = s_j | q_t = s_i), \quad A \in \mathbb{R}^{N\times N}$$

B: Emission probabilities of observation symbols:

$$b_i(o_t) = P(o_t = v_k | q_t = s_i), \qquad B \in \mathbb{R}^{N\times M}$$

For gesture recognition, there are two main tasks to complete. First, given an observation sequence $O = (o_1,\ o_2, \ldots, o_t)$ and a model », the probability that O was generated by » has to be calculated efficiently, which is called the *classification problem*. Second, given a set of observation sequences, a model has to be generated that represents these sequences, which is known as the *training problem* (for further details, refer to (Rabiner, 1989)).

In order to perform the first task, the *forward algorithm* is an efficient method to calculate the probability $P(O|»)$ that a specific observation sequence O has been generated by a particular model ». In order to calculate the desired probability, so called forward variables $\pm_t(i)$ are computed recursively. Thus, $\pm_t(i)$ represents the probability to be in a particular state s_i at a specific time t given an observation sequence O. The algorithm can be described using the following three terms:

Initialization:

$$\pm_1(i) = p_i \cdot b_i(o_1),\ 1 \le i \le N \tag{1}$$

Recursion:

$$\pm_{t+1}(j) = \sum_{i=1}^{N} \pm_t(i) \cdot a_{ij} \cdot b_j(o_{t+1}), \tag{2}$$

$$1 \le i \le N \wedge 1 \le t \le T - 1$$

Termination:

$$P(O|») = \sum_{i=1}^{N} \pm_T(i) \tag{3}$$

Computer-aided implementations of the forward algorithm usually lead to arithmetic underflow caused by repeated multiplications of probabilities, which require an ongoing scaling of the forward variable. The common approach is to divide by the sum of all forward values. Using division operations, however, is computationally expensive and therefore inapplicable for cost-efficient embedded controllers. Zappi et al. (2009) have presented a forward algorithm that has been optimized for fixed-point arithmetic of embedded controllers. The approach was to use computationally inexpensive bit-shifts instead of costly divisions. If after a recursion step all forward variables $\pm_t(i)$ are smaller than 0.5, the $\pm_t(i)$ are left-shifted until one variable is greater than or equal 0.5. Because of the scaling, the termination step does not deliver the probability $P(O|»)$ but a scaled forward variable $\hat{\pm}_T(i)$. However, $P(O|»)$ can be derived easily using the following formula:

$$\sum_{i=1}^{N} \hat{\pm}_T(i) = \prod_{t=1}^{T} 2^{l_t} \cdot \sum_{i=1}^{N} \pm_T(i) = \prod_{t=1}^{T} 2^{l_t} \cdot P(O|») \tag{4}$$

Or logarithmically:

$$\log P(O|») = \log \sum_{i=1}^{N} \hat{\pm}_T(i) - \log \prod_{t=1}^{T} 2^{l_t} \tag{5}$$

Using the binary logarithm, the second addend dissolves in the sum of the bit-shifts. Due to the fact, that the first addend usually is several orders of magnitude smaller than the second one, only the number of bit shifts of two models has to be compared to decide which model is more probable. Using this approach, it is possible to implement highly resource-efficient HMM-based recognition algorithms on controllers without dedicated floating point unit (FPU).

The second task, the training of HMMs, does not have to take place on the embedded device.

Once the data records of all gestures of a gesture set have been captured, the models can be generated on a more powerful device. The Baum-Welch algorithm is a common choice to generate the gesture models, e.g. using the HMM Toolbox for Matlab by Kevin Murphy (1998). The complete set of gesture models can then be transferred to the recognition system. Using the proposed approaches and tools, it is possible to realize efficient and robust gestural user interfaces on cost-efficient, low-performance embedded devices without the need for remote sensing or processing power – even on 8 or 16-bit RISC architectures.

Design Considerations for Gesture Recognition Algorithms

The architecture of a typical gesture recognition system is shown in Figure 2. It consists of the algorithm for sensor data preprocessing, the online classifier and the offline HMM training algorithm (Milosevic et al. 2010). Gesture recognition is usually done in four steps. First, the raw data of the sensors is preprocessed in order to optimize the data stream for the subsequent classifier. Second, the input stream is segmented into single gestures. Third, features are extracted from each segment, and fourth, the features are classified (Zappi et al. 2009).

Accelerations, rotations and the gravity vector are suitable sensor input for HMM-based classifiers. In the preprocessing step, the measured values from each sensor are first combined to a measurement vector. It is possible to transform the measurement vectors to simplify subsequent processing steps. The number of measurement vectors per time unit depends on the sampling rate. As the required computing power is directly proportional to the sampling rate, it should be set to the lowest possible value. In previous work, sampling rates between 20 Hz (Pylvänäinen, 2005) and 90 Hz (Mäntyjärvi, 2004) have been used successfully.

Afterwards, it is necessary to quantize the measurement vectors to reduce the input space of the classifier. Therefore, the desired number of symbols has to be defined. This number corresponds with the number of observations of the HMM. Further, the locations of the initial cluster centers have to be determined. Research has shown that locating the initial cluster centers on a sphere yields the best results (Pylvänäinen, 2005). An effective approach is to distribute the cluster centers uniformly on the unitary sphere, and then to use an adaptive clustering algorithm to adapt the distribution on the unitary sphere to the actual training data (Ziegler et. al, 2012). Each recorded measurement vector is then assigned to the cluster with the lowest distance, giving the quantization symbol. In literature, the number of cluster centers varies between 6 and 18. Figure 3 shows four exemplary distributions on the unitary

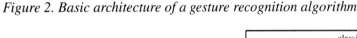

Figure 2. Basic architecture of a gesture recognition algorithm

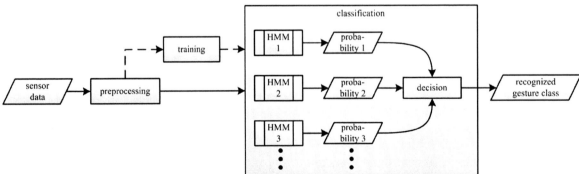

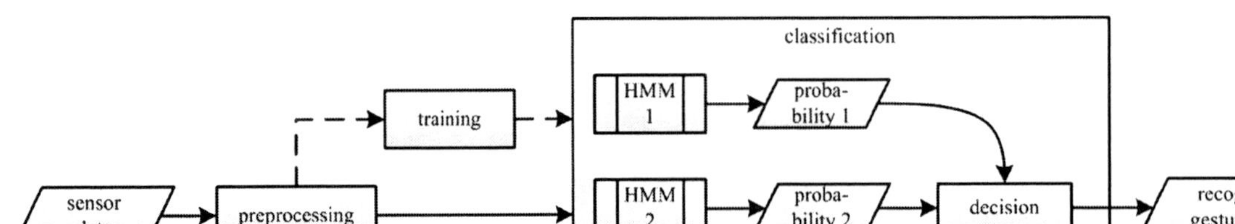

Figure 3. Initial distribution on the unitary sphere for 6, 10, 14 and 18 cluster centers

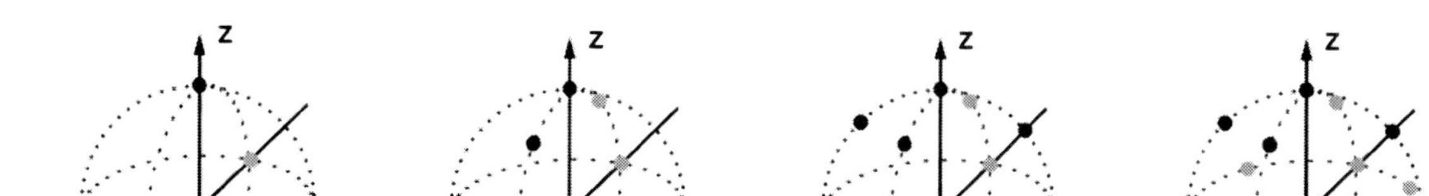

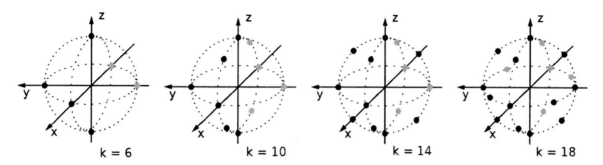

sphere. Research has shown that more than 14 cluster centers do not lead to further improvement of the correct classification ratio (Schlömer et al., 2008; Ziegler et al. 2012). In order to improve the robustness of the models against outliers, a minimal emission probability can be defined for each quantization symbol.

Next, the continuous input data stream has to be segmented into single gestures, because HMM classifiers require a bounded input sequence for classification. Apart of using a manual trigger (as done by Milosevic et al., 2010) the easiest way to segment the input data stream is to check for a defined start and end position as demanded by *design guideline 3*, and to assume a mean execution time per gesture. The input sequence for the classifier is bounded by the repeated occurrence of this predefined position and a fixed time frame. The required computing costs for this segmentation method are comparatively low, as only distances between subsequent vectors have to be calculated.

In the classification step, one HMM is generated per gesture. The probability that the observation sequence representing the gesture was generated by the respective model is calculated for each class by the forward algorithm to classify an unknown gesture. The calculation of the forward variables is performed in real-time. This means, with each new measured vector the recursion step is performed before the next measurement is taken. Thus, the result is available directly after the end of the performed gesture.

In the decision step, the algorithm has to decide which gesture class was actually observed. The result of the classification step is a vector of probabilities for each gesture class representing the probability that an observed sequence matches the particular model. Usually, the decision algorithm treats the model with the highest probability as correct if this decision is sufficiently reliable. Otherwise, e.g. in case of unknown or unclear gestures, the algorithm rejects the classification in order to avoid incorrect matches. A strong indicator of incorrect matching is a small difference between the highest and second-highest probability. An acceptance threshold thus avoids incorrect matches caused by unknown or unclear gestures, which decreases false recognitions. When using a fixed-point algorithm that compares bit-shifts rather than probabilities, the decision problem can be solved by empirically determining a suitable threshold difference between the number of bit-shifts of the two highest probabilities.

Design Considerations for Gestural Interfaces

Creating convenient user experience with gestural interfaces is a difficult task. Inaccurate or unreliable recognition may undermine the trust held in the system. Heavy, bulky or hindering recognition systems may lower the acceptance of the system. For example, Mitra & Acharia (2007) argue that "glove-based gestural interfaces typically require [...] a cumbersome device" which "hinders the ease and naturalness of the user's interaction" (p. 312). In addition complex or oversized recognition systems tend to be expensive, error-prone and therefore impractical for daily use. Complex or confusing gesture vocabularies, on the other hand, may be hard-to-use and physically demanding (Geer, 2004). Convenient hand gesture recognition systems should thus meet the following requirements:

1. Gesture classification should be robust, reliable, accurate and user-independent.
2. Gesture recognition should be self-contained and in real-time.
3. The gesture recognition system should not disturb, distract or restrict users in their activities, and cause no fatigue or harm in any way.
4. The gesture set should be easy to learn, memorable and in accordance to the users' expectations.

CASE STUDY: A WEARABLE DYNAMIC HAND GESTURE RECOGNITION SYSTEM

Implementation of the Sensor Platform

The sensor platform consists of a dual-axis gyroscope with 12 bit resolution, a three-axis accelerometer with 8 bit resolution, a single button and a two-colored LED that indicates correct rest position and successful gesture recognition. The component layout is shown in Figure 4. A low-cost 8 bit RISC microcontroller (Atmel ATmega644P) is used for data processing. The sensor platform is designed to be worn under industrial working gloves and can be fixed to an under-glove on the back of the right hand. It is connected to a small driver unit that provides wireless connectivity and a battery driven power supply. The driver unit can be fixed at the lower arm. The sensor platform has a total weight of 60 g. The weight of the driver unit is 130 g. The overall system is shown in Figure 5. The gesture recognition system is connected wirelessly to a Bluetooth-enabled mobile device that runs the application software.

Parameterization of the Gesture Recognition Algorithm

The architecture of the gesture recognition algorithm is based on Milosevic et al. (2010). Improvements were made to the quantization, segmentation and decision steps. The presented implementation also uses the fixed-point forward algorithm by Zappi et al. (2009).

The main parameters to be set for the gesture recognition algorithm are the topology of the HMM, the number of states, and the number of cluster centers for quantization. Main technical constraints are processing width and sampling

Figure 4. Component layout of the sensor platform

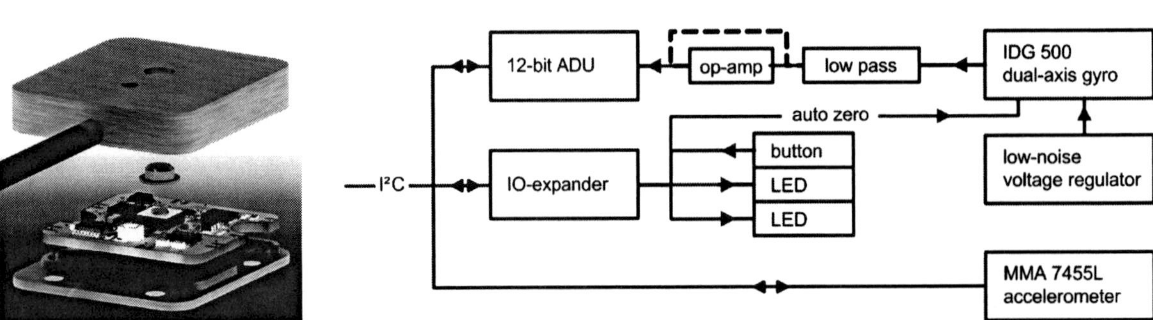

Figure 5. Setup of the gesture recognition system

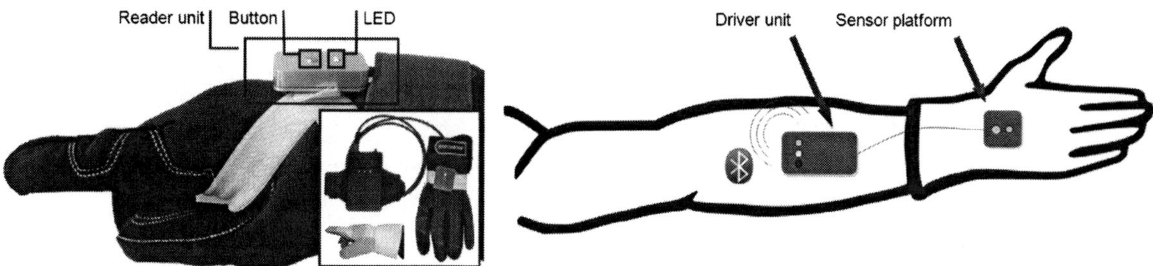

rate. Higher values generally lead to more accurate classification results. However, computing and memory costs rise proportionally while the recognition rate eventually reaches a maximum. Further, all thresholds need to be defined properly in order to reach sufficient recognition accuracy. Higher thresholds lead to low recognition rates, whereas low thresholds may cause many false recognitions. Thus, all these parameters should be chosen carefully based on empirical estimates on the target system. The following tests were conducted in an office environment during the development and evaluation of the recognition system. Initially, recordings from a previous study with an earlier prototype of the recognition hardware were used as test data. Later, the results were verified with the training data of the gesture set presented in this chapter.

Tests with HMMs with 4 to 16 states have shown little to no difference in the recognition rate for more than 6 states. Also, the topology of an HMM (ergodic vs. left-to-right topology) had no significant impact. Thus, the gesture recognition algorithm uses discrete 6-state left-to-right models. Tests with sampling rates from 10 to100 Hz have shown that the algorithm provides reasonable results at a minimum sampling rate of 25 Hz. To empirically estimate the number of cluster centers, values of 6, 10, 14 and 18 centers were evaluated. The results have confirmed previous findings by Schlömer et al. (2008) that more than 14 centers do not lead to further improvement of the correct classification ratio. Thus, 14 initial cluster centers were uniformly distributed on the unitary sphere in the current implementation. The distribution is then optimized online using a k-means-algorithm that iteratively calculates the optimal cluster centers from the training data. The training data for the gesture models was captured offline using the Baum-Welch algorithm.

The minimal emission probability for each quantization symbol was empirically determined to be 2^{-8}. Tests with acceptance thresholds from 0 to 10 bit-shifts revealed that a minimum difference of 5 bit-shifts between the number of bit-shifts of the two highest probabilities was an optimal compromise regarding false recognitions and false rejections. All parameters were chosen based on values from literature and optimized by test series with the given setup. For other setups, additional tests may be necessary.

The proper processing width was determined by a cross validation of the algorithm with the actual gesture set. Zappi et al. (2009) have shown that their fixed-point forward algorithm provides comparable results for floating-point arithmetic and 16 bit and 32 bit fixed-point arithmetic. However, the authors have made no statement on the dependency of their results on the applied gesture set. A cross validation with training data from four participants (all male; aged between 22 and 24) with 15 samples per person and gesture has shown that the mean correct classification ratio was comparable even for 8 bit fixed-point operation, however, showing a decreasing reliability of the classification for some gestures. For this reason, 16 bit fixed-point arithmetic was used in the current implementationThe results are listed in Table 1.

Design of the Application Software

The presented case study was conducted as part of the development of a mobile information system for industrial maintenance. The system was designed to support maintenance workers at their daily work in the facility or plant, which includes servicing, inspection, repair, and overhaul of the plant equipment. The system provides workflow support, access to relevant information and tracking of user activities. The application consists of three menus and an action bar providing quick shortcuts to all menus and to different dialogs. The first menu offers a piping & instrumentation diagram (*P&ID*), which is a typical graphical information source in this domain. A zoomable image view is used to display the diagrams. The second menu offers workflow support providing information on necessary activities, required results and possible input values for each task in a list view. The third menu offers access to the document repository of the plant including equipment manuals in form of a tree view. At the time of the case study, there was no fully functional prototype available. Instead, an interactive mockup prototype designed with the rapid prototyping tool *MS Sketchflow* was used. The mockup is interactive and can be controlled by mouse or keyboard. It is based on *MS Silverlight* and can be executed in any supported browser. Screenshots of the main menus are shown in Figure 6.

Table 1. Results of the cross validation of the fixed-point HMM algorithm compared to the floating-point version (recognition rate)

	8 Bit	16 Bit	32 Bit	Float
Average	0.933	0.958	0.958	0.957
Variance	0.031	0.015	0.015	0.018

Design of the Dynamic Hand Gesture Set

A gesture set to operate the maintenance support application was designed using a two-step participatory design process. First, participatory design sessions were conducted with potential end users to develop different gesture sets. Second, an expert session was conducted with domain experts and future customers to evaluate the usability of the gesture sets. In order to limit the design space to normalized dynamic gestures and to align it with all requirements and technical constraints, a morphologic analysis was carried out to define all possible and reasonable combinations of design attributes prior to the design session (Ritchey, 2011).

In the participatory design session, 9 potential end-users (7 male, 2 female; aged from 24 to 46) were asked to design a gesture set for the maintenance support application using the given morphologic frame. Each session was designed as a Wizard-of-Oz experiment in which each participant completed a mobile maintenance scenario containing several tasks.

The participants were then asked to design a gesture set and to accomplish the given tasks using the interactive mockup prototype and their designed set. The evaluator acted as wizard that interactively simulated the system behavior according to the gestures made by the participant. The participants could refine their gesture set until they were completely satisfied with their design. The session took about 90 minutes per participant in average. The Wizard-of-Oz experiment was repeated after one week in order to evaluate the memorability and learnability of the gesture set.

Afterwards, the user-generated gesture sets were reviewed by 5 experts (all male; aged between 27 and 48; 2 domain experts, 2 interaction experts, and 1 software engineer) with focus on ergonomic and technical design issues. After patching the remaining issues identified by the reviewer, the classifier was trained with the gesture

Figure 6. Screenshots of the three menus provided by the application. Left: Zoomable image view showing the P&ID. Center: List view showing the tasks of the workflow. Right: Tree view of the document repository

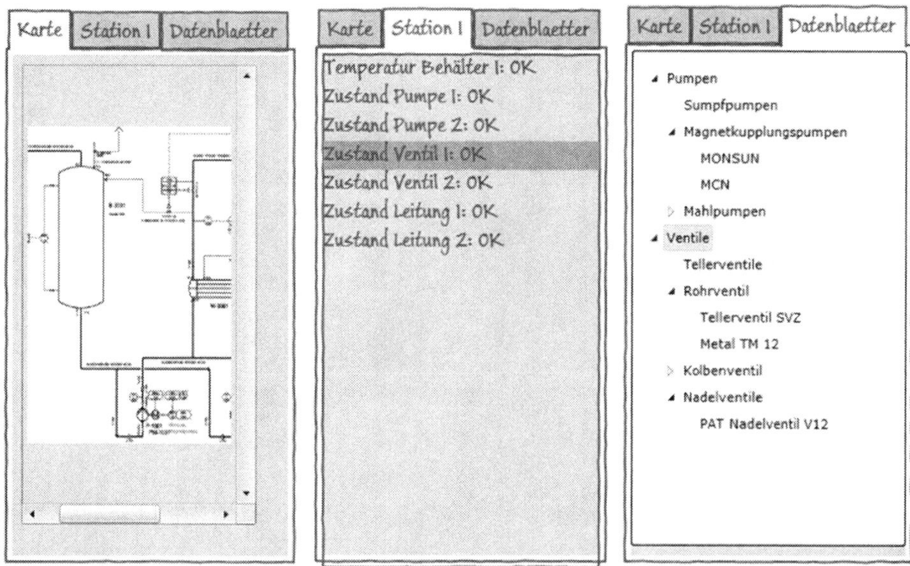

set that had performed best. The final gesture set resulting from this process is shown in Table 2. Gestures 1 to 6 build the core vocabulary which is required to operate the application. They can be supplemented by gestures 7 to 10 as extended vocabulary which provides shortcuts to functions or menus.

Evaluation of the Hand Gesture Recognition System

Design and Procedure

The performance of the recognition system with the final gesture set was evaluated in a formative evaluation. Two main hypotheses were formulated as follows:

1. **The Gesture Set is Effective:** Verified by the ratio of gestures correctly used by the users to the total number of gestures used and by the classification accuracy of the system.
2. **The Gesture Set is Efficient:** Verified by the time between gesture request and gesture execution.

The hypotheses were operationalized as follows:

1. The ratio of correctly used gestures is higher than 90%.
2. The average correct classification ratio is higher than 90%.
3. Average execution time is shorter than 1.5 s.

The target figures have been chosen based on the requirements analysis that was carried out initially. Eight potential end-users (7 male, 1 female; aged between 18 and 44; all right-handed) were asked to use the recognition system to perform any gesture that was requested by a special software. That means, the participants were standing in front of a monitor using the recognition system completely out of the context of the mobile infor-

Table 2. Hand gesture set for interaction with the maintenance support application

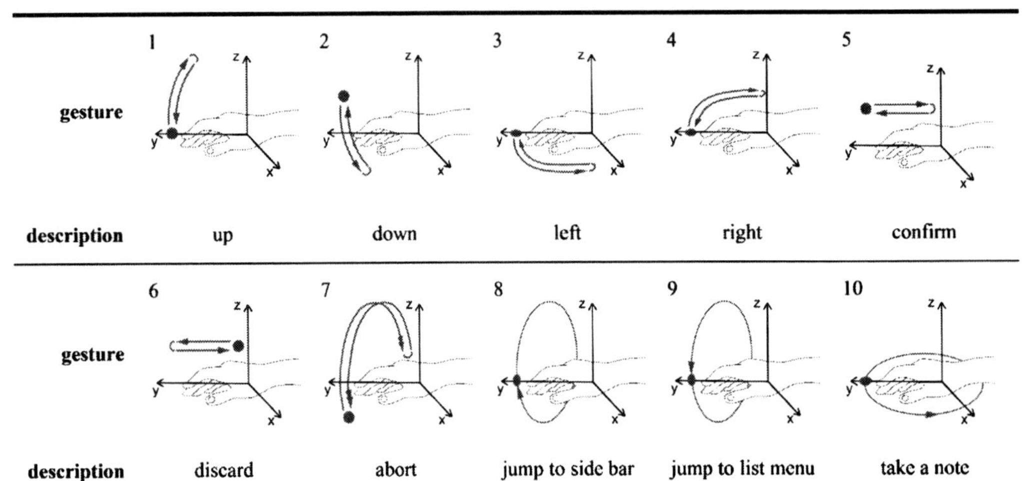

	1	2	3	4	5
gesture					
description	up	down	left	right	confirm

	6	7	8	9	10
gesture					
description	discard	abort	jump to side bar	jump to list menu	take a note

mation system. This evaluation design avoids any influences that may result from the quality of the application software or the task model. The evaluation software requested gestures in a specified order, and recorded recognized gestures and the elapsed time (regardless of whether the gesture was correct or not). Video-taping was used to monitor if a gesture was used or recognized incorrectly.

First, the participants received an introduction on the gesture recognition system and the gesture set until they were familiar with both. Afterwards, the participants were asked to execute 50 gestures in a random order requested by the PC-software. There was a time limit of 5 seconds for each gesture, and no feedback was given whether the used gesture was correct or not. The procedure was then repeated with a different order of gestures. The results of the second round were then analyzed. For each participant the whole evaluation was completed within about 30 minutes.

Results

First, the computational and memory cost has been assessed for different parameterizations. The memory usage originates from the size of the three matrices that describe an HMM and can be calculated directly from the chosen parameters, where Q represents the number of states and O represents the number of clusters:

$\left(Q + Q^2 + Q * O\right) * 2$ Bytes per model (factor 2 is required for 16 bit fixed-point operation)

Further, the required execution time is directly proportional to the number of gestures in the gesture set and to the number of states in the HMM. The current parameter set (6 states, 14 clusters, 10 models, 25 Hz sampling rate, 16 bit processing width) leads to a flash memory consumption for the models of 2,520 Bytes of flash memory and a worst case execution time of 85,000 cycles (average case: 72,000), whereof 74,000 (64,000) cycles account for the forward algorithm. The remaining cycles account for the preprocessing. Processor load at a clock frequency of 11.56 MHz and flash memory consumption including 10 models both remain below 20%. Table 3 compares the computational cost of the forward algorithm for a single model and the overall execution time for ten models including sensor data preprocessing for different parameter sets.

Second, the classification accuracy has been assessed using the metrics established by Zappi et al. (2009):

Table 3. Execution time for different parameter sets (average case / worst case number of cycles) for 16 bit fixed-point operation

Parameters [States/Clusters]	Execution Time of the Forward Algorithm [Cycles]	Overall Execution Time for 10 Models [Cycles]
6 / 14	6400 / 7400	72000 / 85000
6 / 18	6400 / 7400	74000 / 87000
8 / 14	10000 / 11200	108000 / 121400
10 / 14	14500 / 15800	153000 / 168000

- **Correct Classification Ratio (CCR):** The ratio of number of correctly classified instances to the total number of instances.
- **Precision (PR_i):** The ratio of the number of instances correctly classified for class i to the total number of instances classified as class i.
- **Recall (RC_i):** The ratio of the number of instances correctly classified for class i to total number of instances from class i.

The results of the formative evaluation are listed in Table 4. Due to possible learning effects we only analyzed the second round. All results are normally-distributed (verified using a Kolmogorov-Smirnov-Test). A t-test has confirmed both hypotheses at a significance level of $p = 5\%$. On average, participants used the correct gesture in 97.4% of all cases and needed 920 ms for gesture execution. The mean recognition rate was 93.7%, while 54.0% of the incorrect recognitions were caused by unclassified gestures. The remaining incorrect recognitions were classified incorrectly. More details on the evaluation results can be found in Ziegler et al. (2012).

Table 5 shows the results of the classification accuracy estimation captured during the second round of the formative evaluation and averaged over all participants. As can be seen, the precision is near the optimum of 100% for most gestures. The recall ratio is slightly lower, since gestures are sometimes rejected as unclassified. The correct classification ratio is 93.7%, while 54% of the incorrect recognitions were caused by unclassified gestures. The remaining recognitions were incorrectly classified. Table 5 also gives the number of incorrectly used gestures and false recognitions. Gestures 4 and 9 have caused most of the problems. The problems with gesture 4 turned out to be caused by insufficient training, whereas the problems with gesture 9 revealed a usability flaw. Obviously, the design of the gestures 8 and 9 violates *design guideline 5*.

Discussion

The results of the formative evaluation have shown that the proposed system performs well on 8 bit architectures and 16 bit processing width. The results indicate a high applicability of the wearable

Table 4. Results of the formative evaluation

Round	Result	Correct Execution Ratio	Execution Time [s]	Correct Classification Ratio
1	average	0.960	0.974	0.883
	variance	0.023	0.094	0.075
2	average	0.976	0.920	0.937
	variance	0.022	0.063	0.039

Table 5. Classification accuracy for the gesture set

Gesture	Precision	Recall	Incorrect Use	False Recognition
1	1.00	1.00	0	3
2	0.97	1.00	0	0
3	1.00	0.94	3	6
4	0.97	0.78	1	20
5	1.00	0.89	3	6
6	1.00	0.94	3	6
7	1.00	1.00	4	1
8	1.00	1.00	0	1
9	0.90	0.81	8	19
10	0.95	1.00	2	4
CCR:		**0.937**		

recognition system and the designed gesture set. Using more training data from a larger population may increase the robustness of the system against user-dependent effects. The system is extremely resource-efficient and optimized for fixed-point arithmetic of low-cost embedded controllers. This enables engineers to realize fast, resource-efficient and completely self-contained gestural user interfaces, which are especially suitable in environments were energy autarky is a requirement. Because of the low memory and performance requirements, the recognition hardware can be easily miniaturized and highly embedded into human movement without obstructing or harming the user.

The results have further shown that the designed gesture set was easy to learn and memorable for the users, and suitable for automatic online recognition on a hardware platform with limited capabilities. The proposed two-step participatory design process enables designers to create usable, convenient and technically feasible gesture vocabularies in a participatory, task-oriented manner.

FUTURE RESEARCH DIRECTIONS

Currently, the presented system is lacking a summative evaluation in the real context of use. This was by intention, since such studies are hardly generalizable and thus have only reduced scientific value. Nevertheless, a comprehensive summary and comparison of conducted summative evaluations of systems that have been designed using the proposed participatory design process would be a valuable starting point for researchers and engineers who want to conduct their own evaluation. It is conceivable to extend the evaluation with measures for workload analysis. Since hand gestures are known to be physically demanding, the assessment of the individual workload for each developed gesture set would be very informative and could uncover ergonomic problems early in the development.

The gesture recognition algorithm currently uses static segmentation with a defined trigger based on the rest position. These constraints could be removed, if the recognition system was to continuously analyze the data stream. Each sampling step would then trigger a new classification and all active classifications would run in parallel. This should lead to a huge increase of computational and memory cost, but would allow the recognition of arbitrary gestures, regardless of their start and end position and their duration. Even non-disjunctive gestures could be recognized. Different online algorithms for segmenting time series can, for example, be found in Keogh et al. (2001).

From the hardware point of view, there is still great potential for further sensing techniques. First, there are some drawbacks to the current solution. Accelerometer-based gesture recognition is not independent from the orientation of the hand, which means that it is not possible to change the rest position without training new models. The only way to overcome this limitation is to use sensors that are independent from the gravitation vector. Second, additional sensing techniques may enhance the possible gesture space. For example, surface electromyography (SEMG) (Zhiyuan, 2011) is capable of recognizing various finger gestures with high accuracy at low cost and minimal intrusiveness to the user. Of course, it is also possible to equip both hands with a gesture recognition system and to define two hand gesture sets.

The presented gesture set is, by design, specific to the given context of use and the technical constraints of the system. However, it is conceivable that it is possible to identify invariants in the design of gestures that may facilitate the design of future gesture sets. These invariants could be justified with human cognition and biomechanics (Gibet, Kamp & Poirier, 2004) and be formulated as design guidelines.

The scope of the gesture recognition system is of course not limited to the use as a self-contained user interface, but could also be integrated into a multimodal, distributed user interface that provides a combination of special interaction styles, e.g. tactile interfaces, RFID or speech recognition. On the other hand, the gesture recognition system could be combined with special visual displays such as head mounted displays, pico projectors or wearable flexible display screens in relevant professional applications. In particular, in the domain of aircraft maintenance, in which head mounted displays have already been evaluated successfully, this might lead to valuable improvements of current systems. The recognition system could also become a part of an extensive interaction scenario that includes vision-based systems or multiple screens, e.g. smart home control (Greenberg et al, 2011) or in the control room of the future (Schwarz, Oortmann & Reiterer, 2012). Further, the gesture recognition system is not only applicable for hand gestures, but is suitable for the assessment of gestures of all moving body parts. A larger number of gesture recognition systems could thus be fused with the corresponding algorithms to reveal a whole-body gesture, which was, for example, researched by Zappi et al. (2007). Based on this preliminary work new applications could be developed.

CONCLUSION

This book chapter has covered the conceptual, methodological and pragmatic aspects of the design and evaluation of efficient and reliable hand gesture based user interfaces. It has shown that gestural interfaces are a suitable alternative means for interaction in professional working environments, and has given deep insights into the implementation and parameterization of HMM based gesture recognition algorithms. A two-step participatory design process has been presented that can be used as a pattern for participatory, task-oriented design, implementation and evaluation of gesture recognition systems and gesture vocabularies. Finally, this book chapter has focused on potential future research directions for hand gesture based interaction.

There is no doubt that further research is necessary in both the theoretical and conceptual foundations of gesture based interaction in the IT-supported work as well as in a consistent design methodology for such interfaces. This book chapter is a first step in this direction. It can be seen as a methodological and architectural framework for development of resource-efficient, robust and reliable gestural user interfaces for professional working environments. It can either be used directly or serve as a starting point for further research. Mobile accessibility will become a key factor for commercial success of information systems, and innovative user interfaces such as hand gesture recognition systems may leverage the spread of the necessary mobile systems in professional working environments – even in those with adverse environmental conditions.

ACKNOWLEDGMENT

The research leading to these results was partially funded by the European Community's Seventh Framework Programme under grant agreement no. FP7-284928 ComVantage.

REFERENCES

Bailador, G., Roggen, D., Tröster, G., & Trivino, G. (2007). Real time gesture recognition using continuous time recurrent neural networks. In *Proceedings of the 2nd International Conference on Body Area Networks BodyNets* (pp. 15.1-15.8). Brussels, Belgium: ICST.

CyberGloveSystems. (n.d.). Retrieved October 30, 2012, from http://www.cyberglovesystems.com

Geer, D. (2004). Will gesture-recognition technology point the way? *Computer*, *37*(10), 20–23. doi:10.1109/MC.2004.184.

Gibet, S., Kamp, J. F., & Poirier, F. (2004). Gesture analysis: Invariant laws in movement. In *Gesture-Based Communication in Human-Computer Interaction (LNCS)* (Vol. 2915, pp. 451–452). Berlin: Springer. doi:10.1007/978-3-540-24598-8_1.

Greenberg, S., Marquardt, N., Ballendat, T., Diaz-Marino, R., & Wang, M. (2011). Proxemic interactions. *Interaction*, *18*(1), 42–50. doi:10.1145/1897239.1897250.

Henze, N., Löcken, A., Boll, S., Hesselmann, T., & Pielot, M. (2010). Free-hand gestures for music playback: Deriving gestures with a user-centred process. In *Proceedings of the 9th International Conference on Mobile and Ubiquitous Multimedia MUM* (pp. 1-10). New York, NY: ACM Press.

Hofmann, F., Heyer, P., & Hommel, G. (1998). Velocity profile based recognition of dynamic gestures with discrete hidden Markov models. In *Proceedings of the International Gesture Workshop on Gesture and Sign Language in Human-Computer Interaction* (pp. 81-95). Berlin: Springer.

Hurtienne, J., Stößel, C., Sturm, C., Maus, A., Rötting, M., Langdon, P., & Clarkson, J. (2010). Physical gestures for abstract concepts: Inclusive design with primary metaphors. *Interacting with Computers*, *22*(6), 475–484. doi:10.1016/j.intcom.2010.08.009.

Kallio, S., Kela, J., & Mäntyjärvi, J. (2003). Online gesture recognition system for mobile interaction. In *Proceedings of the International Conference on Systems, Man and Cybernetics SMC* (pp. 2070-2076). IEEE.

Kendon, A. (1996). An agenda for gesture studies. *Semiotic Review of Books*, *7*(3), 8–12.

Keogh, E., Chu, S., Hart, D., & Pazzani, M. (2001). An online algorithm for segmenting time series. In *Proceedings of the IEEE International Conference on Data Mining ICDM* (pp. 289-296). IEEE.

Klingmann, M. (2009). *Accelerometer-based gesture recognition with the iphone*. (Master thesis). Goldsmiths University of London, London, UK.

Kratz, S., & Rohs, M. (2010). A $3 gesture recognizer – Simple gesture recognition for devices equipped with 3D acceleration sensors. In *Proceedings of the 15th International Conference on Intelligent User Interfaces IUI* (pp. 341-344). New York, NY: ACM Press.

Kurtenbach, G., & Hulteen, E. A. (1990). Gestures in human-computer communication. In B. Laurel (Ed.), *The Art of Human-Computer Interface Design* (pp. 309–317). Reading, MA: Addison-Wesley Publishing Co..

Liu, J., Wang, Z., Zhong, L., Wickramasuriya, J., & Vasudevan, V. (2009). uWave: Accelerometer–based personalized gesture recognition and its applications. *Journal Pervasive and Mobile Computing*, *5*(6), 657–675. doi:10.1016/j.pmcj.2009.07.007.

Mäntyjärvi, J., Kela, J., Korpipää, P., & Kallio, S. (2004). Enabling fast and effortless customisation in accelerometer based gesture interaction. In *Proceedings of the Third International Conference on Mobile and Ubiquitous Multimedia MUM* (pp. 25-31). New York, NY: ACM Press.

Milosevic, B., Farella, E., & Benini, L. (2010). Continuous gesture recognition for resource constrained smart objects. In *Proceedings of the Fourth International Conference on Mobile Ubiquitous Computing, Systems, Services and Technologies UBICOMM* (pp. 391-396). Xpert Publishing Services.

Min, J.-K., Choe, B., & Cho, S.-B. (2010). A selective template matching algorithm for short and intuitive gesture UI of accelerometer-builtin mobile phones. In *Proceedings of the 2nd World Congress on Nature and Biologically Inspired Computing NaBIC* (pp. 660-665). IEEE.

Mitra, S., & Acharya, T. (2007). Gesture recognition: A survey. *IEEE Transactions on Systems, Man, and Cybernetics – Part C: Applications and Reviews Publication Information*, *37*(3), 311–324. doi:10.1109/TSMCC.2007.893280.

Murphy, K. (1998). *Hidden Markov model (HMM) toolbox for matlab*. Retrieved October 30, 2012, from http://people.cs.ubc.ca/~murphyk/Software/HMM/hmm

Pylvänäinen, T. (2005). Accelerometer based gesture recognition using continuous HMMs. In J. S. Marques, N. P. de la Blanca, & P. Pina (Eds.), *Pattern Recognition and Image Analysis, (LNCS)* (Vol. 3522, pp. 413–430). Berlin: Springer. doi:10.1007/11492429_77.

Rabiner, L. R. (1989). A tutorial on hidden Markov models and selected applications in speech recognition. *Proceedings of the IEEE*, *77*(2), 257–286. doi:10.1109/5.18626.

Rao, J., Gao, T., Gong, Z., & Jiang, Z. (2009). Low cost hand gesture learning and recognition system based on hidden Markov model. In *Proceedings of the 2nd International Symposium on Information Science and Engineering ISISE* (pp. 433-438). IEEE.

Rigoll, G., Kosmala, A., & Eickeler, S. (1998). High performance real–time gesture recognition using hidden Markov models. In *Gesture and Sign Language in Human-Computer Interaction, (LNCS)* (Vol. 1371, pp. 69–80). Berlin: Springer Press. doi:10.1007/BFb0052990.

Ritchey, T. (2011). *Wicked problems/social messes: Decision support modelling with morphological analysis*. Berlin: Springer. doi:10.1007/978-3-642-19653-9.

Rubine, D. H. (1991). *The automatic recognition of gestures*. (Doctoral thesis). Carnegie-Mellon University, Pittsburgh, PA.

Ruiz, J., Li, Y., & Lank, E. (2011). User-defined motion gestures for mobile interaction. In *Proceedings of the 29th International Conference on Human Factors in Computing Systems CHI* (pp. 197-206). New York, NY: ACM Press.

Schlömer, T., Poppinga, B., Henze, N., & Boll, S. (2008). Gesture recognition with a Wii controller. In *Proceedings of the Second International Conference on Tangible and Embedded Interaction TEI* (pp. 11-14). New York, NY: ACM Press.

Schuler, D., & Namioka, A. (1993). *Participatory design: Principles and practices*. Boca Raton, FL: CRC Press Llc.

Schwarz, T., Oortmann, H., & Reiterer, H. (2012). Holistic workspace - Wie neue technologien die operatoren unterstützen. In Automatisieren! by ATP. Oldenbourg Verlag.

Witt, H. (2007). *Human-computer interfaces for wearable computers – A systematic approach to development and evaluation*. (Doctoral thesis). Bremen, Germany: Universität Bremen.

Zappi, P., Milosevic, B., Farella, E., & Benini, L. (2009). Hidden Markov model based gesture recognition on low-cost, low-power tangible user interfaces. *Entertainment Computing*, *1*(2), 75–84. doi:10.1016/j.entcom.2009.09.005.

Zappi, P., Stiefmeier, T., Farella, E., Roggen, D., Benini, L., & Tröster, G. (2007). Activity recognition from on-body sensors by classifier fusion: sensor scalability and robustness. In *Proceedings of the Third International Conference on Intelligent Sensors, Sensor Networks and Information Processing ISSNIP* (pp. 281-286). IEEE.

Zhang, X., Chen, X., Wang, W., Yang, J., Lantz, V., & Wang, K. (2009). Hand gesture recognition and virtual game control based on 3D accelerometer and EMG sensors. In *Proceedings of the 14th International Conference on Intelligent User Interfaces IUI* (pp. 401-406). New York, NY: ACM Press.

Zhiyuan, L., Xiang, C., Kongqiao, W., & Zhangyan, Z. (2011). A prototype of gesture-based interface. In *Proceedings of the 13th International Conference on Human Computer Interaction with Mobile Devices and Services MobileHCI* (pp. 33-36). New York, NY: ACM Press.

Zhou, R., Jingjing, M., Junsong, Y., & Zhengyou, Z. (2011). Robust hand gesture recognition with kinect sensor. In *Proceedings of the 19th International Conference on Multimedia MM* (pp. 759-760). New York, NY: ACM Press.

Ziegler, J., Döring, R., Pfeffer, J., & Urbas, L. (2013). Autonomous dynamic hand gesture recognition in industrial settings. In *Proceedings of IADIS International Conference Interfaces and Human Computer Interaction IHCI*. IADIS.

ADDITIONAL READING

Amma, C., Georgi, M., & Schultz, T. (2012). Airwriting: Hands-free mobile text input by spotting and continuous recognition of 3D-space handwriting with inertial sensors. In *Proceedings of the 16th International Symposium on Wearable Computers ISWC* (pp. 52-59). IEEE.

W. Barfield, & T. Caudell (Eds.). (2001). *Fundamentals of wearable computers and augmented reality*. Boca Raton, FL: CRC Press Llc.

Cassell, J. (1998). *A framework for gesture generation and interpretation: Computer vision in human-machine interaction*. Cambridge, UK: Cambridge University Press.

Dourish, P. (2004). *Where the action is: The foundations of embodied interaction*. Cambridge, MA: The MIT Press.

Kendon, A. (2004). *Gesture: Visible action as utterance*. Cambridge, UK: Cambridge University Press.

Kensing, F., & Blomberg, J. (1998). Participatory design: Issues and concerns. *Computer Supported Cooperative Work*, *7*(3-4), 167–185. doi:10.1023/A:1008689307411.

Kortum, P. (2008). *HCI beyond the GUI: Design for haptic, speech, olfactory, and other nontraditional interfaces*. San Francisco, CA: Morgan Kaufmann.

Kratz, L., Morris, D., & Saponas, T. S. (2012). Making gestural input from arm-worn inertial sensors more practical. In *Proceedings of the 2012 ACM Annual Conference on Human Factors in Computing Systems* (pp. 1747-1750). New York, NY: ACM Press.

Lee, H. C., Shih, C. Y., & Lin, T. M. (2013). Computer-vision based hand gesture recognition and its application in iphone. In *Advances in Intelligent Systems and Applications* (Vol. 2, pp. 487–497). Berlin: Springer. doi:10.1007/978-3-642-35473-1_49.

Lumsden, J., & Brewster, S. (2003). A paradigm shift: Alternative interaction techniques for use with mobile & wearable devices. In *Proceedings of the 2003 Conference of the Centre for Advanced Studies on Collaborative research* (pp. 197-210). IBM Press.

McNeill, D. (1992). *Hand and mind: What gestures reveal about thought*. Chicago: University of Chicago Press.

McNeill, D. (2008). *Gesture and thought*. Chicago: University of Chicago Press.

Montero, C. S., Alexander, J., Marshall, M. T., & Subramanian, S. (2010). Would you do that? Understanding social acceptance of gestural interfaces. In *Proceedings of the 12th International Conference on Human Computer Interaction with Mobile Devices and Services MobileHCI* (pp. 275-278). New York, NY: ACM Press.

Parvini, F., McLeod, D., Shahabi, C., Navai, B., Zali, B., & Ghandeharizadeh, S. (2009). An approach to glove-based gesture recognition. In *Human-Computer Interaction: Novel Interaction Methods and Techniques* (pp. 236–245). Berlin: Springer. doi:10.1007/978-3-642-02577-8_26.

Rico, J., & Brewster, S. (2010). Usable gestures for mobile interfaces: Evaluating social acceptability. In *Proceedings of the 28th International Conference on Human Factors in Computing Systems CHI* (pp. 887-896). New York, NY: ACM Press.

Saffer, D. (2008). *Designing gestural interfaces*. Sebastopol, CA: O'Reilly Media.

Salvendy, G. (2012). *Handbook of human factors and ergonomics*. Hoboken, NJ: Wiley. doi:10.1002/9781118131350.

Schuler, D. (1993). *Participatory design: Principles and practices*. Hillsdale, NJ: L. Erlbaum Associates.

Sturman, D. J. (1991). *Whole-hand input*. (Doctoral dissertation). Massachusetts Institute of Technology, Cambridge, MA.

Weiser, M. (1991). The computer for the 21st century. *Scientific American*, *265*(3), 94–104. doi:10.1038/scientificamerican0991-94 PMID:1675486.

York, J., & Pendharkar, P. C. (2004). Human–computer interaction issues for mobile computing in a variable work context. *International Journal of Human-Computer Studies*, *60*(5), 771–797. doi:10.1016/j.ijhcs.2003.07.004.

KEY TERMS AND DEFINITIONS

Adverse Working Environments: Working environments that confront the worker with adverse environmental conditions with challenging features such as changing light, high humidity, dirt, dust, grease and liquids. There is often a lack of appropriate workstations with desks, seats, storage place and sufficient space for movement. Usually, there are special occupational safety and health provisions to ensure healthy working conditions.

Gesture Recognition: The process in which the gestures performed by the sender are recognized by the receiver. While the sender is typically a human, the receiver can either also be a human or a technical system that is able to perceive, identify and interpret a set of gestures.

Mobile IT-Supported Work: Mobile work in non-office environments that is supported by associated information and communication technology (ICT). Work is performed on the move using laptops, tablets and/or smart phones in changing locations outside the office or even the company's premises, sometimes under adverse environmental conditions.

Normalized Dynamic Hand Gestures: Normalized dynamic hand gestures include motions of the arm and the hand of a human being. They may also include finger motion. They always start from and return to a rest position have a peak structure, in which the part containing the information is located in the middle of the sequence, are well-bounded having clear onsets and offsets, and are disjunctive to other gestures. Gesture phrases are organized symmetrically.

Chapter 18
The Axiomatic Usability Evaluation Method

Yinni Guo
Purdue University, USA

ABSTRACT

This chapter introduces a new usability evaluation method, the axiomatic evaluation method, which is developed based on the axiomatic design theory – a formalized design methodology that can be used to solve a variety of design problems. This new evaluation method examines three domains of a product: customer domain, functional domain, and control domain. This method investigates not only usability problems reported by the users, but also usability problems related to customer requirements and usability problems related to control through checking the mapping matrix between the three domains. To determine how well this new usability evaluation method works, a between-subject experiment was conducted to compare the axiomatic evaluation method with the think aloud method. Sixty participants were randomly assigned to use either method to evaluate three popular consumer electronic devices (music player, digital camera, mobile phone) that represented different levels of complexity. Number of usability problems discovered, completion time, and overall user satisfaction were collected. Results show that the axiomatic evaluation method performed better in finding usability problems for the mobile phone. The axiomatic evaluation method was also better at finding usability problems about user expectation and control than the think aloud method. Benefits and drawbacks of using the axiomatic evaluation method are discussed.This chapter introduces a new usability evaluation method, the axiomatic evaluation method, which is developed based on the axiomatic design theory – a formalized design methodology that can be used to solve a variety of design problems. This new evaluation method examines three domains of a product: customer domain, functional domain, and control domain. This method investigates not only usability problems reported by the users, but also usability problems related to customer requirements and usability problems related to control through checking the mapping matrix between the three domains. To determine how well this new usability evaluation method works, a between-subject experiment was conducted to compare the axiomatic evaluation method with the think aloud method. Sixty participants were randomly assigned to use either method to evaluate three popular consumer electronic devices (music player, digital camera, mobile phone) that represented different levels of complexity. Number of usability problems discovered, completion time, and overall user satisfaction

DOI: 10.4018/978-1-4666-4623-0.ch018

were collected. Results show that the axiomatic evaluation method performed better in finding usability problems for the mobile phone. The axiomatic evaluation method was also better at finding usability problems about user expectation and control than the think aloud method. Benefits and drawbacks of using the axiomatic evaluation method are discussed.

INTRODUCTION

Today usability is a ubiquitous term used in human-computer interaction and commonly used without definition (Hertzum, 2010). The document ISO 9241-11 (1998) defines usability as: the extent to which a product can be used by specified users to achieve specified goals with effectiveness, efficiency and satisfaction in a specified context of use. Here effectiveness is defined as the accuracy and the completeness with which users achieve goals in particular environments; efficiency refers to the resources expended in relation to the accuracy and completeness of the goals achieved; and satisfaction is defined as the comfort and the acceptability of the system for its users and other people affected by its use. Nielsen (1993) also considered usability as a measurable construct, and identified five attributes: learnability, efficiency, memorability, errors, and satisfaction. Learnability refers to how easily novice users can learn a new system to reach a reasonable level of usage proficiency within a short time; efficiency means the expert user's steady-state level of performance that can be obtained once the user has learned the system; memorability refers to how easy it is to remember the system without relearning it again when casual users return to the system after not using it for some time; errors are defined as actions that do not accomplish the desired goals when performing the specified tasks; satisfaction refers to how pleasant and satisfying it is for users to use the system. These definitions of usability have been the basis for many usability evaluation studies that try to find usability problems. In recent years, researchers and designers aim at a more holistic understanding and evaluation of user experience, beyond mere cognitive or ergonomic issues, for example enjoyment, pleasure, emotional and cultural aspects (Macaulay et al., 2006; Wright & McCarthy, 2004). Hertzum (2010) introduces 6 images of usability: universal usability (the systems can be used by everybody), situational usability (quality-in-use of a system in a specified situation with its users, tasks, and wider context of use), perceived usability (user's subjective experience of a system based on his or her interaction with it), hedonic usability (joy of use), organizational usability (groups of people collaborating in an organizational setting), and cultural usability (usability has different meanings depending on the users' cultural background).

The term usability evaluation method was popularized by Gray and Salzman (1998). It refers to any method or technique that performs formative usability evaluation of a human-computer interaction design at any stage of the design's development. Hilbert and Redmiles (2000, pp. 388) defined usability evaluation as "the act of measuring (or identifying potential issues affecting) usability attributes of a system or device with respect to particular users, performing particular tasks, in particular contexts." The essential characteristic of usability evaluation methods is that every method, when applied to an interaction design, produces a list of potential usability problems as its output. Several methods, including cognitive walkthrough, heuristic evaluation, think aloud, interview, and experience prototyping have been developed and used broadly to discover usability problems (Andre et al., 2003; Buchenau & Fulton, 2000; Gray & Salzman, 1998).

These methods have been used to detect usability problems mostly for websites and software, but also for other products including consumer electronic products. Yet some authors have suggested that it is not appropriate to apply the same concept of software usability directly to consumer electronic products (Han et al., 1998a-b; Han et al., 2001; Kwahk et al., 1997). For example, Han et al. (2000) stated, "It is not appropriate to apply the same concept of software usability developed in the HCI research directly to the consumer electronic products". One possible reason to question the appropriateness of applying the concept of software usability to consumer electronic devices is that there are a number of aspects of the interfaces and interactions with electronic devices that are different from those of desktop and laptop interfaces (Zhang et al., 2010). Compared to using software and web sites on consumer electronic devices, users have access to bigger screen and more flexible control tools (keyboard and mouse) when they're using software and web sites on computers (Venkatesh et al., 2003). Though more and more consumer electronic products are adapting touch screen techniques, which allows more flexible control, the experience of performing a task on a touch screen device is still different from that of performing the same task on a computer. As Apple iOS Human Interface Guidelines states (Apple, 2012), people use iOS-based devices (touch screen enabled consumer electronics) very differently than they use desktop and laptop computers, and they have different expectations for the user experience. Touch screen allows users to control the device more directly, but there are still problems like touch responsiveness, touch accuracy, and difficult to type on the touch screen that are degrading the user experience. Not to mention when using consumer electronic products without touch screen, users need to control the device through a compact control panel. Sometimes users do not even know how to operate the device because there is not enough information about how to do so or the design of operation does not fit the users' mental model (Han et al., 2000). Users may encounter situations of pressing the buttons more times than needed and then have to spend additional time pressing the keys again. A typical example is how users change their television or monitor settings. As more and more complicated functions become available on consumer electronics, new usability problems about how to control will continue to emerge.

Because of these differences, researchers have tried to define usability metrics and build usability evaluation methods for consumer electronic products. Ziefle (2002) indicated that predictability, familiarity and generalizability were crucial criteria for the user's selection of a mobile phone. Ciavarella and Paterno (2003) addressed the usability criteria for graphical user interface design of mobile guide applications with five concerns: web metaphors, navigation feedback, orientation support in the surrounding environment, minimal graphical interaction and no redundancy in input commands. Ji et al. (2006) developed a usability checklist for mobile phone user interfaces based on 21 usability principles. Gebauer (2008) summarized the results of a series of research studies conducted to explore the technology requirements of mobile professionals. Kim and Han (2008) established a methodology for developing a usability index for consumer electronic products and a case study on DVD player was conducted to demonstrate the usefulness of the method. Morris (2008) developed a graphical user interface that improves the usability of cell phones, PDAs, and other mobile devices. Geven et al. (2008) employed card-sorting techniques for predefined services and applications with personalization and customization aspects, followed by specific brainstorming to generate additional ideas. Zhang et al. (2009) used an online survey and identified nine critical factors that predicate the handset's perceived usability.

In this chapter, we present a new usability evaluation method—the axiomatic evaluation method, which is able to discover more usability problems about customer requirement and control of the device. In the second section of this chapter, we introduce how the axiomatic evaluation method is developed based on the axiomatic design theory.

The third part of this chapter describes how we validate the new method through a comparison study with the think aloud method. The last part of this chapter summarizes the benefits and drawbacks of using the axiomatic evaluation method and proposes future research as well.

CONCEPTUAL FRAMEWORK

Axiomatic Design Theory

The axiomatic evaluation method is a usability evaluation method developed based on the axiomatic design theory (Guo et al., 2011). The axiomatic design theory (Suh, 1990) is a formalized methodology that can be used to solve a variety of design problems. In the past, engineers design their products according to their experience and intuition. Products are designed, built into prototypes or manufactured and then get requests for redesign because the original design could not meet the customer expectation. The undisciplined design process results not only in poor customer satisfaction, but also with respect to missed schedules, cost overruns and failed products. To be efficient and to generate a design that meets the perceived needs, the designer must specifically state the design goals before the design process begins. Therefore, a rigorous design approach must start with an explicit statement of "what we want to achieve" and end with a clear description of "how we will achieve it" (Lee & Suh, 2005). Once what the customers need is understood, these needs must be transformed into a minimum set of specifications, or functional requirements, that adequately describes "what we want to achieve" to satisfy the customers' needs. The descriptor of "how to achieve it" may be in the form of design parameters.

The ultimate goal of axiomatic design is to establish a scientific basis for design and to improve the expertise of the designer by providing a theoretical foundation based on logical, rational thought processes and tools. The theory helps to overcome shortcomings of the product development process based on a recursive "design/build/test" cycle, which requires continuing modifications and changes as design flaws are discovered through the testing (Suh, 2011).

The axiomatic design consists of four domains and two axioms. The four domains, ordered in consideration are customer domain ([CA]), functional domain ([FR]), physical domain ([DP]) and process domain ([PV]). Customer domain ([CA]) consists of the needs (or attributes) that the customers are looking for in a product, process, systems or material. Functional domain ([FR]) consists of functional requirement which is the minimum set of independent requirements that completely characterizes the functional needs of the product. Physical domain ([DP]) consists of design parameters which are the key physical variables in the physical domain that characterizes the design that satisfies the specified functional requirements. Process domain ([PV]) consists of process variables which are the key variables in the process domain that characterizes the process that can generate the specified design parameters. An earlier domain represents "what we want to achieve", whereas the subsequent adjacent domain represents the design solution of "how we propose to satisfy the requirements specified in the prior domain." The design flow suggested by axiomatic design theory consists of mapping from one domain to the other (Figure 1).

The mapping process between domains can be expressed mathematically in terms of vectors. For example, a set of functional requirements in the functional domain can be written into a functional requirement vector ([FR]). Similarly, a set of design parameters in the physical domain that has been chosen to satisfy the functional requirements constitutes the design parameter vector ([DP]). The mathematical expression can be then written as $[FR] = [A][DP]$, where $[A]$ is the design matrix that characterizes the product design. The design matrix is of the following form for a design

Figure 1. Four domains and the mapping procedure

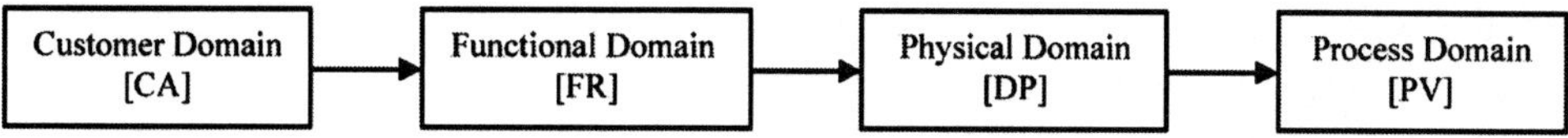

that has three functional requirements and three design parameters:

$$\begin{bmatrix} FR_1 \\ FR_2 \\ FR_3 \end{bmatrix} = \begin{bmatrix} A_{11} & A_{12} & A_{13} \\ A_{21} & A_{22} & A_{23} \\ A_{31} & A_{32} & A_{33} \end{bmatrix} \begin{bmatrix} DP_1 \\ DP_2 \\ DP_3 \end{bmatrix} \quad (1)$$

The axiomatic design theory examines the design quality by two axioms. The two axioms were identified by examining common elements always present in good designs. The axiomatic approach has had a powerful impact in many fields of science and technology (e.g., Euclid's axioms for geometry and the first and second laws of thermodynamics are axioms). The first axiom, the independence axiom, states that the independence of functional requirements that characterizes the design goals must always be maintained. In other words, when there are two or more functional requirements, the design solution must be such that each functional requirement can be satisfied without affecting others. A correct set of design parameters ([DP]) must be chosen to satisfy all functional requirements ([FR]) and maintain their independence; and the design matrix [A] must be either a diagonal matrix or triangular matrix (Suh, 1991). When the design matrix [A] is a diagonal matrix, each of the functional requirement ([FR]) can be satisfied independently by one of the design parameter ([DP]). Such design is called an uncoupled design. When the design matrix [A] is a triangular matrix, the independence of FRs can be guaranteed if and only if the design parameters ([DP]) are determined in a proper sequence. Such a design is called a decoupled design. Any other form of the design matrix is called a full matrix and results in a coupled design, which will result in conflicting control. Examples of diagonal matrix, triangular matrix and full matrix are listed below:

- **Diagonal Matrix (uncoupled design):**
  $$\begin{bmatrix} A_{11} & 0 & 0 \\ 0 & A_{22} & 0 \\ 0 & 0 & A_{33} \end{bmatrix}$$
- **Triangular Matrix (decoupled design):**
  $$\begin{bmatrix} A_{11} & 0 & 0 \\ A_{21} & A_{22} & 0 \\ A_{31} & A_{32} & A_{33} \end{bmatrix}$$
- **Full Matrix (coupled design):**
  $$\begin{bmatrix} A_{11} & A_{12} & 0 \\ A_{21} & A_{22} & A_{23} \\ 0 & A_{32} & A_{33} \end{bmatrix}$$

The second axiom, the information axiom states that among those designs that satisfy the independence axiom, the design that has the smallest information content is the best. The information amount should be estimated by the users. In a real design scenario, there can be many designs that satisfy the independence axiom. However, one of these designs is likely to be superior. The information axiom provides a quantitative measure of the merits of a given design, and it is useful in selecting the best among those designs that are acceptable.

Suh (1995) compares axiomatic design to other design methods. He divides designs into two categories: algorithmic design and axiomatic design. In algorithmic design, designers first need to identify the design process to deliver a design embodiment that satisfies the design goals. This design method can be effective if the design has to satisfy one or just a few functional requirements, but when many functional requirements must be satisfied at the same time, they are not very effective. The algorithmic design approach is more useful at the final stages of detailed design than at the conceptual stage or at higher levels of design hierarchy. Conversely, the axiomatic approach begins with a different premise: there are generalizable principles that govern the underlying behavior axioms are general principles or self-evident truths that cannot be derived or proven to be true except that there are no counter-examples or exceptions (Suh, 1995). Moreover, it has been found that axiomatic design can provide a framework for understanding projects. People working in the same project now have a shared understanding about requirements, constraints, solutions, etc.

The axiomatic design theory has been applied to a variety of products and systems such as mechanical design, system design and control, software design, organizations management, materials design and more. Many innovations have been made and commercialized based on the use of axiomatic design, such as microcellular plastics and woven electrical connectors (Suh, 2001). Although the meanings of the four domains are quite different from one product area to another, the axiomatic design theory successfully enhances the design quality in different fields. As many case studies presented in Suh's (2001) book suggest, the performance, robustness, reliability and functionality of products, process, software, systems and organizations are significantly improved when the axioms are satisfied. In recent years, the axiomatic design theory has been applied in human factors design like ergonomic microscope workstation design (Helander & Lin, 2000), biomechanical hand tools (Helander & Lin, 2002), information visual design (Quill et al., 2001) and e-commerce website (Yenisey, 2007).

Axiomatic Evaluation Method

As discussed in the last section, the core idea of the axiomatic design theory is to start designing from understanding "what do the customers need", to specifying "how could we achieve it" through providing the right functions, the appropriate design parameters for the functions, and the proper process variables for the design parameters. Similarly, in usability evaluation we try answer the questions of "what do the users want in the product" and "how well does the product satisfy user requirements". Therefore it is feasible to apply the framework of axiomatic design theory to usability evaluation, and three domains are set up for the usability evaluation process: customer domain ([CA]), functional domain ([FR]) and control domain ([CT]). Customer domain ([CA]) consists of customer requirements of the product and can be retrieved by an open-ended questionnaire. Functional domain ([FR]) consists of existing functions of the product and can be easily retrieved by reading the product manual. Control domain ([CT]) consists of the control keys of the product, and also can be retrieved by examining the product or reading the product manual. The use of the two axioms are similar, but the axiomatic evaluation method has also included constraints for human-computer interaction design to examine the mapping matrix, such as maintaining stimulus-response compatibility (Proctor & Vu, 2006) and following Hick's Law (Schneider & Anderson, 2011), for which response time increases as a function of the amount of uncertainty among alternatives. The biggest difference between the original axiomatic design theory and the axiomatic evaluation method is that in the evaluation method the third domain is the control domain ([CT]) instead of the physical domain ([DP]). The main reason for this change is that, in the evaluation process, we are more interested in evaluating how the existing design parameters with which users interact (the control keys) support the functions, rather than in figuring out how the design parameters with which users will not interact perform.

Usability problems can be found by examining the mapping between the three domains. The mapping can be expressed as matrices [X] and [Y]:

[CA]=[X][FR]

[Customer Requirements] = [X] [Functions]

[FR]=[Y][CT]

[Functions] = [Y] [Control Keys] (2)

The mapping matrix [X] between customer domain ([CA]) and functional domain ([FR]) can provide an index of function sufficiency, which can be beneficial to prototypes at the beginning stage of product development. If the index is high, the current product could satisfy most customers. If the index is low, designers may want to reconsider the design direction. The mapping between functional domain ([FR]) and control domain ([CT]) shows how easy it is to control the device. Usability problems can be found by checking the mapping matrix [Y] between functional domain and control domain, which is determined by users' operation. According to the independence axiom, an ideal mapping matrix should be a diagonal matrix or a triangular matrix. The former means that users need only one step to control the function, and each function has its own control key. The latter means that the user may need more than one step (press more than one key) to complete the task, but the keys used are not conflicting with the ones used in other functions. So if the [Y] matrix is a diagonal matrix or a triangular matrix, it means there are no conflicting controls between different functions. If the [Y] matrix is neither a diagonal matrix nor a triangular matrix, the designers should reconsider the control design to avoid possible usability problems (e.g., high error rate caused by using the same combination of keys for two functions).

However, only meeting the requirement of a diagonal matrix or a triangular matrix is not enough. According to the information axiom, the design that has the smallest information content is the best design. Therefore, designers should also make sure that users do not need to take too many steps in order to complete a certain task. Other constraints like Fitts's law for movement times (Guiard & Beaudouin-Lafon, 2004), stimulus-response compatibility and Hick's Law can be used to determine usability problems as well. For instance, Hick's law describes the time it takes for a person to make a decision as a result of the possible choices he or she has. In axiomatic evaluation, if the mapping matrix [Y] shows that there are too many options under one menu, it may take users quite some time to find the option they want. When the experimenter examines the video, he will pay more attention to tasks used that menu. Another example is Fitts' law, which is used to model the act of pointing, either by physically touching an object with a hand or finger, or virtually, by pointing to an object on a monitor using a pointing device. In axiomatic evaluation, if the mapping matrix [Y] shows that the keys used for one function locate far away from each other, it is possible that Fitts's law wasn't followed well. When the experimenter examines the video, he will pay more attention to that function.

The proposed axiomatic evaluation method could be used in the formative stage of product development before a final design accepted for release. Compared to traditional usability evaluation methods, the axiomatic evaluation method is more likely to discover more usability problems related to user requirement and control. Examining the mapping matrix between customer domain ([CA]) and functional domain ([FR]) will reveal what the customers need and what is barely needed. Examining the mapping matrix between functional domain ([FR]) and control domain ([CT]) will reveal the problems about control.

THE EXPERIMENT

Since we considered the axiomatic evaluation method as a better tool in discovering usability problems of customer requirement and device control, we conducted an experiment to assess how well this evaluation method worked and in which aspect it would perform better or worse than other usability evaluation methods. We also used this experiment to demonstrate how to use the axiomatic evaluation method to evaluate consumer electronic products. Because the axiomatic evaluation method was a task-specific method used in the formative stage before the design is finalized, we chose another task-specific evaluation method used at the same stage for comparison, the think aloud method. This method was selected also because it did not require participants to have much knowledge about usability. The experiment used a between-subjects design: 60 participants were recruited and randomly assigned to the group using the think aloud method or the group using the axiomatic evaluation method. Three popular consumer electronic devices: music player, digital camera and mobile phone representing different levels of complexity were evaluated by each participant in a randomized order.

Using the Think Aloud Method

The think aloud method is widely used in the same stage of product development in laboratories and industries. This method, developed by Lewis (1982) and refined by Ericsson and Simon (1987), has proved to be successful in collecting qualitative data from a small number of users (Nielsen, 1997). The think aloud procedure involves participants thinking aloud as they perform a set of specified tasks. In a think aloud evaluation experiment, users describe whatever they are looking at, thinking, doing, and feeling, as they go through their task. This enables the experimenter to see how a task is completed. The experimenter records everything the participant says, without attempting to interpret the actions and words. Test sessions are usually videotaped or audiotaped so that experimenter can go back and refer to what participants did and how they reacted. However, there is a limitation of the think aloud method: it seems unnatural to test users and may influence users' problem-solving behavior.

Think aloud method has been adopted in different variations. Boren and Ramey first found that no evidence of a standard think aloud method being used in usability practice (Boren & Ramey, 2000). They observed usability professionals working in two companies and found practitioners frequently deviating from Ericsson and Simon's methodological recommendations by failing to give participants instructions in the prescribed manner, or the opportunity to practice thinking aloud. Nørgaard and Hornbæk (2006) conducted a study of 14 usability tests based in seven different organizations. They found that evaluators frequently engaged in interventions and questions that went beyond the user's actual experience with the system to hypothetical situations. McDonald, Edwards and Zhao did an exploratory, qualitative survey with 207 usability evaluators and found that a range of interventions was used to better understand participant actions and verbalizations (McDonald et al., 2012). Gill and Nonnecke interviewed 20 usability practitioners and found different types of probes were used in real study rather than simple "keep talking" reminders (Gill & Nonnecke, 2012). Think aloud method has also been used with other methods in usability testing. Li and a group of researchers successfully combined think-aloud with "near-live" clinical simulations in a usability evaluation of a new primary care CDS (clinical decision support) tool (Li et al., 2012). The findings suggest the importance of using complementary testing methods.

In this study, we employed the think aloud procedure that has been used in more than 30 studies (e.g. Magliano & Millis, 2003). Participants were first settled comfortably in a quiet room. After the experimenter introduced the purpose of the study, participants were asked to fill out a background questionnaire which asked about their gender, age group, experience of using the three consumer electronic devices, and how important they thought user experience was. Then, printed instruction of how to perform "thinking aloud" was given to the participants. The instruction was based on the methodology developed by Lewis (1982, pp. 83): "The basic idea of thinking aloud is that you ask your users to perform a test task, but you also ask them to talk to you while they are working on it. Ask them to tell you what they are thinking: what they are trying to do, questions that arise as they work, things they read." After this, participants were asked to watch a video of how to perform the think aloud method and to do a warm-up practice. When the experiment formally started, participants were given a list of tasks to perform—to use a set of functions of a product. The set of functions were the major functions listed in the product manual. The experimenter videotaped the whole procedure, and took notes of the thinking reported by the participant. The participants' thinking included not just the problems they encountered, but also whether they thought a certain function was well designed, or what kind of design they liked, or their suggestion for the product. After the participants finished evaluating each task, they were asked to fill out a satisfaction questionnaire. After the experiment, the experimenter went through the notes, collected and categorized the usability problems.

Using the Axiomatic Evaluation Method

Participants in the axiomatic evaluation group were asked to complete the same background questionnaire before the experiment. Unlike the think aloud group, there was no training session. The experimenter introduced the purpose of the study and encouraged the participants to raise any problem or question regarding to the test products. Although the participants were not required to tell the experimenter everything in their mind like the think aloud method, they were encouraged to speak out any problem or question regarding to the test device. This way, the experimenter could collect usability problems found by the participants without interfering them performing the tasks. As the experiment started, participants were first asked to fill out a questionnaire of what functions they really used and their expectations of the product. After that, participants were asked to evaluate the functions they said they would really use. The order of the tasks was randomized for each participant. The evaluating procedure was video-taped and the problems raised by the participants were written down by the experimenter. After evaluating each test product, participants were asked to fill out the same satisfaction questionnaire as used in the think aloud group. After the experiment was completed, the experimenter went through the videos to fill out the mapping matrix [A] between function and control keys according to participants' action—which keys did they click in order to perform a certain task. By examining the mapping matrix according to the independent axiom, information axiom, Hicks's law (Schneider & Anderson, 2011), Fitts's law (Guiard & Beaudouin-Lafon, 2004), and stimulus-response compatibility (Proctor & Vu, 2006), the experimenter can find out usability problems not reported by the participants and the reason of the usability problems. After the experiment, the experimenter sorted the usability problems into the right categories.

Independent and Dependent Variables

The independent variables of this experiment included two testing methods, three testing devices, and participants' background. Dependent variables included number of usability problems found, and completion time. The number of usability problems found was the total number of different usability problems found by all participants using the same evaluation method. To obtain this number, the experimenter first collected all usability problems found by all participants using the same evaluation method and then filtered out all the different ones. Each usability problem may have different weight, but in this study we weighted them equally. The completion time was measured by the timer line on the video recorder. When the participants were ready to perform a task, the experimenter started the recording and then stopped it when the participants said that they were finished. The lapsed time then was the completion time. The overall satisfaction score was measured by a questionnaire using a 5-point Likert scale including satisfaction of the content, the interface, the control panel, the control, and overall satisfaction.

Participants

The number of participants was determined by statistical power analysis and experiment design requirements. In this experiment, each participant would use one of the two methods to evaluate all three products in one of the six testing orders (of the three products). Assuming the standard deviation of the number of usability problems found would be approximately 5, and the maximum difference between the means of usability problems found would be 20, we calculated that having 4 participants in each testing order can give us a power value of 0.9 (given $\alpha=0.05$). Thus, we decided to have 5 participants in each of the 6 testing orders for both evaluation methods, 60 participants in total.

Participants with experience of at least 2 of the 3 consumer electronic products (music player, mobile phone and digital camera) were recruited through e-mail from an electronic product company located in Xiamen, China. A summary table of participants' background is available in the Appendix. More than 90% of the participants had used more than 1 music player for at least 2 years, and over 70% of them had used at least 3 mobile phones for more than 5 years. The participants had less experience of using digital cameras, but still more than half of them had used at least 2 models for more than 2 years. Most of the participants' jobs fell into three main categories: engineering, management and sales. When asked about the importance of usability compared to the other five factors (brand, quality, cost-effectiveness, fashion design, multi-functional design), over 70% of the participants considered usability as being important or very important. Participants in the think aloud group and the axiomatic evaluation group had similar though not exactly the same distribution in gender, age, education, job category, and experience of using the 3 consumer electronic products.

Test Products

Three widely used information appliances representing different levels of complexity were chosen as the test products: music player, mobile phone and digital camera. The music player had eight major functions: playing music, recording, playing recorded soundtrack, radio, games, e-book, picture display, and address book. The music player had one button for power on/off and six buttons for controlling. The labels of the buttons were marked on the back of the music player. The digital camera offered multiple picture taking modes: automatic, manual, portrait, landscape, moving mode and night mode. Besides, this camera can also be used to record videos. The button for shooting was located on top of the camera. The dial of shooting modes was on the left side of the shooting key and labeled with icons. The power key was located at the center of the dial. On the right hand side of the display, there were several function buttons from the upper part to the lower part: zoom in and zoom out, display, menu, delete, function dial and the confirm key. The mobile phone had all common smart phone features. It had a touch screen and a key pad of 21 keys. The 12 number keys were located at the lower part of the keypad, whereas the nine function keys were on the upper side. The function keys are labeled with icons but not text. There were two keys located on the upper right side of the mobile phone to control volume.

RESULTS ANALYSIS

Typically, comparison of the effectiveness of different usability evaluation methods is done by comparing the number of usability problems found by each method. In this study, we compared the two evaluation methods by two criteria: effectiveness through comparison of usability problems found, and efficiency through comparison of completion time. We also examined the satisfaction score of each device and each function.

Number of Usability Problems Found

After the experiment, usability problems found by the two evaluation methods were sorted into eight main categories: content, menu, panel, display, control, functions, technology and appearance. Content category included problems like lack of information, incorrect information, ambiguous information, too much information and lack of description in Chinese. Menu problems were those that involve sorting of menu items and priority of menu options. Panel problems included incorrect positions of keys, awkward shape of buttons, unpleasant feelings of buttons, lack of label on keys and lack of keys. Display problems consisted of font size/style/color problems, screen problems, icon and format issues. Control problems were about whether users do not know which key to press in order to operate a certain function, control bug, as well as non-convenient design. Function problems usually consisted of requirements about major utilities of the device, accessorial functions, or redundant functions. Technology problems included shortage of speed, resolution, sound quality. Appearance problems usually were related to the material, shape, size, weight and looking. If a collected problem was related to more than one category, then the problem was put in all related categories.

A summary of usability problems is shown in Table 1. Because our concern was the total number of different usability problems found by each group of participants, statistical analysis of comparing the average number of usability problems found by each participant in each evaluation method group was not listed here. For the music player, the axiomatic evaluation method found 245 problems, which is slightly more than the think aloud method (212 problems). For the digital camera, the axiomatic evaluation method found 193 problems, a value slightly smaller than the think aloud method (215 problems). For the mobile phone, the axiomatic evaluation method found more than twice as many problems as the think aloud method (404 vs 161). A closer look reveals that the "extra" usability problems found with the axiomatic evaluation method found were mainly from four categories: content (lack of information, incorrect information, ambiguous information), panel (location of the keys, shape of the keys), display, control (don't know which key to press, control bug) and functions. The comparison of using two evaluation methods for mobile phone provided evidence of an advantage of the axiomatic evaluation method in finding usability problems of user requirement (what kind of functions do they need or not) and usability problems about control. This advantage was not evident for the music player and digital camera. One possible reason is that in recent years mobile phone has become more complex device than music player or digital camera and is likely to have more usability problems. Also, nowadays people use mobile phones so much that users become more stringent on their evaluation. It means that people may point out more usability problems, or more detailed/trivial usability problems. Both reasons lead to the conclusion that participants would discover more usability problems in mobile phone than music player and digital camera (and data in Table 1 supports this point). According to Ericsson and Simon's research (Ericsson & Simon, 1993), think aloud participants retrieve information from the short term memory. When evaluating a mobile phone (a complex device with more usability problems), a participant could have noticed several usability problems while performing a task, but he/she was not able to report all of them, due to either speaking out all the problems could break the flow of performing the task, or that he/she forgot some usability problems after he/she explained the first few usability problems (limit of short term memory). While a participant was evaluating a complex device using the axiomatic evaluation method, similar to the think aloud method, not all of the usability problems he/she noticed could be spoke out, but some of the hidden usability problems were caught by examining the mapping matrix (how the participant interacted with the device) recorded in the video. That's why the axiomatic evaluation method could find more usability problems than the think aloud method on a complex device.

Completion Time

Statistical analysis of the completion time is listed in Table 2. Normality test has been conducted on distributions of the total time, the time to fill out background questionnaire, the time to evaluate music player, the time to evaluate mobile phone, the time to evaluate digital camera, and the time to complete the satisfaction questionnaire before ANOVA has been applied. P value of the test results are all larger than 0.1. For the think aloud method, the completion time consists of the time of training, evaluating (three) products and filling out the overall user satisfaction questions. The average time to complete the whole experiment was 51'8", with standard deviation of 4'45". For the axiomatic evaluation method, the completion time consists of the time of evaluating (three) products, filling out the overall user satisfaction questions, and the time for the experimenter to go through the videos and catch usability problems from the mapping matrix. The average time to complete the whole experiment was 52'51", with standard deviation of 7'6".

An ANOVA of the total completion time of the two methods showed nonsignificant result, F-value = 1.19, p = 0.280. Therefore, there is no difference between the completion times of the two methods. However, when comparing the time needed for participant to evaluate one product, the axiomatic evaluation method requires significantly shorter time than the think aloud method ($p<0.05$). Therefore, from the participant's point of view, the axiomatic evaluation method is more efficient.

Satisfaction Score

The satisfaction score was retrieved through a questionnaire after the participant finished each task. Participants were asked five questions including satisfaction of the content, the interface, the control panel, the control, and overall satisfaction. By comparing the satisfaction score of participants in two groups, we discovered some statistical significant difference. For example, for music player, participants in the axiomatic evaluation group rated the satisfaction score lower than the think aloud group participants in functions of music play, radio, e-book and picture display. For mobile phone, the axiomatic evaluation group's satisfaction score is lower for the function of making phone calls. However, for the digital camera, participants in the axiomatic evaluation group had higher satisfaction score on display and menu design with very significant difference ($p < .001$). We can conclude that based on this experiment, the evaluation method would influence the user satisfaction in some way, and it is not related to how much usability problems they find. The participants showed lower satisfaction in the music player while they were using the axiomatic evaluation method, but they did not figure out more usability problems than the think aloud method (Table 3,

Table 1. Summary of Total Number of Problems Found

Category	Sub Category	Music Player		Digital Camera		Mobile Phone	
		TA*	AE**	TA	AE	TA	AE
Content	Lack of information	14	5	12	9	2	18
	Incorrect information	0	1	2	2	0	5
	Ambiguous information	3	5	5	9	3	12
	Redundant information	0	1	0	0	8	16
	Lack of description in Chinese	0	3	5	7	0	0
	Sub-total	17	15	24	27	13	51
Menu	The sorting	8	7	1	1	21	29
	The order or priority	0	0	0	0	0	7
	Sub-total	8	7	1	1	21	36
Panel	Position/location of the keys	5	17	6	13	0	7
	Shape	3	3	3	3	0	4
	Material/touch feeling	16	9	15	10	6	9
	Label on the keys	19	12	9	8	3	4
	Lack of keys	0	1	4	2	3	5
	Sub-total	43	42	37	36	12	29
Display	Font size, style, color	8	9	2	2	3	10
	Screen or display	3	3	1	1	0	3
	Icon	5	1	1	1	3	3
	Format	11	10	0	0	2	7
	Sub-total	27	23	4	4	8	23
Control	Don't know which key to press	41	38	3	7	14	23
	Control bug	16	17	1	3	14	37
	Not convenient design	22	16	6	6	33	47
	Sub-total	79	71	10	16	61	107
Functions	- ***	11	42	16	20	20	121
Technology	- ***	27	35	62	59	20	36
Appearance	- ***	0	10	61	30	6	1
Total	-	212	245	215	193	**161**	**404**

*: TA stands for the group using think aloud evaluation method.

**: AE stands for the group using the axiomatic evaluation method.

***: it is hard to categorize problems about functions, technology and appearance into the same sub-categories for three different consumer electronic products. Therefore we present the total number of problems of this category.

4, 5). Similarly, though participants discovered much more usability problems when using the axiomatic evaluation method on mobile phone, there is no big difference on the satisfaction score except for one item (make phone calls).

Other Findings

A lot more data analysis and modeling have been done (e.g. the generalized linear model of number usability problems, completion time and complexity of test product), but not included in this

Table 2. Statistic Summary of Completion time

Test Segment	TA*		AE**		% of difference	F	p-value
	Mean	Std	Mean	Std			
Training	5'28"	41"	-	-	-	-	-
Background questionnaire	48"	12"	50"	12"	4.17	0.27	0.626
Music player	15'40"	2'48"	9'47"	2'50"	60.14	59.80	<0.0001
Mobile phone	20'45"	3'2"	15'56"	2'47"	30.23	35.86	<0.0001
Digital camera	6'20"	41"	5'4"	1'16"	25.00	16.17	0.0002
Satisfaction questionnaire	2'3"	20"	2'14"	13"	8.94	2.40	0.1266
Experiment review	-	-	20'12"	5'23"	-	-	-
Total	51'8"	4'45"	52'51"	7'6"	3.36	1.19	0.2791

*: TA stands for the group using think aloud evaluation method.

**: AE stands for the group using the axiomatic evaluation method.

Table 3. Summary of Satisfaction Score of Music Player

	Think Aloud		Axiomatic Evaluation		*t*	*p*
	Mean	Std	Mean	Std		
Music play	4.67	0.96	4.10	1.06	2.17	**0.034**
Radio	4.83	1.12	3.70	1.26	3.68	**0.001**
Recorder	4.73	0.64	4.50	0.86	1.19	0.239
Game	3.20	1.19	3.13	1.31	0.21	0.837
E-book	4.63	1.47	3.80	1.10	2.49	**0.016**
Picture display	4.63	1.25	3.77	1.25	2.69	**0.009**
Display	4.20	1.32	3.70	0.99	1.66	0.103
Menu design	3.90	1.64	3.90	1.11	0.19	0.849
Content	4.00	1.25	3.90	1.11	0.33	0.744
Control	3.10	1.31	3.10	0.84	0.12	0.907
General	3.60	1.50	3.40	1.00	0.71	0.481

Table 4. Summary of Satisfaction Score of Digital Camera

	Think Aloud		Axiomatic Evaluation		*t*	*p*
	Mean	Std	Mean	Std		
Picture	3.93	0.98	4.10	0.89	-0.69	0.492
Display	3.83	0.70	4.83	0.65	-5.75	**0.000**
Menu design	3.67	0.92	4.57	0.90	-3.83	**0.000**
Content	4.30	1.18	4.53	0.73	-0.92	0.361
Control	4.10	1.06	4.43	0.82	-1.36	0.179
General	4.00	0.91	4.40	0.81	-1.80	0.078

Table 5. Summary of Satisfaction Score of Mobile Phone

	Think Aloud		Axiomatic Evaluation		*t*	*p*
	Mean	Std	Mean	Std		
Make phone calls	5.33	0.48	5.20	0.89	2.69	**0.009**
Phone book	4.13	1.36	4.47	1.57	-0.88	0.383
Message	3.73	1.44	4.37	1.83	-1.49	0.142
Camera	4.73	1.17	4.23	1.07	1.72	0.090
Video camera	4.67	1.30	4.33	1.06	1.09	0.280
Music player	4.73	0.69	5.07	0.94	-1.56	0.125
Calendar	4.27	1.80	4.40	1.00	-0.35	0.725
Display	4.37	1.40	4.57	1.17	-0.60	0.550
Menu design	4.10	1.32	4.70	1.12	-1.90	0.063
Content	4.20	1.27	4.67	1.12	-1.51	0.137
Control	4.10	1.30	4.53	1.20	-1.35	0.184
General	4.10	1.52	4.30	1.12	-0.58	0.564

chapter because the main goal of this chapter is to introduce a new usability evaluation method. Here we just present some interesting findings when we compare participants of different background.

- Older participants found the font size of button label and text on screen too small, while younger participants found the font size was larger than needed.
- Older participants had much fewer functional requirements than younger users. They usually selected the most basic functions, such as only using the phone calls function and address book function for mobile phone. On the other hand, younger users used almost every function, and required more accessorial and multi-media functions.
- Male users reported more usability problems of panel design. They tended to point out more detailed and technical design problems. They also liked to compare the testing product with their own devices to give the experimenter an idea of why the design was good or bad.
- Participants who considered usability as important or very important reported more usability problems.

CONCLUSION

This experiment showed that the axiomatic evaluation method performed better in finding usability problems for a mobile phone than the think aloud method. But the axiomatic evaluation method did not show advantages in finding usability problems for music player or digital camera. When used to evaluate mobile phone, the axiomatic evaluation method was able to find more usability problems about user requirement and control, which was consistent with what we hypothesized. This experiment also compared the completion time of the two evaluation methods. Although there was no statistically significant difference between the total accomplish time of the two methods, when comparing the time needed for participants to evaluate each product, the axiomatic evaluation method required significantly shorter time than the think aloud method. Therefore, from the participant's point of view, the axiomatic evaluation method is more efficient.

DISCUSSION AND FUTURE RESEARCH

The ultimate goal of usability evaluation is to improve user experience of products. Previous studies provide guidelines for design and several ways to detect usability problems. What is unique about the present research is that it develops and validates a systematic evaluation method that can discover usability problems from "what do the users want" to "how well does the product satisfy user requirements". This type of evaluation procedure could reduce the time and energy of the "design-test-redesign" cycle. The new evaluation method also complements finding usability problems about control.

Theoretical contributions of this study include extension of the application domain for the axiomatic design theory and development of an effective axiomatic evaluation method for usability. Practical contributions include validation of the axiomatic evaluation method for consumer electronic products. One limitation of the study is that only two usability evaluation methods with three products were compared. Also the axiomatic evaluation method didn't discover much feedback about joy of use or emotion which was becoming more important in user experience. The strength of this method is that it can find more usability problems about control and user requirement in complex system or device. In the future, the axiomatic evaluation method needs to be applied to more products with a larger range of complexity, and compared with other evaluation methods on more devices.

REFERENCES

Andre, T. S., Hartson, H. R., & Williges, R. C. (2003). Determining the effectiveness of the usability problem inspector: A theory-based model and tool for finding usability problems. *Human Factors*, *45*(3), 455–482. doi:10.1518/hfes.45.3.455.27255 PMID:14702996.

Apple, Inc. (2012). *Case studies: Transitioning to ios, Apple iOS human interface guidelines*. Retrieved Apr 20, 2012, from http://developer.apple.com/library/ios/#documentation/UserExperience/Conceptual/MobileHIG/TranslateApp/TranslateApp.html#//apple_ref/doc/uid/TP40006556-CH10-SW38

Boren, M. T., & Ramey, J. (2000). Thinking aloud: Reconciling theory and practice. *IEEE Transactions on Professional Communication*, *43*(3), 261–278. doi:10.1109/47.867942.

Buchenau, M., & Suri, J. F. (2000). Experience prototyping. In *Proceedings of the 3rd Conference on Designing Interactive Systems: Processes, Practices, Methods, and Techniques* (pp. 424-433). ACM.

Ciavarella, C., & Paternò, F. (2003). Design criteria for location-aware, indoor, PDA applications. In *Human-Computer Interaction with Mobile Devices and Services* (pp. 131–144). Academic Press. doi:10.1007/978-3-540-45233-1_11.

Ericsson, K., & Simon, H. (1987). Verbal reports on thinking. In C. Faerch, & G. Kasper (Eds.), *Introspection in second language research* (pp. 24–54). Clevedon, UK: Multilingual Matters.

Ericsson, K. A., & Simon, H. A. (1993). *Protocol analysis: Verbal reports as data*. Cambridge, MA: The MIT Press.

Gebauer, J. (2008). User requirements of mobile technology: A summary of research results. *Information, Knowledge. Systems Management*, *7*(1), 101–119.

Geven, A., Sefelin, R., Höller, N., Tscheligi, M., & Mayer, M. (2008). Always-on information: Services and applications on the mobile desktop. In *Proceedings of the 10th International Conference on Human Computer Interaction with Mobile Devices and Services* (pp. 23-32). ACM.

Gill, A. M., & Nonnecke, B. (2012). Think aloud: Effects and validity. In *Proceedings of the 30th ACM International Conference on Design of Communication* (pp. 31-36). ACM.

Gray, W. D., & Salzman, M. C. (1998). Damaged merchandise? A review of experiments that compare usability evaluation methods. *Human-Computer Interaction*, *13*(3), 203–261. doi:10.1207/s15327051hci1303_2.

Guiard, Y., & Beaudouin-Lafon, M. (2004). Fitts' law 50 years later: Applications and contributions from human–computer interaction. *International Journal of Human-Computer Studies*, *61*, 747–750. doi:10.1016/j.ijhcs.2004.09.003.

Guo, Y., Proctor, R., & Salvendy, G. (2011). A conceptual model of the axiomatic usability evaluation method. In M. Smith, & G. Salvendy (Eds.), *Human interface and the management of information: Interacting with information (LNCS)* (Vol. 6671, pp. 93–102). Berlin, Germany: Springer. doi:10.1007/978-3-642-21793-7_11.

Han, S. H., Jung, E. S., Jung, M., Kwahk, J., & Park, S. (1998a). Psychophysical methods and passenger preferences of interior designs. *Applied Ergonomics*, *29*(6), 499–506. doi:10.1016/S0003-6870(97)00009-4 PMID:9796796.

Han, S. H., Yun, M. H., Kim, K., & Cho, S. J. (1998b). *Development of a usability evaluation method. Pohang University of Science and Technology (POSTECH)*. Ministry of Science and Technology.

Han, S. H., Yun, M. H., Kim, K.-J., & Kwahk, J. (2000). Evaluation of product usability: Development and validation of usability dimensions and design elements based on empirical models. *International Journal of Industrial Ergonomics*, *26*, 477–488. doi:10.1016/S0169-8141(00)00019-6.

Han, S. H., Yun, M. H., Kwahk, J., & Hong, S. W. (2001). Usability of consumer electronic products. *International Journal of Industrial Ergonomics*, *28*(3), 143–151. doi:10.1016/S0169-8141(01)00025-7.

Helander, M., & Lin, L. (2002). Axiomatic approach in ergonomics design with an extension of the information axiom. *Journal of Engineering Design*, *13*(4), 321–339. doi:10.1080/09544820 21000050794.

Helander, M. G., & Lin, L. (2000). Anthropometric design of workstations. In D. Tate (Ed.), *Proceedings of the First International Conference on Axiomatic Design* (pp. 130-138). Cambridge, MA: Institute for Axiomatic Design.

Hertzum, M. (2010). Images of usability. *International Journal of Human-Computer Interaction*, *26*(6), 567–600. doi:10.1080/10447311003781300.

Hilbert, D. M., & Redmiles, D. F. (2000). Extracting usability information from user interface events. *ACM Computing Surveys*, *32*(4), 384–421. doi:10.1145/371578.371593.

ISO. (1998). *ISO 9241-11: Ergonomic requirements for office work with visual display terminals (VDTs), part 11: Guidance on usability*. Geneva, Switzerland: ISO.

Ji, Y. G., Park, J. H., Lee, C., & Yun, M. H. (2006). A usability checklist for the usability evaluation of mobile phone user interface. *International Journal of Human-Computer Interaction*, *20*(3), 207–231. doi:10.1207/s15327590ijhc2003_3.

Kim, J., & Han, S. H. (2008). A methodology for developing a usability index of consumer electronic products. *International Journal of Industrial Ergonomics*, *38*(3), 333–345. doi:10.1016/j.ergon.2007.12.002.

Kwahk, J., Han, S. H., Yun, M. H., Hong, S. W., Chung, M. K., & Lee, K. S. (1997). Selection and classification of the usability attributes for evaluating consumer electronic products. In *Proceedings of Human Factors and Ergonomics Society Annual Meeting* (Vol. 41, pp. 432-436). Human Factors and Ergonomics Society.

Lee, D. G., & Suh, N. P. (2005). *Axiomatic design and fabrication of composite structures-applications in robots, machine tools, and automobiles*. New York: Oxford University Press.

Lewis, C. (1982). *Using the thinking-aloud method in cognitive interface design (IBM Research Report RC 9265)*. Yorktown Heights, NY: IBM TJ Watson Research Center.

Li, A. C., Kannry, J. L., Kushniruk, A., Chrimes, D., McGinn, T. G., Edonyabo, D., & Mann, D. M. (2012). Integrating usability testing and think-aloud protocol analysis with near-live clinical simulations in evaluating clinical decision support. *International Journal of Medical Informatics*, *81*(11), 761–772. doi:10.1016/j.ijmedinf.2012.02.009 PMID:22456088.

Macaulay, C., & Jacucci, G., ONeill, S., Kankainen, T., & Simpson, M. (2006). The emerging roles of performance within HCI and interaction design. *Interacting with Computers*, *18*(5), 942–955. doi:10.1016/j.intcom.2006.07.001.

Magliano, J., & Millis, K. (2003). Assessing reading skill with a think-aloud procedure and latent semantic analysis. *Cognition and Instruction*, *21*(3), 251–283. doi:10.1207/S1532690XCI2103_02.

McCarthy, J., & Wright, P. (2004). Technology as experience. *Interaction*, *11*(5), 42–43. doi:10.1145/1015530.1015549.

McDonald, S., Edwards, H. M., & Zhao, T. (2012). Exploring think-alouds in usability testing: An international survey. *IEEE Transactions on Professional Communication*, *55*(1), 2–19. doi:10.1109/TPC.2011.2182569.

Morris, R. P., & Tomlinson, J. J. (2008). A mobile device user interface with a simple, classic design. *IEEE Transactions on Consumer Electronics*, *54*(3), 1252–1258. doi:10.1109/TCE.2008.4637614.

Nielsen, J. (1997). Usability testing. In G. Salvendy (Ed.), *Handbook of human factors and ergonomics* (pp. 1543–1568). New York: John Wiley & Sons.

Nørgaard, M., & Hornbæk, K. (2006). What do usability evaluators do in practice: An explorative study of think-aloud testing. In *Proceedings of 6th Conference of Design Interact System* (pp. 209 - 218). IEEE.

Proctor, R. W., & Vu, K.-P. L. (2006). Selection and control of action. In G. Salvendy (Ed.), *Handbook of human factors and ergonomics* (pp. 89–110). Hoboken, NJ: John Wiley. doi:10.1002/0470048204.ch4.

Quill, L. L., Kancler, D. E., Revels, A. R., & Batchelor, C. (2001). Application of information visualization principles at various stages of system development. In *Proceedings of the Human Factors and Ergonomics Society Annual Meeting* (Vol. 45, pp. 1713-1717). SAGE Publications.

Schneider, D. W., & Anderson, J. R. (2011). A memory-based model of Hick's law. *Cognitive Psychology*, *62*, 193–222. doi:10.1016/j.cogpsych.2010.11.001 PMID:21293788.

Suh, N. P. (1990). *The principles of design*. New York: Oxford University Press.

Suh, N. P. (1995). Designing-in quality through axiomatic design. *IEEE Transactions on Reliability*, *44*(2), 256–264. doi:10.1109/24.387380.

Suh, N. P. (2001). *Axiomatic design: advances and applications*. New York: Oxford University Press.

Venkatesh, V., Ramesh, V., & Massey, A. P. (2003). Understanding usability in mobile commerce. *Communications of the ACM*, *46*(12), 53–56. doi:10.1145/953460.953488.

Yenisey, M. (2007). Axiomatic design approach for e-commercial web sites. In J. Jacko (Ed.), *Human-computer interaction: Interaction design and usability (LNCS)* (Vol. 4550, pp. 308–315). Berlin: Springer. doi:10.1007/978-3-540-73105-4_34.

Zhang, T., Rau, P.-L. P., & Salvendy, G. (2010). Exploring critical usability factors for handsets. *Behaviour & Information Technology*, *29*(1), 45–55. doi:10.1080/01449290802666747.

Ziefle, M. (2002). The influence of user expertise and phone complexity on performance, ease of use and learnability of different mobile phones. *Behaviour & Information Technology*, *21*(5), 303–311. doi:10.1080/0144929021000048538.

ADDITIONAL READING

Almström, P., & Märtensson, P. (2002). A categorization of functional couplings in manufacturing systems. *Proceedings of the Institution of Mechanical Engineers. Part B, Journal of Engineering Manufacture*, *216*(4), 623–626. doi:10.1243/0954405021520120.

Babic, B. (1999). Axiomatic design of flexible manufacturing systems. *International Journal of Production Research*, *37*(5), 1159–1173. doi:10.1080/002075499191454.

Chan, L. W., & Leung, T. P. (1997). Optimization of an electrical interconnect system using axiomatics and fuzzy sets. *Journal of Engineering Design*, *8*(4), 371–387. doi:10.1080/09544829708907972.

Chen, K. Z. (2000). Designing-in of high value for manufacturers in the new millennium. *Integrated Manufacturing Systems*, *11*(6), 417–427. doi:10.1108/09576060010345905.

Engelhardt, F. (2000). Improving systems by combining axiomatic design, quality control tools and designed experiments. *Research in Engineering Design*, *12*(4), 204–219. doi:10.1007/s001630050034.

Guenov, M. (2008). Covariance structural models of the relationship between the design and customer domains. *Journal of Engineering Design*, *19*(1), 75–95. doi:10.1080/09544820701213378.

Helander, M. G. (2007). Using design equations to identify sources of complexity in human–machine interaction. *Theoretical Issues in Ergonomics Science*, *8*(2), 123–146. doi:10.1080/14639220601092442.

Helander, M. G., & Jiao, J. (2002). Research on E-product development (ePD) for mass customization. *Technovation*, *22*(11), 717–724. doi:10.1016/S0166-4972(01)00074-8.

Helander, M. G., & Lin, L. (2002). Axiomatc design in ergonomics and an extension of the information axiom. *Journal of Engineering Design*, *13*(4), 321–339. doi:10.1080/0954482021000050794.

Kulak, O., Kahraman, C., Öztaysi, B., & Tanyas, M. (2005). Multi-attribute information technology project selection using fuzzy axiomatic design. *Journal of Enterprise Information Management*, *18*(3), 275–288. doi:10.1108/17410390510591978.

Li, H. X., Tso, S. K., & Deng, H. (2001). A conceptual approach to integrate design and control for the epoxy dispensing process. *International Journal of Advanced Manufacturing Technology*, *17*(9), 677–682. doi:10.1007/s001700170133.

Lo, S., & Helander, M. G. (2007). Use of axiomatic design principles for analysing the complexity of human–machine systems. *Theoretical Issues in Ergonomics Science*, *8*(2), 147–169. doi:10.1080/14639220601092475.

Park, K. J., Kang, B. S., Song, K. N., & Park, G. J. (2003). Design of a spacer grid using axiomatic design. *Journal of Nuclear Science and Technology*, *40*(12), 989–997. doi:10.3327/jnst.40.989.

Suh, N. P. (1998). Axiomatic design theory for systems. *Research in Engineering Design*, *10*(4), 189–209. doi:10.1007/s001639870001.

Suh, N. P. (2007). Ergonomics, axiomatic design and complexity theory. *Theoretical Issues in Ergonomics Science*, *8*(2), 101–121. doi:10.1080/14639220601092509.

Walvis, T. (2003). Avoiding advertising research disaster: Advertising and the uncertainty principle. *The Journal of Brand Management*, *10*(6), 403–409. doi:10.1057/palgrave.bm.2540137.

KEY TERMS AND DEFINITIONS

Axiomatic Design Theory: A formalized methodology that can be used to solve a variety of design problems. The axiomatic design consists of four domains and two axioms. The four domains, ordered in consideration are customer domain, functional domain, physical domain and process domain. The axiomatic design theory examines the design quality by two axioms, the independence axiom and the information axiom. The two axioms were identified by examining common elements always present in good designs.

Axiomatic Evaluation Method: A usability evaluation method examines three domains of a product: customer domain, functional domain and control domain using the independence axiom, the information axiom and other human-computer interaction design constraints.

Customer Domain: A domain consists of the needs or attributes that the customers are looking for in a product, process, systems or material.

Functional Domain: A domain consists of functional requirement which is the minimum set of independent requirements that completely characterizes the functional needs of the product.

The Independence Axiom: An axiom used in axiomatic design theory states that the independence of functional requirements that characterizes the design goals must always be maintained. When there are two or more functional requirements, the design solution must be such that each functional requirement can be satisfied without affecting others.

The Information Axiom: An axiom used in axiomatic design theory states that among the designs that satisfy the independence axiom, the design that has the smallest information content is the best. The information amount should be estimated by the users.

Physical Domain: A domain consists of design parameters which are the key physical variables in the physical domain that characterizes the design that satisfies the specified functional requirements.

Process Domain: A domain consists of process variables which are the key variables in the process domain that characterizes the process that can generate the specified design parameters.

APPENDIX

Table 6. Participants' Background Information

		Think Aloud Group (N=30)	Axiomatic Evaluation Group (N=30)
Gender	Female	10	10
	Male	20	20
Age	20 to 29	18	20
	30 to 39	7	5
	40 and above	5	5
Education level	High school & associate degree	9	9
	Bachelor degree	17	18
	Master degree and higher	4	3
Job category	Engineer	7	8
	Manager	12	10
	Sales	6	5
	Others	5	7
Attitude to usability (Ranking of usability among 5 parameters that may influence buying decision: brand, price, quality, design, usability)	Not important (rank usability as 4th or 5th)	7	6
	Important (rank usability as 2nd or 3rd)	12	14
	Very important (rank usability as the 1st)	11	10
Experience of using music player	Never used	2	1
	1 model	13	11
	2 models	14	15
	More than 2 models	1	3
Experience of using music player (in years)	Less than 1 years	2	2
	2 to 5 years	23	21
	More than 6 years	5	7
Experience of using cell phone	1 to 2 models	9	7
	3 to 5 models	16	19
	More than 5 models	5	4
Experience of using cell phone (in years)	Less than 5 years	5	6
	6 to 10 years	19	16
	More than 10 years	6	8
Experience of using digital camera	1 model	15	13
	2 to 3 models	13	12
	More than 3 models	2	5
Experience of using digital camera (in years)	1 to 2 years	6	5
	3 to 7 years	16	16
	More than 8 years	8	9

Section 5
Supporting Learning

Chapter 19
Promoting Human-Computer Interaction and Usability Guidelines and Principles Through Reflective Journal Assessment

Tomayess Issa
Curtin University, Australia

Pedro Isaias
Portuguese Open University, Portugal

ABSTRACT

This chapter aims to examine the challenges to, and opportunities for, promoting Human Computer Interaction (HCI) and usability guidelines and principles through reflective journal assessment by information systems students from the Australian and Portuguese higher education sectors. In order to raise students' awareness of HCI and aspects of usability, especially in the Web development process, a new unit was developed by the first researcher called Information Systems 650 (IS650) in Australia. From this unit was derived the Web Site Planning and Development (WSPD) course introduced in Portugal. The reflective journal assessment approach was employed to enhance students' learning and knowledge of HCI and its usability aspects. This study provides empirical evidence from 64 students from Australia and Portugal, based on quantitative and qualitative data derived from three sources: students' formal and informal feedback and an online survey. Students confirmed that the use of reflective journal assessment consolidated their understanding of HCI and usability guidelines and principles and improved their reading, searching, researching, and writing skills, and their proficiency with the endnote software.

DOI: 10.4018/978-1-4666-4623-0.ch019

INTRODUCTION

The Internet (Cyberspace or Information Superhighway) is a network of thousands of computer systems utilizing a common set of technical protocols to create a worldwide communication medium. These massive groups of users reach the Internet through their computers and terminals via educational institutions, commercial Internet access providers and other organizations. The Internet provides numerous benefits to consumers regarding access to information, entertainment, research, business and marketing. The Internet allows users to educate themselves and acquire knowledge at their own pace, and website information can be easily accessed by consumers who can readily obtain only the information which is relevant to their needs (Cappel & Huang, 2007; Issa, 1999; Issa & Turk, 2012; Y. Lee & Kozar, 2012).

Although the Internet offers huge opportunities, there are also many potential problems. A website must meet the users' expectations in terms of content and ease of use. Websites which meet users' expectations will enjoy many advantages as a result of their effective design. According to Donahue (cited in McCracken and Wolfe, 2004) the four most important advantages are: 'Gaining a competitive edge; reducing development and maintenance costs; improving productivity; lowering support costs' (McCracken & Wolfe, 2004, p. 1). Other advantages of good website design are that they allow the users to enjoy working with websites with minimal frustration and aggravation. Studies and research have indicated that usable websites consistently have the highest conversion rates (completion of sales and repeat visits). If users have a gratifying and enjoyable experience, this will encourage them to visit the website more frequently.

In contrast, some users search websites for an item or ways to buy it, quickly become frustrated and leave a website and most probably will never return to it, if the site is not user-friendly and easy to navigate. Website designers should anticipate their target users' needs in order to prevent the frustrations which often occur. Frustration can result from failure to complete a task when working with a website or a system, or when goals are not achieved. This failure can be take place if the users: 'spend a lot of time hitting the wrong buttons; get error messages; feel confused; curse at the screen; and need to ask customer support for help' (McCracken et al. 2004, p. xii). Website design should be driven by two key intentions: to assist people to locate information quickly, and to provide information that is well presented, readable and readily available by adopting the usability and HCI principles and guidelines (Issa & Turk, 2012; Leung & Law, 2012; Sørum, Andersen, & Vatrapu, 2011). Moreover, designers should provide clear instructions to the users concerning the purpose and limitations of the site.

However, if a website has poor usability and its design is not according to HCI principles and guidelines, the users might well ask how the creators of the website could possibly think that it would be acceptable (McCracken et al. 2004, p. xii). Often this happens because the designers are inexperienced or they disregard the users' needs. Perhaps the designer focused on the technical aspects of the project and did not pay any attention to the users' expectations and requirements. Some designers try to mimic successful sites by copying attractive images from the Internet and create their home page without a basic knowledge of design principles. Hence, the website will lack cohesion since the graphics and the texts were written and created by different writers and designers, and it will 'stay a jumble of loose parts.' However, 'If you make your own site, it is your work. It will radiate something of your personality, your preferences and your taste' (Hoekstra, 2000). For these reasons, the first researcher developed a new unit IS650 to raise awareness of usability and HCI principles and guidelines among the Information Systems students, especially in higher education sectors in Australia and Portugal. For the same reason, the IS650 unit is offered in Universidade Aberta as the Web Site Planning and Development (WSPD) unit.

To improve students' understanding, a reflective journal assessment was employed as a pedagogic tool to encourage reflection, critique and self-analysis by students and to make them aware of the importance of usability and HCI principles and guidelines. The units were intended to make students understand that a website developed using the principles and guidelines was more likely to be successful and encourage users to revisit the website as it made them comfortable, confident and satisfied by working with the site. The principle behind integrating reflective journal assessment in the IS650 and WSPD units was to allow the students to understand the importance of usability and HCI in the web development process, and to improve students' skills gained from reading, writing, searching, researching, critical thinking and using the Endnote software.

The outcomes from this chapter will contribute a new and significant theoretical, practical and methodological approach to implementing reflective journal assessment in the higher education sector, and effectively conveying to students of Information Systems in Australia and Portugal, the importance of the concepts of HCI and usability. These findings will be of benefit to both academics and practitioners in the field of information systems/technology. The researchers acknowledge that the study has limitations since it was conducted only in Australia and Portugal.

The aim of this chapter is to ascertain whether the reflective journal assessment improves students' understanding of the principles of HCI and usability, especially in the website development process and to promote professional learning, and communication skills. Furthermore, this chapter addresses ways to encourage students to think critically about usability and HCI issues. Currently, the majority of educationalists indicate that employing reflective journal assessment in the master's degree would enhance students' confidence in their ability, mainly in terms of communication skills as this assessment approach promotes independent research and self-teaching. This chapter is organized as follows: 1) Introduction; 2) HCI and Usability; 3) HCI and Usability design and guidelines; 4) Reflective Journal; 5) Methodology and Research Question; 6) Participants and Assessments; 7) Results; 8) Discussion and Recommendations; 9) Conclusion.

HCI AND USABILITY

In order for computer-based systems -including websites- to be widely accepted and used effectively, they need to be well designed via a "user-centred" approach. This is not to say that all systems/websites have to be designed to accommodate everyone, but that computer-based systems/websites should be designed for the needs and capabilities of the people for whom they are intended. In the end, users should not even have to think about the complexity of how to use a computer/website. For that reason, computers and related devices including websites have to be designed with an understanding that people with specific tasks in mind will want to use them in a way that is seamless with respect to their work. Additionally, it is very important to 'define style, norms, roles and even mores of human and computer relationship that each side can live with, as computers become more complex, smarter and more capable,' and as we allow them to 'take on autonomous or semi-autonomous control of more critical aspects of our lives and society' (Miller, 2004,p. 34).

Systems designers need to know how to think in terms of future users' tasks and how to translate that knowledge into an executable system. This can be accomplished by creating a good interface design to let the user interact and deal with the computer without any difficulties and to have more control of the system. Alice Head (1999, p.9) stated that good interface design 'is a reliable and effective intermediary, sending us the right cues so that tasks get done – regardless of how trivial, incidental, or artful the design might seem to be'.

Recently, as we know, user-centred design has become an important 'concept in the design of interactive system[s] [including the websites]. It is primarily concerned with the design of socio-technical systems that take into account not only their users, but also the use of technologies in users' everyday activities; it can be thought of as the design of spaces for human communications and interaction'(DePaula, 2003, p. 219).

HCI 'is recognized as an interdisciplinary subject'(Dix, Finlay, Abowd, & Beale, 2004, p.4) and therefore requires input from a range of disciplines such as 'computer science (application design and engineering of human interfaces), psychology (the application of theories of cognitive processes and the empirical analysis of user behavior), sociology and anthropology (interactions between technology, work, and organization), and industrial design (interactive products)'. Therefore, HCI comprises 'science, engineering and design aspects' (Hewett et al., 1992).

The purpose of HCI is to design a computer system -including website- to match the needs and requirements of the users. The HCI specialists need to think about the above factors in order to produce an outstanding system/website. To achieve the goals of HCI, a number of approaches can be utilized. These approaches need to be studied very carefully in order to develop a system/website which provides the user with productivity and efficiency. These approaches are (Preece, Rogers, Benyon, Holland, & Carey, 1994, p. 46-47): Involving the user (involve the user as much as possible so that s/he can influence the system design); Integrating different kinds of knowledge and expertise (integrate knowledge and expertise from the different disciplines that contribute to HCI design)'; and Making the design process iterative (testing can be done to check that the design does indeed meet users' requirements).

Hence, it is obvious that HCI design should be user-centred, integrate knowledge from different disciplines, and be highly iterative. In addition, it is important to undertake effective usability evaluation. This will provide feedback regarding negative and positive aspects of prototypes. It is important that the way in which people interact with computers/websites is intuitive and clear. However, designing appropriate HCI is not always straightforward, as the many poorly designed computer systems testify.

One of the challenges of HCI design is to keep abreast of technological developments and to ensure that these are harnessed for maximum human benefit. Recent studies (Dillahunt, Mankoff, & Forlizzi, 2010; DiSalvo, Sengers, & Hronn Brynjarsdottir, 2010; Issa & Turk, 2012; Joshi, Sarda, & Tripathi, 2010; Shi, 2011; Silberman & Tomlinson, 2010) confirm that HCI design, especially in the web development process, will enhance the website presentation, layout and contents, and will meet the diversity of users who will potentially and most likely be using the website. By adopting the above concepts in the web's development process the website will be easy to use and this will encourage users to visit this website frequently.

Usability refers to the 'quality of the interaction in terms of parameters such as time taken to perform tasks, number of errors made and the time to become a competent user' (Benyon, Turner, & Turner, 2005, p. 52). Alternatively, usability 'is a quality attribute that assesses how easy user interfaces are to use. The word "usability" also refers to methods for improving ease-of-use during the design process' (Nielsen, 2003). The usability evaluation stage is crucial as it is here that a software development team can establish the positive and negative aspects of its prototype releases, and make the required changes before the system is delivered to the target users. Several studies (Davis & Shipman, 2011; Hertzum & Clemmensen, 2012; Lavie, Oron-Gilad, & Meyer, 2011; Leung & Law, 2012; Sauer, Seibel, &

Rüttinger, 2010) indicated that usability evaluation can assist designers to observe users to identify what can be improved and what type of new aspects should include in the design, including the websites. HCI specialists 'observe and talk with participants as they try to accomplish true-to-life tasks on a site (or system), and this allows them to form a detailed picture of the site as experienced by the user' (Carroll, 2004).

From the user's perspective, usability is a very important aspect of the web development process as it can mean the difference between completing a task precisely and completely or not, and the user appreciating the process or being frustrated. Alternatively, if usability is not a priority in website design, then users will become very frustrated working with it. The main goal of a usable website is to provide users with a positive response to their research; if the website design is not user-friendly, users are likely to become frustrated (Lazar, Jones, & Shneiderman, 2006; S. Lee & Koubek, 2010; Y. Lee & Kozar, 2012; Tuzovic, 2010). A recent study by Lee and Kozar (2012) confirmed that usability can bring several benefits to the website development process or any application, including effectiveness, efficiency and satisfaction.

Effective HCI and usability design include using appropriate design elements and making the system easy to use. Nowadays, much research goes into the development and improvement of HCI and advances have been made particularly with the use of graphics and animation components – also referred to as multimedia (de Castro Lozano et al., 2011). There are several benefits of adhering to the principles of HCI and usability. These include: the interfaces are more pleasant for the users; communicability is improved because the user interface design is better able to convey the intended meaning or feeling to the target user; and lastly, a website with good usability and HCI will promote users' trust and satisfaction, and this will encourage users to revisit the website. Such a website is successful and manages to convey its message or promote its activities effectively.

HCI AND USABILITY DESIGN PRINCIPLES AND GUIDELINES

To understand the importance of HCI and Usability aspects in the web development process, it is worth examining the design principles and guidelines suggested by Te'eni, Carey, & Zhang (2007). The adoption of these principles and guidelines when developing a user interface, including a website, will improve the performance, functionality, learnability, efficiency, effectiveness, usefulness or utility; it will produce fewer errors and improve users' satisfaction and achievement of goals (Davis & Shipman, 2011; Fernandez, Insfran, & Abrahão, 2011; Leung & Law, 2012; Oztekin, 2011).

To allow our students to understand the HCI and usability concepts in the web development process, design principles and guidelines are introduced. Principles are used to formalize the high level and widely appropriate design goals, while guidelines are essential to the designers to achieve the principles. (Te'eni et al., 2007; Zhang, Carey, Te'eni, & Tremaine, 2005). The design principles are divided into seven stages (see Figure 1); each principle is mainly focused on a specific concept which should be considered initially by the designers and users in order to develop a successful user interface including a website.

The principles are:

1. **Improve Users' Task Performance and Reduce Their Effort:** This principle aims to achieve high functionality along with high usability (i.e. efficiency, ease of use, and comfort in using the system, given that the functionality has been established).
2. **Strive for Fit Between the Information Representation Needed and Presented:**
   a. **Representation:** A simplified description of a real-world phenomenon.

Figure 1. Design Principles – prepared by the researchers

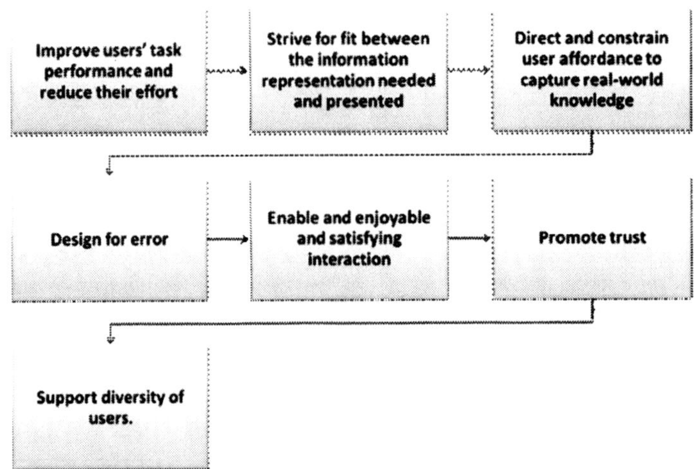

   b. **Functionality:** The set of activities.
   c. **Usability:** A measure of ease.
   d. **Cognitive Fit:** System's representation of the problem supports the user's strategies for performing the task.
3. **Direct and Constrain User Affordance to Capture Real-World Knowledge:** The general idea here is that the knowledge required to act effectively resides both in the person's head and in the real world around him/her.
4. **Design for Error:** A faulty action due to incorrect intention (mistake) or to incorrect or accidental implementation of the intention (slip).
5. **Designing for an Enjoyable and Satisfying Interaction:** The design of the interface or website should make the interaction enjoyable for both the designer and users.
6. **Promote Trust:** Is a critical component in developing interface or website, especially the e-commerce systems where the interactions translate directly into revenue.
7. **Support Diversity of Users:** This principle should take into consideration the diversity of populations of users.

To ensure that the user interface or website is popular and meets users' needs, users and designers must consider these design principles to prevent user frustration and to attract more users to visit the website.

Furthermore, to complete the interface or website design, designers and users must consider the design guidelines which are essential in the web development process. The design guidelines comprise five steps (see Figure 2).

1. **Consistency Guidelines:** If the interface is consistent (even if poorly designed), the end user can adapt to it.
2. **Control and Feedback go Hand in Hand:** Providing feedback is probably the most accepted guideline in the design of any interaction.
3. **Metaphor:** The use of familiar terms and associations to represent a new concept.
4. **Direct Manipulation:** An interaction style in which objects are represented and manipulated in a manner analogous to the real world.

Figure 2. Design Guidelines - prepared by the researchers

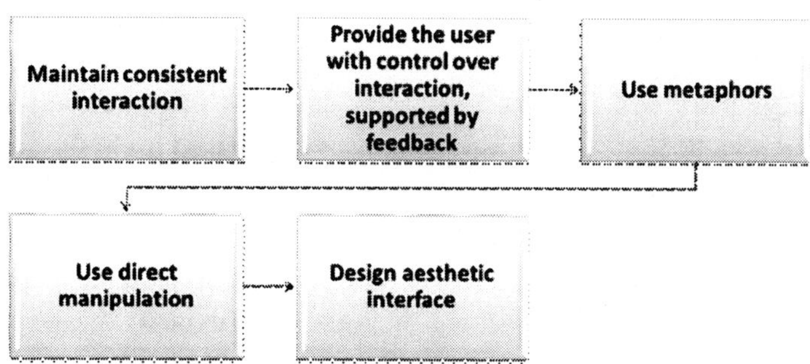

5. **Design Aesthetic Interface:** Aesthetic appeal concerns the overall appearance of an application.

The integration of design principles and guidelines in the web development process will ensure that websites are successful, since they will improve functionality, learnability, efficiency, effectiveness, and accuracy; most importantly, using these websites will increase users' satisfaction. This was confirmed by students from the IS650 and WSPD units. Student 1 confirmed that learning these principles and guidelines 'allow me to think differently and be more critical when I visit any new website now. In the end, the unit made me more aware of this field and the concepts within it'. Another student (Student 2) stated '...which in my opinion are the pinnacle of the unit as it presents detailed elements to enable a high quality interaction with users and provide designers with a framework to guide their developments'.

REFLECTIVE JOURNALS

Currently, teaching in the higher education sector is a challenging exercise, as teachers attempt to use the best approaches to teaching and assessment methods, using the latest, cutting edge technology to develop and enhance students' communication, reflective thinking, research, search, critical thinking, decision making, writing and reading skills, and proficiency in using the endnote software. These skills are essential for both the academic environment and the future workplace. The reflective journal idea was introduced and developed by Dewey (1933) who maintained that reflection 'was a deliberate cognitive process, which addressed problem solving before a solution was reached' (Clarke, 2003, p.4). Several studies indicated (Bailes, Hulsebosch, & Martin, 2010; Scott, 2011; Titus & Gremler, 2010) that integrating reflective journal assessment in a higher education curriculum is essential since this assessment will enhance the level of student performance especially the critical thinking and writing skills, and this assessment will change their learning events and improve students' confidence in their communication skills (e.g. writing, research, citing). In this respect, the majority of educators indicated and confirmed that this assessment approach is considered ideal as an independent method of research and self-teaching.

Recent studies (Anderson, 2012; Clarkeburn & Kettula, 2012; Gadsby & Cronin, 2012; Knapp, 2012; Power, 2012) confirmed that using reflective journals in higher education will encourage the students to engage in critical evaluation and 'becoming more actively involved in their own professional accountability'(Gadsby & Cronin, 2012, p.2). Therefore, this assessment offers many advantages to students and teachers simultaneously since students will acquire or refine several skills and develop their confidence by completing these assessments; on the other hand, teachers will better understand what they already know by reconsidering what they have already learnt (Loughran, 2002). This will lead as to Dewey (1933, p. 78) argument that 'we do not learn from experience, we learn from reflecting on experience'. This statement confirmed that using the reflective journal assessment in IS60 and WSPD units will assist students to learn the HCI and usability concepts by using reflecting and reproducing.

To assist our students to write the reflective journal, the researchers adopted the analysis and evaluation of a reflective journal template (which was developed by the communication skills centre at the Australian University); this template contains the following steps. 1) Reading (full citation required, including author, title, date, publication details, and page numbers). 2) What is the subject/theme of this article, (3) Argument/Findings (What is the author's argument?), (4) Evidence (How do this author's views compare with what others have said on the same or a similar topic?), (5) Observations (What are your own thoughts on the subject?), and (6) Conclusion. Figure 3 demonstrate the steps which are required to write a reflective journal.

The reflective journal is marked using the following criteria developed by the researchers: 1) Reading (well presented; accurate acknowledgement of sources); 2)What is the subject/theme of this article (well presented, listing the important themes of the article(s); 3) Argument/Findings (evidence of understanding; adding up-to-date references to support evidence(s); 4) Observations (student's observations and perspective were presented, explained and demonstrated well); 5) Conclusion (sound and appropriate conclusion(s) is drawn; a full and well-written conclusion is provided based upon the foundation in the argument construction section); 6) Structure and quality of writing (well-structured, e.g. paragraphing, sentence structure, spacing; above-average standard of expression and presentation, excellent overall expression and presentation). Students use the template when completing their journal entries and refer to the assessment criteria to ensure that each is met before the final submission. In addition, although a marking guide is used for this assessment, the marking criteria focus on the ability to reflect instead of what is reflected upon; this avoids plagiarism, unlike other assessment methods (MacFarland & Gourlary, 2009). However, the assessment of the reflective journals must follow the university's policy on plagiarism; therefore, Turnitin software (http://turnitin.com/) is used to detect plagiarism in this assessment.

Therefore to improve the effectiveness of the IS650 and WSPD units in conveying HCI and Usability principles to Information Systems students, the researchers integrated the reflective journal assessment in their curriculum and course work. This method of assessment is considered to be an appropriate means of enhancing communication skills and critical thinking. Most importantly, the intention is to promote Human Computer Interaction and Usability Guidelines and Principles among Information Systems students in Australia and Portugal, who are considered our future developers.

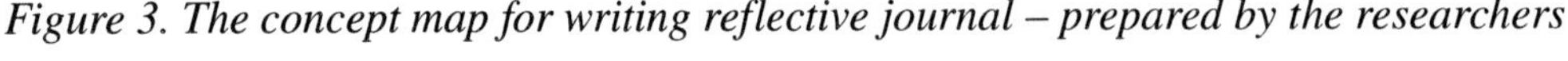
Figure 3. The concept map for writing reflective journal – prepared by the researchers

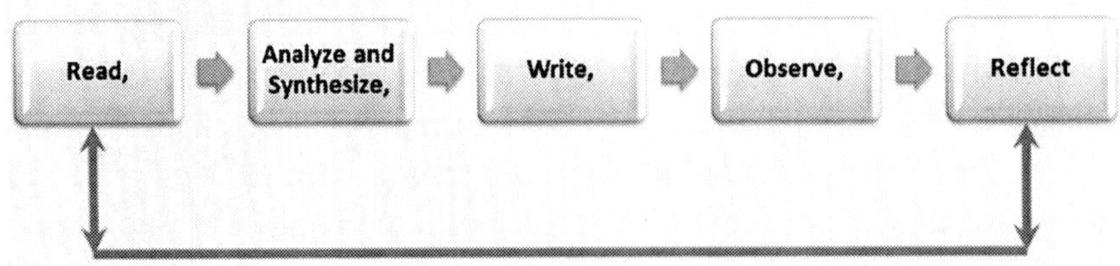

IS650 AND WSPD UNITS; UNIT PROGRAM AND ASSESSMENTS

In this chapter, the researchers intend to examine whether the use of reflective journals assessment can improve students' understanding of the concepts behind usability and HCI principles and guidelines for the web development process. To achieve this, the first researcher developed the IS650 unit program based on her PhD research and results, the Te'eni et al. (2007) textbook, and an up-to-date literature review of journals, e-journals, books and e-books to ensure that up-to-date knowledge and cutting edge development are delivered to the students to promote and enhance their understanding of the design and development of successful, effective websites. Teaching HCI and Usability are a challenge exercise for both authors, since these units need a lot of preparation and planning to ensure that the materials and exercises are cutting edge and enlightened. Several literature reviews (Koehne & Redmiles, 2012; Kybartaite, Nousiainen, Marozas, & Jegelavicius, 2007; Odrakiewicz, 2010) confirmed that teaching these aspects will allow students to obtain new knowledge and skills in dealing with the brand-new technology from iPad to websites. The unit program comprises the following topics: physical, cognitive and affective engineering; evaluation; task analysis; colour; navigation; prototyping; HCI methodologies; social networking and a new topic was introduced is sustainable design. As indicated previously, to convey the same principles as those contained in the IS650 unit, the second researcher is currently running the IS650 unit in his university as the WSPD unit.

To promote HCI and usability aspects in IS650 and WSPD units, students must complete the following assessments: 1) mini tests, reflective journal and contribution to group discussion forum under the blackboard and Moodle respectively. These assessment methods are chosen carefully to develop students' skills of reflective thinking, research, communication, debating, writing and presenting skills using technology and information skills. These skills are essential for university life and the demands of the workplace in future. A series of recommendations is made to ensure that the completion of this unit at the university level will achieve several benefits, including: understanding the principles and guidelines of usability and HCI, which are required to develop websites successfully, analysing and synthesizing journal articles and publications and providing a literature review to identify the gaps in the literature; improving students' communication and personal skills, and matching the unit, degree and university aims and objectives. The units' assessments and syllabus are designed with mainly university graduate attributes in mind (see Table 1). In 2013, slight modifications will be made to the assessment approaches especially for IS650 unit; the three assessments are: Final Test (Individual Assessment) 40%; Reflective Journal (3) – 30% and finally, Wiki – 30%.

Table 1. Assessment activities for postgraduate units - Australia and Portugal (2009 – 2012)

Unit	Assessments	Unit Syllabus
IS650	Mini Tests 25% Reflective Journal (7 Individual and 3 Teamwork) 40% Contribution to Group Discussions – Blackboard (10%)	The IS unit focuses primarily on the principals of usability and human-computer interaction (HCI) design of users' interface including websites
WSPD	Six Group Activities (10% for each activity) 60% overall One final individual work 40%	The WSPD unit is mainly focused on issues relating to Website Planning and Development through a Human-Computer Interaction approach and other related issues.

PARTICIPANTS

This study focused on two postgraduate units in Australia and Portugal: the IS650 unit in Australia and the WSPD unit in Portugal. The 64 participants are mainly from Australia, Asia (Including India), and Europe, Middle East, America (North and South) Mauritius and Africa. A mixture of different nationalities and cultures plays an important role in these units, as each participant interacts and shares his/her knowledge and skills, experience, and cultural perspective with their colleagues in person or via online discussion. The participant group comprised 27% females and 73% males. The researchers noted that both genders took equal part in various activities including discussions, debates, presentations, teamwork activities, and the exchange of ideas. Table 2 provides the demographic details of the IS650 and WSPD students for the 2009-2012 periods.

RESEARCH METHODS AND QUESTION

This chapter aims to examine whether the use of reflective journal assessment will enhance students' understanding of the concepts of HCI and usability in the web development process. This chapter provides experimental evidence based on quantitative and qualitative data derived from three sources: online survey, informal and formal students' feedback from 64 student evaluations and attitudes toward the IS650/WSPD units (respectively at Curtin University and at Universidade Aberta). Both informal and formal feedback was collected during the semester to report students' perceptions of the learning experience at the university, including feedback about the unit and teaching. Informal feedback is a teaching and learning innovation. During week four of the semester, students are asked to provide their anonymous feedback regarding the unit structure, layout and assessments via an online survey. This feedback assists the lecturers to enhance/improve their teaching of the unit before the end of the semester. The second method is formal feedback, which is collected at the end of the semester through the university's formal feedback process. Students have the opportunity to provide feedback anonymously on their learning experiences and on the unit and teaching evaluation.

Finally, the third method is the online survey. This survey is divided into five parts. The purpose of each part of the survey was explained to students. The first part pertains to background information such as participant's level of formal education; main field(s) of study, and gender. Part two aims to examine students' reactions to the unit's program; part three is intended to evaluate students' attitudes to the units' assessment approach; part four seeks students' perception of the lecturer's feedback on the various methods of assessment including the reflective journals, exam and the discussion board. Finally, part five aims to examine whether students' skills (oral presentation, writing, reading, critical thinking, research and search, use of the Endnote software,

Table 2. Postgraduate units participants – Australia and Portugal (2009 – 2012)

Unit	Students #	Gender		Nationality						
		Female	Male	Australia	Asia (Including India)	Europe	Middle East	America (A)/ North (N) and South (S)	Mauritius	Africa
IS650	52	15	37	1	37	0	6	1(NA), 1 (SA)	2	4
WSPD	12	2	10	0	0	9	0	1(SA)	0	2
Total	***64***	***17***	***47***	***1***	***37***	***9***	***6***	***2***	***2***	***6***

collaboration and communication) are promoted and improved after completing the IS650 and WSPD units. In the following section, the researchers discuss the results from part five of the survey. The authors used a five-point Likert scale ranging from "Strongly disagree" to "Strongly agree" for parts two to five. Besides using the Likert five-point scale for this survey, the authors provided a section where students could write down other comments regarding each part. The online survey response rate from IS650, and WSPD was 61.5% and 90% respectively.

RESULTS

To confirm the study's aims and objectives, this section presents the results from the informal and formal feedback and the results from part five of the survey. It was noted from the informal feedback (see Table 3) that students were satisfied with both the lectures (classes) and lecturer (instructor) for both IS650 and WSPD units.

Students confirmed that their lecturers had a good knowledge of HCI and usability and that the classes were engaging and not boring as lecturers used various types of teaching styles in their classes. Furthermore, students were very generous in their comments about their lecturers:

Quick response, willingness to help, friendly and approachable (Student 1)

Enthusiasm, understanding and compromise, asks our opinions (Student 2)

Lecturers are more focused on the knowledge and hot the information (Student 3)

Very detailed when explaining, give good feedback that can help study improve (Student 4)

Good communications, cooperative, solves student's problems (Student 5)

Helpful, kindness (Student 6)

Lecturers give feedback and those help to improve the writing, reading and referencing skills ... thank you (Student 7)

Excellent teaching style and presentation slides (Student 8)

Lecturers use many unique teaching styles to other lecturers. e.g. mp3, class activities, mind maps (Student 9)

Table 3. Informal feedback – IS650 and WSPD

Year	Unit	Question	SD/D	N	A/SA
2009	IS650	I am satisfied with the Lectures (Classes)		1	18
		I am satisfied with the Lecturer (Instructor)		1	18
2010	IS650	I am satisfied with the Lectures (Classes)		1	14
		I am satisfied with the Lecturer (Instructor)			15
2011	IS650	I am satisfied with the Lectures (Classes)		1	15
		I am satisfied with the Lecturer (Instructor)			16
2012	IS650	I am satisfied with the Lectures (Classes)	1	1	11
		I am satisfied with the Lecturer (Instructor)	1	1	11
2011	WSPD	I am satisfied with the Lectures (Classes)			10
		I am satisfied with the Lecturer (Instructor)			10

Sharing and inform interesting issues related with HCI, such as Usability and Satisfaction, using mind map for material summarizing (Student 10)

Using different activities related to the lecture such as exercises for each week and challenge exercises and so on (Student 11)

Group discuss is really a powerful weapon, learn things quick & it is good to share ideas with each other (Student 12).

This feedback confirmed that researchers have unique teaching methods for HCI and Usability concepts, as the majority of the students acknowledged that the activities, the unit program and, most importantly, the approach to assessment including the reflective journals intended to assist them to understand the concepts of HCI and usability, together with the lecturers' feedback, all play a major role in improving their learning journey.

The informal feedback from students was invariably positive:

The journals are very dynamic as they force us to be resourceful, using textbooks, websites, and articles. Also in class reading and analysis keeps class interesting, especially cause me get to discuss in group. (Student 13)

Better understanding of HCI, information about new technologies via the reflective journals (Student 14)

I have learnt to write reflective reviews of the articles I read therefore increased my learning toward HCI and usability (Student 15)

The home work journals is a step in the right direction (Student 16)

I like the journal writing every week, bush us to study hard (Student 17)

Understand the complexity behind HCI and Usability via exercises and reflective journals (Student 18)

Practical approach to teaching than a conventional way (Student 19)

Makes are feeling like doing a post-grad course by encouraging reading articles which are related to our unit in line to write the reflective journals. (Student 20)

Class activities keep the classes interesting. The assessment style of reflective journals have helped in applying knowledge learned in class to real world occurrences (Student 21)

Involving students to read articles that related to the lecture topic to understand the unit program (Student 22)

The journal articles writing are very good to improve our reading, writing knowledge about HCI (Student 23)

I learned huge knowledge from this unit especially Human computer interaction, which I was not aware of before (Student 24)

Personal contact with the unit coordinator, interaction through presentations, improving our thinking and knowledge to HCI and Usability through critical reflection reports (Student 25)

Students were very satisfied and pleased with the reflective journal assessment and recognized that this assessment assisted them to: 1) improve their understanding and knowledge of HCI and Usability by critically reflecting on their reading; and 2) it improved their communication skills as well as their level of critical thinking.

By the same token, the results from part five for the online survey confirmed that completing IS650 and WSPD units (see Tables 4 and 5)

Table 4. IS650 Students 2012 – Part five – online survey (Response rate 61.5%)

Question	Strongly Disagree	Disagree	Neutral	Agree	Strongly Agree	Mean	Standard Deviation
Collaboration skills	0	0	1	3	4	4.38	0.74
Writing skills	0	0	0	2	6	4.75	0.46
Reading skills	0	0	0	2	6	4.75	0.46
Critical skills	0	0	0	2	6	4.75	0.46
Research skills	0	0	0	3	5	4.63	0.52
Search skills	0	0	1	4	3	4.25	0.71
Communication skills	0	0	1	4	3	4.25	0.71

Table 5. WSPD Students 2012 – part five – online survey (Response rate 90%)

Question	Strongly Disagree	Disagree	Neutral	Agree	Strongly Agree	Mean	Standard Deviation
Collaboration skills	0	1	1	5	2	3.89	0.93
Writing skills	0	1	4	3	1	3.44	0.88
Reading skills	0	0	4	4	1	3.67	0.71
Critical skills	0	0	1	6	2	4.11	0.60
Research skills	0	0	1	5	3	4.22	0.67
Search skills	0	0	1	6	2	4.11	0.60
Communication skills	0	0	3	5	1	3.78	0.67

improved and developed a number of students' skills including oral presentation, writing, reading, critical thinking, research and search, use of the Endnote software, collaboration and communication. The online survey was used for units IS650 and WSPD during 2012.

Results depicted in Tables 4 and 5 confirm that the completion of the IS650 and WSPD units allowed the students to acquire valuable skills as a result of collaboration, writing, reading, critical thinking, research, search and communication, all of which skills are essential for university studies and life in general. Students confirmed and emphasized that IS650 and WPDS units were quite challenging and 'it improves my overall quality' and 'Very useful and interesting Units' (Student 26). By the same token, several studies (Diggins, 2004; Gadsby & Cronin, 2012; Lanning, Brickhouse, Gunsolley, Ranson, & Willett, 2011; Worley, 2008) indicate that effective communications skills will help students to build trust, respect, foster learning and attain their goals. It was acknowledged that both writing and oral skills are essential for sharing ideas, feelings and commitments. Therefore, productive communication skills will assist students to understand the assessments, including the reflective journals. Students are given the opportunity to perform well in their studies as well in the workplace, since businesses seek graduates with effective communication and collaboration skills (Cunliffe, 2004; Lanning et al., 2011; Woei & White, 2010).

DISCUSSION

The results from the informal, formal and online survey reveal that the use of reflective journal assessments in IS650 and WSPD gives students a better understanding and knowledge of Human-

Computer Interaction and Usability principles and guidelines. This assessment approach is considered to be the new professional learning method in higher education intended to educate students and impart the skills which are required for both current study and the workforce in future. Moreover, students were satisfied and gratified with the unit assessments since their communication, collaboration, interpersonal, writing, reading, oral presentation, search/research, problem-solving and decision-making skills, which are required for this study and real life in the future, were improved. Also, the findings indicated that the weekly reflective journals assist students to keep track of the unit work throughout the course, as it acts as a revision of material presented during lectures and laboratory sessions.

Furthermore, students confirmed that reflective journal's assessment was one of the ways to enhance their understanding of HCI and Usability. For example, one of the students indicated that 'the first of the journal genres, analysis of current research of the HCI community' required a critical analysis of journal documents. To produce these journals, a structure was provided, which firstly required a brief account of the findings in each individual article. These findings were critically analyzed to enable students to gain an understanding of the relationship between the given articles while providing supporting evidence to justify these relationships. Following this, observations were needed, which required further polishing of current understandings of HCI. This structure represents a methodology that anyone can reproduce to construct a critical working document for a given subject matter. Student 27 endorsed that 'It was noted that through the continuous reflective journals' assessment of the academic writing, a clear improvement was achieved. Students were not only required to reach some standards, but also pushed to improve our coherence and completeness, which are fundamental for being a successful postgraduate. Although it was a great challenge writing the reflective journals, but was fundamental to allow higher performance not only in the IS650 unit, but in other units as well'. The majority of students observed that the IS650 and WSPD units gave them a new insight into HCI and usability which is essential in the web development process as most of them were previously unaware of these issues. Finally, an understanding of all aspects related to HCI and usability in the development of any information systems/technology is an incredible asset that every Information professional should possess.

Despite its challenges, the integration of the reflective journal in IS650 and WSPD units proved to be an interesting and outstanding achievement from the researchers' perspective, as the majority of the students indicated in their formal and informal feedback, as well the online survey, that this assessment approach in their units allowed them to, firstly, raise their awareness of aspects of Usability and HCI especially in the web development process, as the majority of students confirmed that these concepts are essential in the website development process. Student 28 signposted: 'I did not know and aware that HCI and Usability is a thoroughly studied and well-researched field within Information Systems'. While Student 29 pointed out that 'Conducting this subject is very important because I believe every system/web designer should know about HCI and usability how it can be adapted in the design especially the website'. By the same token, Student 30 noted that 'The journals have taught me a lot of Human Computer Interaction aspects such as the complexity of Human Computer Interaction, the importance of user involvement in the system design, the necessity of measuring usability to improve the current usability, the role of trust in e-commercial, etc. While some journals are easy to read, some of them are targeted for more experienced audience'.

Secondly, the students' comments confirmed and revealed that this assessment approach in both IS650 and WSPD units allowed them to understand the concepts behind the unit program, and that the completion of the journals was an excellent experience. Student 31stated that 'the journal assignments have been a very satisfying experience for me, I have to learn the latest issue of Human Computer Interactions. Please keep doing the journal assignments in the future, as it will help the students to improve their reading and writing skills as well as learning new concepts of Human Computer Interactions'. However, this was not the only benefit to be derived from the reflective journals. This approach also gave students the opportunity to acquire and improve upon a wide range of communication skills which are necessary for the purposes of study and future workplace requirements as the majority of organizations seek graduates with excellent communication skills to match the needs of both business and society in general. Finally, student 32 commented: 'I enjoyed the lecturer's teachings because it seemed obvious to me that this particular topic was of a big interest to her. I enjoy studying with lecturers who seem passionate about the field they are teaching as the enthusiasm reaches me, at least during the class. She also listened to the student feedback regarding workload and activities we wanted. Lastly, I appreciated the presentation on her thesis as, again, I like to see practical and concrete work relating to the unit I am learning. It makes the unit feel much more useful in the real world'.

In the IS650 and WSPD units, reflective journal assessment is designed to improve student(s) experience from critically, creatively and reflectively, reviewing, synthesising, analysing and recording the main key points and thoughts about material from textbook(s), journal articles and the Internet. In addition, this assessment encourages student(s) to keep up to date with their readings and their visits to WWW sites which are related to the unit. A reflective journal should not only contain a summary of the reading; it also seeks to encourage students to reflect upon the information acquired from reading these articles, to add their personal record of their educational experiences after having read these articles, and to consider how these experiences assist them to understand and follow the curriculum of units IS650 and WSPD. Lastly, on the basis of the students' outstanding overall satisfaction, the first author is now considered as a teacher-leader in reflective journal assessment in her school, and she now works with her colleagues to support and implement this assessment in the school curriculum strategy to reflect the desirable attributes of university graduates and to promote and improve students' learning skills.

The research aims were confirmed by strong student satisfaction and gratification with the reflective journal assessments in the IS650 and WSPD units. Students were very delighted with this assessment approach; student 31 expressed that 'writing journal is good way of learning as we read the articles, then try to understand what it is about, try to find the linkage between different authors view on the subject and then write how different authors were agreeing or arguing on the same topic supporting our own point of view'. In addition, 'It is all about giving extra justification to your point of view or your way of thinking by supporting it with the articles and giving additional explanation in order to make your answer justifiable and more meaningful'. Finally, there is no doubt that this assessment approach offers numerous many benefits for higher education since students endorsed and confirmed that they learned the principles and guidelines behind HCI and Usability and above all, that their communication skills improved dramatically.

RECOMMENDATIONS FOR INTEGRATING REFLECTIVE JOURNAL IN HIGHER EDUCATION

Reflective journal assessment in higher education is considered a vehicle for reflection, acquiring new knowledge (i.e. HCI and Usability) and, most importantly, prompting and improving students' communications skills for their current studies as well as the workforce in future. This assessment enables students to document their experiences, thoughts, questions, ideas and conclusion that signboard their learning journey when undertaking the IS650 and WSPD units.

The researchers hold that reflective journal assessment is a unique tool that allows students to express their opinions and observations and later to reflect on what they learn from these articles. This assessment process will encourage students to become active learners; it fosters independent learners, since they read, analyze and synthesize, write, observe and later reflect. To ensure the smooth integration of reflective journal assessment in a unit, the following guidelines which are based on the researchers' experience, should be followed: 1) introduce the reflective journal analysis and evaluation template to assist students to organize their ideas, thoughts, and reflection following their reading; 2) keep track of journal submissions, the first journal in particular, to ensure that students have followed the template, especially the observation section; 3) check the marking guide for the reflective journals before the final submission, to ensure that the final submission meets the marking guide and the lecturer' criteria; 4) indicate students' strengths and weaknesses of the current journal entry in order to improve the subsequent journal entry; 5) in order to promote this method of assessment among the students, especially in the first week of the semester, introduce some class exercises based on the template; students present these to the class for peer assessment and feedback from the lecturer regarding the presentation in general and any new thoughts and ideas that have emerged.

Finally, these guidelines are based on the lecturers' perspectives after implementing reflective journal assessment in IS650 and WSPD. Finally, the current studies (Bailes et al., 2010; Clarke, 2003; Lin, Hong, Wang, & Lee, 2011; Power, 2012 ; Sengers, McCarthy, & Dourish, 2006; Titus & Gremler, 2010) indicate that this form of assessment is common-used in the higher education sector as it helps to develop self-empowerment, creativity, writing skills, self-expression, and critical thinking; moreover, it encourages reflection which is associated with deep learning and metacognition. Therefore, the researchers' perception is that this assessment approach should and must be integrated in the higher education curriculum to foster students' learning and shift it away from - traditional teaching-learning practices to the independent learning to learn method.

CONCLUSION

This chapter aims to examine and investigate the employment of reflective journal assessment in the IS650 and WSPD units. This form of assessment was introduced in these units based on both university and business needs since university graduates should develop the communication and critical thinking skills necessary for both their current studies and for their future place in the workforce. The researchers used three sources to collect the data for this study, namely: formal and informal students' feedback, and an online survey. The study outcomes confirmed the research question and study aims, as the majority of students indicated that this method of assessment assisted them to understand the HCI and usability principles and guidelines as these concepts are essential in the web development process, especially to satisfy the users from generations X, Y, and Z. In addition, the IS650 and WSPD units provide significant knowledge regarding the HCI and Usability topics, expanding students' horizons and giving them a greater understanding of the unit program and the rationale for this approach to assessment. Furthermore, this assessment method significantly improved students' communication and time management skills, which are needed for their current studies as well as the workforce in future. A set of recommendations was developed by the researchers to implement the reflective journal as a means of assessment in the higher education sector. This study was limited to two university units; researchers are planning to employ the reflective journal assessments in other units in order to further study and compare students' attitudes to this type of assessment.

REFERENCES

Anderson, J. (2012). Reflective journals as a tool for auto-ethnographic learning: A case study of student experiences with individualized sustainability. *Journal of Geography in Higher Education*, *36*(4), 613–623. doi:10.1080/03098265.2012.692157.

Bailes, C., Hulsebosch, P., & Martin, D. (2010). Reflective journal writing: Deaf pre-service teachers with hearing children. *Teacher Education and Special Education*, *33*(3), 234–247. doi:10.1177/0888406409356763.

Benyon, D., Turner, P., & Turner, S. (2005). *Designing interactive systems*. Englewood Cliffs, NJ: Pearson Education Limited.

Cappel, J. J., & Huang, Z. (2007). A usability analysis of company websites. *Journal of Computer Information Systems*, *48*(1), 117–123.

Carroll, M. (2004). *Usability testing leads to better ROI*. Retrieved from http://www.theusabilitycompany.com/news/media_coverage/pdfs/2003/NewMediaAge_270303.pdf

Clarke, M. (2003). *Reflection: Journals and reflective questions a strategy for professional learning*. Paper presented at the NZARE/AARE Conference. Auckland, New Zealand.

Clarkeburn, H., & Kettula, K. (2012). Fairness and using reflective journals in assessment. *Teaching in Higher Education*, *17*(4), 439–452. doi:10.1080/13562517.2011.641000.

Cunliffe, A. (2004). On becoming a critically reflexive practitioner. *Journal of Management Education*, *28*(4), 407–425. doi:10.1177/1052562904264440.

Davis, P., & Shipman, F. (2011). *Learning usability assessment models for web sites*. Paper presented at the IUI 2011. Palo Alto, CA.

DePaula, R. (2003). *A new era in human computer interaction: The challenges of technology as a social proxy*. Paper presented at the Latin American Conference on HCI. New York, NY.

Dewey, J. (1933). *How we think: A restatement of the relation of reflective thinking to the educative process*. Boston: D. C. Heath.

Dillahunt, T., Mankoff, J., & Forlizzi, J. (2010). *A proposed framework for assessing environmental sustainability in the HCI community*. Paper presented at the CHI 2010. Atlanta, GA.

DiSalvo, C., Sengers, P., & Hronn Brynjarsdottir, P. (2010). *Mapping the landscape of sustainable HCI*. Paper presented at the CHI 2010. Atlanta, GA.

Dix, A., Finlay, J., Abowd, G., & Beale, R. (2004). *Human-computer interaction* (3rd ed.). Englewood Cliffs, NJ: Pearson Education Limited.

Fernandez, A., Insfran, E., & Abrahão, S. (2011). Usability evaluation methods for the web: A systematic mapping study. *Information and Software Technology*, *53*(8), 789–817. Retrieved from http://www.sciencedirect.com/science/article/pii/S0950584911000607 doi:10.1016/j.infsof.2011.02.007.

Gadsby, H., & Cronin, S. (2012). To what extent can reflective journaling help beginning teachers develop Masters level writing skills? *Reflective Practice: International and Multidisciplinary Perspectives*, *13*(1), 1–12. doi:10.1080/14623943.2011.616885.

Head, A. J. (1999). *Design wise*. Thomas H Hogan Sr.

Hertzum, M., & Clemmensen, T. (2012). How do usability professionals construe usability? *International Journal of Human-Computer Studies*, *70*(1), 26–42. Retrieved from http://www.sciencedirect.com/science/article/pii/S1071581911001030 doi:10.1016/j.ijhcs.2011.08.001.

Hewett, T., Baecker, R., Card, C., Carey, T., Gasen, J., Mantei, M., et al. (1992). *Human-computer interaction*. Retrieved from http://old.sigchi.org/cdg/

Hoekstra, G. (2000). *History of web design*. Retrieved from http://www.weballey.net/webdesign/history.html

Issa, T. (1999). *Online shopping and human factors*. Unpublished.

Issa, T., & Turk, A. (2012). Applying usability and HCI principles in developing marketing websites. *International Journal of Computer Information Systems and Industrial Management Applications*, *4*, 76–82.

Joshi, A., Sarda, N. L., & Tripathi, S. (2010). Measuring effectiveness of HCI integration in software development processes. *Journal of Systems and Software*, *83*(11), 2045–2058. doi:10.1016/j.jss.2010.03.078.

Knapp, N. F. (2012). Reflective journals: Making constructive use of the apprenticeship of observation in preservice teacher education. *Teaching Education*, *23*(3), 323–340. doi:10.1080/10476210.2012.686487.

Koehne, B., & Redmiles, D. F. (2012). *Envisioning distributed usability evaluation through a virtual world platform*. Paper presented at the Cooperative and Human Aspects of Software Engineering (CHASE). New York, NY.

Kybartaite, A., Nousiainen, J., Marozas, V., & Jegelavicius, D. (2007). *Review of e-teaching/e-learning practices and technologies*. Retrieved from http://hlab.ee.tut.fi/video/bme/evicab/astore/delivera/wp4revie.pdf

Lanning, S. K., Brickhouse, T. H., Gunsolley, J. C., Ranson, S. L., & Willett, R. M. (2011). Communication skills instruction: An analysis of self, peer-group, student instructors and faculty assessment. *Patient Education and Counseling*, *83*, 145–151. doi:10.1016/j.pec.2010.06.024 PMID:20638816.

Lavie, T., Oron-Gilad, T., & Meyer, J. (2011). Aesthetics and usability of in-vehicle navigation displays. *International Journal of Human-Computer Studies*, *69*(1-2), 80–99. doi:10.1016/j.ijhcs.2010.10.002.

Lazar, J., Jones, A., & Shneiderman, B. (2006). Workplace user frustration with computers: An exploratory investigation of the causes and severity. *Behaviour & Information Technology*, *25*(3), 239–251. doi:10.1080/01449290500196963.

Lee, S., & Koubek, R. J. (2010). The effects of usability and web design attributes on user preference for e-commerce web sites. *Computers in Industry*, *61*(4), 329–341. doi:10.1016/j.compind.2009.12.004.

Lee, Y., & Kozar, K. (2012). Understanding of website usability: Specifying and measuring constructs and their relationships. *Decision Support Systems*, *52*(2), 450–463. Retrieved from http://www.sciencedirect.com/science/article/pii/S0167923611001679 doi:10.1016/j.dss.2011.10.004.

Lin, H.-S., Hong, Z.-R., Wang, H.-H., & Lee, S.-T. (2011). Using reflective peer assessment to promote students' conceptual understanding through asynchronous discussions. *Journal of Educational Technology & Society*, *14*(3), 178–189.

Loughran, J. (2002). Effective reflective practice: In search of meaning in learning about teaching. *Journal of Teacher Education*, *53*(1), 33–43. doi:10.1177/0022487102053001004.

MacFarland, B., & Gourlary, L. (2009). Points of departure - The reflection game: Enacting the penitent self. *Teaching in Higher Education*, *14*(4), 455–459. doi:10.1080/13562510903050244.

McCracken, D. D., & Wolfe, R. J. (2004). *User-centered website development a human-computer interaction approach*. Hillsdale, NJ: Pearson Education, Inc..

Miller, C. A. (2004). Human-computer etiquette: Managing expectations with intentional agents. *Communications of the ACM*, *47*(4), 31–34.

Nielsen, J. (2003). *Usability 101*. Retrieved from http://www.useit.com/alertbox/20030825.html

Odrakiewicz, P. (2010). Managing complexity in higher education through innovative ways of integrity teaching and integrity education management using innovative case studies. *Global Management Journal*, *2*(2), 122–130.

Oztekin, A. (2011). A decision support system for usability evaluation of web-based information systems. *Expert Systems with Applications*, *38*(3), 2110–2118. Retrieved from http://www.sciencedirect.com/science/article/pii/S0957417410007797 doi:10.1016/j.eswa.2010.07.151.

Power, J. B. (2012). Towards a greater understanding of the effectiveness of reflective journals in a university language program. *Reflective Practice: International and Multidisciplinary Perspectives*, *13*(5), 637–649. doi:10.1080/14623943.2012.697889.

Preece, J., Rogers, Y., Benyon, D., Holland, S., & Carey, T. (1994). *Human computer interaction*. Reading, MA: Addison-Wesley.

Sauer, J., Seibel, K., & Rüttinger, B. (2010). The influence of user expertise and prototype fidelity in usability tests. *Applied Ergonomics*, *41*(1), 130–140. doi:10.1016/j.apergo.2009.06.003 PMID:19632666.

Scott, I. (2011). The learning outcome in higher education: Time to think again? *Worcester Journal of Learning and Teaching*, *5*, 1–8.

Sengers, P., McCarthy, J., & Dourish, P. (2006). *Reflective HCI: Articulating an agenda for critical practice*. Paper presented at the CHI' 06. New York, NY.

Shi, M. (2011). *Website characteristics and their influences: A review on web design*. Paper presented at the ABIS 2011. New York, NY.

Silberman, M. S., & Tomlinson, B. (2010). *Toward an ecological sensibility: Tools for evaluating sustainable HCI*. Paper presented at the CHI 2010. Atlanta, GA.

Sørum, H., Andersen, K. N., & Vatrapu, R. (2011). *Public websites and human–computer interaction: An empirical study of measurement of website quality and user satisfaction*. Retrieved from http://dx.doi.org/10.1080/0144929X.2011.577191

Te'eni, D., Carey, J., & Zhang, P. (2007). *Human computer interaction: Developing effective organizational information systems*. Hoboken, NJ: John Wiley & Sons, Inc..

Titus, P., & Gremler, D. (2010). Guiding reflective practice: An auditing framework to assess teaching. *Philosophy and Style Journal of Marketing Education*, *32*(2), 182–196. doi:10.1177/0273475309360161.

Tuzovic, S. (2010). Frequent (flier) frustration and the dark side of word-of-web: Exploring online dysfunctional behavior in online feedback forums. *Journal of Services Marketing*, *24*(6), 446–457. doi:10.1108/08876041011072564.

Woei, L., & White, G. (2010). *The promotion of critical thinking through the use of an online discussion board: Asking the right questions?* Paper presented at the Global Learn Asia Pacific. New York, NY.

Worley, P. (2008). Writing skills essential in tech ed today. *Tech Directions*, *68*(2), 17–19.

Zhang, P., Carey, J., Te'eni, D., & Tremaine, M. (2005). Integrating human-computer interaction development into the systems development life cycle: A methodology. *Communications of the Association for Information Systems*, *15*, 512–543.

KEY TERMS AND DEFINITIONS

Design Guidelines: Are essential to the designers to achieve the principles.[2]

Design Principles: Are used to formalize the high level and widely appropriate design goals.[2]

Human Computer Interaction: Allocate, users, analysts, and designers (internal and external) to identify that the website design is practical. There are many specific issues that need to be taken into consideration when designing website pages, such as text style, fonts, layout, graphics, and color. (Issa 2008)[1]

Method- Formal Feedback: Is collected at the end of the semester through the university's formal feedback process.[2]

Method –Informal Feedback: Is a teaching and learning innovation to examine students' attitudes toward the unit structure, layout and assessments via an online survey.[2]

Reflective Journal: Is an essential assessment to develop students' critical thinking and communication skills, writing, reading, research, search, and using endnote software. [2]

Usability: Allow users, analysts, and designers (internal and external) to confirm that the website design is efficient, effective, safe, has utility, is easy to learn, easy to remember, easy to use and to evaluate, practical, visible, and provides job satisfaction (Issa 2008)

ENDNOTES

1 Issa, T. (2008). *Development and Evaluation of a Methodology for Developing Websites - PhD Thesis, Curtin University, Western Australia.* Retrieved from http://espace.library.curtin.edu.au:1802/view/action/nmets.do?DOCCHOICE=17908.xml&dvs=1235702350272~864&locale=en_US&search_terms=17908&usePid1=true&usePid2=true

2 Prepared by the authors

Chapter 20
The Impact of Visual Complexity on Children's Learning Websites in Relation to Aesthetic Preference and Learning Motivation

Hsiu-Feng Wang
National Chiayi University, Taiwan

Julian Bowerman
Loughborough University, UK

ABSTRACT

Websites in addition to being usable must also be pleasurable to look at. However, although much research has been conducted into usability, subjective issues have been far less explored. The purpose of this research is to look at the relationship between visual complexity, aesthetics, and learning motivation in children's learning websites. An experiment was set up that involved 132 11-12 year-old children using homepages taken from Websites designed for children as test materials. In the experiment, the children were randomly assigned into 3 groups and given a different visual complexity Website according to their group. The Websites given were: homepage with a low degree of visual complexity; homepage with a moderate degree of visual complexity; and homepage with a high degree of visual complexity. This study is guided by Berlyne's experimental theory, which suggests that there is an inverted-U shaped relationship between preference for a stimulus and its complexity. The study applies his theory and aims to understand the relationship between visual complexity, aesthetic preference, and learning motivation. The findings show that children prefer aesthetics of a medium level of perceived complexity, supporting Berlyne's theory. It also shows that children's aesthetic preferences and learning motivation are correlated. The findings have implications for Web designers working on children's Websites as they suggest that by manipulating visual complexity viewing pleasure can be enhanced or depreciated.

DOI: 10.4018/978-1-4666-4623-0.ch020

1. INTRODUCTION

In recent years, the use of the World Wide Web (WWW) as a resource for learning has increased. As the Internet keeps expanding, it is becoming increasingly important for educational organizations that host websites deliver a good user experience for people. Although much research has been conducted in this area with respect to usability (Lindgaard, Fernandes, Dudek, & Brown, 2006), many subjective aspects have, until recently, been neglected. One subjective aspect which has started to receive attention is that of visual appearance. Research conducted in this area includes studies into: first impressions (Lindgaard et al., 2006); the prototype related to first impressions (Tuch, Presslaber, Stocklin, Opwisa, & Bargas-Avila, 2012); and the importance of aesthetics with respect to mode of use (Schaik & Ling, 2009). Although much of this research is still in its infancy, there does seem to be evidence that visual aesthetics critically affect how a user perceives a website in terms of interaction enjoyment (Van de Heijden, 2003; Schenkman & Jönsson, 2000).

One of those factors which severely influence visual aesthetic preference is visual complexity. Its impact on aesthetic preference is very well documented in numerous publications (Pandir & Knight, 2006; Tuch, Bargas-Avila, & Opwis, 2010; Michailidou, Harper, & Bechhofer, 2008), but knowledge about the influence of visual complexity on children's learning websites, and their aesthetic preference, is limited. Another point that needs clarification is whether there is any correlation between aesthetic preference and learning motivation.

The importance of affective variables was already well recognised as factors influence learning motivation and achievement (Dweck, Mangels, & Good, 2004; Hidi, 2006). Aesthetic preference was acknowledged to be one of the critical affective variables that influence people's emotions and feelings. There are studies on learning motivation, primarily covering topics such as interest (e.g. Bergin, 1999; Pintrich, 2003), self-efficacy (e.g. Hidi & Renninger, 2006; Gaffney, 2011), and self-determination (e.g., Deci & Ryan, 1985; Deci, Koestner, & Ryan, 1999). Nevertheless, studies investigating aesthetic preference with respect to learning motivation are rare. Thus, it is important that researchers and practitioners examine possible interactions between aesthetic variables and learning motivation. In this study, we therefore investigate the effect of visual complexity on learning website aesthetics in relation to learning motivation.

1.1. Visual Complexity

Psychologist Berlyne (1974) made an important theory contribution to experimental aesthetics. According to Berlyne's theory, aesthetics relates to a number of so-called 'collative variables', where each person's pleasure is related to the arousal potential of a stimulus. This relationship is linked to the Wundt (inverted-U shape) curve for pleasure, with a linearly increasing line for the arousal potential of a stimulus (see Figure 1). One prediction of the model is that medium levels of stimulus would be preferred, whereas stimuli with low and high arousal potentials are less pleasant. In line with his theory, arousal potential is linked to collative properties such as complexity, novelty, and hedonic value. These are the most important predictors for visual aesthetic preference. Among those properties, visual complexity plays a crucial role in the perceived aesthetic preference (Tuch et al., 2010).

A number of experiments have been conducted with respect to users' preference and perceived visual complexity. However, the experimental support for this inverted U-curve relationship is mixed. In a study of children's aesthetic preferences for websites, Wang and Bowerman (2012) showed that children preferred both classical and expressive aesthetics of a medium level of perceived visual complexity, supporting Berlyne's theory. A similar result was

Figure 1.The expected relationship between an image's complexity and aesthetic preference in the shape of an inverted U-curve

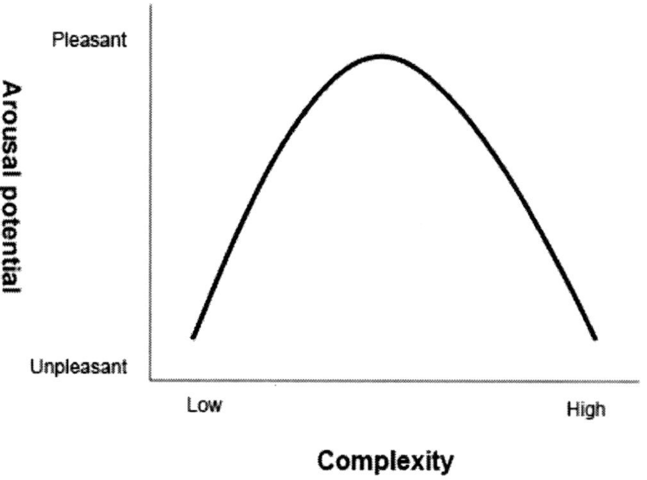

found in research by Geissler, Zinkhan, and Watson (2006), who tested Berlyne's theory in a study of users' attitudes towards home pages with respect to perceived visual complexity. The researchers found that users responded more favourably to websites with a medium level of perceived complexity than to those with a high or low level of perceived complexity and concluded that the findings of their study supported Berlyne's theory. However, in another study that also tested Berlyne's theory, Pandir and Knight (2006) emphasized the effects of individual differences in personal interests and tastes on preferences through an experiment using screenshots of twelve homepages. Their results showed a negative correlation between complexity and pleasure in website perception; therefore, they could not directly support Berlyne's theory. The study also indicated that individual differences in taste and lifestyle are highly personal factors that influence aesthetic preference. Chang, Lin, and Lee (2005) conducted an experiment to test childrens' preference for the complexity of images used in learning English vocabulary. They found that children preferred a more complex image. In a recent study, Tuch, Bargas-Avila, and Opwis (2009), in a test that looked at both cognitive and emotional issues, found that websites with a low level of perceived complexity were preferred. Furthermore, Stevenson, Bruner and Kumar (2000) provided a demonstration of the user's attitude to viewing webpages. They found that webpage complexity plays a key role which influences users' attitudes and intentions. This result was consistent with that of another study by Schaik and Ling (2009). They investigated the effect of context in webpages on aesthetic perception and found that the perceived aesthetics value increased when the website provided context. These disparate findings arguably limit the use of previous research when attempting to predict the aesthetic preferences of children when visual complexity is a factor on learning websites, and suggest that more research in this area is needed.

1.2. Measuring the Visual Complexity of Websites

Numerous studies have shown the influence of aesthetics on website usability, trust and credibility. Besides the importance of aesthetics in the domain of Human-Computer Interaction (HCI), researchers should know how users perceive aesthetic preference. Therefore, it is important to give a general definition of aesthetics. Most of the literature aggresses that aesthetics are the combination of objective and subjective elements (Martindale, Moore, & Borkum, 1990). For instance, when people describe a painting, they can mention the colour, line, and shape of the painting, which can be perceived by anyone. These are the objective elements in aesthetics (Hanfling, 1992). On the other hand, the subjective elements are the preferences for the painting which are the physiological and psychological aspects of the viewing experience. Subjective elements depend on individual difference and will change over time. Tilghman (2004) suggests that to closely evaluate subjective elements we need to base our analysis on people's sensibility, education and taste. Despite the differences between objective and subjective elements of aesthetics, one should view them holistically. In this research, we tried to evaluate children's preferences with regard to the subjective elements of aesthetics for a children's website, and we chose some websites which contained different levels of the objective elements (complexity), in an attempt to assess aesthetic preference. One way to assess the complexity of an image is to analyse the elements of that image and to manipulate the number of elements according to the level of complexity. Michailidou et al. (2008) developed a metric to count the different levels of visual complexity of a website. According to their research, visual complexity is the degree of difficulty in providing a verbal description of an image. Therefore, descriptions of the complexity of an image might include the number of objects, clutter, openness, symmetry, organization, and variety of colours. Based on this theory, they analyse the website's visual complexity in terms of the density and diversity of the elements on the page. The current experiment employed this same metric to divide the sampled children's learning websites into three levels of visual complexity (high, medium, and low).

1.3. Learning Motivation

The importance of learning motivation has been well recognised in educational research. Pintrich and Schunk (1996), for example, stated that motivation influences how and why people learn and how they perform, while Sachs (2001) conducted a study which suggested that there was a positive relationship between achievement motivation and performance. Many educational and psychological studies have developed frameworks and theories which explored the relationship between learning and motivation (Pintrich & Schunk, 1996). In general, motivation can be described as an emotion or sense of feeling that captivates positive senses in our brain by employing extrinsic and intrinsic factors. Research in psychology distinguishes between intrinsic and extrinsic motivation. Intrinsic motivation reflects an activity that is undertaken by individuals for their own sake, enjoyment, or for personal interest. In other words, intrinsic motivation is what a person feels when he is motivated by his own attitudes and interests. In contrast, extrinsic motivation reflects an activity that is undertaken for instrumental assessment or for external reasons. Research from the area of self-determination theory (SDT) has also demonstrated the importance of intrinsic motivation (Deci & Ryan, 1985), focusing on the intrinsic motivation in driving human behaviour. According to Deci and Ryan (1985), intrinsic motivation refers to situations in which an individual is pleased to perform an action. The variations of these different motivational styles, from extrinsic to intrinsic, can lead to different outcomes with various experimental treatments. Therefore, there was a need for more research into how learners internalized the different styles of reading material.

In order to explore children's learning motivation toward the perceived visual complexity of websites, the ARCS model (Attention, Relevance, Confidence and Satisfaction) was employed in the current study of student motivation. The model is designed to motivate people towards success in their learning objectives. According to Small (2000), the model measures the amount of effect invested by learners to achieve the learning goal. In order to assist students to achieve their goal, the instructional situation has to be presented in a way that is engaging and meaningful for students. In this model, there are four important strategy components for motivational instruction: attention, relevance, confidence and satisfaction. Attention strategies are those used to maintain interest and curiosity. Relevance strategies are those that link topics to students' needs, goals and motives. Confidence strategies are those that foster a personal belief in oneself. Satisfaction strategies are those that deliver reinforcement, both intrinsically and extrinsically, for effort. In order to facilitate the implementation of the ARCS model for instructional design, Keller (1983) proposed a measurement instrument named the Instructional Material Motivational Survey (IMMS) in the form of a questionnaire which evaluates people's learning motivation based on the model.

1.4. Research Questions

This study aims to explore the relationship between visual complexity, aesthetic preferences and learning motivation in children's learning websites. It was conducted to test Berlyne's theory on aesthetic preference which suggests that people prefer medium stimuli to high or low stimuli. It also tests how this treatment would affect children's learning motivation. The research questions in this study are:

1. Do the different levels of visual complexity have an impact upon children's aesthetic preferences with regard to children's learning websites?
2. Do the different levels of visual complexity have an impact upon children's learning motivation with regard to children's learning websites?
3. Are the children's aesthetic preferences related to their learning motivation when using children's learning websites?

In the following sections, an overview of the influence of visual complexity on aesthetic preference is given, and a brief introduction to Berlyne's experimental aesthetic theory; this is followed by the measurement of the impact of visual complexity on aesthetic preference and learning motivation. The paper ends with a discussion, conclusion and some suggestions for future research.

2.1. Method

2.1.1. Participants

One hundred and thirty-two primary school children volunteered for this study (70 boys and 62 girls). They were all Taiwanese and ranged from 11 to 12 years old (M=11.53, SD=0.50). All the children could read Chinese and had normal vision. They had received computer lessons at least once a week and reported that they often used computers for gaming and browsing the Internet at home. This indicated that the participants were familiar with computers. After each participant had completed the experiment, they were given a toy as a reward.

2.1.2. Experimental Design

The experiment used a one-factor-at-three-levels between-subjects design. The factor was perceived visual complexity and the three levels were: low, medium and high. The dependent variables were aesthetic preference and learning motivation.

2.1.3. Materials

Twelve websites selected from amongst websites aimed at children were evaluated in the experiment (see Table 1). The websites were taken from do-

Table 1. Different levels of visual complexity learning websites used in this experiment

High level of visual complexity	
VCH1	http://www.kmnp.gov.tw/child/index.php?option=com_content&view=frontpage&Itemid=29
VCH2	http://www.nstm.gov.tw/kids/index.asp
VCH3	http://dspc.moi.gov.tw/web_kid/index.htm
VCH4	http://www.zi1234.com
Medium level of visual complexity	
VCM1	http://www.ylib.com/kids/index.asp
VCM2	http://qihou.sinotech-eng.com/children/default.html
VCM3	http://www.kidsworld.com.tw/
VCM4	http://content.edu.tw/primary/chinese/tp_sd/200006edu/home.htm
Low level of visual complexity	
VCL1	http://tbc.yam.org.tw/
VCL2	http://www.nfa.gov.tw/nfa_c/index.html
VCL3	http://www.apc.gov.tw/portal/kids/index.htm?CID=7CD5E8B1F25E669D
VCL4	http://turing.csie.ntu.edu.tw/ncnudlm/

mains such as museums, libraries and educational establishments. Four of the websites had a high level of perceived visual complexity, four had a medium level of perceived visual complexity and four had a low level of perceived visual complexity.

The websites had been chosen from an original 30 using a two stage selection process. The first stage involved dividing the 30 websites into three sets according to their perceived visual complexity (high, medium and low) using Michailidou et al.'s (2008) ranking system. The number of websites in each set was then reduced to four by six children, aged 11, who did not participate in the experiment. The children were asked to look at printed A4 images of all the websites in each set and choose the four websites from each which best represented the category of perceived visual complexity.

2.2. Measurement Tools

The survey instrument consisted of a three-part questionnaire. The first part collected subjective measures on participants' perceptions of aesthetic preference. The second part collected information on participants' motivations with respect to the learning website. The third part collected information on the participants' gender, age, level of education, reasons for using computers, and time spent on computers per week. These three parts are described in more detail below:

Part 1: Perceptions of Aesthetic Preference

This part of the questionnaire used questions based on those by Lavie and Tractinsky (2004) in an experiment that looked at perceived website aesthetics. The questionnaire employed Likert scales, ranging from 1 (very strongly disagree) to 7 (very strongly agree), to capture each child's level of agreement with statements about the website's aesthetics. The scale consisted of the following four dimensions:

1. **Classical Aesthetics:** The statements on classical aesthetics were about four topics, namely pleasantness, clarity, beauty and symmetry. The scale measured the children's perception of the aesthetics of the website, with sentences such as: *I feel this website is well ordered.* Cronbach's α indicated that the scale was reliable (α= .778).
2. **Expressive Aesthetics:** The statements were about four topics, namely originality, creativity, fascinating design and sophistication. The scale measured the children's perception of the aesthetics of the website, with sentences such as: *I feel this website is creative.* Cronbach's α indicated that the scale was reliable (α= .837).

3. **Pleasure:** The statements were about five topics which measured the participants' perception of the pleasure derived from the website, namely joy, pleasure, gratification, satisfaction and relaxation. Cronbach's ∝ indicated that the scale was reliable (∝= .704).
4. **Playfulness:** The statements were about four topics which measured the participants' perception of the website's playfulness. The scale consisted of the following items: spontaneity, imagination, innovation, and happiness. Cronbach's ∝ indicated that the scale was reliable (∝= .674).

Part 2: Instructional Material Motivational Survey (IMMS)

This part of the questionnaire used questions that were a modification of the Instructional Material Motivational Survey (IMMS), which was developed by Huang, Huang, Diefes-Dux, and Imbrie (2006) in a study that looked at motivation in computer-based learning. The original questionnaire comprised of a 36-item measurement, which was derived as part of a study aimed at reducing in order to reduce children's cognitive load. It was decided to remove 9 items related to relevance. Therefore, this part of the questionnaire was comprised of 27 items which were designed to evaluate a child's satisfaction, confidence and attention. The questionnaire employed Likert scales, ranging from 1 (very strongly disagree) to 7 (very strongly agree), to capture each child's level of agreement with statements about the website's learning motivation. Cronbach's ∝ reliabilities for the scale were reliable, they were: satisfaction (∝= .883), confidence (∝= .814) and attention (∝= .850).

2.3. Procedure

The experiment was carried out in a computer lab with groups of 20 children who were tested independently. It was conducted over a total of 18 sessions. The children were told that they were going to be shown four websites and would be asked a few questions about them. No restrictions were placed on how far away the children sat from their computer screens.

Each session commenced with a practice trial. The trial was performed to ensure that the children understood the computer programme they were to use in the experiment. The children were all shown one homepage from a website on their computer screens and asked to answer two multiple choice questions about it that were displayed below. Both questions were simple; for example, one read: 'How many mice are on the website?' The questions were asked solely to ensure that each child looked carefully at the screen. To answer the questions, the children needed to click a checkbox next to the appropriate answer. Once the children felt that they had answered both questions correctly they were instructed to click a button labelled 'Done'.

When the practice trial had been successfully completed the experiment commenced. In the experiment each time the 'Done' button was clicked a new website and a new set of questions were shown. In total each child saw four websites and answered four sets of questions. Each child saw websites of the same level of perceived visual complexity (high, medium or low). The websites and their respective questions were shown in a random order for each child.

After everyone had seen their four websites, the aesthetics rating questionnaire was handed out. All the children filled out the questionnaire at the same time and each question was explained by the experimenter. Finally the children were given a form to collect their demographic details.

3. RESULTS

In order to analyse the results, the data were divided into aesthetic preferences and learning motivations which were each examined in terms of rating. Analysis of variance (ANOVA) was employed to evaluate the effect of visual complexity in terms of differences in mean scores; and a post-hoc comparison was used to test for differences between the different levels of visual complexity.

3.1. Overall Aesthetic Preference

The mean and standard deviation for the ratings of aesthetic preference are shown in Table 2. The results also showed that there was a significant difference between children's aesthetic preference and three levels of perceived visual complexity ($F_{2,131}$ =10.565, *p*=.000, see Table 3). The multiple comparisons with Scheffé showed that the aesthetic preference ratings for the websites that had a medium level of perceived visual complexity were significantly higher than for those that had a low level of perceived visual complexity (*p*=.000); and the rating for those that had a high level of perceived visual complexity were significantly higher than for those that had a low level of perceived visual complexity (*p*=.005). No significant difference was found between the aesthetic ratings for the websites that had a high level of perceived visual complexity and those that had a medium level of perceived visual complexity (*p*=.722).

Table 2. Descriptive statistics for aesthetic preference and visual complexity (n=132)

Independent variables	Effects	*M*	*SD*
Overall aesthetic	High level of visual complexity	4.56	.90
	Medium level of visual complexity	4.68	.56
	Low level of visual complexity	4.05	.52
Classical aesthetic	High level of visual complexity	4.71	1.31
	Medium level of visual complexity	4.52	1.15
	Low level of visual complexity	4.01	.79
Expressive aesthetic	High level of visual complexity	4.41	1.47
	Medium level of visual complexity	4.65	1.17
	Low level of visual complexity	3.81	1.46
Pleasure	High level of visual complexity	4.78	1.19
	Medium level of visual complexity	5.02	.85
	Low level of visual complexity	4.45	1.01
Playfulness	High level of visual complexity	4.32	1.20
	Medium level of visual complexity	4.53	1.05
	Low level of visual complexity	3.93	.90

3.2. Classical Aesthetic

The results showed that there was a significant difference between children's classical aesthetic preference and three levels of perceived visual complexity ($F_{2,131}$ =4.646, *p*=.011). The multiple comparisons with Scheffé showed that the classical aesthetic preference ratings for the websites that had a high level of perceived visual complexity were significantly higher than for those that had a low level of perceived visual complexity (*p*=.015). No significant difference was found between the websites that had a medium level of perceived visual complexity and those that had a low level of perceived visual complexity (*p*=.102). Also no significant difference was found between the websites that had a high level of perceived visual complexity and those that had a medium level of perceived visual complexity (*p*=.733).

Table 3. ANOVA results for aesthetic preference and visual complexity

Dependent variables		SS	df	MS	F	P
Overall aesthetics	Between groups	9.861	2	4.931	10.565	.000 **
	Within groups	60.203	129	.467		
	Total	70.064	131			
Classical aesthetics	Between Groups	11.404	2	5.702	4.646	.011 **
	Within Groups	158.325	129	1.227		
	Total	169.730	131			
Expressive aesthetics	Between Groups	16.588	2	8.294	4.391	.014 **
	Within Groups	243.641	129	1.889		
	Total	260.229	131			
Pleasure	Between Groups	7.169	2	3.585	3.417	.036 **
	Within Groups	135.341	129	1.049		
	Total	142.510	131			
Playfulness	Between Groups	8.389	2	4.195	3.758	.026**
	Within Groups	143.969	129	1.116		
	Total	152.358	131			

Notes: *significant at the 0.05 level ** significant at the 0.01 level

3.3. Expressive Aesthetic

The results showed that there was a significant difference between children's expressive aesthetic preference and three levels of perceived visual complexity ($F_{2,131}$ =4.391, p=.014). The multiple comparisons with Scheffé showed that the expressive aesthetic preference ratings for the websites that had a medium level of perceived visual complexity were significantly higher than for those that had a low level of perceived visual complexity (p=.018). No significant difference was found between the websites that had a high level of perceived visual complexity and those that had a low level of perceived visual complexity (p=.120). Also no significant difference was found between the websites that had a high level of perceived visual complexity and those that had a medium level of perceived visual complexity (p=.730).

3.4. Pleasure

The results showed that there was a significant difference between children's expressive aesthetic preference and three levels of perceived visual complexity ($F_{2,131}$ =3.417, p=.036). The multiple comparisons with Scheffé showed that the pleasure ratings for the websites that had a medium level of perceived visual complexity were significantly higher than for those that had a low level of perceived visual complexity (p=.037). No significant difference was found between the websites that had a high level of perceived visual complexity and those that had a low level of perceived visual complexity (p=.318). Also no significant difference was found between the websites that had a high level of perceived visual complexity and those that had a medium level of perceived visual complexity (p=.558).

3.5. Playfulness

The results showed that there was a significant difference between children's playfulness and three levels of perceived visual complexity ($F_{2,131}$ =3.758, p=.026). The multiple comparisons with Scheffé showed that the playfulness ratings for the websites that had a medium level of perceived visual complexity were significantly higher than for those that had a high level of perceived visual complexity (p=.029). No significant difference was found between the websites that had a high level of perceived visual complexity and those that had a low level of perceived visual complexity (p=.214). Also no significant difference was found between the websites that had a high level of perceived visual complexity and those that had a medium level of perceived visual complexity (p=.648).

3.6. Overall Learning Motivation

The mean and standard deviation for the ratings of learning motivation are shown in Table 4. The results also showed that there was a significant difference between children's learning motivation and three levels of perceived visual complexity ($F_{2,131}$=4.242, p=.016). The multiple comparisons with Scheffé showed that the learning motivation ratings for the websites that had a medium level of perceived visual complexity were significantly higher than for those that had a low level of perceived visual complexity (p=.028). No significant difference was found between the learning motivation ratings for the websites that had a high level of perceived visual complexity and those that had a low level of perceived visual complexity (p=.081). Also no significant difference was found between the websites that had a high level of perceived visual complexity and those that had a medium level of perceived visual complexity (p=.903) (Table 5).

Table 4. Descriptive statistics for learning motivation and visual complexity

Independent variables	Effects	*M*	*SD*
Overall learning	High level of visual complexity	4.56	1.05
	Medium level of visual complexity	4.65	1.10
	Low level of visual complexity	4.06	.91
Satisfaction	High level of visual complexity	4.36	1.97
	Medium level of visual complexity	5.02	1.39
	Low level of visual complexity	4.16	1.45
Confidence	High level of visual complexity	4.74	1.40
	Medium level of visual complexity	4.47	1.55
	Low level of visual complexity	4.03	1.19
Attention	High level of visual complexity	4.55	1.33
	Medium level of visual complexity	4.45	1.51
	Low level of visual complexity	3.98	1.14

3.7. Satisfaction

The results showed that there was a significant difference between children's satisfaction and three levels of perceived visual complexity ($F_{2,131}$ =3.410, p=.036). The multiple comparisons with Games-Howell showed that the satisfaction ratings for the websites that had a medium level of perceived visual complexity were significantly higher than for those that had a low level of perceived visual complexity (p=.015). No significant difference was found between the learning motivation ratings for the websites that had a high level of perceived visual complexity and those that had a low level of perceived visual complexity (p=.844). Also no significant difference was found between

Table 5. ANOVA results for learning motivation and visual complexity

Dependent variables		*SS*	*df*	*MS*	*F*	*P*
Overall motivation	Between Groups	8.887	2	4.443	4.242	.016 *
	Within Groups	135.121	129	1.047		
	Total	144.008	131			
Satisfaction	Between Groups	17.924	2	8.962	3.410	.036 *
	Within Groups	339.045	129	2.628		
	Total	356.970	131			
Confidence	Between Groups	11.228	2	5.614	2.920	.057
	Within Groups	247.997	129	1.922		
	Total	247.997	131			
Attention	Between Groups	8.229	2	4.114	2.308	.104
	Within Groups	230.003	129	1.783		
	Total	238.231	131			

Notes: *significant at the 0.05 level ** significant at the 0.01 level

the websites that had a high level of perceived visual complexity and those that had a medium level of perceived visual complexity (p=.171).

3.8. Confidence and Attention

The results showed that there was no significant difference between children's confidence and three levels of perceived visual complexity ($F_{2,131}$ =2.920, p=.057). Also no significant difference was found between children's attention and three levels of perceived visual complexity ($F_{2,131}$ =2.308, p=.104).

3.9. Correlation Between Aesthetic Preference and Learning Motivation

In order to determine the correlation between variables, Spearman's correlation analysis was employed. The correlation coefficients matrix for aesthetic preference and learning motivation showed in Table 6. The results showed that there was a significant correlation between children's aesthetic preference and learning motivation (*rho*=.373, p=.000). The results also showed that there was a high correlation between satisfaction and all other learning motivation factors. Satisfaction factors were significantly related to expressive aesthetic factors (r=.452, p =.000), and playfulness and confidence were also correlated (r=.346, p =.000). The correlation between the playfulness and attention factors was significant (r=.321, p =.000). In addition, the correlation between the playfulness and satisfaction factors was also significant (r=.281, p =.001).

The correlations among the other factors are positive but not as high as with the satisfaction factors. This indicated that children felt more satisfied when the design of a website included the aesthetic factors: classical aesthetics, expressive aesthetics, pleasure and playfulness. The satisfaction factors was correlated with classical aesthetics (r=.190, p=.029) and pleasure (r=.200, p =.022). This showed that when the design of a website considered the classical aesthetic, children were pleased with it, thus they felt more satisfied about the learning experience. The remaining correlations were not significant.

Table 6. Correlation coefficients matrix for aesthetic preference and learning motivation

	Classical aesthetic	Expressive aesthetic	Pleasure	Playfulness	Satisfaction	Confidence	Attention
Classical aesthetic	1						
Expressive aesthetic	.403*	1					
Pleasure	.133	-.055	1				
Playfulness	.142	.325**	.108	1			
Satisfaction	.190*	.452**	.200*	.281**	1		
Confidence	.102	.036	-085	.346**	.068	1	
Attention	.147	-.031	-.064	.321**	-.034	.844**	1

Notes: *significant at the 0.05 level ** significant at the 0.01 level

4. DISCUSSION

This experiment explored the relationship between visual complexity, aesthetic preferences and learning motivation in children's learning websites. It tested Berlyne's theory on aesthetic preference which claims that people prefer medium stimuli to high or low level stimuli. It showed that visual complexity had an impact on aesthetic preferences: children preferred a medium level of perceived visual complexity with respect to *expressive aesthetics, pleasure* and *playfulness*, but a high level of perceived visual complexity with respect to *classical aesthetics* and *playfulness*. It also showed that visual complexity had an impact on learning motivation: children preferred a medium level of perceived complexity with respect to *satisfaction*.

The findings of this experiment suggested that the level of perceived visual complexity in websites influenced children's preference for those websites; this is in line with Geissler et al. (2006) and Roberts (2007) who also found a correlation between perceived visual complexity and preference. Also, in common with Geissler et al. (2006) the findings revealed that a medium level of perceived visual complexity is preferred to a high or low level. The findings of this experiment thus support Berlyne's theory and suggest that, when creating webpages for children, designers should use a medium level of visual complexity to deliver the most pleasurable visual experience. The findings from this experiment also indicated that children preferred a high level of perceived visual complexity with respect to *classical aesthetics*. This is in line with Tractinsky, Cokhavi, Kirschenbaum, and Sharfi (2006), who stated that the classical dimension of aesthetic perception refers to a traditional notion of aesthetics, including attributes like aesthetics and symmetry. In other words, children considered that the learning websites with higher levels of visual complexity were more aesthetically appealing. When we looked at *expressive aesthetics*, the results indicated that children preferred a medium level of perceived visual complexity in learning websites. According to Lavie and Tractinsky (2004), expressive aesthetics are concerned with four topics: originality, creativity, fascinating design and sophistication. This result indicated that the children considered the learning websites with medium levels of visual complexity were more original, creative, fascinating and sophisticated than those with other levels of visual complexity. This is consistent with earlier work by Ochsner (2000), who found a positive correlation between visual complexity and arousal in photographs of the IAPS. Other aesthetic dimensions, *pleasure*, and *playfulness*, showed the same trend as the *expressive aesthetic*, which indicated that children who perceived a medium level of visual complexity in a learning website received more pleasure than they received from other levels of visual complexity.

There are very few studies that look at the relationship between a user's aesthetic preference for a website and his/her learning motivation (see Hassenzahl, 2004). This study, however, indicates that aesthetic preference plays more than a minor role in learning motivation. The findings of this experiment suggested that aesthetic preference and learning motivation are correlated. The findings also indicated that the impacts of different levels of visual complexity in websites influenced children's learning motivation with respect to those websites; in other words, children are motivated by a medium level of visual complexity of the learning website. Research into learning motivation has pointed out that emotions have a major impact on students' motivation to engage in learning tasks (Pekrun, 2005). Moreover, positive emotions are directly linked to learning and achievement, for example enjoyment of learning, or pride in success (Pekrun, Goetz, Titz, & Perry, 2002). The results of this research support Pekrun (2002, 2005), and also provide empirical evidence to support the idea that websites with positive emotional factors (for example, the appealing aesthetic in this research) can increase children's learning motivation. According to Huang et al. (2006), learning motivation can be assessed in terms of learners' *attention* to, *confidence* in and *satisfaction* with learning materials. The outcomes from this research revealed that children preferred a medium level of perceived visual complexity with respect to *satisfaction*. This is also supported by Berlyne's theory on aesthetic preference which claims that people prefer medium stimuli to high or low level stimuli.

5. CONCLUSION

This experiment clearly identified that different levels of visual complexity significantly impact the aesthetic preferences and learning motivation of children. The data plainly showed that aesthetic preferences and learning motivation were correlated. In other words, children will increase their learning motivation, if a learning website is aesthetically appealing. These findings should be taken into consideration by practical educators, instructional designers and web designers to create better learning websites for children, especially when they aim to design for learning materials.

It remains unclear to what extent the visual complexity effect in learning websites can be generalised among other user groups (for example, age groups or grade levels, different cultures, and social backgrounds). Further studies with larger and more varied samples are needed. Moreover, it should be noted that participants' classification of website samples can be prejudiced by their preference rather than visual complexity. In order to avoid such bias, the matrix devised by Michaelidou et al. (2008) was employed. Therefore, the final twelve website samples used in this experiment may not be the ones selected by researchers conducting similar experiments.

Finally, the current findings are limited to children's learning websites. Further studies may benefit if the methodology employed in this study were used to investigate other kinds of user interface.

ACKNOWLEDGMENT

This experiment was kindly supported by a grant from the National Science Council of Taiwan. (Contract number: NSC100-2410-H-415-042).

REFERENCES

Bergin, D. (1999). Influences on classroom interest. *Educational Psychologist, 34*, 87–98. doi:10.1207/s15326985ep3402_2.

Berlyne, D. E. (1974). *Studies in the new experimental aesthetics*. Washington, DC: Hemisphere.

Chang, Y.-M., Lin, C.-Y., & Lee, Y.-K. (2005). The preferences of young children for images used in dynamic graphical interfaces in computer-assisted English vocabulary learning. *Displays, 26*, 147–152. doi:10.1016/j.displa.2005.06.002.

Deci, E. L., Koestner, R., & Ryan, R. M. (1999). A meta-analytic review of experiments examining the effects of extrinsic rewards on intrinsic motivation. *Psychological Bulletin, 125*, 627–668. doi:10.1037/0033-2909.125.6.627 PMID:10589297.

Deci, E. L., & Ryan, R. M. (1985). *Intrinsic motivation and self-determination in human behaviour*. New York: Plenum. doi:10.1007/978-1-4899-2271-7.

Dweck, C. S., Mangels, J. A., & Good, C. (2004). Motivational effects on attention, cognition, and performance. In D. Y. Dai, & R. J. Sternberg (Eds.), *Motivation, emotion, and cognition: Integrative perspectives on intellectual functioning and development* (pp. 41–55). London: Lawrence Erlbaum Associates.

Gaffney, A. L. (2011). Measuring students' self-efficacy for communication. *International Journal of Art & Design Education, 30*(2), 211–225. doi:10.1111/j.1476-8070.2011.01702.x.

Geissler, G. L., Zinkhan, M. Z., & Watson, R. T. (2006). The influence of website complexity on consumer attention, attitudes, and purchase intent. *Journal of Advertising, 35*(2), 69–80. doi:10.1080/00913367.2006.10639232.

Hanfling, O. (1992). Aesthetic qualities. In O. Hanfling (Ed.), *Philosophical Aesthetics: An Introduction* (pp. 41–73). Oxford, UK: Blackwell Publishers.

Hassenzahl, M. (2004). The interplay of beauty, goodness, and usability in interactive products. *Human-Computer Interaction, 19*(4), 319–349. doi:10.1207/s15327051hci1904_2.

Hidi, S. (2006). Interest: A unique motivational variable. *Educational Research Review, 1*, 69–82. doi:10.1016/j.edurev.2006.09.001.

Hidi, S., & Renninger, A. (2006). The four-phrase model of interest development. *Educational Psychologist, 41*, 111–127. doi:10.1207/s15326985ep4102_4.

Huang, W., Huang, W., Diefes-Dux, H., & Imbrie, P. K. (2006). A preliminary validation of attention, relevance, confidence and satisfaction model-based instructional material motivational survey in a computer-based tutorial setting. *British Journal of Educational Technology, 37*(2), 243–259. doi:10.1111/j.1467-8535.2005.00582.x.

Keller, J. M. (1983). Motivational design of instruction. In C. M. Reigeluth (Ed.), *Instructional Design Theories and Models: An Overview of their Current Status* (pp. 383–434). Hillsdale, NJ: Lawrence Erlbaum Association.

Lavie, T., & Tractinsky, N. (2004). Assessing dimensions of perceived visual aesthetics of web sites. *International Journal of Human-Computer Studies, 60*, 269–298. doi:10.1016/j.ijhcs.2003.09.002.

Leder, H., Belke, B., Oeberst, A., & Augustin, D. (2004). A model of aesthetic appreciation and aesthetic judgments. *The British Psychological Society, 95*(4), 489–508. PMID:15527534.

Lindgaard, G., Fernandes, G., Dudek, C., & Brown, J. (2006). Attention web designers: You have 50 milliseconds to make a good first impression! *Behaviour & Information Technology*, *25*(2), 115–126. doi:10.1080/01449290500330448.

Martindale, C., Moore, K., & Borkum, J. (1990). Aesthetic preference: Anomalous findings for Berlyne's psychobiological theory. *The American Journal of Psychology*, *103*(1), 53–80. doi:10.2307/1423259.

Michailidou, E., Harper, S., & Bechhofer, S. (2008). Visual complexity and aesthetic perception of web pages. In H. O'Neill, M. Aparicio, C. J. Costa, & A. Protopsaltis (Eds.), *Proceedings of the 26th Annual ACM International Conference on Design of Communication* (pp. 215-224). New York: ACM.

Ochsner, K. (2000). Are affective events richly recollected or simply familiar? The experience and process of recognizing feelings past. *Journal of Experimental Psychology. General*, *129*(2), 242–261. doi:10.1037/0096-3445.129.2.242 PMID:10868336.

Pandir, M., & Knight, J. (2006). Homepage aesthetics: The search for preference factors and the challenges of subjectivity. *Interacting with Computers*, *18*(6), 1351–1370. doi:10.1016/j.intcom.2006.03.007.

Pekrun, R. (2005). Progress and open problems in educational emotion research. *Learning and Instruction*, *15*, 497–506. doi:10.1016/j.learninstruc.2005.07.014.

Pekrun, R., Goetz, T., Titz, W., & Perry, R. P. (2002). Academic emotions in student's self-regulated learning and achievement: A problem of quantitative and qualitative research. *Educational Psychologist*, *37*, 91–106. doi:10.1207/S15326985EP3702_4.

Pintrich, P. (2003). A motivational science perspective on the role of student motivation in learning and teaching contexts. *Journal of Educational Psychology*, *95*(4), 667–686. doi:10.1037/0022-0663.95.4.667.

Pintrich, P., & Schunk, D. (1996). The role of expectancy and self-efficacy beliefs. In *Motivation in Education: Theory, Research & Applications*. Upper Saddle River, NJ: Prentice-Hall.

Roberts, M. N. (2007). *Complexity and aesthetic preference for diverse visual stimuli*. (Unpublished Doctoral Dissertation). Universitat de les Illes Balears.

Sachs, J. (2001). A path model for adult learner feedback. *Educational Psychology*, *21*, 267–275. doi:10.1080/01443410120065478.

Schaik, P., & Ling, J. (2009). The role of context in perceptions of the aesthetics of web pages over time. *Journal of Human-Computer Studies*, *67*, 79–89. doi:10.1016/j.ijhcs.2008.09.012.

Schenkman, B. N., & Jönsson, F. U. (2000). Aesthetics and preferences of web pages. *Behaviour & Information Technology*, *19*, 367–377. doi:10.1080/014492900750000063.

Small, R. (2000). Motivation in instructional design. *Teacher Librarian*, *27*(5), 29–31.

Stevenson, J. S., Bruner, G. C., & Kumar, A. (2000). Webpage background and viewer attitudes. *Journal of Advertising Research*, *40*(1), 29–34.

Tilghman, B. R. (2004). Reflections on aesthetic judgment. *British Journal of Aesthetics*, *44*(3), 248–260. doi:10.1093/aesthj/44.3.248.

Tractinsky, N., Cokhavi, A., Kirschenbaum, M., & Sharfi, T. (2006). Evaluating the consistency of immediate aesthetic perceptions of web pages. *International Journal of Human-Computer Studies*, *64*, 1071–1083. doi:10.1016/j.ijhcs.2006.06.009.

Tuch, A. N., Bargas-Avila, J. A., & Opwis, K. (2009). Visual complexity of websites: Effects on users' experience, physiology, performance, and memory. *International Journal of Human-Computer Studies*, *67*(9), 703–715. doi:10.1016/j.ijhcs.2009.04.002.

Tuch, A. N., Bargas-Avila, J. A., & Opwis, K. (2010). Symmetry and aesthetics in website design: It's a man's business. *Computers in Human Behavior*, *26*, 1831–1837. doi:10.1016/j.chb.2010.07.016.

Tuch, A. N., Presslaber, E. E., Stocklin, M., Opwisa, K., & Bargas-Avila, J. (2012). The role of visual complexity and prototypicality regarding first impression of websites: Working towards understanding aesthetic judgments. *International Journal of Human-Computer Studies*, *70*, 794–811. doi:10.1016/j.ijhcs.2012.06.003.

Van de Heijden, H. (2003). Factors influencing the usage of websites: The case of a generic portal in The Netherlands. *Information & Management*, *40*, 541–549. doi:10.1016/S0378-7206(02)00079-4.

Wang, H. F., & Bowerman, C. J. (2012). The impact of perceived visual complexity on children's websites in relation to classical and expressive aesthetics. In P. K. Blashki (Ed.), *IADIS International Conference IADIS Interfaces and Human Computer Interaction 2012* (pp. 269-273). Lisbon, Portugal: Inderscience Publishers.

ADDITIONAL READING

Bandura, A. (1997). *Self-efficacy: The exercise of control*. New York: Freeman.

Berlyne, D. E. (1960). *Conflict, arousal and curiosity*. New York: McGraw-Hill. doi:10.1037/11164-000.

Colman, A. M., Sluckin, W., & Hargreaves, D. J. (1981). The effect of familiarity on preferences for surnames. *The British Journal of Psychology*, *72*, 363–369. doi:10.1111/j.2044-8295.1981.tb02195.x.

Cyr, D., & Bonanni, C. (2005). Gender and website design in e-business. *International Journal of Electronic Business*, *3*(6), 565–582. doi:10.1504/IJEB.2005.008536.

Fenner, D. E. W. (1996). *Introduction to the aesthetic attitude*. New York: Humanities Press.

Fidel, R., Davies, R. K., Douglass, M. H., Holder, J. K., Hopkins, C. J., & Kushner, E. J. et al. (1999). A visit to the information mall: Web searching behavior of high school students. *Journal of the American Society for Information Science American Society for Information Science*, *50*(1), 24–37. doi:10.1002/(SICI)1097-4571(1999)50:1<24::AID-ASI5>3.0.CO;2-W.

Frumkin, R. (1963). Sex, familiarity and dogmatism as factors in painting preferences. *Perceptual and Motor Skills*, *17*, 12. doi:10.2466/pms.1963.17.1.12 PMID:14045724.

Hidi, S. (2001). Interest, reading and learning: theoretical and practical considerations. *Educational Psychology Review*, *13*(3), 191–209. doi:10.1023/A:1016667621114.

Jordan, P. W. (1998). Human factors for pleasure in product use. *Applied Ergonomics*, *29*(1), 25–33. doi:10.1016/S0003-6870(97)00022-7 PMID:9769086.

Keller, J. M. (1987). Development and use of the ARCS model of instructional design. *Journal of Instructional Development*, *10*(3), 2–10. doi:10.1007/BF02905780.

Lindgarrd, G., & Dudek, C. (2002). User satisfaction, aesthetics and usability: Beyond reductionism. In *Proceedings IFIP 17th World Computer Congress*. Montreal, Canada: IFIP.

Liu, C., & Arnet, K. P. (2000). Exploring the factors associated with site success in the context of electronic commerce. *Information & Management*, *38*, 23–33. doi:10.1016/S0378-7206(00)00049-5.

Mayer, R. E. (1999). *The promise of educational psychology*. Upper Saddle River, NJ: Prentice Hall/Merrill.

Mayer, R. E. (2001). *Multimedia learning*. Cambridge, UK: Cambridge University Press. doi:10.1017/CBO9781139164603.

R. E. Mayer (Ed.). (2005). *The call1bridge handbook of multimedia learning*. New York: Cambridge University Press. doi:10.1017/CBO9780511816819.

Nasar, J. L. (1988). *Environmental aesthetics: Theory, research, and applications*. Cambridge, UK: Cambridge University Press.

Nielsen, J. (1993). *Usability engineering*. Boston: Academic Press.

Nielsen, J. (2000). *Designing web usability: The practice of simplicity*. New York: New Riders Publishing.

Norman, D. A. (1988). *The psychology of everyday things*. New York: Basic Books.

Norman, D. A. (2002, July-August). Emotion and design: Attractive things work better. *Interaction*, 36–42. doi:10.1145/543434.543435.

Ryan, A. (2000). Peer groups as a context for the socialization of adolescents' motivation, engagement, and achievement in school. *Educational Psychologist*, *35*, 101–111. doi:10.1207/S15326985EP3502_4.

Ryan, A. (2001). The peer group as a context for the development of young adolescent motivation and achievement. *Child Development*, *72*, 1135–1150. doi:10.1111/1467-8624.00338 PMID:11480938.

Ryan, R. M., & Deci, E. L. (2000). Self-determination theory and the facilitation of intrinsic motivation, social development, and well-being. *The American Psychologist*, *55*, 68–78. doi:10.1037/0003-066X.55.1.68 PMID:11392867.

Sansone, C., & Harackiewicz, J. (2000). *Intrinsic and extrinsic motivation: The search for optimal motivation and performance*. San Diego, CA: Academic Press.

Whitney, D. E. (1988). Manufacturing by design. *Harvard Business Review*, *66*(4), 83–90.

Wolters, C. (1998). Self-regulated learning and college students' regulation of motivation. *Journal of Educational Psychology*, *90*, 224–235. doi:10.1037/0022-0663.90.2.224.

Zeidner, M. (1998). *Test anxiety: The state of the art*. New York: Plenum.

Zimmerman, B. J., & Kitsantas, A. (1997). Developmental phases in self-regulation: Shifting from process to outcome goals. *Journal of Educational Psychology*, *89*, 29–36. doi:10.1037/0022-0663.89.1.29.

Zusho, A., & Pintrich, P. R. (2001). Motivation in the second decade of life: The role of multiple developmental trajectories. In T. Urdan, & F. Pajares (Eds.), *Adolescence in context* (pp. 163–200). Greenwich, CT: Information Age Press.

KEY TERMS AND DEFINITIONS

Aesthetic Preference: Aesthetic preference refers to someone's predilection towards a particular aesthetic over another.

Berlyne's Experimental Theory: Berlyne's experimental theory suggests that an inverted-U shaped relationship exists between the preference for a stimuli and its arousal potential. Berlyne proposed that complexity, hedonic value and novelty affect arousal potential.

Classical Aesthetics: Classical aesthetics relates to design that is both clear, clean and orderly. It often employs standard usability principles such as symmetry.

Expressive Aesthetics: Expressive aesthetics relates to design that is creative, visually rich and original.

Learning Motivation: Learning motivation is the drive to expend effort to acquire knowledge and/or gain instructional rewards such good grades and positive instructor feedback.

Self-Determination Theory (SDT): Self-determination theory, initially developed by Deci and Ryan (1985), is a theory of human motivation. It suggests that people are motivated both by intrinsic and extrinsic factors.

The ARCS Model: The ARCS model is a model that explains learning motivation. It has four components: Attention, Relevance, Confidence and Satisfaction. The model was developed by Keller (1987).

Chapter 21
Adapting Chatterbots' Interaction for Use in Children's Education

Antonio F. L. Jacob Junior
Federal University of Pará, Brazil

Eulália C. da Mata
Federal University of Pará, Brazil

Ádamo L. Santana
Federal University of Pará, Brazil

Carlos R. L. Francês
Federal University of Pará, Brazil

João C. W. A. Costa
Federal University of Pará, Brazil

Flávia de A. Barros
Federal University of Pernambuco, Brazil

ABSTRACT

The Web is providing greater freedom for users to create and obtain information in a more dynamic and appropriate way. One means of obtaining information on this platform, which complements or replaces other forms, is the use of conversation robots or Chatterbots. Several factors must be taken into account for the effective use of this technology; the first of which is the need to employ a team of professionals from various fields to build the knowledge base of the system and be provided with a wide range of responses, i.e. interactions. It is a multidisciplinary task to ensure that the use of this system can be targeted to children. In this context, this chapter carries out a study of the technology of Chatterbots and shows some of the changes that have been implemented for the effective use of this technology for children. It also highlights the need for a shift away from traditional methods of interaction so that an affective computing model can be implemented.

INTRODUCTION

The first created system that simulated a conversation in natural language was ELIZA (Weizenbaum, 1966). Following this, "dialogues machine" or "Chatterbots" began to be developed for various applications. On the Internet, Chatterbots can be found in chat rooms, and online stores to help consumers, as well as being used by tutors in distance learning systems, FAQ's, Web searches, etc. (Mikic, Burguillo, Rodríguez, Rodríguez & Llamas, 2008).

DOI: 10.4018/978-1-4666-4623-0.ch021

With the increasing use of conversational robots in the WEB, a new form of communication is becoming evident, which is supplementing or replacing other forms of access to information. This can now be conducted by means of direct answers to questions asked by the user through a coherent dialogue.

This form of communications is applicable as a new way of accessing information and can assist in online teaching and learning activities, by reducing the feeling of isolation and dealing with users in a more personal way. Chatterbots is responsible for making the environment more attractive and dynamic and is called the Virtual Companion of Learning.

When a dialogue is conducted through a textual medium, one can lose important aspects of the speech, and this can lead to the meaning of the message being misinterpreted (Jaimes & Sebe, 2007). In view of this, there is a need to use mechanisms to assist in the interaction between the user and chatterbot.

The concept of Embodied Conversational Agents (ECA) was developed to meet this need. These are animated agents (in this case, chatbots) who act out the dialogue through speech, facial expressions, gestures, intonation and other non-verbal methods, to simulate the experience of a face-to-face conversation between humans, that can allow a relationship of trust to be established between both parties (Bickmore & Cassell, 2001).

When considering how to use this type of system for children, one concern is with making it appropriate to the age of the users, since it is often necessary to adjust the language used and employ strategies to encourage interaction with this type of communication. In attempting to do this, the systems adopted for this audience must follow human behaviour, so that it can be incorporated in the activity; this is important since technologies become invisible as they become familiar (Kenski, 2008).

The aim of this chapter is to introduce the changes that are needed to enable Chatterbots to be used for children. This can only be achieved by making a change in the user-system interaction and creating a model of Affective Computing, which uses computational models of emotion and personality.

To test the proposed changes, a prototype was devised to assist in the prevention of cardiovascular problems in children. The stages followed in constructing the model were supervised by two psychologists.

BACKGROUND

In an article "Computing Machinery and Intelligence", Alan Turing (1950) discusses the possibility of devising a thinking machine. He put forward a simple test to evaluate the "intelligence" of the machine, if a human interviewer cannot tell whether he is talking to a person or a machine, and they are indistinguishable, the machine should be considered to be intelligent. This form of assessment is called the "Turing Test" (or "Imitation Game"). In this section, we will outline the technology that has emerged from the "Imitation Game", the techniques used in developing this type of system, and also how the user-system interaction operates.

Chatterbots

Although there have been numerous criticisms of the test proposed by Turing (eg, Searle (1980) by means of the theory of the "Chinese Room"), countless dialogue systems have been developed with the aim of "passing the Turing Test." These systems are currently known as Chatterbots (or chatbots – dialogue robots), and various techniques of Natural Language Processing and Artificial Intelligence are employed in their implementation (Schumaker & Chen, 2010).

The first Chatterbot recorded in literature was ELIZA (Weizenbaum, 1966). Weizenbaum demonstrated how a simple computer program could successfully play an "Imitation Game" just by using some "tricks", such as answering a question with another question. ELIZA is considered to be the first stage toward the spread of dialogue robot systems (Neves; Barros & Hodges, 2006; Zdravkova, 2000).

So far, no system has been able to pass the unrestricted Turing test. As a result, the current goal of these systems is to simulate a dialogue with the purpose of only temporarily deceiving a human, and leading him to think he is talking to another person and not to a machine (Angeli & Coventry, 2001). Periodically, there are competitions to test the performance of robots (e.g. Loebner Prize[1] and ChatterBox Challenge[2]), where the Chatterbot that is able to fool the judges for the longest period of time, is awarded the prize.

Historically, studies in the area of Artificial Intelligence (AI) have been divided into two distinct areas, (Whitby, 2003): "strong" AI, which are concerned with the creation of techniques and methods that involve real problem- solving; and "weak" AI, whose objective is the simulation of the solving process.

Some authors, e.g. (Whitby, 2003, L'Abbate, 2005) think that Chatterbots are one of the most striking examples of "weak" AI, because they simulate a conversation with a human by means of a bank of answers to serve the numerous user inputs. This is one of the main criticisms of some of the techniques used to implement Chatterbots. This is, however, a line of thought that needs further investigation, since several authors have divergent ideas.

Neves, Barros & Hodges (2006) propose classifying the techniques used to implement chatterbots into three "generations": the first is based on simple pattern- matching techniques (e.g. ELIZA) (Weizenbaum, 1966); the second includes Artificial Intelligence techniques (Mauldin, 1994); and the third generation employs more complex techniques of pattern-matching using text mark-up languages, such as AIML (Artificial Intelligence Mark-up Language) (Wallace, 2007). The latter will not be adopted, since mark-up languages can also be regarded as a pattern matching technique.

Some of the techniques used for developing Chatterbots are as follows:

- **Pattern Matching:** Forming an association between pre-selected keywords and group responses, where the user gets a response based on the priority and order of the keywords. This technique can be employed by using simple pattern matching algorithms or through the use of a text markup language.
- **Activation Networks and the Markov Chain:** Each node in the network is represented by a set of patterns, a simple answer and a list of stimulated and inhibited nodes. On receiving the user input, the system evaluates which pattern has been triggered, and the nodes that contain this pattern will be stimulated, returning the node (response) with the highest level to the user. The Markov model is built to simulate the delay between sentences when typing, and simulates human typing behaviour.
- **Fuzzy Logic:** This is used to construct a set of rules to map keywords and regular expressions, which are required for the pattern matching of the user's sentences.
- **Machine Learning:** By means of interaction with the user, the chatterbot can absorb relevant and useful information, and rebuild the database.
- **Case-Based Reasoning:** The answer is based on previous cases which it might be possible to adapt to the current case.

Among these techniques, Pattern Matching should be highlighted, with ELIZA and ALICE at the forefront.

Eliza

This is the oldest and most popular artificial intelligence system, and was created by Joseph Weinzenbaum (1966). Simulating a psychoanalyst, it encourages patients to talk about their lives, by directing the conversation (Figure 1). The Eliza chatbot was created from simple pattern matching techniques.

A.L.I.C.E

The Artificial Linguistic Internet Computer Entity (ALICE) chatterbot was developed by using pattern matching techniques with markup language, and introduced innovations by including a good graphical interface and a large dialogue database (Figure 2); it won three Loebner Prizes.

Traditional User Interaction With Chatterbots

When the chatterbots Eliza and ALICE are examined, it can be observed that the start of the chat is different. In the first, the system introduces itself and attempts to communicate with the user to see if he/she needs any help, while in the second system, it is the user who starts the conversation, although an initial identification is required.

Figure 1. Talk about jealousy with ELIZA

Eliza: Hello. I am ELIZA. How can I help you?

User: I can't say what I want because my girlfriend is jealouss.

Eliza: Why do you say your girlfriend is jealouss?

User: Because she fights with me all the time that a beautiful woman is passing by.

Eliza: Do any other reasons not come to mind?

User: No, I don't give any reason to her.

Eliza: You are being a bit negative.

Moreover, it is important for the user to be motivated and curious to interact with the Virtual Companion of Learning, that is, the chatbot needs to have a nice user interface. The type of user must also be taken into account, as children and adults interact with virtual characters in different ways, with virtual characters being more effective for children´s learning than the simple use of audio (Looije et al, 2008).

PERSONALITY AND EMOTION: PSYCHOLOGICAL AND COMPUTATIONAL MODELS

One of the main objectives of Artificial Intelligence (AI) is to provide techniques for developing computer systems that express intelligent behaviour and can carry out certain activities (Mikic, Burguillo, Rodríguez, Rodrígues & Llamas, 2008). Embedded Conversational Agents are an example of a system that tries to achieve this goal.

Researchers have been building models and simulating some human features, like personality and emotions, with a view to increasing the realism of the virtual dialogues with their peers. The area of AI that studies the computational modelling of emotional influences, or other types of affective phenomena, is known as Affective Computing (Picard, 1997).

Before a cohesive and coherent model of personality and emotion in ECA agents could be created, it was necessary to investigate some of the basic psychological theories used in Affective Computing. With respect to psychological models of personality, several researchers have constructed theories to model personality, and each of these theories has different explanations of the behaviour pattern of each individual.

Revelle (2007) points out that the taxonomic approach is the most widely employed for this purpose. This approach classifies the characteristics of individuals through different categories. For example, adjectives like "quiet", "shy" and

Figure 2. A.L.I.C.E. Interface

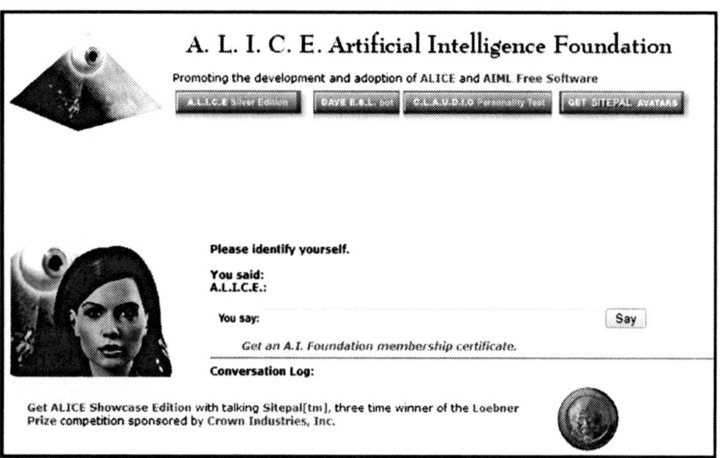

"reserved" classify an individual as introverted. In the literature, two theories can be highlighted that have evolved from this approach: (1) the theory of Eysenck (1970), based on theories of biological substantiation of introversion-extroversion, neuroticism-stability and socialization-psychoticism; and (2) the Theory of Features (Allport, 1998), which determines which traits (factors) can characterize the behaviour of an individual.

The Big Five Model

On the basis of the Theory of Traits, reduced models were created that can be used in computational modelling for Affective Computing. The main models used as a generic taxonomy of personality are the Big Five (Saucier & Goldberg 1998) and the Five Factor (McCrae & Costa Jr., 1998).

Although there are differences between them, the two models are known, in the literature, by the term Big Five, without distinction. Both operate through a process of t distribution and catalogued reduction (Allport, 1998) in five factors/dimensions, known by the acronym OCEAN (McCrae & Costa Jr., 1998): Openness, Conscientiousness, Extraversion, agreeableness, and neuroticism.

These five dimensions (personality types) have strong (high) and weak (low) features which can enable them to classify the personality more clearly. For example, in the Extraversion dimension, individuals who are sociable and interactive have strong personality traits; in contrast, people who are quiet and reserved have weak personality traits. All these structures form a cohesive model and are readily applicable to computational modelling. Later in this chapter there will be an example of a system that is used with this model.

The OCC Model

Just as there is a wide range of models in the literature to represent personality, there are also several models that can be employed to assess the nature of emotions by providing a framework (e.g. (Roseman; Antoniou & Lose, 1996, Ortony et al. 1988]).

The OCC model (Ortony; Clore & Collins, 1988) can be highlighted as a standard model for the computational representation of emotions, since it has been used in various applications (Bates, 1994, Bartneck, 2002). This model consists of 22 emotional categories such as: anger, contentment, love, shame, admiration, hope, etc. As a way of simplifying the selection process and interaction between the different emotional categories, Bartneck (2002) divides this process into five phases: Classification, Quantification, Interaction, Expression and Mapping.

One advantage of the OCC model is that it is not necessary to use all the 22 categories of emotion (Bartneck, 2002). Moreover, the model does not reveal the influence of other personality traits with regard to emotions, so that one is free to adapt different models.

Models of Personality and emotion are not mutually exclusive and can be used in a complementary way when modelling individuals or artificial agents.

RELATED WORK

AIML (Artificial Intelligence Markup Language) (Wallace, 2007) is currently the language most widely used in the construction of Chatterbots, because it is extensible and easy to use (and allows the inclusion of models of personality and emotion).

Neves (2005) developed an extension of the AIML called iAIML (Intentional AIML), which incorporates a mechanism for dealing with intentions in dialogues with Chatterbots. iAIML is based on the Theory of Conversation Analysis (Marcuschi, 1994), a linguistic theory which deals with both the organizational and communicative aspects of a conversation. According to this theory, dialogues are organized into "adjacency pairs" that are linked to intentions (e.g. greet each other; invite: accept/refuse; ask/answer; say goodbye).

The major benefits of iAIML in the context of Chatterbots are as follows: an ability to control the overall structure of the dialogues (thus providing more natural dialogues); and its treatment of unknown sentences. Thus iAIML improves the fluency and coherence of the dialogue in its formation of adjacent pairs, by choosing appropriate Chatterbots responses to stimulate the users. iAIML was adopted in constructing the model outlined in this work, so that the controls that it offered, along with the personality traits and emotions, could be used to build more natural dialogues.

With regard to the application of personality models in the creation of intelligent agents, we highlight the BotCom (Tatai, 2003) and CSIEC (Jia, 2009) applications because of their ability to implement complex features of computational personality models.

Regarding the use of the Big Five model in chatterbots, we highlight the work of Galvão et al. (2004), whose main achievement was the Persona-AIML architecture, which enables the creation of different and coherent models of personality.

Finally, on the question of implementing a system that can convey emotion, we highlight the work of Zong et al. (2000), as this is a good example of how the model in OCC chatterbots can be deployed. In this study, the chatterbot seeks to provide the user with the desired information, and express one of the 22 emotions of the OCC model. The system expresses emotion by executing different human expressions (gestures and facial), and changing the parameters of speech such as volume, speed and stress of certain words.

VIRTUAL LEARNING COMPANION

There are several educational projects and technologies that can be used to support education with the aim of overcoming geographical or social barriers and stimulating learning. The virtual learning environments employ software to predict the interaction between people and objects of knowledge, produce material, socialize with the user and personalize learning (Kenski, 2008).

When used for education, Chatterbots can be integrated into a Virtual Learning Environment. This kind of integration provides an environment that is more attractive and dynamic to the student.

Buti, the chatterbot that has been created in this study, was developed in the context of the research project "Building a Virtual Learning Companion Program for the Promotion of Cardiovascular Health in Childhood and Adolescence" (CVA-PSCV). The purpose of this virtual companion is to monitor the treatment of cardiovascular disease and encourage children and adolescents to think about their eating habits and sedentary lifestyle. The target audience for Buti is children aged 7 to 10.

Development

The development team of the project was formed by professionals and students from the areas of cardiology, psychology, nutrition, physical education and computer science, all of whom followed the various stages of the process. The construction of the virtual learning companion was based on two technologies:

- The iAIML markup language, created to support the control of the overall structure of the dialogues (and provide more natural dialogues), deal with unknown sentences and improve the fluency and coherence of the dialogue by choosing appropriate responses.
- The use of Affective Computing (Piccard, 1997) with the OCC computational model of emotion (Ortony, 1988) in conjunction with the Big Five personality model for synthetic actors (McCrae, 1998).

The next section will explore in detail how the Affective Computing Model was created for the target audience studied.

MCAChat–A Model for Affective Computing in Chatterbots

Conceptually, this model is capable of dealing with emotions and personality traits. However, the current model focuses on the modeling of *emotion*. This decision was taken together with the psychologists who assisted in carrying out this project, for the reasons given below.

The emotions are responsible for modifying physical expression and/or the oral agents (human or artificial) and adjusting their degree of intensity in accordance with the emotion being experienced during an activity (e.g. a dialogue). Furthermore, the emotion expressed is also influenced by several factors, such as the personality traits of those involved in the interaction. From the dialogue that is acted out, it can be seen that this facet influences all the stages of building a dialogue and is indispensable when forming dialogues in a fluent and natural way.

With regard to personality, Allport (1998) states that a psychologist or an individual who knows someone, can predict his activities by taking account of his personality traits. However, the concept of personality is confusing since there is no consensus on this subject among specialists in the area. This is an obstacle to characterization, especially by people with little knowledge in psychology. Thus, personality modeling has been undertaken by means of extensions of the current model.

Initially, we will examine the stages in which the base model of emotion is constructed. The stages for constructing the model, proposed here in CA, were assisted and supervised by two psychologists who participated in the overall project. At the end of this study, we will outline the way this model has been implemented, using the language iAIML.

The Model Structure

This stage of the study was based on the selection of emotion models proposed by Bartneck (2002), which is divided into five categories - classification, quantification, interaction, mapping and expression.

This stage was carried out by adapting, models of personality and emotion to the context of the project (for a CVA chatterbot dialogue with children and teenagers), under the supervision of psychologists. As a result, the Bartneck´s model (2002) was revised, and the modeling of our system is basically divided into four stages:

1. Selecting the emotions that are applicable to the context in question.
2. Finding a means of expressing emotion (text, gesture and facial expressions).
3. Selection of the emotion to be expressed based on the user's intention.
4. Determining how and with what intensity the personality influences emotion.

Each stage has an important role in designing the architecture based on Affective Computing and the modeling and definition of the functioning that is expected when implementing virtual learning companion chatterbot.

Selection and Characterization of Emotions

Initially, we selected the 18 emotions that were most appropriate to our context. Below, the emotions are specified in accordance with the OCC model. In this stage, we observed specific details of the modeling of emotions that are not covered by the OCC model. Stress should be laid on the mechanism for varying the intensity of an emotion, and the degree of usefulness of each emotion in the scope of the project.

The usefulness of each emotion was analysed on the basis of its applicability in the context of the project. Some emotions were rejected by the psychologists, on the grounds that they were unsuitable for the aims of the study. The main criterion for the avoidance of emotions such as "resentment" or "gloating" was that when these negative feelings are seen by children, it might discourage them from using Buti.

We defined a mechanism to control the intensity levels of each emotion (eg, very strong, strong, weak, very weak). Like the procedure put forward by Bartneck (2002), this mechanism also controls the way changes from level to level for each emotion occur (eg, a person starts out by admiring another person, and the degree of admiration increases or decreases as the facts of the situation succeed each other).

Each emotion is different for different levels of intensity, so that one quickly reaches the maximum intensity (a ¨gross¨ type of variation), and others undergo slower variations (a ¨refined¨ type of variation). Each emotion was analysed with the help of psychologists to achieve a definition of this characteristic. The emotion "Pride" is a fine example of change, since it has six different levels, ranging from no emotion ("0"), intermediate range ("1 ", "2", "3 " and "4") to demonstration and maximum (5 "). In turn, the emotion "Sadness" is a gross example of the kind, since it only has four levels of variation: out of control – a state without an emotion ("0") and expressed in only two levels ("1" and "2") until it achieves the maximum index ("4").

On the basis of the current intention of the dialogue (more details given below), the selection is made of the emotion, along with the definition of the variation (which can assume a positive value with an increasing intensity in the expression of the emotion, or negative, if there is an opposite emotion to the emotion selected). One of the means of measuring this variation is to help influence the personality mechanism, which causes a change in the emotion when it reaches maximum intensity. An example of this is shown below.

Means of Expressing Emotion

Earlier, we stressed the importance of providing chatterbots with other means of communicating with the user, apart from through text. In fact, gestures and facial expressions show emotions more clearly than written text can. Examples of these applications can be found at Zabaware[3] and SitePal[4].

Thus, we conducted a study of applications using gestures and facial expressions, so that we could form a better design of our chatterbot (face and body), and allow all the emotions present in their conceptual model to be expressed. We analyzed facial expressions and gestures of people to show certain emotions. These gestures and expressions were adapted to the design of our chatterbot.

Selection of the Emotion to be Expressed

If the model proposed by Bartneck (2002) is employed, a classification must be carried out to evaluate which emotion is likely to be affected by an event, action or object. In our case, this evaluation is effected via iAIML technology.

The iAIML, as shown earlier, is able to identify the user intention in every section of the dialogue (adjacent pairs of sentences). Thus, you can determine what emotion is being expressed by the speaker, by taking account of the user's intention. For example, if the user intends to compliment the Chatterbot for any information he provided to the user, the bot should express the emotion of "pride."

Thus a mapping of intention and emotion was carried out. We use the 54 intentions outlined by Neves (2005), along with some additional intentions to adapt the language to the context of the project. Figure 1 shows some examples of mapping intentions in emotions.

As can be seen in Table 1, the emotion of the chatterbot is determined by the user's intention, the user´s inputs and the possible responses of the chatterbot. In the example of intention "greet", there is no change in the emotional state of the robot, since this action/intention does not trigger any emotion. In other examples, apart from the emotion directly related to caused by the intention (primary emotion), another emotion is displayed with the attribute "MAX", which deals with the emotion created by the influence of the personality of the robot.

Table 1. Mapping intentions: dialogue in emotion (Neves, 2005)

User's Intention	Example of User's Input	Chatbot's Response	Chatbot's Emotion
Greeting	How are you doing ?	I'm fine and you?	Normal
Complaining anout having been insulted	* Are you calling me illiterate ?	I didn´t mean to offend you	Shame
			MAX: Sadness
Praise	* I really enjoyed talking to you	Thanks for the compliment	Pride
			MAX: Shame

Influence of Personality on Emotions

The interaction stage involving the selection process of emotions proposed by Bartneck (2002), defines the extent to which the current emotion can undergo significant changes, depending on external events. Here, these modifications are made on the basis of an analysis of the influence of personality on emotion.

Initially, we selected the traits (strong or weak) of each dimension of personality (OCEAN model) which could be used in the context of the project. It should be noted that the features and weaknesses of each dimension represent almost opposite personalities, such as extraversion, where the strong lines represent the personality of an extrovert, and the weak lines, an introverted person.

After the selection of traits, we analyzed the influence of each dimension of personality on emotions. This analysis assessed whether personality influences the intensity of emotion in a positive ("+"), negative ("-") or neutral ("0") way. For example, we considered the influence of strong features (an extraverted individual) and the extraversion dimension with respect to some of person´s emotions. The following emotions were influenced positively (e.g. became more intense): wonder, joy, relief, love, contentment, gratification, and pride. On the other hand, the following emotions experienced negative influence (became less intense): sadness and fear.

When the emotion is not at the highest level of intensity, it only undergoes a variation in degree, depending on the influence of personality. However, when its intensity is already at a maximum level, there is no other emotion (that is linked to the user's intention) which can express a feeling stronger than the current emotion and that emotion will be replaced by the maximized emotion. Table 1 has an example of maximization of excitement; when the user praises (intention) the Chatterbot excessively, instead of showing pride (primary emotion), it begins to show the emotion of shame (maximized emotion).

Architecture

Figure 3 shows the general architecture of the chatterbot with Affective Computing, with its modules and data flow, during the processing of a sentence that is provided as input by the user. This architecture meets all the characteristics listed above.

First of all, the user enters his input sentence (Figure 3a). A manager component of the interpreter receives this sentence, and starts the process of pattern matching with the entries in the "Dialog Base" component (Figure 3b). If the entry includes a characteristic (intention) that generates an emotion, the "Dialog Base" makes a call to the "Emotions module" (Figure 3c).

The Emotions module, in turn, checks the variation of emotional intensity and requests information about the influence of personality on the given emotion (Figure 3d) and returns another emotion or only a variation in the emotion's intensity (Figure 3e).

The Emotions Module processes the emotion to be expressed, and directs the response on the basis of the dialogues (Figure 3f). When the answer is found that corresponds to the emotion, the dialogue base sends it to the manager (Figure 3g), records the whole process in a log (Figure 4h.) and sends the response to the user (Figure 3i).

The modules were adapted from Emotions and Personality of Persona-AIML architecture (Galvan et al., 2004). The original Personality Component that was responsible for monitoring the influence of personality on the design of Galvan et al. (2004), was divided into two specific modules, - one responsible for the control of the emotion, and the other for the caring personality.

Figure 3. Chatterbots architecture with Affective Computing

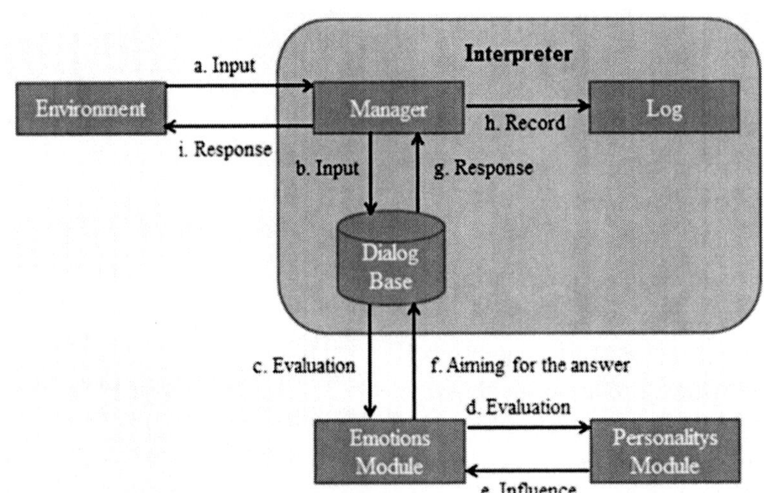

Figure 4. Expressions of some emotions of Buti

The Buti

Initially, the emotions to be used were chosen from the area of healthy living. The following evaluations were made of the degrees of variation of intensity (Fine or Gross) and the degrees of usefulness of each emotion in the scope of the project.

The next step was to design the visual expressions of emotion (Figure 3). This is an important factor in ensuring interaction with children, since Chatterbots that have a nice graphical interface, are considered to be a new way of transmitting information and marketing products for this age group.

We try to include in Buti, the characteristics of a conversational agent by deploying the methods of nonverbal speech through gestures and glances. We used Flash technology for this. The project team decided that it should include features such as the Buti robot merged with the child (to form a humanoid). The intention was to prevent the child from viewing the Buti as a perfect child, and then becoming disheartened when this was compared with a picture of himself/herself.

We used the language of iAIML for the construction of the Base Dialogues project, (Neves 2005), with 54 issues of a general nature with different intentions, after more entries had been added to the topic of healthy living.

As previously stated, before assessing the influence of personality on emotions, we selected the traits of the personality best suited to the situation of the project. May discourage an appropriate interaction between the child and Buti and thus only the strong features of the dimensions (Opening Experience, Conscientiousness, Extraversion and Agreeableness) were chosen for the analysis. The traits in the Neuroticism scale were not selected.

Each personality dimension influences emotions in different ways. Owing to the complexity of dealing with conflicts between the different traits of the personality dimensions, and the difficulty of making an assessment of variations, the psychologists advised that Buti should only have one dimension of personality at a time.

Interaction with Children

There are changes in different phases of human development that interfere with children's learning, since they affect their cognitive maturity, such as: their relationship with the outside world; cultural, historical and instrumental kinds of interference; and mental capacity. Thus, when adapting the learning system, psycho-pedagogical factors must be taken into account..

After conducting a survey of Chatterbots applications, it was observed that, on the whole, it was, the user who directed the conversation. In this context, the first prototype that was created (Figure 5), maintained the main features of this type of interaction.

This initial test was conducted with three children. It was observed that, after initiating the dialogue, no more than three interactions were carried out without the help of the psychologists, who had monitored the entire process. These psychologists confirmed that the children felt intimidated when conducting the dialogue. After obtaining these results, it was found that there was a need to adapt the interface of the virtual learning companion to allow a longer interaction session with children.

After the experiment, the interaction was adapted to the structure framework of the system (Figure 6). In the updated version, the chatterbot initiates the dialogue; in addition, links have been incorporated with representative figures of the possible topics of conversation, since children appreciate the graphics components and are driven by curiosity (Lobstein, 2006).

Six children took part in the second test: four between 7 and 10 years old; and two outside the age range defined for the project (one 6 and another 12 years old). The inclusion of these two children, who did not belong to the target audience of the project, was to see whether the choice of the age range for the project had been done properly.

Furthermore, the main objective was to assess whether, with the expression of emotion by the Buti, users would have more interest in talking with the bot. The tests were conducted through two interactions with the system: (1) only on the basis of dialogues containing information about healthy living; (2) dialogues held on same basis, coupled with the use of the expression of emotions.

The assessment of the tests were undertaken in two ways: by means of questionnaires administered by the psychologists of the project, and by analyzing video tapes of computer interaction involving the children, and observing their attitudes during the interactions. The completion of the questionnaire was conducted in two stages: after the first repetition (no emotion), and soon after the second repetition (with emotion). The questions in the questionnaire assessed the degree of acceptance of the system, and if the users perceived the differences in these repetitions.

The analysis of the system logs revealed that children in this age group tend to write in the way they talk. This prevented these inputs from being properly processed, and as a result affected the responses from the Base Dialogues. However, the problem was solved by making a change in the interaction with the system, where the user is redirected to another topic without losing the flow of the conversation.

Figure 5. Initial Interaction Prototype Centered on Children

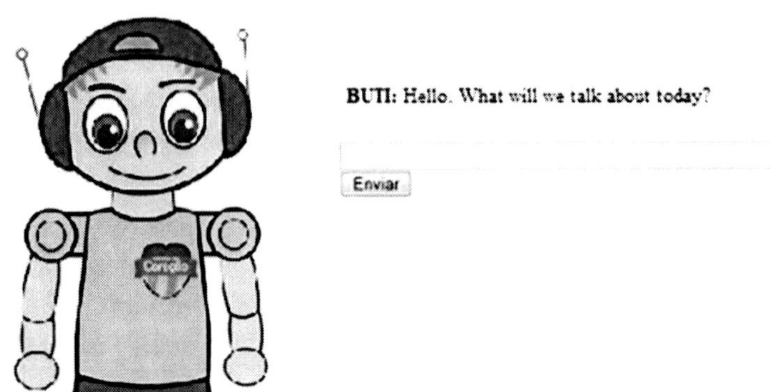
BUTI: Hello. What will we talk about today?
Enviar

Figure 6. Changes in the Interaction with the System

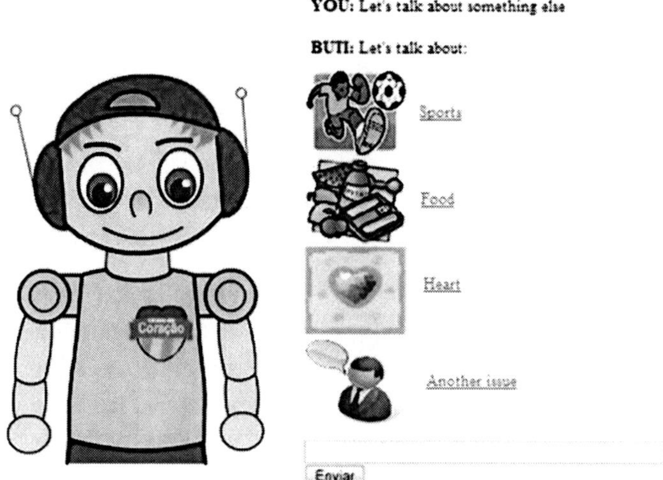

As a result of these changes and from an analysis of the systems logs, it was observed that children, were able to converse about all the topics on the project in which they were based (sports, the heart, food, etc.), with an average of 15 interactions lasting 20 minutes; that is, five times more interactions than the initial tests.

The psychologists confirmed that the children enjoyed talking to Buti, and wished to talk to him again. The child of 12 years, (according to the professional who interviewed him), felt out of place since all the other children were younger than him doing the tests.

In turn, the children expressed what aspects of Buti they liked best: the fact of having a character to speak to (even if only in the tutorial for explanation) who was "cute", nice, smart and loyal. In addition, children stated that they found the use of the system was very interesting, and said that Buti provided them with a good deal of exciting knowledge about the heart, health, sports, food, and other topics. The children also noted the difference in versions with and without emotion, and identified emotions such as joy, sadness, happiness and love.

FUTURE RESEARCH DIRECTIONS

The increasing spread of information via digital media has bought new realities to the world stage. These phenomena have led to a convergence of new technologies that are designed to spread information and improve the quality of life. Good examples of this unprecedented dissemination are mobiles, tablets and digital TV systems.

In this scenario, Interactive Digital TV (IDTV) applications are emerging as a new tool with the ability to leverage many other sectors. For example, the development of interactive applications can complement education in a valuable way.

Since this technology is still in the stage of gaining popularity, especially in third- world countries, the research that has been conducted on its usability for IDTV is mainly concentrated on the requirements of adult audiences.

As explained in this chapter, most usability strategies adopted in systems for adults do not apply when the audience comprises children and pre-teens. This problem becomes more evident when account is taken of studies in educational applications, in IDTV, for children. The reason for this is that, for this type of user, television is not seen as an informative or educational environment, but only as a means of entertainment.

As a result, it is necessary for new studies to adapt systems of interaction with Chatterbots and implement them in these different technologies; which are now being much more widely used b by children (NY Daily News, 2012).

CONCLUSION

The collaboration of psychologists was paramount at all stages of this project, due to their theoretical and practical experience in the area, and with their aid, it was possible to intensify the motivation, learning, interaction and use of the technology leading to a more effective and efficient kind of education

The suitability of the interaction arises because the children are still in a state of growing maturity particularly with regard to language, reflection and logic. The changes achieved better results than those obtained with the traditional use of chatterbot for this public.

Moreover, children showed more interest in interacting with the system when Affective Computing techniques were implemented, with one the most positive factors being the increase in feedback from the children, regarding possible changes in the system's interface and new features that could be included.

REFERENCES

Allport, G. W. (1998). Traits revisited. In *Personality: Critical concepts*. Academic Press.

Angeli de. A., Johnson, G. I., & Coventry, L. (2001). The unfriendly user: Exploring social reactions to chatterbots. In *Proceedings of the International Conference on Affective Human Factor Design* (pp. 467–474). IEEE.

Bartneck, C. (2002). Integrating the OCC model of emotions in embodied characters. In *Proceedings of the Workshop on Virtual Conversational Characters: Applications, Methods and Research Challenges*. Melbourne, Australia: IEEE.

Bates, J. (1994). The role of emotion in believable agents. *Communications of the ACM*, *37*(7), 122–125. doi:10.1145/176789.176803.

Bickmore, T., & Cassell, J. (2001). Relational agents: A model and implementation of building user trust. In *Proceedings of the Conference on Human Factors in Computing Systems – SIGCHI* (pp. 396–403). ACM.

Eyesenck, H. J. (1970). *The structure of human personality*. London: Academic Press.

Galvão, A. M., et al. (2004). Persona-AIML: An architecture developing chatterbots with personality. In *Proceedings of the Joint Conference on Autonomous Agents and Multiagent Systems* (pp. 1266–1267). Washington, DC: IEEE Computer Society.

Jaimes, A., & Sebe, N. (2007). Multimodal human-computer interaction: A survey. *Computer Vision and Image Understanding*, *108*(1-2), 116–134. doi:10.1016/j.cviu.2006.10.019.

Jaques, P. A., & Viccari, R. M. (2006). Considering students' emotions in computer-mediated learning environments. In Z. Ma (Ed.), *Web-based intelligent e-learning systems: Technologies and applications* (pp. 122–138). Hershey, PA: Information Science Publishing.

Jia, J. (2009). An AI framework to teach English as a foreign language: CSIEC. *AI Magazine*, *30*(2), 59–71.

Kenski, V. M. (2008). *Education and technology: The new pace of information*. São Paulo: Papirus.

L'Abbate, M., Thiel, U., & Kamps, T. (2005). Can proactive behavior turn chatterbots into conversational agents? In *Proceedings of the IEEE/WIC/ACM International Conference on Intelligent Agent Technology – IAT* (pp. 173–179). Washington, DC: IEEE Computer Society.

Looije, R. et al. (2008). Children's responses and opinion on three bots that motivate, educate and play. *Journal of Physical Agents*, *2*(2), 13–20.

Marcuschi, M. L. (1994). *Conversational analysis*. São Paulo: Ática.

Mauldin, M. L. (1994). Chatterbots, tinymuds, and the turing test: Entering the loebner prize competition. In *Proceedings of the Nacional Conference on Artificial Intelligence,* (pp. 16–21). Seattle, WA: IEEE.

McCrae, R. R., & Costa, P. T. Jr. (1998). A five-factor theory of personality. In *Personality: Critical concepts*. London: Routledge.

Mikic, F. A., Burguillo, J. C., Rodríguez, D. A., Rodríguez, E., & Llamas, M. (2008). T-bot and Q-bot: A couple of AIML-based bots for tutoring courses and evaluating students. In *Frontiers in Education Conference.* doi: 10.1109/FIE.2008.4720469

Neves, A. M. M., Barros, F. A., & Hodges, C. (2006). iAIML: A mechanism to treat intentionality in AIML chatterbots. In *Proceedings of the IEEE International Conference on Tools with Artificial Intelligence* (pp. 225-231). IEEE.

NY Daily News. (2012). *Are iPads and other tablets bad for children?* Retrieved October 31, 2012, from http://articles.nydailynews.com/2012-04-02/news/31276908_1_electronic-tablets-ipad-electronic-babysitter

Ortony, A., Clore, G. L., & Collins, A. (1988). *The cognitive structure of emotions*. Cambridge, UK: Cambridge University Press. doi:10.1017/CBO9780511571299.

Picard, R. (1997). *Affective computing*. Cambridge, MA: MIT Press.

Revelle, W. (2007). *The personality project.* Retrieved October 31, 2012 from http://www.personalityproject.org

Roseman, I. J., Antoniou, A. A., & Lose, P. E. (1996). Appraisal determinants of emotions: Constructing a more accurate and comprehensive theory. *Cognition and Emotion*, *10*(3), 241–277. doi:10.1080/026999396380240.

Saucier, G., & Goldberg, L. (1998). What is beyond the big five. *Journal of Personality*, *66*, 495–524. doi:10.1111/1467-6494.00022 PMID:9728415.

Schumaker, R. P., & Chen, H. (2010). Interaction analysis of the ALICE chatterbot: A two-study investigation of dialog and domain questioning. *IEEE Transactions on Systems, Man, and Cybernetics. Part A, Systems and Humans*, *40*(1), 40–51. doi:10.1109/TSMCA.2009.2029603.

Searle, J. R. (1980). Minds, brains, and programs. *The Behavioral and Brain Sciences*, 3.

Tatai, G., et al. (2003). Happy chatbot, happy user. In *Proceedings of the International Workshop Intelligent Virtual Agents* (pp. 5-12). IEEE.

Turing, A. (1950). Computing machinery and intelligence. *MIND - The Journal of the Mind Association, 59*(236), 433–460.

Weizenbaum, J. (1966). Eliza: A computer program for the study of natural language communication between man and machine. *Communications of the ACM*, *9*(1), 35–36. doi:10.1145/365153.365168.

Whitby, B. (2003). *Artificial intelligence: A beginner's guide*. OneWorld.

Zdravkova, K. (2000). Conceptual framework for an intelligent chatterbot. In *Proceedings of the International Conference Information Technology Interfaces*. IEEE.

Zong, Y., et al. (2000). Multimodal presentation markup language mpml with emotion expression functions attached. In *Proceedings of the International Conference on Microelectronic Systems Education*. IEEE.

KEY TERMS AND DEFINITIONS

Affective Computing: Is a field of computing that addresses recognition of human emotions and covers other areas for scientific understanding of the answers given by people.

AIML: Markup language that simulates human intelligence to create dialogues in natural language.

Chatterbot or Chatbot: Robot or virtual agent that interacts with humans, simulating conversations. The agent usually has a graphical representation.

Emotion: Express the sensations and feelings in relationship interactions.

Personality: A set of individual characteristics developed from interactions with the environment, defining the way we think, feel and act.

Turing Test or Imitation Game: Test created by Alan Turing to realise whether a machine can intelligently interact with a human, so it would not be recognised as a machine.

Virtual Learning Companion: Is a partner designed to help a human being in the task of understanding a given subject. Created from computational techniques for interact with people.

ENDNOTES

1 http://www.loebner.net/Prizef/loebner-prize.html
2 http://www.chatterboxchallenge.com
3 http://zabaware.com
4 http://www.sitepal.com

Chapter 22
A Framework for Designing Interactive Digital Learning Environments for Young People

Virgínia Tiradentes Souto
University of Brasilia, Brazil

ABSTRACT

In this chapter a descriptive framework for designing interactive digital learning environments for young people is proposed. The proposed framework aims to analyse and compare interactive digital learning environments. This framework may be useful to guide the design of digital learning environments for young people and also to provide a structure for understanding the interface characteristics of such environments and how users interact with them. Young people's characteristics are briefly discussed in relation to the learning process. The approach to creating the framework is presented with the related literature. The framework is described and consists of three main components: learning, user interaction, and visual. Finally, conclusions on the design of interactive digital learning environments are drawn.

INTRODUCTION

The production of digital learning environments has been increasing considerably, especially with the rise in the number of users with a fast Internet connection, new devices, new technological possibilities, among other aspects. Online learning resources, such as content modules, learning objects and online learning communities, have become very popular (Oblinger, 2008).

Students have been taking advantage of these digital environments in order to improve their learning. Governments, organizations, private institutions, and teachers are providing interactive digital educational materials (paid or free) that aim to offer students additional educational resources for their learning process.

Many authors claim that the new generation, born from the 1990s onwards, has a different experience with digital environments because they have had experience in using digital media since they were very young. Researchers claim that different ways of teaching are needed in order to meet the needs of this new generation.

Interactive digital learning environments are therefore part of the learning process in the life of many children and young people nowadays. Among the positive characteristics of this type of

DOI: 10.4018/978-1-4666-4623-0.ch022

learning environment are: they can be of different sizes (a module or an entire course); they can be reused many times in different contexts; they can be used simultaneously by many people; and new versions can benefit people immediately (Wiley, 2000). Examples of these kinds of learning material are: e-books, online games, presentations, applications, exercises, websites, and visualization information. These materials are available from different devices and platforms such as computers, tablets, mobiles, interactive environments in museums, or even in public and private organizations.

According to Trinidad et al. (2005) digital learning environments "can facilitate cognitive, as well as social scaffolding, enabling educators and students to become progressively more involved in the community and sustain their commitment and interests". Oblinger (2008) argues that immersive and authentic learning environments, such as simulations, visualizations, and augmented reality can engage and motivate the students. As he states: "there is a significant difference between learning about physics and learning to be a physicist, for example. Isolated facts and formulae do not take on meaning and relevance until learners discover what these tools can do for them".

Interactive designers have recently faced a new challenge: to design learning environments that answer the demands and expectations of this group of people and at the same time to understand the environment's possibilities, their usability and how users interact with them. Although much has been written and researched on many subjects related to the design of interactive environments, it seems that a great deal of research is still needed on how to create an effective, efficient and pleasant interactive learning environment for this new generation of users.

In this paper, a framework for designing interactive digital learning environments for young people is proposed. This framework is useful to guide design of digital learning environments for young people, and also to provide a structure for understanding interface characteristics of such environments and how users interact with them. It can also be used to evaluate the environment result. Good frameworks are believed to enhance the understanding of the environments at a higher level (Zhang et al. 2005c).

Young people's characteristics are briefly discussed in relation to the learning process. In this study, 'young people' refers to the age-group of around 9 to 19 years old. First, definitions of framework, e-learning and design are presented. Then, the approach to creating the framework is presented with the related literature. The framework is described. Finally conclusions on the design of interactive digital learning environments are drawn.

FRAMEWORK, E-LEARNING AND DESIGN DEFINITIONS

Frameworks

The concepts of framework, e-learning and design vary considerably in the literature. Therefore, it is important to define them for the purpose of this study. Frameworks have been frequently used in different subject areas with different purposes, such as to provide explanatory accounts, models and guidance (Rogers and Muller, 2006). Frameworks may also be used to understand the correlations across concepts, events, ideas, interpretations, knowledge, observations and other components of experience (Svinicki, 2008). In the context of learning, a framework can provide "a basis for examining how developers' intentions are realized in performance assessments that purport to measure reasoning, understanding, and complex problem solving" (Bransford et al., 1999, p. 143).

It is also important to distinguish the concept of framework from that of theory as they are sometimes mixed up. The difference between theories and frameworks is that the first aims to produce testable hypotheses, enabling expansion of the scope, whereas the latter provides a set of constructs for understanding a domain (Rogers, 2004).

Frameworks have been presented in different forms such as concepts, heuristics, principles, problems, questions and steps (Rogers and Muller, 2006). There are also different types of frameworks being used in E-learning, HCI and Design fields, such as analytical (e.g. Lim and Rogers, 2008), descriptive (Walker, 2003), conceptual (Rogers et al., 2002), theoretical (Spink et al., 2002), and interface design (Lin and Zhang, 2003). For example, interface design frameworks are responsible for establishing the kind of content that should be displayed, and when and how to display it (Lin and Zhang, 2003).

It is usual to use a conceptual framework in interactive environments. Conceptual frameworks are defined "as a visual or written product, one that "explains, either graphically or in narrative form, the main things to be studied—the key factors, concepts, or variables—and the presumed relationships among them" Miles and Huberman (1994, p. 18).

Within HCI, design and education domains of conceptual frameworks may be useful for developers, designers or researchers. For example, the conceptual framework proposed by Piccoli et al. (2001), which identifies the primary dimensions of a VLE and their relationship to learning effectiveness, was developed to be "most useful to researchers investigating VLE effectiveness". In contrast, the conceptual framework for mixed reality environments (Rogers et al., 2002) is used as a structure to inform the design of kinds of activity spaces (digital and physical) for children to experiment with.

Another commonly used conceptual framework in the HCI field is activity theory. Originally created by the psychologist Aleksei Leontiev, it has been commonly applied, discussed or modified within the HCI field (e.g. Bødker, 1989; Kuutti, 1996; Rogers, 2008; Kaptelinin, 2012). Activity theory considers that activity is central to describe human work (Leontiev, 1978, Kuutti 1996). It is defined as a "cross-disciplinary framework for studying different forms of human practices as development processes, with both individual and social levels interlinked at the same time" Kuutti (1996). Applying activity theory is relevant because it informs the thinking about the process of designing educational technology (Bellamy, 1996).

It seems that in the HCI field, framework is usually used to inform design and analysis through a guide form (Rogers and Muller, 2006). This definition fits with the proposed framework. The aim of this descriptive framework is to analyze, compare and evaluate interactive digital learning environments.

E-Learning

E-Learning is considered difficult to define as the concept is understood from many angles and meanings (Sangrá et. al. 2012). Sangrá et al. (2012) identified four general categories of definitions from the literature. They are: technology-driven, delivery-system-oriented, communication-oriented, and educational-paradigm-oriented. According to them, an agreement on e-learning definition is important because it could help researchers to identify models and practices for applying e-learning as well as to determine the main factors for better and more effective use of e-learning environments.

Salmon (2005) argues that E-learning has to do with time, motivation, knowledge and good appropriate teaching, and "almost nothing to do with computers" (pp. 214–215). Nevertheless, most material related to e-learning is technical and not on how to translate motivation, excitement and other personal reactions into teaching and learning opportunities (Stein et al., 2011).

Studies about the perception of experts on e-learning definitions have been conducted by some researchers. Moore et al. (2011) investigated the difference between definitions of e-Learning, online learning, and distance learning environments. According to them, the relevant literature (over the last two decades) showed inconsistent definitions of distance learning. The term distance learning is described in many ways, such as e-Learning, online learning, virtual learning and web-based learning. The commonalities found in all the definitions are that the instruction occurs between a learner and an instructor, happens in different places and/or times and uses different forms of instructional materials Moore et al. (2011).

Moore et al. (2011) argue that besides the fact that it is not clear what exactly the e-learning characteristics are, it is clear that all forms of e-learning (e.g. applications, programs, objects, websites) can provide learning opportunities for individuals. They concluded that "there seemed to be some agreement that there was a difference between each of the terms and that this difference was somehow attributed to the characteristics of each of the environments" (p. 133).

In another study about the definition of e-learning, Sangrá et. al. (2012) applied online questionnaires with 33 recognised experts in the field of education and ICT in order to gather their opinions on this definition, with a view to reaching a final consensus. They concluded that it is difficult to provide a single and inclusive e-learning definition that would be accepted by the majority of researchers because of the different perspectives on this concept by authors with different academic backgrounds. Based on their results they concluded that e-learning concepts merge different disciplines, such as computer science, communication technology and pedagogy.

Sangrá et. al. (2012) proposed an inclusive definition based on the study described above and asked experts to use a Likert scale to check the level of acceptance of the definition proposed. The definition investigated is: "E-learning is an approach to teaching and learning, representing all or part of the educational model applied, that is based on the use of electronic media and devices as tools for improving access to training, communication and interaction and that facilitates the adoption of new ways of understanding and developing learning". The found a high level of acceptance of this definition with 31 out of the 33 participants evaluating it positively.

Design

Although there are many studies that deal with "framework design" or "the design of the framework", most of them have different meanings from the one here. They are in most cases related to the verb "design" and not the field "Design". According to Baynes (1994), design generally has "to do with bringing about change"; it may be characterized as an intentional activity, and more specifically (in the field Design) it "relates also to the specific area in which it is used, and by whom".

In the context of education, Archer (2005) defines design as the field of human experience that reflects man's concern with assessing and adapting to his environment depending on his needs. With a different approach, the International Council of Societies of Industrial Design (ICSID) presents a design concept related to activity. According to the ICSID (2012), design is a creative activity that aims to "establish the multi-faceted qualities of objects, processes, services and their systems in whole life cycles." Fallman (2004) discuss the role of design in the HCI field. According to him, the role of design in HCI is not simply a question of problem-solving or an art-form, but as an "unfolding activity which demands deep involvement from the designer".

Bonsiepe (2011) explains that despite the differences in the definition of design, there are two commonly accepted design features: the use of quality orientation and formal-aesthetic quality. Bonsiepe (2011) argues that the main difference between design and other disciplines is the concern for the user from an integrative approach.

In this study, the word design is related to the Design field. Therefore, the main aspects dealt with by the designer's activity in an e-learning development project are those related to user-characteristics and the aesthetic and formal quality of the project (Bonsiepe, 2011).

YOUNG PEOPLE AND DIGITAL LEARNING: A BRIEF OVERVIEW OF CHARACTERISTICS

Much research and discussion has taken place about different generations and their relationship with learning (e.g. Tapscott, 2009; Buckingham, 2006). Young people are usually considered to be aged 9 to 19 years old. They also belong to the 'Net Generation' (Tapscott, 1998) and are known as 'Digital Natives' (Prensky, 2001). These labels have arisen because this age-group has had Internet access and contact with digital media products since they were very young. Ito (2009) claims that young people are usually earlier adopters of digital media than adults, and that they are interacting with complex new media with increasing frequency. Buckingham (2006), in his chapter "Is there a digital generation?", argues that although technological changes affect both young people and adults, there may be broad systematic differences in what they do with technology. While many authors argue that young people learn differently from older people (Prensky, 2001; Barnes, Marateo, and Ferris, 2008; Oblinger, 2008) there are some authors that claim that it is dangerous to make this assumption considering only age or experience with new technology (Bennett and Maton, 2010). Livingstone and Bovill (2008) claim that children and young people are particularly enthusiastic about using new forms of media; however, they believe that young people are not only distinct from adults, but they also vary in gender, age, social class, cultural background, etc. and so "they are not easily reduced to simple categories of 'the child' or 'youth'." Some of the characteristics of young people related to digital learning are presented.

Among the differences between young people and previous generations is the more frequent use of images than text. Oblinger (2008) states that: "visual literacy is an important part of digital literacy". According to her, students are more at home with images than with text.

Jenkins et al (2006) claim that the development of social skills through collaboration and networking for new literacies is relevant. According to them, the new skills include: play, performance, simulation, appropriation, multitasking, distributed cognition, collective intelligence, judgment, transmedia navigation, networking, and negotiation. They argue that there is a need for a systemic approach to media education in order to teach these social skills and cultural competencies. Oblinger and Hagner (2005) observed that digital age students express a need for more varied forms of communication and report being easily bored with traditional learning methods.

According to Buckingham et al. (2004) children can develop competence in handling the media as a result of their "overall level of cognitive, emotional, and social development; their experience of the world in general; and their specific experience of the media". He made a review of research literature on the development of children's abilities in three areas: access, understand and create. He concludes that media literacy, like print literacy, involves cognitive skills, emotional response, enjoyment and cultural appreciation. According to him, "different social groups may have very different orientations to the media, and develop different kinds of literacy that reflect this."

Tapscott (2009) argues that Net Geners are active receivers, as they also leave comments and add content in blog and social media environments. He describes eight "norms" that unify them as a generation: freedom; customization, scrutiny, integrity, collaboration, entertainment, speed, and innovation. He also claims that the brains of Net Geners have been changed by their interaction with computer technology. Examples of these changes are the fact that they are more visually acute and have better spatial awareness (because of their experience with tracking multimedia) and that they are better at hand-eye coordination and more effective collaborators and decision makers (as a result of their use of video games).

Hollingworth et al. (2009) investigated the influence of new media technologies used in learning on young people's career aspirations among students from 14 to 16 years old; they found that students "perceive their learning in media as being 'practical', 'independent' and 'fun'.

Siriaraya et al (2011) investigated the differences between teenagers and older people's behaviour using online support communities. They concluded that young people write with more emotional emphasis in an online community and at a more personal level when compared to older people. Young people also demonstrated less concern when expressing empathy online compared to older people.

Some authors claim that young people engaged in multi-tasking activities (e.g. Livingstone, 2003; Rideout, Foehr, Roberts, 2010). Rideout, Foehr, Roberts (2010) published the third Kaiser Family Foundation Study (first in 1994, second 2004), named "Generation M2: Media in the Lives of 8- to 18-Year-Olds", with data about 2000 young people's use of media in the USA. The survey aimed to understand the use of media by young people and "to provide a more solid base from which to examine media's effects on children". Among other things, they found that young people are doing different tasks at the same time (e.g. listening to music, using the computer, or watching TV) for longer than in previous surveys.

Bennett, Maton and Kervin (2008) and Bennett and Maton (2010) disagree with the aforementioned authors. They think that assumptions about young people should be viewed with caution. They claim that some statements lack empirical evidence and that findings in some studies are contradictory. They affirm that it is problematic to generalise about the whole population. According to learning theories and previous research, there are significant differences between individuals, and their approach to learning depends on various factors such as task perception. Bennett and Maton (2010) concluded that there is still no consensus on the effects on young people of digital technology. They believe that the debate on digital natives should be transferred to a debate on the development of more understanding on the users' experience with technology.

The main point that this discussion on designing interactive digital learning environments reveals is that young users must be considered inside their context of use, taking into account their own characteristics, experiences and wishes. New technologies, new possibilities of interaction and visual appeal can help students to improve their skills and learning if they are well developed and consider all relevant aspects related to the environment. Designers must make use of the resources needed to create effective and outstanding learning environments. As mentioned by Rideout, Foehr, Roberts (2010), knowledge of media's influence on young people's lives is very important for educators, parents and others concerned with promoting their healthy development.

AN APPROACH TO DEVELOPING THE FRAMEWORK: A REVIEW OF THE LITERATURE

In order to develop the proposed framework, concepts related to designing interactive digital learning environments and previous frameworks related to this area were investigated. Ten frameworks briefly described below were chosen because they are related to the learning aspects of interactive digital learning environments, the user interaction design aspects and/or the visual elements of such interfaces. These frameworks have been created and used in different subject areas with different purposes. Some frameworks have been proposed to provide a structure that may guide design or, alternatively, to evaluate a product or even to help understand some concepts. They are divided into: frameworks related to learning aspects; frameworks related to interaction design aspects; and frameworks related to visual elements aspects. Note that they may use different aspects in the same framework. At the end of this review, there is a short discussion on their similarities and differences.

Samples of Framework Related to Learning Aspects

In the context of learning, the American Psychological Association's Board of Educational Affairs (1997) proposed a framework "for developing and incorporating the components of new designs for schooling". They created 14 principles that reflect the nature of learning and learners. The framework is divided into four main factors: cognitive and metacognitive factors, motivational and affective factors, developmental and social factors, and individual differences. Although this framework was not developed focusing on e-learning environments, it presents some principles strongly connected to the new digital era. For instance, the principle that should be stressed is "learning and diversity". It affirms the relevance of considering the linguistic, cultural and social backgrounds of the learners. In this new era with people around the world using the same learning environments and devices these differences should be considered in learning tasks and contexts in order to enhance learning. From the same perspective, there is an important principle that says that learning context is relevant. This means that different environmental, cultural and technological practices can influence learning. Figure 1 shows the principles.

Laurillard (1993, 2002) proposed the well-known Conversational Framework for the effective use of educational technology. The framework incorporates effective teaching and learning practices into an e-learning environment. Although Laurillard discusses her framework in relation to academic students, her framework approach is very interesting for those working with an interactive learning environment. She developed it through the analysis of the findings from research on 'what it takes to learn' in different forms of learning such as conventional, distance, and digital. The Conversational Framework operates on two levels: the discursive level with a focus on theory, concepts, and description-building; and the experiential level with focus on practice, activity and procedure-building. The framework defines an iterative dialogic process between teacher and student with four main components: teacher's conception, student's conception, teacher's constructed environment, and student's actions. The Conversational Framework for learning can be "used to test how various applications of technology measure up to the requirements of a more

Figure 1. A Framework for School Reform & Redesign by the American Psychological Association (adapted from the American Psychological Association's Board of Education, 1997)

Cognitive and Metacognitive Factors	Motivational and Affective Factors	Developmental and Social Factors	Individual Differences Factors
Nature of the learning process	Motivational and emotional influences on learning	Developmental influences on learning	Individual differences in learning
Goals of the learning process	Intrinsic motivation to learn	Social influences on learning	Learning and diversity
Construction of knowledge	Effects of motivation on effort		Standards and assessment
Strategic thinking			
Thinking about thinking			
Context of learning			

progressive teaching model". Figure 2 shows the Conversational Framework.

Unlike the creators of previous frameworks, Khan (2001, 2003) proposed one that addresses many specific aspects of an e-learning environment. He created "a framework for e-learning" in order to find out what it takes "to provide the best and most meaningful open, flexible, and distributed learning environments for learners worldwide". His framework has eight dimensions: institutional (i.e. concerned with issues of administrative and academic affairs and student services), pedagogical (refers to teaching and learning), technological, interface design, evaluation, management, resource support, and ethical. Khan believes that the issues proposed might guide planning, designing, evaluating and implementing e-learning environments, as the framework provides "a sketch of what it takes to create a successful e-learning experience for diverse learners" (2001). He argues that the use of this framework in the design of e-learning environments can ensure that all important aspects are considered independent of the scope and complexity (Khan, 2003). Figure 3 shows the framework for e-learning.

The remainder of this paper demonstrates this approach, describing how we designed a prototype interactive multimedia program to assist the emergent understanding of historical chronology in young children aged five to seven.

Figure 2. The main components of Conversational Framework by Laurillard (adapted from Laurillard, 2002, p. 30)

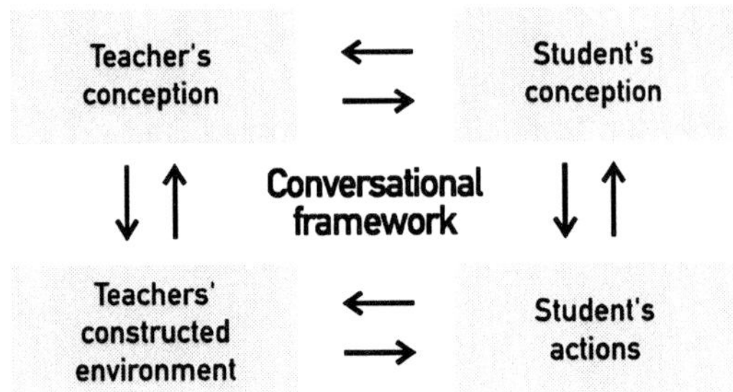

Figure 3. Framework for e-learning by Khan (adapted from Khan, 2001)

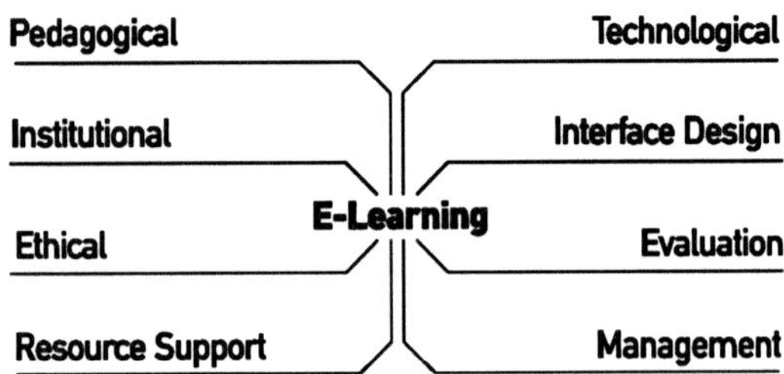

Samples of Framework Related to Interface Design Aspects

Dealing with both learning and user interface design aspects, Good and Robertson (2006) presented a framework for the participatory design of interactive learning environments involving children. This framework consists of five components: context (context in which the design activities take place), activities (sequence of events which occur), roles (the functions of a team member), stakeholders (individuals who have a vested interest in the design process), and skills (personal attributes and dispositions to conduct design sessions). They argue that the framework is useful for three purposes: to offer a 'set of issues to consider when planning to use a child-centred design approach', to offer a number of ideas for appropriate activities at each stage of the design process, and a consideration of the skills necessary to ensure a successful design outcome.' Figure 4 shows the framework for participatory design.

In the context of user interface design, Dyson et al. (1995) created a framework to identify many aspects of multimedia systems in museums. The framework is composed of fourteen main characteristics, divided into two main parts: global and operational characteristics. Global characteristics describe the material included in the multimedia system, its purpose and the genre that is used. The main characteristics are: title, content, function and format. Operational characteristics define the means by which the material is presented, giving

Figure 4. Framework for the participatory design of interactive learning environments involving children by Good and Robertson (adapted from Good and Robertson, 2006, p. 386)

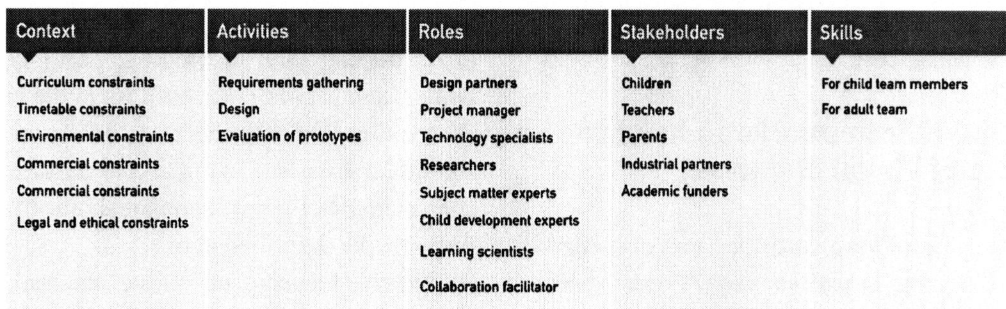

Context	Activities	Roles	Stakeholders	Skills
Curriculum constraints	Requirements gathering	Design partners	Children	For child team members
Timetable constraints	Design	Project manager	Teachers	For adult team
Environmental constraints	Evaluation of prototypes	Technology specialists	Parents	
Commercial constraints		Researchers	Industrial partners	
Commercial constraints		Subject matter experts	Academic funders	
Legal and ethical constraints		Child development experts		
		Learning scientists		
		Collaboration facilitator		

technical and design specifications. The main characteristics are: number of users, storage, input, output, visual modes, auditory modes, operational aids and time constraints, navigational structure and control. Dyson, Andrews, and Leontopolou (1995) state that the framework 'may form a useful general tool for comparing the characteristics of different computer-based interactive systems'. Figure 5 shows the framework.

Garrett (2002) proposes a conceptual framework with five elements to understand how users make decisions on websites. They are: the surface plane (images and text), the skeleton plane (the arrangement of buttons, tabs, photos, and blocks of text), the structure plane (the way in which the features and functions of the site fit together), the scope plane (what the features and functions of the site are), and the strategy plane (what both site owner and users want to get out of the site). According to him, these five planes cover user problems and the tools used to solve them. Figure 6 shows the framework.

In contrast to the previous frameworks related to user interface design, Rogers and Muller (2006) proposed a framework for designing sensor-based interactions. According to them, the focus of this framework is to promote creative design (that seeks to exploit the various properties of sensor-based interactions) not usable design in the traditional HCI sense. The aim of this framework 'is to outline the core dimensions of sensor-based

Figure 5. Framework to describe multimedia by Dyson et al. (adapted from Dyson, Andrews and Leontopoulou, 1995, p. 111)

Global Characteristics	Operational Characteristics
Title	Number of users
Content	Storage
Function	Input
Format	Output
	Visual modes
	Auditory modes
	Operational aids
	Time constraints
	Navigational structure
	Control

Figure 6. Conceptual framework for websites by Garrett (adapted from Garrett, 2002)

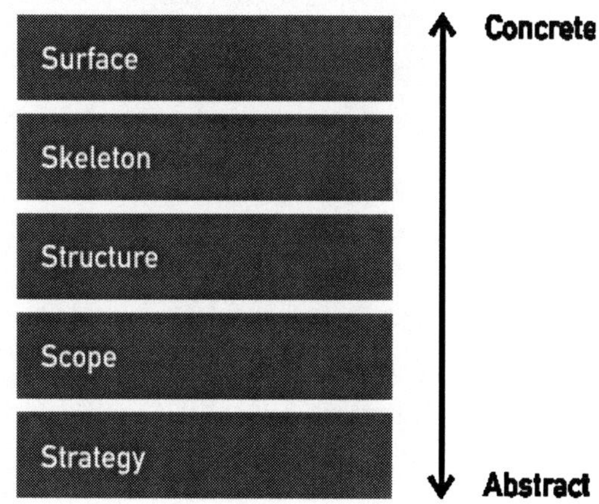

interactions in relation to how people perceive what is going on and how this affects their understanding and subsequent behaviours'. Figure 7 shows the framework.

Samples of Frameworks Related to Aspects of Visual Elements

Different authors have described and classified graphic language in various ways. Focusing on children's printed books, Walker (2003) developed a descriptive framework of the visual characteristics of children's reading and information books. Her framework is divided into three levels: micro (letterforms and their articulation), macro (navigation, layout) and artefact (the material attributes of the books). The framework aimed to identify typical visual characteristics of reading books from a particular period and changes over periods of time. Walker concludes that the visual characteristics are influenced by context of use and production.

More recently, Walker (2006) proposed a framework for describing book design. In contrast to the previous framework, this description places both the macro and micro levels in three categories: document structure and articulation of content (navigation systems, configuration, rhetorical devices, and kinds of content in relation to information unit), typography (letterforms and their articulation) and material attributes (size; format; kind of binding; paper type and colour; and printing process). As in the previous description Walker states that contextual factors should be discussed in relation to the descriptive characteristics. Figure 8 compares both of Walker's frameworks described above.

Finally, focusing on online material, Souto (2008) developed a descriptive framework to analyse and compare online language courses. (See Figure 9.) The framework is divided into four main characteristics: audiovisual, content, navigational and visual. According to the author, the findings show that the framework is useful for identifying and categorising different characteristics related to the interface. Figure 10 shows the framework.

Brief Discussion of the Samples' Frameworks

This review has shown different approaches and types of frameworks that are in some way related to design of interactive digital learning environments. It can be seen that these approaches differ quite a lot, and it is therefore difficult to make comparisons

Figure 7. Sense-making experience framework by Rogers and Muller (adaptation from generalized version of the sense-making experience framework by Rogers and Muller, 2006, p. 13)

Transforms	Activities to consider (examples)	Sensor properties to consider
The phenomenological processes involved are: perceiving understanding reflecting Take into account: uncertainty unexpectedness	looking, collecting, searching, chasing (exploratory and discovery-based activities); eliciting awareness, promoting reflection, (desirable aspects of user experience); walking, waving, dancing (how to couple continuous actions); multi-modal, audio, visual, tactile (kinds of effects).	Discrete– continuous Precision Explicit– implicit

Figure 8. Descriptive framework of the visual characteristics of children's reading and information books Description of book design by Walker (adapted from Walker, 2003 and Walker, 2006, p. 2)

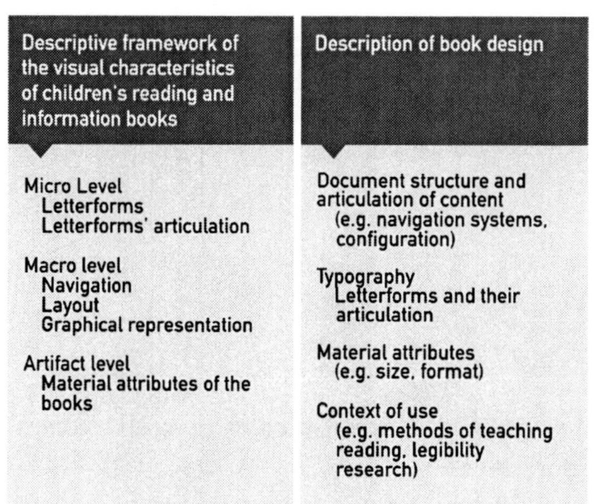

among them. However, this review has noted many interesting aspects, concepts, and characteristics of interactive e-learning environments.

The framework review helped to provide insights and ideas for the proposed framework. Although these frameworks do relate to some extent to the environment studied here they do not focus on the design of interactive digital learning for young people. Most of them focused either on learning aspects of an interface or on user interface design. Just one study focused on the visual elements of an interactive digital learning environment (Souto, 2008), but it did not focus on young people. Therefore, it is considered that there is a need for a descriptive framework for designing an interactive digital learning environment for young people. This should be a framework that can help designers in the development of interactive interfaces that are more creative and usable.

FRAMEWORK FOR DESIGNING INTERACTIVE DIGITAL LEARNING ENVIRONMENTS FOR YOUNG PEOPLE

As mentioned above, the aim of this descriptive framework is to analyze and compare interactive digital learning environments. The framework was derived from the previous frameworks summarized above and from principles for user interface design, and some guidelines such as Android User Interface Guidelines, IOS Human Interface Guidelines and W3C accessibility guidelines. The framework aims to help in the design of more creative and usable learning environments for young people. It also aims to guide the design of digital learning environments for young people, help in the understanding of interface characteristics of these environments and how users interact with them. This is because the proposed framework

Figure 9. Descriptive framework for analysis and comparison of online language courses by Souto (adapted from Souto, 2008)

Audiovisual characteristics	Content characteristics	Navigational characteristics	Visual characteristics
Sound modes	Skills, format	Methods of manipulation	Grid
Visual modes	Levels of details	Types of links, position of links	Images
		Number of links, group of links	Text

Figure 10. The proposed framework with the main components and their sub-components

Learning	User Interaction	Visual
Content	Accessibility	Typography
User characteristics	Interaction	Icons
Skills	Platform requirements	Images
	Usability	Information visualization
		Interface structure

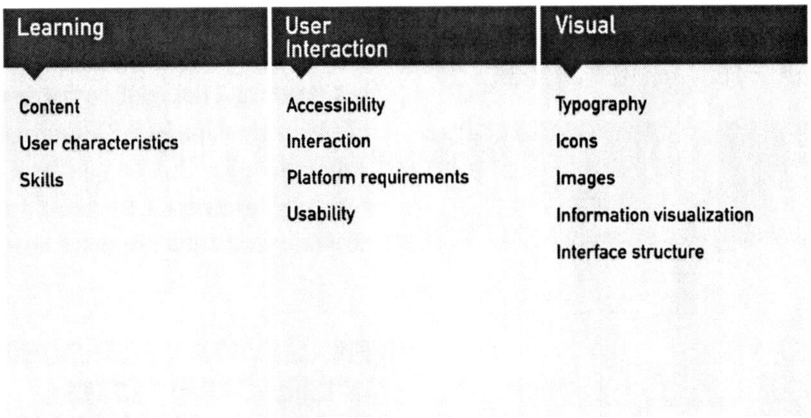

identifies different characteristics of the interface and can be used as a tool during the design process. The framework was divided into three main components: learning, user interaction and visual, with twelve sub-components in total. The framework also takes into account the description of the components and the various ways they can be presented. Figure 10 shows the framework with the main components and their sub-components. The description topic is where the characteristics of the studied environment will fit in order to provide the whole picture of it. The explanations of the components are divided according to the framework structure: learning, user interaction and visual components.

Learning Components

The first component is related to the learning aspects of the interface. The sub-components of the learning component are: user characteristics, skills, and content. 'User characteristics' relates to the users' gender, age, social class, cultural background and experience with the digital environment.

Apart from these, it is important to consider the users' characteristics related to young people, such as: their visual literacy, their need for more forms of communication, their tendency to be easily bored by traditional learning methods, and their emotional response, enjoyment, and cultural appreciation.

Skills are defined "as a capacity to perform a given type of task or activity with a given degree of effectiveness, efficiency, speed, or other measure of quantity or quality" (Romiszowski, 2009, p. 203).

The learning skills most relevant to young people include traditional literacy, research skills, technical skills, critical analysis skills and the new ones related to media technology: play, performance, simulation, appropriation, multitasking, distributed cognition, collective intelligence, judgment, transmedia navigation, networking, and negotiation, as presented by Jenkins et al (2006).

Content refers to the levels of both details and format. In relation to level of details it is important to consider if the content is: superficial, broad, focused or detailed. The format of the content is related to its type, be it dialogue, exercises, texts, videos, games, etc.

The learning components are critical to the design of digital learning environments. In order to develop more usable and better interfaces for young people, designers have to consider their characteristics. As has been previously discussed, young people must be considered inside their context of use, their own characteristics, experiences and wishes.

User Interaction

The second component, user interaction, refers to the technological platform used with all the requirements and characteristics of such platforms and the user's interaction with it. Aspects related to the accessibility (i.e. access by all target public regardless of disability), usability (i.e. efficiency, effectiveness, and satisfaction with the interface) and interaction (structure of the interface, how the interaction works, and the methods of interaction) are sub-components of user interaction.

When considering user interaction among young people it is important to analyze how they interact with the interface, what kind of method of interaction they prefer and under which circumstances they are using the interface. It is more accurate to create interfaces that fulfil young people's needs when their behaviour is known and understood by the designers. The visual interface of a learning environment is a complex area that can offer various solutions, and it contributes strongly to allowing these environments to function effectively. Many aspects should be considered when developing the visual interface of interactive digital learning environments. Aspects related to the legibility of the elements, the function of each element, and their harmony should be carefully decided. Furthermore, due to the fact that one of the main purposes is to learn in a pleasant environment, the aesthetic aspect should also be carefully considered.

Visual Components

The last component is the visual elements of an interface. Its sub-components are: typographic aspects (e.g. typeface, text alignment, line length, line spacing, colour), images (e.g. 2D drawing, 3D drawing, photography, texture), icons (e.g. representation - pictorial, alphanumeric characters, abstract, diagram; type - pure icon, explicate icon, aid icon; shape; size; colour; complexity; localization; movement; clicking resources) and other graphic elements. In addition, another sub-component, called "interface structure", includes aspects such as the existence of a grid among different pages, how the interface elements are organized, the number of elements, interface impression, layout structure, and also falls into the category of visual components. Finally, the sub-component "information visualization" includes different types of visual representation of information, such as bubble chart, tag clouds, word tree.

Although the visual elements are one of the main aspects that make an interface successful, they are often not mentioned or are weakly explored in the frameworks. The knowledge of all possible visual elements that can be used in the interface, the understanding of how these elements work, and how young people feel in relation to them are essential to build appropriate and outstanding interactive digital learning environments.

The Complete Framework with Main Components, Sub-Components and Issues

The complete framework is presented below (Figure 11). The issues related to each sub-component are illustrated. Not all issues are addressed, but the framework presents samples of many of them, which developers of the environment can use as a guide to help them fit in with the environment's characteristics.

When to Use the Proposed Framework and Examples of Use

As mentioned above, the aim of the proposed framework is to analyse and compare interactive digital learning environments. In addition, it may be useful to guide design of digital learning environments for young people, by which is meant that the framework can build design concepts. According to Roger and Scaife (1998), design concepts are "issues which designers need to con-

Figure 11. The complete framework with the main components and their sub-components

Main components	Sub-components	Description
Learning	Content	level of details (superficial, broad, focused or detailed); format of the content (type, be it dialogue, exercises, texts, videos, games, etc)
	Skills	traditional literacy, research skills, technical skills, critical analysis skills, play, performance, simulation, appropriation, multitasking, distributed cognition, collective intelligence, judgment, transmedia navigation, networking, and negotiation
	User characteristics	users' gender, age, social class, cultural background, visual literacy, need for more forms of communication, tendency to be easily bored with traditional learning methods, emotional response, enjoyment, and cultural appreciation
User interaction	Accessibility	access by all target public regardless of disability.
	Interaction	structure of the interface, how the interaction works, and the methods of interaction
	Platform requirements	display, devices, software
	Usability	effectiveness, efficiency and satisfaction with the environment
Visual	Typography	typeface, text alignment, line length, line spacing, colour, etc.
	Icons	representation (e.g. pictorial, alphanumeric characters, abstract, diagram), type (pure icon, explicate icon, aid icon), shape, size, colour, complexity, localization, movement, clicking resources
	Images	2D drawing, 3D drawing, photography, texture
	Information visualization	different types of visual representation of information, such as bubble chart, tag clouds, word tree
	Interface structure	the existence of a grid among different pages, how the interface elements are organized, the number of elements, interface impression, layout structure

sider when developing interactive multimedia". Through these issues designers can frame questions on how to achieve particular goals or how to create displays that improve learning (Rogers and Scaife, 1998).

For example, let us suppose that in an interactive digital environment for learning mathematics students will need to deal with math symbols and other types of icons within the interface. By trying to fill the descriptions of components of the framework the designers will deal with many questions in the development of such signs. In the sub-component user characteristics, within learning component, the designer will need to research the users' visual literacy and cultural background, among other aspects, in order to make their decisions. In relation to the visual components the designers will need to make many decisions in relation to icon representations (e.g. pictorial, alphanumeric), types (e.g. pure icon, explicate icon), and other aspects, such as shape, size and colour. These visual components are also related to other components. For example, while deciding the size of the icon the designers will need to consider user interaction aspects, such as: which are the methods of manipulation of the interface (e.g. touching, linking) and the platform requirements (display size, display resolution). Therefore, it is important to consider how these design decisions are related to each other in order to find solutions that combine effectively with all the aspects.

The example illustrated above is related to the process of designing a learning environment (during the development stage). Another way of using this framework is to analyse and compare different learning environments for young people that have been completed. In this case, the framework can be used to check whether there are similarities and differences among different environments, how they occur and their frequency. For example, the framework may be used in order to verify whether there are similarities among the placement (e.g. left, right, centre, top, down) of some interface elements. This is important because there may be commonalities in, for example, the placement of the back button of an environment, and therefore it is important that this button be located in the place that is already familiar to users, so that the environment under development can be intuitive for them.

Apart from showing the commonalties and differences among the analysed environments, the framework can also be useful to show different techniques and/or technologies that are being used in such environments. As an example, we can illustrate the case of learning environments used to help students to learn historical facts. In addition to the text content, it is helpful if the environment provides images, infographics and even games/exercises to help students to understand and fix the content. In order to create an effective interface for such an environment, the designers will need to consider many aspects, such as what type of exercise should be presented, the quantity of information on each screen, how the content and exercises should be linked to each other, and the navigation of the content. These decisions may be made based on users' mental model or based on research findings on such subjects.

The proposed framework may also be used to help to evaluate learning environment interfaces. The framework may be used to identify the issues that will be evaluated through different types of methods, such as heuristics, thinking-aloud or usability tests. For example, the proposed framework combined with the heuristics proposed by Nielsen (1995) or the Eight Golden Rules proposed by Shneiderman (1997) can be used to identify problems with some design elements. The Nielsen heuristic "consistency and standards" can be combined with the sub-component "interface structure" of the framework to check whether the layout structure is consistent within the environment, for example.

The framework can also be used by Human-Computer Interaction researchers interested in specific design problems. It may be used to identify some design variables that should be investigated using an empirical research method. This is because the framework consists of a set of issues that designers have to consider while developing an interactive learning environment for young people, and therefore the investigation of these issues is required in order to create effective environments. The framework used as an analytical tool can help researchers to have insights into some particular design elements that should be investigated. For example, based on the results of an analysis of 50 interactive literature environments for secondary school students in which differences in menu types were found, researchers may find it relevant to investigate which of these different menus most help the user to find information on screen. Therefore, it can be said that the proposed framework can be used as a basis to investigate user behaviour, performance and preference for some interface design elements.

CONCLUSION

As said, the aim of this descriptive framework is to analyse and compare interactive digital learning environments. It seems that frameworks of this nature are important because of the complexity of interactive digital learning environments. The relevance of the creation of a descriptive framework is related to the need to categorise and classify learning environments in order to create more usable interfaces. The framework can also guide design of digital learning environments for young people, and help in the understanding of the interface characteristics of such environments and how users interact with them.

Unlike previous frameworks for interactive design environments, the framework proposed here presents a structure that focuses on the design aspects of the development of such environments. In addition, it focuses on young people's environments. The framework is intended to help designers to create a more interesting and intuitive learning environment by identifying different characteristics of the interface. It also provides a means for reflection and may be used to evaluate the design of e-learning environments. This is because by using this framework it is possible to create a big picture of the environment. Furthermore, the framework can provide researchers with a set of all characteristics of the environment for investigation.

Future work will focus on applying the framework during the development of interactive digital learning environments in order to see whether it is useful to guide the design of such environments. It is also important to mention that this proposed framework might need to be reviewed with future new technologies and newer means of user interaction.

Depending on the project and its purpose, different levels of detail in the framework should be applied. However, it is important to highlight that a descriptive framework is not enough by itself to evaluate learning environment characteristics. A great deal of research should be carried out for a good understanding and evaluation of the characteristics of an interactive digital learning environment for young people. Although the proposed framework is meant to be used in environments for young people it seems that it can also be adapted to be applied to other types of users by revising the description of the components.

Young people, unquestionably, like to use interactive digital environments. This kind of environment seems to require and produce new intellectual characteristics and brain connections and makes young people have a different set of skills for accessing and navigating through information (Tapscott, 2009). Although there is an increase in the number of studies on the role of new media in young people's lives, much research still needs to be done to provide a whole picture of it (Ito, 2009). The challenge is to create interactive digital learning environments that engage, motivate and help in the learning process by creating exciting content and appealing interactive designs. The framework to guide design of digital learning environments may help in this task.

ACKNOWLEDGMENT

Thanks to the Foundation for Research Support of the Federal District – FAP-DF and the University de Brasília – UnB.

REFERENCES

American Psychological Association's Board of Educational Affairs. (1997). *Learner-centered psychological principles: A framework for school reform & redesign*. Washington, DC: American Psychological Association.

Archer, B. (2005). The three Rs. In *A Framework for Design and Design Education*. Wellesbourne: The Design and Technology Association.

Barnes, K., Marateo, R., & Ferris, S. (2007). Teaching and learning with the net generation. *Innovate, 3*(4).

Baynes, K. (1994). *Designerly play*. Loughborough, UK: Loughborough University.

Bennett, S., & Maton, K. (2010). Beyond the 'digital natives' debate: Towards a more nuanced understanding of students' technology experiences. *Journal of Computer Assisted Learning, 26*(5), 321–331. doi:10.1111/j.1365-2729.2010.00360.x.

Bennett, S., Maton, K., & Kervin, L. (2008). The 'digital natives' debate: A critical review of the evidence. *British Journal of Educational Technology, 39*(5), 775–786. doi:10.1111/j.1467-8535.2007.00793.x.

Bødker, S. (1987). *Through the interface – A human activity approach to user interface design*. Aarhus, Denmark: Aarhus University.

Bonsiepe, G. (2011). *Design, cultura e sociedade*. São Paulo: Blucher.

Buckingham, D. (2004). *The media literacy of children and young people: A review of the research literature on behalf of Ofcom*. London: University of London, Youth and Media Institute of Education.

D. Buckingham, & R. Willett (Eds.). (2006). *Digital generations: Children, young people and new media*. Mahwah, NJ: Erlbaum.

Dyson, M. C., Andrews, M., & Leontopoulou, S. (1995). Multimedia in museums: The need for a descriptive framework. *Convergence (London), 1*(2), 105–124. doi:10.1177/135485659500100210.

Fallman, D. (2003). Design-oriented human-computer interaction. In *Proceedings of CHI 2003*. Ft. Lauderdale, FL: ACM.

Garrett, J. J. (2002). *The elements of user experience: User-centered design for the web*. Berkeley, CA: Peachpit Press.

Good, J., & Robertson, J. (2006). CARSS: A framework for learner-centred design with children. *International Journal of Artificial Intelligence in Education, 16*(4), 381–413.

Hollingworth, S., Allen, K., & Kuyok, K. A. (2009). *The influence of new media technologies used in learning on young people's career aspirations*. London: Institute for Policy Studies in Education, Metropolitan University.

ICSID. (2012). *Definition of design*. Retrieved October 20, 2012, from http://www.icsid.org/about/about/articles31.htm.

Jenkins, H., Clinton, K., Purushotma, R., Robison, A. J., & Weigel, M. (2006). *Confronting the challenges of participatory culture: Media education for the 21st century*. Chicago: The MacArthur Foundation.

Kaptelinin, V. (2012). Activity theory. In *Encyclopedia of Human-Computer Interaction*. Aarhus, Denmark: The Interaction Design Foundation. Retrieved October 20, 2012. http://www.interaction-design.org/encyclopedia/activity_theory.html

Khan, B. H. (2001). A framework for e-learning. *E-Learning: Content, Technology & Services for Corporate, Government & Higher Education*. Retrieved October 20, 2012, from http://lomo.kyberia.net/diplomovka/webdownload/partial/elearningmag.com/E-Learning%20-%20A%20Framework%20for%20E-learning.pdf

Khan, B. H. (2003). A framework for open, flexible and distributed e-learning. *Magazine eLearn*, (2).

Kuutti, K. (1995). Activity theory as a potential framework for human- computer interaction research. In B. Nardi (Ed.), *Context and Consciousness: Activity Theory and Human Computer Interaction* (pp. 17–44). Cambridge, MA: MIT Press.

Laurillard, D. (2001). *Rethinking university teaching: A framework for the effective use of educational technology*. London: Routledge.

Laurillard, D. (2002). Rethinking university teaching in the digital age. In *Futures Forum 2002*. Retrieved October 20, 2012, from http://net.educause.edu/ir/library/pdf/ffp0205s.pdf

Leontiev, A. N. (2009). *Activity and consciousness*. Marxists Internet Archive. Retrieved October 20, 2012, from http://www.marxists.org/archive/leontev/works/activity-consciousness.pdf

Lim, Y., & Rogers, Y. (2008). A framework and an environment for collaborative analysis of user experience. *Journal of Human–Computer Interaction*, *24*(6), 529–555. doi:10.1080/10447310801971204.

Lin, Y., & Zhang, W. J. (2004). Towards a novel interface design framework: Function–behavior–state paradigm. *International Journal of Human-Computer Studies*, *61*, 259–297. doi:10.1016/j.ijhcs.2003.11.008.

Livingstone, S., & Bovill, M. (1999). *Young people, new media: Report of the research project children young people and the changing media environment*. London: Department of Media and Communications, London School of Economics and Political Science.

Miles, M. B., & Huberman, A. M. (1994). *Qualitative data analysis: An expanded sourcebook* (2nd ed.). Thousand Oaks, CA: Sage.

Moore, J. L., Dickson-Deane, C., & Galyen, K. (2010). e-Learning, online learning, and distance learning environments: Are they the same? *The Internet and Higher Education*, *14*, 129–135. doi:10.1016/j.iheduc.2010.10.001.

Nielsen, J. (1995). 10 usability heuristics. *Alertbox*. Retrieved January 31, 2013, from http://www.nngroup.com/articles/ten-usability-heuristics/

Oblinger, D. G., & Hagner, P. (2005). *Seminar on educating the net generation*. Retrieved October 20, 2012, from http://www.educause.edu/section_params/conf/esem052/OneDayv2-HO.ppt#3

Piccoli, G., Ahmad, R., & Ives, B. (2001). Web-based virtual learning environments: A research framework and a preliminary assessment of effectiveness in basic IT skills training. *Management Information Systems Quarterly*, *25*(4), 401–426. doi:10.2307/3250989.

Prensky, M. (2001). Digital natives, digital immigrants. *Horizon*, *9*(5). doi:10.1108/10748120110424816.

Rideout, V. J., Foehr, M. A., Ulla, G., & Roberts, D. F. (2010). Generation M2 media in the lives of 8- to 18-year-olds. *A Kaiser Family Foundation Study*. Retrieved October 20, 2012, from http://www.kff.org/entmedia/upload/8010.pdf

Rogers, Y., & Muller, H. (2006). A framework for designing sensor-based interactions to promote exploration and reflection in play. *International Journal of Human-Computer Studies*, *64*, 1–14. doi:10.1016/j.ijhcs.2005.05.004.

Rogers, Y., & Scaife, M. (1998). How can interactive multimedia facilitate learning? In J. Lee (Ed.), *Intelligence and Multimodality in Multimedia Interfaces: Research and Applications. AAAI*. Press.

Rogers, Y., Scaife, M., Gabrielli, S., Smith, H., & Harris, E. (2002). A conceptual framework for mixed reality environments: Designing novel learning activities for young children. *Journal Presence: Teleoperators and Virtual Environments*, *11*(6), 677–686. doi:10.1162/105474602321050776.

Romiszowski, A. (2009). Fostering skill development outcomes. In *Instructional-Design Theories and Models* (Vol. 3, pp. 19–224). New York: Routledge.

Salmon, G. (2005). Flying not flapping: A strategic framework for e-learning and pedagogical innovation in higher education institutions. *ALT-J*, *13*(3), 201–218. doi:10.1080/09687760500376439.

Sangrà, A., Vlachopoulos, D., & Cabrera, N. (2012). Building an inclusive definition of e-learning: An approach to the conceptual framework. *International Review of Research in Open and Distance Learning*, *13*(2), 145–159.

Shneiderman, B. (1997). *Designing the user interface: Strategies for effective human-computer interaction* (3rd ed.). Boston: Addison-Wesley Longman Publishing Co., Inc..

Siriaraya, P., Tang, C., Ang, C. S., Pfeil, U., & Zaphiris, P. (2011). A comparison of empathic communication pattern for teenagers and older people in online support communities. *Behaviour & IT*, *30*(5), 617–628.

Souto, V. T. (2008). Descriptive framework for analysis and comparison of online language courses. In *Proceedings of the ED-MEDIA 2008 –World Conference on Educational Multimedia, Hypermedia & Telecommunications*. Association for the Advancement of Computing in Education.

Spink, A., Wilson, T. D., Ford, N., Foster, A., & Ellis, D. (2002). Information-seeking and mediated searching: Part 1: Theoretical framework and research design. *Journal of the American Society for Information Science and Technology*, *53*(9), 695–703. doi:10.1002/asi.10081.

Stein, S., Shephard, K., & Harris, I. (2011). Conceptions of e-learning and professional development for e-learning held by tertiary educators in New Zealand. *British Journal of Educational Technology*, *42*(1), 145–165. doi:10.1111/j.1467-8535.2009.00997.x.

Svinicki, M. D. (2008). *A guidebook on conceptual frameworks for research in engineering education*. Retrieved October 20, 2012, from http://www.ce.umn.edu/~smith/docs/RREE-Research_Frameworks-Svinicki.pdf

Tapscott, D. (1998). *Growing up digital: The rise of the net generation*. New York: McGraw Hill.

Tapscott, D. (2009). *Grown up digital: How the net generation is changing your world*. New York: McGraw-Hill.

Trinidad, S. (2006). Constructive solutions: Improving teaching and learning in e-learning environments. In *Proceedings of AARE 2005 International Education Research Conference: UWS Parramatta*. Retrieved October 20, 2012, http://www.aare.edu.au/05pap/tri05058.pdf.

Walker, S. (2003). Towards a method for describing the visual characteristics of children's readers and information books. In *Proceedings of the Information Design International Conference*. Sociedade Brasileira de Design da Informação.

Walker, S. (2006). An approach to describing the design of children's reading and information books. *InfoDesign Revista Brasileira de Design da Informação*, *3*(1/2), 1–10.

Wiley, D. A. (2000). Connecting learning objects to instructional design theory: A definition, a metaphor, and a taxonomy. *Learning Technology*, *2830*(435), 1–35.

KEY TERMS AND DEFINITIONS

Design: Creative activity that is concerned, among other things, with user-characteristics and the aesthetic and formal quality of the project.

Digital Learning Environments: Digital environments (e.g. e-books, online games, applications) that provide learning opportunities for people.

E-Learning: Electronic media that provide learning opportunities for people.

Framework: Structure that aims to guide the design of digital learning environments.

Interaction design: process of designing the structure and interaction behaviours of environments.

Interface Design: Process of designing the user's visual interface.

Young People: people aged 9 to 19 years old.

Section 6
Reflection

Chapter 23
The Conceptual Pond:
A Persuasive Tool for Quantifiable Qualitative Assessment

Christian Grund Sørensen
Aalborg University, Denmark

Mathias Grund Sørensen
Aalborg University, Denmark

ABSTRACT

"The Conceptual Pond" is a persuasive application designed to gather qualitative input through a multi-platform assessment interface. The process of using the application serves as a conceptual aid for personal reflection as well as providing a compilation and evaluation system with the ability to transform this input into quantitative data. In this chapter, a pilot study of this application is presented and discussed. The aim of this chapter is the discussion of central issues in the system, the use of semantic fields, user freedom vs. default options, graphical interface, persuasive technology design, and the epistemological potential of the application. In this discourse, contextualized rhetorical and persuasive technology theories are implemented. Functionality and epistemological impact is exemplified through several use cases, one of these linked to the EUROPlot project. In a more comprehensive scope, this chapter adds to the discussion of the role of IT systems in experiencing the world and reflecting on it, thus breaking new ground for designing persuasive applications supporting human recognition.

INTRODUCTION

How can qualitative data be collected and transformed into quantitative data? This is a challenge in many fields, including development, research and evaluation. This chapter suggests an approach to utilizing persuasive technology, graphic interface and intuitive design to fulfill this.

In the course of developing persuasive learning objects in an EU research project on IT supported learning it has become evident to the authors that reliable assessment and monitoring of impressions and opinions is a very important factor. *Evaluation* and *assessment* is a central part of most pedagogical theories. Nevertheless there is often not much consensus concerning how this observation and assessments should be performed and optimized.

It is essential that the challenges of evaluation are met in a way that respects human nature and cognition. For a system to be truly persuasive and

DOI: 10.4018/978-1-4666-4623-0.ch023

create satisfaction and ownership with the users it will need both intuitive handling and considerable user freedom. It is obvious that the questions of bias and validity are essential.

At the same time the increasing use of different digital devices in education supports the possibility of utilizing these technologies in creating contextually relevant evaluation processes.

The Conceptual Pond is designed to solve tasks primarily in the field of learning, social sciences and human sciences. The theoretical background and functionality however makes it no less relevant in other sectors such as human computer interaction, psychology, or social sciences. The need for analyzing humanly expressed thoughts is central in a broad variety of academic, pedagogic, cultural or societal projects.

Collecting reliable *qualitative* data and analyzing it has always been a time consuming challenge. Could a persuasive evaluation system support this process and even open doors to possibilities hitherto less explored? The Conceptual Pond suggests a new approach to assessment facilitating the quantification of the qualitative.

The purpose of this chapter it to present The Conceptual Pond as a framework for performing quantifiable qualitative assessments supported field studies demonstrating its potential. We first analyze the background and conditions of the assessment challenge. We then present the semantics and interface of The Conceptual Pond, including a discussion of important implementation concerns. Next, we present case studies of The Conceptual Pond and suggest further possible domains for the application of The Conceptual Pond. Finally, we discuss persuasive properties and potential of the application, followed by suggestions for further work and finally our conclusion.

BACKGROUND

This chapter serves to present a pilot study of The Conceptual pond. Before digging into the concept and the potential it is however important to address a number of background questions related to the origin and nature of the application.

The Conceptual Pond was originally developed to meet challenges in the environment of the EUROPlot-project (www.eplot.eu). The objective of this research project is to facilitate e-learning and blended learning supported by a framework of persuasive, pedagogical tools. The scope of The Conceptual Pond is nevertheless more comprehensive and should support assessment, creativity and productivity in numerous contexts in the areas of learning and research.

In more detail the aim of the EUROPlot project is to create and develop generative learning designs and educational applications with the use of primarily GLOmaker (www.glomaker.org), Plotlearner and Plotlearner for Munk software, including an EMDROS database (www.emdros.org) of searchable and annotated full texts (Gram-Hansen et al., 2011; Gram-Hansen et al., 2012). The overall task in the relevant part of the project is the mediation of knowledge about Danish playwright and vicar Kaj Munk (1898-1944). Such cultural discourse displays specific characteristics as stated by e.g. Hooper-Greenhill (2004). A central challenge to cultural mediation is evaluating impressions and outcomes that are frequently too complex to fit meaningfully in predesigned response patterns. In the Munk Case the central mediation aims at the following goals:

1. It should enhance interest and engagement in the biography and contemporary time of Kaj Munk.
2. It should offer easy access to Munk's literary works and support reading and semantic searches in relevant archives.
3. It should generate engagement and discussion about topics related to Munk's ideology, thoughts and beliefs. This should be done in a reflective process.
4. It should facilitate these objectives for recipients ranging from primary school children to academics.

5. Systems should cooperate with the Kaj Munk Research Center, Vedersø Vicarage Museum, and schools at various levels.

The focus of The Conceptual Pond is to support several aspects of the learning experience: The self-assessment and evaluation aspect. At the same time, it may be argued that the use of the application may facilitate a deeper immersion into the subject through activating the user with the application. Obviously, an interactive activity like this requires reflection and registration thus facilitating a deeper level of learning. Finally, the wide targeted range of participants imposes strong requirements to the design of the framework. The Conceptual Pond has been designed to provide the participant with a high level of expressiveness through a simple and intuitive interface in order to facilitate the needs of wide range of participants.

In the design process it has become evident that the potential of The Conceptual Pond is much broader than the original project and it is now in the process of being implemented in a variety of environments featuring an agile development method in programming and a constructive hermeneutic method in project development and evaluation.

Assessment in Learning

Generally recognized theories of learning such as the *cognitive domain* of Blooms Taxonomy (Bloom, 1956) and the SOLO Taxonomy of Jonathan Biggs (Biggs & Tang, 2007) (Structure of Observed Learning Outcomes) have an emphasis on *evaluation* and *assessment*. This preference for evaluation and assessment is more dominant in an Anglo-Saxon learning paradigm than in Scandinavian school tradition. However, since evaluation is an integrated part of contemporary educational practice. It is necessary also for e.g. the EUROPlot-project to develop and present suitable assessment tools for the evaluation of the individual student as well as groups.

A number of decisions must be made in the evaluation process, as "Abstract principles have to be translated into real tests for real students ... "How" decisions include question format: *selected-response* tasks, in which the student selects from among answers that are provided on the test, or *constructed-response* tasks, in which the student generates a product or performance." (Odendahl, 2011, p. 8). The process is usually of a two-step nature needing both stage 1, the gathering of qualitative input, and subsequently stage 2, the adaptation of these data into an environment suitable for further analysis (Rossman & Rallis, 2012).

Assessment in Persuasive Technology

In the field of *persuasive technology, assessment* and *evaluation* obviously is a centerpiece. In many cases this is based on automatized system feedback facilitating self-assessment, such as e.g. fitness monitoring apps like Endomondo. In other cases the scope is on persuasion through some kind of surveillance, ranging from positive teacher attention to an approach conceptually inspired by Jeremy Bentham's concept of the *Panopticon*. In this concept the Panopticon is an original design for a prison structure in which all cells may be monitored at any time unseen by the inmate, thus creating unspoken behavioral control. The Panopticon is used also as a societal metaphor by Michel Foucault (Foucault, 1977; Jespersen et al. 2007).

The basic discourse in the persuasive technology field is rooted in the research of behavioral psychologist B.J. Fogg. In his book "Persuasive Technology – Using Computers to Change what we Say and Do" (2003) he combines observations in the human computer interaction field with a psychological understanding offering a number of methods or devices to persuade the user into adapting a certain attitude or behavior "without coercion or deception" (Fogg, 2003).

Many of these "classic" persuasive devices require a certain kind of monitoring, assessment or feedback to function as intended. This also goes for B.J. Foggs' persuasive tools, namely tailoring, conditioning, reduction (to some extent), and in some cases also tunneling, and suggestion. These persuasive devices most often function with the assistance of interactive feedback that allows for proactive agency decided by the feedback of past choice, such as product recommendation systems utilizing past user purchases. Assessment and evaluation is even more at the center of technologies related to self-monitoring and surveillance (Oinas-Kukkonen, 2008).

Assessment is in this context the process of collecting input from the user and analyzing this, most commonly in order to present a result. This may be the result for a single individual (a pupil at school), but may also be relevant for a group (a class) or contribute to a more comprehensive discourse (a common understanding of something).

Much research has been done in the field of exploring the possibilities of using persuasive technology in assessment. Most studies have been made in the areas of health-care and prevention. This goes for the classic example of the heart-rate monitor in Fogg's "Persuasive Technology" (2003, p. 44). In an extended form it plays a role in the studies of Munson, Lauterbach, Newman, and Resnick (2010) where the role of assessment is linked with a social network site in order to benefit from the persuasive power of social comparison and peer support. Another example is the studies of weight loss websites by Lehto and Oinas-Kukkonen (2010). They underscore the worth of assessment in the context of *social facilitation*, which is closely related to self-monitoring and social comparison.

Assessing the Uncountable

In Persuasive Technology studies there is a tendency towards focusing on systems that generate *quantitative* outcomes. This is not surprising, as quantitative results are often easily transferrable into digital behavior support systems. In many contexts this makes good sense. However, in some contexts a different approach to assessment is needed.

Tools for evaluation and assessment in the form of multiple-choice-tests, questionnaires and game-like applications with timelines and similar objects are available in many forms. But they are not always sufficiently advanced to acquire and store the necessary information. This goes for instance for traditional *qualitative* surveys such as opinions and emotions. Also, many sources of error are present in the digital assessment. Respondents may misinterpret the wording of a question or they may experience manipulation due to biased questions or the absence of possibilities for relevant answers. At the same time, the concept of "measuring everything that counts" is an important factor in society, as sociological and management studies reveal (Petersen, 1999). In spite of the obvious advantages of quantitative assessment, it is just as obvious that these assessments may imply a reductionist approach.

Assessing the uncountable, one must be open to a variety of different expressions. Since The Conceptual Pond empowers the user to utilize any words or phrases she wants, there is no limit to the complexity. This is fully in line with a traditional rhetorical approach that leaves any words open in description or argument.

Recognizing that the wording must be free to embrace the complexity of human expression, the question remains which kind of expression the application will contain? As we shall see from the use cases, it is clear that user input comprise both denotations and connotations. Realizing this may problematize the stringent distinctions between these two styles of expression, but it should not undermine the actual quality and credibility of the expressions collected by The Conceptual Pond.

Classical rhetoric categorizes arguments from different *topoi* (Greek: places). These are the realms from which information, arguments and examples are collected, such as law, literature, or technology. Depending on the context and matter of a discourse, arguments and examples may be taken from different contexts using a *topological* approach. This acknowledgement of variety in argument and expression supports the underlying thesis for The Conceptual Pond, that in many cases all expressions are valid and valuable, be they of an emotional or a purely rational nature.

Empowering Data

Though the primary reason for using The Conceptual Pond may be connected to reflection, self-assessment, creation of portfolio or individual evaluation, the design is also made for data to be analyzed and vitalized.

The application design supports searches in relation to parameters such as user ID, user-generated content in the graphical interface (e.g. reflections on a certain drama), number of words, time-lapse, age and gender. The data facilitate access to typical patterns of expression, e.g. typical understandings of a drama. A fully searchable database with the possibility of positive and negative segmentation, e.g. excluding from the searches pupils in primary school who have filled out the The Conceptual Pond in a very short time and with very few words.

Searches may be visualized in table-format or in a graphic presentation, visualizing clusters of semantic expressions to facilitate a more intuitive overview through the reduction of the cognitive load and adaption to individual *learning strategies*.

With a personal log-on, the individual may gain access to the portfolio of recent activities and expressions. This portfolio can also be linked with other portfolio material deriving from e.g. the EUROPlot-project creating a personalized, virtual learning environment.

In summary, The Conceptual Pond like many other applications has a history of origin. The general need for assessment and evaluation however suggests that the concept may be applicable in a number of contexts and thus exceeds the original framework. This pilot study should reveal whether the application offers new functionality and greater insight through the process of gathering and empowering of data.

THE SEMANTIC POND OF CONCEPTS

The Conceptual Pond is an application designed to *assess* the outcome of an experience, an impression or an opinion. The strategy is to collect data in a simple and intuitive system, thus facilitating both self-monitoring and external assessment. The time factor is important, as *kairos*, the opportune moment for gathering this information is frequently evanescent.

The central cognitive element of the application is words. These words are understood in the sense of *semantic fields* containing meaning and expressions in themselves. This is not quite the same as keywords. Keywords mainly have a referential function leaving the semantic content to some degree irrelevant. They are helpful, conceptual links, but the emphasis with keywords is not to express or mediate a very specific meaning but rather to contribute to a collective understanding of the overall subject.

The use of semantics in The Conceptual Pond is dependent on the actual meaning of the words as understood by the user. Words in this application are self-contained and express a complete meaning on its own. Obviously, since the application exploits words in this sense there is room for a subjective understanding. People define and use words with some difference, leaving a fleeting or gradually changing understanding in society. In spite of this subjectivity aspect that may give rise to concern in terms of validity, this use of a semantic approach offers other advantages.

First, that the exact wording in the application is the most reliable and exact expression of the thoughts of the user. Second, that the user must not adhere to certain terms defined by the inquirer.

As specified later in this chapter the element of *user freedom* is crucial to the persuasive design of this application. Using semantics in this way as *statements of expression* may be problematized for the absence of syntactical awareness. Complex thoughts may need a combination of words to be expressed convincingly. Due to the application design and due to considerations of usability and persuasive impact, the use of syntax should be limited. A syntactical approach featuring full sentences would complicate the quantification of data and challenge the element of comparison.

Concepts often present themselves with airy and rather subjective definitions. Still, concepts are popular for expressing thoughts that are not described helpfully through more technical and well-defined terms. They leave room for some interpretation, but on the other side not arbitrary or random understandings. For this reason, the use of semantics in The Conceptual Pond is nevertheless valid. The function of the application is to help the user codify her impression and personal judgment as well as storing denotation and connotation.

Though The Conceptual Pond is primarily a text-based application, the concepts and expressions may be given in the form of visual markers such as photos, drawings, colors or symbols. These diverse types of input may be helpful in relation to illiterate people, children or people with cognitive disabilities. It is also possible to imagine situations, where certain psychological, pedagogical or cognitive considerations may require words to be substituted with other conceptual representations.

We will now continue to describe in details the graphical interface of The Conceptual Pond followed by a discussion on main challenges of the implementation (Figure 1). These challenges are important to address properly in order to ensure the fairness of the resulting data as well as to ensure easy quantitative analysis of the data.

The Graphical Interface

The Conceptual Pond is designed with a simple graphical interface. This is important, as the application should be intuitive and easy to navigate even for primary school children and the technologically challenged. Navigation is a simple drag-and-drop movement and the user is always able to alter her choice and change position of the marker. The user has the command of a virtually unlimited number of markers, each of them marked with a word or a short sentence. Empty markers are also available, so the user can insert non-pre-designed words of her choice. Unused markers stay in the right side of the screen, unless the user chooses to leave them otherwise. The markers are clearly marked as moveable boxes and have a clear inscription of the corresponding word. In special situations the markers could be substituted with pictures, colors or symbols as previously mentioned.

The left and center part of the assessment screen is dominated by a *circle of relevance*. This *circle of relevance* marks the area in which the words relevant to the user, describing her denotations and connotations related to the subject, are dragged and dropped at will. The center of the *circle of relevance* is a marked in a clear color fading slowly into a lighter color. The position relative to the center signals the strength and importance of the expression. Using gradients of the colors green enhances the intuitive impact of the interface. As noted by Ham and Midden (2010) the color green is intuitively recognized as something positive and thereby reduces the cognitive load of the user.

Another reason for choosing a simplistic, graphical interface is the observations in the field of cognitive style by Riding & Raynor and others. It comprises two fundamental aspects: "First, *cognitive style*, which reflects the way in which the individual person thinks; second, *learning strategy*, which reflects those processes which are used by the learner to respond to the demands of a learning activity" (Riding & Rayner, 2010).

Figure 1. The graphical interface of The Conceptual Pond

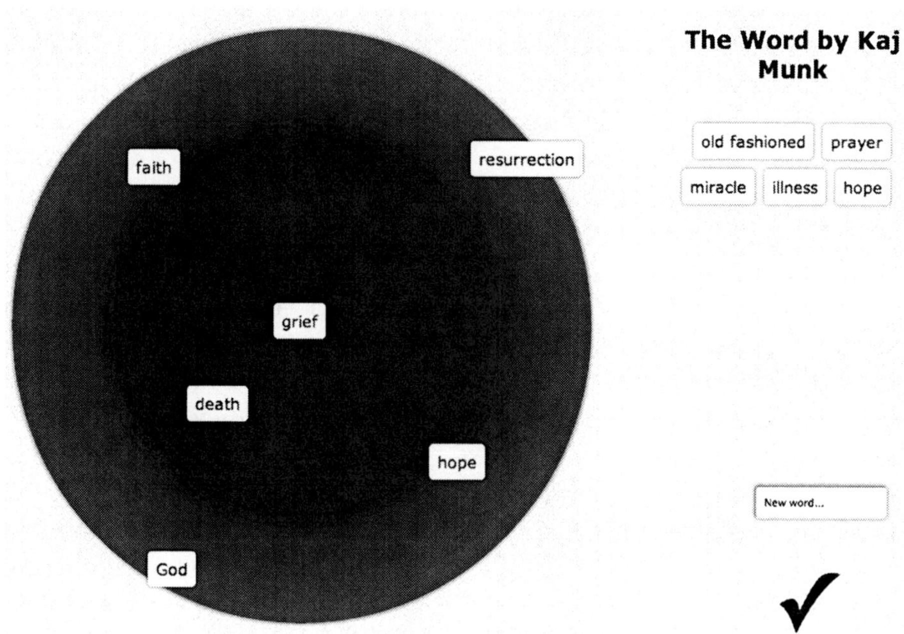

Assuming that the *cognitive style* of the individual user reflects the general distribution in society and that this results in a preferred learning strategy the graphical interface is chosen to cover the presumed learning strategies of most people.

The interface combining both semantic labels and visual action should acknowledge a variety of *learning strategies*. Another possibility would be a text-based interface with strength-markers for every word to be clicked in boxes, as it is often done in questionnaires. This design is ruled out for reasons mentioned above. A combination of the visual interface and click boxes or numeric strength markers would be counterproductive to the overall intuitive experience.

Implementation Complexity of User Freedom

One of the important focuses of The Conceptual Pond is *user freedom*. However, from a practical perspective, it introduces multiple complications to allow the user complete freedom of expression. One such problem is the potential of multiple words with the same meaning in the system. This problem does arise from the fact that variations of the same phrase can be present in the system. These can be introduced from various sources, e.g. words spelled differently or different phrasings with the same meanings. As the user of the system can only be presented with a fixed-size, limited set of the (potentially large) set of previous inputs and predefined suggestions, different users are likely to be suggested different phrasings of the same meaning. Thus, the result will be a diverged representation of a given opinion in the resulting data.

Surely one could just merge diverged phrasings in the resulting data, however, this will happen at the risk of losing valuable differences in the expression of the phrasings and in the end risking biasing the dataset. A better approach would be to catch the diverged phrasings when it occurs, thus allowing the user to determine whether it agrees with the correction. This could be realized with the help of features such as spell checking, autosuggestion from previous entries or even a semantic analysis of the inputted phrasing.

Another problem is that of malicious users potentially providing random, incorrect or offensive new phrases. Such phrases can be eliminated from the resulting data, but as previous entries are presented to new users, one might risk presenting new users with bad or offensive suggestions. To prevent this, one could successfully apply techniques as those proposed for the former problem in order to filter the acceptable inputs, however, it is an ethical question whether this limits the users freedom of expressiveness. Alternatively, the same approaches could be applied only to filter which suggestions are presented to new users, however, this happens at a risk of biasing the resulting data.

Bias of Suggestions

As previously mentioned, one should be careful in the design of pre-emptive techniques not to *bias* the resulting data. However, also the way suggestions are generated must be carefully designed in order to prevent biasing the resulting data.

The approach used in the prototype uses a randomized selection of suggestions based on how commonly they are used. That is, each suggestion is represented in a random drawing a weight equal to number of times it has been selected by users. Initial suggestions are simply represented with a weight further increased by one. The same phrase can only appear once in the suggestions.

This approach has several advantages. Firstly, it ensures that the most commonly used phrases are also more likely to occur in the suggestions for the user, thus ensuring a more consistent resulting dataset. Secondly, it strives to prevent biasing the resulting data by providing a fair drawing of suggestions to display. Thirdly, it minimizes the risk of the initial suggestions biasing the resulting data, as these are not assigned any priority or higher probability to be displayed.

However, experiments with the prototype reveal that the initial suggestions are by far the most commonly selected phrases by the user, thus indicating that biased initial suggestions could bias the entire resulting data. Same experiments also suggest that when a non-initial phrase has been used, it is as likely to be selected in the succeeding submissions as the initial suggestions. This finding can be expected from the fact that under the current selection criteria, when phrases are added incrementally, the total expected frequency of being shown as an initial suggestion is still higher for initial suggestions than for subsequent suggestions (as they are introduced earlier). This indicates a general problem with this approach; that early-added phrases are more likely to be frequently selected by users than phrases added later.

It is an important topic of further research to construct a suggestion algorithm, which entirely prevents bias from the initial suggestions. A suggestion for a better algorithm could be to weight the phrases in a randomized drawing by the time they have not been suggested out of the total amount of suggestions[1] (that is, the sum of number of suggestions over all phrases subtracted the number of suggestions of this phrase), so that less suggested phrases are more likely to be suggested to subsequent participants. This algorithm ensures a more fair total expected frequency of suggestion, however would still suffer for frequency differences, especially with late suggestions, as the frequency requires time to stabilize due to the randomized selection. Alternatively, one could replace the probabilistic choice of suggestions with a deterministic choice, ensuring a minimal time to stabilize frequencies. This, however, has the consequence that new phrases would always be suggested to immediately following participants of the proposer of the phrase. This is potentially problematic in the case of homogeneous groups of immediately following participants, e.g. a school class evaluating a movie at the same time.

Quantification

The Conceptual Pond is a framework for *quantifiable data assessment* thus the quantifiable measures of the assessment are vital. We will now present pilot studies on the quantification of data collected by The Conceptual Pond. Further research should aim at a more systematic approach to data analysis and quantification.

The main data collected by The Conceptual Pond is *phrase valuations*, that is, a numerical value showing correctness of the phrase as assessed by the user. The *phrase frequency*, the number of times a given phrase has been chosen to be of relevance (despite the valuation). An example of aggregated phrase valuations and frequencies can be seen in Figure 2.

While phrase valuations are the main quantifiable measure and word frequencies are subject to bias (as previously discussed), it is however relevant to consider both the valuations and frequencies of phrases. To see this, consider e.g. the word "anger" in Figure 2, which has been assigned a very large valuation but has only been selected once. Considering only the valuation would suggest this phrase to be most significant, whereas the frequency reveals otherwise. For this reason, we consider the default measure to be a combination of phrase valuations and frequencies (as we will see in Figure 3). The combination can be weighted to e.g. lessen the impact of frequencies in the case of a known bias in the suggested phrases.

Finally, The Conceptual Pond also supports the collection of meta-data (e.g. gender, age, time taken to perform the assessment) of the users to facilitate filtering of data as well as comparison among user groups. It should be noticed that it is possible to filter the data to the level of individual responses, in which case it is possible to obtain a qualitative response consisting of phrases selected by the participant as well as a valuation (i.e. confidence) in these.

USE CASES

We will now present two use cases showing the potential of The Conceptual Pond. We also propose a third case study to show the diverse application domains of The Conceptual Pond. To give the reader an impression of the output of the framework, we present examples of results obtainable from the use cases. Acknowledging that this

Figure 2. Aggregated phrase valuations and frequencies based on the case study of "The Word" by Kaj Munk

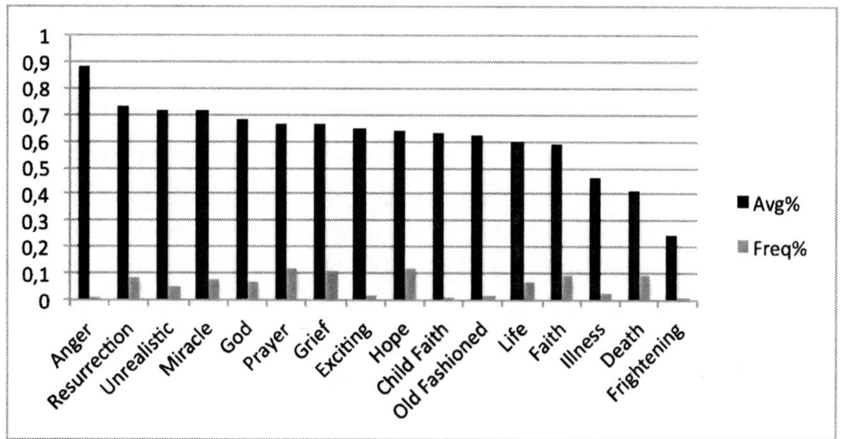

Figure 3. Results from the evaluation of "The Word" by Kaj Munk. The graph shows the combined average phrase valuation and frequency in percent by word. The uncombined aggregated values can be seen in Figure 2.

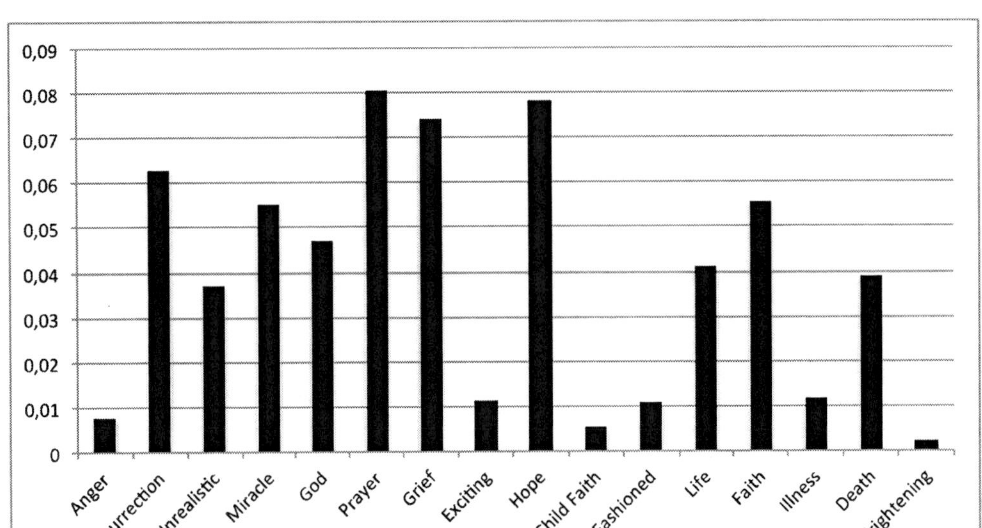

chapter presents a pilot study the resulting data will not be analyzed as thoroughly as in the case of a regular survey in which a larger quantity of users may be preferred. Nevertheless the functionality and qualities of The Conceptual Pond should be recognizable and evident.

Case Study: Cultural Mediation and Evaluation of Learning Outcomes and Reflection

A group of 23 teenagers (13-14 years old) viewed a selected scene of the play "The Word" by Kaj Munk (1962) in a well-known 1955 movie adaptation of Carl Th. Dreyer. The movie was rewarded the Golden Lion Award at the 1955 Venice Film Festival. Despite an antiquated visual language featuring slow dialogue and black/white aesthetics the scene of the resurrection of a woman deceased in childbirth proves to be very moving and is an iconic moment in Danish dramatic tradition. Though this scene is religious in nature it is not kerugmatik (Greek: *Kerygma*, a heralded message) in a theological or homiletic sense.

Question was, however, how would this group of teenagers react to the screening? What are their impressions and reflections? At the same time it was vital not to influence the participants in the survey. Immediately after the screening the teenagers were given a very brief introduction to The Conceptual Pond (2 minutes). Remaining in silence they accessed the system individually contributing with their observations and reflections. The interface was accessed on a laptop PC similar to devices used at school thus eliminating cognitive stress in operation. The laptop was placed in a kiosk setup with the screen turned away in order to secure privacy of the users and avoid possible peer pressure that could bias the results.

Each of the 23 teenagers initiated their session filling out a few pieces of generic information (name, gender, age). Subsequently all contributors accessed the interface and reported their impressions to the system. This process was monitored from some distance to respect privacy and at the same time record the time lapse.

Average operating time was 105 seconds ranging from 25 seconds to 180 seconds. All participants except 2 performed between 75 and 135 seconds. Only one user displayed any hesitation in using the system. None required additional instruction. All 23 participants explicitly preferred The Conceptual Pond to a paper questionnaire. 9 users had specific comments. 2 suggested minor changes in design. 7 applauded the user freedom compared to other evaluation methods (such as questionnaires and qualitative interviews).

A graphical representation of the main results of the evaluation is found in Figure 3. The graph is based on the data available in Appendix 1 and generated from the valuation and frequency of phrases as previously discussed. The graph shows in an easily accessible manner the main phrases associated with this scene of the play as expressed by the participants. Figure 4 shows the same results, only grouped by gender. This allows for a visual comparison between the phrases selected by on male and female participants thus highlighting gender specific differences.

Subsequently the same group of teenagers was presented with a Biblical paraphrase of the fishing expedition of Peter in Luke 5 (results omitted in this chapter). The Conceptual Pond was used in the same way as before displaying only small improvements in speed compared to previous survey (estimated 10 seconds). This is promising, since it suggests that the cognitive load when using the system is concentrated on content reflection rather than operating the system. It is obvious that system operation skills are enhanced at a second application whereas cognitive effort should remain mostly unchanged.

After processing the research results have been discussed with a number of educators. Most notable is the fact that the teenagers did not perceive the movie as old fashioned or frightening, which was the general expectation. On the contrary it is clear that despite of the time span of 87 years (the original play) or 57 years (the movie) the presentation creates connotations coherent with the presumed original intention. From a pedagogy of religion approach it is interesting to note the focus on hope, grief and prayer that seem to indicate a personal reflection rather than a simple retelling of the narrative.

Gender seems to be a less determining factor though a slightly higher occupation with emotionally engaging subjects such as death and anger is present with the female respondents.

Figure 4. Results from the evaluation of "The Word" by Kaj Munk. The graph shows combined average phrase valuation and frequency in percent by word grouped by gender.

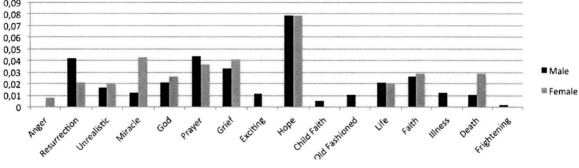

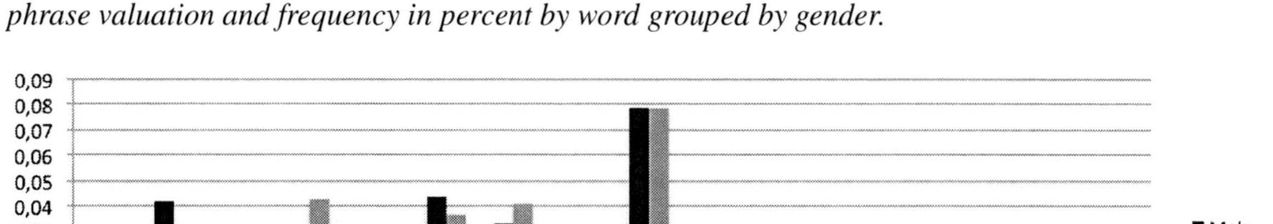

Case Study: Evaluation in the Field of Library Science

A group of 25 users was chosen randomly from users at a rural municipal library (Figure 5). The age of the users ranged from 8 to 76 years of age. The test was performed during regular opening hours in the afternoon, which should support the attendance of a variety of different users in relation to age, gender and interests. A laptop PC was used placed on a table in a quiet corner close to the reception. The screen was turned away from the public and adult users preferred sitting on a chair. The laptop was fitted with a standard mouse to complement the touchpad.

The objective of the survey was to clarify which media types and services from the library were preferred. Default suggestions were defined by the head librarian focusing on types of material such as music, novels, games and nonfiction. There was also an interest in evaluating user appreciation of the library being open to unstaffed services.

Operating the system took a while longer than with the test group of teenagers. 140 seconds on average, ranging from 60 to 240 seconds. 3 users used more than 180 seconds. This is not surprising as many of the participants where children or old age pensioners.

Though the users found no problem in understanding the system, the handling of both the touchpad and the external mouse presented problems for several of the participants over 60 years of age. This suggests that a touch device should be preferred for this diverse group for motoric reasons. In comparison it presented no problem for the teenagers. Except for the motorically challenged users all users expressed satisfaction – especially with the fact, that they were not limited to default options thus creating their own survey environment if desired.

The head librarian praised the survey for being "easy accessible and quick to complete", stressing that "one can use the survey method to acquire new and different descriptions than those thought out by the initiator of the survey himself. That is interesting and perhaps the most important." At the same time he found it in some cases unhelpful that users may interfere with the survey design by changing the agenda through contributing alternative suggestions. This was indeed the case in this survey. While the librarian focused on types of media the users also expressed their interest in genres such as horror and memoirs revealing another bias in conceptualizing the library experience.

The survey results in this case mirror as well the original categorization made by the head librarian as the expressions added by the users.

Figure 5. Results from the survey of preferred media types at a rural municipal library. The graph shows combined average phrase valuation and frequency in percent by word grouped by age.

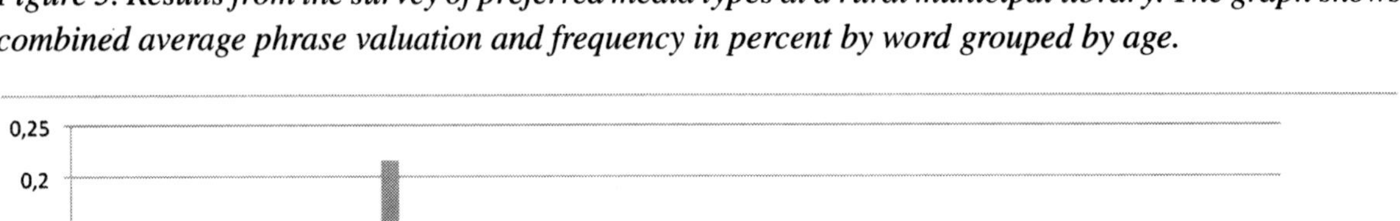

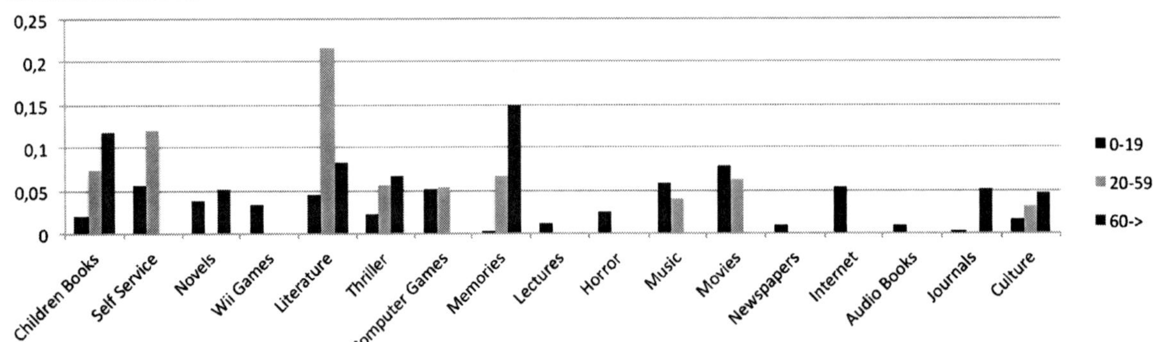

In this example data is presented divided into certain age groups, which is a relevant interest for the library. The survey clearly confirms quite different values and interests amongst the user groups. The older users prefer memoirs and – more surprising – children's books. They have no interest in digital media and they do not enjoy the self-service system that leaves the library often unstaffed. The younger adult users that supposedly have a job during the daytime value the self-service system. The youngest users have an interest in movies, music and games but not least the accessible Internet connection, which is available at the library computers. They value the self service system but probably to a high degree because it allows them to hang out in the library using their favorite category of media – which is in this case most probable not a genre of literature but the internet.

Through this pilot survey it is possible for the library to have a fairly well supported understanding of user preferences and to be able better to allocate staff and investments for the benefit of the different user groups.

Suggested Case Study: Reflective Self-Evaluation in Psychological Treatment

This experiment has not yet been carried out, as it will need to undergo a preliminary ethical screening process. At the same time it has a temporal aspect that will require a user involvement of approx. one year. The potential of The Conceptual Pond is in facilitating self-evaluation and biography reflection in a process of psychological healing. When undergoing a psychological reflection process supervised by a psychologist a challenge often is, that the client does not recognize in depth the changes in emotions and attitudes happening over time. So it may be beneficial for the healing process to possess a chart of previous thoughts and emotions. If such a charting is done through The Conceptual Pond it may be repeated at various intervals thus creating a log of the clients psychology while still allowing a complete freedom of expression for the client. These charts may in be merged into a dynamic dataset that allows for a graphic representation of a temporal process. Thereby both enabling enhanced insight in the client's personal dynamic psychological biography and thus empowering the client for further change for the better. Drawing on the insights of e.g. Riding & Raynor: "The learning performance is likely to be affected by an interaction between cognitive style, and the way the instructional material is structured its mode of presentation its type of content" (2010, p. 140). It is therefore likely that clients with a more visual cognitive style will benefit more from a visual presentation of their psychological development than a simple summary made by the psychologist. Used in such a way the evaluation tool may not only fulfill descriptive purposes, but also serve as a helpful device in enhancing the self-insight of the client thus contributing to the reflection process.

DESIGNING FOR PERSUASION

The persuasive design of The Conceptual Pond is rooted in a combination of several *macrosuasive* and *microsuasive* (Fogg, 2003, p. 18) strategies. They comply with an understanding of effective persuasion as something more complex than the sheer implementation of a number of persuasive tools. Effective persuasion must be developed in the light of the actual aim, conditions and interaction environment.

On the *macrosuasion* level the principles of freedom, self-monitoring and epistemological impact are central factors. The concept of freedom is an underlying value in the system design. Ethical principles are important in this understanding, as elaborated later in the chapter. But freedom is also a crucial factor in persuasion. In contrast to most questionnaires and similar materials used in empirical studies, the user of The Conceptual Pond is free to express herself in any semantic style. This freedom of interaction and user empowerment creates system credibility by allowing the individual considerable autonomy.

Though the principle of user freedom is crucial, it must be balanced with other considerations, such as ease of use and cognitive accessibility. For this reason, a number of predefined markers are instantly available. This is suggestion technology implemented to balance different interests.

The role of self-monitoring and self-assessment is to some extent related to ownership as well. Following Fogg's formula for credibility "perceived trustworthiness + perceived expertise → perceived credibility" (2003, p. 123) the *trustworthiness* supported by the freedom-centered design needs the *expertise* on a functional level. In rhetorical terms, the personal ethos of the application is important but the discursive argument also needs credibility in the enthymeme for the rhetorical agency to succeed. The understanding of this is tied to the twofold Aristotelian approach to epistemology. Recognition may evolve in one of two ways: Either the logic recognition related to the syllogisms or the rhetorical recognition of the enthymeme. Syllogistic logic is connected with undisputable and recognizable facts, logical arguments and mathematics. The rhetorical enthymeme is connected with everyday decisions such as determining the level of trust in another person or determining the probability of rain the next day. In the epistemological framework trustworthiness is a vital factor with the concept of the enthymeme (in fact the root of epistemology is *pistis*, Greek: faith).

Self-assessment is supported by the possibility of comparing with previous visits. Comparing results with other users facilitates social comparison, and this feature may be extended to a broad context in social media or in a narrow context e.g. the virtual Kaj Munk Research Lab, which is an online toolbox for research in Kaj Munk.

Facilitating self-assessment and the creation of a personal portfolio The Conceptual Pond proves to support an epistemological process. Using the application adds definition, codification and reflection to the experience in question. The choice of words in the semantic expression and the positioning of the markers on the graphic interface entail a cognitive process and is prompted by the persuasive design. Using the application is similar to using an authoring tool with a creative impact.

In a less fundamental level, though perhaps not quite microsuasive, persuasive strategies are connected to the interface design. The interface is simple and offers instant overview. Navigation is intuitive, using a comfortable drag-and-drop function to choose semantic content. The movement is persuasive due to the tangible impression of functionality and the instant gratification of watching the application be filled out in a short time.

Kairos

Bringing the ancient rhetorical concept of *kairos* into play in a postmodern paradigm facilitates a three-dimensional view to the potential of The Conceptual Pond. Reaching kairos is the art of designing and applying technology at exactly the right time, at exactly the right place and in the exact right manner. This suggests an ecological approach focusing on adaptable systems design suitable for any learning environment.

The kairos approach also offers guidelines for evaluation of the evaluation system itself; is the system consistent in its adaptability confronted with the requirements of adaptability in time, place and mode?

The Opportune Moment

Designing a system to embrace input that is also of a reflective or emotional nature requires that the system may be present at the *opportune moment.* Is this the case with The Conceptual Pond? It may be argued that it is actually the case. This IT-supported mode of assessment is available at all times of day and night and does not require the presence of a supporting helper such as a teacher or a guide. It may be performed in the solitude of the night or in a crowd by day.

From a perspective of reflection it is imperative that some acts of evaluation are carried out immediately after receiving the impression. In the use case of the teenagers evaluation of impressions from viewing the Kaj Munk play, they still had the experience in vivid memory when accessing the survey.

Another aspect of kairos is the time elapsing carrying out a task. In relation to this it is promising that tests displayed response times between 95 and 140 sec. on average which appears considerably less time consuming than comparable questionnaires.

The Opportune Location

Since learning and reflection takes place in a number of environments it is imperative that the evaluation system may be available everywhere. This is the case since The Conceptual Pond is accessible through all kind of devices such as smartphones, tablets or pc. This allows for it being used in the open country by the Kaj Munk Vicarage Museum, at a kiosk at the library or at a school computer.

Location might also point to geographical or language barriers. Since the surveys may be configured to any language using Latin letters it may be applied in almost any setting.

The Opportune Manner

The third aspect of kairos refers to the function and characteristics of the system itself. Does it offer content in a contextually relevant way? In relation to The Conceptual Pond the question primarily is one of mediation. As shown in the use cases the choice of technology and mode proves to be convincing. Apart from the few motorical problems handling a non-touch device the system seems fully sustainable. Offering the use of The Conceptual Pond on a generous number of touch devices should facilitate reflection and assessment in a helpful way thus mediating in the opportune manner.

Ethical Considerations

Ethical considerations are relevant in the development of The Conceptual Pond. These considerations are implemented in the design process with the focus on two essential questions:

First, the problem of the *unbiased assessment:* German Philosopher Jürgen Habermas is probably best known for his *discourse ethics* with the understanding, that truth is the result of an unbiased conversation, *communicative rationality*. In The Conceptual Pond design process it is helpful to implement Habermas' ideas of "dominance free dialogue" and "dominance free space" (Habermas, 2008). The underlying principle is the understanding of *free speech* as a central prerequisite for approaching truth.

Second, another, yet kindred question is the question of freedom. Danish Theologian K.E. Løgstrup expresses this. He claims to identify a number of "sovereign expressions of life" (Løgstrup, 1997); trust, compassion, love and the *open speech*. Though some of Løgstrup's basic philosophical premises may be problematized (as he is sometimes accused of committing the naturalistic fallacy), the concept of *open speech* is a vital ethical consideration also here (Gram-Hansen, 2009).

Both of these philosophical ethical standards support the personal integrity of the user. Though a totally unbiased application may be utopian the ethical standards should contribute to enhanced user freedom. Some concrete choices in the design process must therefore be taken with an active implementation of ethical standards working towards an unbiased and open system.

These deontological approaches to ethics do not rest unchallenged. From a utilitarian perspective the focus on bias or freedom should in necessary yield in recognition of the common good, thus presenting a less individualistic approach.

Complying with Fogg's comment that "Identifying intent is a key step in making evaluation about ethics" (2003, p. 221) the intent of the application is obviously a consideration. The intent may be divided in four use scenarios.

The first is the use for self-evaluation, e.g. through using the application for clarifying thoughts or a personal portfolio. This use is unproblematic.

The second use is the functionality in relation to legitimate assessment and evaluation in the education sector. The Conceptual Pond may be a valuable tool and the use is unproblematic, since it merely substitutes the writing of essays expressing the same information.

The third use is linked to analyzing anonymized data sets. Since this is in the public interest and presents no indiscretion for the user it is unproblematic.

The fourth use entails an aspect of surveillance. Personal opinions and judgments may be of interest to certain persons, but with no legitimate reasons this is highly problematic and requires a system design, that guards the privacy of the user.

LESSONS LEARNED

We have learned that The Conceptual Pond is well suited for many areas of application, as well for a wide range of participants. It seems evident that the good results achieved in this pilot study may lead to a larger scale implementation.

We have also learned that it is important to tailor the actual survey environment for optimizing the experience for the user and the benefit of the survey.

Thirdly we have observed that The Conceptual Pond through its open structure collects data of a good quality. This data may be reviewed and presented favorably through combined qualities from qualitative research and qualities of quantitative comparison.

These positive results do by no means extinguish the need for further research and the clarification and refinement of the process.

FURTHER RESEARCH

Further research is needed to clarify the potential of The Conceptual Pond and possible pitfalls. The first step will be to implement the system in a number of use cases, including the Kaj Munk-case of EUROPlot. The health and prevention sector has already been mentioned, and the engaging, persuasive principles of the design should be directly applicable in many health care and prevention contexts.

As previously mentioned, it is also a topic of further research how the general suggestions of words should be carried out in order to impose as little bias in the survey as possible. Multiple approaches have already been suggested and should be implemented and evaluated. It should furthermore be examined if more strict requirements for the amount, diversity and semantic fields of suggestions should be introduced in order to limit the bias of the survey.

Data analysis and quantifications should be approached more systematically than what has been done in these pilot studies. The approach should relate to existing frameworks.

We would also like to explore the potential of using graphically based input rather than textual input. This approach could be feasible in evaluating and creating reflections for children and other individuals, for whom a textual interaction seems not applicable. Multiple topics of further research arise from this regarding both the validity of the approach, possible technical limitations and establishing a visual rhetoric.

Finally, it may be argued that more work needs to be done in the field of semantic categorization in order to achieve optimal accuracy. This research is at present undertaken at Aalborg University in relation to searchable texts related to the EMDROS Database and the Kaj Munk Research Center. The process of developing semantic searches should provide relevant tools for adding a semantic layer to The Conceptual Pond for the benefit of registration and evaluation.

CONCLUSION

The Conceptual Pond is a novel and innovative design implementing persuasive technologies to the solution of a very concrete assignment. The application seems to present the quality of being transferrable to a multitude of other contexts and environments, in which persuasive design strategies until now have not been a dominant factor. For these reasons, the design should be explored further and refined.

The intuitive interface and persuasive design of The Conceptual Pond has shown to facilitate easy interaction with the system and can even be extended to allow evaluation and reflections for groups that are not generally reachable with traditional assessment approaches. Combined with the strong focus on freedom of expression, The Conceptual Pond is applicable in a large variety of situations and for a broad audience.

Working with The Conceptual Pond project has given rise to several interesting discourses and recognitions. First of all, may we argue convincingly that assessment is as much a part of perception as it is a tool for accountability? In Odenberg's *constructed-response* tasks (Odendahl, 2011) the tasks have a primary focus on assessment. The dynamics of The Conceptual Pond should be directed more towards an epistemological impact. On the basis of the pilot study it seems reasonable to argue that completing a suitable evaluation process should enhance the learning outcomes and the level of reflection for the benefit of deeper learning.

It does not mean that this chapter aims to endorse a very proactive test-focused pedagogical thinking. There is a difference between assessment as a tool for reflection and self-evaluation and testing in a Benthamian Panopticon. While testing and grading are essential pillars in society it is questionable whether a stronger focus on testing and evaluation might increase the already considerable cognitive load of expectations haunting symbol analysts from kindergarten all through working life.

Would this uneasiness about a high level of assessment be an argument not to employ The Conceptual Pond too often? On the contrary. Assessment, evaluation, and surveys are valuable tools in a varied epistemological approach. The question should be formulated differently: How do we apply assessment so that it does not only capture factual knowledge or unargumented opinion in a datasheet but does indeed add the extra value of reflection and inner experience to the process of expressing your personal impressions and inner discourse?

The Conceptual Pond is breaking new ground in utilizing a virtual assessment system for qualitative experiences in a systematized way that may contribute valid quantitative feedback. The rise of social media, applications for interpersonal communication as well as the games industry has opened new perspectives, namely for the computer to be a partner in discovering and experiencing the world. The binary codes of the technical architecture have often shaped the format of input into binary slots thus limiting the actual cognitive and emotional potential of the system. The Conceptual Pond demonstrates that this is not a law of nature. Perhaps the crucial difference to traditional survey methods is the level of freedom that is ascribed in the expressions of the user.

Could you share the sensation of hearing the first bird singing in a silent morning of spring? Could this experience be expressed meaningfully and reflected upon within a virtual architecture? Could you reflect upon it and allow these impressions and reflections to be shared and understood in the framework of a system of evaluation and assessment? All these approaches seem possible.

This chapter calls for an interdisciplinary approach to applied computer science. Through The Conceptual Pond project the authors of this chapter have combined skills of technical computer science with insights from human and technical sciences. This common effort resulted in The Conceptual Pond – suggesting a framework for connecting the paradigms of quality and quantity since a sustainable understanding of life and the world requires both.

REFERENCES

Biggs, J., & Tang, C. (2007). *Teaching for quality learning at university* (3rd ed.). Buckingham, UK: SRHE and Open University Press.

Bloom, B. (1956). *Taxonomy of educational objectives, the classification of educational goals – Handbook I: Cognitive domain.* New York: Academic Press.

Fogg, B. (2003). *Persuasive technology – Using computers to change what we say and do.* San Francisco, CA: Academic Press.

Gram-Hansen, S. B. (2009). Towards an approach to ethics and HCI development based on Løgstrup's ideas. *Lecture Notes in Computer Science, 5726*, 200–203. doi:10.1007/978-3-642-03655-2_24.

Gram-Hansen, S. B., Schärfe, H., & Dinesen, J. W. (2011). Towards a context oriented approach to ethical evaluation of interactive technologies. *Lecture Notes in Computer Science, 6949*, 628–631. doi:10.1007/978-3-642-23768-3_99.

Gram-Hansen, S. B., Schärfe, H., & Dinesen, J. W. (2012). Plotting to persuade – Exploring the theoretical cross field between persuasion and learning. *Lecture Notes in Computer Science, 7284*, 262–267. doi:10.1007/978-3-642-31037-9_24.

Habermas, J. (2008). *Diskursetik.* Copenhagen, Denmark: Academic Press.

Ham, J., & Midden, C. (2010). Ambient persuasive technology needs little cognitive effort: The differential effects of cognitive load on lighting feedback versus factual feedback. *Lecture Notes in Computer Science*, 6137.

Hooper-Greenhil, E. (2004). Measuring learning outcomes in museums, archives and libraries: The learning impact research project. *International Journal of Heritage Studies, 10*(2). doi:10.1080/13527250410001692877.

Jespersen, J. L., Albrechtslund, A., Øhrstrøm, P., Hasle, P., & Albretsen, J. (2007). Surveillance, persuasion, and panopticon. *Lecture Notes in Computer Science.* doi:10.1007/978-3-540-77006-0_15.

Lehto, T., & Oinas-Kukkonen, H. (2010). Persuasive features in six weight loss websites: A qualitative evaluation. *Lecture Notes in Computer Science*, 6137.

Løgstrup, K. (1997). *The ethical demand.* South Bend, IN: University of Notre Dame Press.

Munk, K. (1962). *Kærlighed og andre skuespil.* Copenhagen: Academic Press.

Munson, S., Lauterbach, D., Newman, M., & Resnick, P. (2010). Happier together: Integrating a wellness application into a social network site. *Lecture Notes in Computer Science*, 6137.

Odendahl, N. V. (2011). Testwise - Understanding educational assessment. Lanham.

Oinas-Kukkonen, H. (2008). A systematic framework for designing and evaluating persuasive systems. In *Proceedings of Persuasive 2008.* Springer. doi:10.1007/978-3-540-68504-3_15.

Oinas-Kunnonen, H. (2010). Behavior change support systems: A research model and agenda. *Lecture Notes in Computer Science*, 6137.

Petersen, V. (1999). Modern scientific management - Or the attempt to measure everything that counts. Aarhus.

Riding, R., & Rayner, S. (2010). *Cognitive styles and learning strategies*. London: Academic Press.

Rossman, G. B., & Rallis, S. F. (2012). *Learning in the field*. Thousand Oaks, CA: SAGE.

KEY TERMS AND DEFINITIONS

Conceptual: Based on a concept, an understanding, an impression or an interpretation of an experience, a thought or an object.

Cultural Mediation: The mediation of cultural content in areas such as museums, libraries, churches, heritage.

Kairos: The opportune moment. Term from classic rhetoric depicting the appropriate temporal, locational or modal position.

Qualitative Data: Data of an unstructured or less structured nature such as interviews or focus group observations gathered for research purposes.

Quantification: Transforming qualitative data into generic data that will fit into conventional quantitative cross tabulation and presentations such as graphs.

Quantitative Data: Data of a primarily structured nature such as predefined questionnaires or countable observations gathered for research purposes.

Semantic Fields: The denotations of a word and its close connotations defining the meaning of the word.

User Freedom: The empowerment of the user to navigate and interact with the system according to his own preferences.

APPENDIX 1

Table 1 contains the resulting data from the use case of "The Word" by Kaj Munk. Columns that are not used in figures in this chapter have been omitted.

Table 1. The resulting data from the use case analysis of "The Word" by Kaj Munk

Gender	(Phrase, Valuation 0-100)
Male	(Death, 28.81156), (Grief, 85.60890), (Prayer, 89.58404), (Hope, 66.68017)
Female	(Death, 88.76616), (Prayer, 95.37834), (God, 88.44012), (Hope, 79.71120), (Miracle, 39.31037), (Life, 51.75873)
Female	(Miracle, 79.99728), (Death, 67.47018), (Grief, 3.097346), (Life, 40.44142), (Prayer, 27.40861), (Hope, 7.590925), (Faith, 44.43596), (Hope, 51.50396)
Female	(Unrealistic, 94.04557)
Male	(Resurrection, 99.64448), (Life, 63.77109), (Prayer, 54.75897), (Exciting, 46.49599), (God, 39.96900), (Hope, 49.36021), (Faith, 21.56138), (Illness, 14.96827), (Unrealistic, 12.78089), (Frightening, 24.27796)
Male	(Life, 91.54958), (Prayer, 85.06427), (Death, 54.98245)
Male	(Resurrection, 81.88793), (Grief, 73.67429)
Male	(Hope, 54.55868), (Faith, 67.07583), (Life, 26.09457), (God, 23.72386), (Resurrection, 75.41538)
Male	(Faith, 82.84448), (Resurrection, 92.49541), (Life, 58.35849), (Prayer, 73.83954), (Miracle, 64.42003), (Child Faith, 63.45185), (Old Fashioned, 53.15762)
Female	(Miracle, 79.57338), (Grief, 66.72814), (Death, 21.31205), (Faith, 75.78151), (Hope, 24.69843)
Female	(Hope, 52.57853), (Life, 51.82165), (Grief, 76.30459), (Death, 32.44966), (Prayer, 31.57962), (Faith, 29.82334)
Male	(Miracle, 75.39072), (God, 97.75154), (Prayer, 67.12697)
Female	(Faith, 83.52714), (Prayer, 81.61725), (God, 93.84132), (Grief, 53.69207)
Male	(Hope, 96.26289), (Grief, 75.67762), (Exciting, 82.84309)
Female	(Grief, 45.25161), (God, 63.58996), (Miracle, 61.18663), (Faith, 47.98809)
Female	(Grief, 87.17186), (Anger, 87.99798), (Resurrection, 68.52465), (Death, 34.77447), (God, 54.36551), (Miracle, 65.94129), (Hope, 59.66091)
Female	(Resurrection, 87.91260), (Death, 66.14452), (Miracle, 84.39873), (Hope, 67.66249), (Grief, 69.99761), (Prayer, 73.40329), (Resurrection, 90.74439)
Male	(Resurrection, 24.14607), (Hope, 47.50328), (Faith, 80.29064)
Male	(Old Fashioned, 71.58105), (Unrealistic, 86.29722), (Hope, 91.33469), (God, 84.71050), (Illness, 66.71048), (Resurrection, 53.47030), (Faith, 57.10985), (Prayer, 72.74427), (Grief, 66.61210)
Male	(Illness, 56.04239), (Unrealistic, 95.18645), (Prayer, 62.11204), (Resurrection, 57.48087)
Female	(Miracle, 89.97167), (Death, 7.325220), (Prayer, 52.57040), (Hope, 56.59085), (Unrealistic, 50.89066)
Female	(Faith, 54.87488), (Life, 92.10635), (Hope, 62.33235), (Grief, 76.06815), (Prayer, 67.28421), (Death, 13.49607), (Unrealistic, 90.76541)
Male	(Death, 36.22745), (Hope, 80.71139), (Grief, 79.48285)

APPENDIX 2

Table 2 contains the resulting data from the survey of preferred media types at a rural municipal library. Columns that are not used in figures in this chapter have been omitted.

Table 2. The resulting data from the survey of preferred media types at a rural municipal library

Age Group	(Phrase, Valuation 0-100)
20-59	(Literature, 95.69809), (Movies, 15.51044), (Self Service, 84.41606), (Culture, 41.83938)
20-59	(Computer Games, 71.00207), (Music, 53.95853), (Movies, 67.01657), (Self Service, 71.26016)
0-19	(Computer Games, 97.46051), (Internet, 35.64565), (Movies, 31.02280)
0-19	(Computer Games, 91.45481), (Horror, 62.33603), (Movies, 50.85374), (Literature, 39.10599)
0-19	(Music, 82.28102), (Wii Games, 61.54103), (Movies, 69.33388), (Internet, 83.59581), (Self Service, 57.99506), (Thriller, 47.91879)
60->	(Children Books, 84.44620), (Thriller, 79.73083), (Memories, 83.75112)
60->	(Memories, 52.93877), (Literature, 77.17258), (Culture, 26.32355)
0-19	(Movies, 25.79153), (Music, 34.53512), (Novels, 76.05468), (Internet, 42.71665), (Literature, 75.66671), (Culture, 18.43988)
60->	(Literature, 21.47660), (Culture, 30.79916), (Memories, 44.32441), (Journals, 62.22592), (Children Books, 58.79788), (Novels, 60.87346)
20-59	(Literature, 97.09816), (Memories, 87.89536)
0-19	(Literature, 86.07217), (Horror, 43.81461), (Journals, 8.299223), (Lectures, 53.63929), (Thriller, 50.45511), (Music, 39.98416), (Computer Games, 27.82906), (Audio Books, 39.16092), (Memories, 12.17087), (Self Service, 96.84765), (Newspapers, 41.25751), (Movies, 73.63543), (Internet, 32.73548), (Culture, 56.27157)
0-19	(Children Books, 88.78924), (Novels, 97.06567), (Movies, 15.36964), (Computer Games, 11.64023), (Internet, 41.71272), (Music, 16.86170)
20-59	(Children Books, 95.34564), (Thriller, 71.80071), (Literature, 87.55137)
0-19	(Music, 81.97818), (Movies, 76.80004), (Self Service, 91.09282), (Internet, 4.587579), (Wii Games, 91.56618)

[1]The first suggestions could be handled individually to prevent all phrases to be assigned a weight of 0.

Section 7

The Future

Chapter 24
Playful Interfaces for Scientific Image Data:
A Case for Storytelling

Amalia Kallergi
Leiden University, The Netherlands

Fons J. Verbeek
Leiden University, The Netherlands

ABSTRACT

Recent developments in the field of HCI draw our attention to the potential of playful interfaces, play, and games. This chapter identifies a new but relevant application domain for playful interfaces (i.e. scientific practice involving image data). Given the thesis that play and playfulness are relevant for a researcher's interaction with scientific images, the question remains: How do we design playful interfaces that support meaningful ways to playfully engage with scientific images? This chapter introduces, investigates, and implements storytelling with scientific images as a worthwhile instance of playful interaction with scientific images. To better understand and further exemplify the potential of storytelling with scientific images, the chapter contributes both a review of utilitarian usages of storytelling with images and findings from a case study storytelling game.

INTRODUCTION

This chapter considers recent Human Computer Interaction (HCI) developments regarding play and playfulness and their applicability for the design of interfaces for scientific data. Scientific practice is a particularly important human activity, both economically and socially, and a data-intensive practice that can be extensively and diversely supported by computerized systems. We believe that interfaces to scientific data can facilitate interactions that go beyond the stereotypical use of computers as data processing machines. Well-designed interfaces, effective displays and interactive tools can potentially empower the human researcher by easing her tasks and amplifying her cognitive capacities. And yet, scientific practice is somewhat neglected by the field of HCI, with interfaces to scientific data often lacking behind current developments in the field. The toolkit of the state-of-the-art HCI has been extended with powerful constructs such as innovative hardware,

DOI: 10.4018/978-1-4666-4623-0.ch024

new visualization techniques and interdisciplinary concepts such as serious games. Motivated by the enormous interest of HCI in play and games, this study considers play and playfulness as a means to interact and engage with scientific data.

The need for playful interfaces in the sciences becomes even more prominent when considering the creative nature of scientific inquiry. Scientists are professionals who engage daily in creative problem posing and solving. There is nothing mystical or romantic here, no muse visitations or bursts of inspiration: Scientific practice is creative for it "involves slow, methodical work, with mini-insights occurring every day" (Sawyer, 2006, p. 269). Such mini-insights vary from new ideas to new observations to new realizations and new inferences and can be based on or derived by scientific data. We believe that such creative responses to data can be facilitated by a more open-minded and playful attitude of the researcher. Creative responses to data can inform everyday scientific practice but, for such responses to occur, a moment of openness, playfulness and exploration may be required.

If play and playfulness are relevant for scientific practice and if play and playfulness are relevant for the design of interfaces, how do we design playful interfaces that support relevant ways to playfully engage with scientific data? This chapter introduces, investigates and implements storytelling with scientific images as a worthwhile instance of playful interaction. We conduct a broad review of practices and products involving storytelling with images and further implement a case study game that promotes storytelling with scientific images. Our major contribution is the investigation of storytelling as a means to playfully engage with scientific images. Nonetheless, our take on playful interfaces revisits current practices in playful and game-ful design by encouraging an understanding of playful interfaces as interfaces that are playful not because of added playful elements but because of playfulness embedded in the interaction.

BACKGROUND

Definitions

This subsection will briefly define the core topics of this chapter. Note that we aim at providing a general understanding and a common ground in terminology; formal or finite definitions of the concepts involved are out of the scope of this subsection.

Play and Playfulness

Delineating the concept of play is a difficult task and any attempt to do so will unavoidably start from the seminal writings of Huizinga (1955) and Caillois (2001). For a compilation of major formal definitions of play and of game the reader is referred to Salen and Zimmerman (2004). Confronted with the ambiguity of play, Salen and Zimmerman (2004) propose three families of activities, each a superset of the previous:

- Game play, i.e. activities that involve games.
- Ludic activities, i.e. activities commonly understood as play.
- Playful activities, i.e. ordinary activities exercised in a playful manner.

Eventually, the authors propose a definition of play as 'free movement within a more rigid structure'. This definition, complemented with the aforementioned families of play-related activities, should be sufficient for our discussion.

We define playfulness as the inclination to be less serious, i.e. either more humorous or more experimental or looking for fun and amusement. Playfulness can be understood as the inclination to play; this definition, however, requires us to demarcate what play is. On the contrary, playfulness as the inclination to be less serious allows us to reconsider what engaging in play may amount to. To quote Fullerton et al. (2008, p. 92), "a playful approach can be applied to even the most serious of difficult subject because playfulness is a state of mind rather than an action". Note that we consider playfulness as an attitude, not as a personality trait, and one that can be induced. Finally, we will be using the term 'playful' as in 'playful interface' and 'playful interaction' to refer to interfaces that are both an invitation to play and an invitation to adopt a playful attitude. However, as we shall see, the term 'playful interface' is not without its cultural baggage within the field of HCI.

Stories and Storytelling

A story is an account of events; these events can be "either true or false" (Polkinghorne, 1988, chapter II). Everyone's got a story to tell, and it need not be one of a literary value. Stories and narratives can be treated as either synonym or distinct terms depending on whether a story is understood as distinct from its rendering (Abbott, 2007). We use the term 'story' and 'narrative' interchangeably, with story being the account of a sequence of events rather than only the sequence of events accounted. This definition is closer to an everyday understanding of the term 'story' but it still allows us to consult the extensive field of narratology, i.e. the study of narratives. However, here be dragons! The field of narratology is a fearsome one, perturbed by its own definition wars, including ones on the definition of narrative. An account of a sequence of events may not always demonstrate a satisfying degree of 'narrativity'; a typical example given is the chronicle.

For the remainder of this chapter, the term 'storytelling' will refer to the telling of a story that is actively generated by the storyteller, rather than the reciting of an existing story. Story-making need not be mediated by an artefact, but there exists a long tradition of 'user-generated' stories, i.e. stories unfolded or produced by the user's interaction with a tool or platform. Numerous environments or strategies have been attributed a capacity to support or engage a reader or player into the production of narratives: Hypertext fiction, interactive storytelling and videogames, mainly adventure and role-playing games, are a few typical examples, all distinct in their mechanics and aesthetics and yet alike in their ascribed potentials to transform 'traditional' narratives. From a cybertext theory (Aarseth, 1997) perspective, user-generated stories will involve 'non-trivial effort' and interaction with a mechanism/algorithm operating on a set of building tokens. We are aware of this tradition of interactive and playable stories and acknowledge the impact of technologies and interactivity on the way stories emerge. Technically, the use of small units of information to be assembled by the user in a meaningful storyline is a theme we adhere to. However, we are less interested on the trails of the user as an output (cf. hypertext) or the choices of the player on particular forking or decision points (cf. interactive storytelling).

HCI Ludens: Meeting Points of HCI and Play

This subsection will summarize recent HCI developments regarding play, games and playfulness. Such developments have motivated our interest in play and playfulness as elements of interfaces to scientific data.

Playful Interfaces

Kuts (2009) reviews HCI literature on 'playful interfaces' and reports the following notion of playfulness within HCI: "The definition of playfulness in user experience can be crystallized as elements of a design that engage people's attention or involve them into activity for play, amusement, or creative enjoyment". In a sense, playful interfaces are interfaces that invoke positive affect by playful features. The interest of HCI in playful interfaces has been, in times, preceded, intertwined or running in parallel with an interest in issues of fun and pleasure. Draper (1999), Monk et al. (2002), Carroll (2004), Blythe et al. (2004) and

Shneiderman (2004) have all argued in favor of fun and pleasure as components of the user experience that are relevant for the design of interfaces. Today, user experience research is a prominent and well established subject within HCI. Various suggestions and guidelines for the design of fun/playful/enjoyable interfaces have been articulated: In a classic work, Malone (1982) proposes heuristics for the design of enjoyable interfaces, namely challenge, fantasy and curiosity, by examining how players of video games experience fun. More recently, Shneiderman (2004) proposes a toolkit of fun features consisting of graphics, animations, sounds, alluring metaphors and compelling content. Finally, Kuts (2009) reports on aspects of the interface that are considered playful, such as exploration, customization and feedback, and proposes a set of user interface components to promote them.

Gamification

Gamification as "the use of game design elements in nongame contexts" (Deterding et al., 2011) is a relatively new development in the design of application software. Deterding et al. (2011) acknowledge that gamification approximates the tradition of 'playful interfaces' and previous initiatives of HCI to learn from video games but are confident that gamification can serve as a research topic of its own sake. The trend has already been heavily criticized by game scholars and game designers alike, who observe a tendency to superficially gamify applications: Much too often, application designers have advocated gamification of applications by means of extrinsic rewards resulting in an abuse of game elements such as points and badges. At present, the HCI community remains active in discussing and better understanding the issues raised by gamification, especially the issue of motivation via game elements.

Serious Games

Serious games are games for purposes other than mere entertainment (Alvarez & Michaud, 2008; Susi et al., 2007). The underlying idea is that educational or other objectives can be successfully conveyed via the medium of video games. Serious games have found applications in a variety of fields and industries such as education, marketing, training and social awareness but their success and quality varies. For example, instruction games with drill and practice exercises have been heavily criticized as the worst of both worlds, i.e. bad education and bad gameplay (Charsky, 2010). On the contrary, simulations and games that train the corresponding skills, be it motor skills or problem solving skills, may have more promising potential.

Games with a Purpose

Games with a purpose (von Ahn, 2006) are games that harvest human effort during play. As such, they provide an effective mechanism to utilize humans for traditionally challenging areas of computation. The underlying idea is that we can engage humans in tedious tasks, and bring human computation and crowd-sourcing to a new level, if we transform these tasks into games. The paradigm has been applied successfully at numerous occasions for problems that are either computationally challenging or simply tedious. For example, the 'ESP game' (von Ahn & Dabbish, 2004) was a pioneering example in producing semantic image annotations, i.e. annotations about the content of an image, via game play. Siorpaes and Hepp (2008) review more game examples relevant to the field of semantic web technologies, an area that traditionally requires painstaking effort in capturing human knowledge. Another significant example of human computation via play can be found in the domain of biological sciences. The game 'fold-it' is a puzzle game for predicting protein structures. Players of the game have collectively outperformed state-of-the art algorithms while, at the same time, suggesting new solution strategies (Cooper et al., 2010).

INTRODUCING STORYTELLING AS PLAYFUL INTERACTION WITH SCIENTIFIC IMAGE DATA

Motivated by recent developments in HCI regarding play and games, our study emphasizes the potential role of playful interfaces to scientific data as a means to stimulate creative responses to scientific data. In the previous section, we provided an overview of relevant HCI traditions and trends regarding the notion of play and games. These traditions inform us that play and games have considerable potentials for learning, user engagement and motivation and that enjoyment is a considerable part of the user experience. The potentials of play and games are relevant: Openness, playfulness and positive affect are essential components of an attitude that favors exploration and creativity. However, if we are to design playful interfaces and games for the sake of creative responses to scientific data, we need to consider the creative processes involved and desired. We also believe that playfulness can not be an added feature of the interface but should emerge from what is inherently playful and creative in scientific practice involving scientific data. Finally, if we are to design playful interfaces or games that are of relevance, we must carefully consider the particularities of the data in question and the workflows of the scientists in question.

Our study specializes on data repositories of a specific domain of science, i.e. the life sciences, and of a particular type of data, i.e. image data. Partially motivated by our research expertise, the choice of subject is not without its justification: Biological research is an excellent example of a data-intensive scientific practice, with an increasing number of research databases available. Furthermore, biology is a science typically oriented around visual clues. The production, inspection and analysis of image-based observations is an indispensable part of contemporary biological research. From the various functions and roles of images in the research workflow and scientific discourse of the biologist, we focus on images as preliminary or intermediate findings used to guide and refine research choices. Consider the following, simplified take on biological imaging for research purposes: Biologists make images in order to study biological phenomena; they design experiments and image their samples in order to test hypotheses, to track biological entities or processes or to model organisms. Image data are to be observed, discussed, reflected upon and further tested by designing new or refined experiments. Note that the processes involved are often social and collaborative. They may also require comparing or contrasting the acquired image data to other reference images. Via such processes, image data become significant signposts in directing research and decision-making. In a sense, we understand ongoing research involving image data as a process of refining research experiments and choices by incorporating image-based observations. Such observations can be facilitated by various mechanisms such as a new look into one's own images, a new association between one's own images and one's repository of background knowledge, or a new association between one's own data and the data of another researcher. In other words, creative responses to image data, be it new ideas, questions or insights, can further inform a research path and, for such responses to occur, it is often useful to re-consider and re-interpret one's own images under a new light, under the light of other images and under the light of new, even non-obvious and unexpected, associations.

What kind of play can we devise that will invite a playful and creative (re)consideration of scientific images? Our work investigates a particular instance of playful interaction that we find worthwhile, i.e. storytelling with images. Our understanding of creative responses to images emphasizes the role of associations, the possibility to re-view data under a new light or under the light of other data and the role of imagination as a way to articulate potentially useful ideas and create new associations. We suggest that storytelling may provide a valid strategy to ignite similar processes: By creating opportunities for storytelling and confronting the player with the challenges of story composition, we hope to create opportunities for a great deal of re-consideration, re-interpretation, imagination and filling-in of gaps to be at work. Note that we focus on the processes active during story-making rather than on the output stories. Potentially, storytelling and the processes we associate with it can be exercised in a shared or social context.

UNDERSTANDING STORYTELLING WITH IMAGES

This section provides an overview of well-established functions and applications of storytelling in general and of storytelling with images in particular. Essentially, storytelling involves a process of articulation and of synthesis which we find particularly valuable. In addition, the considerable playful and social dimensions of storytelling are of equal relevance.

Functions of Storytelling as Found in Literature

There is a substantial tradition on storytelling as a means to understanding. Firstly, stories have been long acknowledged as carriers of information and as a means to transmit know-how, beliefs and values across generations. Their cultural significance aside, stories are powerful communication tools. This applies to the domain of science as well: As most science communicators would confirm, stories about famous scientists, significant scientific discoveries and even complex scientific phenomena are powerful and engaging educational aids. An extensive overview of the applicability of narratives for science education and science communication is provided by Avraamidou and Osborne (2009). Clearly, stories help transmit a message and make a speaker easier understood. But can a story make a speaker easier understood to the speaker herself? In other words, can the composition of a story contribute to understanding? Several practices would support the case as stories have been frequently used to either elicit or organize information. Consider as an example the use of narratives in social science research: Stories have been repeatedly used as the means for human subjects to articulate about their experiences. What is more, narrative inquiry as a methodology engages with stories as both the subject and the means of the inquiry. That is to say, stories are either the collected material to be analyzed or a medium for the researcher to make sense out of her own observations (Pinnegar & Daynes, 2007; Polkinghorne, 1988, chapter VII). In a similar fashion, storytelling has been applied for knowledge management in organizations, e.g. as a way to verbalize tacit knowledge about a task or about the organization (Hannabuss, 2000.; Rhodes & Brown, 2005). Similar practices are to be found in the field of HCI, with storytelling being used as a tool for brainstorming or user-centered research. In all of the above cases, storytelling is employed to stimulate and facilitate the articulation of useful information and knowledge that would otherwise remain implicit.

Storytelling seems to be a natural and comfortable way for humans to cope with information and complexity. The idea of a narrative way of thinking which qualifies as a distinct mode of reasoning was pioneered by Bruner (1986) and Polkinghorne (1988). The exact nature of narrative knowing and narrative reasoning as well as the exact relation of narrative reasoning to paradigmatic (or logico-scientific) mode of reasoning are discussions we will refrain from. However, we find it fascinating that the way we process stories requires a particular way of connectivity between parts. Firstly, it requires some connectivity: Parts of a story become meaningful because they contribute to a plot. To quote Polkinghorne (1988, p. 18), "narrative ordering makes individual events comprehensible by identifying the whole to which they contribute". Secondly, the connectivity involved is of peculiar nature. The causal relation between parts is by far not necessary, but it is still sufficient. As Worth (2005) summarizes, "narrative lines of reasoning do not generally prove anything, but they do show how something might have come to be the case". In a way, what makes stories particularly attractive is exactly the need to devise or imagine explanations that impose coherence over discrete items.

A word of mention is now due to the types of texts or stories specifically produced by scientists. As already mentioned, narrative inquiry and science communication are straightforward examples of the use of stories in scientific practice. At the same time, scientists produce a variety of written texts which may or may not be understood as stories. The various scientific writing 'genres', e.g. the research article or the conference presentation, are definitely worth analyzing in terms of language and rhetoric devices employed. Such purely argumentative scientific texts have been in times examined under the lens of traditional narratives (Dubois, 1992; Sheehan & Rode, 1999; de Waard, 2010). Then again, debates over the narrativity of scientific texts are irrelevant to our purposes as we are motivated by the processes of verbalizing, composing and articulating, not by the nature of the output text. As regards the act and process of writing, it is useful to observe that scientific writing can be integral to scientific inquiry as opposed to ensuing it. Holmes (1987) studied manuscripts of prominent scientific figures to suggest that the act of writing may have played an active role in the conduction of research. Specifically, the need to formulate one's research into a legible and coherent whole for an informed and critical audience may help the researcher identify gaps, synthesize ideas and conceive new experiments. Naturally, we wonder if verbal articulation for the sake of storytelling with research material can have a similar impact.

Functions of Storytelling as Found in HCI Products and Practices

This subsection examines the ways that the field of HCI has approached, incorporated or facilitated the act of storytelling. Focus is on storytelling that includes and initiates from images. The act of storytelling is internal to all the activities and artifacts discussed but the means employed range from purely analogue, e.g. card-based storytelling, to entirely digital. Digital storytelling tends to refer to storytelling for educational purposes as assisted by productivity software (Meadows, 2003; Robin, 2006), but we use the term for any method/activity that utilizes a digital tool or environment and involves humans in the making of a story. Such activities may vary from the authoring of multimedia narratives to interactive storytelling in gaming environments.

Playing with Stories

Children play and storytelling are not interchangeable notions (Nicolopoulou, 2005) but every child knows that making up stories is (part of the) fun. Given the significance of storytelling for the development of a child's literacy and the close relation between play and storytelling, the field of Children Computer Interaction has shown proliferating interest on storytelling for play and learning. Children specific products are outside of the scope of this chapter but the overwhelming research on digital storytelling for children must be mentioned. Within the field of Children Computer Interaction, common understandings of digital storytelling range from multimedia stories authoring, to playing with smart storytelling toys, to interactive storytelling. An overview of digital storytelling from an educational perspective is provided by Farmer (2007); for an HCI perspective, see the review by Garzotto et al. (2010). Finally, a useful summary of digital storytelling interfaces for children is provided by Göttel (2011). Although particular to a subset of HCI literature, i.e. Computer Supported Collaborative Learning, the themes of remote authoring, co-located authoring and enriched experience are indicative.

Constructing a story, usually in collaboration with other players, is a valid way for all ages to play as demonstrated by various games dedicated to storytelling. The relations between storytelling and gaming are many and perplexing but we only consider straightforward storytelling games that are explicitly about composing stories. In particular, let us examine the gameplay of two storytelling games using imagery, namely "Once upon a time" and "Rory's Story cubes". "Once upon a time" (Atlas Games, 1993) is a popular storytelling card game based on the fairytale genre. Players are dealt storytelling cards, depicting common fairytale elements, and one 'happy ever after' card each. The storyteller uses her cards to create a fairytale story, working her way toward her ending card. However, the storyteller may be interrupted by another player who then picks up the task of storytelling. The first player to finish her cards, concluding the story with her ending card is the winner. "Once upon a time" is a typical example of storytelling out of the combination of randomly distributed tokens (combinatory). Moreover, it employs formal elements (in this case, fairytale motifs) and some knowledge of narrative theory to aid the storyteller. On the other hand, "Rory's story cubes" (The Creativity Hub Ltd., 2007) is a purely combinatory storytelling game without any additional support for the player. The player rolls 9 icon-sided dice and creates a story with the pictograms tossed. Note that the "Rory's story cubes" game is also advertised by its designers as a creative exercise, an aid for inspiration and a creative problem solving tool.

Storytelling as a Design Methodology

Storytelling is an attractive design methodology as it can stimulate the imagination, ease communication and facilitate verbalization of ideas or knowledge. The field of interaction design has employed the practice of storytelling in various stages and in various ways, from producing user case scenarios to fostering collaboration (Erickson, 1996; Gruen et al., 2002). When it comes to collaborative brainstorming, storytelling and playing are often intertwined: Various design games, such as the ones discussed by Brandt and Messeter (2004), Johansson and Linde (2005) and Johansson (2006), are simple card games that require verbal articulation. On the other hand, with interaction design and HCI taking a true participatory approach, storytelling is also a tool to elicit and collect valuable information from the user. As such, it is exercised by the user rather than by the designer. Consider also the practice of HCI probes, initially proposed by Gaver et al. (1999), i.e. the use of physical artifacts as prompts to elicit and collect user responses that can further inform and inspire the design process. One of the qualities of HCI probes, among others, is their capacity to capture information that is often unreported or deem irrelevant by the user. Probes come in a variety of forms but photo-collages, diaries and postcards are frequently included in probe kits. Sometimes, storytelling is also employed as a means to discuss with the users the material they collected using the probes (Mattelmäki, 2006). The notion of probes as physical triggers and their potential to articulate often unreported information is particularly attractive. In a way, we imagine a storytelling artifact that functions in a similar probing fashion.

Storytelling as an Interaction Metaphor

Storytelling provides a compelling metaphor for the design of interfaces. Let us repeat here that we, humans, naturally use stories to organize our experience. This is particularly prominent in the way we interact with images: Storytelling based on photographs is a very natural way of interacting with personal photos. Formal research by Chalfen (1987) on how people interact with printed photographs confirms that printed photos quickly turn us into storytellers. Frohlich et al. (2002) distinguish between storytelling with images and reminiscing talk with images, but do not dismiss the importance of storytelling as a means to co-present sharing. Systems for the management of personal digital photo collections have attempted to either include and facilitate storytelling or exploit the stories of the photos as a more intuitive organization of the collection. The widely cited work of Balanovic et al. (2000) aids the authoring and sharing of stories with digital photos in a fashion that resembles yet augments common interactions with printed photos. Other systems have explicitly included storytelling as a mechanism to annotate and organize material. Landry and Guzdial (2006) and Kuijk et al. (2010) employ story annotations as a means to improve image sharing, while Kuchinsky et al. (1999) and Ames and Manguy (2006) as a means to intuitive management and retrieval. The idea of data organization by narrative has been applied to generic documents as well. Gonçalves and Jorge (2008) propose organizing and querying personal documents by story elements such as time, place, purpose etc. In this case, the story about and around the document is exploited for annotation and retrieval. Finally, of particular relevance to our purposes is the work of Kuchinsky et al. (2002): The authors propose a biological storytelling metaphor as a means to organize various data about biological entities (genes, proteins, etc). We endorse the propositions by Kuchinsky et al. (2002) on the relevance of storytelling for scientific reasoning and practice; their notion of synthesis as a necessary part of hypothesis formulation greatly corresponds to our notion of a synthesis via the establishment of associations. However, their work does not consider the particularities of image data and of image-based storytelling, which have been the focal point of our study.

IMPLEMENTING STORYTELLING WITH IMAGES

As seen in the previous section, stories and storytelling have been extensively used as a means to probe articulation, to invite creative play and to impose coherence and structure. Stories provide humans with a mechanism to synthesize parts into an intelligible whole and a faculty to articulate about their experiences or their ideas. We attempt to probe similar processes of synthesis and articulation during a researcher's interaction with images by creating a game that supports storytelling with scientific images. This section describes LABBOOK, our collaborative storytelling game for biologists and their images. The game should be understood as an opportunity for creative play with scientific images as well as an opportunity for playful exposure to one another's images and to one another.

Concept Design

Despite the widespread applications of storytelling with images, storytelling with scientific images is a novel and somehow unconventional practice for researchers in the life sciences. Certainly, the context of scientific practice imposes additional requirements for the design of a storytelling game. For example, while storytelling with personal photos is a natural response, storytelling with research images might be not; thus, our game may need to stimulate our players towards the right mindset and tone. To make the most out of the potential of storytelling as a creative exercise and to emphasize the social aspects of scientific creativity, our game should operate on a multi-player game mode.

In putting forth our requirements for a game concept, use case scenarios were of particular help. The major aim of our game is to stimulate collaborative storytelling. But how and under which circumstances do we envision our game to be played? Considering the workflow and actual routines of a practicing scientist, how do we create opportunities for storytelling that are not artificial and do no introduce hassle for the researchers? Providing realistic answers to these questions is crucial for the adoption of our product. With these in mind, we provide the following use case scenarios:

1. The coffee table scenario: Colleagues of the same research group use the game as a pastime activity during coffee breaks. They play a couple of rounds with one another's images while at the coffee room of the institute. The game may be laying around at the shared facilities or be owned by one of the group members.
2. The ice breaker scenario: Collaborators in an interdisciplinary project use the game as an introductory activity during a project meeting. They play a couple of rounds with one another's images to get acquainted to the work or research interests of each collaborating party.

Note that both of the above mentioned scenarios expect the players to be co-located.

LABBOOK- The Game

LABBOOK (Figure 1) is a collaborative storytelling game for biologists and their images. It is played by a group of players on a tablet computer shared among the players. The aim of the game is to collectively construct a story around a collection of research images and within a set time limit. Stories unfold image by image with the players taking turns in the same story: The player whose turn is due draws the next image/storymove that she attaches with her narration to the ongoing story. One storymove (Figure 2) is a combination of a random image from the image set and a random utility card. The progression of the story is linear: A new move connects to the previous move and new moves are drawn by shaking the

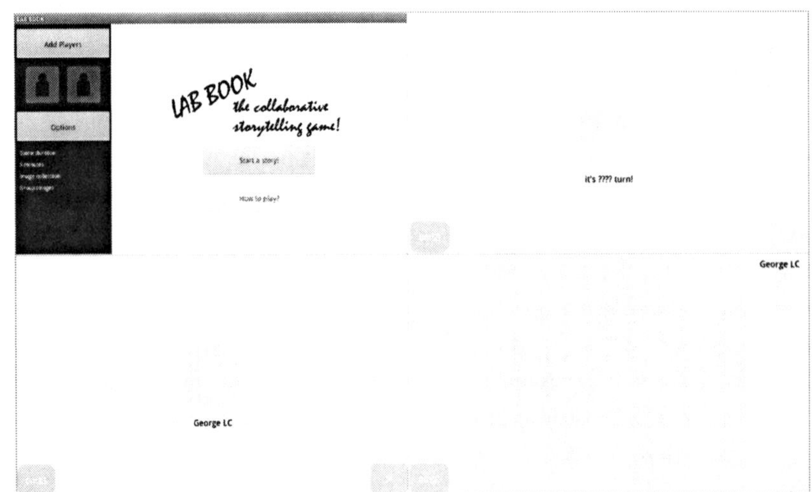

Figure 1. Screenshots of LABBOOK, the game. Players play in random order and the new next player is drawn by shaking the tablet. Stories unfold storymove by storymove and the new storymove is drawn by shaking the tablet.

Figure 2. One storymove is a combination of a random image from the image set and a random utility card. The player whose turn is due (highlighted at the top right corner) attaches the storymove to the ongoing story using hints from both the image and the utility card. Utility cards provide various suggestions including characters, places, literary genres or annotation terms from the image collection.

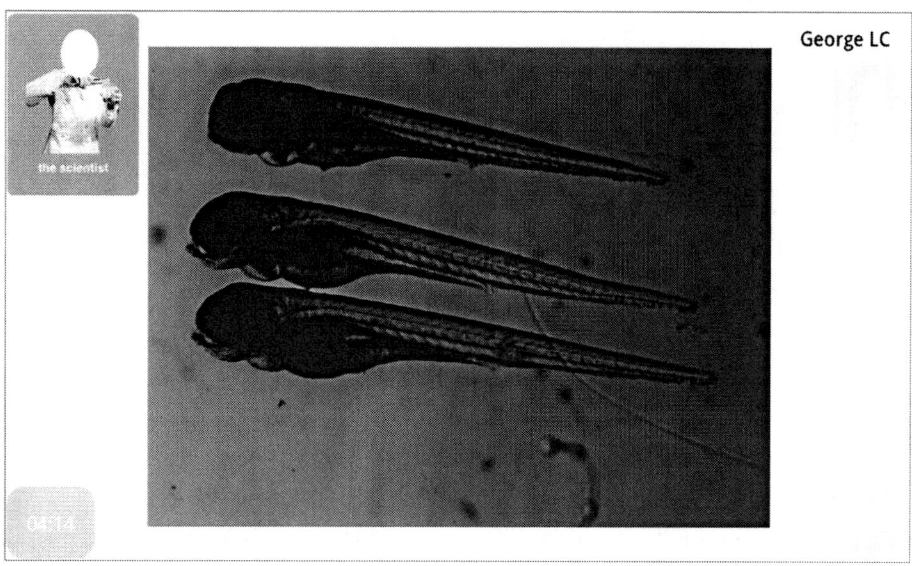

tablet. The sequence of the players is arbitrary: Players play in random order instead of in turns and the new next player is drawn by shaking the tablet. The story ends when the time is up with a random closing line. The player's narration is automatically audio-recorded and can be played back at the end of the game. There is no (extrinsic) reward other than enjoying the process, the company and the generated story.

At the core of LABBOOK is collaborative storytelling with scientific images. Thus, the fundamental elements of the game are the players and their images. In addition, LABBOOK employs numerous constructs to assist story construction such as cliché phrases and utility cards with characters, places and literary genres. Another essential component of the game is the platform it is played on. The tablet computer meets our requirement for a shared, collaborative and fluent story development by supporting a shared space and a shared story timeline. Then again, the hardware itself, i.e. a portable tablet with a touchscreen, microphone, speakers and accelerometer, introduced new opportunities for game design. The tablet allowed us to introduce a shake control which we hope to evoke a feeling of chance and to highlight the randomness involved in each storymove. The size and mobility of the display, as opposed to a tabletop, could potentially increase physical interaction with or around the display; we attempt to capitalize on such an opportunity by introducing a random play order.

Preliminary Results

LABBOOK has been evaluated in laboratory conditions only and with a small sample of players and images. More specifically, we asked four novice users (4 life science students/ 2 male, 2 female) to play the game first in pairs (2 groups) and then in a group of four (1 group). The game was played with a set of 15 images out of two research projects previously presented to the players (Figure 3). That is to say, the users had prior exposure

Figure 3. Representative images used in the LABBOOK user evaluation game sessions. (a) EGFR-induced breast cancer cells visualized with a confocal laser microscope. Image courtesy of Division of Toxicology, Leiden Amsterdam Centre for Drug Research (LACDR). (b) Bright field image containing a zebrafish larva imaged with a Leica DC500 microscope. Image courtesy of Department of Molecular Cell Biology, Institute of Biology Leiden (IBL).

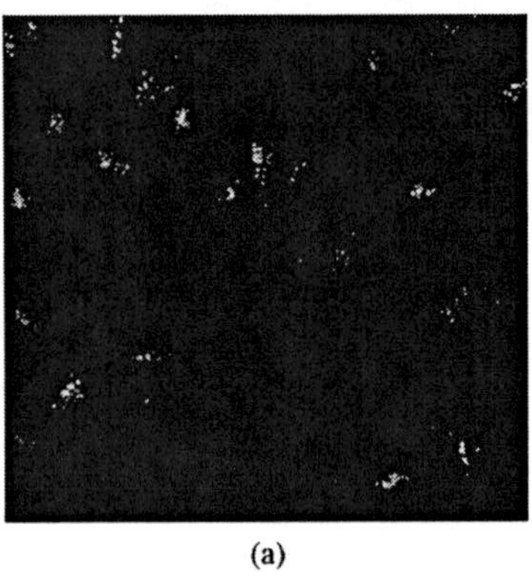

(a)

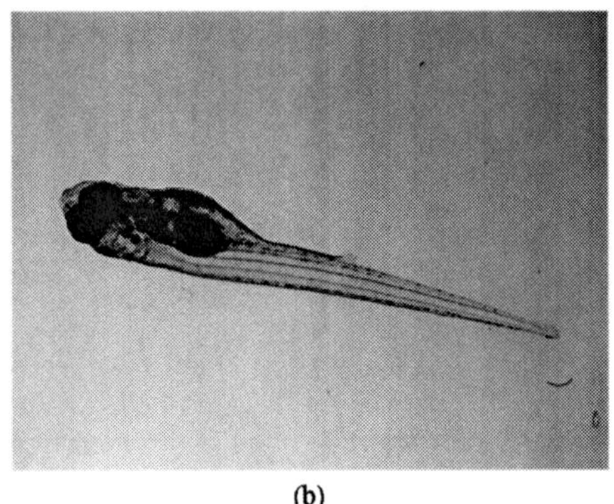

(b)

to the images and a thorough introduction to the research topics involved but were not the ones producing or researching the images involved. The sessions were audio-recorded (51 minutes of audio). Players were encouraged to play the game in their native language, i.e. Dutch.

Table 1 summarizes relevant quotes as extracted from play sessions and questionnaires. Overall, our players reported that the game rules and in-game interface were straightforward and easy to resolve. When it comes to story construction, the aids incorporated in LABBOOK were overall appreciated. Utility cards were well-noticed with players frequently starting their sentences with the utility card text. Noticeably, all players highly appreciated the input of other players as a source of inspiration (cf. Table 1). All in all, LABBOOK seems to successfully integrate playful elements, narrative aids and the multi-player mode. Then again, our players were of the opinion that it is the image set that governs story construction. All players asked for more diverse images in the game; they were fatigued by the reoccurring images feeling unable to come up with new ideas. Nevertheless, players clearly valued LABBOOK as a creative exercise and as a platform for conversation (Table 1).

The stories produced with LABBOOK demonstrate a capacity of storytelling to engage players with visual details in the images. Players appropriate visual details for the sake of story composition; as a matter of fact, they are very attentive to the image content. Green, red and pink specks in the image, the orientation of the fish and the positioning of the cells are repeatedly captured in the players' narration. The players' capacity of finding and utilizing patterns in the images is impressive. For example, players very often group cells together and propose that (groups of) cells move away or towards each other (cf. Table 2). Players were also able to make associations between subsequent images. For example, they often include in their narration the increase or decrease in the number of cells or fish depicted; multiplication, death and joining/being joined by other members of the same type were some reoccurring themes. Another frequently used strategy was zooming in or out in content when images of fish were followed by images of cells and vice versa (Table 2).

Table 1. Relevant quotes extracted from play sessions and questionnaires (player id indicated as A# for the first pair and B# for the second pair)

Topic	Quotes
Support: Interface	"sometimes when you are in a game or something you think what do I need to do now? this explains itself" [B1], "there shouldn't be much more in the screen because you are thinking about what you are going to say and shouldn't be distracted by more things" [B2]
Support: Other Players	"I think it's nicer to play with 4 people instead of 2 [...] more ideas, different people know more things, so you can just adapt to someone else's story when you don't know what to say" [B1], "more different, more inspiration, we have different points of view, although it got less because we got it a couple of times" [A2]
Support: Image Set	"There has to be a bigger variation in the pictures, I think that's also something that really matters, because right now they are all the same, so we can't talk for hours about it any more..." [A2], "[B2] It is nice if there are different pictures ... [B1] you make a story and then the same pictures come back so you can't continue with your story [B2] but it is a good thing that sometime the same pictures come back..." [B1, B2]
Impact: Potential Use	"it's more like a game for people who want to be creative, because you need to be creative to keep coming up with something new" [B1], "maybe it's a good exercise when you are afraid to talk spontaneous in a group, and you just pass on the tablet and everybody says something, it gives you a subject to talk about" [B2]

Table 2. Story fragments extracted from audio recordings translated from Dutch (story id indicated as A for the first pair, B for the second pair and AB_# for the joined group)

topic	fragment
patterns: grouping, movement	"the cells were afraid of each other and flew to the other side" [AB_1] "they all went off to different directions" [AB_2] "then they all decided to go line dancing" [A]
transitions: zoom in/out	"the computer analyst saw in the zebrafish [...] that a cluster emerged" [A] "the tragedy was that the fish had only two cells" [B] "and the cells were actually one big zebrafish..." [AB_1]

FUTURE RESEARCH DIRECTIONS

LABBOOK is a prototype game meant to both illustrate and further clarify storytelling with scientific images. In its current implementation, LABBOOK is a well-functioning and well-received platform for collaborative storytelling with images. The game's interface is straightforward, the game rules are clear and unproblematic and story construction is stimulated by narrative, playful and social elements. Certainly, there is a lot to be done for LABBOOK to be released as a complete product. Functionality aside, some algorithmic aspects of the game require attention: Variation in the image set, the total number of images included and variation between storymoves are parameters the impact and range of which should be further researched. Eventually, we can always consider more elaborate ways to regulate either the initial image set or the transitions between storymoves. Potentially, we can also consider incorporating computational support for story composition or employing formal narrative elements as aids to story construction.

While we examined the stories produced by our players attentively, our appreciation of them has been only subjective. At present, we lack a metric to evaluate the produced stories on either their quality or their usefulness. Such a metric may or may not measure the story's narrative quality and may or may not consider its scientific content. Nonetheless, a metric will be needed if we are to compare different prototypes or different games on the stories they facilitate. Note that our examination of the produced stories focused on (attributes of) the story-making process, particularly the strategies, creative solutions and inspirations of our players. Moreover, we have been attentive for straightforward references to the image content as well as straightforward references to transitions between images. Regardless of the value of the stories themselves, such references allow us to raise a case for the value of story-making as a trigger for an active look into and in between images.

LABBOOK was conceived as a platform that creates opportunities for storytelling in a shared and social context. The game mode implemented, i.e. a multi-player game for players that are co-located, was a means to stimulate both storytelling and social interaction and we are confident that the game can accommodate the use case scenarios proposed. During this work, we have been increasingly aware of the importance of social exchange and conversation during a research trajectory. Our storytelling paradigm, thus, must expand to address both storytelling with other images as a process of synthesis and articulation and storytelling together with other researchers as a process of conversation. Similarly, we suggest that future instances of playful interactions with scientific (image) data should better examine the role of social interaction and exchange.

CONCLUSION

This chapter considered storytelling with scientific images as a worthwhile instance of playful interaction with scientific images. By means of literature review and the development of a storytelling game we attempt to better understand and further exemplify the potential of storytelling with scientific images.

Our review of existing and well-established products and practices involving storytelling and storytelling with images identified a number of reoccurring functions of storytelling. Storytelling is extensively used as a means to probe articulation, of both new and existing knowledge, to invite creative play and to impose coherence and structure. Used as an organization metaphor in interfaces, storytelling is generally utilized to either facilitate image sharing or to facilitate image retrieval. All things considered, storytelling allows participants to make explicit, to make coherent, to play, to share, to organize. Storytelling with images spans across a variety of applications, from analogue games to video games to story editors, and a variety of story construction methods, with or without a narrative theory backdrop and with or without generative capacities.

Our storytelling game has invited players to playfully engage with scientific images in ways that could potentially stimulate creative responses to scientific images. We confronted players with the challenges of story composition and invited them to imagine associations between images, review data under a new light/context, fill-in the gaps and participate in social exchange and conversation. Our game has resulted in a number of encouraging observations and responses that further motivate our interest in storytelling with scientific images. An active look into and in between images and a shared conversation space appear to be two of the major contributions of storytelling with images. Formally evaluating the creative potential of our game is a cumbersome task but, at minimum, the game was valued as a creative exercise and a platform for conversation.

Our interest in storytelling with scientific images originated from an interest to introduce playfulness in a scientist's interaction with images. Our approach in designing and providing a playful interface for scientific images has been diametrically opposed to superficially layering playful or game-ful elements in an existing application. Instead, we devised a way to literally play with images by engaging in an activity, i.e. storytelling, that is playful, creative and relevant. And while LABBOOK is comparable to a serious game, we acknowledge that making playful interfaces does not necessarily equal with making games. Nor is making games a panacea when playfulness is the objective. Making games that focus on what is intrinsically valuable, relevant and playful may be a step to the right direction.

REFERENCES

Aarseth, E. (1997). *Cybertext: Perspectives on ergodic literature*. Baltimore, MD: Johns Hopkins University Press.

Abbott, H. (2007). Story, plot, and narration. In *The Cambridge Companion to Narrative* (pp. 39–51). Cambridge, UK: Cambridge University Press. doi:10.1017/CCOL0521856965.003.

Alvarez, J., & Michaud, L. (2008). *Serious games, advergaming, edugaming, training and more (Technical report)*. IDATE.

Ames, M., & Manguy, L. (2006). Photoarcs: Ludic tools for sharing photographs. In *Proceedings of the 14th Annual ACM International Conference on Multimedia* (pp. 615–618). ACM.

Avraamidou, L., & Osborne, J. (2009). The role of narrative in communicating science. *International Journal of Science Education, 31*(12), 1683–1707. doi:10.1080/09500690802380695.

Balabanovíc, M., Chu, L., & Wolff, G. (2000). Storytelling with digital photographs. In *Proceedings of the SIGCHI Conference on Human Factors in Computing Systems* (pp. 564–571). ACM.

Blythe, M., Overbeeke, K., Monk, A., & Wright, P. (2004). *Funology: From usability to enjoyment*. Berlin: Springer.

Brandt, E., & Messeter, J. (2004). Facilitating collaboration through design games. In *Proceedings of the Eighth Conference on Participatory Design: Artful Integration: Interweaving Media, Materials and Practices-Volume 1* (pp. 121–131). ACM.

Bruner, J. (1986). *Actual minds, possible worlds*. Boston: Harvard University Press.

Caillois, R. (2001). *Man, play and games*. Champaign-Urbana: IL: University of Illinois Press.

Carroll, J. (2004). Beyond fun. *Interactions (New York, N.Y.), 11*(5), 38–40. doi:10.1145/1015530.1015547.

Chalfen, R. (1987). *Snapshot versions of life*. Popular Press.

Charsky, D. (2010). From edutainment to serious games: A change in the use of game characteristics. *Games and Culture, 5*(2), 177–198. doi:10.1177/1555412009354727.

Cooper, S., Khatib, F., Treuille, A., Barbero, J., Lee, J., & Beenen, M. et al. (2010). Predicting protein structures with a multiplayer online game. *Nature, 466*(7307), 756–760. doi:10.1038/nature09304 PMID:20686574.

de Waard, A. (2010). From proteins to fairytales: Directions in semantic publishing. *IEEE Intelligent Systems, 25*(2), 83–88. doi:10.1109/MIS.2010.49.

Deterding, S., Dixon, D., & Khaled, R. (2011). Gamification: Toward a definition. In *Proceedings of CHI 2011* (pp. 12–15). ACM.

Draper, S. (1999). Analysing fun as a candidate software requirement. *Personal and Ubiquitous Computing, 3*(3), 117–122.

Dubois, B. (1992). From narrative toward exposition: Materials and methods sections of biomedical journal articles. In Language in context: Essays for Robert E. Longacre (pp. 157–188). Summer Institute of Linguistics.

Erickson, T. (1996). Design as storytelling. *Interactions (New York, N.Y.)*, *3*(4), 30–35. doi:10.1145/234813.234817.

Farmer, L. (2004). Using technology for storytelling: Tools for children. *New Review of Children's Literature and Librarianship*, *10*(2), 155–168. doi:10.1080/1361454042000312275.

Frohlich, D., Kuchinsky, A., Pering, C., Don, A., & Ariss, S. (2002). Requirements for photoware. In *Proceedings of the 2002 ACM Conference on Computer Supported Cooperative Work* (pp. 166–175). ACM.

Fullerton, T., Swain, C., & Hoffman, S. (2008). *Game design workshop: A playcentric approach to creating innovative games*. San Francisco, CA: Morgan Kaufmann.

Garzotto, F., Paolini, P., & Sabiescu, A. (2010). Interactive storytelling for children. In *Proceedings of the 9th International Conference on Interaction Design and Children* (pp. 356–359). ACM.

Gaver, W., Dunne, T., & Pacenti, E. (1999). Design: Cultural probes. *Interactions (New York, N.Y.)*, *6*(1), 21–29. doi:10.1145/291224.291235.

Gonçalves, D., & Jorge, J. (2008). In search of personal information: Narrative-based interfaces. In *Proceedings of the 13th International Conference on Intelligent User Interfaces* (pp. 179–188). ACM.

Göttel, T. (2011). Reviewing children's collaboration practices in storytelling environments. In *Proceedings of the 10th International Conference on Interaction Design and Children* (pp. 153–156). ACM.

Gruen, D., Rauch, T., Redpath, S., & Ruettinger, S. (2002). The use of stories in user experience design. *International Journal of Human-Computer Interaction*, *14*(3-4), 503–534. doi:10.1080/10447318.2002.9669132.

Hannabuss, S. (2000). Narrative knowledge: Eliciting organisational knowledge from storytelling. [). ASLIB.]. *Aslib Proceedings*, *52*, 402–413. doi:10.1108/EUM0000000007031.

Holmes, F. (1987). Scientific writing and scientific discovery. *Isis*, *78*(2), 220–235. doi:10.1086/354391 PMID:3316115.

Huizinga, J. (1955). *Homo ludens: A study of the play element in human culture*. Boston: Beacon Press.

Johansson, M. (2006). Design games: Reinstalling the designer in collaborative design. In *Proceedings of DRS06 Wonderground*. DRS.

Johansson, M., & Linde, P. (2005). Playful collaborative exploration: New research practice in participatory design. *Journal of Research Practice*, *1*(1).

Kuchinsky, A., Graham, K., Moh, D., Adler, A., Babaria, K., & Creech, M. (2002). Biological storytelling: A software tool for biological information organization based upon narrative structure. In *Proceedings of the Working Conference on Advanced Visual Interfaces* (pp. 331–341). ACM.

Kuchinsky, A., Pering, C., Creech, M., Freeze, D., Serra, B., & Gwizdka, J. (1999). Fotofile: A consumer multimedia organization and retrieval system. In *Proceedings of the SIGCHI Conference on Human Factors in Computing Systems: The CHI is the Limit* (pp. 496–503). ACM.

Kuijk, F., Guimarães, R., Cesar, P., & Bulterman, D. (2010). From photos to memories: A user-centric authoring tool for telling stories with your photos. In *User Centric Media* (pp. 13–20). Springer. doi:10.1007/978-3-642-12630-7_2.

Kuts, E. (2009). Playful user interfaces: Literature review and model for analysis. In *Breaking New Ground: Innovation in Games, Play, Practice and Theory: Proceedings of the 2009 Digital Games Research Association Conference*. London: IEEE.

Landry, B., & Guzdial, M. (2006). Itell: Supporting retrospective storytelling with digital photos. In *Proceedings of the 6th Conference on Designing Interactive Systems* (pp. 160–168). ACM.

Malone, T. W. (1982). Heuristics for designing enjoyable user interfaces: Lessons from computer games. In *Proceedings of the 1982 Conference on Human Factors in Computing Systems,* (pp. 63–68). ACM.

Mattelmäki, T. (2006). *Design probes*. Helsinki, Finland: University of Art and Design Helsinki.

Meadows, D. (2003). Digital storytelling: Research-based practice in new media. *Visual Communication*, *2*(2), 189–193. doi:10.1177/1470357203002002004.

Monk, A., Hassenzahl, M., Blythe, M., & Reed, D. (2002). Funology: Designing enjoyment. In *Proceedings of CHI '02 Extended Abstracts on Human Factors in Computing Systems* (pp. 924–925). ACM.

Nicolopoulou, A. (2005). Play and narrative in the process of development: Commonalities, differences, and interrelations. *Cognitive Development*, *20*, 495–502. doi:10.1016/j.cogdev.2005.09.001.

Pinnegar, S., & Daynes, J. (2007). Locating narrative inquiry historically. In *Handbook of narrative inquiry: Mapping a methodology*. Thousand Oaks, CA: Sage Publications, Inc. doi:10.4135/9781452226552.n1.

Polkinghorne, D. (1988). *Narrative knowing and the human sciences*. New York: State University of New York Press.

Rhodes, C., & Brown, A. (2005). Narrative, organizations and research. *International Journal of Management Reviews*, *7*(3), 167–188. doi:10.1111/j.1468-2370.2005.00112.x.

Robin, B. (2006). The educational uses of digital storytelling. [Orlando, FL: AACE.]. *Proceedings of Society for Information Technology & Teacher Education International Conference, 2006*, 709–716.

Salen, K., & Zimmerman, E. (2004). *Rules of play: Game design fundamentals*. Cambridge, MA: The MIT Press.

Sawyer, R. (2006). *Explaining creativity: The science of human innovation*. Oxford, UK: Oxford University Press.

Sheehan, R., & Rode, S. (1999). On scientific narrative stories of light by Newton and Einstein. *Journal of Business and Technical Communication*, *13*(3), 336–358. doi:10.1177/105065199901300306.

Shneiderman, B. (2004). Designing for fun: How can we design user interfaces to be more fun? *Interactions (New York, N.Y.)*, *11*(5), 48–50. doi:10.1145/1015530.1015552.

Siorpaes, K., & Hepp, M. (2008). Games with a purpose for the semantic web. *IEEE Intelligent Systems*, *23*(3), 50–60. doi:10.1109/MIS.2008.45.

Susi, T., Johannesson, M., & Backlund, P. (2007). *Serious games: An overview (Technical report, GLS)*. Madison, WI: University of Wisconsin-Madison.

von Ahn, L. (2006). Games with a purpose. *Computer*, *39*(6), 92–94. doi:10.1109/MC.2006.196.

von Ahn, L., & Dabbish, L. (2004). Labeling images with a computer game. In *Proceedings of the SIGCHI Conference on Human Factors in Computing Systems* (pp. 319–326). ACM.

Worth, S. (2005). Narrative knowledge: Knowing through storytelling. In *Proceedings of the Fourth Media in Transition*. IEEE.

ADDITIONAL READING

Bawden, D. (1986). Information systems and the stimulation of creativity. *Journal of Information Science, 12*(5), 203. doi:10.1177/016555158601200501.

Boden, M. (2004). *The creative mind: Myths and mechanisms*. Psychology Press.

D. Clandinin (Ed.). (2007). *Handbook of narrative inquiry: Mapping a methodology*. Thousand Oaks, CA: Sage Publications, Inc..

Costello, B., & Edmonds, E. (2007). A study in play, pleasure and interaction design. In *Proceedings of the 2007 Conference on Designing Pleasurable Products and Interfaces* (pp. 76–91). ACM.

Csikszentmihalyi, M. (1991). *Flow: The psychology of optimal experience*. New York: Harper Perennial.

Dunbar, K. (1995). How scientists really reason: Scientific reasoning in real-world laboratories. In *The nature of insight* (pp. 365–395). Cambridge, MA: The MIT Press.

Dunbar, K., & Fugelsang, J. (2005). Scientific thinking and reasoning. In *The Cambridge Handbook of Thinking and Reasoning*. Cambridge, UK: Cambridge University Press.

D. Herman (Ed.). (2007). *The Cambridge companion to narrative*. Cambridge, UK: Cambridge University Press. doi:10.1017/CCOL0521856965.

Klahr, D., & Simon, H. (1999). Studies of scientific discovery: Complementary approaches and convergent findings. *Psychological Bulletin, 125*(5), 524–543. doi:10.1037/0033-2909.125.5.524.

Knorr-Cetina, K., & Amann, K. (1990). Image dissection in natural scientific inquiry. *Science, Technology & Human Values, 15*(3), 259. doi:10.1177/016224399001500301.

Murray, J. H. (1998). *Hamlet on the holodeck: The future of narrative in cyberspace*. Cambridge, MA: The MIT Press.

Norris, S. P., Guilbert, S. M., Smith, M. L., Hakimelahi, S., & Phillips, L. M. (2005). A theoretical framework for narrative explanation in science. *Science Education, 89*(4), 535–563. doi:10.1002/sce.20063.

O'Connor, B. (1988). Fostering creativity: Enhancing the browsing environment. *International Journal of Information Management, 8*(3), 203–210. doi:10.1016/0268-4012(88)90063-1.

Pauwels, L. (2008). An integrated model for conceptualising visual competence in scientific research and communication. *Visual Studies, 23*(2), 147–161. doi:10.1080/14725860802276305.

Pope, R. (2005). *Creativity: Theory, history, practice*. London: Routledge.

Runco, M. A. (2004). Creativity. *Annual Review of Psychology, 55*(1), 657–687. doi:10.1146/annurev.psych.55.090902.141502 PMID:14744230.

Ryan, M.-L. (2001). Beyond myth and metaphor: The case of narrative in digital media. *Game Studies, 1*(1).

Simons, J. (2007). Narrative, games, and theory. *Game Studies, 7*(1).

Sternberg, R. (1999). *Handbook of creativity*. Cambridge, UK: Cambridge University Press.

Zimmerman, E. (2004). Narrative, interactivity, play, and games: Four naughty concepts in need of discipline. In *First person: New media as story, performance, and game* (pp. 154–164). Cambridge, MA: The MIT Press.

KEY TERMS AND DEFINITIONS

Creativity: The ability to come up with ideas or artefacts that are new, surprising and valuable (Boden, 2004).

Creative Responses to Scientific Image Data: New ideas, observations, realizations or inferences based on or derived by scientific image data; can inform everyday scientific practice and may be facilitated by an open-minded and playful attitude of the researcher.

Games with a Purpose: Games that harvest human effort during play.

Gamification: The use of game design elements in nongame contexts (Deterding et al., 2011).

Playful Interfaces: Interfaces that attempt to invoke play and a playful attitude.

Playfulness: The inclination to be less serious, i.e. either more humorous or more experimental or looking for fun and amusement.

Serious Games: Games for purposes other than mere entertainment.

Story: An account of a sequence of events; can be either true or false.

Storytelling: The telling of a story that is actively generated by the storyteller.

Compilation of References

Aarseth, E. (1997). *Cybertext: Perspectives on ergodic literature*. Baltimore, MD: Johns Hopkins University Press.

Abbott, H. (2007). Story, plot, and narration. In *The Cambridge Companion to Narrative* (pp. 39–51). Cambridge, UK: Cambridge University Press. doi:10.1017/CCOL0521856965.003.

Abdelnour-Nocera, J., Kurosu, M., Clemmensen, T., Bidwell, N., Vatrapu, R., Winschiers-Theophilus, H., & Yeo, A. (2011). *Re-framing HCI through local and indigenous perspectives*. Paper presented at the Lecture Notes in Computer Science. Berlin, Germany.

Abdullah, R., & Hübner, R. (2006). *Pictograms, icons, and signs*. London, UK: Thames & Hudson.

Abowd, G.D., & Myatt. (2000). Charting past, present and future research in ubiquitous computing. *ACM Transactions*.

Adams, E. (2010). *Fundamentals of game design* (2nd ed.). Berkeley, CA: New Riders.

Adams, L., Gouvousis, A., vanLue, M., & Waldron, C. (2004). Social story intervention: Improving communication skills in a child with an autism spectrum disorder. *Focus on Autism and Other Developmental Disabilities*, *19*, 87–94. doi:10.1177/10883576040190020301.

Agosta, E., Graetz, J. E., Mastropieri, M. A., & Scruggs, T. E. (2004). Teacher-researcher partnership to improve social behavior through social stories. *Intervention in School and Clinic*, *39*(5), 276–287. doi:10.1177/10534512040390050401.

Ahmed, A. S., & Seong, D. S. K. (2006). *SignWriting on mobile phones for the deaf*. Paper presented at Mobility 06. Bangkok, Thailand.

Ahonen, M., Launis, M., & Kuorinka, T. (1989). *Ergonomic workplace analysis*. Helsinki, Finland: Finnish Institute of Occupational Health.

Aiello, G., & Gendelman, I. (2008). Seattle's pike place market (de) constructed: An analysis of tourist narratives about a public space. *Journal of Tourism and Cultural Change*, *5*(3), 158–185. doi:10.2167/jtcc093.0.

Ali, S. N. S., Razali, A. M., Suradi, N. R., Abu Bakar, A., & Ramli, S. A. (2010). A framework for continuous outpatient health care delivery improvement through treatment plan support. In *Proceedings of the Regional Conference on Statistical Sciences*, (pp. 93-102). IEEE.

Allport, G. W. (1998). Traits revisited. In *Personality: Critical concepts*. Academic Press.

Alvarez, J., & Michaud, L. (2008). *Serious games, advergaming, edugaming, training and more (Technical report)*. IDATE.

Alves, N. S., & Prietch, S. S. (2012). *Analysis and discussion of methods for assessment of emotional experience with deaf people: A practical approach (Tech. Rep.)*. Rondonópolis, Brazil: Universidade Federal de Mato Grosso.

Amar, R. A., & Stasko, J. T. (2005). Knowledge precepts for design and evaluation of information visualizations. *IEEE Transactions on Visualization and Computer Graphics*, *11*(4), 432–442. doi:10.1109/TVCG.2005.63 PMID:16138553.

American Psychological Association's Board of Educational Affairs. (1997). *Learner-centered psychological principles: A framework for school reform & redesign*. Washington, DC: American Psychological Association.

Ames, M., & Manguy, L. (2006). Photoarcs: Ludic tools for sharing photographs. In *Proceedings of the 14th Annual ACM International Conference on Multimedia* (pp. 615–618). ACM.

Anderson, J. (2012). Reflective journals as a tool for auto-ethnographic learning: A case study of student experiences with individualized sustainability. *Journal of Geography in Higher Education*, *36*(4), 613–623. doi:10.1080/03098265.2012.692157.

Andre, T. S., Hartson, H. R., & Williges, R. C. (2003). Determining the effectiveness of the usability problem inspector: A theory-based model and tool for finding usability problems. *Human Factors*, *45*(3), 455–482. doi:10.1518/hfes.45.3.455.27255 PMID:14702996.

Andrienko, G., Andrienko, N., Keim, D., MacEachren, A. M., & Wrobel, S. (2011). Challenging problems of geospatial visual analytics. *Journal of Visual Languages and Computing*, *22*(4), 251–256. doi:10.1016/j.jvlc.2011.04.001.

Angeli de. A., Johnson, G. I., & Coventry, L. (2001). The unfriendly user: Exploring social reactions to chatterbots. In *Proceedings of the International Conference on Affective Human Factor Design* (pp. 467–474). IEEE.

Apostolopoulos, G., Peris, V., & Saha, D. (1999). Transport layer security: How much does it really cost? In *Proceedings of the Conf. on Computer Communications (IEEE Infocom)*. IEEE Computer Society.

Apple, Inc. (2012). *Case studies: Transitioning to ios, Apple iOS human interface guidelines*. Retrieved Apr 20, 2012, from http://developer.apple.com/library/ios/#documentation/UserExperience/Conceptual/MobileHIG/TranslateApp/TranslateApp.html#//apple_ref/doc/uid/TP40006556-CH10-SW38

Apter, M. J. (1991). A structural-phenomenology of play. In *Adult Play: A Reversal Theory Approach* (pp. 13–22). Amsterdam: Swets & Zeitlinger.

Archer, B. (2005). The three Rs. In *A Framework for Design and Design Education*. Wellesbourne: The Design and Technology Association.

Arnkil, H. (2004). The Finnish workplace development programme — A small giant? *Concepts and Transformation*, *9*(3), 249–278. doi:10.1075/cat.9.3.03arn.

Arwood, E. L., & Brown, M. M. (1999). *A guide to cartooning and flowcharting*. Portland, OR: Apricot Inc..

ASD Concepts LLC. (2009). *Social story: How to greet someone at school*. Available at http://www.child-autism-parent-cafe.com/How-To-Greet-Someone-At-School.html

Ashbrook, D., & Starner, T. (2002). Learning significant locations and predicting user movement with GPS. In *Proceedings of the Sixth International Symposium on Wearable Computers*, (pp. 101-108). IEEE.

Attwood, T. (2000). Strategies for improving the social integration of children with Asperger syndrome. *Autism*, *4*(1), 85–100. doi:10.1177/1362361300004001006.

Avedon, E., & Sutton-Smith, B. (1971). *The study of games*. New York: John Wiley & Sons.

Avraamidou, L., & Osborne, J. (2009). The role of narrative in communicating science. *International Journal of Science Education*, *31*(12), 1683–1707. doi:10.1080/09500690802380695.

Axtell, R. E. (1998). *Gestures: The DO's and TABOOs of body language around the world*. New York, NY: John Wiley & Sons, Inc..

Aykin, N. (2005). *Usability and internationalization of information technology*. Mahwah, NJ: Erlbaum.

N. Aykin (Ed.). (2004). *Usability and internationalization of information technology*. Mahwah, NJ: Lawrence Erlbaum Associates Inc..

Baader, F., Calvanese, D., McGuinness, D. L., Nardi, D., & Patel-Schneider, P. F. (2010). *The description logic handbook* (2nd ed.). Cambridge, UK: Cambridge University Press.

Badre, A. (2000). The effects of cross cultural interface design orientation on world wide web user performance. *GVU Technical Report*, 1-30.

Badre, A., & Barber, W. (1998). Culturabilty: The merging of culture and usabilty. In *Proceedings of the 4th Conference on Human Factors and the Web*. Basking Ridge.

Bailador, G., Roggen, D., Tröster, G., & Trivino, G. (2007). Real time gesture recognition using continuous time recurrent neural networks. In *Proceedings of the 2nd International Conference on Body Area Networks BodyNets* (pp. 15.1-15.8). Brussels, Belgium: ICST.

Bailes, C., Hulsebosch, P., & Martin, D. (2010). Reflective journal writing: Deaf pre-service teachers with hearing children. *Teacher Education and Special Education, 33*(3), 234–247. doi:10.1177/0888406409356763.

Baillie, L., Benyon, D., Bodker, S., & Macaulay, C. (2003). Special Issue on Interacting with technology in household environments. *Cognition Technology and Work, 5*(1), 2–3.

Balabanovíc, M., Chu, L., & Wolff, G. (2000). Storytelling with digital photographs. In *Proceedings of the SIGCHI Conference on Human Factors in Computing Systems* (pp. 564–571). ACM.

Ball, J. (2008). *Early intervention and autism: real-life questions, real-life answers.* Arlington, TX: Future Horizons.

Banerjee, A., Burstyn, J., Girouard, A., & Vertegaal, R. (2012). Multipoint: Comparing laser and manual pointing as remote input in large display interactions. *International Journal of Human-Computer Studies, 70*(10), 690–702. doi:10.1016/j.ijhcs.2012.05.009.

Bargas-Avila, J., & Hornbæk, K. (2011). Old wine in new bottles or novel challenges? A critical analysis of empirical studies of user experience. In *Proceedings of CHI 2011, User Experience*. ACM.

Barnes, K., Marateo, R., & Ferris, S. (2007). Teaching and learning with the net generation. *Innovate, 3*(4).

Baron-Cohen, S., Golan, O., Chapman, E., & Granader, Y. (2007). Trasported to a world of emotion. *The Psychologist UK.* Available at http://www.the-psychologist.org.uk/archive/archive_home.cfm/volumeID_20-Ed.ID_144-ArticleID_1140-getfile_get-PDF/thepsychologist%5C0207baro.pdf

Baron-Cohen, S., Golan, O., & Ashwin, E. (2009). Can emotion recognition be taught to children with autism spectrum conditions? *Philosophical Transactions of the Royal Society of Biological Sciences, 364*, 3567–3574. doi:10.1098/rstb.2009.0191 PMID:19884151.

Bar-Shalom, Y., Li, X. R., & Kirubarajan, T. (2001). *Estimation with applications to tracking and navigation: Theory, algorithms, and software.* New York: Wiley. doi:10.1002/0471221279.

Bartle, R. (2005). Hearts, clubs, diamonds, spades: Players who suit MUDs (1996). In K. Salen, & E. Zimmerman (Eds.), *The Game Design Reader: A Rules of Play Anthology.* Cambridge, MA: The MIT Press.

Bartneck, C. (2002). Integrating the OCC model of emotions in embodied characters. In *Proceedings of the Workshop on Virtual Conversational Characters: Applications, Methods and Research Challenges.* Melbourne, Australia: IEEE.

Bastien, J. M. C., & Scapin, D. L. (1993). Ergonomic criteria for the evaluation of human-computer interfaces. *International Journal of Human-Computer Interaction, 4*(156), 183–196.

Bateman, J., Kleinz, J., Kamps, T., & Reichenberger, K. (2001). Towards constructive text, diagram, and layout generation for information presentation. *Computational Linguistics, 27*, 409–449. doi:10.1162/089120101317066131.

Bates, J. (1994). The role of emotion in believable agents. *Communications of the ACM, 37*(7), 122–125. doi:10.1145/176789.176803.

Battarbee, K. (2003). Co-experience: The social user experience. In *Proceedings of CHI 2003.* ACM.

Baumgartner, V.-J. (2003). *A practical set of cultural dimensions for global user-interface analysis and design.* Retrieved from http://www.mavas.at/val/education05_thesis00.asp

Baynes, K. (1994). *Designerly play.* Loughborough, UK: Loughborough University.

Bedwell., et al. (2009). In support of city exploration. In *Proceedings of the 27th International Conference on Human Factors in Computing Systems.* ACM.

Bennett, S., & Maton, K. (2010). Beyond the 'digital natives' debate: Towards a more nuanced understanding of students' technology experiences. *Journal of Computer Assisted Learning, 26*(5), 321–331. doi:10.1111/j.1365-2729.2010.00360.x.

Bennett, S., Maton, K., & Kervin, L. (2008). The 'digital natives' debate: A critical review of the evidence. *British Journal of Educational Technology, 39*(5), 775–786. doi:10.1111/j.1467-8535.2007.00793.x.

Benyon, D., Turner, P., & Turner, S. (2005). *Designing interactive systems*. Englewood Cliffs, NJ: Pearson Education Limited.

Berelson, B. (1952). *Content analysis in communication research*. Free Press.

Bernard-Opitz, V., Sriram, N., & Nakhoda-Sapuan, S. (2001). Enhancing social problem solving in children with autism and normal children through computer-assisted instruction. *Journal of Autism and Developmental Disorders, 31*(4), 377–384. doi:10.1023/A:1010660502130 PMID:11569584.

Bernsen, N. O., Dybkjær, H., & Dybkjær, L. (1998). *Designing interactive speech systems* (2nd ed.). London: Springer. doi:10.1007/978-1-4471-0897-9.

Bevan, N. (2009). Extending quality in use to provide a framework for usability measurement. In *Proceedings of HCI International 2009*. San Diego, CA: ACM.

Bevan, N. (2001). International standards for HCI and usability. *International Journal of Human-Computer Studies International Journal of Human-Computer Studies, 55*(4), 533–552. doi:10.1006/ijhc.2001.0483.

Bianchini, C. S., Borgia, F., Bottoni, P., & de Marsico, M. (2012). *Swift – A signwriting improved fast transcriber*. Paper presented at AVI '12. Capri Island, Italy.

Bickmore, T., & Cassell, J. (2001). Relational agents: A model and implementation of building user trust. In *Proceedings of the Conference on Human Factors in Computing Systems – SIGCHI* (pp. 396–403). ACM.

Bidwell, N. J., Winschiers-Theophilus, H., Koch Kapuire, G., & Rehm, M. (2011b). Pushing personhood into place: Situating media in the transfer of rural knowledge in Africa. *International Journal of Human-Computer Studies, 69*(10), 618–631. doi:10.1016/j.ijhcs.2011.02.002.

Biesterfeldt, J., & Capra, M. (2011). Leading international UX research projects design, user experience, and usability. In A. Marcus (Ed.), *Theory, Methods, Tools and Practice* (Vol. 6769, pp. 368–377). Springer.

Biggs, J., & Tang, C. (2007). *Teaching for quality learning at university* (3rd ed.). Buckingham, UK: SRHE and Open University Press.

Biswas, P., Robinson, P., & Langdon, P. (2012). Designing inclusive interfaces through user modeling and simulation. *International Journal of Human-Computer Interaction, 28*(1), 1–33. doi:10.1080/10447318.2011.565718.

Bledsoe, R., Myles, B. S., & Simpson, R. L. (2003). Use of a social story intervention to improve mealtime skills of an adolescent with Asperger Syndrome. *Autism, 7*, 289–295. doi:10.1177/13623613030073005 PMID:14516061.

Bloom, B. (1956). *Taxonomy of educational objectives, the classification of educational goals – Handbook I: Cognitive domain*. New York: Academic Press.

Blythe, M., Overbeeke, K., Monk, A., & Wright, P. (2004). *Funology: From usability to enjoyment*. Berlin: Springer.

Bødker, K., Kensing, F., & Simonsen, J. (2004). *Participatory IT design: Designing for Business and Workplace Realities*. Cambridge, MA: MIT Press.

Bødker, S. (1987). *Through the interface – A human activity approach to user interface design*. Aarhus, Denmark: Aarhus University.

Boess, S., Saakes, D. P., & Hummels, C. (2007). When is role-playing really experiential? Case studies. In *Proceedings of Tangible and Embedded Interaction* (pp. 279–282). IEEE. doi:10.1145/1226969.1227025.

Bogdashina, O. (2006). *Theory of mind and the triad of perspective on autism and Asperger Syndrome: A view from the bridge*. London: Jessica Kingsley Publishers.

Bogost, I. (2011). *Gamification is bullshit*. Retrieved April 2, 2012 from http://www.bogost.com/blog/Gamification_is_ bullshit.shtml

Bonsiepe, G. (2011). *Design, cultura e sociedade*. São Paulo: Blucher.

Boraston, Z., Blakemore, S., Chilvers, R., & Skuse, D. (2007). Impaired sadness recognition is linked to social interaction deficit in autism. *Neuropsychologia, 45*(7), 1501–1510. doi:10.1016/j.neuropsychologia.2006.11.010 PMID:17196998.

Boren, M. T., & Ramey, J. (2000). Thinking aloud: Reconciling theory and practice. *IEEE Transactions on Professional Communication*, *43*(3), 261–278. doi:10.1109/47.867942.

Bosselar, A., & Massaro, D. W. (2003). Development and evaluation of a computer-animated tutor for vocabulary and language learning in children with autism. *Journal of Autism and Developmental Disorders*, *33*(6). PMID:14714934.

Boucher, J. (2009). *The autistic spectrum: Characteristics, causes, and practical issues*. London: SAGE Publications Limited.

Bourges-Waldegg, P., & Scrivener, S. A. R. (1998). Meaning, the central issue in cross-cultural HCI design. *Interacting with Computers: The Interdisciplinary Journal of Human-Computer Interaction*, *9*(3), 287–309. doi:10.1016/S0953-5438(97)00032-5.

Bourguet, M.-L., & Ando, A. (1998). Synchronization of speech and hand gestures during multimodal human-computer interaction. In *Proceedings of the Conference Summary on Human Factors in Computing Systems*, (pp. 241 – 242). doi: 10.1145/286498.286726

Bowen, M., & Plimley, L. (2008). *The autism inclusion toolkit: Training materials and facilitator notes*. London: SAGE Publications Limited.

Bowler, L., He, D., & Hong, W. Y. (2011). Who is referring teens to health information on the web? Hyperlinks between blogs and health web sites for teens. In *Proceedings of the 2011 iConference*, (pp. 238-243). iConference.

Bradley, M. M., & Lang, P. J. (1994). Measuring emotion: The self-assessment manikin and the semantic differential. *Journal of Behavior Therapy and Experimental Psychiatry*, *25*(1). doi:10.1016/0005-7916(94)90063-9 PMID:7962581.

Brandt, E., & Messeter, J. (2004). Facilitating collaboration through design games. In *Proceedings of the Eighth Conference on Participatory Design: Artful Integration: Interweaving Media, Materials and Practices-Volume 1* (pp. 121–131). ACM.

Brangier, E., & Bastien, J. M. C. (2010). L'évolution de l'ergonomie des produits informatiques: Accessibilité, utilisabilité, émotionnalité et persuasivité. In G. Vallery, M. C. Le Port, & M. Zouinar (Eds.), *Ergonomie des produits et des services médiatisés: Nouveaux territoires, nouveaux enjeux* (pp. 307–328). Paris: Presses Universitaires de France.

Brangier, E., Hammes-Adelé, S., & Bastien, J.-M. C. (2010). Analyse critique des approches de l'acceptation des technologies: De l'utilisabilité à la symbiose humain-technologie-organisation. *Revue Européenne de Psychologie Appliquée*, *60*(2), 129–146. doi:10.1016/j.erap.2009.11.002.

Brassard, M. R., & Boehm, A. E. (2007). *Preschool assessment: Principal and practices*. New York: The Guilford Press.

Braun, B.-M., Röse, K., & Rößger, P. (2007). Localizing for the Korean market: Actually being there with a multi-method approach. In V. Evers, C. Sturm, M. Alberto, M. Rocha, E. Cambranes Martinez & T. Mandl (Eds.), *Proceedings of the Eighth International Workshop on Internationalisation of Products and Systems* (pp. 55-62). Product & Systems Internationalisation, Inc.

Bringay, S., Barry, C., & Charlet, J. (2006). Annotations: A functionality to support cooperation, coordination and awareness in the electronic medical record. In *Proceedings of the 7th International Conference on the Design of Cooperative Systems*. COOP.

Broekens, J., Pronker, A., & Neuteboom, M. (2010). Real time labeling of affect in music using the affectbutton. In *Proceedings of AFFINE'10*. AFFINE.

Brownell, M. D. (2002). Musically adapted social stories to modify behaviours in students with autism: four case studies'. *Journal of Music Therapy*, *39*(2), 117–144. PMID:12213082.

Broy, M., & Stølen, K. (2001). *Specification and development of interactive systems: Focus on streams, interfaces, and refinement*. Berlin: Springer. doi:10.1007/978-1-4613-0091-5.

Bruner, J. (1986). *Actual minds, possible worlds*. Boston: Harvard University Press.

Bryan, N. B., McLean, E. R., Smits, S. J., & Burn, J. (1994). The structure of work perceptions among Hong Kong and United States IS professionals: A multidimensional scaling test of the Hofstede cultural paradigm. In *Proceedings of the 1994 Computer Personnel Research Conference on Reinventing IS: Managing Information Technology in Changing Organizations* (pp. 219-230). Alexandria, VA: ACM.

Buchenau, M., & Suri, J. F. (2000). Experience prototyping. In *Proceedings of the Conference on Designing Interactive Systems Processes, Practices, Methods, and Techniques*. DIS.

Buckingham, D. (2004). *The media literacy of children and young people: A review of the research literature on behalf of Ofcom*. London: University of London, Youth and Media Institute of Education.

D. Buckingham, & R. Willett (Eds.). (2006). *Digital generations: Children, young people and new media*. Mahwah, NJ: Erlbaum.

Burmester, M., Mast, M., Jäger, K., & Homans, H. (2010). *Valence method for formative evaluation of user experience*. Paper presented at DIS 2010. Aarhus, Denmark.

Buur, J., & Larsen, H. (2010). The quality of conversations in participatory innovation. *CoDesign: International Journal of CoCreation in Design and the Arts*, *6*(3), 121–138.

Buur, J., & Matthews, B. (2008). Participatory innovation. *International Journal of Innovation Management*, *12*, 255–273. doi:10.1142/S1363919608001996.

Cabitza, F., & Gesso, I. (2011). Web of active documents: An architecture for flexible electronic patient records. In A. Fred, J. Filipe, & H. Gamboa (Eds.), *Biomedical Engineering Systems and Technologies: Third International Joint Conference, BIOSTEC 2010,* (Vol. 127, pp. 44–56). Springer.

Cabitza, F., Gesso, I., & Corna, S. (2011). Tailorable flexibility: Making end-users autonomous in the design of active interfaces. In K. Blashki (Ed.), *MCCSIS 2011: IADIS Multi Conference on Computer Science and Information Systems*. IADIS.

Cabitza, F., Simone, C., & Locatelli, M. P. (2012). Supporting artifact-mediated discourses through a recursive annotation tool. In *Proceedings of the 17th ACM International Conference on Supporting Group Work* (pp. 253–262). New York, NY: ACM.

Cabitza, F., Colombo, G., & Simone, C. (2013). Leveraging underspecification in knowledge artifacts to foster collaborative activities in professional communities. *International Journal of Human-Computer Studies*, *71*(1), 24–45. doi:10.1016/j.ijhcs.2012.02.005.

Cabitza, F., & Simone, C. (2010). WOAD: A framework to enable the end-user development of coordination oriented functionalities. *Journal of Organizational and End User Computing*, *22*(2), 1–20. doi:10.4018/joeuc.2010101905.

Cabitza, F., & Simone, C. (2012). Affording mechanisms: An integrated view of coordination and knowledge management. *Computer Supported Cooperative Work*, *21*(2), 227–260. doi:10.1007/s10606-011-9153-z.

Cabitza, F., Simone, C., & Sarini, M. (2009). Leveraging coordinative conventions to promote collaboration awareness. *Computer Supported Cooperative Work*, *18*(4), 301–330. doi:10.1007/s10606-009-9093-z.

Cacciabue, P. C. (2008). Role and challenges of ergonomics in modern societal contexts. *Ergonomics*, *51*(1), 42–48. doi:10.1080/00140130701800878 PMID:18097829.

Cagiltay, K. (1999). Culture and its effects on human-computer-interaction. In B. Collis & R. Oliver (Eds.), *Proceedings of World Conference on Educational Multimedia, Hypermedia and Telecommunications 1999* (pp. 1626-1626). Chesapeake, VA: AACE.

Caillois, R. (1967). *Les jeux et les hommes*. Paris: Gallimard.

Caillois, R. (2001). *Man, play and games*. Champaign-Urbana: IL: University of Illinois Press.

Callahan, E. (2005). Cultural similarities and differences in the design of university web sites. *Journal of Computer-Mediated Communication*, *11*(1), 239–273. doi:10.1111/j.1083-6101.2006.tb00312.x.

Cambra, C. (2005). Feelings and emotions in deaf adolescents. *Deafness & Education International*, *7*(4), 195–205.

Caple, D. C. (2010). The IEA contribution to the transition of ergonomics from research to practice. *Applied Ergonomics, 41*, 731–737. doi:10.1016/j.apergo.2010.03.002 PMID:20392433.

Capovilla, F., Raphael, W., & Mauricio, A. (2010). *Dicionário enciclopédico ilustrado trilíngue*. São Paulo, Brazil: EdUSP.

Cappel, J. J., & Huang, Z. (2007). A usability analysis of company websites. *Journal of Computer Information Systems, 48*(1), 117–123.

Card, S., Mackinlay, J., & Shneiderman, B. (1999). *Readings in information visualization: Using vision to think*. San Fransisco, CA: Morgan Kaufmann.

Carr, D. B. (2001). Designing linked micromap plots for states with many counties. *Statistics in Medicine, 20*(9-10), 1331–1339. doi:10.1002/sim.670 PMID:11343354.

Carroll, M. (2004). *Usability testing leads to better ROI*. Retrieved from http://www.theusabilitycompany.com/news/media_coverage/pdfs/2003/NewMediaAge_270303.pdf

Carroll, J. (2004). Beyond fun. *Interactions (New York, N.Y.), 11*(5), 38–40. doi:10.1145/1015530.1015547.

Castro Salgado, L. C., Leitão, C. F., & Souza, C. S. (2013). Semiotic engineering and culture. In *A Journey Through Cultures* (pp. 19–42). Springer. doi:10.1007/978-1-4471-4114-3_2.

Casual Games Association. (2011). *Smart gamification: Seven core concepts for creating compelling experiences*. Retrieved February 2, 2012 from http://casualconnect.org/lectures/business/smart-Gamification-seven-core-concepts-for-creating-compelling-experiences-amy-jo-kim

Cesario, M., Jervis, M., Luz, S., Masoodian, M., & Rogers, B. (2012). Time-based geographical mapping of communicable diseases. In *Proceedings of the 6th International Conference on Information Visualization*, (pp. 118-123). IEEE.

Chalfen, R. (1987). *Snapshot versions of life*. Popular Press.

Chalmeta, R. (2006). Methodology for customer relationship management. *Journal of Systems and Software, 79*, 1015–1024. doi:10.1016/j.jss.2005.10.018.

Charsky, D. (2010). From edutainment to serious games: A change in the use of game characteristics. *Games and Culture, 5*(2), 177–198. doi:10.1177/1555412009354727.

Chen, E. (2008). *Autism aspergers myths – The theory of mind*. Retrieved from http://iautistic.com/autism-myths-theory-of-mind.php

Chen, H.-T., Ma, W.-C., & Liou, D.-M. (2002). Design and implementation of a real-time clinical alerting system for intensive care unit. In *Proceedings of the AMIA Symposium* (p. 131). AMIA.

Chen, L., Achrekar, H., Liu, B., & Lazarus, R. (2010). Vision: Towards real time epidemic vigilance through online social networks: introducing SNEFT - Social network enabled flu trends. In *Proceedings of the 1st ACM Workshop on Mobile Cloud Computing & Services: Social Networks and Beyond*. ACM.

Chen, Q. (2001). *Human computer interaction issues and challenges*. Retrieved from http://search.ebscohost.com/login.aspx?direct=true&scope=site&db=nlebk&db=nlabk&AN=60706

Chen, J., Roth, R. E., Naito, A. T., Lengerich, E. J., & MacEachren, A. M. (2008). Geovisual analytics to enhance spatial scan statistics interpretation: an analysis of U.S cervical cancer mortality. *International Journal of Health Geographics, 7*(57).

Chen, W., & Akay, M. (2011). Developing EMRs in developing countries. *IEEE Transactions on Information Technology in Biomedicine, 15*(1), 62–65. doi:10.1109/TITB.2010.2091509 PMID:21075735.

Chien, S., Tran, D., Davies, A., Johnston, M., Doubleday, J., Castano, R., et al. (2007). Lights out autonomous operation of an earth observing sensorweb. In *Proceedings of the 7th International Symposium on Reducing the Cost of Spacecraft Ground Systems and Operations*. Moscow, Russia: AIAA.

Cho, H., Ishida, T., Yamashita, N., Inaba, R., Mori, Y., & Koda, T. (2007). Culturally-situated pictogram retrieval. In *Proceedings of the 1st International Conference on Intercultural Collaboration* (IWIC'07). Berlin: Springer-Verlag.

Choong, Y.-Y., & Salvendy, G. (1998). Design of icons for use by Chinese in mainland China. *Interacting with Computers*, *9*(4), 417–430. doi:10.1016/S0953-5438(97)00026-X.

Choset, H., Lynch, K. M., Hutchinson, S., Kantor, G., Burgard, W., Kavraki, L. E., & Thrun, S. (2005). *Principles of robot motion*. London: MIT Press.

Ciavarella, C., & Paternò, F. (2003). Design criteria for location-aware, indoor, PDA applications. In *Human-Computer Interaction with Mobile Devices and Services* (pp. 131–144). Academic Press. doi:10.1007/978-3-540-45233-1_11.

Ciolfi, L., & Bannon, L. (2005). *Space, place and the design of technologically enhanced physical environments: Spaces spatiality and technology*. Boston: Kluwer.

Clarke, M. (2003). *Reflection: Journals and reflective questions a strategy for professional learning*. Paper presented at the NZARE/AARE Conference. Auckland, New Zealand.

Clarkeburn, H., & Kettula, K. (2012). Fairness and using reflective journals in assessment. *Teaching in Higher Education*, *17*(4), 439–452. doi:10.1080/13562517.2011.641000.

Clemmensen, T. (2008). *Interaction design & usability from an Indian perspective - Talks with: Apala Chavan, Anirudha Joshi, Dinesh Katre, Devashish Pandya, Sammeer Chabukswar, Pradeep Yammiyavar*. Retrieved from /z-wcorg/ database

Clemmensen, T. (2010). A comparison of what is part of usability testing in three countries. *International Federation for Information Processing,* (316), 31-45.

Clemmensen, T., & Clemmensen, T. (2009a). *A framework for thinking about the maturity of cultural usability*. Retrieved from http://openarchive.cbs.dk/cbsweb/handle/10398/7949

Clemmensen, T., & Clemmensen, T. (2009b). Towards a theory of cultural usability. *A Comparison of ADA and CM-U Theory,*(5619), 416-425.

Clemmensen, T., & Clemmensen, T. (2010). Regional styles of human-computer interaction. In *Proccedings of the 3rd ACM International Conference on Intercultural Collaboration (ICIS),* (pp. 219-222). Association for Computing Machinery.

Clemmensen, T., & Goyal, S. (2005). *Cross cultural usability testing: The relationship between evaluator and test user*. Retrieved from http://openarchive.cbs.dk/cbsweb/handle/10398/6474

Clemmensen, T. (2009). Towards a theory of cultural usability: A comparison of ADA and CMU theory. *IFIP Advances in Information and Communication Technology*, *316*, 98–112. doi:10.1007/978-3-642-11762-6_9.

Clemmensen, T. (2012). Usability problem identification in culturally diverse settings. *Information Systems Journal*, *22*(2), 151–175. doi:10.1111/j.1365-2575.2011.00381.x.

Clemmensen, T., & Clemmensen, T. (2011). Templates for cross-cultural and culturally specific usability testing. *Results from Field Studies and Ethnographic Interviewing in Three Countries*, *27*(7), 634–669. doi: doi:10.1080/10447318.2011.555303.

Clemmensen, T., & Clemmensen, T. (2012). *The human-computer domain relation in UX models*. Academic Press.

Clemmensen, T., & Goyal, S. (2004). *Studying cross cultural think-aloud usability testing: Some suggestions for an experimental paradigm*. Academic Press.

Clemmensen, T., Hertzum, M., Hornbæk, K., Kumar, J., Shi, Q., & Yammiyavar, P. (2007). *Usability constructs: A cross-cultural study of how users and developers experience their use of information systems*. Academic Press.

Clemmensen, T., Hertzum, M., Hornbæk, K., Shi, Q., & Yammiyavar, P. (2009). Cultural cognition in usability evaluation. *Interacting with Computers*, *21*(3), 212–220. doi:10.1016/j.intcom.2009.05.003.

Clemmensen, T., & Roese, K. (2010). An overview of a decade of journal publications about culture and human-computer interaction (HCI). *IFIP Advances in Information and Communication Technology*, *316*, 98–112. doi:10.1007/978-3-642-11762-6_9.

Coelho, J., Duarte, C., Feiteira, P., Costa, D., & Costa, D. (2012). Building bridges between elderly and TV application developers. In *Proceedings of the International Conference on Advances in Computer-Human Interactions*, (pp. 53-59). IEEE.

Coelho, J., Duarte, C., Langdon, P., & Biswas, P. (2011). Developing accessible TV applications. In *Proceedings of the International ACM SIGACCESS Conference on Computers and Accessibility,* (pp. 131– 138). ACM. doi:10.1145/2049536.2049561

Conradi, B., Serényi, B., Kranz, M., & Hussmann, H. (2010). SourceBinder: Community-based visual and physical prototyping. In V. Pipek, M. Rohde, S. Budweg, S. Draxler, S. Lohmann, A. Rashid, & G. Stevens (Eds.), *ODS 2010: Proceedings of the 2nd International Workshop on Open Design Spaces*, (Vol. 7, pp. 23–35). International Institute for Socio-Informatics.

Constantine, L. L., & Lockwood, L. A. D. (2002). Usage-centered engineering for web applications. In *Proceedings of IEEE Software*. IEEE.

Constantine, L. (2003). Canonical abstract prototypes for abstract visual and interaction design. In *Proceedings of Interactive Systems: Design, Specification, and Verification* (Vol. 2844). Berlin: Springer. doi:10.1007/978-3-540-39929-2_1.

Constantine, L. (2009). *Human activity modeling: Toward a pragmatic integration of activity theory and usage-centered design human-centered software engineering*. Springer.

Constantine, L., & Lockwood, L. A. D. (1999). *Software for use: A practical guide to the models and methods of usage-centered design*. Reading, MA: Addison Wesley.

Cooper, S., Khatib, F., Treuille, A., Barbero, J., Lee, J., & Beenen, M. et al. (2010). Predicting protein structures with a multiplayer online game. *Nature*, *466*(7307), 756–760. doi:10.1038/nature09304 PMID:20686574.

Costa, D. (2011). *Self-adaptation of multimodal systems*. (Master Thesis). University of Lisbon, Lisbon, Portugal.

Costa, D., & Duarte, C. (2011a). Self-adapting TV based applications. In C. Stephanidis (Ed.), *Universal Access in Human-Computer Interaction: Design for All and eInclusion* (pp. 357–364). Springer. doi:10.1007/978-3-642-21672-5_39.

Costa, D., & Duarte, C. (2011b). Adapting multimodal fission to user's abilities. In C. Stephanidis (Ed.), *Universal Access in Human-Computer Interaction: Design for All and eInclusion* (pp. 347–354). Springer. doi:10.1007/978-3-642-21672-5_38.

Crozier, S., & Tincani, M. J. (2005). Using a modified social story to decrease disruptive behavior of a child with autism. *Focus on Autism and Other Developmental Disabilities*, *20*, 150–157. doi:10.1177/10883576050200030301.

Crozier, S., & Tincani, M. J. (2007). Effects of social stories on prosocial behaviors of preschool children with autism spectrum disorders. *Journal of Autism and Developmental Disorders*, *37*, 1803–1814. doi:10.1007/s10803-006-0315-7 PMID:17165149.

Csikszentmihalyi, M. (1990). *Flow: The psychology of optimal experience*. New York: Harper and Row.

Cunliffe, A. (2004). On becoming a critically reflexive practitioner. *Journal of Management Education*, *28*(4), 407–425. doi:10.1177/1052562904264440.

Cunningham, A., Close, B., Thomas, B., & Hutterer, P. (2010). Design and impressions of a multi-user tabletop interaction device. In *Proceedings of the Eleventh Australasian Conference on User Interface* (pp. 71 – 79). IEEE.

Currie, N. J., & Peacock, B. (2002). *International space station robotic systems operations: A human factors perspective*. Academic Press. doi:10.1177/154193120204600106.

CyberGloveSystems. (n.d.). Retrieved October 30, 2012, from http://www.cyberglovesystems.com

Cyr, D., & Trevor-Smith, H. (2004). Localization of web design: An empirical comparison of German, Japanese, and United States web site characteristics. *Journal of the American Society for Information Science and Technology*, *55*(13), 1199–1208. doi:10.1002/asi.20075.

Cziksentimihalyi, M., & Rochberg-Halton, E. (1981). *The meaning of things*. Cambridge, UK: Cambridge University.

Danado, J., & Paternò, F. (2012). Puzzle: A visual-based environment for end user development in touch-based mobile phones. In M. Winckler, P. Forbrig, & R. Bernhaupt (Eds.), *Human-Centered Software Engineering, (LNCS)* (Vol. 7623, pp. 199–216). Berlin: Springer. doi:10.1007/978-3-642-34347-6_12.

Dang, C. T., Straub, M., & André, E. (2009). Hand distinction for multi-touch tabletop interaction. In *Proceedings of the ACM International Conference on Interactive Tabletops and Surfaces,* (pp. 101 – 108). ACM. doi:10.1145/1731903.1731925

Dasgupta, S., & Gupta, B. (2010). *Organizational culture and technology use in a developing country: An empirical study.* Paper presented at the SIG GlobDev Third Annual Workshop. Saint Louis, MO.

Davis, P., & Shipman, F. (2011). *Learning usability assessment models for web sites.* Paper presented at the IUI 2011. Palo Alto, CA.

Davis, F. D. (1989). Perceived usefulness, perceived ease of use, and user acceptance of information technology. *Management Information Systems Quarterly, 13,* 319–340. doi:10.2307/249008.

Dawson, G., Rogers, S., Munson, J., Smith, M., Winter, J., & Greenson, J. et al. (2006). The effects of social stories on the social engagement of children with autism. *Journal of Positive Behavior Interventions, 8,* 29–42. doi:10.1177/10983007060080010501.

Day, D. L. (1991). *The cross-cultural study of human-computer interaction: A review of research methodology, technology transfer, and the diffusion of innovation.* Academic Press.

de Lemos, R., Giese, H., Müller, H. A., Shaw, M., Andersson, J., & Baresi, L. et al. (2012). *Software engineering for self-adaptive systems: A second research roadmap. Software Engineering for Self-Adaptive Systems II.* Dagstuhl, Germany: Schloss Dagstuhl - Leibniz-Zentrum fuer Informatik, Germany.

De Souza, C. S., Barbosa, S. D. J., & Prates, R. O. (2001). *A semiotic engineering approach to HCI.* Paper presented at the CHI 2001. New York, NY.

De Souza, C. S. (1993). The semiotic engineering of user interface languages. *International Journal of Man-Machine Studies, 39,* 753–773. doi:10.1006/imms.1993.1082.

de Waard, A. (2010). From proteins to fairytales: Directions in semantic publishing. *IEEE Intelligent Systems, 25*(2), 83–88. doi:10.1109/MIS.2010.49.

Dearman, D., Kellar, M., & Truong, K. N. (2008). An examination of daily information needs and sharing opportunities. In *Proceedings of the 2008 ACM Conference on Computer Supported Cooperative Work,* (pp. 679-688). ACM.

Deci, E., Koestner, R., & Ryan, R. (2001). Extrinsic rewards and intrinsic motivations in education: Reconsidered once again. *Review of Educational Research, 71*(1), 1–27. doi:10.3102/00346543071001001.

Dejoux, C., & Wechtler, H. (2011). Diversité générationnelle: Implications, principes et outils de management. *Management et Avenir, 43,* 227–238. doi:10.3917/mav.043.0227.

Del Galdo, E. M., & Nielsen, J. (1996). *International user interfaces.* New York: Wiley.

Delius, D. M., Plagemann, C., & Burgard, W. (2009). Probabilistic situation recognition for vehicular traffic scenarios. In *Proceedings of the IEEE International Conference on Robotics and Automation.* IEEE.

Demiri, V. (2004). *Teaching social story to children with autism using social stories: An empirical study.* (PhD Thesis). Hofstra University, Hempstead, NY.

DePaula, R. (2003). *A new era in human computer interaction: The challenges of technology as a social proxy.* Paper presented at the Latin American Conference on HCI. New York, NY.

Desmet, P. M. A. (2002). *Designing emotions.* (Doctoral Thesis). Technical University of Delft, Delft, The Netherlands.

Desmet, P. M. A., Hekkert, P., & Hillen, M. G. (2004). *Values and emotions, an empirical investigation in the relationship between emotional responses to products and human values.* Paper presented at Techné: Design Wisdom 5th European Academy of Design conference. Barcelona, Spain.

Desmet, P. M. A. (2003). *Measuring emotions: Development and application of an instrument to measure emotional responses to products.* Boston: Kluwer Academic Pub..

Desurvire, H., & Wiberg, C. (2008). Master of the game: Assessing approachability in future game design. In *Proceedings of CHI '08 Extended Abstracts on Human Factors in Computing Systems (CHI EA '08)*. ACM.

Deterding, S., Dixon, D., & Khaled, R. (2011). Gamification: Toward a definition. In *Proceedings of CHI 2011* (pp. 12–15). ACM.

Deterding, S., Khaled, R., Nacke, L., & Dixon, D. (2011a). Gamification: Toward a definition. In *Proceedings of CHI 2011 Workshop Gamification: Using Game Design Elements in Non-Game Contexts* (pp. 6-9). Vancouver, Canada: ACM.

Deterding, S., Sicart, M., Nacke, L., O'Hara, K., & Dixon, D. (2011b). Gamification: Using game design elements in non-gaming contexts. In *Proceedings of CHI 2011 Workshop Gamification: Using Game Design Elements in Non-Game Contexts* (pp. 2-5). Vancouver, Canada: ACM.

Dewey, J. (1933). *How we think: A restatement of the relation of reflective thinking to the educative process*. Boston: D. C. Heath.

Dewey, J. (1980). *Experience and education*. New York: Perigee.

Dhillon, B. (2004). *Engineering usability: Fundamentals, applications, human factors, and human error*. American Scientific Publishers.

Dickey, M. D. (2005). Engaging By design: How engagement strategies in population computer and video games can inform instructional design. *Education Teach Research Dev., 53*(2), 67–83. doi:10.1007/BF02504866.

Dillahunt, T., Mankoff, J., & Forlizzi, J. (2010). *A proposed framework for assessing environmental sustainability in the HCI community*. Paper presented at the CHI 2010. Atlanta, GA.

DIN. (2010). *DIN EN ISO 9241-210 ergonomische anforderungen der mensch-system-interaktion teil 210: Prozess zur gestaltung gebrauchstauglicher systeme*. Berlin: BeuthVerlag.

Dinet, J., Vivian, R., & Brangier, E. (2011). Towards future methods to take into account cross-cultural differences in design: An example with the expert community staff (ECS). In *Proceedings of the 1st International Conference on Design, User Experience and Usability: Theory, Methods, Tools and Practice* (LNCS), (vol. 6769 LNCS, pp. 53-61). Berlin: Springer.

DiSalvo, C., Sengers, P., & Hronn Brynjarsdottir, P. (2010). *Mapping the landscape of sustainable HCI*. Paper presented at the CHI 2010. Atlanta, GA.

Dix, A., Finlay, J., Abowd, G., & Beale, R. (2004). *Human-computer interaction* (3rd ed.). Englewood Cliffs, NJ: Pearson Education Limited.

Dodd, S. (2005). *Understanding autism*. London: Elsevier.

Doherty, M. J. (2009). *Theory of mind: How children understand others' thoughts and feelings*. New York: Taylor & Francis.

Donaldson, A., & Varley, J. (2010). Randomized, controlled trial of an intervention for toddlers with autism: The early start Denver model. *Pediatrics, 125*, e17–e23. doi:10.1542/peds.2009-0958 PMID:19948568.

Dong, W., & Fu, W.-T. (2010). *Toward a cultural-sensitive image tagging interface*. Paper presented at the 15th International Conference on Intelligent User Interfaces. Hong Kong, China.

Dong, Y., & Lee, K. (2008). A cross-cultural comparative study of users' perceptions of a webpage: With a focus on the cognitive styles of Chinese, Koreans and Americans. *International Journal of Design*. Retrieved from http://www.ijdesign.org/ojs/index.php/IJDesign/article/view/267/163

Dong, J., & Salvendy, G. (1999). Designing menus for the Chinese population: Horizontal or vertical? *Behaviour & Information Technology, 18*(6), 467–471. doi:10.1080/014492999118887.

Dormann, C. (2006). Cultural representations in web design: Differences in emotions and values. In T. McEwan, D. Benyon, & J. Gulliksen (Eds.), *People and computers XIX - The bigger picture* (pp. 285–299). London: Academic Press. doi:10.1007/1-84628-249-7_18.

Dormann, C., & Chisalita, C. (2002). *Cultural values in web site design*. Academic Press.

Dourish, P., & Mainwaring, S. D. (2012). *Ubicomp's colonial impulse*. Paper presented at the 2012 ACM Conference on Ubiquitous Computing. Pittsburgh, PA.

Dourish, P., & Bell, G. (2011). *Divining a digital future: Mess and mythology in ubiquitous computing*. Cambridge, MA: MIT Press.

Draper, S. (1999). Analysing fun as a candidate software requirement. *Personal and Ubiquitous Computing*, *3*(3), 117–122.

Duarte, C. (2008). *Design and evaluation of adaptive multimodal systems*. (Doctoral Dissertation). University of Lisbon, Lisbon, Portugal.

Duarte, C., & Carriço, L. (2006). A conceptual framework for developing adaptive multimodal applications. In *Proceedings of the International Conference on Intelligent User Interfaces*, (pp. 132–139). IEEE. doi: 10.1145/1111449.1111481

Duarte, C., Coelho, J., Feiteira, P., Costa, D., & Costa, D. (2011). Eliciting interaction requirements for adaptive multimodal TV based applications. In C. Stephanidis (Ed.), *Universal Access in Human-Computer Interaction: Design for All and eInclusion* (pp. 42–50). Springer. doi:10.1007/978-3-642-21672-5_6.

Dubois, B. (1992). From narrative toward exposition: Materials and methods sections of biomedical journal articles. In Language in context: Essays for Robert E. Longacre (pp. 157–188). Summer Institute of Linguistics.

Dul, J., & Neumann, W. P. (2009). Ergonomics contributions to company strategies. *Applied Ergonomics*, *40*, 745–752. doi:10.1016/j.apergo.2008.07.001 PMID:18775532.

Dumas, B., Lalanne, D., & Oviatt, S. (2009). Multimodal interfaces: A survey of principles, models and frameworks. In D. Lalanne, & J. Kohlas (Eds.), *Human Machine Interaction* (pp. 3–26). Springer. doi:10.1007/978-3-642-00437-7_1.

Dyck, J., Pinelle, D., Brown, B., & Gutwin, C. (2003). Learning from games: HCI design innovations in entertainment software. In *Proceedings of Graphics Interface*. IEEE.

Dyck, M. J. (2011). The ability to understand the experience of other people: Development and validation of the emotion recognition scales. *Australian Psychologist*.

Dye, M. W. G., Hauser, P. C., & Bavelier, D. (2009, May). Is visual selective attention in deaf individuals enhanced or deficient? The case of the useful field of view. *PLoS ONE. Visual Attention and Deafness*, *4*(5), e5640. PMID:19462009.

Dyer, M. (2004). *The essential guide to geocaching, tracking treasure with your GPS*. Golden, CO: Fulcrum Publishing.

Dyson, M. C., Andrews, M., & Leontopoulou, S. (1995). Multimedia in museums: The need for a descriptive framework. *Convergence (London)*, *1*(2), 105–124. doi: 10.1177/135485659500100210.

Easterbrooks, S. R., & Huston, S. G. (2008). The signed reading fluency of students who are deaf/hard of hearing. *Journal of Deaf Studies and Deaf Education*, *13*(1). PMID:17607020.

Eigenbrode, S. D., O'Rourke, M., Wulfhorst, J. D., Althoff, D. M., Goldberg, C. S., Merrill, K., & Bosque-Pérez, N. A. (2007). Employing philosophical dialogue in collaborative science. *Bioscience*, *57*(1), 55–64. doi:10.1641/B570109.

Ekahau. (2008). *Positioning engine 4.2 datasheet*. Retrieved from http://www.ekahau.com/file.php?id=99419

Ekman, P. (2003). *Emotions revealed: Recognizing faces and feelings to improve communication and emotional life* (2nd ed.). New York, NY: St. Martin's Press.

Eliasz, A. W. (2009). Not just teaching robotics but teaching through robotics. In J. H. Kim, S. S. Ge, P. Vadakkepat, N. Jesse, & A. Al Manum (Eds.), *Proceedings of communication in computer and information sciences series*. Springer. doi:10.1007/978-3-642-03986-7_25.

Elmezain, M., Al-Hamadi, A., & Michaelis, B. (2009). Improving hand gesture recognition using 3D combined features. In *Proceedings of 2nd International Conference on Machine Vision*. IEEE.

Elmezain, M., Al-Hamadi, A., Appenrodt, J., & Michaelis, B. (2008). A hidden Markov model-based continuous gesture recognition system for hand motion trajectory. In *Proceedings of the 19th International Conference on Pattern Recognition*. IEEE.

Elokla, N., Hirai, Y., & Morita, Y. (2010). A proposal for measuring user's kansei. In *Proceedings of the International Conference on Kansei Engineering and Emotion Research (KEER2010)*. KEER.

Elzouki, S., Fabri, M., & Moore, D. (2007). Teaching severely autistic children to recognise emotions: Finding a methodology. In *Proceedings of the twenty-first British Computer Society on Human Computer Interaction Group Conference,* (vol. 2, pp. 137-140). IEEE.

Endrass, B., Rehm, M., André, E., & Nakano, Y. (2008). *Talk is silver, silence is golden: A cross cultural study on the usage of pauses in speech.* Academic Press.

Epps, J., Lichman, S., & Wu, M. (2006). A study of hand shape use in tabletop gesture interaction. In Proceedings of Extended Abstracts on Human Factors in Computing Systems, (pp. 748–753). doi: doi:10.1145/1125451.1125601.

Erickson, T. (1993). From interface to interplace: The spatial environment as medium for interaction. In *Proceedings of Conference on Spatial Information Theory.* Cupertino, CA: Kluwer.

Erickson, T. (1996). Design as storytelling. *Interactions (New York, N.Y.)*, *3*(4), 30–35. doi:10.1145/234813.234817.

Ericsson, K. A., & Simon, H. A. (1993). *Protocol analysis: Verbal reports as data.* Cambridge, MA: The MIT Press.

Ericsson, K., & Simon, H. (1987). Verbal reports on thinking. In C. Faerch, & G. Kasper (Eds.), *Introspection in second language research* (pp. 24–54). Clevedon, UK: Multilingual Matters.

Eriksson, E., & Arnkil, T. A. (2009). *Taking up one's worries: A handbook on early dialogues.* Jyväskylä: Gummerus.

Ermi, L., & Mäyrä, F. (2005). Fundamental components of the gameplay experience: analysing immersion. In *Proceedings of DIGRA 2005 Conference: Changing Views – World in Play*. DIGRA.

Esselink, B. (1998). *A practical guide to software localization: For translators, engineers and project managers* (Vol. 3). Amsterdam: Benjamins.

Ester, M., Kriegel, H. P., Sander, J., & Xu, X. (1996). A density-based algorithm for discovering clusters in large spatial databases with noise. In *Proceedings of the 2nd Int. Conf. on Knowledge Discovery and Data Mining (KDD-96).* AAAI Press.

Evers, V. (2003). Cross-cultural aspects of user understanding and behaviour: Evaluation of a virtual campus website by user from North America, England, The Netherlands and Japan. In V. Evers, K. Röse, P. Honold, J. Coronado & D. Day (Eds.), *Proceedings of the Fifth International Workshop on Internationalisation of Products and Systems* (pp. 189-210). Kaiserslautern, Germany: University of Kaiserslautern.

Evers, V., & Day, D. (1997). The role of culture in interface acceptance. In *Proceedings of the IFIP TC13 Interantional Conference on Human-Computer Interaction* (pp. 260-267). London: Chapman & Hall, Ltd.

Evers, V., Kukulska-Hulme, A., & Jones, A. (1999). *Cross-cultural understanding of interface design: A cross-cultural analysis of icon recognition.* Paper presented at the International Workshop on Internationalization of Products and Systems. Rochester, NY.

Evers, V. (1998). Cross-cultural understanding of metaphors in interface design. In *Proceedings of Attitudes toward Technology and Communication.* CATAC.

Evers, V., Kukulska-Hulme, A., & Jones, A. (1999). *Cross-cultural understanding of interface design: A cross-cultural analysis of icon recognition.* Academic Press.

Eyal, G. (2010). *The autism matrix.* Cambridge, MA: Polity Press.

Eyesenck, H. J. (1970). *The structure of human personality.* London: Academic Press.

Faiola, A. (2006). *Toward an HCI theory of cultural cognition.* Academic Press.

Fallman, D. (2003). Design-oriented human-computer interaction. In *Proceedings of CHI 2003.* Ft. Lauderdale, FL: ACM.

Fambonne, E. (2003). The prevalence of autism. *Journal of the American Medical Association, 289*(1), 87–89. doi:10.1001/jama.289.1.87 PMID:12503982.

Farmer, L. (2004). Using technology for storytelling: Tools for children. *New Review of Children's Literature and Librarianship*, *10*(2), 155–168. doi:10.1080/1361454042000312275.

Fasciano, M., & Lapalme, G. (2000). Intentions in the coordinated generation of graphics and text from tabular data. *Knowledge and Information Systems*, *2*, 310–339. doi:10.1007/PL00011645.

Fayyad, U., Grinstein, G., & Wierse, A. (2001). *Information visualization in data mining and knowledge discovery*. San Francisco, CA: Morgan Kaufmann.

Feilkas, M., Fleischmann, A., Hölzl, F., Pfaller, C., Scheidemann, K., Spichkova, M., & Trachtenherz, D. (2009). *A top-down methodology for the development of automotive software* (Technical Report TUM-I0902). Munich, Germany: TU München.

Feilkas, M., Hölzl, F., Pfaller, C., Rittmann, S., Schätz, B., Schwitzer, W., et al. (2011). *A refined top-down methodology for the development of automotive software systems – The keylessentry system case study* (Technical Report TUM-I1103). Munich, Germany: TU München.

Feiner, S., & McKeown, K. (1993). Automating the generation of coordinated multimedia explanations. In M. T. Maybury (Ed.), *Intelligent multimedia interfaces* (pp. 117–138). American Association for Artificial Intelligence.

Feinstein, A. (2010). *A history of autism: Conversations with the pioneers*. Hoboken, NJ: John Wiley and Sons. doi:10.1002/9781444325461.

Feiteira, P., & Duarte, C. (2011). Adaptive multimodal fusion. In C. Stephanidis (Ed.), *Universal Access in Human-Computer Interaction: Design for All and eInclusion* (pp. 373–380). Springer. doi:10.1007/978-3-642-21672-5_41.

Fernandes, T. (1995). *Global interface design*. Boston: AP Professional.

Fernandez, A., Insfran, E., & Abrahão, S. (2011). Usability evaluation methods for the web: A systematic mapping study. *Information and Software Technology*, *53*(8), 789–817. Retrieved from http://www.sciencedirect.com/science/article/pii/S0950584911000607 doi:10.1016/j.infsof.2011.02.007.

Fisher, G. (1998). Beyond couch potatoes: From consumers to designers. In *Proceeding of the Third Asian Pacific Computer and Human Interaction*. AMC.

Fitzgerald, W. (2004). *Models for cross-cultural communications for cross-cultural website design*. Ottawa, Canada: National Research Council Canada.

Flatla, D., Gutwin, C., Nacke, L. E., Bateman, S., & Mandryk, R. L. (2011). Calibration games: Making calibration tasks enjoyable by adding motivating game elements. In *Proceedings of the 24th Annual ACM Symposium on User Interface Software and Technology 2011*. Santa Barbara, CA: ACM.

Flintman, M. (2007). *Supporting mobile mixed-reality experiences*. (Doctoral dissertation). The University of Nottingham, Nottingham, UK.

Fogg, B. J. (2003). *Persuasive technology: Using computers to change what we think and do*. San Francisco, CA: Morgan Kaufmann.

Folmer, E., & Bosch, J. (2004). Architecting for usability: A survey. *Journal of Systems and Software*, *70*, 61–78. doi:10.1016/S0164-1212(02)00159-0.

Følstad, A., Law, E., & Hornbæk, K. (2012). Analysis in practical usability evaluation: A survey study. In *Proceedings of the SIGCHI Conference on Human Factors in Computing Systems*. ACM.

Forlizzi, J., & Shannon, F. (2000). The building blocks of experience: An early framework for interaction designers. In *Proceedings of DIS'00*. Brooklyn, NY: DIS.

Foxall, G. R., & Goldsmith, R. E. (1994). *Consumer psychology for marketing*. New York, NY: Routledge Chapman & Hall Inc..

Fox, B. (2005). *Game interface design*. Boston: Thomson Course Technology PTR.

Friedman, C. P., & Wyatt, J. (2006). Evaluation methods in biomedical informatics. In K. J. Hannah, & M. J. Ball (Eds.), *Health Informatics* (2nd ed.). Berlin: Springer.

Frohlich, D., Kuchinsky, A., Pering, C., Don, A., & Ariss, S. (2002). Requirements for photoware. In *Proceedings of the 2002 ACM Conference on Computer Supported Cooperative Work* (pp. 166–175). ACM.

Fuchs, E. N., & Schwitter, R. (1995). Specifying logic programs in controlled natural language. In *Proceedings CLNLP 95, ELSNET/COMPULOG-NET/EAGLES Workshop on Computational Logic for Natural Language Processing*. Edinburgh, UK: University of Edinburgh.

Fuchs, E. N., & Schwitter, R. (2007). Web-annotations for humans and machines. In *Proceedings of the 4th European Semantic Web Conference (ESWC 2007)*, (LNCS). Berlin: Springer.

Fullerton, T., Swain, C., & Hoffman, S. (2008). *Game design workshop: A playcentric approach to creating innovative games*. San Francisco, CA: Morgan Kaufmann.

Gabbert, C. (2010). *Using social stories to teach kids with Asperger's disorder: The hub for bright minds*. Retrieved from http://www.brighthub.com/education/special/articles/29487.aspx

Gadsby, H., & Cronin, S. (2012). To what extent can reflective journaling help beginning teachers develop Masters level writing skills? *Reflective Practice: International and Multidisciplinary Perspectives*, *13*(1), 1–12. doi:10.1080/14623943.2011.616885.

Gajos, K. Z., Weld, D. S., & Wobbrock, J. O. (2008). Decision-theoretic user interface generation. In *Proceedings of the National Conference on Artificial Intelligence* (vol. 3, pp. 1532–1536). IEEE.

Gallagher, H. L., & Frith, C. D. (2003). Functional imaging of theory of mind. *Trends in Cognitive Sciences*, *7*, 77–83. doi:10.1016/S1364-6613(02)00025-6 PMID:12584026.

Galtung, J. (1981). Structure, culture, and intellectual style: An essay comparing saxonic, teutonic, gallic and nipponic approaches. *Social Sciences Information. Information Sur les Sciences Sociales*, *20*(6), 817. doi:10.1177/053901848102000601.

Galvão, A. M., et al. (2004). Persona-AIML: An architecture developing chatterbots with personality. In *Proceedings of the Joint Conference on Autonomous Agents and Multiagent Systems* (pp. 1266–1267). Washington, DC: IEEE Computer Society.

Garrett, J. J. (2002). *The elements of user experience: User-centered design for the web*. Berkeley, CA: Peachpit Press.

Gartner. (2011). *Gartner says by 2015, more than 50 percent of organizations that manage innovation processes will gamify those processes*. Retrieved February 2, 2012 from http://www.gartner.com/it/page.jsp?id=1629214

Garzotto, F., Paolini, P., & Sabiescu, A. (2010). Interactive storytelling for children. In *Proceedings of the 9th International Conference on Interaction Design and Children* (pp. 356–359). ACM.

Gaver, et al. (1999). Cultural probes. *Interaction*, *6*(1), 21–29. doi:10.1145/291224.291235.

Gaver, et al. (2001). *The presence project*. London: Royal College of Art.

Gaver, et al. (2004). Cultural probes and the value of uncertainty. *Interaction*, *9*(5), 53–56. doi:10.1145/1015530.1015555.

Gaver., et al. (2003). Ambiguity as a resource for design. In *Proceedings of the Conference on Human Factors in Computing Systems*. ACM.

Gaver, W., Dunne, T., & Pacenti, E. (1999). Design: Cultural probes. *Interactions (New York, N.Y.)*, *6*(1), 21–29. doi:10.1145/291224.291235.

Gavgani, V. Z. (2010). Health information need and seeking behavior of patients in developing countries' context, an Iranian experience. In *Proceedings of the 1st ACM International Health Informatics Symposium*, (pp. 575-579). ACM.

Gebauer, J. (2008). User requirements of mobile technology: A summary of research results. *Information, Knowledge. Systems Management*, *7*(1), 101–119.

Geer, D. (2004). Will gesture-recognition technology point the way? *Computer*, *37*(10), 20–23. doi:10.1109/MC.2004.184.

Geven, A., Sefelin, R., Höller, N., Tscheligi, M., & Mayer, M. (2008). Always-on information: Services and applications on the mobile desktop. In *Proceedings of the 10th International Conference on Human Computer Interaction with Mobile Devices and Services* (pp. 23-32). ACM.

Gibet, S., Kamp, J. F., & Poirier, F. (2004). Gesture analysis: Invariant laws in movement. In *Gesture-Based Communication in Human-Computer Interaction (LNCS)* (Vol. 2915, pp. 451–452). Berlin: Springer. doi:10.1007/978-3-540-24598-8_1.

Gill, A. M., & Nonnecke, B. (2012). Think aloud: Effects and validity. In *Proceedings of the 30th ACM International Conference on Design of Communication* (pp. 31-36). ACM.

Gnauk, B., Dannecker, L., & Hahmann, M. (2012). Leveraging gamification in demand dispatch systems. In *Proceedings of the 1st Workshop on Energy Data Management, 15th International Conference on Extending Database Technology*. Berlin, Germany: IEEE.

Goguen, J. A., & Linde, C. (1993). *Techniques for requirements elicitation.* Paper presented at the Requirements Engineering, 1993. New York, NY.

Golan, O., Ashwin, E., Granader, Y., McClintock, S., Day, K., Leggett, V., & Baron-Cohen, S. (2009). Enhancing emotion recognition in children with autism spectrum conditions: an intervention using animated vehicles with real emotional faces. *Journal of Autism and Developmental Disorders*, *40*(3), 269–279. doi:10.1007/s10803-009-0862-9 PMID:19763807.

Goldstein, N. E., Sexton, J., & Feldman, R. S. (2000). Encoding of facial expressions of emotion and knowledge of american sign language. *Journal of Applied Social Psychology*, *30*(1). doi:10.1111/j.1559-1816.2000.tb02305.x.

Gonçalves, D., & Jorge, J. (2008). In search of personal information: Narrative-based interfaces. In *Proceedings of the 13th International Conference on Intelligent User Interfaces* (pp. 179–188). ACM.

Good, J., & Robertson, J. (2006). CARSS: A framework for learner-centred design with children. *International Journal of Artificial Intelligence in Education*, *16*(4), 381–413.

Google Correlate. (n.d.). Retrieved November 5, 2012 from http://www.google.com/trends/correlate

Google Flu Trends. (n.d.). *How does this work?* Retrieved November 5, 2012 from http://www.google.org/flutrends/about/how.html

Göttel, T. (2011). Reviewing children's collaboration practices in storytelling environments. In *Proceedings of the 10th International Conference on Interaction Design and Children* (pp. 153–156). ACM.

Gould, E., & Marcus, A. (2011). Company culture audit to improve development team's collaboration, communication, and cooperation design, user experience, and usability. In *Proceedings of Theory, Methods, Tools and Practice (LNCS)* (Vol. 6769, pp. 415–424). Berlin: Springer.

Graf, J., & Wörn, H. (2009). Safe human-robot interaction using 3D sensor. In *Proceedings of VDI Automation*, (pp. 445-456). VDI.

Graf, J., Puls, S., & Wörn, H. (2010). Recognition and understanding situations and activities with description logics for safe human-robot cooperation. In *Proceedings of Cognitive* (pp. 90–96). Cognitive.

Gram-Hansen, L. B. (2009). Geocaching in a persuasive perspective. In *Proceedings of Persuasive '09*. Persuasive. doi:10.1145/1541948.1541993.

Gram-Hansen, S. B. (2009). Towards an approach to ethics and HCI development based on Løgstrup's ideas. *Lecture Notes in Computer Science*, *5726*, 200–203. doi:10.1007/978-3-642-03655-2_24.

Gram-Hansen, S. B., Schärfe, H., & Dinesen, J. W. (2011). Towards a context oriented approach to ethical evaluation of interactive technologies. *Lecture Notes in Computer Science*, *6949*, 628–631. doi:10.1007/978-3-642-23768-3_99.

Gram-Hansen, S. B., Schärfe, H., & Dinesen, J. W. (2012). Plotting to persuade – Exploring the theoretical cross field between persuasion and learning. *Lecture Notes in Computer Science*, *7284*, 262–267. doi:10.1007/978-3-642-31037-9_24.

Grandin, T. (1992). An inside view of autism. In E. Schopler, & G. B. Mesibov (Eds.), *High-functioning individuals with autism*. New York: Plenum Press. doi:10.1007/978-1-4899-2456-8_6.

Gray Center. (2010). *The gray center*. Retrieved from http://www.thegraycenter.org/

Gray, C. A. (1994). *Comic strip conversations*. Future Horizons.

Gray, C. A. (1998). Social stories and comic strip conversation with students with Asperger syndrome and high functioning autism. In *Asperger Syndrome or High-Functioning Autism?* New York: Plenum. doi:10.1007/978-1-4615-5369-4_9.

Gray, C. A., & Garand, J. D. (1993). Social stories: Improving responses of students with autism with accurate social information. *Focus on Autistic Behavior, 8*(1), 1–10.

Gray, W. D., & Salzman, M. C. (1998). Damaged merchandise? A review of experiments that compare usability evaluation methods. *Human-Computer Interaction, 13*(3), 203–261. doi:10.1207/s15327051hci1303_2.

Greenberg, S., Marquardt, N., Ballendat, T., Diaz-Marino, R., & Wang, M. (2011). Proxemic interactions. *Interaction, 18*(1), 42–50. doi:10.1145/1897239.1897250.

Grelotti, D. J., Klin, A. J., Gauthier, I., Skudlarski, P., Cohen, D. J., & Gore, J. C. et al. (2005). fMRI activation of the fusiform gyrus and amygdala to cartoon characters but not to faces in a boy with autism. *Neuropsychologia, 43*(3), 373–385. doi:10.1016/j.neuropsychologia.2004.06.015 PMID:15707614.

Gruen, D., Rauch, T., Redpath, S., & Ruettinger, S. (2002). The use of stories in user experience design. *International Journal of Human-Computer Interaction, 14*(3-4), 503–534. doi:10.1080/10447318.2002.9669132.

Guiard, Y., & Beaudouin-Lafon, M. (2004). Fitts' law 50 years later: Applications and contributions from human–computer interaction. *International Journal of Human-Computer Studies, 61*, 747–750. doi:10.1016/j.ijhcs.2004.09.003.

Guo, Y., Proctor, R., & Salvendy, G. (2011). A conceptual model of the axiomatic usability evaluation method. In M. Smith, & G. Salvendy (Eds.), *Human interface and the management of information: Interacting with information (LNCS)* (Vol. 6671, pp. 93–102). Berlin, Germany: Springer. doi:10.1007/978-3-642-21793-7_11.

Gustavsen, B. (2011). Theory and practice: the mediating discourse. In P. Reason, & H. Bradbury (Eds.), *The Handbook of Action Research*. London: Sage.

Gutwin, C., & Greenberg, S. (1997). Workspace awareness, position paper. In S. E. McDaniel & T. Brinck (Eds.), *Proceedings of the ACM CHI'97 Workshop on Awareness in Collaborative Systems*. Atlanta, GA: ACM.

Habermas, J. (2008). *Diskursetik*. Copenhagen, Denmark: Academic Press.

Hagiwara, T., & Myles, B. S. (1999). A multimedia social story intervention: Teaching skills to children with autism. *Focus on Autism and Other Developmental Disabilities, 14*, 82–95. doi:10.1177/108835769901400203.

Hakkarainen, P., Ketola, R., & Nevala, N. (2011). Reliability and usability of the ergonomic workplace method for assessing working environments. *Theoretical Issues in Ergonomics Science, 12*(4), 367–378. doi:10.1080/14639221003736339.

Hall, E. T. (1959). *The silent language*. New York: Doubleday.

Hall, E. T. (1976). *Beyond culture*. New York: Anchor Books.

Hall, E. T., & Hall, M. R. (1990). *Understanding cultural differences*. Yarmouth, ME: Intercultural Press.

Hall, E. T., & Hall, M. R. (2004). *Understanding cultural differences*. Yarmouth, ME: Intercultural Press.

Hamacher, N. A. (2006). *Automatische kriterienorientierte bewertung der gebrauchstauglichkeit interaktiver systeme*. München, Germany: Dr. Hut.

Ham, J., & Midden, C. (2010). Ambient persuasive technology needs little cognitive effort: The differential effects of cognitive load on lighting feedback versus factual feedback. *Lecture Notes in Computer Science*, 6137.

Hampe-Neteler, W. (1994). *Software-ergonomische bewertung zwischen arbeitsgestaltung und softwareentwicklung* (Vol. 2). Frankfurt am Main, Germany: Lang.

Hanley-Hochdorfer, K., Bray, M. A., Kehle, T. J., & Elinoff, M. J. (2010). Social stories to increase verbal initiation in children with autism and Asperger's disorder. *School Psychology Review, 39*(3), 484–492.

Hannabuss, S. (2000). Narrative knowledge: Eliciting organisational knowledge from storytelling.[). ASLIB.]. *Aslib Proceedings, 52*, 402–413. doi:10.1108/EUM0000000007031.

Han, S. H., Jung, E. S., Jung, M., Kwahk, J., & Park, S. (1998a). Psychophysical methods and passenger preferences of interior designs. *Applied Ergonomics, 29*(6), 499–506. doi:10.1016/S0003-6870(97)00009-4 PMID:9796796.

Han, S. H., Yun, M. H., Kim, K., & Cho, S. J. (1998b). *Development of a usability evaluation method. Pohang University of Science and Technology (POSTECH)*. Ministry of Science and Technology.

Han, S. H., Yun, M. H., Kim, K.-J., & Kwahk, J. (2000). Evaluation of product usability: Development and validation of usability dimensions and design elements based on empirical models. *International Journal of Industrial Ergonomics*, *26*, 477–488. doi:10.1016/S0169-8141(00)00019-6.

Han, S. H., Yun, M. H., Kwahk, J., & Hong, S. W. (2001). Usability of consumer electronic products. *International Journal of Industrial Ergonomics*, *28*(3), 143–151. doi:10.1016/S0169-8141(01)00025-7.

Hansen, T. E., Hourcade, J. P., Segre, A., Hlady, C., Polgreen, P., & Wyman, C. (2010). Interactive visualization of hospital contact network data on multi-touch displays. In *Proceedings of the 3rd Mexican Workshop on Human Computer Interaction*, (pp. 15-22). ACM.

Han, Y., & Zukerman, I. (1997). A mechanism for multimodal presentation planning based on agent cooperation and negotiation. *Human-Computer Interaction*, *12*, 187–226. doi:10.1207/s15327051hci1201&2_6.

Harle, C. A., Neill, D. B., & Padman, R. (2012). Information visualization for chronic disease risk assessment. *IEEE Intelligent Systems*, *27*(6), 81–85. doi:10.1109/MIS.2012.112.

Harrison, S., & Dourish, P. (1996). Re-place-ing space: The roles of place and space in collaborative systems. In *Proceedings of the ACM Conference on Computer Supported Cooperative Work*. ACM.

Hassenzahl, M. (2003). The thing and I: Understanding the relationship between user and product. In *Funology: From Usability to Enjoyment*. Dordrecht, The Netherlands: Kluwer Academic Publishers.

Hassenzahl, M. (2004). Emotions can be quite ephemeral: We cannot design them. *Interaction*, *11*(5), 46–48. doi:10.1145/1015530.1015551.

Hassenzahl, M. (2005). The quality of interactive products: Hedonic needs, emotions and experience. In *Encyclopaedia of Human Computer Interaction*. Hershey, PA: Idea Group Inc. doi:10.4018/978-1-59140-562-7.ch042.

Hassenzahl, M., & Tractinsky, N. (2006). User experience–A research agenda. *Behaviour & Information Technology*, *25*(2), 91–97. doi:10.1080/01449290500330331.

Hawker, J., Begg, N., Blair, I., Reintjes, R., & Weinberg, J. (2000). *Communicable disease control handbook*. Boston: Wiley-Blackwell.

Hawking, P., Stein, A., Zeleznikow, J., Pramod, S., Devon, N., Dawson, L., & Foster, S. (2005). Emerging issues in location based tourism systems. In *Proceedings of the International Conference on Mobile Business*, (pp. 75-81). IEEE.

Hayashi, E. C. S., & Baranauskas, M. C. C. (2010). Meta-communication in inclusive scenarios: Issues and alternatives. In *Proceedings of the IX Simpósio de Fatores Humanos em Sistemas Computacionais*. Academic Press.

Head, A. J. (1999). *Design wise*. Thomas H Hogan Sr.

Hedlund, A., Åteg, M., Andersson, I. M., & Rosén, G. (2010). Assessing motivation for work environment improvements: Internal consistency, reliability and factorial structure. *Journal of Safety Research*, *41*, 145–151. doi:10.1016/j.jsr.2009.12.005 PMID:20497800.

Heimgärtner, R. (2005b). Research in progress: Towards cross-cultural adaptive human-machine-interaction in automotive navigation systems. In D. Day & E. M. del Galdo (Eds.), *Proceedings of the Seventh International Workshop on Internationalisation of Products and Systems (IWIPS 2005)* (pp. 97-111). Amsterdam: Grafisch Centrum Amsterdam.

Heimgärtner, R. (2007). *Cultural differences in human computer interaction: Results from two online surveys*. Paper presented at the Open innovation. Konstanz, Germany.

Heimgärtner, R. (2010). *Cultural differences in human-computer interaction - Towards culturally adaptive human-machine interaction*. (PhD Dissertation). Universitätsbibliothek der Universität Regensburg, Regensburg, Germany.

Heimgärtner, R., Tiede, L.-W., & Windl, H. (2011). *Empathy as key factor for successful intercultural HCI design*. Paper presented at the 14th International Conference on Human-Computer Interaction. Orlando, FL.

Heimgärtner, R. (2008). A tool for getting cultural differences in HCI. In K. Asai (Ed.), *Human Computer Interaction: New Developments* (pp. 343–368). Rijeka, Germany: InTech. doi:10.5772/5870.

Heimgärtner, R. (2012). *Cultural differences in human-computer interaction. Oldenbourg*. Germany: Verlag.

Heimgärtner, R. (2013). Reflections on a model of culturally influenced human computer interaction to cover cultural contexts in HCI design. *International Journal of Human-Computer Interaction*. doi:10.1080/10447318.2013.765761.

Heimgärtner, R., & Tiede, L. W. (2008). Technik und kultur: Interkulturelle erfahrungen bei der produktentwicklung für China. In O. Rösch (Ed.), *Interkulturelle Kommunikation* (Vol. 6, pp. 149–162). Berlin: Verlag News & Media.

Helander, M. G., & Lin, L. (2000). Anthropometric design of workstations. In D. Tate (Ed.), *Proceedings of the First International Conference on Axiomatic Design* (pp. 130-138). Cambridge, MA: Institute for Axiomatic Design.

Helander, M., & Lin, L. (2002). Axiomatic approach in ergonomics design with an extension of the information axiom. *Journal of Engineering Design, 13*(4), 321–339. doi:10.1080/09544820210000050794.

Henze, N., Löcken, A., Boll, S., Hesselmann, T., & Pielot, M. (2010). Free-hand gestures for music playback: Deriving gestures with a user-centred process. In *Proceedings of the 9th International Conference on Mobile and Ubiquitous Multimedia MUM* (pp. 1-10). New York, NY: ACM Press.

Hermeking, M. (2001). *Kulturen und technik*. München, Germany: Waxmann.

Herskowitz, V. (2009). *Autism and computers: Maximizing independence through technology*. Researcher House.

Hertzum, M. (2010). Images of usability. *International Journal of Human-Computer Interaction, 26*(6), 567–600. doi:10.1080/10447311003781300.

Hertzum, M., & Clemmensen, T. (2012). How do usability professionals construe usability? *International Journal of Human-Computer Studies, 70*(1), 26–42. Retrieved from http://www.sciencedirect.com/science/article/pii/S1071581911001030 doi:10.1016/j.ijhcs.2011.08.001.

Heumann, J. (2002). Use cases, usability requirements, and user interfaces. In *Proceedings of Object-Oriented Programming, Systems, Languages, and Applications (OOPSLA 2002)*. ACM.

Hewett, T., Baecker, R., Card, C., Carey, T., Gasen, J., Mantei, M., et al. (1992). *Human-computer interaction*. Retrieved from http://old.sigchi.org/cdg/

Hickson, L., & Khemka, I. (1999). Decision making and mental retardation. In L. M. Glidden (Ed.), *International Review of Research in Mental Retardation*. Academic Press.

Hilbert, D. M., & Redmiles, D. F. (2000). Extracting usability information from user interface events. *ACM Computing Surveys, 32*(4), 384–421. doi:10.1145/371578.371593.

Himanen, P. (2012). *Sininen kirja: Suomen kestävän kasvun malli: Luonnos kansalliseksi tulevaisuushankkeeksi*. Retrieved from http://valtioneuvosto.fi/tiedostot/julkinen/pdf/2012/sininen-kirja/fi.pdf.

Hinrichs, U., & Carpendale, S. (2011). Gestures in the wild: studying multi-touch gesture sequences on interactive tabletop exhibits. In *Proceedings of the SIGCHI Conference on Human Factors in Computing Systems*, (pp. 3023 – 3032). ACM. doi: 10.1145/1978942.1979391

Hiraga, R., & Kato, N. (2009). Is visual information useful for music communication? In *Proceedings of MSIADU'09*. Beijing, China: MSIADU.

Hodemacher, D., Jarman, F., & Mandl, T. (2005). *Kultur und web-design: Ein empirischer vergleich zwischen grossbritannien und deutschland*. Paper presented at the Mensch & Computer 2005: Kunst und Wissenschaft – Grenzüberschreitungen der interaktiven ART., Wien, Austria.

Hodicová, R. (2007). *Psychische distanz und internationalisierung von KMU: Empirische untersuchung am beispiel des sächsisch-tschechischen grenzraumes*. Duv.

Hoekstra, G. (2000). *History of web design*. Retrieved from http://www.weballey.net/webdesign/history.html

Hofmann, F., Heyer, P., & Hommel, G. (1998). Velocity profile based recognition of dynamic gestures with discrete hidden Markov models. In *Proceedings of the International Gesture Workshop on Gesture and Sign Language in Human-Computer Interaction* (pp. 81-95). Berlin: Springer.

Hofstede, G., Hofstede, G. J., Minkov, M., & Vinken, H. (2008). *Announcing a new version of the values survey module: The VSM 08*. Retrieved September 12, 2009, from http://stuwww.uvt.nl/~csmeets/VSM08.html

Hofstede, G. (1984). *Culture's consequences: International differences in work-related values*. Beverly Hills, CA: Sage.

Hofstede, G. (1994). *VSM94: Values survey module 1994 manual*. Tilberg, Netherlands: IRIC.

Hofstede, G. (2006). What did GLOBE really measure? Researchers' minds versus respondents' minds. *Journal of International Business Studies*, *37*(6), 882. doi:10.1057/palgrave.jibs.8400233.

Hofstede, G. H. (1991). *Cultures and organizations: Software of the mind*. London: McGraw-Hill.

Hofstede, G. H., Hofstede, G. J., & Minkov, M. (2010). *Cultures and organizations: Software of the mind* (3rd ed.). Maidenhead, UK: McGraw-Hill.

Hoft, N. L. (1996). Developing a cultural model. In E. M. Del Galdo, & J. Nielsen (Eds.), *International users interface* (pp. 41–73). Hoboken, NJ: John Wiley & Sons, Inc..

Hollingworth, S., Allen, K., & Kuyok, K. A. (2009). *The influence of new media technologies used in learning on young people's career aspirations*. London: Institute for Policy Studies in Education, Metropolitan University.

Holmes, F. (1987). Scientific writing and scientific discovery. *Isis*, *78*(2), 220–235. doi:10.1086/354391 PMID:3316115.

Holzinger, A. (2005). Usability engineering methods for software developers. *Communications of the ACM*, *48*(1), 71–74. doi:10.1145/1039539.1039541.

Hölzl, F., & Spichkova, M. & Trachtenherz. D. (2010). *Safety-critical system development methodology* (Technical Report TUM-I1020). Munich, Germany: TU München.

Honold, P. (1999). Cross-cultural or intercultural - Some findings on international usability testing. In G. V. Prabhu & E. M. Del Galdo (Eds.), *Designing for Global Markets 1, First International Workshop on Internationalisation of Products and Systems* (pp. 107-122). Rochester, NY: Backhouse Press.

Honold, P. (2000a). Intercultural usability engineering: Barriers and challenges from a German point of view. In D. Day, E. D. Galdo, & G. V. Prabhu (Eds.), *Designing for Global Markets 2* (pp. 137–147). Academic Press.

Honold, P. (2000b). Culture and context: An empirical study for the development of a framework for the elicitation of cultural influence in product usage. *International Journal of Human-Computer Interaction*, *12*(3-4), 327–345. doi:10.1080/10447318.2000.9669062.

Honold, P. (2000c). *Interkulturelles usability engineering: Eine untersuchung zu kulturellen einflüssen auf die gestaltung und nutzung technischer produkte*. Düsseldorf, Germany: VDI Verl.

Hooper-Greenhil, E. (2004). Measuring learning outcomes in museums, archives and libraries: The learning impact research project. *International Journal of Heritage Studies*, *10*(2). doi:10.1080/13527250410001692877.

Hopkins, W. G. (2000). Quantitative research design. *Sportscience*, *4*(1). Retrieved from http://sportsci.org/jour/0001/wghdesign.html

Horner, R. H., Carr, E. G., Halle, J., McGee, F., Odom, S., & Wolery, M. (2005). The use of single-subject research to identify evidence-based practice in special education. *Exceptional Children*, *71*(2), 165–179.

House, R. J. (2004). *Culture, leadership, and organizations: The globe study of 62 societies*. Thousand Oaks, CA: Sage.

House, R. J., & Aditya, R. N. (1997). The social scientific study of leadership: quo vadis? *Journal of Management*, *23*(3), 409. doi:10.1177/014920639702300306.

Howlin, P. (2003). Outcome in high-functioning adults with autism with and without early language delays: Implications for the differentiation between autism and Asperger syndrome. *Journal of Autism and Developmental Disorders*, *33*(1), 3–13. doi:10.1023/A:1022270118899 PMID:12708575.

Howlin, P., Baron-Cohen, S., & Hadwin, J. (1999). *Teaching children with autism to mind-read: A practical guide for teachers and parents*. Hoboken, NJ: John Wiley and Sons.

Huber, F., Schätz, B., Schmidt, A., & Spies, K. (1996). AutoFocus - A tool for distributed systems specification. In *Proceedings of of FTRTFT'96, (LNCS)* (Vol. 1135). Berlin: Springer.

Huizinga, J. (1955). *Homo ludens: A study of the play element in human culture*. Boston: Beacon Press.

Hummel, B., Thiemann, W., & Lulcheva, I. (2007). Description logics for vision-based intersection understanding. In Proceedings of Cognitive Systems with Interactive Sensors. Stanford.

Hunicke, R., Leblanc, M., & Zubek, R. (2004). MDA: A formal approach to game design and game research. In *Proceedings of the Challenges in Games AI Workshop, Nineteenth National Conference of Artificial Intelligence* (pp. 1-5). San Jose, CA: IEEE.

Hurtienne, J., Stößel, C., Sturm, C., Maus, A., Rötting, M., Langdon, P., & Clarkson, J. (2010). Physical gestures for abstract concepts: Inclusive design with primary metaphors. *Interacting with Computers*, *22*(6), 475–484. doi:10.1016/j.intcom.2010.08.009.

Hwang, Y. K., & Ahuja, N. (1992). A potential field approach to path planning. *IEEE Transactions on Robotics and Automation*, *8*(1). doi:10.1109/70.127236.

IActionable. (2012). *What is gamification?* Retrieved January 16, 2013 from http://iactionable.com/gamification/what-is-gamification/

Iacucci, G., & Kuutti, K. (2002). Everyday life as a stage in creating and performing scenarios for wireless devices. *Personal and Ubiquitous Computing Journal*, *6*, 299–306. doi:10.1007/s007790200031.

ICSID. (2012). *Definition of design*. Retrieved October 20, 2012, from http://www.icsid.org/about/about/articles31.htm.

Ihamäki, P. (2012a). Geocaching: Interactive communication instruments around the game. *Eludamos Journal for Computer Game Culture, 5*(2).

Ihamäki, P. (2007). Geocaching at the institute of paasikivi – New ways of teaching GPS Technology & basics of orientation in local geography. In *New Trends in Information and Communication Technology & Accessibility*. Academic Press.

Ihamäki, P. (2008). Geocaching – A new experience for sport tourism. In *Selling or Telling? Paradoxes in tourism, culture and heritage*. Atlas Reflections.

Ihamäki, P. (2012b). Geocachers the creative tourism experience. *Journal of Hospitality and Tourism Technology*, *3*(3). doi:10.1108/17579881211264468.

Ihamäki, P., & Tuomi, P. (2009). Understanding 21st century's mobile games within boundaries. In *Breaking New Ground: Innovation in Games, Play, Practice and Theory*. Brunel University.

Inayatullah, S. (2006). Anticipatory action learning: Theory and practices. *Futures*, *38*, 656–666. doi:10.1016/j.futures.2005.10.003.

Ingalls, D., Wallace, S., Chow, Y.-Y., Ludolph, F., & Doyle, K. (1988). Fabrik: A visual programming environment. In *Proceedings on Object-Oriented Programming Systems, Languages and Applications* (pp. 176–190). New York, NY: ACM.

Instone, K. (2005). User experience: An umbrella topic. In *Proceedings of CHI '05 Extended Abstracts on Human Factors in Computing Systems* (pp. 1087-1088). New York, NY: ACM.

International, D. (2003). Developing international software (2. ed. ed.). Redmond, WA: Microsoft Press.

Irani, L. (2010). HCI on the move: Methods, culture, values. In *Proceedings of the Conference on Human Factors in Computing Systems*, (pp. 2939-2942). IEEE.

Isa, W. A. W. M., Noor, N. L. M., & Mehad, S. (2009). *Cultural prescription vs. user perception of information architecture for culture centred website: A case study on Muslim online user*. Paper presented at the 3rd International Conference on Online Communities and Social Computing: Held as Part of HCI International 2009. San Diego, CA.

ISO. (1998). *ISO 9241-11: Ergonomic requirements for office work with visual display terminals (VDTs), part 11: Guidance on usability*. Geneva, Switzerland: ISO.

ISO. (1999). *Human-centred design processes for interactive systems*. Geneva: international Standards Organisation.

Issa, T. (1999). *Online shopping and human factors.* Unpublished.

Issa, T., & Turk, A. (2012). Applying usability and HCI principles in developing marketing websites. *International Journal of Computer Information Systems and Industrial Management Applications*, *4*, 76–82.

Jääskeläinen, K. (2001). *Strategic questions in the development of interactive television programs.* (Doctoral Dissertation). University of Art and Design Helsinki, Helsinki, Finland.

Jacko, J. A. (Ed.). (2007). Human-Computer interaction: Interaction design and usability. In *Proceedings of the 12th International Conference, HCI International 2007,* (Vol. 4550). Berlin: Springer.

Jagne, J., & Smith-Atakan, A. (2006). Cross-cultural interface design strategy. *Universal Access in the Information Society*, *5*(3), 299–305. doi:10.1007/s10209-006-0048-6.

Jaimes, A., & Sebe, N. (2007). Multimodal human-computer interaction: A survey. *Computer Vision and Image Understanding*, *108*(1-2), 116–134. doi:10.1016/j.cviu.2006.10.019.

Janz, N. K., & Becker, M. H. (1984). The health belief model: A decade later. *Health Education & Behavior*, *11*(1), 1–47. doi:10.1177/109019818401100101 PMID:6392204.

Jaques, P. A., & Viccari, R. M. (2006). Considering students' emotions in computer-mediated learning environments. In Z. Ma (Ed.), *Web-based intelligent e-learning systems: Technologies and applications* (pp. 122–138). Hershey, PA: Information Science Publishing.

Järvinen, A. (2008). *Games without frontiers: Theories ans methods for game studies and design.* (Doctoral Dissertation). University of Tampere, Tampere, Finland. Retrieved April 2, 2012 from http://ocw.metu.edu.tr/pluginfile.php/4468/mod_resource/content/0/ceit706/week3_new/AkiJarvinen_Dissertation.pdf

Jenkins, H., Clinton, K., Purushotma, R., Robison, A. J., & Weigel, M. (2006). *Confronting the challenges of participatory culture: Media education for the 21st century.* Chicago: The MacArthur Foundation.

Jensen, R. E., & Bjørn, P. (2012). Divergence and convergence in global software development: Cultural complexities as social worlds. In J. Dugdale, C. Masclet, M. A. Grasso, J.-F. Boujut, & P. Hassanaly (Eds.), *From Research to Practice in the Design of Cooperative Systems: Results and Open Challenges* (pp. 123–136). London: Springer. doi:10.1007/978-1-4471-4093-1_9.

Jespersen, J. L., Albrechtslund, A., Øhrstrøm, P., Hasle, P., & Albretsen, J. (2007). Surveillance, persuasion, and panopticon. *Lecture Notes in Computer Science.* doi:10.1007/978-3-540-77006-0_15.

Jetter, H.-C. (2004). *Interkulturelles UI design und UI evaluation.* Universität Konstanz.

Jia, J. (2009). An AI framework to teach English as a foreign language: CSIEC. *AI Magazine*, *30*(2), 59–71.

Jin, H., & Liu, H. (2009). Research on visualization techniques in data mining. In *Proceedings of the International Conference on Computational Intelligence and Software Engineering.* IEEE.

Ji, Y. G., Park, J. H., Lee, C., & Yun, M. H. (2006). A usability checklist for the usability evaluation of mobile phone user interface. *International Journal of Human-Computer Interaction*, *20*(3), 207–231. doi:10.1207/s15327590ijhc2003_3.

Joan, S., & Rich, R. (1999). *Facing learning disabilities in the adult years: Understanding dyslexia, ADHD, assessment, intervention, and research.* Oxford, UK: Oxford University Press.

Johansson, M. (2006). Design games: Reinstalling the designer in collaborative design. In *Proceedings of DRS06 Wonderground.* DRS.

Johansson, M., & Linde, P. (2005). Playful collaborative exploration: New research practice in participatory design. *Journal of Research Practice*, *1*(1).

Johnson, D., & Wiles, J. (2003). Effective affective user interface design in games. *Ergonomics*, *46*, 1332–1345. doi:10.1080/00140130310001610865 PMID:14612323.

Jones, N. A., Ross, H., Lynam, T., Perez, P., & Leitch, A. (2011). Mental models: An interdisciplinary synthesis of theory and methods. *Ecology and Society*, *16*(1), 46.

Jordan, P. W. (1999). Pleasure with products: Human factors for body, mind and soul. In W. S. Green, & P. W. Jordan (Eds.), *Humans factors in Product Design: Current practice and future trends* (pp. 206–217). London: Taylor & Francis.

Joshi, A., Sarda, N. L., & Tripathi, S. (2010). Measuring effectiveness of HCI integration in software development processes. *Journal of Systems and Software, 83*(11), 2045–2058. doi:10.1016/j.jss.2010.03.078.

Jungk, R., & Müllert, N. (1987). *Futures workshops: How to create desirable futures*. London: Institute for Social Inventions.

Junxia, G., Xiaoqing, D., Shengjin, W., & Wu Youshou, W. (2008). Full body tracking-based human action recognition. In *Proceedings of the 19th International Conference on Pattern Recognition.* Tampa, Finland: IEEE.

Juul, J. (2005). *Half-real: Video games between real rules and fictional worlds*. Cambridge, MA: The MIT Press.

E. Kaasinen, & L. Norros (Eds.). (2007). *Älykkäiden ympäristöjen suunnittelu: Kohti ekologista systeemiajattelua*. Helsinki: Teknologiateollisuus.

Kabassi, K., & Virvou, M. (2003). Adaptive help for e-mail users. In J. Jacko, & C. Stephanidis (Eds.), *Human-Computer Interaction: Theory and Practice* (pp. 405–409). CRC Press.

Kallio, S., Kela, J., & Mäntyjärvi, J. (2003). Online gesture recognition system for mobile interaction. In *Proceedings of the International Conference on Systems, Man and Cybernetics SMC* (pp. 2070-2076). IEEE.

Kamal, N., Fels, S., & Ho, K. (2010). Online social networks for personal informatics to promote positive health behavior. In *Proceedings of the 2nd ACM SIGMM Workshop on Social Media,* (pp. 47-52). ACM.

Kamentz, E. (2006). *Adaptivität von hypermedialen Lernsystemen: Ein Vorgehensmodell für die Konzeption einer Benutzermodellierungskomponente unter Berücksichtigung kulturbedingter Benutzereigenschaften*. Retrieved from http://d-nb.info/986457256/34

Kankanhalli, A., Tan, B. C. Y., Wei, K.-K., & Holmes, M. C. (2004). Cross-cultural differences and information systems developer values. *Decision Support Systems, 38*(2), 183–195. doi:10.1016/S0167-9236(03)00101-5.

Kantardzic, M. (2002). *Data mining: Concepts, models, methods, and algorithms*. New York, NY: IEEE Press & John Wiley. doi:10.1109/9780470544341.

Kappos, A., & Rivard, S. (2008). A three-perspective model of culture, information systems, and their development and use. *Management Information Systems Quarterly, 32*(3), 601–634.

Kaptelinin, V. (2012). Activity theory. In *Encyclopedia of Human-Computer Interaction*. Aarhus, Denmark: The Interaction Design Foundation. Retrieved October 20, 2012. http://www.interaction-design.org/encyclopedia/activity_theory.html

Kaptelinin, V., & Nardi, B. (2006). *Acting with technologie: Activity theory and interaction design*. Cambridge, MA: MIT Press.

Kaufmann, W. E., & Silverman, W. (2010). Searching for the causes of autism. *Exceptional Parent, 40*(2), 32–33.

Kay, R. H., & Loverock, S. (2008). Assessing emotions related to learning new software: The computer emotion scale. *Computers in Human Behavior*, 24.

Kazdin, A. (1982). *Single-case research designs: Methods for clinical and applied settings*. New York: Oxford University Press.

Kendall, L., Hartzler, A., Klasnja, P., & Pratt, W. (2011). Descriptive analysis of physical activity conversations on Twitter. In *Proceedings of CHI '11 Extended Abstracts on Human Factors in Computing Systems*, (pp. 1555-1560). ACM.

Kendon, A. (1996). An agenda for gesture studies. *Semiotic Review of Books, 7*(3), 8–12.

Kensing, F. (1998, January-February). Prompted reflections: A technique for understanding complex work. *Interaction.* doi:10.1145/268986.268988.

Kensing, F., & Madsen, K. H. (1991). Generating visions: Future workshops and metaphorical design. In J. Greenbaum, & M. Kyng (Eds.), *Design at work: Cooperative design of computer systems*. Mahwah, NJ: Lawrence Erlbaum.

Kenski, V. M. (2008). *Education and technology: The new pace of information*. São Paulo: Papirus.

Keogh, E., Chu, S., Hart, D., & Pazzani, M. (2001). An online algorithm for segmenting time series. In *Proceedings of the IEEE International Conference on Data Mining ICDM* (pp. 289-296). IEEE.

Kersten, G. E., Kersten, M. A., & Rakowski, W. M. (2002). Software and culture: Beyond the internationalization of the interface. *Journal of Global Information Management*, *10*(4), 86–101. doi:10.4018/jgim.2002100105.

Kettenring, J. R. (2009). Massive datasets. *Wiley Interdisciplinary Reviews: Computational Statistics*, *1*(1), 25–32. doi:10.1002/wics.15.

Khalid, H. M., & Helander, G. H. (2004). A framework for affective customer needs in product design. *Theoretical Issues in Ergonomics Science*, *5*(1), 27–42. doi:10.1080/14639220310000086744.

Khan, B. H. (2001). A framework for e-learning. *E-Learning: Content, Technology & Services for Corporate, Government & Higher Education*. Retrieved October 20, 2012, from http://lomo.kyberia.net/diplomovka/webdownload/partial/elearningmag.com/E-Learning%20-%20A%20Framework%20for%20E-learning.pdf

Khan, B. H. (2003). A framework for open, flexible and distributed e-learning. *Magazine eLearn*, (2).

Kim, J., & Han, S. H. (2008). A methodology for developing a usability index of consumer electronic products. *International Journal of Industrial Ergonomics*, *38*(3), 333–345. doi:10.1016/j.ergon.2007.12.002.

Klare, G. R. (2000). Readable computer documentation. *ACM Journal of Computer Documentation*, *24*(3), 148–168. doi:10.1145/344599.344645.

Klingmann, M. (2009). *Accelerometer-based gesture recognition with the iphone*. (Master thesis). Goldsmiths University of London, London, UK.

Kluwe, R. H., & Haider, H. (1990). Models of internal representations of complex systems. *Sprache & Kognition*, *4*, 173–190.

Knapp, N. F. (2012). Reflective journals: Making constructive use of the apprenticeship of observation in preservice teacher education. *Teaching Education*, *23*(3), 323–340. doi:10.1080/10476210.2012.686487.

Knautz, K., Guschauski, D., Miskovic, D., Siebenlist, T., Terliesner, J., & Stock, W. (2012). Incentives for emotional multimedia tagging. In *Proceedings of the ACM 2012 Conference on Computer Supported Cooperative Work Companion*. New York, NY: ACM.

Koda, T., Rehm, M., & Andre, E. (2008). Cross-cultural evaluations of avatar facial expressions designed by western designers. *Lecture Notes in Computer Science*, *5208*, 245–252. doi:10.1007/978-3-540-85483-8_25.

Koehne, B., & Redmiles, D. F. (2012). *Envisioning distributed usability evaluation through a virtual world platform*. Paper presented at the Cooperative and Human Aspects of Software Engineering (CHASE). New York, NY.

Koivisto, E. M. I., & Wenninger, C. V. (2005). Enhancing player experience in MMORPGs with mobile features. In *Proceedings of DIGRA 2005 Conference: Changing Views – Worlds in Play*. DIGRA.

Komischke, T., McGee, A., Wang, N., & Wissmann, K. (2003). Mobile phone usability and cultural dimensions: China, Germany & USA. In L. Mühlbach (Ed.), *Human Factors in Telecommunication: Proceedings of the 19th International Symposium on Human Factors in Telecommunication (HFT 03)*. Berlin, Germany: Springer.

Komlodi, A. (2005). *Cross-cultural study of information seeking*. Paper presented at the International Conference on Human-Computer Interaction (HCII 2005). Las Vegas, NV.

Koning, H., Dormann, C., & van Vliet, H. (2002). *Practical guidelines for the readability of IT-architecture diagrams*. Academic Press. doi:10.1145/584955.584969.

Korhonen, H., Montola, M., & Arrasvuori, J. (2009). Understanding playful user experience through digital games. In *Proceedings of the International Conference on Designing Pleasurable Products and Interfaces*. DPPI.

Kralisch, A. (2006). *The impact of culture and language on the use of the internet empirical analyses of behaviour and attitudes*. (Dissertation). Berlin.

Kramsch, C. J. (1998). *Language and culture*. Oxford, UK: Oxford University Press.

Kratz, S., & Rohs, M. (2010). A $3 gesture recognizer – Simple gesture recognition for devices equipped with 3D acceleration sensors. In *Proceedings of the 15th International Conference on Intelligent User Interfaces IUI* (pp. 341-344). New York, NY: ACM Press.

Krebs, D., Conrad, A., & Wang, J. (2012). Combining visual block programming and graph manipulation for clinical alert rule building. In *Proceedings of the 2012 ACM Annual Conference Extended Abstracts on Human Factors in Computing Systems Extended Abstracts*, (pp. 2453–2458). New York, NY: ACM.

Krömker, H. (2000). Introduction. *International Journal of Human-Computer Interaction, 12*(3&4), 281–284.

Krüger, V., Kragic, D., Ude, A., & Geib, C. (2007). The meaning of action: A review on action recognition and mapping. *Proceedings of Advanced Robotics, 21*, 1473–1501.

Kuchinsky, A., Graham, K., Moh, D., Adler, A., Babaria, K., & Creech, M. (2002). Biological storytelling: A software tool for biological information organization based upon narrative structure. In *Proceedings of the Working Conference on Advanced Visual Interfaces* (pp. 331–341). ACM.

Kuchinsky, A., Pering, C., Creech, M., Freeze, D., Serra, B., & Gwizdka, J. (1999). Fotofile: A consumer multimedia organization and retrieval system. In *Proceedings of the SIGCHI Conference on Human Factors in Computing Systems: The CHI is the Limit* (pp. 496–503). ACM.

Kuhn, T. (2010). *Controlled English for knowledge representation*. (PhD Thesis). University of Zurich, Zurich, Switzerland.

Kuijk, F., Guimarães, R., Cesar, P., & Bulterman, D. (2010). From photos to memories: A user-centric authoring tool for telling stories with your photos. In *User Centric Media* (pp. 13–20). Springer. doi:10.1007/978-3-642-12630-7_2.

Kuoch, H., & Mirenda, P. (2003). Social story interventions for young children with autism spectrum disorder. *Focus on Autism and Other Developmental Disabilities, 18*, 219–227. doi:10.1177/10883576030180040301.

Kurdyukova, E., Redlin, M., & André, E. (2012). Studying user-defined ipad gestures for interaction in multi-display environment. In *Proceedings of the ACM International Conference on Intelligent User Interfaces*, (pp. 93 – 96). ACM. doi: 10.1145/2166966.2166984

Kurtenbach, G., & Hulteen, E. A. (1990). Gestures in human-computer communication. In B. Laurel (Ed.), *The Art of Human-Computer Interface Design* (pp. 309–317). Reading, MA: Addison-Wesley Publishing Co..

Kuts, E. (2009). Playful user interfaces: Literature review and model for analysis. In *Breaking New Ground: Innovation in Games, Play, Practice and Theory: Proceedings of the 2009 Digital Games Research Association Conference*. London: IEEE.

Kuutti, K. (1995). Activity theory as a potential framework for human- computer interaction research. In B. Nardi (Ed.), *Context and Consciousness: Activity Theory and Human Computer Interaction* (pp. 17–44). Cambridge, MA: MIT Press.

Kwahk, J., Han, S. H., Yun, M. H., Hong, S. W., Chung, M. K., & Lee, K. S. (1997). Selection and classification of the usability attributes for evaluating consumer electronic products. In *Proceedings of Human Factors and Ergonomics Society Annual Meeting* (Vol. 41, pp. 432-436). Human Factors and Ergonomics Society.

Kybartaite, A., Nousiainen, J., Marozas, V., & Jegelavicius, D. (2007). *Review of e-teaching/ e- learning practices and technologies*. Retrieved from http://hlab.ee.tut.fi/video/bme/evicab/astore/delivera/wp4revie.pdf

L'Abbate, M., Thiel, U., & Kamps, T. (2005). Can proactive behavior turn chatterbots into conversational agents? In *Proceedings of the IEEE/WIC/ACM International Conference on Intelligent Agent Technology – IAT* (pp. 173–179). Washington, DC: IEEE Computer Society.

Laarni, J., Koskinen, H., & Norros, L. (2008). *Activity-driven design of collaborative tools for nuclear power plant control rooms*. Paper presented at International Ergonomic Association Symposium. Helsinki, Finland.

Lakoff, G., & Johnson, M. (1980). *Metaphors we live by*. Chicago: University of Chicago Press.

Landry, B., & Guzdial, M. (2006). Itell: Supporting retrospective storytelling with digital photos. In *Proceedings of the 6th Conference on Designing Interactive Systems* (pp. 160–168). ACM.

Lang, P. J., Bradley, M. M., & Cuthbert, B. N. (1999). *International affective picture system (IAPS), instruction manual and affective ratings* (Tech. Rep. A-4). Gaithersburg, FL: The Center for Research in Psychophysiology, University of Florida.

Lanning, S. K., Brickhouse, T. H., Gunsolley, J. C., Ranson, S. L., & Willett, R. M. (2011). Communication skills instruction: An analysis of self, peer-group, student instructors and faculty assessment. *Patient Education and Counseling*, *83*, 145–151. doi:10.1016/j.pec.2010.06.024 PMID:20638816.

Lantz, J. (2002). Theory of mind in autism: development, implications, and interventions. *The Reporter*, *7*(3), 18–25.

Laurillard, D. (2002). Rethinking university teaching in the digital age. In *Futures Forum 2002*. Retrieved October 20, 2012, from http://net.educause.edu/ir/library/pdf/ffp0205s.pdf

Laurillard, D. (2001). *Rethinking university teaching: A framework for the effective use of educational technology*. London: Routledge.

Lavee, G., Rivlin, E., & Rudzsky, M. (2009). Understanding video events: A survey of methods for automatic interpretation of semantic occurrences in video. *IEEE Transactions on Systems, Man and Cybernetics. Part C, Applications and Reviews*, *39*(5), 489–504. doi:10.1109/TSMCC.2009.2023380.

Lavie, T., Oron-Gilad, T., & Meyer, J. (2011). Aesthetics and usability of in-vehicle navigation displays. *International Journal of Human-Computer Studies*, *69*(1-2), 80–99. doi:10.1016/j.ijhcs.2010.10.002.

Law, Kasirun, & Gan. (2011). Gamification towards sustainable mobile application. In *Proceedings of the 5th Malaysian Conference in Software Engineering* (pp. 349-353). IEEE.

Law, W. K., & Perez, K. (2005). Cross-cultural implementation of information system. *Journal of Cases on Information Technology*, *7*(2), 121–130. doi:10.4018/jcit.2005040108.

Lazar, J., Jones, A., & Shneiderman, B. (2006). Workplace user frustration with computers: An exploratory investigation of the causes and severity. *Behaviour & Information Technology*, *25*(3), 239–251. doi:10.1080/01449290500196963.

LeBlanc, R., & Volkers, H. (2007). *What you should know about Autism spectrum disorders: Signs, symptoms, diagnosis, treatment and effects on life*. Cranendonck Coaching.

Lee, I., Choi, G. W., Kim, J., Kim, S., Lee, K., Kim, D.,... An, Y. (2008). Cultural dimensions for user experience: Cross-country and cross-product analysis of users' cultural characteristics. *People and Computers, 1*(Edit 22), 3-12.

Lee, K.-P. (2007). *Culture and its effects on human interaction with design: With the emphasis on cross-cultural perspectives between Korea and Japan*. Retrieved from http://hdl.handle.net/2241/5979

Lee, Y. (2002). *Introduction*. Retrieved from http://www.csulb.edu/web/journals/jecr/issues/20024/paper3.pdf

Lee, D. G., & Suh, N. P. (2005). *Axiomatic design and fabrication of composite structures-applications in robots, machine tools, and automobiles*. New York: Oxford University Press.

Lee, K. W., & Lee, Y. C. (2012). Design and validation of an improved graphical user interface with the 'Tool ball'. *Applied Ergonomics*, *43*(1), 57–68. doi:10.1016/j.apergo.2011.03.004 PMID:21555114.

Lee, S., & Koubek, R. J. (2010). The effects of usability and web design attributes on user preference for e-commerce web sites. *Computers in Industry*, *61*(4), 329–341. doi:10.1016/j.compind.2009.12.004.

Lee, Y., & Kozar, K. (2012). Understanding of website usability: Specifying and measuring constructs and their relationships. *Decision Support Systems*, *52*(2), 450–463. Retrieved from http://www.sciencedirect.com/science/article/pii/S0167923611001679 doi:10.1016/j.dss.2011.10.004.

Lefevre, R. (2011). *Rude hand gestures of the world*. San Francisco, CA: Chronicle Books.

Lehto, T., & Oinas-Kukkonen, H. (2010). Persuasive features in six weight loss websites: A qualitative evaluation. *Lecture Notes in Computer Science*, 6137.

Leidner, D. E., & Kayworth, T. (2006). Review: A review of culture in information systems research: toward a theory of information technology culture conflict. *Management Information Systems Quarterly*, *30*(2), 357–399.

Leong., et al. (2010). Understanding experience using dialogical methods: The case of serendipity. In *Proceedings of OZCHI*. Brisbane, Australia: OZCHI.

Leontiev, A. N. (2009). *Activity and consciousness*. Marxists Internet Archive. Retrieved October 20, 2012, from http://www.marxists.org/archive/leontev/works/activity-consciousness.pdf

Lera, E., & Garreta-Domingo, M. (2007). Ten emotion heuristics: Guidelines for assessing the user's affective dimension easily and cost-effectivelly. In *Proceedings of the 21st BCS HCI Group Conference*. BCI. Freitas-Magalhães, A. (2011). *A psicologia das emoções: O fascínio do rosto humano*. Porto, Portugal: Universidade Fernando Pessoa.

Leuxner, C., Sitou, W., & Spanfelner, B. (2010). A formal model for work flows. In *Proceedings of the 8th IEEE International Conference on Software Engineering and Formal Method* (pp. 135–144). IEEE.

Leveson, N. G., & Turner, C. S. (1993). An investigation of the therac-25 accidents. *IEEE Computer*, *26*(7), 18–41. doi:10.1109/MC.1993.274940.

Lewandowitz, L., Rößger, P., & Vöhringer-Kuhnt, T. (2006). Asiatische vs. europäische HMI Lösungen von Fahrerinformationssystemen. In *Proceedings of Useware 2006* (Vol. 1946, pp. 279–287). Düsseldorf, Germany: VDI.

Lewandowski, T. A. (2010). Evolving understanding of the relationship between mercury exposure and autism. In L. I. Simeonov, M. V. Kochubovski, & B. G. Simeonova (Eds.), *Environmental heavy metal pollution and effects on child mental development: Risk assessment and prevention strategies*. Springer. doi:10.1007/978-94-007-0253-0_4.

Lewis, C. (1982). *Using the thinking-aloud method in cognitive interface design (IBM Research Report RC 9265)*. Yorktown Heights, NY: IBM TJ Watson Research Center.

Li, A. C., Kannry, J. L., Kushniruk, A., Chrimes, D., McGinn, T. G., Edonyabo, D., & Mann, D. M. (2012). Integrating usability testing and think-aloud protocol analysis with near-live clinical simulations in evaluating clinical decision support. *International Journal of Medical Informatics*, *81*(11), 761–772. doi:10.1016/j.ijmedinf.2012.02.009 PMID:22456088.

H. Lieberman, F. Paternò, & V. Wulf (Eds.). (2006). *End user development*. Springer Netherlands. doi:10.1007/1-4020-5386-X.

Lim, Y., & Rogers, Y. (2008). A framework and an environment for collaborative analysis of user experience. *Journal of Human–Computer Interaction*, *24*(6), 529–555. doi:10.1080/10447310801971204.

Lincke, J., Krahn, R., Ingalls, D., & Hirschfeld, R. (2009). Lively fabrik - A web-based end-user programming environment. In *Proceedings of the 2009 Seventh International Conference on Creating, Connecting and Collaborating through Computing*, (pp. 11–19). IEEE.

Linde, C. (1993). *Life stories, the creation of coherence*. Oxford, UK: Oxford University Press.

Lin, H.-S., Hong, Z.-R., Wang, H.-H., & Lee, S.-T. (2011). Using reflective peer assessment to promote students' conceptual understanding through asynchronous discussions. *Journal of Educational Technology & Society*, *14*(3), 178–189.

Lin, Y., & Zhang, W. J. (2004). Towards a novel interface design framework: Function–behavior–state paradigm. *International Journal of Human-Computer Studies*, *61*, 259–297. doi:10.1016/j.ijhcs.2003.11.008.

Lippard, L. (1997). *The lure of the local: Senses of place in a multicentered society*. New York: New Press.

List, D. (2006). Action research cycles for multiple futures perspectives. *Futures*, *38*, 673–684. doi:10.1016/j.futures.2005.10.001.

Liu, X., & Fujimura, K. (2004). Hand gesture recognition using depth data. In *Proceedings of the IEEE International Conference on Automatic Face and Gesture Recognition*, (pp. 529 – 534). IEEE.

Liu, Y., Alexandrova, T., & Nakajima, T. (2011). Gamifying intelligent environments. In *Proceedings of the 2011 International ACM Workshop on Ubiquitous Meta User Interfaces, Ubi-MUI '11* (pp. 7-12). ACM.

Liu, C.-H., Wang, Y.-M., Yu, G.-L., & Wang, Y.-J. (2009). Related theories and exploration on dynamic model of empathy. *Advances in Psychological Science*, *5*, 14.

Liu, J., Wang, Z., Zhong, L., Wickramasuriya, J., & Vasudevan, V. (2009). uWave: Accelerometer–based personalized gesture recognition and its applications. *Journal Pervasive and Mobile Computing*, *5*(6), 657–675. doi:10.1016/j.pmcj.2009.07.007.

Livingstone, S., & Bovill, M. (1999). *Young people, new media: Report of the research project children young people and the changing media environment*. London: Department of Media and Communications, London School of Economics and Political Science.

Locatelli, M. P., Ardesia, V., & Cabitza, F. (2010). Supporting learning by doing in archaeology with active process maps. In *Proceedings of the IADIS International Conference on e-Learning*, (Vol. 1, pp. 218–225). IADIS.

Loccoz, N. M., Brémond, F., & Thonnat, M. (2003). Recurrent Bayesian network for the recognition of human behaviours from video. In *Proceedings of the 3rd International Conference on Computer Vision Systems (ICVS'03)*. Graz, Austria: ICVS.

Lockton, D., Harrison, D., & Stanton, N. (2010). The design with intent method: A design tool for influencing user behaviour. *Applied Ergonomics*, *41*(3), 382–392. doi:10.1016/j.apergo.2009.09.001 PMID:19822311.

Løgstrup, K. (1997). *The ethical demand*. South Bend, IN: University of Notre Dame Press.

Looije, R. et al. (2008). Children's responses and opinion on three bots that motivate, educate and play. *Journal of Physical Agents*, *2*(2), 13–20.

Lorimer, P. A., Simpson, R. L., Myles, B. S., & Ganz, J. B. (2002). The use of social stories as a preventative behavioral intervention in a home setting with a child with autism. *Journal of Positive Behavior Interventions*, *4*(1), 53–60. doi:10.1177/109830070200400109.

Loughran, J. (2002). Effective reflective practice: In search of meaning in learning about teaching. *Journal of Teacher Education*, *53*(1), 33–43. doi:10.1177/0022487102053001004.

Loureiro, I., Leão, C. P., & Arezes, P. (2012). Ergonomic tridimensional analysis: Critical ergonomic factors identification in a commercial environmental. *Work (Reading, Mass.)*, *41*(S1), 636–641. PMID:22316794.

Loureiro, I., Leão, C. P., & Arezes, P. M. (2010a). Management of the benefits on the client's involvement on ergonomic analysis. In T. de Magalhães et al. (Eds.), *Communications in Computer and Information Science* (pp. 1–8). Berlin, Germany: Springer. doi:10.1007/978-3-642-15717-2_1.

Loureiro, I., Leão, C. P., & Arezes, P. M. (2010b). Tabela de ponderação: Construção de uma metodologia para intervenção ergonómica. In P. Arezes et al. (Eds.), *SHO 2010: Occupational Safety and Hygiene* (pp. 299–303). Guimarães, Portugal: Academic Press.

Lu, X. (2009). Web GIS based information visualization for infectious disease prevention. In *Proceedings of the Third International Symposium on Intelligent Information Technology Application*, (pp. 148-151). IEEE.

Luimula, M., Pieskä, S., Pitkäaho, T., & Tervonen, J. (2009). Ambient intelligence in mobile field work. In *Proceedings of the 8th International Conference and Workshop on Ambient Intelligence and Embedded Systems*. IEEE.

Luimula, M., Sääskilahti, K., Partala, T., & Saukko, O. (2007). A field comparison of techniques for location selection on a mobile device. In *Proceedings of the Wireless Applications and Computing, International IADIS Conference*. Lisbon, Portugal: IADIS.

Ma, X., Chen, G., & Xiao, J. (2010). Analysis of an online health social network. In *Proceedings of the 1st ACM International Health Informatics Symposium* (IHI '10), (pp. 297-306). ACM.

Macaulay, C., & Jacucci, G., ONeill, S., Kankainen, T., & Simpson, M. (2006). The emerging roles of performance within HCI and interaction design. *Interacting with Computers*, *18*(5), 942–955. doi:10.1016/j.intcom.2006.07.001.

Macdonald, W., & Bendak, S. (2000). Effects of workload level and 8- versus 12-h workday duration on test battery performance. *International Journal of Industrial Ergonomics, 26*(3), 399–416. doi:10.1016/S0169-8141(00)00015-9.

MacFarland, B., & Gourlary, L. (2009). Points of departure - The reflection game: Enacting the penitent self. *Teaching in Higher Education, 14*(4), 455–459. doi:10.1080/13562510903050244.

Macias, B., & Pulman, S. (1993). Natural language processing for requirements specifications. In F. Redmill, & T. Anderson (Eds.), *Safety-Critical Systems, Current Issues, Techniques and Standards*. London: Chapman & Hall.

Macintyre, M. S. (2009). *Play for children with special needs: Supporting children with learning differences*. New York: Taylor & Francis.

Magliano, J., & Millis, K. (2003). Assessing reading skill with a think-aloud procedure and latent semantic analysis. *Cognition and Instruction, 21*(3), 251–283. doi:10.1207/S1532690XCI2103_02.

Maguire, M. (2011). Guidelines on website design and colour selection for international acceptance design, user experience, and usability. In *Theory, Methods, Tools and Practice* (Vol. 6769, pp. 162–171). Berlin: Springer.

Mahajan, D., Kwatra, N., Jain, S., Kalra, P., & Banerjee, S. (2004). A framework for activity recognition and detection of unusual activities. In *Proceedings of ICVGIP*. Kolkata, India: ICVGIP.

Maier, E. (2005). Activity theory as a framework foraccommodating cultural factors in HCI studies. In A. Auinger (Ed.), *Workshops-Proceedings der 5: Fachübergreifenden Konferenz Mensch und Computer 2005: Internationalisierung von Informationssystemen: Kulturelle Aspekte der Mensch-Maschine-Interaktion* (pp. 69–79). Wien, Austria: Springer.

Maier, E., Mandl, T., Röse, K., Womser-Hacker, C., & Yetim, F. (2005). Internationalisierung von informationssystemen: Kulturelle aspekte der mensch-maschine-interaktion. In A. Auinger (Ed.), *Workshops-Proceedings der 5. fachübergreifenden Konferenz Mensch und Computer 2005* (pp. 57–58). Wien, Austria: Springer.

Malone, T. W. (1982). Heuristics for designing enjoyable user interfaces: Lessons from computer games. In *Proceedings of the 1982 Conference on Human Factors in Computing Systems,* (pp. 63–68). ACM.

Malone, T. W. (1984). Heuristics for designing enjoyable user interfaces: Lessons from computer games. In J. C. Thomas, & M. L. Schneider (Eds.), *Human Factors in Computer Systems*. Norwood, NJ: Ablex.

Maloney, J., Resnick, M., Rusk, N., Silverman, B., & Eastmond, E. (2010). The scratch programming language and environment. *Transactions on Computing Education, 10*(4), 16:1–16:15.

Mamlin, B. W., Biondich, P. G., Wolfe, B. A., Fraser, H., Jazayeri, D., Allen, C., et al. (2006). Cooking up an open source EMR for developing countries: OpenMRS - A recipe for successful collaboration. In *Proceedings of AMIA Annual Symposium* (p. 529). AMIA.

Mandasari, V. (2012). *Learning social story with 2D animated social stories for children with autism spectrum disorders*. (Dissertation for Masters of Science by Research). Swinburne University of Technology.

Mandryk, R. L., Atkins, M. S., & Inkpen, K. M. (2006). A continuous and objective evaluation of emotional experience with interactive play environments. In *Proceedings of CHI 2006*. ACM.

Mäntyjärvi, J., Kela, J., Korpipää, P., & Kallio, S. (2004). Enabling fast and effortless customisation in accelerometer based gesture interaction. In *Proceedings of the Third International Conference on Mobile and Ubiquitous Multimedia MUM* (pp. 25-31). New York, NY: ACM Press.

Marcus, A., & Baumgartner, V.-J. (2004). A practical set of culture dimensions for global user-interface development. In *Proceedings of Computer Human Interaction, 6th Asia Pacific Conference, APCHI 2004,* (pp. 252-261). APCHI.

Marcus, A., & Gould, E. W. (2000). *Cultural dimensions and global web user-interface design: What? So what? Now what?* Retrieved from http://www.amanda.com

Marcus, A. (2001). Cross-cultural user-interface design. In M. J. S. G. Smith (Ed.), *Proceedings Human-Computer Interface Internat. (HCII)* (Vol. 2, pp. 502–505). New Orleans, LA: Lawrence Erlbaum Associates.

Marcus, A. (2001). International and intercultural user interfaces. In C. Stephanidis (Ed.), *User Interfaces for All: Concepts, Methods, and Tools* (pp. 47–63). Mahwah, NJ: Lawrence Erlbaum.

Marcus, A. (2003). User-interface design and China: A great leap forward. *Interaction*, *10*(1), 21–25. doi:10.1145/604575.604588.

Marcus, A. (2006). Cross-cultural user-experience design. In *Diagrammatic Representation and Inference* (pp. 16–24). Academic Press. doi:10.1007/11783183_4.

Marcus, A., & Gould, E. W. (2000). Crosscurrents: Cultural dimensions and global web user-interface design. *Interaction*, *7*(4), 32–46. doi:10.1145/345190.345238.

Marcuschi, M. L. (1994). *Conversational analysis*. São Paulo: Ática.

Marmasse, N., & Schmandt, C. (2002). A user-centered location model. *Personal and Ubiquitous Computing*, *6*, 318–321. doi:10.1007/s007790200035.

Marschark, M. (2007). *Raising and educating a deaf child: A comprehensive guide to the choices, controversies, and decisions faced by parents and educators* (2nd ed.). Oxford, UK: Oxford University Press.

Martins, S., & Filgueiras, L. V. L. (2010). Avaliando modelos de interação para comunicação de deficientes auditivos. In *Proceedings of IHC 2010 – IX Simpósio de Fatores Humanos em Sistemas Computacionais*. Belo Horizonte, Brazil: IHC.

Martinsons, M. G., & Westwood, R. I. (1997). Management information systems in the Chinese business culture: An explanatory theory. *Information & Management*, *32*(5), 215–228. doi:10.1016/S0378-7206(96)00009-2.

Masip, L., Oliva, M., & Granolles, T. (2011). User experience specification through quality attributes. In P. Campos et al. (Eds.), *INTERACT 2011, (LNCS)* (Vol. 6949). Berlin: Springer. doi:10.1007/978-3-642-23768-3_106.

Maslow, A. H. (1970). *Motivation and personality* (3rd ed.). New York, NY: Harper & Row.

Mattelmäki, T. (2006). *Design probes*. Helsinki, Finland: University of Art and Design Helsinki.

Mauldin, M. L. (1994). Chatterbots, tinymuds, and the turing test: Entering the loebner prize competition. In *Proceedings of the Nacional Conference on Artificial Intelligence*, (pp. 16–21). Seattle, WA: IEEE.

Mayer, R. E. (2003). The promise of multimedia learning: Using the same instructional design methods across different media. *Learning and Instruction*, *13*(2), 125–139. doi:10.1016/S0959-4752(02)00016-6.

Mayer, R. E., & Moreno, R. (2002). Animation as an aid to multimedia learning. *Educational Psychology Review*, *14*(1), 87–99. doi:10.1023/A:1013184611077.

McCarthy, J., & Wright, P. (2004). Technology as experience. *Interaction*, *11*(5), 42–43. doi:10.1145/1015530.1015549.

McCracken, D. D., & Wolfe, R. J. (2004). *User-centered website development a human-computer interaction approach*. Hillsdale, NJ: Pearson Education, Inc..

McCrae, R. R., & Costa, P. T. Jr. (1998). A five-factor theory of personality. In *Personality: Critical concepts*. London: Routledge.

McCullough, M. (2005). *Digital ground, architecture, pervasive computing, and environmental knowing*. Cambridge, MA: MIT Press.

McCullough, S., & Emmorey, K. (1997). *Face processing by deaf ASL signers: Evidence for expertise in distinguishing local features*. Oxford, UK: Oxford University Press. doi:10.1093/oxfordjournals.deafed.a014327.

McDonald, S., Edwards, H. M., & Zhao, T. (2012). Exploring think-alouds in usability testing: An international survey. *IEEE Transactions on Professional Communication*, *55*(1), 2–19. doi:10.1109/TPC.2011.2182569.

McGonigal, J. (2011). *Reality is broken*. New York: The Penguin Press.

Meadows, D. (2003). Digital storytelling: Research-based practice in new media. *Visual Communication*, *2*(2), 189–193. doi:10.1177/1470357203002002004.

Merler, S., Jurman, G., & Furlanello, C. (2006). Strategies for containing an influenza pandemic: The case of Italy. In *Proceedings of the 1st International Conference on Bio-Inspired Models of Network, Information and Computing Systems*, (pp. 1-7). IEEE.

Miki, M., Miyajima, C., Nishino, T., Kitaoka, N., & Takeda, K. (2008). An integrative recognition method for speech and gestures. In *Proceedings of the International Conference on Multimodal Interfaces,* (pp. 93 – 96). IEEE. doi: 10.1145/1452392.1452411

Mikic, F. A., Burguillo, J. C., Rodríguez, D. A., Rodríguez, E., & Llamas, M. (2008). T-bot and Q-bot: A couple of AIML-based bots for tutoring courses and evaluating students. In *Frontiers in Education Conference.* doi: 10.1109/FIE.2008.4720469

Miles, M. B., & Huberman, A. M. (1994). *Qualitative data analysis: An expanded sourcebook* (2nd ed.). Thousand Oaks, CA: Sage.

Miller, E. (1987). The therac-25 experience. In *Proceedings of the Conf. State Radiation Control Program Directors.* IEEE.

Miller, C. A. (2004). Human-computer etiquette: Managing expectations with intentional agents. *Communications of the ACM, 47*(4), 31–34.

Milosevic, B., Farella, E., & Benini, L. (2010). Continuous gesture recognition for resource constrained smart objects. In *Proceedings of the Fourth International Conference on Mobile Ubiquitous Computing, Systems, Services and Technologies UBICOMM* (pp. 391-396). Xpert Publishing Services.

Min, J.-K., Choe, B., & Cho, S.-B. (2010). A selective template matching algorithm for short and intuitive gesture UI of accelerometer-builtin mobile phones. In *Proceedings of the 2nd World Congress on Nature and Biologically Inspired Computing NaBIC* (pp. 660-665). IEEE.

Minnen, D., Essa, I., & Starner, T. (2003). Expectation grammars: Leveraging high-level expectations for activity recognition.[CVPR]. *Proceedings of Computer Vision and Pattern Recognition, 2,* 626–632.

Miskelly, C., & Cater, K. (2005). *Locating story: Collaborative community-based located media production.* Cambridge, MA: MIT.

Mitra, S., & Acharya, T. (2007). Gesture recognition: A survey. *IEEE Transactions on Systems, Man, and Cybernetics – Part C: Applications and Reviews Publication Information, 37*(3), 311–324. doi:10.1109/TSMCC.2007.893280.

Möller, R., & Neumann, B. (2008). Ontology-based reasoning techniques for multimedia interpretation and retrieval. In *Semantic Multimedia and Ontologies* (pp. 55–98). London: Springer. doi:10.1007/978-1-84800-076-6_3.

Monk, A., Hassenzahl, M., Blythe, M., & Reed, D. (2002). Funology: Designing enjoyment. In *Proceedings of CHI '02 Extended Abstracts on Human Factors in Computing Systems* (pp. 924–925). ACM.

Montola, M., Stenros, J., & Waern, A. (2009). *Pervasive games, theory and design.* San Francisco, CA: Morgan Kaufmann Publishers.

Moore, J. L., Dickson-Deane, C., & Galyen, K. (2010). e-Learning, online learning, and distance learning environments: Are they the same? *The Internet and Higher Education, 14,* 129–135. doi:10.1016/j.iheduc.2010.10.001.

Morris, M. R., Wobbrock, J. O., & Wilson, A. D. (2010). Understanding users' preferences for surface gestures. In *Proceedings of Graphics Interface* (pp. 261–268). IEEE.

Morrison, C., & Blackwell, A. (2009). Observing end-user customisation of electronic patient records. In V. Pipek, M. Rosson, B. de Ruyter, & V. Wulf (Eds.), In *Proceedings of the 2nd International Symposium on End-User Development,* (LNCS), (Vol. 5435, pp. 275–284). Springer.

Morrison, T. (2006). *Kiss, bow, or shake hands.* Avon, MA: Adams Media. Barber, W., & Badre, A. (1998). Culturability: The merging of culture and usability. In *Proceedings of the 4th Human Factors and the Web Conference.* IEEE.

Morris, R. P., & Tomlinson, J. J. (2008). A mobile device user interface with a simple, classic design. *IEEE Transactions on Consumer Electronics, 54*(3), 1252–1258. doi:10.1109/TCE.2008.4637614.

Muessig, K., & Price, J. G. (2007). *International viewpoint and news.* Berlin: Springer-Verlag.

Muller, M. J. (2003). Participatory design: The third space in HCI. In J. A. Jacko, & A. Sears (Eds.), *The Human-Computer Interaction Handbook: Fundamentals, Evolving Technologies and Emerging Applications.* Mahwah, NJ: Lawrence Erlbaum.

Müller-Tomfelde, C., Cheng, K., & Li, J. (2011). Pseudo-direct touch: interaction for collaboration in large and high-resolution displays environments. In *Proceedings of the Australian Computer-Human Interaction Conference,* (pp. 225 – 228). IEEE. doi: 10.1145/2071536.2071572

Munk, K. (1962). *Kærlighed og andre skuespil.* Copenhagen: Academic Press.

Munson, S., Lauterbach, D., Newman, M., & Resnick, P. (2010). Happier together: Integrating a wellness application into a social network site. *Lecture Notes in Computer Science*, 6137.

Murphy, K. (1998). *Hidden Markov model (HMM) toolbox for matlab.* Retrieved October 30, 2012, from http://people.cs.ubc.ca/~murphyk/Software/HMM/hmm

Mutschler, B., & Reichert, M. (2004). *Usability-metriken als nachweis der wirtschaftlichkeit von verbesserungen der mensch-maschine-schnittstelle.* Academic Press.

Myles, B. S., Trautman, M. L., & Schelvan, R. L. (2004). *The hidden curriculum: Practical solutions for understanding unstated rules in social situations.* Autism Asperger Publishing Company.

Nardi, B. A. (1993). *A small matter of programming: perspectives on end user computing.* Cambridge, MA: MIT Press.

Nardi, B. A. (1996). *Context and consciousness: Activity theory and human-computer interaction.* Cambridge, MA: MIT Press.

Nardi, B., & O'Day, V. L. (1999). *Information ecologies: Using technology with heart.* Cambridge, MA: MIT Press.

Navarro-Prieto, R., & Cañas, J. J. (2001). Are visual programming languages better? The role of imagery in program comprehension. *International Journal of Human-Computer Studies, 54*(6), 799–829. doi:10.1006/ijhc.2000.0465.

Neca, J., & Duarte, C. (2011). Evaluation of gestural interaction with and without voice commands. In *Proceedings of IADIS International Conference Interfaces and Human Computer Interaction,* (pp. 69 – 76). IADIS.

Nemery, A., Brangier, E., & Kopp, S. (2010). Proposition d'une grille de critères d'analyses ergonomiques des formes de persuasion interactive In B. David, M. Noirhomme, & A. Tricot (Eds.), *Proceedings of IHM 2010.* New York: ACM.

Nemery, A., Brangier, E., & Kopp, S. (2011). First validation of persuasive criteria for designing and evaluating the social influence of user interfaces: justification of a guideline. In A. Marcus (Ed.), *Design, User Experience, and Usability, (LNCS)* (Vol. 6770, pp. 616–624). Berlin: Springer. doi:10.1007/978-3-642-21708-1_69.

Neumann, B., & Möller, R. (2008). On scene interpretation with description logics. *Image and Vision Computing, 26,* 81–101. doi:10.1016/j.imavis.2007.08.013.

Neves, A. M. M., Barros, F. A., & Hodges, C. (2006). iAIML: A mechanism to treat intentionality in AIML chatterbots. In *Proceedings of the IEEE International Conference on Tools with Artificial Intelligence* (pp. 225-231). IEEE.

Newman, J. (2001). *Reconfiguring the videogame player.* Paper presented at GameCulture International Computer and Videogame Conference. Bristol, UK.

Newman, J. (2002). In search of the videogame player: The lives of Mario. *New Media & Society, 4,* 405.

Nicholson, S. (2012). A user-centered theoretical framework for meaningful gamification. Paper Presented at Games+Learning+Society 8.0. Madison, WI.

Nicolopoulou, A. (2005). Play and narrative in the process of development: Commonalities, differences, and interrelations. *Cognitive Development, 20,* 495–502. doi:10.1016/j.cogdev.2005.09.001.

Nielsen, J. (1995). 10 usability heuristics. *Alertbox.* Retrieved January 31, 2013, from http://www.nngroup.com/articles/ten-usability-heuristics/

Nielsen, J. (2003). *Usability 101.* Retrieved from http://www.useit.com/alertbox/20030825.html

Nielsen, J. (1990). *Designing user interfaces for international use* (Vol. 13). Amsterdam: Elsevier.

Nielsen, J. (1997). Usability testing. In G. Salvendy (Ed.), *Handbook of human factors and ergonomics* (pp. 1543–1568). New York: John Wiley & Sons.

Nielsen, J. (2006a). *Designing web usability*. Berkeley, CA: New Riders.

Nielsen, J. (2006b). *Usability engineering*. Amsterdam: Kaufmann.

Nisbett, R. E. (2003). *The geography of thought: How Asians and Westerners think differently..., & why*. New York: Free Press.

Nisbett, R. E., Peng, K., Choi, I., & Norenzayan, A. (2001). Culture and systems of thought: Holistic versus analytic cognition. *Psychological Review*, *108*, 291–310. doi:10.1037/0033-295X.108.2.291 PMID:11381831.

Nørgaard, M., & Hornbæk, K. (2006). What do usability evaluators do in practice: An explorative study of think-aloud testing. In *Proceedings of 6th Conference of Design Interact System* (pp. 209 - 218). IEEE.

Norman, D. A. (2004). *Emotional design: Why we love (or hate) everyday things*. New York, NY: Perseus Books Group.

D. A. Norman, & S. Draper (Eds.). (1986). *User centered system design: New perspectives on human-computer interaction*. Hoboken, NJ: Lawrence Erlbaum Associates.

Norris, C., & Datillo, J. (1999). Evaluating effects of a social story intervention on a young girl with autism. *Focus on Autism and Other Developmental Disabilities*, *14*(3), 180–186. doi:10.1177/108835769901400307.

Nunes, M., & O'Neill, H. (2000). *Fundamental de UML*. Lisbon, Portugal: FCA - Editora de Informática.

NY Daily News. (2012). *Are iPads and other tablets bad for children?* Retrieved October 31, 2012, from http://articles.nydailynews.com/2012-04-02/news/31276908_1_electronic-tablets-ipad-electronic-babysitter

O'Hara, K. (2008). Understanding geocaching practices and motivations. In *Proceedings of CHI 2008*. ACM.

Oblinger, D. G., & Hagner, P. (2005). *Seminar on educating the net generation*. Retrieved October 20, 2012, from http://www.educause.edu/section_params/conf/esem052/OneDayv2-HO.ppt#3

Odendahl, N. V. (2011). Testwise - Understanding educational assessment. Lanham.

Odom, S. L., & Watts, P. S. (1991). Reducing teacher prompts in peer-initiation interventions through visual feedback and corresponding training. *The Journal of Special Education*, *25*, 26–43. doi:10.1177/002246699102500103.

Odrakiewicz, P. (2010). Managing complexity in higher education through innovative ways of integrity teaching and integrity education management using innovative case studies. *Global Management Journal*, *2*(2), 122–130.

Oinas-Kukkonen, H. (2008). A systematic framework for designing and evaluating persuasive systems. In *Proceedings of Persuasive 2008*. Springer. doi:10.1007/978-3-540-68504-3_15.

Oinas-Kukkonen, H., & Harjumaa, M. (2009). Persuasive systems design: Key issues, process model, and system features. *Communications of the Association for Information Systems*, *24*(1), 485–500.

Oinas-Kunnonen, H. (2010). Behavior change support systems: A research model and agenda. *Lecture Notes in Computer Science*, 6137.

Olaverri-Monreal, C., Draxler, C., & Bengler, K. J. (2011). *Variable menus for the local adaptation of graphical user interfaces*. Paper presented at the Information Systems and Technologies (CISTI). New York, NY.

Olivier, P., Xu, G., Monk, A., & Hoey, J. (2009). Ambient kitchen: Designing situated services using a high fidelity prototyping environment. In *Proceedings of the International Conference on Pervasive Technologies Related to Assistive Environments,* (pp. 47:1 – 47:7). doi:10.1145/1579114.1579161

Omar, S. (2007). *Geographical information system for dengue management system*. (Final Year Dissertation). Universiti Teknologi Petronas, Petronas, Malaysia.

Ortony, A., Clore, G. L., & Collins, A. (1988). *The cognitive structure of emotions*. Cambridge, UK: Cambridge University Press. doi:10.1017/CBO9780511571299.

Osterling, J., & Dawson, G. (1994). Early recognition of children with autism: A study of first birthday home videotapes. *Journal of Autism and Developmental Disorders*, *24*(3), 247–257. doi:10.1007/BF02172225 PMID:8050980.

Ou, L. C., Luo, M. R., Woodcock, A., & Wright, A. (2004). A study of colour emotion and colour preference: Part I: Colour emotions for single colours. *Color Research and Application*, *29*(3). doi:10.1002/col.20010.

Oviatt, S. (2003). Multimodal interfaces. In J. Jacko, & A. Sears (Eds.), *The Human-Computer Interaction Handbook: Fundamentals, Evolving Technologies and Emerging Applications* (pp. 286–304). Lawrence Erlbaum Associates Inc..

Ozdemir, S. (2008). The effectiveness of social stories on decreasing disruptive behaviors of children with autism: Three case studies. *Journal of Autism and Developmental Disorders*, *38*, 1689–1696. doi:10.1007/s10803-008-0551-0 PMID:18373187.

Oztekin, A. (2011). A decision support system for usability evaluation of web-based information systems. *Expert Systems with Applications*, *38*(3), 2110–2118. Retrieved from http://www.sciencedirect.com/science/article/pii/S0957417410007797 doi:10.1016/j.eswa.2010.07.151.

Paay, J. (2005). Where we met last time. In *Proceedings of OZCHI*. Canberra, Australia: OZCHI.

Pagulayan, R. J., & Steury, K. R. Fulton, B., & Romero, R.L. (2004). Designing for fun: User-testing case studies. In M. Blythe, K. Overbeeke, A. Monk, & P. Wright (Eds.), Funology: Form Usability to Enjoyment. Boston: Kluwer Academic Publishers.

Pagulayan, R., Keeker, K., Wixon, D., Romero, R., & Fuller, T. (2003). User-centered design in games. In J. A. Jacko, & A. Sears (Eds.), *The Human-Computer Interaction Handbook: Fundamentals, Evolving Techniques and Emerging Applications*. Mahwah, NJ: Lawrence Eribaum Associates.

Palaniappan, S., & Awang, R. (2008). Intelligent heart disease prediction system using data mining techniques. In *Proceedings of the International Conference on Computer Systems and Applications,* (pp. 108-115). IEEE.

Park, S., & Aggarwal, J. K. (2004). A hierarchical Bayesian network for event recognition of human actions and interactions. *Multimedia Systems*, *10*(2), 164–179. doi:10.1007/s00530-004-0148-1.

Parsons, S., & Mitchell, P. (2002). The potential of virtual reality in social story training for people with autistic spectrum disorders. *Journal of Intellectual Disability Research*, *46*(5), 430–443. doi:10.1046/j.1365-2788.2002.00425.x PMID:12031025.

Paterson, B., Winschiers-Theophilus, H., Dunne, T. T., Schinzel, B., & Underhill, L. G. (2011). Interpretation of a cross-cultural usability evaluation: A case study based on a hypermedia system for rare species management in Namibia. *Interacting with Computers*, *23*(3), 239–246. doi:10.1016/j.intcom.2011.03.002.

PD-Downloads: Pejabat Kesihatan Wilayah Persekutuan Putrajaya. (n.d.). Retrieved November 5, 2012 from http://pkpj.moh.gov.my/modules/PDdownloads/viewcat.php?cid=2

Peesapati, S. T., Wang, H.-C., & Cosley, D. (2010). Intercultural human-photo encounters: How cultural similarity affects perceiving and tagging photographs. In *Proceedings of ACM International Conference on Intercultural Collaboration* (ICIC 2010). ACM.

Perry, D. E., Porter, A. A., & Votta, L. G. (2000). Empirical studies of software engineering: A roadmap. In *Proceedings of the Conference on The Future of Software Engineering*, (pp. 345–355). New York, NY: ACM.

Peter, J. W. (2004). The complete idiot's guide to geocaching. New York: Peguin Group (USA), Inc.

Petersen, V. (1999). Modern scientific management - Or the attempt to measure everything that counts. Aarhus.

Picard, R. (1997). *Affective computing*. Cambridge, MA: MIT Press.

Piccoli, G., Ahmad, R., & Ives, B. (2001). Web-based virtual learning environments: A research framework and a preliminary assessment of effectiveness in basic IT skills training. *Management Information Systems Quarterly*, *25*(4), 401–426. doi:10.2307/3250989.

Pinnegar, S., & Daynes, J. (2007). Locating narrative inquiry historically. In *Handbook of narrative inquiry: Mapping a methodology*. Thousand Oaks, CA: Sage Publications, Inc. doi:10.4135/9781452226552.n1.

Plocher, T., Patrick Rau, P.-L., & Choong, Y.-Y. (2012). Cross-cultural design. In *Handbook of Human Factors and Ergonomics* (pp. 162–191). Hoboken, NJ: John Wiley & Sons, Inc. doi:10.1002/9781118131350.ch6.

Polkinghorne, D. (1988). *Narrative knowing and the human sciences*. New York: State University of New York Press.

Poppe, R. (2010). A survey on vision-based human action recognition. *Image and Vision Computing*, *28*, 976–990. doi:10.1016/j.imavis.2009.11.014.

Pôrto, W. G. (2066). *Emoção e memória*. São Paulo, Brazil: Artes Médicas.

Power, J. B. (2012). Towards a greater understanding of the effectiveness of reflective journals in a university language program. *Reflective Practice: International and Multidisciplinary Perspectives*, *13*(5), 637–649. doi:10.1080/14623943.2012.697889.

Prabhu, G., & Harel, D. (1999). *GUI design preference validation for Japan and China - A case for KANSEI engineering?* Paper presented at the HCI International (the 8th International Conference on Human-Computer Interaction) on Human-Computer Interaction: Ergonomics and User Interfaces. New York, NY.

Prates, R. O., de Souza, C. S., & Barbosa, S. D. J. (2000). Methods and tools: A method for evaluating the communicability of user interfaces. *Interaction*, *7*(1), 31–38. doi:10.1145/328595.328608.

Preece, J., Rogers, Y., Benyon, D., Holland, S., & Carey, T. (1994). *Human computer interaction*. Reading, MA: Addison-Wesley.

Preim, B., & Dachselt, R. (2010). Interaktive systeme: Vol. I. *Grundlagen, graphical user interfaces, informationsvisualisierung*. Berlin, Germany: Springer Verlag.

Prensky, M. (2001). Digital natives, digital immigrants. *Horizon*, *9*(5). doi:10.1108/10748120110424816.

Prietch, S. S., & Filgueiras, L. V. L. (2012a). Assistive technology in the classroom taking into account the deaf student-centered design: the TApES project. In *Proceedings of Educational Interfaces, Software, and Technology (EIST)/ ACM SIGCHI Conference on Human Factors in Computing Systems (CHI)*. Austin, TX: ACM.

Prietch, S. S., & Filgueiras, L. V. L. (2012b). Emotional quality evaluation method for interviewing people with hearing disabilities (emotion-libras). In *Proceedings of IADIS International Conference Interfaces and Human Computer Interaction (ICHI)*. Lisbon, Portugal: IADIS.

Proctor, R. W., & Vu, K.-P. L. (2006). Selection and control of action. In G. Salvendy (Ed.), *Handbook of human factors and ergonomics* (pp. 89–110). Hoboken, NJ: John Wiley. doi:10.1002/0470048204.ch4.

Puckette, M. (1996). Pure data: Another integrated computer music environment. In *Proceedings of the Second Intercollege Computer Music Concerts*, (pp. 37–41). IEEE.

Pulkkis, A., & Ala-Laurinaho, A. (2007). Dialogiset menetelmät suunnittelussa. In E. Kaasinen, & L. Norros (Eds.), *Älykkäiden ympäristöjen suunnittelu: Kohti ekologista systeemiajattelua* (pp. 215–220). Helsinki: Teknologiateollisuus.

Puls, S., & Wörn, H. (2012). Combining HMM-based continuous human action recognition and spatio-temporal reasoning for augmented situation awareness. In *Proceedings of the IADIS International Conference on Interfaces and Human Computer Interaction* (pp. 133-140). IADIS.

Puls, S., Betz, P., Wyden, M., & Wörn, H. (2012b). Path planning for industrial robots in human-robot interaction. *IEEE/RSJ IROS Workshop on Robot Motion Planning: Online, Reactive, and in Real-Time*.

Puls, S., Graf, J., & Wörn, H. (2011). Design and evaluation of description logics based recognition and understanding of situations and activities for safe human-robot cooperation. *International Journal on Advances in Intelligent Systems*, *4*, 218–227.

Puls, S., Graf, J., & Wörn, H. (2012a). Cognitive robotics in industrial environments. In *Human Machine Interaction – Getting Closer*. Rijeka, Croatia: Academic Press. doi:10.5772/28130.

Pylvänäinen, T. (2005). Accelerometer based gesture recognition using continuous HMMs. In J. S. Marques, N. P. de la Blanca, & P. Pina (Eds.), *Pattern Recognition and Image Analysis, (LNCS)* (Vol. 3522, pp. 413–430). Berlin: Springer. doi:10.1007/11492429_77.

Quek, F., McNeill, D., Bryll, R., Duncan, S., Ma, X.-F., & Kirbas, C. et al. (2002). Multimodal human discourse: gesture and speech. *ACM Transactions on Computer-Human Interaction*, *9*(3), 171–193. doi:10.1145/568513.568514.

Quill, L. L., Kancler, D. E., Revels, A. R., & Batchelor, C. (2001). Application of information visualization principles at various stages of system development. In *Proceedings of the Human Factors and Ergonomics Society Annual Meeting* (Vol. 45, pp. 1713-1717). SAGE Publications.

Quill, K. A. (1995). Visually cued instruction for children with autism and pervasive developmental disorders. *Focus on Autism and Other Developmental Disabilities*, *10*(3), 10–20. doi:10.1177/108835769501000302.

Quill, K. A. (1997). Instructional consideration for young children with autism: The rationale for visually cued instruction. *Journal of Autism and Developmental Disorders*, *27*(6), 697–714. doi:10.1023/A:1025806900162 PMID:9455729.

Rabiner, L. R. (1989). A tutorial on hidden Markov models and selected applications in speech recognition. *Proceedings of the IEEE*, *77*(2), 257–286. doi:10.1109/5.18626.

Ramos, J. (2002). Action research as foresight methodology. *Journal of Futures Studies*, *7*, 1–24.

Rao, J., Gao, T., Gong, Z., & Jiang, Z. (2009). Low cost hand gesture learning and recognition system based on hidden Markov model. In *Proceedings of the 2nd International Symposium on Information Science and Engineering ISISE* (pp. 433-438). IEEE.

Rathje, S. (2003). Ist wenig kulturelles Verständnis besser als gar keins? Problematik der verwendung von dimensionsmodellen zur kulturbeschreibung. *Interculture-Online*. Retrieved from www.interculture-online.info

Rätzmann, M. (2004). *Software-testing & internationalisierung* (2nd ed.). Bonn, Germany: Galileo Press.

Rau, P.-L. P., & Plocher, T. A. et al. (2012). *Cross-cultural design for IT products and services*. Boca Raton, FL: Taylor & Francis. doi:10.1201/b12679.

Redmill, F., & Rajan, J. (1997). *Human factors in safety-critical systems*. London: Butterworth-Heinemann.

Rehm, M., Bee, N., Endrass, B., Wissner, M., & André, E. (2007). *Too close for comfort? Adapting to the user's cultural background*. Academic Press. doi:10.1145/1290128.1290142.

Reinecke, K., Reif, G., & Bernstein, A. (2007). Cultural user modeling with CUMO: An approach to overcome the personalization bootstrapping problem. In *Proceedings of the First International Workshop on Cultural Heritage on the Semantic Web at the 6th International Semantic Web Conference (ISWC 2007)*. Busan, South Korea: ISWC.

Reiterer, H. (2008). *Seminar reader: Future challenges and trends in HCI*. University of Konstanz.

Reithinger, N., Alexandersson, J., Becker, T., Blocher, A., Engel, R., & Lockelt, M. … Tschernomas, V. (2003). Smartkom: Adaptive and flexible multimodal access to multiple applications. In *Proceedings of the International Conference on Multimodal Interfaces*, (pp. 101–108). IEEE. doi:10.1145/958432.958454

Reithinger, N., Fedeler, D., Kumar, A., Lauer, C., Pecourt, E., & Romary, L. (2005). Miamm – A multimodal dialogue system using haptics. In J. Kuppevelt, L. Dybkjaer, N. Bernsen, & N. Ide (Eds.), *Advances in Natural Multimodal Dialogue Systems* (Vol. 30, pp. 307–332). Springer. doi:10.1007/1-4020-3933-6_14.

Repenning, A., Ahmadi, N., Repenning, N., Ioannidou, A., Webb, D., & Marshall, K. (2011). Collective programming: Making end-user programming (more) social. In M. Costabile, Y. Dittrich, G. Fischer, & A. Piccinno (Eds.), *End-User Development, (LNCS)* (Vol. 6654, pp. 325–330). Springer. doi:10.1007/978-3-642-21530-8_34.

Revelle, W. (2007). *The personality project*. Retrieved October 31, 2012 from http://www.personalityproject.org

Rhodes, C., & Brown, A. (2005). Narrative, organizations and research. *International Journal of Management Reviews*, *7*(3), 167–188. doi:10.1111/j.1468-2370.2005.00112.x.

Ribeiro, P., Silva, T., José, R., & Iurgel, I. (2010). Combining explicit and implicit interaction modes with virtual characters in public spaces. In *Proceedings of the Joint Conference on Interactive Digital Storytelling*, (pp. 244-247). IEEE.

Richards, G. (2004). Don't panic![control medical]. *Engineering & Technology*, *4*(10), 45–47. doi:10.1049/et.2009.1007.

Rideout, V. J., Foehr, M. A., Ulla, G., & Roberts, D. F. (2010). Generation M2 media in the lives of 8- to 18-year-olds. *A Kaiser Family Foundation Study*. Retrieved October 20, 2012, from http://www.kff.org/entmedia/upload/8010.pdf

Riding, R., & Rayner, S. (2010). *Cognitive styles and learning strategies*. London: Academic Press.

Rigoll, G., Kosmala, A., & Eickeler, S. (1998). High performance real–time gesture recognition using hidden Markov models. In *Gesture and Sign Language in Human-Computer Interaction, (LNCS)* (Vol. 1371, pp. 69–80). Berlin: Springer Press. doi:10.1007/BFb0052990.

Ritchey, T. (2011). *Wicked problems/social messes: Decision support modelling with morphological analysis*. Berlin: Springer. doi:10.1007/978-3-642-19653-9.

Rızvanoğlu, K., & Öztürk, Ö. (2009). *Cross-cultural understanding of the dual structure of metaphorical icons: An explorative study with French and Turkish users on an e-learning site*. Paper presented at the 3rd International Conference on Internationalization, Design and Global Development: Held as Part of HCI International 2009, San Diego, CA.

Robert, T. (2011). *Gamification: La slideshareatture*. Retrieved February 2, 2012 from http://www.ludicite.ca/2011/10/ Gamification-la-slideshareatture

Robertson, C., Nelson, T. A., MacNab, Y. C., & Lawson, A. B. (2010). Review of methods for space-time disease surveillance. *Spatial and Spatio-temporal Epidemiology*, *1*(23), 105–116. doi:10.1016/j.sste.2009.12.001 PMID:22749467.

Röbig, S., Didier, M., & Bruder, R. (2010). *Internationales verständnis von usability sowie methodenanwendung im bereich der usability*. Paper presented at the Grundlagen - Methoden - Technologien, 5. VDI Fachtagung USEWARE 2010, Baden-Baden. Retrieved from http://tubiblio.ulb.tu-darmstadt.de/46312/

Robin, B. (2006). The educational uses of digital storytelling.[Orlando, FL: AACE.]. *Proceedings of Society for Information Technology & Teacher Education International Conference, 2006*, 709–716.

Robinson, J. (1988). Unlearning and backcasting: Rethinking some of the questions we ask about the future. *Technological Forecasting and Social Change*, *33*, 325–338. doi:10.1016/0040-1625(88)90029-7.

Rogers, M. F., & Myles, M. F. (2001). Using social stories and comic strip conversations to interprest social situations for an adolescent with Asperger syndrome. *Intervention in School and Clinic*, *36*(5), 310–313. doi:10.1177/105345120103600510.

Rogers, S. J. (2000). Interventions that facilitate socialization in chldren with autism. *Journal of Autism and Developmental Disorders*, *30*(5), 399–409. doi:10.1023/A:1005543321840 PMID:11098875.

Rogers, Y., & Muller, H. (2006). A framework for designing sensor-based interactions to promote exploration and reflection in play. *International Journal of Human-Computer Studies*, *64*, 1–14. doi:10.1016/j.ijhcs.2005.05.004.

Rogers, Y., & Scaife, M. (1998). How can interactive multimedia facilitate learning? In J. Lee (Ed.), *Intelligence and Multimodality in Multimedia Interfaces: Research and Applications. AAAI.* Press.

Rogers, Y., Scaife, M., Gabrielli, S., Smith, H., & Harris, E. (2002). A conceptual framework for mixed reality environments: Designing novel learning activities for young children. *Journal Presence: Teleoperators and Virtual Environments*, *11*(6), 677–686. doi:10.1162/105474602321050776.

Romiszowski, A. (2009). Fostering skill development outcomes. In *Instructional-Design Theories and Models* (Vol. 3, pp. 19–224). New York: Routledge.

Roque, R. V. (2007). *OpenBlocks: An extendable framework for graphical block programming systems*. (Master Thesis). Massachusetts Institute of Technology, Cambridge, MA.

Röse, K. (2001). *Kultur als variable des UI design*. Paper presented at the Mensch & Computer 2001. Stuttgart, Germany.

Röse, K. (2002). *Methodik zur gestaltung interkultureller mensch-maschine-systeme in der produktionstechnik* (Vol. 5). Kaiserslautern: Univ.

Röse, K., & Zühlke, D. (2001). *Culture-oriented design: Developers' knowledge gaps in this area.* Paper Presented at the 8th IFAC/IFIPS/IFORS/IEA Symposium on Analysis, Design, and Evaluation of Human-Machine Systems. Kassel, Germany.

Röse, K., Liu, L., & Zühlke, D. (2001). Design issues in mainland china: demands for a localized human-machine-interaction design. In G. Johannsen (Ed.), *8th IFAC/IFIPS/IFORS/IEA Symposium on Analysis, Design, and Evaluation of Human-Machine Systems* (pp. 17-22). Kassel: Preprints.

Röse, K., Zühlke, D., & Liu, L. (2001). Similarities and dissimilarities of German and Chinese users. In G. Johannsen (Ed.), *Preprints of 8th IFAC/IFIP/IFORS/IEA Symposium on Analysis, Design, and Evaluation of Human-Machine Systems* (pp. 24-29). Germany, Kassel: IFIP.

Röse, K. (2002). Kulturmodelle und ihre anwendbarkeit beim user interface design. *Bedienen und Verstehen*, *4*, 305–317.

Roseman, I. J., Antoniou, A. A., & Lose, P. E. (1996). Appraisal determinants of emotions: Constructing a more accurate and comprehensive theory. *Cognition and Emotion*, *10*(3), 241–277. doi:10.1080/026999396380240.

Rosset, D. B., Rondan, C., Da Fonseca, D., Santos, A., Assouline, B., & Deruelle, C. (2008). Typical emotion processing for cartoon but not for real faces in children with autistic spectrum disorders. *Journal of Autism and Developmental Disorders*, *38*, 919–925. doi:10.1007/s10803-007-0465-2 PMID:17952583.

Rößger, P. (2003). An international comparison of the usability of driver-information-systems. In *Proceedings of the Fifth International Workshop on Internationalisation of Products and Systems* (pp. 129-134). University of Kaiserslautern.

Rößger, P., & Hofmeister, J. (2003). Cross cultural usability: An international study on driver information systems. *Human-Computer Interaction.*

Rossman, G. B., & Rallis, S. F. (2012). *Learning in the field.* Thousand Oaks, CA: SAGE.

Roullet, F. I., & Crawley, J. N. (2011). Mouse models of autism: Testing hypothesis about molecular mechanisms. *Current Topics in Behavioral Neurosciences*, *7*, 187–212. doi:10.1007/7854_2010_113 PMID:21225409.

Rousseau, C., Bellik, Y., & Vernier, F. (2005). WWHT: Un modéle conceptuel pour la présentation multimodale d'information. In *Proceedings of the 17th International Conference on Francophone sur l'Interaction Homme-Machine*, (pp. 59–66). IEEE. doi:10.1145/1148550.1148558

Rowe, C. (1999). Do social stories benefit children with autism in mainstream primary schools? *British Journal of Special Education*, *26*(1), 12–14. doi:10.1111/1467-8527.t01-1-00094.

Rubine, D. H. (1991). *The automatic recognition of gestures.* (Doctoral thesis). Carnegie-Mellon University, Pittsburgh, PA.

Ruiz, J., Li, Y., & Lank, E. (2011). User-defined motion gestures for mobile interaction. In *Proceedings of the 29th International Conference on Human Factors in Computing Systems CHI* (pp. 197-206). New York, NY: ACM Press.

Russell, J. A. (1980). A circumplex model of affect. *Journal of Personality and Social Psychology*, *39*(6), 1161–1178. doi:10.1037/h0077714.

Rust, J., & Smith, A. (2006). How should the effectiveness of social stories to modify the behaviour of children on the autistic spectrum be tested? Lessons from the literature. *Autism*, *10*(2), 125–138. doi:10.1177/1362361306062019 PMID:16613863.

Saha, D., & Mukherjee, A. (2003). Pervasive computing: A paradigm for the 21st century. *Computer*, *36*(3), 25–31. doi:10.1109/MC.2003.1185214.

Salen, K., & Zimmerman, E. (2004). *Rules of play: Game design fundamentals.* Cambridge, MA: The MIT Press.

Salgado, L. C. de C., Leito, C. F., & de Souza, C. S. (2012). *A journey through cultures: Metaphors for guiding the design of cross-cultural interactive systems.* Berlin: Springer Publishing Company, Incorporated.

Salmon, G. (2005). Flying not flapping: A strategic framework for e-learning and pedagogical innovation in higher education institutions. *ALT-J*, *13*(3), 201–218. doi:10.1080/09687760500376439.

Sangrà, A., Vlachopoulos, D., & Cabrera, N. (2012). Building an inclusive definition of e-learning: An approach to the conceptual framework. *International Review of Research in Open and Distance Learning*, *13*(2), 145–159.

Sansosti, F. J., & Powell-Smith, K. A. (2006). Using social stories to improve the social behavior of children with Asperger syndrome. *Journal of Positive Behavior Interventions*, *8*, 43–57. doi:10.1177/10983007060080010601.

Sansosti, F. J., & Powel-Smith, K. A. (2008). Using computer-presented social stories and video models to increase the social communication skills of children with high-functioning autism spectrum disorders. *Journal of Positive Behavior Interventions*, *10*(3), 162–178. doi:10.1177/1098300708316259.

Sarasohn-Kahn, J. (2008). *The wisdom of patients: Health care meets online social media*. Retrieved November 5, 2012 from http://www.chcf.org/publications/2008/04/the-wisdom-of-patients-health-care-meets-online-social-media

Saucier, G., & Goldberg, L. (1998). What is beyond the big five. *Journal of Personality*, *66*, 495–524. doi:10.1111/1467-6494.00022 PMID:9728415.

Sauer, J., Seibel, K., & Rüttinger, B. (2010). The influence of user expertise and prototype fidelity in usability tests. *Applied Ergonomics*, *41*(1), 130–140. doi:10.1016/j.apergo.2009.06.003 PMID:19632666.

Sawyer, R. (2006). *Explaining creativity: The science of human innovation*. Oxford, UK: Oxford University Press.

Scanfeld, D., Scanfeld, V., & Larson, E. (2010). Dissemination of health information through social networks: Twitter and antibiotics. *American Journal of Infection Control*, *38*(3), 182–188. doi:10.1016/j.ajic.2009.11.004 PMID:20347636.

Scattone, D., Tingstrom, D. H., & Wilczynski, S. M. (2006). Increasing appropriate social interaction of children with autism spectrum disorders using social stories. *Focus on Autism and Other Developmental Disabilities*, *21*(4), 211–222. doi:10.1177/10883576060210040201.

Scattone, D., Wilczynski, S. M., Edwards, R. P., & Rabian, B. (2002). Decreasing disruptive behaviors of children with autism using social stories. *Journal of Autism and Developmental Disorders*, *32*(6), 535–543. doi:10.1023/A:1021250813367 PMID:12553590.

Schank, R. (1998, July-August). Narrative and intelligence economy. *Harvard Business Review*, 97.

Schätz, B. (2004). Mastering the complexity of reactive systems: The AUTOFOCUS approach. In *Formal Methods for Embedded Distributed Systems: How to Master the Complexity* (pp. 215–258). Boston: Kluwer Academic Publishers. doi:10.1007/1-4020-7997-4_7.

Schell, J. (2008). *The art of game design: A book of lenses*. Burlington, MA: Morgan Kaufmann.

Scherer, K. R. (2005). *What are emotions? And how can they be measured?* Thousand Oaks, CA: SAGE Publications. doi:10.1177/0539018405058216.

Schlögl, C. (2005). Information and knowledge management: dimensions and approaches. *Information Research*, *10*(4), 10–14.

Schlömer, T., Poppinga, B., Henze, N., & Boll, S. (2008). Gesture recognition with a Wii controller. In *Proceedings of the Second International Conference on Tangible and Embedded Interaction TEI* (pp. 11-14). New York, NY: ACM Press.

Schmidt, D., Block, F., & Gellersen, H. (2009). A comparison of direct and indirect multi-touch input for large surfaces. In *Proceedings of the IFIP TC 13 International Conference on Human-Computer Interaction: Part I*, (pp. 582 – 594). IFIP. doi: 10.1007/978-3-642-03655-2_65

Schmitz, K.-D., & Wahle, K. (2000). *Softwarelokalisierung*. Tübingen: Stauffenburg-Verl.

Schneider, D. W., & Anderson, J. R. (2011). A memory-based model of Hick's law. *Cognitive Psychology*, *62*, 193–222. doi:10.1016/j.cogpsych.2010.11.001 PMID:21293788.

Schneider, N., & Goldstein, H. (2009). Using social stories and visual schedules to improve socially appropriate behaviors in children with autism. *Journal of Positive Behavior Interventions*, *11*, 1–12.

E. Schopler, & G. B. Mesibov (Eds.). (1986). *Social behavior in autism*. New York: Plenum Press. doi:10.1007/978-1-4899-2242-7.

Schreibman, L. E. (2005). *The science and fiction of autism*. Boston: Harvard University Press.

Schreibman, L. E. (2008). Treatment controversies in autism. *Zero to Three*, *28*(4), 38–45.

Schro¨der. S., & Ziefle, M. (2006). Evaluating the usability of cellular phones' menu structure in a cross-cultural society. In E.A. Konigsveld (Ed.), *Proceedings IEA 2006: Meeting Diversity in Ergonomics*. Elsevier.

Schuler, D., & Namioka, A. (1993). *Participatory design: Principles and practices*. Boca Raton, FL: CRC Press Llc.

Schumaker, R. P., & Chen, H. (2010). Interaction analysis of the ALICE chatterbot: A two-study investigation of dialog and domain questioning. *IEEE Transactions on Systems, Man, and Cybernetics. Part A, Systems and Humans*, *40*(1), 40–51. doi:10.1109/TSMCA.2009.2029603.

Schwartz, S. H. (2004). Mapping and interpreting cultural differences around the world. In H. Vinken, J. Soeters, & P. Ester (Eds.), *Comparing cultures, Dimensions of culture in a comparative perspective* (pp. 43–73). Leiden, The Netherlands: Brill.

Schwarz, T., Oortmann, H., & Reiterer, H. (2012). Holistic workspace - Wie neue technologien die operatoren unterstützen. In Automatisieren! by ATP. Oldenbourg Verlag.

Scott, I. (2011). The learning outcome in higher education: Time to think again? *Worcester Journal of Learning and Teaching*, *5*, 1–8.

Scurlock, M. (2008). *Using social stories with children with Asperger syndrome*. (MSc thesis). Ohio University, Athens, OH.

Searle, J. R. (1980). Minds, brains, and programs. *The Behavioral and Brain Sciences*, 3.

Seikkula, J., Arnkil, T. E., & Eriksson, E. (2003). Postmodern society and social networks: Open and anticipation dialogues in network meetings. *Family Process*, *42*, 185–203. doi:10.1111/j.1545-5300.2003.42201.x PMID:12879593.

Seland, G. (2006). System designer assessments of role play as a design method: A qualitative study. In *Proceedings of the 4th Nordic Conference on Human-Computer Interaction: Changing Roles* (NordiCHI '06) (pp. 222-231). ACM.

Seligman, M. E. P. (2011). *Flourish: A new understanding of happiness and well-being - And how to achieve them*. New York, NY: Free Press.

Sengers, P., McCarthy, J., & Dourish, P. (2006). *Reflective HCI: Articulating an agenda for critical practice*. Paper presented at the CHI' 06. New York, NY.

Seto, E., Leonard, K. J., Cafazzo, J. A., Barnsley, J., Masino, C., & Ross, H. J. (2012). Developing healthcare rule-based expert systems: Case study of a heart failure telemonitoring system. *International Journal of Medical Informatics*, *81*(8), 556–565. doi:10.1016/j.ijmedinf.2012.03.001 PMID:22465288.

Shackel, B., & Richardson, S. J. (1991). *Human factors for informatics usability*. Cambridge, UK: Cambridge University Press.

Shaer, O., Strait, M., Valdes, C., Feng, T., Lintz, M., & Wang, H. (2011). Enhancing genomic learning through tabletop interaction. In *Proceedings of the SIGCHI Conference on Human Factors in Computing Systems*, (pp. 2817 – 2826). ACM. doi: 10.1145/1978942.1979361

Shah, H., Nersessian, N. J., Harrold, M. J., & Newstetter, W. (2012). *Studying the influence of culture in global software engineering: thinking in terms of cultural models*. Paper presented at the 4th international conference on Intercultural Collaboration. Bengaluru, India.

Shahriar, S. D. (2011). *A comparative study on evaluation of methods in capturing emotion*. (Master Degree Thesis). UMEA Universitet, Umea, Sweden.

Sharmin, M. A., Rahman, M. M., Ahmed, S. I., Rahman, M. M., & Ferdous, S. M. (2011). Teaching intelligible speech to the autistic children by interactive computer games. In *Proceedings of the Twenty-Sixth ACM Symposium on Applied Computing*. Tai Chung, Taiwan: ACM.

Sheehan, R., & Rode, S. (1999). On scientific narrative stories of light by Newton and Einstein. *Journal of Business and Technical Communication*, *13*(3), 336–358. doi:10.1177/105065199901300306.

Shen, S.-T., Prior, S. D., Chen, K., & Fang, T. (2009). Chinese users' preference for web browser icons. *Design Principles and Practices*, *3*(1), 115–128.

Shen, S.-T., Woolley, M., & Prior, S. (2006). Towards culture-centred design. *Interacting with Computers*, *18*(4), 820–852. doi:10.1016/j.intcom.2005.11.014.

Shenson, J., & Joshi, A. (2012). Visualizing disease incidence in the context of socioeconomic factors. In *Proceedings of the 5th International Symposium on Visual Information Communication and Interaction*, (pp. 29-38). IEEE.

Sherman, E. (2004). *Geocaching hike and seek with your GPS*. New York: Springer.

Shi, M. (2011). *Website characteristics and their influences: A review on web design*. Paper presented at the ABIS 2011. New York, NY.

Shi, Q., & Clemmensen, T. (2007). Relationship model in cultural usability testing usability and internationalization. In *Proceedings of HCI and Culture*, (Vol. 4559, pp. 422-431). Berlin: Springer.

Shi, Y., Huang, Y., Minnen, D., Bobick, A., & Essa, I. (2004). Propagation networks for recognition of partially ordered sequential action.[CVPR]. *Proceedings of Computer Vision and Pattern Recognition*, *2*, 862–869.

Shneiderman, B. (1996). The eyes have it: A task by data type taxonomy for information visualizations. In *Proceedings of the IEEE Symposium on Visual Languages*, (pp. 336-343). IEEE.

Shneiderman, B. (2008). Extreme visualization: Squeezing a billion records into a million pixels. In *Proceedings of the 2008 ACM SIGMOD International Conference on Management of Data*, (pp. 3-12). ACM.

Shneiderman, B. (1997). *Designing the user interface: Strategies for effective human-computer interaction* (3rd ed.). Boston: Addison-Wesley Longman Publishing Co., Inc..

Shneiderman, B. (2004). Designing for fun: How can we design user interfaces to be more fun? *Interactions (New York, N.Y.)*, *11*(5), 48–50. doi:10.1145/1015530.1015552.

Shneiderman, B., Plaisant, C., Cohen, M., & Jacobs, S. (2009). *Designing the user interface: Strategies for effective human-computer interaction*. Reading, MA: Addison-Wesley Publishing Company.

Shotter, J., & Gustavsen, B. (1999). *The role of dialogue conferences in the development of learning regions: Doing from within our lives together what we cannot do apart*. Stockholm: Centre for Advanced Studies in Leadership, Stockholm School of Economics.

Sicile-Kira, C. (2004). *Autism spectrum disorders: The complete guide to understanding autism, Asperger's syndrome, pervasive developmental disorder, and other ASDs*. New York: Penguin.

Sicile-Kira, C., & Grandin, T. (2006). *Adolescents on the autism spectrum: A parent's guide to the cognitive, social, physical and transition needs of teenagers with Autism Spectrum Disorders*. New York: Penguin.

Silberman, M. S., & Tomlinson, B. (2010). *Toward an ecological sensibility: Tools for evaluating sustainable HCI*. Paper presented at the CHI 2010. Atlanta, GA.

Silva, M. G., & Bowman, D. A. (2009). *Body-based interaction for desktop games* (pp. 4249–4254). Extended Abstracts on Human Factors in Computing Systems.

Simon, S. J. (2000). The impact of culture and gender on web sites: An empirical study. *SIGMIS Database*, *32*(1), 18–37. doi:10.1145/506740.506744.

Singer, L., & Schneider, K. (2012). It was a bit of a race: Gamification of version control. In *Proceedings of the 2nd International Workshop on Games and Software Engineering (GAS)*. Zürich, Switzerland: GAS.

Single-Subject Research . (2011). Retrieved form http://en.wikipedia.org/wiki/Single-subject_research

Siorpaes, K., & Hepp, M. (2008). Games with a purpose for the semantic web. *IEEE Intelligent Systems*, *23*(3), 50–60. doi:10.1109/MIS.2008.45.

Siriaraya, P., Tang, C., Ang, C. S., Pfeil, U., & Zaphiris, P. (2011). A comparison of empathic communication pattern for teenagers and older people in online support communities. *Behaviour & IT*, *30*(5), 617–628.

Slater, A., & Bremner, J. G. (2003). *An introduction to developmental psychology*. London: Wiley-Blackwell Publishing.

SmartKids. (2012). *Passatempo: Alfabeto em libras*. Retrieved June, 18, 2012, from http://www.smartkids.com.br/

Smith, A., & Chang, Y. (2003). Quantifying hofstede and developing cultural fingerprints for website acceptability. In *Proceedings of the Fifth International Workshop on Internationalisation of Products and Systems* (pp. 89-102). University of Kaiserslautern.

Smith, A., Dunckley, L., French, T., Minocha, S., & Chang, Y. (2004). A process model for developing usable crosscultural websites. *Interacting with Computers, 16*(1), 63–91. doi:10.1016/j.intcom.2003.11.005.

Sommerville, I. (2006). *Software engineering*. Harlow, UK: Pearson Education.

Sørum, H., Andersen, K. N., & Vatrapu, R. (2011). *Public websites and human–computer interaction: An empirical study of measurement of website quality and user satisfaction*. Retrieved from http://dx.doi.org/10.1080/0144929X.2011.577191

Souto, V. T. (2008). Descriptive framework for analysis and comparison of online language courses. In *Proceedings of the ED-MEDIA 2008 – World Conference on Educational Multimedia, Hypermedia & Telecommunications*. Association for the Advancement of Computing in Education.

Spichkova, M. (2007). *Specification and seamless verification of embedded real-time systems: Focus on isabelle*. (PhD Thesis). Munich, Germany: TU München.

Spichkova, M. (2011). Architecture: Requirements + decomposition + refinement. *Softwaretechnik-Trends, 32*(4).

Spichkova, M. (2011). *Focus on processes* (Technical Report TUM-I1115). Munich, Germany: TU München.

Spichkova, M. (2012). *Component composition: Formal specification and verification of cryptographic properties* (Technical Report TUM-I124). Munich, Germany: TU München.

Spichkova, M., Hölzl, F., & Trachtenherz, D. (2012). Verified system development with the autofocus tool chain. In *Proceedings of the 2nd Workshop on Formal Methods in the Development of Software (WS-FMDS)*. WS-FMDS.

Spichkova, M., Zhu, X., & Mou, D. (2013). Do we really need to write documentation for a system? CASE tool add-ons: Generator+editor for a precise documentation. In *Proceedings of the International Conference on Model-Driven Engineering and Software Development (MODELSWARD'13)*. MODELSWARD.

Spink, A., Wilson, T. D., Ford, N., Foster, A., & Ellis, D. (2002). Information-seeking and mediated searching: Part 1: Theoretical framework and research design. *Journal of the American Society for Information Science and Technology, 53*(9), 695–703. doi:10.1002/asi.10081.

Springer, T., Wustmann, P., Braun, I., Dargie, W., & Berger, M. (2010). A comprehensive approach for situation-awareness based on sensing and reasoning about context. *Lecture Notes in Computer Science, 5061*, 143–157. doi:10.1007/978-3-540-69293-5_13.

Stanton, N. A., Hedge, A., Brookhuis, K., Salas, E., & Hendrick, H. (2005). *Handbook of human factors and ergonomics methods*. Boca Raton, FL: CRC Press.

Stanton, N. A., & Young, M. S. (2003). Giving ergonomics away? The application of ergonomics methods by novices. *Applied Ergonomics, 34*(5), 479–490. doi:10.1016/S0003-6870(03)00067-X PMID:12963333.

Stein, S., Shephard, K., & Harris, I. (2011). Conceptions of e-learning and professional development for e-learning held by tertiary educators in New Zealand. *British Journal of Educational Technology, 42*(1), 145–165. doi:10.1111/j.1467-8535.2009.00997.x.

Stengers, H., Troyer, O., Baetens, M., Boers, F., & Mushtaha, A. (2004). *Localization of web sites: Is there still a need for it?* Paper presented at the International Workshop on Web Engineering. Santa Cruz, CA.

Stephanidis, C. (2009). Universal access in the information society. Universal Access in the Information Society, 8(2).

Stevenson, T. (2002). Anticipatory action learning: conversations about the future. *Futures, 34*, 417–425. doi:10.1016/S0016-3287(01)00068-4.

Stevenson, T. (2006). From vision into action. *Futures, 38*, 667–672. doi:10.1016/j.futures.2005.10.009.

Stilan, E., Chen, A., & Bezuayehu, L. (2011). Accessible icon design in enterprise applications. In *Proceedings of the International Cross-Disciplinary Conference on Web Accessibility* (W4A '11). New York: ACM.

Stillman, W. (2009). *Empowered autism parenting: Celebrating (and defending) your child's place in the world.* San Francisco, CA: Jossey-Bass.

Stokoe, W. C. Jr. (2005). Sign language structure: An outline of the visual communication systems of the American deaf. *Journal of Deaf Studies and Deaf Education, 10*(1). doi:10.1093/deafed/eni001 PMID:15585746.

Stolee, K. T., & Fristoe, T. (2011). Expressing computer science concepts through Kodu game lab. In *Proceedings of the 42nd ACM Technical Symposium on Computer Science Education*, (pp. 99–104). New York, NY: ACM.

Strickland, D. (1997). Virtual reality for the treatment of autism. In G. Riva (Ed.), *Virtual reality in neuro-psycho-physiology: Cognitive, clinical, and methodological issues in assessment and rehabilitation.* Amsterdam: IOS Press.

Strömberg, H., Pirttilä, V., & Ikonen, V. (2004). Interactive scenarios—Building ubiquitous computing concepts in the spirit of participatory design. *Personal and Ubiquitous Computing, 8*(3), 200–207.

Sturm, C. (2002). *TLCC-towards a framework for systematic and successful product internationalization.* Paper presented at the International Workshop on Internationalisation of Products and Systems. Austin, TX.

Sturm, C., & Mueller, C. H. (2003). Putting theory into practice: How to apply cross-cultural differences to user interface design? In M. Rauterberg, M. Menozzi, & J. Wesson (Eds.), *Human-computer interaction: INTERACT '03, IFIP TC13 International Conference on Human-Computer Interaction, 1st-5th September 2003* (pp. 1051-1052), International Federation for Information Processing.

Suh, N. P. (1990). *The principles of design.* New York: Oxford University Press.

Suh, N. P. (1995). Designing-in quality through axiomatic design. *IEEE Transactions on Reliability, 44*(2), 256–264. doi:10.1109/24.387380.

Suh, N. P. (2001). *Axiomatic design: advances and applications.* New York: Oxford University Press.

Suits, B. (1990). *Grasshopper: Games, life, and utopia.* Boston: David R. Godine.

Sun, H. (2001). Building a culturally-competent corporate web site: An exploratory study of cultural markers in multilingual web design In *Proceedings of the 19th Annual International Conference on Computer Documentation* (pp. 95-102). Sante Fe, NM: ACM.

Sun, X., & Shi, Q. (2007). *Language issues in cross cultural usability testing: A pilot study in china.* Paper presented at the 2nd International Conference on Usability and Internationalization. Beijing, China.

Sun, X., & Wang, J. (2010). Human action recognition based on projection and mass center movement features. In *Proceedings of the 8th World Congress on Intelligent Control and Automation.* Jinan, China: IEEE.

Sung, J., Grinter, R. E., & Christensen, H. I. (2009). Pimp my roomba: Designing for personalization. In *Proceedings of the SIGCHI Conference on Human Factors in Computing Systems,* (pp. 193 – 196). ACM. doi: 10.1145/1518701.1518732

Sun, H. (2012). *Cross-cultural technology design: Creating culture-sensitive technology for local users.* Oxford, UK: Oxford University Press. doi:10.1093/acprof:oso/9780199744763.001.0001.

Susi, T., Johannesson, M., & Backlund, P. (2007). *Serious games: An overview (Technical report, GLS).* Madison, WI: University of Wisconsin-Madison.

Sutton, V. (2004). *The signwriting site.* Retrieved June, 18, 2012, from www.signwriting.org

Svinicki, M. D. (2008). *A guidebook on conceptual frameworks for research in engineering education.* Retrieved October 20, 2012, from http://www.ce.umn.edu/~smith/docs/RREE-Research_Frameworks-Svinicki.pdf

Sweetser, P., & Wyeth, P. (2005). GameFlow: A model for evaluating player enjoyment in games. *ACM Computers in Entertainment, 3*(3).

Syahman, A. M. (2006). *GIS for dengue epidemic management for ipoh/ batu gajah.* (Final Year Dissertation). Universiti Teknologi Petronas, Petronas, Malaysia.

Symanzik, J., Klinke, G., Klinke, S., Schmelzer, S., Cook, D., & Lewin, N. (1997). The acrview/xgobi/xplore environment: Technical details and applications for spatial data analysis. In *Proceedings of the Section on Statistical Graphics American Statistical Association,* (pp. 73-78). ASA.

Tadokoro, S., Takebe, T., Ishikawa, Y., & Takamori, T. (1993). Control of human cooperative robots based on stochastic prediction of human motion. In *Proceedings of the 2nd IEEE International Workshop on Robot and Human Communication* (pp. 387-392). IEEE.

Tang, A., Tory, M., Po, B., Neumann, P., & Carpendale, S. (2006). Collaborative coupling over tabletop displays. In *Proceedings of the SIGCHI Conference on Human Factors in Computing Systems,* (pp. 1181 – 1190). ACM. doi: 10.1145/1124772.1124950

Tapscott, D. (1998). *Growing up digital: The rise of the net generation.* New York: McGraw Hill.

Tapscott, D. (2009). *Grown up digital: How the net generation is changing your world.* New York: McGraw-Hill.

Tartaro, A. (2007). Authorable virtual peers for children with autism. In *Proceedings of the Conference on Human Factors in Computing Systems.* ACM.

Tartaro, A., & Cassell, J. (2008). Playing with virtual peers: Bootstrapping contingent discourse in children with autism. In *Proceedings of the Eighth International Conference for Learning Sciences,* (vol. 2, pp. 382-389). IEEE.

Tatai, G., et al. (2003). Happy chatbot, happy user. In *Proceedings of the International Workshop Intelligent Virtual Agents* (pp. 5-12). IEEE.

Tateishi, M., & Toma, T. (2010). *A cross-cultural comparative study of user interface in social media: Why social media can cross seas but not nationalisms.* Retrieved from http://koara.lib.keio.ac.jp/xoonips/modules/xoonips/detail.php?koara_id=KO40002001-00002010-0037

Te'eni, D., Carey, J., & Zhang, P. (2007). *Human computer interaction: Developing effective organizational information systems.* Hoboken, NJ: John Wiley & Sons, Inc..

T-Engine Forum. (2007). *Ucode tag lineup significantly expanded.* Ubiquitous ID Center.

Tenorth, M., & Beetz, M. (2009). KNOWROB – Knowledge processing for autonomous personal robots. *IEEE International Conf. on Intelligent Robots and Systems (IROS).* IEEE.

Thiemann, K. S., & Goldstein, H. (2001). Social stories, written text cues, and video feedback: Effects on social communication of children with autism. *Journal of Applied Science, 34*(4), 425–446. PMID:11800183.

Thissen, F. (2008). Interkulturelles informationsdesign. In W. Weber (Ed.), *Kompendium Informationsdesign* (pp. 387–424). Berlin, Germany: Springer. doi:10.1007/978-3-540-69818-0_15.

Thom, J., Millen, D. R., & DiMicco, J. (n.d.). Removing gamification from an enterprise SNS. In *Proceedings of the Fifteenth Conference on Computer Supported Cooperative Work2012.* Seattle, WA: IEEE.

Thomas, A. (1996). *Psychologie interkulturellen Handelns.* Göttingen, Germany: Hogrefe.

Titus, P., & Gremler, D. (2010). Guiding reflective practice: An auditing framework to assess teaching. *Philosophy and Style Journal of Marketing Education, 32*(2), 182–196. doi:10.1177/0273475309360161.

Triclot, M. (2011). *Philosophie des jeux vidéo.* Paris: La Découverte.

Trinidad, S. (2006). Constructive solutions: Improving teaching and learning in e-learning environments. In *Proceedings of AARE 2005 International Education Research Conference: UWS Parramatta.* Retrieved October 20, 2012, http://www.aare.edu.au/05pap/tri05058.pdf.

Trompenaars, F., & Hampden-Turner, C. (2012). *Riding the waves of culture: Understanding diversity in business* (3rd ed.). London: Nicholas Brealey Publ..

Tse, E., Greenberg, S., & Shen, C. (2006). GSI demo: Multiuser gesture/speech interaction over digital tables by wrapping single user applications. In *Proceedings of the International Conference on Multimodal Interfaces,* (pp. 76 – 83). doi: 10.1145/1180995.1181012

Tse, E., Greenberg, S., Shen, C., Forlines, C., & Kodama, R. (2008). Exploring true multi-user multimodal interaction over a digital table. In *Proceedings of the ACM Conference on Designing Interactive Systems,* (pp. 109 – 118). ACM. doi: 10.1145/1394445.1394457

Tsui, K. L., Goldsman, D., Jiang, W., & Wong, S. Y. (2010). Recent research in public health surveillance and health management. In *Proceedings of the Prognostics and Health Management Conference.* IEEE.

Tuddenham, P., Kirk, D., & Izadi, S. (2010). Graspables revisited: Multi-touch vs. tangible input for tabletop displays in acquisition and manipulation tasks. In *Proceedings of the SIGCHI Conference on Human Factors in Computing Systems,* (pp. 2223 – 2232). ACM. doi: 10.1145/1753326.1753662

Turing, A. (1950). Computing machinery and intelligence. *MIND - The Journal of the Mind Association, 59*(236), 433–460.

Tuzovic, S. (2010). Frequent (flier) frustration and the dark side of word-of-web: Exploring online dysfunctional behavior in online feedback forums. *Journal of Services Marketing, 24*(6), 446–457. doi:10.1108/08876041011072564.

Twachtman-Reilly, J., Amaral, S. C., & Zebrowski, P. P. (2008). Addressing feeding disorders in children on the autism spectrum in school-based setting: Physiological and behavioral issues. *Language, Speech, and Hearing Services in Schools, 39*, 261–272. doi:10.1044/0161-1461(2008/025) PMID:18420528.

Van der Beek, A. J., Mathiassen, S. E., & Burdorf, A. (2013). Efficient assessment of exposure to manual lifting using company data. *Applied Ergonomics, 44*(3), 360–365. doi:10.1016/j.apergo.2012.09.006 PMID:23069188.

Van der Geest, J. N., Kemner, C., Camfferman, G., Verbaten, M. N., & van Engeland, H. (2002). Looking at images with human figures: Comparison between autistic and normal children. *Journal of Autism and Developmental Disorders, 32*(2). doi:10.1023/A:1014832420206 PMID:12058845.

van der Veer, G. (2011). Culture centered design. In Proceedings of the 9th ACM SIGCHI Italian Chapter International Conference on Computer-Human Interaction: Facing Complexity (CHItaly). ACM.

Van Gorp, T., & Adams, E. (2012). *Design for emotion.* Waltham, MA: Morgan Kaufmann.

Van House. N., Davis, M., Ames, M., Finn, M., & Viswanathan, V. (2005). The uses of personal networked digital imaging: an empirical study of cameraphone photos and sharing. In *Proceedings of CHI '05 Extended Abstracts on Human Factors in Computing Systems* (CHI EA '05). ACM.

van Vliet, M., Kok, K., Veldkamp, A., & Sarkki, S. (2012). Structure in creativity: An exploration study to analyse the effects of structuring tools on scenario workshop results. *Futures, 44*, 746–760. doi:10.1016/j.futures.2012.05.002.

Vatrapu, R., & Suthers, D. (2007). Culture and computers: A review of the concept of culture and implications for intercultural collaborative online learning. *Lecture Notes in Computer Science, 4568*, 260. doi:10.1007/978-3-540-74000-1_20.

Vavoula, G. N., & Sharples, M. (2007). Future technology workshop: A collaborative method for the design of new learning technologies and activities. *Computer-Supported Collaborative Learning, 2*, 393–419. doi:10.1007/s11412-007-9026-0.

VDMA. (2009). *Software-Internationalisierung Leitfaden.* VDMA Fachverband Software.

Venkatesh, V., Ramesh, V., & Massey, A. P. (2003). Understanding usability in mobile commerce. *Communications of the ACM, 46*(12), 53–56. doi:10.1145/953460.953488.

Vöhringer-Kuhnt, T. (2002). *The Influence Of Culture On Usability.* (M.A. master Thesis). Freie Universität, Berlin, Germany.

Voida, S., Tobiasz, M., Stromer, J., Isenberg, P., & Carpendale, S. (2009). Getting practical with interactive tabletop displays: Designing for dense data, fat fingers, diverse interactions, and face-to-face collaboration. In *Proceedings of the ACM International Conference on Interactive Tabletops and Surfaces,* (pp. 109 – 116). ACM. doi: 10.1145/1731903.1731926

Volpert, W. (1991). Work design for human development. In C. Floyd et al. (Eds.), *Software Development and Reality Construction.* Berlin: Springer-Verlag.

von Ahn, L., & Dabbish, L. (2004). Labeling images with a computer game. In *Proceedings of the SIGCHI Conference on Human Factors in Computing Systems* (pp. 319–326). ACM.

von Ahn, L. (2006). Games with a purpose. *Computer, 39*(6), 92–94. doi:10.1109/MC.2006.196.

Wahlster, W., André, E., Finkler, W., Profitlich, H.-J., & Rist, T. (1993). Plan-based integration of natural language and graphics generation. *Artificial Intelligence, 63*, 387–427. doi:10.1016/0004-3702(93)90022-4.

Walker, S. (2003). Towards a method for describing the visual characteristics of children's readers and information books. In *Proceedings of the Information Design International Conference*. Sociedade Brasileira de Design da Informação.

Walker, S. (2006). An approach to describing the design of children's reading and information books. *InfoDesign Revista Brasileira de Design da Informação*, *3*(1/2), 1–10.

Wallbott, H. G., & Seithe, W. (1993). Sensitivity of persons with hearing impairment to visual emotional expression: Compensation or deficit? *European Journal of Social Psychology*, 23.

Wallin, J. M. (n.d.). *Social stories: An introduction to social stories*. Retrieved from http://www.polyxo.com/socialstories/introduction.html

Weber, G., & Specht, M. (1997). User modeling and adaptive navigation support in www-based tutoring systems. In *Proceedings of the International Conference on User Modeling*, (pp. 289-300). IEEE.

Weibelzahl, S., & Weber, G. (2002). Advantages, opportunities, and limits of empirical evaluations: Evaluating adaptive systems. *Künstliche Intelligenz*, *3*, 17–20.

Weiser, M. (1991). The computer for the 21st century. *Scientific American*, *265*(3), 94–104. doi:10.1038/scientificamerican0991-94 PMID:1675486.

Weiser, M. (1999). The computer for the 21st century. *Mobile Computing and Communications Review*, *3*(3), 3–11. doi:10.1145/329124.329126.

Weiss, M. J., LaRue, R. H., & Newcomer, A. (2009). Social story and autism: Understanding and addressing the deficits. In J. L. Matson (Ed.), *Applied Behavior Analysis for Children with Autism Spectrum Disorders*. Springer. doi:10.1007/978-1-4419-0088-3_7.

Weizenbaum, J. (1966). Eliza: A computer program for the study of natural language communication between man and machine. *Communications of the ACM*, *9*(1), 35–36. doi:10.1145/365153.365168.

Wells, P. (n.d.). *Undestanding animation*. London: Routledge.

Weyns, D., Malek, S., & Andersson, J. (2010). FORMS: A formal reference model for self-adaptation. In *Proceedings of the 7th International Conference on Autonomic Computing*, (pp. 205–214). New York, NY: ACM.

Whitby, B. (2003). *Artificial intelligence: A beginner's guide*. OneWorld.

Whitley, K. N., & Blackwell, A. F. (2001). Visual programming in the wild: A survey of LabVIEW programmers. *Journal of Visual Languages and Computing*, *12*(4), 435–472. doi:10.1006/jvlc.2000.0198.

Wickens, C. D., & Hollands, J. G. (2000). *Engineering psychology and human performance*. Englewood Cliffs, NJ: Prentice Hall.

Wiley, D. A. (2000). Connecting learning objects to instructional design theory: A definition, a metaphor, and a taxonomy. *Learning Technology*, *2830*(435), 1–35.

Williams, B. F., & Williams, R. L. (2011). *Effective programs for treating autism spectrum disorder: Applied behavior analysis models*. New York: Taylor & Francis.

Windl, H., & Heimgärtner, R. (2013). *Intercultural design for use - Extending usage-centered design by cultural aspects*. Paper presented at the HCII 2013. Las Vegas, NV.

Wing, L. (1981). Asperger's syndrome: A clinical account. *Psychological Medicine*, *11*(1), 115–129. doi:10.1017/S0033291700053332 PMID:7208735.

Wing, L. (1988). The continuum of autistic characteristics. In E. Schopler, & G. B. Mesibov (Eds.), *Diagnosis and assessment in autism*. New York: Plenum Press. doi:10.1007/978-1-4899-0792-9_7.

Wing, L. (1998). The history of Asperger syndrome. In E. Schopler, G. B. Mesibov, & L. J. Kunce (Eds.), *Asperger syndrome or high-functioning autism?* New York: Springer. doi:10.1007/978-1-4615-5369-4_2.

Wing, L. (2006). *What's so special about autism?* National Autistic Society.

Wing, L., & Gould, J. (1979). Severe impairments of social interaction and associated abnormalities in children: Epidemiology and classification. *Journal of Autism and Developmental Disorders*, *9*(1), 11–29. doi:10.1007/BF01531288 PMID:155684.

Wing, L., & Wing, J. K. (1976). *Early childhood autism: Clinical, educational, and social aspects*. Pergamon Press.

Winnicott, D. W. (1971). *Playing and reality*. New York: Basic Books.

Witkin, H. A., Moore, C. A., Goodenough, D. R., & Cox, P. W. (1977). Field-dependent and field-independent cognitive styles and their educational implications. *Review of Educational Research, 47*(1), 1. doi:10.3102/00346543047001001.

Witt, H. (2007). *Human-computer interfaces for wearable computers – A systematic approach to development and evaluation*. (Doctoral thesis). Bremen, Germany: Universität Bremen.

Witt, M., Scheiner, C., & Robra-Bissantz, S. (2011). Gamification of online idea competitions: Insights from an explorative case. In H.-U. Heiß, P. Pepper, B.-H. Schlingloff, & J. Schneider (Eds.), *Informatik schafft Communities, (LNIS)* (p. 192). Berlin: Springer.

Wobbrock, J. O., Morris, M. R., & Wilson, A. D. (2009). User-defined gestures for surface computing. In *Proceedings of the SIGCHI Conference on Human Factors in Computing Systems,* (pp. 1083 – 1092). ACM. doi: 10.1145/1518701.1518866

Woei, L., & White, G. (2010). *The promotion of critical thinking through the use of an online discussion board: Asking the right questions?* Paper presented at the Global Learn Asia Pacific. New York, NY.

Wong, W.-K., Moore, A., Cooper, G., & Wagner, M. (2002). Rule-based anomaly pattern detection for detecting disease outbreaks. In *Proceedings of the Eighteenth National Conference on Artificial Intelligence* (pp. 217–223). Menlo Park, CA: American Association for Artificial Intelligence.

World Health Organization. (2010). *Country cooperation strategy at a glance – Malaysia*. Retrieved 22nd March 2012 from http://www.who.int/countries/mys/en/

Worley, P. (2008). Writing skills essential in tech ed today. *Tech Directions, 68*(2), 17–19.

Worth, S. (2005). Narrative knowledge: Knowing through storytelling. In *Proceedings of the Fourth Media in Transition*. IEEE.

Wu, Y. C., Chen, H. S., Tsai, W. J., Lee, S. Y., & Yu, J. Y. (2008). Human action recognition based on layered-HMM. In *Proceedings of the IEEE International Conference on Multimedia and Expo*. Hannover, Germany: IEEE.

Wyer, R. S., Chiu, C.-Y., & Hong, Y.-Y. (2009). *Understanding culture: Theory, research, and application*. New York: Psychology Press.

Yamada, N., Sakamoto, K., Kunito, G., Isoda, Y., Yamazaki, K., & Tanaka, S. (2007). Applying ontology and probabilistic model to human activity recognition from surrounding things. *IPSJ Digital Courier, 3*.

Yammiyavar, P., Clemmensen, T., & Kumar, J. (2008). Influence of cultural background on non-verbal communication in a usability testing situation. *International Journal of Design*. Retrieved from http://www.ijdesign.org/ojs/index.php/IJDesign/article/view/313

Yau, N. (2011). *Visualize this – The flowingdata guide to design, visualization and statistics*. Indianapolis, IN: Wiley.

Yenisey, M. (2007). Axiomatic design approach for e-commercial web sites. In J. Jacko (Ed.), *Human-computer interaction: Interaction design and usability (LNCS)* (Vol. 4550, pp. 308–315). Berlin: Springer. doi:10.1007/978-3-540-73105-4_34.

Yeo, A. W. (2001). *Global-software development lifecycle: An exploratory study*. Paper presented at the SIGCHI Conference on Human Factors in Computing Systems. Seattle, WA.

Yin, Y., & Davis, R. (2010). Toward natural interaction in the real world: Real-time gesture recognition. In *Proceedings of the International Conference on Multimodal Interfaces and the Workshop on Machine Learning for Multimodal Interaction,* (pp. 15:1 – 15:8). doi: 10.1145/1891903.1891924

Young, M. S., Bisset, F. J., Grant, L., Williams, B., Sell, R., & Haslam, R. (2012). An ergonomically designed ergonomics exhibition: Lessons from and for public engagement. *Theoretical Issues in Ergonomics Science, 13*(1), 75–91. doi:10.1080/1463922X.2010.491875.

Zahedi, F., & Bansal, G. (2011). Cultural signifiers of web site images. *Journal of Management Information Systems, 28*(1), 147–200. doi:10.2753/MIS0742-1222280106.

Zaidenberg, S., Brdiczka, O., Reignier, P., & Crowley, J. (2006). Learning context models for the recognition of scenarios. In *Artificial Intelligence Applications and Innovations*. Boston: Springer. doi:10.1007/0-387-34224-9_11.

Zappi, P., Stiefmeier, T., Farella, E., Roggen, D., Benini, L., & Tröster, G. (2007). Activity recognition from on-body sensors by classifier fusion: sensor scalability and robustness. In *Proceedings of the Third International Conference on Intelligent Sensors, Sensor Networks and Information Processing ISSNIP* (pp. 281-286). IEEE.

Zappi, P., Milosevic, B., Farella, E., & Benini, L. (2009). Hidden Markov model based gesture recognition on low-cost, low-power tangible user interfaces. *Entertainment Computing*, *1*(2), 75–84. doi:10.1016/j.entcom.2009.09.005.

Zdravkova, K. (2000). Conceptual framework for an intelligent chatterbot. In *Proceedings of the International Conference Information Technology Interfaces*. IEEE.

Zeng, D., Chen, H., Tseng, C., Larson, C. A., Eidson, M., & Gotham, I. … Ascher, M. (2004). Towards a national infectious disease information infrastructure: A case study in west nile virus and botulism. In *Proceedings of the 2004 Annual National Conference on Digital Government Research*, (pp. 1-10). IEEE.

Zeng, W., Cui, X., Liu, X., Cui, H., & Wang, P. (2006). Remote sensing and GIS for identifying and monitoring the environmental factors associated with vector-borne disease: An overview. In *Proceedings of the IEEE International Conference on Geoscience and Remote Sensing Symposium 2006*, (pp. 1443-1446). IEEE.

Zhang, N., Hong, W., Zheng, S., & Tao, L. (2012). A solution for an application of information visualization in telemedicine. In *Proceedings of the 7th International Conference on Computer Science & Education (ICCSE)*, (pp. 407-411). ICCSE.

Zhang, X., Chen, X., Wang, W., Yang, J., Lantz, V., & Wang, K. (2009). Hand gesture recognition and virtual game control based on 3D accelerometer and EMG sensors. In *Proceedings of the 14th International Conference on Intelligent User Interfaces IUI* (pp. 401-406). New York, NY: ACM Press.

Zhang, P., Carey, J., Te'eni, D., & Tremaine, M. (2005). Integrating human-computer interaction development into the systems development life cycle: A methodology. *Communications of the Association for Information Systems*, *15*, 512–543.

Zhang, Q., Chintakovid, T., Sun, X., Ge, Y., & Zhang, K. (2006). Saving face or sharing personal information? A cross-cultural study on knowledge sharing. *Journal of Information and Knowledge Management*, *5*(1), 73–80. doi:10.1142/S0219649206001335.

Zhang, T., Rau, P.-L. P., & Salvendy, G. (2010). Exploring critical usability factors for handsets. *Behaviour & Information Technology*, *29*(1), 45–55. doi:10.1080/01449290802666747.

Zhiyuan, L., Xiang, C., Kongqiao, W., & Zhangyan, Z. (2011). A prototype of gesture-based interface. In *Proceedings of the 13th International Conference on Human Computer Interaction with Mobile Devices and Services MobileHCI* (pp. 33-36). New York, NY: ACM Press.

Zhou, R., Jingjing, M., Junsong, Y., & Zhengyou, Z. (2011). Robust hand gesture recognition with kinect sensor. In *Proceedings of the 19th International Conference on Multimedia MM* (pp. 759-760). New York, NY: ACM Press.

Zichermann, G., & Cunningham, C. (2011). *Gamification by design: Implementing game mechanics in web and mobile apps*. Sebastopol, CA: O'Reilly Media, Inc..

Ziefle, M. (2002). The influence of user expertise and phone complexity on performance, ease of use and learnability of different mobile phones. *Behaviour & Information Technology*, *21*(5), 303–311. doi:10.1080/0144929021000048538.

Ziegler, J., Döring, R., Pfeffer, J., & Urbas, L. (2013). Autonomous dynamic hand gesture recognition in industrial settings. In *Proceedings of IADIS International Conference Interfaces and Human Computer Interaction IHCI*. IADIS.

Zimmerman., et al. (2007). Research through design as a method for interaction design research in HCI. In *Proceedings of SIGCHI Conference on Human Factors in Computing Systems*. ACM.

Zink, K. (2000). Ergonomics in the past and the future: From a German perspective to an international one. *Ergonomics, 43*(7), 920–930. doi:10.1080/001401300409116 PMID:10929827.

Zong, Y., et al. (2000). Multimodal presentation markup language mpml with emotion expression functions attached. In *Proceedings of the International Conference on Microelectronic Systems Education*. IEEE.

Zühlke, D., & Röse, K. (2000). Design of global user-interfaces: Living with the challenge. In *Proceedings of the IEA 2000/HFES 2000 Congress,* (Vol. 6, pp. 154-157). San Diego, CA: IEA.

Zühlke, D. (2004). Useware-systeme für internationale märkte. In *Useware-Engineering für Technische Systeme* (pp. 142–164). Berlin, Germany: Springer.

About the Contributors

Katherine Blashki, with a recognised background in the communication, arts and information technology faculties at numerous universities, including Monash and Deakin Universities in Australia and Noroff University College in Norway, is also acknowledged for her extensive experience in the creative industries sector with a focus on game-based learning, creating narrative, and systems development. Previously Head of School of Multimedia Systems, Faculty of Information Technology at Monash University, Chair of New Media Technologies, a collaboration between the Faculties of Arts, and Science & Technology, both at Deakin University, and Director of Research and Education at AFTRS, Katherine now consults to aspiring higher education institutions across the world. With a demonstrated commitment to encouraging industry innovation, her research and writing credits include more than 110 papers and journals together with participation in community, industry, and international consultancies in communication, IT, and the creative industries. Katherine is currently Program Chair for the IADIS Games and Entertainment Technologies and Human Computer Interfaces conferences, held since 2005, and a past board member for Film Victoria based in Australia.

Pedro Isaías is an associate professor at the Universidade Aberta (Portuguese Open University) in Lisbon, Portugal, responsible for several courses and director of the master degree program in Electronic Commerce and Internet since its start in 2003. He holds a PhD in Information Management (in the speciality of information and decision systems) from the New University of Lisbon. Author of several books, book chapters, papers, and research reports, all in the information systems area, he has headed several conferences and workshops within the mentioned area. He has also been responsible for the scientific coordination of several EU-funded research projects. He is also a member of the editorial board of several journals and program committee member of several conferences and workshops. At the moment, he conducts research activity related to Information Systems in general, E-Learning, E-Commerce, and WWW related areas.

* * *

Lina Aaltonen, M.Sc. (Tech.), is Research Scientist at the Systems Research Centre of VTT in the Human Activity and Systems Usability team. She received her M.Sc. degree in electrical engineering in 2005 at Helsinki University of Technology, TKK, Finland. Her main subject was cognitive technology and minor automation technology. Before joining VTT in 2008, she did research on multisensory integration, brain imaging, and simulated brain processes at the department of Biomedical Engineering and Computational Science, TKK. She is currently working towards her doctoral degree at Aalto University School of Science, Finland. Her research interests include usability evaluation and smart evolving technological solutions in complex working environments. In this project, Iina will mainly contribute to WP2 and WP3 with focus on ICT solutions and tools.

Pedro M. Arezes holds a PhD in Production and Systems Engineering from the University of Minho (Portugal) and he is an Associate Professor (with Habilitation) at the same university, where he coordinates the Human Engineering Research Group. In 2005, he was appointed as Director of the Ergonomics Laboratory at the University of Minho, and he is also the Chairman of the Board of the Human Engineering MSc course and member of the board of the Doctoral Programme in Industrial Engineering and Systems. He has authored more than 150 papers in peer-reviewed papers published in international journals and congress proceedings.

Ismael Avila has a bachelor's degree in electronics and electrical engineering (1992) from the Federal University of Minas Gerais (Brazil) and a master's degree in Intelligent Systems from the State University of Campinas – Unicamp (Brazil). Since 1994 works as an engineer and consultant at the CPqD R&D Center in Telecommunications and has participated in several IT projects for the Brazilian Telecommunications Ministry in the areas of HCI, usability and ICT appropriation, during which has developed service acceptance and technological innovation diffusion models in scenarios of digital divide and digital television deployment and proposed icon-based solutions both for improving ICT intelligibility for low-literacy users and for authentication solutions in mobile phones. Is author or co-author of several papers and technical reports and is currently involved in projects in the area of smart grid and telecommunications.

Flávia de Almeida Barros graduated in Computer Science at Federal University Pernambuco (1984), Master's degree in Computer Science from Federal University of Pernambuco (1990), and PhD in Computer Science - University of Essex (1995). She is currently Associate Professor 1 Federal University of Pernambuco (Center for Informatics). Member of the project Construction of a Virtual Learning Companion for a Program to Promote Cardiovascular Health in Childhood and Adolescence (2006 - 2008). Has experience in Computer Science with emphasis in Artificial Intelligence, acting on the following themes: natural language processing, information retrieval and information systems to Web.

Lau Bee Theng completed her PhD in 2006. Presently, she is a senior lecturer and ICT program coordinator at Faculty of Engineering, Computing and Science, Swinburne University of Technology, Sarawak Campus. Her research interest is mainly on assistive technologies utilizing ICT for the special people. She has published more than 40 articles in peer reviewed journals, book chapters and conference papers. She has successfully supervised 4 Masters of Science students and coordinated a few research projects on assistive technologies for special children, injury recognition and activity monitoring using multi depth sensors.

Lulit Bezuayehu is an expert in human-computer interface testing and evaluation with almost 20 years of user research experience. Having lived in a few countries (England, Ethiopia, and Thailand) and traveled extensively, Lulit is interested in understanding the global user experience and has conducted research with diverse users from around the world. Lulit is a User Experience Architect at Oracle, focusing on user research for Oracle's Human Resources applications. She has a B.A. in Mathematics and Computer Science from the University of St. Thomas, a B.S. in Electrical Engineering from the University of Minnesota, and a MBA from Capella University.

Julian Bowerman is a PhD student at Loughborough Design School, Loughborough University, United Kingdom, where he is a member of the Design Ergonomics Research Group. He received his bachelor's degree in Engineering Product Design from South Bank University, London, after which he worked in industry in various design related companies and as a self-employed designer. He is interested in applying ergonomics to enhance both product usability and user experience and in the development of tools that enable designers to understand people more comprehensively so that designers can design better products for them. He also has an interest in culture with respect to product design.

Alexandre Melo Braga holds a BS in computer science and a Master's degree in computer science. He is PhD student in computer security and cryptography at the State University of Campinas – Unicamp (Brazil). Since 2000, he has been working as a consultant and researcher in information security, software security, secure software development, and applied cryptography, and has published several papers on those subjects. He is a part-time lecturer in cryptography, information security, and software development. He holds various professional certifications, including PMP, CSSLP, CISSP, SCJP, SCWCD, SCMAD.

Eric Brangier received his Ph. D. in 1991 in Psychology. After spending four years as a research engineer in a computer company, he was assistant professor, then Full Professor at the University of Lorraine. His research deals with the topics of ergonomics of products, ergonomics of complex systems, psychology of new technologies, cognitive ergonomics, user experience. His recent international scientific responsibilities were to be chairman of three scientific conferences (HCI Human Computer Interaction French meeting and Ergo'IA International conference). Pr. Eric Brangier has also been working as an expert for different committees (National Research and Safety Institute, INRS, Department of research and technology of a French ministry, Research founding society in Quebec). He has participated in 50 committees of international conferences. He was invited in Canada, Swiss, Portugal, Poland and Norway. He is the author of 2 books and more than 300 scientific papers and communications.

Federico Cabitza, BSc MEng PhD, got his master degree at the Politecnico of Milan in 2001. From 2001 to 2004, he worked as a software analyst in the private sector. In February 2007, he received the PhD in computer science with a thesis on computational models and architectures supporting collaboration and knowledge work in corporate domains. Currently, he is an assistant professor at the Università degli Studi di Milano-Bicocca where he teaches computing formalisms, socio-technical analysis of collaborative systems and knowledge management. His current research interests regard ICT-oriented domain analysis, user requirement elicitation and prioritization, and the design of computer-based support for cooperative work and knowledge management, with a focus on applications for the medical domain.

Yoke Yie Chen obtained her MSc in Business Information Technology from University of Manchester, UK, in 2007. She is currently working as a Lecturer in the Department of Computer and Information Sciences, Universiti Teknologi Petronas, Malaysia. Her field of interest includes text mining and intelligent system. She has published technical papers in international, national journals and conferences.

Cheah Hui Chow obtained her degree in Information and Communication Technology from Universiti Teknologi Petronas in 2011. She joined Shell Business Service Centre in August 2011 as part of their graduate program, which entitles her to switch between different roles within the organization in her first 3 years. Her first role under the Shell graduate program is a Downstream Application Support analyst supporting Shell's downstream business on SAP supply chain area. She is now in her second role which is a Performance Reporting analyst looking after the End User Computing bundle's performance.

David Costa is a Human-Computer Interaction researcher at LaSIGE. He is originally from Lisbon, Portugal, where he studied Computer Engineering in the Faculty of Sciences of the University of Lisbon. David currently holds a master's degree for his research on multimodal outputs (2011). During his period in LaSIGE research group, he was involved in an European project named "Gentle User Interfaces for Elderly People" (GUIDE), where he developed a multimodal adaptive fission engine for that system. From this collaboration resulted several publications on national and international conferences. With the GUIDE project recently completed, David is now working on a new project still focused on the elderly people named "Smartphones for Seniors" (S4S). His main research interests are multimodal interaction, mobile devices, and adaptive interfaces.

Fábio Costa completed his Bachelor degree in Informatics Engineering in 2011 from the University of Minho. Since then, he is attending the Master degree in Network Engineering and Communication Services in the same University. In 2012, he was integrated in a research group at the school of engineering from University of Minho called Algoritmi center. Currently, he is doing the final year of his master degree in the University of Pisa in Italy, thanks to the Erasmus programme, where is developing his Master's thesis on Network Tomography. Thanks to his work developed so far, he was invited to stay at the University of Pisa as a PhD student.

Joao Crisóstomo Weyl Albuquerque Costa received his Electronic Engineering degree at Federal do Pará (1981), Master's degree in Electrical Engineering - Telecommunications - Pontifical Catholic University of Rio de Janeiro (1989), and Ph.D. in Electrical Engineering - Telecommunications - State University of Campinas (1994). Currently, he is an associate professor at the Faculty of Computer Engineering Institute of Technology. He is vice-president of the Brazilian Microwave and Optoelectronics 2010-2012, member of the Brazilian Society of Telecommunications and CNPq Researcher (since 1994). He works as a researcher at the Graduate Program in Computer Science and the Graduate Program in Electrical Engineering in the areas of communications networks, applied electromagnetics and computer science, with research interests that include modeling of high-frequency devices, performance evaluation of mobile communication networks and optical access networks and communication solutions for monitoring systems, and those areas, coordinated and participated in several projects funded (CNPq, FINEP, CAPES, SECTAM) and for public and private companies (Ericsson, Brasilsat, Eletronorte).

Eulália Carvalho da Mata received a degree in Technical Data Processing by the Pará State Technical School (1998), Bacharel's degree in Computer Engineering at Institute Higher Studies in Amazonia - IESAM (2009), Specialization in Planning, Implementation and Management of Distance Education at the Open University partnership between Brazil and Federal University Fluminense (2012). Currently, she is a Master's degree candidate at the Federal University of Pará, in Electrical Engineering (Applied Computing). She has experience in assisting in the development and management of information systems, performing online support, managing activities, resources, and people involved. She teaches: Distance Education, Technology, Project Management, Virtual Learning Environment, and Digital Inclusion.

Ádamo Lima de Santana received a Bacharel's degree in Computer Science at the University of Amazonia (2002) and Master's degree (2005) and Ph.D. (2008) in Electrical Engineering (Applied Computing) Federal University of Pará (UFPA) and University College Cork. Currently, he is Adjunct Professor II and Director of the School of Computer Engineering and Telecommunications UFPA and advisor of the Graduate Program in Electrical Engineering (PPGEE-UFPA). He has experience in the area of Computer Engineering, with emphasis in Computational Intelligence, Data Mining and Business Intelligence, acting on the following topics: game theory, prediction of load optimization, pattern discovery, and decision support.

Randy Döring studied Information System Technology at Dresden University of Technology and obtained his master degree in 2012. His main research area is hardware-in-the-loop simulation of embedded systems. Today, he works as system engineer at TraceTronic GmbH, an international operating company specialized in hardware and software development for the automotive industry.

Carlos Duarte holds a PhD (2008) in Computer Science, from the University of Lisbon, and an MsC in Electronic and Computers Engineering from the Instituto Superior Técnico, Technical University of Lisbon, where he also graduated in Electronic and Computers Engineering. He is currently a Professor at the Department of Informatics, Faculty of Sciences of the University of Lisbon, and a senior researcher at LaSIGE, as a member of the HCIM Group since 2000. His main research interests include multimodal and adaptive interfaces, with a special emphasis on accessibility, usability evaluation, mobile devices, UI design, hypermedia, digital books, and eLearning. He has participated in several research projects, both European (e.g. GUIDE, ACCESSIBLE) and national, some as coordinator. He has published over 60 refereed technical and scientific papers and book chapters, and served on the editorial board, scientific committees and as a reviewer for several journals and conferences.

Carlos Renato Lisboa Francês received the Colleger Research Productivity 2, Bacharel's degreein Computer Science at Federal University of Pará (1995), Master's degree in Computer Science and Computational Mathematics at the University of São Paulo (1998), and Ph.D. in Computer Science and Computational Mathematics at the University of São Paulo (2001). He is currently an adjunct professor at the Faculty of Computer Engineering, Federal University of Pará, was president of the Data Processing Company of the State of Pará (period 01/2007 and Dec/2010), and member of the advisory committee of the National Institute of computing studies and Research (INEP-MEC). Has experience in Computer Science, with an emphasis on Performance Evaluation, acting on the following topics: Digital TV, access technologies, performance Markov Models and simulation, correlation techniques (Bayesian networks), and optimization.

Lucia Filgueiras has a PhD in Electrical Engineering from University of Sao Paulo (USP), Brazil, where she works as Assistant Professor in the Computer Engineering Department at Escola Politecnica. She leads Grupo i, a research group on Human-Computer Interaction and User Experience. The group has studied HCI-UX since the eighties, from human reliability in critical system operation to crossmedia narratives. The current focus of research are assistive technologies and their applications. Prof. Filgueiras presently manages accessibility initiatives in USP, working as executive coordinator of Programa USP Legal. In past years, she has worked as a usability consultant, when she founded the Brazilian chapter of Usability Professionals' Association and two usability laboratories.

Iade Gesso received the BSc and the MSc degrees in Computer Science from the University of Milano-Bicocca in 2006 and 2009, respectively, attending the courses of the curricula "Design and Development of Information Systems." He obtained his PhD in Computer Science from the University of Milano-Bicocca in the February 2013 with a thesis titled "Making End-Users Autonomous in the Design of their Active Documents." Currently, he has as a post doctoral fellowship from the Department of Informatics, Systems and Communication (DISCo) of the University of Milano-Bicocca within the project "Communication Supports in Corporate Social Networks." His research interests range from the Computer-Supported Cooperative Work (CSCW) to the End-User Development (EUD) and Visual Languages, with the aim to support collaboration through digital artifacts making them flexible as their paper-based counterparts. In 2012, he worked as intern at the Xerox Research Centre Europe (XRCE).

Kim Nee Goh obtained her MSc in Human-Computer Interaction from University of Michigan, USA, in 2007. She is currently working as a Lecturer in the Department of Computer and Information Sciences, Universiti Teknologi PETRONAS, Malaysia. Her research interest includes persuasive technologies and interface and interaction design especially in the health domain. She has published technical papers in international, national journals and conferences.

Yinni Guo got her PhD in 2010 from School of Industrial Engineering, Purdue University in the area of HCI. Her research focused on development of a new usability evaluation method for consumer electronics, the axiomatic evaluation method. This chapter presents the essential part of the research of axiomatic evaluation method. In graduate school, she also conducted research on how to design content for consumer electronics and online services. She has authored or co-authored more than 10 research papers in internationally referred journals and conference proceedings. She is also frequent reviewer for top journals/conferences in the field. Now she is a human factors engineer in Intel Labs in Santa Clara, USA.

Rüdiger Heimgärtner studied information science, linguistics and philosophy in combination with religious studies, as well as intercultural decision-making and responsibility. He worked as an electronics technician and hardware developer, later in international software and HCI projects as developer, designer, software architect, and project manager at Siemens and Continental. Following his doctoral thesis project at Siemens VDO (today Continental Automotive GmbH), he concentrated research on training and advising developers, designers and managers in the areas of user interface design, usability engineering, as well as project, process and quality management for the intercultural context. He is the founder and managing director of the company Intercultural User Interface Consulting (IUIC), which offers research, coaching and training for universal and Intercultural User Interface Design (IUID). Dr. Rüdiger Heimgärtner is member in the usability professionals association and in several research groups including internationalization of software as well as standardization of usability and accessibility engineering.

Pirita Ihamäki holds a MA Degree and M.Sc. (Economy) Degree in University of Turku from the Department of Cultural Production and Landscape Studies, Finland. She is PhD student of Digital Culture. Currently, she is working for concept designer with Coppersky Ldt. She research interests include: human-computer interaction, user centred design, adventure tourist services, mixed reality applications, social media and digital education applications. She has authored many conference papers and journal articles in these areas.

Antonio Fernando Lavareda Jacob Junior graduated in Bachelor of Computer Science from University of Amazonia (2005) and Master's degree in Computer Science from Federal University of Pernambuco (2008). He is currently a scholar - Brazil Computational Intelligence Services, a doctoral student at the Federal University of Pará and adjunct professor at the University of Amazonia. He has experience in Computer Science, with emphasis in the areas of Computing in Education, Artificial Intelligence and Software Engineering mainly in the following areas: Natural Language Processing, Affective Computing, Human-Computer Interaction Design, Applications for Children and TV digital interactive.

Tomayess Issa is a Senior Lecturer at the School of Information Systems at Curtin University, Australia? She joined the School of Information Systems – Curtin University in 2001. She received her Ph.D. from the School of Information Systems, Curtin University in 2008. Her PhD research was mainly about Web development and Human Factors. Tomayess has vast experience in Australian tertiary education, teaching in Information Systems area. Tomayess published several journal and conference papers in her research interest, and she is a member of an international conference program committee. Currently, she conducts research locally and globally in information systems, Usability and Human-Computer Interaction, Social Network (including web 2.0 and web 3.0), Sustainability and Green IT, Cloud Computing, Networking and Operating systems.

Amalia Kallergi is a Human Computer Interaction researcher with a soft spot for data in collections. Educated as a computer scientist (BSc) and as a media-technologist (MSc), she conducted her PhD research on playful interfaces for scientific image data in collections at the Imaging & BioInformatics group of Leiden University, the Netherlands. Next to making video games and other toys for biologists to explore their images, Amalia has been frequenting classrooms, laboratories and other exciting places as a researcher, teacher, student and honours class coordinator.

Ken Keane, as a Senior Researcher at Madeira Interactive Technologies Institute, currently investigates the use of social media technologies in providing innovative social interaction between tourists and residents in the Madeira region of Portugal. He has an interest in the design spaces that are offered by mobile technologies, social media, and local communities and how they may increase social opportunities around culture, community, traditions, environment, and identity within the context of tourism. Currently in his third year as a PhD candidate at the University of Madeira, he is specializing in Human Computer Interaction with a focus on the role of Narrative in User Experience Design. He has strong interest in Qualitative research methods within a User centered design process, adopting techniques from the fields of Ethnography, Participatory design, User Experience Design, and Interaction design.

Jari Laarni, Ph.D., is Principal Scientist at the Systems Research Centre of VTT Technical Research Centre of Finland. He received a Ph.D. in psychology from the University of Helsinki in 1997. He is specialized in the areas of visual perception, cognitive psychology, usability evaluation and user experience analysis, and he has researched on the issues involved in visual attention and search, user interface evaluation, sense of presence in media environments, operator work analysis, human well-being an stress In these areas he has published over 80 papers in international journals or conference proceedings. He has participated in several national and international research projects on the above-mentioned topics.

Celina P. Leão is an Assistant Professor at the Production and Systems Department of School of Engineering of University of Minho. She received her MSc degree in industrial Mathematics from University of Strathclyde/Glasgow Caledonian University, Scotland, in 1994, and in 2003 her PhD in Engineering Science from Porto University, Portugal. Her research work in the R&D Centro Algoritmi focuses her main interests in modeling and simulation of processes, and in the application of new methodologies in the learning process of numerical methods and statistics in engineering. Currently she supervises PhD and MSc projects in these areas, being co-author of several scientific papers published in international journals and conferences.

Isabel F. Loureiro received her graduation in Pharmacy from the University of Porto and her PhD in Industrial and Systems Engineering from the University of Minho, Portugal. Presently, she is an Invited Assistant Professor at the Department of Production and Systems, School of Engineering, University of Minho and in the Allied Health Sciences School of Polytechnic of Porto. She is also a member of the Research Center for Industrial and Technology Management (CGIT) and Algoritmi Centro, University of Minho. Her research work focuses her main interests in Ergonomics and Occupational Safety and Hygiene.

Mika Luimula is a Principal Lecturer and a Head of the Media Laboratory in the Degree Programme of Information Technology at Turku University of Applied Sciences. He holds a PhD in information processing sciences and a MSc in mathematics. He is leading game development R&D activities in Game Tech&Arts Laboratory. His research interests include game development, serious games, health informatics, and location-aware systems. Dr. Luimula has published around 50 scientific papers in above mentioned research areas.

Vivi Mandasari completed her Master of Science by research at Swinburne University of Technology in 2012. Prior to her Master degree, she completed a Bachelor degree in Multimedia Software Development from the same University in 2009. Her research interests include application in helping the children with Autism Spectrum Disorders and 2D animations for teaching and learning.

Cathie Marache-Francisco is an Ergonomist Researcher. She is currently working under a PhD convention at Lorraine University (Metz, Fr) under the supervision of Pr. Eric Brangier. This work is financed by SAP (Levallois-Perret, Fr), an international software company that develops professional systems. Her main interest is Gamification and the way it can be applied to the professional context of Business Intelligence. Indeed, she is part of a research team in SAP that works on a mobile Dashboard application and she is in charge of the user interface design of that project. Her researches also deal with Ergonomics, User Experience, Emotional Design, and Persuasive Technology, which are topics that she teaches to engineer students in Paris.

Ewerton Martins de Menezes has a bachelor's degree in computer engineering (2011) from the State University of Campinas – Unicamp (Brazil). Has been working as a researcher at CPqD Foundation for 2 years on R&D projects and consulting for the Brazilian Telecommunications Ministry, utilities, banks, and other business areas. As part of innovative services and applications development, he is mostly focused on user experience, usability, and accessibility aspects in mobile devices, in the Web and in digital TV platforms. He has been responsible for the conception and execution of UX evaluations by end-users, considering also eye tracking data in the analysis. Is author and co-author of papers published in international conferences in the human-computer interaction, multimedia, and mobile communication fields.

Valentina Nisi's background covers Fine Arts, Multimedia, and Interaction Design. Valentina's main area of expertise is Digital Media Art and Design of digitally mediated experiences. In particular designing and producing experiences and services that connect people, content, and real spaces through the use of digital technologies. Beside research and design work, Valentina also enjoys writing stories for trans-media platforms, as well as for traditional cinema. In the last years, Valentina has been researching and publishing in the areas of Interaction Design, Digital Art and Entertainment as well as teaching graduate and undergraduate Students. Her teaching covers Service Design and Interaction Design, Visual Communication, Interactive Narrative and Industry sponsored Capstone Projects in the area of HCI.

Rafael Nunes is a MSc student at the Faculty of Sciences of the University of Lisbon, where he also graduated in Computer Science. He is a junior researcher at the LASIGE research group. His research interests are centered in the field of Human Computer Interaction with specific focus on multimodality, interfaces and improving user experience.

S. Tejaswi Peesapati is an information scientist with an interest in human-computer interaction. He has extensive experience designing, deploying and analyzing surveys as a tool for conducting global user research. He is currently a user researcher at Oracle, focusing on both desktop and mobile user experience for the Human Resources applications. Tejaswi previously worked as a Research Scientist with the Interaction Design Lab and Human-Computer Interaction Group at Cornell University. While at Cornell, Tejaswi worked on various research projects funded by National Science Foundation that focused on using technologies to support 'reminiscence'. Tejaswi has a B.S. in Computer Science from Jawaharlal Nehru Technological University in India, and a M.S. in Computer Science from Louisiana Tech University.

Johannes Pfeffer is a research scientist and PhD-student at Faculty of Electrical and Computer Engineering at TU Dresden. In 2010, he obtained a Master degree in Mechatronics. His research focuses on model driven app orchestration for industrial use. Other research topics related to this subject are model transformation, usability on mobile devices, mobile solutions for supervisory control, and industrial maintenance support.

Soraia Silva Prietch is a doctoral student at the Department of Digital Systems in the Escola Politécnica da Universidade de São Paulo, Brazil. She is an Assistant Professor at Universidade Federal de Mato Grosso, *Campus* de Rondonópolis, since 2004. Soraia currently coordinates a research project titled "TEA-Club," whose name plays with the perspective of relationship between researcher and friend with the subjects (deaf participants), to address questions about the use of assistive technologies in educational. Her areas of interest are human-computer interaction, computers in education, and assistive technologies. A complete curriculum of her formation, professional activities and publications can be found at the Plataforma Lattes/CNPq.

Stephan Puls studied Informatics at the Karlsruhe Institute of Technology (KIT). Since 2010, he is scientific researcher at the Institute for Process Control and Robotics at KIT. Besides teaching fundamentals of computer science to undergraduate students, his research interests center around human-robot cooperation including sensor data analysis, object and action recognition, and reasoning about situations.

Andreia Ribeiro holds a Master degree in Computer Science from the Faculty of Sciences of the University of Lisbon. She is a junior researcher at LaSIGE, the Large Scale Informatics Systems Laboratory, working in the HCIM group. Her main research interests are gestural interaction and designing multimodal, multiuser and multiple surface applications.

Virginia Tiradentes Souto is a senior lecturer in the Design department at the University of Brasilia, Brazil. She has both a master's (1998) and a PhD (2006) in Typography and Graphic Communication from the University of Reading, UK. She has been working as a designer since 1995, including at the National Council for Scientific and Technological Development (CNPq), and the National Education and Research Network (RNP). She has written a number of papers about design, especially the design of electronic media. Her main areas of research interest are information design and interaction design.

Christian Grund Sørensen is a Master of Theology, University of Copenhagen. Master of Science (IT), Aalborg University, Doctoral researcher at Center for Computer Mediated Epistemology, Aalborg University, Vicar in Danish Lutheran Church, and social media advisor. He is affiliated with EUROPLOT (EU project funded by EACEA), Kaj Munk Research Center, and Theological Pedagogical Center, Denmark. Born in 1968 and father of five., his academic interests are in several fields and focused on interdisciplinary approach: Persuasive technology, information architecture, HCI, multimedia learning, cultural mediation, museum research, system theory, rhetoric, rhetorical epistemology, logic, renaissance thinking, Søren Kierkegaard, Kaj Munk, philosophy, theology, homiletics, religious communication, ethics, and social media. He believes that interdisciplinarity and creative thinking fertilize academic episteme and allow us to facilitate new groundbreaking through multifaceted inspiration.

Mathias Grund Sørensen is an elite master-student of Computer Science in the Embedded Software group at Aalborg University. His primary work concerns formal model checking and he has in particular worked with discrete time model checking on Timed-Arc Petri Nets and extensions to the model checking tool TAPAAL. He also has a strong interest in machine intelligence and human-computer interaction and is in particular interested in the new possibilities emerging from recent shifts in mobile technology and interaction.

Maria Spichkova was born in 1980 in Moscow, Russia, obtained a Bachelor Degree in Computer Science at Moscow Power Engineering Institute (Technical University, Russia) in 2000 and a Master Degree in Computer Science at Dresden University of Technology (Germany) in 2003. Since 2003, she has been working in a researcher and lecturer role at Technical University Munich (Germany), where she received a Ph.D. in Computer Science in 2007 and has been involved, both as participant and as project leader, in a large number of research industrial projects in collaboration with AVL, DENSO Automotive, Robert Bosch GmbH, BMW Car IT, etc. Author of several journal and conference papers and research reports, all in the area of Software & Systems Engineering. At the moment she conducts research activity related to specification, modelling, testing, and verification of safety-critical systems as well as to human factor related areas.

Eric Stilan has over 20 years of experience as a designer, illustrator, and Clio award-winning animator. He is an advocate for users with disabilities, focusing on low vision and color blindness, and strives to make his designs accessible for these users. Eric researches the cultural implications of icons and their use in existing and emerging technologies. He is a Principal Visual Designer for Oracle, where he has been instrumental in the visual design of PeopleSoft and Fusion applications. Eric was a key partner in developing methodologies to measure and evaluate the effectiveness of icons in Oracle's enterprise applications. Eric has a BA in Visual Design and Animation from the State University of New York at Purchase.

José Teixeira earned his Bachelor of Engineering degree in Informatics Engineering from Minho University in 2011. He has been taking a master degree in Computer Networks and Services from Minho University since then. From 2012, he has integrated a research unit of the School of Engineering from University of Minho called Centro ALGORITMI, where his work lead him to present a paper at an international conference. Thanks to the ERASMUS programme he is currently doing the final year of his master degree abroad in University of Pisa - Italy, where he has been developing work related to Software Defined Networks. Due to the relevance of the work developed, he has been invited to remain in University of Pisa as a PhD student.

Leon Urbas is Chair for Process Control Systems Engineering at the Technische Universität Dresden. His main areas of research are the Engineering of distributed safety-critical systems including function integration, model-driven engineering, modularization, information modeling for the process industries, and middleware in automation. He is further devoted to the design of usable mobile information systems in the process industries, the analysis, design and evaluation of alarm and supports systems, and the user modeling for prospective HMI design.

Fons J. Verbeek is Group Leader of the section Imaging & BioInformatics at the Leiden Institute of Advanced Computer Science (LIACS) at Leiden University, the Netherlands. He obtained his PhD at the Pattern Recognition group of the Delft University of Technology on 3D Image Analysis and Visualization in Microscopy. The research in the section Imaging & BioInformatics is concerned with analysis of biomedical images ranging from cells and sub-cellular structures to whole organisms. In addition, attention is paid to annotation of images with ontologies and interaction paradigms with images. Besides image analysis, he is active in Human Computer Interaction research.

Hsiu-Feng Wang is an assistant professor in the Department of e-Learning Design and Management, at National Chiayi University, Taiwan. She studied for a bachelor's degree in Graphic Communication in the Department of Graphic Design at Ming Chuan University, Taiwan. She then completed a Master's Degree at Middlesex University, UK, before reading for her PhD in the Department of Typography and Graphic Communication at Reading University, UK. She is interested in graphic icon design, information design, the legibility of Traditional Chinese writing and user-centred design. Her current research is concerned with how design variables influence the effectiveness of online teaching materials for children.

Heinz Wörn studied electrical engineering and obtained his PhD in control of machine tools at the University of Stuttgart. He then worked in industry for KUKA Schweißanlagen und Roboter GmbH where he advanced to a leading position in research and development. Since 1997, he heads the Institute for Process Control and Robotics at the Karlsruhe Institute of Technology as Professor for Complex Systems in Automation and Robotics. His research interests include distributed automation, fault tolerant robot controls, diagnosis techniques, and modular software architectures for automation.

Jens Ziegler is a research scientist and PhD-student at Faculty of Electrical and Computer Engineering at TU Dresden. He obtained a Master degree in Electrical Engineering in 2008. Since 2010, he is the head of the Mobile Information Systems research group at the Chair of Control Systems Engineering. His research focuses on requirements engineering including task & context analysis and customer inquiry techniques, mobile interaction design for industrial environments, and the design and evaluation of mobile solutions for supervisory control and industrial maintenance support.

Index

E

F

G

H

I

K

L

M

N

O

P

Q

R

S

T

U

V

W

Y

CPSIA information can be obtained at www.ICGtesting.com
Printed in the USA
BVOW05*2043021013

R5442300001B/R54423PG332151BVX2B/3/P